NATIONAL CENTER FOR EDUCATIO

Digest of Education Statistics 1996

Thomas D. Snyder
Project Director

Charlene M. Hoffman
Production Manager

Claire M. Geddes
Program Analyst

U.S. Department of Education
Office of Educational Research and Improvement   **NCES 96-133**

U.S. Department of Education
Richard W. Riley
Secretary

Office of Educational Research and Improvement
Sharon P. Robinson
Assistant Secretary

National Center for Education Statistics
Pascal D. Forgione, Jr.
Commissioner

The National Center for Education Statistics (NCES) is the primary federal entity for collecting, analyzing, and reporting data related to education in the United States and other nations. It fulfills a congressional mandate to collect, collate, analyze, and report full and complete statistics on the condition of education in the United States; conduct and publish reports and specialized analyses of the meaning and significance of such statistics; assist state and local education agencies in improving their statistical systems; and review and report on education activities in foreign countries.

NCES activities are designed to address high priority education data needs; provide consistent, reliable, complete, and accurate indicators of education status and trends; and report timely, useful, and high quality data to the U.S. Department of Education, the Congress, the states, other education policymakers, practitioners, data users, and the general public.

We strive to make our products available in a variety of formats and in language that is appropriate to a variety of audiences. You, as our customer, are the best judge of our success in communicating information effectively. If you have any comments or suggestions about this or any other NCES product or report, we would like to hear from you. Please direct your comments to:

> National Center for Education Statistics
> Office of Educational Research and Improvement
> U.S. Department of Education
> 555 New Jersey Avenue NW
> Washington, DC 20208–5574

November 1996

The NCES World Wide Web Home Page is
http://www.ed.gov/NCES/

Suggested Citation

U.S. Department of Education. National Center for Education Statistics. *Digest of Education Statistics 1996,* NCES 96–133, by Thomas D. Snyder. Production Manager, Charlene M. Hoffman. Program Analyst, Claire M. Geddes. Washington, DC: 1996.

For sale by the U.S. Government Printing Office
Superintendent of Documents, Mail Stop: SSOP, Washington, DC 20402-9328
ISBN 0-16-048916-4

FOREWORD

This 1996 edition of the *Digest of Education Statistics* is the 32nd in a series of publications initiated in 1962. (The *Digest* has been issued annually except for combined editions for the years 1977–78, 1983–84, and 1985–86.) Its primary purpose is to provide a compilation of statistical information covering the broad field of American education from kindergarten through graduate school. The *Digest* includes a selection of data from many sources, both government and private, and draws especially on the results of surveys and activities carried out by the National Center for Education Statistics (NCES). The publication contains information on a variety of subjects in the field of education statistics, including the number of schools and colleges, teachers, enrollments, and graduates, in addition to educational attainment, finances, federal funds for education, employment and income of graduates, libraries, and international education. Supplemental information on population trends, attitudes on education comparisons, education characteristics of the labor force, government finances, and economic trends provides background for evaluating education data. Although the *Digest* contains important information on federal education funding, more detailed information on federal activities is available from federal education program offices. For example, the Office of Bilingual Education and Minority Languages Affairs supports the National Clearinghouse on Bilingual Education, which compiles information on students and teachers involved in bilingual education.

The *Digest* is divided into seven chapters: "All Levels of Education," "Elementary and Secondary Education," "Postsecondary Education," "Federal Programs for Education and Related Activities," "Outcomes of Education," "International Comparisons of Education," and "Learning Resources and Technology." To qualify for inclusion, material must be nationwide in scope and of current interest and value. The introduction includes a brief overview of current trends in American education, which supplements the tabular materials in chapters 1 through 7. Information on the structure of the statistical tables is contained in the "Guide to Tabular Presentation." The "Guide to Sources" provides a brief synopsis of the surveys used to generate the tabulations for the *Digest*. Also, a "Definitions" section is included to help readers understand terms.

In addition to updating many of the statistics that have appeared in previous years, this edition contains a significant amount of new material, including:

- Percent of students in grades 4, 8, and 12 at various geography proficiency levels in 1994, table 115;

- Sources of funding for state education agencies, table 158;

- Staff and student/staff ratios in institutions of higher education, by type and control of institution and state, table 219;

- Percent of public schools and school classrooms with Internet access, table 411.

Mary Frase
Acting Associate Commissioner,
Data Development and Longitudinal Studies
  Group
National Center for Education Statistics
November 1996

ACKNOWLEDGMENTS

Many people have contributed in one way or another to the development of the *Digest*. Thomas D. Snyder was responsible for the overall development and preparation of this *Digest* which was prepared under the general direction of Jeanne E. Griffith.

Charlene M. Hoffman provided technical assistance in all phases of its preparation and was responsible for Chapter 4, "Federal Programs for Education and Related Activities," and for tables on degrees conferred. Claire Geddes developed the text for chapter introductions and was responsible for materials dealing with higher education enrollment, finance, and faculty characteristics. William Sonnenberg provided statistical computing consultation on all phases of the report. Celestine Davis provided statistical assistance on materials dealing with educational attainment and student assessment. Debra Gerald and William Hussar prepared projections of school enrollment and finance statistics.

A number of individuals outside the Center also expended large amounts of time and effort on the *Digest*. Sherrie Aitken, Carla Claycomb, Peter Eisenberg, John Powell, William Scarbrough, Linda Shafer, and Patricia Thomson of CSR, Inc., provided research and statistical assistance. Robert Craig and Michelle Brown of Pinkerton Computer Consultants, Inc., provided computer support. In the Office of Media and Information Services, Robert LeGrand and Simone Miranda provided editorial assistance and Phil Carr designed the cover. Jerry Fairbanks of the U.S. Government Printing Office managed the typesetting.

This year's edition of the *Digest* has received extensive reviews by individuals within and outside the Department of Education. We wish to thank them for their time and expert advice. In the Office of Educational Research and Improvement (OERI), W. Vance Grant, Mary Frase, and Shelley Burns reviewed the entire manuscript. Rosemary Clark (U.S. Bureau of the Census) also reviewed the entire document. OERI staff who reviewed portions of the manuscript were: Susan Ahmed, Sam Barbett, Jonaki Bose, Patricia Q. Brown, Susan Broyles, Adrienne Chute, Mike Cohen, Rosa Fernandez, Debra Gerald, Arnold Goldstein, Steven Gorman, Kerry Gruber, Frank Johnson, Austin Lin, Marilyn McMillen, Frank Morgan, Jeffrey Owings, John Sietsema, Shi-Chang Wu, and Linda Zimbler. Agency reviews were conducted by the Office of Bilingual Education and Minority Languages Affairs and the Planning and Evaluation Service.

Contents

Figures

Tables

1. All Levels of Education

Enrollment, Teachers, and Schools

Enrollment Rates

Educational Attainment

2. Elementary and Secondary Education

Enrollment

Schools and School Districts

High School Seniors, Completions, and Dropouts

Educational Achievement

3–A. Postsecondary Education: College and University Education

Enrollment

Staff

Expenditures

Property

3–B. Postsecondary Education: Vocational and Adult Education

Adult Education

Vocational Education

4. Federal Programs for Education and Related Activities

5. Outcomes of Education

Educational Characteristics of the Workforce

Recent High School and College Graduates

6. International Comparisons of Education '

INTRODUCTION

In the fall of 1996, about 66.1 million persons were enrolled in American schools and colleges (table 1). About 4.0 million were employed as elementary and secondary school teachers and as college faculty. Other professional, administrative, and support staff of educational institutions numbered 4.4 million. Thus about 74 million people were involved, directly or indirectly, in providing or receiving formal education. In a nation with a population of about 265 million, more than 1 out of every 4 persons participated in formal education.

Elementary/Secondary Enrollment

Since the enrollment rates of kindergarten and elementary school age children have not changed in many years, increases in elementary school enrollment have been driven by increases in the number of young people. Enrollment in public elementary and secondary schools rose 16 percent between 1985 and 1996. The fastest growth occurred in the elementary grades, where enrollment rose 21 percent over the same period, from 27.0 million to a record high of 32.8 million in 1996 (table 2). Secondary enrollments declined 8 percent from 1985 to 1990, but then rose by 15 percent from 1990 to 1996, for a net increase of 5 percent.

Private school enrollment grew more slowly than public school enrollment over this period, rising 4 percent, from 5.6 million in 1985 to 5.8 million in 1996. As a result, the percentage of students enrolled in private schools declined from 12 percent in 1985 to 11 percent in 1996.

The National Center for Education Statistics (NCES) forecasts record levels of enrollment during the late 1990s. It is anticipated that by the year 1997, public school enrollments will surpass the previous high set in 1971 and will continue to climb into the next century. Public elementary school enrollment is expected to reach 33.2 million in 1997 and 33.9 million in 2000 (table 3). Between fall 1996 and fall 2000, public elementary enrollment is projected to grow by 3 percent, while public secondary school enrollment is expected to rise by 6 percent.

Higher Education

College enrollment rose to a record level of 14.5 million in fall 1992 and is expected to return to nearly that level in 1996, after falling slightly between 1993 and 1995 (table 3). Despite decreases in the traditional college-age population during the 1980s and early 1990s, total enrollment has remained relatively high because of the increased participation of older women students and a high rate of college attendance for recent high school graduates (tables 171 and 180). The number of part-time students has generally increased at a faster rate than full-time students (table 169).

Teachers

An estimated 3.1 million elementary and secondary school teachers will be engaged in classroom instruction in the fall of 1996 (table 4). This number has risen in recent years, up about 18 percent since 1986. The number of public school teachers in 1996 will be about 2.7 million and the number in private schools will be about 0.4 million. About 1.9 million teachers are expected to teach in elementary schools, while about 1.2 million will teach at the secondary level (table 4).

The number of public school teachers has risen at a slightly faster rate than the number of students over the past 10 years, resulting in a small decrease in the pupil/teacher ratio. The lower pupil/teacher ratio reflects the trend toward more specialized education programs. In the fall of 1996, there were 17.4 public school pupils per teacher compared with 17.7 public school pupils per teacher 10 years earlier. During the same time period, the pupil/teacher ratio in private schools fell from 15.7 to 15.1 (table 63). Despite the historical trend towards lower pupil/teacher ratios, the fluctuations since 1990 suggest stability or an increase in the pupil/teacher ratio.

The salaries of public school teachers, which lost purchasing power to inflation during the 1970s, rose faster than the inflation rate in the 1980s. The rising salaries reflect an interest by state and local education agencies in boosting teacher salary schedules and, to some extent, an increase in teachers' experience and education levels (tables 68 and 76). The value of teachers' salaries, after adjustment for inflation, rose about 6 percent between 1985–86 and 1995–96. Virtually all of this increase occurred during the mid 1980s. Since 1990–91, the average salary for teachers actually fell slightly after adjusting for inflation. The average salary for teachers in 1995–96 was $37,846 (table 76).

Public perception about problems facing the local public schools has shifted in the past several years. Between 1986 and 1990, an increasing number of people believed that drug use was a major problem, but the proportion of people with this opinion dropped to 7 percent in 1995. The most frequently cited problem in 1995 was lack of discipline (15 percent). Fighting, gangs, and violence was cited by 9 percent of the population. The lack of financial support was cited as a major problem by 11 percent of the public (table 22).

Faculty and Staff

During the fall of 1992, there were 905,000 instructional faculty and staff members teaching in higher education institutions. Making up this figure were 528,000 full-time, and 377,000 part-time instructors who varied in number of hours and students taught. Full-time instructors generally taught more hours and more students, with 61 percent teaching eight or more hours per week, and two-thirds teaching 50 or more students. About 30 percent of part-time instructors taught eight or more hours per week, and 30 percent taught 50 or more students (tables 223 and 224).

Another defining feature of college faculty is that it is disproportionately composed of white males. For full-time faculty, the percentage of white males is 58 percent, and it is slightly less than half, at 49 percent, for part-time faculty (table 227).

Student Performance

Student achievement has improved in many areas, especially for minority children in mathematics and science. Improvements for all students during the 1980 to 1992 period were more consistent in the areas of mathematics and science than in reading.

Reading

Overall, the reading achievement scores for the country's 9-, 13- and 17-year-old students are mixed. Many of the advancements in performance that had been made in earlier years among black students, as well as among 9-year-olds and 17-year-olds from disadvantaged urban communities, have not continued or have reversed. For example, while 9-year-olds in the bottom quartile of the distribution were as proficient in 1992 as those in 1971, their performance has not returned to the higher level that was obtained in 1980. Those in the 75th percentile showed no difference from the first assessment. For 13-year-olds, overall gains were seen only for students in the top and middle of the distribution, while those in the low end failed to maintain gains they had made between 1971 and 1988. At age 17, middle and lower end students had proficiencies higher in 1992 than in

1971. The average performance for the top performing students returned to the 1971 level, reflecting an increase since 1980 (tables 105 and 106).

Mathematics

Results from assessments of mathematics proficiency indicate that students have made some improvements in their skill with basic computations. However, the performance of older students on advanced mathematical operations has shown little change. The proportion of 9-year-olds who showed beginning skills and understanding rose from 70 percent in 1978 to 81 percent in 1992. The proportion of 9-year-olds demonstrating skill with numerical operations and beginning problem solving rose from 20 percent to 28 percent during the same time period (table 117).

At ages 9 and 13, significant improvement was observed between 1978 and 1992. For 17-year-old students, performance did not change between 1978 and 1982, but an upturn occurred during the following decade. For all ages, there were significant increases in average proficiency between 1982 and 1992. Sizable increases also were registered by minority students, with increases among black and Hispanics at all three age groups.

A 1992 voluntary assessment of the states found that mathematics proficiency varied widely among eighth-graders in the 44 jurisdictions (41 states, 2 territories, and the District of Columbia) that participated in the program (table 118). In 1992, student performance was significantly better than in 1990 in 17 of the jurisdictions participating in both assessments. No state experienced a significant decline in achievement.

Science

Improvements also were registered in science proficiency between 1977 and 1992. The proportion of 9-year-olds who understood simple scientific principles rose from 68 percent in 1977 to 78 percent in 1992. Also, the proportion of 9-year-olds who were able to apply basic scientific information rose. The percentage of 13-year-olds demonstrating the ability to apply basic scientific information rose from 49 to 61 percent between 1977 and 1992, but no improvement was registered at the higher levels of achievement. No significant changes occurred in the overall achievement of 17-year-olds between 1977 and 1992 with the exception of the ability to analyze scientific procedures and data. For this skill, the percentage of 17-year-old students who demonstrated success increased significantly. Black and Hispanic students at all three ages performed significantly better in 1992 than in 1977 (tables 122 and 123).

International Comparisons

On an international assessment of reading literacy, U.S. students scored in the top performing group at ages 9 and 14 (tables 401 and 402). However, in mathematics and science the results of international comparisons are less encouraging. Recent international assessments of mathematics and science have highlighted the relatively low level of achievement of U.S. students, particularly older students, compared with their peers in other countries (tables 393 to 400). In a 1991 science assessment that was administered to nationally representative groups of 9-year-olds in 10 different countries, U.S. students scored lower than Korean students but about the same as students from Taiwan, Canada, Hungary, Spain, and the former Soviet Union. In a mathematics assessment, U.S. 9-year-olds had averages that were below 5 of the 9 other countries (tables 393 and 394). The U.S. 13-year-olds placed in the middle group of countries with nationally representative science achievement data (table 399). In the mathematics assessment of 13-year-olds, the U.S. students were higher than only 1 of 14 countries (Jordan) and about the same as Slovenia and Spain. The remaining 11 countries all had average test scores that were significantly higher than the U.S. (table 396).

Graduates and Degrees

The number of high school graduates in 1994–95 totaled about 2.6 million. Approximately 2.3 million graduated from public schools and less than 0.3 million graduated from private schools. The number of high school graduates has declined from its peak in 1976–77 when 3.2 million people earned their diplomas. The dropout rate declined over this period, from 14 percent of all 16- to 24-year-olds in 1977 to 12 percent in 1995 (table 101).

The number of degrees conferred by institutions of higher education is estimated to have been at an all-time high during the 1994–95 school year: 530,000 associate degrees; 1,192,000 bachelor's degrees; 405,000 master's degrees; 77,000 first-professional degrees; and 43,000 doctor's degrees (table 239).

The Bureau of the Census has collected annual statistics on the educational attainment of the population in terms of years of school completed. These data indicate that, between 1980 and 1995, the proportion of the adult population 25 years of age and over with 4 years of high school or more rose from 69 percent to 82 percent and the proportion of adults with at least 4 years of college increased from 17 percent to 23 percent. In contrast, the proportion of young adults (25- to 29-year-olds) completing high school remained virtually unchanged, and the proportion completing college rose only slightly (table 8).

Expenditures

Expenditures for public and private education, from preprimary through graduate school, are estimated at $530 billion for 1995–96. The expenditures of elementary and secondary schools are expected to total about $318 billion for 1995–96, while those for institutions of higher education will be about $211 billion. Viewed in another context, the total expenditures for education are expected to amount to about 7.3 percent of the gross domestic product in 1995–96, about the same percentage as in the recent past (table 30).

Summary

The statistical highlights in this section of the report provide a quantitative description of the current American education scene. Clearly, from the large number of participants, the number of years that people spend in school, and the large sums expended by educational institutions, it is evident that the American people have a high regard for education. Assessment data indicate that there have been improvements in mathematics and science performance between 1982 and 1992. A higher proportion of high school graduates are going on to college. Yet, wide variations in student proficiency from state to state and mediocre scores of American students in international assessments pose challenges.

NOTE: Readers should be aware of the limitations of statistics. These limitations vary with the exact nature of a particular survey. For example, estimates based on a sample of institutions will differ somewhat from the figures that would have been obtained if a complete census had been taken using the same survey procedures. Although some of the surveys conducted by the National Center for Education Statistics are complete, census-type surveys, all surveys are subject to design, reporting, and processing errors and errors due to nonresponse. More information on survey methodologies can be found in the "Guide to Sources" in the appendix. Price indexes for inflation adjustments can be found in table 37.

CHAPTER 1
All Levels of Education

This chapter provides a broad overview of education in the United States. It brings together material from preprimary, elementary, secondary, and post-secondary education and from the general population to present a composite picture of the American educational system. Tables illustrate the total number of persons enrolled in school, the number of teachers, the number of schools, and total expenditures for education at all levels. This chapter also includes statistics on education-related topics such as educational attainment, family characteristics, population, and opinions about schools. Economic indicators and price indexes have been added to assist researchers in preparing comparative analyses.

Figure 1 shows the structure of education in the United States. It presents the three levels of education (elementary, secondary, and postsecondary) and gives the approximate age-range of persons at each level. Pupils ordinarily spend from 6 to 8 years in the elementary grades, which may be preceded by 1 or 2 years in nursery school and kindergarten. The elementary school program is followed by a 4- to 6-year program in secondary school. Pupils normally complete the entire program through grade 12 by age 17 or 18.

High school graduates who decide to continue their education may enter a technical or vocational institution, a 2-year college, or a 4-year college or university. A 2-year college normally offers the first 2 years of a standard 4-year college curriculum and a selection of terminal-vocational programs. Academic courses completed at a 2-year college are usually transferable for credit at a 4-year college or university. A technical or vocational institution offers postsecondary technical training leading to a specific career.

An associate degree requires at least 2 years of college-level work, and a bachelor's degree normally can be earned in 4 years. At least 1 year beyond the bachelor's is necessary for a master's degree, while a doctor's degree usually requires a minimum of 3 or 4 years beyond the bachelor's.

Professional schools differ widely in admission requirements and in program length. Medical students, for example, generally complete a 4-year program of premedical studies at a college or university before they can enter the 4-year program at a medical school. Law programs normally require 3 years of coursework beyond the bachelor's degree level.

Many of the statistics in this chapter are derived from the statistical activities of the National Center for Education Statistics. In addition, substantial contributions have been drawn from the work of other groups, both government and nongovernment, as shown in the source notes of the appropriate tables. Information on survey methodologies is in the "Guide to Sources" in the appendix and in the publications cited in the source notes.

Enrollment, Teachers, and Schools

Enrollment in elementary and secondary schools grew rapidly during the 1950s and 1960s and peaked in 1971 (table 3). This enrollment rise was caused by what is known as the "baby boom," a dramatic increase in births following World War II. From 1971 to 1984, total elementary and secondary school enrollment decreased every year, reflecting the decline in the school-age population over that period. After these years of decline, enrollment in elementary and secondary schools showed a small increase in the fall of 1985 (table 3).

Public school enrollment in kindergarten through grade eight rose from 27.4 million in fall 1986 to an estimated 32.8 million in fall 1996. Enrollment in the upper grades declined from 12.3 million in 1986 to 11.3 million in 1990, before showing increases in the early 1990s. The net result of these trends was an overall increase in both the secondary and elementary levels.

The increase from 1986 to 1996 was concentrated in the elementary grades, but this pattern is expected to change. The growing numbers of young pupils that have been filling the elementary schools will cause significant increases at the secondary school level during the mid-1990s. Between fall 1996 and fall 2006, public elementary enrollment is projected to grow by 2 percent, while public secondary school enrollment is expected to rise by 15 percent. Moreover, by 1997, public school enrollment is projected to surpass the previous high set in 1971 and is expected to continue to increase into the next century.

The proportion of students in private schools and colleges has changed little over the past 10 years. The percentage of private elementary and secondary students decreased slightly, from 12 percent in 1986 to 11 percent in 1996, and the percentage of college students who attended private colleges and universities remained at 22 percent. In 1996, about 5.8 million students were enrolled in private schools at the elementary and secondary levels and 3.1 million students in institutions of higher education (table 3).

College enrollment fell from 14.5 in fall 1992 to 14.3 million in fall 1994, but estimates indicate that enrollment rose slightly in 1996. Total college enrollment is expected to increase slowly during the remainder of the 1990s, as increasing numbers of high school graduates pursue higher education.

Although school attendance rates among 5- to 17-year-olds have remained relatively steady over the past 10 years, the proportion of 18- and 19-year-olds attending high school or college rose rapidly from 52 percent in 1985 to 59 percent in 1995. The proportion of 20- to 24-year-olds enrolled in school rose from 24 percent to 32 percent during the same time period (table 6).

Americans have become more educated. In 1995, 82 percent of the population 25 years old and over had completed high school and 23 percent had completed 4 or more years of college. This represents an increase from 1980, when 69 percent had completed high school and 17 percent had 4 years of college (table 8). In 1995, about 5 percent of persons, 25 years old or over, held a master's degree, slightly more than 1 percent held a professional degree (e.g., medicine or law), and 1 percent held a doctor's degree (table 9).

An estimated 3.1 million elementary and secondary school teachers were engaged in classroom instruction in the fall of 1996 (table 4). This number has risen about 18 percent since 1986. The number of public school teachers in 1996 was about 2.7 million and the number in private schools was estimated at 0.4 million. About 1.9 million teachers were teaching in elementary schools, while about 1.2 million were employed at the secondary level (table 4).

Expenditures

Education expenditures rose to an estimated high of $530 billion in the 1995–96 school year. Elementary and secondary schools spent about 60 percent of this total, and colleges and universities accounted for the remaining 40 percent (table 31). An estimated 7.3 percent of the gross domestic product was spent by elementary and secondary schools and colleges and universities in 1995–96 (table 30).

The proportion of total state and local government funds spent on education declined during the 1980s, at least partly as a result of the drop in elementary and secondary enrollment and the expansion of other governmental services. During this same time period, the proportion of federal funds spent on education rose (table 33). Of the 1991–92 state and local funds spent on education, about 70 percent went to elementary and secondary schools, 26 percent to colleges and universities, and 4 percent to other education programs (table 35).

Figure 1.—The structure of education in the United States

NOTE—Adult education programs, while not separately delineated above, may provide instruction at the elementary, secondary, or higher education level. Chart reflects typical patterns of progression rather than all possible variations.

SOURCE: U.S. Department of Education, National Center for Education Statistics.

Figure 2.-Enrollment and total expenditures in current and constant dollars, by level of education: 1960–61 to 1995–96

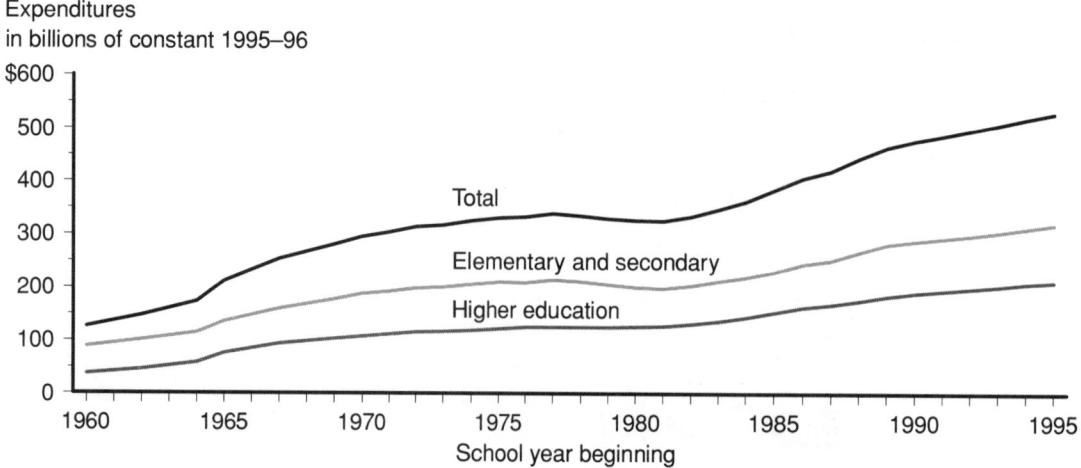

SOURCE: U.S. Department of Education, National Center for Education Statistics, *Statistics of State School Systems; Statistics of Public Elementary and Secondary School Systems; Statistics of Nonpublic Secondary Schools; Statistics of Nonpublic Elementary and Secondary Schools; Revenues and Expenditures for Public Elementary and Secondary Education; Fall Enrollment in Institutions of Higher Education; Financial Statistics of Institutions of Higher Education;* Common Core of Data surveys; and Integrated Postsecondary Education Data System surveys.

Figure 3.- Years of school completed by persons 25 years old and over: 1940 to 1995

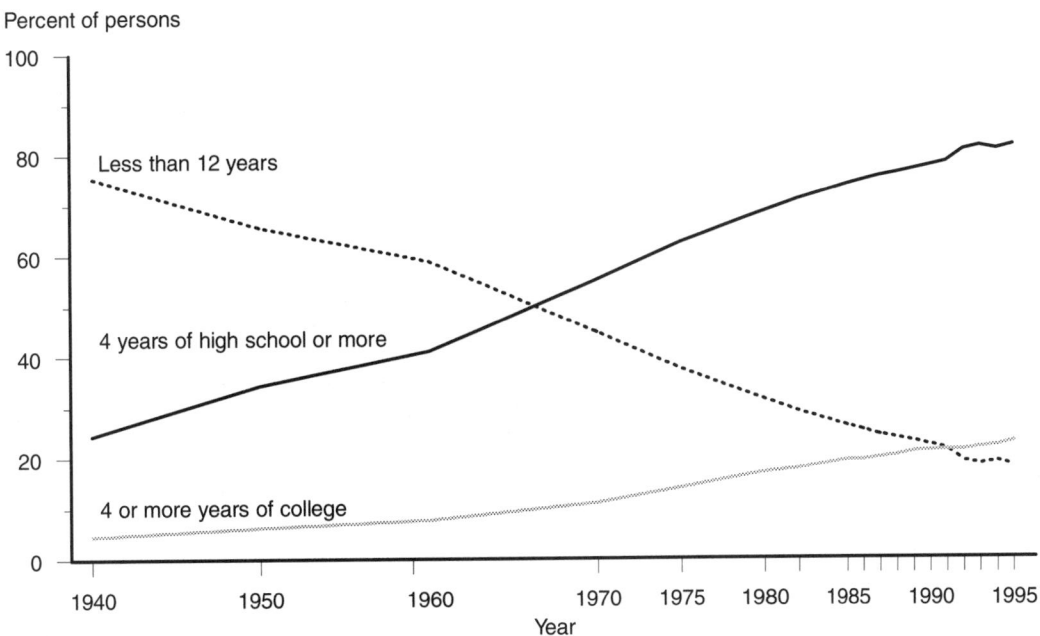

SOURCE: U.S. Department of Commerce, Bureau of the Census, *1960 Census of Population,* Vol. 1, part 1; and *Current Population Reports,* Series P-20; and Current Population Survey, unpublished data.

Figure 4.-Years of school completed by persons 25 to 29 years of age: 1940 to 1995

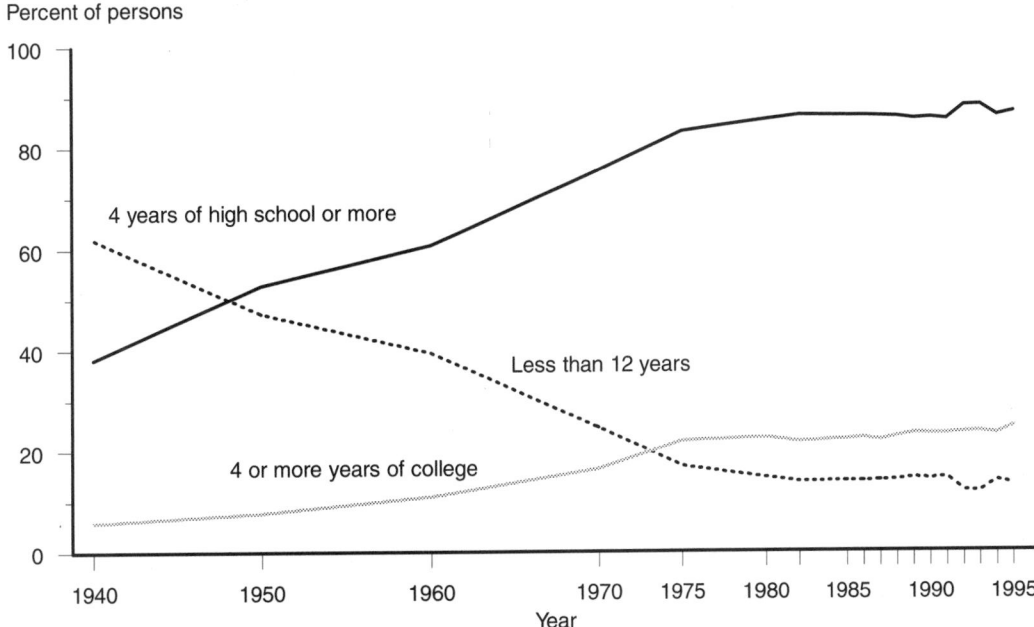

SOURCE: U.S. Department of Commerce, Bureau of the Census, *1960 Census of Population,* Vol. 1, part 1; and *Current Population Reports,* Series P-20; and Current Population Survey, unpublished data.

Figure 5.–Highest degree earned by persons 25 years old and over: March 1995

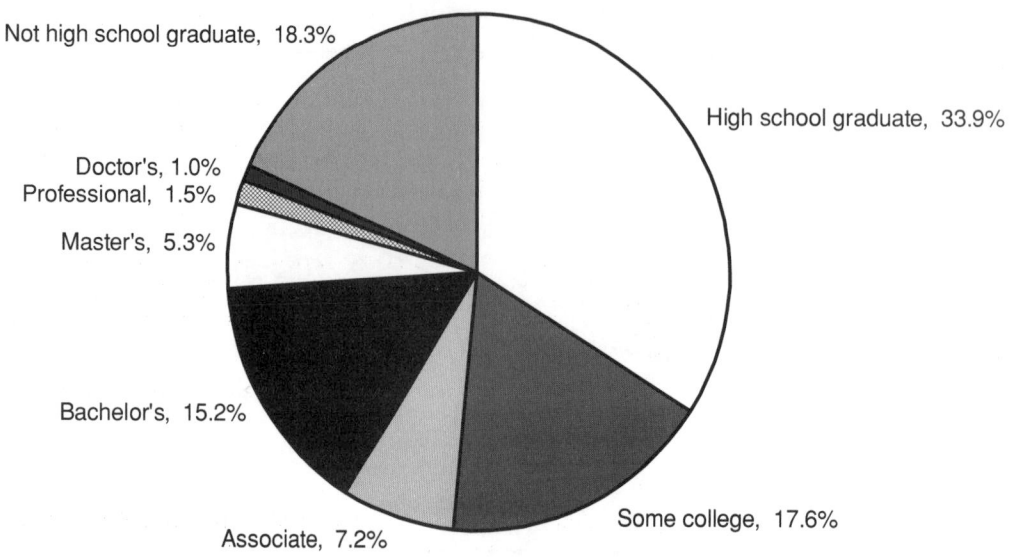

Not high school graduate, 18.3%

High school graduate, 33.9%

Doctor's, 1.0%
Professional, 1.5%

Master's, 5.3%

Bachelor's, 15.2%

Some college, 17.6%

Associate, 7.2%

Total persons age 25 and over = 166.4 million

SOURCE: U.S. Department of Commerce, Bureau of the Census, Current Population Survey, unpublished data.

Figure 6.–Items most frequently cited by the public as a major problem facing the local public schools: 1980 to 1995

Percent citing problem

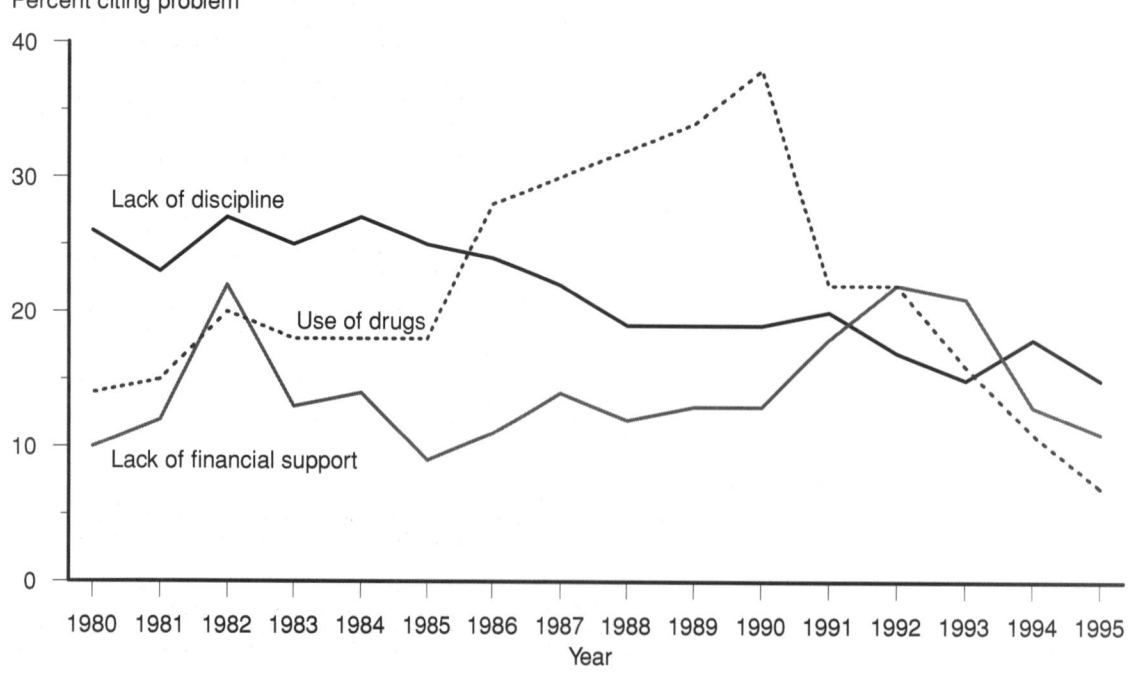

Lack of discipline

Use of drugs

Lack of financial support

Year

SOURCE: "The Annual Gallup Poll of the Public's Attitudes Toward the Public Schools," *Phi Delta Kappan*, various years.

Table 1.—Estimated number of participants in elementary and secondary education and in higher education: Fall 1996

[In millions]

Participants	All levels (elementary, secondary, and higher education)	Elementary and secondary schools			Institutions of higher education		
		Total	Public	Private	Total	Public	Private
1	2	3	4	5	6	7	8
Total	74.5	57.5	51.0	6.4	17.0	13.1	3.9
Enrollment [1]	66.1	51.7	45.9	5.8	14.4	11.3	3.1
Teachers and faculty	4.0	3.1	2.7	0.4	0.9	0.7	0.3
Other professional, administrative, and support staff	4.4	2.7	2.5	0.2	1.7	1.2	0.5

[1] Includes enrollments in local public school systems and in most private schools (religiously affiliated and nonsectarian). Excludes subcollegiate departments of institutions of higher education, residential schools for exceptional children, and federal schools. Elementary and secondary includes most kindergarten and some nursery school enrollment. Excludes preprimary enrollment in schools that do not offer first grade or above. Higher education comprises full-time and part-time students enrolled in degree-credit and nondegree-credit programs in universities, other 4-year colleges, and 2-year colleges.

NOTE.—The enrollment figures include all students in elementary and secondary schools and colleges and universities. However, the data for teachers and other staff in public and private elementary and secondary schools and colleges and universities are reported in terms of full-time equivalents. Because of rounding, details may not add to totals.

SOURCE: U.S. Department of Education, National Center for Education Statistics, unpublished projections and estimates. (This table was prepared June 1996.)

Table 2.—Enrollment in educational institutions, by level and control of institution: Fall 1980 to fall 2000

[In thousands]

Level of instruction and type of control	Fall 1980	Fall 1985	Fall 1989	Fall 1990	Fall 1991	Fall 1992	Fall 1993	Fall 1994 [1]	Fall 1995 [2]	Projected fall 1996	Projected fall 1997	Projected fall 1998	Projected fall 1999	Projected fall 2000
1	2	3	4	5	6	7	8	9	10	11	12	13	14	15
All levels	58,305	57,226	59,436	60,267	61,605	62,686	63,241	63,984	64,572	66,081	66,996	67,807	68,570	69,165
Public	50,335	48,901	51,121	52,061	53,356	54,208	54,654	55,242	55,770	57,139	57,929	58,615	59,251	59,747
Private	7,971	8,325	8,316	8,206	8,248	8,478	8,587	8,741	8,801	8,943	9,067	9,192	9,319	9,418
Elementary and secondary education [3]	46,208	44,979	45,898	46,448	47,246	48,198	48,936	49,705	50,362	51,683	52,400	52,921	53,342	53,668
Public	40,877	39,422	40,543	41,217	42,047	42,823	43,465	44,109	44,662	45,885	46,524	46,988	47,365	47,656
Private	5,331	5,557	5,355	5,232	5,199	5,375	5,471	[4] 5,596	5,700	5,798	5,876	5,933	5,977	6,012
Grades K-8 [5]	31,639	31,229	33,314	33,973	34,580	35,300	35,784	36,254	36,516	37,330	37,772	38,109	38,303	38,484
Public	27,647	27,034	29,152	29,878	30,506	31,088	31,504	31,894	32,085	32,837	33,226	33,522	33,692	33,852
Private	3,992	4,195	[4] 4,162	4,095	[4] 4,074	[4] 4,212	[4] 4,280	[4] 4,360	4,431	4,493	4,547	4,587	4,610	4,632
Grades 9–12	14,570	13,750	12,583	12,475	12,666	12,898	13,152	13,450	13,845	14,353	14,628	14,811	15,039	15,184
Public	13,231	12,388	11,390	11,338	11,541	11,735	11,961	12,214	12,576	13,049	13,299	13,466	13,673	13,804
Private	1,339	1,362	[4] 1,193	1,137	[4] 1,125	[4] 1,163	[4] 1,191	[4] 1,236	1,269	1,304	1,329	1,346	1,367	1,380
Higher education [6]	12,097	12,247	13,539	13,819	14,359	14,487	14,305	14,279	14,210	14,398	14,596	14,886	15,228	15,497
Public	9,457	9,479	10,578	10,845	11,310	11,385	11,189	11,134	11,108	11,254	11,405	11,627	11,886	12,091
Undergraduate [7]	8,442	8,477	9,488	9,710	10,148	10,216	10,012	9,945	9,884	10,016	10,159	10,368	10,603	10,797
First-professional	114	112	113	112	111	111	114	114	120	122	124	127	131	133
Graduate [8]	901	890	978	1,023	1,050	1,058	1,064	1,075	1,104	1,115	1,123	1,133	1,153	1,161
Private	2,640	2,768	2,961	2,974	3,049	3,103	3,116	3,145	3,101	3,145	3,191	3,259	3,342	3,406
Undergraduate [7]	2,033	2,120	2,255	2,250	2,291	2,321	2,312	2,317	2,286	2,320	2,360	2,419	2,483	2,539
First-professional	163	162	162	162	169	170	179	181	183	186	188	192	199	202
Graduate [8]	443	486	544	563	589	611	625	647	632	639	643	649	660	665

[1] Preliminary.

[2] Based on "Early Estimates" surveys for public elementary and secondary schools.

[3] Includes enrollments in local public school systems and in most private schools (religiously affiliated and nonsectarian). Excludes subcollegiate departments of institutions of higher education, residential schools for exceptional children, and federal schools. Excludes preprimary pupils in schools that do not offer first grade or above.

[4] Estimated.

[5] Includes kindergarten and some nursery school pupils.

[6] Includes full-time and part-time students enrolled in degree-credit and nondegree-credit programs in universities and 2-year and 4-year colleges.

[7] Includes unclassified students below the baccalaureate level.

[8] Includes unclassified postbaccalaureate students.

NOTE.—Higher education enrollment projections are based on the middle alternative projections published by the National Center for Education Statistics. Because of rounding, details may not add to totals. Some data have been revised from previously published figures.

SOURCE: U.S. Department of Education, National Center for Education Statistics, Common Core of Data and "Fall Enrollment in Institutions of Higher Education" surveys; Integrated Postsecondary Education Data System (IPEDS), "Fall Enrollment" surveys, and *Projections of Education Statistics to 2006*. (This table was prepared August 1996.)

Table 3.—Enrollment in educational institutions, by level and by control of institution: 1869–70 to fall 2006

[In thousands]

Year	Total enrollment, all levels	Elementary and secondary, total	Public elementary and secondary schools			Private elementary and secondary schools [1]			Higher education [2]		
			Total	Kinder-garten through grade 8	Grades 9 through 12	Total	Kinder-garten through grade 8	Grades 9 through 12	Total	Public	Private
1	2	3	4	5	6	7	8	9	10	11	12
1869–70	—	—	6,872	6,792	80	—	—	—	52	—	—
1879–80	—	—	9,868	9,757	110	—	—	—	116	—	—
1889–90	14,491	14,334	12,723	12,520	203	1,611	1,516	95	157	—	—
1899–1900	17,092	16,855	15,503	14,984	519	1,352	1,241	111	238	—	—
1909–10	19,728	19,372	17,814	16,899	915	1,558	1,441	117	355	—	—
1919–20	23,876	23,278	21,578	19,378	2,200	1,699	1,486	214	598	—	—
1929–30	29,430	28,329	25,678	21,279	4,399	2,651	2,310	341	1,101	—	—
1939–40	29,539	28,045	25,434	18,832	6,601	2,611	2,153	458	1,494	797	698
1949–50	31,151	28,492	25,111	19,387	5,725	3,380	2,708	672	2,659	1,355	1,304
Fall 1959	44,497	40,857	35,182	26,911	8,271	5,675	4,640	1,035	3,640	2,181	1,459
Fall 1964	52,996	47,716	41,416	30,025	11,391	[3]6,300	[3]5,000	1,300	5,280	3,468	1,812
Fall 1965	54,394	48,473	42,173	30,563	11,610	6,300	4,900	1,400	5,921	3,970	1,951
Fall 1966	55,629	49,239	43,039	31,145	11,894	[3]6,200	[3]4,800	[3]1,400	6,390	4,349	2,041
Fall 1967	56,803	49,891	43,891	31,641	12,250	[3]6,000	[3]4,600	[3]1,400	6,912	4,816	2,096
Fall 1968	58,257	50,744	44,944	32,226	12,718	5,800	4,400	1,400	7,513	5,431	2,082
Fall 1969	59,055	51,050	45,550	32,513	13,037	[3]5,500	[3]4,200	[3]1,300	8,005	5,897	2,108
Fall 1970	59,838	51,257	45,894	32,558	13,336	5,363	4,052	1,311	8,581	6,428	2,153
Fall 1971	60,220	51,271	46,071	32,318	13,753	[3]5,200	[3]3,900	[3]1,300	8,949	6,804	2,144
Fall 1972	59,941	50,726	45,726	31,879	13,848	[3]5,000	[3]3,700	[3]1,300	9,215	7,071	2,144
Fall 1973	60,047	50,445	45,445	31,401	14,044	[3]5,000	[3]3,700	[3]1,300	9,602	7,420	2,183
Fall 1974	60,297	50,073	45,073	30,971	14,103	[3]5,000	[3]3,700	[3]1,300	10,224	7,989	2,235
Fall 1975	61,004	49,819	44,819	30,515	14,304	[3]5,000	[3]3,700	[3]1,300	11,185	8,835	2,350
Fall 1976	60,490	49,478	44,311	29,997	14,314	5,167	3,825	1,342	11,012	8,653	2,359
Fall 1977	60,003	48,717	43,577	29,375	14,203	5,140	3,797	1,343	11,286	8,847	2,439
Fall 1978	58,897	47,637	42,551	28,463	14,088	5,086	3,732	1,353	11,260	8,786	2,474
Fall 1979	58,221	46,651	41,651	28,034	13,616	[3]5,000	[3]3,700	[3]1,300	11,570	9,037	2,533
Fall 1980	58,305	46,208	40,877	27,647	13,231	5,331	3,992	1,339	12,097	9,457	2,640
Fall 1981	57,916	45,544	40,044	27,280	12,764	[3]5,500	[3]4,100	[3]1,400	12,372	9,647	2,725
Fall 1982	57,591	45,166	39,566	27,161	12,405	[3]5,600	[3]4,200	[3]1,400	12,426	9,696	2,730
Fall 1983	57,432	44,967	39,252	26,981	12,271	5,715	4,315	1,400	12,465	9,683	2,782
Fall 1984	57,150	44,908	39,208	26,905	12,304	[3]5,700	[3]4,300	[3]1,400	12,242	9,477	2,765
Fall 1985	57,226	44,979	39,422	27,034	12,388	5,557	4,195	1,362	12,247	9,479	2,768
Fall 1986	57,709	45,205	39,753	27,420	12,333	[3]5,452	[3]4,116	[3]1,336	12,504	9,714	2,790
Fall 1987	58,254	45,488	40,008	27,933	12,076	5,479	4,232	1,247	12,767	9,973	2,793
Fall 1988	58,485	45,430	40,189	28,501	11,687	5,241	[3]4,036	[3]1,206	13,055	10,161	2,894
Fall 1989	59,436	45,898	40,543	29,152	11,390	5,355	[3]4,162	[3]1,193	13,539	10,578	2,961
Fall 1990	60,267	46,448	41,217	29,878	11,338	5,232	4,095	1,137	13,819	10,845	2,974
Fall 1991	61,605	47,246	42,047	30,506	11,541	5,199	[3]4,074	[3]1,125	14,359	11,310	3,049
Fall 1992	62,686	48,198	42,823	31,088	11,735	5,375	[3]4,212	[3]1,163	14,487	11,385	3,103
Fall 1993	63,241	48,936	43,465	31,504	11,961	5,471	[3]4,280	[3]1,191	14,305	11,189	3,116
Fall 1994 [4]	63,984	49,705	44,109	31,894	12,214	5,596	4,360	1,236	14,279	11,134	3,145
Fall 1995 [5]	64,572	50,362	44,662	32,085	12,576	5,700	4,431	1,269	14,210	11,108	3,101
Fall 1996 [6]	66,081	51,683	45,885	32,837	13,049	5,798	4,493	1,304	14,398	11,254	3,145
Fall 1997 [6]	66,996	52,400	46,524	33,226	13,299	5,876	4,547	1,329	14,596	11,405	3,191
Fall 1998 [6]	67,807	52,921	46,988	33,522	13,466	5,933	4,587	1,346	14,886	11,627	3,259
Fall 1999 [6]	68,570	53,342	47,365	33,692	13,673	5,977	4,610	1,367	15,228	11,886	3,342
Fall 2000 [6]	69,165	53,668	47,656	33,852	13,804	6,012	4,632	1,380	15,497	12,091	3,406
Fall 2001 [6]	69,604	53,933	47,891	34,029	13,862	6,042	4,656	1,386	15,671	12,225	3,446
Fall 2002 [6]	69,966	54,168	48,102	34,098	14,004	6,066	4,666	1,400	15,798	12,319	3,479
Fall 2003 [6]	70,244	54,312	48,234	34,065	14,169	6,078	4,661	1,416	15,932	12,420	3,512
Fall 2004 [6]	70,527	54,449	48,365	33,882	14,483	6,084	4,636	1,448	16,078	12,531	3,547
Fall 2005 [6]	70,816	54,587	48,497	33,680	14,818	6,090	4,609	1,481	16,229	12,646	3,582
Fall 2006 [6]	71,004	54,615	48,528	33,507	15,021	6,086	4,585	1,501	16,389	12,768	3,621

[1] Beginning in fall 1980, data include estimates for an expanded universe of private schools. Therefore, these totals may differ from figures shown in other tables, and direct comparisons with earlier years should be avoided.

[2] Data for 1869–70 through 1949–50 include resident degree-credit students enrolled at any time during the academic year. Beginning in 1959, data include all resident and extension students enrolled at the beginning of the fall term.

[3] Estimated.

[4] Preliminary data.

[5] Public elementary and secondary data are based on "Early Estimates" surveys. Other data are projected.

[6] Projected.

—Data not available.

NOTE.—Elementary and secondary enrollment includes pupils in local public school systems and in most private schools (religiously affiliated and nonsectarian), but generally excludes pupils in subcollegiate departments of institutions of higher education, residential schools for exceptional children, and federal schools. Elementary enrollment includes some nursery school pupils. Higher education enrollment includes students in colleges, universities, professional schools, teachers colleges, and 2-year colleges. Higher education enrollment projections are based on the middle alternative projections published by the National Center for Education Statistics. Some data have been revised from previously published figures. Because of rounding, details may not add to totals.

SOURCE: U.S. Department of Education, National Center for Education Statistics, *Statistics of State School Systems; Statistics of Public Elementary and Secondary School Systems; Statistics of Nonpublic Elementary and Secondary Schools; Projections of Education Statistics to 2006;* Common Core of Data; "Fall Enrollment in Institutions of Higher Education" surveys; and Integrated Postsecondary Education Data System (IPEDS), "Fall Enrollment" surveys. (This table was prepared August 1996.)

Table 4.—Teachers in elementary and secondary schools, and senior instructional staff in institutions of higher education, by control of institution: Fall 1970 to fall 2006

[In thousands]

Fall	All levels			Elementary and secondary teachers [1]									Higher education senior instructional staff [2]		
	Total	Public	Private	Total			Elementary teachers			Secondary teachers			Total	Public	Private
				Total	Public	Private	Total	Public	Private	Total	Public	Private			
1	2	3	4	5	6	7	8	9	10	11	12	13	14	15	16
1970	2,766	2,373	393	2,292	2,059	233	1,283	1,130	153	1,009	929	80	474	314	160
1975	3,081	2,641	440	2,453	2,198	[3]255	1,353	1,181	[3]172	1,100	1,017	[3]83	628	443	185
1980	3,171	2,679	492	2,485	2,184	301	1,401	1,189	212	1,084	995	89	[3]686	[3]495	[3]191
1981	3,145	2,636	509	2,440	2,127	[3]313	1,404	1,183	[3]221	1,037	945	[3]92	705	509	196
1982	3,168	2,639	529	2,458	2,133	[3]325	1,413	1,182	[3]231	1,045	951	[3]94	[3]710	[3]506	[3]204
1983	3,200	2,651	549	2,476	2,139	337	1,426	1,186	240	1,050	953	97	724	512	212
1984	3,225	2,673	552	2,508	2,168	[3]340	1,451	1,208	[3]243	1,057	960	[3]97	[3]717	[3]505	[3]212
1985	3,264	2,709	555	2,549	2,206	343	1,483	1,237	246	1,066	969	97	[3]715	[3]503	[3]212
1986	3,314	2,754	560	2,592	2,244	[3]348	1,521	1,271	[3]250	1,071	973	[3]98	[3]722	[3]510	[3]212
1987	3,425	2,832	593	2,632	2,279	[3]353	1,564	1,307	[3]257	1,068	973	[3]95	[4]793	[4]553	[4]240
1988	3,472	2,882	590	2,668	2,323	[3]345	1,604	1,353	[3]251	1,064	970	[3]94	[3]804	[3]559	[3]245
1989	3,558	2,934	624	2,734	2,357	[3]377	1,662	1,387	[3]275	1,072	970	[3]102	[4]824	[4]577	[4]247
1990	3,570	2,972	599	2,753	2,398	[3]355	1,680	1,426	[3]254	1,073	972	[3]101	[3]817	[3]574	[3]244
1991	3,613	3,013	600	2,787	2,432	[3]355	1,713	1,459	[3]254	1,074	973	[3]101	[4]826	[4]581	[4]245
1992	3,699	3,080	620	2,822	2,459	[3]363	1,746	1,486	[3]260	1,075	972	[3]103	[3]877	[3]621	[3]257
1993	3,785	3,154	631	2,870	2,504	[3]366	1,777	1,515	[3]262	1,093	989	[3]104	915	650	265
1994[5]	3,846	3,199	647	2,931	2,552	379	1,777	1,510	267	1,153	1,041	112	915	647	268
1995[3]	3,882	3,232	650	2,972	2,586	386	1,800	1,529	272	1,172	1,058	114	910	646	264
1996[6]	3,993	3,333	660	3,071	2,679	392	1,851	1,576	276	1,220	1,103	117	922	654	268
1997[6]	4,052	3,383	669	3,118	2,720	398	1,876	1,597	279	1,242	1,123	119	934	663	271
1998[6]	4,115	3,434	681	3,161	2,758	404	1,899	1,616	283	1,262	1,142	121	953	676	277
1999[6]	4,177	3,484	693	3,202	2,793	409	1,920	1,634	286	1,282	1,159	123	975	691	284
2000[6]	4,232	3,529	703	3,239	2,826	413	1,938	1,649	288	1,301	1,177	125	993	703	290
2001[6]	—	—	—	3,272	2,855	417	1,954	1,663	291	1,318	1,191	126	—	—	—
2002[6]	—	—	—	3,304	2,883	421	1,965	1,673	293	1,338	1,210	128	—	—	—
2003[6]	—	—	—	3,334	2,910	424	1,975	1,681	294	1,359	1,229	130	—	—	—
2004[6]	—	—	—	3,368	2,940	428	1,985	1,690	295	1,383	1,250	132	—	—	—
2005[6]	—	—	—	3,403	2,971	432	1,997	1,700	297	1,406	1,272	135	—	—	—
2006[6]	—	—	—	3,431	2,996	435	2,009	1,710	299	1,422	1,286	136	—	—	—

[1] Includes teachers in local public school systems and in most private schools (religiously affiliated and nonsectarian). Excludes subcollegiate departments of institutions of higher education, residential schools for exceptional children, and federal schools. Teachers are reported in terms of full-time equivalents.

[2] Includes full-time and part-time faculty with the rank of instructor or above in colleges, universities, professional schools, teachers colleges, and 2–year colleges. Excludes teaching assistants.

[3] Estimated.

[4] Based on actual survey data. Methodology for this year and later years is not consistent with figures for earlier years.

[5] Preliminary data.

[6] Projected.

—Data not available.

NOTE.—Because of rounding, details may not add to totals. Some data have been revised from previously published figures.

SOURCE: U.S. Department of Education, National Center for Education Statistics, Common Core of Data; *Projections of Education Statistics,* various years; Integrated Postsecondary Education Data System (IPEDS), "Staff" survey; and Equal Employment Opportunity Commission, unpublished data. (This table was prepared June 1996.)

Table 5.—Educational institutions, by level and control of institution: 1978–79 to 1994–95

Level and control of institution	1980–81	1982–83	1984–85	1986–87	1987–88	1988–89	1989–90	1990–91	1991–92	1992–93	1993–94	1994–95
1	2	3	4	5	6	7	8	9	10	11	12	13
All institutions	117,707	—	—	121,433	122,111	—	—	119,242	—	—	121,855	—
Elementary and secondary schools .	106,746	—	—	109,071	110,055	—	—	109,228	—	—	111,486	—
Elementary	72,659	—	—	74,104	76,247	—	—	74,716	—	—	75,591	—
Secondary	24,856	—	—	23,844	23,153	—	—	22,873	—	—	22,610	—
Combined	5,202	—	—	6,932	8,202	—	—	8,847	—	—	10,678	—
Other [1]	4,029	—	—	4,191	2,453	—	—	2,792	—	—	2,608	—
Public schools	85,982	84,740	84,007	83,455	83,248	83,165	83,425	84,538	84,578	84,501	85,393	86,221
Elementary	59,326	58,051	57,231	58,801	59,311	59,296	59,757	59,015	59,258	59,680	60,052	60,808
Secondary	22,619	22,383	22,320	21,406	20,758	20,550	20,359	20,406	20,120	19,995	20,059	20,282
Combined	1,743	1,605	1,596	1,983	2,179	2,235	2,280	2,325	2,481	2,549	2,674	2,764
Other [1]	2,294	2,701	2,860	1,265	1,000	1,084	1,029	2,792	2,719	2,277	2,608	2,367
Private schools	20,764	—	—	[2]25,616	26,807	—	—	24,690	25,998	—	26,093	—
Elementary	13,333	—	—	[2]15,303	16,936	—	—	15,701	15,716	—	15,539	—
Secondary	2,237	—	—	[2]2,438	2,395	—	—	2,467	2,475	—	2,551	—
Combined	3,459	—	—	[2]4,949	6,023	—	—	6,522	7,807	—	8,004	—
Other [1]	1,735	—	—	[2]2,926	1,453	—	—	(3)	(3)	—	(3)	—
Postsecondary institutions	[4]10,961	—	—	12,362	12,056	11,389	10,606	10,014	9,983	10,601	10,369	10,246
Public	[4]2,393	—	—	2,363	2,250	2,169	2,120	2,096	2,129	2,146	2,152	2,179
Private nonprofit	[4]2,359	—	—	3,432	3,254	3,092	2,942	2,808	2,810	2,926	2,890	2,916
Proprietary	[4]6,209	—	—	6,567	6,552	6,128	5,544	5,110	5,044	5,529	5,327	5,151
Noncollegiate institutions	[4]7,730	—	—	8,956	8,469	7,824	7,071	6,455	6,382	6,963	6,737	6,558
Public	[4]896	—	—	830	659	587	557	529	531	522	527	538
Private nonprofit	[4]790	—	—	1,797	1,581	1,434	1,286	1,159	1,148	1,254	1,203	1,214
Proprietary	[4]6,044	—	—	6,329	6,229	5,803	5,228	4,767	4,703	5,187	5,007	4,806
Institutions of higher education [5] ..	3,231	3,280	3,331	3,406	3,587	3,565	3,535	3,559	3,601	3,638	3,632	3,688
2–year colleges	1,274	1,296	1,306	1,336	1,452	1,436	1,408	1,418	1,444	1,469	1,442	1,473
Public	945	933	935	960	992	984	968	972	999	1,024	1,021	1,036
Private nonprofit	182	363	186	173	186	180	177	167	176	179	181	192
Proprietary	147	(6)	185	203	274	272	263	279	269	266	240	245
4-year colleges	1,957	1,984	2,025	2,070	2,135	2,129	2,127	2,141	2,157	2,169	2,190	2,215
Public	552	560	566	573	599	598	595	595	599	600	604	605
Private nonprofit	1,387	1,424	1,430	1,462	1,487	1,478	1,479	1,482	1,486	1,493	1,506	1,510
Proprietary	18	(6)	29	35	49	53	53	64	72	76	80	100

[1] Includes special education, alternative, and other schools not classified by grade span. Because of changes in survey definitions, figures for "other" schools are not comparable from year to year.

[2] Data are for 1985–86. Data were collected from a sample survey that differed significantly from earlier surveys. The sample survey was designed to correct an undercount of about 10 percent that was known to have occurred in earlier surveys.

[3] Included in other categories.

[4] Because of changes in survey procedures, figures are not directly comparable with data for later years.

[5] Includes those colleges designated as institutions of higher education by the Higher Education General Information Survey system, even if they have a less than 2–year pro-gram. Includes branch campuses. Beginning in 1980, total includes some schools accredited by the Accrediting Commission of Career Schools and Colleges of Technology.

[6] Included under "private nonprofit."

—Data not available.

SOURCE: U.S. Department of Education, National Center for Education Statistics, Common Core of Data and Private School surveys; Higher Education General Information Survey, "Institutional Characteristics of Colleges and Universities;" and Integrated Postsecondary Education Data System, "Institutional Characteristics" surveys. (This table was prepared October 1996.)

Table 6.—Percent of the population 3 to 34 years old enrolled in school,[1] by age:
April 1940 to October 1995

| Year | Total, 3 to 34 years | 3 and 4 years | 5 and 6 years | 7 to 13 years | 14 to 17 years | 18 and 19 years | 20 to 24 years | | | 25 to 29 years | 30 to 34 years |
							Total	20 and 21 years	22 to 24 years		
1	2	3	4	5	6	7	8	9	10	11	12
1940[2]	—	—	—	95.0	79.3	28.9	6.6	—	—	—	—
1945	—	—	—	98.1	78.4	20.7	3.9	—	—	—	—
1947	—	—	73.8	98.5	79.3	24.3	10.2	—	—	3.0	—
1948	—	—	74.7	98.1	81.8	26.9	9.7	—	—	2.6	—
1949	—	—	76.2	98.6	81.6	25.3	9.2	—	—	3.8	—
1950	—	—	74.4	98.7	83.7	29.4	9.0	—	—	3.0	0.9
1951	—	—	73.6	99.1	85.2	26.2	8.6	—	—	2.5	—
1952	—	—	75.2	98.8	85.2	28.8	9.7	—	—	2.6	1.2
1953	—	—	78.6	99.4	85.9	31.2	11.1	—	—	2.9	1.7
1954	—	—	77.3	99.4	87.1	32.4	11.2	—	—	4.1	1.5
1955	—	—	78.1	99.2	86.9	31.5	11.1	—	—	4.2	1.6
1956	—	—	77.6	99.3	88.2	35.4	12.8	—	—	5.1	1.9
1957	—	—	78.6	99.5	89.5	34.9	14.0	—	—	—	—
1958	—	—	80.4	99.5	89.2	37.6	13.4	—	—	—	—
1959	—	—	80.0	99.4	90.2	36.8	12.7	—	—	—	—
1960	—	—	80.7	99.5	90.3	38.4	13.1	—	—	4.9	2.4
1961	—	—	81.7	99.3	91.4	38.0	13.7	—	—	—	—
1962	—	—	82.2	99.3	92.0	41.8	15.6	—	—	—	—
1963	—	—	82.7	99.3	92.9	40.9	17.3	—	—	—	—
1964	—	—	83.3	99.0	93.1	41.6	16.8	—	—	5.2	2.6
1965	55.5	10.6	84.9	99.4	93.2	46.3	19.0	27.6	13.2	6.1	3.2
1966	56.1	12.5	85.8	99.3	93.7	47.2	19.9	29.9	13.2	6.5	2.7
1967	56.6	14.2	87.4	99.3	93.7	47.6	22.0	33.3	13.6	6.6	4.0
1968	56.7	15.7	87.6	99.1	94.2	50.4	21.4	31.2	13.8	7.0	3.9
1969	57.0	16.1	88.4	99.2	94.0	50.2	23.0	34.1	15.4	7.9	4.8
1970	56.4	20.5	89.5	99.2	94.1	47.7	21.5	31.9	14.9	7.5	4.2
1971	56.2	21.2	91.6	99.1	94.5	49.2	21.9	32.2	15.4	8.0	4.9
1972	54.9	24.4	91.9	99.2	93.3	46.3	21.6	31.4	14.8	8.6	4.6
1973	53.5	24.2	92.5	99.2	92.9	42.9	20.8	30.1	14.5	8.5	4.5
1974	53.6	28.8	94.2	99.3	92.9	43.1	21.4	30.2	15.1	9.6	5.7
1975	53.7	31.5	94.7	99.3	93.6	46.9	22.4	31.2	16.2	10.1	6.6
1976	53.1	31.3	95.5	99.2	93.7	46.2	23.3	32.0	17.1	10.0	6.0
1977	52.5	32.0	95.8	99.4	93.6	46.2	22.9	31.8	16.5	10.8	6.9
1978	51.2	34.2	95.3	99.1	93.7	45.4	21.8	29.5	16.3	9.4	6.4
1979	50.3	35.1	95.8	99.2	93.6	45.0	21.7	30.2	15.8	9.6	6.4
1980	49.7	36.7	95.7	99.3	93.4	46.4	22.3	31.0	16.3	9.3	6.4
1981	48.9	36.0	94.0	99.2	94.1	49.0	22.5	31.6	16.5	9.0	6.9
1982	48.6	36.4	95.0	99.2	94.4	47.8	23.5	34.0	16.8	9.6	6.3
1983	48.4	37.5	95.4	99.2	95.0	50.4	22.7	32.5	16.6	9.6	6.4
1984	47.9	36.3	94.5	99.2	94.7	50.1	23.7	33.9	17.3	9.1	6.3
1985	48.3	38.9	96.1	99.2	94.9	51.6	24.0	35.3	16.9	9.2	6.1
1986	48.2	38.9	95.3	99.2	94.9	54.6	23.6	33.0	17.9	8.8	6.0
1987	48.6	38.3	95.1	99.5	95.0	55.6	25.5	38.7	17.5	9.0	5.8
1988	48.7	38.2	96.0	99.7	95.1	55.6	26.1	39.1	18.2	8.3	5.9
1989	49.1	39.1	95.2	99.3	95.7	56.0	27.0	38.5	19.9	9.3	5.7
1990	50.2	44.4	96.5	99.6	95.8	57.2	28.6	39.7	21.0	9.7	5.8
1991	50.7	40.5	95.4	99.6	96.0	59.6	30.2	42.0	22.2	10.2	6.2
1992	51.4	39.7	95.5	99.4	96.7	61.4	31.6	44.0	23.7	9.8	6.1
1993	51.8	40.4	95.4	99.5	96.5	61.6	30.8	42.7	23.6	10.2	5.9
1994[3]	53.3	[4]47.3	96.7	99.4	96.6	60.2	32.0	44.9	24.0	10.8	6.7
1995	53.7	[4]48.7	96.0	98.9	96.3	59.4	31.5	44.9	23.2	11.6	5.9

[1] Includes enrollment in any type of graded public, parochial, or other private schools. Includes nursery schools, kindergartens, elementary schools, high schools, colleges, universities, and professional schools. Attendance may be on either a full-time or part-time basis and during the day or night. Enrollments in "special" schools, such as trade schools, business colleges, or correspondence schools, are not included.
[2] Data are as of April 1940. Data for all other years are as of October.
[3] Revised from previously published figures.
[4] Preprimary enrollment collected using new procedures. May not be comparable to figures for earlier years.

—Data not available.

NOTE.—Data are based upon sample surveys of the civilian noninstitutional population.

SOURCE: U.S. Department of Commerce, Bureau of the Census, *Historical Statistics of the United States, Colonial Times to 1970; Current Population Reports,* Series P-20, various years; and Current Population Survey, unpublished data. (This table was prepared August 1996.)

Table 7.—Percent of the population 3 to 34 years old enrolled in school, [1] by race/ethnicity, sex, and age: October 1975 to October 1995

Year and age	Total				Male				Female			
	All races	White, non-Hispanic	Black, non-Hispanic	Hispanic origin	All races	White, non-Hispanic	Black, non-Hispanic	Hispanic origin	All races	White, non-Hispanic	Black, non-Hispanic	Hispanic origin
1	2	3	4	5	6	7	8	9	10	11	12	13
1975												
Total, 3 to 34 years	53.7	53.0	57.7	54.8	56.1	55.2	60.4	58.1	51.5	50.8	55.3	51.7
3 and 4 years	31.5	31.0	34.4	27.3	30.9	31.1	31.4	26.7	32.1	30.9	37.5	27.9
5 and 6 years	94.7	95.1	94.4	92.1	94.4	94.8	94.8	89.7	95.1	95.4	94.0	94.4
7 to 9 years	99.3	99.4	99.3	99.6	99.2	99.2	99.4	99.6	99.5	99.6	99.2	99.5
10 to 13 years	99.3	99.3	99.1	99.2	98.9	99.0	98.9	98.8	99.6	99.6	99.3	99.7
14 and 15 years	98.2	98.5	97.4	95.6	98.4	98.6	97.6	97.4	98.0	98.4	97.2	93.8
16 and 17 years	89.0	89.5	86.8	86.2	90.7	91.2	88.1	88.3	87.2	87.8	85.5	84.0
18 and 19 years	46.9	46.8	46.9	44.0	49.9	49.4	49.6	51.9	44.2	44.2	44.6	37.1
20 and 21 years	31.2	32.1	26.7	27.5	35.3	36.7	28.4	31.3	27.4	27.8	25.3	24.3
22 to 24 years	16.2	16.4	13.9	14.1	20.0	20.8	14.5	15.9	12.6	12.2	13.4	12.5
25 to 29 years	10.1	10.1	9.4	8.3	13.1	13.2	11.6	11.9	7.2	7.2	7.6	5.3
30 to 34 years	6.6	6.6	7.1	5.5	7.7	7.5	8.7	7.2	5.6	5.8	5.9	4.1
1980												
Total, 3 to 34 years	49.7	48.8	54.0	49.8	50.9	50.0	56.2	49.9	48.5	47.7	52.1	49.8
3 and 4 years	36.7	37.4	38.2	28.5	37.8	39.2	36.4	30.1	35.5	35.5	40.0	26.6
5 and 6 years	95.7	95.9	95.5	94.5	95.0	95.4	94.1	94.0	96.4	96.5	97.0	94.9
7 to 9 years	99.1	99.1	99.4	98.4	99.0	99.0	99.5	97.7	99.2	99.2	99.3	99.0
10 to 13 years	99.4	99.4	99.4	99.7	99.4	99.4	99.4	99.4	99.4	99.3	99.3	99.9
14 and 15 years	98.2	98.7	97.9	94.3	98.7	98.9	98.4	96.7	97.7	98.5	97.3	92.1
16 and 17 years	89.0	89.2	90.7	81.8	89.1	89.4	90.7	81.5	88.8	89.0	90.6	82.2
18 and 19 years	46.4	47.0	45.8	37.8	47.0	48.5	42.9	36.9	45.8	45.7	48.3	38.8
20 and 21 years	31.0	33.0	23.3	19.5	32.6	34.8	22.8	21.4	29.5	31.3	23.7	17.6
22 to 24 years	16.3	16.8	13.6	11.7	17.8	18.7	13.4	10.7	14.9	15.0	13.7	12.6
25 to 29 years	9.3	9.4	8.8	6.9	9.8	9.8	10.6	6.8	8.8	9.1	7.5	6.9
30 to 34 years	6.4	6.4	6.9	5.1	5.9	5.6	7.2	6.2	7.0	7.2	6.6	4.1
1985												
Total, 3 to 34 years	48.3	47.8	50.8	47.7	49.2	48.7	52.6	47.5	47.4	46.9	49.2	47.9
3 and 4 years	38.9	40.3	42.8	27.0	36.7	39.1	34.6	26.4	41.2	41.6	50.3	27.7
5 and 6 years	96.1	96.6	95.7	94.5	95.3	95.6	94.5	95.3	97.0	97.6	97.1	93.7
7 to 9 years	99.1	99.4	98.6	98.4	99.0	99.3	98.4	98.9	99.2	99.4	98.9	98.0
10 to 13 years	99.3	99.3	99.5	99.4	99.2	99.2	99.1	99.1	99.4	99.3	99.9	99.7
14 and 15 years	98.1	98.3	98.1	96.1	98.3	98.4	98.5	96.2	97.9	98.1	97.6	96.0
16 and 17 years	91.7	92.5	91.8	84.5	92.4	92.9	92.0	88.9	90.9	92.2	91.6	80.0
18 and 19 years	51.6	53.7	43.5	41.8	52.2	53.4	49.4	38.6	51.0	54.0	37.8	44.7
20 and 21 years	35.3	37.2	27.7	24.0	36.5	38.8	29.9	20.3	34.1	35.7	25.8	27.4
22 to 24 years	16.9	17.5	13.8	11.6	18.8	19.8	13.5	12.6	15.1	15.4	14.0	10.4
25 to 29 years	9.2	9.6	7.4	6.6	9.4	9.7	5.8	8.2	9.1	9.4	8.7	4.9
30 to 34 years	6.1	6.2	5.2	5.7	5.4	5.6	3.9	4.0	6.8	6.9	6.2	7.5
1990												
Total, 3 to 34 years	50.2	49.8	52.2	47.2	50.9	50.4	54.3	46.8	49.5	49.2	50.3	47.7
3 and 4 years	44.4	47.2	41.8	30.7	43.9	47.9	38.1	28.0	44.9	46.6	45.5	33.6
5 and 6 years	96.5	96.7	96.5	94.9	96.5	96.8	96.2	95.8	96.4	96.7	96.9	93.9
7 to 9 years	99.7	99.7	99.8	99.5	99.7	99.7	99.9	99.5	99.6	99.7	99.8	99.4
10 to 13 years	99.6	99.7	99.9	99.1	99.6	99.6	99.9	99.0	99.7	99.7	99.8	99.1
14 and 15 years	99.0	99.0	99.4	99.0	99.1	99.2	99.7	99.1	98.9	98.9	99.1	98.8
16 and 17 years	92.5	93.5	91.7	85.4	92.6	93.4	93.0	85.5	92.4	93.7	90.5	85.3
18 and 19 years	57.2	59.1	55.0	44.0	58.2	59.7	60.4	40.7	56.3	58.5	49.8	47.2
20 and 21 years	39.7	43.1	28.3	27.2	40.3	44.2	31.0	21.7	39.2	42.0	25.8	33.1
22 to 24 years	21.0	21.9	19.7	9.9	22.3	23.7	19.3	11.2	19.9	20.3	20.0	8.4
25 to 29 years	9.7	10.4	6.1	6.3	9.2	10.0	4.7	4.6	10.2	10.7	7.3	8.1
30 to 34 years	5.8	6.2	4.5	3.6	4.8	5.0	2.3	4.0	6.9	7.4	6.3	3.1
1995												
Total, 3 to 34 years	53.7	53.8	56.3	49.7	54.3	54.2	58.6	49.1	53.2	53.4	54.1	50.3
3 and 4 years [2]	48.7	52.2	47.8	36.9	49.4	51.1	52.4	40.8	48.1	53.5	43.4	32.7
5 and 6 years	96.0	96.6	95.4	93.9	95.3	95.9	94.6	93.6	96.8	97.4	96.3	94.3
7 to 9 years	98.7	98.9	97.7	98.5	98.9	99.0	98.1	98.8	98.5	98.9	97.2	98.2
10 to 13 years	99.1	99.0	99.2	99.2	99.1	99.0	99.5	98.8	99.0	98.9	98.9	99.5
14 and 15 years	98.9	98.8	99.0	98.9	99.0	98.9	99.6	98.4	98.8	98.7	98.3	99.4
16 and 17 years	93.6	94.4	93.0	88.2	94.5	95.0	95.6	88.4	92.6	93.8	90.3	88.0
18 and 19 years	59.4	61.8	57.5	46.1	59.5	61.9	59.2	47.4	59.2	61.8	56.1	44.8
20 and 21 years	44.9	49.7	37.8	27.1	44.7	50.0	36.7	24.8	45.1	49.3	38.7	29.2
22 to 24 years	23.2	24.4	20.0	15.6	22.8	24.1	20.6	14.8	23.6	24.8	19.5	16.6
25 to 29 years	11.6	12.3	10.0	7.1	11.0	12.2	6.3	5.6	12.2	12.3	13.0	8.7
30 to 34 years	5.9	5.7	7.7	4.7	5.4	5.0	6.9	4.5	6.5	6.3	8.3	4.9

[1] Includes enrollment in any type of graded public, parochial, or other private schools. Includes nursery schools, kindergartens, elementary schools, high schools, colleges, universities, and professional schools. Attendance may be on either a full-time or part-time basis and during the day or night. Enrollments in "special" schools, such as trade schools, business colleges, or correspondence schools, are not included.

[2] Preprimary enrollment collected using new procedures. May not be comparable to figures for earlier years.

NOTE.—Data are based upon sample surveys of the civilian noninstitutional population.

SOURCE: U.S. Department of Commerce, Bureau of the Census, Current Population Survey, unpublished data. (This table was prepared August 1996.)

Table 8.—Years of school completed by persons age 25 and over and 25 to 29, by race and sex: 1910 to 1995

Age and year	All races				White [1]				Black and other races [1]			
	Percent, by years of school completed			Median years of school completed	Percent, by years of school completed			Median years of school completed	Percent, by years of school completed			Median years of school completed
	Less than 5 years of elementary school	4 years of high school or more	4 or more years of college		Less than 5 years of elementary school	4 years of high school or more	4 or more years of college		Less than 5 years of elementary school	4 years of high school or more	4 or more years of college	
1	2	3	4	5	6	7	8	9	10	11	12	13
Males and females												
25 and over												
1910 [2]	23.8	13.5	2.7	8.1	—	—	—	—	—	—	—	—
1920 [2]	22.0	16.4	3.3	8.2	—	—	—	—	—	—	—	—
1930 [2]	17.5	19.1	3.9	8.4	—	—	—	—	—	—	—	—
April 1940	13.7	24.5	4.6	8.6	10.9	26.1	4.9	8.7	41.8	7.7	1.3	5.7
April 1950	11.1	34.3	6.2	9.3	8.9	36.4	6.6	9.7	32.6	13.7	2.2	6.9
April 1960	8.3	41.1	7.7	10.5	6.7	43.2	8.1	10.8	23.5	21.7	3.5	8.2
March 1970	5.3	55.2	11.0	12.2	4.2	57.4	11.6	12.2	14.7	36.1	6.1	10.1
March 1975	4.2	62.5	13.9	12.3	3.3	64.5	14.5	12.4	11.7	46.4	9.2	11.4
March 1980	3.4	68.6	17.0	12.5	2.6	70.5	17.8	12.5	8.8	54.6	11.1	12.2
March 1982	3.0	71.0	17.7	12.6	2.4	72.8	18.5	12.6	7.4	58.1	12.4	12.3
March 1985	2.7	73.9	19.4	12.6	2.2	75.5	20.0	12.7	6.0	63.2	15.4	12.4
March 1986	2.7	74.7	19.4	12.6	2.2	76.2	20.1	12.7	5.5	65.3	15.2	12.4
March 1987	2.4	75.6	19.9	12.7	2.0	77.0	20.5	12.7	5.1	66.7	15.7	12.4
March 1988	2.4	76.2	20.3	12.7	2.0	77.7	20.9	12.7	5.1	66.7	16.4	12.5
March 1989	2.5	76.9	21.1	12.7	2.0	78.4	21.8	12.7	5.6	67.3	16.9	12.5
March 1990	2.4	77.6	21.3	12.7	2.0	79.1	22.0	12.7	5.4	68.7	16.5	12.5
March 1991	2.4	78.4	21.4	12.7	2.0	79.9	22.2	12.8	5.0	69.6	16.7	12.5
March 1992	2.8	80.8	21.4	12.8	1.8	82.2	22.1	12.9	4.1	72.9	17.2	12.6
March 1993	2.1	81.5	21.9	12.9	1.7	82.7	22.6	12.9	4.1	74.7	17.7	12.7
March 1994	1.9	80.9	22.2	—	1.7	82.0	22.9	—	3.3	74.5	18.1	—
March 1995	1.8	81.7	23.0	—	1.6	83.0	24.0	—	3.3	74.2	17.4	—
25 to 29												
1920 [2]	—	—	—	—	12.9	22.0	4.5	8.5	44.6	6.3	1.2	5.4
April 1940	5.9	38.1	5.9	10.3	3.4	41.2	6.4	10.7	27.0	12.3	1.6	7.1
April 1950	4.6	52.8	7.7	12.1	3.3	56.3	8.2	12.2	16.1	23.6	2.8	8.7
April 1960	2.8	60.7	11.0	12.3	2.2	63.7	11.8	12.3	7.2	38.6	5.4	10.8
March 1970	1.1	75.4	16.4	12.6	0.9	77.8	17.3	12.6	2.2	58.4	10.0	12.2
March 1975	1.0	83.1	21.9	12.8	1.0	84.4	22.8	12.8	0.7	73.8	15.4	12.6
March 1980	0.8	85.4	22.5	12.9	0.8	86.9	23.7	12.9	1.0	77.0	15.2	12.7
March 1982	0.8	86.2	21.7	12.8	0.8	86.9	22.7	12.9	0.7	82.2	15.8	12.8
March 1985	0.7	86.1	22.2	12.9	0.8	86.8	23.2	12.9	0.5	82.4	16.7	12.8
March 1986	0.9	86.1	22.4	12.9	0.9	86.5	23.5	12.9	0.9	84.3	16.3	12.8
March 1987	0.9	86.0	22.0	12.8	0.8	86.3	23.0	12.9	1.1	84.1	16.9	12.8
March 1988	1.0	85.9	22.7	12.8	1.0	86.6	23.5	12.9	1.2	82.0	18.1	12.6
March 1989	1.0	85.5	23.4	12.9	0.9	86.0	24.4	12.9	1.2	83.1	18.1	12.8
March 1990	1.2	85.7	23.2	12.9	1.2	86.3	24.2	12.9	1.1	82.5	18.2	12.8
March 1991	1.0	85.4	23.2	12.9	1.0	85.8	24.6	12.9	0.6	83.1	16.4	12.8
March 1992	0.9	88.1	23.6	13.0	0.9	88.5	25.0	13.0	0.9	85.7	16.9	12.8
March 1993	0.7	88.2	23.7	13.0	0.7	88.5	24.7	13.0	0.5	87.0	18.7	12.9
March 1994	0.8	86.1	23.3	—	0.8	86.5	24.2	—	0.9	84.2	19.1	—
March 1995	0.9	86.8	24.7	—	1.0	87.4	26.0	—	0.8	84.6	19.4	—
Males												
25 and over												
April 1940	15.1	22.7	5.5	8.6	12.0	24.2	5.9	8.7	46.2	6.9	1.4	5.4
April 1950	12.2	32.6	7.3	9.0	9.8	34.6	7.9	9.3	36.9	12.6	2.1	6.4
April 1960	9.4	39.5	9.7	10.3	7.4	41.6	10.3	10.6	27.7	20.0	3.5	7.9
March 1970	5.9	55.0	14.1	12.2	4.5	57.2	15.0	12.2	17.9	35.4	6.8	9.9
March 1980	3.6	69.2	20.9	12.6	2.7	71.0	22.1	12.6	10.3	55.3	11.9	12.2
March 1990	2.7	77.7	24.4	12.8	2.2	79.1	25.3	12.8	5.9	69.1	18.3	12.6
March 1991	2.7	78.5	24.3	12.8	2.2	79.8	25.4	12.8	6.0	70.1	17.8	12.6
March 1992	2.3	81.0	24.3	12.9	1.9	82.3	25.2	12.9	4.5	73.0	18.8	12.6
March 1993	2.2	81.8	24.8	12.9	1.8	83.0	25.7	13.0	4.7	74.9	19.0	12.7
March 1994	2.1	81.0	25.1	—	1.8	82.1	26.1	—	4.0	74.5	19.0	—
March 1995	2.0	81.7	26.0	—	1.7	83.0	27.2	—	3.9	74.3	18.6	—
Females												
25 and over												
April 1940	12.4	26.3	3.8	8.7	9.8	28.1	4.0	8.8	37.5	8.4	1.2	6.1
April 1950	10.0	36.0	5.2	9.6	8.1	38.2	5.4	10.0	28.6	14.7	2.4	7.2
April 1960	7.4	42.5	5.8	10.7	6.0	44.7	6.0	11.0	19.7	23.1	3.6	8.5
March 1970	4.7	55.4	8.2	12.1	3.9	57.7	8.6	12.2	11.9	36.6	5.6	10.3
March 1980	3.2	68.1	13.6	12.4	2.5	70.1	14.0	12.5	7.6	54.1	10.4	12.1
March 1990	2.2	77.5	18.4	12.7	1.8	79.0	19.0	12.7	5.0	68.4	15.1	12.5
March 1991	2.1	78.3	18.8	12.7	1.8	79.9	19.3	12.7	4.1	69.1	15.8	12.5
March 1992	2.0	80.6	18.6	12.8	1.7	82.0	19.1	12.8	3.8	72.9	15.9	12.6
March 1993	2.0	81.3	19.2	12.8	1.7	82.5	19.7	12.8	3.5	74.5	16.5	12.7
March 1994	1.7	80.7	19.6	—	1.5	81.9	20.0	—	2.8	74.6	17.4	—
March 1995	1.7	81.6	20.2	—	1.5	83.0	21.0	—	2.8	74.2	16.3	—

[1] Persons of Hispanic origin are included, as appropriate, in the "white" or in the "black and other races" category.

[2] Estimates based on retrojection, by the Bureau of the Census, of 1940 census data on education by age.

—Data not available.

NOTE.—Data for 1975 and subsequent years are for the noninstitutional population.

SOURCE: U.S. Department of Commerce, Bureau of the Census, U.S. Census of Population, 1960, Vol. 1, part 1; Current Population Reports, Series P-20; Series P-19, No. 4; 1960 Census Monograph, "Education of the American Population," by John K. Folger and Charles B. Nam; and unpublished data from the Current Population Survey; and U.S. Department of Labor, Bureau of Labor Statistics, Office of Employment and Unemployment Statistics, "Educational Attainment of Workers, March 1991," and unpublished data. (This table was prepared June 1996.)

Table 9.—Highest level of education attained by persons age 18 and over, by age, sex, and race/ethnicity: 1995

[In thousands]

Age, sex, and race	Total population [1]	Elementary level		High school			College					
		Less than 7 years	7 or 8 years	1 to 3 years	4 years	Grad-uate	Some college	Associ-ate	Bach-elor's	Master's	First-profes-sional	Doctor-ate
1	2	3	4	5	6	7	8	9	10	11	12	13
Total												
18 and over	191,596	7,156	7,639	19,025	2,426	64,228	38,014	12,927	27,189	8,887	2,432	1,673
18 and 19 years old	7,016	72	118	2,530	384	2,034	1,858	17	2	—	—	—
20 to 24 years old	18,142	390	267	1,645	327	5,744	6,801	1,015	1,874	70	4	5
25 years old and over	166,438	6,694	7,253	14,850	1,715	56,450	29,355	11,894	25,313	8,817	2,428	1,668
25 to 29 years old	19,400	494	299	1,528	229	6,361	4,083	1,617	3,910	649	175	55
30 to 34 years old	21,988	560	304	1,697	213	7,700	4,012	1,947	4,150	978	296	129
35 to 39 years old	22,241	559	312	1,529	192	7,683	4,305	1,985	3,882	1,182	393	218
40 to 49 years old	37,411	1,017	714	2,343	334	11,804	7,116	3,261	6,618	2,938	753	513
50 to 59 years old	24,220	902	973	2,230	235	8,662	4,144	1,506	3,182	1,650	362	375
60 to 64 years old	9,911	586	662	1,186	105	3,666	1,447	496	1,004	472	152	136
65 years old and over	31,267	2,575	3,989	4,336	406	10,575	4,249	1,083	2,566	948	298	242
Men												
18 and over	92,008	3,742	3,554	9,036	1,283	29,491	17,890	5,575	13,909	4,620	1,713	1,195
18 and 19 years old	3,522	44	51	1,353	242	1,028	798	4	2	—	—	—
20 to 24 years old	9,023	241	132	857	175	3,084	3,297	432	775	29	—	—
25 years old and over	79,463	3,458	3,371	6,826	866	25,378	13,795	5,138	13,132	4,591	1,713	1,195
25 to 29 years old	9,689	276	163	770	117	3,296	1,959	737	1,893	342	96	41
30 to 34 years old	10,900	355	143	906	138	3,880	1,865	812	2,042	507	175	78
35 to 39 years old	11,041	299	177	747	123	3,907	2,014	841	1,926	616	249	142
40 to 49 years old	18,435	547	403	1,178	167	5,286	3,454	1,479	3,569	1,461	548	344
50 to 59 years old	11,681	477	487	1,019	97	3,723	1,917	717	1,792	897	277	277
60 to 64 years old	4,714	322	325	493	50	1,487	700	213	599	274	129	122
65 years old and over	13,003	1,181	1,674	1,714	173	3,799	1,886	340	1,311	494	240	192
Women												
18 and over	99,588	3,414	4,085	9,989	1,143	34,738	20,124	7,352	13,280	4,267	719	478
18 and 19 years old	3,494	29	67	1,176	143	1,006	1,059	13	—	—	—	—
20 to 24 years old	9,119	149	136	788	151	2,660	3,504	583	1,099	40	4	5
25 years old and over	86,975	3,236	3,882	8,025	850	31,072	15,561	6,756	12,181	4,226	715	472
25 to 29 years old	9,712	218	136	759	112	3,065	2,123	880	2,017	308	79	14
30 to 34 years old	11,088	205	162	791	75	3,820	2,148	1,135	2,108	471	122	51
35 to 39 years old	11,200	260	135	783	69	3,776	2,290	1,144	1,956	566	144	77
40 to 49 years old	18,976	470	311	1,165	167	6,518	3,663	1,782	3,049	1,476	205	169
50 to 59 years old	12,538	425	486	1,211	137	4,938	2,227	789	1,390	753	85	98
60 to 64 years old	5,198	264	337	693	55	2,179	748	283	405	198	23	14
65 years old and over	18,264	1,394	2,315	2,622	234	6,776	2,363	743	1,255	454	58	50
White, non-Hispanic												
18 and over	145,875	2,103	5,348	12,295	1,391	50,157	29,750	10,510	23,031	7,780	2,102	1,408
18 and 19 years old	4,763	7	68	1,553	208	1,450	1,469	7	2	—	—	—
20 to 24 years old	12,406	39	121	818	134	3,958	4,903	788	1,582	58	4	2
25 years old and over	128,707	2,057	5,159	9,924	1,050	44,749	23,378	9,716	21,447	7,722	2,098	1,406
25 to 29 years old	13,416	54	109	746	100	4,387	2,885	1,268	3,156	533	137	41
30 to 34 years old	15,807	43	133	945	92	5,595	2,918	1,470	3,424	829	245	112
35 to 39 years old	16,514	74	166	945	113	5,689	3,220	1,575	3,229	1,005	334	165
40 to 49 years old	28,881	202	385	1,337	174	9,171	5,629	2,711	5,601	2,604	656	410
50 to 59 years old	19,312	240	601	1,534	156	7,165	3,511	1,254	2,736	1,461	317	338
60 to 64 years old	8,093	214	470	866	77	3,158	1,287	425	902	430	140	124
65 years old and over	26,684	1,231	3,296	3,551	337	9,584	3,928	1,011	2,399	860	270	216
Black, non-Hispanic												
18 and over	21,807	917	888	3,498	476	7,826	4,395	1,248	1,889	501	84	85
18 and 19 years old	1,056	4	6	481	77	306	178	5	—	—	—	—
20 to 24 years old	2,541	15	23	326	82	920	939	98	137	1	—	—
25 years old and over	18,210	898	859	2,692	317	6,600	3,278	1,146	1,752	500	84	85
25 to 29 years old	2,606	5	6	295	39	1,086	589	184	355	32	15	—
30 to 34 years old	2,779	22	23	331	56	1,134	564	259	336	47	5	2
35 to 39 years old	2,738	33	32	280	20	1,165	597	204	294	67	28	18
40 to 49 years old	4,194	70	103	594	97	1,450	905	308	437	179	22	28
50 to 59 years old	2,434	96	175	412	52	893	351	125	203	106	5	17
60 to 64 years old	932	107	92	215	15	304	85	36	54	16	2	6
65 years old and over	2,528	565	427	565	38	569	188	30	72	54	6	15
Hispanic												
18 and over	17,619	3,723	1,260	2,740	463	4,678	2,616	753	995	237	103	50
18 and 19 years old	970	61	41	408	79	227	149	5	—	—	—	—
20 to 24 years old	2,479	324	122	452	92	724	598	94	69	2	—	3
25 years old and over	14,171	3,338	1,097	1,881	292	3,728	1,869	654	927	235	103	47
25 to 29 years old	2,600	411	170	450	83	738	409	107	189	34	7	1
30 to 34 years old	2,616	471	146	391	58	746	389	146	208	37	19	4
35 to 39 years old	2,168	405	109	262	56	631	356	127	151	42	18	11
40 to 49 years old	2,959	673	203	323	48	834	402	159	201	64	31	21
50 to 59 years old	1,738	520	167	216	23	388	202	76	103	32	10	2
60 to 64 years old	661	236	91	83	8	133	51	13	28	12	4	2
65 years old and over	1,428	622	212	155	16	257	59	26	46	15	14	6

[1] Civilian noninstitutional population.
—Data not applicable or not available.

NOTE.—Data are based on a sample survey of the noninstitutional population. Although cells with fewer than 75,000 people are subject to relatively wide sampling vari-ation, they are included in the table to permit various types of aggregations. Because of rounding, details may not add to totals.

SOURCE: U.S. Department of Commerce, Bureau of the Census, Current Population Survey, unpublished data. (This table was prepared June 1996.)

Table 10.—Number of persons age 18 and over who hold a bachelor's or higher degree, by field of study, sex, race, and age: Spring 1993

[Numbers in thousands]

Field of study	Total	Sex		Race		Age					
		Men	Women	White [1]	Black [1]	18 to 24 years old	25 to 34 years old	35 to 44 years old	45 to 54 years old	55 to 64 years old	65 years old and over
1	2	3	4	5	6	7	8	9	10	11	12
Total population, 18 and over	188,683	90,555	98,128	159,940	21,391	25,507	42,162	41,094	28,657	20,524	30,739
Number of persons with bachelor's or higher degree	36,786	19,352	17,436	32,280	2,314	2,456	9,635	10,691	6,869	3,470	3,664
Percent of population	19.5	21.4	17.8	20.2	10.8	9.6	22.9	26.0	24.0	16.9	11.9
Agriculture and forestry	543	437	107	517	11	39	94	198	103	56	53
Biology	827	525	302	674	59	102	190	283	156	65	30
Business and management	6,739	4,524	2,215	5,947	458	472	2,091	1,839	1,250	595	490
Economics	815	551	263	695	42	58	236	213	144	96	67
Education	6,078	1,482	4,597	5,493	409	268	965	1,764	1,438	798	845
Engineering	3,425	2,986	439	2,874	164	197	1,165	906	489	353	315
English and journalism	1,356	519	837	1,163	97	109	363	383	285	86	130
Home economics	375	17	358	329	27	6	61	113	49	60	86
Law	1,167	865	301	1,045	53	56	279	372	226	110	124
Liberal arts and humanities	2,855	1,228	1,629	2,570	132	242	690	855	518	236	315
Mathematics and statistics	754	477	276	637	80	44	223	188	146	54	99
Medicine and dentistry	1,119	825	294	900	27	22	253	413	187	85	159
Nursing, pharmacy, and health technologies	2,166	352	1,814	1,845	137	156	649	665	329	180	186
Physical and earth sciences	918	650	270	837	31	48	270	198	192	77	133
Police science and law enforcement	363	251	112	309	30	19	149	114	57	14	9
Psychology	1,342	531	811	1,216	63	138	364	415	243	75	107
Religion and theology	577	484	93	525	48	9	112	172	95	88	101
Social sciences	2,341	1,023	1,318	2,028	232	226	576	689	440	210	200
Vocational and technical studies	202	140	62	165	17	20	82	38	29	20	13
Other fields	2,825	1,487	1,338	2,507	198	226	824	872	492	213	199
Percentage distribution of degree holders, by field											
Total	100.0	100.0	100.0	100.0	100.0	100.0	100.0	100.0	100.0	100.0	100.0
Agriculture and forestry	1.5	2.3	0.6	1.6	0.5	1.6	1.0	1.9	1.5	1.6	1.4
Biology	2.2	2.7	1.7	2.1	2.5	4.2	2.0	2.6	2.3	1.9	0.8
Business and management	18.3	23.4	12.7	18.4	19.8	19.2	21.7	17.2	18.2	17.1	13.4
Economics	2.2	2.8	1.5	2.2	1.8	2.4	2.4	2.0	2.1	2.8	1.8
Education	16.5	7.7	26.4	17.0	17.7	10.9	10.0	16.5	20.9	23.0	23.1
Engineering	9.3	15.4	2.5	8.9	7.1	8.0	12.1	8.5	7.1	10.2	8.6
English and journalism	3.7	2.7	4.8	3.6	4.2	4.4	3.8	3.6	4.1	2.5	3.5
Home economics	1.0	0.1	2.1	1.0	1.2	0.2	0.6	1.1	0.7	1.7	2.3
Law	3.2	4.5	1.7	3.2	2.3	2.3	2.9	3.5	3.3	3.2	3.4
Liberal arts and humanities	7.8	6.3	9.3	8.0	5.7	9.9	7.2	8.0	7.5	6.8	8.6
Mathematics and statistics	2.0	2.5	1.6	2.0	3.5	1.8	2.3	1.8	2.1	1.6	2.7
Medicine and dentistry	3.0	4.3	1.7	2.8	1.2	0.9	2.6	3.9	2.7	2.4	4.3
Nursing, pharmacy, and health technologies	5.9	1.8	10.4	5.7	5.9	6.4	6.7	6.2	4.8	5.2	5.1
Physical and earth sciences	2.5	3.4	1.5	2.6	1.3	2.0	2.8	1.9	2.8	2.2	3.6
Police science and law enforcement	1.0	1.3	0.6	1.0	1.3	0.8	1.5	1.1	0.8	0.4	0.2
Psychology	3.6	2.7	4.7	3.8	2.7	5.6	3.8	3.9	3.5	2.2	2.9
Religion and theology	1.6	2.5	0.5	1.6	2.1	0.4	1.2	1.6	1.4	2.5	2.8
Social sciences	6.4	5.3	7.6	6.3	10.0	9.2	6.0	6.4	6.4	6.1	5.5
Vocational and technical studies	0.5	0.7	0.4	0.5	0.7	0.8	0.9	0.4	0.4	0.6	0.4
Other fields	7.7	7.7	7.7	7.8	8.6	9.2	8.6	8.2	7.2	6.1	5.4

[1] Includes persons of Hispanic origin.

NOTE.—Data are based on a sample survey of the civilian noninstitutional population. Because of rounding, details may not add to totals.

SOURCE: U.S. Department of Commerce, Bureau of the Census, *Current Population Reports*, Series P-70, No. 51, "What's It Worth? Educational Background and Economic Status: Spring 1993." (This table was prepared April 1996.)

Table 11.—Educational attainment of persons 25 years old and over, by state: April 1990

State	Number of persons 25 years old and over	Distribution of population, by highest level of education attained						
		Less than 9th grade	9th to 12th grade, no diploma	High school graduate	Some college, no degree	Associate degree	Bachelor's degree	Graduate or professional degree
1	2	3	4	5	6	7	8	9
United States	**158,868,436**	**10.4**	**14.4**	**30.0**	**18.7**	**6.2**	**13.1**	**7.2**
Alabama	2,545,969	13.7	19.4	29.4	16.8	5.0	10.1	5.5
Alaska	323,429	5.1	8.2	28.7	27.6	7.2	15.0	8.0
Arizona	2,301,177	9.0	12.3	26.1	25.4	6.8	13.3	7.0
Arkansas	1,496,150	15.2	18.4	32.7	16.6	3.7	8.9	4.5
California	18,695,499	11.2	12.6	22.3	22.6	7.9	15.3	8.1
Colorado	2,107,072	5.6	10.0	26.5	24.0	6.9	18.0	9.0
Connecticut	2,198,963	8.4	12.4	29.5	15.9	6.6	16.2	11.0
Delaware	428,499	7.2	15.3	32.7	16.9	6.5	13.7	7.7
District of Columbia	409,131	9.6	17.3	21.2	15.6	3.1	16.1	17.2
Florida	8,887,168	9.5	16.1	30.1	19.4	6.6	12.0	6.3
Georgia	4,023,420	12.0	17.1	29.6	17.0	5.0	12.9	6.4
Hawaii	709,820	10.1	9.8	28.7	20.1	8.3	15.8	7.1
Idaho	601,292	7.4	12.9	30.4	24.2	7.5	12.4	5.3
Illinois	7,293,930	10.3	13.5	30.0	19.4	5.8	13.6	7.5
Indiana	3,489,470	8.5	15.8	38.2	16.6	5.3	9.2	6.4
Iowa	1,776,798	9.2	10.7	38.5	17.0	7.7	11.7	5.2
Kansas	1,565,936	7.7	11.0	32.8	21.9	5.4	14.1	7.0
Kentucky	2,333,833	19.0	16.4	31.8	15.2	4.1	8.1	5.5
Louisiana	2,536,994	14.7	17.0	31.7	17.2	3.3	10.5	5.6
Maine	795,613	8.8	12.4	37.1	16.1	6.9	12.7	6.1
Maryland	3,122,665	7.9	13.7	28.1	18.6	5.2	15.6	10.9
Massachusetts	3,962,223	8.0	12.0	29.7	15.8	7.2	16.6	10.6
Michigan	5,842,642	7.8	15.5	32.3	20.4	6.7	10.9	6.4
Minnesota	2,770,562	8.6	9.0	33.0	19.0	8.6	15.6	6.3
Mississippi	1,538,997	15.6	20.1	27.5	16.9	5.2	9.7	5.1
Missouri	3,291,579	11.6	14.5	33.1	18.4	4.5	11.7	6.1
Montana	507,851	8.1	10.9	33.5	22.1	5.6	14.1	5.7
Nebraska	996,049	8.0	10.2	34.7	21.1	7.1	13.1	5.9
Nevada	789,638	6.0	15.2	31.5	25.8	6.2	10.1	5.2
New Hampshire	713,894	6.7	11.2	31.7	18.0	8.1	16.4	7.9
New Jersey	5,166,233	9.4	13.9	31.1	15.5	5.2	16.0	8.8
New Mexico	922,590	11.4	13.5	28.7	20.9	5.0	12.1	8.3
New York	11,818,569	10.2	15.0	29.5	15.7	6.5	13.2	9.9
North Carolina	4,253,494	12.7	17.3	29.0	16.8	6.8	12.0	5.4
North Dakota	396,550	15.0	8.3	28.0	20.5	10.0	13.5	4.5
Ohio	6,924,764	7.9	16.4	36.3	17.0	5.3	11.1	5.9
Oklahoma	1,995,424	9.8	15.6	30.5	21.3	5.0	11.8	6.0
Oregon	1,855,369	6.2	12.3	28.9	25.0	6.9	13.6	7.0
Pennsylvania	7,872,932	9.4	15.9	38.6	12.9	5.2	11.3	6.6
Rhode Island	658,956	11.1	16.9	29.5	15.0	6.3	13.5	7.8
South Carolina	2,167,590	13.6	18.1	29.5	15.8	6.3	11.2	5.4
South Dakota	430,500	13.4	9.5	33.7	18.8	7.4	12.3	4.9
Tennessee	3,139,066	16.0	17.0	30.0	16.9	4.2	10.5	5.4
Texas	10,310,605	13.5	14.4	25.6	21.1	5.2	13.9	6.5
Utah	897,321	3.4	11.5	27.2	27.9	7.8	15.4	6.8
Vermont	357,245	8.7	10.6	34.6	14.7	7.2	15.4	8.9
Virginia	3,974,814	11.2	13.7	26.6	18.5	5.5	15.4	9.1
Washington	3,126,390	5.5	10.7	27.9	25.0	7.9	15.9	7.0
West Virginia	1,171,766	16.8	17.3	36.6	13.2	3.8	7.5	4.8
Wisconsin	3,094,226	9.5	11.9	37.1	16.7	7.1	12.1	5.6
Wyoming	277,769	5.7	11.2	33.2	24.2	6.9	13.1	5.7

SOURCE: U.S. Department of Commerce, Bureau of the Census, Decennial Census, Minority Economic Profiles, unpublished data. (This table was prepared June 1993.)

Table 12.—Educational attainment of persons 25 years old and over, by state and race/ethnicity: April 1990

State	Percent with high school diploma or higher						Percent with bachelor's degree or higher					
	Total	White [1]	Black [1]	His-panic [2]	Asian/ Pacific Islander [1]	American Indian or Alaskan Native [1]	Total	White [1]	Black [1]	His-panic [2]	Asian/ Pacific Islander [1]	American Indian or Alaskan Native [1]
1	2	3	4	5	6	7	8	9	10	11	12	13
United States	**75.2**	**77.9**	**63.1**	**49.8**	**77.5**	**65.5**	**20.3**	**21.5**	**11.4**	**9.2**	**36.6**	**9.3**
Alabama	66.9	70.3	54.6	73.8	78.9	64.9	15.7	17.3	9.3	20.1	43.7	11.6
Alaska	86.6	91.1	88.2	80.4	75.4	63.1	23.0	26.8	14.1	14.6	20.5	4.1
Arizona	78.7	82.4	75.1	51.7	80.2	52.1	20.3	22.2	14.3	6.9	37.5	4.6
Arkansas	66.3	68.6	51.5	59.1	66.4	65.4	13.3	14.1	8.4	11.1	24.6	9.8
California	76.2	81.1	75.6	45.0	77.2	71.4	23.4	25.4	14.8	7.1	34.1	11.1
Colorado	84.4	86.1	80.8	58.3	78.3	73.9	27.0	28.3	17.1	8.6	32.1	12.1
Connecticut	79.2	80.9	67.0	53.5	81.9	68.9	27.2	28.5	12.3	12.1	50.8	12.5
Delaware	77.5	80.3	63.2	60.1	86.1	62.0	21.4	23.0	10.6	16.5	55.9	10.2
District of Columbia	73.1	93.1	63.8	52.6	80.2	66.3	33.3	69.0	15.3	24.0	50.9	17.7
Florida	74.4	77.0	56.4	57.2	77.8	68.2	18.3	19.3	9.8	14.2	33.6	11.5
Georgia	70.9	74.9	58.6	66.2	77.5	71.6	19.3	21.8	11.0	20.5	38.6	12.5
Hawaii	80.1	89.3	94.2	73.9	74.7	84.4	22.9	30.2	15.2	10.3	19.4	17.7
Idaho	79.7	80.9	82.8	43.4	80.3	68.1	17.7	18.0	15.8	6.6	27.6	7.2
Illinois	76.2	79.1	65.2	45.0	83.9	71.4	21.0	22.4	11.4	8.0	49.8	13.4
Indiana	75.6	76.5	65.4	62.6	85.8	65.0	15.6	17.6	9.3	10.8	53.1	8.4
Iowa	80.1	80.3	70.1	64.2	76.4	67.6	16.9	16.7	12.8	13.7	47.3	9.7
Kansas	81.3	82.4	71.0	58.1	73.6	75.4	21.1	21.7	11.6	10.1	39.9	10.8
Kentucky	64.6	64.7	61.7	74.0	77.9	59.8	13.6	13.9	7.7	18.9	44.2	8.0
Louisiana	68.3	74.2	53.1	67.6	68.1	49.1	16.1	18.7	9.1	16.6	31.4	5.5
Maine	78.8	78.9	87.6	83.8	74.3	69.9	18.8	18.8	22.3	23.6	44.9	7.7
Maryland	78.4	80.8	70.6	70.3	84.8	73.4	26.5	28.9	16.1	25.2	50.3	19.7
Massachusetts	80.0	81.2	70.0	52.0	74.1	71.1	27.2	27.7	17.0	13.6	44.9	14.9
Michigan	76.8	78.6	64.9	60.9	83.3	67.8	17.4	18.1	10.1	11.6	54.1	7.6
Minnesota	82.4	82.8	76.2	71.1	69.7	68.2	21.8	21.9	17.5	17.2	33.5	7.7
Mississippi	64.3	71.7	47.3	67.7	68.2	57.4	14.7	17.2	8.8	17.1	35.1	8.1
Missouri	73.9	74.9	65.1	71.0	81.5	65.1	17.8	18.3	11.2	18.0	47.3	11.0
Montana	81.0	81.7	80.9	66.4	78.5	68.1	19.8	20.3	18.4	10.9	32.1	7.9
Nebraska	81.8	82.4	73.2	60.0	80.0	69.0	18.9	19.2	12.4	9.4	39.5	8.8
Nevada	78.8	80.9	70.8	53.7	74.1	69.8	15.3	15.9	9.0	7.0	21.9	8.0
New Hampshire	82.2	82.2	86.1	78.2	82.7	65.9	24.4	24.2	25.7	25.5	26.1	16.0
New Jersey	76.7	78.6	67.0	53.9	86.8	66.9	24.9	25.8	13.6	10.8	57.1	14.8
New Mexico	75.1	78.6	74.7	59.6	80.8	58.2	20.4	23.4	14.2	8.7	38.7	5.8
New York	76.7	78.5	64.7	50.4	72.4	65.2	23.1	25.3	12.6	9.3	38.7	13.4
North Carolina	70.0	73.1	58.1	71.0	77.9	51.5	17.4	19.3	9.5	17.9	39.3	7.9
North Dakota	76.7	76.9	95.9	75.2	83.7	64.3	18.1	18.3	17.1	15.9	37.8	8.3
Ohio	75.7	76.9	64.6	63.3	83.5	65.3	17.0	17.6	9.1	14.2	53.2	8.3
Oklahoma	74.6	75.7	70.1	55.9	76.1	68.1	17.8	18.7	12.0	10.5	34.7	10.8
Oregon	81.5	82.3	75.0	53.0	79.4	71.0	20.6	20.8	9.1	10.1	32.3	8.3
Pennsylvania	74.7	75.9	63.5	52.2	77.1	67.8	17.9	18.5	10.0	11.8	45.2	12.0
Rhode Island	72.0	73.0	65.9	46.8	59.6	64.5	21.3	21.8	12.7	8.9	30.6	8.3
South Carolina	68.3	73.6	53.3	71.8	77.4	62.5	16.6	19.8	7.6	19.8	34.4	10.9
South Dakota	77.1	77.8	82.2	71.3	74.3	62.5	17.2	17.6	24.1	13.4	33.1	6.8
Tennessee	67.1	68.2	59.4	71.5	79.3	63.1	16.0	16.7	10.2	21.9	42.6	10.5
Texas	72.1	76.2	66.1	44.6	79.1	70.9	20.3	22.6	12.0	7.3	41.3	13.9
Utah	85.1	86.2	77.0	61.0	80.7	59.3	22.3	22.7	15.9	9.1	29.4	6.4
Vermont	80.8	80.8	82.9	84.7	87.1	66.8	24.3	24.2	30.5	28.2	52.1	11.1
Virginia	75.2	78.3	60.3	70.5	82.1	70.7	24.5	27.0	11.1	22.4	40.2	14.7
Washington	83.8	85.0	81.2	56.7	77.3	72.3	22.9	23.3	15.4	11.0	30.2	9.1
West Virginia	66.0	66.0	64.7	70.3	88.8	57.9	12.3	12.2	10.9	17.6	63.3	6.5
Wisconsin	78.6	79.6	61.3	54.1	71.5	66.8	17.7	18.1	8.3	10.0	40.4	5.5
Wyoming	83.0	83.9	81.2	59.3	77.5	68.2	18.8	19.3	9.5	4.8	28.6	6.2

[1] Includes persons of Hispanic origin.
[2] Persons of Hispanic origin may be of any race.

SOURCE: U.S. Department of Commerce, Bureau of the Census, Decennial Census, Minority Economic Profiles, unpublished data. (This table was prepared June 1993.)

Table 13.—Years of school completed by persons age 25 and over in the 15 largest states and the 15 largest metropolitan areas: March 1993

State	Percent completing—			Metropolitan area [1]	Percent completing—		
	Less than high school diploma	High school diploma	Bachelor's degree or more		Less than high school diploma	High school diploma	Bachelor's degree or more
1	2	3	4	1	2	3	4
United States [2]	**19.8**	**80.2**	**21.9**				
California	20.3	79.7	25.0	Atlanta, GA	15.9	84.1	31.3
Florida	20.4	79.6	19.8	Boston, MA	13.0	87.0	34.9
Georgia	25.3	74.7	21.1	Chicago, IL	21.4	78.6	25.0
Illinois	20.8	79.2	22.1	Cleveland, OH	14.0	86.0	21.9
Indiana	20.8	79.2	14.1	Dallas, TX	19.1	80.9	27.2
Massachusetts	15.4	84.6	30.0	Detroit, MI	18.3	81.7	22.1
Michigan	18.5	81.5	19.1	Houston, TX	16.7	83.3	30.7
Missouri	19.7	80.3	20.3	Los Angeles/Anaheim/Riverside, CA	23.4	76.6	23.6
New Jersey	17.9	82.1	27.9	Miami, FL	24.6	75.4	21.2
New York	19.3	80.7	24.2	New York, NY	19.7	80.3	27.7
North Carolina	25.2	74.8	18.5	Philadelphia, PA/NJ	20.4	79.6	23.4
Ohio	17.2	82.8	19.5	Pittsburgh, PA	17.7	82.3	20.5
Pennsylvania	20.2	79.8	18.7	San Francisco, CA	16.0	86.3	33.0
Texas	22.7	77.3	22.1	St. Louis, MO	19.1	80.9	21.2
Virginia	19.3	80.7	25.8	Washington, DC/MD/VA	12.0	88.0	38.2

[1] Metropolitan Statistical Area.
[2] Includes data for all states and the District of Columbia.

SOURCE: U.S. Department of Commerce, Bureau of the Census, *Current Population Reports*, Series P-20, No. 476, *Educational Attainment in the United States: March 1993 and 1992*. (This table was prepared July 1995.)

Table 14.—Estimates of resident population, by age group: July 1, 1960 to July 1, 1995

[In thousands]

Year	Total, all ages	Total, 3 to 34 years	3 and 4 years	5 and 6 years	7 to 13 years	14 to 17 years	18 and 19 years	20 and 21 years	22 to 24 years	25 to 29 years	30 to 34 years
1	2	3	4	5	6	7	8	9	10	11	12
1960	179,979	90,722	8,063	7,811	25,155	11,211	4,886	4,443	6,425	10,823	11,905
1961	182,992	92,597	8,207	7,924	25,293	12,046	5,411	4,635	6,587	10,756	11,738
1962	185,771	94,396	8,190	8,108	25,790	12,751	5,617	4,943	6,710	10,740	11,547
1963	188,483	96,275	8,152	8,251	26,326	13,492	5,461	5,467	6,930	10,848	11,348
1964	191,141	98,281	8,206	8,233	27,011	14,264	5,429	5,685	7,258	11,051	11,144
1965	193,526	100,210	8,190	8,190	27,563	14,146	6,450	5,503	7,902	11,226	11,040
1966	195,576	101,993	8,031	8,251	28,032	14,398	7,183	5,417	8,198	11,521	10,962
1967	197,457	103,635	7,888	8,237	28,392	14,727	6,928	6,289	8,278	11,943	10,953
1968	199,399	105,363	7,645	8,074	28,732	15,170	6,988	6,972	8,082	12,624	11,076
1969	201,385	106,931	7,253	7,930	28,907	15,549	7,119	6,787	8,980	13,119	11,287
1970	203,984	108,653	6,962	7,703	28,969	15,921	7,410	6,850	9,728	13,604	11,505
1971	206,827	110,482	6,805	7,344	28,892	16,326	7,644	7,106	10,596	13,927	11,842
1972	209,284	112,287	6,789	7,051	28,628	16,637	7,854	7,447	10,418	15,142	12,321
1973	211,357	113,954	6,938	6,888	28,159	16,864	8,044	7,658	10,615	15,694	13,094
1974	213,342	115,641	7,117	6,864	27,599	17,033	8,196	7,893	10,864	16,428	13,644
1975	215,465	117,006	6,912	7,014	26,904	17,125	8,418	8,089	11,228	17,183	14,131
1976	217,563	118,073	6,437	7,194	26,321	17,117	8,604	8,240	11,554	18,177	14,428
1977	219,760	118,853	6,190	6,978	25,878	17,042	8,613	8,456	11,856	18,180	15,661
1978	222,095	119,414	6,208	6,499	25,593	16,944	8,617	8,628	12,120	18,585	16,218
1979	224,567	120,126	6,252	6,256	25,174	16,610	8,698	8,653	12,443	19,077	16,961
1980	227,225	121,132	6,366	6,291	24,800	16,143	8,718	8,669	12,716	19,686	17,743
1981	229,466	121,999	6,535	6,315	24,396	15,609	8,582	8,759	12,903	20,169	18,731
1982	231,664	121,823	6,658	6,407	24,121	15,057	8,480	8,768	12,914	20,704	18,714
1983	233,792	122,302	6,877	6,572	23,709	14,740	8,290	8,652	12,981	21,414	19,067
1984	235,825	122,254	7,045	6,694	23,367	14,725	7,932	8,567	12,962	21,459	19,503
1985	237,924	122,512	7,134	6,916	22,976	14,888	7,637	8,370	12,895	21,671	20,025
1986	240,133	122,688	7,187	7,086	22,992	14,824	7,483	8,024	12,720	21,893	20,479
1987	242,289	122,672	7,132	7,178	23,325	14,502	7,502	7,742	12,450	21,857	20,984
1988	244,499	122,713	7,176	7,238	23,791	14,023	7,701	7,606	12,048	21,739	21,391
1989	246,819	122,655	7,315	7,184	24,228	13,536	7,898	7,651	11,607	21,560	21,676
1990	249,402	122,627	7,355	7,240	24,756	13,310	7,693	7,883	11,251	21,232	21,907
1991	252,131	122,580	7,434	7,383	25,113	13,418	7,173	8,013	11,156	20,732	22,158
1992	255,028	122,622	7,591	7,429	25,579	13,653	6,889	7,756	11,295	20,179	22,251
1993	257,783	122,801	7,844	7,518	25,973	13,928	6,899	7,265	11,498	19,625	22,251
1994	260,341	122,931	8,022	7,676	26,188	14,427	6,937	6,972	11,354	19,177	22,177
1995	262,755	122,975	8,021	7,927	26,456	14,765	7,050	6,982	10,901	19,005	21,868

NOTE.—Some data have been revised from previously published figures. Because of rounding, details may not add to totals.

SOURCE: U.S. Department of Commerce, Bureau of the Census, *Current Population Reports*, Series P-25, Nos. 519, 917, 1000, 1022, 1045, 1057, 1059, 1092, 1095, and

U.S. Population Estimates, by Age, Sex, Race, and Hispanic Origin: 1990–1995, PPL-41; and unpublished data. (This table was prepared April 1996.)

Table 15.—Estimates of school-age [1] resident population, by race and sex: July 1, 1960 to July 1, 1995

[In thousands]

Year	Total			White [2]			Black [2]			Other races [2]		
	Total	Male	Female	Total	Male	Female	Total	Male	Female	Total	Male	Female
1	2	3	4	5	6	7	8	9	10	11	12	13
1960	44,176	22,437	21,739	38,366	19,532	18,832	5,366	2,677	2,690	446	228	217
1961	45,263	22,995	22,269	39,220	19,975	19,246	5,575	2,782	2,792	469	238	232
1962	46,648	23,706	22,941	40,352	20,560	19,791	5,802	2,897	2,906	496	251	244
1963	48,070	24,438	23,633	41,524	21,164	20,361	6,025	3,009	3,016	520	264	257
1964	49,509	25,174	24,336	42,692	21,765	20,929	6,272	3,135	3,137	545	275	270
1965	49,900	25,377	24,522	42,891	21,872	21,019	6,440	3,220	3,221	567	285	281
1966	50,681	25,784	24,898	43,469	22,176	21,293	6,619	3,308	3,311	594	300	295
1967	51,357	26,135	25,224	43,969	22,438	21,529	6,768	3,383	3,384	622	314	310
1968	51,974	26,456	25,517	44,422	22,677	21,744	6,903	3,453	3,450	649	325	323
1969	52,386	26,675	25,711	44,697	22,826	21,871	7,016	3,511	3,505	673	338	336
1970	52,593	26,793	25,801	44,783	22,877	21,906	7,108	3,561	3,547	703	355	349
1971	52,562	26,780	25,782	44,644	22,809	21,834	7,182	3,600	3,583	737	371	365
1972	52,316	26,658	25,658	44,336	22,655	21,681	7,211	3,615	3,596	768	388	380
1973	51,910	26,456	25,455	43,898	22,434	21,464	7,213	3,617	3,596	799	405	394
1974	51,498	26,249	25,249	43,454	22,210	21,244	7,213	3,618	3,596	830	420	409
1975	51,044	26,022	25,022	42,950	21,956	20,994	7,199	3,611	3,588	895	456	440
1976	50,633	25,822	24,811	42,477	21,721	20,755	7,208	3,617	3,591	948	483	465
1977	49,897	25,456	24,441	41,737	21,350	20,386	7,167	3,600	3,568	994	506	487
1978	49,038	25,024	24,013	40,883	20,919	19,964	7,116	3,576	3,540	1,039	530	509
1979	48,041	24,524	23,517	39,910	20,427	19,484	7,037	3,538	3,498	1,094	560	536
1980	47,232	24,135	23,097	39,002	19,982	19,020	6,989	3,520	3,469	1,241	633	608
1981	46,319	23,676	22,643	38,105	19,527	18,578	6,872	3,474	3,398	1,342	675	667
1982	45,585	23,309	22,276	37,365	19,153	18,212	6,826	3,442	3,384	1,394	714	680
1983	45,020	23,031	21,989	36,800	18,873	17,927	6,762	3,412	3,350	1,458	746	712
1984	44,788	22,920	21,868	36,509	18,731	17,778	6,743	3,404	3,339	1,536	785	751
1985	44,782	22,927	21,855	36,393	18,679	17,714	6,729	3,400	3,329	1,660	848	812
1986	44,903	22,996	21,907	36,408	18,701	17,707	6,802	3,438	3,364	1,693	857	836
1987	45,005	23,056	21,949	36,361	18,674	17,687	6,841	3,460	3,381	1,803	922	881
1988	45,051	23,086	21,965	36,279	18,637	17,642	6,881	3,482	3,399	1,891	967	924
1989	44,947	23,036	21,911	36,122	18,550	17,572	6,867	3,475	3,392	1,958	1,011	947
1990	45,306	23,224	22,082	36,320	18,667	17,653	6,916	3,501	3,415	2,070	1,056	1,014
1991	45,917	23,536	22,381	36,759	18,892	17,867	7,012	3,552	3,460	2,143	1,090	1,053
1992	46,662	23,918	22,744	37,288	19,162	18,126	7,147	3,624	3,523	2,226	1,133	1,093
1993	47,419	24,303	23,116	37,802	19,422	18,380	7,297	3,702	3,595	2,319	1,178	1,141
1994	48,291	24,751	23,539	38,406	19,732	18,674	7,474	3,794	3,680	2,411	1,226	1,185
1995	49,149	25,191	23,957	39,013	20,042	18,969	7,631	3,876	3,756	2,505	1,273	1,230

[1] Includes persons 5 to 17 years of age.
[2] Includes persons of Hispanic origin.

NOTE.—Some data have been revised from previously published figures. Because of rounding, details may not add to totals.

SOURCE: U.S. Department of Commerce, Bureau of the Census, *Current Population Reports*, Series P-25, Nos. 519, 917, 1000, 1022, 1045, 1057, 1092, and *U.S. Population Estimates, by Age, Sex, Race, and Hispanic Origin: 1990–1995*, PPL-41; and unpublished data. (This table was prepared April 1996.)

Table 16.—Estimated total and school-age resident population, by state: [1] 1970 to 1995

[In thousands]

State	1970 [2] Total, all ages	1970 [2] 5- to 17-year-olds	1980 [2] Total, all ages	1980 [2] 5- to 17-year-olds	1985 [3] Total, all ages	1985 [3] 5- to 17-year-olds	1990 [2] Total, all ages	1990 [2] 5- to 17-year-olds	1993 [3] Total, all ages	1993 [3] 5- to 17-year-olds	1994 [3] Total, all ages	1994 [3] 5- to 17-year-olds	1995 [3] Total, all ages	1995 [3] 5- to 17-year-olds
1	2	3	4	5	6	7	8	9	10	11	12	13	14	15
United States	203,302	52,540	226,546	47,407	237,924	44,782	248,710	45,166	257,783	47,419	260,341	48,291	262,755	49,149
Alabama	3,444	934	3,894	866	3,973	798	4,041	774	4,181	771	4,219	778	4,253	779
Alaska	303	88	402	92	532	112	550	117	598	132	606	136	604	136
Arizona	1,775	486	2,718	578	3,184	601	3,665	686	3,945	762	4,075	795	4,218	837
Arkansas	1,923	498	2,286	496	2,327	461	2,351	455	2,426	464	2,453	468	2,484	477
California	19,971	4,999	23,668	4,681	26,441	4,752	29,760	5,337	31,217	5,734	31,431	5,844	31,589	5,984
Colorado	2,210	589	2,890	592	3,209	599	3,294	607	3,564	677	3,656	700	3,747	712
Connecticut	3,032	768	3,108	638	3,201	549	3,287	520	3,278	545	3,275	557	3,275	570
Delaware	548	148	594	125	618	113	666	114	698	122	706	124	717	127
District of Columbia ..	757	164	638	109	635	88	607	80	579	75	570	76	554	75
Florida	6,791	1,609	9,746	1,789	11,351	1,792	12,938	2,011	13,726	2,230	13,953	2,300	14,166	2,403
Georgia	4,588	1,223	5,463	1,231	5,963	1,195	6,478	1,230	6,902	1,308	7,055	1,344	7,201	1,372
Hawaii	770	204	965	198	1,040	194	1,108	196	1,166	205	1,179	209	1,187	213
Idaho	713	200	944	213	994	223	1,007	228	1,100	245	1,133	252	1,163	258
Illinois	11,110	2,859	11,427	2,401	11,400	2,192	11,431	2,095	11,686	2,144	11,752	2,168	11,830	2,205
Indiana	5,195	1,386	5,490	1,200	5,459	1,087	5,544	1,056	5,706	1,056	5,752	1,066	5,803	1,079
Iowa	2,825	743	2,914	604	2,830	543	2,777	525	2,821	536	2,829	541	2,842	541
Kansas	2,249	573	2,364	468	2,427	452	2,478	472	2,535	497	2,554	506	2,565	510
Kentucky	3,221	844	3,661	800	3,695	745	3,685	703	3,794	705	3,827	709	3,860	712
Louisiana	3,645	1,041	4,206	969	4,408	937	4,220	890	4,290	893	4,315	898	4,342	903
Maine	994	260	1,125	243	1,163	222	1,228	223	1,240	226	1,240	228	1,241	230
Maryland	3,924	1,038	4,217	895	4,413	788	4,781	803	4,958	864	5,006	884	5,042	904
Massachusetts	5,689	1,407	5,737	1,153	5,881	989	6,016	940	6,018	978	6,041	1,001	6,074	1,019
Michigan	8,882	2,450	9,262	2,067	9,076	1,824	9,295	1,754	9,460	1,798	9,496	1,824	9,549	1,837
Minnesota	3,806	1,051	4,076	865	4,184	796	4,375	828	4,524	893	4,567	914	4,610	925
Mississippi	2,217	635	2,521	599	2,588	576	2,573	550	2,640	545	2,669	549	2,697	553
Missouri	4,678	1,183	4,917	1,008	5,000	941	5,117	944	5,235	984	5,278	1,003	5,324	1,012
Montana	694	197	787	167	822	167	799	163	841	174	856	179	870	179
Nebraska	1,485	389	1,570	324	1,585	305	1,578	309	1,613	321	1,623	326	1,637	329
Nevada	489	127	800	160	951	166	1,202	204	1,382	246	1,457	261	1,530	279
New Hampshire	738	189	921	196	997	182	1,109	194	1,124	206	1,137	212	1,148	219
New Jersey	7,171	1,797	7,365	1,528	7,566	1,340	7,730	1,265	7,859	1,326	7,904	1,352	7,945	1,386
New Mexico	1,017	311	1,303	303	1,438	304	1,515	320	1,616	347	1,654	358	1,685	362
New York	18,241	4,358	17,558	3,552	17,792	3,173	17,990	3,000	18,153	3,094	18,169	3,129	18,136	3,177
North Carolina	5,084	1,323	5,882	1,254	6,254	1,175	6,629	1,147	6,952	1,214	7,070	1,246	7,195	1,285
North Dakota	618	175	653	136	677	133	639	127	637	128	638	129	641	129
Ohio	10,657	2,820	10,798	2,307	10,735	2,090	10,847	2,012	11,061	2,048	11,102	2,070	11,151	2,087
Oklahoma	2,559	640	3,025	622	3,271	635	3,146	609	3,233	633	3,258	643	3,278	648
Oregon	2,092	534	2,633	525	2,673	504	2,842	521	3,035	564	3,086	574	3,141	587
Pennsylvania	11,801	2,925	11,864	2,376	11,771	2,079	11,882	1,996	12,030	2,067	12,052	2,099	12,072	2,125
Rhode Island	950	225	947	186	969	163	1,003	159	1,000	165	997	169	990	170
South Carolina	2,591	720	3,122	703	3,303	663	3,487	663	3,630	672	3,664	678	3,673	682
South Dakota	666	187	691	147	698	139	696	144	716	152	721	154	729	154
Tennessee	3,926	1,002	4,591	972	4,715	903	4,877	882	5,094	912	5,175	931	5,256	945
Texas	11,199	3,002	14,229	3,137	16,273	3,318	16,987	3,437	18,022	3,660	18,378	3,742	18,724	3,819
Utah	1,059	312	1,461	350	1,643	418	1,723	457	1,860	482	1,908	491	1,951	491
Vermont	445	118	511	109	530	100	563	102	576	106	580	108	585	110
Virginia	4,651	1,197	5,347	1,114	5,715	1,039	6,187	1,060	6,473	1,115	6,552	1,134	6,618	1,149
Washington	3,413	881	4,132	826	4,400	816	4,867	893	5,259	990	5,343	1,014	5,431	1,033
West Virginia	1,744	442	1,950	414	1,907	383	1,793	337	1,818	323	1,822	321	1,828	315
Wisconsin	4,418	1,203	4,706	1,011	4,748	908	4,892	927	5,044	981	5,082	997	5,123	1,009
Wyoming	332	92	470	101	500	108	454	101	470	103	476	104	480	104

[1] Includes Armed Forces residing in each state.
[2] As of April 1.
[3] Estimates as of July 1.

NOTE.—Some data have been revised from previously published figures. Because of rounding, details may not add to totals.

SOURCE: U.S. Department of Commerce, Bureau of the Census, *Current Population Reports*, Series P-25, No. 1095 at the national level, CPH-L-74 (1990 data); and forthcoming state level P-25 Reports. (This table was prepared July 1996.)

Table 17.—Families, by family status and presence of own children under 18: 1970 to 1994

Family status	1970	1980	1985	1988	1989	1990	1991	1992	1993	1994	Change, 1970 to 1980	Change, 1980 to 1994
1	2	3	4	5	6	7	8	9	10	11	12	13
	In thousands										Percent change	
All families	**51,456**	**59,550**	**62,706**	**65,133**	**65,837**	**66,090**	**66,322**	**67,173**	**68,144**	**68,490**	**15.7**	**15.0**
Married-couple family	44,728	49,112	50,350	51,809	52,100	52,317	52,147	52,457	53,171	53,171	9.8	8.3
No own children under 18	19,196	24,151	26,140	27,209	27,365	27,780	27,750	28,037	28,464	28,113	25.8	16.4
With own children under 18	25,532	24,961	24,210	24,600	24,735	24,537	24,397	24,420	24,707	25,058	−2.2	0.4
One own child under 18	8,163	9,671	9,640	9,904	9,829	9,583	9,319	9,520	9,466	9,452	18.5	−2.3
Two own children under 18	8,045	9,488	9,456	9,576	9,870	9,784	9,721	9,728	10,007	10,188	17.9	7.4
Three or more own children under 18	9,325	5,802	5,115	5,120	5,035	5,170	5,357	5,173	5,234	5,418	−37.8	−6.6
Other family, male householder, no spouse present	1,228	1,733	2,228	2,715	2,847	2,884	2,907	3,025	3,026	2,913	41.1	68.1
No own children under 18	887	1,117	1,331	1,669	1,779	1,731	1,725	1,742	1,702	1,599	25.9	43.2
With own children under 18	341	616	896	1,047	1,068	1,153	1,181	1,283	1,324	1,314	80.6	113.3
One own child under 18	179	374	584	657	619	723	701	768	799	805	108.9	115.2
Two own children under 18	87	165	213	296	326	307	363	391	397	368	89.7	123.0
Three or more own children under 18	75	77	100	94	121	123	117	123	128	141	2.7	83.1
Other family, female householder, no spouse present	5,500	8,705	10,129	10,608	10,890	10,890	11,268	11,692	11,947	12,406	58.3	42.5
No own children under 18	2,642	3,261	4,123	4,335	4,371	4,290	4,445	4,648	4,721	4,759	23.4	45.9
With own children under 18	2,858	5,445	6,006	6,273	6,519	6,599	6,823	7,043	7,226	7,647	90.5	40.4
One own child under 18	1,008	2,398	2,885	3,017	3,164	3,225	3,283	3,327	3,425	3,566	137.9	48.7
Two own children under 18	810	1,817	1,977	2,039	2,095	2,173	2,203	2,244	2,400	2,531	124.3	39.3
Three or more own children under 18	1,040	1,230	1,144	1,217	1,260	1,202	1,335	1,472	1,400	1,550	18.3	26.0
	Percent of all families										Change in percentage points	
All families	**100.0**	**100.0**	**100.0**	**100.0**	**100.0**	**100.0**	**100.0**	**100.0**	**100.0**	**100.0**	—	—
Married-couple family	86.9	82.5	80.3	79.5	79.1	79.2	78.6	78.1	78.0	77.6	−4.5	−4.8
No own children under 18	37.3	40.6	41.7	41.8	41.6	42.0	41.8	41.7	41.8	41.0	3.3	0.5
With own children under 18	49.6	41.9	38.6	37.8	37.6	37.1	36.8	36.4	36.3	36.6	−7.7	−5.3
One own child under 18	15.9	16.2	15.4	15.2	14.9	14.5	14.1	14.2	13.9	13.8	0.4	−2.4
Two own children under 18	15.6	15.9	15.1	14.7	15.0	14.8	14.7	14.5	14.7	14.9	0.3	−1.1
Three or more own children under 18	18.1	9.7	8.2	7.9	7.6	7.8	8.1	7.7	7.7	7.9	−8.4	−1.8
Other family, male householder, no spouse present	2.4	2.9	3.6	4.2	4.3	4.4	4.4	4.5	4.4	4.3	0.5	1.3
No own children under 18	1.7	1.9	2.1	2.6	2.7	2.6	2.6	2.6	2.5	2.3	0.2	0.5
With own children under 18	0.7	1.0	1.4	1.6	1.6	1.7	1.8	1.9	1.9	1.9	0.4	0.9
One own child under 18	0.3	0.6	0.9	1.0	0.9	1.1	1.1	1.1	1.2	1.2	0.3	0.5
Two own children under 18	0.2	0.3	0.3	0.5	0.5	0.5	0.5	0.6	0.6	0.5	0.1	0.3
Three or more own children under 18	0.1	0.1	0.2	0.1	0.2	0.2	0.2	0.2	0.2	0.2	(1)	0.1
Other family, female householder, no spouse present	10.7	14.6	16.2	16.3	16.5	16.5	17.0	17.4	17.5	18.1	3.9	3.5
No own children under 18	5.1	5.5	6.6	6.7	6.6	6.5	6.7	6.9	6.9	6.9	0.3	1.5
With own children under 18	5.6	9.1	9.6	9.6	9.9	10.0	10.3	10.5	10.6	11.2	3.6	2.0
One own child under 18	2.0	4.0	4.6	4.6	4.8	4.9	5.0	5.0	5.0	5.2	2.1	1.2
Two own children under 18	1.6	3.1	3.2	3.1	3.2	3.3	3.3	3.3	3.5	3.7	1.5	0.6
Three or more own children under 18	2.0	2.1	1.8	1.9	1.9	1.8	2.0	2.2	2.1	2.3	(1)	0.2

1 Less than .05 percent.
—Not applicable.

NOTE.—Because of rounding, details may not add to totals.

SOURCE: U.S. Department of Commerce, Bureau of the Census, *Current Population Reports*, Series P-20, *Household and Family Characteristics*, various years; and unpublished data. (This table was prepared April 1996.)

Table 18.—Characteristics of families with own children under 18, by family status and race/ethnicity:[1] 1994

[Numbers in thousands]

Family characteristics	All races				White[2]				Black[2]				Hispanic origin[3]			
	Total	Married-couple families	Other families		Total	Married-couple families	Other families		Total	Married-couple families	Other families		Total	Married-couple families	Other families	
			Male householder, no spouse present	Female householder, no spouse present			Male householder, no spouse present	Female householder, no spouse present			Male householder, no spouse present	Female householder, no spouse present			Male householder, no spouse present	Female householder, no spouse present
1	2	3	4	5	6	7	8	9	10	11	12	13	14	15	16	17
Total families	**68,490**	**53,171**	**2,913**	**12,406**	**57,870**	**47,443**	**2,297**	**8,130**	**7,989**	**3,714**	**450**	**3,825**	**5,940**	**4,033**	**410**	**1,498**
Total families with own children under 18	34,018	25,058	1,314	7,647	27,642	21,884	1,010	4,748	4,793	1,924	238	2,630	3,790	2,609	175	1,006
Percent of all families	49.7	47.1	45.1	61.6	47.8	46.1	44.0	58.4	60.0	51.8	52.9	68.8	63.8	64.7	42.7	67.2
Percent distribution	100.0	73.7	3.9	22.5	100.0	79.2	3.7	17.2	100.0	40.1	5.0	54.9	100.0	68.8	4.6	26.5
Families with—																
1 child under 18	13,824	9,452	805	3,566	11,229	8,240	627	2,362	1,983	771	144	1,068	1,299	821	95	383
2 children under 18	13,086	10,188	368	2,531	10,846	8,981	279	1,586	1,630	696	63	871	1,357	966	52	339
3 children under 18	5,193	4,016	115	1,062	4,200	3,510	83	607	755	309	29	417	766	558	21	187
4 children under 18	1,409	1,032	22	356	1,021	848	17	155	301	110	3	188	258	177	7	74
5 children under 18	316	229	4	82	220	187	4	29	70	23	—	48	70	51	—	18
6 or more under 18	190	141	—	50	127	118	—	9	53	16	—	38	41	36	—	5
Total own children under 18	62,582	47,231	1,955	13,397	50,750	41,249	1,487	8,014	8,884	3,602	375	4,907	8,266	5,865	305	2,097
Average number of children per family with children	1.84	1.88	1.49	1.75	1.84	1.88	1.47	1.69	1.85	1.87	1.57	1.87	2.18	2.25	1.74	2.08
Total families with own children under 6	15,909	12,117	555	3,236	12,841	10,594	409	1,838	2,266	873	117	1,277	2,000	1,419	92	489
Percent of all families	23.2	22.8	19.1	26.1	22.2	22.3	17.8	22.6	28.4	23.5	26.0	33.4	33.7	35.2	22.4	32.6
Percent distribution	100.0	76.2	3.5	20.3	100.0	82.5	3.2	14.3	100.0	38.5	5.2	56.4	100.0	71.0	4.6	24.5
Families with—																
1 child under 6	10,711	8,088	426	2,196	8,669	7,046	322	1,301	1,494	610	76	808	1,298	908	64	326
2 children under 6	4,471	3,527	108	835	3,664	3,125	69	470	588	210	38	340	601	447	20	135
3 children under 6	644	449	19	175	466	390	16	60	145	35	3	107	87	58	9	20
4 or more under 6	84	53	1	30	41	33	1	7	40	18	—	22	14	6	—	8
Total own children under 6	21,238	16,303	686	4,249	17,215	14,336	504	2,375	3,005	1,133	157	1,715	3,060	2,174	141	745
Average number of children per family with children	1.33	1.35	1.23	1.31	1.34	1.35	1.23	1.29	1.33	1.30	1.35	1.34	1.53	1.53	1.53	1.52
Total families with own children under 3	9,251	7,161	374	1,716	7,501	6,284	270	948	1,306	511	87	708	1,228	899	67	262
Percent of all families	13.5	13.5	12.8	13.8	13.0	13.2	11.8	11.7	16.3	13.8	19.3	18.5	20.7	22.3	16.3	17.5
Percent distribution	100.0	77.4	4.0	18.5	100.0	83.8	3.6	12.6	100.0	39.1	6.7	54.2	100.0	73.2	5.5	21.3
Families with—																
1 child under 3	8,106	6,313	343	1,451	6,643	5,550	252	841	1,074	442	76	557	1,066	788	56	222
2 or more under 3	1,145	848	31	265	859	733	18	107	232	69	11	151	162	111	11	40
Total own children under 3	10,415	8,092	406	1,917	8,487	7,141	295	1,051	1,460	561	97	802	1,571	1,141	89	341
Average number of children per family with children	1.13	1.13	1.09	1.12	1.13	1.14	1.09	1.11	1.12	1.10	1.11	1.13	1.28	1.27	(4)	1.30

[1] Race of family is defined as race of head of household.
[2] Includes persons of Hispanic origin.
[3] Persons of Hispanic origin may be of any race.
[4] Averages and percents are shown only when the base is 75,000 or greater.
—Less than 500.

NOTE.—Because of rounding, details may not add to totals.

SOURCE: U.S. Department of Commerce, Bureau of the Census, *Current Population Reports*, Series P-20, No. 483, *Household and Family Characteristics: March 1994*. (This table was prepared April 1996.)

Table 19.—Household income and poverty rates, by state: 1990, 1993, and 1994

State	Median household income [1]			Percent of persons below the poverty level										Poverty status of 5- to 17-year-olds, 1994			
				1990 [2]								1994		Number in poverty		Percent in poverty	
	1990 [2]	1993	1994	Total	Under 5 years	5 years	6 to 11 years	12 to 17 years	18 to 64 years	65 to 74 years	75 years and over	Total	Standard error	Number (in thousands)	Standard error	Percent	Standard error
1	2	3	4	5	6	7	8	9	10	11	12	13	14	15	16	17	18
United States	$34,080	$32,041	$32,264	13.1	20.1	19.7	18.3	16.3	11.0	10.4	16.5	14.5	0.21	9,974	251	20.1	0.46
Alabama	26,757	25,724	27,196	18.3	26.1	25.8	24.3	22.3	14.6	19.2	31.1	16.4	1.87	157	34	19.5	3.83
Alaska	46,952	44,030	45,367	9.0	13.6	10.6	10.9	9.8	7.9	6.4	10.6	10.2	1.38	15	4	11.7	2.62
Arizona	31,227	31,291	31,293	15.7	24.9	24.2	21.8	19.1	14.0	9.3	13.2	15.9	1.79	189	35	23.4	3.94
Arkansas	23,978	23,629	25,565	19.1	28.5	26.6	25.2	22.7	15.3	18.0	29.9	15.3	1.83	87	19	20.4	4.07
California	40,591	34,945	35,331	12.5	19.0	19.3	18.3	17.1	10.9	6.5	9.5	17.9	0.74	1,550	110	25.3	1.59
Colorado	34,176	35,371	37,833	11.7	17.9	16.5	15.3	12.5	10.3	8.5	15.1	9.0	1.48	69	22	9.9	2.98
Connecticut	47,307	40,528	41,097	6.8	11.7	11.9	11.2	8.9	5.3	5.6	9.7	10.8	1.85	100	28	18.6	4.72
Delaware	39,545	36,987	35,873	8.7	13.3	12.7	11.8	10.8	7.2	8.2	13.5	8.3	1.56	10	4	9.8	3.52
District of Columbia	34,841	28,003	30,116	16.9	27.0	25.5	25.0	24.4	14.3	15.5	19.7	21.2	2.45	29	6	30.0	5.75
Florida	31,163	29,281	29,294	12.7	20.3	20.1	18.8	16.8	11.0	9.0	13.5	14.9	0.87	563	56	22.1	2.00
Georgia	32,907	32,474	31,467	14.7	22.1	21.3	20.1	18.1	11.4	16.5	26.7	14.0	1.68	267	55	18.5	3.50
Hawaii	44,028	43,754	42,255	8.3	12.6	12.6	11.2	10.8	6.9	6.7	10.4	8.7	1.55	21	7	12.0	3.75
Idaho	28,639	31,804	31,536	13.3	19.6	18.9	15.9	13.3	12.0	8.7	15.6	12.0	1.51	39	8	15.5	2.99
Illinois	36,570	33,698	35,081	11.9	18.9	18.7	17.0	15.0	10.0	8.9	13.4	12.4	0.90	405	49	18.0	2.00
Indiana	32,653	30,230	27,858	10.7	16.8	15.8	14.1	11.8	9.1	8.7	14.0	13.7	1.79	164	42	13.7	3.33
Iowa	29,741	29,397	33,079	11.5	17.5	15.4	14.1	11.7	10.3	8.1	15.3	10.7	1.57	74	19	13.5	3.27
Kansas	30,945	30,532	28,322	11.5	16.8	16.5	14.1	11.6	10.1	8.5	16.8	14.9	1.77	97	20	19.5	3.70
Kentucky	25,551	25,000	26,595	19.0	27.9	26.5	24.6	22.4	16.2	17.5	25.3	18.5	1.99	200	36	26.6	4.26
Louisiana	24,888	26,986	25,676	23.6	33.4	33.0	31.1	29.7	19.6	20.5	30.1	25.7	2.32	337	51	36.8	4.64
Maine	31,583	28,141	30,316	10.8	15.7	15.9	14.0	11.5	8.9	11.0	18.3	9.4	1.58	20	7	9.6	3.17
Maryland	44,660	40,962	39,198	8.3	11.9	11.9	11.5	10.2	6.8	8.8	13.6	10.7	1.65	143	37	17.2	4.15
Massachusetts	41,900	38,013	40,500	8.9	14.5	14.8	13.8	11.0	7.3	7.3	12.6	9.7	0.83	121	20	12.2	1.86
Michigan	35,173	33,498	35,284	13.1	22.1	20.4	18.1	15.7	11.2	8.7	14.3	14.1	0.94	326	39	17.9	1.97
Minnesota	35,048	34,544	33,644	10.2	14.8	14.6	12.5	10.6	8.8	8.4	17.2	11.7	1.69	115	31	13.7	3.49
Mississippi	22,832	22,759	25,400	25.2	35.8	35.1	33.5	31.9	20.0	24.0	37.1	19.9	1.97	138	24	28.2	4.24
Missouri	29,892	29,416	30,190	13.3	20.4	19.2	17.8	15.1	11.1	11.3	19.7	15.6	1.96	204	45	23.6	4.64
Montana	26,066	27,148	27,631	16.1	24.3	23.0	20.3	17.1	14.7	9.9	16.6	11.5	1.59	20	5	12.3	3.06
Nebraska	29,499	31,802	31,794	11.1	17.3	15.4	13.4	10.8	9.7	8.6	16.8	8.8	1.38	43	11	12.5	2.93
Nevada	35,163	36,731	35,871	10.2	15.1	14.4	12.6	11.9	9.1	8.4	12.3	11.1	1.49	45	10	16.2	3.39
New Hampshire	41,193	38,936	35,245	6.4	8.5	8.7	7.3	6.2	5.4	7.7	13.9	7.7	1.57	23	8	12.2	3.92
New Jersey	46,407	41,537	42,280	7.6	11.7	12.6	11.7	10.4	6.0	6.8	11.3	9.2	0.78	211	29	14.6	1.86
New Mexico	27,312	27,443	26,905	20.6	30.3	30.6	27.6	25.2	17.8	13.7	21.2	21.1	1.96	111	17	29.2	3.83
New York	37,379	32,509	31,899	13.0	20.6	21.2	19.6	17.0	11.0	10.0	14.7	17.0	0.77	769	62	23.5	1.70
North Carolina	30,215	29,558	30,114	13.0	19.2	18.5	17.2	15.3	10.1	15.7	25.9	14.2	0.91	206	25	18.4	2.08
North Dakota	26,321	28,838	28,278	14.4	19.6	18.4	17.2	14.7	13.0	10.8	19.5	10.4	1.50	15	4	11.6	2.85
Ohio	32,550	32,086	31,855	12.5	21.1	19.9	17.8	14.6	10.7	8.7	13.8	14.1	0.93	448	48	19.5	1.93
Oklahoma	26,734	26,932	26,991	16.7	25.3	23.4	21.7	18.5	14.2	13.5	24.1	16.7	1.90	140	28	21.5	3.87
Oregon	30,899	33,987	31,456	12.4	19.7	16.1	14.8	13.3	11.5	8.1	13.1	11.8	1.73	81	22	13.7	3.54
Pennsylvania	32,961	31,789	32,066	11.1	17.5	17.0	15.7	13.8	9.5	8.7	13.5	12.5	0.88	400	48	19.0	2.08
Rhode Island	36,490	34,367	31,928	9.6	16.3	16.1	13.8	11.0	7.6	8.9	15.6	10.3	1.78	24	7	13.3	3.85
South Carolina	29,772	26,720	29,846	15.4	22.8	21.8	21.2	19.1	12.0	17.3	26.5	13.8	1.59	121	25	18.7	3.54
South Dakota	25,516	28,447	29,733	15.9	23.6	22.2	20.2	17.3	13.6	11.1	21.3	14.5	1.60	32	6	18.2	2.96
Tennessee	28,129	25,745	28,639	15.7	23.9	22.5	20.8	18.5	12.5	17.2	26.7	14.6	1.69	206	41	20.1	3.64
Texas	30,633	29,463	30,755	18.1	25.6	25.5	24.2	23.0	15.2	14.9	23.8	19.1	0.99	1,084	92	26.8	2.00
Utah	33,416	36,702	35,716	11.4	15.8	14.4	12.0	10.0	11.0	6.4	12.5	8.0	1.29	46	12	9.9	2.40
Vermont	33,781	31,860	35,802	9.9	13.5	13.7	12.5	9.8	8.5	9.7	16.3	7.6	1.51	7	3	7.0	2.86
Virginia	37,790	37,366	37,647	10.2	14.5	14.5	13.5	11.9	8.4	11.6	18.5	10.7	1.38	157	37	12.6	2.85
Washington	35,358	36,568	33,533	10.9	17.0	16.4	14.3	12.2	9.8	7.0	12.4	11.7	1.60	146	36	14.6	3.35
West Virginia	23,579	22,995	23,564	19.7	31.7	30.3	25.9	22.4	17.7	14.1	20.8	18.6	2.04	66	15	22.0	4.41
Wisconsin	33,384	32,579	35,388	10.7	17.7	16.4	15.0	11.9	9.2	6.6	12.6	9.0	1.39	120	31	12.1	2.95
Wyoming	30,724	30,196	33,140	11.9	18.3	16.2	14.1	11.2	10.8	8.4	14.3	9.3	1.73	12	4	10.7	3.22

[1] In 1994 dollars adjusted by the Consumer Price Index for all urban consumers.
[2] Based on 1989 incomes collected in the 1990 Census. May differ from data derived from the Current Population Survey.

SOURCE: U.S. Department of Commerce, Bureau of the Census, *Decennial Census, Minority Economic Profiles,* unpublished data; and *Current Population Reports,* Series P-60, "Poverty in the United States," "Money Income of Households, Families, and Persons in the United States," and "Income, Poverty, and Valuation of Noncash Benefits," various years. (This table was prepared June 1996.)

Table 20.—Poverty status of persons, families, and children under 18, by race/ethnicity: 1959 to 1994

Year and race/ ethnicity	Number below the poverty level, in thousands						Percent below the poverty level					
	All persons	In all families			In families with female householder, no husband present		All persons	In all families			In families with female householder, no husband present	
		Total	House-holder	Related children under 18	Total	Related children under 18		Total	House-holder	Related children under 18	Total	Related children under 18
1	2	3	4	5	6	7	8	9	10	11	12	13
All races												
1959	39,490	34,562	8,320	17,208	7,014	4,145	22.4	20.8	18.5	26.9	49.4	72.2
1960	39,851	34,925	8,243	17,288	7,247	4,095	22.2	20.7	18.1	26.5	48.9	68.4
1965	33,185	28,358	6,721	14,388	7,524	4,562	17.3	15.8	13.9	20.7	46.0	64.2
1970	25,420	20,330	5,260	10,235	7,503	4,689	12.6	10.9	10.1	14.9	38.1	53.0
1971	25,559	20,405	5,303	10,344	7,797	4,850	12.5	10.8	10.0	15.1	38.7	53.1
1972	24,460	19,577	5,075	10,082	8,114	5,094	11.9	10.3	9.3	14.9	38.2	53.1
1973	22,973	18,299	4,828	9,453	8,178	5,171	11.1	9.7	8.8	14.2	37.5	52.1
1974	23,370	18,817	4,922	9,967	8,462	5,361	11.2	9.9	8.8	15.1	36.5	51.5
1975	25,877	20,789	5,450	10,882	8,846	5,597	12.3	10.9	9.7	16.8	37.5	52.7
1976	24,975	19,632	5,311	10,081	9,029	5,583	11.8	10.3	9.4	15.8	37.3	52.0
1977	24,720	19,505	5,311	10,028	9,205	5,658	11.6	10.2	9.3	16.0	36.2	50.3
1978	24,497	19,062	5,280	9,722	9,269	5,687	11.4	10.0	9.1	15.7	35.6	50.6
1979	26,072	19,964	5,461	9,993	9,400	5,635	11.7	10.2	9.2	16.0	34.9	48.6
1980	29,272	22,601	6,217	11,114	10,120	5,866	13.0	11.5	10.3	17.9	36.7	50.8
1981	31,822	24,850	6,851	12,068	11,051	6,305	14.0	12.5	11.2	19.5	38.7	52.3
1982	34,398	27,349	7,512	13,139	11,701	6,696	15.0	13.6	12.2	21.3	40.6	56.0
1983	35,303	27,933	7,647	13,427	12,072	6,747	15.2	13.9	12.3	21.8	40.2	55.4
1984	33,700	26,458	7,277	12,929	11,831	6,772	14.4	13.1	11.6	21.0	38.4	54.0
1985	33,064	25,729	7,223	12,483	11,600	6,716	14.0	12.6	11.4	20.1	37.6	53.6
1986	32,370	24,754	7,023	12,257	11,944	6,943	13.6	12.0	10.9	19.8	38.3	54.4
1987	32,221	24,725	7,005	12,275	12,148	7,074	13.4	12.0	10.7	19.7	38.1	54.7
1988	31,745	24,048	6,876	11,935	11,972	6,742	13.0	11.6	10.4	19.0	37.2	50.6
1989	31,528	24,066	6,784	12,001	11,668	6,808	12.8	11.5	10.3	19.0	35.9	51.1
1990	33,585	25,232	7,098	12,715	12,578	7,363	13.5	12.0	10.7	19.9	37.2	53.4
1991	35,708	27,143	7,712	13,658	13,824	8,065	14.2	12.8	11.5	21.1	39.7	55.5
1992	36,880	27,947	7,960	13,876	13,716	8,032	14.8	13.3	11.7	21.1	39.0	54.3
1993	39,265	29,927	8,393	14,961	14,636	8,503	15.1	13.6	12.3	22.0	38.7	53.7
1994	38,059	28,985	8,053	14,610	14,380	8,427	14.5	13.1	11.6	21.2	38.6	52.9
White [1]												
1960	28,309	24,262	6,115	11,229	4,296	2,357	17.8	16.2	14.9	20.0	39.0	59.9
1965	22,496	18,508	4,824	8,595	4,092	2,321	13.3	11.7	11.1	14.4	35.4	52.9
1970	17,484	13,323	3,708	6,138	3,761	2,247	9.9	8.1	8.0	10.5	28.4	43.1
1975	17,770	13,799	3,838	6,748	4,577	2,813	9.7	8.3	7.7	12.5	29.4	44.2
1980	19,699	14,587	4,195	6,817	4,940	2,813	10.2	8.6	8.0	13.4	28.0	41.6
1985	22,860	17,125	4,983	7,838	5,990	3,372	11.4	9.9	9.1	15.6	29.8	45.2
1987	21,195	15,593	4,567	7,398	5,989	3,474	10.4	8.9	8.1	14.7	29.6	45.8
1988	20,715	15,001	4,471	7,095	5,950	3,385	10.1	8.6	7.9	14.0	29.2	43.0
1989	20,785	15,179	4,409	7,164	5,723	3,320	10.0	8.6	7.8	14.1	28.1	42.8
1990	22,326	15,916	4,622	7,696	6,210	3,597	10.7	9.0	8.1	15.1	29.8	45.9
1991	23,747	17,268	5,022	8,316	6,806	3,941	11.3	9.7	8.8	16.1	31.5	47.1
1992	25,259	18,294	5,160	8,333	6,907	3,783	11.9	10.1	8.9	16.0	30.8	45.3
1993	26,226	18,968	5,452	9,123	7,199	4,102	12.2	10.5	9.4	17.0	31.0	45.6
1994	25,379	18,474	5,312	8,826	7,228	4,099	11.7	10.1	9.1	16.3	31.8	45.7
Black [1]												
1959	9,927	9,112	1,860	5,022	2,416	1,475	55.1	54.9	48.1	65.5	70.6	81.6
1966	8,867	8,090	1,620	4,774	3,160	2,107	41.8	40.9	35.5	50.6	65.3	76.6
1970	7,548	6,683	1,481	3,922	3,656	2,383	33.5	32.2	29.5	41.5	58.7	67.7
1975	7,545	6,533	1,513	3,884	4,168	2,724	31.3	30.1	27.1	41.4	54.3	66.0
1980	8,579	7,190	1,826	3,906	4,984	2,944	32.5	31.1	28.9	42.1	53.4	64.8
1985	8,926	7,504	1,983	4,057	5,342	3,181	31.3	30.5	28.7	43.1	53.2	66.9
1987	9,520	7,848	2,117	4,234	5,789	3,394	32.4	31.2	29.4	44.4	54.1	68.3
1988	9,356	7,650	2,090	4,148	5,601	3,130	31.3	30.0	28.2	42.8	51.9	61.8
1989	9,302	7,704	2,077	4,257	5,530	3,256	30.7	29.7	27.8	43.2	49.4	62.9
1990	9,837	8,160	2,193	4,412	6,005	3,543	31.9	31.0	29.3	44.2	50.6	64.7
1991	10,242	8,504	2,343	4,637	6,557	3,853	32.7	32.0	30.4	45.6	54.8	68.2
1992	10,827	9,134	2,435	4,850	6,799	3,967	33.4	32.9	30.9	46.3	54.0	67.1
1993	10,877	9,242	2,499	5,030	6,955	4,104	33.1	32.9	31.3	45.9	53.0	65.9
1994	10,196	8,447	2,212	4,787	6,489	3,935	30.6	29.6	27.3	43.3	50.2	63.2
Hispanic origin [2]												
1975	2,991	2,755	627	1,619	1,053	694	26.9	26.3	25.1	33.1	57.2	68.4
1980	3,491	3,143	751	1,718	1,319	809	25.7	25.1	23.2	33.0	54.5	65.0
1985	5,236	4,605	1,074	2,512	1,983	1,247	29.0	28.3	25.5	39.6	55.7	72.4
1987	5,422	4,761	1,168	2,606	2,045	1,241	28.0	27.5	25.5	38.9	55.6	70.1
1988	5,357	4,700	1,141	2,576	2,052	1,208	26.7	26.0	23.7	37.3	55.0	65.5
1989	5,430	4,659	1,133	2,496	1,902	1,163	26.2	25.2	23.4	35.5	50.6	65.0
1990	6,006	5,091	1,244	2,750	2,115	1,314	28.1	26.9	25.0	37.7	53.0	68.4
1991	6,339	5,541	1,372	2,977	2,282	1,398	28.7	28.2	26.5	39.8	52.7	68.6
1992	7,592	6,455	1,395	2,946	2,474	1,289	29.6	28.4	26.2	38.8	51.5	65.7
1993	8,126	6,876	1,625	3,666	2,837	1,673	30.6	29.3	27.3	39.9	53.2	66.1
1994	8,416	7,357	1,724	3,956	2,920	1,804	30.7	30.2	27.8	41.1	54.8	68.3

[1] Includes persons of Hispanic origin.
[2] Persons of Hispanic origin may be of any race.

SOURCE: U.S. Department of Commerce, Bureau of the Census, *Current Population Reports*, Series P-60, "Poverty in the United States" and "Income, Poverty, and Valuation of Noncash Benefits," various years. (This table was prepared June 1996.)

Table 21.—Average grade that the public would give the schools in their community and in the nation at large: 1974 to 1995

Year	All adults			No children in school			Public school parents			Private school parents		
	Nation	Local community	Local neighborhood	Nation	Local community	Local neighborhood	Nation	Local community	Local neighborhood	Nation	Local community	Local neighborhood
1	2	3	4	5	6	7	8	9	10	11	12	13
1974	—	2.63	—	—	2.57	—	—	2.80	—	—	2.15	—
1975	—	2.38	—	—	2.31	—	—	2.49	—	—	1.81	—
1976	—	2.38	—	—	2.34	—	—	2.48	—	—	2.22	—
1977	—	2.33	—	—	2.25	—	—	2.59	—	—	2.05	—
1978	—	2.21	—	—	2.11	—	—	2.47	—	—	1.69	—
1979	—	2.21	—	—	2.15	—	—	2.38	—	—	1.88	—
1980	—	2.26	—	—	—	—	—	—	—	—	—	—
1981	1.94	2.20	—	—	2.12	—	—	2.36	—	—	1.88	—
1982	2.01	2.24	—	2.04	2.18	—	2.01	2.35	—	2.02	2.20	—
1983	1.91	2.12	—	1.92	2.10	—	1.92	2.31	—	1.82	1.89	—
1984	2.09	2.36	—	2.11	2.30	—	2.11	2.49	—	2.04	2.17	—
1985	2.14	2.39	—	2.16	2.36	—	2.20	2.44	—	1.93	2.00	—
1986	2.13	2.36	—	—	2.29	—	—	2.55	—	—	2.14	—
1987	2.18	2.44	—	2.20	2.38	—	2.22	2.61	—	2.03	2.01	—
1988	2.08	2.35	—	2.02	2.32	—	2.13	2.48	—	2.00	2.13	—
1989	2.01	2.35	—	1.99	2.27	—	2.06	2.56	—	1.93	2.12	—
1990	1.99	2.29	—	1.98	2.27	—	2.03	2.44	—	1.85	2.09	—
1991	2.00	2.36	—	—	—	—	—	—	—	—	—	—
1992	1.93	2.30	—	1.92	—	—	1.94	2.73	—	1.85	—	—
1993	1.95	2.41	—	1.97	2.40	—	1.97	2.48	—	1.80	2.11	—
1994	1.95	2.26	2.43	1.95	2.16	2.34	1.90	2.55	2.64	1.86	1.90	2.23
1995	1.97	2.28	2.47	1.98	2.25	2.43	1.93	2.41	2.56	1.81	1.85	2.09

—Data not available.

NOTE.—Average based on a scale where A=4, B=3, C=2, D=1, and F=0.

SOURCE: "The Annual Gallup Poll of the Public's Attitudes Toward the Public Schools," *Phi Delta Kappan,* various years. (This table was prepared April 1996.)

Table 22.—Items most frequently cited by the general public as a major problem facing the local public schools: 1970 to 1995

Problems	Percent																	
	1970	1975	1980	1981	1982	1983	1984	1985	1986	1987	1988	1989	1990	1991	1992	1993	1994	1995
1	2	3	4	5	6	7	8	9	10	11	12	13	14	15	16	17	18	19
Lack of discipline	18	23	26	23	27	25	27	25	24	22	19	19	19	20	17	15	18	15
Lack of financial support	17	14	10	12	22	13	14	9	11	14	12	13	13	18	22	21	13	11
Fighting/violence/gangs	—	—	—	—	—	—	—	—	—	—	—	—	—	—	9	13	18	9
Use of drugs	11	9	14	15	20	18	18	18	28	30	32	34	38	22	22	16	11	7
Standards/quality of education	—	—	—	—	—	—	—	—	—	—	—	—	—	—	—	—	8	4
Large schools/overcrowding	—	10	7	5	4	3	4	5	5	8	6	8	7	9	9	8	7	3
Lack of respect	—	—	—	—	—	—	—	—	—	—	—	—	—	—	—	—	3	3
Lack of family structure/problems of home life	—	—	—	—	—	—	—	—	—	—	—	—	—	—	—	—	5	3
Crime/vandalism	—	—	—	—	—	—	—	—	—	—	—	—	—	—	—	—	4	2
Getting good teachers	12	11	6	11	10	8	14	10	6	9	11	7	7	11	5	5	3	2
Parents' lack of interest	3	2	6	5	5	6	5	3	4	6	7	6	4	7	5	4	3	2
Poor curriculum/standards	6	5	11	14	11	14	15	11	8	8	11	8	8	10	9	9	3	2
Pupils' lack of interest/truancy	—	3	5	4	5	5	4	5	3	6	5	3	6	5	3	4	3	2
Integration/segregation/racial discrimination	17	15	10	11	6	5	6	4	3	4	4	4	5	5	4	4	3	2
Management of funds/programs	—	—	—	—	—	—	—	—	—	—	—	—	—	—	—	—	(1)	2
Moral standards	—	—	—	1	2	4	1	2	5	7	6	3	3	3	4	3	—	—
Low teacher pay	—	—	—	—	—	—	4	2	3	5	4	4	6	4	3	3	—	—
Teachers' lack of interest	—	—	6	4	7	8	5	4	4	5	3	4	4	2	2	—	—	—
Drinking/alcoholism	—	—	2	2	3	3	4	3	5	6	5	4	4	2	2	—	—	—
Lack of proper facilities	11	3	2	2	2	1	2	1	1	2	1	1	2	—	—	—	—	—

—Data not available.
[1] Less than .05 percent.

SOURCE: "The Annual Gallup Poll of the Public's Attitudes Toward the Public Schools," *Phi Delta Kappan,* various years. (This table was prepared April 1996.)

Table 23.—Public opinion of public and private school choice: 1989 to 1995

	Percent who favor position							
					1995			
Question	1989	1990	1991	1993	Total	No children in school	Public school parents	Nonpublic school parents
1	2	3	4	5	6	7	8	9
Do you favor or oppose allowing students and their parents to choose which public schools in the community the students attend regardless of where they live?	60	62	62	65	69	69	69	78
Do you favor or oppose allowing students and parents to choose a private school to attend at public expense?	—	—	26	24	33	30	38	44
Do you think private schools that accept government tuition payments for these students should be accountable to public authorities or not?								
Yes, should be accountable	—	—	—	63	73	—	—	—
No, should not be accountable	—	—	—	34	24	—	—	—
Don't know	—	—	—	3	3	—	—	—

—Not applicable.

SOURCE: *Phi Delta Kappan,* "The Annual Gallup Poll of the Public's Attitudes Toward the Public Schools," September 1995. (This table was prepared April 1996.)

Table 24.—Parental involvement in 8th graders' school-related activities, by selected parental characteristics: 1988

Characteristics of parents	Percent of parents [1] who talk with child regularly about			Percent of parents [1] who report family rules about			Percent of parents [1] who report that they			Percent of parents [1] who have contacted school about child's	
	Current school experiences	High school plans	Plans after high school	Number of hours of television watched on school days	Doing homework	Maintaining certain grade average	Never or seldom help with homework	Belong to a parent-teacher organization	Attend the parent-teacher organization meeting	Academic performance	Academic program
1	2	3	4	5	6	7	8	9	10	11	12
Total	79.4	47.1	38.3	61.7	92.0	72.7	29.4	31.9	36.2	52.5	34.8
Race/ethnicity											
Asian/Pacific Islander	59.8	41.7	36.5	67.1	89.3	74.7	42.8	29.4	41.2	36.0	29.4
Hispanic	67.1	52.7	44.8	68.7	92.3	79.8	44.7	15.5	43.0	48.3	34.5
Black, non-Hispanic	75.0	57.8	51.4	75.3	95.5	82.3	31.4	30.4	47.8	52.1	34.2
White, non-Hispanic	82.3	45.0	35.4	58.5	91.4	70.1	26.8	34.3	33.3	53.7	35.1
American Indian/Alaskan Native	72.5	44.6	39.9	62.9	95.9	75.7	35.5	16.6	35.0	52.5	42.5
Socioeconomic status [2]											
Lower quartile	66.3	43.0	33.5	64.0	92.2	74.2	41.7	12.2	29.2	38.1	24.2
Middle two quartiles	80.7	46.5	38.4	60.8	93.0	74.9	27.5	29.8	35.2	54.1	34.8
Highest quartile	89.0	52.7	42.9	61.6	89.9	66.9	21.9	54.0	44.4	61.9	44.1
Highest education level of parents											
Two-parent families											
Neither completed high school	60.0	40.7	29.6	64.0	92.6	75.2	47.6	10.6	32.7	32.3	21.2
One did not complete high school	72.9	45.7	34.7	61.6	92.6	74.8	33.7	15.4	28.7	42.8	28.6
Both completed high school ..	81.9	46.0	37.7	61.3	93.3	75.5	26.6	30.8	35.8	53.6	35.1
One graduated college [3]	87.2	51.8	42.4	61.1	91.5	69.9	21.8	48.6	42.7	60.9	41.1
Both graduated college	89.5	52.3	40.8	63.0	88.1	61.1	20.5	60.7	46.9	61.5	46.4
Single-parent families (female)											
Did not complete high school	61.0	47.1	34.6	64.3	91.2	73.2	50.3	9.7	25.1	33.9	19.0
Completed high school	77.0	48.1	42.1	62.5	92.7	75.1	33.8	24.6	33.0	53.5	32.7
Graduated college	84.0	51.8	44.8	60.1	87.0	66.3	28.3	46.7	43.9	67.8	45.6
Family composition											
Two-parent family	81.0	47.4	38.0	61.7	92.2	72.6	27.6	34.2	37.3	52.9	35.7
One-parent family	74.2	47.0	40.2	62.1	91.2	73.3	36.2	23.6	32.0	52.0	31.6

[1] The respondent was the parent most knowledgeable about the child's education. The responding parents reported on their own and their spouses' activities.

[2] Socioeconomic status was measured by a composite score on parental education and occupations, and family income.

[3] Includes a small number of cases where one parent was a high school dropout.

NOTE.—Because of rounding, details may not add to totals.

SOURCE: U.S. Department of Education, National Center for Education Statistics, National Education Longitudinal Study of 1988, "Base Year Parent Survey." (This table was prepared July 1990.)

Table 25.—Teachers' opinions about the most important goals for education, by type and control of school: 1990–91

Goal	Percent of teachers indicating item is the most important goal							
	Public school teachers				Private school teachers			
	Total	Elementary schools	Secondary schools	Combined schools	Total	Elementary schools	Secondary schools	Combined schools
1	2	3	4	5	6	7	8	9
Building basic literacy skills	49.9	52.4	45.7	49.1	32.4	34.6	26.6	32.6
Encouraging academic excellence	11.1	8.8	15.5	8.9	13.0	8.9	20.4	14.3
Promoting occupational or vocational skills	1.9	0.7	3.6	4.7	0.2	0.2	0.5	0.2
Promoting good work habits and self-discipline	13.2	11.8	15.7	12.2	8.9	8.6	10.1	8.7
Promoting personal growth	20.4	23.3	15.2	20.4	19.7	21.1	19.3	18.5
Promoting human relations	1.6	1.6	1.7	2.0	1.4	0.7	2.0	1.8
Promoting specific moral values	1.4	1.2	1.6	2.4	3.1	3.1	4.9	2.3
Promoting multicultural awareness or understanding	0.5	0.3	0.9	0.4	—	—	—	—
Fostering religious or spiritual development	—	—	—	—	21.2	22.8	16.1	21.7

—Data not available.

SOURCE: U.S. Department of Education, National Center for Education Statistics, "Schools and Staffing Survey, 1990–91." (This table was prepared May 1993.)

Table 26.—Teachers' perceptions about serious problems in their schools, by type and control of school: 1990–91 and 1993–94

Problem area	Percent of teachers indicating item is a serious problem									
	Public school teachers					Private school teachers				
	1990–91	1993–94				1990–91	1993–94			
	Total	Total	Elementary schools	Secondary schools	Combined schools	Total	Total	Elementary schools	Secondary schools	Combined schools
1	2	3	4	5	6	7	8	9	10	11
Student tardiness	11.2	10.5	6.3	18.3	7.8	3.4	2.6	1.8	4.3	2.6
Student absenteeism	14.1	14.4	7.2	27.1	15.0	2.6	2.2	0.8	5.2	2.7
Teacher absenteeism	1.6	1.5	1.3	1.9	2.0	0.7	0.8	0.7	1.2	0.9
Students cutting class	4.6	5.1	1.3	11.9	4.6	0.7	0.7	0.2	2.4	0.7
Physical conflicts among students	6.5	8.2	7.8	8.6	8.1	1.1	1.5	0.9	2.1	2.1
Robbery or theft	3.4	4.1	3.0	5.8	3.6	0.8	0.8	0.4	1.4	1.1
Vandalism of school property	5.4	6.7	5.2	9.0	5.9	0.9	1.2	0.9	2.0	1.2
Student pregnancy	6.4	7.3	1.1	18.4	10.1	0.3	0.4	0.2	1.1	0.4
Student use of alcohol	8.2	9.3	1.6	23.1	14.2	2.4	3.1	0.3	11.0	2.7
Student drug abuse	4.2	5.7	1.0	14.2	7.1	0.5	1.3	0.2	4.0	1.4
Student possession of weapons	1.2	2.8	1.2	5.6	2.7	0.1	0.3	0.2	0.6	0.3
Verbal abuse of teachers	7.5	11.1	8.6	14.8	14.3	1.7	2.3	0.7	2.8	4.4
Student disrespect for teachers	13.0	18.5	15.3	23.6	20.3	2.9	3.4	2.2	4.2	4.7
Students dropping out	6.3	5.8	1.2	14.1	7.7	0.2	0.6	0.3	1.3	0.7
Student apathy	20.6	23.6	15.6	38.0	28.9	4.1	4.5	2.2	9.7	5.1
Lack of academic challenge	5.7	6.5	4.2	10.4	9.9	1.3	1.5	1.0	2.5	1.6
Lack of parental involvement	25.4	27.6	23.0	34.5	35.5	4.3	4.0	2.8	7.1	4.7
Parental alcoholism/drug abuse	12.0	13.1	12.9	12.3	18.7	2.2	2.6	1.6	4.2	3.4
Poverty	17.1	19.5	20.8	15.9	26.8	2.0	2.7	2.2	3.2	3.0
Racial tension	3.8	5.1	4.0	6.7	5.5	0.7	0.9	0.6	1.7	0.8
Students come unprepad to learn ...	—	28.8	24.3	36.0	30.9	—	4.1	2.6	7.6	4.6

—Data not available.

SOURCE: U.S. Department of Education, National Center for Education Statistics, "Schools and Staffing Survey," 1990–91, and 1993–94. (This table was prepared September 1996.)

Table 27.—Teachers' perceptions about teaching and school conditions, by type and control of school: 1993–94

Statement	Percent of teachers somewhat agreeing or strongly agreeing with statement							
	Public school teachers				Private school teachers			
	Total	Elementary schools	Secondary schools	Combined schools	Total	Elementary schools	Secondary schools	Combined schools
1	2	3	4	5	6	7	8	9
The school administration's behavior toward the staff is supportive	79.2	80.7	76.8	77.0	88.2	89.4	83.3	88.7
My principal enforces school rules for student conduct and backs me up when I need it	80.8	82.0	78.6	81.4	88.4	89.3	84.4	88.5
The principal lets staff members know what is expected of them	85.6	86.9	83.5	82.1	88.2	89.1	86.6	88.2
Principal talks to me frequently about my instructional practices	44.3	49.0	35.6	45.7	54.0	58.3	41.2	53.7
Goals and priorities for the school are clear	82.8	85.4	78.1	79.3	90.2	90.9	88.3	90.2
Teachers in this school are evaluated fairly	87.9	88.6	86.6	85.3	89.8	90.4	87.3	90.3
In this school, staff members are recognized for a job well done	67.9	71.7	61.7	62.6	81.1	82.4	74.7	82.1
Principal knows what kind of school he/she wants and has communicated it to the staff	80.5	82.8	76.7	77.1	88.6	89.1	85.5	89.9
Principal does a poor job in getting resources for this school	16.1	15.1	18.1	19.6	10.5	10.6	12.9	8.7
Most of my colleagues share my beliefs and values about what the central mission of the school should be	84.2	87.3	79.1	81.4	93.2	95.0	88.4	93.7
Teachers participate in making most of the important education decisions in this school	58.3	62.8	50.3	58.4	74.0	75.1	66.1	75.3
There is a great deal of cooperative effort among staff	77.5	80.9	71.8	76.3	90.5	90.3	86.2	93.0
I receive a great deal of support from parents for the work I do	52.5	58.4	43.2	47.4	84.6	87.3	77.7	83.1
I make a conscious effort to coordinate the content of my courses with that of other teachers	85.0	88.0	79.8	82.9	85.2	86.6	78.5	86.1
Routine duties and paperwork interfere with my job of teaching	70.8	70.9	71.4	65.7	40.1	40.5	45.2	36.2
I have to follow rules in this school that conflict with my best professional judgement	24.2	22.0	27.4	26.4	15.0	15.1	19.1	13.0
Level of student misbehavior in this school interferes with my teaching	44.1	42.9	45.5	43.9	22.4	22.7	20.2	25.1
Amount of student tardiness and class cutting in this school interferes with my teaching	27.9	18.4	45.3	24.6	8.6	6.4	13.4	9.2
Rules for student behavior are consistently enforced by teachers in this school, even for students who are not in their classes	61.8	70.9	45.8	59.5	77.6	83.1	63.6	77.0
I am satisfied with my class sizes	64.9	62.9	68.2	78.1	84.4	82.2	84.0	89.3
I am satisfied with my teaching salary	44.9	44.1	47.2	43.1	41.6	35.5	43.6	49.5
I sometimes feel it is a waste of time to try to do my best as a teacher	26.8	23.4	32.6	30.8	13.4	12.1	16.5	13.7
I plan with the librarian/media specialist for the integration of services into my teaching	66.9	67.8	65.8	64.5	60.6	58.6	65.4	61.2
Library/media materials are adequate to support my instructional objectives	65.6	64.9	67.7	59.9	61.0	56.4	67.2	63.4
Necessary materials are available as needed by staff	73.1	73.7	73.0	72.3	85.7	84.5	85.3	87.3

SOURCE: U.S. Department of Education, National Center for Education Statistics, "Schools and Staffing Survey, 1993–94." (This table was prepared September 1996.)

Table 28.—Public's level of confidence in various institutions: 1994

Institution	Percent of respondents by levels of confidence				
	A great deal	Quite a lot	Some	Very little	Can't say
1	2	3	4	5	6
Small businesses	16.2	36.7	36.8	7.2	3.2
Religious organizations	21.3	28.3	30.9	16.7	2.8
The military	15.8	32.8	34.0	14.1	3.2
Private higher education	14.4	33.9	30.9	12.4	8.4
Youth development and recreation	13.8	33.0	35.6	12.1	5.5
Private elementary or secondary education	13.4	31.9	34.7	13.9	6.2
Public higher education	11.4	33.9	39.2	10.7	4.8
Public elementary or secondary education	11.3	30.7	40.6	14.7	2.7
Federated charitable appeals, e.g., United Way	11.3	26.1	36.1	21.2	5.3
Health organizations	11.2	24.4	43.0	16.6	4.7
Environmental organizations	10.7	22.9	40.3	20.5	5.6
Human services organizations	10.3	22.9	45.0	15.4	6.5
Private and community foundations	8.0	22.5	43.9	16.7	8.9
Recreation for adults	8.6	21.7	43.4	15.0	11.3
Arts, culture, and humanities organizations	8.1	21.2	40.5	18.7	11.6
Work-related organizations	5.5	22.6	48.8	14.6	8.6
Media, e.g., newspapers, TV, radio	6.1	19.8	40.5	32.0	1.6
Public/society benefit, e.g., civil rights, social justice, community improvement organizations	6.0	17.9	45.5	24.4	6.1
Local government	3.8	19.4	45.6	29.0	2.1
Organized labor	6.7	15.9	43.9	29.1	4.4
Major corporations	5.1	17.2	50.6	22.7	4.4
State government	4.4	16.4	46.0	31.2	1.9
Federal government	3.5	15.5	44.2	34.8	1.9
International/foreign, e.g., culture exchange, relief organizations	3.7	14.9	38.3	30.7	12.5
Political organizations, e.g., Republican or Democratic parties	3.9	12.7	40.3	39.7	3.4
Organizations that advocate a particular cause	3.9	12.5	39.5	37.6	6.6
Congress	3.2	12.0	40.9	41.3	2.6

NOTE.—Institutions are listed in rank order as determined by the combined responses of "a great deal" and "quite a lot" of confidence.

SOURCE: Independent Sector, The Gallup Organization, *Giving and Volunteering in the United States, 1994.* (This table was prepared April 1995.)

Table 29.—Percentage of households contributing to education and other charitable organizations and average annual donation, by type of charity: 1989, 1991, and 1993

Type of charity	1989			1991			1993		
	Percentage of total households[1]	Average annual contribution		Percentage of total households[1]	Average annual contribution		Percentage of total households[1]	Average annual contribution	
		Per contributing household	Per total household		Per contributing household	Per total household		Per contributing household	Per total household
1	2	3	4	5	6	7	8	9	10
Total	75.1	$978	$734	72.2	$899	$649	73.4	$880	$646
Religious	53.2	896	477	51.3	800	410	49.2	817	402
Health	32.4	143	46	32.9	154	51	25.7	139	36
Human services	23.0	263	60	27.5	260	71	26.7	208	56
Youth development	21.6	129	28	22.1	114	25	17.9	106	19
Education	19.1	291	56	21.1	225	47	17.5	424	74
Environment	13.4	88	12	16.3	99	16	11.6	89	10
Arts, culture, and humanities	9.6	193	19	9.4	194	18	8.1	139	11
Public and societal benefit	11.2	120	13	11.2	132	15	11.2	160	18
Private and community foundations	6.4	116	7	6.0	113	7	5.3	144	8
Recreation, adults	6.2	135	8	6.3	164	10	4.6	193	9
International, foreign	4.2	202	8	3.5	198	7	2.8	(2)	(2)
Other	3.0	195	6	2.8	233	7	4.7	81	4

[1] Percents do not add to total because of respondents giving to more than one type of charity.

[2] Sample size too small for reliable data.

NOTE.—Details for total households do not add to total because details only include households which reported a donation amount for the particular type of charity. The percentage of total includes households who reported giving donations, but did not specify amount.

SOURCE: Independent Sector, The Gallup Organization, *Giving and Volunteering in the United States, 1989, 1991, and 1993.* (This table was prepared April 1995.)

Table 30.—Total expenditures of educational institutions related to the gross domestic product, by level of institution: 1959–60 to 1995–96

Year	Gross domestic product (in billions)	School year	Total expenditures for education (amounts in millions of current dollars)					
			All educational institutions		All elementary and secondary schools		All colleges and universities	
			Amount	As a percent of gross domestic product	Amount	As a percent of gross domestic product	Amount	As a percent of gross domestic product
1	2	3	4	5	6	7	8	9
1959	$507.2	1959–60	$23,860	4.7	$16,713	3.3	$7,147	1.4
1961	544.8	1961–62	28,503	5.2	19,673	3.6	8,830	1.6
1963	617.4	1963–64	34,440	5.6	22,825	3.7	11,615	1.9
1965	719.1	1965–66	43,682	6.1	28,048	3.9	15,634	2.2
1967	833.6	1967–68	55,652	6.7	35,077	4.2	20,575	2.5
1969	982.2	1969–70	68,459	7.0	43,183	4.4	25,276	2.6
1970	1,035.6	1970–71	75,741	7.3	48,200	4.7	27,541	2.7
1971	1,125.4	1971–72	80,672	7.2	50,950	4.5	29,722	2.6
1972	1,237.3	1972–73	86,875	7.0	54,952	4.4	31,923	2.6
1973	1,382.6	1973–74	95,396	6.9	60,370	4.4	35,026	2.5
1974	1,496.9	1974–75	108,664	7.3	68,846	4.6	39,818	2.7
1975	1,630.6	1975–76	118,706	7.3	75,101	4.6	43,605	2.7
1976	1,819.0	1976–77	126,417	6.9	79,194	4.4	47,223	2.6
1977	2,026.9	1977–78	137,042	6.8	86,544	4.3	50,498	2.5
1978	2,291.4	1978–79	148,308	6.5	93,012	4.1	55,296	2.4
1979	2,557.5	1979–80	165,627	6.5	103,162	4.0	62,465	2.4
1980	2,784.2	1980–81	182,849	6.6	112,325	4.0	70,524	2.5
1981	3,115.9	1981–82	197,801	6.3	120,486	3.9	77,315	2.5
1982	3,242.1	1982–83	212,081	6.5	128,725	4.0	83,356	2.6
1983	3,514.5	1983–84	228,597	6.5	139,000	4.0	89,597	2.5
1984	3,902.4	1984–85	247,657	6.3	149,400	3.8	98,257	2.5
1985	4,180.7	1985–86	269,485	6.4	161,800	3.9	107,685	2.6
1986	4,422.2	1986–87	291,974	6.6	175,200	4.0	116,774	2.6
1987	4,692.3	1987–88	313,375	6.7	187,999	4.0	125,376	2.7
1988	5,049.6	1988–89	346,883	6.9	209,377	4.1	137,506	2.7
1989	5,438.7	1989–90	381,228	7.0	230,673	4.2	150,555	2.8
1990	5,743.8	1990–91	412,652	7.2	248,930	4.3	163,722	2.9
1991	5,916.7	1991–92	434,102	7.3	261,262	4.4	172,840	2.9
1992	6,244.4	1992–93 [1]	457,124	7.3	274,435	4.4	182,689	2.9
1993	6,550.2	1993–94 [2]	479,069	7.3	287,485	4.4	191,584	2.9
1994	6,931.4	1994–95 [3]	504,500	7.3	302,900	4.4	201,600	2.9
1995	7,245.8	1995–96 [3]	529,600	7.3	318,400	4.4	211,200	2.9

[1] Revised from previously published data.
[2] Preliminary.
[3] Estimated.

NOTE.—Total expenditures for public elementary and secondary schools include current expenditures, interest on school debt, and capital outlay. Data for private elementary and secondary schools are estimated. Total expenditures for colleges and universities include current-fund expenditures and additions to plant value. Excludes expenditures of noncollegiate postsecondary institutions. Because of rounding, details may not add to totals.

SOURCE: U.S. Department of Education, National Center for Education Statistics, *Statistics of State School Systems; Revenues and Expenditures for Public Elementary and Secondary Education; Financial Statistics of Institutions of Higher Education;* Common Core of Data survey; "Financial Statistics of Institutions of Higher Education" survey, Integrated Postsecondary Education Data System (IPEDS) "Finance" survey, and unpublished data; Council of Economic Advisers, *Economic Indicators;* and National Education Association, *Estimates of School Statistics,* various years. (This table was prepared June 1996.)

Table 31.—Total expenditures of educational institutions, by level and control of institution:
1899–1900 to 1995–96
[In millions of current dollars]

School year	Total	Elementary and secondary schools			Colleges and universities		
		Total	Public	Private [1]	Total	Public	Private
1	2	3	4	5	6	7	8
1899–1900	—	—	$215	—	—	—	—
1909–10	—	—	426	—	—	—	—
1919–20	—	—	1,036	—	—	—	—
1929–30	—	—	2,317	—	$632	$292	$341
1939–40	—	—	2,344	—	758	392	367
1949–50	$8,911	$6,249	5,838	$411	2,662	1,430	1,233
1951–52	10,735	7,861	7,344	517	2,874	1,565	1,309
1953–54	13,147	9,733	9,092	641	3,414	1,912	1,502
1955–56	15,907	11,727	10,955	772	4,180	2,348	1,832
1957–58	20,055	14,525	13,569	956	5,530	3,237	2,293
1959–60	23,860	16,713	15,613	1,100	7,147	3,904	3,244
1961–62	28,503	19,673	18,373	1,300	8,830	4,919	3,911
1963–64	34,440	22,825	21,325	1,500	11,615	6,558	5,057
1965–66	43,682	28,048	26,248	1,800	15,634	9,047	6,588
1967–68	55,652	35,077	32,977	2,100	20,575	12,750	7,824
1969–70	68,459	43,183	40,683	2,500	25,276	16,234	9,041
1970–71	75,741	48,200	45,500	2,700	27,541	18,028	9,513
1971–72	80,672	50,950	48,050	2,900	29,722	19,538	10,184
1972–73	86,875	54,952	51,852	3,100	31,923	21,144	10,779
1973–74	95,396	60,370	56,970	3,400	35,026	23,542	11,484
1974–75	108,664	68,846	64,846	4,000	39,818	26,966	12,852
1975–76	118,706	75,101	70,601	4,500	43,605	29,736	13,869
1976–77	126,417	79,194	74,194	5,000	47,223	31,997	15,226
1977–78	137,042	86,544	80,844	5,700	50,498	34,031	16,467
1978–79	148,308	93,012	86,712	6,300	55,296	37,110	18,187
1979–80	165,627	103,162	95,962	7,200	62,465	41,434	21,031
1980–81	182,849	112,325	104,125	8,200	70,524	46,559	23,965
1981–82	197,801	120,486	111,186	9,300	77,315	50,813	26,502
1982–83	212,081	128,725	118,425	10,300	83,356	54,338	29,018
1983–84	228,597	139,000	127,500	11,500	89,597	58,124	31,473
1984–85	247,657	149,400	137,000	12,400	98,257	63,705	34,553
1985–86	269,485	161,800	148,600	13,200	107,685	70,069	37,616
1986–87	291,974	175,200	160,900	14,300	116,774	74,552	42,222
1987–88	313,375	187,999	172,699	15,300	125,376	79,859	45,516
1988–89	346,883	209,377	192,977	16,400	137,506	87,107	50,398
1989–90	381,228	230,673	212,473	18,200	150,555	96,387	54,169
1990–91	412,652	248,930	229,430	19,500	163,722	104,433	59,288
1991–92	434,102	261,262	241,062	20,200	172,840	109,026	63,814
1992–93	457,124	274,435	252,935	21,500	182,689	115,470	67,220
1993–94 [2]	479,069	287,485	265,285	22,200	191,584	120,700	70,884
1994–95 [1]	504,500	302,900	279,400	23,500	201,600	126,700	74,900
1995–96 [1]	529,600	318,400	293,700	24,800	211,200	132,700	78,400

[1] Estimated.
[2] Preliminary.
—Data not available.

NOTE.—Total expenditures for public elementary and secondary schools include current expenditures, interest on school debt, and capital outlay. Data for private elementary and secondary schools are estimated. Total expenditures for colleges and universities include current-fund expenditures and additions to plant value. Excludes expenditures of noncollegiate postsecondary institutions. Some data have been revised from previously published figures. Because of rounding, details may not add to totals.

SOURCE: U.S. Department of Education, National Center for Education Statistics, *Statistics of State School Systems; Revenues and Expenditures for Public Elementary and Secondary Education; Financial Statistics of Institutions of Higher Education;* Common Core of Data survey; "Financial Statistics of Institutions of Higher Education" survey; Integrated Postsecondary Education Data System (IPEDS) "Finance" survey; and National Education Association, *Estimates of School Statistics,* various years. (This table was prepared June 1996.)

Table 32.—Estimated total expenditures of educational institutions, by level, control of institution, and source of funds: 1979–80 to 1993–94

[In billions of current dollars]

Level and control of institution and source of funds	1979–80 Amount	1979–80 Percent	1984–85 Amount	1984–85 Percent	1989–90 Amount	1989–90 Percent	1990–91 Amount	1990–91 Percent	1992–93[1] Amount	1992–93[1] Percent	1993–94[2] Amount	1993–94[2] Percent
1	2	3	4	5	6	7	8	9	10	11	12	13
All levels												
Total public and private	$165.6	100.0	$247.7	100.0	$381.2	100.0	$412.7	100.0	$457.1	100.0	$479.1	100.0
Federal	18.9	11.4	21.3	8.6	31.6	8.3	34.1	8.3	40.1	8.8	42.3	8.8
State	64.3	38.8	96.1	38.8	142.0	37.3	151.6	36.7	159.9	35.0	164.6	34.3
Local	43.3	26.1	63.3	25.6	97.8	25.7	105.5	25.6	117.4	25.7	125.1	26.1
All other	39.1	23.6	66.9	27.0	109.8	28.8	121.5	29.4	139.8	30.6	147.1	30.7
Total public	137.4	100.0	200.7	100.0	308.9	100.0	333.9	100.0	368.4	100.0	386.0	100.0
Federal	14.8	10.8	15.8	7.9	22.9	7.4	24.9	7.5	30.1	8.2	32.0	8.3
State	63.9	46.5	95.5	47.6	140.6	45.5	150.3	45.0	158.3	43.0	163.1	42.3
Local	43.1	31.4	63.1	31.4	97.4	31.5	105.0	31.5	116.9	31.7	124.6	32.3
All other	15.6	11.3	26.3	13.1	47.9	15.5	53.7	16.1	63.1	17.1	66.3	17.2
Total private	28.2	100.0	47.0	100.0	72.4	100.0	78.8	100.0	88.7	100.0	93.2	100.0
Federal	4.1	14.5	5.5	11.7	8.6	11.9	9.2	11.6	10.0	11.3	10.3	11.0
State	0.4	1.6	0.7	1.4	1.4	1.9	1.3	1.7	1.6	1.8	1.5	1.6
Local	0.2	0.6	0.2	0.5	0.4	0.6	0.4	0.5	0.4	0.5	0.5	0.6
All other	23.5	83.4	40.6	86.4	62.0	85.6	67.9	86.1	76.7	86.4	80.8	86.7
Elementary and secondary schools												
Total public and private	103.2	100.0	149.4	100.0	230.7	100.0	248.9	100.0	274.4	100.0	287.5	100.0
Federal	9.4	9.1	9.1	6.1	13.0	5.6	14.2	5.7	17.6	6.4	18.7	6.5
State	44.7	43.3	66.8	44.7	100.5	43.6	108.2	43.5	115.8	42.2	119.8	41.7
Local	41.6	40.3	60.8	40.7	93.9	40.7	101.2	40.6	112.6	41.0	119.7	41.7
All other	7.5	7.3	12.8	8.6	23.3	10.1	25.4	10.2	28.3	10.3	29.3	10.2
Total public	96.0	100.0	137.0	100.0	212.5	100.0	229.4	100.0	252.9	100.0	265.3	100.0
Federal	9.4	9.8	9.1	6.6	13.0	6.1	14.2	6.2	17.6	7.0	18.7	7.0
State	44.7	46.6	66.8	48.7	100.5	47.3	108.2	47.2	115.8	45.8	119.8	45.2
Local	41.6	43.3	60.8	44.3	93.9	44.2	101.2	44.1	112.6	44.5	119.7	45.1
All other	0.3	0.3	0.4	0.3	[3]5.1	[3]2.4	[3]5.9	[3]2.6	[3]6.8	[3]2.7	[3]7.1	[3]2.7
Total private[4]	7.2	100.0	12.4	100.0	18.2	100.0	19.5	100.0	21.5	100.0	22.2	100.0
All other	7.2	100.0	12.4	100.0	18.2	100.0	19.5	100.0	21.5	100.0	22.2	100.0
Institutions of higher education												
Total public and private	62.5	100.0	98.3	100.0	150.6	100.0	163.7	100.0	182.7	100.0	191.6	100.0
Federal	9.5	15.2	12.2	12.4	18.6	12.3	19.9	12.2	22.5	12.3	23.6	12.3
State	19.6	31.4	29.4	29.9	41.6	27.6	43.4	26.5	44.0	24.1	44.8	23.4
Local	1.7	2.7	2.5	2.6	3.9	2.6	4.3	2.6	4.7	2.6	5.3	2.8
All other	31.6	50.6	54.1	55.1	86.5	57.4	96.1	58.7	111.4	61.0	117.9	61.5
Total public	41.4	100.0	63.7	100.0	96.4	100.0	104.4	100.0	115.5	100.0	120.7	100.0
Federal	5.4	13.1	6.7	10.6	9.9	10.3	10.7	10.3	12.4	10.8	13.3	11.0
State	19.2	46.3	28.7	45.1	40.2	41.7	42.1	40.3	42.5	36.8	43.3	35.9
Local	1.5	3.7	2.3	3.6	3.5	3.7	3.9	3.7	4.3	3.7	4.8	4.0
All other	15.3	36.9	25.9	40.7	42.7	44.3	47.7	45.7	56.2	48.7	59.3	49.1
Total private	21.0	100.0	34.6	100.0	54.2	100.0	59.3	100.0	67.2	100.0	70.9	100.0
Federal	4.1	19.4	5.5	15.9	8.6	15.9	9.2	15.4	10.0	14.9	10.3	14.5
State	0.4	2.1	0.7	1.9	1.4	2.6	1.3	2.3	1.6	2.3	1.5	2.1
Local	0.2	0.8	0.2	0.6	0.4	0.7	0.4	0.7	0.4	0.6	0.5	0.7
All other	16.3	77.7	28.2	81.6	43.8	80.8	48.4	81.6	55.2	82.1	58.6	82.7

[1] Revised from previously published data.

[2] Preliminary data.

[3] Revenues from individuals including fees for transportation and books and food service receipts. This expenditure includes only the individual contributions for these categories and excludes contributions from public sources.

[4] Some private elementary and secondary school revenues come from federal, state, and local sources. However, comprehensive data are not available to delineate the sources of revenues for private schools.

NOTE.—Estimated distribution of expenditures by source of funds are obtained from distribution of revenue sources for current funds. Federally-supported student aid that goes to higher education institutions through students' tuition payments is shown under "All other" rather than "federal." Such payments would add substantial amounts and several percentage points to the federal share. Other federal programs, not included in this table because they do not support regular educational institutions, would increase the federal share even further. Typical examples of these payments would be federal support for libraries and museums. Additionally, the federal contribution to education through tax expenditures is not reflected in this table. Because of rounding, details may not add to totals.

SOURCE: U.S. Department of Education, National Center for Education Statistics, Common Core of Data; "Financial Statistics of Institutions of Higher Education" survey; Integrated Postsecondary Education Data System (IPEDS) "Finance" survey, unpublished data. (This table was prepared June 1996.)

Table 33.—Governmental expenditures, by level of government and function: 1970–71 to 1991–92

In millions

Expenditure, by function	All governments [1]							Federal government				State and local governments [2]			
	1970–71	1980–81	1987–88	1988–89	1989–90	1990–91	1991–92	1970–71	1980–81	1990–91	1991–92	1970–71	1980–81	1990–91	1991–92
1	2	3	4	5	6	7	8	9	10	11	12	13	14	15	16
General expenditures [2]	$301,096	$827,877	$1,461,880	$1,542,620	$1,686,807	$1,804,005	$1,858,760	$150,422	$422,301	$1,059,508	$1,072,581	$150,674	$407,449	$908,108	$975,848
Selected federal programs															
National defense and international relations	80,910	174,564	329,993	346,338	344,069	366,112	351,684	80,910	174,564	366,112	351,684	—	—	—	—
Postal service	8,683	20,466	33,892	36,472	39,065	43,102	44,890	8,683	20,466	43,102	44,890	—	—	—	—
Space research and technology	3,334	5,523	8,866	10,806	12,063	13,514	13,550	3,334	5,523	13,514	13,550	—	—	—	—
Education and libraries	64,042	158,012	260,736	284,963	310,080	334,333	353,399	4,629	12,408	45,256	49,622	60,174	147,649	313,744	330,785
Social services and income maintenance															
Public welfare	20,446	74,643	115,113	126,132	140,734	167,681	202,364	2,220	22,395	119,135	142,482	18,226	54,121	130,402	158,212
Hospitals and health	14,835	47,378	78,789	85,091	92,487	102,817	108,166	3,630	11,277	28,207	27,679	11,205	36,101	81,110	88,112
Social insurance administration	2,031	5,075	7,166	7,352	7,716	8,193	9,172	1,086	2,799	7,995	9,020	945	2,276	3,250	3,717
Transportation	23,722	46,578	70,536	74,289	78,539	84,048	87,360	4,062	7,724	24,768	26,554	19,819	39,231	75,410	77,955
Public safety															
Police protection	5,706	16,851	30,934	32,723	35,921	38,942	41,248	478	1,904	6,725	7,400	5,228	14,947	32,772	34,545
Correction	1,979	7,806	20,154	22,500	26,229	29,297	31,112	94	413	2,122	2,646	1,885	7,393	27,356	28,701
Environment and housing															
Natural resources	13,740	43,599	90,119	64,353	80,915	56,949	64,550	10,658	38,896	46,549	53,938	3,082	6,175	12,575	13,049
Housing and community development	4,467	13,894	25,224	28,230	32,430	33,346	32,549	1,913	6,808	30,199	31,887	2,554	7,086	16,648	17,067
Governmental administration															
Financial administration	3,612	10,944	20,454	22,125	24,200	27,204	28,852	1,341	3,714	10,308	10,843	2,271	7,230	16,995	18,090
General control [3]	3,567	11,514	27,656	30,088	33,346	36,977	38,327	540	1,973	7,900	9,045	4,432	12,771	31,466	32,244
Interest on general debt	21,688	97,641	202,437	220,883	237,691	247,376	254,968	16,599	80,510	195,142	199,713	5,089	17,131	52,234	55,255
Other and unallocable	28,334	93,389	139,812	150,274	191,322	214,115	196,569	10,245	30,927	112,474	91,628	15,764	55,338	114,147	118,116

Percentage distribution

Expenditure, by function	All governments [1]							Federal government				State and local governments [2]			
	1970–71	1980–81	1987–88	1988–89	1989–90	1990–91	1991–92	1970–71	1980–81	1990–91	1991–92	1970–71	1980–81	1990–91	1991–92
General expenditures [2]	100.0	100.0	100.0	100.0	100.0	100.0	100.0	100.0	100.0	100.0	100.0	100.0	100.0	100.0	100.0
Selected federal programs															
National defense and international relations	26.9	21.1	22.6	22.5	20.4	20.3	18.9	53.8	41.3	34.6	32.8	—	—	—	—
Postal service	2.9	2.5	2.3	2.4	2.3	2.4	2.4	5.8	4.8	4.1	4.2	—	—	—	—
Space research and technology	1.1	0.7	0.6	0.7	0.7	0.7	0.7	2.2	1.3	1.3	1.3	—	—	—	—
Education and libraries	21.3	19.1	17.8	18.5	18.4	18.5	19.0	3.1	2.9	4.3	4.6	39.9	36.2	34.5	33.9
Social services and income maintenance															
Public welfare	6.8	9.0	7.9	8.2	8.3	9.3	10.9	1.5	5.3	11.2	13.3	12.1	13.3	14.4	16.2
Hospitals and health	4.9	5.7	5.4	5.5	5.5	5.7	5.8	2.4	2.7	2.7	2.6	7.4	8.9	8.9	9.0
Social insurance administration	0.7	0.6	0.5	0.5	0.5	0.5	0.5	0.7	0.7	0.8	0.8	0.6	0.6	0.4	0.4
Transportation	7.9	5.6	4.8	4.8	4.7	4.7	4.7	2.7	1.8	2.3	2.5	13.2	9.6	8.3	8.0
Public safety															
Police protection	1.9	2.0	2.1	2.1	2.1	2.2	2.2	0.3	0.5	0.6	0.7	3.5	3.7	3.6	3.5
Correction	0.7	0.9	1.4	1.5	1.6	1.6	1.7	0.1	0.1	0.2	0.2	1.3	1.8	3.0	2.9
Environment and housing															
Natural resources	4.6	5.3	6.2	4.2	4.8	3.2	3.5	7.1	9.2	4.4	5.0	2.0	1.5	1.4	1.3
Housing and community development	1.5	1.7	1.7	1.8	1.9	1.8	1.8	1.3	1.6	2.9	3.0	1.7	1.7	1.8	1.7
Governmental administration															
Financial administration	1.2	1.3	1.4	1.4	1.4	1.5	1.6	0.9	0.9	1.0	1.0	1.5	1.8	1.9	1.9
General control [3]	1.2	1.4	1.9	2.0	2.0	2.0	2.1	0.4	0.5	0.7	0.8	2.9	3.1	3.5	3.3
Interest on general debt	7.2	11.8	13.8	14.3	14.1	13.7	13.7	11.0	19.1	18.4	18.6	3.4	4.2	5.8	5.7
Other and unallocable	9.4	11.3	9.6	9.7	11.3	11.9	10.6	6.8	7.3	10.6	8.5	10.5	13.6	12.6	12.1

— Not applicable.

[1] Excludes duplicative intergovernmental transactions.
[2] General expenditures include expenditures through the federal government ($3,466,000 in 1990–91), which are excluded from direct general expenditures.
[3] Includes judicial and legal expenditures and expenditures on general and public buildings and other governmental administration.

SOURCE: U.S. Department of Commerce, Bureau of the Census, Government Finances, 1991–92, Series GF92–5. (This table was prepared April 1996.)

Table 34.—Direct general expenditures of state and local governments for all functions and for education, by level and state: 1991–92

[In millions]

State	Total direct general expenditures [1]	Education expenditures							
		Total	Elementary and secondary education			Higher education			Other education [3]
			Total	Current expenditure	Capital outlay [2]	Total	Current expenditure	Capital outlay	
1	2	3	4	5	6	7	8	9	10
United States	$1,150,484.7	$320,547.8	$228,695.0	$207,030.1	$21,664.9	$84,328.9	$75,148.6	$9,180.3	$7,523.9
Alabama	15,089.8	4,202.8	2,420.8	2,238.3	182.5	1,437.8	1310.7	127.0	344.2
Alaska	6,690.3	1,361.3	1,006.0	914.5	91.6	296.2	263.4	32.8	59.1
Arizona	15,910.4	4,750.4	3,202.3	2,591.8	610.5	1,476.9	1359.8	117.1	71.2
Arkansas	7,324.4	2,617.5	1,691.5	1,541.6	149.9	766.4	667.5	99.0	159.6
California	162,653.9	38,589.0	26,806.2	24,758.0	2,048.2	11,066.6	10116.1	950.4	716.2
Colorado	15,131.1	4,619.2	3,125.0	2,758.4	366.6	1,457.3	1315.0	142.4	36.9
Connecticut	17,235.2	4,579.8	3,688.8	3,355.8	333.0	765.7	749.8	15.9	125.3
Delaware	3,273.0	1,068.6	624.0	592.8	31.2	389.3	361.8	27.5	55.3
District of Columbia	5,823.0	742.9	623.7	576.7	47.0	119.1	99.1	20.1	—
Florida	54,289.1	14,482.9	11,050.7	9,375.0	1,675.7	3,070.8	2560.2	510.5	361.4
Georgia	26,081.1	7,278.2	5,440.3	4,897.8	542.5	1,569.9	1390.0	179.6	268.0
Hawaii	6,684.5	1,340.2	814.5	699.9	114.6	511.5	456.2	55.3	14.2
Idaho	3,647.4	1,236.5	827.7	714.3	113.3	364.1	326.9	37.2	44.7
Illinois	46,781.2	12,985.4	9,323.8	8,574.1	749.7	3,350.1	2959.4	390.7	311.5
Indiana	19,889.2	7,158.7	4,857.3	4,303.9	553.4	2,186.8	1937.6	249.1	114.7
Iowa	11,207.3	3,887.6	2,578.9	2,356.5	222.4	1,251.0	1146.5	104.5	57.7
Kansas	9,605.0	3,455.3	2,160.8	2,002.2	158.6	1,223.2	945.1	278.1	71.4
Kentucky	13,565.5	3,939.5	2,458.2	2,295.5	162.6	1,191.7	1073.7	118.0	289.6
Louisiana	17,608.9	4,920.0	3,490.5	3,353.2	137.4	1,240.0	1143.9	96.1	189.4
Maine	5,235.6	1,582.0	1,189.0	1,070.8	118.2	356.5	317.6	38.9	36.5
Maryland	20,609.9	6,144.9	4,306.7	3,952.3	354.4	1,704.0	1527.6	176.4	134.1
Massachusetts	30,623.7	6,326.4	4,870.2	4,636.8	233.4	1,297.1	1186.3	110.8	159.1
Michigan	41,406.3	13,593.0	9,557.7	8,731.2	826.5	3,935.1	3623.0	312.1	100.2
Minnesota	22,630.9	6,547.1	4,752.6	4,263.3	489.3	1,663.8	1533.7	130.2	130.7
Mississippi	8,428.1	2,624.2	1,671.8	1,537.3	134.6	851.9	781.3	70.6	100.5
Missouri	16,994.7	5,459.5	4,060.3	3,581.8	478.5	1,289.5	1189.3	100.2	109.7
Montana	3,325.4	1,074.0	770.4	703.4	67.0	247.3	235.2	12.1	56.2
Nebraska	7,415.3	2,224.4	1,484.8	1,349.3	135.5	690.9	621.8	69.1	48.7
Nevada	6,404.0	1,592.9	1,190.6	941.2	249.4	377.1	316.8	60.3	25.3
New Hampshire	4,569.4	1,285.6	988.3	914.5	73.8	274	273.1	1.0	23.2
New Jersey	42,421.7	12,126.3	9,838.8	9,369.7	469.1	2,179.1	1949.3	229.8	108.3
New Mexico	6,589.3	2,111.2	1,308.2	1,167.8	140.4	751.0	687.5	63.5	52.0
New York	124,386.5	27,668.4	22,184.7	20,529.9	1,654.8	5,080.8	4507.4	573.4	402.9
North Carolina	25,374.1	8,136.0	5,397.5	4,609.8	787.7	2,556.0	2338.8	217.2	182.5
North Dakota	2,699.6	928.0	529.4	493.9	35.5	370.3	328.4	41.8	28.3
Ohio	45,382.7	12,724.4	8,962.8	8,163.4	799.4	3,555.9	2998.0	557.9	205.7
Oklahoma	11,662.5	3,672.1	2,499.5	2,302.1	197.4	1,085.1	1010.6	74.5	87.6
Oregon	13,726.4	4,089.0	2,848.9	2,616.3	232.5	1,174.3	1039.5	134.8	65.9
Pennsylvania	52,921.7	15,550.7	10,939.3	9,876.5	1,062.8	3,992.6	3060.1	932.5	618.7
Rhode Island	5,145.9	1,234.5	868.7	833.7	35.0	288.4	270.1	18.3	77.4
South Carolina	14,230.3	4,269.5	2,883.2	2,607.7	275.5	1,257.8	1081.0	176.8	128.4
South Dakota	2,450.1	797.3	582.4	515.7	66.7	183.7	168.7	15.0	31.2
Tennessee	19,750.1	4,680.2	2,945.3	2,688.2	257.1	1,508.0	1194.7	313.3	226.9
Texas	64,926.2	21,660.3	15,633.8	13,791.7	1,842.1	5,733.3	5281.3	452.0	293.2
Utah	7,262.0	2,444.9	1,506.5	1,352.2	154.2	880.0	794.4	85.7	58.4
Vermont	2,591.2	934.8	638.5	612.4	26.1	268.6	251.8	16.8	27.8
Virginia	23,527.6	7,777.0	5,448.2	4,989.8	458.4	2,086.1	1906.3	179.8	242.8
Washington	27,702.3	7,612.1	5,371.0	4,311.4	1,059.7	2,023.2	1822.7	200.6	217.8
West Virginia	6,822.2	2,210.1	1,568.8	1,399.3	169.6	551.3	519.2	32.1	90.0
Wisconsin	22,046.7	7,372.5	5,086.9	4,658.8	428.1	2,137.3	1928.1	209.3	148.3
Wyoming	2,731.8	878.5	619.0	557.7	61.3	244.4	222.4	22.0	15.2

[1] Includes state and local government expenditures for education services, social services and income maintenance, transportation, public safety, environment and housing, governmental administration, interest on general debt, and other general expenditures. Includes intergovernmental expenditure to the federal government.

[2] Includes outlays for "other education."

[3] Includes assistance and subsidies to individuals and private institutions for elementary, secondary, and higher education, as well as miscellaneous education expenditures.

—Not applicable.

NOTE.—Current expenditure data in this table differ from figures appearing in other tables because of slightly varying definitions used in the Governmental Finances and Common Core of Data surveys. Because of rounding, details may not add to totals.

SOURCE: U.S. Department of Commerce, Bureau of the Census, *Government Finances: 1991–92*, Series GF/92–5. (This table was prepared April 1996.)

Table 35.—Direct general expenditures per capita of state and local governments for all functions and for education, by level and state: 1991–92

State	Total, all direct general expenditures per capita [1]	Education expenditures per capita							
		Total		Elementary and secondary education		Higher education		Other education [2]	
		Amount	As a percent of all functions	Amount	As a percent of all functions	Amount	As a percent of all functions	Amount	As a percent of all functions
1	2	3	4	5	6	7	8	9	10
United States	$3,811.44	$1,279.12	33.6	$896.57	23.5	$330.60	8.7	$51.95	1.4
Alabama	3,110.68	1,031.80	33.2	585.31	18.8	347.63	11.2	98.87	3.2
Alaska	9,893.08	2,324.66	23.5	1,713.81	17.3	504.59	5.1	106.26	1.1
Arizona	3,509.48	1,259.20	35.9	835.69	23.8	385.42	11.0	38.09	1.1
Arkansas	2,750.56	1,106.23	40.2	705.09	25.6	319.48	11.6	81.67	3.0
California	4,214.59	1,274.76	30.2	868.44	20.6	358.52	8.5	47.79	1.1
Colorado	3,696.73	1,347.56	36.5	900.58	24.4	419.97	11.4	27.01	0.7
Connecticut	4,591.40	1,410.57	30.7	1,124.30	24.5	233.37	5.1	52.91	1.2
Delaware	4,249.52	1,584.31	37.3	905.69	21.3	565.05	13.3	113.58	2.7
District of Columbia	7,561.24	1,269.90	16.8	1,066.24	14.1	203.66	2.7	—	—
Florida	3,504.12	1,090.13	31.1	819.30	23.4	227.67	6.5	43.17	1.2
Georgia	3,310.99	1,084.12	32.7	805.85	24.3	232.54	7.0	45.73	1.4
Hawaii	5,203.28	1,158.98	22.3	702.20	13.5	440.93	8.5	15.86	0.3
Idaho	3,060.38	1,168.54	38.2	775.69	25.3	341.25	11.2	51.59	1.7
Illinois	3,466.72	1,147.55	33.1	801.64	23.1	288.03	8.3	57.88	1.7
Indiana	3,188.63	1,292.71	40.5	857.87	26.9	386.22	12.1	48.63	1.5
Iowa	3,620.82	1,418.67	39.2	917.11	25.3	444.88	12.3	56.69	1.6
Kansas	3,391.51	1,387.29	40.9	856.45	25.3	484.83	14.3	46.01	1.4
Kentucky	3,183.59	1,068.51	33.6	654.64	20.6	317.38	10.0	96.50	3.0
Louisiana	3,680.89	1,163.94	31.6	814.21	22.1	289.25	7.9	60.47	1.6
Maine	3,761.99	1,297.19	34.5	962.73	25.6	288.66	7.7	45.81	1.2
Maryland	3,656.33	1,274.92	34.9	877.49	24.0	347.19	9.5	50.24	1.4
Massachusetts	4,117.21	1,069.68	26.0	811.98	19.7	216.25	5.3	41.44	1.0
Michigan	3,771.26	1,468.24	38.9	1,012.79	26.9	416.99	11.1	38.46	1.0
Minnesota	4,494.03	1,495.19	33.3	1,060.85	23.6	371.39	8.3	62.95	1.4
Mississippi	2,869.54	1,019.49	35.5	639.56	22.3	325.89	11.4	54.04	1.9
Missouri	2,883.94	1,065.27	36.9	781.87	27.1	248.31	8.6	35.09	1.2
Montana	3,552.63	1,320.89	37.2	934.99	26.3	300.16	8.4	85.75	2.4
Nebraska	3,442.55	1,401.05	40.7	924.51	26.9	430.23	12.5	46.31	1.3
Nevada	3,997.62	1,206.49	30.2	897.18	22.4	284.14	7.1	25.17	0.6
New Hampshire	3,677.05	1,175.79	32.0	889.57	24.2	246.73	6.7	39.50	1.1
New Jersey	4,693.27	1,583.82	33.7	1,263.17	26.9	279.77	6.0	40.89	0.9
New Mexico	3,787.72	1,351.94	35.7	827.45	21.8	475.03	12.5	49.46	1.3
New York	5,642.40	1,569.77	27.8	1,224.39	21.7	280.41	5.0	64.97	1.2
North Carolina	3,107.79	1,200.19	38.6	788.77	25.4	373.52	12.0	37.90	1.2
North Dakota	3,897.90	1,482.61	38.0	832.42	21.4	582.16	14.9	68.03	1.7
Ohio	3,384.90	1,183.73	35.0	813.62	24.0	322.79	9.5	47.32	1.4
Oklahoma	3,125.12	1,161.24	37.2	778.17	24.9	337.81	10.8	45.25	1.4
Oregon	3,952.97	1,391.45	35.2	956.96	24.2	394.45	10.0	40.04	1.0
Pennsylvania	3,757.95	1,324.44	35.2	910.93	24.2	332.47	8.8	81.05	2.2
Rhode Island	4,375.54	1,254.75	28.7	864.33	19.8	286.96	6.6	103.46	2.4
South Carolina	3,313.13	1,197.79	36.2	800.23	24.2	349.11	10.5	48.46	1.5
South Dakota	3,178.73	1,128.70	35.5	819.08	25.8	258.34	8.1	51.27	1.6
Tennessee	3,005.36	924.24	30.8	586.25	19.5	300.15	10.0	55.85	1.9
Texas	3,150.63	1,238.64	39.3	885.47	28.1	324.72	10.3	28.45	0.9
Utah	3,199.44	1,362.80	42.6	830.92	26.0	485.40	15.2	46.49	1.5
Vermont	4,076.35	1,693.22	41.5	1,120.15	27.5	471.24	11.6	101.83	2.5
Virginia	3,310.88	1,240.76	37.5	854.34	25.8	327.13	9.9	59.28	1.8
Washington	4,210.58	1,511.73	35.9	1,045.76	24.8	393.93	9.4	72.04	1.7
West Virginia	3,212.93	1,234.02	38.4	865.80	26.9	304.23	9.5	63.99	2.0
Wisconsin	3,963.88	1,501.13	37.9	1,015.96	25.6	426.86	10.8	58.30	1.5
Wyoming	5,281.93	1,923.07	36.4	1,328.26	25.1	524.36	9.9	70.45	1.3

[1] Includes state and local government expenditures for education services, social services and income maintenance, transportation, public safety, environment and housing, governmental administration, interest on general debt, and other general expenditures. Includes intergovernmental expenditure to the federal government.

[2] Includes assistance and subsidies to individuals and private institutions for elementary, secondary, and higher education, as well as miscellaneous education expenditures.

—Not applicable.

NOTE.—Per capita amounts are based on population figures as of April 1, 1991, and are computed on the basis of amounts rounded to the nearest thousand. Because of rounding, details may not add to totals.

SOURCE: U.S. Department of Commerce, Bureau of the Census, Governments Division, *Government Finances: 1991–92*, Series GF/92–5. (This table was prepared April 1996.)

Table 36.—Gross domestic product, state and local expenditures, personal income, disposable personal income, median family income, and population: 1929 to 1995

Year	Gross domestic product, in billions		State and local expenditures,[1] in millions		Personal income, in billions	Disposable personal income, in billions of 1992 dollars	Disposable personal income per capita		Median family income	Total population in thousands	
	Current dollars	Constant 1992 dollars	All general expenditures	Education expenditures			Current dollars	Constant 1992 dollars		Annual averages of quarterly data[2]	As of July 1[3]
1	2	3	4	5	6	7	8	9	10	11	12
1929	—	—	—	—	—	—	—	—	—	—	121,878
1933	—	—	—	—	—	—	—	—	—	—	125,690
1939	—	—	—	—	—	—	—	—	—	—	131,028
1940	—	—	$9,229	$2,638	—	—	—	—	—	—	132,122
1941	—	—	—	—	—	—	—	—	—	—	133,402
1942	—	—	9,190	2,586	—	—	—	—	—	—	134,860
1943	—	—	—	—	—	—	—	—	—	—	136,739
1944	—	—	8,863	2,793	—	—	—	—	—	—	138,397
1945	—	—	—	—	—	—	—	—	—	—	139,928
1946	—	—	11,028	3,356	—	—	—	—	—	—	141,389
1947	—	—	—	—	—	—	—	—	$3,031	—	144,126
1948	—	—	17,684	5,379	—	—	—	—	3,187	—	146,631
1949	—	—	—	—	—	—	—	—	3,107	—	149,188
1950	—	—	22,787	7,177	—	—	—	—	3,319	—	151,684
1951	—	—	—	—	—	—	—	—	3,709	—	154,287
1952	—	—	26,098	8,318	—	—	—	—	3,890	—	156,954
1953	—	—	27,910	9,390	—	—	—	—	4,242	—	159,565
1954	—	—	30,701	10,557	—	—	—	—	4,167	—	162,391
1955	—	—	33,724	11,907	—	—	—	—	4,418	—	165,275
1956	—	—	36,711	13,220	—	—	—	—	4,780	—	168,221
1957	—	—	40,375	14,134	—	—	—	—	4,966	—	171,274
1958	—	—	44,851	15,919	—	—	—	—	5,087	—	174,882
1959	$507.2	$2,212.3	48,887	17,283	$393.5	$1,530.1	$1,971	$8,641	5,417	177,073	177,830
1960	526.6	2,261.7	51,876	18,719	411.7	1,565.4	2,008	8,660	5,620	180,760	180,671
1961	544.8	2,309.8	56,201	20,574	429.1	1,615.8	2,062	8,794	5,735	183,742	183,691
1962	585.2	2,449.1	60,206	22,216	456.1	1,693.7	2,151	9,077	5,956	186,590	186,538
1963	617.4	2,554.0	63,977	23,729	479.1	1,755.5	2,225	9,274	6,249	189,300	189,242
1964	663.0	2,702.9	69,302	26,286	513.5	1,881.9	2,384	9,805	6,569	191,927	191,889
1965	719.1	2,874.8	74,678	28,563	555.8	2,000.2	2,541	10,292	6,957	194,347	194,303
1966	787.8	3,060.2	82,843	33,287	604.7	2,106.6	2,715	10,715	7,532	196,599	196,560
1967	833.6	3,140.2	93,350	37,919	649.7	2,198.4	2,877	11,061	7,933	198,752	198,712
1968	910.6	3,288.6	102,411	41,158	713.5	2,298.2	3,096	11,448	8,632	200,745	200,706
1969	982.2	3,388.0	116,728	47,238	778.2	2,373.6	3,297	11,708	9,433	202,736	202,677
1970	1,035.6	3,388.2	131,332	52,718	836.1	2,465.6	3,545	12,022	9,867	205,089	205,052
1971	1,125.4	3,500.1	150,674	59,413	898.9	2,564.0	3,805	12,345	10,285	207,692	207,661
1972	1,237.3	3,690.3	168,550	65,814	987.3	2,680.8	4,074	12,770	11,116	209,924	209,896
1973	1,382.6	3,902.3	181,357	69,714	1,105.6	2,869.4	4,553	13,539	12,051	211,939	211,909
1974	1,496.9	3,888.2	198,959	75,833	1,213.3	2,847.0	4,928	13,310	12,902	213,898	213,854
1975	1,630.6	3,865.1	230,721	87,858	1,315.6	2,895.0	5,367	13,404	13,719	215,981	215,973
1976	1,819.0	4,081.1	256,731	97,216	1,455.4	3,008.0	5,837	13,793	14,958	218,086	218,035
1977	2,026.9	4,279.3	274,215	102,780	1,611.4	3,105.1	6,362	14,095	16,009	220,289	220,239
1978	2,291.4	4,493.7	296,983	110,758	1,820.2	3,264.2	7,097	14,662	17,640	222,629	222,585
1979	2,557.5	4,624.0	327,517	119,448	2,049.7	3,353.9	7,861	14,899	19,587	225,106	225,055
1980	2,784.2	4,611.9	369,086	133,211	2,285.7	3,373.3	8,665	14,813	21,023	227,726	227,726
1981	3,115.9	4,724.9	407,449	145,784	2,560.4	3,452.3	9,566	15,009	22,388	230,008	229,966
1982	3,242.1	4,623.6	436,896	154,282	2,718.7	3,483.0	10,108	14,999	23,433	232,218	232,188
1983	3,514.5	4,810.0	466,421	163,876	2,891.7	3,579.9	10,764	15,277	24,674	234,332	234,307
1984	3,902.4	5,138.2	505,008	176,108	3,205.5	3,841.9	11,887	16,252	26,433	236,394	236,348
1985	4,180.7	5,329.5	553,899	192,686	3,439.6	3,958.6	12,587	16,597	27,735	238,506	238,466
1986	4,422.2	5,489.9	605,623	210,819	3,647.5	4,087.0	13,244	16,981	29,458	240,682	240,651
1987	4,692.3	5,648.4	657,134	226,619	3,877.3	4,154.1	13,849	17,106	[4] 30,970	242,842	242,804
1988	5,049.6	5,862.9	704,921	242,683	4,172.8	4,318.1	14,857	17,621	[4] 32,191	245,061	245,021
1989	5,438.7	6,060.4	762,360	263,898	4,489.3	4,403.7	15,742	17,801	[4] 34,213	247,387	247,342
1990	5,743.8	6,138.7	834,818	288,148	4,791.6	4,484.6	16,670	17,942	[4] 35,353	249,956	249,913
1991	5,916.7	6,079.0	908,108	309,302	4,968.5	4,486.4	17,191	17,755	[4] 35,939	252,680	252,650
1992	6,244.4	6,244.4	975,848	326,275	5,264.2	4,613.7	18,062	18,062	[4] 36,573	255,432	255,419
1993	6,550.2	6,383.8	—	—	5,479.2	4,666.2	18,552	18,075	[4] 36,959	258,159	258,137
1994	6,931.4	6,604.2	—	—	5,750.2	4,775.6	19,253	18,320	[4] 38,782	260,681	260,660
1995	7,245.8	6,739.0	—	—	6,101.7	4,934.7	20,174	18,757	—	263,090	263,034

[1] Data for years prior to 1963 include expenditures for government fiscal years ending during that particular calendar year. Data for 1963 and later years are the aggregations of expenditures for government fiscal years which ended on June 30 of the stated year. General expenditures exclude expenditures of publicly owned utilities and liquor stores, and of insurance-trust activities. Intergovernmental payments between state and local governments are excluded. Payments to the federal government are included.

[2] Population of the United States including Armed Forces overseas; includes Alaska and Hawaii beginning 1960. Quarterly data are averages for the period.

[3] Population of the United States including Armed Forces overseas; includes Alaska and Hawaii beginning 1958. Includes revisions based on the 1990 Census.

[4] Revised methodology.
—Data not available.

NOTE.—Gross domestic product data are adjusted by the GDP chain weight price deflator. Personal income data are adjusted by the personal consumption deflator. Some data have been revised from previously published figures.

SOURCE: Executive Office of the President, *Economic Report of the President*, February 1996, and *Economic Indicators*, May 1996; and U.S. Department of Commerce, Bureau of the Census, *Consumer Income*, Series P-60, No. 174; and U.S. Census Bureau, News Release, December 30, 1991. (This table was prepared July 1996.)

Table 37.—Gross domestic product deflator, Consumer Price Index, education price indexes, and federal budget composite deflator: 1919 to 1996

Calendar year			School year						Federal fiscal year	
Year	Gross domestic product chain weight deflator	Consumer Price Index [1]	Year	Consumer Price Index [2]	Elementary/ Secondary Price Index	Higher Education Price Index	Research and Development Index	Academic Library Operations Index	Year	Federal budget composite deflator
1	2	3	4	5	6	7	8	9	10	11
1919	—	17.3	1919–20	19.1	—	—	—	—	1919	—
1929	—	17.1	1929–30	17.1	—	—	—	—	1929	—
1934	—	13.4	1934–35	13.6	—	—	—	—	1934	—
1939	—	13.9	1939–40	14.0	—	—	—	—	1939	—
1940	—	14.0	1940–41	14.2	—	—	—	—	1940	0.0978
1941	—	14.7	1941–42	15.6	—	—	—	—	1941	0.1009
1942	—	16.3	1942–43	16.9	—	—	—	—	1942	0.1115
1943	—	17.3	1943–44	17.4	—	—	—	—	1943	0.1199
1944	—	17.6	1944–45	17.8	—	—	—	—	1944	0.1160
1945	—	18.0	1945–46	18.2	—	—	—	—	1945	0.1141
1946	—	19.5	1946–47	21.2	—	—	—	—	1946	0.1193
1947	—	22.3	1947–48	23.3	—	—	—	—	1947	0.1496
1948	—	24.1	1948–49	24.1	—	—	—	—	1948	0.1543
1949	—	23.8	1949–50	23.7	—	—	—	—	1949	0.1582
1950	—	24.1	1950–51	25.1	—	—	—	—	1950	0.1634
1951	—	26.0	1951–52	26.3	—	—	—	—	1951	0.1592
1952	—	26.5	1952–53	26.7	—	—	—	—	1952	0.1627
1953	—	26.7	1953–54	26.9	—	—	—	—	1953	0.1712
1954	—	26.9	1954–55	26.8	—	—	—	—	1954	0.1765
1955	—	26.8	1955–56	26.9	—	—	—	—	1955	0.1801
1956	—	27.2	1956–57	27.7	—	—	—	—	1956	0.1907
1957	—	28.1	1957–58	28.6	—	—	—	—	1957	0.2017
1958	—	28.9	1958–59	29.0	—	—	—	—	1958	0.2124
1959	23.0	29.1	1959–60	29.4	—	—	—	—	1959	0.2249
1960	23.3	29.6	1960–61	29.8	—	25.6	26.7	—	1960	0.2351
1961	23.6	29.9	1961–62	30.1	—	26.5	27.5	—	1961	0.2407
1962	23.9	30.2	1962–63	30.4	—	27.6	28.5	—	1962	0.2450
1963	24.2	30.6	1963–64	30.8	—	28.6	29.5	—	1963	0.2544
1964	24.6	31.0	1964–65	31.2	—	29.8	30.7	—	1964	0.2596
1965	25.0	31.5	1965–66	31.9	—	31.3	32.0	—	1965	0.2650
1966	25.7	32.4	1966–67	32.9	—	32.9	33.8	—	1966	0.2732
1967	26.6	33.4	1967–68	34.0	—	34.9	35.7	—	1967	0.2812
1968	27.7	34.8	1968–69	35.7	—	37.1	38.0	—	1968	0.2927
1969	29.0	36.7	1969–70	37.8	—	39.5	40.3	—	1969	0.3092
1970	30.6	38.8	1970–71	39.7	—	42.1	42.7	—	1970	0.3282
1971	32.1	40.5	1971–72	41.2	—	44.3	45.0	—	1971	0.3508
1972	33.5	41.8	1972–73	42.8	—	46.7	47.1	—	1972	0.3736
1973	35.4	44.4	1973–74	46.6	—	49.9	50.1	—	1973	0.3961
1974	38.5	49.3	1974–75	51.8	52.7	54.3	54.8	—	1974	0.4307
1975	42.2	53.8	1975–76	55.5	57.3	57.8	59.0	57.3	1975	0.4758
1976	44.6	56.9	1976–77	58.7	60.9	61.5	62.7	61.6	1976	0.5098
1977	47.5	60.6	1977–78	62.6	64.8	65.7	66.8	65.8	1977	0.5523
1978	50.9	65.2	1978–79	68.5	70.5	70.5	71.7	71.4	1978	0.5928
1979	55.3	72.6	1979–80	77.6	76.6	77.5	78.3	78.5	1979	0.6441
1980	60.4	82.4	1980–81	86.6	85.9	85.8	86.6	86.1	1980	0.7102
1981	66.1	90.9	1981–82	94.1	93.7	93.9	94.0	94.0	1981	0.7817
1982	70.2	96.5	1982–83	98.2	100.0	100.0	100.0	100.0	1982	0.8369
1983	73.2	99.6	1983–84	101.8	105.0	104.8	104.5	105.1	1983	0.8776
1984	75.9	103.9	1984–85	105.8	111.9	110.7	109.9	111.2	1984	0.9125
1985	78.6	107.6	1985–86	108.8	118.4	116.2	115.3	117.6	1985	0.9452
1986	80.6	109.6	1986–87	111.2	123.0	120.7	120.0	124.1	1986	0.9735
1987	83.1	113.6	1987–88	115.8	129.7	126.0	126.8	129.9	1987	1.0000
1988	86.1	118.3	1988–89	121.2	136.1	132.6	132.2	138.5	1988	1.0361
1989	89.7	124.0	1989–90	127.0	144.1	140.7	139.4	147.2	1989	1.0813
1990	93.6	130.7	1990–91	133.9	152.2	148.1	146.1	155.6	1990	1.1282
1991	97.3	136.2	1991–92	138.2	158.2	153.2	151.1	163.0	1991	1.1783
1992	100.0	140.3	1992–93	142.5	161.8	157.9	155.8	169.9	1992	1.2183
1993	102.6	144.5	1993–94	146.2	166.8	163.2	160.4	177.1	1993	1.2513
1994	105.0	148.2	1994–95	150.4	—	—	—	—	1994	1.2813
1995	107.5	152.4	1995–96	154.5	—	—	—	—	1995	1.3104
1996	—	—	1996–97	—	—	—	—	—	1996	1.3434

[1] Index for urban wage earners and clerical workers through 1977; 1978 and later figures are for all urban consumers.

[2] Consumer Price Index adjusted to a school-year basis (July through June).

—Data not available.

NOTE.—Some data have been revised from previously published figures.

SOURCE: Council of Economic Advisers, *Economic Indicators,* February 1991 and May 1996, and *Economic Report of the President,* February 1996; U.S. Department of Education, National Institute of Education, *Inflation Measures for Schools and Colleges;* U.S. Department of Labor, Bureau of Labor Statistics, Consumer Price Index; Research Associates of Washington, "Inflation Measures for Schools and Colleges, 1990 Update," and unpublished data; and U.S. Office of Management and Budget, *Budget of the U.S. Government, Fiscal Year 1997.* (This table was prepared July 1996.)

CHAPTER 2
Elementary and Secondary Education

This chapter contains a variety of statistics on public and private elementary and secondary education. Data are presented for enrollments, teachers, schools, student performance, graduates, and expenditures. These data are derived from surveys conducted by the National Center for Education Statistics (NCES) and other public and private organizations.

Enrollments

Public elementary and secondary school enrollments increased by 13 percent from 1985 to 1995, but elementary and secondary enrollment exhibited different patterns. Between 1985 and 1995, public elementary enrollment rose by 19 percent while secondary enrollment increased by 2 percent. Secondary enrollment declined in most years during this period (tables 3 and 39).

Preprimary education enrollment has grown substantially. Between 1985 and 1995, preprimary enrollment of 3- to 5-year-olds rose by 32 percent. An important feature of the increasing participation of young children in preprimary schools is the increasing proportion in full-day programs. In 1995 about 48 percent of the children attended school all day compared with 37 percent in 1985 (table 45).

Slightly increasing numbers and proportions of children are being served in programs for the disabled. During the 1980–81 school year, 10 percent of students were served in these programs compared with 12 percent in 1993–94. Much of the rise since 1980–81 may be attributed to the increasing proportion of children identified as learning disabled, which rose from 4 percent of enrollment in 1980–81 to 6 percent of enrollment in 1993–94 (table 51).

Tuition at Private Schools

The average full tuition (highest tuition charged) for private schools was $3,116 in 1993–94. Schools with religious orientation charged significantly lower tuition than nonsectarian schools. Students at Catholic schools paid $2,178 on average and students at schools with other religious orientations paid $2,915 on average, compared with the average tuition of $6,631 for nonsectarian private schools. Mean tuition paid by private elementary school students was lower than that paid by other schools' students, with Catholic school students paying $1,628. Students at schools with other religious orientations paid $2,606, and students at nonsectarian schools paid $4,693. Mean tuition paid by private secondary school students was substantially higher than that for private elementary school students, averaging $3,643 at Catholic schools, $5,261 at other religiously oriented schools, and $9,525 at nonsectarian schools (table 60).

Teachers and Other School Staff

During the 1970s and early 1980s, public school enrollment decreased, while the number of teachers rose. As a result, the pupil/teacher ratio fell from 22.3 in 1970 to 17.9 in 1985. After 1985, the number of pupils per teacher continued downward, reaching 17.2 in 1990. Between 1990 and 1995, enrollment rose slightly faster than the number of teachers, and the pupil/teacher ratio increased to an estimated 17.4 in fall 1995 (table 63).

In 1993–94, 73 percent of public school teachers were women, 48 percent were under 40, and more than 47 percent had a master's degree or above. By comparison, about 75 percent of the 378,000 full-time and part-time private school teachers were women. About 56 percent of the private school teachers were under age 40, and 34 percent had a master's or higher degree (table 66).

Principals tended to be older and have higher level credentials than teachers. Also, they were more likely to be male. About 7 percent of the public school principals were under age 40 and 99 percent had a master's degree or above. About 35 percent of the principals were women (table 86).

In general, public school teachers have higher salaries than private school teachers. In 1993–94, the average base salary for public school teachers was $34,153, compared with $21,968 for private school teachers (table 72). The average salary for public school teachers grew slowly during the 1990s, reaching $37,846 in 1995–96. After adjustment for inflation, teachers' salaries rose 6 percent between 1985–86 and 1995–96 (table 76).

The number of nonteaching staff employed by public schools grew at a faster rate than the number of pupils and teachers in the 1970s. During the 1970s, the proportion of the total staff who were teachers declined from 60 percent to 52 percent in fall 1980. In the 1980s and early 1990s, the number of teachers grew at about the same rate as other public school staff. In 1980, there were 9.8 pupils per staff member (total staff) compared with 9.0 pupils per staff member in 1994. In 1993–94, the number of pupils per staff member at private schools was 9.3 (tables 59 and 81).

Schools

Over the past decades, the trend to consolidate small schools has brought a large decline in the total number of public schools in the United States. In 1930, there were more than 247,000 public schools, compared with around 87,000 today. But the number of schools has grown in recent years, with an increase of 1,720 schools between 1992–93 and 1994–95 (table 88).

The shift in structure of public school systems toward middle schools (grades 4, 5, or 6 to 6, 7, or 8) is continuing. The number of elementary schools rose by 6 percent to 61,000 between 1984–85 and 1994–95, but middle schools accounted for a disproportionate share of this increase, rising by 44 percent. Meanwhile, the number of junior high schools (grades 7 to 8 and 7 to 9) declined by 35 percent (table 93). During this 1984–85 to 1994–95 period, the proportion of elementary schools with traditional 1–6 and 1–8 grade spans dropped, and the proportion with formerly atypical 1–5 spans rose (table 96).

Elementary enrollment has risen faster than the number of schools and the average elementary school size has increased. Elementary schools grew from an average of 403 students in 1984–85 to 471 in 1994–95. During the same time period, the average secondary school size fell from 721 to 697. Schools tend to be smaller in predominantly rural states, such as Nebraska, South Dakota, and Montana, and larger in states with large urban populations, such as California, Hawaii, and Florida (tables 94, 96, and 97).

Completions and Achievement

The dropout rate among 16- to 24-year-olds (which counts GED recipients and special program completers as graduates) suggest some improvements have been made over the past quarter century. Between 1968 and 1990, the dropout rate for 16- to 24-year-olds fell from 16.2 percent to 12.1 percent. The dropout rate for 1995 was 12.0 percent, which is not significantly different from 1990. The dropout rate statistic is based on the civilian noninstitutionalized population, which excludes persons in prisons and persons not living in households (table 101). Comparisons of the number of public

and private high school graduates with the 17-year-old population suggest that the proportion of young people earning regular high school diplomas has not increased over the past 20 years. At its highest point in 1968–69, there were 77 graduates for every 100 persons 17 years of age. This ratio declined during the 1970s, falling to 71 in 1979–80. The ratio has risen slightly in the 1990s, reaching 72 in 1995–96. This indicator is not a graduation rate because many students complete their high school education through alternative programs, such as night schools and the General Educational Development (GED) program (table 98).

Student achievement has improved in a number of areas. An overall increase was seen in reading proficiency scores for 13- and 17-year-olds since 1971, with some leveling off in the performance of 17-year-olds since 1984. After significant gains between 1971 and 1980, 9-year-old reading proficiency fell, but rose again in 1994 to pass 1971 levels. The increase in reading ability was supported by an overall trend across assessments in other subjects toward higher average proficiencies for 13-year-old students. Significant gaps in performance continue to exist between racial/ethnic subgroups and between male and female students. In the case of racial/ethnic differences, trends toward some narrowing of the gap observed in earlier assessments have stalled since 1988 at all three ages assessed. Gender gaps favoring female students in reading were essentially the same in 1992 as in the 1971 (table 105). Gender gaps favoring 13-year-old and 17-year-old males in science did not narrow significantly between 1977 and 1992. (table 123).

The results of assessments in average writing achievement from 1984 to 1992 reveal a dramatic shift at grade 8. After declining between 1984 and 1990, average performance increased in 1992 beyond the original 1984 level. There were no significant changes in overall writing performance at grade 11. At grade 4 there was an increase in performance between 1990 and 1992, countering downward fluctuations in the 1980s, so that performance was essentially unchanged between 1984 and 1992 (table 111).

Results from national assessments of mathematics achievement found that at ages 9 and 13, significant improvement was observed between 1978 and 1992. For in-school 17-year-olds, performance declined between 1978 and 1982, but an upturn during the past decade has increased performance levels. For all three ages, there were increases in average mathematics proficiency between 1982 and 1992, with particularly large increases among black and Hispanic 13- and 17-year-olds (table 116).

On a national assessment of educational progress administered to the states on a voluntary basis in both 1990 and 1992, 15 states and 2 territories that participated both years showed significant improvement in eighth grade mathematics performance. Of the 35 jurisdictions participating in both years, none showed a significant decline. (table 118).

Average science proficiency increased for white and minority students between 1977 and 1992. Although the average science proficiency of white students at all three age groups (ages 9, 13, and 17) remained significantly higher than the average proficiencies of black and Hispanic students, there was some evidence of gaps narrowing between 1977 and 1992. The performance gap between white and black students decreased for 9-year-olds and 17-year-olds between 1977 and 1992, but the gaps for 13-year-olds remained relatively stable. Since 1977, the performance gap between white and Hispanic students remained essentially the same for 9- and 17-year-olds, but decreased for 13-year-olds (table 123).

The Scholastic Assessment Test (SAT, formerly known as the Scholastic Aptitude Test) was not designed as an indicator of student achievement, but rather to help predict how well students will do in college. Between 1984–85 and 1994–95, mathematics SAT scores increased by 7 points, while verbal scores fell by 3 points. Although considerable differences exist among students from different racial/ethnic groups, these differences narrowed between 1984–85 and 1994–95. Combined mathematics and verbal scores for white students rose by only 7 points compared with an increase of 22 points for black students and 34 points for Asian American students (table 126).

Over the past 10 years, the average number of science and mathematics courses completed by public high school graduates increased substantially. The mean number of mathematics courses (Carnegie units) completed in high school rose from 2.6 in 1982 to 3.4 in 1992, and the number of science courses rose from 2.2 to 2.9. The average number of courses in vocational-technical areas completed by all high school graduates dropped gradually, from 4.6 units in 1982 to 3.8 units in 1992. As a result of the increased academic course load, the proportion of students completing the recommendations of the National Commission on Excellence (4 units of English, 3 units of social studies, 3 units of science, 3 units of mathematics, and .5 units of computer science) rose from 2.7 percent in 1982 to 29.2 percent in 1992 (tables 133, 134, and 136).

Drugs and Violence

Twelfth-grade students at public schools were less likely to feel safe at school and were more likely to report fights between racial/ethnic groups and gangs at school than students at Catholic and other private schools. About 10 percent of all 1992 high school seniors reported that they did not feel safe at school and 23 percent reported that there were often fights between different racial/ethnic groups (table 139). The proportion of public and private high school seniors who reported ever using an illicit drug rose from 55 percent in 1975 to 66 percent in 1981. After 1981, the proportion of seniors who had ever used drugs fell. After reaching 41 percent in 1992, the proportion rose again to 48 percent in 1995. Also, the proportion of high school seniors who had ever used cocaine fell from 17 percent in 1985 to 6 percent in 1995. Alcohol remained the most often used drug. The proportion of seniors who had used alcohol within the previous 30 days declined from 72 percent in 1980 to 51 percent in 1995 (table 147).

Resources and Expenditures

The state share of revenues for public elementary and secondary schools had grown steadily for many decades, but this trend began to reverse in the late 1980s. Between 1986–87 and 1993–94, the state share declined from 49.7 percent of all revenues to 45.2 percent, while the local share rose from 43.9 percent to 47.8 percent. The federal share also rose slightly over this period, from 6.4 percent to 7.0 percent (table 155).

The expenditure per student in public schools rose significantly during the late 1980s, but there has been relatively little change during the first half of the 1990s. Between 1985–86 and 1990–91, current expenditures per student in average daily attendance grew 14 percent, after adjustment for inflation. From 1990–91 to 1995–96, expenditures per student grew by 2 percent. In 1995–96, the estimated current expenditure per student in average daily attendance was $6,213 (table 166).

Figure 7.-Preprimary enrollment of 3- to 5-year-olds, by attendance status: October 1970 to October 1995

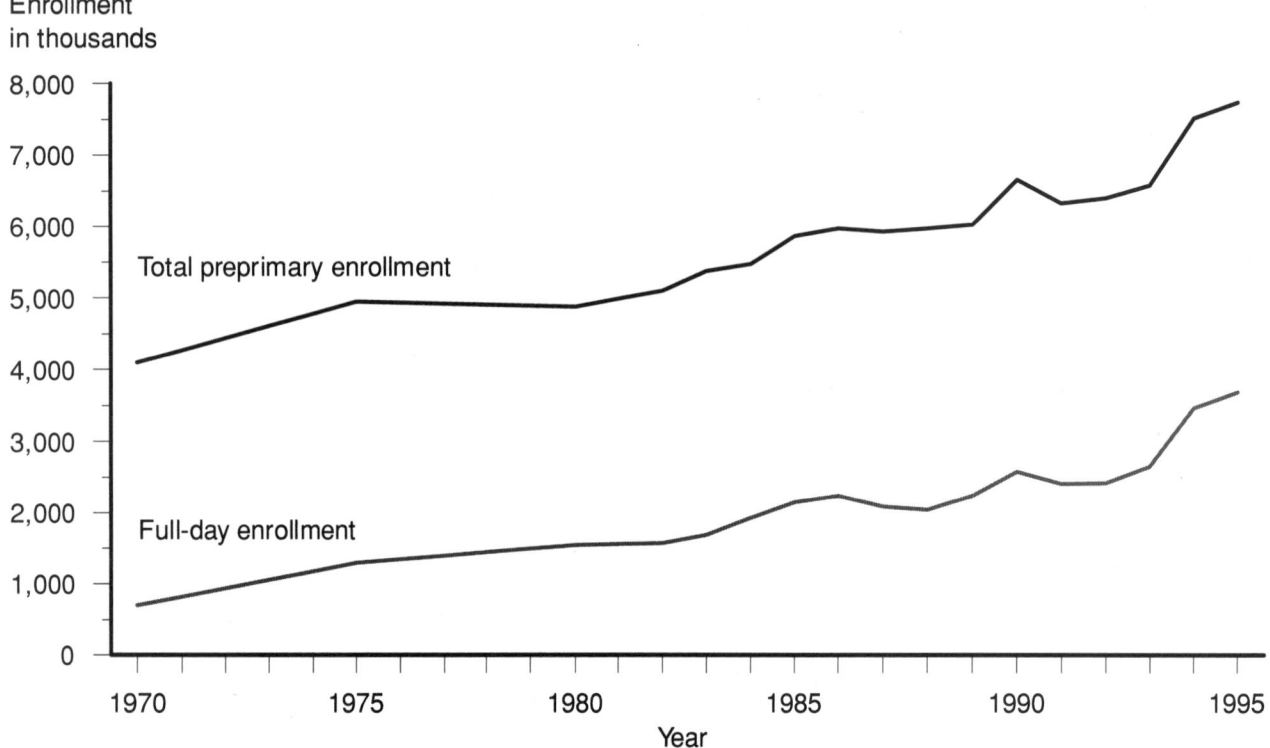

NOTE.—Data for 1994 and 1995 were collected using new procedures and may not be comparable with figures for earlier years.

SOURCE: U.S. Department of Education, National Center for Education Statistics, *Preprimary Enrollment,* various years; and U.S. Department of Commerce, Bureau of the Census, Current Population Survey, unpublished data.

Figure 8.-Enrollment, number of teachers, pupil/teacher ratios, and expenditures in public schools: 1960–61 to 1995–96

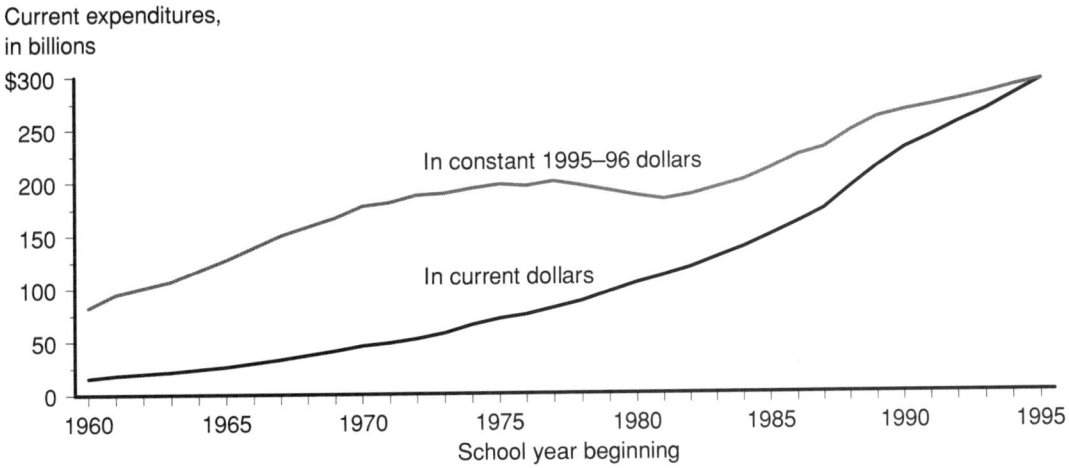

SOURCE: U.S. Department of Education, National Center for Education Statistics, *Statistics of State School Systems; Statistics of Public Elementary and Secondary School Systems; Revenues and Expenditures for Public Elementary and Secondary Education;* and Common Core of Data surveys.

Figure 9.–Percentage change in public elementary and secondary enrollment, by state: Fall 1990 to fall 1995

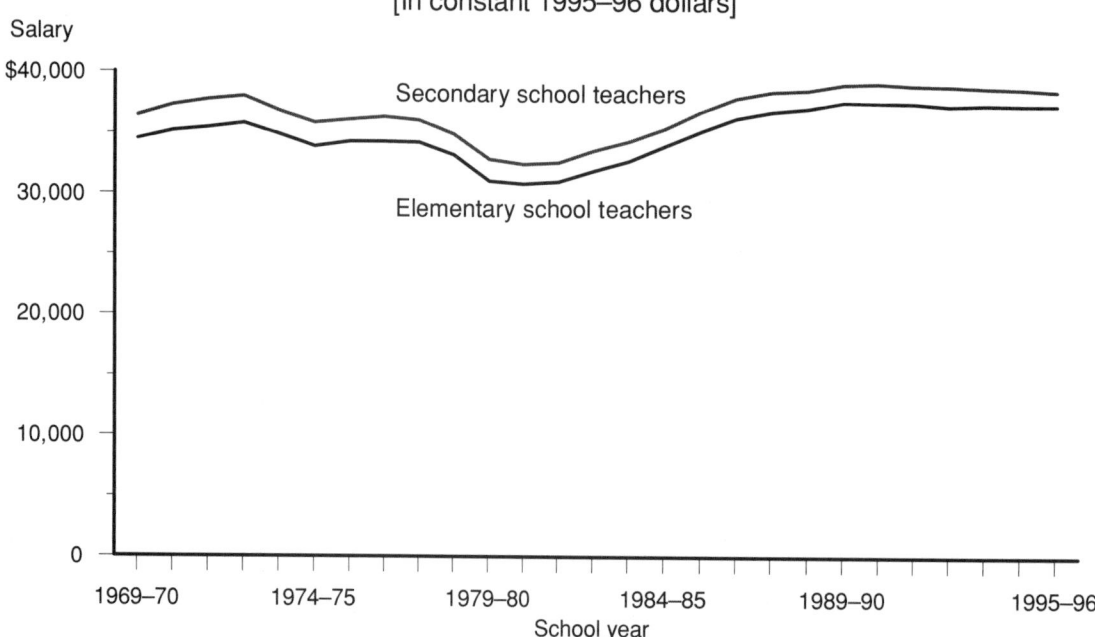

SOURCE: U.S. Department of Education, National Center for Education Statistics, Common Core of Data surveys.

Figure 10.–Average annual salary for public elementary and secondary school teachers: 1969–70 to 1995–96

[In constant 1995–96 dollars]

SOURCE: National Education Association, *Estimates of School Statistics*, latest edition 1995–96. Copyright 1996 by the National Education Association. (All rights reserved.)

Figure 11.-Sources of revenue for public elementary and secondary schools: 1970–71 to 1993–94

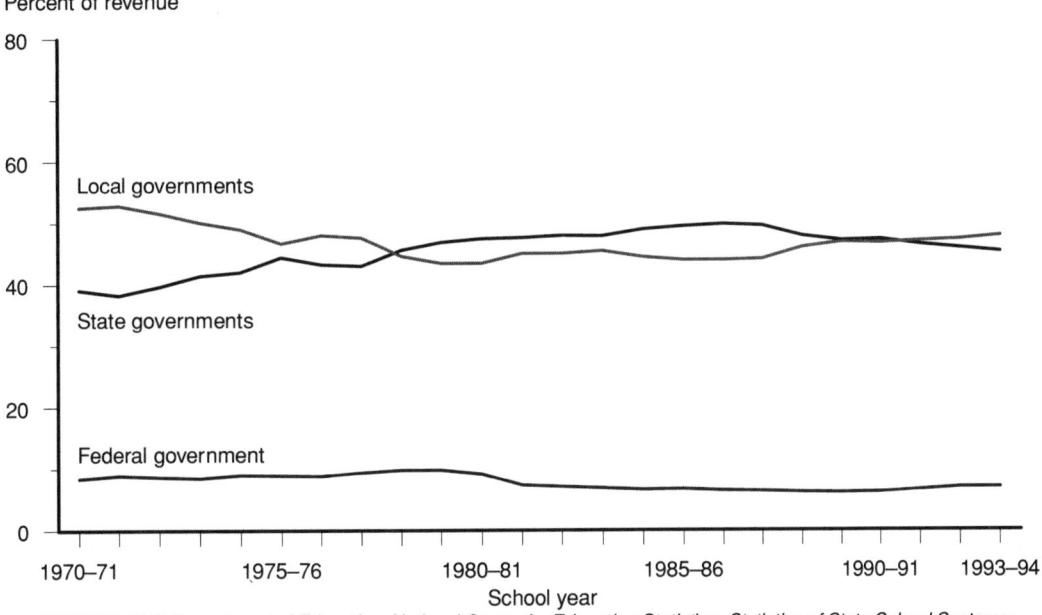

SOURCE: U.S. Department of Education, National Center for Education Statistics, *Statistics of State School Systems; Revenues and Expenditures for Public Elementary and Secondary Education;* and Common Core of Data surveys.

Figure 12.-Current expenditure per pupil in average daily attendance in public elementary and secondary schools: 1970-71 to 1995–96

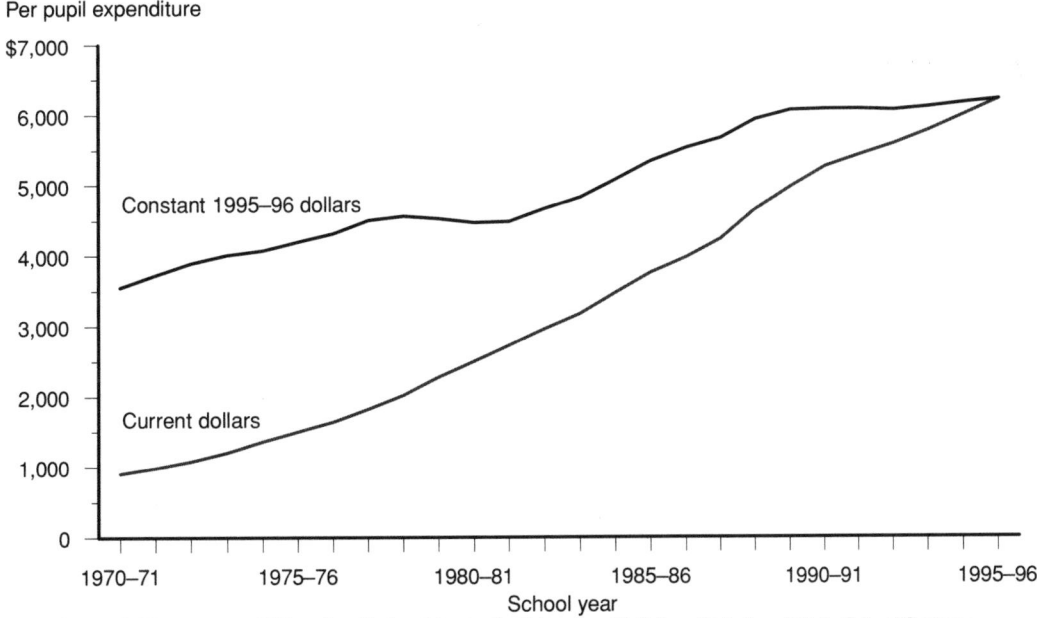

SOURCE: U.S. Department of Education, National Center for Education Statistics, *Statistics of State School Systems; Revenues and Expenditures for Public Elementary and Secondary Education;* and Common Core of Data surveys.

Table 38.—Historical summary of public elementary and secondary school statistics: 1869–70 to 1993–94

Item	1869–70	1879–80	1889–90	1899–1900	1909–10	1919–20	1929–30	1939–40	1949–50	1959–60	1969–70	1979–80	1989–90	1990–91	1992–93	1993–94
1	2	3	4	5	6	7	8	9	10	11	12	13	14	15	16	17
Population, pupils, and instructional staff																
Total population,[1] in thousands	38,558	50,156	62,622	75,995	90,490	104,514	121,767	130,880	149,199	179,323	201,385	224,567	246,819	249,402	255,028	257,783
Population aged 5–17 years,[1] in thousands	11,683	15,066	18,473	21,573	24,011	27,571	31,414	30,151	30,223	43,881	52,386	48,041	44,947	45,306	46,662	47,419
Percent of total population 5–17	30.3	30.0	29.5	28.4	26.5	26.4	25.8	23.0	20.3	24.5	26.0	21.4	18.2	18.2	18.3	18.4
Total enrollment in elementary and secondary schools, in thousands[2]	[3]7,562	9,867	12,723	15,503	17,814	21,578	25,678	25,434	25,112	36,087	45,550	41,651	40,543	41,217	42,823	43,465
Kindergarten and grades 1–8, in thousands	[3]7,481	9,757	12,520	14,984	16,899	19,378	21,279	18,833	19,387	27,602	32,513	28,034	29,152	29,878	31,088	31,504
Grades 9–12, in thousands	[3]80	110	203	519	915	2,200	4,399	6,601	5,725	8,485	13,037	13,616	11,390	11,338	11,735	11,961
Enrollment as a percent of total population	[3]19.6	19.7	20.3	20.4	19.7	20.6	21.1	19.4	16.8	20.1	22.6	18.5	16.4	16.5	16.8	16.9
Enrollment as a percent of 5- to 17-year-olds	[3]64.7	65.5	68.9	71.9	74.2	78.3	81.7	84.4	83.1	82.2	87.0	86.7	90.2	91.0	91.8	91.7
Percent of total enrollment in high schools (grades 9–12 and postgraduate)	[3]1.1	1.1	1.6	3.3	5.1	10.2	17.1	26.0	22.8	23.5	28.6	32.7	28.1	27.5	27.4	27.5
High school graduates, in thousands	—	—	22	62	111	231	592	1,143	1,063	1,627	2,589	2,748	2,320	2,235	2,233	2,221
Average daily attendance, in thousands	4,077	6,144	8,154	10,633	12,827	16,150	21,265	22,042	22,284	32,477	41,934	38,289	37,799	38,427	39,570	40,146
Average number of days attended by pupils enrolled, in millions	539	801	1,098	1,535	2,011	2,615	3,673	3,858	3,964	5,782	7,501	[4]6,835	—	—	—	—
Percent of enrolled pupils attending daily	59.3	62.3	64.1	68.6	72.1	74.8	82.8	86.7	88.7	90.0	90.4	[4]90.1	—	—	—	—
Average length of school term, in days	132.2	130.3	134.7	144.3	157.5	161.9	172.7	175.0	177.9	178.0	178.9	[4]178.5	—	179.8	—	—
Average number of days attended per pupil	78.4	81.1	86.3	99.0	113	121.2	143	151.7	157.9	160.2	161.7	[4]160.8	—	—	—	—
Total instructional staff, in thousands	—	—	—	—	—	678	880	912	963	1,457	2,286	2,406	2,986	3,051	3,140	3,209
Supervisors, in thousands	—	—	—	—	—	7	7	5	5	64	91	106	126	127	122	121
Principals, in thousands	—	—	—	—	—	14	31	32	43	—	—	—	—	—	—	—
Teachers, librarians, and other nonsupervisory instructional staff,[5] in thousands	201	287	364	423	523	657	843	875	920	1,393	2,195	2,300	2,860	2,924	3,017	3,088
Men, in thousands	78	123	126	127	110	93	140	195	196	[4]404	[4]711	[4]782	—	—	—	—
Women, in thousands	123	164	238	296	413	564	703	681	724	[4]989	[4]1,484	[4]1,518	—	—	—	—
Percent men	38.7	42.8	34.5	29.9	21.1	14.1	16.6	22.2	21.3	[4]29.0	[4]32.4	[4]34.0	—	—	—	—
Finance *(Amounts in millions of current dollars)*																
Total revenue receipts	—	—	$143	$220	$433	$970	$2,089	$2,261	$5,437	$14,747	$40,267	$96,881	$208,548	$223,341	$247,626	$260,142
Federal government	—	—	—	—	—	2	7	40	156	652	3,220	9,504	12,701	13,776	17,261	18,336
State governments	—	—	—	—	—	160	354	684	2,166	5,768	16,063	45,349	98,239	105,325	113,403	117,462
Local sources, including intermediate	—	—	—	—	—	808	1,728	1,536	3,116	8,327	20,985	42,029	97,608	104,240	116,961	124,344
Percent of revenue receipts from																
Federal government	—	—	—	—	—	0.3	0.4	1.8	2.9	4.4	8.0	9.8	6.1	6.2	7.0	7.0
State governments	—	—	—	—	—	16.5	16.9	30.3	39.8	39.1	39.9	46.8	47.1	47.2	45.8	45.2
Local sources, including intermediate	—	—	—	—	—	83.2	82.7	68.0	57.3	56.5	52.1	43.4	46.8	46.7	47.2	47.8
Total expenditures for public schools	$63	$78	$141	$215	$426	$1,036	$2,317	$2,344	$5,838	$15,613	$40,683	$95,962	$212,473	$229,430	$252,935	$265,285
Current expenditures[6]	—	—	114	180	356	861	1,844	1,942	4,687	[7]12,329	[7]34,218	[7]86,984	[7]187,933	[7]202,038	[7]220,948	[7]231,521
Capital outlay[8]	—	—	26	35	70	154	371	258	1,014	2,662	4,659	6,506	17,781	19,771	22,172	23,747
Interest on school debt	—	—	—	—	—	18	93	131	101	490	1,171	1,874	3,776	4,325	5,437	5,335
Other current expenditures[9]	—	—	—	—	—	3	10	13	36	133	636	[10]598	2,983	3,296	4,379	4,682
Percent of total expenditures devoted to:																
Current expenditures[6]	—	81.3	83.5	83.6	83.1	79.6	82.8	80.3	[7]79.0	[7]84.1	[7]90.6	[7]88.5	[7]88.1	[7]87.4	[7]87.3	
Capital outlay[8]	—	18.7	16.5	16.4	14.8	16.0	11.0	17.4	17.0	11.5	6.8	8.4	8.6	8.8	9.0	
Interest on school debt	—	—	—	—	1.8	4.0	5.6	1.7	3.1	2.0	1.8	1.9	2.1	2.0		
Other current expenditures[9]	—	—	—	—	0.3	0.4	0.6	0.6	0.8	1.6	[10]0.6	1.4	1.4	1.7	1.8	

Table 38.—Historical summary of public elementary and secondary school statistics: 1869–70 to 1993–94—Continued

Item	1869–70	1879–80	1889–90	1899–1900	1909–10	1919–20	1929–30	1939–40	1949–50	1959–60	1969–70	1979–80	1989–90	1990–91	1992–93	1993–94
1	2	3	4	5	6	7	8	9	10	11	12	13	14	15	16	17
Amounts in current dollars																
Annual salary of instructional staff[11]	$189	$195	$252	$325	$485	$871	$1,420	$1,441	$3,010	$5,174	$9,047	[12]$16,715	[12]$32,638	[12]$34,412	[12]$36,454	[12]$37,383
Personal income per member of labor force[1]	—	—	—	—	—	—	1,634	1,356	3,400	5,756	9,639	19,528	36,242	38,398	41,456	42,793
Total school expenditures per capita of total population	1.59	1.56	2.23	2.83	4.71	9.91	19.03	17.91	39	87	202	427	861	920	992	1,029
National income[1] per capita	—	—	—	—	—	—	667	587	1,520	2,289	3,977	9,143	17,673	18,492	19,413	20,150
Current expenditure[6,13] per pupil in ADA[14]	—	—	13.99	16.67	27.85	53.32	86.70	88.09	210	375	816	2,272	4,972	5,258	5,584	5,767
Total expenditure[15] per pupil in ADA	15.55	12.71	17.23	20.21	33.23	64.16	108.49	105.74	260	471	955	2,491	5,542	5,885	6,281	6,491
National income per pupil in ADA	—	—	—	—	—	—	3,845	3,502	10,312	12,637	19,099	53,626	115,402	120,019	125,114	129,386
Current expenditure per day[16] per pupil in ADA[6]	—	—	0.10	0.12	0.18	0.33	0.50	0.50	1.17	2.11	4.56	12.73	—	—	—	—
Total expenditure per day per pupil in ADA	0.12	0.10	0.13	0.14	0.21	0.40	0.63	0.60	1.46	2.65	5.34	13.95	—	—	—	—
Amounts in constant 1993–94 dollars																
Annual salary of instructional staff[11]	—	—	—	—	—	$6,682	$12,130	$15,077	$18,584	$25,747	$35,019	[12]$31,482	[12]$37,584	[12]$37,573	[12]$37,398	[12]$37,383
Personal income per member of labor force[1]	—	—	—	—	—	—	13,958	14,187	20,991	28,641	37,310	36,780	41,735	41,925	42,530	42,793
Total school expenditures per capita of total population	—	—	—	—	—	76	163	187	242	433	782	805	991	1,004	1,017	1,029
National income[1] per capita	—	—	—	—	—	—	5,698	6,142	9,384	11,389	15,394	17,221	20,352	20,190	19,916	20,150
Current expenditure[6,13] per pupil in ADA[14]	—	—	—	—	—	409	741	922	1,297	1,867	3,158	4,279	5,725	5,741	5,728	5,767
Total expenditure[15] per pupil in ADA	—	—	—	—	—	492	927	1,106	1,607	2,344	3,697	4,692	6,382	6,425	6,444	6,491
National income per pupil in ADA	—	—	—	—	—	—	32,845	36,641	63,665	62,883	73,927	101,002	132,890	131,042	128,354	129,386
Current expenditure per day[16] per pupil in ADA[6]	—	—	—	—	—	2.53	4.27	5.23	7.22	10.50	17.65	23.98	—	—	—	—
Total expenditure per day per pupil in ADA	—	—	—	—	—	2.81	4.93	5.75	8.26	12.08	18.93	24.06	—	—	—	—

[1] Data on population and labor force are from the Bureau of the Census, and data on personal income and national income are from the Bureau of Economic Analysis, U.S. Department of Commerce. Population data through 1900 are based on total population from the decennial census. From 1909–10 to 1959–60, population data are total population, including armed forces overseas, as of July 1. Data for later years are for resident population that excludes armed forces overseas.

[2] Data for 1869–70 through 1959–60 are school year enrollment. Data for later years are fall enrollment.

[3] Data for 1870–71.

[4] Estimated by the National Center for Education Statistics.

[5] Prior to 1919–20, data are for the number of different persons employed rather than number of positions.

[6] Prior to 1919–20, includes interest on school debt.

[7] Because of the modification of the scope of "current expenditures for elementary and secondary schools," data for 1959–60 and later years are not entirely comparable with prior years.

[8] Beginning in 1969–70, includes capital outlay by state and local school building authorities.

[9] Includes summer schools, community colleges, and adult education. Beginning in 1959–60, also includes community services, formerly classified with "current expenditures for elementary and secondary schools."

[10] Excludes community colleges and adult education.

[11] Average includes supervisors, principals, teachers, and other nonsupervisory instructional staff.

[12] Estimated by the National Education Association.

[13] Excludes current expenditures not allocable to pupil costs.

[14] "ADA" means average daily attendance in elementary and secondary schools.

[15] The expenditure figure used here is the sum of current expenditures allocable to pupil costs, capital outlay, and interest on school debt.

[16] Per-day rates derived by dividing annual rates by average length of term.

—Data not collected.

NOTE.—Kindergarten enrollment includes a relatively small number of nursery school pupils. Because of rounding, details may not add to totals. Some data have been revised from previously published figures. Beginning in 1959–60, data include Alaska and Hawaii.

SOURCE: U.S. Department of Education, National Center for Education Statistics, *Statistics of State School Systems*; *Statistics of Public Elementary and Secondary School Systems*; *Revenues and Expenditures for Public Elementary and Secondary Education, FY 1980*; Common Core of Data surveys; and Council of Economic Advisers, *Economic Report of the President*. (This table was prepared August 1996.)

Table 39.—Enrollment in public elementary and secondary schools, by level and state: Fall 1980 to fall 1995

State or other area	Fall 1980 Total	Fall 1981 Total	Fall 1982 Total	Fall 1983 Total	Fall 1984 Total	Fall 1985 Total	Fall 1986 Total	Fall 1987 Total	Fall 1988 Total	Fall 1989 Total	Fall 1990 Total
1	2	3	4	5	6	7	8	9	10	11	12
United States	**40,877,481**	**40,044,093**	**39,565,610**	**39,252,308**	**39,208,252**	**39,421,961**	**39,753,172**	**40,008,213**	**40,188,690**	**40,542,707**	**41,216,683**
Alabama	758,721	743,448	724,037	721,901	712,586	730,460	733,735	729,234	724,751	723,743	721,806
Alaska [4]	86,514	90,858	89,413	98,206	104,599	107,345	107,848	106,869	106,481	109,280	113,903
Arizona	513,790	507,199	510,296	506,682	530,062	548,252	534,538	572,421	574,890	607,615	639,853
Arkansas	447,700	437,121	432,565	432,120	432,668	433,410	437,438	437,036	436,387	434,960	436,286
California	4,076,421	4,046,156	4,065,486	4,089,017	4,151,110	4,255,554	4,377,989	4,488,398	4,618,120	4,771,978	4,950,474
Colorado	546,033	544,174	545,209	542,196	545,427	550,642	558,415	560,236	560,081	562,755	574,213
Connecticut [6]	531,459	505,386	486,470	477,585	468,145	462,026	468,847	465,465	460,637	461,560	469,123
Delaware	99,403	95,072	92,646	91,406	91,767	92,901	94,410	95,659	96,678	97,808	99,658
District of Columbia	100,049	94,975	91,105	88,843	87,397	87,092	85,612	86,435	84,792	81,301	80,694
Florida	1,510,225	1,487,721	1,484,734	1,495,543	1,524,107	1,562,283	1,607,320	1,664,774	1,720,930	1,789,925	1,861,592
Georgia	1,068,737	1,056,117	1,053,689	1,050,859	1,062,315	1,079,594	1,096,425	1,110,947	1,107,994	1,126,535	1,151,687
Hawaii	165,068	162,805	162,024	162,241	163,860	164,169	164,640	166,160	167,488	169,493	171,708
Idaho	203,247	204,524	202,973	206,352	208,080	208,669	208,391	212,444	214,615	214,932	220,840
Illinois	1,983,463	1,924,084	1,880,289	1,853,316	1,834,355	1,826,478	1,825,185	1,811,446	1,794,916	1,797,355	1,821,407
Indiana	1,055,589	1,025,172	999,542	984,384	972,659	966,106	966,780	964,129	960,994	954,165	954,525
Iowa	533,857	516,216	504,983	497,287	491,011	485,332	481,286	480,826	478,200	478,486	483,652
Kansas	415,291	409,909	407,074	405,222	405,347	410,229	416,091	421,112	426,596	430,864	437,034
Kentucky	669,798	658,350	651,084	647,414	644,421	643,833	642,778	642,696	637,627	630,688	636,401
Louisiana	777,560	782,053	784,027	800,193	800,941	788,349	795,188	793,093	786,683	783,025	784,757
Maine	222,497	216,293	211,986	209,753	207,537	206,101	211,752	211,817	212,902	213,775	215,149
Maryland	750,665	721,841	699,201	683,491	673,840	671,560	675,747	683,797	688,947	698,806	715,176
Massachusetts	1,021,885	947,037	908,984	878,844	859,391	844,330	833,918	825,320	823,428	825,588	834,314
Michigan	1,797,052	1,724,787	1,674,697	1,635,963	1,609,448	1,602,747	1,597,154	1,589,287	1,582,785	1,576,785	1,584,431
Minnesota	754,318	733,741	715,190	705,236	701,697	705,140	711,134	721,481	726,950	739,553	756,374
Mississippi	477,059	471,615	468,294	467,744	466,058	471,195	498,639	505,550	503,326	502,020	502,417
Missouri	844,648	818,705	802,535	795,453	793,793	795,107	800,606	802,060	806,639	807,934	816,558
Montana	155,193	153,435	152,335	153,646	154,412	153,869	153,327	152,207	152,191	151,265	152,974
Nebraska	280,430	273,340	269,009	266,998	265,599	265,819	267,139	268,100	269,434	270,920	274,081
Nevada	149,481	151,339	151,104	150,442	151,633	154,948	161,239	168,353	176,474	186,834	201,316
New Hampshire	167,232	163,827	160,197	159,030	158,614	160,974	163,717	166,045	169,413	171,696	172,785
New Jersey	1,246,008	1,199,643	1,172,520	1,147,841	1,129,223	1,116,194	1,107,467	1,092,982	1,080,871	1,076,005	1,089,646
New Mexico	271,198	268,091	268,632	269,711	272,478	277,551	281,943	287,229	292,425	296,057	301,881
New York	2,871,724	2,783,017	2,718,678	2,674,818	2,645,811	2,621,378	2,607,719	2,594,070	2,573,715	2,565,841	2,598,337
North Carolina	1,129,376	1,108,960	1,096,815	1,089,606	1,088,724	1,086,165	1,085,248	1,085,976	1,083,156	1,080,744	1,086,871
North Dakota	116,885	117,708	117,078	117,213	118,711	118,570	118,703	119,004	118,809	117,816	117,825
Ohio	1,957,381	1,898,501	1,860,245	1,827,300	1,805,440	1,793,965	1,793,508	1,793,431	1,778,544	1,764,410	1,771,089
Oklahoma	577,807	582,572	593,825	591,389	589,690	592,327	593,183	584,212	580,426	578,580	579,087
Oregon	464,599	457,165	448,184	447,109	446,884	447,527	449,307	455,895	461,752	472,394	472,394
Pennsylvania	1,909,292	1,839,015	1,783,969	1,737,952	1,701,880	1,683,221	1,674,161	1,668,542	1,659,714	1,655,279	1,667,834
Rhode Island	148,956	143,414	139,959	136,412	134,610	133,949	134,690	134,800	133,585	135,729	138,813
South Carolina	619,223	609,158	608,518	604,553	602,718	606,643	611,629	614,921	615,774	616,177	622,112
South Dakota	128,507	125,657	123,897	123,060	123,314	124,291	125,458	126,817	126,910	127,329	129,164
Tennessee	853,569	838,297	828,264	822,057	817,212	813,753	818,073	823,783	821,580	819,660	824,595
Texas	2,900,073	2,935,547	2,985,659	2,989,796	3,040,305	3,131,705	3,209,515	3,236,787	3,283,707	3,328,514	3,382,887
Utah	343,618	355,554	370,183	378,208	390,141	403,305	415,994	423,386	431,119	438,554	446,652
Vermont	95,815	93,183	91,454	90,416	90,089	90,157	92,112	92,755	93,381	94,779	95,762
Virginia	1,010,371	989,548	975,727	966,110	965,222	968,104	975,135	979,417	982,393	985,346	998,601
Washington	757,639	750,188	739,215	736,239	741,177	749,706	761,428	775,755	790,918	810,232	839,709
West Virginia	383,503	377,772	375,115	371,251	362,941	357,923	351,837	344,236	335,912	327,540	322,389
Wisconsin	830,247	804,262	784,830	774,646	767,542	768,234	767,819	772,363	774,857	782,905	797,621
Wyoming	98,305	99,541	101,665	99,254	101,261	102,779	100,955	98,455	97,793	97,172	98,226
Outlying areas											
American Samoa	9,647	9,896	—	10,124	—	—	11,055	11,248	11,764	12,258	12,463
Guam	26,420	25,084	25,676	26,249	—	26,043	25,676	25,936	26,041	26,493	26,391
Northern Marianas	—	5,300	—	4,499	4,841	—	—	5,819	6,079	6,101	6,449
Puerto Rico	712,880	721,419	708,794	701,925	692,923	686,914	679,489	672,837	661,693	651,225	644,734
Virgin Islands	25,201	25,525	25,699	26,126	26,122	25,448	24,435	24,020	23,492	21,193	21,750

Table 39.—Enrollment in public elementary and secondary schools, by level and state: Fall 1980 to fall 1995—Continued

State or other areas	Fall 1991 Total	Fall 1992 Total	Fall 1992 Kindergarten through grade 8[2]	Fall 1992 Grades 9 to 12	Fall 1993 Total	Fall 1993 Kindergarten through grade 8[2]	Fall 1993 Grades 9 to 12	Fall 1994 Total	Fall 1994 Kindergarten through grade 8[2]	Fall 1994 Grades 9 to 12	Estimated fall 1995[1] Total
1	13	14	15	16	17	18	19	20	21	22	23
United States	42,046,878	42,823,312	31,088,304	11,735,008	43,464,916	31,504,032	11,960,884	44,108,775	31,894,333	12,214,442	44,661,558
Alabama	722,004	731,634	535,248	196,386	734,288	535,637	198,651	736,472	535,187	201,285	[3]735,947
Alaska[4]	118,680	122,487	91,640	30,847	125,948	93,601	32,347	127,057	93,719	33,338	[3]125,257
Arizona	656,980	673,477	497,917	175,560	709,453	526,412	183,041	737,424	542,904	194,520	[5]766,498
Arkansas	438,518	441,490	317,598	123,892	444,271	317,713	126,558	447,565	319,282	128,283	[3]454,278
California	5,107,145	5,254,844	3,850,790	1,404,054	5,327,231	3,903,137	1,424,094	5,407,043	3,955,434	1,451,609	5,447,846
Colorado	593,030	612,635	451,321	161,314	625,062	459,930	165,132	640,521	469,755	170,766	[3]656,279
Connecticut[6]	481,050	488,476	361,548	126,928	496,298	368,632	127,666	506,824	375,638	131,186	[3]514,627
Delaware	102,196	104,321	75,983	28,338	105,547	76,617	28,930	106,813	76,819	29,994	[3]108,461
District of Columbia	80,618	80,937	61,133	19,804	80,678	61,434	19,244	80,450	62,126	18,324	[3]79,802
Florida	1,932,131	1,981,407	1,469,850	511,557	2,040,763	1,515,194	525,569	2,108,968	1,567,328	541,640	2,172,794
Georgia	1,177,569	1,207,186	891,647	315,539	1,235,304	910,425	324,879	1,270,948	934,650	336,298	[3]1,311,126
Hawaii	174,747	177,448	128,610	48,838	180,410	131,638	48,772	183,795	133,675	50,120	[3]186,574
Idaho	225,680	231,668	164,634	67,034	236,774	166,999	69,775	240,448	168,887	71,561	[3]243,097
Illinois	1,848,166	1,873,567	1,344,549	529,018	1,893,078	1,356,329	536,749	1,916,172	1,368,041	548,131	1,927,519
Indiana	956,988	960,630	677,249	283,381	965,633	679,066	286,567	968,933	678,943	289,990	980,198
Iowa	491,363	494,839	348,648	146,191	498,519	348,006	150,513	499,550	344,754	154,796	[3]502,301
Kansas	445,390	451,536	328,244	123,292	457,614	329,708	127,906	460,838	329,211	131,627	464,088
Kentucky	646,024	655,041	469,897	185,144	655,265	467,315	187,950	657,642	467,005	190,637	638,634
Louisiana	794,128	797,985	590,824	207,161	800,560	587,490	213,070	797,933	583,892	214,041	[3]781,142
Maine	216,400	216,453	156,368	60,085	216,995	156,528	60,467	212,601	155,903	56,698	[3]219,225
Maryland	736,238	751,850	555,565	196,285	772,638	569,497	203,141	790,938	580,903	210,035	[5]810,020
Massachusetts	846,155	859,948	629,649	230,299	877,726	645,518	232,208	893,727	658,507	235,220	910,020
Michigan	1,593,561	1,603,610	1,164,879	438,731	1,599,377	1,159,968	439,409	1,614,784	1,170,251	444,533	1,643,100
Minnesota	773,571	793,724	569,298	224,426	810,233	576,980	233,253	821,693	581,426	240,267	835,418
Mississippi	504,127	506,668	370,006	136,662	505,907	368,688	137,219	505,962	366,846	139,116	[3]503,602
Missouri	842,965	859,357	621,712	237,645	866,378	622,171	244,207	878,541	628,286	250,255	[3]873,638
Montana	155,779	160,011	115,315	44,696	163,009	116,668	46,341	164,341	116,748	47,593	[3]165,499
Nebraska	279,552	282,414	202,439	79,975	285,097	203,426	81,671	287,100	203,055	84,045	[3]289,733
Nevada	211,810	222,974	165,348	57,626	235,800	175,054	60,746	250,747	185,336	65,411	[3]265,041
New Hampshire	177,138	181,247	133,182	48,065	185,360	136,211	49,149	189,319	138,851	50,468	190,450
New Jersey	1,109,796	1,130,560	817,661	312,899	1,151,307	843,526	307,781	1,174,206	862,331	311,875	[5]1,197,560
New Mexico	308,667	315,668	217,418	98,250	322,292	226,287	96,005	327,248	229,168	98,080	328,463
New York	2,643,993	2,689,686	1,893,303	796,383	2,733,813	1,920,609	813,204	2,766,208	1,949,245	816,963	2,830,000
North Carolina	1,097,598	1,114,083	810,576	303,507	1,133,231	828,171	305,060	1,156,767	847,463	309,304	[3]1,165,385
North Dakota	118,376	118,734	84,569	34,165	119,127	84,127	35,000	119,288	83,419	35,869	[3]119,090
Ohio	1,783,767	1,795,199	1,283,869	511,330	1,807,319	1,290,197	517,122	1,814,290	1,295,289	519,001	[3]1,838,411
Oklahoma	588,263	597,096	438,796	158,300	604,076	441,094	162,982	609,718	442,607	167,111	[5]616,497
Oregon	498,614	510,122	365,416	144,706	516,611	368,141	148,470	521,945	371,967	149,978	[3]527,914
Pennsylvania	1,692,797	1,717,613	1,215,974	501,639	1,744,082	1,233,113	510,969	1,765,891	1,244,103	521,788	1,801,970
Rhode Island	142,144	143,798	105,677	38,121	145,676	107,047	38,629	147,487	107,913	39,574	[3]148,978
South Carolina	627,470	640,464	467,305	173,159	643,696	466,951	176,745	648,673	468,798	179,875	[3]637,519
South Dakota	131,576	134,573	97,882	36,691	142,825	102,281	40,544	143,482	101,805	41,677	[3]144,114
Tennessee	833,651	855,231	621,801	233,430	866,557	630,015	236,542	881,355	640,534	240,821	[3]880,960
Texas	3,464,371	3,541,769	2,634,346	907,423	3,608,262	2,681,053	927,209	3,677,171	2,720,623	956,548	[3]3,740,260
Utah	456,430	463,870	329,883	133,987	471,365	329,926	141,439	474,675	328,482	146,193	[3]473,666
Vermont	97,137	98,558	73,865	24,693	102,755	74,828	27,927	104,533	75,590	28,943	[3]105,965
Virginia	1,016,204	1,031,925	757,847	274,078	1,045,471	767,347	278,124	1,060,809	774,319	286,490	[3]1,079,854
Washington	869,327	896,475	651,743	244,732	915,952	660,424	255,528	938,314	673,107	265,207	[3]951,696
West Virginia	320,249	318,296	219,037	99,259	314,383	215,784	98,599	310,511	212,808	97,703	[3]306,451
Wisconsin	814,671	829,415	588,447	240,968	844,001	595,717	248,284	860,686	601,215	259,471	869,172
Wyoming	102,074	100,313	71,798	28,515	100,899	71,402	29,497	100,369	70,185	30,184	[3]99,859
Outlying areas											
American Samoa	13,365	13,994	10,582	3,412	14,484	10,974	3,510	14,445	11,054	3,391	[5]14,406
Guam	28,334	30,077	22,428	7,649	30,920	23,153	7,767	32,185	24,189	7,996	[5]33,502
Northern Marianas	7,096	8,086	6,133	1,953	8,188	6,380	1,808	8,429	6,559	1,870	[3]10,634
Puerto Rico	642,392	637,034	469,764	167,270	631,460	464,117	167,343	621,121	455,653	165,468	[3]621,370
Virgin Islands	22,346	22,887	16,804	6,083	22,752	16,706	6,046	23,126	16,659	6,467	[3]22,221

[1] Data estimated by state education agencies.
[2] Includes a relatively small number of prekindergarten students.
[3] Actual data.
[4] Beginning in 1983, data include students enrolled in public schools on federal bases and other special arrangements.
[5] Data estimated by the National Center for Education Statistics.
[6] Beginning in 1986, data include state vocational/technical schools.
—Data not available.

NOTE.—Some data have been revised from previously published figures.

SOURCE: U.S. Department of Education, National Center for Education Statistics, Common Core of Data surveys. (This table was prepared August 1996.)

Table 40.—Enrollment in public elementary and secondary schools, by grade and state: Fall 1994

State or other area	Total, all levels	Prekindergarten through grade 8 and elementary unclassified							
		Total	Prekinder-garten [1]	Kindergarten	Grade 1	Grade 2	Grade 3	Grade 4	Grade 5
1	2	3	4	5	6	7	8	9	10
United States	44,108,775	31,894,333	598,861	3,444,168	3,593,323	3,439,802	3,438,988	3,425,869	3,371,777
Alabama	736,472	535,187	8,992	57,723	60,366	56,502	57,259	56,773	57,923
Alaska	127,057	93,719	2,593	10,309	10,679	10,194	10,420	10,318	10,086
Arizona	737,424	542,904	3,540	59,545	63,198	60,274	60,591	60,032	58,579
Arkansas	447,565	319,282	1,652	35,620	35,359	33,615	33,626	34,488	34,620
California	5,407,043	3,955,434	66,018	448,237	457,886	438,672	431,169	426,919	416,333
Colorado	640,521	469,755	9,853	48,673	51,634	51,229	52,191	51,877	51,311
Connecticut	506,824	375,638	7,601	43,511	44,869	42,023	41,225	40,737	39,693
Delaware	106,813	76,819	618	7,523	9,097	8,450	8,595	8,367	8,402
District of Columbia ...	80,450	62,126	5,508	7,628	7,184	6,515	6,365	5,783	5,457
Florida	2,108,968	1,567,328	46,389	172,001	175,017	169,558	170,564	173,191	170,288
Georgia	1,270,948	934,650	12,859	108,398	105,961	102,495	101,656	101,054	100,813
Hawaii	183,795	133,675	631	15,678	15,696	15,208	15,052	14,572	14,828
Idaho	240,448	168,887	1,501	17,260	18,324	17,665	17,326	18,361	19,116
Illinois	1,916,172	1,368,041	42,938	146,314	152,229	143,486	143,029	143,030	138,902
Indiana	968,933	678,943	4,651	71,588	78,451	71,305	71,884	72,400	73,132
Iowa	499,550	344,754	4,453	37,434	35,338	34,813	36,351	36,992	36,586
Kansas	460,838	329,211	2,640	33,445	36,070	35,191	35,915	36,488	36,115
Kentucky	657,642	467,005	17,934	44,191	45,866	46,173	55,697	48,233	48,778
Louisiana	797,933	583,892	19,292	60,705	63,448	60,476	61,849	62,461	60,139
Maine	212,601	155,903	1,006	16,569	17,524	16,583	17,351	17,397	17,154
Maryland	790,938	580,903	18,834	62,341	65,377	64,160	62,270	61,982	61,010
Massachusetts	893,727	658,507	13,982	77,777	77,583	73,836	71,606	71,131	68,837
Michigan	1,614,784	1,170,251	4,409	136,353	129,951	125,664	123,321	123,829	119,821
Minnesota	821,693	581,426	8,060	62,908	62,446	61,956	63,873	64,605	63,660
Mississippi	505,962	366,846	1,146	38,528	41,762	37,940	38,135	38,606	39,004
Missouri	878,541	628,286	16,002	66,607	67,874	66,607	67,802	68,457	67,020
Montana	164,341	116,748	483	11,820	12,852	12,391	12,845	13,009	13,113
Nebraska	287,100	203,055	3,985	21,752	21,275	21,223	21,705	22,144	22,496
Nevada	250,747	185,336	1,424	20,462	21,827	21,062	20,941	20,573	20,048
New Hampshire	189,319	138,851	1,210	8,325	18,014	16,411	16,185	16,352	15,678
New Jersey	1,174,206	862,331	10,283	92,316	99,907	92,142	89,159	87,374	85,007
New Mexico	327,248	229,168	4,174	24,055	25,770	24,912	24,554	24,294	24,033
New York	2,766,208	1,949,245	32,227	212,239	225,269	212,486	205,740	202,024	196,405
North Carolina	1,156,767	847,463	8,949	97,508	97,339	91,560	90,471	89,492	87,139
North Dakota	119,288	83,419	639	8,677	8,893	8,634	8,966	9,236	9,292
Ohio	1,814,290	1,295,289	17,505	141,284	144,280	141,064	141,329	136,834	138,552
Oklahoma	609,718	442,607	5,367	46,355	53,654	46,476	47,234	47,929	48,221
Oregon	521,945	371,967	1,069	38,930	40,710	40,348	41,248	41,739	41,623
Pennsylvania	1,765,891	1,244,103	3,583	132,132	146,636	137,635	137,533	135,061	131,944
Rhode Island	147,487	107,913	469	10,701	13,721	12,154	11,707	11,549	11,504
South Carolina	648,673	468,798	7,920	46,859	54,602	50,731	51,139	51,268	50,585
South Dakota	143,482	101,805	1,244	10,618	10,615	10,649	10,917	11,116	11,138
Tennessee	881,355	640,534	10,761	71,413	73,170	66,964	67,349	67,339	65,872
Texas	3,677,171	2,720,623	128,736	272,065	300,731	290,911	289,548	291,604	286,219
Utah	474,675	328,482	3,273	33,750	34,790	33,734	34,515	34,837	35,668
Vermont	104,533	75,590	1,903	8,040	8,176	8,183	8,224	8,396	8,430
Virginia	1,060,809	774,319	3,115	85,160	84,678	82,663	82,990	84,103	81,212
Washington	938,314	673,107	6,155	71,637	73,594	73,187	74,642	75,299	74,861
West Virginia	310,511	212,808	2,754	22,377	22,186	22,123	22,210	22,236	22,651
Wisconsin	860,686	601,215	18,531	61,898	64,040	64,247	65,127	65,996	64,380
Wyoming	100,369	70,185	—	6,929	7,405	7,322	7,588	7,982	8,099
Outlying areas									
American Samoa	14,445	11,054	1,570	1,126	1,173	1,184	1,094	1,071	1,045
Guam	32,185	24,189	465	2,931	2,981	2,835	2,753	2,587	2,531
Northern Marianas	8,429	6,559	510	556	793	805	695	681	630
Puerto Rico	621,121	455,653	143	39,962	53,773	49,955	48,958	50,311	49,778
Virgin Islands	23,126	16,659	—	1,487	1,816	1,837	1,732	1,745	1,702

Table 40.—Enrollment in public elementary and secondary schools, by grade and state: Fall 1994—Continued

State or other area	Prekindergarten through grade 8 and elementary unclassified				Grades 9 through 12 and secondary unclassified					
	Grade 6	Grade 7	Grade 8	Elementary unclassified	Total	Grade 9	Grade 10	Grade 11	Grade 12	Secondary unclassified
1	11	12	13	14	15	16	17	18	19	20
United States	3,381,438	3,403,533	3,302,290	494,284	12,214,442	3,604,068	3,131,438	2,748,677	2,487,928	242,331
Alabama	58,719	61,765	59,165	—	201,285	63,656	50,929	44,970	41,730	—
Alaska	9,674	9,943	9,503	—	33,338	9,947	8,692	7,642	7,057	—
Arizona	58,791	58,676	55,334	4,344	194,520	59,150	51,564	43,363	40,119	324
Arkansas	35,024	36,795	36,437	2,046	128,283	36,689	34,158	29,429	27,161	846
California	409,387	403,367	388,561	68,885	1,451,609	420,643	381,364	334,408	285,132	30,062
Colorado	51,775	51,103	49,332	777	170,766	50,078	44,702	39,956	35,464	566
Connecticut	38,110	37,577	35,665	4,627	131,186	38,001	33,780	30,760	28,640	5
Delaware	8,416	8,788	8,563	—	29,994	9,469	7,979	6,681	5,865	—
District of Columbia ...	4,978	5,244	5,031	2,433	18,324	4,923	4,904	3,920	3,203	1,374
Florida	169,018	165,489	155,813	—	541,640	172,850	147,925	120,030	100,835	—
Georgia	101,974	100,458	98,982	—	336,298	114,176	85,636	71,880	64,606	—
Hawaii	14,540	13,832	13,592	46	50,120	15,597	11,979	12,034	10,473	37
Idaho	19,478	20,176	19,680	—	71,561	19,777	19,098	16,906	15,780	—
Illinois	133,142	134,518	135,134	55,319	548,131	148,944	135,955	119,266	109,360	34,606
Indiana	75,449	78,369	77,779	3,935	289,990	83,123	73,535	67,167	62,699	3,466
Iowa	38,082	38,504	39,091	7,110	154,796	40,647	37,925	35,453	34,125	6,646
Kansas	36,981	37,116	36,757	2,493	131,627	38,007	33,574	30,338	28,811	897
Kentucky	49,973	51,190	50,562	8,408	190,637	55,758	48,521	43,371	39,482	3,505
Louisiana	62,011	63,214	57,747	12,550	214,041	68,599	54,796	45,167	40,666	4,813
Maine	17,112	16,867	16,571	1,769	56,698	15,503	14,674	13,434	12,534	553
Maryland	60,953	60,049	57,222	6,705	210,035	63,067	51,978	45,585	43,223	6,182
Massachusetts	66,869	66,447	64,097	6,342	235,220	66,707	60,669	56,226	51,618	—
Michigan	118,795	120,642	117,380	50,086	444,533	128,383	109,751	98,671	88,136	19,592
Minnesota	63,918	65,393	64,607	—	240,267	65,149	61,728	57,408	55,982	—
Mississippi	39,174	42,294	39,970	10,287	139,116	43,434	33,918	28,584	26,436	6,744
Missouri	68,357	66,705	66,025	6,830	250,255	72,584	65,084	57,447	52,654	2,486
Montana	13,194	13,329	13,229	483	47,593	13,309	12,148	11,286	10,681	169
Nebraska	22,511	22,927	23,037	—	84,045	23,281	21,958	19,662	19,144	—
Nevada	19,920	19,524	18,881	674	65,411	18,685	17,463	15,586	13,659	18
New Hampshire	15,732	15,473	14,926	545	50,468	14,564	12,969	11,965	10,919	51
New Jersey	83,410	83,350	80,901	58,482	311,875	83,256	74,858	68,708	65,662	19,391
New Mexico	25,831	26,102	25,443	—	98,080	28,547	23,885	20,114	16,925	8,609
New York	197,222	197,519	191,181	76,933	816,963	227,040	202,906	172,751	144,139	70,127
North Carolina	87,733	88,336	86,344	22,592	309,304	97,534	81,618	67,828	62,324	—
North Dakota	9,526	9,862	9,694	—	35,869	9,564	9,091	8,796	8,418	—
Ohio	141,349	146,443	142,132	4,517	519,001	151,879	132,103	122,753	112,266	—
Oklahoma	49,524	49,377	47,149	1,321	167,111	48,838	43,273	38,583	35,899	518
Oregon	42,276	41,973	40,473	1,578	149,978	41,301	39,088	35,667	33,356	566
Pennsylvania	134,201	136,184	132,994	16,200	521,788	147,352	131,782	119,328	109,885	13,441
Rhode Island	11,114	11,324	10,747	2,923	39,574	11,534	10,318	9,124	8,440	158
South Carolina	51,743	53,152	50,799	—	179,875	60,058	46,796	37,645	35,376	—
South Dakota	11,226	11,800	11,604	878	41,677	12,077	10,794	9,560	8,925	321
Tennessee	66,194	68,508	65,598	17,366	240,821	72,593	63,757	55,070	49,401	—
Texas	288,987	290,713	281,109	—	956,548	323,162	243,914	205,735	183,737	—
Utah	36,499	38,163	37,519	5,734	146,193	38,356	37,318	32,978	33,337	4,204
Vermont	8,349	8,063	7,826	—	28,943	7,993	7,311	6,669	6,458	512
Virginia	81,313	81,795	79,929	27,361	286,490	84,447	73,958	65,077	62,899	109
Washington	75,442	75,308	72,982	—	265,207	75,684	69,532	61,841	58,150	—
West Virginia	23,904	25,517	25,200	1,650	97,703	26,766	24,415	23,031	22,058	1,433
Wisconsin	65,362	65,844	65,790	—	259,471	73,083	67,255	61,696	57,437	—
Wyoming	8,176	8,426	8,203	55	30,184	8,304	8,110	7,128	6,642	—
Outlying areas										
American Samoa	945	943	903	—	3,391	885	869	829	746	62
Guam	2,396	2,433	2,275	2	7,996	2,795	2,266	1,666	1,262	7
Northern Marianas	647	692	550	—	1,870	625	429	410	406	—
Puerto Rico	49,129	54,180	49,774	9,690	165,468	45,789	44,240	38,239	32,935	4,265
Virgin Islands	1,715	2,197	1,585	843	6,467	1,935	1,553	1,210	1,140	629

[1] Data include imputations for nonrespondents.
—Data not reported or not applicable.

SOURCE: U.S. Department of Education, National Center for Education Statistics, Common Core of Data survey. (This table was prepared March 1996.)

Table 41.—Enrollment in public elementary and secondary schools, by grade and state: Fall 1993

State or other area	Total, all levels	Prekindergarten through grade 8 and elementary unclassified							
		Total	Prekinder-garten [1]	Kindergarten	Grade 1	Grade 2	Grade 3	Grade 4	Grade 5
1	2	3	4	5	6	7	8	9	10
United States	43,464,916	31,504,032	545,135	3,376,998	3,529,072	3,429,243	3,436,978	3,361,110	3,350,453
Alabama	734,288	535,637	8,264	56,598	59,239	55,781	58,612	57,497	58,098
Alaska	125,948	93,601	2,787	10,329	10,663	10,549	10,479	10,156	9,809
Arizona	709,453	526,412	3,164	57,656	60,628	59,285	59,098	57,701	58,110
Arkansas	444,271	317,713	1,248	34,337	34,586	33,737	34,398	34,255	34,834
California	5,327,231	3,903,137	59,954	444,104	444,346	435,329	431,107	420,233	413,420
Colorado	625,062	459,930	7,249	47,598	51,410	51,673	51,222	50,807	51,307
Connecticut	496,298	368,632	6,216	42,338	43,961	41,289	40,244	39,093	37,639
Delaware	105,547	76,617	565	8,153	8,816	8,703	8,455	8,285	8,335
District of Columbia ...	80,678	61,434	5,216	6,986	7,195	6,728	6,149	5,870	5,435
Florida	2,040,763	1,515,194	34,793	167,140	169,039	168,302	170,860	168,509	166,144
Georgia	1,235,304	910,425	5,534	103,365	103,346	100,224	100,082	99,802	100,493
Hawaii	180,410	131,638	532	15,199	15,158	15,038	14,713	14,813	14,770
Idaho	236,774	166,999	1,389	17,039	17,464	16,872	17,788	18,665	19,015
Illinois	1,893,078	1,356,329	42,359	144,758	147,148	143,397	143,349	138,827	132,833
Indiana	965,633	679,066	3,960	70,226	74,695	71,896	72,476	72,841	74,494
Iowa	498,519	348,006	5,430	36,348	35,131	36,217	36,994	36,370	37,530
Kansas	457,614	329,708	2,432	34,575	36,063	35,896	36,393	35,975	36,525
Kentucky	655,265	467,315	15,732	43,340	46,083	46,151	57,522	48,083	49,333
Louisiana	800,560	587,490	12,857	61,133	63,742	61,535	61,709	60,077	59,614
Maine	216,995	156,528	1,036	17,536	16,995	17,637	17,514	17,237	17,018
Maryland	772,638	569,497	17,984	60,378	64,504	62,421	62,141	61,199	60,377
Massachusetts	877,726	645,518	13,178	76,494	76,002	72,068	71,381	69,111	66,902
Michigan	1,599,377	1,159,968	11,704	132,658	130,499	124,979	124,837	120,049	118,276
Minnesota	810,233	576,980	6,656	62,345	62,208	63,724	64,244	63,194	63,288
Mississippi	505,907	368,688	2,197	37,622	40,553	38,640	38,589	39,236	39,662
Missouri	866,378	622,171	13,950	65,679	67,707	67,595	67,969	66,445	67,607
Montana	163,009	116,668	483	12,021	12,779	12,715	12,894	12,967	12,902
Nebraska	285,097	203,426	3,577	21,374	21,429	21,770	22,097	22,391	22,319
Nevada	235,800	175,054	1,237	19,179	20,487	20,202	19,725	19,305	19,153
New Hampshire	185,360	136,211	1,292	8,194	18,156	16,038	16,237	15,630	15,614
New Jersey	1,151,307	843,526	9,225	90,827	96,030	89,592	87,454	84,767	83,173
New Mexico	322,292	226,287	1,933	23,723	26,035	24,975	24,605	24,182	24,676
New York	2,733,813	1,920,609	31,687	205,238	220,578	209,649	204,260	198,259	196,767
North Carolina	1,133,231	828,171	8,469	93,406	92,701	89,371	90,875	85,989	85,721
North Dakota	119,127	84,127	615	8,752	8,990	8,969	9,223	9,266	9,583
Ohio	1,807,319	1,290,197	17,210	140,778	143,737	140,554	140,822	136,317	138,011
Oklahoma	604,076	441,094	5,456	44,864	53,724	47,482	47,788	48,242	49,154
Oregon	516,611	368,141	837	37,859	40,259	40,704	41,454	41,290	41,885
Pennsylvania	1,744,082	1,233,113	4,181	131,842	145,111	138,527	134,504	131,575	131,962
Rhode Island	145,676	107,047	465	11,348	13,041	11,858	11,659	11,603	11,208
South Carolina	643,696	466,951	7,244	45,490	53,676	51,226	51,457	50,357	50,992
South Dakota	142,825	102,281	612	10,574	10,818	10,908	11,068	11,086	11,084
Tennessee	866,557	630,015	9,542	68,462	70,638	67,305	66,952	65,646	65,662
Texas	3,608,262	2,681,053	120,446	268,646	299,513	288,258	289,284	284,394	284,342
Utah	471,365	329,926	2,690	33,623	33,634	34,245	34,634	35,467	36,281
Vermont	102,755	74,828	2,024	7,766	8,454	8,227	8,284	8,457	8,318
Virginia	1,045,471	767,347	3,186	81,787	84,318	83,296	84,146	81,615	79,683
Washington	915,952	660,424	5,087	68,908	72,729	73,380	73,746	73,824	74,884
West Virginia	314,383	215,784	3,981	20,077	22,623	22,254	22,181	22,349	23,623
Wisconsin	844,001	595,717	17,270	61,136	64,779	64,467	65,336	63,756	64,435
Wyoming	100,899	71,402	—	7,190	7,652	7,605	7,968	8,046	8,153
Outlying areas									
American Samoa	14,484	10,974	1,663	1,056	1,240	1,143	1,093	1,056	987
Guam	30,920	23,153	486	2,866	2,806	2,761	2,585	2,517	2,476
Northern Marianas	8,188	6,380	421	656	809	700	677	633	626
Puerto Rico	631,460	464,117	281	38,305	55,003	50,180	50,072	51,411	51,786
Virgin Islands	22,752	16,706	—	1,624	1,870	1,757	1,745	1,755	1,782

Table 41.—Enrollment in public elementary and secondary schools, by grade and state: Fall 1993—Continued

State or other area	Prekindergarten through grade 8 and elementary unclassified				Grades 9 through 12 and secondary unclassified					
	Grade 6	Grade 7	Grade 8	Elementary unclassified	Total	Grade 9	Grade 10	Grade 11	Grade 12	Secondary unclassified
1	11	12	13	14	15	16	17	18	19	20
United States	3,355,633	3,355,288	3,249,266	514,856	11,960,884	3,486,958	3,050,404	2,751,227	2,424,031	248,264
Alabama	59,400	62,144	60,004	—	198,651	62,141	50,543	46,067	39,900	—
Alaska	9,817	9,852	9,160	—	32,347	9,608	8,514	7,250	6,975	—
Arizona	57,242	55,834	53,500	4,194	183,041	54,878	48,281	41,964	37,614	304
Arkansas	35,107	36,892	36,471	1,848	126,558	36,045	32,711	29,876	27,169	757
California	405,416	398,553	380,223	70,452	1,424,094	406,551	375,992	333,716	277,271	30,564
Colorado	50,619	49,168	47,665	1,212	165,132	47,344	42,536	39,610	34,770	872
Connecticut	37,007	36,127	34,662	10,056	127,666	36,481	32,802	30,393	27,979	11
Delaware	8,302	8,738	8,265	—	28,930	8,930	7,867	6,251	5,882	—
District of Columbia ...	5,211	5,394	4,935	2,315	19,244	5,003	5,403	4,145	3,303	1,390
Florida	163,447	157,906	149,054	—	525,569	164,978	140,271	119,674	100,646	—
Georgia	100,824	99,401	97,354	—	324,879	107,625	82,822	71,728	62,704	—
Hawaii	14,507	13,608	13,245	55	48,772	14,219	12,351	11,957	10,201	44
Idaho	19,444	19,356	19,185	782	69,775	19,537	18,139	16,567	15,044	488
Illinois	134,201	136,363	138,518	54,576	536,749	143,950	131,770	120,785	106,519	33,725
Indiana	76,961	78,388	78,125	5,004	286,567	81,632	72,611	67,005	60,971	4,348
Iowa	37,744	38,861	38,548	8,833	150,513	38,637	36,483	34,893	32,588	7,912
Kansas	36,672	36,913	35,902	2,362	127,906	35,955	32,721	30,761	27,644	825
Kentucky	49,483	51,533	51,306	8,749	187,950	54,502	48,467	43,758	37,629	3,594
Louisiana	60,283	61,553	56,522	28,465	213,070	66,376	51,405	44,676	39,826	10,787
Maine	16,663	16,537	15,844	2,511	60,467	16,630	15,317	14,239	13,446	835
Maryland	60,127	58,407	55,285	6,674	203,141	60,213	50,116	46,082	40,661	6,069
Massachusetts	66,295	64,679	62,412	6,996	232,208	64,643	60,303	55,953	51,309	—
Michigan	118,991	119,423	116,702	41,850	439,409	126,933	110,107	98,594	87,447	16,328
Minnesota	63,677	64,539	63,105	—	233,253	62,353	59,909	56,349	54,642	—
Mississippi	40,203	42,696	39,815	9,475	137,219	41,660	33,709	29,587	26,156	6,107
Missouri	65,691	66,654	66,371	6,503	244,207	71,288	63,148	57,243	50,195	2,333
Montana	13,112	13,285	12,834	676	46,341	12,737	11,935	11,114	10,325	230
Nebraska	22,720	23,138	22,611	—	81,671	22,627	20,770	19,696	18,578	—
Nevada	18,796	18,419	17,825	726	60,746	17,014	16,065	14,899	12,749	19
New Hampshire	15,383	14,997	14,118	552	49,149	14,039	12,499	11,925	10,635	51
New Jersey	82,715	81,942	79,459	58,342	307,781	81,629	73,124	69,108	64,402	19,518
New Mexico	25,403	25,856	24,899	—	96,005	27,115	23,706	20,180	16,767	8,237
New York	195,714	194,988	188,274	75,195	813,204	225,243	200,597	175,038	143,055	69,271
North Carolina	88,232	86,428	86,093	20,886	305,060	94,369	79,553	70,282	60,856	—
North Dakota	9,671	9,729	9,329	—	35,000	9,230	8,971	8,733	8,066	—
Ohio	140,855	145,856	141,534	4,523	517,122	151,241	131,594	122,355	111,932	—
Oklahoma	49,281	47,724	46,153	1,226	162,982	46,597	42,337	38,833	34,744	471
Oregon	41,932	40,605	39,500	1,816	148,470	41,129	38,344	35,518	32,828	651
Pennsylvania	132,960	134,423	130,209	17,819	510,969	143,719	127,919	117,500	107,244	14,587
Rhode Island	11,100	11,136	10,650	2,979	38,629	11,060	10,111	9,205	8,094	159
South Carolina	52,875	53,043	50,591	—	176,745	58,795	45,611	38,390	33,949	—
South Dakota	11,485	11,604	11,427	1,615	40,544	11,276	10,264	9,495	8,936	573
Tennessee	66,547	67,705	64,124	17,432	236,542	71,363	62,534	54,977	47,668	—
Texas	285,414	286,548	274,208	—	927,209	308,461	234,566	205,293	178,889	—
Utah	37,837	37,528	38,031	5,956	141,439	37,270	33,749	34,524	31,692	4,204
Vermont	7,988	7,814	7,496	—	27,927	7,515	6,962	6,673	6,227	550
Virginia	80,889	80,496	78,443	29,488	278,124	80,277	71,469	65,949	60,314	115
Washington	74,094	73,106	70,666	—	255,528	72,322	65,967	61,392	55,847	—
West Virginia	24,649	25,657	25,677	2,713	98,599	26,196	25,214	23,347	21,507	2,335
Wisconsin	64,374	65,495	64,669	—	248,284	69,407	64,586	60,603	53,688	—
Wyoming	8,273	8,247	8,268	—	29,497	8,215	7,659	7,075	6,548	—
Outlying areas										
American Samoa	959	904	873	—	3,510	907	914	821	809	59
Guam	2,338	2,231	2,085	2	7,767	2,964	2,029	1,605	1,154	15
Northern Marianas	612	636	610	—	1,808	480	514	430	384	—
Puerto Rico	51,290	56,314	50,711	8,764	167,343	46,689	45,341	38,871	32,610	3,832
Virgin Islands	1,705	2,130	1,568	770	6,046	1,801	1,343	1,267	1,097	538

[1] Data include imputations for nonrespondents.
—Data not reported or not applicable.

SOURCE: U.S. Department of Education, National Center for Education Statistics, Common Core of Data survey. (This table was prepared March 1996.)

Table 42.—Enrollment in public elementary and secondary schools, by grade: Fall 1980 to fall 1994

Grade	Fall 1980	Fall 1981	Fall 1982	Fall 1983	Fall 1984	Fall 1985	Fall 1986	Fall 1987	Fall 1988	Fall 1989	Fall 1990	Fall 1991	Fall 1992	Fall 1993	Fall 1994
1	2	3	4	5	6	7	8	9	10	11	12	13	14	15	16
In thousands															
All grades	40,877	40,044	39,566	39,252	39,208	39,422	39,753	40,008	40,189	40,543	41,217	42,047	42,823	43,465	44,109
Elementary	27,647	27,280	27,161	26,981	26,905	27,034	27,420	27,933	28,501	29,152	29,878	30,506	31,088	31,504	31,894
Kindergarten [1]	2,689	2,687	2,845	2,859	3,010	3,192	3,310	3,388	3,433	3,486	3,610	3,686	3,817	3,922	4,043
1st grade	2,894	2,951	2,937	3,080	3,113	3,239	3,358	3,407	3,460	3,485	3,499	3,556	3,542	3,529	3,593
2nd grade	2,800	2,782	2,790	2,781	2,904	2,941	3,054	3,173	3,223	3,289	3,327	3,360	3,431	3,429	3,440
3rd grade	2,893	2,806	2,763	2,772	2,765	2,895	2,933	3,046	3,167	3,235	3,297	3,334	3,361	3,437	3,439
4th grade	3,107	2,918	2,798	2,758	2,772	2,771	2,896	2,938	3,051	3,182	3,248	3,315	3,342	3,361	3,426
5th grade	3,130	3,127	2,912	2,798	2,761	2,776	2,775	2,901	2,945	3,067	3,197	3,268	3,325	3,350	3,372
6th grade	3,038	3,180	3,142	2,928	2,831	2,789	2,806	2,811	2,937	2,987	3,110	3,239	3,303	3,356	3,381
7th grade	3,085	3,183	3,288	3,247	3,036	2,938	2,899	2,910	2,905	3,027	3,067	3,181	3,299	3,355	3,404
8th grade	3,086	3,059	3,123	3,222	3,186	2,982	2,870	2,839	2,853	2,853	2,979	3,020	3,129	3,249	3,302
Elementary ungraded	924	587	563	535	528	511	520	520	527	540	543	545	539	515	494
Secondary	13,231	12,764	12,405	12,271	12,304	12,388	12,333	12,076	11,687	11,390	11,338	11,541	11,735	11,961	12,214
9th grade	3,377	3,286	3,248	3,330	3,440	3,439	3,256	3,143	3,106	3,141	3,169	3,313	3,352	3,487	3,604
10th grade	3,368	3,218	3,137	3,103	3,145	3,230	3,215	3,020	2,895	2,868	2,896	2,915	3,027	3,050	3,131
11th grade	3,195	3,039	2,917	2,861	2,819	2,866	2,954	2,936	2,749	2,629	2,612	2,645	2,656	2,751	2,749
12th grade	2,925	2,907	2,787	2,678	2,599	2,550	2,601	2,681	2,650	2,473	2,381	2,392	2,431	2,424	2,488
Secondary ungraded	366	314	315	299	300	303	308	296	288	279	282	275	269	248	242
Percent															
All grades	100.0	100.0	100.0	100.0	100.0	100.0	100.0	100.0	100.0	100.0	100.0	100.0	100.0	100.0	100.0
Elementary	67.6	68.1	68.6	68.7	68.6	68.6	69.0	69.8	70.9	71.9	72.5	72.6	72.6	72.5	72.3
Kindergarten [1]	6.6	6.7	7.2	7.3	7.7	8.1	8.3	8.5	8.5	8.6	8.8	8.8	8.9	9.0	9.2
1st grade	7.1	7.4	7.4	7.8	7.9	8.2	8.4	8.5	8.6	8.6	8.5	8.5	8.3	8.1	8.1
2nd grade	6.8	6.9	7.1	7.1	7.4	7.5	7.7	7.9	8.0	8.1	8.1	8.0	8.0	7.9	7.8
3rd grade	7.1	7.0	7.0	7.1	7.1	7.3	7.4	7.6	7.9	8.0	8.0	7.9	7.8	7.9	7.8
4th grade	7.6	7.3	7.1	7.0	7.1	7.0	7.3	7.3	7.6	7.8	7.9	7.9	7.8	7.7	7.8
5th grade	7.7	7.8	7.4	7.1	7.0	7.0	7.0	7.2	7.3	7.6	7.8	7.8	7.8	7.7	7.6
6th grade	7.4	7.9	7.9	7.5	7.2	7.1	7.1	7.0	7.3	7.4	7.5	7.7	7.7	7.7	7.7
7th grade	7.5	7.9	8.3	8.3	7.7	7.5	7.3	7.3	7.2	7.5	7.4	7.6	7.7	7.7	7.7
8th grade	7.5	7.6	7.9	8.2	8.1	7.6	7.2	7.1	7.1	7.0	7.2	7.2	7.3	7.5	7.5
Elementary ungraded	2.3	1.5	1.4	1.4	1.3	1.3	1.3	1.3	1.3	1.3	1.3	1.3	1.3	1.2	1.1
Secondary	32.4	31.9	31.4	31.3	31.4	31.4	31.0	30.2	29.1	28.1	27.5	27.4	27.4	27.5	27.7
9th grade	8.3	8.2	8.2	8.5	8.8	8.7	8.2	7.9	7.7	7.7	7.7	7.9	7.8	8.0	8.2
10th grade	8.2	8.0	7.9	7.9	8.0	8.2	8.1	7.5	7.2	7.1	7.0	6.9	7.1	7.0	7.1
11th grade	7.8	7.6	7.4	7.3	7.2	7.3	7.4	7.3	6.8	6.5	6.3	6.3	6.2	6.3	6.2
12th grade	7.2	7.3	7.0	6.8	6.6	6.5	6.5	6.7	6.6	6.1	5.8	5.7	5.7	5.6	5.6
Secondary ungraded	0.9	0.8	0.8	0.8	0.8	0.8	0.8	0.7	0.7	0.7	0.7	0.7	0.6	0.6	0.5

[1] Includes a relatively small number of prekindergarten pupils. Beginning in fall 1992, includes total prekindergarten pupils.

NOTE.—Some data have been revised from previously published figures. Because of rounding, details may not add to totals.

SOURCE: U.S. Department of Education, National Center for Education Statistics, Statistics of Public Elementary and Secondary School Systems; and Common Core of Data surveys. (This table was prepared August 1996.)

Table 43.—Average daily attendance in public elementary and secondary schools, by state: 1969–70 to 1993–94

State or other area	1969–70	1979–80	1980–81	1985–86	1989–90	1990–91	1991–92	1992–93	1993–94
1	2	3	4	5	6	7	8	9	10
United States	41,934,376	38,288,911	37,703,744	36,523,103	37,799,296	38,426,543	38,960,783	39,570,462	40,146,393
Alabama	777,123	711,432	701,925	686,716	683,833	682,524	681,840	694,078	696,071
Alaska	72,489	79,945	83,745	98,535	98,213	102,585	110,277	110,797	112,869
Arizona	391,526	481,905	476,149	494,504	557,252	573,140	593,413	610,558	631,450
Arkansas	414,158	423,610	417,080	408,601	403,025	408,145	410,902	413,076	416,479
California [1]	4,418,423	4,044,736	4,014,917	4,245,090	4,893,341	5,065,647	4,993,009	5,066,708	5,108,907
Colorado	500,388	513,475	508,750	507,876	519,419	521,899	532,525	568,158	579,682
Connecticut	618,881	507,362	501,085	452,058	439,524	450,808	457,476	468,992	465,487
Delaware	120,819	94,058	89,609	84,936	89,838	91,052	93,909	95,660	97,247
District of Columbia ...	138,600	91,576	85,773	76,241	71,468	69,092	70,939	71,201	70,079
Florida	1,312,693	1,464,461	1,389,487	1,442,921	1,646,583	1,714,394	1,776,539	1,818,011	1,873,199
Georgia	1,019,427	989,433	988,612	1,004,799	1,054,097	1,075,728	1,098,966	1,125,385	1,148,319
Hawaii	168,140	151,563	151,713	151,174	157,360	160,193	163,212	165,851	169,779
Idaho	170,920	189,199	190,144	198,141	203,987	209,085	213,843	217,933	223,489
Illinois	2,084,844	1,770,435	1,765,357	1,604,265	1,587,733	1,618,101	1,630,534	1,685,678	1,709,915
Indiana	1,111,043	983,444	944,424	870,463	884,568	888,177	895,794	897,799	899,585
Iowa	624,403	510,081	501,403	454,341	450,224	456,614	462,360	467,788	477,916
Kansas	470,296	382,019	374,451	371,655	388,986	397,609	405,083	408,689	410,862
Kentucky	647,970	619,868	614,676	577,190	569,795	569,713	574,226	579,446	578,020
Louisiana	776,555	727,601	715,844	732,230	727,125	720,551	732,485	722,626	732,202
Maine	225,146	211,400	207,554	198,358	195,089	196,229	198,413	200,462	199,125
Maryland	785,989	686,336	664,866	592,383	620,617	637,370	653,203	668,778	687,455
Massachusetts	1,056,207	935,960	950,675	745,991	763,231	770,802	785,840	796,897	810,028
Michigan	1,991,235	1,758,427	1,711,139	1,481,068	1,446,996	1,452,700	1,460,795	1,467,900	1,474,413
Minnesota	864,595	748,606	710,836	669,385	699,001	714,072	727,838	744,567	756,725
Mississippi	524,623	454,401	446,515	448,117	476,048	474,029	473,398	473,262	471,367
Missouri	906,132	777,269	756,536	714,230	729,693	733,680	747,760	759,529	778,605
Montana	162,664	144,608	141,641	138,829	135,406	138,341	141,316	144,718	146,849
Nebraska	314,516	270,524	263,797	250,975	254,754	257,587	262,429	267,975	267,931
Nevada	113,421	134,995	138,481	143,941	173,149	185,755	195,463	204,440	217,681
New Hampshire	140,203	154,187	150,316	147,561	154,915	156,579	160,203	172,376	175,968
New Jersey	1,322,124	1,140,111	1,121,272	1,029,797	997,561	1,016,159	1,036,885	1,053,135	1,079,653
New Mexico	259,997	253,453	240,496	252,892	290,245	291,215	321,955	304,661	310,610
New York	3,099,192	2,530,289	2,475,055	2,276,842	2,244,110	2,278,531	2,319,738	2,347,468	2,404,426
North Carolina	1,104,295	1,072,150	1,055,651	1,014,795	1,012,274	1,012,613	1,023,186	1,035,258	1,051,295
North Dakota	141,961	118,986	111,759	108,947	109,659	109,691	110,635	111,174	111,770
Ohio	2,246,282	1,849,283	1,801,914	1,660,718	1,584,735	1,603,025	1,602,418	1,594,191	1,609,855
Oklahoma	560,993	548,065	542,800	553,370	543,170	548,387	556,609	560,744	566,155
Oregon	436,736	418,593	417,009	401,476	419,771	431,806	444,272	452,509	455,492
Pennsylvania	2,169,225	1,808,630	1,754,782	1,560,746	1,524,839	1,542,077	1,568,279	1,588,514	1,609,125
Rhode Island	163,205	139,195	135,096	122,109	125,934	129,856	132,278	134,736	135,016
South Carolina	600,292	569,612	580,132	558,716	569,029	573,138	578,236	581,775	586,178
South Dakota	158,543	124,934	121,663	118,269	119,823	121,403	124,171	126,916	127,550
Tennessee	836,010	806,696	797,237	762,225	761,766	767,738	774,596	786,146	796,744
Texas	2,432,420	2,608,817	2,647,288	2,923,741	3,075,333	3,085,648	3,175,400	3,237,958	3,306,297
Utah	287,405	312,813	323,048	379,249	408,917	417,609	426,507	432,781	439,484
Vermont	97,772	95,045	90,884	85,875	87,832	88,901	90,908	96,121	97,550
Virginia	995,580	955,105	938,794	904,347	989,197	1,011,513	1,023,683	1,049,901	1,065,071
Washington	764,735	710,929	704,655	696,372	755,141	781,371	808,090	833,641	850,813
West Virginia	372,278	353,264	351,823	330,145	301,947	300,067	296,191	294,202	291,238
Wisconsin	880,609	770,554	743,505	694,351	711,466	731,088	748,830	765,184	769,717
Wyoming	81,293	89,471	91,381	95,547	91,277	92,506	93,926	94,109	94,650
Outlying areas									
American Samoa	—	—	—	10,816	11,448	12,272	12,935	14,150	14,094
Guam	20,315	—	22,343	23,220	23,883	25,330	25,330	30,417	31,711
Northern Marianas	—	—	—	4,921	6,809	6,062	6,194	7,334	7,278
Puerto Rico	—	656,709	671,661	636,268	597,436	597,418	558,515	548,067	588,484
Virgin Islands	—	—	23,312	23,811	18,924	19,984	20,498	20,624	20,381

[1] Data for California are not strictly comparable with those for other states because California's attendance figures through 1990–91 include excused absences.

—Data not available.

SOURCE: U.S. Department of Education, National Center for Education Statistics, *Revenues and Expenditures for Public Elementary and Secondary Education; Statistics of State School Systems;* and Common Core of Data survey. (This table was prepared May 1996.)

Table 44.—Enrollment in public elementary and secondary schools, by race or ethnicity and state: Fall 1986 and fall 1994

State or other area	Percent distribution, fall 1986						Percent distribution, fall 1994					
	Total	White [1]	Black [1]	Hispanic	Asian or Pacific Islander	American Indian/ Alaskan Native	Total	White [1]	Black [1]	Hispanic	Asian or Pacific Islander	American Indian/ Alaskan Native
1	2	3	4	5	6	7	8	9	10	11	12	13
United States	**100.0**	**70.4**	**16.1**	**9.9**	**2.8**	**0.9**	**100.0**	**[2]65.6**	**[2]16.7**	**[2]13.0**	**[2]3.6**	**[2]1.1**
Alabama	100.0	62.0	37.0	0.1	0.4	0.5	100.0	62.3	35.8	0.4	0.6	0.8
Alaska	100.0	65.7	4.3	1.7	3.3	25.1	100.0	64.7	4.8	2.6	4.1	23.8
Arizona	100.0	62.2	4.0	26.4	1.3	6.1	100.0	58.4	4.3	28.7	1.7	7.0
Arkansas	100.0	74.7	24.2	0.4	0.6	0.2	100.0	73.9	23.9	1.1	0.7	0.3
California	100.0	53.7	9.0	27.5	9.1	0.7	100.0	41.4	8.7	37.9	11.2	0.9
Colorado	100.0	78.7	4.5	13.7	2.0	1.0	100.0	73.5	5.4	17.6	2.5	1.0
Connecticut	100.0	77.2	12.1	8.9	1.5	0.2	100.0	72.7	13.3	11.4	2.4	0.2
Delaware	100.0	68.3	27.7	2.5	1.4	0.2	100.0	65.4	29.1	3.6	1.7	0.2
District of Columbia	100.0	4.0	91.1	3.9	0.9	0.1	100.0	4.0	88.0	6.6	1.3	[3]
Florida	100.0	65.4	23.7	9.5	1.2	0.2	100.0	58.7	25.0	14.4	1.7	0.2
Georgia	100.0	60.7	37.9	0.6	0.8	[3]	100.0	59.1	37.5	1.8	1.5	0.1
Hawaii	100.0	23.5	2.3	2.2	71.7	0.3	100.0	23.2	2.7	4.9	68.8	0.4
Idaho	100.0	92.6	0.3	4.9	0.8	1.3	—	—	—	—	—	—
Illinois	100.0	69.8	18.7	9.2	2.3	0.1	100.0	64.4	21.0	11.6	3.0	0.1
Indiana	100.0	88.7	9.0	1.7	0.5	0.1	100.0	85.7	11.2	2.2	0.8	0.2
Iowa	100.0	94.6	3.0	0.9	1.2	0.3	100.0	93.1	3.2	1.8	1.5	0.4
Kansas	100.0	85.6	7.6	4.4	1.9	0.6	100.0	83.0	8.4	5.7	1.9	1.0
Kentucky	100.0	89.2	10.2	0.1	0.5	[3]	100.0	89.3	9.7	0.3	0.6	0.1
Louisiana	100.0	56.5	41.3	0.8	1.1	0.3	100.0	51.5	45.7	1.1	1.3	0.5
Maine	100.0	98.3	0.5	0.2	0.8	0.2	100.0	97.5	0.7	0.4	0.8	0.5
Maryland	100.0	59.7	35.3	1.7	3.1	0.2	100.0	58.1	34.7	3.1	3.8	0.3
Massachusetts	100.0	83.7	7.4	6.0	2.8	0.1	100.0	79.1	8.0	9.0	3.7	0.2
Michigan	100.0	76.4	19.8	1.8	1.2	0.8	100.0	77.4	17.5	2.6	1.5	1.1
Minnesota	100.0	93.9	2.1	0.9	1.7	1.5	100.0	88.1	4.5	1.8	3.7	1.9
Mississippi	100.0	43.9	55.5	0.1	0.4	0.1	100.0	47.8	50.9	0.3	0.5	0.4
Missouri	100.0	83.4	14.9	0.7	0.8	0.2	100.0	82.2	15.8	0.9	1.0	0.2
Montana	100.0	92.7	0.3	0.9	0.5	5.5	100.0	87.7	0.5	1.4	0.8	9.6
Nebraska	100.0	91.4	4.4	2.4	0.8	1.0	100.0	87.8	5.8	3.8	1.2	1.3
Nevada	100.0	77.4	9.6	7.5	3.2	2.3	100.0	69.0	9.3	15.5	4.2	2.0
New Hampshire	100.0	98.0	0.7	0.5	0.8	0.1	100.0	96.8	0.8	1.1	1.0	0.2
New Jersey	100.0	69.1	17.4	10.7	2.7	0.1	100.0	63.0	18.6	13.1	5.2	0.2
New Mexico	100.0	43.1	2.3	45.1	0.8	8.7	100.0	39.9	2.4	46.4	1.0	10.4
New York	100.0	68.4	16.5	12.3	2.7	0.2	100.0	57.7	20.2	16.9	4.8	0.4
North Carolina	100.0	68.4	28.9	0.4	0.6	1.7	100.0	65.2	30.5	1.5	1.2	1.5
North Dakota	100.0	92.4	0.6	1.1	0.8	5.0	100.0	90.1	0.8	0.8	0.7	7.6
Ohio	100.0	83.1	15.0	1.0	0.7	0.1	100.0	82.5	15.1	1.4	1.0	0.1
Oklahoma	100.0	79.0	7.8	1.6	1.0	10.6	100.0	70.4	10.4	3.7	1.2	14.3
Oregon	100.0	89.8	2.2	3.9	2.4	1.7	100.0	86.0	2.5	6.3	3.2	1.9
Pennsylvania	100.0	84.4	12.6	1.8	1.2	0.1	100.0	80.9	13.9	3.4	1.7	0.1
Rhode Island	100.0	87.9	5.6	3.7	2.4	0.3	100.0	79.9	7.0	9.5	3.2	0.5
South Carolina	100.0	54.6	44.5	0.2	0.6	0.1	100.0	56.8	41.7	0.6	0.7	0.2
South Dakota	100.0	90.6	0.5	0.6	0.7	7.6	100.0	84.2	0.8	0.7	0.8	13.6
Tennessee	100.0	76.5	22.6	0.2	0.6	[3]	100.0	75.4	23.0	0.6	0.9	0.1
Texas	100.0	51.0	14.4	32.5	2.0	0.2	100.0	47.1	14.3	36.1	2.3	0.2
Utah	100.0	93.7	0.4	3.0	1.5	1.5	100.0	91.0	0.7	4.8	2.1	1.4
Vermont	100.0	98.4	0.3	0.2	0.6	0.6	100.0	97.5	0.7	0.3	0.9	0.5
Virginia	100.0	72.6	23.7	1.0	2.6	0.1	100.0	67.2	26.2	3.0	3.4	0.2
Washington	100.0	84.5	4.2	3.8	5.1	2.3	100.0	79.1	4.6	7.4	6.3	2.6
West Virginia	100.0	95.9	3.7	0.1	0.3	[3]	100.0	95.3	3.9	0.2	0.4	0.1
Wisconsin	100.0	86.6	8.9	1.9	1.7	1.0	100.0	83.7	9.3	3.1	2.6	1.3
Wyoming	100.0	90.7	0.9	5.9	0.6	1.9	100.0	89.4	1.0	6.1	0.8	2.8
Other areas												
American Samoa	—	—	—	—	—	—	100.0	[3]	[3]	[3]	100.0	[3]
Guam	—	—	—	—	—	—	100.0	8.3	1.8	0.5	89.3	0.1
Northern Marianas	—	—	—	—	—	—	100.0	1.0	[3]	[3]	98.2	0.8
Puerto Rico	—	—	—	—	—	—	100.0	[3]	[3]	100.0	[3]	[3]
Virgin Islands	—	—	—	—	—	—	100.0	1.1	85.4	13.1	0.5	[3]

[1] Excludes persons of Hispanic origin.
[2] Includes estimate for nonresponding state.
[3] Less than 0.05 percent.
—Data not available.

NOTE.—The 1986–87 data were derived from the 1986 Elementary and Secondary School Civil Rights sample survey of public school districts. Because of rounding, details may not add to totals.

SOURCE: U.S. Department of Education, Office for Civil Rights, 1986 State Summaries of Elementary and Secondary School Civil Rights Survey; and National Center for Education Statistics, Common Core of Data survey. (This table was prepared September 1996.)

Table 45.—Enrollment of 3-, 4-, and 5-year-old children in preprimary programs, by level and control of program and by attendance status: October 1965 to October 1995

[In thousands]

Year and age	Total population, 3 to 5 years old	Enrollment by level and control						Enrollment by attendance		
		Total	Percent enrolled	Nursery school		Kindergarten		Full-day	Part-day	Percent full-day
				Public	Private	Public	Private			
1	2	3	4	5	6	7	8	9	10	11
Total, 3 to 5 years old										
1965	12,549	3,407	27.1	127	393	2,291	596	—	—	—
1970	10,949	4,104	37.5	332	762	2,498	511	698	3,405	17.0
1975	10,185	4,955	48.7	570	1,174	2,682	528	1,295	3,659	26.1
1980	9,284	4,878	52.5	628	1,353	2,438	459	1,551	3,327	31.8
1983	10,254	5,384	52.5	809	1,538	2,416	623	1,686	3,700	31.3
1984	10,612	5,480	51.6	742	1,593	2,668	476	1,929	3,550	35.2
1985	10,733	5,865	54.6	846	1,631	2,847	541	2,144	3,722	36.6
1986	10,866	5,971	55.0	829	1,715	2,859	567	2,241	3,730	37.5
1987	10,872	5,931	54.6	819	1,736	2,842	534	2,090	3,841	35.2
1988	10,993	5,978	54.4	851	1,770	2,875	481	2,044	3,935	34.2
1989	11,039	6,026	54.6	930	1,894	2,704	497	2,238	3,789	37.1
1990	11,207	6,659	59.4	1,199	2,180	2,772	509	2,577	4,082	38.7
1991	11,370	6,334	55.7	996	1,828	2,967	543	2,408	3,926	38.0
1992	11,545	6,402	55.5	1,073	1,783	2,995	550	2,410	3,992	37.6
1993	11,954	6,581	55.1	1,205	1,779	3,020	577	2,642	3,939	40.1
1994 [1]	12,328	7,514	61.0	1,848	2,314	2,819	534	3,468	4,046	46.2
1995 [1]	12,518	7,739	61.8	1,950	2,381	2,800	608	3,689	4,051	47.7
3 years old										
1965	4,149	203	4.9	41	153	5	4	—	—	—
1970	3,516	454	12.9	110	322	12	10	142	312	31.3
1975	3,177	683	21.5	179	474	11	18	259	423	37.9
1980	3,143	857	27.3	221	604	16	17	321	536	37.5
1983	3,574	1,004	28.1	314	631	21	39	357	648	35.5
1984	3,609	1,004	27.8	295	658	30	22	401	603	39.9
1985	3,594	1,035	28.8	278	679	52	26	350	685	33.8
1986	3,607	1,041	28.9	257	737	26	21	399	642	38.3
1987	3,569	1,022	28.6	264	703	24	31	378	644	37.0
1988	3,719	1,027	27.6	298	678	24	26	369	658	35.9
1989	3,713	1,005	27.1	277	707	3	18	390	615	38.8
1990	3,692	1,205	32.6	347	840	11	7	447	758	37.1
1991	3,811	1,074	28.2	313	702	38	22	388	687	36.1
1992	3,905	1,081	27.7	336	685	26	34	371	711	34.3
1993	4,053	1,097	27.1	369	687	20	20	426	670	38.9
1994 [1]	4,081	1,385	33.9	469	887	19	9	670	715	48.4
1995 [1]	4,148	1,489	35.9	511	947	15	17	754	736	50.6
4 years old										
1965	4,238	683	16.1	68	213	284	118	—	—	—
1970	3,620	1,007	27.8	176	395	318	117	230	776	22.8
1975	3,499	1,418	40.5	332	644	313	129	411	1,008	29.0
1980	3,072	1,423	46.3	363	701	239	120	467	956	32.8
1983	3,414	1,619	47.4	402	813	231	173	442	1,177	27.3
1984	3,579	1,603	44.8	376	860	257	110	521	1,082	32.5
1985	3,598	1,766	49.1	496	859	276	135	643	1,123	36.4
1986	3,616	1,772	49.0	498	903	257	115	622	1,150	35.1
1987	3,597	1,717	47.7	431	881	280	125	548	1,169	31.9
1988	3,598	1,768	49.1	481	922	261	104	519	1,249	29.4
1989	3,692	1,882	51.0	524	1,055	202	100	592	1,290	31.4
1990	3,723	2,087	56.1	695	1,144	157	91	716	1,371	34.3
1991	3,763	1,994	53.0	584	982	287	140	667	1,326	33.5
1992	3,807	1,982	52.1	602	971	282	126	632	1,350	31.9
1993	4,044	2,178	53.9	719	957	349	154	765	1,413	35.1
1994 [1]	4,202	2,532	60.3	1,020	1,232	198	82	1,095	1,438	43.2
1995 [1]	4,145	2,553	61.6	1,054	1,208	207	84	1,104	1,449	43.3
5 years old										
1965	4,162	2,521	60.6	18	27	2,002	474	—	—	—
1970	3,814	2,643	69.3	45	45	2,168	384	326	2,317	12.3
1975	3,509	2,854	81.3	59	57	2,358	381	625	2,228	21.9
1980	3,069	2,598	84.7	44	48	2,183	322	763	1,835	29.4
1983	3,266	2,761	84.5	93	94	2,164	410	887	1,875	32.1
1984	3,423	2,872	83.9	72	76	2,381	344	1,007	1,865	35.1
1985	3,542	3,065	86.5	73	94	2,519	379	1,151	1,914	37.6
1986	3,643	3,157	86.7	75	75	2,576	432	1,220	1,937	38.6
1987	3,706	3,192	86.1	124	152	2,538	378	1,163	2,028	36.4
1988	3,676	3,184	86.6	72	170	2,590	351	1,155	2,028	36.3
1989	3,633	3,139	86.4	129	132	2,499	378	1,255	1,883	40.0
1990	3,792	3,367	88.8	157	196	2,604	411	1,414	1,953	42.0
1991	3,796	3,267	86.0	100	143	2,642	382	1,354	1,913	41.4
1992	3,832	3,339	87.1	135	127	2,688	390	1,408	1,931	42.2
1993	3,857	3,306	85.7	116	136	2,651	403	1,451	1,856	43.9
1994 [1]	4,044	3,597	88.9	359	194	2,601	442	1,704	1,893	47.4
1995 [1]	4,224	3,697	87.5	385	226	2,578	507	1,830	1,867	49.5

[1] Data collected using new procedures. May not be comparable with figures for earlier years.

—Data not available.

NOTE.—Data are based on sample surveys of the civilian noninstitutional population. Although cells with fewer than 75,000 children are subject to wide sampling variation, they are included in the table to permit various types of aggregations. Enrollment data for 5-year-olds include only those students in preprimary programs. Because of rounding, details may not add to totals.

SOURCE: U.S. Department of Education, National Center for Education Statistics, *Preprimary Enrollment,* various years; and U.S. Department of Commerce, Bureau of the Census, Current Population Survey, unpublished data. (This table was prepared July 1996.)

Table 46.—Child care, nursery school, and kindergarten experiences prior to first grade, by educational attainment of parents: 1991

Educational experiences	Total	Parents' highest level of educational attainment [1]					
		Less than high school	High school or equivalency	Vocational/ technical or some college	College graduate	Graduate or professional school	No parent in household
1	2	3	4	5	6	7	8
Use of nonparental home-based child care prior to starting first grade							
Number of 1st and 2nd grade children, in thousands	7,547	791	2,393	2,288	1,051	947	78
Percent using child care by relatives	28	28	34	34	20	17	24
In own home [2]	10	12	11	12	8	8	6
In other home	18	16	23	22	12	9	18
Percent using child care by nonrelatives	27	11	22	31	32	37	12
In own home [2]	6	3	4	5	8	11	4
In other home	21	8	18	26	24	26	8
Attendance at day care centers, nursery schools, prekindergarten, and Head Start on a regular basis prior to starting first grade							
Total	100	100	100	100	100	100	100
Percent attending day care center, not nursery school ..	15	8	15	17	16	12	18
Percent attending nursery school, not day care center	34	27	32	31	40	48	29
Percent attending day care center and nursery school ..	22	11	18	27	23	23	19
Percent not attending day care center or nursery school	29	53	34	25	21	16	34
Attendance at kindergarten programs							
Total	100	100	100	100	100	100	100
Percent attending kindergarten	98	95	98	99	99	98	99
Public kindergartens	84	92	90	83	79	73	85
Full-day	33	45	38	31	23	23	46
Part-day	51	47	52	52	56	50	39
Private kindergartens	14	3	8	16	20	25	14
Full-day	7	1	4	8	11	14	8
Part-day	7	2	4	8	9	11	6
Percent not attending kindergarten	2	4	2	1	1	2	1

[1] Highest level of schooling completed by either parent or guardian in the household or the only parent or guardian in the household.

[2] Includes those in own home as well as those in both own and other home.

SOURCE: U.S. Department of Education, National Center for Education Statistics, "Experiences in Child Care and Early Childhood Progams of First and Second Graders." (This table was prepared April 1992.)

Table 47.—Child care arrangements of preschool children, by age and household characteristics: 1991 and 1995

Characteristics	Children [1]		Percent in nonparental arrangements [2]			Percent with parental care only
	Number, in thousands	Percent	Relative care	Nonrelative care	Center based program [3]	
1	2	3	4	5	6	7
1991						
Age, total	8,428	100.0	16.9	14.8	52.8	31.0
3 years old	3,749	44.5	16.1	14.8	42.3	37.8
4 years old	3,636	43.1	18.1	14.8	60.4	25.9
5 years old	1,044	12.4	15.6	15.0	63.9	24.3
Race/ethnicity						
White, non-hispanic	5,867	69.6	14.8	17.3	54.0	30.6
Black, non-hispanic	1,239	14.7	24.1	7.9	58.2	25.0
Hispanic	1,002	11.9	19.5	9.7	38.9	40.6
Other	319	3.8	19.3	12.1	53.2	32.6
Household income						
$10,000 or less	1,495	17.7	16.8	6.3	44.9	42.4
10,001 to 20,000	1,437	17.0	19.3	11.8	44.5	35.9
20,001 to 30,000	1,711	20.3	18.9	12.9	44.5	38.5
30,001 to 40,000	1,319	15.7	15.9	15.7	53.2	29.7
40,001 to 50,000	936	11.1	16.6	21.4	60.0	23.1
50,001 to 75,000	974	11.6	15.6	21.9	68.4	15.2
More than 75,000	556	6.6	9.6	25.9	80.4	8.8
1995						
Age, total	9,232	100.0	19.4	16.9	55.1	25.9
3 years old	4,126	44.7	21.4	18.5	40.7	32.0
4 years old	4,065	44.0	18.3	15.3	64.7	22.2
5 years old	1,041	11.3	15.1	17.2	74.5	16.2
Race/ethnicity						
White, non-hispanic	6,337	68.6	16.5	19.4	56.9	25.2
Black, non-hispanic	1,396	15.1	28.6	11.3	59.5	20.3
Hispanic	1,042	11.3	22.8	12.5	37.4	38.4
Other	457	5.0	22.6	10.5	56.7	24.2
Household income						
$10,000 or less	1,795	19.4	18.1	10.5	48.8	34.4
10,001 to 20,000	1,204	13.0	25.2	15.1	44.6	32.7
20,001 to 30,000	1,484	16.1	20.7	13.5	45.5	34.2
30,001 to 40,000	1,319	14.3	20.0	20.3	46.1	29.7
40,001 to 50,000	1,037	11.2	18.1	19.8	55.5	23.1
50,001 to 75,000	1,381	15.0	18.8	19.1	71.1	11.8
More than 75,000	1,012	11.0	13.7	25.2	82.2	7.8

[1] Estimates are based only on children 3 to 5 years old who have not entered kindergarten.
[2] Columns do not add up to total because some children participated in more than one type of nonparental arrangement.
[3] Center based programs include day care centers, nursery schools, prekindergarten, preschools and Head Start programs.

SOURCE: U.S. Department of Education, National Center for Education Statistics, National Household Education Survey (NHES), 1991 and 1995. (This table was prepared July 1996.)

Table 48.—Percent of public school kindergarten teachers indicating the importance of various factors for kindergarten readiness: Spring 1993

Kindergarten readiness factors	Not at all important	Not very important	Somewhat important	Very important	Essential	Percent rating readiness factor as "Very important" or "Essential," by percentage of school's students eligible for free or reduced-price lunches		
						Less than 20 percent	20 to 49 percent	50 percent or more
1	2	3	4	5	6	7	8	9
Is physically healthy, rested, and well nourished	0	(1)	4	24	72	97	95	95
Finishes tasks	3	11	47	31	9	43	40	37
Can count to 20 or more	33	34	26	5	3	8	6	9
Takes turns and shares	2	8	34	37	19	64	55	52
Has good problem-solving skills	8	23	44	20	5	29	23	23
Is enthusiastic and curious in approaching new activities	1	3	19	43	33	83	76	73
Is able to use pencils or paint brushes	15	27	38	16	5	23	21	19
Is not disruptive of the class	2	8	30	36	24	61	58	61
Knows the English language	13	12	33	24	17	40	45	39
Is sensitive to other children's feelings	1	6	35	41	17	61	58	56
Sits still and pays attention	3	12	43	30	12	46	37	43
Knows the letters of the alphabet	27	30	33	6	4	7	9	13
Can follow directions	2	7	31	41	19	61	61	58
Identifies primary colors and basic shapes	13	24	40	17	7	22	21	27
Communicates needs, wants, and thoughts verbally in child's primary language	1	1	15	41	43	85	84	83

[1] Less than 0.5 percent.

SOURCE: U.S. Department of Education, National Center for Education Statistics, Kindergarten Teacher Survey on Student Readiness. (This table was prepared April 1994.)

Table 49.—Participation of public kindergarten children in selected activities 5 days a week, by length and size of class and teacher preparation: Spring 1993

Activity	Total	Percent of kindergarten classes participating in activity every day						
		Length of kindergarten class		Size of kindergarten class			Teacher majored in early childhood education	
		Full-day	Half-day	Less than 20	20 to 25	More than 25	Yes	No
1	2	3	4	5	6	7	8	9
Listening to stories read aloud	90	91	90	87	92	91	91	89
Running, climbing, jumping, and other gross motor activities	58	72	48	55	57	64	60	56
Free play	66	72	62	64	67	67	67	66
Choosing from a set of specific options (like building blocks, objects, or books)	69	72	67	69	71	65	72	66
Using objects for math or science	49	61	41	48	51	48	53	45
Dramatic play, arts and crafts, music (creative activities)	64	66	63	62	65	66	68	60
Using worksheets for literary skills	14	25	13	21	18	17	19	18
Using worksheets for math or science	18	20	9	17	12	15	16	12

SOURCE: U.S. Department of Education, National Center for Education Statistics, Kindergarten Teacher Survey on Student Readiness. (This table was prepared April 1994.)

Table 50.—Public school pupils transported at public expense and current expenditures for transportation: 1929–30 to 1993–94

School year	Average daily attendance, all students	Pupils transported at public expense		Expenditures for transportation (in current dollars)		Expenditures for transportation (in constant 1993–94 dollars)	
		Number	Percent of total	Total[1] (in thousands)	Average per pupil transported	Total[1] (in thousands)	Average per pupil transported
1	2	3	4	5	6	7	8
1929–30	21,265,000	1,902,826	8.9	$54,823	$29	$456,485	$246
1931–32	22,245,000	2,419,173	10.9	58,078	24	574,153	243
1933–34	22,458,000	2,794,724	12.4	53,908	19	580,217	213
1935–36	22,299,000	3,250,658	14.6	62,653	19	649,805	205
1937–38	22,298,000	3,769,242	16.9	75,637	20	752,542	205
1939–40	22,042,000	4,144,161	18.8	83,283	20	849,367	210
1941–42	21,031,000	4,503,081	21.4	92,922	21	849,391	194
1943–44	19,603,000	4,512,412	23.0	107,754	24	881,357	200
1945–46	19,849,000	5,056,966	25.5	129,756	26	1,013,785	206
1947–48	20,910,000	5,854,041	28.0	176,265	30	1,078,205	189
1949–50	22,284,000	6,947,384	31.2	214,504	31	1,290,891	191
1951–52	23,257,000	7,697,130	33.1	268,827	35	1,457,770	194
1953–54	25,643,871	8,411,719	32.8	307,437	37	1,629,386	199
1955–56	27,740,149	9,695,819	35.0	353,972	37	1,876,645	199
1957–58	29,722,275	10,861,689	36.5	416,491	38	2,078,590	196
1959–60	32,477,440	12,225,142	37.6	486,338	40	2,359,028	198
1961–62	34,682,340	13,222,667	38.1	576,361	44	2,732,911	212
1963–64	37,405,058	14,475,778	38.7	673,845	47	3,113,928	221
1965–66	39,154,497	15,536,567	39.7	787,358	51	3,516,930	232
1967–68	40,827,965	17,130,873	42.0	981,006	57	4,111,323	246
1969–70	41,934,376	18,198,577	43.4	1,218,557	67	4,597,613	259
1971–72	42,254,272	19,474,355	46.1	1,507,830	77	5,222,442	275
1973–74	41,438,054	21,347,039	51.5	1,858,141	87	5,680,033	273
1975–76	41,269,720	21,772,483	52.8	2,377,313	109	6,109,606	288
1977–78	40,079,590	[2]21,800,000	54.4	2,731,041	125	6,214,641	[2]292
1979–80	38,288,911	21,713,515	56.7	3,833,145	177	7,037,201	332
1980–81	37,703,744	[2]22,272,000	59.1	[2]4,408,000	198	[2]7,253,000	[2]334
1981–82	37,094,652	[2]22,246,000	60.0	[2]4,793,000	215	[2]7,259,000	[2]335
1982–83	36,635,868	[2]22,199,000	60.6	[2]5,000,000	225	[2]7,261,000	[2]336
1983–84	36,362,978	[2]22,031,000	60.6	[2]5,284,000	240	[2]7,399,000	[2]345
1984–85	36,404,261	[2]22,320,000	61.3	[2]5,722,000	256	[2]7,711,000	[2]354
1985–86	36,523,103	[2]22,041,000	60.3	[2]6,123,000	278	[2]8,020,000	[2]373
1986–87	36,863,867	[2]22,397,000	60.8	[2]6,551,000	292	[2]8,394,000	[2]384
1987–88	37,050,707	[2]22,158,000	59.8	[2]6,888,000	311	[2]8,475,000	[2]392
1988–89	37,268,072	[2]22,635,000	60.7	[2]7,550,000	334	[2]8,879,000	[2]402
1989–90	37,799,296	[2]22,459,000	59.4	8,030,990	358	9,014,506	[2]412
1990–91	38,426,543	[2]22,000,000	57.3	8,678,954	394	9,236,826	[2]431
1991–92	38,960,783	[2]23,165,000	59.5	8,789,770	379	9,064,323	[2]401
1992–93	39,570,462	[2]23,439,000	59.2	9,252,300	395	9,252,300	[2]405
1993–94	40,146,393	[2]23,857,752	59.4	9,627,190	404	9,384,102	[2]404

[1] Excludes capital outlay for years through 1979–80, and 1989–90 to 1993–94. From 1980–81 to 1988–89 total transportation figures include capital outlay.

[2] Estimate based on data appearing in January issues of School Bus Fleet.

NOTE.—Constant dollars are adjusted for inflation using the Consumer Price Index computed on a school year basis. Some data have been revised from previously published figures.

SOURCE: U.S. Department of Education, National Center for Education Statistics, Statistics of State School Systems; Revenues and Expenditures for Public Elementary and Secondary Education, and unpublished data; and Bobbit Publishing Co., School Bus Fleet, January issues. (This table was prepared June 1996.)

Table 51.—Children 0 to 21 years old served in federally supported programs for the disabled, by type of disability: 1976–77 to 1993–94

Type of disability	1976–77	1980–81	1982–83	1983–84	1984–85	1985–86	1986–87	1987–88	1988–89	1989–90	1990–91	1991–92	1992–93	1993–94
1	2	3	4	5	6	7	8	9	10	11	12	13	14	15
	Number served,[1] in thousands													
All disabilities	3,692	4,142	4,255	4,298	4,315	4,317	4,374	4,447	4,544	4,641	4,762	4,949	5,125	5,318
Specific learning disabilities	796	1,462	1,741	1,806	1,832	1,862	1,914	1,928	1,987	2,050	2,130	2,234	2,354	2,424
Speech or language impairments	1,302	1,168	1,131	1,128	1,126	1,125	1,136	953	967	973	985	997	996	1,005
Mental retardation	959	829	757	727	694	660	643	582	564	548	534	538	519	536
Serious emotional disturbance	283	346	352	361	372	375	383	373	376	381	390	399	401	413
Hearing impairments	87	79	73	72	69	66	65	56	56	57	58	60	60	63
Orthopedic impairments	87	58	57	56	56	57	57	47	47	48	49	51	52	56
Other health impairments	141	98	50	53	68	57	52	45	43	52	55	58	65	82
Visual impairments	38	31	28	29	28	27	26	22	23	22	23	24	23	24
Multiple disabilities	—	68	63	65	69	86	97	77	85	86	96	97	102	108
Deaf-blindness	—	3	2	2	2	2	2	1	2	2	1	1	1	1
Autism and other	—	—	—	—	—	—	—	—	—	—	—	5	19	24
Preschool disabled[2]	(3)	(3)	(3)	(3)	(3)	(3)	(3)	363	394	422	441	484	531	582
	Percentage distribution of children served													
All disabilities	100.0	100.0	100.0	100.0	100.0	100.0	100.0	100.0	100.0	100.0	100.0	100.0	100.0	100.0
Specific learning disabilities	21.6	35.3	40.9	42.0	42.4	43.1	43.8	43.4	43.6	44.2	44.7	45.1	45.9	45.6
Speech or language impairments	35.3	28.2	26.6	26.2	26.1	26.1	26.0	21.4	21.1	21.0	20.7	20.2	19.4	18.9
Mental retardation	26.0	20.0	17.8	16.9	16.1	15.3	14.7	13.1	12.7	11.8	11.2	10.9	10.1	10.1
Serious emotional disturbance	7.7	8.4	8.3	8.4	8.6	8.7	8.8	8.4	8.3	8.2	8.2	8.1	7.8	7.8
Hearing impairments	2.4	1.9	1.7	1.7	1.6	1.5	1.5	1.3	1.3	1.2	1.2	1.2	1.2	1.2
Orthopedic impairments	2.4	1.4	1.3	1.3	1.3	1.3	1.3	1.1	1.1	1.0	1.0	1.0	1.0	1.1
Other health impairments	3.8	2.4	1.2	1.2	1.6	1.3	1.2	1.0	1.0	1.1	1.2	1.2	1.3	1.5
Visual impairments	1.0	0.7	0.7	0.7	0.7	0.6	0.6	0.5	0.5	0.5	0.5	0.5	0.5	0.5
Multiple disabilities	—	1.6	1.5	1.5	1.6	2.0	2.2	1.7	1.8	1.9	2.0	2.0	2.0	2.0
Deaf-blindness	—	0.1	(4)	0.1	(4)	(4)	(4)	(4)	(4)	(4)	(4)	(4)	(4)	(4)
Autism and other	—	—	—	—	—	—	—	—	—	—	—	0.1	0.4	0.4
Preschool disabled[2]	(3)	(3)	(3)	(3)	(3)	(3)	(3)	8.2	8.7	9.1	9.3	9.8	10.4	10.9
	Number served as a percent of total enrollment[5]													
All disabilities	8.33	10.13	10.75	10.95	11.00	10.95	11.00	11.11	11.30	11.44	11.55	11.77	11.97	12.23
Specific learning disabilities	1.80	3.58	4.40	4.60	4.67	4.72	4.81	4.82	4.94	5.06	5.17	5.31	5.50	5.57
Speech or language impairments	2.94	2.86	2.86	2.87	2.87	2.85	2.86	2.38	2.41	2.40	2.39	2.37	2.33	2.31
Mental retardation	2.16	2.03	1.91	1.85	1.77	1.68	1.62	1.45	1.40	1.35	1.30	1.28	1.21	1.23
Serious emotional disturbance	0.64	0.85	0.89	0.92	0.95	0.95	0.96	0.93	0.94	0.94	0.95	0.95	0.94	0.95
Hearing impairments	0.20	0.19	0.18	0.18	0.18	0.17	0.16	0.14	0.14	0.14	0.14	0.14	0.14	0.15
Orthopedic impairments	0.20	0.14	0.14	0.14	0.14	0.14	0.14	0.12	0.12	0.12	0.12	0.12	0.12	0.13
Other health impairments	0.32	0.24	0.13	0.13	0.17	0.14	0.13	0.11	0.11	0.13	0.13	0.14	0.15	0.19
Visual impairments	0.09	0.08	0.07	0.07	0.07	0.07	0.07	0.05	0.06	0.06	0.06	0.06	0.05	0.06
Multiple disabilities	—	0.17	0.16	0.17	0.17	0.22	0.24	0.19	0.21	0.21	0.23	0.23	0.24	0.25
Deaf-blindness	—	0.01	0.01	0.01	(6)	0.01	(6)	(6)	(6)	(6)	(6)	(6)	(6)	(6)
Autism and other	—	—	—	—	—	—	—	—	—	—	—	0.01	0.04	0.05
Preschool disabled[2]	(3)	(3)	(3)	(3)	(3)	(3)	(3)	0.91	0.98	1.04	1.07	1.15	1.24	1.34

[1] Includes students served under Chapter I and Individuals with Disabilities Education Act (IDEA), formerly the Education of the Handicapped Act.

[2] Includes preschool children 3–5 years and 0–5 years served under Chapter I and IDEA, respectively.

[3] Prior to 1987–88, these students were included in the counts by handicapping condition. Beginning in 1987–88, states were no longer required to report preschool handicapped students (0–5 years) by handicapping condition.

[4] Less than .05 percent.

[5] Based on the enrollment in public schools, kindergarten through 12th grade, including a relatively small number of prekindergarten students.

[6] Less than .005 percent.

—Data not available.

NOTE.—Counts are based on reports from the 50 states and District of Columbia only (i.e., figures from U.S. territories are not included). Increases since 1987–88 are due in part to new legislation enacted fall 1986, which mandates public school special education services for all handicapped children ages 3 through 5. Some data have been revised from previously published figures. Because of rounding, details may not add to totals.

SOURCE: U.S. Department of Education, Office of Special Education and Rehabilitative Services, *Annual Report to Congress on the Implementation of The Individuals with Disabilities Education Act*, various years, and unpublished tabulations; and National Center for Education Statistics, Common Core of Data survey. (This table was prepared April 1996.)

Table 52.—Percentage distribution of disabled persons 3 to 21 years old receiving education services for the disabled, by age group and educational environment: 1992–93

Type of disability	All environments	Regular class	Resource room	Separate class	Public separate school facility	Private separate school facility	Public residential facility	Private residential facility	Homebound/hospital environment
1	2	3	4	5	6	7	8	9	10
All persons, 3 to 21 years old	**100.0**	**40.5**	**29.9**	**24.1**	**2.7**	**1.4**	**0.6**	**0.2**	**0.6**
3 to 5 years old	100.0	47.5	12.2	30.6	4.8	2.9	0.3	0.1	1.6
6 to 21 years old	100.0	39.8	31.7	23.5	2.4	1.2	0.6	0.3	0.5
Mental retardation	100.0	7.1	26.8	56.8	6.8	1.1	0.6	0.3	0.5
Speech or language impairments	100.0	81.7	10.7	6.0	0.2	1.1	0.1	(¹)	0.1
Visual impairments	100.0	45.4	21.0	18.0	3.9	1.7	8.6	0.8	0.5
Serious emotional disturbance	100.0	19.6	26.7	35.2	8.5	5.3	1.8	1.7	1.3
Orthopedic impairments	100.0	35.1	20.0	34.1	5.2	1.5	0.4	0.2	3.5
Other health impairments	100.0	40.0	27.4	20.6	1.7	0.8	0.3	0.2	9.1
Specific learning disabilities	100.0	34.8	43.9	20.1	0.4	0.3	0.1	(¹)	0.2
Deaf-blindness	100.0	12.5	9.9	31.5	15.6	5.7	22.1	1.6	1.0
Multiple disabilities	100.0	7.5	19.0	44.6	17.9	5.8	2.2	1.3	1.8
Hearing impairments	100.0	29.5	19.7	28.1	5.6	2.7	13.2	0.9	0.4

¹ Less than 0.05 percent.

NOTE.—This table reflects a compilation of data reported by the states as of October 1, 1994. There are some reporting variations, e.g., estimated or incomplete data and nonstandard definitions, from state to state. Data include Puerto Rico. Data for 3- to 5- year-old children are no longer collected by type of disability. Because of rounding, details may not add to totals.

SOURCE: U.S. Department of Education, Office of Special Education and Rehabilitative Services, *Seventeenth Annual Report to Congress on the Implementation of The Individuals with Disabilities Education Act, 1995.* (This table was prepared April 1996.)

Table 53.—State legislation on gifted and talented programs and number and percent of students receiving services in public elementary and secondary schools, by state: 1993–94

State	State-mandated gifted and talented programs[1]	Discretionary state-supported gifted and talented programs[2]	Gifted and talented students receiving services	Gifted and talented students as a percent of enrollment	State	State-mandated gifted and talented programs[1]	Discretionary state-supported gifted and talented programs[2]	Gifted and talented students receiving services	Gifted and talented students as a percent of enrollment
1	2	3	4	5	1	2	3	4	5
Alabama			16,522	2.4	Missouri	X		24,877	5.0
Alaska	X		4,696	4.0	Montana	X		—	—
Arizona	X		39,200	—	Nebraska		X	18,600	10.0
Arkansas	X		34,710	8.0	Nevada	X	X	8,343	2.0
California		X	290,000	5.0	New Hampshire	X		—	—
Colorado	X		—	—	New Jersey	X		—	—
Connecticut	X		16,871	3.5	New Mexico	X		—	—
Delaware	X		—	³5.0	New York	X		135,000	6.0
District of Columbia	X		—	9.0	North Carolina	X		88,450	8.0
Florida	X		74,572	3.5	North Dakota		X	1,107	1.0
Georgia	X		—	5.0	Ohio	X		244,670	13.0
Hawaii	X		18,000	11.0	Oklahoma	X		61,082	10.0
Idaho	X		—	1.3	Oregon	X		—	8.5
Illinois	X		⁴166,234	5.0	Pennsylvania	X		79,756	4.6
Indiana		X	85,192	8.9	Rhode Island		X	—	3.5–5.0
Iowa	X		—	4.0	South Carolina	X		52,000	10.0
Kansas	X		—	3.1	South Dakota	X		6,515	4.4
Kentucky	X		52,600	5.0	Tennessee	X		18,626	2.0
Louisiana	X		24,000	3.2	Texas	X		248,769	7.0
Maine	X		10,100	5.0	Utah	X		—	—
Maryland		X	90,222	12.0	Vermont		X	—	—
Massachusetts		X	—	—	Virginia	X		121,598	9.2
Michigan		X	225,154	14.0	Washington		X	38,781	1.5
Minnesota		X	55,467	7.2	West Virginia	X		—	3.5
Mississippi	X		21,678	4.3	Wisconsin	X		—	15.0
					Wyoming		X	—	3.0

[1] Mandate requiring identification of and/or services for gifted/talented students.
[2] No mandate requiring identification of or services for gifted/talented students.
[3] Grades 2 through 6 only.
[4] Data for 1991–92.

—Data not available.

SOURCE: Council of State Directors of Programs for the Gifted, *The 1994 State of the States Gifted and Talented Education Report.* (This table was prepared May 1996.)

Table 54.—Number of children served under Individuals with Disabilities Education Act and Chapter 1 of the Education Consolidation and Improvement Act, State Operated Programs, by age group and state: 1990–91, 1991–92, and 1993–94

State	Birth to age 21			Ages 0 to 5			Percent change, birth to 21, 1990–91 to 1993–94
	1990–91	1991–92	1993–94	1990–91	1991–92	1993–94	
1	2	3	4	5	6	7	8
United States	4,761,742	4,948,601	5,318,021	440,661	483,824	581,683	11.7
Alabama	94,945	96,975	99,760	7,498	8,344	9,161	5.1
Alaska	14,745	16,106	18,006	1,813	2,089	2,633	22.1
Arizona	57,235	61,076	69,530	4,936	5,784	7,685	21.5
Arkansas	47,835	49,018	53,187	5,274	5,648	6,972	11.2
California	469,282	494,058	533,807	40,489	44,351	52,061	13.7
Colorado	57,102	60,357	66,595	4,894	5,444	7,011	16.6
Connecticut	64,562	66,192	71,863	6,142	6,471	7,875	11.3
Delaware	14,294	14,435	15,196	1,579	1,677	1,953	6.3
District of Columbia	6,290	7,104	6,994	411	588	600	11.2
Florida	236,013	253,606	289,539	16,387	18,289	31,017	22.7
Georgia	101,997	107,660	123,143	7,333	8,378	11,869	20.7
Hawaii	13,169	14,163	15,248	1,273	1,577	1,890	15.8
Idaho	22,017	22,755	23,536	3,129	3,209	3,654	6.9
Illinois	239,185	245,931	257,986	26,122	27,353	30,346	7.9
Indiana	114,643	118,924	127,961	8,937	9,874	12,874	11.6
Iowa	60,695	61,510	63,373	6,329	6,391	6,633	4.4
Kansas	45,212	47,063	50,438	4,308	4,952	6,421	11.6
Kentucky	79,421	81,681	80,539	11,008	12,989	13,668	1.4
Louisiana	73,663	78,760	86,931	7,541	8,600	11,083	18.0
Maine	27,987	27,891	29,350	2,895	2,497	2,873	4.9
Maryland	91,940	92,520	97,998	10,409	10,615	12,018	6.6
Massachusetts	154,616	156,633	160,275	17,014	18,293	21,163	3.7
Michigan	166,927	172,238	181,251	14,963	18,370	19,748	8.6
Minnesota	80,896	83,028	90,918	10,529	11,205	12,725	12.4
Mississippi	60,934	61,197	64,153	5,704	4,731	5,896	5.3
Missouri	101,955	105,521	114,008	4,889	6,491	9,108	11.8
Montana	17,204	18,038	18,401	1,934	2,071	2,131	7.0
Nebraska	32,761	35,975	37,112	2,961	3,356	3,728	13.3
Nevada	18,440	20,530	25,242	1,742	2,364	3,215	36.9
New Hampshire	19,658	21,047	23,354	2,077	2,153	2,561	18.8
New Jersey	181,319	184,621	190,003	17,190	17,445	18,025	4.8
New Mexico	36,037	38,207	43,474	2,247	2,652	3,631	20.6
New York	307,458	324,677	365,697	26,353	31,511	46,243	18.9
North Carolina	123,126	127,867	136,513	10,700	11,984	15,042	10.9
North Dakota	12,504	12,679	12,440	1,374	1,377	1,336	−0.5
Ohio	205,440	210,268	219,875	12,487	13,629	16,347	7.0
Oklahoma	65,653	68,576	73,130	5,359	5,983	6,627	11.4
Oregon	55,149	56,702	63,212	3,581	3,943	5,859	14.6
Pennsylvania	219,428	214,035	210,826	23,156	22,236	24,248	−3.9
Rhode Island	21,076	21,588	23,582	2,112	2,263	2,798	11.9
South Carolina	77,765	79,872	81,930	8,346	9,199	10,571	5.4
South Dakota	14,987	15,284	15,907	2,366	2,463	2,518	6.1
Tennessee	104,898	111,315	119,146	7,536	10,926	11,799	13.6
Texas	350,636	367,860	411,917	30,955	33,082	38,059	17.5
Utah	47,747	50,009	51,950	4,565	5,043	5,256	8.8
Vermont	12,263	11,101	10,452	1,200	1,130	1,232	−14.8
Virginia	113,971	122,647	131,599	11,791	13,359	14,271	15.5
Washington	85,395	91,286	101,254	11,409	12,462	14,392	18.6
West Virginia	43,135	44,338	44,528	3,630	4,372	5,298	3.2
Wisconsin	86,930	91,742	102,412	12,213	12,885	15,648	17.8
Wyoming	11,202	11,935	12,480	1,571	1,726	1,911	11.4

NOTE.—Individuals with Disabilities Education Act (IDEA), formerly known as the Education of the Handicapped Act, now extends the right to a free and appropriate education to 3- to 5-year-old disabled children.

SOURCE: U.S. Department of Education, Office of Special Education and Rehabilitative Services, Annual Report to Congress on the Implementation of The Individuals with Disabilities Education Act, various years, and unpublished tabulations. (This table was prepared April 1996.)

Table 55.—Enrollment in grades 9 to 12 in public and private schools compared with population 14 to 17 years of age: 1889–90 to fall 1995

[Numbers in thousands]

Year	Enrollment, grades 9 to 12[1]			Population 14 to 17 years of age[3]	Enrollment as a percent of population 14 to 17 years of age[4]
	All schools	Public schools	Private schools[2]		
1	2	3	4	5	6
1889–90	298	203	95	5,355	5.6
1899–1900	630	519	111	6,152	10.2
1909–10	1,032	915	117	7,220	14.3
1919–20	2,414	2,200	214	7,736	31.2
1929–30	4,741	4,399	[5]341	9,341	50.7
1939–40	7,059	6,601	[6]458	9,720	72.6
1949–50	6,397	5,725	672	8,405	76.1
1951–52	6,538	5,882	656	8,516	76.8
1953–54	7,038	6,290	747	8,861	79.4
1955–56	7,696	6,873	823	9,207	83.6
1957–58	8,790	7,860	931	10,139	86.7
Fall 1959	9,306	8,271	1,035	11,155	83.4
Fall 1961	10,489	9,369	1,120	12,046	87.1
Fall 1963	12,170	10,883	1,287	13,492	90.2
Fall 1965	13,010	11,610	1,400	14,146	92.0
Fall 1966	13,294	11,894	1,400	14,398	92.3
Fall 1967	13,650	12,250	1,400	14,727	92.7
Fall 1968	14,118	12,718	1,400	15,170	93.1
Fall 1969	14,337	13,037	1,300	15,549	92.2
Fall 1970	14,647	13,336	1,311	15,921	92.0
Fall 1971	15,053	13,753	[7]1,300	16,326	92.2
Fall 1972	15,148	13,848	[7]1,300	16,637	91.0
Fall 1973	15,344	14,044	[7]1,300	16,864	91.0
Fall 1974	15,403	14,103	[7]1,300	17,033	90.4
Fall 1975	15,604	14,304	[7]1,300	17,125	91.1
Fall 1976	15,656	14,314	1,342	17,117	91.5
Fall 1977	15,546	14,203	1,343	17,042	91.2
Fall 1978	15,441	14,088	1,353	16,944	91.1
Fall 1979	14,916	13,616	[7]1,300	16,610	89.8
Fall 1980	14,570	13,231	1,339	16,143	90.3
Fall 1981	14,164	12,764	[7]1,400	15,609	90.7
Fall 1982	13,805	12,405	[7]1,400	15,057	91.7
Fall 1983	13,671	12,271	[7]1,400	14,740	92.7
Fall 1984	13,704	12,304	[7]1,400	14,725	93.1
Fall 1985	13,750	12,388	1,362	14,888	92.4
Fall 1986	13,669	12,333	[7]1,336	14,824	92.2
Fall 1987	13,323	12,076	1,247	14,502	91.9
Fall 1988	12,893	11,687	[7]1,206	14,023	91.9
Fall 1989	12,583	11,390	[7]1,193	13,536	93.0
Fall 1990	12,475	11,338	[7]1,137	13,310	93.7
Fall 1991	12,666	11,541	[7]1,125	13,418	94.4
Fall 1992	12,898	11,735	[7]1,163	13,653	94.5
Fall 1993	13,152	11,961	[7]1,191	13,928	94.4
Fall 1994	13,450	12,214	[7]1,236	14,427	93.2
Fall 1995	13,845	12,576	[7]1,269	14,765	93.8

[1] Includes a relatively small number of secondary ungraded and postgraduate students.

[2] Data for most years are partly estimated.

[3] Data for 1890 through 1950 and for 1960 are from the decennial censuses of population. The other figures are Bureau of the Census estimates as of July 1 preceding the opening of the school year.

[4] Gross enrollment ratio based on school enrollment of all ages in grades 9 to 12 divided by the 14- to 17-year-old population. Differs from enrollment rates in other tables which are based on the enrollment of persons in the given age group only.

[5] Data are for 1927–28.

[6] Data are for 1940–41.

[7] Estimated.

NOTE.—Includes enrollment in public schools that are a part of state and local school systems and also in most private schools, both religiously affiliated and nonsectarian. Excludes enrollment in subcollegiate departments of institutions of higher education, residential schools for exceptional children, and federal schools. Because of rounding, details may not add to totals. Some data have been revised from previously published figures.

SOURCE: U.S. Department of Education, National Center for Education Statistics, *Statistics of State School Systems; Statistics of Public Elementary and Secondary School Systems; Statistics of Nonpublic Elementary and Secondary Schools;* Common Core of Data survey; and *Projections of Education Statistics to 2006.* (This table was prepared July 1996.)

Table 56.—Enrollment in foreign language courses compared with enrollment in grades 9 to 12 of public secondary schools: Fall 1948 to fall 1990

[In thousands]

Language	Fall 1948	Fall 1960	Fall 1965	Fall 1968	Fall 1970	Fall 1974	Fall 1976	Fall 1978	Fall 1982	Fall 1985	Fall 1990	Percent change in enrollment	
												1976 to 1985	1985 to 1990
1	2	3	4	5	6	7	8	9	10	11	12	13	14
Total enrollment, grades 9 to 12	[1]**5,602**	**8,589**	**11,610**	**12,718**	**13,336**	**14,103**	**14,314**	**14,088**	**12,405**	**12,388**	**11,338**	**−13.5**	**−8.5**
All foreign languages[2]													
Number enrolled	1,170	2,522	3,659	3,890	3,779	3,295	3,174	3,200	2,910	4,029	4,257	26.9	5.7
Percent of all students	20.9	29.4	31.5	30.6	28.3	23.3	22.2	22.7	23.3	32.2	37.5	—	—
Modern foreign languages													
Number enrolled	741	1,867	3,068	3,518	3,514	3,127	3,023	3,048	2,740	3,852	4,093	27.4	6.3
Percent of all students	13.2	21.7	26.4	27.7	26.4	22.1	21.1	21.6	21.9	31.1	36.1	—	—
Spanish													
Number enrolled	443	933	1,427	1,698	1,811	1,678	1,717	1,631	1,563	2,334	2,611	35.9	11.9
Percent of all students	7.9	10.9	12.3	13.4	13.6	11.9	12.0	11.6	12.5	18.8	23.0	—	—
French													
Number enrolled	254	744	1,251	1,328	1,231	978	888	856	858	1,134	1,089	27.7	−3.9
Percent of all students	4.5	8.7	10.8	10.4	9.2	6.9	6.2	6.1	6.9	9.2	9.6	—	—
German													
Number enrolled	43	151	328	423	411	393	353	331	267	312	295	−11.5	−5.3
Percent of all students	0.8	1.8	2.8	3.3	3.1	2.8	2.5	2.3	2.1	2.5	2.6	—	—
Russian													
Number enrolled	—	10	27	24	20	15	11	9	6	6	16	−46.7	174.9
Percent of all students	—	0.1	0.2	0.2	0.2	0.1	0.1	0.1	[3]	[3]	0.1	—	—
Italian													
Number enrolled	—	20	25	27	27	40	46	46	44	47	40	3.1	−14.0
Percent of all students	—	0.2	0.2	0.2	0.2	0.3	0.3	0.3	0.4	0.4	0.4	—	—
Other modern foreign languages[4]													
Number enrolled	1	9	9	18	15	23	9	176	3	18	40	—	—
Percent of all students	[3]	0.1	0.1	0.1	0.1	0.2	0.1	1.2	[3]	0.1	0.4	—	—
Latin													
Number enrolled	429	655	591	372	265	167	150	152	170	177	164	17.6	−7.4
Percent of all students	7.7	7.6	5.1	2.9	2.0	1.2	1.1	1.1	1.4	1.4	1.4	—	—

[1] Estimated.

[2] Includes enrollment in ancient Greek (not shown separately). Fewer than 1,000 students were enrolled in this language in each of the years shown.

[3] Less than 0.05 percent.

[4] Includes students enrolled in unspecified modern foreign languages. In 1978, a relatively large number of students were not identified by field of study.

—Data not reported, not available, or not applicable.

NOTE.—Because of rounding, details may not add to totals.

SOURCE: U.S. Department of Education, National Center for Education Statistics, Common Core of Data survey; and American Council on the Teaching of Foreign Languages, *Foreign Language Enrollments in Public Secondary Schools, Fall 1989 and Fall 1990.* (This table was prepared April 1992.)

Table 57.—Student participation in school programs and services, by control, level of school, and type of community: 1993–94

Control, level, and community type	Total students		Percent of students participating in program or service							
	Number	Percent distribution	Bilingual education	English as a second language	Remedial reading	Remedial mathematics	Programs for the disabled	Programs for the gifted and talented	Diagnostic and prescriptive	Extended day
1	2	3	4	5	6	7	8	9	10	11
Public total	**41,621,660**	**100.0**	**3.07**	**3.97**	**10.88**	**6.90**	**6.88**	**6.43**	**0.27**	**2.50**
School level [1]										
Elementary	26,886,026	64.6	3.98	4.75	13.46	7.77	6.76	6.25	0.31	3.58
Secondary	13,757,801	33.1	1.39	2.58	5.63	5.03	6.54	6.90	0.20	0.48
Combined	977,833	2.3	1.80	1.88	13.70	9.39	14.84	4.72	0.44	1.31
Community type										
Central city	12,163,036	29.2	6.30	7.13	12.86	8.34	7.05	6.55	0.23	3.82
Urban fringe/large town	13,559,662	32.6	2.04	3.90	8.84	5.60	6.34	7.26	0.23	2.69
Rural/small town	15,898,962	38.2	1.48	1.60	11.09	6.90	7.20	5.63	0.35	1.33
Private total	**4,970,548**	**100.0**	**0.81**	**0.58**	**6.35**	**4.16**	**2.98**	**4.93**	**0.89**	**9.20**
School level [1]										
Elementary	2,803,359	56.4	0.77	0.45	7.22	4.33	0.93	3.34	0.94	12.48
Secondary	811,087	16.3	0.19	0.62	4.24	3.06	3.43	8.56	0.47	0.23
Combined	1,356,102	27.3	1.25	0.83	5.82	4.46	6.95	6.05	1.03	7.76
Community type										
Central city	2,261,125	45.5	0.83	0.71	7.33	4.77	2.68	5.56	0.72	11.36
Urban fringe/large town	1,810,230	36.4	0.97	0.57	5.98	4.15	3.58	5.24	0.85	8.89
Rural/small town	899,193	18.1	0.42	0.27	4.63	2.62	2.50	2.75	1.48	4.39

[1] Elementary schools have grade 6 or lower or a low grade of ungraded and no grade higher than 8. Secondary schools have no grade lower than 7. Combined schools have grades lower than 7 and higher than 8.

NOTE.—Students may participate in more than one program or service. Includes only kindergarten pupils who attend schools that offer first grade or above. Excludes pre-kindergarten students. Totals differ from data appearing in other tables because of vary-ing survey processing procedures and time period coverages.

SOURCE: U.S. Department of Education, National Center for Education Statistics, "Schools and Staffing Survey, 1993–94." (This table was prepared September 1996.)

Table 58.—Private elementary and secondary enrollment and schools, by selected characteristics: 1993–94

Selected characteristics	Kindergarten through 12th grade enrollment [1]				Schools			
	Total	Catholic	Other religious	Non-sectarian	Total	Catholic	Other religious	Non-sectarian
1	2	3	4	5	6	7	8	9
Total	**4,970,646**	**2,516,130**	**1,686,064**	**768,451**	**26,093**	**8,351**	**12,180**	**5,563**
School enrollment								
Less than 150	890,343	168,200	509,028	213,115	14,155	1,572	8,499	4,084
150 to 299	1,482,210	853,139	467,749	161,322	6,820	3,815	2,232	773
300 to 499	1,243,578	719,037	359,278	165,263	3,272	1,885	973	414
500 to 749	736,057	432,557	196,751	106,749	1,228	729	327	172
750 or more	618,457	343,197	153,257	122,003	619	350	149	120
Percent minority students								
Less than 5%	1,855,365	876,589	774,050	204,726	10,750	3,152	6,137	1,461
5%, but less than 20%	1,620,369	761,747	502,822	355,800	7,482	2,376	3,070	2,036
20%, but less than 50%	704,432	375,825	189,615	138,992	3,785	1,095	1,395	1,295
50% or more	790,479	501,969	219,577	68,933	4,076	1,727	1,578	771
Community type								
Central city	2,261,124	1,179,765	754,308	327,051	9,707	3,543	4,061	2,103
Urban fringe/large town	1,810,231	995,081	529,918	285,232	8,583	2,963	3,399	2,221
Rural/small town	899,192	341,182	401,843	156,168	7,803	1,844	4,720	1,239

[1] Includes only kindergarten pupils who attend schools that offer first grade.

NOTE.—Data are based upon a sample survey and may not be strictly comparable with data reported elsewhere. Includes only schools that offer first grade or above. Ex-cludes prekindergarten students. Because of rounding, details may not add to totals.

SOURCE: U.S. Department of Education, National Center for Education Statistics, "Schools and Staffing Survey, 1993–94." (This table was prepared September 1996.)

Table 59.—Private elementary and secondary staff and student-staff ratios, by level and orientation of school: 1993–94

Orientation and type of staff	Full-time equivalent staff				Students per full-time equivalent staff member			
	Total	Elementary [1]	Secondary [2]	Combined [3]	Total	Elementary [1]	Secondary [2]	Combined [3]
1	2	3	4	5	6	7	8	9
Total	534,636	240,894	104,213	189,529	9.3	11.6	7.8	7.2
Principals	23,589	13,180	2,459	7,950	210.7	212.7	329.8	170.6
Assistant principals	8,361	3,094	2,113	3,154	594.5	906.1	383.9	430.0
Other managers	7,801	1,510	3,483	2,808	637.2	1,856.5	232.9	483.0
Instruction coordinators	6,063	1,837	1,293	2,933	819.8	1,526.1	627.3	462.4
Teachers	330,838	155,220	60,644	114,974	15.0	18.1	13.4	11.8
Teacher aides	33,905	16,516	2,566	14,823	146.6	169.7	316.1	91.5
Guidance counselors	8,640	1,713	3,758	3,169	575.3	1,636.5	215.8	428.0
Librarians/media specialists	8,946	4,320	1,950	2,676	555.6	648.9	415.9	506.8
Library/media center aides	3,768	1,942	588	1,238	1,319.2	1,443.5	1,379.4	1,095.5
Student support staff [4]	11,003	2,207	2,684	6,112	451.8	1,270.2	302.2	221.9
Secretaries/clerical staff	37,634	15,170	9,061	13,403	132.1	184.8	89.5	101.2
Other employees [5]	54,092	24,187	13,615	16,290	91.9	115.9	59.6	83.3
Catholic								
Total	206,094	135,831	59,239	11,024	12.2	13.6	10.0	6.9
Principals	8,186	6,702	1,177	307	307.4	275.8	503.0	247.1
Assistant principals	2,854	1,210	1,475	169	881.6	1,527.5	401.4	448.9
Other managers	3,139	717	2,168	254	801.6	2,577.8	273.1	298.7
Instruction coordinators	1,138	619	477	42	2,211.0	2,985.9	1,241.1	1,806.2
Teachers	132,240	88,524	37,132	6,584	19.0	20.9	15.9	11.5
Teacher aides	9,078	8,144	176	758	277.2	226.9	3,363.7	100.1
Guidance counselors	3,843	1,144	2,341	358	654.7	1,615.6	252.9	211.9
Librarians/media specialists	4,291	2,836	1,230	225	586.4	651.7	481.3	337.2
Library/media center aides	1,969	1,489	363	117	1,277.9	1,241.3	1,630.9	648.4
Student support staff [4]	2,287	1,418	568	301	1,100.2	1,303.4	1,042.3	252.0
Secretaries/clerical staff	13,731	8,139	4,841	751	183.2	227.1	122.3	101.0
Other employees [5]	23,338	14,889	7,291	1,158	107.8	124.1	81.2	65.5
Other religious orientation								
Total	184,521	72,798	16,970	94,753	9.1	9.9	7.3	8.9
Principals	9,917	4,535	573	4,809	170.0	158.4	217.2	175.4
Assistant principals	3,184	1,102	278	1,804	529.5	651.7	447.7	467.5
Other managers	1,932	584	340	1,008	872.7	1,229.7	366.0	836.8
Instruction coordinators	2,298	775	153	1,370	733.7	926.7	813.4	615.7
Teachers	120,253	46,973	10,366	62,914	14.0	15.3	12.0	13.4
Teacher aides	10,021	4,827	171	5,023	168.3	148.8	727.8	167.9
Guidance counselors	2,001	473	403	1,125	842.6	1,518.3	308.8	749.7
Librarians/media specialists	2,596	977	349	1,270	649.5	735.1	356.6	664.1
Library/media center aides	990	330	112	548	1,703.1	2,176.3	1,111.1	1,539.1
Student support staff [4]	1,318	489	231	598	1,279.3	1,468.7	538.7	1,410.4
Secretaries/clerical staff	13,551	5,033	1,637	6,881	124.4	142.7	76.0	122.6
Other employees [5]	16,460	6,700	2,357	7,403	102.4	107.2	52.8	113.9
Non-sectarian								
Total	144,025	32,267	28,005	83,753	5.3	7.3	3.4	5.2
Principals	5,486	1,943	709	2,834	140.1	121.9	133.5	154.2
Assistant principals	2,323	782	360	1,181	330.8	303.0	262.9	369.9
Other managers	2,730	209	975	1,546	281.5	1,133.6	97.1	282.6
Instruction coordinators	2,627	443	663	1,521	292.5	534.8	142.7	287.2
Teachers	78,345	19,723	13,146	45,476	9.8	12.0	7.2	9.6
Teacher aides	14,806	3,545	2,219	9,042	51.9	66.8	42.6	48.3
Guidance counselors	2,796	96	1,014	1,686	274.8	2,468.0	93.3	259.1
Librarians/media specialists	2,059	507	371	1,181	373.2	467.3	255.1	369.9
Library/media center aides	809	123	113	573	949.9	1,926.3	837.4	762.5
Student support staff [4]	7,398	300	1,885	5,213	103.9	789.8	50.2	83.8
Secretaries/clerical staff	10,352	1,998	2,583	5,771	74.2	118.6	36.6	75.7
Other employees [5]	14,294	2,598	3,967	7,729	53.8	91.2	23.9	56.5

[1] Includes schools beginning with grade 6 or below and with no grade higher than 8.
[2] Schools have no grade lower than 7.
[3] Schools have grades lower than 7 and higher than 8.
[4] Includes student support services professional staff, such as school psychologists, social workers, occupational therapists, speech therapists, and nurses.
[5] Includes cafeteria workers and maintenance staff.

NOTE.—Data are based upon a sample survey and may not be strictly comparable with data reported elsewhere. Includes only schools that offer first grade or above.

SOURCE: U.S. Department of Education, National Center for Education Statistics, "Schools and Staffing Survey, 1993–94." (This table was prepared August 1995.)

Table 60.—Private elementary and secondary enrollment and schools, by amount of tuition, level, and orientation of school: 1993–94

Orientation and tuition	Kindergarten through 12th grade enrollment [1]				Schools				Average tuition paid by students [2]			
	Total	Elementary	Secondary	Combined	Total	Elementary	Secondary	Combined	Total	Elementary	Secondary	Combined
1	2	3	4	5	6	7	8	9	10	11	12	13
Total	4,970,646	2,803,359	811,087	1,356,199	26,093	15,538	2,551	8,004	$3,116	$2,138	$4,578	$4,266
Catholic	2,516,130	1,848,257	592,011	75,862	8,351	6,924	1,161	266	2,178	1,628	3,643	4,153
Less then $1,000	393,901	378,724	(3)	(3)	1,786	1,706	(3)	(3)	—	—	—	—
$1,000 to $2,499	1,368,046	1,274,601	81,955	(3)	4,834	4,542	235	(3)	—	—	—	—
$2,500 to $4,999	675,708	188,123	452,901	(3)	1,533	642	782	(3)	—	—	—	—
$5,000 or more	71,929	(3)	(3)	(3)	(3)	(3)	(3)	(3)	—	—	—	—
Other religious	1,686,064	718,170	124,447	843,448	12,180	6,328	612	5,240	2,915	2,606	5,261	2,831
Less then $1,000	113,382	66,259	(3)	45,878	2,435	1,386	(3)	1,044	—	—	—	—
$1,000 to $2,499	839,447	387,917	(3)	435,788	6,759	3,645	(3)	3,012	—	—	—	—
$2,500 to $4,999	513,773	187,164	62,993	263,615	2,198	970	316	913	—	—	—	—
$5,000 or more	203,014	68,255	38,655	96,104	738	303	172	263	—	—	—	—
Non-sectarian	768,451	236,932	94,629	436,890	5,563	2,287	778	2,498	6,631	4,693	9,525	7,056
Less then $1,000	49,128	(3)	(3)	(3)	912	(3)	(3)	(3)	—	—	—	—
$1,000 to $2,499	121,869	(3)	(3)	(3)	666	(3)	(3)	(3)	—	—	—	—
$2,500 to $4,999	200,857	119,326	(3)	74,395	1,810	1,301	(3)	465	—	—	—	—
$5,000 or more	396,244	82,596	74,283	239,364	2,166	456	408	1,302	—	—	—	—

[1] Only includes kindergarten students who attend schools that offer first grade or above.
[2] Tuition weighted by the number of students enrolled in schools.
[3] Too few sample cases (fewer than 30 schools) for reliable estimates.
—Data not applicable.

NOTE.—Data are based upon a sample survey and may not be strictly comparable with data reported elsewhere. Elementary schools have grade 6 or lower and no grade higher than 8. Secondary schools have no grade lower than 7. Combined schools have grades lower than 7 and higher than 8. Excludes prekindergarten students. Because of rounding and missing values in cells with too few sample cases, details may not add to totals.

SOURCE: U.S. Department of Education, National Center for Education Statistics, "Schools and Staffing Survey, 1993–94." (This table was prepared August 1995.)

Table 61.—Summary statistics on Catholic elementary and secondary schools, by level: 1919–20 to 1995–96

School year	Number of schools			Enrollment			Instructional staff		
	Total	Elementary	Secondary	Total	Elementary	Secondary	Total	Elementary	Secondary
1	2	3	4	5	6	7	8	9	10
1919–20	8,103	6,551	1,552	1,925,521	1,795,673	129,848	[1] 49,516	[1] 41,592	[1] 7,924
1929–30	10,046	7,923	2,123	2,464,467	2,222,598	241,869	[1] 72,552	[1] 58,245	[1] 14,307
1939–40	10,049	7,944	2,105	2,396,305	2,035,182	361,123	[1] 81,057	[1] 60,081	[1] 20,976
1949–50	10,778	8,589	2,189	3,066,387	2,560,815	505,572	[1] 94,295	[1] 66,525	[1] 27,770
Fall 1960	12,893	10,501	2,392	5,253,791	4,373,422	880,369	[1] 151,902	[1] 108,169	[1] 43,733
1969–70	11,771	9,695	2,076	4,658,098	3,607,168	1,050,930	[2] 195,400	[2] 133,200	[2] 62,200
1970–71	11,350	9,370	1,980	4,363,566	3,355,478	1,008,088	166,208	112,750	53,458
1974–75	10,127	8,437	1,690	3,504,000	2,602,000	902,000	150,179	100,011	50,168
1975–76	9,993	8,340	1,653	3,415,000	2,525,000	890,000	149,276	99,319	49,957
1979–80	9,640	8,100	1,540	3,139,000	2,293,000	846,000	147,294	97,724	49,570
1980–81	9,559	8,043	1,516	3,106,000	2,269,000	837,000	145,777	96,739	49,038
1981–82	9,494	7,996	1,498	3,094,000	2,266,000	828,000	146,172	96,847	49,325
1982–83	9,432	7,950	1,482	3,007,189	2,211,412	795,777	146,460	97,337	49,123
1983–84	9,401	7,937	1,464	2,969,000	2,179,000	790,000	146,913	98,591	48,322
1984–85	9,325	7,876	1,449	2,903,000	2,119,000	784,000	149,888	99,820	50,068
1985–86	9,220	7,790	1,430	2,821,000	2,061,000	760,000	146,594	96,741	49,853
1986–87	9,102	7,693	1,409	2,726,000	1,998,000	728,000	141,930	93,554	48,376
1987–88	8,992	7,601	1,391	2,623,000	1,942,000	681,000	139,887	93,199	46,688
1988–89	8,867	7,505	1,362	2,551,000	1,912,000	639,000	137,700	93,154	44,546
1989–90	8,719	7,395	1,324	2,499,000	1,894,000	606,000	136,900	94,197	42,703
1990–91	8,587	7,291	1,296	2,475,439	1,883,906	591,533	131,198	91,039	40,159
1991–92	8,508	7,239	1,269	2,442,924	1,856,302	586,622	153,334	109,084	44,250
1992–93	8,423	7,174	1,249	2,444,842	1,860,937	583,905	154,816	109,825	44,991
1993–94	8,345	7,114	1,231	2,444,609	1,859,947	584,662	157,201	112,199	45,002
1994–95	8,293	7,055	1,238	2,475,207	1,877,782	597,425	[3] 164,219	[3] 117,620	[3] 46,599
1995–96	8,243	7,015	1,228	2,491,111	1,884,461	606,650	[3] 166,759	[3] 118,753	[3] 48,006

[1] Includes part-time teachers.
[2] Includes estimates for the nonreporting schools.
[3] Full-time equivalent

NOTE.—Data reported by the National Catholic Educational Association and data reported by the National Center for Education Statistics are not directly comparable because survey procedures and definitions differ. Excludes prekindergarten enrollment.

SOURCE: National Catholic Educational Association, *A Statistical Report on Catholic Elementary and Secondary Schools for the Years 1967–68 to 1969–70*, as compiled from the Official Catholic Directory (Copyright © 1970 by the National Catholic Educational Association); *Catholic Schools in America* (1978 edition, Copyright © 1978 by the Franklin Press); and *United States Catholic Elementary and Secondary Schools, 1989–90, 1990–91, 1991–92, 1992–93, 1993–94, 1994–95, and 1995–96* (Copyright © 1990, 1991, 1992, 1993, 1994, 1995, and 1996 by the National Catholic Educational Association. All rights reserved.) (This table was prepared June 1996.)

Table 62.—Private elementary and secondary schools, enrollment, teachers, and high school graduates, by state:[1] Fall 1993

State	Number of schools		Enrollment		Teachers		High school graduates, 1992–93	
	Total	Standard error	Total	Standard error	Total	Standard error	Total	Standard error
1	2	3	4	5	6	7	8	9
United States[2]	**26,093**	**205**	**4,836,442**	**12,875**	**338,162**	**1,319**	**247,278**	**697**
Alabama	410	79	72,630	4,724	5,424	456	4,174	348
Alaska	66	—	5,884	0	476	—	213	—
Arizona	263	—	41,957	—	2,796	—	2,415	—
Arkansas	179	30	29,011	3,995	2,023	335	1,023	—
California	3,145	65	569,062	1,987	35,170	248	24,436	65
Colorado	391	68	53,732	7,798	4,115	632	1,826	283
Connecticut	360	22	70,198	1,875	6,345	125	6,291	46
Delaware	90	—	22,308	—	1,780	—	1,446	—
District of Columbia	80	—	15,854	—	1,544	—	1,054	—
Florida	1,262	83	233,743	3,789	16,842	424	9,820	54
Georgia	580	81	97,726	3,586	8,283	300	5,630	127
Hawaii	121	—	30,537	—	2,144	—	1,886	—
Idaho	78	—	8,019	—	552	—	341	—
Illinois	1,347	12	293,038	794	17,550	70	14,724	98
Indiana	619	—	91,986	—	6,139	—	4,061	—
Iowa	290	30	50,602	211	3,291	34	2,495	—
Kansas	206	—	37,045	—	2,382	—	1,668	—
Kentucky	296	—	58,058	—	3,815	—	2,949	—
Louisiana	458	19	145,512	4,036	9,286	301	7,844	—
Maine	140	—	16,999	—	1,535	—	1,914	—
Maryland	522	—	112,481	—	8,646	—	5,648	—
Massachusetts	648	29	126,744	1,362	11,329	168	10,281	—
Michigan	1,075	—	187,741	—	11,322	—	8,925	—
Minnesota	542	—	86,051	—	5,595	—	3,453	—
Mississippi	221	30	58,655	1,564	3,995	150	3,901	180
Missouri	719	69	117,466	616	7,973	85	5,839	212
Montana	82	—	9,111	—	684	—	355	—
Nebraska	223	—	39,564	—	2,575	—	1,904	—
Nevada	58	—	10,723	—	654	—	646	—
New Hampshire	130	—	18,386	—	1,742	—	1,730	—
New Jersey	878	—	195,921	—	14,281	—	11,025	—
New Mexico	166	—	20,007	—	1,569	—	1,029	—
New York	1,985	59	473,119	4,776	34,771	482	26,625	125
North Carolina	463	18	69,000	1,803	5,746	147	2,983	—
North Dakota	59	—	7,577	—	529	—	332	—
Ohio	1,016	58	246,805	3,480	14,872	306	12,398	172
Oklahoma	190	62	25,837	3,584	2,250	450	1,536	288
Oregon	250	—	34,092	—	2,254	—	1,700	—
Pennsylvania	1,846	54	342,298	4,260	21,880	235	18,532	304
Rhode Island	112	—	23,153	—	1,835	—	1,408	—
South Carolina	297	21	51,600	1,819	3,989	155	2,383	—
South Dakota	96	—	9,575	—	707	—	254	—
Tennessee	496	54	84,538	2,909	6,684	162	4,970	—
Texas	1,353	98	211,337	7,591	16,726	708	8,447	469
Utah	66	—	9,793	—	749	—	590	—
Vermont	85	—	9,107	—	945	—	1,120	—
Virginia	515	55	84,438	4,584	7,391	621	4,580	—
Washington	486	53	70,205	1,858	4,798	348	2,644	—
West Virginia	145	—	13,539	—	1,085	—	672	—
Wisconsin	954	—	141,762	—	8,927	—	5,129	—
Wyoming	35	—	1,919	—	167	—	31	—

[1] Includes special education, vocational/technical education, and alternative schools. Excludes prekindergarten enrollment.

[2] The National Center for Education Statistics employed an area frame sample to account for noninclusion of schools at the national level. However, caution should be exercised in interpreting state by state characteristics since the samples were not designed to produce such numbers.

—Insufficient data to compute a standard error.

NOTE.—Tabulation includes only schools that offer first grade or above.

SOURCE: U.S. Department of Education, National Center for Education Statistics, "Private School Survey, 1993–94." (This table was prepared August 1995.)

Table 63.—Public and private elementary and secondary teachers and pupil-teacher ratios, by level: Fall 1955 to fall 1996

Year	Public and private elementary and secondary			Public elementary and secondary			Private elementary and secondary		
	Kindergarten to grade 12	Elementary	Secondary	Kindergarten to grade 12	Elementary	Secondary	Kindergarten to grade 12	Elementary	Secondary
1	2	3	4	5	6	7	8	9	10
Number of teachers, in thousands									
1955	1,286	827	459	1,141	733	408	[1]145	[1]94	[1]51
1960	1,600	991	609	1,408	858	550	[1]192	[1]133	[1]59
1964	1,865	1,086	779	1,648	940	708	[1]217	[1]146	[1]71
1965	1,933	1,112	822	1,710	965	746	223	147	76
1966	2,012	1,153	859	1,789	1,006	783	[1]223	[1]147	[1]76
1967	2,079	1,188	891	1,855	1,040	815	[1]224	[1]148	[1]76
1968	2,161	1,223	938	1,936	1,076	860	225	147	78
1969	2,245	1,260	986	2,016	1,109	908	[1]229	[1]151	[1]78
1970	2,292	1,283	1,009	2,059	1,130	929	233	153	80
1971	2,293	1,263	1,030	2,063	1,111	952	[1]230	[1]152	[1]78
1972	2,337	1,296	1,041	2,106	1,142	964	[1]231	[1]154	[1]77
1973	2,372	1,308	1,064	2,136	1,151	985	[1]236	[1]157	[1]79
1974	2,410	1,330	1,079	2,165	1,166	998	[1]245	[1]164	[1]81
1975	2,453	1,353	1,100	2,198	1,181	1,017	[1]255	[1]172	[1]83
1976	2,457	1,351	1,106	2,189	1,168	1,021	268	183	85
1977	2,488	1,375	1,113	2,209	1,185	1,024	279	190	89
1978	2,479	1,376	1,103	2,207	1,191	1,016	272	185	87
1979	2,461	1,379	1,082	2,185	1,191	994	[1]276	[1]188	[1]88
1980	2,485	1,401	1,084	2,184	1,189	995	301	212	89
1981	2,440	1,404	1,037	2,127	1,183	945	[1]313	[1]221	[1]92
1982	2,458	1,413	1,045	2,133	1,182	951	[1]325	[1]231	[1]94
1983	2,476	1,426	1,050	2,139	1,186	953	337	240	97
1984	2,508	1,451	1,057	2,168	1,208	960	[1]340	[1]243	[1]97
1985	2,549	1,483	1,066	2,206	1,237	969	343	246	97
1986	2,592	1,521	1,071	2,244	1,271	973	[1]348	[1]250	[1]98
1987	2,632	1,564	1,068	2,279	1,307	973	[1]353	[1]257	[1]95
1988	2,668	1,604	1,064	2,323	1,353	970	[1]345	[1]251	[1]94
1989	2,734	1,662	1,072	2,357	1,387	970	[1]377	[1]275	[1]102
1990	2,753	1,680	1,073	2,398	1,426	972	[1]355	[1]254	[1]101
1991	2,787	1,713	1,074	2,432	1,459	973	[1]355	[1]254	[1]101
1992	2,822	1,746	1,075	2,459	1,486	972	[1]363	[1]260	[1]103
1993	2,870	1,777	1,093	2,504	1,515	989	[1]366	[1]262	[1]104
1994[2]	2,931	1,777	1,153	2,552	1,510	1,041	379	267	112
1995[2]	2,972	1,800	1,172	2,586	1,529	1,058	386	272	114
1996[3]	3,071	1,851	1,220	2,679	1,576	1,103	392	276	117
Pupil-teacher ratios									
1955	27.4	31.4	20.3	26.9	30.2	20.9	[1]31.7	[1]40.4	[1]15.7
1960	26.4	29.4	21.4	25.8	28.4	21.7	[1]30.7	[1]36.1	[1]18.6
1964	25.6	28.7	21.2	25.1	27.9	21.5	[1]29.0	[1]34.2	[1]18.3
1965	25.1	28.4	20.6	24.7	27.6	20.8	28.3	33.3	18.4
1966	24.5	27.7	20.2	24.1	26.9	20.3	[1]27.8	[1]32.7	[1]18.4
1967	24.0	26.9	20.1	23.7	26.3	20.3	[1]26.8	[1]31.1	[1]18.4
1968	23.5	26.0	20.2	23.2	25.4	20.4	25.8	29.9	17.9
1969	22.7	25.1	19.7	22.6	24.7	20.0	[1]24.0	[1]27.8	[1]16.7
1970	22.4	24.6	19.5	22.3	24.3	19.8	23.0	26.5	16.4
1971	22.4	25.0	19.1	22.3	24.9	19.3	[1]22.6	[1]25.7	[1]16.7
1972	21.7	23.9	18.9	21.7	23.9	19.1	[1]21.6	[1]24.0	[1]16.9
1973	21.3	23.0	19.1	21.3	23.0	19.3	[1]21.2	[1]23.6	[1]16.5
1974	20.8	22.6	18.5	20.8	22.6	18.7	[1]20.4	[1]22.6	[1]16.0
1975	20.3	21.7	18.6	20.4	21.7	18.8	[1]19.6	[1]21.5	[1]15.7
1976	20.1	21.7	18.3	20.2	21.8	18.5	19.3	20.9	15.8
1977	19.6	20.9	17.9	19.7	21.1	18.2	18.4	20.0	15.1
1978	19.2	20.9	17.1	19.3	21.0	17.3	18.7	20.2	15.6
1979	19.0	20.5	17.0	19.1	20.6	17.2	[1]18.1	[1]19.7	[1]14.8
1980	18.6	20.1	16.6	18.7	20.4	16.8	17.7	18.8	15.0
1981	18.7	20.0	16.8	18.8	20.3	16.9	[1]17.6	[1]18.6	[1]15.2
1982	18.4	19.8	16.4	18.6	20.2	16.6	[1]17.2	[1]18.2	[1]14.9
1983	18.2	19.6	16.2	18.4	19.9	16.4	17.0	18.0	14.4
1984	17.9	19.3	16.0	18.1	19.7	16.1	[1]16.8	[1]17.7	[1]14.4
1985	17.6	19.1	15.6	17.9	19.5	15.8	16.2	17.1	14.0
1986	17.4	18.8	15.5	17.7	19.3	15.7	[1]15.7	[1]16.5	[1]13.6
1987	17.3	18.8	15.0	17.6	19.3	15.2	[1]15.5	[1]16.4	[1]13.1
1988	17.0	18.6	14.7	17.3	19.0	14.9	[1]15.2	[1]16.1	[1]12.8
1989	16.8	18.4	14.3	17.2	19.0	14.6	[1]14.2	[1]15.1	[1]11.7
1990	16.9	18.5	14.3	17.2	19.0	14.6	[1]14.7	[1]16.1	[1]11.3
1991	17.0	18.5	14.5	17.3	18.9	14.9	[1]14.6	[1]16.0	[1]11.1
1992	17.1	18.5	14.8	17.4	18.9	15.1	[1]14.8	[1]16.2	[1]11.3
1993	17.1	18.4	14.8	17.4	18.8	15.2	[1]14.9	[1]16.3	[1]11.5
1994[2]	17.0	18.7	14.5	17.3	19.0	14.9	15.2	16.8	11.2
1995[2]	17.1	18.7	14.6	17.4	19.1	14.9	15.1	16.7	11.3
1996[3]	17.1	18.7	14.6	17.4	19.1	14.9	15.1	16.7	11.3

[1] Estimated.

[2] Preliminary data.

[3] Projected.

NOTE.—Data for teachers are expressed in full-time equivalents. Distribution of unclassified teachers by level is estimated. Distribution of elementary and secondary school teachers by level is determined by reporting units. Kindergarten includes a relatively small number of nursery school teachers and students. Some data have been revised from previously published figures. Because of rounding, details may not add to totals.

SOURCE: U.S. Department of Education, National Center for Education Statistics, *Statistics of Public Elementary and Secondary Day Schools;* Common Core of Data surveys; and *Projections of Education Statistics to 2006.* (This table was prepared June 1996.)

Table 64.—Public elementary and secondary teachers, by level and state: Fall 1990 to fall 1995

[In full-time equivalents]

State or other area	Fall 1990	Fall 1991	Fall 1992	Fall 1993 [1]				Fall 1994				Estimated, 1995
				Total	Elementary	Secondary	Unclassified	Total	Elementary	Secondary	Unclassified	
1	2	3	4	5	6	7	8	9	10	11	12	13
United States	**2,398,169**	**2,432,243**	**2,458,956**	**2,503,901**	**1,397,223**	**893,541**	**213,137**	**2,552,199**	**1,419,351**	**912,386**	**220,463**	**2,586,497**
Alabama	36,266	40,480	41,961	43,003	23,930	19,073	—	42,789	24,168	18,423	198	[2]44,056
Alaska	6,710	7,118	7,282	7,193	4,702	2,491	—	7,205	4,666	2,539	—	7,421
Arizona	32,987	33,978	36,076	37,493	27,188	10,305	—	38,132	27,595	10,537	—	[3]39,624
Arkansas	25,984	25,785	26,017	26,014	13,706	12,208	100	26,181	13,884	12,160	137	[2]29,193
California	217,228	224,000	218,566	221,787	142,444	56,384	22,959	225,001	142,795	58,586	23,620	225,025
Colorado	32,342	33,093	33,419	33,661	17,439	16,222	—	34,894	18,008	16,886	—	35,184
Connecticut	34,785	34,383	34,193	34,526	20,132	9,345	5,049	35,316	20,745	9,340	5,231	35,950
Delaware	5,961	6,095	6,252	6,380	3,259	3,121	—	6,416	3,215	3,201	—	[2]6,463
District of Columbia	5,950	6,346	6,064	6,056	3,353	2,259	444	6,110	3,497	2,173	440	[3]6,432
Florida	108,088	109,939	107,590	110,653	48,139	40,876	21,638	110,674	48,150	40,893	21,631	116,837
Georgia	63,058	63,816	66,942	74,172	54,210	19,962	—	77,914	56,211	21,703	—	[3]80,171
Hawaii	9,083	9,451	10,083	10,111	5,739	4,328	44	10,240	5,770	4,425	45	10,241
Idaho	11,254	11,626	11,827	12,007	6,185	5,642	180	12,582	6,388	6,018	176	[3]12,780
Illinois	108,775	110,153	111,461	110,874	65,188	28,207	17,479	110,830	66,462	28,619	15,749	113,005
Indiana	54,806	54,509	54,552	55,107	27,649	24,948	2,510	55,496	27,527	25,251	2,718	55,625
Iowa	31,045	31,395	31,403	31,616	18,321	12,188	1,107	31,775	18,663	12,021	1,091	[2]32,451
Kansas	29,140	29,324	29,753	30,283	14,712	12,561	3,010	30,579	14,823	12,763	2,993	30,878
Kentucky	36,777	37,571	37,868	37,324	26,178	11,146	—	38,784	27,054	11,730	—	37,240
Louisiana	45,401	46,170	46,904	46,913	26,556	10,377	9,980	47,599	26,916	12,176	8,507	[2]47,634
Maine	15,513	15,416	15,375	15,344	10,440	4,904	—	15,404	10,524	4,880	—	14,609
Maryland	42,562	43,616	44,495	44,171	25,027	19,144	—	46,565	25,792	20,773	—	[2]46,200
Massachusetts	54,003	55,963	57,225	58,766	21,480	29,367	7,919	60,489	22,342	29,922	8,225	[3]61,574
Michigan	80,008	82,967	82,301	80,267	34,136	36,419	9,712	80,522	34,846	36,701	8,975	80,800
Minnesota	43,574	44,903	45,050	46,956	23,981	22,949	26	46,958	23,980	22,948	30	48,386
Mississippi	28,062	28,111	27,829	28,376	18,592	9,184	600	28,866	15,071	8,864	4,931	[2]28,796
Missouri	52,359	52,643	52,984	54,860	28,339	25,775	746	56,606	29,054	26,782	770	[2]57,718
Montana	9,613	9,883	10,135	9,949	6,913	3,036	—	10,079	7,009	3,070	—	[2]10,100
Nebraska	18,764	19,069	19,323	19,616	11,244	8,372	—	19,774	11,368	8,406	—	[2]19,970
Nevada	10,373	11,409	11,953	12,579	6,563	4,648	1,368	13,414	6,784	5,058	1,572	[2]13,685
New Hampshire	10,637	11,464	11,654	11,972	8,059	3,913	—	12,109	8,158	3,951	—	12,208
New Jersey	79,886	80,515	83,057	84,564	46,855	26,509	11,200	85,258	47,280	26,439	11,539	[3]86,929
New Mexico	16,703	17,498	17,912	18,404	10,570	4,564	3,270	19,025	11,265	4,342	3,418	[2]19,325
New York	176,390	171,914	176,375	179,413	90,022	63,453	25,938	182,273	91,408	63,928	26,937	[2]185,918
North Carolina	64,283	65,326	66,630	69,421	40,237	24,935	4,249	71,592	42,480	24,700	4,412	[2]71,814
North Dakota	7,591	7,733	7,794	7,755	5,211	2,544	—	7,796	5,223	2,573	—	[2]7,503
Ohio	103,088	103,372	106,233	107,444	71,186	36,103	155	109,085	72,005	36,912	168	[2]104,189
Oklahoma	37,221	37,650	38,433	39,031	18,735	16,180	4,116	39,406	18,735	16,517	4,154	[2]39,335
Oregon	26,174	26,745	26,634	26,488	14,386	8,716	3,386	26,208	14,128	8,484	3,596	[2]26,679
Pennsylvania	100,275	100,475	100,912	101,302	45,975	43,358	11,969	102,988	46,919	43,798	12,272	[2]104,650
Rhode Island	9,522	9,709	10,069	9,823	4,404	4,103	1,316	10,066	4,597	4,090	1,379	10,209
South Carolina	36,963	37,115	37,295	38,620	26,252	12,368	—	39,437	26,820	12,617	—	[2]39,240
South Dakota	8,511	8,868	8,767	9,557	5,897	2,589	1,071	9,985	6,098	2,738	1,149	[2]9,300
Tennessee	43,051	43,062	43,566	46,066	32,072	12,398	1,596	47,406	33,039	12,795	1,572	[2]50,723
Texas	219,298	219,192	219,385	224,830	113,630	82,139	29,061	234,213	116,999	85,987	31,227	[2]240,207
Utah	17,884	18,305	19,191	19,053	8,918	7,780	2,355	19,524	9,041	8,056	2,427	[2]20,077
Vermont	7,257	7,031	7,521	7,330	3,123	2,947	1,260	7,566	3,131	2,952	1,483	7,683
Virginia	63,638	64,537	68,181	70,859	42,844	28,015	—	72,853	43,905	28,948	—	[3]73,328
Washington	41,764	42,931	44,295	45,524	24,232	17,533	3,759	46,439	24,077	18,247	4,115	[2]45,345
West Virginia	21,476	20,997	20,961	21,029	10,070	7,394	3,565	21,024	10,212	7,244	3,568	[2]20,915
Wisconsin	49,302	52,028	53,387	52,822	35,585	17,237	—	54,054	37,235	16,819	—	56,172
Wyoming	6,784	6,564	5,821	6,537	3,215	3,322	—	6,698	3,289	3,401	8	[2]6,700
Outlying areas												
American Samoa	662	671	725	656	455	182	19	698	484	196	18	[3]696
Guam	1,543	1,499	1,628	1,644	794	845	5	1,826	870	784	172	[3]1,900
Northern Marianas	416	430	425	431	265	166	—	406	224	182	—	[2]534
Puerto Rico	34,260	37,291	38,381	39,816	21,935	14,596	3,285	39,933	22,001	14,617	3,315	[2]40,003
Virgin Islands	1,575	1,581	1,595	1,570	773	722	75	1,528	757	703	68	[2]1,550

[1] Data have been revised from previously published figures.
[2] Estimated by the National Center for Education Statistics.
[3] Actual fall data.
—Data not available, not reported, or not applicable.

NOTE.—Distribution of elementary and secondary teachers determined by reporting units. Teachers reported in full-time equivalents.

SOURCE: U.S. Department of Education, National Center for Education Statistics, Common Core of Data surveys. (This table was prepared August 1996.)

Table 65.—Teachers, enrollment, and pupil-teacher ratios in public elementary and secondary schools, by state: Fall 1989 to fall 1994

State or other area	Pupil-teacher ratio, fall 1989	Pupil-teacher ratio, fall 1990	Pupil-teacher ratio, fall 1991	Fall 1992			Fall 1993			Fall 1994		
				Teachers	Enrollment	Pupil-teacher ratio	Teachers	Enrollment	Pupil-teacher ratio	Teachers	Enrollment	Pupil-teacher ratio
1	2	3	4	5	6	7	8	9	10	11	12	13
United States	17.2	17.2	17.3	2,458,956	42,823,312	17.4	2,503,901	43,464,916	17.4	2,552,199	44,108,775	17.3
Alabama	18.1	19.9	17.8	41,961	731,634	17.4	43,003	734,288	17.1	42,789	736,472	17.2
Alaska	16.8	17.0	16.7	7,282	122,487	16.8	7,193	125,948	17.5	7,205	127,057	17.6
Arizona	18.9	19.4	19.3	36,076	673,477	18.7	37,493	709,453	18.9	38,132	737,424	19.3
Arkansas	17.0	16.8	17.0	26,017	441,490	17.0	26,014	444,271	17.1	26,181	447,565	17.1
California	22.4	22.8	22.8	218,566	5,254,844	24.0	221,787	5,327,231	24.0	225,001	5,407,043	24.0
Colorado	17.6	17.8	17.9	33,419	612,635	18.3	33,661	625,062	18.6	34,894	640,521	18.4
Connecticut	13.3	13.5	14.0	34,193	488,476	14.3	34,526	496,298	14.4	35,316	506,824	14.4
Delaware	16.4	16.7	16.8	6,252	104,321	16.7	6,380	105,547	16.5	6,416	106,813	16.6
District of Columbia	13.4	13.6	12.7	6,064	80,937	13.3	6,056	80,678	13.3	6,110	80,450	13.2
Florida	17.2	17.2	17.6	107,590	1,981,407	18.4	110,653	2,040,763	18.4	110,674	2,108,968	19.1
Georgia	18.3	18.3	18.5	66,942	1,207,186	18.0	74,172	1,235,304	16.7	77,914	1,270,948	16.3
Hawaii	19.1	18.9	18.5	10,083	177,448	17.6	10,111	180,410	17.8	10,240	183,795	17.9
Idaho	20.1	19.6	19.4	11,827	231,668	19.6	12,007	236,774	19.7	12,582	240,448	19.1
Illinois	16.9	16.7	16.8	111,461	1,873,567	16.8	110,874	1,893,078	17.1	110,830	1,916,172	17.3
Indiana	17.5	17.4	17.6	54,552	960,630	17.6	55,107	965,633	17.5	55,496	968,933	17.5
Iowa	15.7	15.6	15.7	31,403	494,839	15.8	31,616	498,519	15.8	31,775	499,550	15.7
Kansas	15.0	15.0	15.2	29,753	451,536	15.2	30,283	457,614	15.1	30,579	460,838	15.1
Kentucky	17.7	17.3	17.2	37,868	655,041	17.3	37,324	655,265	17.6	38,784	657,642	17.0
Louisiana	17.6	17.3	16.6	46,904	797,985	17.0	46,913	800,560	17.1	47,599	797,933	16.6
Maine	14.1	13.9	14.0	15,375	216,453	14.1	15,344	216,995	14.1	15,404	212,601	13.8
Maryland	16.8	16.8	16.9	44,495	751,850	16.9	44,171	772,638	17.5	46,565	790,938	17.0
Massachusetts	14.0	15.4	15.1	57,225	859,948	15.0	58,766	877,726	14.9	60,489	893,727	14.8
Michigan	19.7	19.8	19.2	82,301	1,603,610	19.5	80,267	1,599,377	19.9	80,522	1,614,784	20.1
Minnesota	17.2	17.4	17.2	45,050	793,724	17.6	46,956	810,233	17.3	46,958	821,693	17.5
Mississippi	18.2	17.9	17.9	27,829	506,668	18.2	28,376	505,907	17.8	28,866	505,962	17.5
Missouri	15.7	15.6	16.0	52,984	859,357	16.2	54,860	866,378	15.8	56,606	878,541	15.5
Montana	15.7	15.9	15.8	10,135	160,011	15.8	9,949	163,009	16.4	10,079	164,341	16.3
Nebraska	14.7	14.6	14.7	19,323	282,414	14.6	19,616	285,097	14.5	19,774	287,100	14.5
Nevada	20.4	19.4	18.6	11,953	222,974	18.7	12,579	235,800	18.7	13,414	250,747	18.7
New Hampshire	16.2	16.2	15.5	11,654	181,247	15.6	11,972	185,360	15.5	12,109	189,319	15.6
New Jersey	13.5	13.6	13.8	83,057	1,130,560	13.6	84,564	1,151,307	13.6	85,258	1,174,206	13.8
New Mexico	18.3	18.1	17.6	17,912	315,668	17.6	18,404	322,292	17.5	19,025	327,248	17.2
New York	14.7	14.7	15.4	176,375	2,689,686	15.2	179,413	2,733,813	15.2	182,273	2,766,208	15.2
North Carolina	17.1	16.9	16.8	66,630	1,114,083	16.7	69,421	1,133,231	16.3	71,592	1,156,767	16.2
North Dakota	15.1	15.5	15.3	7,794	118,734	15.2	7,755	119,127	15.4	7,796	119,288	15.3
Ohio	17.4	17.2	17.3	106,233	1,795,199	16.9	107,444	1,807,319	16.8	109,085	1,814,290	16.6
Oklahoma	16.2	15.6	15.6	38,433	597,096	15.5	39,031	604,076	15.5	39,406	609,718	15.5
Oregon	18.4	18.0	18.6	26,634	510,122	19.2	26,488	516,611	19.5	26,208	521,945	19.9
Pennsylvania	15.7	16.6	16.8	100,912	1,717,613	17.0	101,302	1,744,082	17.2	102,988	1,765,891	17.1
Rhode Island	14.5	14.6	14.6	10,069	143,798	14.3	9,823	145,676	14.8	10,066	147,487	14.7
South Carolina	17.0	16.8	16.9	37,295	640,464	17.2	38,620	643,696	16.7	39,437	648,673	16.4
South Dakota	15.5	15.2	14.8	8,767	134,573	15.3	9,557	142,825	14.9	9,985	143,482	14.4
Tennessee	19.1	19.2	19.4	43,566	855,231	19.6	46,066	866,557	18.8	47,406	881,355	18.6
Texas	16.7	15.4	15.8	219,385	3,541,769	16.1	224,830	3,608,262	16.0	234,213	3,677,171	15.7
Utah	24.9	25.0	24.9	19,191	463,870	24.2	19,053	471,365	24.7	19,524	474,675	24.3
Vermont	13.8	13.2	13.8	7,521	98,558	13.1	7,330	102,755	14.0	7,566	104,533	13.8
Virginia	15.9	15.7	15.7	68,181	1,031,925	15.1	70,859	1,045,471	14.8	72,853	1,060,809	14.6
Washington	20.1	20.1	20.2	44,295	896,475	20.2	45,524	915,952	20.1	46,439	938,314	20.2
West Virginia	15.1	15.0	15.3	20,961	318,296	15.2	21,029	314,383	14.9	21,024	310,511	14.8
Wisconsin	15.9	16.2	15.7	53,387	829,415	15.5	52,822	844,001	16.0	54,054	860,686	15.9
Wyoming	14.5	14.5	15.6	5,821	100,313	17.2	6,537	100,899	15.4	6,698	100,369	15.0
Outlying areas												
American Samoa	18.6	18.8	19.9	725	13,994	19.3	656	14,484	22.1	698	14,445	20.7
Guam	16.3	17.1	18.9	1,628	30,077	18.5	1,644	30,920	18.8	1,826	32,185	17.6
Northern Marianas	17.0	15.5	16.5	425	8,086	19.0	431	8,188	19.0	406	8,429	20.8
Puerto Rico	19.5	18.8	17.2	38,381	637,034	16.6	39,816	631,460	15.9	39,933	621,121	15.6
Virgin Islands	13.3	13.8	14.1	1,595	22,887	14.3	1,570	22,752	14.5	1,528	23,126	15.1

NOTE.—Some data have been revised from previously published figures. Teachers reported in full-time equivalents.

SOURCE: U.S. Department of Education, National Center for Education Statistics, Common Core of Data surveys. (This table was prepared August 1996.)

Table 66.—Teachers in public and private elementary and secondary schools, by selected characteristics: 1993–94

Selected characteristics	Total [1]	Percent of teachers, by highest degree earned						Percent of teachers, by years of full-time teaching experience			
		No degree	Associate	Bachelor's	Master's	Education specialist	Doctor's	Less than 3	3 to 9	10 to 20	Over 20
1	2	3	4	5	6	7	8	9	10	11	12
Public schools											
Total	**2,561,294**	**0.6**	**0.2**	**52.0**	**42.0**	**4.6**	**0.7**	**9.7**	**25.5**	**35.0**	**29.8**
Men	694,098	1.3	0.4	46.2	45.7	5.1	1.3	8.9	21.6	29.9	39.6
Women	1,867,195	0.3	0.1	54.1	40.6	4.4	0.5	10.0	26.9	37.0	26.1
Race/ethnicity											
White, non-Hispanic	2,216,605	0.5	0.1	51.8	42.5	4.4	0.7	9.4	25.5	35.2	30.0
Black, non-Hispanic	188,371	0.5	0.2	48.4	44.6	5.4	0.9	8.5	20.9	35.6	35.3
Hispanic	108,744	0.9	0.5	62.8	29.8	4.6	1.4	16.7	32.1	34.1	17.1
Asian or Pacific Islander	27,510	0.9	0.4	49.3	34.7	13.1	1.7	14.9	29.7	29.2	26.2
American Indian or Alaskan Native	20,064	0.8	0.3	54.9	39.1	4.3	0.6	11.4	27.7	34.6	26.6
Age											
Less than 30	479,413	0.6	0.1	76.3	21.5	1.5	0.1	33.9	61.8	4.3	(2)
30 to 39	761,670	0.4	0.2	52.8	42.0	4.0	0.5	7.0	28.5	62.3	2.2
40 to 49	980,923	0.5	0.2	43.1	49.6	5.8	0.8	3.0	12.2	33.5	51.3
50 or more	339,265	1.1	0.2	41.4	48.8	6.7	1.9	1.0	5.8	21.8	71.5
School type											
Elementary	1,500,106	0.2	0.0	54.6	40.5	4.2	0.5	9.9	26.6	35.7	27.8
Secondary	813,348	1.2	0.4	46.7	45.5	5.1	1.1	9.0	22.8	34.3	33.9
Combined	68,235	0.9	0.3	54.7	37.8	5.6	0.8	12.6	27.2	35.4	24.8
Private schools											
Total	**378,365**	**5.2**	**1.5**	**59.0**	**29.8**	**2.9**	**1.7**	**20.9**	**33.9**	**29.6**	**15.6**
Men	93,130	4.4	0.9	47.3	40.6	2.6	4.3	21.7	28.2	28.7	21.4
Women	285,235	5.4	1.7	62.8	26.3	3.0	0.8	20.6	35.8	29.9	13.7
Race/ethnicity											
White, non-Hispanic	347,811	4.8	1.3	59.4	30.2	2.6	1.6	20.4	33.6	30.0	16.0
Black, non-Hispanic	11,664	8.3	3.7	55.8	26.4	4.8	1.0	26.9	34.9	27.9	10.3
Hispanic	12,221	11.1	4.9	57.4	19.9	4.4	2.3	25.5	41.8	21.6	11.1
Asian or Pacific Islander	5,167	6.8	0.9	46.1	36.8	5.7	3.6	26.1	34.6	26.6	12.7
American Indian or Alaskan Native	1,502	3.4	6.0	49.4	16.1	25.1	0.0	29.4	42.8	17.9	9.9
Age											
Less than 30	102,157	7.2	1.3	74.5	14.9	1.7	0.5	42.9	54.3	2.7	(2)
30 to 39	108,748	5.0	1.6	57.7	31.0	3.1	1.6	19.1	35.3	44.6	1.0
40 to 49	115,812	3.6	1.9	53.1	35.9	3.4	2.2	9.5	25.2	42.1	23.2
50 or more	51,648	5.0	1.0	44.0	43.3	3.7	3.0	6.6	10.2	22.9	60.3
School type											
Elementary	171,754	4.9	1.8	67.0	23.0	2.6	0.7	22.5	35.2	28.4	13.9
Secondary	61,787	1.2	0.6	46.5	45.6	3.0	3.2	19.0	28.2	30.2	22.6
Combined	106,106	7.9	1.9	54.4	30.4	3.4	2.1	20.2	35.9	30.4	13.5

[1] Data are based upon a sample survey and may not be strictly comparable with data reported elsewhere.

[2] Less than .05 percent.

NOTE.—Excludes prekindergarten teachers. Details may not add to totals because of survey item nonresponse and rounding.

SOURCE: U.S. Department of Education, National Center for Education Statistics, "Schools and Staffing Survey, 1993–94." (This table was prepared August 1995.)

Table 67.—Highest degree earned and number of years teaching experience for teachers in public elementary and secondary schools, by state: 1993–94

State	Total[1]	Percent of teachers, by highest degree[2]				Percent of teachers, by years of full-time teaching experience			
		Bachelor's	Master's	Education specialist	Doctor's	Less than 3	3 to 9	10 to 20	Over 20
1	2	3	4	5	6	7	8	9	10
United States	2,561,294	52.0	42.0	4.6	0.7	9.7	25.5	35.0	29.8
Alabama	44,791	38.5	52.6	7.8	0.7	11.1	22.0	42.2	24.7
Alaska	8,152	59.0	35.3	4.2	(3)	8.0	29.3	42.7	20.0
Arizona	37,600	51.4	43.3	4.0	0.7	13.1	29.1	38.1	19.8
Arkansas	30,621	64.9	32.5	1.8	0.5	9.2	27.3	40.2	23.3
California	209,032	58.6	32.6	6.8	1.0	9.8	27.8	31.8	30.7
Colorado	35,723	46.5	49.4	2.5	0.5	9.4	26.1	38.7	25.7
Connecticut	35,465	19.6	62.4	15.7	1.4	6.4	19.8	35.5	38.3
Delaware	7,027	46.0	48.3	5.1	—	7.7	24.1	36.2	32.0
District of Columbia	5,185	41.2	54.4	2.4	2.0	10.8	14.7	30.6	43.9
Florida	106,535	57.2	37.0	3.3	1.4	8.7	29.4	37.8	24.0
Georgia	74,907	48.9	42.5	7.7	(3)	13.3	28.3	35.6	22.8
Hawaii	11,137	47.8	21.7	27.5	1.0	16.2	28.1	22.0	33.7
Idaho	12,166	74.4	21.7	2.6	0.6	12.4	33.3	33.7	20.6
Illinois	111,511	49.7	46.1	3.4	0.5	9.0	25.1	30.8	35.1
Indiana	57,732	21.4	72.9	4.9	—	5.6	24.7	37.1	32.6
Iowa	35,861	67.3	31.3	1.2	(3)	10.1	23.3	32.1	34.5
Kansas	31,164	53.5	42.8	2.3	1.1	12.3	28.2	35.2	24.3
Kentucky	41,571	23.4	56.8	18.7	0.8	9.5	26.8	32.9	30.8
Louisiana	48,948	60.5	31.2	6.9	0.5	9.7	29.8	35.1	25.5
Maine	15,658	68.4	28.4	1.6	(3)	7.0	28.7	37.4	26.9
Maryland	43,862	43.3	49.6	6.2	0.6	11.7	23.6	32.4	32.4
Massachusetts	58,416	38.8	54.8	3.9	0.9	8.4	17.1	33.6	41.0
Michigan	83,288	46.6	48.1	4.7	0.6	7.4	21.5	29.4	41.9
Minnesota	44,150	63.4	33.6	2.6	(3)	13.0	20.0	33.0	34.0
Mississippi	29,851	56.3	37.5	4.3	(3)	10.5	22.8	39.8	26.9
Missouri	62,454	54.3	42.4	2.2	0.6	10.6	26.9	37.2	25.3
Montana	12,851	71.3	26.0	1.8	0.5	11.1	27.5	39.0	22.5
Nebraska	20,411	61.5	36.0	1.9	(3)	10.1	24.4	39.0	26.5
Nevada	12,822	50.5	42.8	5.7	0.6	12.0	33.2	35.0	19.8
New Hampshire	12,299	60.2	35.9	2.6	0.7	10.6	26.8	38.2	24.4
New Jersey	83,935	56.2	37.4	4.8	1.0	5.8	21.1	34.6	38.5
New Mexico	19,265	53.2	43.6	2.2	(3)	12.5	32.5	33.9	21.1
New York	178,701	25.0	68.1	5.3	1.5	10.3	23.9	29.7	36.1
North Carolina	72,305	61.8	35.0	1.2	0.5	9.7	26.6	38.8	25.0
North Dakota	8,404	79.3	18.0	1.6	—	12.1	27.2	37.7	23.0
Ohio	111,518	53.2	41.8	3.1	(3)	6.8	23.2	38.6	31.4
Oklahoma	42,220	56.9	39.5	3.2	(3)	10.4	27.0	41.2	21.5
Oregon	25,706	51.5	43.1	4.0	0.8	7.4	27.0	39.6	26.0
Pennsylvania	114,571	46.7	45.6	6.9	(3)	6.9	18.3	33.0	41.8
Rhode Island	9,217	40.1	53.3	5.7	1.0	7.2	21.9	28.6	42.3
South Carolina	39,623	48.8	43.4	5.6	0.7	10.5	25.1	42.3	22.1
South Dakota	10,579	75.1	23.2	1.5	—	10.4	28.6	37.3	23.8
Tennessee	47,662	51.2	42.0	4.8	1.2	12.4	22.9	35.5	29.2
Texas	223,800	69.7	26.8	1.8	0.9	12.1	30.1	37.5	20.4
Utah	19,884	70.6	23.5	4.2	(3)	12.7	32.8	36.1	18.3
Vermont	7,327	49.4	47.5	2.1	—	12.3	25.3	34.4	28.0
Virginia	64,937	64.4	31.3	2.4	0.5	10.5	26.0	37.5	26.1
Washington	48,452	56.3	37.5	3.6	1.0	10.8	30.1	32.2	26.9
West Virginia	21,473	41.7	53.1	4.3	—	4.4	21.6	42.7	31.4
Wisconsin	62,958	59.3	38.1	1.7	0.6	9.1	24.7	29.5	36.7
Wyoming	7,567	71.3	26.5	1.4	(3)	9.4	22.6	41.6	26.5

[1] Data are based on a head count of all teachers rather than on the number of full-time equivalent teachers appearing in other tables.

[2] Teachers with less than a bachelor's degree are not shown.

[3] Less than 0.05 percent.

—Data not available.

NOTE.—Excludes prekindergarten teachers. Details may not add to totals due to rounding or item nonresponse.

SOURCE: U.S. Department of Education, National Center for Education Statistics, "Schools and Staffing Survey, 1993–94." (This table was prepared June 1995.)

Table 68.—Selected characteristics of public school teachers: Spring 1961 to spring 1991

Item	1961	1966	1971	1976	1981	1986	1991
1	2	3	4	5	6	7	8
Number of teachers, in thousands	**1,408**	**1,710**	**2,055**	**2,196**	**2,185**	**2,206**	**2,398**
Sex (percent)							
Men	31.3	31.1	34.3	32.9	33.1	31.2	27.9
Women	68.7	68.9	65.7	67.1	66.9	68.8	72.1
Median age (years)							
All teachers	41	36	35	33	37	41	42
Men	34	33	33	33	38	42	43
Women	46	40	37	33	36	41	42
Race (percent)							
White	—	—	88.3	90.8	91.6	89.6	86.8
Black	—	—	8.1	8.0	7.8	6.9	8.0
Other	—	—	3.6	1.2	0.7	3.4	5.2
Marital status (percent)							
Single	22.3	22.0	19.5	20.1	18.5	12.9	11.7
Married	68.0	69.1	71.9	71.3	73.0	75.7	75.7
Widowed, divorced, or separated	9.7	9.0	8.6	8.6	8.5	11.4	12.6
Highest degree held (percent) [1]							
Less than bachelor's	14.6	7.0	2.9	0.9	0.4	0.3	0.6
Bachelor's	61.9	69.6	69.6	61.6	50.1	48.3	46.3
Master's or specialist degree	23.1	23.2	27.1	37.1	49.3	50.7	52.6
Doctor's	0.4	0.1	0.4	0.4	0.3	0.7	0.5
College credits earned in last 3 years							
Percent who earned credits	—	—	60.7	63.2	56.1	53.1	50.3
Mean number of credits earned [2]	—	—	14	—	9	4	4
Median years of teaching experience	11	8	8	8	12	15	15
Teaching for first year (percent)	8.0	9.1	9.1	5.5	2.4	3.1	3.0
Average number of pupils per class							
Elementary teachers, not departmentalized	29	28	27	25	25	24	24
Elementary teachers, departmentalized	—	—	25	23	22	—	—
Secondary teachers	28	26	27	25	23	25	26
Mean number of students taught per day by secondary teachers	138	132	134	126	118	94	93
Average number of hours in required school day	7.4	7.3	7.3	7.3	7.3	7.3	7.2
Average number of hours per week spent on all teaching duties							
All teachers	47	47	47	46	46	49	47
Elementary teachers	49	47	46	44	44	47	44
Secondary teachers	46	48	48	48	48	51	50
Average number of days of classroom teaching in school year	—	181	181	180	180	180	180
Average number of nonteaching days in school year	—	5	4	5	6	5	5
Average annual salary as classroom teacher	[3] $5,264	$6,253	$9,261	$12,005	$17,209	$24,504	$31,790
Total income, including spouse's (if married)	—	—	$15,021	$19,957	$29,831	$43,413	$55,491
Willingness to teach again (percent)							
Certainly would	49.9	52.6	44.9	37.5	21.8	22.7	28.6
Probably would	26.9	25.4	29.5	26.1	24.6	26.3	30.5
Chances about even	12.5	12.9	13.0	17.5	17.6	19.8	18.5
Probably would not	7.9	7.1	8.9	13.4	24.0	22.0	17.0
Certainly would not	2.8	2.0	3.7	5.6	12.0	9.3	5.4

[1] Figures for curriculum specialist or professional diploma based on six years of college study are not included.

[2] Measured in semester hours.

[3] Includes extra pay for extra duties.

—Data not available.

NOTE.—Data are based upon sample surveys of public school teachers. Data differ from figures appearing in other tables because of varying processing procedures and time period coverages. Because of rounding, percents may not add to 100.0.

SOURCE: National Education Association, "Status of the American Public School Teacher, 1990–91." (Copyright © 1992 by the National Education Association. All rights reserved.) (This table was prepared January 1993.)

Table 69.—Public secondary school teachers, by subject taught: Spring 1966 to spring 1991

[Percentage distribution]

Teaching field in which largest portion of time was spent	1966	1971	1976	1981	1986	1991
1	2	3	4	5	6	7
Total secondary school teachers, in thousands	**746**	**927**	**1,016**	**995**	**970**	**1,012**
All fields	100.0	100.0	100.0	100.0	100.0	100.0
Agriculture	1.6	0.6	0.6	1.1	0.6	0.3
Art	2.0	3.7	2.4	3.1	1.5	2.6
Business education	7.0	5.9	4.6	6.2	6.5	3.5
English	18.1	20.4	19.9	23.8	21.8	25.0
Foreign language	6.4	4.8	4.2	2.8	3.7	3.8
Health and physical education	6.9	8.3	7.9	6.5	5.6	7.5
Home economics	5.9	5.1	2.8	3.6	2.6	3.1
Industrial arts	5.1	4.1	3.9	5.2	2.2	2.1
Mathematics	13.9	14.4	18.2	15.3	19.2	14.5
Music	4.7	3.8	3.0	3.7	4.8	4.2
Science	10.8	10.6	13.1	12.1	11.0	13.3
Social studies	15.3	14.0	12.4	11.2	13.6	11.0
Special education	0.4	1.1	3.0	2.1	3.5	5.2
Other	1.9	3.1	4.0	3.3	3.4	3.9

NOTE.—Because of rounding, percents may not add to 100.0. Data are based upon sample surveys of public school teachers.

SOURCE: National Education Association, *Status of the American Public School Teacher, 1990–91.* (Copyright © 1992 by the National Education Association. All rights reserved.) (This table was prepared January 1993.)

Table 70.—Percent of vocational and nonvocational public school teachers of grades 9 to 12, by selected demographic and educational characteristics: 1993–94

Characteristics of teachers	Total	Teacher type		Characteristics of teachers	Total	Teacher type	
		Nonvocational	Vocational			Nonvocational	Vocational
1	2	3	4	1	2	3	4
Total	**100.0**	**100.0**	**100.0**	Major field of study			
				Business and management	1.1	0.7	6.5
Sex				Education	52.4	50.3	75.2
Male	48.3	46.2	63.2	Academic area	26.7	28.6	5.3
Female	51.7	53.8	36.8	English education	5.2	5.7	0.3
				Music education	3.4	3.7	0.2
				Physical education	9.1	9.5	3.8
Race/ethnicity				Other academic area	9.0	9.7	1.0
White	88.8	88.9	88.5	Administration	5.3	5.1	7.0
Black	6.0	5.9	7.1	General	4.5	4.6	3.3
Hispanic	3.4	3.5	2.8	Special education	6.8	7.3	1.3
Asian	0.9	0.9	0.8	Vocational education	6.5	3.7	37.2
American Indian or Alaskan Native	0.8	0.8	0.8	Other education	7.9	6.7	21.5
				English	4.1	4.4	0.3
Age				Foreign language	4.7	5.1	0.1
Under 30 years	9.8	10.3	6.4	Mathematics	3.2	3.5	0.6
30 to 39 years	22.1	22.3	20.8	Sciences	7.8	8.1	4.3
40 to 49 years	40.7	40.7	40.6	Social sciences and history	10.0	10.7	1.8
50 years and over	27.5	26.8	32.2	Visual and performing arts	2.6	2.7	1.0
				Other	6.1	6.2	5.5
Highest college degree				Age at which first began to teach full-time or part-time			
Less than a bachelor's degree	1.7	0.5	10.3	25 or under	75.7	75.6	76.5
Bachelor's degree	46.6	47.0	43.5	26 to 35	22.1	22.1	21.7
Master's degree	45.4	46.2	39.8	36 to 45	2.2	2.2	1.9
Education specialist [1]	5.3	5.2	5.6	46 to 55	0.1	0.1	0.0
Doctorate or first professional	1.1	1.1	0.7				

[1] Education specialist degrees or certificates are generally awarded for one year's work beyond the master's level.

SOURCE: U.S. Department of Education, National Center for Education Statistics, "Schools and Staffing Survey, 1993–94." (This table was prepared September 1996.)

Table 71.—Mobility of public and private elementary and secondary teachers, by selected school and teacher characteristics: 1988–89 and 1991–92

Characteristic	Percentage distribution of public school teachers						Percentage distribution of private school teachers					
	1987–88 to 1988–89			1990–91 to 1991–92			1987–88 to 1988–89			1990–91 to 1991–92		
	Remained teaching in the same school	Remained in teaching but changed schools	Left teaching	Remained teaching in the same school	Remained in teaching but changed schools	Left teaching	Remained teaching in the same school	Remained in teaching but changed schools	Left teaching	Remained teaching in the same school	Remained in teaching but changed schools	Left teaching
1	2	3	4	5	6	7	8	9	10	11	12	13
Total	**86.5**	**7.9**	**5.6**	**87.6**	**7.3**	**5.1**	**77.8**	**9.5**	**12.7**	**81.1**	**6.6**	**12.3**
Sex												
Male	87.7	7.3	5.1	89.1	6.4	4.5	83.7	6.1	10.2	81.6	6.3	12.1
Female	86.1	8.1	5.8	87.1	7.6	5.3	76.2	10.4	13.4	81.0	6.6	12.3
Race/ethnicity												
White, non-Hispanic	86.5	7.8	5.7	87.6	7.3	5.1	78.7	9.2	12.1	81.3	6.7	12.0
Total minority	87.0	8.6	4.4	87.5	7.1	5.3	64.4	14.2	21.4	79.3	5.3	15.4
Black, non-Hispanic	86.2	8.8	5.1	85.5	8.3	6.1	29.6	35.7	34.7	78.4	2.4	19.3
Hispanic	88.9	8.2	2.9	89.6	6.0	4.4	68.6	10.2	21.3	77.4	9.0	13.6
Age												
Less than 25	78.7	17.0	4.3	73.8	17.2	9.1	63.2	17.9	19.0	62.4	13.8	23.8
25 to 29	75.0	16.1	9.0	76.6	14.3	9.0	64.8	17.5	17.6	70.4	11.8	17.8
30 to 39	85.2	9.0	5.8	85.9	9.9	4.2	78.5	9.1	12.4	78.7	7.5	13.7
40 to 49	91.2	6.4	2.4	92.5	5.5	2.0	82.0	7.5	10.5	87.2	5.2	7.7
50 to 59	90.4	3.9	5.7	89.3	4.0	6.7	82.3	6.4	11.3	87.0	3.3	9.6
60 to 64	72.0	4.5	23.4	71.0	2.2	26.8	79.8	3.3	16.9	81.1	1.1	17.8
65 and over	83.3	0.0	16.7	48.9	10.3	40.9	88.2	3.9	7.9	73.4	5.9	20.7
Full-time teaching experience												
Less than 1 year	76.9	11.5	11.6	51.5	31.3	17.2	67.0	5.6	27.4	67.0	4.6	28.4
1 to 3 years	77.4	14.3	8.3	79.7	13.1	7.2	70.6	13.5	15.9	73.5	9.8	16.7
1 year	77.3	14.2	8.5	79.0	12.6	8.4	64.1	17.0	18.8	71.2	10.0	18.8
2 years	78.8	13.6	7.6	78.7	14.1	7.1	73.5	12.0	14.6	75.0	9.2	15.8
3 years	76.0	15.2	8.8	81.6	12.4	5.9	74.0	11.7	14.3	75.1	10.2	14.7
4 to 9 years	82.9	11.1	6.0	84.8	9.9	5.3	75.7	11.6	12.8	79.2	8.1	12.7
10 to 19 years	89.3	6.7	4.0	91.0	6.5	2.4	81.1	7.5	11.4	88.6	5.3	6.2
20 to 24 years	93.6	4.1	2.2	93.3	3.3	3.4	85.5	7.1	7.4	92.3	3.0	4.7
25 years or more	84.9	4.1	11.0	85.9	3.1	11.0	88.3	4.3	7.4	83.0	2.4	14.6
Level taught												
Elementary	85.0	9.5	5.5	87.1	8.1	4.8	76.7	10.8	12.5	81.9	6.7	11.3
Secondary	88.1	6.2	5.6	88.2	6.4	5.5	78.9	8.2	12.9	80.3	6.4	13.3
School size												
Less than 150	85.6	9.8	4.5	86.6	8.1	5.3	64.4	16.2	19.4	72.6	10.3	17.0
150 to 299	84.6	9.9	5.4	88.0	7.7	4.3	79.6	8.4	12.1	79.4	6.8	13.8
300 to 499	86.9	7.5	5.6	85.8	8.5	5.7	80.3	9.5	10.2	86.4	5.9	7.7
500 to 749	86.8	7.5	5.7	87.7	7.6	4.7	84.9	5.9	9.2	85.5	4.7	9.8
750 or more	87.7	7.4	4.9	88.6	6.1	5.4	82.2	4.9	12.8	91.0	2.3	6.7
Percent minority enrollment												
Less than 5%	88.0	6.9	5.1	89.6	5.7	4.6	77.6	9.2	13.2	81.2	7.3	11.5
5 to 19%	86.6	7.6	5.8	88.1	6.4	5.5	82.2	7.4	10.3	82.0	5.8	12.2
20 to 49%	87.3	7.6	5.2	85.6	8.6	5.9	71.8	9.3	18.9	82.4	5.3	12.2
50% or more	85.0	9.7	5.3	86.2	8.9	4.9	69.6	16.8	13.6	76.7	10.2	13.1
Community type												
Central city	—	—	—	88.8	6.4	4.8	—	—	—	80.6	6.3	13.1
Urban fringe/small town ..	—	—	—	87.0	7.4	5.6	—	—	—	84.0	6.5	9.4
Rural/small town	—	—	—	86.0	8.7	5.3	—	—	—	78.5	7.7	13.8

—Data not available or not applicable.

NOTE.—Details may not add to 100 percent due to rounding.

SOURCES: U.S. Department of Education, National Center for Education Statistics, *Characteristics of Stayers, Movers, and Leavers: Results from the Teacher Followup Survey: 1991–92.* (This table was prepared May 1994.)

Table 72.—Average salaries for full-time teachers in public and private elementary and secondary schools, by selected characteristics: 1993–94

Selected characteristics	Total earned income	Base salary	Number of full-time teachers	School year supplemental contract		Supplemental contract during summer		Number of teachers with nonschool employment		
				Number of teachers	Supplemental salary	Number of teachers	Supplemental salary	Teaching or tutor	Education related	Not education related
1	2	3	4	5	6	7	8	9	10	11
Public schools										
Total	$35,924	$34,153	2,340,182	815,827	$2,075	401,505	$2,070	118,369	80,014	237,177
Men	39,591	36,182	642,803	348,855	2,922	147,294	2,530	37,293	39,150	124,487
Women	34,536	33,384	1,697,380	466,972	1,442	254,210	1,803	81,076	40,863	112,689
Race/ethnicity										
White, non-Hispanic	36,000	34,221	2,011,889	722,694	2,067	328,487	2,015	99,783	68,991	208,306
Black, non-Hispanic	35,548	33,889	181,896	48,968	2,325	40,819	2,221	10,734	5,490	16,336
Hispanic	34,837	32,996	102,965	31,653	1,930	24,122	2,477	5,817	3,644	7,337
Asian or Pacific Islander	37,701	36,134	25,383	6,391	1,873	5,381	2,285	1,298	910	2,327
American Indian or Alaskan Native ...	34,945	32,994	18,050	6,121	2,068	2,696	2,310	737	979	2,871
Age										
Less than 30	27,974	25,966	440,029	193,398	1,930	91,979	1,880	20,334	15,319	45,970
30 to 39	33,448	31,737	684,515	242,075	2,146	120,762	1,891	33,174	24,735	66,564
40 to 49	39,586	37,803	901,801	301,456	2,115	150,854	2,273	48,720	30,658	96,996
50 or more	41,951	40,414	313,838	78,898	2,064	37,910	2,290	16,141	9,303	27,647
Level										
Elementary	34,611	33,517	1,193,249	254,890	1,503	170,052	1,801	47,820	27,084	90,749
Secondary	37,291	34,815	1,146,933	560,937	2,335	231,453	2,267	70,549	52,930	146,427
Private schools										
Total	$23,395	$21,968	301,440	64,064	$1,894	62,810	$2,122	20,202	11,424	33,880
Men	28,948	26,120	71,854	27,419	2,408	21,317	2,584	3,993	4,969	14,126
Women	21,657	20,669	229,586	36,645	1,509	41,493	1,885	16,209	6,456	19,754
Race/ethnicity										
White, non-Hispanic	23,415	22,000	277,853	59,475	1,903	55,913	2,109	18,426	10,677	31,505
Black, non-Hispanic	22,532	20,796	8,927	1,350	2,451	3,024	2,173	(¹)	(¹)	(¹)
Hispanic	22,013	20,672	9,786	2,013	1,209	2,269	2,298	(¹)	(¹)	(¹)
Asian or Pacific Islander	27,611	25,861	3,786	997	2,054	1,185	2,643	(¹)	(¹)	(¹)
American Indian or Alaskan Native ...	23,130	21,625	1,088	(¹)	(¹)	(¹)	(¹)	(¹)	(¹)	(¹)
Age										
Less than 30	19,776	18,052	86,939	22,069	1,719	23,361	1,959	6,532	3,967	13,391
30 to 39	23,700	22,193	82,809	19,182	1,922	18,856	2,165	5,466	3,708	9,895
40 to 49	25,225	23,999	91,749	17,251	2,047	16,365	2,274	5,925	3,098	7,892
50 or more	26,437	25,362	39,943	5,562	2,013	4,228	2,248	2,279	(¹)	2,702
Level										
Elementary	20,962	19,977	179,373	23,015	1,514	33,301	1,846	11,805	5,645	18,074
Secondary	26,970	24,896	122,068	41,048	2,106	29,509	2,435	8,397	5,780	15,805

¹ Too few sample cases (fewer than 30) for a reliable estimate.

NOTE.—Details may not add to totals because of rounding or missing values in cells with too few cases, or survey item nonresponse.

SOURCE: U.S. Department of Education, National Center for Education Statistics, "Schools and Staffing Survey, 1993–94." (This table was prepared August 1995.)

Table 73.—Percent of public school teachers who agree strongly or agree somewhat with specific aspects of job satisfaction: 1984 and 1995

Item	1984		1995	
	Total teachers	Teachers with fewer than five years experience	Total teachers	Teachers with fewer than five years experience
1	2	3	4	5
I love to teach	97	98	97	99
I am usually recognized for good performance	70	72	77	80
I have to spend too much time on administrative tasks	73	65	74	72
I would advise a young person to pursue a career in teaching	45	63	67	77
My job allows me the opportunity to earn a decent salary	37	31	63	43
The training and preparation teachers receive today does a good job preparing them for the classroom	46	58	57	64
I sometimes feel pressure to promote students even when I know they have not mastered minimum requirements	—	—	54	59
As a teacher, I feel respected in today's society	47	49	54	57

—Not available.

SOURCE: Metropolitan Life/Louis Harris Associates, Inc., *The Metropolitan Life Survey of The American Teacher, 1984–1995*. (This table was prepared April 1996.)

Table 74.—Public school teachers' ratings of their schools and whether suggested changes will have a positive effect on education (in percent): 1984 and 1995

Item	1984		1995	
	Total teachers	Teachers with fewer than five years experience	Total teachers	Teachers with fewer than five years experience
1	2	3	4	5
Ratings of schools				
Excellent	42	33	47	43
Good	49	56	45	45
Fair	7	7	6	11
Poor	1	2	1	1
Suggested changes that would have a positive effect				
Emphasize basic skills, such as reading, writing, math	97	96	96	97
Emphasize school discipline and safety	95	96	96	100
Broaden the curriculum to include such things as computer literacy and foreign languages	92	93	94	93
Tighten graduation requirements to include more academically stringent subjects	91	91	81	82
Establish minimum competency tests for students at predetermined grade levels	87	93	78	76
Increase the amount of homework required of students	73	72	62	60

SOURCE: Metropolitan Life/Louis Harris Associates, Inc., *The Metropolitan Life Survey of The American Teacher, 1984–1995*. (This table was prepared April 1996.)

Table 75.—Percent of public school teachers who think about leaving: 1985 and 1995

Item	1985		1995	
	Total teachers	Teachers with fewer than five years experience	Total teachers	Teachers with fewer than five years experience
1	2	3	4	5
Ever seriously considered leaving				
Yes, considered	51	38	41	42
No, not considered	49	62	59	58
Likely to leave within the next 5 years				
Very likely	12	10	12	13
Fairly likely	14	9	12	23
Not too likely	26	29	24	21
Not at all likely	47	50	51	43

SOURCE: Metropolitan Life/Louis Harris Associates, Inc., *The Metropolitan Life Survey of The American Teacher, 1984–1995*. (This table was prepared April 1996.)

Table 76.—Estimated average annual salary of teachers in public elementary and secondary schools: 1959–60 to 1995–96

School year	Current dollars			Constant 1995–96 dollars [1]		
	All teachers	Elementary teachers	Secondary teachers	All teachers	Elementary teachers	Secondary teachers
1	2	3	4	5	6	7
1959–60	$4,995	$4,815	$5,276	$26,309	$25,361	$27,790
1961–62	5,515	5,340	5,775	28,396	27,495	29,735
1963–64	5,995	5,805	6,266	30,083	29,129	31,443
1965–66	6,485	6,279	6,761	31,455	30,455	32,793
1967–68	7,423	7,208	7,692	33,781	32,802	35,005
1969–70	8,626	8,412	8,891	35,341	34,464	36,427
1970–71	9,268	9,021	9,568	36,107	35,145	37,276
1971–72	9,705	9,424	10,031	36,500	35,444	37,727
1972–73	10,174	9,893	10,507	36,782	35,766	37,986
1973–74	10,770	10,507	11,077	35,749	34,876	36,769
1974–75	11,641	11,334	12,000	34,786	33,868	35,858
1975–76	12,600	12,280	12,937	35,162	34,269	36,103
1976–77	13,354	12,989	13,776	35,213	34,251	36,326
1977–78	14,198	13,845	14,602	35,083	34,211	36,081
1978–79	15,032	14,681	15,450	33,962	33,169	34,907
1979–80	15,970	15,569	16,459	31,837	31,038	32,812
1980–81	17,644	17,230	18,142	31,523	30,783	32,413
1981–82	19,274	18,853	19,805	31,697	31,005	32,570
1982–83	20,695	20,227	21,291	32,632	31,894	33,572
1983–84	21,935	21,487	22,554	33,353	32,672	34,294
1984–85	23,600	23,200	24,187	34,533	33,948	35,392
1985–86	25,199	24,718	25,846	35,839	35,155	36,759
1986–87	26,569	26,057	27,244	36,967	36,255	37,906
1987–88	28,034	27,519	28,798	37,453	36,765	38,474
1988–89	29,564	29,022	30,218	37,754	37,062	38,589
1989–90	31,367	30,832	32,049	38,232	37,580	39,063
1990–91	33,085	32,491	33,897	38,236	37,549	39,174
1991–92	34,063	33,479	34,824	38,144	37,490	38,996
1992–93	35,029	34,337	35,880	38,037	37,286	38,961
1993–94	35,819	35,298	36,671	37,913	37,362	38,815
1994–95	36,802	36,275	37,621	37,868	37,326	38,711
1995–96	37,846	37,336	38,563	37,846	37,336	38,563

[1] Based on the Consumer Price Index, prepared by the Bureau of Labor Statistics, U.S. Department of Labor.

NOTE.—Some data have been revised from previously published figures.

SOURCE: National Education Association, *Estimates of School Statistics;* and unpublished data. (Latest edition 1995–96. Copyright © 1996 by the National Education Association. All rights reserved.) (This table was prepared July 1996.)

Table 77.—Estimated average annual salary of teachers in public elementary and secondary schools, by state: 1969–70 to 1995–96

State	Current dollars							Constant 1995–96 dollars [1]							Percent change, 1979–80 to 1995–96 in constant dollars
	1969–70	1979–80	1989–90	1992–93	1993–94	1994–95	1995–96	1969–70	1979–80	1989–90	1992–93	1993–94	1994–95	
1	2	3	4	5	6	7	8	9	10	11	12	13	14	15
United States	$8,626	$15,970	$31,367	$35,029	$35,819	$36,802	$37,846	$35,341	$31,837	$38,232	$38,037	$37,913	$37,868	18.9
Alabama	6,818	13,060	24,828	26,953	28,705	31,144	31,307	27,933	26,036	30,262	29,268	30,383	32,046	20.2
Alaska	10,560	27,210	43,153	46,701	47,512	47,951	[2]49,620	43,265	54,244	52,598	50,712	50,290	49,340	−8.5
Arizona	8,711	15,054	29,402	31,352	31,800	32,175	[2]32,484	35,689	30,011	35,837	34,044	33,659	33,107	8.2
Arkansas	6,307	12,299	22,352	27,433	28,098	28,934	29,322	25,840	24,519	27,244	29,789	29,741	29,772	19.6
California	10,315	18,020	37,998	40,035	40,264	41,078	[2]42,516	42,261	35,924	46,314	43,473	42,618	42,268	18.4
Colorado	7,761	16,205	30,758	33,541	33,826	34,571	35,364	31,797	32,305	37,490	36,421	35,804	35,572	9.5
Connecticut	9,262	16,229	40,461	48,343	49,769	50,045	50,400	37,947	32,353	49,316	52,495	52,679	51,495	55.8
Delaware	9,015	16,148	33,377	36,217	37,469	39,076	40,533	36,935	32,192	40,682	39,327	39,659	40,208	25.9
District of Columbia	10,285	22,190	38,402	38,702	42,543	43,700	[2]43,700	42,138	44,237	46,807	42,026	45,030	44,966	−1.2
Florida	8,412	14,149	28,803	31,172	31,944	32,588	33,320	34,464	28,207	35,107	33,849	33,811	33,532	18.1
Georgia	7,276	13,853	28,006	30,223	30,712	32,633	34,307	29,810	27,617	34,135	32,819	32,507	33,578	24.2
Hawaii	9,453	19,920	32,047	36,470	36,564	38,518	35,807	38,729	39,711	39,061	39,602	38,702	39,634	−9.8
Idaho	6,890	13,611	23,861	27,011	27,756	29,783	30,891	28,228	27,134	29,083	29,331	29,379	30,646	13.8
Illinois	9,569	17,601	32,794	38,632	39,387	39,431	41,008	39,204	35,088	39,971	41,950	41,690	40,573	16.9
Indiana	8,833	15,599	30,902	35,066	35,712	36,785	37,805	36,189	31,097	37,665	38,077	37,800	37,851	21.6
Iowa	8,355	15,203	26,747	30,130	30,760	31,511	32,376	34,231	30,308	32,601	32,718	32,558	32,424	6.8
Kansas	7,612	13,690	28,744	32,863	33,919	34,652	35,518	31,187	27,292	35,035	35,685	35,902	35,656	30.1
Kentucky	6,953	14,520	26,292	31,115	31,625	32,257	[2]33,018	28,487	28,946	32,046	33,787	33,474	33,191	14.1
Louisiana	7,028	13,760	24,300	26,102	26,285	26,461	26,800	28,794	27,431	29,618	28,344	27,822	27,228	−2.3
Maine	7,572	13,071	26,881	30,250	30,996	31,972	32,869	31,023	26,058	32,764	32,848	32,808	32,898	26.1
Maryland	9,383	17,558	36,319	38,753	39,453	40,661	41,215	38,442	35,003	44,268	42,081	41,759	41,839	17.7
Massachusetts	8,764	17,253	34,712	38,774	40,852	42,174	[2]43,756	35,906	34,395	42,309	42,104	43,240	43,396	27.2
Michigan	9,826	19,663	37,072	43,901	[2]45,186	[2]47,360	[2]49,168	40,257	39,199	45,186	47,671	47,828	48,732	25.4
Minnesota	8,658	15,912	32,190	35,093	36,146	35,948	[2]36,937	35,472	31,721	39,235	38,107	38,259	36,989	16.4
Mississippi	5,798	11,850	24,292	24,367	25,153	26,818	27,689	23,755	23,624	29,609	26,460	26,623	27,595	17.2
Missouri	7,799	13,682	27,094	29,382	30,310	31,189	33,341	31,953	27,276	33,024	31,905	32,082	32,092	22.2
Montana	7,606	14,537	25,081	27,617	28,200	28,785	29,364	31,162	28,980	30,570	29,989	29,849	29,619	1.3
Nebraska	7,375	13,516	25,522	28,768	29,564	30,922	31,496	30,216	26,945	31,108	31,239	31,292	31,818	16.9
Nevada	9,215	16,295	30,590	34,119	33,955	34,836	36,167	37,754	32,485	37,285	37,049	35,940	35,845	11.3
New Hampshire	7,771	13,017	28,986	33,931	34,121	34,720	35,792	31,838	25,950	35,330	36,845	36,116	35,726	37.9
New Jersey	9,130	17,161	35,676	42,680	44,693	46,087	47,910	37,406	34,211	43,484	46,345	47,306	47,422	40.0
New Mexico	7,796	14,887	24,756	26,532	27,922	28,491	29,349	31,940	29,678	30,174	28,811	29,554	29,316	−1.1
New York	10,336	19,812	38,925	44,999	45,772	47,612	[2]48,115	42,347	39,496	47,444	48,863	48,448	48,991	21.8
North Carolina	7,494	14,117	27,883	29,315	29,728	30,793	30,564	30,703	28,143	33,986	31,833	31,466	31,685	8.6
North Dakota	6,696	13,263	23,016	25,211	25,506	26,327	26,969	27,434	26,440	28,053	27,376	26,997	27,090	2.0
Ohio	8,300	15,269	31,218	34,519	35,678	36,802	37,835	34,005	30,439	38,050	37,483	37,764	37,868	24.3
Oklahoma	6,882	13,107	23,070	25,918	27,009	28,172	[2]28,900	28,196	26,129	28,119	28,144	28,588	28,988	10.6
Oregon	8,818	16,266	30,840	35,880	37,590	38,590	39,650	36,128	32,427	37,590	38,961	39,788	39,708	22.3
Pennsylvania	8,858	16,515	33,338	41,215	42,411	44,510	46,916	36,291	32,923	40,634	44,755	44,890	45,799	42.5
Rhode Island	8,776	18,002	36,057	37,933	39,261	40,729	[2]42,160	35,955	35,888	43,949	41,191	41,556	41,909	17.5
South Carolina	6,927	13,063	27,217	29,224	29,566	30,279	31,568	28,380	26,042	33,174	31,734	31,294	31,156	21.2
South Dakota	6,403	12,348	21,300	24,289	25,259	25,994	26,346	26,233	24,616	25,962	26,375	26,736	26,747	7.0
Tennessee	7,050	13,972	27,052	28,960	30,514	32,477	33,451	28,884	27,854	32,973	31,447	32,298	33,418	20.1
Texas	7,255	14,132	27,496	29,935	30,519	31,223	32,000	29,724	28,173	33,514	32,506	32,303	32,127	13.6
Utah	7,644	14,909	23,686	27,239	27,706	29,082	30,452	31,318	29,722	28,870	29,578	29,326	29,924	2.5
Vermont	7,968	12,484	29,012	34,824	34,517	35,406	36,295	32,645	24,887	35,362	37,815	36,535	36,432	45.8
Virginia	8,070	14,060	30,938	33,212	33,009	33,998	34,687	33,063	28,029	37,709	36,064	34,939	34,983	23.8
Washington	9,225	18,820	30,457	35,759	35,863	36,151	38,025	37,795	37,519	37,123	38,830	37,960	37,198	1.3
West Virginia	7,650	13,710	22,842	30,301	30,549	31,944	32,155	31,342	27,332	27,841	32,903	32,335	32,869	17.6
Wisconsin	8,963	16,006	31,921	35,926	35,990	37,746	[2]38,571	36,722	31,909	38,907	39,011	38,094	38,839	20.9
Wyoming	8,232	16,012	28,141	30,080	30,952	31,285	31,571	33,727	31,921	34,300	32,663	32,761	32,191	−1.1

[1] Based on the Consumer Price Index prepared by the Bureau of Labor Statistics, U.S. Department of Labor. Price index does not account for different rates of change in the cost of living among states.

[2] Estimated by the National Education Association.

NOTE.—Some data have been revised from previously published figures.

SOURCE: National Education Association, *Estimates of School Statistics;* and unpublished data. (Latest edition 1995–96. Copyright © 1996 by the National Education Association. All rights reserved.) (This table was prepared July 1996.)

Table 78.—Minimum and average teacher salaries, by state: 1990–91, 1993–94, and 1994–95

State	1990–91				1993–94				1994–95			Percent change, 1990–91 to 1994–95 (constant dollars)[1]	
	Minimum (beginning) salary	Average salary	Minimum (beginning) salary (in 1994–95 dollars)[1]	Average salary (in 1994–95 dollars)[1]	Minimum (beginning) salary	Average salary	Minimum (beginning) salary (in 1994–95 dollars)[1]	Average salary (in 1994–95 dollars)[1]	Minimum (beginning) salary	Average salary	Minimum (beginning) salary as a percent of average salary	Minimum salary	Average salary
1	2	3	4	5	6	7	8	9	10	11	12	13	14
United States	$21,542	$32,880	$24,195	$36,929	$23,258	$35,813	$23,925	$36,840	$23,915	$36,744	65.1	−1.2	−0.5
Alabama	22,114	26,846	24,837	30,152	[2]22,500	28,659	23,145	[2]29,480	24,818	30,545	81.3	−0.1	1.3
Alaska	[3]29,950	43,406	33,638	48,751	[3]31,800	[2]47,902	32,711	[3]49,275	[3]31,709	47,864	66.2	−5.7	−1.8
Arizona	[3]21,375	30,773	24,007	34,562	21,825	31,825	22,451	32,737	[3]22,152	32,223	68.7	−7.7	−6.8
Arkansas	[4]17,458	[2]23,735	19,608	26,658	[2]19,694	[2]28,312	20,258	[2]29,124	[2]28,950	[2]28,950	72.1	6.5	8.6
California	[3]24,570	[3]39,118	27,596	[1]43,935	[3]25,500	[3]40,636	26,231	[3]41,801	[3]25,500	[3]40,667	62.7	−7.6	−7.4
Colorado	19,786	31,819	22,223	35,737	20,091	33,826	20,667	34,796	20,888	34,571	60.4	−6.0	−3.3
Connecticut	25,312	43,398	28,429	48,742	28,052	50,389	28,856	51,833	28,549	50,598	56.4	0.4	3.8
Delaware	21,112	35,246	23,712	39,586	22,795	37,469	23,448	38,543	23,746	39,076	60.8	0.1	−1.3
District of Columbia .	23,327	[3]39,362	26,200	44,209	25,825	43,014	26,565	44,247	25,937	43,142	60.1	−1.0	−2.4
Florida	21,368	30,555	23,999	34,318	23,171	31,944	23,835	32,860	23,941	32,590	73.5	−0.2	−5.0
Georgia	20,471	[2]28,950	22,992	32,515	21,885	[5]29,214	22,512	30,051	23,486	[5]32,198	72.9	2.1	−1.0
Hawaii	23,792	33,548	26,722	37,679	25,100	36,564	25,819	37,612	25,436	37,443	67.9	−4.8	−0.6
Idaho	15,685	25,510	17,617	28,651	[2]18,700	27,756	19,236	[2]28,552	19,411	29,784	65.2	10.2	4.0
Illinois	[2]21,954	[2]34,642	24,657	38,908	[6]25,171	[6]39,416	25,892	[6]40,546	[6]25,616	[6]39,445	64.9	3.9	1.4
Indiana	[2]20,247	[2]32,931	22,740	[3]36,986	22,021	[2]35,741	22,652	36,765	[2]22,680	[2]36,799	61.6	−0.3	−0.5
Iowa	19,404	27,949	21,793	31,391	20,709	30,760	21,303	31,642	21,803	31,511	69.2	(7)	0.4
Kansas	[8]18,954	[8]28,188	21,288	31,659	[2]22,624	[8]31,700	23,272	[2]32,609	[8]21,325	[8]32,085	66.5	0.2	1.3
Kentucky	19,311	29,115	21,689	32,700	[3]21,257	31,639	21,866	[3]32,546	[3]21,682	32,272	67.2	(7)	−1.3
Louisiana	17,486	26,170	19,639	29,393	18,195	26,243	18,717	26,995	18,551	[3]26,811	69.2	−5.5	−8.8
Maine	18,878	28,531	21,203	32,044	19,840	30,996	20,409	31,884	20,001	31,972	62.6	−5.7	−0.2
Maryland	23,548	[2]38,312	26,448	43,030	24,703	39,475	25,411	40,606	[6]26,813	40,661	65.9	1.4	−5.5
Massachusetts	[3]21,800	36,090	24,485	[1]40,534	[3]23,000	38,960	23,659	[3]40,077	[3]24,150	40,976	58.9	−1.4	1.1
Michigan	[3]22,400	[3]37,800	25,158	[1]42,455	24,400	[3]45,218	25,099	46,514	[3]25,132	[3]46,575	54.0	−0.1	9.7
Minnesota	[2]21,029	33,128	23,619	[3]37,207	[5]23,408	[2]36,146	24,079	[5]37,182	23,413	35,948	65.1	−0.9	−3.4
Mississippi	[3]18,950	[3]24,609	21,284	[3]27,639	18,833	25,153	19,373	25,874	19,650	26,818	73.3	−7.7	−3.0
Missouri	[3]20,293	[3]27,636	22,792	31,039	21,078	30,324	21,682	31,193	21,653	31,209	69.4	−5.0	0.5
Montana	[3]18,400	26,696	20,666	29,983	[3]18,750	28,200	19,287	[3]29,008	[3]19,589	28,785	68.1	−5.2	−4.0
Nebraska	18,344	26,592	20,603	[1]29,867	[3]20,804	29,564	21,400	[3]30,411	20,958	30,922	67.8	1.7	3.5
Nevada	[9]24,358	[9]35,269	27,358	39,612	[9]24,155	[9]37,181	24,847	[9]38,247	[9]24,640	[9]38,010	64.8	−9.9	−4.0
New Hampshire	[3]20,635	31,273	23,176	35,124	[3]22,400	34,121	23,042	[3]35,099	[3]22,803	34,721	65.7	−1.6	−1.1
New Jersey	24,500	38,411	27,517	[3]43,141	29,346	45,582	30,187	46,889	[3]30,226	47,038	64.3	9.8	9.0
New Mexico	19,124	[2]25,800	21,479	[3]28,977	22,057	27,922	22,689	28,722	22,731	28,394	80.1	5.8	−2.0
New York	[10]26,375	[10]42,080	29,623	[3]47,262	[10]26,903	[10]45,772	27,674	[10]47,084	28,298	47,612	59.4	−4.5	0.7
North Carolina	19,810	29,165	22,249	[3]32,756	20,002	29,727	20,575	30,579	[3,10]20,620	[2]30,793	67.0	−7.3	−6.0
North Dakota	16,274	23,574	18,278	26,477	17,453	25,506	17,953	26,237	17,933	26,317	68.1	−1.9	−0.6
Ohio	18,452	31,964	20,724	35,900	19,553	35,912	20,113	36,941	[2]20,059	[2]36,971	54.3	−3.2	3.0
Oklahoma	[8]18,575	[8]24,378	20,862	[3]27,380	22,181	27,612	22,817	28,403	24,015	[8]28,745	83.5	15.1	5.0
Oregon	[9]20,357	[9]32,295	22,864	36,272	[9]23,186	[9]37,589	23,851	[9]38,666	[9]24,366	[9]38,871	62.7	6.6	7.2
Pennsylvania	[3]23,250	[2]36,057	26,113	40,497	28,231	42,411	29,040	43,627	29,416	44,510	66.1	12.6	9.9
Rhode Island	20,887	[3]38,220	23,459	[3]42,927	23,365	39,261	24,035	40,386	24,095	40,729	59.2	2.7	−5.1
South Carolina	[2]19,757	[2]28,174	22,190	31,643	20,533	[2]29,414	21,122	30,257	20,878	[2]30,366	68.8	−5.9	−4.0
South Dakota	16,676	22,363	18,730	25,117	18,935	25,259	19,478	25,983	19,328	26,037	74.2	3.2	3.7
Tennessee	20,150	28,248	22,631	31,727	19,625	30,514	20,188	31,389	21,115	[2]31,270	67.5	−6.7	−1.4
Texas	[3]20,150	[3]28,100	22,631	[1]31,560	21,806	[11]30,519	22,431	31,394	22,510	[11]31,223	72.1	−0.5	−1.1
Utah	17,234	[2]25,415	19,356	[3]28,545	18,787	[2]28,056	19,325	28,860	19,605	28,919	67.8	1.3	1.3
Vermont	[3]18,509	[3]29,714	20,788	33,373	22,982	34,517	23,641	35,506	[3]23,442	[3]35,207	66.6	12.8	5.5
Virginia	[2]22,206	[2]32,692	24,941	[3]36,718	23,273	33,472	23,940	34,431	[3]23,971	33,907	70.7	−3.9	−7.7
Washington	[2]20,612	[2]32,975	23,150	[3]37,036	[5]23,183	35,860	23,847	[5]36,888	[2]21,814	[2]36,160	60.3	−5.8	−2.4
West Virginia	18,728	25,966	21,034	29,164	21,450	30,549	22,065	31,425	21,960	31,944	68.7	4.4	9.5
Wisconsin	20,689	33,077	23,237	37,150	22,809	36,644	24,356	37,694	24,293	[3]37,617	64.6	4.5	1.3
Wyoming	19,238	28,996	21,607	32,567	[3]20,416	30,954	21,001	[3]31,841	[3]20,722	31,285	66.2	−4.1	−3.9

[1] Based on the Consumer Price Index prepared by the Bureau of Labor Statistics, U.S. Department of Labor. Price index does not account for different rates of change in the cost of living among states.
[2] Preliminary or state estimate.
[3] Estimated by the American Federation of Teachers. See NOTE.
[4] Excludes state-paid health insurance.
[5] Reflects the redefinition of classroom teacher.
[6] Preliminary or state estimate. Includes pay for extra duties.
[7] Change of less than .05 percent.
[8] Estimated to exclude fringe benefits.
[9] Includes 6 percent pension pick-up in Oregon and 9.5 percent in Nevada.

[10] Median salary.
[11] Including incentive pay or career ladder stipends and revision of classroom teacher definition.

NOTE.—Data in this table reflect results of surveys conducted by the American Federation of Teachers. Because of differing survey and estimation methods, these data are not entirely comparable with figures appearing in other tables.

SOURCE: American Federation of Teachers, *Survey and Analysis of Salary Trends,* various years. (This table was prepared August 1996.)

Table 79.—Average annual salary of instructional staff[1] in public elementary and secondary schools, by state: 1939–40 to 1995–96

State or other area	Current dollars									Constant 1995–96 dollars[2]				
	1939–40	1949–50	1959–60	1969–70	1979–80	1989–90	1993–94	1994–95	1995–96	1969–70	1979–80	1989–90	1993–94	1994–95
1	2	3	4	5	6	7	8	9	10	11	12	13	14	15
United States	$1,441	$3,010	$5,174	$9,047	$16,715	$32,638	$37,383	$38,501	$39,662	$37,066	$33,322	$39,781	$39,568	$39,616
Alabama	744	2,111	4,002	6,954	13,338	26,200	30,015	32,597	32,453	28,491	26,590	31,934	31,770	33,541
Alaska	—	—	6,859	10,993	27,697	[3]43,161	[3]47,679	[3]48,929	[3]50,516	45,039	55,215	52,607	50,466	50,346
Arizona	1,544	3,556	5,590	8,975	16,180	33,592	[3]39,794	[3]41,325	[3]42,870	36,771	32,256	40,944	42,120	42,522
Arkansas	584	1,801	3,295	6,461	12,704	22,296	29,189	30,103	30,607	26,471	25,326	27,176	30,895	30,975
California	2,351	—	[3]6,600	10,950	18,626	[3]39,309	42,116	[3]42,538	[3]44,027	44,862	37,132	47,912	44,578	43,770
Colorado	1,393	2,821	4,997	8,105	16,840	31,832	34,975	35,712	[3]36,430	33,206	33,571	38,799	37,020	36,747
Connecticut	1,861	3,558	6,008	9,597	16,989	41,888	51,418	51,770	52,200	39,319	33,868	51,056	54,424	53,270
Delaware	1,684	3,273	[3]5,800	9,387	16,845	34,620	39,031	40,668	42,177	38,459	33,581	42,197	41,313	41,846
District of Columbia	2,350	3,920	6,280	10,700	23,027	43,637	39,257	39,663	[3]39,663	43,838	45,905	53,187	41,552	40,812
Florida	1,012	2,958	5,080	8,785	14,875	30,275	33,350	[3]33,617	34,365	35,992	29,654	36,901	35,300	34,591
Georgia	770	1,963	[4]3,904	7,520	14,547	29,541	32,283	34,816	37,102	30,810	29,000	36,006	34,170	35,825
Hawaii	—	—	5,390	9,600	20,436	32,956	37,671	37,319	37,057	39,331	40,740	40,169	39,873	38,400
Idaho	1,057	2,481	4,216	7,081	14,110	24,758	28,928	31,063	32,285	29,011	28,129	30,177	30,619	31,963
Illinois	1,700	3,458	[5]5,814	9,789	18,271	33,912	40,737	40,855	42,489	40,106	36,424	41,334	43,119	42,038
Indiana	1,433	3,401	5,542	9,239	16,256	31,905	36,743	37,922	38,924	37,852	32,407	38,888	38,891	39,021
Iowa	1,017	2,420	[3]4,030	8,779	15,776	27,619	31,830	32,622	33,534	35,968	31,450	33,664	33,691	33,567
Kansas	1,014	2,628	[3]4,450	7,811	14,513	30,154	35,640	36,709	37,626	32,002	28,932	36,754	37,724	37,772
Kentucky	826	1,936	3,327	7,325	15,350	27,482	33,561	34,232	[3]35,324	30,011	30,601	33,497	35,523	35,224
Louisiana	1,006	2,983	4,978	7,264	14,020	25,036	30,560	27,631	28,167	29,761	27,950	30,515	32,347	28,431
Maine	894	2,115	3,694	8,059	13,743	27,831	32,049	33,050	33,994	33,018	27,397	33,922	33,923	34,007
Maryland	1,642	3,594	5,557	9,885	18,308	37,520	40,878	42,300	42,702	40,499	36,498	45,732	43,268	43,525
Massachusetts	2,037	3,338	[6]5,545	9,347	18,900	40,175	47,893	51,116	[3]53,033	38,295	37,678	48,968	50,693	52,597
Michigan	1,576	3,420	5,654	10,125	20,682	[3]37,286	[3]46,392	[3]48,507	[3]50,764	41,482	41,231	45,446	49,104	49,912
Minnesota	1,276	3,013	5,275	9,250	16,654	33,340	37,309	37,145	[3]37,680	37,897	33,201	40,637	39,490	38,221
Mississippi	559	1,416	3,314	5,959	12,274	25,079	26,070	27,764	28,710	24,414	24,469	30,568	27,594	28,568
Missouri	1,159	2,581	4,536	8,064	14,543	28,166	31,521	32,725	33,870	33,038	28,992	34,330	33,364	33,673
Montana	1,184	2,962	[3]4,425	7,875	15,080	29,526	29,040	30,052	30,908	32,264	30,063	35,988	30,738	30,923
Nebraska	829	2,292	3,876	7,633	14,236	27,024	31,595	[3]32,803	[3]34,023	31,273	28,380	32,939	33,442	33,753
Nevada	1,557	3,209	5,693	9,615	17,290	31,970	35,603	36,553	37,879	39,393	34,468	38,967	37,684	37,612
New Hampshire	1,258	2,712	4,455	8,016	13,508	[3]29,798	38,599	[3]39,564	42,188	32,842	26,929	36,320	40,856	40,710
New Jersey	2,093	3,511	5,871	9,650	18,851	37,485	46,979	48,463	50,435	39,536	37,580	45,689	49,725	49,867
New Mexico	1,144	3,215	5,382	10,021	15,406	25,790	28,611	28,866	[3]29,389	41,056	30,713	31,434	30,284	29,702
New York	2,604	3,706	6,537	11,240	20,400	40,000	46,900	48,500	[3]49,690	46,051	40,668	48,754	49,642	49,905
North Carolina	946	2,688	4,178	7,762	14,445	28,952	30,968	32,070	31,778	31,801	28,797	35,288	32,778	32,999
North Dakota	745	2,324	3,695	6,840	13,684	23,788	25,692	26,515	27,153	28,024	27,280	28,994	27,194	27,283
Ohio	1,587	3,088	5,124	8,594	16,100	32,467	36,853	37,988	39,038	35,210	32,096	39,573	39,007	39,088
Oklahoma	1,014	2,736	4,659	7,257	13,500	23,944	27,981	29,129	[3]29,894	29,732	26,913	29,184	29,617	29,973
Oregon	1,333	3,323	5,535	9,200	16,996	32,100	38,920	39,800	40,900	37,693	33,882	39,125	41,195	40,953
Pennsylvania	1,640	3,006	5,308	8,899	17,060	34,110	43,300	45,456	47,911	36,459	34,010	41,575	45,831	46,773
Rhode Island	1,809	3,294	[7]5,499	9,030	18,425	36,704	39,992	41,464	[3]42,900	36,996	36,731	44,737	42,330	42,665
South Carolina	743	1,891	3,450	7,069	13,670	28,453	30,970	31,748	33,100	28,962	27,252	34,680	32,781	32,668
South Dakota	807	2,064	3,725	7,200	13,010	22,120	24,977	26,037	27,354	29,499	25,936	26,961	26,437	26,791
Tennessee	862	2,302	3,929	7,187	14,193	27,949	31,685	33,724	34,735	29,445	28,294	34,066	33,537	34,701
Texas	1,079	3,122	4,708	7,598	14,729	28,549	31,046	33,164	33,861	31,129	29,363	34,797	32,861	34,125
Utah	1,394	3,103	5,096	8,049	17,403	24,591	28,669	30,145	31,565	32,977	34,694	29,973	30,345	31,018
Vermont	981	2,348	4,466	8,225	13,300	29,012	35,691	36,375	37,054	33,698	26,514	35,362	37,778	37,429
Virginia	899	2,328	4,312	8,364	14,655	31,656	33,826	34,840	35,535	34,267	29,215	38,584	35,804	35,849
Washington	1,706	3,487	[7]5,643	9,792	19,735	31,828	37,490	37,807	39,741	40,118	39,343	38,794	39,682	38,902
West Virginia	1,170	2,425	3,952	7,954	14,395	23,842	31,656	33,070	33,296	32,588	28,697	29,060	33,507	34,028
Wisconsin	1,379	3,007	[8]4,870	9,150	16,335	32,445	36,040	38,952	[3]39,498	37,488	32,565	39,546	38,147	40,080
Wyoming	1,169	2,798	4,937	8,496	16,830	29,047	31,832	32,181	32,493	34,808	33,551	35,404	33,693	33,113
Outlying areas														
American Samoa	—	—	852	5,130	—	—	—	—	—	21,018	—	—	—	— —
Guam	—	—	4,107	7,800	—	—	—	—	—	31,957	—	—	—	— —
Puerto Rico	—	—	[9]2,360	—	—	—	—	—	—	—	—	—	—	— —
Virgin Islands	—	—	3,407	—	—	—	—	—	—	—	—	—	—	— —

[1] Includes supervisors, principals, classroom teachers, and other instructional staff.
[2] Based on the Consumer Price Index prepared by the Bureau of Labor Statistics, U.S. Department of Labor. Price index does not account for different rates of change in the cost of living among states.
[3] Estimated by National Education Association.
[4] Excludes kindergarten teachers.
[5] Includes administrators.
[6] Includes clerical assistants to instructional personnel.
[7] Includes attendance personnel.

[8] Excludes vocational schools not operated as part of the regular public school system.
[9] Median salary.
—Data not available.

NOTE.—Some data have been revised from previously published data.

SOURCE: U.S. Department of Education, National Center for Education Statistics, *Statistics of State School Systems;* National Education Association, *Estimates of School Statistics;* (Latest edition 1995–96. Copyright © 1996 by the National Education Association. All rights reserved.) and unpublished data. (This table was prepared June 1996.)

Table 80.—Estimated average annual salary of instructional staff [1] in public elementary and secondary schools and average annual earnings of full-time employees in all industries: 1929–30 to 1995–96

School year	Current dollars		Constant 1995–96 dollars [2]		
	Average salary of instructional staff	Earnings per full-time employee working for wages or salary [3]	Average salary of instructional staff	Earnings per full-time employee working for wages or salary [3]	Ratio of instructional staff salary to salary for all full-time employees
1	2	3	4	5	6
1929–30	$1,420	$1,386	$12,839	$12,532	1.02
1931–32	1,417	1,198	15,211	12,860	1.18
1933–34	1,227	1,070	14,340	12,506	1.15
1935–36	1,283	1,160	14,449	13,064	1.11
1937–38	1,374	1,224	14,844	13,224	1.12
1939–40	1,441	1,282	15,958	14,197	1.12
1941–42	1,507	1,576	14,958	15,643	0.96
1943–44	1,728	2,030	15,348	18,030	0.85
1945–46	1,995	2,272	16,926	19,276	0.88
1947–48	2,639	2,692	17,529	17,881	0.98
1949–50	3,010	2,930	19,670	19,147	1.03
1951–52	3,450	3,322	20,315	19,561	1.04
1953–54	3,825	3,628	22,013	20,879	1.05
1955–56	4,156	3,924	23,926	22,590	1.06
1957–58	4,702	4,276	25,482	23,173	1.10
1959–60	5,174	4,632	27,252	24,397	1.12
1961–62	5,700	4,928	29,349	25,374	1.16
1963–64	6,240	5,373	31,312	26,962	1.16
1965–66	6,935	5,838	33,637	28,316	1.19
1967–68	7,630	6,444	34,723	29,326	1.18
1969–70	9,047	7,334	37,066	30,048	1.23
1970–71	9,698	7,815	37,783	30,447	1.24
1971–72	10,213	8,334	38,411	31,344	1.23
1972–73	10,634	8,858	38,445	32,025	1.20
1973–74	11,254	9,647	37,356	32,022	1.17
1974–75	12,167	10,420	36,357	31,137	1.17
1975–76	13,124	11,218	36,625	31,306	1.17
1976–77	13,840	11,991	36,495	31,619	1.15
1977–78	14,698	12,829	36,318	31,699	1.15
1978–79	15,764	13,851	35,616	31,294	1.14
1979–80	16,715	15,095	33,322	30,092	1.11
1980–81	18,404	16,495	32,881	29,470	1.12
1981–82	20,327	17,818	33,429	29,303	1.14
1982–83	21,641	18,883	34,124	29,774	1.15
1983–84	23,005	19,749	34,980	30,029	1.16
1984–85	24,666	20,626	36,093	30,181	1.20
1985–86	26,362	21,518	37,493	30,603	1.23
1986–87	27,706	22,432	38,549	31,211	1.24
1987–88	29,219	23,467	39,037	31,352	1.25
1988–89	30,850	24,502	39,396	31,289	1.26
1989–90	32,638	25,555	39,781	31,148	1.28
1990–91	34,412	26,668	39,769	30,820	1.29
1991–92	35,550	27,829	39,809	31,163	1.28
1992–93	36,454	28,937	39,585	31,422	1.26
1993–94	37,383	—	39,568	—	—
1994–95	38,501	—	39,616	—	—
1995–96	39,662	—	39,662	—	—

[1] Includes supervisors, principals, classroom teachers, and other instructional staff.
[2] Based on the Consumer Price Index prepared by the Bureau of Labor Statistics, U.S. Department of Labor.
[3] Calendar-year data from the U.S. Department of Commerce have been converted to a school-year basis by averaging the two appropriate calendar years in each case.
—Data not available.

NOTE.—Some data have been revised from previously published figures.

SOURCE: U.S. Department of Education, National Center for Education Statistics, Statistics of State School Systems, and unpublished data; National Education Association, Estimates of State School Statistics, 1995–96, (Copyright © 1996 by the National Education Association. All rights reserved.), unpublished data; and U.S. Department of Commerce, Survey of Current Business, July and August issues. (This table was prepared July 1996.)

Table 81.—Staff employed in public elementary and secondary school systems, by functional area: 1949–50 to fall 1994

[In full-time equivalents]

Number

School year	Total	School district administrative staff					Instructional staff								Support staff						
		Total	Inter-mediate district staff	School district superintendents	Assistants to superintendents	Instruction coordinators	Total	Principals and assistant principals	Teachers	Instructional aides	Librarians	Guidance counselors	Psychological personnel	Other instructional staff	Total	Secretarial and clerical personnel	Transportation staff	Food service	Plant operation and maintenance	Health	Recreational and other staff
1	2	3	4	5	6	7	8	9	10	11	12	13	14	15	16	17	18	19	20	21	22
1949–50	1,300,031	33,642	5,843	18,025	(1)	9,774	963,110	43,137	913,671	(2)	(2)	(2)	(2)	6,302	303,280	31,824	81,626	68,814	105,874	9,412	5,730
1959–60	2,089,283	42,423	9,901	13,361	5,386	13,775	1,457,329	63,554	1,353,372	(2)	17,363	14,643	2,121	6,277	589,531	75,930	113,111	161,925	192,655	16,104	29,807
1969–70	3,360,763	65,282	7,113	13,014	13,618	31,537	2,285,568	90,593	2,016,244	57,418	42,689	48,763	6,168	23,693	1,009,913	164,476	175,351	270,338	273,395	26,562	99,791
Fall 1980	4,168,286	78,784	—	13,269	44,961	20,554	2,859,573	107,061	2,184,216	325,755	48,018	63,973	14,033	116,517	1,229,929	223,647	(4)	(4)	(4)	(4)	1,006,282
Fall 1984	4,062,271	[3]65,222	—	—	—	—	[3]2,691,787	124,536	2,167,950	288,967	47,024	63,310	(5)	(5)	[3]1,305,262	(5)	(5)	(5)	(5)	(5)	(5)
Fall 1985	4,159,624	[3]67,404	—	—	—	—	[3]2,756,232	129,297	2,205,987	306,860	47,442	66,646	(5)	(5)	[3]1,335,988	(5)	(5)	(5)	(5)	(5)	(5)
Fall 1986	4,232,805	[3]74,541	—	—	—	—	[3]2,822,059	131,564	2,243,579	330,398	47,938	68,580	(5)	(5)	[3]1,336,205	(5)	(5)	(5)	(5)	(5)	(5)
Fall 1987	4,311,941	74,191	—	—	—	—	[3]2,859,626	125,927	2,279,241	335,991	48,185	70,282	(5)	(5)	[3]1,378,124	(5)	(5)	(5)	(5)	(5)	(5)
Fall 1988	4,319,356	[3]69,334	—	—	—	—	[3]2,930,547	126,609	2,323,213	356,682	48,980	75,063	(5)	(5)	[3]1,319,475	(5)	(5)	(5)	(5)	(5)	(5)
Fall 1989	4,431,033	70,302	—	—	—	—	[3]2,985,851	125,594	2,356,702	374,172	49,769	79,614	(5)	(5)	[3]1,374,880	(5)	(5)	(5)	(5)	(5)	(5)
Fall 1990	4,494,076	[3]75,868	—	—	—	—	[3]3,051,404	127,417	2,398,169	395,959	49,909	79,950	(5)	(5)	[3]1,366,804	(5)	(5)	(5)	(5)	(5)	(5)
Fall 1991	4,559,359	[3]76,084	—	—	—	—	[3]3,103,939	121,936	2,432,243	410,538	49,917	81,049	(5)	(5)	[3]1,379,336	(5)	(5)	(5)	(5)	(5)	(5)
Fall 1992	4,708,286	[6]78,414	(7)	(7)	45,712	32,702	[3]3,139,544	121,486	2,458,956	427,279	50,324	81,937	(5)	(5)	[3]1,490,328	(5)	(5)	(5)	(5)	(5)	(5)
Fall 1993	4,808,080	[6]80,862	(7)	(7)	47,614	33,248	[3]3,209,381	123,918	2,503,901	450,519	50,511	82,964	(5)	(5)	[3]1,517,837	(5)	(5)	(5)	(5)	(5)	(5)
Fall 1994	4,907,996	[6]81,838	(7)	(7)	48,900	32,938	[3]3,285,099		2,552,199	473,408	50,687	84,887	(5)	(5)	[3]1,541,059	(5)	(5)	(5)	(5)	(5)	(5)

Percentage distribution

School year	Total	Total	Inter-mediate district staff	School district superintendents	Assistants to superintendents	Instruction coordinators	Total	Principals and assistant principals	Teachers	Instructional aides	Librarians	Guidance counselors	Psychological personnel	Other instructional staff	Total	Secretarial and clerical personnel	Transportation staff	Food service	Plant operation and maintenance	Health	Recreational and other staff
1949–50	100.0	2.6	0.4	1.4	(1)	0.8	74.1	3.3	70.3	(2)	(2)	(2)	(2)	0.5	23.3	2.4	6.3	5.3	8.1	0.7	0.4
1959–60	100.0	2.0	0.5	0.6	0.3	0.7	69.8	3.0	64.8	(2)	0.8	0.7	0.1	0.3	28.2	3.6	5.4	7.8	9.2	0.8	1.4
1969–70	100.0	1.9	0.2	0.4	0.4	0.9	68.0	2.7	60.0	1.7	1.3	1.5	0.2	0.7	30.1	4.9	5.2	8.0	8.1	0.8	3.0
Fall 1980	100.0	1.9	—	0.3	1.1	0.5	68.6	2.6	52.4	7.8	1.2	1.5	0.3	2.8	29.5	5.4	(4)	(4)	(4)	(4)	24.1
Fall 1984	100.0	[3]1.6	—	—	—	—	[3]66.3	3.1	53.4	7.1	1.1	1.6	(5)	(5)	[3]32.1	(5)	(5)	(5)	(5)	(5)	(5)
Fall 1985	100.0	[3]1.6	—	—	—	—	[3]66.3	3.1	53.0	7.4	1.1	1.6	(5)	(5)	[3]32.1	(5)	(5)	(5)	(5)	(5)	(5)
Fall 1986	100.0	[3]1.8	—	—	—	—	[3]66.7	2.9	53.0	7.8	1.1	1.6	(5)	(5)	[3]31.6	(5)	(5)	(5)	(5)	(5)	(5)
Fall 1987	100.0	[3]1.7	—	—	—	—	[3]67.8	2.9	52.9	7.8	1.1	1.6	(5)	(5)	[3]32.0	(5)	(5)	(5)	(5)	(5)	(5)
Fall 1988	100.0	[3]1.6	—	—	—	—	[3]67.9	2.8	53.8	8.3	1.1	1.7	(5)	(5)	[3]30.5	(5)	(5)	(5)	(5)	(5)	(5)
Fall 1989	100.0	[3]1.7	—	—	—	—	[3]68.1	2.8	53.4	8.4	1.1	1.8	(5)	(5)	[3]31.0	(5)	(5)	(5)	(5)	(5)	(5)
Fall 1990	100.0	[3]1.7	—	—	—	—	[3]66.7	2.8	53.3	8.8	1.1	1.8	(5)	(5)	[3]30.4	(5)	(5)	(5)	(5)	(5)	(5)
Fall 1991	100.0	[3]1.7	—	—	—	—	[3]66.7	2.6	52.2	9.0	1.1	1.8	(5)	(5)	[3]30.3	(5)	(5)	(5)	(5)	(5)	(5)
Fall 1992	100.0	[6]1.7	(7)	(7)	1.0	0.7	[3]66.3	2.5	52.1	9.1	1.1	1.7	(5)	(5)	[3]31.7	(5)	(5)	(5)	(5)	(5)	(5)
Fall 1993	100.0	[6]1.7	(7)	(7)	1.0	0.7	[3]66.7	2.5	52.0	9.4	1.1	1.7	(5)	(5)	[3]31.6	(5)	(5)	(5)	(5)	(5)	(5)
Fall 1994	100.0	[6]1.7	(7)	(7)	1.0	0.7	[3]66.9			9.6	1.1	1.7	(5)	(5)	[3]31.4	(5)	(5)	(5)	(5)	(5)	(5)

Pupils per staff member

School year	Total	Total	Inter-mediate district staff	School district superintendents	Assistants to superintendents	Instruction coordinators	Total	Principals and assistant principals	Teachers	Instructional aides	Librarians	Guidance counselors	Psychological personnel	Other instructional staff	Total	Secretarial and clerical personnel	Transportation staff	Food service	Plant operation and maintenance	Health	Recreational and other staff
1949–50	19.3	746.4	4,297.7	1,393.1	(1)	2,569.2	26.1	582.1	27.5	(2)	(2)	(2)	(2)	3,984.9	82.8	789.1	307.6	364.9	237.2	2,668.0	4,382.4
1959–60	16.8	829.3	3,553.4	2,633.2	6,532.2	2,554.1	24.1	553.6	26.0	(2)	2,026.3	2,402.7	16,589.1	5,605.1	59.7	463.4	311.0	217.3	182.6	2,184.7	1,180.3
1969–70	13.6	697.7	6,403.8	3,500.1	3,344.9	1,444.3	19.9	502.8	22.6	793.3	1,067.0	934.1	7,384.9	1,922.5	45.1	276.9	259.8	168.5	166.6	1,714.9	456.5
Fall 1980	9.8	518.9	—	3,080.7	909.2	1,988.8	14.3	381.8	18.7	125.5	833.8	639.0	2,913.0	350.8	33.2	182.8	(4)	(4)	(4)	(4)	40.6
Fall 1984	9.7	[3]601.2	—	—	—	—	[3]14.6	314.8	18.1	135.7	851.3	619.3	(5)	(5)	30.0	(5)	(5)	(5)	(5)	(5)	(5)
Fall 1985	9.5	[3]584.9	—	—	—	—	[3]14.3	304.9	17.9	128.5	831.0	591.5	(5)	(5)	29.5	(5)	(5)	(5)	(5)	(5)	(5)
Fall 1986	9.4	[3]533.3	—	—	—	—	[3]14.1	302.2	17.7	120.3	829.3	579.7	(5)	(5)	29.8	(5)	(5)	(5)	(5)	(5)	(5)
Fall 1987	9.3	[3]539.3	—	—	—	—	[3]14.0	317.7	17.6	119.1	830.3	569.3	(5)	(5)	29.0	(5)	(5)	(5)	(5)	(5)	(5)
Fall 1988	9.3	[3]579.6	—	—	—	—	[3]13.7	320.5	17.3	112.7	820.5	535.4	(5)	(5)	30.5	(5)	(5)	(5)	(5)	(5)	(5)
Fall 1989	9.1	[3]576.7	—	—	—	—	[3]13.6	322.8	17.2	108.4	814.6	509.2	(5)	(5)	29.5	(5)	(5)	(5)	(5)	(5)	(5)
Fall 1990	9.2	[3]543.3	—	—	—	—	[3]13.5	323.5	17.2	104.1	825.8	515.5	(5)	(5)	30.2	(5)	(5)	(5)	(5)	(5)	(5)
Fall 1991	9.2	[3]552.6	—	—	—	—	[3]13.5	325.2	17.3	102.4	842.3	513.2	(5)	(5)	30.5	(5)	(5)	(5)	(5)	(5)	(5)
Fall 1992	9.1	[6]546.1	(7)	(7)	936.8	1,309.5	[3]13.6	351.2	17.4	100.2	851.0	528.4	(5)	(5)	28.7	(5)	(5)	(5)	(5)	(5)	(5)
Fall 1993	9.0	[6]537.5	(7)	(7)	912.9	1,307.3	[3]13.5	357.8	17.4	96.5	860.5	523.9	(5)	(5)	28.6	(5)	(5)	(5)	(5)	(5)	(5)
Fall 1994	9.0	[6]539.0	(7)	(7)	902.0	1,339.1	[3]13.4	356.0	17.3	93.2	870.2	519.6	(5)	(5)	28.6	(5)	(5)	(5)	(5)	(5)	(5)

1 Data included in column 5.
2 Data included in column 10.
3 Data not comparable with figures for years prior to 1984.
4 Data included in column 22.
5 Data included in column 16.
6 Because of classification revisions, data are not directly comparable with figures for prior years.
7 Data included in column 6.
— Data not available.

NOTE.—Some data have been revised from previously published figures. Because of variations in data collection instruments, some categories are only roughly comparable over time. Because of rounding, details may not add to totals.

SOURCE: U.S. Department of Education, National Center for Education Statistics, *Statistics of State School Systems*, Common Core of Data surveys, and unpublished estimates. (This table was prepared August 1996.)

Table 82.—Staff employed in public school systems, by type of assignment and state: Fall 1994

[In full-time equivalents]

State or other area	Total	School district staff			School staff						Student support staff	Other support services staff
		Officials and administrators	Administrative support staff	Instruction coordinators	Principals and assistant principals	School and library support staff	Teachers	Instructional aides	Guidance counselors	Librarians		
1	2	3	4	5	6	7	8	9	10	11	12	13
United States [1]	4,907,996	48,900	147,041	32,938	123,918	235,815	2,552,199	473,408	84,887	50,687	138,212	1,019,991
Alabama [2]	81,542	406	1,085	957	2,163	2,651	42,789	6,678	1,643	1,215	455	21,500
Alaska [3]	15,151	195	533	113	428	891	7,205	1,842	229	148	561	3,006
Arizona	74,540	420	681	198	1,689	5,877	38,132	9,049	1,009	771	7,036	9,678
Arkansas	50,201	563	993	754	1,435	1,747	26,181	2,572	1,212	949	1,286	12,509
California [2]	436,125	2,048	20,256	4,314	10,352	27,766	225,001	56,391	4,999	850	9,600	74,548
Colorado	64,985	812	2,180	729	1,772	4,382	34,894	5,440	1,066	709	1,503	11,498
Connecticut	64,743	1,160	1,753	451	1,531	3,217	35,316	6,822	1,115	653	3,182	9,543
Delaware	11,759	90	381	55	406	473	6,416	829	214	120	477	2,298
District of Columbia	10,507	438	331	161	305	442	6,110	359	264	176	61	1,860
Florida	226,975	1,673	11,666	801	5,768	11,588	110,674	22,243	4,585	2,512	6,523	48,942
Georgia [4]	161,390	2,136	3,771	649	3,777	7,391	77,914	21,172	2,338	1,986	1,494	38,762
Hawaii	16,567	152	296	456	471	678	10,240	790	532	288	494	2,170
Idaho	21,194	121	433	202	633	830	12,582	1,805	478	180	375	3,555
Illinois	204,414	3,274	5,422	1,624	4,980	9,982	110,830	19,470	2,757	1,910	6,270	37,895
Indiana	115,441	874	513	1,307	2,719	7,814	55,496	14,372	1,650	1,028	1,585	28,083
Iowa	60,526	512	764	377	1,737	4,364	31,775	5,346	1,302	652	2,159	11,538
Kansas	56,790	473	2,399	163	1,659	2,449	30,579	4,451	1,073	968	1,839	10,737
Kentucky	81,720	1,197	1,658	622	1,728	3,110	38,784	9,784	1,254	1,136	2,854	19,593
Louisiana	96,124	1,531	1,903	97	2,391	3,011	47,599	10,177	1,068	1,206	2,072	25,069
Maine	29,264	449	697	117	844	1,316	15,404	3,726	591	235	1,015	4,870
Maryland	84,699	789	759	677	2,607	3,568	46,565	7,255	1,719	1,055	1,533	18,172
Massachusetts	108,281	954	5,626	1,010	2,126	3,059	60,489	11,714	2,004	579	1,792	18,928
Michigan	164,766	1,331	2,602	579	4,995	7,466	80,522	13,412	2,876	1,445	6,014	43,524
Minnesota	74,914	1,278	1,730	487	1,593	3,372	46,958	6,088	901	984	2,859	8,664
Mississippi	60,708	900	1,390	450	1,492	2,161	28,866	8,930	794	704	2,079	12,942
Missouri	116,974	650	4,492	1,288	2,516	7,796	56,606	6,909	2,483	1,317	1,635	31,282
Montana [4],[5]	18,446	161	495	149	484	903	10,079	1,841	398	341	66	3,529
Nebraska	37,144	616	699	217	938	1,418	19,774	3,370	728	567	975	7,842
Nevada	23,098	178	505	110	660	1,375	13,414	1,643	452	241	557	3,963
New Hampshire	22,336	353	453	140	476	793	12,109	3,098	617	261	441	3,595
New Jersey	161,586	1,691	7,029	1,336	4,427	8,212	85,258	13,274	3,130	1,785	8,632	26,812
New Mexico	38,642	496	1,297	543	851	2,774	19,025	4,269	641	249	849	7,648
New York	356,386	2,813	23,618	1,399	6,944	7,467	182,273	27,390	5,770	3,061	8,642	87,009
North Carolina [4]	137,792	1,281	3,119	725	3,967	5,723	71,592	21,766	2,926	2,154	2,743	21,796
North Dakota	13,919	268	330	58	392	467	7,796	1,343	246	179	350	2,490
Ohio	204,043	5,497	9,513	434	4,903	14,277	109,085	9,884	3,510	1,753	1,304	43,883
Oklahoma [4]	78,270	548	186	625	2,375	5,572	39,406	7,205	1,368	899	11,801	8,285
Oregon	50,377	710	1,359	344	1,565	3,378	26,208	5,501	1,278	658	1,468	7,908
Pennsylvania	193,696	1,335	6,575	1,580	4,021	9,953	102,988	13,680	3,626	2,190	9,639	38,109
Rhode Island	15,438	157	315	79	370	791	10,066	1,272	306	76	185	1,821
South Carolina [4],[5]	74,174	260	1,954	502	2,182	3,566	39,437	7,268	1,514	1,103	2,460	13,928
South Dakota [4]	17,989	337	765	23	654	758	9,985	1,905	394	213	271	2,684
Tennessee	96,282	960	2,810	728	4,560	4,499	47,406	9,574	1,389	1,363	3,412	19,581
Texas	450,462	2,554	2,393	1,168	11,010	18,048	234,213	41,317	8,026	4,201	3,520	124,012
Utah	36,186	107	677	449	885	1,998	19,524	4,665	529	279	386	6,687
Vermont [6]	15,337	146	245	337	428	720	7,566	2,776	353	224	1,556	986
Virginia [3]	133,192	1,783	1,790	1,168	3,453	5,576	72,853	11,692	3,130	1,967	3,162	26,618
Washington [3],[4]	90,440	1,053	2,535	836	2,469	4,721	46,439	8,480	1,735	1,259	3,558	17,355
West Virginia	38,481	271	1,883	327	1,100	371	21,024	2,867	596	364	940	8,738
Wisconsin	100,996	782	2,023	977	2,359	4,337	54,054	8,442	1,914	1,387	3,836	20,885
Wyoming	12,984	117	159	46	328	717	6,698	1,260	155	137	706	2,661
Outlying areas												
American Samoa	1,340	26	38	38	59	84	698	13	24	7	43	310
Guam	4,730	20	115	26	65	47	1,826	499	79	34	181	1,838
Northern Marianas	1,051	9	99	18	28	57	406	231	23	3	88	89
Puerto Rico	68,868	286	144	629	1,339	4,394	39,933	—	954	897	2,050	18,242
Virgin Islands	3,193	101	300	—	78	126	1,528	314	76	35	285	350

[1] Includes imputations for undercounts in designated states.
[2] Includes imputation for prekindergarten teachers.
[3] Includes imputation for instruction coordinators.
[4] Includes imputation for support staff.
[5] Includes imputation for instruction aides.
[6] All staff, except teachers, estimated by the National Center for Education Statistics.

—Data not available or not applicable.

SOURCE: U.S. Department of Education, National Center for Education Statistics, Common Core of Data survey; and unpublished estimates. (This table was prepared August 1996.)

Table 83.—Staff employed in public school systems, by type of assignment and state: Fall 1993

[In full-time equivalents]

| State or other area | Total | School district staff | | | School staff | | | | | | Student support staff | Other support services staff |
		Officials and administrators	Administrative support staff	Instruction coordinators	Principals and assistant principals	School and library support staff	Teachers	Instructional aides	Guidance counselors	Librarians		
1	2	3	4	5	6	7	8	9	10	11	12	13
United States [1]	4,808,080	47,614	145,680	33,248	121,486	230,861	2,503,901	450,519	82,964	50,511	123,924	1,017,372
Alabama [2]	80,923	251	1,084	393	2,133	2,339	43,003	3,897	1,607	1,194	488	24,534
Alaska	15,689	188	524	427	415	1,084	7,193	2,146	226	156	382	2,948
Arizona	74,679	407	683	180	1,633	5,846	37,493	9,519	972	773	7,022	10,151
Arkansas	50,502	656	1,012	784	1,420	1,608	26,014	2,501	1,203	948	1,297	13,059
California [2]	431,093	2,036	20,337	4,248	10,195	27,676	221,787	55,984	4,976	928	9,434	73,492
Colorado	62,927	775	2,059	577	1,817	4,298	33,661	4,995	1,024	704	1,421	11,596
Connecticut	62,014	906	1,586	416	1,536	3,151	34,526	6,178	1,108	654	2,864	9,089
Delaware	11,640	93	374	61	398	463	6,380	846	203	116	455	2,251
District of Columbia	10,591	420	298	168	379	450	6,056	366	261	173	68	1,952
Florida	226,911	1,676	11,659	801	5,760	11,584	110,653	22,238	4,584	2,513	6,517	48,926
Georgia [3]	156,005	2,055	3,762	1,000	3,688	7,111	74,172	20,043	2,110	2,051	4,060	35,953
Hawaii	18,292	142	334	226	467	699	10,111	2,203	531	286	450	2,843
Idaho	19,983	116	433	185	593	774	12,007	1,709	387	168	348	3,263
Illinois	198,862	1,623	5,392	1,507	4,408	9,379	110,874	17,609	2,756	1,973	5,172	38,169
Indiana	113,892	870	417	1,293	2,741	7,736	55,107	13,633	1,651	1,047	1,590	27,807
Iowa	60,267	759	788	372	1,737	4,424	31,616	4,945	1,305	652	2,133	11,536
Kansas	55,783	473	2,142	166	1,630	2,412	30,283	4,178	1,054	973	1,784	10,688
Kentucky	81,279	1,141	1,630	626	1,804	3,194	37,324	9,322	1,271	1,187	2,911	20,869
Louisiana	93,197	1,469	1,836	496	1,847	2,921	46,913	9,431	1,027	1,217	3,258	22,782
Maine	28,865	444	691	118	843	1,255	15,344	3,452	597	241	991	4,889
Maryland	82,753	627	488	669	2,528	3,692	44,171	7,277	1,724	1,078	1,993	18,506
Massachusetts	104,196	968	5,395	957	2,075	2,748	58,766	10,611	1,886	567	1,667	18,556
Michigan	169,283	1,922	2,713	915	4,677	6,933	80,267	12,629	2,826	1,500	8,150	46,751
Minnesota	74,859	1,278	1,730	487	1,594	3,318	46,956	6,089	901	984	2,859	8,663
Mississippi	59,853	833	1,334	399	1,478	2,245	28,376	8,886	814	640	1,856	12,992
Missouri [3]	112,810	629	4,299	1,990	2,419	7,248	54,860	6,430	2,365	1,272	1,482	29,816
Montana [3,4]	18,717	173	506	139	480	885	9,949	1,745	395	339	481	3,625
Nebraska [3]	36,832	607	772	212	933	1,104	19,616	3,325	702	558	949	8,054
Nevada [3]	22,418	309	529	87	610	1,327	12,579	1,257	443	239	358	4,680
New Hampshire	21,913	329	442	148	478	843	11,972	2,902	576	254	384	3,585
New Jersey	160,202	1,728	6,923	1,378	4,508	8,212	84,564	12,806	3,135	1,800	8,556	26,592
New Mexico	36,694	441	910	468	837	2,251	18,404	4,066	557	243	851	7,666
New York	353,603	2,825	24,421	2,176	6,930	8,802	179,413	26,272	5,688	2,983	8,563	85,530
North Carolina [3]	133,059	1,319	3,067	767	3,909	5,171	69,421	20,721	2,726	2,151	2,533	21,274
North Dakota	13,780	268	328	58	386	461	7,755	1,290	235	179	336	2,484
Ohio	201,828	5,443	8,991	383	4,868	14,114	107,444	9,804	3,754	1,776	1,310	43,941
Oklahoma	73,067	622	1,350	435	1,974	4,773	39,031	6,172	1,270	860	400	16,180
Oregon	50,392	716	1,372	338	1,576	3,380	26,488	5,236	1,300	665	1,370	7,951
Pennsylvania	190,885	1,267	5,926	1,576	3,866	9,898	101,302	12,676	3,523	2,170	9,666	39,015
Rhode Island	15,442	158	487	78	366	701	9,823	1,320	279	82	333	1,815
South Carolina	71,433	263	1,996	503	2,166	3,491	38,620	6,891	1,476	1,085	628	14,314
South Dakota	17,201	326	726	14	621	455	9,557	1,801	371	208	545	2,577
Tennessee	92,349	870	2,669	659	4,267	5,123	46,066	8,981	1,310	1,280	2,539	18,585
Texas	433,102	2,564	2,260	1,257	10,722	16,988	224,830	38,816	7,676	4,143	3,306	120,540
Utah	35,301	105	650	411	875	1,998	19,053	4,309	513	267	426	6,694
Vermont	14,928	479	167	309	510	761	7,330	2,139	319	200	513	2,201
Virginia	130,033	1,794	1,742	1,077	3,389	5,451	70,859	11,209	3,039	1,945	3,015	26,513
Washington	87,734	1,029	2,448	636	2,426	4,551	45,524	7,940	1,663	1,255	2,365	17,897
West Virginia	38,486	268	1,862	334	1,120	408	21,029	2,858	584	360	844	8,819
Wisconsin	88,640	835	1,662	314	3,138	4,389	52,822	7,565	1,788	1,339	2,662	12,126
Wyoming	12,893	119	474	30	316	736	6,537	1,301	273	135	339	2,633
Outlying areas												
American Samoa	1,339	25	48	32	56	81	656	11	18	6	40	366
Guam	3,839	14	97	20	57	166	1,644	471	77	50	108	1,135
Northern Marianas	1,101	9	51	8	29	42	431	233	18	4	167	109
Puerto Rico	68,005	297	89	672	1,298	4,090	39,816	0	909	857	2,058	17,919
Virgin Islands	3,324	36	375	0	79	88	1,570	353	75	44	325	379

[1] Includes imputations for undercounts in designated states.
[2] Includes imputation for prekindergarten teachers.
[3] Includes imputation for support staff.
[4] Includes imputation for instruction aides.

NOTE.—Some data have been revised from previously published figures.

SOURCE: U.S. Department of Education, National Center for Education Statistics, Common Core of Data survey; and unpublished estimates. (This table was prepared March 1996.)

Table 84.—Staff and teachers in public elementary and secondary schools, by state: Fall 1988 to fall 1994

State or other area	Teachers as a percent of staff				Fall 1992 [1]			Fall 1993 [1]			Fall 1994		
	Fall 1988	Fall 1989	Fall 1990	Fall 1991	Staff	Teachers	Teachers as a percent of staff	Staff	Teachers	Teachers as a percent of staff	Staff	Teachers	Teachers as a percent of staff
1	2	3	4	5	6	7	8	9	10	11	12	13	14
United States [2]	53.8	53.2	53.4	53.3	4,708,286	2,458,956	52.2	4,808,080	2,503,901	52.1	4,907,996	2,552,199	52.0
Alabama	53.2	50.0	48.7	49.4	[3]78,882	[3]41,961	[3]53.2	[3]80,923	[3]43,003	[3]53.1	[3]81,542	[3]42,789	[3]52.5
Alaska	46.5	48.3	50.3	50.9	14,792	7,282	49.2	15,689	7,193	45.8	[3]15,151	7,205	[3]47.6
Arizona	52.7	52.7	52.0	51.9	71,591	36,076	50.4	74,679	37,493	50.2	74,540	38,132	51.2
Arkansas	54.7	51.8	52.2	49.9	48,880	26,017	53.2	50,502	26,014	51.5	50,201	26,181	52.2
California	50.2	50.7	51.7	52.2	[3]427,610	[3]218,566	[3]51.1	[3]431,093	[3]221,787	[3]51.4	[3]436,125	[3]225,001	[3]51.6
Colorado	52.5	52.7	52.6	52.9	62,785	33,419	53.2	62,927	33,661	53.5	64,985	34,894	53.7
Connecticut	[5]86.9	55.5	56.3	56.8	63,648	34,193	53.7	62,014	34,526	55.7	64,743	35,316	54.5
Delaware	54.8	54.8	55.2	55.5	11,390	6,252	54.9	11,640	6,380	54.8	11,759	6,416	54.6
District of Columbia	58.4	57.0	58.3	57.0	10,567	6,064	57.4	10,591	6,056	57.2	10,507	6,110	58.2
Florida	50.8	50.5	49.8	50.0	217,356	107,590	49.5	226,911	110,653	48.8	226,975	110,674	48.8
Georgia	49.7	48.8	48.9	48.0	[3]142,840	66,942	[3]46.9	[3]156,005	74,172	[3]47.5	[3]161,390	77,914	[3]48.3
Hawaii	42.1	60.2	59.9	60.7	17,731	10,083	56.9	18,292	10,111	55.3	16,567	10,240	61.8
Idaho	63.0	62.4	62.3	62.4	19,571	11,827	60.4	19,983	12,007	60.1	21,194	12,582	59.4
Illinois	56.4	56.6	56.7	55.9	199,380	111,461	55.9	198,862	110,874	55.8	204,414	110,830	54.2
Indiana	51.2	50.9	50.7	50.1	111,919	54,552	48.7	113,892	55,107	48.4	115,441	55,496	48.1
Iowa	53.9	53.4	53.0	52.1	60,208	31,403	52.2	60,267	31,616	52.5	60,526	31,775	52.5
Kansas	57.6	57.3	56.8	56.8	54,185	29,753	54.9	55,783	30,283	54.3	56,790	30,579	53.8
Kentucky	49.9	50.1	49.5	48.7	79,191	37,868	47.8	81,279	37,324	45.9	81,720	38,784	47.5
Louisiana	48.9	49.9	49.8	69.6	92,180	46,904	50.9	93,197	46,913	50.3	96,124	47,599	49.5
Maine	57.3	57.8	57.3	56.9	28,937	15,375	53.1	28,865	15,344	53.2	29,264	15,404	52.6
Maryland	54.4	54.4	53.9	54.6	80,861	44,495	55.0	82,753	44,171	53.4	84,699	46,565	55.0
Massachusetts	56.5	56.7	57.2	56.5	101,278	57,225	56.5	104,196	58,766	56.4	108,281	60,489	55.9
Michigan	47.1	46.9	46.4	46.6	173,863	82,301	47.3	169,283	80,267	47.4	164,766	80,522	48.9
Minnesota	56.3	56.5	56.2	57.4	79,215	45,050	56.9	74,859	46,956	62.7	74,914	46,958	62.7
Mississippi	[4]63.1	49.0	48.3	47.5	57,876	27,829	48.1	59,853	28,376	47.4	60,708	28,866	47.5
Missouri	51.8	50.6	50.6	52.3	[3]109,417	52,984	[3]48.4	112,810	54,860	48.6	116,974	56,606	48.4
Montana	[4]77.5	[4]76.8	[4]76.4	[4]75.6	[3]18,760	10,135	[3]54.0	[3]18,717	9,949	[3]53.2	[3]18,446	10,079	[3]54.6
Nebraska	55.8	55.4	53.4	55.0	[3]35,648	19,323	[3]54.2	[3]36,832	19,616	[3]53.3	37,144	19,774	53.2
Nevada	[4]85.8	[4]89.0	[4]89.4	[4]86.8	[3]21,452	11,953	[3]55.7	22,418	12,579	56.1	23,098	13,414	58.1
New Hampshire	54.4	51.4	51.8	56.0	21,262	11,654	54.8	21,913	11,972	54.6	22,336	12,109	54.2
New Jersey	55.3	54.3	54.2	54.2	151,460	83,057	54.8	160,202	84,564	52.8	161,586	85,258	52.8
New Mexico	52.3	50.2	50.3	50.7	34,803	17,912	51.5	36,694	18,404	50.2	38,642	19,025	49.2
New York	55.3	50.6	50.9	50.8	343,900	176,375	51.3	353,603	179,413	50.7	356,386	182,273	51.1
North Carolina	52.0	51.6	51.2	51.7	[3]129,445	66,630	[3]51.5	133,059	69,421	52.2	[3]137,792	71,592	[3]52.0
North Dakota	56.1	55.3	54.5	56.9	13,797	7,794	56.5	13,780	7,755	56.3	13,919	7,796	56.0
Ohio	54.1	54.0	54.0	53.1	200,793	106,233	52.9	201,828	107,444	53.2	204,043	109,085	53.5
Oklahoma	54.8	54.2	54.2	54.0	72,166	38,433	53.3	73,067	39,031	53.4	[3]78,270	39,406	[3]50.3
Oregon	53.1	53.1	53.2	53.0	51,681	26,634	51.5	50,392	26,488	52.6	50,377	26,208	52.0
Pennsylvania	55.4	55.4	52.5	52.7	191,370	100,912	52.7	190,885	101,302	53.1	193,696	102,988	53.2
Rhode Island	62.3	61.7	60.2	62.8	15,833	10,069	63.6	15,442	9,823	63.6	15,438	10,066	65.2
South Carolina	58.0	57.4	56.0	55.7	67,106	37,295	55.6	[3]71,433	38,620	[3]54.1	[3]74,174	39,437	[3]53.2
South Dakota	59.4	58.0	56.3	60.1	15,671	8,767	55.9	17,201	9,557	55.6	[3]17,989	9,985	[3]55.5
Tennessee	50.5	49.8	49.4	51.0	86,790	43,566	50.2	[3]92,349	46,066	[3]49.9	96,282	47,406	49.2
Texas	60.1	59.9	66.0	65.0	420,243	219,385	52.2	433,102	224,830	51.9	450,462	234,213	52.0
Utah	57.2	56.2	55.2	55.0	34,838	19,191	55.1	35,301	19,053	54.0	36,186	19,524	54.0
Vermont	57.3	57.3	53.6	50.5	14,970	7,521	50.2	[3]14,928	7,330	[3]49.1	[3]15,337	7,566	[3]49.3
Virginia	51.9	51.7	49.0	[5]49.4	126,619	68,181	53.8	130,033	70,859	54.5	[3]133,192	[3]72,853	[3]54.7
Washington	55.7	55.5	55.1	55.0	81,398	44,295	54.4	87,734	45,524	51.9	[3]90,440	46,439	[3]51.3
West Virginia	54.8	54.9	54.9	54.5	38,487	20,961	54.5	38,486	21,029	54.6	38,481	21,024	54.6
Wisconsin	59.0	59.0	58.1	59.0	92,139	53,387	57.9	88,640	52,822	59.6	100,996	54,054	53.5
Wyoming	50.4	49.9	53.1	50.0	11,502	5,821	50.6	12,893	6,537	50.7	12,984	6,698	51.6
Outlying areas													
American Samoa	53.7	53.1	52.6	52.5	1,350	725	53.7	1,339	656	49.0	1,340	698	52.1
Guam	50.5	54.3	52.6	50.6	3,517	1,628	46.3	3,839	1,644	42.8	4,730	1,826	38.6
Northern Marianas	51.9	52.0	51.1	47.5	1,096	425	38.8	1,101	431	39.1	1,051	406	38.6
Puerto Rico	53.5	53.5	55.4	54.9	67,643	38,381	56.7	68,005	39,816	58.5	68,868	39,933	58.0
Virgin Islands	48.1	48.0	48.0	48.1	3,353	1,595	47.6	3,324	1,570	47.2	3,193	1,528	47.9

[1] Some data have been revised from previously published figures.
[2] U.S. totals include imputations for underreporting and nonreporting states.
[3] Includes imputations for underreporting.
[4] Support staff underreported.
[5] Data estimated by the National Center for Education Statistics.

SOURCE: U.S. Department of Education, National Center for Education Statistics, Common Core of Data survey; and unpublished estimates. (This table was prepared August 1996.)

Table 85.—Staff, enrollment, and pupil-staff ratios in public elementary and secondary schools, by state: Fall 1988 to fall 1994

State or other area	Pupil-staff ratio				Fall 1992 [1]			Fall 1993 [1]			Fall 1994		
	Fall 1988	Fall 1989	Fall 1990	Fall 1991	Staff	Enrollment	Pupil-staff ratio	Staff	Enrollment	Pupil-staff ratio	Staff	Enrollment	Pupil-staff ratio
1	2	3	4	5	6	7	8	9	10	11	12	13	14
United States	[2]9.3	[2]9.1	[2]9.2	[2]9.2	[2]4,708,286	42,823,312	[2]9.1	[2]4,808,080	43,464,916	[2]9.0	[2]4,907,996	44,108,775	[2]9.0
Alabama	9.9	9.1	9.7	8.8	[3]78,882	731,634	[3]9.3	[3]80,923	734,288	[3]9.1	[3]81,542	736,472	[3]9.0
Alaska	7.9	8.1	8.5	8.5	14,792	122,487	8.3	15,689	125,948	8.0	[3]15,151	127,057	[3]8.4
Arizona	9.6	10.0	10.1	10.0	71,591	673,477	9.4	74,679	709,453	9.5	74,540	737,424	9.9
Arkansas	8.6	8.8	8.8	8.5	48,880	441,490	9.0	50,502	444,271	8.8	50,201	447,565	8.9
California	11.4	11.4	11.8	11.9	[3]427,610	5,254,844	[3]12.3	[3]431,093	5,327,231	[3]12.4	[3]436,125	5,407,043	[3]12.4
Colorado	9.4	9.3	9.3	9.5	62,785	612,635	9.8	62,927	625,062	9.9	64,985	640,521	9.9
Connecticut	[5]11.3	7.4	7.6	8.0	63,648	488,476	7.7	62,014	496,298	8.0	64,743	506,824	7.8
Delaware	9.0	9.0	9.2	9.3	11,390	104,321	9.2	11,640	105,547	9.1	11,759	106,813	9.1
District of Columbia	8.3	7.7	7.9	7.2	10,567	80,937	7.7	10,591	80,678	7.6	10,507	80,450	7.7
Florida	8.7	8.7	8.6	8.8	217,356	1,981,407	9.1	226,911	2,040,763	9.0	226,975	2,108,968	9.3
Georgia	9.2	8.9	8.9	8.9	[3]142,840	1,207,186	[3]8.5	[3]156,005	1,235,304	[3]7.9	[3]161,390	1,270,948	[3]7.9
Hawaii	8.1	11.5	11.3	11.2	17,731	177,448	10.0	18,292	180,410	9.9	16,567	183,795	11.1
Idaho	13.0	12.5	12.2	12.1	19,571	231,668	11.8	19,983	236,774	11.8	21,194	240,448	11.3
Illinois	9.6	9.6	9.5	9.4	199,380	1,873,567	9.4	198,862	1,893,078	9.5	204,414	1,916,172	9.4
Indiana	9.1	8.9	8.8	8.8	111,919	960,630	8.6	113,892	965,633	8.5	115,441	968,933	8.4
Iowa	8.5	8.4	8.3	8.1	60,208	494,839	8.2	60,267	498,519	8.3	60,526	499,550	8.3
Kansas	8.7	8.6	8.5	8.6	54,185	451,536	8.3	55,783	457,614	8.2	56,790	460,838	8.1
Kentucky	8.9	8.8	8.6	8.4	79,191	655,041	8.3	81,279	655,265	8.1	81,720	657,642	8.0
Louisiana	8.9	8.8	8.6	[4]12.0	92,180	797,985	[4]8.7	93,197	800,560	8.6	96,124	797,933	8.3
Maine	8.4	8.1	8.0	8.0	28,937	216,453	7.5	28,865	216,995	7.5	29,264	212,601	7.3
Maryland	9.2	9.1	9.1	9.2	80,861	751,850	9.3	82,753	772,638	9.3	84,699	790,938	9.3
Massachusetts	7.7	7.9	8.8	8.5	101,278	859,948	8.5	104,196	877,726	8.4	108,281	893,727	8.3
Michigan	9.3	9.2	9.2	8.9	173,863	1,603,610	9.2	169,283	1,599,377	9.4	164,766	1,614,784	9.8
Minnesota	9.6	9.7	9.8	9.9	79,215	793,724	10.0	74,859	810,233	10.8	74,914	821,693	11.0
Mississippi	[4]11.6	8.9	8.6	8.5	57,876	506,668	8.8	59,853	505,907	8.5	60,708	505,962	8.3
Missouri	8.2	8.0	7.9	8.4	[3]109,417	859,357	[3]7.9	112,810	866,378	7.7	116,974	878,541	7.5
Montana	[4]12.3	[4]12.1	[4]12.2	[4]11.9	[3]18,760	160,011	[3]8.5	[3]18,717	163,009	8.7	[3]18,446	164,341	[3]8.9
Nebraska	8.3	8.1	7.8	8.1	[3]35,648	282,414	[3]7.9	[3]36,832	285,097	7.7	37,144	287,100	7.7
Nevada	[4]17.4	[4]18.1	[4]17.3	[4]16.1	[3]21,452	222,974	[3]10.4	22,418	235,800	10.5	23,098	250,747	10.9
New Hampshire	8.8	8.4	8.4	8.6	21,262	181,247	8.5	21,913	185,360	8.5	22,336	189,319	8.5
New Jersey	7.5	7.3	7.4	7.5	151,460	1,130,560	7.5	160,202	1,151,307	7.2	161,586	1,174,206	7.3
New Mexico	9.7	9.2	9.1	8.9	34,803	315,668	9.1	36,694	322,292	8.8	38,642	327,248	8.5
New York	8.2	7.4	7.5	7.8	343,900	2,689,686	7.8	353,603	2,733,813	7.7	356,386	2,766,208	7.8
North Carolina	9.1	8.8	8.7	8.7	[3]129,445	1,114,083	[3]8.6	133,059	1,133,231	8.5	[3]137,792	1,156,767	[3]8.4
North Dakota	8.6	8.3	8.5	8.7	13,797	118,734	8.6	13,780	119,127	8.6	13,919	119,288	8.6
Ohio	9.5	9.4	9.3	9.2	200,793	1,795,199	8.9	201,828	1,807,319	9.0	204,043	1,814,290	8.9
Oklahoma	9.1	8.8	8.4	8.4	72,166	597,096	8.3	73,067	604,076	8.3	[3]78,270	609,718	[3]7.8
Oregon	9.8	9.8	9.6	9.9	51,681	510,122	9.9	50,392	516,611	10.3	50,377	521,945	10.4
Pennsylvania	8.8	8.7	8.7	8.9	191,370	1,717,613	9.0	190,885	1,744,082	9.1	193,696	1,765,891	9.1
Rhode Island	9.0	8.9	8.8	9.2	15,833	143,798	9.1	15,442	145,676	9.4	15,438	147,487	9.6
South Carolina	9.9	9.7	9.4	9.4	67,106	640,464	9.5	[3]71,433	643,696	[3]9.0	[3]74,174	648,673	[3]8.7
South Dakota	9.1	9.0	8.5	8.9	15,671	134,573	8.6	17,201	142,825	8.3	[3]17,989	143,482	[3]8.0
Tennessee	9.7	9.5	9.5	9.9	86,790	855,231	9.9	[3]92,349	866,557	[3]9.4	96,282	881,355	9.2
Texas	10.0	10.0	10.2	10.3	420,243	3,541,769	8.4	433,102	3,608,262	8.3	450,462	3,677,171	8.2
Utah	14.0	14.0	13.8	13.7	34,838	463,870	13.3	35,301	471,365	13.4	36,186	474,675	13.1
Vermont	7.8	7.9	7.1	7.0	14,970	98,558	6.6	[3]14,928	102,755	[3]6.9	15,337	104,533	6.8
Virginia	8.4	8.2	7.7	[6]7.8	126,619	1,031,925	[6]8.1	130,033	1,045,471	8.0	[3]133,192	1,060,809	[3]8.0
Washington	11.4	11.2	11.1	11.1	81,398	896,475	11.0	87,734	915,952	10.4	[3]90,440	938,314	[3]10.4
West Virginia	8.3	8.3	8.2	8.3	38,487	318,296	8.3	38,486	314,383	8.2	38,481	310,511	8.1
Wisconsin	9.4	9.4	9.4	9.2	92,139	829,415	9.0	88,640	844,001	9.5	100,996	860,686	8.5
Wyoming	7.4	7.2	7.7	7.8	11,502	100,313	8.7	12,893	100,899	7.8	12,984	100,369	7.7
Outlying areas													
American Samoa	9.4	9.9	9.9	10.5	1,350	13,994	10.4	1,339	14,484	10.8	1,340	14,445	10.8
Guam	9.4	8.9	9.0	9.6	3,517	30,077	8.6	3,839	30,920	8.1	4,730	32,185	6.8
Northern Marianas	9.5	8.9	7.9	7.8	1,096	8,086	7.4	1,101	8,188	7.4	1,051	8,429	8.0
Puerto Rico	10.6	10.4	10.4	9.5	67,643	637,034	9.4	68,005	631,460	9.3	68,868	621,121	9.0
Virgin Islands	7.1	6.4	6.6	6.8	3,353	22,887	6.8	3,324	22,752	6.8	3,193	23,126	7.2

[1] Some data have been revised from previously published figures.
[2] U.S. totals include imputations for underreporting and nonreporting states.
[3] Includes imputations for underreporting.
[4] Support staff underreported.
[5] Support staff not reported.

[6] Estimated by the National Center for Education Statistics.

SOURCE: U.S. Department of Education, National Center for Education Statistics, Common Core of Data survey; and unpublished estimates. (This table was prepared August 1996.)

Table 86.—Principals in public and private elementary and secondary schools, by selected characteristics: 1993–94

Selected characteristics	Total [1]	Percent of principals, by highest degree earned [2]				Average years of experience		Average annual salary of principals, by length of school year [3]			
		Bachelor's	Master's	Education specialist	Doctor's and first-professional	As a principal	Prior teaching experience	Total	10 months or less	11 months	12 months
1	2	3	4	5	6	7	8	9	10	11	12
					Public schools						
Total	79,618	1.4	63.4	25.8	9.3	8.7	11.0	$54,858	$50,103	$53,117	$58,399
Men	52,114	1.1	65.1	24.7	9.1	10.3	10.0	54,922	49,545	52,946	58,492
Women	27,505	2.0	60.2	27.9	9.8	5.6	13.0	54,736	50,908	53,439	58,195
Race/ethnicity											
White, non-Hispanic ..	67,081	1.5	62.8	26.5	9.2	9.0	10.8	54,466	48,797	52,893	58,311
Black, non-Hispanic ...	8,018	0.0	64.3	23.7	11.9	7.1	12.7	57,669	58,346	54,061	58,836
Hispanic	3,269	2.7	74.5	17.3	5.5	6.3	11.3	55,862	50,035	54,898	59,597
Asian or Pacific Islander	620	6.7	50.9	25.4	17.0	5.6	11.7	59,447	56,916	(4)	(4)
American Indian or Alaskan Native	631	1.1	65.8	24.8	8.2	8.2	9.9	51,117	46,401	49,121	55,337
Age											
Under 40	5,936	4.5	71.2	18.9	5.3	2.8	7.8	46,542	41,817	46,877	49,779
40 to 44	14,571	1.6	65.4	26.2	6.7	5.0	10.3	52,038	48,033	49,581	55,443
45 to 49	25,427	0.9	59.8	30.0	9.3	7.1	11.4	55,423	50,663	53,705	58,872
50 to 54	18,868	1.0	63.9	24.9	10.3	10.3	11.8	56,559	52,464	54,279	59,643
55 or over	14,817	1.4	63.8	22.4	12.4	15.1	11.6	57,826	52,414	56,355	62,148
Type of school											
Elementary	53,684	1.5	64.1	25.7	8.6	8.9	11.2	54,161	50,306	52,930	57,620
Secondary	18,262	1.2	63.1	25.4	10.3	8.0	10.6	56,601	47,100	53,982	60,204
Combined	2,747	2.6	60.2	27.8	9.4	7.5	10.9	52,825	50,729	51,879	54,040
					Private schools						
Total	25,015	25.9	51.6	8.2	5.9	8.8	9.4	32,075	21,994	32,215	35,295
Men	11,606	23.1	49.6	6.8	9.2	9.0	7.6	35,597	21,144	41,663	38,350
Women	13,410	28.3	53.3	9.4	3.0	8.6	11.1	29,185	22,537	27,818	32,231
Race/ethnicity											
White, non-Hispanic ..	23,133	25.6	52.1	8.1	5.8	8.7	9.5	31,969	21,289	32,071	35,283
Black, non-Hispanic ...	1,060	26.5	43.6	11.0	4.6	8.3	7.4	34,383	(4)	(4)	35,801
Hispanic	524	34.5	44.0	9.2	12.1	10.1	12.1	31,350	(4)	(4)	(4)
Age											
Under 40	4,794	38.1	36.6	8.2	1.4	3.5	5.0	26,308	17,903	33,527	29,420
40 to 44	4,403	35.9	45.5	8.5	5.3	5.3	7.9	30,486	20,004	30,127	33,044
45 to 49	5,144	22.2	59.0	8.1	5.5	8.3	9.9	34,641	23,945	31,812	38,932
50 to 54	4,120	15.1	59.1	7.7	11.0	9.6	11.1	37,727	27,338	35,421	40,097
55 or over	6,553	20.0	56.0	8.3	6.8	14.8	12.4	31,781	23,679	31,308	35,144
Type of school											
Elementary	13,354	26.1	54.2	8.0	4.7	9.4	10.4	28,779	23,427	30,050	30,687
Secondary	2,304	6.0	67.4	14.0	12.4	7.8	10.5	43,683	(4)	40,018	45,195
Combined	6,772	29.4	44.2	6.6	5.5	8.0	7.5	33,634	17,957	39,884	37,490

[1] Total differs from data appearing in other tables because of varying survey processing procedures and time period coverages.

[2] Percentages for those with less than a bachelor's degree are not shown.

[3] Excludes principals reporting a salary of $0. About 7.4 percent of private school principals had $0 salary. If these principals are included in the average annual salary calculations, the average for all private school principals is $29,714.

[4] Too few cases for reliable estimate.

NOTE.—Details may not add to 100.0 percent because of rounding and survey item nonresponse. Data revised from previously published figures.

SOURCE: U.S. Department of Education, National Center for Education Statistics, "Schools and Staffing Survey, 1993–94." (This table was prepared November 1996.)

Table 87.—Public elementary and secondary students, schools, pupil-teacher ratios, and finances, by type of locale: 1993

Characteristic	Total[1]	Large central city[2]	Mid-size central city[3]	Urban fringe of large city[4]	Urban fringe of mid-size city[5]	Large town[6]	Small town[7]	Rural[8]	Unknown[9]
1	2	3	4	5	6	7	8	9	10
Schools, enrollment, and teachers, 1993–94									
Enrollment, in thousands	44,082	6,197	8,124	7,453	4,970	1,303	5,679	9,682	673
Schools	87,110	8,677	13,562	12,279	8,321	2,553	12,224	27,415	2,079
Average school size[10]	512	724	610	630	615	526	486	314	324
Pupil-teacher ratio[11]	17.8	19.0	17.9	18.6	18.3	17.7	17.2	16.7	20.5
Enrollment (percent distribution)	100.0	14.1	18.4	16.9	11.3	3.0	12.9	22.0	1.5
Schools (percent distribution)	100.0	10.0	15.6	14.1	9.6	2.9	14.0	31.5	2.4
Revenues and expenditures, 1992–93 (in millions)									
Total revenue	$223,291	$36,428	$39,787	$41,589	$26,467	$6,398	$27,672	$44,644	$304
Federal	15,426	3,649	3,096	1,628	1,353	427	1,795	3,429	49
Impact aid	549	36	96	37	82	26	81	192	0
Bilingual education	20	6	4	1	2	1	2	4	0
Indian education	34	1	3	1	0	1	5	22	0
Children with disabilites	1,603	404	372	255	159	47	142	218	6
Eisenhower science awards	34	9	7	4	3	1	3	7	0
Drug Free schools	102	18	25	12	11	3	9	22	1
Chapter 2 (block grants)	246	64	56	30	26	8	19	42	1
Vocational education	327	83	76	36	33	9	28	51	11
Chapter 1	3,458	1,159	760	273	315	100	252	595	4
Other and unclassified	9,052	1,869	1,697	980	722	231	1,252	2,277	25
State	103,301	17,190	19,174	15,073	12,363	3,017	13,046	23,365	74
State school lunch programs	233	64	46	30	42	5	15	31	0
Local	104,563	15,589	17,517	24,889	12,751	2,955	12,830	17,851	182
Property tax[12]	18,743	5,272	2,859	4,524	1,647	751	1,533	2,157	0
Parent government contribution[12]	56,325	7,906	11,383	15,216	7,870	1,405	5,509	6,900	136
Lunch sales	2,936	302	625	639	406	98	310	552	4
Transportation	42	8	9	13	3	1	4	3	0
Other and unclassified	26,517	2,102	2,640	4,497	2,825	699	5,474	8,238	41
Total revenue (percent distribution)	100.0	100.0	100.0	100.0	100.0	100.0	100.0	100.0	100.0
Federal	6.9	10.0	7.8	3.9	5.1	6.7	6.5	7.7	16.0
State	46.3	47.2	48.2	36.2	46.7	47.2	47.1	52.3	24.2
Local	46.8	42.8	44.0	59.8	48.2	46.2	46.4	40.0	59.8
Total expenditures	215,242	34,972	38,424	40,357	25,442	6,204	26,666	42,733	444
Current expenditures	203,273	33,551	36,212	38,109	24,013	5,804	25,095	40,067	422
Instruction	100,706	20,226	20,671	20,263	12,726	3,043	9,140	14,431	206
Operation and maintenance	16,554	3,292	3,492	3,414	2,042	499	1,453	2,316	47
Food service	6,816	1,438	1,524	1,026	802	209	596	1,213	8
Other	79,197	8,594	10,525	13,406	8,443	2,054	13,906	22,107	161
Other current	1,266	171	280	247	217	65	133	148	5
Capital outlay	6,411	675	1,188	1,138	750	219	850	1,576	15
Interest on debt	4,292	575	744	862	461	116	589	942	3
Current expenditures (percent distribution)	100.0	100.0	100.0	100.0	100.0	100.0	100.0	100.0	100.0
Instruction	49.5	60.3	57.1	53.2	53.0	52.4	36.4	36.0	48.8
Operation and maintenance	8.1	9.8	9.6	9.0	8.5	8.6	5.8	5.8	11.0
Food service	3.4	4.3	4.2	2.7	3.3	3.6	2.4	3.0	2.0
Other	39.0	25.6	29.1	35.2	35.2	35.4	55.4	55.2	38.2
Current expenditure per student	4,901	5,560	4,652	5,477	5,053	4,484	4,612	4,358	19,612
Instruction expenditure per student	2,428	3,352	2,656	2,912	2,678	2,350	1,680	1,570	9,563

[1] Includes data for districts not identified by locale.
[2] Central city of metropolitan statistical area (MSA) with population of 400,000 or more or a population density of 6,000 or more persons per square mile.
[3] Central city of an MSA but not designated as a large central city.
[4] Place within the MSA of a large central city.
[5] Place within the MSA of a mid-size central city.
[6] Place not within an MSA but with population of 25,000 or more and defined as urban.
[7] Place not within an MSA with a population of at least 2,500 but less than 25,000.
[8] Place with a population of less than 2,500.
[9] Urbanicity code was not determined.
[10] Average for schools reporting enrollment.
[11] Ratio for schools reporting both FTE teachers and fall enrollment data.

[12] Property tax and parent government contributions are determined on the basis of independence or dependence of the local school system and are mutually exclusive.

NOTE.—Locale classification procedures not comparable with previous years. Enrollments by locale were used to distribute school district revenue and expenditure amounts by locale classification.

SOURCE: U.S. Department of Education, National Center for Education Statistics, Common Core of Data survey; and U.S. Department of Commerce, Bureau of the Census, *Survey of Local Government Finances*, unpublished data. (This table was prepared July 1995.)

Table 88.—Public school districts and public and private elementary and secondary schools: 1929–30 to 1994–95

School year	Public school districts [1]	Public schools [2]					Private schools [2,3]		
		Total, all schools [4]	Total, regular schools [5]	Elementary schools		Secondary schools	Total [4]	Elementary schools	Secondary schools
				Total	One-teacher				
1	2	3	4	5	6	7	8	9	10
1929–30	—	—	—	238,306	149,282	23,930	—	9,275	3,258
1937–38	119,001	—	—	221,660	121,178	25,467	—	9,992	3,327
1939–40	117,108	—	—	—	113,600	—	—	11,306	3,568
1945–46	101,382	—	—	160,227	86,563	24,314	—	9,863	3,294
1947–48	94,926	—	—	146,760	75,096	25,484	—	10,071	3,292
1949–50	83,718	—	—	128,225	59,652	24,542	—	10,375	3,331
1951–52	71,094	—	—	123,763	50,742	23,746	—	10,666	3,322
1953–54	63,057	—	—	110,875	42,865	25,637	—	11,739	3,913
1955–56	54,859	—	—	104,427	34,964	26,046	—	12,372	3,887
1957–58	47,594	—	—	95,446	25,341	25,507	—	13,065	3,994
1959–60	40,520	—	—	91,853	20,213	25,784	—	13,574	4,061
1961–62	35,676	—	—	81,910	13,333	25,350	—	14,762	4,129
1963–64	31,705	—	—	77,584	9,895	26,431	—	—	4,451
1965–66	26,983	—	—	73,216	6,491	26,597	17,849	15,340	4,606
1967–68	22,010	—	94,197	70,879	4,146	27,011	—	—	—
1970–71	17,995	—	89,372	65,800	1,815	25,352	—	14,372	3,770
1973–74	16,730	—	88,655	65,070	1,365	25,906	—	—	—
1975–76	16,376	88,597	87,034	63,242	1,166	25,330	—	—	—
1976–77	16,271	—	86,501	62,644	1,111	25,378	19,910	16,385	5,904
1978–79	16,014	—	84,816	61,982	1,056	24,504	19,489	16,097	5,766
1980–81	15,912	85,982	83,688	61,069	921	24,362	20,764	16,792	5,678
1982–83	15,824	84,740	82,039	59,656	798	23,988	—	—	—
1983–84	15,747	84,178	81,418	59,082	838	23,947	[6] 27,694	[6] 20,872	[6] 7,862
1984–85	—	84,007	81,147	58,827	825	23,916	—	—	—
1985–86	—	—	—	—	—	—	[6] 25,616	[6] 20,252	[6] 7,387
1986–87	[7] 15,713	83,455	82,190	60,784	763	23,389	—	—	—
1987–88	[7] 15,577	83,248	82,248	61,490	729	22,937	[6] 26,807	[6] 22,959	[6] 8,418
1988–89	[7] 15,376	83,165	82,081	61,531	583	22,785	—	—	—
1989–90	[7] 15,367	83,425	82,396	62,037	630	22,639	—	—	—
1990–91	[7] 15,358	84,538	81,746	61,340	617	22,731	[6] 24,690	[6] 22,223	[6] 8,989
1991–92	[7] 15,173	84,578	81,859	61,739	569	22,601	[6] 25,998	[6] 23,523	[6] 9,282
1992–93	[7] 15,025	84,501	82,224	62,229	430	22,544	—	—	—
1993–94	[7] 14,881	85,393	82,785	62,726	442	22,733	[6] 26,093	[6] 23,543	[6] 10,555
1994–95	[7] 14,772	86,221	83,854	63,572	458	23,046	—	—	—

[1] Includes operating and nonoperating districts.

[2] Schools with both elementary and secondary programs are included under elementary schools and also under secondary schools.

[3] Data for most years are partly estimated.

[4] Includes regular schools and special schools not classified by grade span.

[5] Includes elementary, secondary, and combined elementary/secondary schools.

[6] These data are from sample surveys and should not be compared directly with the data for earlier years.

[7] Because of expanded survey coverage, data are not directly comparable with figures for earlier years.

—Data not available.

SOURCE: U.S. Department of Education, National Center for Education Statistics, *Statistics of State School Systems; Statistics of Public Elementary and Secondary School Systems; Statistics of Nonpublic Elementary and Secondary Schools; Private Schools in American Education;* and Common Core of Data surveys. (This table was prepared October 1996.)

Table 89.—Public school districts and enrollment, by size of district: 1988–89 to 1994–95

Enrollment size of district	1988–89	1989–90	1990–91	1991–92	1992–93			1993–94			1994–95		
	Number of districts	Number of districts	Number of districts	Number of districts	Number of districts	Percent of districts	Percent of students	Number of districts	Percent of districts	Percent of students	Number of districts	Percent of districts	Percent of students
1	2	3	4	5	6	7	8	9	10	11	12	13	14
Total	15,376	15,367	15,358	15,173	15,025	100.0	100.0	14,881	100.0	100.0	14,772	100.0	100.0
25,000 or more	177	179	190	195	202	1.3	29.6	206	1.4	29.9	207	1.4	29.9
10,000 to 24,999	473	479	489	502	510	3.4	18.0	525	3.5	18.2	542	3.7	18.6
5,000 to 9,999	924	913	937	941	955	6.4	15.6	973	6.5	15.6	996	6.7	15.7
2,500 to 4,999	1,907	1,937	1,940	1,981	2,002	13.3	16.5	2,008	13.5	16.3	2,013	13.6	16.1
1,000 to 2,499	3,529	3,547	3,542	3,525	3,530	23.5	13.6	3,570	24.0	13.5	3,579	24.2	13.4
600 to 999	1,813	1,801	1,799	1,793	1,798	12.0	3.3	1,785	12.0	3.2	1,777	12.0	3.2
300 to 599	2,266	2,283	2,275	2,222	2,200	14.6	2.3	2,162	14.5	2.2	2,113	14.3	2.1
1 to 299	3,984	3,910	3,816	3,648	3,465	23.1	1.1	3,294	22.1	1.0	3,173	21.5	1.0
Size not reported [1]	303	318	370	366	363	2.4	—	358	2.4	—	372	2.5	—

[1] Includes school districts reporting enrollment of 0.

—Data not reported.

NOTE.—Because of rounding, details may not add to totals.

SOURCE: U.S. Department of Education, National Center for Education Statistics, Common Core of Data surveys. (This table was prepared October 1996.)

Table 90.—Number and percentage of public elementary and secondary education agencies, by state and type of agency: 1994–95

State or other area	Total agencies	Regular school districts, including supervisory union components		Regional education service agencies and supervisory union administrative centers		State-operated agencies		Federally operated and other agencies	
		Number	Percent	Number	Percent	Number	Percent	Number	Percent
1	2	3	4	5	6	7	8	9	10
United States	16,257	14,772	90.9	1,152	7.1	192	1.2	141	0.9
Alabama	131	127	96.9	0	0.0	1	0.8	3	2.3
Alaska	56	56	100.0	0	0.0	0	0.0	0	0.0
Arizona	242	227	93.8	5	2.1	1	0.4	9	3.7
Arkansas	335	314	93.7	17	5.1	4	1.2	0	0.0
California	1,062	1,001	94.3	58	5.5	3	0.3	0	0.0
Colorado	194	176	90.7	18	9.3	0	0.0	0	0.0
Connecticut	179	166	92.7	6	3.4	4	2.2	3	1.7
Delaware	22	19	86.4	0	0.0	3	13.6	0	0.0
District of Columbia	1	1	100.0	0	0.0	0	0.0	0	0.0
Florida	74	67	90.5	0	0.0	1	1.4	6	8.1
Georgia	184	181	98.4	0	0.0	0	0.0	3	1.6
Hawaii	1	1	100.0	0	0.0	0	0.0	0	0.0
Idaho	113	112	99.1	0	0.0	1	0.9	0	0.0
Illinois	1,035	914	88.3	85	8.2	5	0.5	31	3.0
Indiana	326	294	90.2	28	8.6	3	0.9	1	0.3
Iowa	421	390	92.6	15	3.6	15	3.6	1	0.2
Kansas	304	304	100.0	0	0.0	0	0.0	0	0.0
Kentucky	255	176	69.0	0	0.0	77	30.2	2	0.8
Louisiana	72	66	91.7	0	0.0	5	6.9	1	1.4
Maine	328	285	86.9	42	12.8	1	0.3	0	0.0
Maryland	24	24	100.0	0	0.0	0	0.0	0	0.0
Massachusetts	461	352	76.4	86	18.7	1	0.2	22	4.8
Michigan	619	557	90.0	57	9.2	4	0.6	1	0.2
Minnesota	465	397	85.4	65	14.0	3	0.6	0	0.0
Mississippi	164	153	93.3	0	0.0	10	6.1	1	0.6
Missouri	542	536	98.9	0	0.0	2	0.4	4	0.7
Montana	561	481	85.7	77	13.7	3	0.5	0	0.0
Nebraska	799	680	85.1	112	14.0	7	0.9	0	0.0
Nevada	18	17	94.4	0	0.0	1	5.6	0	0.0
New Hampshire	246	178	72.4	68	27.6	0	0.0	0	0.0
New Jersey	619	607	98.1	12	1.9	0	0.0	0	0.0
New Mexico	89	89	100.0	0	0.0	0	0.0	0	0.0
New York	755	717	95.0	38	5.0	0	0.0	0	0.0
North Carolina	123	119	96.7	0	0.0	2	1.6	2	1.6
North Dakota	289	243	84.1	38	13.1	3	1.0	5	1.7
Ohio	790	661	83.7	102	12.9	3	0.4	24	3.0
Oklahoma	551	551	100.0	0	0.0	0	0.0	0	0.0
Oregon	258	248	96.1	7	2.7	2	0.8	1	0.4
Pennsylvania	612	501	81.9	100	16.3	11	1.8	0	0.0
Rhode Island	37	36	97.3	0	0.0	1	2.7	0	0.0
South Carolina	106	95	89.6	11	10.4	0	0.0	0	0.0
South Dakota	218	177	81.2	17	7.8	5	2.3	19	8.7
Tennessee	140	140	100.0	0	0.0	0	0.0	0	0.0
Texas	1,044	1,044	100.0	0	0.0	0	0.0	0	0.0
Utah	47	40	85.1	5	10.6	2	4.3	0	0.0
Vermont	344	284	82.6	60	17.4	0	0.0	0	0.0
Virginia	161	141	87.6	18	11.2	0	0.0	2	1.2
Washington	296	296	100.0	0	0.0	0	0.0	0	0.0
West Virginia	57	55	96.5	0	0.0	2	3.5	0	0.0
Wisconsin	429	427	99.5	0	0.0	2	0.5	0	0.0
Wyoming	58	49	84.5	5	8.6	4	6.9	0	0.0
Department of Defense dependents schools .	11	0	0.0	0	0.0	0	0.0	11	100.0
Outlying areas									
American Samoa	1	1	100.0	0	0.0	0	0.0	0	0.0
Guam	1	1	100.0	0	0.0	0	0.0	0	0.0
Northern Marianas	1	1	100.0	0	0.0	0	0.0	0	0.0
Puerto Rico	1	1	100.0	0	0.0	0	0.0	0	0.0
Virgin Islands	1	1	100.0	0	0.0	0	0.0	0	0.0

SOURCE: U.S. Department of Education, National Center for Education Statistics, Common Core of Data survey. (This table was prepared October 1996.)

Table 91.—Selected statistics for public school districts enrolling more than 20,000 pupils, by state: 1993–94

Name of district, by state	State	Enrollment, fall 1993	Classroom teachers,[1] fall 1993	Pupils per teacher, fall 1993	Percent minority pupils, fall 1993	Number of schools, 1993-94	Number of 1992-93 graduates[2]	Revenue and expenditures,[3] 1992-93 (in thousands of dollars)									Current expenditure per pupil 1992-93[4]
								Revenue receipts				Total expenditures	Current expenditures			Interest on school debt	
								Total	Federal	State	Local		Total	Instruction	Capital outlay		
1	2	3	4	5	6	7	8	9	10	11	12	13	14	15	16	17	18
Districts with more than 20,000 students	—	14,536,579	—	—	—	20,477	655,424	81,083,789	7,047,765	38,550,426	35,485,598	76,682,319	72,746,705	43,456,091	2,432,391	1,503,223	5,096
Birmingham City	Ala.	42,847	2,463	17.4	91.1	90	1,753	169,344	25,212	100,973	43,159	155,250	152,689	85,628	2,041	520	3,591
Huntsville City	Ala.	25,075	1,532	16.4	40.8	42	1,343	125,194	9,920	60,333	54,941	104,661	100,527	57,992	4,073	61	4,033
Jefferson County	Ala.	40,733	2,368	17.2	15.0	58	2,256	149,848	11,811	97,679	40,358	136,410	132,801	81,812	3,047	562	3,271
Mobile County	Ala.	66,580	3,451	19.3	49.5	88	3,310	233,691	33,446	145,750	54,495	192,442	185,878	115,524	5,481	1,083	2,779
Montgomery County	Ala.	35,244	1,992	17.7	64.7	53	1,723	125,268	18,286	80,642	26,340	109,705	107,668	65,828	1,963	74	3,045
Anchorage	Alaska	47,340	2,142	22.1	29.0	82	2,239	354,841	38,368	241,644	74,829	294,134	286,982	146,234	7,115	37	6,203
Mesa Unified	Ariz.	67,639	—	—	20.5	71	3,265	291,052	13,964	146,264	130,824	258,780	240,676	151,152	10,078	8,026	3,665
Paradise Valley	Ariz.	30,042	1,480	20.3	10.5	33	1,528	134,579	3,567	56,440	74,572	125,253	109,811	69,192	4,380	11,062	3,808
Peoria Unified	Ariz.	24,752	1,172	21.1	21.5	25	1,175	99,742	3,134	53,069	43,539	91,223	81,112	50,545	3,382	6,729	3,514
Phoenix Union High	Ariz.	20,168	1,168	17.3	68.1	15	2,776	151,520	12,239	10,597	128,684	137,527	122,781	65,195	6,114	8,632	6,527
Scottsdale	Ariz.	22,096	1,140	19.4	11.3	26	1,284	102,132	2,758	21,219	78,155	95,756	85,256	48,988	2,621	7,879	4,048
Tucson Unified	Ariz.	60,529	—	—	51.8	110	2,672	264,112	23,151	128,754	112,207	260,504	233,553	132,373	10,213	16,738	4,035
Washington	Ariz.	24,016	1,283	18.7	20.0	32	—	93,510	6,122	51,341	36,047	91,291	87,482	57,518	2,695	1,114	3,702
Little Rock	Ark.	25,543	1,623	15.7	66.9	48	1,590	130,581	9,934	51,815	68,832	134,142	126,398	73,943	3,155	4,589	4,881
Pulaski County Special	Ark.	20,426	1,217	16.8	30.7	36	1,196	92,319	6,700	55,754	29,865	89,279	84,166	51,749	3,124	1,989	3,880
ABC Unified	Calif.	21,243	826	25.7	76.4	30	1,403	100,405	5,596	75,261	19,548	103,138	101,180	61,101	1,849	109	4,752
Anaheim Union High	Calif.	23,466	846	27.7	60.6	20	2,717	114,083	7,603	70,113	36,367	115,980	113,341	66,450	2,639	0	4,898
Bakersfield City Elementary	Calif.	26,366	1,069	24.7	71.4	36	—	130,728	13,375	99,572	17,781	112,574	107,388	65,647	2,780	2,406	4,077
Capistrano Unified	Calif.	31,262	1,240	25.2	21.8	32	1,562	166,755	3,513	76,601	86,641	134,330	131,118	80,746	2,858	354	4,364
Chino Unified	Calif.	26,607	1,094	24.3	45.8	28	1,124	125,160	3,332	82,034	39,794	123,191	114,154	70,485	8,360	677	4,419
Clovis Unified	Calif.	27,416	1,113	24.6	32.8	29	1,388	161,119	49,724	80,464	30,931	159,877	148,071	79,596	7,289	4,517	5,686
Compton Unified	Calif.	28,482	1,001	28.5	99.6	38	606	134,466	18,505	99,831	16,130	139,924	135,622	75,305	4,302	0	4,736
Corona-Norco Unified	Calif.	25,655	987	26.0	46.7	33	1,282	107,534	4,923	71,522	31,089	101,760	96,484	58,631	5,276	0	3,846
East Side Union High	Calif.	22,032	968	22.8	79.7	14	4,363	116,643	7,286	68,799	40,558	115,057	112,143	66,374	2,061	853	4,974
Elk Grove Unified	Calif.	32,038	1,308	24.5	51.8	36	1,543	186,807	7,501	126,770	52,536	152,187	145,061	75,853	6,973	153	4,753
Fairfield-Suisun Joint	Calif.	20,756	843	24.6	50.9	27	965	87,355	4,092	65,315	17,948	78,819	77,571	49,961	1,248	0	3,737
Fontana Unified	Calif.	29,764	1,111	26.8	68.9	32	1,270	139,197	8,418	113,374	17,405	136,388	129,896	70,897	5,206	1,286	4,419
Fremont Unified	Calif.	28,928	1,162	24.9	43.3	40	1,559	133,459	4,724	81,438	47,297	119,357	117,096	78,564	1,461	800	4,112
Fresno Unified	Calif.	76,349	3,158	24.2	73.0	86	2,981	361,702	39,346	252,721	69,635	383,254	375,562	218,984	7,672	20	4,953
Garden Grove Unified	Calif.	41,664	1,608	25.9	71.7	63	2,359	177,929	16,827	106,898	54,204	180,239	178,314	110,645	1,905	20	4,332
Glendale Unified	Calif.	28,742	1,083	26.5	41.0	29	1,649	124,470	11,147	79,909	33,414	115,163	113,084	74,152	2,079	0	3,990
Grossmont Union High	Calif.	20,010	810	24.7	28.0	13	3,424	107,429	4,412	57,187	45,830	108,341	104,915	54,911	3,426	0	5,343
Hacienda La Puente Unified	Calif.	21,831	821	26.6	85.9	35	1,291	135,670	11,603	98,162	25,905	128,824	126,141	60,896	2,655	28	5,736
Hayward Unified	Calif.	20,115	803	25.0	69.4	33	853	94,661	7,742	63,945	22,974	84,089	83,091	48,614	998	0	4,064
Irvine Unified	Calif.	21,519	898	24.0	32.5	30	1,606	107,083	5,444	39,890	61,749	103,554	96,952	62,135	5,432	1,170	4,549
Kern High	Calif.	22,646	844	26.8	49.1	20	3,990	179,308	8,441	76,691	94,176	120,692	118,433	58,366	2,255	4	5,363
Lodi Unified	Calif.	25,155	1,041	24.2	49.6	36	1,089	113,152	7,921	80,754	24,477	104,647	100,783	62,330	3,603	261	4,005
Long Beach Unified	Calif.	76,783	3,018	25.4	77.5	80	3,430	394,557	47,670	271,662	75,225	369,390	361,647	212,602	7,743	0	4,795
Los Angeles Unified	Calif.	639,129	24,933	25.6	87.9	640	25,439	3,451,551	348,942	2,462,366	640,243	3,700,377	3,650,772	2,168,098	49,605	0	5,706
Montebello Unified	Calif.	32,321	1,093	29.6	95.5	30	1,691	149,019	14,527	110,597	23,895	147,845	146,441	84,922	1,404	0	4,470
Moreno Valley Unified	Calif.	31,621	1,263	25.0	53.6	33	1,346	147,372	7,166	118,507	21,699	131,804	126,331	74,087	5,319	154	4,030
Mt. Diablo Unified	Calif.	34,110	1,471	23.2	28.8	54	1,741	148,368	6,574	79,841	61,953	140,405	139,153	83,971	1,232	20	4,143
Oakland Unified	Calif.	51,748	2,187	23.7	93.1	89	1,837	279,738	30,421	198,286	51,031	278,611	269,832	159,616	7,748	1,031	5,267
Ontario-Montclair Elementary	Calif.	22,649	861	26.3	76.9	31	—	92,074	8,228	70,130	13,716	88,966	87,528	55,786	1,438	0	3,912
Orange Unified	Calif.	26,387	1,016	26.0	46.3	38	1,494	113,093	5,518	42,930	64,645	112,958	111,177	66,181	1,722	59	4,221
Pasadena Unified	Calif.	22,032	899	24.5	82.9	31	1,020	116,940	10,220	69,130	37,590	116,029	115,098	69,218	931	0	5,131
Placentia-Yorba Linda Unified	Calif.	22,482	887	25.3	35.5	29	1,276	101,971	3,373	53,276	45,322	99,388	96,227	59,411	3,027	134	4,272
Pomona Unified	Calif.	29,880	1,133	26.4	88.1	35	971	140,867	17,352	102,961	20,554	148,322	144,233	77,375	3,109	980	4,892
Poway Unified	Calif.	28,106	1,113	25.3	25.9	28	1,517	129,465	3,022	69,534	56,909	118,617	110,620	65,996	7,475	522	4,083
Rialto Unified	Calif.	22,427	874	25.7	75.3	21	937	104,707	5,168	84,396	15,143	89,316	82,929	49,200	6,328	59	3,822
Richmond Unified	Calif.	31,329	1,264	24.8	74.4	56	1,477	151,743	16,315	91,236	44,192	141,348	138,586	80,223	2,762	0	4,429
Riverside Unified	Calif.	33,655	1,320	25.5	51.1	39	1,596	148,118	10,439	97,748	39,931	146,555	143,748	85,664	2,771	36	4,338
Sacramento City Unified	Calif.	49,997	1,972	25.4	69.0	75	2,028	230,375	26,220	159,612	44,543	238,089	232,363	135,071	5,726	0	4,600
Saddleback Valley Unified	Calif.	27,720	1,152	24.1	24.2	34	1,652	125,877	2,891	53,508	69,478	123,130	118,925	75,617	3,702	503	4,392
San Bernardino City Unified	Calif.	43,933	1,783	24.6	70.5	57	1,478	205,371	17,515	158,905	28,951	193,233	190,268	111,652	2,965	0	4,366
San Diego City Unified	Calif.	127,258	5,170	24.6	67.8	156	6,106	666,031	57,406	297,671	310,954	656,641	645,010	370,985	11,535	96	5,155
San Francisco Unified	Calif.	61,631	2,851	21.6	86.2	108	3,635	325,128	28,846	156,815	139,467	304,357	300,316	173,417	4,041	0	4,853
San Jose Unified	Calif.	30,905	1,351	22.9	65.0	48	1,654	164,547	12,877	81,928	69,742	158,591	153,174	91,033	5,107	310	5,028

Table 91.—Selected statistics for public school districts enrolling more than 20,000 pupils, by state: 1993-94—Continued

Name of district, by state	State	Enrollment, fall 1993	Classroom teachers,[1] fall 1993	Pupils per teacher, fall 1993	Percent minority pupils, fall 1993	Number of schools, 1993-94	Number of 1992-93 graduates[2]	Revenue and expenditures,[3] 1992-93 (in thousands of dollars)										Current expenditure per pupil 1992-93[4]
								Revenue receipts				Total expenditures	Current expenditures					
								Total	Federal	State	Local		Total	Instruction	Capital outlay	Interest on school debt		
1	2	3	4	5	6	7	8	9	10	11	12	13	14	15	16	17	18
San Juan Unified	Calif.	47,650	1,853	25.7	19.5	87	2,656	226,354	13,291	151,415	61,648	207,757	202,917	124,823	4,840	0	4,237
Santa Ana Unified	Calif.	48,407	1,693	28.6	95.1	46	1,842	218,339	19,870	131,085	67,384	204,427	190,916	123,144	13,145	366	3,975
Stockton City Unified	Calif.	34,337	1,488	23.1	81.3	41	1,065	171,743	20,409	118,121	33,213	183,854	177,401	96,589	6,351	102	5,229
Sweetwater Union High	Calif.	28,769	1,209	23.8	79.8	19	3,579	144,721	9,574	107,236	27,911	144,850	140,638	77,632	4,212	0	4,894
Torrance Unified	Calif.	21,233	826	25.7	47.6	30	1,333	91,807	3,042	55,452	33,313	86,916	84,579	48,962	2,308	29	4,093
Visalia Unified	Calif.	23,369	921	25.4	48.5	31	1,070	102,675	6,885	76,316	19,474	102,596	101,961	61,918	635	0	4,505
Vista Unified	Calif.	21,947	862	25.5	44.7	23	919	108,455	4,914	67,997	35,544	94,001	89,011	52,863	4,982	8	4,286
Adams-Arapahoe	Colo.	27,430	1,472	18.6	36.3	44	1,211	139,920	6,798	84,701	48,421	142,447	132,103	78,569	3,468	6,876	4,838
Boulder Valley	Colo.	24,085	1,353	17.8	15.3	48	1,324	138,130	4,569	19,745	113,816	129,736	122,906	71,977	3,103	3,727	5,211
Cherry Creek	Colo.	33,343	1,834	18.2	14.6	42	1,904	204,919	2,778	56,104	146,037	189,043	170,321	105,066	5,941	12,781	5,329
Colorado Springs	Colo.	31,799	1,522	20.9	25.6	57	1,609	145,947	7,644	71,956	66,347	131,628	129,704	80,212	1,924	0	4,050
Denver	Colo.	62,673	3,584	17.5	69.3	111	2,596	386,894	29,203	78,667	279,024	365,284	316,834	184,114	35,414	13,036	5,034
Jefferson County	Colo.	82,760	3,834	21.6	12.3	129	4,365	433,024	11,007	211,012	211,005	424,421	393,333	231,924	10,698	20,390	4,837
Northglenn-Thornton	Colo.	22,791	1,170	19.5	21.8	38	1,147	122,520	4,873	70,202	47,445	116,870	100,900	60,015	8,125	7,845	4,553
Poudre School District	Colo.	20,485	1,011	20.3	13.4	43	1,118	108,127	3,876	42,230	62,021	99,043	94,890	57,157	3,235	918	4,747
Bridgeport City	Conn.	20,495	1,322	15.5	87.6	38	693	157,774	18,250	99,511	40,013	146,579	141,162	93,508	2,890	2,527	6,899
Hartford	Conn.	25,292	1,791	14.1	93.8	33	846	237,164	21,289	134,766	81,109	228,146	223,760	146,254	2,167	2,219	8,817
D.C. Public Schools	D.C.	80,678	4,530	17.8	96.0	173	3,136	731,548	84,327	0	647,221	695,075	678,385	328,497	16,690	0	8,382
Alachua County	Fla.	28,426	1,594	17.8	40.3	40	1,248	150,948	14,787	88,388	47,773	140,786	126,844	66,488	6,572	7,370	4,552
Bay County	Fla.	23,873	1,442	16.6	19.0	32	1,148	117,486	11,375	71,783	34,328	113,435	110,349	64,632	3,013	73	4,750
Brevard County	Fla.	62,556	3,561	17.6	19.3	78	2,943	318,226	20,323	168,119	129,784	281,624	268,365	159,391	7,480	5,779	4,396
Broward County	Fla.	189,862	9,546	19.9	47.5	184	8,246	1,051,501	73,511	517,651	460,339	1,026,532	930,983	490,008	59,307	36,242	5,228
Clay County	Fla.	23,142	1,288	18.0	11.5	25	1,260	108,087	6,288	71,612	30,187	95,910	91,782	52,801	3,894	234	4,016
Collier County	Fla.	23,924	1,382	17.3	33.4	33	1,001	157,906	13,814	27,421	116,671	145,550	129,278	73,287	6,563	9,709	5,671
Dade County	Fla.	308,465	15,271	20.2	83.9	314	14,555	1,850,267	238,119	950,032	662,116	1,802,305	1,728,572	959,030	40,468	33,265	5,698
Duval County	Fla.	119,785	5,943	20.2	42.9	154	4,606	615,275	54,402	359,187	201,686	521,804	495,827	274,603	17,222	8,755	4,214
Escambia County	Fla.	44,641	2,624	17.0	37.5	70	2,081	242,649	31,540	153,072	58,037	230,725	217,240	118,968	8,808	4,677	4,905
Hillsborough County	Fla.	135,104	8,010	16.9	40.0	170	5,972	749,832	90,795	409,583	249,454	694,197	658,549	353,904	27,589	8,059	4,981
Lake County	Fla.	22,669	1,226	18.5	23.0	40	1,042	114,426	9,810	63,091	41,525	107,215	97,937	51,503	7,225	2,053	4,410
Lee County	Fla.	47,390	2,479	19.1	25.6	70	2,297	277,007	14,457	71,352	181,198	257,601	231,578	118,829	16,095	9,928	5,026
Leon County	Fla.	29,836	1,699	17.6	39.7	45	1,349	167,248	13,658	93,572	60,018	154,344	140,773	72,079	7,786	5,785	4,820
Manatee County	Fla.	29,685	1,640	18.1	27.3	55	1,167	159,238	12,140	68,823	78,275	137,029	131,982	74,102	4,401	646	4,626
Marion County	Fla.	32,702	1,830	17.9	27.4	44	1,431	164,818	14,088	97,734	52,996	151,609	140,848	79,454	6,367	4,394	4,471
Okaloosa County	Fla.	28,856	1,594	18.1	19.1	36	1,656	131,729	11,287	83,213	37,229	119,140	115,904	64,859	1,476	1,760	4,113
Orange County	Fla.	113,638	6,372	17.8	44.4	146	4,951	619,585	43,197	272,254	304,134	565,690	529,060	268,885	19,113	17,517	4,804
Osceola County	Fla.	23,122	1,151	20.1	34.4	28	1,059	108,776	5,397	54,567	48,812	100,637	92,146	49,903	5,209	3,282	4,221
Palm Beach County	Fla.	122,145	6,804	18.0	42.6	125	5,247	769,160	50,052	217,650	501,458	660,077	624,015	370,160	13,192	22,870	5,358
Pasco County	Fla.	38,265	2,079	18.4	10.4	43	1,777	193,985	14,180	103,977	75,828	185,290	167,699	89,604	9,138	8,453	4,591
Pinellas County	Fla.	100,135	5,499	18.2	22.9	142	4,905	570,656	39,848	259,292	271,516	478,893	465,690	262,216	12,422	781	4,750
Polk County	Fla.	69,718	3,826	18.2	29.9	104	3,073	330,689	30,438	199,796	100,455	329,346	310,158	170,851	15,315	3,873	4,580
Saint Lucie County	Fla.	25,250	1,217	20.7	37.9	31	845	136,110	13,566	55,184	67,360	124,877	111,033	60,304	8,765	5,079	4,659
Sarasota County	Fla.	30,205	1,672	18.1	15.9	38	1,591	200,372	12,944	44,735	142,693	182,723	163,906	85,986	9,940	8,877	5,592
Seminole County	Fla.	52,688	2,620	20.1	25.5	51	2,542	255,427	12,436	134,450	108,541	219,439	205,406	121,331	8,629	5,404	3,982
Volusia County	Fla.	53,972	3,031	17.8	23.0	67	2,490	279,882	17,748	137,783	124,351	259,894	231,487	129,438	10,400	18,007	4,403
Atlanta	Ga.	59,244	3,616	16.4	93.1	112	2,555	455,638	52,069	121,427	282,142	386,779	382,392	224,974	4,387	0	6,401
Bibb County	Ga.	25,158	1,519	16.6	64.5	39	1,075	109,891	13,603	62,819	33,469	108,792	103,818	65,302	2,696	2,278	4,133
Chatham County	Ga.	35,358	2,229	15.9	62.1	44	1,434	203,415	18,613	98,302	86,500	179,777	164,041	106,268	11,365	4,371	4,726
Clayton County	Ga.	37,961	2,202	17.2	45.8	42	1,766	178,168	10,845	84,382	82,941	163,268	157,775	94,264	2,903	2,590	4,308
Cobb County	Ga.	77,563	4,761	16.3	19.0	86	4,089	348,015	11,399	157,143	179,473	348,410	324,655	208,719	9,794	13,961	4,344
DeKalb County	Ga.	81,468	5,114	15.9	77.2	106	4,227	435,543	19,952	170,136	245,455	436,983	420,605	281,687	12,846	3,532	5,316
Fulton County	Ga.	50,190	3,060	16.4	48.0	53	2,283	307,257	12,310	84,853	210,094	255,766	239,663	138,942	7,357	8,746	5,057
Gwinnett County	Ga.	76,482	4,334	17.6	15.7	66	3,738	349,315	9,262	161,830	178,223	343,434	313,761	206,471	17,407	12,266	4,348
Muscogee County	Ga.	31,984	2,004	16.0	58.1	51	1,630	228,395	16,736	95,974	115,685	154,756	149,827	90,192	3,458	1,471	4,671
Richmond County	Ga.	35,422	2,064	17.2	64.7	56	1,565	161,407	17,271	88,714	55,422	146,006	140,906	87,515	3,356	1,744	4,049
Hawaii Public Schools	Hawaii	180,529	—	—	76.3	241	9,309	1,065,809	79,517	962,375	23,917	1,016,323	980,659	580,597	35,664	0	5,526
Boise City ISD	Idaho	26,099	1,362	19.2	—	45	1,367	107,794	5,630	51,503	50,661	94,768	90,594	57,858	1,895	2,279	3,607
City of Chicago	Ill.	409,499	21,722	18.9	88.6	609	15,445	2,427,068	360,275	831,124	1,235,669	2,333,374	2,284,616	1,387,464	47,422	1,336	5,551
Elgin Unified	Ill.	29,653	1,465	20.2	34.1	50	1,405	128,700	6,020	41,396	81,284	141,370	134,365	86,871	1,744	5,261	4,656
Rockford	Ill.	27,688	1,623	17.1	33.9	50	1,360	127,630	9,149	47,170	71,311	140,271	135,057	79,343	1,282	3,932	4,814

Table 91.—Selected statistics for public school districts enrolling more than 20,000 pupils, by state: 1993–94—Continued

Name of district, by state	State	Enrollment, fall 1993	Class-room teachers,[1] fall 1993	Pupils per teacher, fall 1993	Percent minority pupils, fall 1993[4]	Number of schools, 1993-94	Number of 1992-93 graduates[2]	Revenue and expenditures,[3] 1992-93 (in thousands of dollars)									
								Revenue receipts				Total expenditures	Current expenditures				Current expenditure per pupil 1992-93[4]
								Total	Federal	State	Local		Total	Instruction	Capital outlay	Interest on school debt	
1	2	3	4	5	6	7	8	9	10	11	12	13	14	15	16	17	18
Evansville-Vanderburgh	Ind.	23,826	1,401	17.0	15.1	38	1,345	130,977	8,821	62,214	59,942	119,041	116,390	72,108	1,936	715	4,926
Fort Wayne Community Schools	Ind.	31,726	1,729	18.3	27.9	53	1,784	169,759	12,472	83,811	73,476	161,759	156,710	94,760	4,152	911	4,906
Gary Community Schools	Ind.	24,150	1,245	19.4	98.7	43	1,269	140,312	15,759	86,029	38,524	134,781	128,888	75,103	3,424	2,469	5,321
Indianapolis Public Schools	Ind.	46,656	2,661	17.5	56.1	92	1,612	335,857	32,241	188,706	114,910	282,748	273,290	151,705	7,793	1,665	5,852
South Bend Community Schools	Ind.	21,469	1,249	17.2	38.3	36	1,231	123,938	5,927	69,012	48,999	107,149	102,274	61,058	3,992	883	4,779
Des Moines Independent Community	Iowa	31,652	2,622	12.1	21.6	65	1,522	177,770	13,223	89,352	75,195	170,385	166,953	108,736	2,616	816	5,334
Kansas City Unified	Kans.	22,096	1,250	17.7	64.5	48	769	122,365	11,635	72,149	38,581	122,341	119,131	66,904	3,201	9	5,415
Shawnee Mission Unified	Kans.	31,827	2,046	15.6	8.8	57	1,986	153,784	3,600	47,565	102,619	177,252	149,744	91,270	25,355	2,153	4,749
Wichita Unified	Kans.	47,132	2,818	16.7	36.7	104	2,171	250,000	13,750	92,152	144,098	258,266	252,934	149,209	5,280	52	5,290
Fayette County	Ky.	33,087	2,042	16.2	25.0	57	1,611	146,427	9,306	65,654	71,467	141,274	134,882	76,629	2,903	3,489	4,119
Jefferson County	Ky.	93,529	5,381	17.4	32.3	150	4,805	470,432	55,779	210,937	203,716	422,239	406,824	248,003	8,764	6,651	4,354
Caddo Parish	La.	51,255	2,955	17.3	60.3	76	2,237	215,528	22,395	117,671	75,462	208,213	200,882	118,756	4,124	3,207	3,878
Calcasieu Parish	La.	34,373	2,094	16.4	31.3	58	1,575	145,001	12,020	74,322	58,659	139,699	130,939	78,683	4,182	4,578	3,855
East Baton Rouge Parish	La.	63,179	3,844	16.4	60.7	103	2,680	276,519	26,832	153,971	95,516	273,383	270,580	161,029	2,803	0	4,286
Jefferson Parish	La.	57,270	3,370	17.0	50.2	82	2,254	274,785	26,635	129,562	118,588	272,875	249,426	155,870	2,932	20,517	4,353
Lafayette Parish	La.	31,108	1,743	17.8	34.5	40	1,463	123,086	11,816	67,385	43,885	117,613	111,509	69,782	3,016	3,088	3,629
Orleans Parish	La.	85,983	4,590	18.7	93.7	121	2,849	376,431	65,740	184,482	126,209	387,001	366,556	232,380	11,310	9,135	4,341
Rapides Parish	La.	24,488	1,603	15.3	42.5	53	1,178	114,785	14,528	62,136	38,121	110,300	103,102	59,800	2,311	4,887	4,144
Saint Tammany Parish	La.	30,487	1,861	16.4	16.5	44	1,300	125,415	7,254	67,606	50,555	123,548	116,401	71,222	3,127	4,020	3,971
Terrebonne Parish	La.	22,033	1,193	18.5	34.3	43	908	73,161	8,864	45,363	18,934	72,623	70,351	42,852	665	1,607	3,242
Anne Arundel County	Md.	69,020	3,884	17.8	20.1	113	3,864	416,890	18,186	162,785	235,919	352,719	344,926	203,014	3,772	4,021	5,116
Baltimore City	Md.	113,354	6,191	18.3	84.2	178	3,315	665,348	85,031	377,347	202,970	558,703	533,834	331,332	20,620	4,249	4,824
Baltimore County	Md.	96,402	5,688	16.9	26.1	156	5,392	595,527	18,181	199,097	378,249	523,315	509,472	303,645	10,892	2,951	5,462
Carroll County	Md.	23,730	1,306	18.2	3.6	36	1,455	139,229	4,309	64,806	70,114	112,951	109,786	64,984	1,747	1,418	4,739
Charles County	Md.	20,101	1,201	16.7	27.3	32	1,117	120,918	5,393	54,715	60,810	103,149	101,570	55,748	1,579		5,196
Frederick County	Md.	30,451	1,817	16.8	10.1	49	1,745	189,441	5,890	76,643	106,908	146,252	139,785	82,570	4,104	2,363	4,771
Harford County	Md.	34,775	2,010	17.3	15.5	47	1,758	193,855	8,356	98,471	87,028	158,368	154,045	93,600	3,717	606	4,558
Howard County	Md.	34,416	2,060	16.7	23.3	55	2,073	263,318	4,093	73,910	185,315	204,628	191,592	110,770	8,261	4,775	5,813
Montgomery County	Md.	113,429	6,551	17.3	42.0	178	6,587	925,026	29,124	187,550	708,352	771,737	732,016	449,220	20,712	19,009	6,652
Prince George's County	Md.	115,918	6,356	18.2	78.2	175	6,240	717,115	42,833	317,520	356,762	616,216	611,422	333,285	4,377	417	5,405
Boston City	Mass.	63,738	—	—	80.7	117	2,840	489,025	49,588	117,680	321,757	455,828	441,600	276,723	3,145	11,083	7,076
Springfield City	Mass.	24,113	—	—	67.6	43	1,018	156,671	13,335	107,307	36,029	110,300	106,797	57,962	745	2,758	4,434
Worcester Public Schools	Mass.	21,924	—	—	40.2	49	757	133,703	14,339	59,684	59,680	117,660	115,273	75,764	584	1,803	5,386
Detroit Public Schools	Mich.	173,295	7,799	22.2	93.4	262	6,751	1,049,094	131,372	631,911	285,811	1,020,988	990,486	536,289	9,145	21,357	5,748
Flint City	Mich.	26,206	1,153	22.7	71.3	43	1,097	174,392	17,209	80,408	76,775	172,618	170,605	73,990	2,013	0	6,410
Grand Rapids Public Schools	Mich.	27,092	1,144	23.7	71.8	75	0	184,484	21,939	49,775	112,770	172,153	162,043	73,131	4,280	5,830	6,019
Lansing City	Mich.	20,503	939	21.8	48.3	42	819	133,744	7,405	41,915	84,424	139,663	134,240	69,615	3,645	1,778	6,438
Utica Community	Mich.	23,350	1,080	21.6	3.9	37	1,667	134,347	2,228	2,630	129,489	132,126	134,327	74,487	3,256	4,543	5,080
Anoka Junction	Minn.	37,777	1,988	19.0	5.9	47	2,140	206,268	5,250	115,757	85,261	216,093	199,679	115,489	12,664	3,750	5,467
Minneapolis Special	Minn.	44,533	2,844	15.7	59.0	138	1,664	320,995	26,030	93,693	201,272	317,073	291,832	174,756	18,699	6,542	6,887
Osseo ISD 279	Minn.	20,998	1,155	18.2	12.6	30	1,051	120,249	2,590	60,699	56,960	121,773	112,638	68,923	3,442	5,693	5,453
Rosemount	Minn.	24,152	1,289	18.7	6.8	27	1,229	117,339	1,967	64,518	50,854	114,594	98,766	63,867	6,759	9,069	4,283
Saint Paul Independent	Minn.	39,239	2,225	17.6	49.4	128	1,566	261,606	23,809	121,737	116,060	252,978	235,038	145,427	13,388	4,552	6,173
Jackson Municipal Schools	Miss.	33,444	—	—	83.8	59	1,439	138,230	16,886	55,187	66,157	132,281	125,182	73,961	2,094	5,005	3,739
Kansas City	Mo.	36,599	2,891	12.7	75.5	83	1,168	338,080	22,087	169,752	146,241	311,388	297,768	135,625	13,401	219	8,316
Parkway	Mo.	22,690	1,259	18.0	25.0	27	1,592	117,815	1,885	27,950	87,980	129,280	125,819	79,713	1,176	2,285	5,552
Saint Louis City	Mo.	41,213	3,105	13.3	80.7	110	1,175	312,624	38,620	148,080	125,924	286,982	274,002	143,693	5,096	7,884	6,706
Springfield	Mo.	24,632	1,372	18.0	6.3	56	1,377	87,626	6,705	31,136	49,785	97,046	92,708	58,028	1,569	2,769	3,813
Lincoln	Neb.	30,017	2,019	14.9	10.9	48	1,668	176,098	9,463	46,435	120,200	162,662	157,821	109,171	3,702	1,139	5,307
Omaha City	Neb.	43,609	2,660	16.4	36.6	82	2,367	238,993	19,427	82,383	137,183	240,481	214,572	133,176	20,946	4,963	4,972
Clark County	Nev.	145,327	7,189	20.2	34.9	193	5,891	448,790	33,473	226,864	188,453	671,517	616,436	363,986	17,080	38,001	4,526
Washoe County	Nev.	43,715	2,289	19.1	23.2	75	1,910	117,869	7,959	52,383	57,527	183,108	174,926	112,429	3,435	4,747	4,159
Jersey City	N.J.	30,697	1,995	15.4	89.5	37	1,133	291,098	27,366	178,019	85,713	258,297	244,200	144,683	7,543	6,554	8,543
Newark	N.J.	46,835	3,428	13.7	90.7	80	1,659	543,953	55,407	401,372	87,174	473,202	455,176	261,353	12,313	5,713	9,501
Paterson City	N.J.	22,617	1,643	13.8	92.4	35	715	232,012	20,957	170,968	40,087	193,284	188,403	114,831	4,881	0	8,522
Albuquerque	N.M.	92,697	5,433	17.1	52.8	130	4,403	379,960	29,355	313,125	37,480	354,514	354,227	202,533	287	0	3,864

Table 91.—Selected statistics for public school districts enrolling more than 20,000 pupils, by state: 1993-94—Continued

Name of district, by state	State	Enrollment, fall 1993	Classroom teachers, fall 1993	Pupils per teacher, fall 1993	Percent minority pupils, fall 1993	Number of schools, 1993-94	Number of 1992-93 graduates[2]	Revenue and expenditures,[3] 1992-93 (in thousands of dollars) — Revenue receipts: Total	Federal	State	Local	Total expenditures	Current expenditures: Total	Instruction	Capital outlay	Interest on school debt	Current expenditure per pupil 1992-93[4]
1	2	3	4	5	6	7	8	9	10	11	12	13	14	15	16	17	18
Las Cruces	N.M.	21,857	1,139	19.2	63.0	33	1,040	86,658	8,628	67,099	10,931	78,082	75,415	40,467	447	2,220	3,582
Buffalo City	N.Y.	48,128	3,153	15.3	62.8	74	2,062	374,384	41,937	253,937	78,510	360,014	352,950	223,137	4,695	2,369	7,308
New York City	N.Y.	1,005,521	55,353	18.2	82.5	1,064	34,765	7,484,189	776,099	3,036,036	3,672,054	7,589,571	7,301,451	5,020,100	74,070	214,050	7,420
Rochester City	N.Y.	35,568	2,461	14.5	76.9	55	842	328,171	28,930	165,054	134,187	314,870	304,705	184,143	8,339	1,826	8,688
Syracuse City	N.Y.	23,337	1,469	15.9	46.4	34	835	194,133	15,905	116,676	61,552	185,635	177,785	109,694	2,960	4,890	7,636
Yonkers City	N.Y.	21,271	1,333	16.0	70.3	33	685	204,176	14,663	63,897	125,616	201,963	194,556	120,826	3,360	4,047	9,610
Buncombe County	N.C.	23,384	1,384	16.9	7.1	35	1,311	112,218	6,568	72,822	32,828	105,563	100,703	62,652	1,625	3,235	4,402
Charlotte-Mecklenburg	N.C.	82,842	4,851	17.1	45.0	121	4,104	414,483	26,265	236,416	151,802	405,667	383,828	227,917	9,795	12,044	4,779
Cumberland County	N.C.	49,247	2,896	17.0	50.2	69	2,614	196,363	24,324	132,388	39,651	196,277	191,760	120,954	4,517	0	4,002
Durham County	N.C.	27,545	1,954	14.1	56.4	44	1,389	155,292	8,617	82,344	64,331	142,059	130,583	78,342	3,998	7,478	4,783
Forsyth County-Winston Salem	N.C.	38,609	2,783	13.9	39.4	57	2,103	194,051	11,422	113,651	68,978	191,294	185,045	115,505	2,940	3,309	4,863
Gaston County	N.C.	28,858	1,770	16.3	19.8	54	1,566	122,775	8,369	84,051	30,355	116,220	112,970	74,137	2,632	618	3,875
Guilford County	N.C.	54,451	3,519	15.5	40.3	92	3,110	134,701	6,006	76,304	52,391	127,496	122,344	73,312	3,743	1,409	4,709
New Hanover County Schools	N.C.	20,363	1,266	16.1	31.2	30	1,194	96,174	7,401	58,160	30,613	85,950	83,402	51,515	1,822	726	4,251
Robeson County	N.C.	23,414	1,389	16.9	76.5	41	1,205	102,531	18,423	68,389	15,719	98,947	96,625	60,388	1,874	448	4,174
Wake County	N.C.	73,263	4,769	15.4	31.0	94	3,740	458,342	15,630	195,076	247,636	327,487	313,059	190,617	3,455	10,973	4,465
Akron City	Ohio	33,495	1,997	16.8	44.4	63	1,767	193,668	15,383	79,549	98,736	176,967	175,257	101,806	1,631	79	5,200
Cincinnati City	Ohio	52,381	3,058	17.1	65.9	83	1,848	481,547	29,701	130,458	321,388	339,785	331,983	202,000	3,390	4,412	6,444
Cleveland City	Ohio	73,633	4,205	17.5	77.6	129	2,254	696,062	64,556	230,558	400,948	498,573	479,861	268,904	6,987	11,725	6,765
Columbus City	Ohio	63,877	4,096	15.6	53.9	144	2,331	432,326	38,604	145,545	248,177	414,247	398,718	213,814	7,385	8,144	6,182
Dayton City	Ohio	28,886	1,775	16.3	64.8	50	838	191,895	24,870	80,921	86,104	172,229	169,752	98,368	2,451	26	5,773
Toledo City	Ohio	39,238	2,287	17.2	47.0	61	1,640	244,221	22,521	113,742	107,958	245,861	240,584	125,453	4,831	446	6,079
Oklahoma City	Okla.	38,052	2,238	17.0	60.0	81	1,271	160,501	18,655	87,853	53,993	156,294	154,242	86,265	1,920	132	4,132
Tulsa	Okla.	41,341	2,458	16.8	43.0	80	1,697	175,902	14,914	86,245	74,743	181,497	168,572	91,044	11,215	1,710	4,057
Beaverton	Oreg.	27,488	1,250	22.0	15.7	40	1,615	143,485	3,728	29,842	109,915	152,021	138,281	84,802	13,171	569	5,091
Portland	Oreg.	54,073	2,810	19.2	30.4	101	2,813	374,192	26,812	113,461	233,919	376,211	363,060	204,134	3,426	9,725	6,604
Salem-Keizer	Oreg.	30,930	1,411	21.9	13.1	48	1,617	164,134	8,714	79,490	75,930	168,448	152,088	94,196	14,302	2,058	5,060
Philadelphia	Penn.	207,667	10,489	19.8	78.3	259	8,590	1,388,395	204,151	654,546	529,698	1,340,118	1,303,730	793,034	6,402	29,986	6,470
Pittsburgh City	Penn.	40,107	2,443	16.4	55.1	83	2,253	365,632	31,867	127,011	206,754	348,402	339,839	187,068	2,405	6,158	8,402
Providence City	R.I.	22,832	—	—	70.6	36	879	140,245	13,774	64,440	62,031	130,375	127,444	85,693	696	2,235	5,785
Aiken County	S.C.	24,802	1,359	18.3	34.6	35	1,382	104,527	8,257	55,523	40,747	97,786	94,085	57,498	2,136	1,565	3,790
Berkeley County	S.C.	28,181	1,503	18.7	34.8	37	1,475	112,039	13,265	64,095	34,679	106,953	102,475	56,200	2,517	1,961	3,611
Charleston County	S.C.	44,883	2,672	16.8	58.9	72	1,870	199,660	22,898	87,506	89,256	191,534	180,909	111,549	4,518	6,107	4,036
Greenville County	S.C.	53,280	3,192	16.7	28.0	92	2,817	233,155	15,315	106,410	111,430	223,937	213,535	127,600	5,258	5,144	4,055
Horry County	S.C.	24,746	1,551	16.0	31.0	36	1,441	122,805	11,870	39,134	71,801	116,022	108,991	65,745	1,284	5,747	4,383
Richland	S.C.	27,014	1,786	15.1	75.9	51	1,336	144,319	14,828	53,650	75,841	135,193	130,252	72,617	2,475	2,466	4,816
Chattanooga City	Tenn.	20,284	1,188	17.1	62.2	37	1,003	93,467	12,253	36,705	44,509	89,707	84,779	54,405	3,485	1,443	4,186
Hamilton County	Tenn.	23,891	1,371	17.4	5.3	40	1,252	87,689	4,974	40,691	42,024	87,660	84,371	57,208	1,523	1,766	3,495
Knox County	Tenn.	51,742	2,979	17.4	14.3	86	2,822	222,555	20,674	89,217	112,664	203,033	197,401	125,152	3,474	2,158	3,827
Memphis City	Tenn.	105,978	5,387	19.7	82.4	162	5,239	444,620	65,070	185,997	193,553	432,227	420,155	277,060	10,371	1,701	3,945
Nashville-Davidson County	Tenn.	72,483	4,439	16.3	44.0	119	2,926	312,339	44,414	114,123	173,802	304,214	292,085	194,065	4,971	7,158	4,199
Shelby County	Tenn.	41,994	2,174	19.3	19.5	41	2,183	133,577	6,019	67,450	60,108	130,670	122,787	84,689	4,169	3,714	2,976
Sumner County	Tenn.	20,424	1,105	18.5	7.7	33	1,285	70,191	3,856	36,032	30,303	67,029	63,693	43,003	808	2,528	3,122
Aldine ISD	Texas	43,539	2,687	16.2	75.3	43	1,530	224,028	15,614	120,889	87,525	185,032	154,041	94,098	26,671	4,320	3,608
Alief ISD	Texas	33,315	1,996	16.7	73.2	29	1,246	178,707	8,356	77,303	93,048	151,100	118,296	72,493	23,736	9,068	3,669
Amarillo ISD	Texas	28,864	1,740	16.6	37.5	49	1,211	134,123	11,760	68,406	53,957	108,947	102,421	61,474	3,232	3,294	3,586
Arlington ISD	Texas	48,667	2,737	17.8	33.9	57	2,258	196,290	9,978	41,308	145,004	197,290	150,813	94,773	33,372	13,105	3,140
Austin ISD	Texas	71,664	4,468	16.0	59.0	102	2,884	407,138	30,524	117,946	258,668	334,088	300,014	166,633	15,938	18,136	4,297
Beaumont ISD	Texas	20,258	1,263	16.0	70.2	34	714	113,458	12,235	36,457	64,766	90,126	87,551	48,466	2,323	252	4,295
Brownsville ISD	Texas	39,402	2,476	15.9	97.2	40	1,628	249,307	38,420	189,129	21,758	183,298	161,348	100,835	19,779	2,171	4,140
Clear Creek ISD	Texas	24,496	1,397	17.5	24.0	27	1,182	112,792	2,468	13,839	96,485	118,743	91,458	58,252	22,124	5,161	3,858
Conroe ISD	Texas	26,140	1,729	15.1	19.1	33	1,151	135,740	5,495	64,070	66,175	128,025	100,863	58,252	20,566	6,596	3,967
Corpus Christi	Texas	42,374	2,564	16.5	74.1	62	1,729	224,888	20,749	126,822	77,317	196,474	172,606	106,379	16,946	6,922	4,113
Cypress-Fairbanks ISD	Texas	48,252	2,925	16.5	29.8	47	2,072	227,156	4,901	72,802	149,453	234,706	204,288	103,387	16,794	13,624	4,408
Dallas ISD	Texas	142,652	8,530	16.7	86.3	196	4,707	757,844	99,140	119,296	539,408	619,032	580,915	338,310	22,025	16,092	4,158
Ector County ISD	Texas	28,188	1,645	17.1	52.5	41	1,071	134,951	12,231	55,199	67,521	105,834	101,060	56,965	3,491	1,283	3,593
El Paso ISD	Texas	64,141	3,877	16.5	80.2	79	3,027	336,098	41,227	202,108	92,763	303,798	262,653	158,697	33,770	7,375	4,088

Table 91.—Selected statistics for public school districts enrolling more than 20,000 pupils, by state: 1993–94—Continued

Name of district, by state	State	Enrollment, fall 1993	Classroom teachers,[1] fall 1993	Pupils per teacher, fall 1993	Percent minority pupils, fall 1993	Number of schools, 1993–94	Number of 1992–93 graduates[2]	Revenue receipts				Total expenditures,[3] 1992–93 (in thousands of dollars)	Current expenditures			Capital outlay	Interest on school debt	Current expenditure per pupil 1992–93[4]
								Total	Federal	State	Local	Total expenditures	Total	Instruction			
1	2	3	4	5	6	7	8	9	10	11	12	13	14	15	16	17	18
Fort Bend ISD	Texas	41,981	2,331	18.0	54.5	39	1,802	185,988	6,623	85,972	93,393	208,669	177,028	93,121	21,668	9,973	4,359
Fort Worth ISD	Texas	72,114	4,063	17.7	69.6	129	2,466	397,554	41,537	185,459	170,558	322,362	302,970	170,664	11,237	8,155	4,263
Garland ISD	Texas	41,134	2,283	18.0	35.7	58	1,851	182,869	8,703	82,993	91,173	159,576	136,828	81,222	13,417	9,331	3,384
Houston ISD	Texas	200,445	11,410	17.6	87.6	256	6,773	1,096,666	120,455	345,368	630,843	946,762	797,767	455,490	130,478	18,517	4,029
Humble ISD	Texas	21,306	1,309	16.3	17.4	24	1,142	104,802	3,149	44,887	56,766	118,687	77,371	45,520	34,876	6,440	3,726
Irving ISD	Texas	25,435	1,439	17.7	47.8	31	978	117,934	7,323	19,263	91,348	129,667	99,894	56,053	21,299	8,474	4,018
Katy ISD	Texas	22,537	1,276	17.7	19.0	24	1,102	104,225	2,919	30,793	70,513	101,261	83,168	49,195	10,667	7,426	3,840
Killeen ISD	Texas	26,793	1,547	17.3	56.2	37	841	122,227	19,461	85,579	17,187	105,444	87,394	51,153	15,846	2,204	3,554
Klein ISD	Texas	28,057	1,742	16.1	28.5	27	1,649	139,581	4,360	69,112	66,109	136,296	109,034	64,856	22,076	5,186	3,932
Laredo ISD	Texas	23,871	1,382	17.3	98.1	28	1,150	140,224	20,956	105,917	13,351	99,374	90,338	50,244	7,737	1,299	3,771
Lewisville ISD	Texas	24,804	1,525	16.3	15.1	32	1,095	107,157	3,674	39,073	64,410	109,767	78,919	48,655	22,479	8,369	3,412
Lubbock ISD	Texas	30,571	2,069	14.8	53.5	58	1,391	170,119	15,560	59,426	95,133	150,406	132,972	77,198	12,308	5,126	4,304
McAllen ISD	Texas	21,691	1,411	15.4	88.3	30	1,087	148,321	13,296	103,987	31,038	99,908	93,067	55,582	4,125	2,716	4,299
Mesquite ISD	Texas	28,185	1,484	19.0	23.6	36	1,183	123,919	5,485	64,615	53,819	99,754	89,143	52,065	1,289	9,322	3,264
Midland ISD	Texas	22,799	1,291	17.7	45.0	35	938	102,713	5,475	38,849	58,389	93,725	78,613	46,664	12,605	2,507	3,537
North East ISD	Texas	43,122	2,641	16.3	41.5	49	2,529	219,290	11,380	78,004	129,906	172,809	163,749	99,236	6,964	2,096	3,873
Northside ISD	Texas	54,992	3,515	15.6	58.2	76	3,010	286,594	17,686	149,071	119,837	239,061	204,247	127,090	20,253	14,561	3,785
Pasadena ISD	Texas	39,265	2,230	17.6	55.7	50	1,586	195,436	13,075	104,123	78,238	173,100	151,679	89,046	17,526	3,895	3,861
Plano ISD	Texas	34,956	2,120	16.5	18.6	44	2,068	180,226	4,417	18,507	157,302	179,357	141,553	87,572	26,038	11,766	4,277
Richardson ISD	Texas	33,495	2,050	16.3	35.2	50	1,992	168,928	5,932	20,380	142,616	152,342	137,451	82,382	8,686	6,205	4,141
Round Rock ISD	Texas	22,887	1,554	14.7	23.2	31	1,162	117,135	4,019	53,599	59,517	106,944	89,304	53,711	11,433	6,207	4,098
San Antonio ISD	Texas	59,544	3,646	16.3	94.1	107	2,063	381,675	56,897	234,935	89,843	302,533	291,702	172,586	8,638	2,193	4,873
Spring Branch ISD	Texas	27,663	1,784	15.5	55.8	36	395	166,326	12,157	22,710	131,459	148,905	135,282	71,075	7,212	6,411	4,937
Ysleta ISD	Texas	49,388	1,298	38.0	86.8	63	2,674	271,494	28,847	189,690	52,957	215,173	196,256	116,256	14,074	5,070	3,978
Alpine	Utah	41,601	1,594	26.1	4.1	47	2,220	133,434	7,606	86,204	39,624	129,152	120,708	71,237	4,568	3,876	2,994
Davis County	Utah	57,933	2,311	25.1	4.8	69	3,319	185,724	12,988	122,459	50,277	181,655	163,938	104,016	9,935	7,782	2,870
Granite	Utah	79,746	3,247	24.6	10.7	100	4,032	249,749	17,646	154,427	77,676	237,874	227,576	147,732	7,029	3,269	2,841
Jordan	Utah	70,256	2,808	25.0	5.4	69	3,749	237,583	10,758	139,246	87,579	221,297	210,427	125,947	8,839	2,031	3,057
Salt Lake City	Utah	26,077	1,157	22.5	28.2	40	1,057	116,239	12,284	37,031	66,924	111,315	102,083	56,970	9,232	0	3,930
Weber County	Utah	26,987	1,093	24.7	5.6	36	1,659	88,373	6,000	56,681	25,692	85,141	79,003	52,471	3,018	3,120	2,961
Chesapeake City	Va.	33,182	—	—	35.4	41	1,695	141,238	9,585	63,583	68,070	153,914	147,519	92,050	4,416	1,979	4,663
Chesterfield County	Va.	47,919	—	—	19.9	53	2,704	208,700	6,787	86,079	115,834	213,219	198,682	123,453	3,143	11,394	4,228
Fairfax County	Va.	135,413	—	—	32.1	198	8,814	854,601	26,262	109,565	718,774	868,404	830,487	467,767	12,664	25,253	6,224
Hampton City	Va.	22,991	—	—	54.0	34	1,272	99,362	9,687	45,341	44,334	105,255	103,145	65,737	1,951	159	4,521
Henrico County	Va.	34,952	—	—	33.4	54	2,106	172,516	6,708	53,334	112,474	180,567	170,942	104,272	4,495	5,130	4,985
Newport News City	Va.	31,894	—	—	54.5	37	1,465	140,532	13,436	64,680	62,416	149,798	144,881	89,210	2,068	2,849	4,808
Norfolk City	Va.	36,450	—	—	66.2	56	1,282	198,500	26,932	77,972	93,596	199,630	193,067	109,461	4,548	2,015	5,209
Prince William County	Va.	44,881	—	—	27.2	61	2,590	241,384	10,105	84,068	147,211	252,032	239,513	140,849	5,025	7,494	5,338
Richmond City	Va.	27,465	—	—	90.8	59	952	208,128	21,361	51,062	135,705	200,727	192,820	107,078	4,507	3,400	7,035
Virginia Beach City	Va.	74,880	—	—	28.8	80	3,680	312,751	25,861	140,694	146,196	339,620	313,479	202,478	17,993	8,148	4,234
Edmonds	Wash.	20,415	988	20.7	17.0	37	—	115,018	4,596	81,856	28,566	115,774	103,305	60,629	8,391	4,078	5,120
Kent	Wash.	23,817	1,153	20.7	18.0	36	—	129,703	4,805	87,889	37,009	126,416	111,992	67,450	7,694	6,730	4,827
Lake Washington	Wash.	23,380	1,097	21.3	13.0	40	—	150,199	3,350	100,461	46,388	136,358	118,155	72,478	8,101	10,102	4,934
Seattle	Wash.	45,159	2,303	19.6	58.0	108	—	309,544	31,506	180,016	98,022	303,017	285,342	156,684	17,610	65	6,416
Spokane	Wash.	31,128	1,601	19.4	12.2	65	—	167,918	11,511	122,798	33,609	168,417	160,978	98,156	3,674	3,765	5,156
Tacoma	Wash.	31,083	1,752	17.7	36.6	69	—	209,615	21,242	132,716	55,657	196,869	184,037	110,099	11,447	1,385	5,897
Kanawha County	W. Va.	33,644	2,080	16.2	10.1	88	2,203	174,558	13,209	102,162	59,187	169,106	186,125	95,828	2,981	0	4,883
Madison Metropolitan	Wis.	24,452	1,710	14.3	25.4	51	1,363	181,782	4,887	31,679	145,216	179,773	173,526	110,849	2,782	3,465	7,151
Milwaukee City	Wis.	95,259	4,936	19.3	73.0	150	3,036	730,107	61,978	366,716	301,413	655,441	648,147	397,020	7,294	0	6,873
Racine Unified	Wis.	22,260	1,379	16.1	34.3	37	1,087	137,804	6,190	66,487	65,127	139,518	135,687	86,988	1,268	2,563	5,961

[1] Data exclude teachers reported as working in school district offices rather than in schools.

[2] Includes all categories of high school completers such as GEDs.

[3] Expenditures by local school districts only. Excludes expenditures by state education agencies for local school districts.

[4] Current expenditure per pupil based on fall enrollment collected by the Bureau of the Census, not the enrollment figure shown in column 3.

ISD—Independent school district.

—Data not available or not applicable.

NOTE.—Data on finances and per pupil expenditures prepared by the Bureau of the Census.

SOURCE: U.S. Department of Education, National Center for Education Statistics, Common Core of Data survey; and U.S. Department of Commerce, "Survey of Local Government Finances." (This table was prepared July 1995.)

Table 92.—Enrollment of the 130 largest public school districts: Fall 1994

Name of school district	State	Rank order [1]	Enrollment, fall 1994	Name of school district	State	Rank order [1]	Enrollment, fall 1994
1	2	3	4	1	2	3	4
New York City	N.Y.	1	1,022,534	Fulton County	Ga.	66	53,143
Los Angeles Unified	Calif.	2	632,973	Cincinnati City	Ohio	67	52,852
City of Chicago Schools	Ill.	3	407,241	Knox County	Tenn.	68	52,285
Dade County	Fla.	4	321,615	Oakland Unified	Calif.	69	51,706
Philadelphia City	Penn.	5	208,710	Arlington	Texas	70	50,293
Houston	Texas	6	202,149	Cumberland County	N.C.	71	49,995
Broward County	Fla.	7	199,255	Caddo Parish	La.	72	49,609
Hawaii	Hawaii	8	183,869	Lee County	Fla.	73	49,413
Detroit City	Mich.	9	170,855	Cypress-Fairbanks	Texas	74	49,364
Clark County	Nev.	10	156,348	Sacramento City Unified	Calif.	75	49,282
Dallas ISD	Texas	11	145,019	Santa Ana Unified	Calif.	76	48,870
Hillsborough County	Fla.	12	138,575	Chesterfield County	Va.	77	48,050
Fairfax County	Va.	13	137,646	Anchorage	Alaska	78	47,655
San Diego City Unified	Calif.	14	128,555	Buffalo City	N.Y.	79	47,595
Palm Beach County	Fla.	15	127,519	Ysleta	Texas	80	47,572
Duval County	Fla.	16	121,362	San Juan Unified	Calif.	81	47,080
Orange County	Fla.	17	118,666	Seattle	Wash.	82	46,565
Prince George's County	Md.	18	118,478	Newark City	N.J.	83	46,541
Montgomery County	Md.	19	117,082	Indianapolis	Ind.	84	46,038
Baltimore City	Md.	20	113,428	Wichita	Kansas	85	46,002
Memphis City	Tenn.	21	108,643	Washoe County	Nevada	86	45,752
Pinellas County	Fla.	22	102,170	Prince William County	Va.	87	45,675
Baltimore County	Md.	23	99,231	Minneapolis	Minn.	88	45,187
Milwaukee	Wisc.	24	98,009	Escambia County	Fla.	89	44,765
Jefferson County	Ky.	25	93,407	Charleston County	S.C.	90	44,669
Albuquerque	N.M.	26	89,001	San Bernardino City Unified	Calif.	91	44,250
Orleans Parish	La.	27	86,028	Shelby County	Tenn.	92	43,843
Charlotte-Mecklenburg	N.C.	28	86,023	Aldine	Texas	93	43,818
Jefferson County	Colo.	29	84,018	Omaha	Nebr.	94	43,577
DeKalb County	Ga.	30	83,722	North East	Texas	95	43,484
Cobb County	Ga.	31	80,479	Fort Bend	Texas	96	43,115
District of Columbia	D.C.	32	80,450	Garland	Texas	97	42,433
Gwinnett County	Ga.	33	80,220	Garden Grove Unified	Calif.	98	42,423
Granite District	Utah	34	78,590	Alpine District	Utah	99	42,014
Long Beach Unified	Calif.	35	78,127	Corpus Christi	Texas	100	41,902
Fresno Unified	Calif.	36	77,023	Birmingham City	Ala.	101	41,839
Wake County Schools	N.C.	37	76,922	St. Louis City	Mo.	102	41,054
Virginia Beach City	Va.	38	75,926	Tulsa	Okla.	103	40,801
Cleveland City	Ohio	39	73,803	St. Paul	Minn.	104	40,732
Austin	Texas	40	73,191	Jefferson County	Ala.	105	40,422
Fort Worth	Texas	41	72,342	Pasco County	Fla.	106	40,114
Nashville-Davidson County	Tenn.	42	71,574	Brownsville	Texas	107	40,111
Polk County	Fla.	43	71,297	Pittsburgh	Penn.	108	39,716
Jordan District	Utah	44	70,761	Forsyth County	N.C.	109	39,554
Anne Arundel County	Md.	45	70,588	Pasadena	Texas	110	39,189
Mesa Unified	Ariz.	46	69,160	Clayton County	Ga.	111	39,149
Columbus City	Ohio	47	65,809	Okla City	Okla.	112	39,053
El Paso	Texas	48	64,880	Toledo City	Ohio	113	39,021
Mobile County	Ala.	49	64,645	Anoka-Hennepin	Minn.	114	38,344
Brevard County	Fla.	50	64,595	Kansas City	Mo.	115	36,598
Denver County	Colo.	51	62,773	Norfolk City	Va.	116	36,479
Tucson Unified District	Ariz.	52	62,624	Plano	Texas	117	36,426
Boston	Mass.	53	61,489	Howard County	Md.	118	36,125
East Baton Rouge Parish	La.	54	61,460	Rochester City	N.Y.	119	36,080
San Francisco Unified	Calif.	55	61,340	Harford County	Md.	120	35,956
San Antonio	Texas	56	60,419	Henrico County	Va.	121	35,934
Atlanta City	Ga.	57	59,560	Richmond County	Ga.	122	35,918
Davis District	Utah	58	58,122	Chatham County	Ga.	123	35,442
Jefferson Parish	La.	59	56,790	Montgomery County	Ala.	124	34,746
Northside	Texas	60	56,117	Cherry Creek	Colo.	125	34,714
Guilford County	N.C.	61	55,688	Alief	Texas	126	34,680
Volusia County	Fla.	62	55,530	Riverside Unified	Calif.	127	34,662
Portland	Oreg.	63	54,849	Calcasieu Parish	La.	128	34,487
Greenville County	S.C.	64	54,064	Mt. Diablo Unified	Calif.	129	34,410
Seminole County	Fla.	65	53,366	Chesapeake City	Va.	130	34,130

[1] Public school districts ranked by size of enrollment in fall 1994.
ISD=Independent School District.

SOURCE: U.S. Department of Education, National Center for Education Statistics, Common Core of Data survey. (This table was prepared September 1996.)

Table 93.—Public elementary and secondary schools, by type of school: 1967–68 to 1994–95

Year	Total, all public schools	Regular schools											Combined elementary/ secondary schools[6]	Other schools[7]
		Total[1]	Elementary schools				Secondary schools							
			Total[2]	Middle schools[3]	One-teacher schools	Other elementary schools	Total[4]	Junior high[5]	3-year or 4-year high schools	5-year or 6-year high schools	Other sec- ondary schools			
1	2	3	4	5	6	7	8	9	10	11	12		13	14
1967–68	—	94,197	67,186	—	4,146	63,040	23,318	7,437	10,751	4,650	480		3,693	—
1970–71	—	89,372	64,020	2,080	1,815	60,125	23,572	7,750	11,265	3,887	670		1,780	—
1972–73	—	88,864	62,942	2,308	1,475	59,159	23,919	7,878	11,550	3,962	529		2,003	—
1974–75	—	87,456	61,759	3,224	1,247	57,288	23,837	7,690	11,480	4,122	545		1,860	—
1975–76	88,597	87,034	61,704	3,916	1,166	56,622	23,792	7,521	11,572	4,113	586		1,538	1,563
1976–77	—	86,501	61,123	4,180	1,111	55,832	23,857	7,434	11,658	4,130	635		1,521	—
1978–79	—	84,816	60,312	5,879	1,056	53,377	22,834	6,282	11,410	4,429	713		1,670	—
1980–81	85,982	83,688	59,326	6,003	921	52,402	22,619	5,890	10,758	4,193	1,778		1,743	2,294
1982–83	84,740	82,039	58,051	6,875	798	50,378	22,383	5,948	11,678	4,067	690		1,605	2,701
1983–84	84,178	81,418	57,471	6,885	838	49,748	22,336	5,936	11,670	4,046	684		1,611	2,760
1984–85	84,007	81,147	57,231	6,893	825	49,513	22,320	5,916	11,671	4,021	712		1,596	2,860
1986–87	83,455	82,190	58,801	7,452	763	50,586	21,406	5,142	11,453	4,197	614		1,983	1,265
1987–88	83,248	82,248	59,311	7,641	729	50,941	20,758	4,900	11,279	4,048	531		2,179	1,000
1988–89	83,165	82,081	59,296	7,957	583	50,756	20,550	4,687	11,350	3,994	519		2,235	1,084
1989–90	83,425	82,396	59,757	8,272	630	50,855	20,359	4,512	11,492	3,812	543		2,280	1,029
1990–91	84,538	81,746	59,015	8,545	617	49,853	20,406	4,561	11,537	3,723	585		2,325	2,792
1991–92	84,578	81,859	59,258	8,829	569	49,860	20,120	4,298	11,528	3,699	595		2,481	2,719
1992–93	84,501	82,224	59,680	9,154	430	50,096	19,995	4,115	11,651	3,613	616		2,549	2,277
1993–94	85,393	82,785	60,052	9,573	442	50,037	20,059	3,970	11,858	3,595	636		2,674	2,608
1994–95	86,221	83,854	60,808	9,954	458	50,396	20,282	3,859	12,058	3,628	737		2,764	2,367

[1] Excludes special education, alternative, and other schools not classified by grade span.
[2] Includes schools beginning with grade 6 or below and with no grade higher than 8.
[3] Includes schools with grade spans beginning with 4, 5, or 6 and ending with grade 6, 7, or 8.
[4] Includes schools with no grade lower than 7.
[5] Includes schools with grades 7 and 8 or grades 7 through 9.
[6] Includes schools beginning with grade 6 or lower and ending with grade 9 or above.

[7] Includes special education, alternative, and other schools not classified by grade span.
[8] Because of revision in data collection procedures, figures not comparable to data for other years.
—Data not available.

SOURCE: U.S. Department of Education, National Center for Education Statistics, *Statistics of State School Systems;* and Common Core of Data surveys. (This table was prepared October 1996.)

Table 94.—Public elementary and secondary schools, by type and size of school: 1994–95

Enrollment size of school	Number of schools, by type					Enrollment, by type of school[1]				
	Total[2]	Elementary[3]	Secondary[4]	Combined elementary/ secondary[5]	Other[2]	Total[2]	Elementary[3]	Secondary[4]	Combined elementary/ secondary[5]	Other[2]
1	2	3	4	5	6	7	8	9	10	11
Total	86,221	60,808	20,282	2,764	2,367	44,031,369	28,619,677	14,138,843	1,139,741	133,108
Percent[6]	100.00	100.00	100.00	100.00	100.00	100.00	100.00	100.00	100.00	100.00
Under 100	8.95	5.93	13.11	29.41	59.34	0.83	0.62	0.92	3.16	16.04
100 to 199	9.65	9.05	10.58	14.22	15.51	2.78	2.92	2.22	5.06	14.20
200 to 299	11.38	12.35	8.67	10.38	10.22	5.52	6.64	3.09	6.26	15.92
300 to 399	13.62	16.00	7.56	8.07	6.11	9.15	11.89	3.77	6.79	13.54
400 to 499	13.43	15.91	7.29	7.02	2.94	11.60	15.19	4.68	7.64	8.42
500 to 599	11.78	13.77	6.94	6.73	1.65	12.40	16.00	5.46	8.89	5.59
600 to 699	8.72	9.75	6.37	5.57	1.29	10.83	13.37	5.92	8.72	5.34
700 to 799	6.05	6.40	5.53	3.91	0.59	8.69	10.14	5.95	7.07	2.74
800 to 999	7.26	6.78	9.18	5.61	0.94	12.39	12.72	11.80	12.15	5.42
1,000 to 1,499	6.12	3.67	13.75	5.79	1.06	14.06	9.01	24.10	16.91	7.71
1,500 to 1,999	1.90	0.33	6.65	2.13	0.24	6.26	1.18	16.36	8.84	2.72
2,000 to 2,999	0.97	0.05	3.79	0.80	0.00	4.39	0.26	12.77	4.48	0.00
3,000 or more	0.15	0.00	0.58	0.36	0.12	1.08	0.04	2.95	4.04	0
Average enrollment[6]	520	471	697	412	156	520	471	697	412	156

[1] These enrollment data should be regarded as approximations only. Totals differ from those reported in other tables because this table represents data reported by schools rather than by states or school districts. Excludes data for schools not reporting enrollment.
[2] Includes special education, alternative, and other schools not classified by grade span.
[3] Includes schools beginning with grade 6 or below and with no grade higher than 8.

[4] Includes schools with no grade lower than 7.
[5] Includes schools beginning with grade 6 or below and ending with grade 9 or above.
[6] Data are for schools reporting their enrollment size.

NOTE.—Because of rounding, details may not add to totals.

SOURCE: U.S. Department of Education, National Center for Education Statistics, Common Core of Data survey. (This table was prepared October 1996.)

Table 95.—Public elementary and secondary schools, by type and state: 1989–90 to 1994–95

State or other area	Total, all schools,[1] 1989–90	Total, all schools,[1] 1990–91	Total, all schools,[1] 1991–92	Total, all schools,[1] 1992–93	Total, all schools,[1] 1993–94	Number of schools, 1994–95							
						Total[1]	Elementary schools[2]	Secondary schools[3]	Combined elementary/secondary schools[4]				Other[5]
									Total	Prekindergarten, kindergarten, or first grade to grade 12	Other schools ending with grade 12	Other combined schools	
1	2	3	4	5	6	7	8	9	10	11	12	13	14
United States	**83,425**	**84,538**	**84,578**	**84,501**	**85,393**	**86,221**	**60,808**	**20,282**	**2,764**	**1,505**	**642**	**617**	**2,367**
Alabama	1,292	1,297	1,291	1,294	1,294	1,309	859	290	160	124	13	23	0
Alaska	495	498	495	494	496	498	185	87	206	157	6	43	20
Arizona	1,026	1,049	1,091	1,118	1,133	1,136	818	250	20	8	7	5	48
Arkansas	1,097	1,098	1,098	1,090	1,070	1,073	647	414	10	6	1	3	2
California	7,433	7,913	7,927	7,665	7,734	7,821	5,695	1,863	183	109	44	30	80
Colorado	1,337	1,344	1,397	1,399	1,419	1,460	1,031	343	22	5	9	8	64
Connecticut	983	985	988	993	1,000	1,045	784	206	48	15	8	25	7
Delaware	170	173	175	176	177	182	121	42	19	13	2	4	0
District of Columbia	184	181	180	181	173	175	120	37	4	0	0	4	14
Florida	2,505	2,516	2,517	2,594	2,615	2,733	1,906	471	350	189	82	79	6
Georgia	1,732	1,734	1,728	1,724	1,755	1,767	1,382	316	69	12	40	17	0
Hawaii	234	235	238	238	241	242	182	47	13	6	1	6	0
Idaho	574	582	597	605	603	608	380	202	19	11	2	6	7
Illinois	4,225	4,239	4,238	4,185	4,195	4,195	3,054	876	28	22	3	3	237
Indiana	1,923	1,915	1,908	1,902	1,912	1,912	1,390	430	33	14	10	9	59
Iowa	1,607	1,588	1,577	1,560	1,556	1,554	1,078	446	22	4	18	0	8
Kansas	1,459	1,477	1,472	1,483	1,482	1,491	1,046	427	14	7	3	4	4
Kentucky	1,385	1,400	1,400	1,395	1,372	1,374	991	338	2	0	1	1	43
Louisiana	1,536	1,533	1,518	1,453	1,459	1,459	999	315	119	94	14	11	26
Maine	748	747	743	742	706	733	552	130	16	9	5	2	35
Maryland	1,217	1,220	1,228	1,263	1,271	1,263	1,029	214	15	11	1	3	5
Massachusetts	1,817	1,842	1,764	1,772	1,791	1,831	1,437	335	27	17	6	4	32
Michigan	3,314	3,313	3,360	3,340	3,356	3,432	2,496	776	67	37	22	8	93
Minnesota	1,564	1,590	1,635	1,622	2,083	2,100	1,166	655	87	13	37	37	192
Mississippi	954	972	973	978	1,009	1,018	569	229	79	65	11	3	141
Missouri	2,151	2,199	2,205	2,188	2,217	2,234	1,432	574	33	3	21	9	195
Montana	758	900	898	899	900	899	537	362	0	0	0	0	0
Nebraska	1,524	1,506	1,495	1,454	1,427	1,419	1,012	363	21	15	3	3	23
Nevada	331	354	375	383	407	421	314	93	9	3	6	0	5
New Hampshire	444	439	449	450	461	458	355	99	4	3	0	1	0
New Jersey	2,264	2,272	2,284	2,292	2,287	2,295	1,786	387	5	2	2	1	117
New Mexico	658	681	686	700	709	715	533	169	4	1	1	2	9
New York	3,996	4,010	4,009	4,032	4,082	4,130	2,948	935	147	88	36	23	100
North Carolina	1,952	1,955	1,950	1,948	1,958	1,968	1,513	397	39	20	8	11	19
North Dakota	679	663	651	642	640	623	356	219	8	3	3	2	40
Ohio	3,715	3,731	3,805	3,821	3,818	3,812	2,696	869	119	46	23	50	128
Oklahoma	1,859	1,880	1,817	1,829	1,820	1,824	1,210	606	0	0	0	0	8
Oregon	1,190	1,199	1,196	1,217	1,219	1,213	904	261	39	29	7	3	9
Pennsylvania	3,276	3,260	3,252	3,197	3,193	3,190	2,362	712	30	9	11	10	86
Rhode Island	294	309	314	313	311	308	242	59	2	2	0	0	5
South Carolina	1,103	1,097	1,102	1,104	1,094	1,094	793	248	10	4	5	1	43
South Dakota	799	802	673	733	777	827	511	299	0	0	0	0	17
Tennessee	1,535	1,543	1,519	1,514	1,523	1,554	1,117	324	55	37	8	10	58
Texas	5,937	5,991	6,052	6,184	6,324	6,465	4,448	1,616	401	207	98	96	0
Utah	718	714	712	714	718	728	473	222	12	5	3	4	21
Vermont	336	397	395	399	400	394	297	55	17	12	5	0	25
Virginia	1,779	1,811	1,810	1,816	1,828	1,851	1,372	339	22	3	11	8	118
Washington	1,858	1,936	1,956	2,017	2,030	2,064	1,290	516	101	47	30	24	157
West Virginia	1,035	1,015	987	949	907	883	626	180	25	10	1	14	52
Wisconsin	2,019	2,018	2,029	2,030	2,032	2,030	1,480	521	29	8	14	7	0
Wyoming	404	415	419	410	409	411	284	118	0	0	0	0	9
Department of Defense dependents schools	—	—	—	—	—	190	132	42	16	12	3	1	0
Outlying areas													
American Samoa	30	30	27	30	31	31	24	6	0	0	0	0	1
Guam	37	35	35	35	35	35	30	5	0	0	0	0	0
Northern Marianas	26	26	24	24	25	25	20	3	0	0	0	0	2
Puerto Rico	1,661	1,619	1,590	1,593	1,584	1,566	994	341	196	4	1	191	35
Virgin Islands	34	33	33	33	32	32	23	8	1	0	0	1	0

[1] Includes special education, alternative, and other schools not classified by grade span.

[2] Includes schools beginning with grade 6 or below and with no grade higher than 8.

[3] Includes schools with no grade lower than 7.

[4] Includes schools beginning with grade 6 or below and ending with grade 9 or above.

[5] Includes special education, alternative, and other schools not classified by grade span.

—Data not available.

SOURCE: U.S. Department of Education, National Center for Education Statistics, Common Core of Data survey. (This table was prepared October 1996.)

Table 96.—Public elementary schools, by grade span and average school size, by state: 1994–95

State or other area	Total	Schools, by grade span						Average number of students per school [1]
		Prekindergarten, kindergarten, or 1st grade to grades 3 or 4	Prekindergarten, kindergarten, or 1st grade to grade 5	Prekindergarten, kindergarten, or 1st grade to grade 6	Prekindergarten, kindergarten, or 1st grade to grade 8	Grades 4, 5, or 6 to 6, 7, or 8	Other grade spans	
1	2	3	4	5	6	7	8	9
United States	60,808	4,876	19,296	16,568	4,508	9,954	5,606	471
Alabama	859	81	245	196	76	175	86	487
Alaska	185	4	24	104	23	14	16	367
Arizona	818	47	161	294	151	103	62	579
Arkansas	647	81	57	369	5	77	58	393
California	5,695	182	1,681	2,406	531	687	208	611
Colorado	1,031	30	471	240	12	198	80	424
Connecticut	784	83	293	144	43	138	83	450
Delaware	121	40	15	8	2	30	26	553
District of Columbia	120	6	7	91	4	8	4	437
Florida	1,906	26	1,169	229	23	357	102	769
Georgia	1,382	44	721	114	22	278	203	634
Hawaii	182	1	33	116	14	14	4	621
Idaho	380	30	80	169	16	49	36	371
Illinois	3,054	335	533	646	717	450	373	416
Indiana	1,390	57	548	455	39	217	74	439
Iowa	1,078	134	308	279	22	208	127	287
Kansas	1,046	78	300	269	140	160	99	286
Kentucky	991	51	405	230	107	176	22	424
Louisiana	999	117	280	217	73	204	108	504
Maine	552	84	88	89	108	89	94	260
Maryland	1,029	20	563	182	13	190	61	543
Massachusetts	1,437	214	442	279	72	231	199	425
Michigan	2,496	217	911	611	66	434	257	425
Minnesota	1,166	140	218	478	33	144	153	430
Mississippi	569	74	88	154	52	108	93	511
Missouri	1,432	89	446	412	113	240	132	384
Montana	537	28	82	251	68	49	59	187
Nebraska	1,012	51	123	483	157	56	142	168
Nevada	314	11	130	83	17	45	28	552
New Hampshire	355	57	68	85	47	64	34	366
New Jersey	1,786	271	424	313	261	309	208	445
New Mexico	533	25	192	156	5	97	58	406
New York	2,948	265	911	841	71	511	349	603
North Carolina	1,513	83	646	231	117	326	110	525
North Dakota	356	16	25	233	40	19	23	193
Ohio	2,696	335	745	809	81	467	259	424
Oklahoma	1,210	54	339	220	300	199	98	340
Oregon	904	48	347	222	95	148	44	370
Pennsylvania	2,362	292	819	639	62	387	163	474
Rhode Island	242	41	46	90	4	32	29	401
South Carolina	793	87	330	90	18	193	75	548
South Dakota	511	35	106	146	87	76	61	182
Tennessee	1,117	104	287	264	226	166	70	503
Texas	4,448	456	1,623	776	92	963	538	551
Utah	473	8	99	317	4	36	9	552
Vermont	297	24	24	118	60	22	49	218
Virginia	1,372	85	675	176	3	266	167	523
Washington	1,290	57	405	491	62	174	101	449
West Virginia	626	60	170	256	39	78	23	295
Wisconsin	1,480	100	520	373	111	249	127	375
Wyoming	284	18	73	124	4	43	22	212
Department of Defense dependents schools	132	5	29	65	15	16	2	456
Outlying areas								
American Samoa	24	0	1	0	21	1	1	461
Guam	30	0	21	0	0	6	3	818
Northern Marianas	20	0	0	10	0	0	10	266
Puerto Rico	994	101	25	757	4	34	73	292
Virgin Islands	23	0	0	22	0	0	1	543

[1] Average for schools reporting enrollment data.

NOTE.—Includes schools beginning with grade 6 or below and with no grade higher than 8. Excludes schools not reported by level, such as special education schools for the disabled.

SOURCE: U.S. Department of Education, National Center for Education Statistics, Common Core of Data survey. (This table was prepared October 1996.)

Table 97.—Public secondary schools, by grade span and average school size, by state: 1994–95

State or other area	Total	Grades 7 to 8 and 7 to 9	Grades 7 to 12	Grades 8 to 12	Grades 9 to 12	Grades 10 to 12	Other spans ending with grade 12	Other grade spans	Average number of students per school [1]
1	2	3	4	5	6	7	8	9	10
United States	20,282	3,859	3,152	476	11,180	878	121	616	697
Alabama	290	31	73	10	152	11	1	12	697
Alaska	87	15	23	4	44	1	0	0	463
Arizona	250	75	5	5	150	9	0	6	973
Arkansas	414	79	213	1	43	63	0	15	440
California	1,863	428	87	45	1,113	112	11	67	939
Colorado	343	55	61	9	195	13	3	7	579
Connecticut	206	34	9	4	152	2	2	3	700
Delaware	42	10	2	0	29	0	0	1	898
District of Columbia	37	16	1	0	18	1	1	0	643
Florida	471	31	51	23	284	21	12	49	1,108
Georgia	316	24	13	32	241	3	0	3	1,097
Hawaii	47	13	8	0	24	0	0	2	1,333
Idaho	202	46	41	4	84	20	1	6	477
Illinois	876	222	30	9	594	10	2	9	700
Indiana	430	77	110	3	230	7	1	2	792
Iowa	446	73	108	2	249	12	1	1	406
Kansas	427	69	60	3	275	13	4	3	368
Kentucky	338	44	51	3	207	5	1	27	647
Louisiana	315	62	46	12	177	9	1	8	762
Maine	130	21	13	2	92	1	0	1	499
Maryland	214	28	11	2	163	2	2	6	1,057
Massachusetts	335	46	47	18	216	6	1	1	777
Michigan	776	117	122	21	472	18	5	21	672
Minnesota	655	91	234	34	185	63	18	30	465
Mississippi	229	48	44	7	106	13	3	8	667
Missouri	574	69	213	11	248	18	1	14	528
Montana	362	185	0	0	174	2	0	1	177
Nebraska	363	42	226	1	79	12	0	3	320
Nevada	93	15	17	4	50	1	0	6	803
New Hampshire	99	25	0	0	72	2	0	0	563
New Jersey	387	71	39	11	252	6	2	6	909
New Mexico	169	35	27	1	91	8	0	7	640
New York	935	145	194	14	488	24	0	70	943
North Carolina	397	66	23	2	271	26	2	7	872
North Dakota	219	18	151	7	30	8	2	3	233
Ohio	869	176	140	28	492	17	3	13	708
Oklahoma	606	126	0	0	368	85	5	22	327
Oregon	261	53	24	9	165	5	0	5	675
Pennsylvania	712	112	181	16	340	46	7	10	850
Rhode Island	59	17	4	1	33	3	0	1	853
South Carolina	248	36	24	7	158	6	1	16	825
South Dakota	299	113	1	1	180	3	0	1	168
Tennessee	324	63	35	4	199	14	1	8	864
Texas	1,616	298	182	28	958	32	18	100	699
Utah	222	80	31	4	52	47	1	7	932
Vermont	55	6	24	1	24	0	0	0	601
Virginia	339	39	12	46	225	9	0	8	981
Washington	516	123	58	18	256	37	7	17	634
West Virginia	180	55	23	2	77	23	0	0	636
Wisconsin	521	94	60	6	340	18	1	2	563
Wyoming	118	42	0	1	63	11	0	1	339
Department of Defense dependents schools	42	2	28	0	11	1	0	0	453
Outlying areas									
American Samoa	6	0	0	0	6	0	0	0	555
Guam	5	0	0	0	5	0	0	0	1,598
Northern Marianas	3	1	1	0	1	0	0	0	961
Puerto Rico	341	166	27	0	3	135	2	8	662
Virgin Islands	8	5	0	0	2	1	0	0	1,245

[1] Average for schools reporting enrollment data.

SOURCE: U.S. Department of Education, National Center for Education Statistics, Common Core of Data survey. (This table was prepared October 1996.)

NOTE.—Includes schools with no grade lower than 7. Excludes schools not reported by level, such as special education schools for the disabled.

Table 98.—High school graduates compared with population 17 years of age, by sex and control of school: 1869–70 to 1995–96

[Numbers in thousands]

School year	Population 17 years old [1]	High school graduates					Graduates as a percent of 17-year-old population
		Total [2]	Sex		Control		
			Male	Female	Public [3]	Private [4]	
1	2	3	4	5	6	7	8
1869–70	815	16	7	9	—	—	2.0
1879–80	946	24	11	13	—	—	2.5
1889–90	1,259	44	19	25	22	22	3.5
1899–1900	1,489	95	38	57	62	33	6.4
1909–10	1,786	156	64	93	111	45	8.8
1919–20	1,855	311	124	188	231	80	16.8
1929–30	2,296	667	300	367	592	75	29.0
1939–40	2,403	1,221	579	643	1,143	78	50.8
1947–48	2,261	1,190	563	627	1,073	117	52.6
1949–50	2,034	1,200	571	629	1,063	136	59.0
1951–52	2,086	1,197	569	627	1,056	141	57.4
1953–54	2,135	1,276	613	664	1,129	147	59.8
1955–56	2,242	1,415	680	735	1,252	163	63.1
1956–57	2,272	1,434	690	744	1,270	164	63.1
1957–58	2,325	1,506	725	781	1,332	174	64.8
1958–59	2,458	1,627	784	843	1,435	192	66.2
1959–60	2,672	1,858	895	963	1,627	231	69.5
1960–61	2,892	1,964	955	1,009	1,725	239	67.9
1961–62	2,768	1,918	938	980	1,678	240	69.3
1962–63	2,740	1,943	956	987	1,710	233	70.9
1963–64	2,978	2,283	1,120	1,163	2,008	275	76.7
1964–65	3,684	2,658	1,311	1,347	2,360	298	72.1
1965–66	3,489	2,665	1,323	1,342	2,367	298	76.4
1966–67	3,500	2,672	1,328	1,344	2,374	298	76.3
1967–68	3,532	2,695	1,338	1,357	2,395	300	76.3
1968–69	3,659	2,822	1,399	1,423	2,522	300	77.1
1969–70	3,757	2,889	1,430	1,459	2,589	300	76.9
1970–71	3,872	2,938	1,454	1,484	2,638	300	75.9
1971–72	3,973	3,002	1,487	1,515	2,700	302	75.6
1972–73	4,049	3,035	1,500	1,535	2,729	306	75.0
1973–74	4,132	3,073	1,512	1,561	2,763	310	74.4
1974–75	4,256	3,133	1,542	1,591	2,823	310	73.6
1975–76	4,272	3,148	1,552	1,596	2,837	311	73.7
1976–77	4,272	3,152	1,548	1,604	2,837	315	73.8
1977–78	4,286	3,127	1,531	1,596	2,825	302	73.0
1978–79	4,327	3,101	1,517	1,584	2,801	300	71.7
1979–80	4,262	3,043	1,491	1,552	2,748	295	71.4
1980–81	4,212	3,020	1,483	1,537	2,725	295	71.7
1981–82	4,134	2,995	1,471	1,524	2,705	290	72.4
1982–83	3,962	2,888	1,437	1,451	2,598	290	72.9
1983–84	3,784	2,767	—	—	2,495	272	73.1
1984–85	3,699	2,677	—	—	2,414	263	72.4
1985–86	3,670	2,643	—	—	2,383	260	72.0
1986–87	3,754	2,694	—	—	2,429	265	71.8
1987–88	3,849	2,773	—	—	2,500	273	72.1
1988–89	3,842	2,727	—	—	2,459	268	71.0
1989–90	3,574	2,586	—	—	2,320	266	72.4
1990–91	3,417	2,503	—	—	2,235	268	73.2
1991–92	3,381	2,482	—	—	2,226	256	73.4
1992–93	3,433	2,490	—	—	2,233	257	72.5
1993–94	3,442	2,479	—	—	2,221	258	72.0
1994–95 [5]	3,571	2,552	—	—	2,288	264	71.5
1995–96 [5]	3,597	2,572	—	—	2,305	267	71.5

[1] Derived from *Current Population Reports*, Series P-25. 17–year-old population adjusted to reflect October 17-year-old population.

[2] Includes graduates of public and private schools.

[3] Data for 1929–30 and preceding years are from *Statistics of Public High Schools* and exclude graduates of high schools which failed to report to the Office of Education.

[4] For most years, private school data have been estimated based on periodic private school surveys. For years through 1957–58, private includes data for subcollegiate departments of institutions of higher education and residential schools for exceptional children.

[5] Public high school graduates based on state estimates.

—Data not available.

NOTE.—Includes graduates of regular day school programs. Excludes graduates of other programs, when separately reported, and recipients of high school equivalency certificates. Some data have been revised from previously published figures. Because of rounding, details may not add to totals.

SOURCE: U.S. Department of Education, National Center for Education Statistics, *Statistics of Public High Schools; Biennial Survey of Education in the United States; Statistics of State School Systems; Statistics of Nonpublic Elementary and Secondary Schools;* Common Core of Data surveys; and U.S. Department of Commerce, Bureau of the Census, *Current Population Reports*, Series P-25. (This table was prepared July 1996.)

Table 99.—Public high school graduates, by state: 1969–70 to 1995–96

State	1969–70	1979–80	1980–81	1985–86	1989–90	1990–91	1992–93	1993–94	Estimated 1994–95	Estimated 1995–96	Percent change, 1990–91 to 1995–96
1	2	3	4	5	6	7	8	9	10	11	12
United States	2,588,639	2,747,678	2,725,285	2,382,616	[1] 2,320,337	2,234,893	2,233,241	2,221,098	[1] 2,287,725	[1] 2,304,722	3.1
Alabama	45,286	45,190	44,894	39,620	40,485	39,042	36,007	34,447	[2] 36,268	36,352	–6.9
Alaska	3,297	5,223	5,343	5,464	5,386	5,458	5,535	5,747	[2] 5,765	6,266	14.8
Arizona	22,040	28,633	28,416	27,533	32,103	31,282	31,747	31,799	[3] 29,468	[3] 30,413	–2.8
Arkansas	26,068	29,052	29,577	26,227	26,475	25,668	25,655	24,990	[2] 26,039	26,429	3.0
California	260,908	249,217	242,172	229,026	236,291	234,164	249,320	253,083	257,385	261,761	11.8
Colorado	30,312	36,804	35,897	32,621	32,967	31,293	31,839	31,867	[2] 32,408	33,449	6.9
Connecticut	34,755	37,683	38,369	33,571	27,878	27,290	26,799	26,330	[2] 26,330	26,446	–3.1
Delaware	6,985	7,582	7,349	5,791	5,550	5,223	5,492	5,230	[2] 5,234	5,543	6.1
District of Columbia [4]	4,980	4,959	4,848	3,875	3,626	3,369	3,136	3,207	[2] 2,974	2,675	–20.6
Florida	70,478	87,324	88,755	83,029	88,934	87,419	89,428	88,032	[2] 89,828	90,617	3.7
Georgia	56,859	61,621	62,963	59,082	56,605	60,088	57,602	56,356	[2] 59,736	59,406	–1.1
Hawaii	10,407	11,493	11,472	9,958	10,325	8,974	8,854	9,369	9,984	9,984	11.3
Idaho	12,296	13,187	12,679	12,059	11,971	11,961	12,974	13,281	[2] 14,198	14,478	21.0
Illinois	126,864	135,579	136,795	114,319	108,119	103,329	103,628	102,126	105,164	105,103	1.7
Indiana	69,984	73,143	73,381	59,817	60,012	57,892	57,559	54,650	[2] 56,629	57,677	–0.4
Iowa	44,063	43,445	42,635	34,279	31,796	28,593	30,677	30,247	31,184	31,641	10.7
Kansas	33,394	30,890	29,397	25,587	25,367	24,414	24,720	25,319	26,367	25,994	6.5
Kentucky	37,473	41,203	41,714	37,288	38,005	35,835	36,361	38,454	36,679	36,162	0.9
Louisiana	43,641	46,297	46,199	39,965	36,053	33,489	33,682	34,822	[2] 36,691	35,576	6.2
Maine	14,003	15,445	15,554	13,006	13,839	13,151	12,103	11,633	[2] 12,950	11,300	–14.1
Maryland	46,462	54,270	54,050	46,700	41,566	39,014	39,523	39,091	[2] 41,841	41,600	6.6
Massachusetts	63,865	73,802	74,831	60,360	[5] 55,941	50,216	48,321	47,453	[3] 49,140	[3] 49,681	–1.1
Michigan	121,000	124,316	124,372	101,042	93,807	88,234	85,302	83,385	84,100	87,400	–0.9
Minnesota	60,480	64,908	64,166	51,988	49,087	46,474	48,002	47,514	49,658	51,615	11.1
Mississippi	29,653	27,586	28,083	25,134	25,182	23,665	23,597	23,379	[2] 23,707	23,129	–2.3
Missouri	55,315	62,265	60,359	49,204	48,957	46,928	46,864	46,566	[2] 48,915	49,230	4.9
Montana	11,520	12,135	11,634	9,761	9,370	9,013	9,389	9,601	[2] 9,965	10,253	13.8
Nebraska	21,280	22,410	21,411	17,845	17,664	16,500	17,569	17,072	[2] 17,969	16,240	–1.6
Nevada	5,449	8,473	9,069	8,784	9,477	9,370	9,042	9,485	[2] 10,038	10,623	13.4
New Hampshire	8,516	11,722	11,552	10,648	10,766	10,059	10,065	9,933	9,101	8,840	–12.1
New Jersey	86,498	94,564	93,168	78,781	69,824	67,003	67,134	66,125	[3] 68,587	[3] 69,456	3.7
New Mexico	16,060	18,424	17,915	15,468	14,884	15,157	15,172	14,892	[2] 14,928	14,957	–1.3
New York	190,000	204,064	198,465	162,165	143,318	133,562	132,963	132,708	135,500	137,200	2.7
North Carolina	68,886	70,862	69,395	65,865	64,782	62,792	60,460	57,738	[2] 59,272	56,424	–10.1
North Dakota	11,150	9,928	9,924	7,610	7,690	7,573	7,310	7,522	[2] 7,817	7,923	4.6
Ohio	142,248	144,169	143,503	119,561	114,513	107,484	109,200	107,700	109,418	110,217	2.5
Oklahoma	36,293	39,305	38,875	34,452	35,606	33,007	30,542	31,872	[2] 33,364	32,864	–0.4
Oregon	32,236	29,939	28,729	26,286	25,473	24,597	26,301	26,338	[2] 26,899	27,100	10.2
Pennsylvania	151,014	146,458	144,645	122,871	110,527	104,770	103,715	101,958	105,380	108,520	3.6
Rhode Island	10,146	10,864	10,719	8,908	7,825	7,744	7,640	7,450	[2] 7,830	7,646	–1.3
South Carolina	34,940	38,697	38,347	34,500	32,483	32,999	31,297	30,603	33,300	32,500	–1.5
South Dakota	11,757	10,689	10,385	7,870	7,650	7,127	7,952	8,442	[2] 8,427	8,747	22.7
Tennessee	49,000	49,845	50,648	43,263	46,094	44,847	44,166	40,643	[2] 40,643	43,525	–2.9
Texas	139,046	171,444	171,665	161,150	172,480	174,306	160,546	163,191	[2] 169,143	168,465	–3.4
Utah	18,395	20,035	19,886	19,774	21,196	22,219	24,197	26,407	[2] 29,093	27,931	25.7
Vermont	6,095	6,733	6,424	5,794	6,127	5,212	5,215	5,414	[2] 5,574	5,344	2.5
Virginia	58,562	66,621	67,126	63,113	60,605	58,441	56,948	56,140	[2] 59,644	59,603	2.0
Washington	50,425	50,402	50,046	45,805	45,941	42,514	45,262	47,235	[2] 48,846	50,788	19.5
West Virginia	26,139	23,369	23,580	21,870	21,854	21,064	20,228	19,884	[2] 20,648	20,720	–1.6
Wisconsin	66,753	69,332	67,743	58,340	52,038	49,340	50,027	48,371	51,808	52,837	7.1
Wyoming	5,363	6,072	6,161	5,587	5,823	5,728	6,174	5,997	[2] 5,889	6,072	6.0
Outlying areas											
American Samoa	[6] 367	—	—	608	703	597	712	738	[3] 749	[3] 741	24.1
Guam	972	—	—	840	1,033	1,014	912	985	[3] 1,043	[3] 1,078	6.3
Northern Marianas	—	—	—	—	227	273	245	328	[2] 386	386	41.4
Puerto Rico	24,917	—	—	31,597	29,049	29,329	29,064	27,718	28,294	28,294	–3.5
Virgin Islands	[6] 432	—	—	1,044	1,260	981	927	886	[2] 995	964	–1.7

[1] National total includes estimates for nonreporting states.

[2] Actual count.

[3] Data estimated by the National Center for Education Statistics.

[4] Beginning in 1985–86, graduates from adult programs are excluded.

[5] Data from *Projections of Education Statistics to 2002* published by the National Center for Education Statistics (NCES).

[6] Data are for 1970–71.

—Data not reported.

NOTE.—Data include graduates of regular day school programs, but exclude graduates of other programs and persons receiving high school equivalency certificates. They also exclude graduates of subcollegiate departments of institutions of higher education, federal schools for American Indians and on federal installations, and residential schools for disabled children. Some data have been revised from previously published figures. All 1994–95 and 1995–96 data are state estimates unless otherwise indicated.

SOURCE: U.S. Department of Education, National Center for Education Statistics, Common Core of Data surveys. (This table was prepared July 1996.)

Table 100.—General Educational Development (GED) credentials issued, and number and age of test takers: United States and outlying areas, 1971 to 1994

Year	Number of credentials issued, in thousands [1]	Number completing test battery, in thousands [2]	Number of test takers, in thousands [3]	Percentage distribution of test takers, by age				
				19 years old or less	20- to 24-year-olds	25- to 29-year-olds	30- to 34-year-olds	35 years old or over
1	2	3	4	5	6	7	8	9
1971	227	—	377	—	—	—	—	—
1972	245	—	419	—	—	—	—	—
1973	249	—	423	—	—	—	—	—
1974	295	412	540	35	27	13	9	17
1975	342	507	652	33	26	14	9	18
1976	337	507	656	31	28	14	10	17
1977	331	488	680	40	24	13	9	14
1978	381	467	641	31	27	13	10	19
1979	435	583	744	35	27	13	8	16
1980	488	708	779	37	27	13	8	15
1981	500	701	770	37	27	13	8	15
1982	494	692	756	37	28	13	8	15
1983	477	678	740	34	29	14	9	15
1984	437	613	676	32	28	15	9	16
1985	427	622	685	33	26	15	10	16
1986	439	648	713	33	26	15	10	16
1987	458	662	729	33	24	15	10	18
1988	421	617	701	36	23	14	10	17
1989	364	554	645	36	24	13	10	16
1990	419	628	727	35	25	14	10	17
1991	471	672	770	33	27	14	10	17
1992	465	653	754	32	28	13	11	16
1993	476	652	757	33	27	14	11	16
1994	498	682	788	35	26	13	10	16

[1] Number of people receiving high school equivalency credentials based on the GED tests.

[2] Number of people completing the entire GED battery of five tests.

[3] Number of people taking the GED tests (one or more subtests).

—Data not available.

NOTE.—Because of rounding, percentages may not add to 100.

SOURCE: American Council on Education, General Educational Development Testing Service. (This table was prepared June 1995.)

Table 101.—Percent of high school dropouts among persons 16 to 24 years old, [1] by sex and race/ethnicity: April 1960 to October 1995

Year	Total				Men				Women			
	All races	White, non-Hispanic	Black, non-Hispanic	Hispanic origin	All races	White, non-Hispanic	Black, non-Hispanic	Hispanic origin	All races	White, non-Hispanic	Black, non-Hispanic	Hispanic origin
1	2	3	4	5	6	7	8	9	10	11	12	13
1960 [2]	27.2	—	—	—	27.8	—	—	—	26.7	—	—	—
1967 [3]	17.0	15.4	28.6	—	16.5	14.7	30.6	—	17.3	16.1	26.9	—
1968 [3]	16.2	14.7	27.4	—	15.8	14.4	27.1	—	16.5	15.0	27.6	—
1969 [3]	15.2	13.6	26.7	—	14.3	12.6	26.9	—	16.0	14.6	26.7	—
1970 [3]	15.0	13.2	27.9	—	14.2	12.2	29.4	—	15.7	14.1	26.6	—
1971 [3]	14.7	13.4	23.7	—	14.2	12.6	25.5	—	15.2	14.2	22.1	—
1972	14.6	12.3	21.3	34.3	14.1	11.7	22.3	33.7	15.1	12.8	20.5	34.9
1973	14.1	11.6	22.2	33.5	13.7	11.5	21.5	30.4	14.5	11.8	22.8	36.4
1974	14.3	11.9	21.2	33.0	14.2	12.0	20.1	33.8	14.4	11.8	22.1	32.2
1975	13.9	11.4	22.9	29.2	13.3	11.0	23.0	26.7	14.5	11.8	22.9	31.6
1976	14.1	12.0	20.5	31.4	14.1	12.1	21.2	30.3	14.2	11.8	19.9	32.3
1977	14.1	11.9	19.8	33.0	14.5	12.6	19.5	31.6	13.8	11.2	20.0	34.3
1978	14.2	11.9	20.2	33.3	14.6	12.2	22.5	33.6	13.9	11.6	18.3	33.1
1979	14.6	12.0	21.1	33.8	15.0	12.6	22.4	33.0	14.2	11.5	20.0	34.5
1980	14.1	11.4	19.1	35.2	15.1	12.3	20.8	37.2	13.1	10.5	17.7	33.2
1981	13.9	11.4	18.4	33.2	15.1	12.5	19.9	36.0	12.8	10.2	17.1	30.4
1982	13.9	11.4	18.4	31.7	14.5	12.1	21.2	30.5	13.3	10.9	15.9	32.8
1983	13.7	11.2	18.0	31.6	14.9	12.2	19.9	34.3	12.5	10.1	16.2	29.1
1984	13.1	11.0	15.5	29.8	14.0	12.0	16.8	30.6	12.3	10.1	14.3	29.0
1985	12.6	10.4	15.2	27.6	13.4	11.1	16.1	29.9	11.8	9.8	14.3	25.2
1986	12.2	9.7	14.2	30.1	13.1	10.3	15.0	32.8	11.4	9.1	13.5	27.2
1987	12.7	10.4	14.1	28.6	13.2	10.8	15.0	29.1	12.1	10.0	13.3	28.1
1988	12.9	9.6	14.5	35.8	13.5	10.4	15.0	36.0	12.2	8.9	14.1	35.4
1989	12.6	9.4	13.9	33.0	13.6	10.3	14.9	34.4	11.7	8.5	13.0	31.6
1990	12.1	9.0	13.2	32.4	12.3	9.3	11.9	34.3	11.8	8.7	14.4	30.3
1991	12.5	8.9	13.6	35.3	13.0	8.9	13.5	39.2	11.9	8.9	13.7	31.1
1992 [4]	11.0	7.7	13.7	29.4	11.3	8.0	12.5	32.1	10.7	7.5	14.8	26.6
1993 [4]	11.0	7.9	13.6	27.5	11.2	8.2	12.6	28.1	10.9	7.7	14.4	26.9
1994 [4,5]	11.5	7.7	12.6	30.0	12.3	8.0	14.1	31.6	10.6	7.5	11.3	28.1
1995 [4]	12.0	8.6	12.1	30.0	12.2	9.0	11.1	30.0	11.7	8.2	12.9	30.0

[1] "Status" dropouts.

[2] Based on the April 1960 decennial census.

[3] White and black include persons of Hispanic origin.

[4] Because of changes in data collection procedures, data may not be comparable with figures for earlier years.

[5] Data have been revised from previously published data.

—Data not available.

NOTE.—"Status" dropouts are persons who are not enrolled in school and who are not high school graduates. People who have received GED credentials are counted as graduates. Data are based upon sample surveys of the civilian noninstitutional population.

SOURCE: U.S. Department of Commerce, Bureau of the Census, Current Population Survey, unpublished tabulations; and U.S. Department of Education, National Center for Education Statistics, Dropout Rates in the United States. (This table was prepared July 1996.)

Table 102.—Percent of high school dropouts among persons 16 to 34 years old,[1] by age, sex, and race/ethnicity: October 1970 to October 1995

Year, race/ethnicity, and sex	16 and 17 years	18 and 19 years	20 and 21 years	22 to 24 years	25 to 29 years	30 to 34 years
1	2	3	4	5	6	7
October 1970						
All races	8.0	16.2	16.6	18.7	22.5	26.5
Male	7.1	16.0	16.1	17.9	21.4	26.2
Female	8.9	16.3	16.9	19.4	23.6	26.8
White [2]	7.3	14.1	14.6	16.3	19.9	24.6
Male	6.3	13.3	14.1	15.3	19.0	24.2
Female	8.4	14.8	15.1	17.2	20.7	24.9
Black [2]	12.8	31.2	29.6	37.8	44.4	43.5
Male	13.3	36.4	29.6	39.5	43.1	45.9
Female	12.4	26.6	29.6	36.4	45.6	41.5
October 1980						
All races	8.9	15.7	16.0	15.2	13.9	14.6
Male	8.9	16.9	17.8	16.4	13.8	14.0
Female	8.8	14.7	14.3	14.0	14.0	15.2
White, non-Hispanic	8.6	12.7	12.1	11.8	10.4	11.0
Male	8.5	13.6	13.5	13.2	10.6	10.7
Female	8.6	11.9	10.9	10.4	10.3	11.3
Black, non-Hispanic	7.0	21.0	24.6	23.6	22.4	23.1
Male	7.2	22.2	30.8	24.6	22.2	21.9
Female	6.8	19.8	19.6	22.8	22.6	24.0
Hispanic origin	16.5	39.0	41.6	40.6	40.9	45.4
Male	18.1	43.1	41.4	42.9	40.1	43.9
Female	15.0	34.6	41.9	38.6	41.7	47.0
October 1990						
All races	6.3	14.2	12.8	13.8	13.9	12.9
Male	6.6	14.6	13.2	14.0	14.5	13.3
Female	6.1	13.8	12.4	13.6	13.4	12.5
White, non-Hispanic	5.4	11.1	9.4	9.5	9.2	8.7
Male	5.9	11.4	9.6	9.8	9.8	9.4
Female	5.0	10.8	9.1	9.1	8.5	8.0
Black, non-Hispanic	6.9	16.6	15.6	13.6	19.3	16.7
Male	6.3	15.5	12.4	13.2	18.9	16.4
Female	7.5	17.6	18.6	13.9	19.6	16.9
Hispanic origin	12.9	34.2	31.6	42.8	41.7	42.4
Male	13.1	39.4	37.9	41.4	42.6	41.4
Female	12.5	29.4	25.0	44.4	40.7	43.5
October 1994 [3]						
All races	5.0	13.4	13.9	12.9	12.8	13.0
Male	5.2	14.3	15.3	13.8	14.0	14.3
Female	4.7	12.4	12.6	12.0	11.7	11.8
White, non-Hispanic	4.1	9.9	9.0	8.0	8.3	8.6
Male	4.0	10.5	9.7	8.1	9.5	9.8
Female	4.2	9.3	8.4	7.9	7.1	7.4
Black, non-Hispanic	4.3	19.8	15.6	12.4	15.0	14.5
Male	4.7	23.6	17.4	12.8	17.0	15.9
Female	3.9	16.2	13.9	12.1	13.5	13.3
Hispanic origin	11.1	25.6	36.7	38.8	37.2	39.2
Male	13.0	26.0	38.3	39.9	37.8	40.2
Female	9.0	25.2	34.6	37.5	36.5	38.1
October 1995 [3]						
All races	5.4	14.6	13.8	13.6	12.4	11.7
Male	4.8	14.7	13.6	14.9	13.9	12.0
Female	6.1	14.5	13.9	12.3	10.9	11.4
White, non-Hispanic	4.7	11.4	9.4	8.9	7.8	7.7
Male	4.2	11.7	9.3	10.4	9.0	7.9
Female	5.2	11.0	9.5	7.4	6.7	7.5
Black, non-Hispanic	5.6	15.7	15.1	12.6	11.6	11.6
Male	4.1	18.1	16.2	9.4	11.3	12.1
Female	7.3	13.7	14.2	15.4	11.8	11.1
Hispanic origin	10.7	30.8	34.4	37.4	39.0	36.6
Male	11.2	27.0	33.4	39.0	42.1	35.5
Female	10.2	35.0	35.4	35.3	35.6	37.8

[1] "Status" dropouts.
[2] Includes persons of Hispanic origin.
[3] Because of changes in data collection procedures, data may not be comparable with figures for earlier years.

NOTE.—"Status" dropouts are persons who are not enrolled in school and who are not high school graduates. People who have received GED credentials are counted as graduates. Data are based upon sample surveys of the civilian noninstitutional population.

SOURCE: U.S. Department of Commerce, Bureau of the Census, Current Population Survey, unpublished data. (This table was prepared July 1996.)

Table 103.—Students with disabilities exiting the educational system, by age, type of disability, and basis of exit: United States and outlying areas, 1991–92 and 1992–93

Student characteristics	1991–92									1992–93[1]		
	Total exiting the system		Graduated with diploma		Graduated through certificate		Reached maximum age[2]	Dropped out[3]	Other reasons for exit[4]	Graduated with diploma	Graduated through certificate	Reached maximum age[2]
	Number	Percent	Number	Percent	Number	Percent	Number	Number	Number	Number	Number	Number
1	2	3	4	5	6	7	8	9	10	11	12	13
Age group												
14 to 21 (and over)	229,368	100.0	100,742	43.9	30,839	13.4	4,337	51,489	41,961	103,801	34,732	5,096
14	11,403	100.0	138	1.2	223	2.0	8	3,460	7,574	130	65	6
15	12,934	100.0	171	1.3	158	1.2	16	4,768	7,821	110	92	51
16	20,634	100.0	505	2.4	217	1.1	44	11,479	8,389	477	143	45
17	36,665	100.0	14,356	39.2	1,929	5.3	70	12,678	7,632	16,178	2,209	91
18	69,081	100.0	45,063	65.2	7,263	10.5	115	11,060	5,580	47,398	8,396	168
19	45,079	100.0	29,325	65.1	7,593	16.8	68	5,461	2,632	28,275	8,596	197
20	18,131	100.0	7,444	41.1	7,190	39.7	588	1,777	1,132	7,572	8,339	727
21 (and over)	15,441	100.0	3,740	24.2	6,266	40.6	3,428	806	1,201	3,661	6,892	3,811
Type of disability												
All disabilities, 14 to 21 and over	229,368	100.0	100,742	43.9	30,839	13.4	4,337	51,489	41,961	103,801	34,732	5,096
Specific learning disabilities	132,497	100.0	65,851	49.7	14,318	10.8	662	28,257	23,409	69,309	17,156	746
Mental retardation	38,993	100.0	14,088	36.1	10,797	27.7	2,359	7,650	4,099	12,718	11,305	2,662
Serious emotional disturbance	34,001	100.0	9,557	28.1	2,217	6.5	338	11,894	9,995	10,411	2,474	583
Speech or language impairments	8,108	100.0	3,562	43.9	596	7.4	87	1,633	2,230	3,516	514	116
Multiple disabilities	4,028	100.0	1,560	38.7	977	24.3	529	546	416	1,494	1,116	642
Other health impairments	3,642	100.0	1,771	48.6	614	16.9	67	606	584	1,815	627	65
Hearing impairments	3,403	100.0	1,900	55.8	587	17.2	69	444	403	1,851	660	41
Orthopedic impairments	2,749	100.0	1,379	50.2	439	16.0	123	252	556	1,451	421	117
Visual impairments	1,449	100.0	879	60.7	172	11.9	55	166	177	872	260	31
Autism	291	100.0	82	28.2	75	25.8	29	27	78	114	110	62
Deaf-blindness	143	100.0	72	50.3	42	29.4	15	6	8	68	64	18
Traumatic brain injury	64	100.0	41	64.1	5	7.8	4	8	6	182	25	13

[1] Data collection forms changed for the 1992–93 period. These three categories are compatible with previous reports.

[2] Upper age limits for service eligibility vary by state.

[3] These figures reflect an estimate of those who were actually known to have dropped out and do not include youth who simply stopped coming to school or whose status was unknown.

[4] Includes students who died or no longer received special education services, but whose exit reason is unknown.

NOTE.—It can be assumed that a substantial proportion of the "Other" category includes students who are no longer in school and have neither graduated nor reached the maximum age. Therefore, the overall dropout figure probably exceeds 23 percent.

SOURCE: U.S. Department of Education, Office of Special Education and Rehabilitative Services, *Sixteenth* and *Seventeenth Annual Reports to Congress on the Implementation of The Individuals with Disabilities Education Act, 1994* and *1995*. (This table was prepared April 1996.)

Table 104.—Postsecondary education and employment status, wages earned, and living arrangements of special education students out of secondary school up to 3 years, by type of disability: 1990

Type of disability	Percent in postsecondary education		Percent currently competitively employed	Average annual total compensation	Percent living independently[1]
	Academic	Vocational			
1	2	3	4	5	6
All disabilities[2]	**16.5**	**14.7**	**55.0**	**$5,524**	**27.8**
Learning disabled	18.7	17.8	63.1	6,932	33.9
Serious emotional disturbance	15.3	13.3	52.0	5,310	21.1
Speech/language impairments	37.0	17.9	58.5	4,389	36.4
Mental retardation	2.5	5.7	40.8	3,078	14.8
Visual impairment	53.9	14.9	30.3	2,027	39.3
Hard of hearing	35.0	20.0	43.6	2,773	25.9
Deaf	28.3	19.9	24.8	1,689	32.3
Orthopedic impairments	30.9	13.4	26.4	1,636	16.6
Other health impairments	35.1	23.5	47.5	4,388	17.2
Multiple disabilities	8.0	4.0	15.8	778	8.0

[1] Living independently includes living alone, with a spouse or roommate, in a college dormitory, or in military housing not as a dependent.

[2] All conditions includes youth in each of the 11 Federal special education disability categories. Percentages are reported separately only for categories with at least 25 youth in the sample.

NOTE.—Data based on students who had been out of school up to three years and had attended special and regular schools in the 1985–86 or 1986–87 school years.

SOURCE: U.S. Department of Education, Office of Special Education and Rehabilitative Services, *The Seventeenth Annual Report to Congress on the Implementation of The Individuals with Disabilities Education Act*, The National Longitudinal Transition Study, 1995. (This table was prepared April 1996.)

Table 105.—Average student proficiency in reading, by age and selected characteristics of students: 1971 to 1992

Selected characteristics of students	9-year-olds						13-year-olds						17-year-olds [1]					
	1971	1980	1984	1988	1990	1992	1971	1980	1984	1988	1990	1992	1971	1980	1984	1988	1990	1992
1	2	3	4	5	6	7	8	9	10	11	12	13	14	15	16	17	18	19
Total	**207.6**	**215.0**	**210.9**	**211.8**	**209.2**	**210.5**	**255.2**	**258.5**	**257.1**	**257.5**	**256.8**	**259.8**	**285.2**	**285.5**	**288.8**	**290.1**	**290.2**	**289.7**
Sex																		
Male	201.2	210.0	207.5	207.5	204.0	205.9	249.6	254.3	252.6	251.8	250.5	254.1	278.9	281.8	283.8	286.0	284.0	284.2
Female	213.9	220.1	214.2	216.3	214.5	215.4	260.8	262.6	261.7	263.0	263.1	265.3	291.3	289.2	293.9	293.8	296.5	295.7
Race/ethnicity																		
White	214.0	221.3	218.2	217.7	217.0	217.9	260.9	264.4	262.6	261.3	262.3	266.4	291.4	292.8	295.2	294.7	296.6	297.4
Black	170.1	189.3	185.7	188.5	181.8	184.5	222.4	232.8	236.3	242.9	241.5	237.6	238.7	243.1	264.3	274.4	267.3	260.6
Hispanic	(²)	190.2	187.2	193.7	189.4	191.7	(²)	237.2	239.6	240.1	237.8	239.2	(²)	261.4	268.1	270.8	274.8	271.2
Parental education																		
Not high school graduate	188.6	194.3	195.1	192.5	192.6	194.9	238.4	238.5	240.0	246.5	240.8	239.2	261.3	262.1	269.4	267.4	269.7	270.8
Graduated high school	207.8	213.0	208.9	210.8	209.1	207.4	255.5	253.5	253.4	252.7	251.4	252.1	283.0	277.5	281.2	282.0	282.9	280.5
Post high school	223.9	226.0	222.9	220.0	217.7	219.5	270.2	270.9	267.6	265.3	266.9	269.9	302.2	298.9	301.2	299.5	299.9	298.6
Control of school																		
Public	—	213.5	209.4	210.2	207.5	208.6	—	256.9	255.2	256.1	255.0	257.2	—	284.4	287.2	288.7	288.6	287.8
Private	—	227.0	222.8	223.4	228.3	224.7	—	270.6	271.2	268.3	269.7	276.3	—	298.4	303.0	299.6	311.0	309.6
Type of community																		
Advantaged urban	229.8	232.5	230.8	222.4	227.1	233.6	272.9	276.8	274.5	266.3	270.1	280.8	305.9	300.8	302.2	301.0	299.9	302.6
Disadvantaged urban	179.2	187.6	191.5	192.0	186.1	183.5	234.3	241.6	238.9	239.0	241.0	230.9	259.7	258.1	265.7	275.0	273.3	266.7
Extreme rural	200.2	211.8	201.2	211.3	209.4	206.5	247.4	254.8	254.9	262.4	251.2	257.2	276.8	279.0	282.7	286.6	289.9	285.3
Other	207.8	214.5	211.3	211.3	209.8	211.6	255.4	257.9	257.1	257.3	257.5	261.2	285.2	286.6	289.6	288.3	290.9	292.6
Region																		
Northeast	213.0	221.1	215.7	215.2	217.4	217.6	261.1	260.0	260.4	258.6	258.9	264.6	291.3	285.9	292.2	294.8	295.7	297.3
Southeast	193.9	210.3	204.3	207.2	197.4	199.3	244.7	252.6	256.4	257.6	255.5	253.8	270.5	280.1	284.7	285.5	285.1	278.4
Central	214.9	216.7	215.3	218.2	212.7	215.8	260.1	264.5	258.8	255.9	257.4	263.5	290.7	287.4	290.0	291.2	293.5	293.8
West	205.0	212.8	207.8	207.9	209.6	209.3	253.6	256.4	253.8	257.9	255.6	257.5	283.7	287.3	288.4	289.0	286.8	290.4

[1] All participants of this age were in school.
[2] Test scores of Hispanics were not tabulated separately.
—Data not available.

NOTE.—These test scores are from the National Assessment of Educational Progress (NAEP). The NAEP scores have been evaluated at certain performance levels. A score of 300 implies an ability to find, understand, summarize, and explain relatively complicated literary and informational material. A score of 250 implies an ability to search for specific information, interrelate ideas, and make generalizations about literature, science, and social studies materials. A score of 200 implies an ability to understand, combine ideas, and make inferences based on short uncomplicated passages about specific or sequentially related information. A score of 150 implies an ability to follow brief written directions and carry out simple, discrete reading tasks. Scale ranges from 0 to 500.

SOURCE: U.S. Department of Education, National Center for Education Statistics, National Assessment of Educational Progress, *The Reading Report Card, 1971–88* and *NAEP 1992 Trends in Academic Progress*, by Educational Testing Service. (This table was prepared April 1994.)

Table 106.—Student proficiency in reading, by percentile and age: 1971 to 1992

Percentile	9-year-olds						13-year-olds						17-year-olds [1]					
	1971	1980	1984	1988	1990	1992	1971	1980	1984	1988	1990	1992	1971	1980	1984	1988	1990	1992
1	2	3	4	5	6	7	8	9	10	11	12	13	14	15	16	17	18	19
Average	**207.6**	**215.0**	**210.9**	**211.8**	**209.2**	**210.5**	**255.2**	**258.5**	**257.1**	**257.5**	**256.8**	**259.8**	**285.2**	**285.5**	**288.8**	**290.1**	**290.2**	**289.7**
Standard deviation	42.1	37.9	41.1	41.2	44.7	40.3	35.7	34.9	35.5	34.7	36.0	39.4	45.8	41.8	40.3	37.1	41.3	43.0
Percentiles																		
5th	134.8	148.5	140.5	141.9	134.8	140.7	192.8	199.1	196.7	199.5	195.7	190.9	206.1	213.0	219.9	226.1	220.0	214.3
10th	151.6	165.1	156.7	156.7	150.1	156.0	207.8	212.8	210.2	212.9	209.8	207.9	225.3	230.6	236.0	241.5	236.9	232.7
25th	180.0	191.1	183.7	184.3	178.7	183.1	232.3	235.3	233.9	234.2	233.2	234.7	255.9	258.7	262.5	265.7	263.5	262.6
50th	209.3	217.2	212.6	213.7	210.3	213.6	257.0	259.6	258.2	257.9	257.3	261.6	287.7	287.5	290.3	291.1	291.1	293.0
75th	236.7	241.3	239.6	240.1	240.3	239.3	279.9	282.8	281.6	281.4	281.5	287.0	316.7	314.6	316.8	316.0	318.6	319.4
90th	260.5	261.7	262.8	263.0	265.7	259.9	299.6	302.3	301.7	301.6	302.0	309.2	341.7	337.5	339.6	336.9	342.7	342.7
95th	274.1	273.3	276.5	277.5	280.4	272.1	310.8	313.9	313.7	313.7	314.4	321.9	356.5	350.9	352.6	348.7	356.0	355.8

[1] All participants of this age were in school.

NOTE.—These test scores are from the National Assessment of Educational Progress (NAEP). The NAEP scores have been evaluated at certain performance levels. A score of 300 implies an ability to find, understand, summarize, and explain relatively complicated literary and informational material. A score of 250 implies an ability to search for specific information, interrelate ideas, and make generalizations about literature, science, and social studies materials. A score of 200 implies an ability to understand, combine ideas, and make inferences based on short uncomplicated passages about specific or sequentially related information. A score of 150 implies an ability to follow brief written directions and carry out simple, discrete reading tasks. Scale ranges from 0 to 500.

SOURCE: U.S. Department of Education, National Center for Education Statistics, National Assessment of Educational Progress, *The Reading Report Card, 1971–88,* and *NAEP 1992 Trends in Academic Progress*, by Educational Testing Service. (This table was prepared April 1994.)

Table 107.—Student proficiency in reading, by age, amount of time spent on homework, reading habits, and reading materials in the home: 1971, 1984, and 1992

Time spent on homework, reading habits, and reading materials in the home	Average proficiency score						Percent					
	9-year-olds		13-year-olds		17-year-olds[1]		9-year-olds		13-year-olds		17-year-olds[1]	
	1984	1992	1984	1992	1984	1992	1984	1992	1984	1992	1984	1992
1	2	3	4	5	6	7	8	9	10	11	12	13
Materials read a few times a year or more												
Poems	211	211	260	264	290	294	70	70	68	74	76	84
Plays	211	208	260	262	290	293	56	54	59	64	63	71
Biographies	213	212	261	263	292	294	45	47	62	72	59	69
Science books	212	211	259	261	289	293	84	88	90	92	70	80
Books about other places	211	211	259	262	289	294	79	81	83	80	81	84
Frequency of reading for fun												
Daily	214	215	264	269	297	304	53	56	35	37	31	27
Weekly	212	212	254	260	290	291	28	28	35	32	34	33
Monthly	204	204	255	257	290	287	7	6	14	13	17	18
Yearly	197	197	252	250	280	282	3	3	7	8	10	12
Never	198	189	239	246	269	268	9	7	8	10	9	11
Time spent on homework each day												
None	212	211	254	253	276	274	36	32	23	21	22	22
Didn't do assignment	198	193	247	251	287	286	4	4	4	4	11	12
Less than 1 hour	218	215	261	260	290	291	42	47	36	36	26	29
1 to 2 hours	216	211	266	269	296	298	13	12	29	29	27	25
More than 2 hours	201	195	264	267	303	308	6	5	9	10	13	12
	1971	1992	1971	1992	1971	1992	1971	1992	1971	1992	1971	1992
Reading materials in the home[2]												
0 to 2	186	197	227	241	246	269	28	37	17	22	11	18
3	208	214	249	256	274	286	33	33	25	31	22	27
4	223	224	267	271	296	299	39	30	58	48	67	55

[1] Excludes persons not enrolled in school.
[2] The 4 items in the scale were: newspaper subscription, magazine subscription, more than 25 books in the home, and encyclopedia in the home.

NOTE.—These test scores are from the National Assessment of Educational Progress (NAEP). The NAEP scores have been evaluated at certain performance levels. A score of 300 implies an ability to find, understand, summarize, and explain relatively complicated literary and informational material. A score of 250 implies an ability to search for specific information, interrelate ideas, and make generalizations about literature, science, and social studies materials. A score of 200 implies an ability to understand, combine ideas, and make inferences based on short uncomplicated passages about specific or sequentially related information. A score of 150 implies an ability to follow brief written directions and carry out simple, discrete reading tasks. Scale ranges from 0 to 500.

SOURCE: U.S. Department of Education, National Center for Education Statistics, National Assessment of Educational Progress, The Reading Report Card, 1971–88, and NAEP 1992 Trends in Academic Progress, by Educational Testing Service. (This table was prepared April 1994.)

Table 108.—Percent of students at or above selected reading proficiency levels,[1] by sex, race/ethnicity, and age: 1971 to 1992

Sex, race/ethnicity, and level	9-year-olds[2]							13-year-olds[2]							17-year-olds[2]						
	1971	1975	1980	1984	1988	1990	1992	1971	1975	1980	1984	1988	1990	1992	1971	1975	1980	1984	1988	1990	1992
1	2	3	4	5	6	7	8	9	10	11	12	13	14	15	16	17	18	19	20	21	22
Total																					
Level 150[3]	90.6	93.1	94.6	92.3	92.7	90.1	92.3	99.8	99.7	99.9	99.8	99.9	99.8	99.5	99.6	99.7	99.9	100.0	100.0	99.9	99.8
Level 200[4]	58.7	62.1	67.7	61.5	62.6	58.9	62.0	93.0	93.2	94.8	93.9	94.9	93.8	92.7	96.0	96.4	97.2	98.3	98.9	98.1	97.1
Level 250[5]	15.6	14.6	17.7	17.2	17.5	18.4	16.2	57.8	58.6	60.7	59.0	58.7	58.7	61.6	78.6	80.1	80.7	83.1	85.7	84.1	82.5
Level 300[6]	0.9	0.6	0.6	1.0	1.4	1.7	0.7	9.8	10.2	11.3	11.0	10.9	11.0	15.3	39.0	38.7	37.8	40.3	40.9	41.4	43.2
Level 350[7]	0.0	0.0	0.0	0.0	0.0	0.0	0.0	0.1	0.2	0.2	0.3	0.2	0.4	0.6	6.8	6.2	5.3	5.7	4.6	7.0	6.8
Male																					
Level 150[3]	87.9	91.0	92.9	90.4	90.4	87.9	90.2	99.6	99.6	99.8	99.7	99.7	99.7	99.2	99.4	99.5	99.8	99.9	100.0	99.8	99.7
Level 200[4]	52.7	56.2	62.7	58.0	58.4	53.8	56.9	90.7	90.9	93.4	92.2	92.8	91.4	90.4	94.7	95.3	96.3	97.6	98.5	97.0	96.3
Level 250[5]	12.0	11.5	14.6	15.9	15.8	16.1	14.2	51.6	51.7	55.9	54.0	52.3	52.4	55.5	74.4	75.6	77.9	79.6	82.9	77.7	78.4
Level 300[6]	0.6	0.3	0.4	0.8	1.1	1.0	0.0	7.3	7.0	9.1	9.0	8.6	7.6	12.8	33.9	33.7	35.0	35.4	37.1	36.1	38.4
Level 350[7]	0.0	0.0	0.0	0.0	0.0	0.0	0.0	0.1	0.1	0.2	0.2	0.1	0.2	0.4	5.2	5.1	4.5	4.8	3.5	5.6	5.3
Female																					
Level 150[3]	93.2	95.3	96.4	94.2	94.9	92.4	94.4	99.9	99.9	99.9	99.9	100.0	99.9	99.8	99.8	99.8	99.9	99.9	100.0	100.0	99.9
Level 200[4]	64.6	68.1	72.7	65.2	66.9	64.2	67.3	95.2	95.5	96.1	95.8	96.9	96.3	95.0	97.3	97.5	98.1	99.0	99.3	99.2	97.9
Level 250[5]	19.2	17.7	20.7	18.4	19.1	20.8	18.2	64.0	65.5	65.4	64.0	65.0	65.0	67.5	82.6	84.3	83.6	86.8	88.2	88.6	86.8
Level 300[6]	1.3	0.9	0.8	1.1	1.6	2.0	0.8	12.3	13.5	13.2	13.2	13.2	14.5	17.7	44.0	43.6	40.7	45.0	44.4	46.8	48.5
Level 350[7]	0.0	0.0	0.0	0.0	0.0	0.1	0.0	0.2	0.3	0.3	0.4	0.4	0.5	0.8	8.4	7.3	6.0	6.7	5.5	8.5	8.4
White[8]																					
Level 150[3]	94.0	96.0	97.1	95.4	95.1	93.5	95.8	99.9	99.9	99.9	99.9	99.9	99.9	99.8	99.9	99.9	100.0	100.0	100.0	100.0	99.9
Level 200[4]	65.0	69.0	74.2	68.6	68.4	66.0	69.3	96.2	96.4	97.1	96.2	96.0	96.0	95.9	97.9	98.6	99.1	99.0	99.3	98.8	98.6
Level 250[5]	18.0	17.4	21.0	20.9	20.3	22.6	19.6	64.2	65.5	67.8	65.3	63.7	64.8	68.5	83.7	86.2	86.9	88.0	88.7	88.3	88.0
Level 300[6]	1.1	0.7	0.8	1.2	1.6	2.0	0.9	11.3	12.1	13.6	13.1	12.4	13.3	18.1	44.0	43.9	43.3	46.3	45.4	47.5	50.1
Level 350[7]	0.0	0.0	0.0	0.0	0.0	0.0	0.0	0.2	0.3	0.3	0.4	0.3	0.5	0.8	7.7	7.2	6.2	6.9	5.5	8.7	8.3
Black[8]																					
Level 150[3]	69.7	80.7	84.9	81.3	83.2	76.9	79.6	98.6	98.4	99.3	99.4	99.8	99.4	98.7	97.6	97.7	99.0	99.9	100.0	99.6	99.1
Level 200[4]	22.0	31.6	41.3	36.6	39.4	33.9	36.6	74.2	76.9	84.1	85.5	91.3	87.7	82.0	81.9	82.0	85.6	95.9	98.0	95.7	91.6
Level 250[5]	1.6	2.0	4.1	4.5	5.6	5.2	4.6	21.1	24.8	30.1	34.6	40.2	41.7	38.4	40.1	43.0	44.0	65.7	75.8	69.1	61.4
Level 300[6]	0.0	0.0	0.0	0.1	0.2	0.3	0.0	0.8	1.5	1.8	2.8	4.6	4.6	5.7	7.7	8.1	7.1	16.2	24.9	19.7	16.9
Level 350[7]	0.0	0.0	0.0	0.0	0.0	0.0	0.0	0.0	0.0	0.0	0.1	0.1	0.1	0.1	0.4	0.4	0.2	0.9	1.4	1.5	1.6
Hispanic																					
Level 150[3]	—	80.8	84.5	82.0	85.6	83.7	83.4	—	99.6	99.7	99.5	99.2	99.1	98.1	—	99.3	99.3	99.8	99.3	99.7	99.8
Level 200[4]	—	34.6	41.6	39.6	45.9	40.9	43.1	—	81.3	86.8	86.7	87.4	85.8	83.4	—	88.7	93.3	95.6	96.3	95.9	93.4
Level 250[5]	—	2.6	5.0	4.3	8.6	5.8	7.2	—	32.0	35.4	39.0	38.0	37.2	40.9	—	52.9	62.2	68.3	71.5	75.2	69.2
Level 300[6]	—	0.0	0.0	0.1	0.4	0.2	0.0	—	2.2	2.3	4.1	4.4	3.9	6.0	—	12.6	16.5	21.2	23.3	27.1	27.3
Level 350[7]	—	0.0	0.0	0.0	0.0	0.0	0.0	—	0.0	0.0	0.1	0.0	0.1	0.0	—	1.2	1.3	2.0	1.3	2.4	2.3

[1] As measured by the National Assessment of Educational Progress (NAEP).
[2] All participants of this age were in school.
[3] Able to follow brief written directions and carry out simple, discrete reading tasks.
[4] Able to understand, combine ideas, and make inferences based on short uncomplicated passages about specific or sequentially related information.
[5] Able to search for specific information, interrelate ideas, and make generalizations about literature, science, and social studies materials.
[6] Able to find, understand, summarize, and explain relatively complicated literary and informational material.
[7] Able to understand the links between ideas even when those links are not explicitly stated and to make appropriate generalizations even when the texts lack clear introductions or explanations.
[8] Data for 1971 include persons of Hispanic origin.
—Data not available.

SOURCE: U.S. Department of Education, National Center for Education Statistics, National Assessment of Educational Progress, The Reading Report Card, 1971–88 and NAEP 1992 Trends in Academic Progress, by Educational Testing Service. (This table was prepared April 1994.)

Table 109.—Average proficiency in reading for 4th graders in public schools,[1] by selected characteristics, region, and state: 1994

Region and state	Average	Race/ethnicity						Sex		Parental education[2]			
		White	Black	His-panic	Asian	Pacific Islander	Amer-ican Indian	Male	Female	Did not finish high school	Grad-uated high school	Some edu-cation after high school	Grad-uated college
1	2	3	4	5	6	7	8	9	10	11	12	13	14
United States	**212**	**223**	**186**	**188**	**231**	**216**	**200**	**207**	**218**	**188**	**206**	**222**	**222**
Region													
Northeast	212	224	184	191	(3)	(3)	(3)	207	216	(3)	202	222	221
Southeast	208	219	188	184	(3)	(3)	(3)	202	215	186	207	222	216
Central	218	225	182	199	(3)	(3)	(3)	212	225	(3)	215	221	226
West	212	222	186	186	5 226	(3)	(3)	207	217	188	201	221	223
State													
Alabama	208	220	188	178	(3)	(3)	(3)	203	213	197	201	217	217
Arizona	206	220	183	188	(3)	(3)	181	201	211	189	200	219	218
Arkansas	209	218	183	192	(3)	(3)	(3)	204	213	196	203	221	215
California	197	211	182	174	211	5 213	(3)	194	200	166	191	207	207
Colorado	213	222	191	193	(3)	(3)	204	209	218	192	213	220	222
Connecticut	222	234	190	190	(3)	(3)	(3)	218	226	204	209	234	231
Delaware	206	215	188	190	(3)	(3)	(3)	200	212	185	202	217	214
Florida	205	218	183	189	(3)	(3)	(3)	199	210	187	195	219	212
Georgia	207	222	185	184	(3)	(3)	(3)	201	212	185	199	219	217
Hawaii	201	219	189	185	219	191	(3)	194	208	192	194	215	208
Indiana	220	225	193	201	(3)	(3)	(3)	216	223	198	216	230	229
Iowa	223	225	5 186	204	(3)	(3)	(3)	219	227	211	219	232	229
Kentucky	212	215	190	196	(3)	(3)	(3)	206	217	195	212	222	218
Louisiana	197	213	180	175	(3)	(3)	(3)	193	200	188	196	209	200
Maine	228	229	(3)	218	(3)	(3)	(3)	225	231	214	225	237	236
Maryland	210	223	185	197	232	(3)	(3)	205	214	195	202	215	217
Massachusetts	223	231	199	194	5 201	(3)	(3)	221	226	206	212	230	232
Minnesota	218	222	173	202	(3)	(3)	196	214	223	(3)	212	220	229
Mississippi	202	220	187	181	(3)	(3)	(3)	196	207	192	199	213	207
Missouri	217	223	192	200	(3)	(3)	212	213	221	199	216	227	225
Montana[4]	222	226	(3)	208	—	—	203	218	227	211	219	227	230
Nebraska[4]	220	224	5 190	205	(3)	(3)	202	216	224	(3)	215	232	231
New Hampshire[4]	223	224	(3)	213	(3)	(3)	(3)	218	229	207	220	236	231
New Jersey	219	231	193	200	237	(3)	(3)	216	222	193	209	225	230
New Mexico	205	219	196	196	(3)	(3)	185	201	208	188	200	220	215
New York	212	226	191	193	230	(3)	(3)	207	216	196	208	224	220
North Carolina	214	225	193	189	(3)	(3)	5 201	209	220	195	204	226	223
North Dakota	225	228	(3)	212	(3)	(3)	5 197	221	230	(3)	217	232	233
Pennsylvania[4]	215	224	180	187	(3)	(3)	(3)	211	220	187	210	221	224
Rhode Island[4]	220	226	197	195	203	(3)	(3)	215	225	203	217	230	228
South Carolina	203	219	184	182	(3)	(3)	(3)	199	208	189	193	216	213
Tennessee[4]	213	220	188	196	(3)	(3)	(3)	208	217	200	213	225	219
Texas	212	227	191	198	(3)	(3)	(3)	210	214	195	207	224	222
Utah	217	221	(3)	199	(3)	(3)	195	213	222	(3)	211	225	226
Virginia	213	224	192	206	(3)	(3)	(3)	208	219	196	207	220	221
Washington	213	217	198	190	220	208	207	209	217	197	209	216	223
West Virginia	213	215	202	192	(3)	(3)	(3)	208	218	196	213	226	221
Wisconsin[4]	224	228	197	203	(3)	(3)	(3)	221	227	212	223	228	233
Wyoming	221	224	(3)	209	(3)	(3)	5 210	218	224	203	215	230	228
Department of Defense Overseas Schools	218	224	205	211	222	215	210	213	223	(3)	209	226	223
Guam	181	192	171	171	180	183	(3)	172	190	164	176	189	185

[1] As measured by the National Assessment of Educational Progress (NAEP). Forty-one states and Guam participated in the test, but the sample size in two states was insufficient to permit a reliable estimate.

[2] Parents' highest level of education. Data not shown for students who did not know parents' level of education.

[3] Sample size is insufficient to permit a reliable estimate

[4] Did not satisfy one or more of the guidelines for school sample participation rates. Data are subject to appreciable nonresponse bias.

[5] The nature of the sample does not allow accurate determination of the variability of this value.

—Data not available.

NOTE.—These test scores are from the National Assessment of Educational Progress (NAEP). The NAEP scores have been evaluated at certain performance levels. A score of 300 implies an ability to find, understand, summarize, and explain relatively complicated literary and informational material. A score of 250 implies an ability to search for specific information, interrelate ideas, and make generalizations about literature, science, and social studies materials. A score of 200 implies an ability to understand, combine ideas, and make inferences based on short uncomplicated passages about specific or sequentially related information. A score of 150 implies an ability to follow brief written directions and carry out simple, discrete reading tasks. Scale ranges from 0 to 500. Excludes states not participating in the survey. Some data have been revised from previously published figures.

SOURCE: U.S. Department of Education, National Center for Education Statistics, National Assessment of Educational Progress, *1994 NAEP Reading, Revised Edition: A First Look*, prepared by Educational Testing Service. (This table was prepared November 1995).

Table 110.—Average proficiency in reading for 4th graders in public schools,[1] by reading and television watching habits, region, and state: 1992

Region and state	Frequency of reading for fun				Amount of television watched each day				
	Almost every day	Once or twice a week	Once or twice a month	Never or hardly ever	Six or more hours	Four to five hours	Three hours	Two hours	One hour or less
1	2	3	4	5	6	7	8	9	10
United States	**223**	**218**	**209**	**199**	**198**	**216**	**223**	**223**	**220**
Region									
Northeast	231	220	211	200	201	221	232	227	229
Southeast	216	214	208	201	198	214	218	217	217
Central	227	220	211	204	199	215	226	228	224
West	219	218	206	191	197	215	218	221	214
State									
Alabama	212	210	205	197	198	209	216	215	210
Arizona	217	211	203	199	201	210	214	217	210
Arkansas	217	213	206	199	200	217	220	217	212
California	212	200	196	190	184	205	208	208	210
Colorado	225	216	215	202	203	218	220	223	220
Connecticut	230	220	219	207	204	219	226	232	233
Delaware [2]	220	215	210	197	198	216	216	225	218
District of Columbia	192	190	184	178	184	190	190	193	193
Florida	214	212	206	195	196	210	214	220	212
Georgia	219	215	206	198	200	216	220	220	215
Hawaii	210	203	202	192	193	208	210	208	205
Idaho	226	220	217	205	206	219	223	225	224
Indiana	229	222	221	206	210	223	227	228	225
Iowa	233	225	218	210	212	224	231	234	229
Kentucky	219	215	214	201	203	218	219	217	213
Louisiana	208	206	206	194	195	207	210	209	209
Maine [2]	234	227	224	213	215	226	233	230	232
Maryland	221	211	207	194	194	213	220	223	220
Massachusetts	234	225	223	211	211	226	230	234	234
Michigan	224	216	209	207	198	217	222	225	225
Minnesota	230	221	212	204	204	220	228	229	227
Mississippi	202	202	200	192	192	202	208	209	195
Missouri	227	222	220	205	208	222	227	229	222
Nebraska [2]	228	223	221	203	204	224	228	227	222
New Hampshire [2]	236	228	224	210	216	229	228	233	235
New Jersey [2]	232	225	220	203	205	225	229	233	235
New Mexico	218	212	214	194	196	212	217	220	211
New York [2]	221	216	214	201	202	214	224	223	221
North Carolina	219	212	207	198	197	214	218	222	217
North Dakota	234	226	222	212	211	226	231	231	229
Ohio	226	217	214	204	204	220	225	224	222
Oklahoma	225	225	221	207	211	224	227	227	220
Pennsylvania	227	221	221	206	202	221	228	230	227
Rhode Island	223	217	216	197	203	217	222	223	223
South Carolina	216	211	210	196	198	212	215	222	215
Tennessee	219	213	208	201	199	218	219	218	214
Texas	218	215	212	202	200	213	220	222	218
Utah	228	222	214	207	209	220	225	224	224
Virginia	228	223	216	204	205	223	228	232	230
West Virginia	224	218	212	201	204	218	223	223	219
Wisconsin	233	222	217	206	211	225	228	230	227
Wyoming	230	224	217	207	210	223	227	229	227
Outlying areas									
Guam	187	186	175	174	176	190	193	184	178

[1] As measured by the National Assessment of Educational Progress (NAEP). Forty-one states, the District of Columbia, and Guam participated in the test.

[2] Did not satisfy one or more of the guidelines for school sample participation rates. Data are subject to appreciable nonresponse bias.

NOTE.—These test scores are from the National Assessment of Educational Progress (NAEP). The NAEP scores have been evaluated at certain performance levels. A score of 300 implies an ability to find, understand, summarize, and explain relatively complicated literary and informational material. A score of 250 implies an ability to search for specific information, interrelate ideas, and make generalizations about literature, science, and social studies materials. A score of 200 implies an ability to understand, combine ideas, and make inferences based on short uncomplicated passages about specific or sequentially related information. A score of 150 implies an ability to follow brief written directions and carry out simple, discrete reading tasks. Scale ranges from 0 to 500.

SOURCE: U.S. Department of Education, National Center for Education Statistics, National Assessment of Educational Progress, *NAEP 1992 Reading Report Card for the Nation and the States*, prepared by Educational Testing Service. (This table was prepared January 1994.)

Table 111.—Average writing performance of 4th, 8th, and 11th graders, by selected characteristics of students: 1984 to 1992

Selected characteristics of students	4th graders				8th graders				11th graders			
	1984	1988	1990	1992	1984	1988	1990	1992	1984	1988	1990	1992
1	2	3	4	5	6	7	8	9	10	11	12	13
All students	**203.8**	**205.7**	**201.7**	**207.1**	**266.7**	**263.7**	**256.6**	**274.4**	**289.7**	**291.3**	**287.1**	**287.3**
Sex												
Male	200.5	199.0	195.0	198.3	257.5	253.7	245.6	263.6	281.1	282.2	276.4	279.4
Female	207.6	212.6	208.7	216.1	276.2	273.5	267.9	285.0	298.6	299.3	298.2	296.4
Race/ethnicity												
White	210.7	214.9	211.0	216.7	271.7	269.1	262.1	279.2	296.8	296.2	292.8	294.1
Black	181.6	173.3	171.4	175.0	247.1	246.0	239.0	258.1	270.3	275.2	268.2	263.2
Hispanic	188.5	190.3	184.1	189.4	246.9	250.4	245.7	265.0	259.1	273.8	276.9	273.6
Parental education												
Not high school graduate	178.7	194.2	185.7	191.2	257.7	254.3	245.6	257.9	273.6	275.8	268.0	271.0
Graduated high school	191.8	199.4	196.6	202.2	260.8	257.6	252.5	267.9	283.5	284.6	278.2	278.4
Post high school	208.0	211.4	213.9	201.4	271.4	275.1	266.9	279.6	297.6	296.1	292.2	292.3
Graduated college	218.1	212.4	209.0	213.7	277.8	270.5	264.9	284.3	299.9	299.0	297.5	295.7
Control of school												
Public	201.9	204.2	200.4	205.2	264.4	262.1	253.6	272.4	287.8	289.9	285.5	286.5
Private	215.4	216.0	216.2	221.6	281.8	275.5	276.7	287.6	305.4	299.7	305.8	295.4
Type of community												
Advantaged urban	221.2	218.4	216.8	235.9	285.7	270.9	279.4	293.5	305.8	295.2	295.2	296.6
Disadvantaged urban	199.2	174.8	175.2	183.9	249.2	245.8	244.5	251.7	267.1	256.1	273.4	270.4
Extreme rural	188.2	202.3	201.9	203.2	259.6	268.3	252.3	267.3	286.8	291.9	285.6	288.5
Other	202.8	207.4	203.2	206.9	266.1	263.7	255.0	275.1	290.0	290.9	287.9	288.9
Region												
Northeast	212.4	204.0	211.1	216.1	273.3	265.1	261.4	284.7	290.9	295.0	295.4	290.2
Southeast	203.5	200.1	192.3	193.0	266.9	268.2	251.8	266.3	287.3	289.4	280.0	277.8
Central	200.8	211.9	203.0	213.9	263.8	258.1	259.1	277.2	291.3	291.8	288.8	291.4
West	200.8	207.3	201.2	205.7	263.5	264.0	255.0	271.3	288.8	289.2	284.8	289.4

NOTE.—These test scores are from the National Assessment of Educational Progress (NAEP). The writing scale score ranges from 0 to 500 and is defined as the average of a respondent's estimated scores on specific writing tasks. The average response method is used to estimate average writing achievement for each participant as if each had performed all 11 writing tasks.

SOURCE: U.S. Department of Education, National Center for Education Statistics, National Assessment of Educational Progress, *The Writing Report Card, 1984–88* and *NAEP 1992 Trends in Academic Progress*, by Educational Testing Service. (This table was prepared April 1994.)

Table 112.—Student values and attitudes toward writing, by grade level: 1984, 1990, and 1992

Statements about writing	Percent of students reporting the statement is true more than half the time								
	Grade 4			Grade 8			Grade 11		
	1984	1990	1992	1984	1990	1992	1984	1990	1992
1	2	3	4	5	6	7	8	9	10
Writing helps me think more clearly	—	—	—	44	46	42	52	47	50
Writing helps me tell others what I think	—	—	—	52	56	52	55	58	57
Writing helps tell others how I feel	—	—	—	50	56	52	55	60	60
Writing helps me understand my own feelings	—	—	—	40	47	44	47	50	49
People who write well have a better chance of getting good jobs	—	—	—	47	53	51	54	58	59
People who write well are more influential	—	—	—	49	55	52	54	60	60
I like to write	55	57	54	39	42	43	40	39	43
I am a good writer	59	62	63	41	44	44	38	44	49
People like what I write	52	56	55	38	39	44	35	42	46
I write on my own outside of school	47	42	46	36	35	37	31	28	33
I don't like to write things that will be graded	37	33	32	31	36	37	27	30	30
If I didn't have to write for school, I wouldn't write anything	33	27	28	17	19	18	15	16	17

—Data not available.

SOURCE: U.S. Department of Education, National Center for Education Statistics, *NAEP 1992 Trends in Academic Progress,* by Educational Testing Service. (This table was prepared April 1994.)

Table 113.—Percent of students at or above selected history proficiency levels, by selected characteristics and grade level: 1994

Selected characteristics of students	Percentage of 4th graders				Percentage of 8th graders				Percentage of 12th graders			
	Below basic	At or above basic	At or above proficient	At or above advanced	Below basic	At or above basic	At or above proficient	At or above advanced	Below basic	At or above basic	At or above proficient	At or above advanced
1	2	3	4	5	6	7	8	9	10	11	12	13
All students	**36**	**64**	**17**	**2**	**39**	**61**	**14**	**1**	**57**	**43**	**11**	**1**
Sex												
Male	38	62	18	2	39	61	15	1	55	45	12	1
Female	35	65	16	2	39	61	13	1	60	40	9	1
Race/ethnicity												
White	26	74	22	3	29	71	17	1	50	50	13	1
Black	64	36	4	0	67	33	4	0	83	17	2	0
Hispanic	59	41	6	1	59	41	5	0	78	22	4	0
Asian	36	64	22	4	28	72	23	2	54	46	16	2
Pacific Islander	41	59	16	3	48	52	11	1	67	33	7	1
American Indian	49	51	9	0	58	42	5	0	70	30	5	0
Region												
Northeast	37	63	18	3	31	69	19	1	54	46	13	1
Southeast	39	61	15	2	49	51	9	0	63	37	8	0
Central	29	71	20	3	31	69	17	1	55	45	11	1
West	39	61	16	1	42	58	11	1	57	43	10	1
Parents' level of education												
Not high school graduate	63	37	2	0	63	37	3	0	85	15	1	0
Graduated high school	43	57	10	1	50	50	7	0	71	29	4	0
Some college	26	74	21	3	32	68	14	0	58	42	8	1
Graduated college	26	74	25	4	26	74	22	1	44	56	17	1

SOURCE: U.S. Department of Education, National Center for Education Statistics, National Assessment of Educational Progress, *NAEP 1994 U.S. History Report Card.* (This table was prepared November 1995.)

Table 114.—Average student proficiency in geography and U.S. history, by student characteristics: 1994

Characteristic	Percentage distribution of 12th graders	Geography scores			History scores		
		4th graders	8th graders	12th graders	4th graders	8th graders	12th graders
1	2	3	4	5	6	7	8
United States ..	100	206	260	285	205	259	286
Sex							
Male	50	208	262	288	203	259	288
Female	50	203	258	281	206	259	285
Race							
White	74	218	270	291	215	267	292
Black	12	168	229	258	177	239	265
Hispanic	8	183	239	268	180	243	267
Region							
Northeast	21	203	266	284	204	266	289
Southeast	23	200	252	278	201	251	282
Central	28	215	268	289	212	266	288
West	29	205	255	286	202	256	286
Type of school							
Public	89	204	258	283	203	257	284
Nonpublic schools	11	221	276	294	222	278	299
Catholic schools	6	222	276	291	221	279	298
Other nonpublic	4	220	276	298	224	277	299
Parents' level of education							
Not high school graduate	7	186	238	263	177	241	263
Graduated high school ..	22	197	250	274	197	251	276
Some college	25	216	265	286	214	264	287
Graduated college	44	216	272	294	216	270	296

—Data not available.

NOTE.—These test scores are from the National Assessment of Educational Progress (NAEP). As with the NAEP reading scale, these scales range from 0 to 500. However, the distribution of scores varies by subject. Therefore, direct score comparisons among the subjects should be avoided.

SOURCE: U.S. Department of Education, National Center for Education Statistics, National Assessment of Educational Progress, *NAEP 1994 U.S. History Report Card*, and *The Geography Report Card*, prepared by Educational Testing Service. (This table was prepared November 1995.)

Table 115.—Percent of students at or above selected geography proficiency levels, by selected characteristics and grade level: 1994

Selected characteristics of students	Percentage of 4th graders				Percentage of 8th graders				Percentage of 12th graders			
	Below basic	At or above basic	At or above proficient	At or above advanced	Below basic	At or above basic	At or above proficient	At or above advanced	Below basic	At or above basic	At or above proficient	At or above advanced
1	2	3	4	5	6	7	8	9	10	11	12	13
All students	**30**	**70**	**22**	**3**	**29**	**71**	**28**	**4**	**30**	**70**	**27**	**2**
Sex												
Male	29	71	26	4	28	72	30	5	27	73	32	2
Female	32	68	19	2	31	69	25	3	33	67	22	1
Race/ethnicity												
White	19	81	29	4	18	82	36	5	22	78	33	2
Black	66	34	3	0	66	34	5	0	68	32	5	0
Hispanic	51	49	10	1	50	50	10	1	52	48	10	0
Asian	21	79	32	5	21	79	40	8	31	69	32	3
Region												
Northeast	33	67	22	3	24	76	33	6	31	69	25	2
Southeast	36	64	17	2	38	62	21	3	40	60	20	1
Central	22	78	28	4	20	80	36	6	25	75	32	2
West	30	70	21	3	33	67	23	3	28	72	29	2
Parents' level of education												
Not high school graduate	48	52	8	0	53	47	8	1	59	41	7	0
Graduated high school	37	63	15	1	38	62	15	1	44	56	14	0
Some college	20	80	30	3	21	79	29	3	25	75	24	1
Graduated college	22	78	31	5	18	82	41	7	19	81	40	3

SOURCE: U.S. Department of Education, National Center for Education Statistics, National Assessment of Educational Progress, *NAEP 1994 Geography Report Card*. (This table was prepared November 1995.)

Table 116.—Average mathematics proficiency, by age and by selected characteristics of students: 1978 to 1992

Selected characteristics of students	9-year-olds					13-year-olds					17-year-olds [1]				
	1978	1982	1986	1990	1992	1978	1982	1986	1990	1992	1978	1982	1986	1990	1992
1	2	3	4	5	6	7	8	9	10	11	12	13	14	15	16
All students	218.6	219.0	221.7	229.6	229.6	264.1	268.6	269.0	270.4	273.1	300.4	298.5	302.0	304.6	306.7
Sex															
Male	217.4	217.1	221.7	229.1	230.8	263.6	269.2	270.0	271.2	274.1	303.8	301.5	304.7	306.3	308.9
Female	219.9	220.8	221.7	230.2	228.4	264.7	268.0	267.9	269.6	272.0	297.1	295.6	299.4	302.9	304.5
Race/ethnicity															
White	224.1	224.0	226.9	235.2	235.1	271.6	274.4	273.6	276.3	278.9	305.9	303.7	307.5	309.5	311.9
Black	192.4	194.9	201.6	208.4	208.0	229.6	240.4	249.2	249.1	250.2	268.4	271.8	278.6	288.5	285.8
Hispanic	202.9	204.0	205.4	213.8	211.9	238.0	252.4	254.3	254.6	259.3	276.3	276.7	283.1	283.5	292.2
Television watched per day															
0 to 2 hours	—	218.0	222.0	231.0	231.0	—	273.0	276.0	277.0	280.0	305.0	303.0	310.0	312.0	314.0
3 to 5 hours	—	227.0	229.0	234.0	233.0	—	269.0	271.0	271.0	273.0	296.0	294.0	299.0	300.0	300.0
6 or more hours	—	214.0	213.0	221.0	219.0	—	256.0	255.0	258.0	255.0	279.0	280.0	282.0	287.0	285.0
Reading materials in the home [2]															
0 to 2 items	201.0	203.0	208.0	196.0	—	239.0	250.0	255.0	240.0	—	277.0	281.0	281.0	271.0	—
3 items	221.0	221.0	224.0	211.0	—	260.0	267.0	266.0	255.0	—	296.0	295.0	297.0	286.0	—
4 items	231.0	231.0	234.0	226.0	—	275.0	279.0	276.0	266.0	—	308.0	306.0	309.0	299.0	—

[1] All participants of this age group were in school.

[2] The 4 items in the scale were: newspaper subscription; magazine subscription; more than 25 books in the home; and encyclopedia in the home.

—Data not available.

NOTE.—These test scores are from the National Assessment of Educational Progress (NAEP). Performers at the 150 level know some basic addition and subtraction facts, and most can add two-digit numbers without regrouping. They recognize simple situations in which addition and subtraction apply. Performers at the 200 level have considerable understanding of two-digit numbers and know some basic multiplication and division facts. Performers at the 250 level have an initial understanding of the four basic operations. They can also compare information from graphs and charts, and are developing an ability to analyze simple logical relations. Performers at the 300 level can compute decimals, simple fractions, and percents. They can identify geometric figures, measure lengths and angles, and calculate areas of rectangles. They are developing the skills to operate with signed numbers, exponents, and square roots. Performers at the 350 level can apply a range of reasoning skills to solve multi-step problems. They can solve routine problems involving fractions and percents, recognize properties of basic geometric figures, and work with exponents and square roots. Scale ranges from 0 to 500.

SOURCE: U.S. Department of Education, National Center for Education Statistics, National Assessment of Educational Progress, *Trends in Academic Progress* and *NAEP 1992 Trends in Academic Progress*, prepared by Educational Testing Service. (This table was prepared April 1994.)

Table 117.—Percent of students at or above selected mathematics proficiency levels, [1] by race/ethnicity and age: 1978 to 1992

Race/ethnicity and year	9-year-olds [2]				13-year-olds [3]				17-year-olds [3]			
	Simple arithmetic facts	Beginning skills and understanding	Numerical operations and beginning problem solving	Moderately complex procedures and reasoning	Beginning skills and understanding	Numerical operations and beginning problem solving	Moderately complex procedures and reasoning	Multi-step problem solving and algebra	Beginning skills and understanding	Numerical operations and beginning problem solving	Moderately complex procedures and reasoning	Multi-step problem solving and algebra
1	2	3	4	5	6	7	8	9	10	11	12	13
All students												
1978	97	70	20	1	95	65	18	1	100	92	52	7
1982	97	71	19	1	98	71	17	0	100	93	48	6
1986	98	74	21	1	99	73	16	0	100	96	52	6
1990	99	82	28	1	98	75	17	0	100	96	56	7
1992	99	81	28	1	99	78	19	0	100	97	59	7
White [4]												
1978	98	76	23	1	98	73	21	1	100	96	58	8
1982	98	77	22	1	99	78	21	1	100	96	55	6
1986	99	80	25	1	99	79	19	0	100	98	59	8
1990	100	87	33	2	99	82	21	0	100	98	63	8
1992	100	87	32	1	100	85	23	0	100	98	66	9
Black [4]												
1978	88	42	4	0	80	29	2	0	99	71	17	0
1982	90	46	4	0	90	38	3	0	100	76	17	1
1986	94	53	6	0	95	49	4	0	100	86	21	0
1990	97	60	9	0	95	49	4	0	100	92	33	2
1992	97	60	10	0	95	51	4	0	100	90	30	1
Hispanic												
1978	93	54	9	0	86	36	4	0	99	78	23	1
1982	94	56	8	0	96	52	6	0	100	81	22	1
1986	96	58	7	0	97	56	6	0	99	89	27	1
1990	98	68	11	0	97	57	6	0	100	86	30	2
1992	97	65	12	0	98	63	7	0	100	94	39	1

[1] As measured by the National Assessment of Educational Progress (NAEP).

[2] Virtually no students were able to perform multi-step problems and algebra.

[3] Virtually all students knew simple arithmetic facts. Data are only for students enrolled in school.

[4] Excludes persons of Hispanic origin.

SOURCE: U.S. Department of Education, National Center for Education Statistics, National Assessment of Educational Progress, *NAEP 1992 Trends in Academic Progress*, prepared by Educational Testing Service. (This table was prepared May 1994.)

Table 118.—Average proficiency in mathematics content areas for 8th graders in public schools, by region and state: 1990 and 1992

Region and state	Average proficiency in content areas												1992 percent of students at or above		
	All areas		Numbers and operations		Measurement		Geometry		Data analysis, statistics, and probability		Algebra and functions		Level 200[1]	Level 250[2]	Level 300[3]
	1990	1992	1990	1992	1990	1992	1990	1992	1990	1992	1990	1992			
1	2	3	4	5	6	7	8	9	10	11	12	13	14	15	16
United States	**262**	**266**	**266**	**270**	**258**	**264**	**259**	**262**	**262**	**267**	**260**	**266**	**96**	**67**	**18**
Region															
Northeast	270	267	272	271	267	265	268	263	273	269	268	266	96	65	21
Southeast	254	258	260	263	248	253	251	253	253	258	256	259	95	58	12
Central	265	273	270	277	262	272	261	269	265	274	262	272	98	75	22
West	261	267	263	270	257	266	260	263	261	267	259	266	96	68	19
State															
Alabama	253	251	259	258	248	245	249	245	251	250	252	253	93	51	9
Arizona	260	[4]265	265	269	257	264	256	260	259	265	258	264	97	68	14
Arkansas	256	255	262	262	254	251	253	250	255	254	253	255	94	58	9
California	256	260	260	263	252	258	256	259	255	258	256	258	93	61	15
Colorado	267	[4]272	269	273	265	273	266	269	270	274	266	270	98	75	20
Connecticut	270	[4]273	274	277	268	275	266	268	271	274	268	270	97	74	24
Delaware	261	262	265	267	259	258	256	257	262	262	259	263	96	64	14
District of Columbia	231	[4]234	239	243	222	221	229	231	223	229	235	237	82	32	4
Florida	255	259	260	264	252	254	251	255	255	259	255	260	94	61	14
Georgia	259	259	263	265	253	253	257	253	260	259	257	259	95	60	12
Hawaii	251	[4]257	257	261	249	254	252	257	243	249	249	256	93	57	13
Idaho	271	[4]274	275	277	269	276	269	271	273	274	270	274	99	80	20
Indiana	267	269	271	272	265	269	264	266	269	273	265	267	98	72	19
Iowa	278	283	282	285	276	287	274	278	280	285	275	280	100	86	29
Kentucky	257	[4]261	261	266	254	259	253	256	258	262	257	260	96	64	13
Louisiana	246	249	253	256	241	242	243	244	243	248	246	249	92	50	7
Maine	—	278	—	280	—	282	—	274	—	282	—	274	99	83	24
Maryland	261	264	264	269	256	261	257	259	261	266	262	264	95	64	19
Massachusetts	—	272	—	276	—	270	—	267	—	274	—	271	98	74	22
Michigan	264	267	269	270	261	266	261	261	265	268	264	267	96	69	18
Minnesota	275	[4]282	279	282	272	285	272	278	279	284	274	281	99	83	29
Mississippi	—	246	—	256	—	236	—	239	—	243	—	245	90	45	6
Missouri	—	270	—	272	—	271	—	266	—	272	—	270	98	74	18
Nebraska	276	277	279	279	273	278	273	274	278	278	273	275	98	81	25
New Hampshire	273	[4]278	275	280	272	280	271	273	275	281	272	274	99	82	23
New Jersey	270	271	274	276	267	268	266	265	270	271	268	272	97	73	22
New Mexico	256	[4]259	259	263	254	257	257	256	253	258	257	257	96	61	10
New York	261	266	264	270	255	262	260	261	263	268	260	265	94	68	19
North Carolina	250	[4]258	256	261	242	253	249	254	248	258	251	259	95	59	11
North Dakota	281	283	286	286	279	285	278	277	285	286	275	279	100	87	28
Ohio	264	267	269	272	259	266	260	262	266	270	262	267	97	70	17
Oklahoma	263	[4]267	268	271	258	266	260	262	264	269	262	267	97	72	16
Pennsylvania	266	271	270	274	264	271	263	265	268	273	265	270	98	73	20
Rhode Island	260	[4]265	264	269	257	263	256	259	259	266	261	266	97	68	15
South Carolina	—	260	—	265	—	257	—	256	—	258	—	259	96	60	14
Tennessee	—	258	—	264	—	253	—	252	—	259	—	257	95	59	11
Texas	258	[4]264	262	267	254	260	258	262	257	263	256	266	96	64	17
Utah	—	274	—	276	—	275	—	269	—	275	—	272	99	78	21
Virginia	264	267	268	272	260	265	261	261	264	268	265	267	97	68	18
West Virginia	256	258	260	263	253	256	254	254	256	260	254	257	97	60	9
Wisconsin	274	277	278	280	273	279	272	272	277	280	271	275	98	80	26
Wyoming	272	[4]274	275	276	270	278	270	272	273	275	270	271	99	79	19
Outlying areas															
Guam	232	[4]234	240	240	229	228	236	239	214	221	230	235	80	34	5
Virgin Islands	219	[4]222	229	231	216	211	223	222	196	214	219	221	76	18	1

[1] Indicates ability to perform simple additive reasoning and problem solving.

[2] Indicates ability to perform simple multiplicative reasoning and 2–step problem solving.

[3] Indicates ability to perform reasoning and problem solving involving fractions, decimals, percents, elementary geometry, and simple algebra.

[4] Statistically significant increases from 1990 to 1992.

—Did not participate in 1990 Trial State Assessment.

NOTE.—These test scores are from the National Assessment of Educational Progress (NAEP). Forty-one states, the District of Columbia, and two outlying areas participated in the 1992 Trial State Assessment of 8th graders. Seven of these states did not participate in the 1990 assessment. Scale ranges from 0 to 500.

SOURCE: U.S. Department of Education, National Center for Education Statistics, National Assessment of Educational Progress, *NAEP 1992 Mathematics Report Card for the Nation and the States*, prepared by Educational Testing Service. (This table was prepared April 1993.)

Table 119.—Average proficiency in mathematics content areas for 4th graders in public schools, by region and state: 1992

Region and state	Average proficiency in content areas							Parental education [1]				Percent of students at or above	
	All areas	Numbers and operations	Meas-ure-ment	Ge-ome-try	Data analysis, statistics, and probability	Algebra and functions	Esti-ma-tion	Did not finish high school	Grad-uated high school	Some edu-cation after high school	Grad-uated col-lege	Level 200 [2]	Level 250 [3]
1	2	3	4	5	6	7	8	9	10	11	12	13	14
United States	217	214	222	220	218	216	206	203	212	223	225	71	16
Region													
Northeast	223	220	227	224	223	222	205	—	215	229	231	75	22
Southeast	209	205	214	212	210	206	195	198	203	217	215	61	10
Central	222	219	228	224	223	220	212	—	218	228	229	77	19
West	217	214	221	222	217	215	213	202	216	218	224	70	15
State													
Alabama	207	204	213	209	209	204	198	202	203	216	211	58	9
Arizona	214	210	219	219	214	213	205	202	210	225	220	68	12
Arkansas	209	205	215	212	211	206	197	198	208	215	213	62	9
California	207	204	210	213	206	208	202	189	200	217	216	60	11
Colorado	220	216	225	227	220	217	212	200	212	228	228	75	17
Connecticut	226	223	230	230	225	225	217	205	218	225	235	79	23
Delaware	217	214	220	219	219	215	203	196	213	219	225	69	15
District of Columbia	191	189	193	198	189	191	171	186	187	198	196	37	5
Florida	212	208	219	215	214	211	200	199	204	221	219	66	12
Georgia	214	211	219	216	218	213	199	202	205	223	221	67	14
Hawaii	213	211	216	218	212	210	199	199	203	219	218	65	14
Idaho	220	216	227	226	219	217	211	200	215	228	227	77	14
Indiana	220	216	226	223	222	218	210	209	216	230	226	75	14
Iowa	229	227	234	229	230	226	221	211	223	235	236	84	24
Kentucky	214	211	218	215	215	212	205	203	210	222	223	67	12
Louisiana	203	199	208	206	204	201	188	194	198	214	207	54	7
Maine	231	227	236	236	231	228	220	215	225	240	240	86	26
Maryland	216	214	220	219	217	215	200	201	206	226	224	67	17
Massachusetts	226	224	229	229	225	222	217	195	219	230	234	80	22
Michigan	219	215	225	222	218	216	209	201	212	224	227	73	17
Minnesota	227	225	233	230	227	225	223	—	220	230	236	81	24
Mississippi	200	198	206	202	199	195	188	193	197	209	205	50	6
Missouri	221	217	226	224	223	220	211	210	216	227	228	76	17
Nebraska	224	221	230	229	225	220	216	—	222	230	230	78	20
New Hampshire	229	225	234	233	229	227	222	211	222	232	236	84	23
New Jersey	226	225	230	226	225	224	213	210	219	230	234	80	23
New Mexico	212	207	216	219	214	210	203	202	207	223	221	65	10
New York	217	215	221	218	221	215	204	210	211	225	227	71	16
North Carolina	211	208	216	215	214	210	198	201	204	220	219	64	12
North Dakota	228	224	235	229	229	225	222	—	224	234	233	85	21
Ohio	217	214	223	221	218	216	210	205	215	221	227	71	15
Oklahoma	219	216	224	220	221	217	211	209	215	225	225	76	13
Pennsylvania	223	221	229	223	223	221	212	211	220	236	230	77	20
Rhode Island	214	212	218	216	213	212	206	200	207	220	224	68	12
South Carolina	211	208	218	215	211	207	195	204	204	219	220	63	12
Tennessee	209	207	213	211	211	209	200	201	205	213	217	63	9
Texas	217	214	220	220	218	216	199	211	213	225	224	71	14
Utah	223	219	229	227	221	221	213	205	216	228	230	79	18
Virginia	220	217	224	222	223	217	206	203	210	219	230	73	18
West Virginia	214	210	223	217	214	211	204	201	210	222	223	68	11
Wisconsin	228	225	234	228	229	225	219	219	225	237	234	83	23
Wyoming	224	221	230	228	224	222	216	215	221	232	229	82	17
Outlying area													
Guam	191	188	192	201	189	192	173	183	186	206	191	40	4

[1] Parents' highest level of education.

[2] Indicates ability to perform simple additive reasoning and problem solving.

[3] Indicates ability to perform simple multiplicative reasoning and 2–step problem solving.

—Sample size insufficient to permit reliable estimate. There were fewer than 62 students.

NOTE.—These test scores are from the National Assessment of Educational Progress (NAEP). Forty-one states, the District of Columbia, and Guam participated in the 1992 Trial State Assessment of 4th graders. Scale ranges from 0 to 500.

SOURCE: U.S. Department of Education, National Center for Education Statistics, National Assessment of Educational Progress, *NAEP 1992 Mathematics Report Card for the Nation and the States*, prepared by Educational Testing Service. (This table was prepared April 1993.)

Table 120.—Selected characteristics of 8th grade students in public schools, by region and state: 1992 [1]

Region and state	Math units required for graduation	Year of revision of state guides with NCTM standards [2]	Length of school year 1989	Length of school year 1992	Passing test in math required for graduation in 1993	Percent of students with 4 or more hours of math instruction each week	Spending 30 minutes or more on math homework each day	Spending 1 or 2 hours on all homework each day	Spending more than 2 hours on all homework each day	Positive attitudes towards math [3]	Both parents living at home	Watching 6 or more hours of television each day
1	2	3	4	5	6	7	8	9	10	11	12	13
United States	—	—	—	—	—	32	64	59	8	59	75	13
Region												
Northeast	—	—	—	—	—	35	59	62	8	56	75	14
Southeast	—	—	—	—	—	37	65	56	7	59	71	17
Central	—	—	—	—	—	24	63	65	6	63	79	11
West	—	—	—	—	—	30	68	56	10	56	75	12
State												
Alabama	2	1989	175	175	Yes	60	65	59	7	62	72	20
Alaska	2	Devel.,1994	—	180	No	—	—	—	—	—	—	—
Arizona	2	1992	175	175	No	34	65	56	5	54	76	9
Arkansas	3	1993	178	178	No	42	61	56	7	60	75	20
California	2	1991	180	180	No	43	67	63	10	56	74	10
Colorado	(4)	1994	180	(5)	No	27	65	61	7	58	77	7
Connecticut	3	Devel.,1995	180	180	No	21	61	70	9	59	79	11
Delaware	2	Devel.,1994	180	180	No	30	57	62	5	63	73	17
District of Columbia	3	1993	190	180	No	52	63	63	10	73	45	31
Florida	3	Devel.,1994	180	180	Yes	40	62	57	7	61	71	15
Georgia	3	1992	180	180	Yes	56	65	59	7	66	71	18
Hawaii	3	Devel.,1994	183	180	Yes	34	68	55	11	54	75	22
Idaho	2	1994	180	180	No	28	63	57	5	56	83	7
Illinois	2	Devel.,1994	180	180	No	—	—	—	—	—	—	—
Indiana	2	1991	180	180	No	32	62	60	6	61	78	9
Iowa	(4)	1987	180	180	No	20	61	63	4	63	83	7
Kansas	2	1991	—	180	No	—	—	—	—	—	—	—
Kentucky	3	1993	175	175	No	47	61	54	6	57	78	13
Louisiana	3	Devel.,1994	180	180	Yes	54	62	61	10	63	71	20
Maine	2	Devel.,1994	—	175	No	12	66	70	8	61	81	8
Maryland	3	1985	180	180	Yes	45	60	65	7	61	73	17
Massachusetts	(4)	1994	—	180	No	28	67	70	9	57	77	8
Michigan	3	Devel.,1994	180	180	Yes	39	67	61	7	60	75	13
Minnesota	1	Devel.,1994	175	175	No	41	64	59	5	57	85	5
Mississippi	2	1993	—	180	Yes	60	68	60	8	67	70	21
Missouri	2	1990	—	174	No	44	66	60	6	60	77	12
Montana	2	Devel.,1995	180	180	No	—	—	—	—	—	—	—
Nebraska	(4)	Devel.,1994	(5)	(5)	No	25	69	61	5	60	81	8
Nevada	2	1993	—	180	Yes	—	—	—	—	—	—	—
New Hampshire	2	1993	180	180	No	38	62	68	9	58	81	7
New Jersey	3	1993	180	180	Yes	28	62	68	10	62	78	13
New Mexico	3	1992	180	180	Yes	26	65	56	7	56	75	11
New York	2	Devel.,1994	180	180	Yes	20	54	66	9	62	75	15
North Carolina	2	1992	180	180	Yes	52	64	64	7	65	73	16
North Dakota	2	1993	180	180	No	44	70	63	6	55	85	5
Ohio	2	1990	182	182	Yes	26	62	62	6	62	74	12
Oklahoma	2	1993	175	175	No	37	69	59	7	58	78	11
Oregon	2	Devel.,1994	175	(5)	No	—	—	—	—	—	—	—
Pennsylvania	3	none	180	180	No	24	58	63	4	59	79	9
Rhode Island	2	Devel.,1994	180	180	No	43	62	67	7	56	78	9
South Carolina	3	1993	—	180	Yes	59	61	61	7	70	73	17
South Dakota	2	Devel.,1994	—	175	No	—	—	—	—	—	—	—
Tennessee	2	1991	—	180	Yes	60	67	62	6	58	73	14
Texas	3	1991	175	175	Yes	38	67	57	8	61	75	12
Utah	2	1993	—	180	No	28	62	56	5	55	85	5
Vermont	(6)	Devel.,1994	—	175	No	—	—	—	—	—	—	—
Virginia	2	1988	180	180	Yes	38	65	63	7	63	77	15
Washington	2	Devel.,1994	—	180	No	—	—	—	—	—	—	—
West Virginia	2	1992	180	180	Yes	40	57	55	5	58	78	13
Wisconsin	2	Devel.,1995	180	180	No	32	59	61	5	59	80	8
Wyoming	(4)	1990	175	175	No	24	60	55	5	58	81	8
Outlying areas												
Guam	—	—	—	—	—	28	68	47	12	50	79	20
Virgin Islands	—	—	—	180	—	31	61	47	11	75	56	32

[1] Data are for 1992 unless otherwise specified.
[2] Standards recommended by the National Council of Teachers of Mathematics.
[3] Percent of students agreeing or strongly agreeing with positive statements about mathematics.
[4] Local board determines.
[5] No statewide policy.
[6] 5 units of math and science combined.

—Data not available or not applicable.

SOURCE: U.S. Department of Education, National Center for Education Statistics, National Assessment of Educational Progress, *The State of Mathematics Achievement,* by Educational Testing Service; and Council of Chief State School Officers, *State Education Indicators.* (This table was prepared June 1994.)

Table 121.— Mathematics proficiency of 17-year-olds, by highest mathematics course taken, sex, and race/ethnicity: 1978, 1990, and 1992

Year, sex, and race/ethnicity	Percent of students	Average proficiency by highest mathematics course taken						Percent of students at or above			
		All areas	Prealgebra or general mathematics	Algebra I	Geom-etry	Algebra II	Precalculus or calculus	200 [1]	250 [2]	300 [3]	350 [4]
1	2	3	4	5	6	7	8	9	10	11	12
1978											
Total	100.0	300.4	267	286	307	321	334	99.8	92.0	51.5	7.3
Male	48.7	303.8	269	289	310	325	337	99.9	93.0	55.1	9.5
Female	51.3	297.1	264	284	304	318	329	99.7	91.0	48.2	5.2
White	83.1	305.9	272	291	310	325	338	100.0	95.6	57.6	8.5
Black	11.8	268.4	247	264	281	292	297	98.8	70.7	16.8	0.5
Hispanic	4.0	276.3	256	273	294	303	306	99.3	78.3	23.4	1.4
Other [5]	1.1	312.9	—	—	—	—	—	100.0	94.5	64.7	15.4
1990											
Total	100.0	304.6	273	288	299	319	344	100.0	96.0	56.1	7.2
Male	48.6	306.3	274	291	302	323	347	99.9	95.8	57.6	8.8
Female	51.4	302.9	271	285	296	316	341	100.0	96.2	54.7	5.6
White	73.3	309.5	277	292	304	323	347	100.0	97.6	63.2	8.3
Black	15.6	288.5	264	278	285	302	329	99.9	92.4	32.8	2.0
Hispanic	6.9	283.5	259	278	286	306	323	99.6	85.8	30.1	1.9
Other [5]	4.2	312.5	—	—	—	—	—	100.0	97.9	61.6	15.9
1992											
Total	100.0	306.7	271	289	302	320	343	100.0	96.6	59.1	7.2
Male	50.7	308.9	275	291	306	323	344	100.0	96.9	60.5	9.1
Female	49.3	304.5	267	287	297	317	341	100.0	96.3	57.7	5.2
White	74.7	311.9	276	293	306	323	347	100.0	98.3	66.4	8.7
Black	14.8	285.8	256	279	283	301	313	100.0	89.6	29.8	0.9
Hispanic	7.4	292.2	269	285	297	312	320	100.0	94.1	39.2	1.2
Other [5]	3.1	317.1	—	—	—	—	—	100.0	96.5	69.8	16.9

[1] Indicates ability to perform simple additive reasoning and problem solving.

[2] Indicates ability to perform simple multiplicative reasoning and 2–step problem solving.

[3] Indicates ability to perform reasoning and problem solving involving fractions, decimals, percents, elementary geometry, and simple algebra.

[4] Indicates ability to perform reasoning and problem solving involving geometry, algebra, and beginning statistics and probability.

[5] Includes Asian/Pacific Islanders and American Indians/Alaskan Natives.

—Data not available.

NOTE.—These test scores are from the National Assessment of Educational Progress (NAEP). Scale ranges from 0 to 500.

SOURCE: U.S. Department of Education, National Center for Education Statistics, National Assessment of Educational Progress, *Trends in Academic Progress* and *NAEP 1992 Trends in Academic Progress,* prepared by Educational Testing Service. (This table was prepared May 1994.)

Table 122.—Percent of students at or above selected science proficiency levels,[1] by race/ethnicity and age: 1977 to 1992

Sex, race/ethnicity, and year	9-year-olds [2]				13-year-olds [3]				17-year-olds [3]			
	Know everyday science facts	Understand simple scientific principles	Apply general scientific information	Analyze scientific procedures and data	Understand simple scientific principles	Apply general scientific information	Analyze scientific procedures and data	Integrate specialized scientific information	Understand simple scientific principles	Apply general scientific information	Analyze scientific procedures and data	Integrate specialized scientific information
1	2	3	4	5	6	7	8	9	10	11	12	13
Total												
1977	93.5	68.0	25.7	3.2	86.0	48.8	11.1	0.7	97.1	81.6	41.7	8.5
1982	95.2	70.7	24.3	2.3	89.8	50.9	9.6	0.4	95.7	76.6	37.3	7.1
1986	96.2	72.0	27.5	3.0	91.6	52.5	9.1	0.2	97.1	80.7	41.3	7.9
1990	97.0	76.4	31.1	3.1	92.3	56.5	11.2	0.4	96.7	81.2	43.3	9.2
1992	97.4	78.0	32.8	3.4	93.1	61.3	12.0	0.2	97.8	83.3	46.6	10.1
Male												
1977	94.3	69.5	27.4	3.7	87.2	52.3	13.1	0.9	97.8	85.2	48.8	11.8
1982	95.0	69.7	25.6	2.5	91.9	56.2	12.6	0.5	96.8	81.2	45.2	10.4
1986	96.8	74.1	29.9	3.8	92.9	57.3	11.9	0.3	97.4	82.4	48.8	11.4
1990	96.8	76.3	33.1	4.2	92.7	59.8	14.0	0.6	96.8	82.5	48.2	13.0
1992	97.7	80.4	37.2	4.6	93.1	62.9	14.2	0.3	98.0	85.0	50.9	13.6
Female												
1977	92.8	66.5	24.0	2.6	84.7	45.4	9.0	0.4	96.4	78.0	34.8	5.3
1982	95.5	71.8	23.0	2.1	87.9	46.0	6.9	0.2	94.6	72.2	29.9	3.9
1986	95.6	70.0	25.1	2.2	90.3	47.7	6.3	0.1	96.9	79.1	34.1	4.5
1990	97.1	76.4	29.1	2.0	92.0	53.3	8.5	0.2	96.6	79.9	38.7	5.5
1992	97.1	75.7	28.6	2.2	93.1	59.6	9.9	0.2	97.5	81.6	42.0	6.6
White [4]												
1977	97.7	76.8	30.8	3.9	92.2	56.5	13.4	0.8	99.2	88.2	47.5	10.0
1982	98.3	78.4	29.4	2.9	94.4	58.3	11.5	0.4	98.6	84.9	43.9	8.6
1986	98.2	78.9	32.7	3.8	96.1	61.0	11.3	0.3	98.8	87.8	48.7	9.6
1990	99.2	84.4	37.5	3.9	96.9	66.5	14.2	0.5	99.0	89.6	51.2	11.4
1992	99.2	85.5	39.4	4.3	97.9	71.1	15.0	0.3	99.3	90.5	55.4	12.8
Black [4]												
1977	72.4	27.2	3.5	0.2	57.3	14.9	1.2	0.0	83.6	40.5	7.7	0.4
1982	82.1	38.9	3.9	0.1	68.6	17.1	0.8	0.0	79.7	35.0	6.5	0.2
1986	88.6	46.2	8.3	0.3	73.6	19.6	1.1	0.0	90.9	52.2	12.5	0.9
1990	88.0	46.4	8.5	0.1	77.6	24.3	1.5	0.1	88.3	51.4	15.7	1.5
1992	90.7	51.3	9.2	0.3	73.8	26.2	1.8	0.0	92.1	55.7	14.1	0.8
Hispanic												
1977	84.6	42.0	8.8	0.3	62.2	18.1	1.8	0.0	93.1	61.5	18.5	1.8
1982	85.1	40.2	4.2	0.0	75.5	24.1	2.4	0.0	86.9	48.0	11.1	1.4
1986	89.6	50.1	10.7	0.2	76.7	24.9	1.5	0.0	93.3	60.0	14.8	1.1
1990	93.6	56.3	11.6	0.4	80.2	30.0	3.3	0.1	91.9	59.9	21.1	2.1
1992	92.4	55.5	11.7	0.4	86.2	36.5	3.3	0.0	94.6	68.3	23.0	2.5

[1] As measured by the National Assessment of Educational Progress (NAEP).

[2] Virtually no students were able to integrate specialized scientific information.

[3] Virtually all students knew everyday science facts. Data exclude persons not enrolled in school.

[4] Excludes persons of Hispanic origin.

SOURCE: U.S. Department of Education, National Assessment of Educational Progress, *Trends in Academic Progress* and *NAEP 1992 Trends in Academic Progress,* prepared by Educational Testing Service. (This table was prepared May 1994.)

Table 123.—Average science proficiency, by age and by selected characteristics of students: 1977 to 1992

Selected characteristics of students	9-year-olds					13-year-olds					17-year-olds [1]				
	1977	1982	1986	1990	1992	1977	1982	1986	1990	1992	1977	1982	1986	1990	1992
1	2	3	4	5	6	7	8	9	10	11	12	13	14	15	16
All students	219.9	220.8	224.3	228.7	230.6	247.4	250.1	251.4	255.2	258.0	289.5	283.3	288.5	290.4	294.1
Sex															
Male	222.1	221.0	227.3	230.3	234.7	251.1	255.6	256.1	258.5	260.1	297.0	291.9	294.9	295.6	299.1
Female	217.6	220.7	221.3	227.1	226.7	243.7	245.0	246.9	251.8	256.0	282.2	275.2	282.3	285.4	289.0
Race/ethnicity															
White, non-Hispanic	229.6	229.0	231.9	237.5	239.1	256.1	257.3	259.2	264.1	267.1	297.7	293.1	297.5	300.9	304.2
Black, non-Hispanic	174.8	187.0	196.2	196.4	200.3	208.1	217.1	221.6	225.7	224.4	240.2	234.7	252.8	253.0	256.2
Hispanic	191.9	189.0	199.4	206.2	204.7	213.4	225.5	226.1	231.6	237.5	262.3	248.7	259.3	261.5	270.2
Parental education															
Not high school graduate	198.5	198.2	203.6	209.8	217.2	223.5	225.3	229.4	232.9	233.8	265.3	258.5	257.5	261.4	262.0
Graduated high school	223.0	218.0	219.6	225.8	222.0	245.3	243.1	244.8	247.3	246.4	284.4	275.2	277.0	276.3	280.2
Some college	237.2	229.1	235.8	237.6	236.6	260.3	258.8	257.8	262.8	265.9	295.6	290.1	295.1	296.5	295.9
Graduated college	232.3	230.5	235.2	236.2	238.9	266.4	263.5	264.4	267.5	269.2	309.3	300.2	303.8	305.5	308.3
Type of school															
Public	218.0	219.7	222.6	227.7	229.1	245.2	248.5	250.9	253.6	257.2	288.2	282.3	287.1	289.0	292.2
Private	234.6	231.5	233.0	236.8	240.2	267.7	263.7	263.1	269.0	264.5	308.4	292.0	321.3	307.8	311.7
Type of community															
Advantaged urban	242.0	243.2	243.1	241.2	252.3	267.9	276.3	267.2	268.3	274.6	304.2	304.5	302.0	304.9	298.4
Disadvantaged urban	180.5	192.2	191.6	208.5	201.6	215.7	222.3	222.7	226.6	224.5	256.3	249.6	241.1	254.0	262.7
Extreme rural	224.5	212.4	224.0	233.0	227.6	244.8	244.9	257.5	249.3	262.3	289.0	283.3	296.2	293.9	295.3
Other	220.2	221.5	222.7	228.6	231.0	247.0	250.8	251.9	258.7	259.7	290.8	284.4	289.8	292.5	298.7
Region															
Northeast	224.4	221.8	228.2	231.1	234.4	255.2	254.1	257.6	256.8	256.8	296.3	284.4	292.2	292.6	300.1
Southeast	205.1	213.9	218.8	219.9	222.8	235.1	238.7	247.1	251.3	254.2	276.4	276.3	283.5	283.6	283.0
Central	225.2	226.3	227.9	234.2	237.5	253.8	253.8	249.4	260.4	262.5	294.0	289.3	294.4	299.6	304.2
West	220.9	219.9	222.1	229.5	227.4	243.0	252.4	252.3	252.6	258.0	286.5	280.9	283.2	285.8	290.4

[1] Excludes persons not enrolled in school.

NOTE.—These test scores are from the National Assessment of Educational Progress (NAEP). Performers at the 150 level know some general scientific facts of the type that could be learned from everyday experiences. Performers at the 200 level are developing some understanding of simple scientific principles, particularly in the life sciences. Performers at the 250 level can interpret data from simple tables and make inferences about the outcomes of experimental procedures. They exhibit knowledge and understanding of the life sciences and also demonstrate some knowledge of basic information from the physical sciences. Performers at the 300 level can evaluate the appropriateness of the design of an experiment and have the skill to apply their scientific knowledge in interpreting information from text and graphs. These students also exhibit a growing understanding of principles from the physical sciences. Performers at the 350 level can infer relationships and draw conclusions using detailed scientific knowledge from the physical sciences, particularly chemistry. They also can apply basic principles of genetics and interpret the societal implications of research in this field. Scale ranges from 0 to 500.

SOURCE: U.S. Department of Education, National Center for Education Statistics, National Assessment of Educational Progress, *NAEP 1992 Trends in Academic Progress*, prepared by Educational Testing Service. (This table was prepared May 1994.)

Table 124.—Twelfth graders' achievement on history, mathematics, reading, and science tests: 1992

Achievement test	Total	Sex		Race/ethnicity					Socioeconomic status [1]			Control of school		
		Male	Female	White	Black	Hispanic	Asian	American Indian	Low	Middle	High	Public	Catholic	Other private
1	2	3	4	5	6	7	8	9	10	11	12	13	14	15
Twelfth graders' achievement, standardized score [2]														
History	51.2	51.9	50.5	52.5	45.9	47.4	52.1	44.5	45.8	50.5	55.9	50.8	55.1	54.9
Mathematics	51.4	51.8	51.0	52.9	44.8	47.3	54.3	45.2	45.5	50.6	56.7	50.9	55.1	56.1
Reading	51.0	49.9	52.2	52.4	45.5	47.2	51.4	45.2	45.9	50.4	55.5	50.6	54.7	55.0
Science	51.1	52.4	49.7	52.9	43.3	46.5	51.8	44.8	45.4	50.5	55.9	50.7	53.9	55.0
Distribution of twelfth graders' achievement, by score quartile [3]														
History	100.0	100.0	100.0	100.0	100.0	100.0	100.0	100.0	100.0	100.0	100.0	100.0	100.0	100.0
Lower quartile	20.2	19.6	20.9	15.5	39.6	32.4	16.8	41.1	37.6	20.5	7.9	21.4	7.1	13.8
Lower middle quartile	24.6	21.5	27.9	23.4	28.1	28.9	25.6	32.5	30.9	26.9	16.5	25.2	21.0	17.2
Upper middle quartile	26.9	26.3	27.4	28.4	21.5	23.5	25.5	13.6	21.1	27.7	29.2	26.8	31.2	22.1
Upper quartile	28.3	32.5	23.8	32.7	10.8	15.3	32.2	12.7	10.3	24.8	46.5	26.6	40.7	46.9
Mathematics	100.0	100.0	100.0	100.0	100.0	100.0	100.0	100.0	100.0	100.0	100.0	100.0	100.0	100.0
Lower quartile	19.7	20.1	19.2	14.8	41.2	31.6	11.9	42.8	37.0	20.4	6.5	20.9	8.2	7.6
Lower middle quartile	24.2	22.4	26.0	22.5	30.0	30.6	21.1	29.8	32.4	26.3	15.2	24.9	17.0	17.3
Upper middle quartile	27.6	26.9	28.4	29.5	20.3	22.9	28.4	18.5	22.4	29.3	28.4	27.2	34.3	28.5
Upper quartile	28.5	30.6	26.3	33.2	8.5	14.9	38.7	8.9	8.3	23.9	50.0	27.0	40.5	46.6
Reading	100.0	100.0	100.0	100.0	100.0	100.0	100.0	100.0	100.0	100.0	100.0	100.0	100.0	100.0
Lower quartile	21.1	25.6	16.4	16.6	38.2	31.6	23.2	41.2	36.3	21.6	9.8	22.3	8.1	14.0
Lower middle quartile	24.6	24.5	24.7	22.6	31.3	32.9	20.0	31.1	32.4	26.8	15.8	25.5	18.1	13.6
Upper middle quartile	26.4	25.0	27.9	28.3	20.7	21.2	24.9	15.5	20.8	27.4	28.6	25.8	36.3	25.2
Upper quartile	27.8	24.9	30.9	32.5	9.8	14.3	31.9	12.2	10.5	24.3	45.9	26.4	37.5	47.2
Science	100.0	100.0	100.0	100.0	100.0	100.0	100.0	100.0	100.0	100.0	100.0	100.0	100.0	100.0
Lower quartile	20.9	18.2	23.6	14.0	52.6	34.3	17.7	37.6	39.0	20.9	8.4	21.9	11.7	10.5
Lower middle quartile	24.5	21.1	28.1	23.0	25.2	33.8	25.2	35.8	31.9	26.8	16.0	25.0	22.0	17.4
Upper middle quartile	26.3	27.1	25.5	29.0	16.0	18.9	26.5	20.9	19.8	28.3	27.4	26.3	27.3	26.1
Upper quartile	28.3	33.6	22.7	33.9	6.2	13.1	30.5	5.7	9.3	24.1	48.3	26.8	39.0	46.0

[1] Socioeconomic status was measured by a composite score on parental education and occupations, and family income. The "Low" SES group is the lowest quartile; the "Middle" SES group is the middle two quartiles; and the "High" SES group is the upper quartile.

[2] In the full data file, the standardized scores have a mean of 50 and a standard deviation of 10. Because dropouts and students who were retained in grades between 8 and 11 were excluded from this tabulation, the scores are slightly higher.

[3] In the full data file, twenty-five percent of all students fall into each one of the quartile groupings. Because dropouts and students who were retained in grades between 8 and 11 were excluded from this tabulation, the scores are slightly higher.

NOTE.—Because of rounding, details may not add to totals.

SOURCE: U.S. Department of Education, National Center for Education Statistics, "National Education Longitudinal Study of 1988, Second Followup" survey. (This table was prepared July 1995.)

Table 125.—Scholastic Assessment Test [1] score averages for college-bound high school seniors, by sex: 1966–67 to 1994–95

School year	Verbal score			Mathematical score		
	Total	Male	Female	Total	Male	Female
1	2	3	4	5	6	7
1966–67	466	463	468	492	514	467
1967–68	466	464	466	492	512	470
1968–69	463	459	466	493	513	470
1969–70	460	459	461	488	509	465
1970–71	455	454	457	488	507	466
1971–72	453	454	452	484	505	461
1972–73	445	446	443	481	502	460
1973–74	444	447	442	480	501	459
1974–75	434	437	431	472	495	449
1975–76	431	433	430	472	497	446
1976–77	429	431	427	470	497	445
1977–78	429	433	425	468	494	444
1978–79	427	431	423	467	493	443
1979–80	424	428	420	466	491	443
1980–81	424	430	418	466	492	443
1981–82	426	431	421	467	493	443
1982–83	425	430	420	468	493	445
1983–84	426	433	420	471	495	449
1984–85	431	437	425	475	499	452
1985–86	431	437	426	475	501	451
1986–87	430	435	425	476	500	453
1987–88	428	435	422	476	498	455
1988–89	427	434	421	476	500	454
1989–90	424	429	419	476	499	455
1990–91	422	426	418	474	497	453
1991–92	423	428	419	476	499	456
1992–93	424	428	420	478	502	457
1993–94	423	425	421	479	501	460
1994–95	428	429	426	482	503	463

[1] Scholastic Aptitude Test revised, 1994.

NOTE.—Possible scores on each part of the SAT range from 200 to 800. Data for the years 1966–67 through 1970–71 are estimates derived from the test scores of all participants.

Table 126.—Scholastic Assessment Test [1] score averages, by race/ethnicity: 1975–76 to 1994–95

Racial/ethnic background	1975–76	1977–78	1978–79	1979–80	1980–81	1981–82	1982–83	1983–84	1984–85	1986–87	1987–88	1988–89	1989–90	1990–91	1991–92	1992–93	1993–94	1994–95
1	2	3	4	5	6	7	8	9	10	11	12	13	14	15	16	17	18	19
SAT-Verbal																		
All students	431	429	427	424	424	426	425	426	431	430	428	427	424	422	423	424	423	428
White	451	446	444	442	442	444	443	445	449	447	445	446	442	441	442	444	443	448
Black	332	332	330	330	332	341	339	342	346	351	353	351	352	351	352	353	352	356
Mexican-American	371	370	370	372	373	377	375	376	382	379	382	381	380	377	372	374	372	376
Puerto Rican	364	349	345	350	353	360	358	358	368	360	355	360	359	361	366	367	367	372
Asian-American	414	401	396	396	397	398	395	398	404	405	408	409	410	411	413	415	416	418
American Indian	388	387	386	390	391	388	388	390	392	393	393	384	388	393	395	400	396	403
Other	410	399	393	394	388	392	386	388	391	405	410	414	410	411	417	422	425	432
SAT-Mathematical																		
All students	472	468	467	466	466	467	468	471	475	476	476	476	476	474	476	478	479	482
White	493	485	483	482	483	483	484	487	490	489	490	491	491	489	491	494	495	498
Black	354	354	358	360	362	366	369	373	376	377	384	386	385	385	385	388	388	388
Mexican-American	410	402	410	413	415	416	417	420	426	424	428	430	429	427	425	428	427	426
Puerto Rican	401	388	388	394	398	403	403	405	409	400	402	406	405	406	406	409	411	411
Asian-American	518	510	511	509	513	513	514	519	518	521	522	525	528	530	532	535	535	538
American Indian	420	419	421	426	425	424	425	427	428	432	435	428	437	437	442	447	441	447
Other	458	450	447	449	447	449	446	450	448	455	460	467	467	466	473	477	480	486

[1] Scholastic Aptitude Test revised, 1994.

NOTE.—Possible scores on each part of the SAT range from 200 to 800. No racial/ethnic group data are available prior to 1975–76. No data are available for 1985–86 due to changes in the Student Descriptive Questionnaire completed when students registered for the test.

Table 127.—Distribution of Scholastic Assessment Test [1] scores, by sex of student: 1975–76 to 1994–95

Year	Number of test takers	200 or higher	250 or higher	300 or higher	350 or higher	400 or higher	450 or higher	500 or higher	550 or higher	600 or higher	650 or higher	700 or higher	750 or higher
1	2	3	4	5	6	7	8	9	10	11	12	13	14

Verbal

Year	Number of test takers	200 or higher	250 or higher	300 or higher	350 or higher	400 or higher	450 or higher	500 or higher	550 or higher	600 or higher	650 or higher	700 or higher	750 or higher
Total													
1975–76	999,809	100.00	96.26	89.26	77.47	60.27	43.01	28.11	15.58	8.20	3.55	1.23	0.25
1980–81	994,046	100.00	95.46	87.32	75.34	58.44	40.64	25.76	13.87	7.00	3.01	1.03	0.21
1985–86	1,000,748	100.00	95.81	88.92	77.55	61.77	43.17	28.03	15.75	7.87	3.25	0.99	0.14
1986–87	1,080,426	100.00	96.08	88.57	76.62	60.18	43.02	27.85	15.44	8.14	3.42	1.07	0.13
1987–88	1,134,364	100.00	95.81	88.62	76.44	60.53	42.38	26.91	14.94	7.32	3.22	0.92	0.09
1988–89	1,088,223	100.00	95.72	88.21	75.39	59.55	42.17	26.77	14.85	7.76	3.16	0.87	0.10
1989–90	1,025,523	100.00	95.20	87.44	74.97	58.70	40.67	25.11	14.41	7.43	3.13	1.00	0.12
1990–91	1,032,685	100.00	94.89	86.96	74.38	57.58	40.38	25.22	14.08	7.25	3.15	1.03	0.13
1991–92	1,034,131	100.00	94.70	86.95	74.29	58.68	40.96	25.42	14.02	7.28	3.18	0.98	0.13
1992–93	1,044,465	100.00	94.85	87.20	74.71	58.70	40.85	25.77	14.87	7.77	3.37	1.00	0.12
1993–94	1,050,386	100.00	94.76	86.97	74.58	57.72	40.26	25.95	14.76	7.58	3.32	1.11	0.14
1994–95	1,067,993	100.00	95.24	87.96	75.60	59.81	41.83	26.52	15.98	8.25	3.65	1.20	0.13
Male													
1975–76	494,626	100.00	96.39	89.54	77.90	60.90	43.65	28.69	16.04	8.49	3.69	1.29	0.26
1980–81	478,448	100.00	95.97	88.50	77.16	60.73	42.89	27.53	15.03	7.67	3.30	1.13	0.23
1985–86	481,477	100.00	96.19	89.87	79.10	63.74	45.17	29.77	17.02	8.71	3.68	1.11	0.15
1986–87	520,326	100.00	96.23	89.12	77.72	61.79	44.91	29.71	16.93	9.22	4.02	1.26	0.15
1987–88	544,065	100.00	96.14	89.54	78.21	62.92	45.04	29.25	16.70	8.44	3.82	1.13	0.11
1988–89	521,229	100.00	96.00	89.06	77.04	61.86	44.81	29.15	16.63	8.93	3.75	1.07	0.12
1989–90	490,420	100.00	95.40	88.00	76.04	60.19	42.62	27.05	15.91	8.40	3.60	1.15	0.14
1990–91	493,252	100.00	95.08	87.45	75.29	58.94	41.99	26.71	15.18	7.98	3.51	1.16	0.14
1991–92	491,748	100.00	94.89	87.46	75.34	60.23	42.68	26.98	15.16	8.00	3.55	1.10	0.15
1992–93	495,086	100.00	94.98	87.55	75.35	59.75	42.21	27.18	16.01	8.60	3.83	1.18	0.15
1993–94	493,063	100.00	94.67	86.93	74.71	58.21	41.15	26.90	15.54	8.10	3.61	1.23	0.15
1994–95	496,016	100.00	95.18	87.98	75.83	60.28	42.47	27.32	16.68	8.78	3.94	1.31	0.15
Female													
1975–76	505,183	100.00	96.14	88.97	77.05	59.65	42.38	27.55	15.13	7.92	3.42	1.17	0.24
1980–81	515,598	100.00	94.99	86.23	73.66	56.32	38.56	24.11	12.80	6.39	2.73	0.94	0.18
1985–86	519,271	100.00	95.46	88.04	76.11	59.95	41.31	26.42	14.57	7.09	2.85	0.88	0.12
1986–87	560,100	100.00	95.93	88.07	75.60	58.67	41.26	26.13	14.05	7.14	2.87	0.90	0.11
1987–88	590,299	100.00	95.50	87.76	74.82	58.33	39.93	24.76	13.32	6.29	2.66	0.74	0.06
1988–89	566,994	100.00	95.45	87.42	73.88	57.42	39.75	24.58	13.21	6.68	2.61	0.69	0.08
1989–90	535,103	100.00	95.01	86.93	73.98	57.34	38.88	23.34	13.04	6.53	2.70	0.86	0.10
1990–91	539,433	100.00	94.71	86.52	73.55	56.33	38.90	23.85	13.08	6.58	2.81	0.92	0.12
1991–92	542,383	100.00	94.53	86.49	73.34	57.28	39.40	24.00	12.98	6.62	2.84	0.87	0.12
1992–93	549,379	100.00	94.74	86.88	74.13	57.76	39.62	24.50	13.84	7.01	2.95	0.83	0.09
1993–94	557,323	100.00	94.84	87.01	74.47	57.28	39.49	25.10	14.06	7.12	3.06	1.00	0.12
1994–95	571,977	100.00	95.29	87.95	75.39	59.40	41.28	25.83	15.38	7.80	3.40	1.10	0.11

Mathematical

Year	Number of test takers	200 or higher	250 or higher	300 or higher	350 or higher	400 or higher	450 or higher	500 or higher	550 or higher	600 or higher	650 or higher	700 or higher	750 or higher
Total													
1975–76	999,776	100.00	98.78	93.65	83.55	70.87	57.16	41.82	26.94	16.34	8.49	3.75	1.16
1980–81	993,672	100.00	98.85	92.99	82.77	70.48	55.57	40.59	25.98	14.45	7.08	2.71	0.66
1985–86	1,000,747	100.00	98.91	93.63	84.64	71.98	57.41	42.32	29.29	17.95	9.56	4.08	1.01
1986–87	1,080,426	100.00	98.91	93.30	84.22	71.61	57.40	42.37	29.67	18.32	9.94	3.86	1.02
1987–88	1,134,364	100.00	99.08	93.93	84.62	72.17	57.43	43.03	29.55	17.60	9.26	3.78	0.91
1988–89	1,088,223	100.00	99.08	94.04	84.57	71.97	57.94	42.81	29.33	18.01	10.07	4.27	1.11
1989–90	1,025,523	100.00	98.89	93.77	84.21	71.57	57.71	43.20	29.59	18.41	10.14	4.23	1.18
1990–91	1,032,685	100.00	98.83	93.63	83.49	70.80	56.63	42.68	29.27	17.85	9.70	4.51	1.32
1991–92	1,034,131	100.00	98.70	93.65	84.25	71.81	57.96	43.36	28.83	18.12	10.10	4.60	1.37
1992–93	1,044,465	100.00	98.49	93.34	84.28	72.33	58.55	44.39	29.78	18.80	10.63	5.11	1.62
1993–94	1,050,386	100.00	98.51	93.75	84.49	72.99	59.13	44.48	30.21	18.90	10.56	4.85	1.42
1994–95	1,067,993	100.00	98.95	94.49	83.96	71.65	57.65	44.37	31.58	21.51	12.44	5.65	1.49
Male													
1975–76	494,619	100.00	99.13	95.37	87.63	77.29	65.30	50.65	34.93	22.71	12.70	6.02	1.99
1980–81	478,301	100.00	99.20	94.98	87.17	77.17	63.99	49.45	33.92	20.38	10.75	4.46	1.17
1985–86	481,477	100.00	99.24	95.38	88.49	78.26	65.53	51.16	37.47	24.49	14.00	6.44	1.73
1986–87	520,326	100.00	99.16	94.91	87.75	77.36	64.90	50.74	37.66	24.82	14.47	6.15	1.75
1987–88	544,065	100.00	99.31	95.37	87.91	77.48	64.40	50.71	36.91	23.63	13.43	5.96	1.57
1988–89	521,229	100.00	99.30	95.45	88.00	77.62	65.19	50.91	37.13	24.43	14.62	6.70	1.89
1989–90	490,420	100.00	99.16	95.17	87.70	77.13	64.71	50.81	36.85	24.40	14.41	6.53	2.00
1990–91	493,252	100.00	99.08	94.91	86.79	76.22	63.65	50.40	36.59	23.82	13.93	6.96	2.23
1991–92	491,748	100.00	98.99	95.05	87.50	77.03	64.73	50.88	36.01	24.05	14.28	6.96	2.24
1992–93	495,086	100.00	98.83	94.73	87.55	77.69	65.50	52.10	37.18	25.00	15.09	7.77	2.69
1993–94	493,063	100.00	98.86	94.97	87.55	77.92	65.65	51.91	37.27	24.78	14.75	7.28	2.29
1994–95	496,016	100.00	99.16	95.56	87.03	76.62	63.97	51.17	38.13	27.22	16.75	8.12	2.34
Female													
1975–76	505,157	100.00	98.45	91.96	79.56	64.59	49.20	33.17	19.12	10.11	4.37	1.53	0.34
1980–81	515,371	100.00	98.53	91.14	78.69	64.27	47.76	32.37	18.60	8.94	3.66	1.09	0.19
1985–86	519,270	100.00	98.61	92.01	81.07	66.16	49.87	34.12	21.70	11.88	5.45	1.89	0.34
1986–87	560,100	100.00	98.67	91.80	80.93	66.26	50.44	34.59	22.25	12.29	5.74	1.73	0.33
1987–88	590,299	100.00	98.87	92.60	81.58	67.28	51.00	35.94	22.78	12.05	5.42	1.77	0.30
1988–89	566,994	100.00	98.87	92.75	81.42	66.77	51.27	35.37	22.15	12.11	5.90	2.03	0.39
1989–90	535,103	100.00	98.65	92.50	81.01	66.47	51.30	36.22	22.94	12.92	6.22	2.12	0.44
1990–91	539,433	100.00	98.60	92.45	80.48	65.85	50.22	35.62	22.57	12.40	5.83	2.26	0.49
1991–92	542,383	100.00	98.45	92.37	81.31	67.07	51.82	36.54	22.32	12.74	6.30	2.45	0.57
1992–93	549,379	100.00	98.18	92.09	81.34	67.50	52.28	37.45	23.11	13.21	6.61	2.72	0.65
1993–94	557,323	100.00	98.25	92.72	81.79	68.64	53.36	37.92	23.96	13.69	6.86	2.69	0.65
1994–95	571,977	100.00	98.76	93.55	81.30	67.34	52.18	38.46	25.89	16.56	8.70	3.50	0.75

[1] Formerly known as the Scholastic Aptitude Test.

NOTE.—Possible scores on each part of the SAT range from 200 to 800. In some years, mathematics and verbal test results were not available for every student.

SOURCE: College Entrance Examination Board, *National Report on College-Bound Seniors*, various years. (Copyright ©1995 by the College Entrance Examination Board. All rights reserved.) (This table was prepared November 1995.)

Table 128.—Scholastic Assessment Test [1] score averages, by intended area of study: [2] 1977–78 to 1994–95

Test and year	Intended area of study [3]									
	Arts and humanities	Biological sciences and related areas	Business, commerce, and communications	Computer and information sciences	Education	Engineering	Mathematics	Physical sciences	Social sciences and related areas	Miscellaneous [4]
1	2	3	4	5	6	7	8	9	10	11
Verbal										
1977–78	439	436	409	420	396	448	464	499	448	422
1978–79	436	435	408	419	392	445	459	498	446	420
1979–80	434	433	406	417	389	444	455	495	448	419
1980–81	434	433	406	416	391	446	456	498	446	420
1981–82	436	434	409	417	394	449	455	496	450	424
1982–83	438	432	409	413	394	448	453	496	451	421
1983–84	440	434	410	411	398	453	457	501	451	423
1984–85	445	439	414	413	404	453	459	506	454	429
1986–87	447	438	415	403	408	456	475	507	452	410
1987–88	444	434	414	400	407	453	468	500	447	409
1988–89	445	433	414	396	406	452	473	504	447	410
1989–90	441	430	410	392	406	449	473	503	441	408
1990–91	440	428	407	390	406	446	469	497	437	410
1991–92	442	428	407	394	407	447	467	497	435	414
1992–93	444	427	407	400	409	448	468	497	435	415
1993–94	441	427	407	406	407	446	471	496	435	414
1994–95	452	431	413	416	409	451	480	500	438	418
Change, 1984–85 to 1994–95	7	–8	–1	3	5	–2	21	–6	–16	–11
Mathematical										
1977–78	454	474	448	499	422	540	585	566	464	461
1978–79	452	472	448	498	420	536	580	561	463	458
1979–80	452	472	446	496	418	535	577	560	463	459
1980–81	453	472	446	492	418	534	572	558	463	459
1981–82	452	470	446	489	419	537	569	558	464	461
1982–83	454	470	445	484	418	539	572	560	466	460
1983–84	456	475	449	483	425	543	578	564	467	463
1984–85	462	480	455	488	432	545	578	569	471	469
1986–87	469	482	459	476	437	554	602	576	472	453
1987–88	471	482	462	470	442	547	596	568	472	455
1988–89	473	481	465	472	440	551	606	577	473	459
1989–90	475	481	465	468	442	550	609	577	471	460
1990–91	473	478	462	467	441	548	605	572	466	463
1991–92	475	479	463	472	443	550	606	573	465	472
1992–93	478	480	465	479	446	553	607	574	464	481
1993–94	480	482	468	488	447	553	611	574	467	472
1994–95	476	486	471	495	446	556	619	580	468	474
Change, 1984–85 to 1994–95	14	6	16	7	14	11	41	11	–3	5

[1] Formerly known as the Scholastic Aptitude Test.
[2] Students indicated their first and second choices of fields of study. Only their first choices are reported here.
[3] Based on classifications reported by College Entrance Examination Board.
[4] Includes "trade and vocational," "other," and "undecided" through 1984–85. Data for 1985–86 to 1994–95 exclude "other."

NOTE.—Possible scores on each part of the SAT range from 200 to 800. No data are available for 1985–86 due to changes in the Student Descriptive Questionnaire completed when students registered for the test.

SOURCE: College Entrance Examination Board, *National Report on College-Bound Seniors,* various years. (Copyright ©1995 by the College Entrance Examination Board. All rights reserved.) (This table was prepared November 1995.)

Table 129.—Scholastic Assessment Test [1] score averages, by class rank: [2] 1976–77 to 1994–95

Year	Top tenth		Second tenth		Second fifth		Third fifth		Fourth fifth		Lowest fifth	
	Verbal	Mathematics	Verbal	Mathematics	Verbal	Mathematics	Verbal	Mathematics	Verbal	Mathematics	Verbal	Mathematics
1	2	3	4	5	6	7	8	9	10	11	12	13
1976–77	518	574	452	499	415	453	372	401	347	374	339	364
1977–78	515	570	450	494	414	451	372	400	349	374	339	364
1978–79	514	568	448	494	413	451	371	400	347	372	337	364
1979–80	510	568	446	494	411	451	370	401	346	373	339	366
1980–81	511	567	447	496	412	453	371	402	348	374	339	368
1981–82	511	568	449	497	415	454	374	404	349	375	343	368
1982–83	508	570	447	498	414	455	374	403	351	375	343	369
1983–84	511	575	450	503	417	459	377	406	353	377	341	365
1984–85	516	577	455	508	421	463	381	411	357	380	346	369
1986–87	518	585	456	511	418	461	380	409	358	380	353	374
1987–88	515	585	454	511	417	463	379	411	358	382	352	373
1988–89	515	585	453	512	416	463	376	410	354	381	346	373
1989–90	512	585	449	512	412	463	373	410	351	381	342	370
1990–91	512	584	448	511	411	462	372	409	350	379	340	368
1991–92	512	585	448	511	412	464	373	411	350	379	338	363
1992–93	513	586	449	513	412	466	373	413	350	380	336	363
1993–94	512	586	447	514	410	467	373	415	349	382	332	363
1994–95	518	594	452	518	414	467	375	413	349	379	334	362

[1] Formerly known as the Scholastic Aptitude Test.
[2] Self-reported class rank.

NOTE.—Possible scores on each part of the SAT range from 200 to 800.

SOURCE: College Entrance Examination Board, *National Report on College-Bound Seniors,* various years. (Copyright ©1995 by the College Entrance Examination Board. All rights reserved.) (This table was prepared November 1995.)

Table 130.—Scholastic Assessment Test [1] score averages, by state: 1974–75 to 1994–95

State	1974–75 Verbal	1974–75 Mathematical	1980–81 Verbal	1980–81 Mathematical	1985–86 Verbal	1985–86 Mathematical	1990–91 Verbal	1990–91 Mathematical	1992–93 Verbal	1992–93 Mathematical	1993–94 Verbal	1993–94 Mathematical	1994–95 Verbal	1994–95 Mathematical	Percent of graduates taking SAT, 1994–95 [2]
1	2	3	4	5	6	7	8	9	10	11	12	13	14	15	16
United States	434	472	424	466	431	475	422	474	424	478	423	479	428	482	41
Alabama	426	457	457	488	476	514	476	515	480	526	482	529	491	538	8
Alaska	461	481	449	486	445	479	439	481	438	477	434	477	445	489	47
Arizona	496	525	476	514	466	509	442	490	444	497	443	496	448	496	27
Arkansas	482	510	477	510	482	519	482	523	478	519	477	518	482	523	6
California	435	473	426	475	423	481	415	482	415	484	413	482	417	485	45
Colorado	479	515	467	513	466	514	453	506	454	509	456	513	462	518	29
Connecticut	442	471	430	463	440	474	429	468	430	474	426	472	431	477	81
Delaware	439	476	429	470	442	475	428	464	429	465	428	464	429	468	68
District of Columbia	—	—	—	—	413	439	405	435	405	441	406	443	412	445	53
Florida	441	474	424	463	426	469	416	466	416	466	413	466	420	469	48
Georgia	397	427	390	426	402	440	400	444	399	445	398	446	406	448	65
Hawaii	414	478	390	464	403	477	405	478	401	478	401	480	407	482	57
Idaho	493	524	486	523	475	512	463	505	465	507	461	508	468	511	15
Illinois	460	510	459	508	466	519	471	535	475	541	478	546	488	560	13
Indiana	418	463	406	451	415	459	408	457	409	460	410	466	415	467	58
Iowa	523	568	515	566	519	576	515	578	520	583	506	574	516	583	5
Kansas	503	540	502	542	498	544	493	546	494	548	494	550	503	557	9
Kentucky	470	507	474	509	483	519	473	520	476	522	474	523	477	522	11
Louisiana	456	491	461	494	474	507	476	518	481	527	481	530	486	535	9
Maine	437	471	426	465	434	466	421	458	422	463	420	463	427	469	68
Maryland	436	471	423	461	436	475	429	475	431	478	429	479	430	479	64
Massachusetts	434	469	422	462	436	473	426	470	427	476	426	475	430	477	80
Michigan	451	498	456	508	462	514	461	519	469	528	472	537	484	549	11
Minnesota	506	552	486	539	482	540	480	543	489	556	495	562	506	579	9
Mississippi	477	503	473	502	485	516	477	520	481	521	485	528	496	540	4
Missouri	465	500	462	504	476	519	476	526	481	532	485	537	495	550	9
Montana	500	547	485	539	485	541	464	518	459	516	463	523	473	536	21
Nebraska	459	507	489	537	493	549	481	543	479	544	482	543	494	556	9
Nevada	465	497	445	487	445	485	435	484	432	488	429	484	434	483	30
New Hampshire	449	485	439	479	450	485	440	481	442	487	438	486	444	491	70
New Jersey	424	454	414	450	424	465	417	469	419	473	418	475	420	478	70
New Mexico	486	516	474	510	489	527	474	522	478	525	475	528	485	530	11
New York	441	484	427	471	427	471	413	468	416	471	416	472	419	473	74
North Carolina	399	428	391	427	399	436	400	444	406	453	405	455	411	454	60
North Dakota	510	554	494	544	508	556	502	571	518	583	497	559	515	592	5
Ohio	456	499	457	500	460	503	450	496	454	505	456	510	460	515	23
Oklahoma	480	514	485	526	487	521	476	521	482	530	482	537	491	536	9
Oregon	440	468	431	469	444	486	439	483	441	492	436	491	448	499	51
Pennsylvania	430	470	421	459	429	465	417	459	418	460	417	462	419	461	70
Rhode Island	432	469	415	452	432	466	421	459	419	464	420	462	425	463	70
South Carolina	382	412	374	406	395	431	395	437	396	442	395	443	401	443	58
South Dakota	523	561	519	561	531	567	496	551	502	558	483	548	505	563	5
Tennessee	477	511	475	514	486	521	487	528	486	531	488	535	497	543	12
Texas	431	467	415	455	419	458	411	463	413	472	412	474	419	474	47
Utah	516	553	511	548	506	541	494	537	500	549	509	558	513	563	4
Vermont	439	476	427	467	442	474	424	466	426	467	427	472	429	472	68
Virginia	431	463	424	461	435	473	424	466	425	469	424	469	428	468	65
Washington	489	522	472	517	461	502	433	480	435	486	434	488	443	494	48
West Virginia	462	502	458	495	462	502	441	485	439	485	439	482	448	484	17
Wisconsin	492	544	477	533	478	536	481	542	485	551	487	557	501	572	9
Wyoming	506	548	478	528	484	534	466	514	463	507	459	521	476	525	10

[1] Formerly known as the Scholastic Aptitude Test.
[2] Based on the number of high school graduates in 1995 as projected by the Western Interstate Commission for Higher Education and the number of 1995 seniors who took the SAT.
—Data not available.

NOTE.—Possible scores on each part of the SAT range from 200 to 800. Rankings of states based on SAT scores alone are invalid because of the varying proportions of students in each state taking the tests.

SOURCE: College Entrance Examination Board, "College-Bound Seniors: 1995 Profile of SAT Program Test Takers," Copyright 1995 by the College Entrance Examination Board. All rights reserved.) (This table was prepared November 1995.)

Table 131.—American College Testing (ACT) score [1] averages, by sex: 1967 to 1995

Type of test and sex	1967	1970	1975	1980	1982	1983	1984	1985	1986	1987	1988	1989	1990[1]	1991[1]	1992[1]	1993[1]	1994[1]	1995[1]
1	2	3	4	5	6	7	8	9	10	11	12	13	14	15	16	17	18	19
Participants:[2]																		
Total (in thousands)	788	714	822	836	805	835	849	739	730	777	842	855	817	796	832	876	892	945
Test scores[3]																		
Composite, total	19.9	18.6	18.5	18.5	18.4	18.3	18.5	18.6	18.8	18.7	18.8	18.6	20.6	20.6	20.6	20.7	20.8	20.8
Male	20.3	19.5	19.3	19.3	19.2	19.1	19.3	19.4	19.6	19.5	19.6	19.3	21.0	20.9	20.9	21.0	20.9	21.0
Female	19.4	17.8	17.9	17.8	17.8	17.6	17.9	17.9	18.1	18.1	18.1	18.0	20.3	20.4	20.5	20.5	20.7	20.7
English, total	18.5	17.7	17.9	17.8	17.9	17.8	18.1	18.1	18.1	18.5	18.4	18.5	18.4	20.5	20.3	20.2	20.3	20.2
Male	17.6	17.1	17.3	17.3	17.3	17.3	17.5	17.6	17.9	17.9	18.0	17.8	20.1	19.8	19.8	19.8	19.8	19.8
Female	19.4	18.3	18.3	18.2	18.4	18.2	18.6	18.6	18.9	18.9	19.0	18.9	20.9	20.7	20.6	20.6	20.7	20.6
Math, total	20.0	17.6	17.4	17.4	17.3	17.2	16.9	17.3	17.2	17.3	17.2	17.1	19.9	20.0	20.0	20.1	20.2	21.3
Male	21.1	19.3	18.9	18.9	18.6	18.4	18.6	18.6	18.8	18.6	18.4	18.3	20.7	20.6	20.7	20.8	20.8	20.9
Female	18.8	16.2	16.2	16.0	16.0	15.7	16.1	16.0	16.0	16.1	16.1	16.1	19.3	19.4	19.5	19.6	19.6	19.7
Social studies, total[4]	19.7	17.4	17.2	17.2	17.3	17.1	17.3	17.4	17.6	17.5	17.4	17.2	—	21.2	21.1	21.2	21.2	21.3
Male	20.3	18.7	18.2	18.1	18.1	18.0	18.1	18.3	18.6	18.4	18.4	18.1	—	21.3	21.1	21.2	21.1	21.1
Female	19.0	16.4	16.4	16.4	16.6	16.4	16.5	16.6	16.9	16.7	16.6	16.4	—	21.1	21.1	21.2	21.4	21.4
Natural science, total[5]	20.8	21.1	21.1	21.0	20.8	20.9	21.0	21.2	21.4	21.4	21.4	21.2	—	20.7	20.7	20.8	20.9	21.0
Male	21.6	22.4	22.4	22.3	22.2	22.4	22.4	22.6	22.7	22.8	22.8	22.6	—	21.3	21.4	21.5	21.6	21.6
Female	20.0	20.0	20.0	20.0	19.7	19.6	19.9	20.0	20.2	20.1	20.2	20.0	—	20.1	20.1	20.3	20.4	20.5
Percent																		
Obtaining composite scores of—																		
26 or above[6]	14	14	13	13	13	13	13	14	14	14	14	14	12	11	12	12	13	13
15 or below[7]	21	33	33	33	34	35	33	32	31	31	31	32	35	35	35	35	34	34
Planned major field of study																		
Business[8]	18	21	20	19	19	18	19	21	22	23	23	22	20	18	15	13	12	12
Engineering[9]	8	6	8	10	11	10	9	9	9	8	9	9	9	10	10	9	9	8
Social science[10]	10	9	6	6	6	6	7	7	8	9	10	11	10	10	10	9	9	8
Education[11]	16	12	9	7	6	6	6	6	7	8	8	8	8	10	5	8	8	8

[1] 1990 and later data are not comparable with previous years because a new version of the ACT was introduced. Estimated average composite scores for the new version for prior years were: 1989, 20.6; 1988, 1987, and 1986, 20.8; and 1982, 20.3.
[2] Beginning in 1985, data are for seniors who graduated in year shown and had taken the ACT in their junior or senior years.
[3] Minimum score, 1; maximum score, 36.
[4] Beginning in 1990, the test was changed to "reading".
[5] Beginning in 1990, the test was changed to "science reasoning".
[6] Beginning in 1990, scores were 27 or above.
[7] As of 1990, scores were 18 or below.

[8] Includes political and persuasive (e.g., sales) fields through 1975; thereafter, business and commerce.
[9] Beginning in 1993, includes engineering and engineering related technologies.
[10] Includes religion through 1975.
[11] Includes education and teacher education.
—Not available.

SOURCE: The American College Testing program, *High School Profile Report,* annual. (This table prepared April 1996.)

Table 132.—Percent of high school seniors reporting they were in general, college preparatory, and vocational programs, by student characteristics: 1982 and 1992

Student characteristics	General [1]		College preparatory or academic		Vocational	
	1982	1992	1982	1992	1982	1992
1	2	3	4	5	6	7
All seniors	35.2	45.3	37.9	43.0	26.9	11.7
Males	38.1	46.3	36.8	41.8	25.1	11.9
Females	32.4	44.2	38.9	44.2	28.7	11.6
Race/ethnicity						
White	34.8	43.3	40.6	45.7	24.6	11.0
Black	35.1	48.9	33.3	35.6	31.6	15.4
Hispanic	37.4	56.4	24.9	30.6	37.7	13.1
Asian	27.5	40.3	55.9	50.9	16.6	8.8
American Indian	55.3	60.8	19.1	22.6	25.6	16.7
Test performance quartile						
Lowest test quartile	42.0	61.5	12.3	15.2	45.6	23.3
Second test quartile	44.6	53.9	20.5	30.0	34.9	16.1
Third test quartile	37.9	39.7	37.6	50.0	24.5	10.4
Highest test quartile	18.9	25.4	73.1	72.0	8.0	2.6
Socioeconomic status [2]						
Low quartile	40.3	55.6	20.5	23.2	39.2	21.2
Middle 2 quartiles	36.2	46.0	36.4	40.9	27.4	13.1
High quartile	27.4	36.2	60.1	60.8	12.5	3.0
Control of school						
Public	36.7	47.1	34.5	40.0	28.8	12.9
Catholic	21.9	24.4	67.4	73.5	10.7	2.2
Other private	22.1	33.1	67.6	65.9	10.3	1.0
Location of school						
Urban	32.2	43.3	37.4	45.5	30.4	11.2
Suburban	33.6	45.5	41.4	44.6	25.0	9.8
Rural/nonmetropolitan area	39.6	46.5	32.6	38.6	27.9	14.9

[1] Includes special education, "other," and "don't know."
[2] Socioeconomic status was measured by a composite score on parental education and occupations, and family income. The "Low" SES group is the lowest quartile; the "Middle" SES group is the middle two quartiles; and the "High" SES group is the upper quartile.

SOURCE: U.S. Department of Education, National Center for Education Statistics, "High School and Beyond," First Followup survey; and "National Education Longitudinal Study of 1988," Second Followup Student survey. (This table was prepared April 1995.)

Table 133.—Average number of Carnegie units earned by public high school graduates in various subject fields, by student characteristics: 1982 to 1992

Student characteristics	Total	English	History/social studies	Mathematics			Science					Foreign languages	Arts	Vocational education[1]	Personal use[2]	Computer science[3]
				Total	Less than algebra	Algebra or higher	Total	General science	Biology	Chemistry	Physics					
1	2	3	4	5	6	7	8	9	10	11	12	13	14	15	16	17
1982 graduates	21.44	3.87	3.16	2.55	0.92	1.62	2.16	0.74	0.93	0.34	0.16	0.96	1.45	4.64	2.64	0.08
Male	21.28	3.84	3.16	2.63	1.01	1.63	2.22	0.78	0.89	0.35	0.21	0.78	1.28	4.62	2.76	0.09
Female	21.58	3.89	3.17	2.46	0.85	1.62	2.11	0.70	0.96	0.33	0.12	1.14	1.62	4.66	2.53	0.07
Race/ethnicity																
White	21.51	3.84	3.19	2.59	0.80	1.79	2.24	0.73	0.96	0.37	0.19	1.02	1.51	4.53	2.59	0.09
Black	21.13	4.06	3.09	2.53	1.39	1.14	2.04	0.81	0.89	0.25	0.09	0.70	1.25	4.82	2.64	0.08
Hispanic	21.19	3.88	3.02	2.26	1.24	1.03	1.79	0.77	0.79	0.16	0.07	0.76	1.30	5.26	2.92	0.04
Asian	22.18	3.82	3.19	3.14	0.74	2.41	2.59	0.51	1.09	0.60	0.39	1.89	1.32	3.12	3.10	0.14
American Indian	21.32	3.92	3.22	2.09	1.14	0.95	1.96	0.72	0.78	0.35	0.11	0.45	1.67	5.09	2.93	0.04
Academic track																
Academic[4]	21.80	4.04	3.34	2.97	0.82	2.15	2.58	0.73	1.10	0.51	0.25	1.43	1.87	2.87	2.69	0.08
Vocational[5]	20.37	3.41	2.67	1.68	1.06	0.63	1.33	0.70	0.56	0.04	0.03	0.18	0.57	8.08	2.45	0.07
Both[6]	22.80	3.99	3.34	2.54	1.04	1.49	2.10	0.83	0.90	0.26	0.11	0.68	1.40	6.29	2.46	0.10
Neither[7]	19.11	3.48	2.72	1.72	1.08	0.64	1.40	0.72	0.62	0.04	0.02	0.21	0.80	5.79	2.99	0.07
1987 graduates	22.77	4.01	3.31	3.02	0.98	2.04	2.51	0.76	1.08	0.47	0.20	1.36	1.42	4.43	2.70	0.31
Male	22.65	3.98	3.30	3.07	1.04	2.03	2.54	0.78	1.04	0.47	0.25	1.16	1.24	4.52	2.84	0.33
Female	22.89	4.03	3.33	2.97	0.93	2.05	2.49	0.73	1.13	0.47	0.16	1.55	1.60	4.36	2.56	0.29
Race/ethnicity																
White	22.91	4.01	3.29	3.03	0.86	2.17	2.58	0.74	1.11	0.50	0.22	1.35	1.49	4.52	2.64	0.33
Black	22.14	4.09	3.32	2.96	1.45	1.51	2.32	0.90	1.00	0.31	0.11	1.09	1.19	4.47	2.71	0.23
Hispanic	22.54	3.97	3.20	2.87	1.45	1.42	2.21	0.77	1.05	0.29	0.10	1.50	1.32	4.27	3.20	0.21
Asian	23.88	3.85	3.50	3.72	0.77	2.95	3.02	0.65	1.11	0.81	0.45	2.49	1.18	2.92	3.21	0.39
American Indian	23.18	4.20	3.19	3.06	1.51	1.56	2.44	0.81	1.22	0.32	0.09	0.75	1.69	4.70	3.13	0.22
Academic track																
Academic[4]	23.08	4.14	3.51	3.34	0.83	2.51	2.85	0.73	1.20	0.64	0.29	1.80	1.75	2.96	2.75	0.31
Vocational[5]	21.11	3.54	2.60	1.96	1.30	0.66	1.50	0.76	0.68	0.05	0.01	0.21	0.43	8.35	2.52	0.25
Both[6]	23.48	4.01	3.28	2.86	1.15	1.71	2.26	0.83	1.04	0.28	0.11	0.92	1.14	6.54	2.49	0.39
Neither[7]	19.30	3.37	2.56	2.00	1.47	0.53	1.52	0.76	0.70	0.05	0.01	0.24	0.73	5.56	3.32	0.15
1990 graduates	23.50	4.09	3.50	3.20	0.99	2.21	2.75	0.84	1.14	0.54	0.23	1.60	1.55	4.10	2.72	0.35
Male	23.34	4.05	3.47	3.22	1.06	2.16	2.78	0.87	1.11	0.53	0.28	1.39	1.31	4.23	2.88	0.36
Female	23.65	4.13	3.52	3.18	0.93	2.25	2.72	0.82	1.17	0.54	0.19	1.78	1.76	3.98	2.57	0.34
Race/ethnicity																
White	23.53	4.08	3.48	3.18	0.89	2.29	2.80	0.83	1.15	0.56	0.25	1.59	1.61	4.13	2.66	0.35
Black	23.30	4.23	3.49	3.23	1.32	1.92	2.67	0.96	1.11	0.44	0.16	1.23	1.34	4.36	2.74	0.39
Hispanic	23.77	4.05	3.44	3.21	1.41	1.81	2.49	0.83	1.10	0.42	0.14	1.97	1.48	4.00	3.13	0.32
Asian	24.06	4.02	3.70	3.64	0.83	2.81	2.97	0.68	1.12	0.74	0.42	2.52	1.30	2.89	3.02	0.34
American Indian	22.63	4.01	3.36	3.17	1.25	1.93	2.48	0.83	1.09	0.42	0.15	1.15	1.11	4.43	2.91	0.37
Academic track																
Academic[4]	23.57	4.17	3.63	3.40	0.84	2.56	2.98	0.82	1.21	0.66	0.30	1.94	1.80	2.84	2.81	0.33
Vocational[5]	22.07	3.52	2.63	2.02	1.52	0.50	1.64	0.88	0.71	0.04	0.01	0.17	0.43	9.17	2.48	0.23
Both[6]	23.95	4.02	3.35	2.98	1.30	1.67	2.41	0.92	1.06	0.31	0.11	0.99	1.10	6.64	2.48	0.44
Neither[7]	20.21	3.49	2.71	1.97	1.56	0.41	1.58	0.82	0.71	0.03	0.02	0.26	0.57	6.58	3.05	0.23
1992 graduates	23.76	4.18	3.58	3.39	0.98	2.41	2.87	0.84	1.19	0.58	0.26	1.67	1.62	3.76	2.69	0.35
Male	23.58	4.13	3.55	3.38	1.06	2.32	2.88	0.88	1.14	0.56	0.30	1.44	1.42	3.91	2.87	0.34
Female	23.95	4.23	3.61	3.40	0.88	2.52	2.90	0.80	1.25	0.61	0.24	1.92	1.81	3.57	2.51	0.38
Race/ethnicity																
White	23.83	4.17	3.61	3.38	0.87	2.51	2.93	0.83	1.21	0.61	0.28	1.70	1.68	3.73	2.63	0.34
Black	23.21	4.20	3.59	3.37	1.35	2.02	2.74	0.94	1.15	0.47	0.18	1.28	1.45	3.92	2.66	0.38
Hispanic	23.62	4.26	3.38	3.36	1.24	2.12	2.60	0.81	1.16	0.47	0.16	1.76	1.44	3.79	3.03	0.41
Asian	24.45	4.14	3.51	3.65	0.74	2.91	3.22	0.73	1.20	0.79	0.50	2.43	1.38	3.18	2.93	0.43
American Indian	23.38	4.09	3.63	3.16	1.55	1.61	2.55	1.03	0.99	0.35	0.18	0.92	1.53	4.53	2.97	0.25
Academic track																
Academic[4]	23.84	4.25	3.69	3.56	0.87	2.69	3.05	0.81	1.24	0.69	0.31	1.97	1.85	2.72	2.75	0.33
Vocational[5]	21.44	3.57	2.69	2.11	1.62	0.49	1.70	0.91	0.75	0.03	0.01	0.10	0.40	8.38	2.49	0.22
Both[6]	24.28	4.11	3.40	3.11	1.23	1.88	2.57	0.95	1.11	0.36	0.15	1.01	1.10	6.48	2.50	0.48
Neither[7]	19.19	3.08	2.59	2.17	1.42	0.75	1.76	0.93	0.78	0.04	0.01	0.14	0.66	5.92	2.87	0.19

[1] Includes nonoccupational vocational education, vocational general introduction, agriculture, business, marketing, health, occupational home economics, trade and industry, and technical courses.

[2] Includes personal and social courses, religion and theology, and courses not included in the other subject fields.

[3] Computer courses are included in mathematics and vocational categories.

[4] Includes students who complete at least 12 Carnegie units in academic courses, but less than 3 Carnegie units in any specific labor market preparation field.

[5] Includes students who complete at least 3 Carnegie units in a specific labor market preparation field, but less than 12 Carnegie units in academic courses.

[6] Includes students who complete at least 12 Carnegie units in academic courses and at least 3 Carnegie units in a specific labor market preparation field.

[7] Includes students who complete less than 12 Carnegie units in academic courses and less than 3 Carnegie units in a specific labor market preparation field.

NOTE.—The Carnegie unit is a standard of measurement that represents one credit for the completion of a 1-year course.

SOURCE: U.S. Department of Education, National Center for Education Statistics, "High School and Beyond," First Followup survey; "1990 High School Transcript Study" and the "National Education Longitudinal Study of 1988," Second Followup survey. (This table was prepared August 1994.)

Table 134.—Average number of Carnegie units earned by public school graduates in vocational education courses, by student characteristics: 1982 to 1992

Student characteristics	Total	General labor market preparation	Consumer and homemaking education	Specific labor market preparation								
				Total	Agriculture	Business	Marketing	Health	Occupational home economics	Trade and industrial	Technical/communications	Other
1	2	3	4	5	6	7	8	9	10	11	12	13
1982 graduates	4.64	1.06	0.68	2.89	0.21	1.03	0.16	0.05	0.17	1.06	0.11	0.10
Male	4.62	1.02	0.31	3.29	0.35	0.48	0.14	0.02	0.05	1.98	0.14	0.13
Female	4.66	1.10	1.03	2.53	0.08	1.54	0.18	0.08	0.29	0.20	0.09	0.07
Race/ethnicity												
White	4.53	1.04	0.63	2.87	0.23	1.06	0.15	0.04	0.17	1.01	0.12	0.09
Black	4.82	1.08	0.92	2.82	0.10	0.97	0.22	0.12	0.23	0.97	0.11	0.10
Hispanic	5.26	1.18	0.87	3.21	0.24	0.98	0.15	0.06	0.20	1.37	0.07	0.14
Asian	3.12	0.98	0.28	1.86	0.05	0.57	0.04	0.03	0.05	0.87	0.16	0.09
American Indian	5.09	1.25	0.53	3.32	0.26	0.72	0.13	0.07	0.10	1.85	0.05	0.14
Academic track												
Academic [1]	2.87	0.93	0.59	1.36	0.06	0.58	0.07	0.03	0.07	0.37	0.11	0.07
Vocational [2]	8.08	1.18	0.66	6.24	0.62	1.81	0.32	0.08	0.41	2.78	0.11	0.11
Both [3]	6.29	0.94	0.51	4.84	0.32	1.75	0.29	0.11	0.26	1.94	0.12	0.05
Neither [4]	5.79	1.76	1.47	2.56	0.16	0.99	0.19	0.05	0.19	0.52	0.10	0.36
1987 graduates	4.43	0.93	0.60	2.90	0.19	0.97	0.16	0.07	0.19	0.96	0.24	0.12
Male	4.52	0.90	0.33	3.29	0.32	0.57	0.13	0.02	0.08	1.74	0.29	0.14
Female	4.36	0.95	0.86	2.55	0.07	1.35	0.19	0.12	0.29	0.23	0.18	0.12
Race/ethnicity												
White	4.52	0.94	0.60	2.99	0.24	0.98	0.15	0.07	0.18	1.01	0.26	0.10
Black	4.47	0.98	0.73	2.77	0.09	0.99	0.17	0.12	0.26	0.75	0.16	0.23
Hispanic	4.27	0.97	0.60	2.70	0.06	0.98	0.16	0.08	0.17	0.97	0.13	0.15
Asian	2.92	0.69	0.34	1.88	0.01	0.65	0.16	0.11	0.08	0.44	0.31	0.12
American Indian	4.70	0.87	0.64	3.19	0.19	1.09	0.08	0.09	0.09	1.30	0.21	0.14
Academic track												
Academic [1]	2.96	0.84	0.57	1.54	0.05	0.61	0.08	0.04	0.07	0.35	0.25	0.09
Vocational [2]	8.35	1.09	0.67	6.59	0.66	1.61	0.35	0.19	0.57	2.88	0.20	0.13
Both [3]	6.54	0.98	0.52	5.04	0.40	1.74	0.30	0.13	0.33	1.85	0.24	0.05
Neither [4]	5.56	1.42	1.24	2.90	0.14	0.78	0.23	0.06	0.27	0.64	0.11	0.67
1990 graduates	4.10	0.83	0.57	2.70	0.20	0.90	0.16	0.04	0.17	0.87	0.22	0.14
Male	4.23	0.78	0.33	3.12	0.31	0.58	0.14	0.02	0.06	1.58	0.27	0.16
Female	3.98	0.87	0.79	2.32	0.09	1.19	0.18	0.06	0.27	0.22	0.18	0.13
Race/ethnicity												
White	4.13	0.80	0.55	2.78	0.24	0.88	0.16	0.04	0.15	0.94	0.22	0.15
Black	4.36	0.96	0.79	2.62	0.06	1.08	0.18	0.04	0.27	0.64	0.23	0.12
Hispanic	4.00	0.85	0.54	2.61	0.15	0.96	0.19	0.02	0.27	0.75	0.17	0.10
Asian	2.89	0.73	0.32	1.85	0.04	0.66	0.05	0.01	0.05	0.73	0.26	0.05
American Indian	4.43	0.84	0.72	2.87	0.36	0.96	0.15	0.0	0.08	0.95	0.16	0.21
Academic track												
Academic [1]	2.84	0.77	0.56	1.51	0.06	0.61	0.08	0.02	0.07	0.34	0.23	0.10
Vocational [2]	9.17	1.12	0.65	7.40	0.96	1.44	0.33	0.11	0.51	3.54	0.14	0.37
Both [3]	6.64	0.83	0.52	5.30	0.46	1.71	0.38	0.10	0.40	1.93	0.22	0.10
Neither [4]	6.58	2.01	1.31	3.25	0.25	0.84	0.18	0.08	0.19	0.70	0.14	0.87
1992 graduates	3.76	0.69	0.54	2.53	0.19	0.85	0.13	0.06	0.18	0.79	0.22	0.11
Male	3.91	0.69	0.36	2.86	0.30	0.59	0.13	0.02	0.07	1.36	0.26	0.13
Female	3.57	0.68	0.70	2.19	0.08	1.10	0.13	0.10	0.28	0.23	0.19	0.09
Race/ethnicity												
White	3.73	0.67	0.53	2.52	0.22	0.84	0.13	0.05	0.15	0.80	0.22	0.11
Black	3.92	0.74	0.68	2.52	0.12	0.93	0.14	0.08	0.35	0.61	0.20	0.09
Hispanic	3.79	0.74	0.46	2.59	0.09	0.92	0.13	0.09	0.21	0.71	0.26	0.18
Asian	3.18	0.56	0.36	2.25	0.03	0.85	0.07	0.07	0.06	0.88	0.26	0.03
American Indian	4.53	0.66	0.50	3.37	0.20	0.75	0.10	0.06	0.35	1.73	0.12	0.06
Academic track												
Academic [1]	2.72	0.63	0.54	1.55	0.07	0.63	0.08	0.03	0.09	0.33	0.21	0.10
Vocational [2]	8.38	1.00	0.61	6.78	1.01	1.17	0.25	0.15	0.65	3.14	0.19	0.21
Both [3]	6.48	0.70	0.47	5.30	0.45	1.61	0.30	0.13	0.43	2.04	0.28	0.08
Neither [4]	5.92	2.22	1.18	2.53	0.51	0.50	0.10	0.07	0.11	0.59	0.16	0.48

[1] Includes students who complete at least 12 Carnegie units in academic courses, but less than 3 Carnegie units in any specific labor market preparation field.

[2] Includes students who complete at least 3 Carnegie units in a specific labor market preparation field, but less than 12 Carnegie units in academic courses.

[3] Includes students who complete at least 12 Carnegie units in academic courses and at least 3 Carnegie units in a specific labor market preparation field.

[4] Includes students who complete less than 12 Carnegie units in academic courses and less than 3 Carnegie units in a specific labor market preparation field.

NOTE.—The Carnegie unit is a standard of measurement that represents one credit for the completion of a 1-year course.

SOURCE: U.S. Department of Education, National Center for Education Statistics, "High School and Beyond," First Followup survey; "1990 High School Transcript Study" and the "National Education Longitudinal Study of 1988," Second Followup survey. (This table was prepared August 1994.)

Table 135.—Percentage of high school graduates taking selected mathematics and science courses in high school, by sex and race/ethnicity: 1982 to 1994

Courses (credits)	1982	1987	1990	1994							
				Total	Sex		Race/ethnicity				
					Men	Women	White	Black	His-panic	Asian/Pacific Islander	American Indian/Alaskan Native
1	2	3	4	5	6	7	8	9	10	11	12
Mathematics [1]											
Any mathematics (1.0)	98.5	98.9	99.6	99.6	99.5	99.6	99.6	99.3	99.2	100.0	98.9
Algebra I (1.0)	53.9	64.0	64.2	66.4	64.7	68.1	67.5	65.0	70.7	61.7	58.7
Geometry (1.0)	45.5	59.7	63.4	70.4	68.3	72.4	72.7	58.1	69.4	75.8	60.0
Algebra II (0.5)	32.2	48.6	51.7	58.6	55.4	61.6	61.6	43.7	51.0	66.6	39.2
Trigonometry (0.5)	12.1	18.6	18.2	17.2	16.6	17.8	18.6	13.6	9.8	25.3	6.7
Analysis/pre-calculus (0.5)	5.9	12.6	13.4	17.3	16.3	18.2	18.2	9.8	13.9	33.9	8.7
Statistics/probability (0.5)	1.0	1.3	1.0	2.0	2.0	2.1	2.3	1.7	1.0	1.1	1.2
Calculus (1.0)	4.6	6.0	6.5	9.2	9.4	9.1	9.6	3.8	6.0	23.4	3.8
AP calculus (1.0)	1.5	3.2	4.1	7.0	7.2	6.8	7.3	2.0	4.6	21.0	2.2
Science											
Any science (1.0)	96.6	98.7	99.4	99.5	99.3	99.8	99.7	99.5	99.3	99.3	99.7
Biology (1.0)	76.4	87.8	91.3	93.5	92.3	94.7	94.4	91.3	94.0	90.9	91.2
AP/honors biology (1.0)	6.6	2.7	4.9	4.6	4.0	5.1	4.6	2.7	3.3	8.3	1.7
Chemistry (1.0)	30.9	43.7	49.0	56.0	53.2	58.7	58.5	43.8	46.5	69.3	41.3
AP/honors chemistry (1.0)	2.9	3.3	3.5	3.9	4.1	3.7	4.3	2.1	2.5	7.7	0.6
Physics (1.0)	14.2	19.2	21.5	24.4	26.9	22.0	26.1	14.7	16.0	42.3	10.3
AP/honors physics (1.0)	1.0	1.6	2.0	2.4	3.0	1.8	2.5	1.4	1.8	6.0	0.3
Engineering (1.0)	0.1	0.1	0.1	0.3	0.4	0.2	0.2	0.4	0.1	1.0	—
Astronomy (0.5)	1.1	1.0	1.2	1.7	2.0	1.5	2.0	0.6	0.4	0.8	2.2
Geology/earth science (0.5)	13.2	14.5	24.8	23.0	22.8	23.2	23.8	23.3	15.3	16.7	23.2
Biology and chemistry (2.0)	28.1	42.1	47.6	53.8	50.9	56.6	56.4	42.2	45.1	64.8	39.6
Biology, chemistry, and physics (3.0)	10.6	16.4	18.8	21.3	23.1	19.6	22.7	13.0	13.4	37.2	8.0

[1] These data only report the percentage of students who earned credit in each mathematics course while in high school and does not count those students who took these courses prior to entering high school. In 1992, approximately 93 percent of graduates had taken algebra I before or during high school, and 70 percent had taken geometry.
—Less than 0.05 percent.

SOURCE: U.S. Department of Education, National Center for Education Statistics, National Assessment of Educational Progress, *The 1994 High School Transcript Study Tabulations: Comparative Data on Credits Earned and Demographics for 1994, 1990, 1987, and 1982 High School Graduates, 1996.* (This table was prepared September 1996.)

Table 136.—Percent of high school graduates earning minimum credits in selected combinations of academic courses, by sex and race/ethnicity: 1982 to 1994

Year of graduation and course combinations taken [1]	All students	Sex		Race/ethnicity				
		Male	Female	White	Black	Hispanic	Asian	American Indian/Alaskan Native
1	2	3	4	5	6	7	8	9
1982 graduates								
4 Eng., 3 S.S., 3 Sci., 3 Math, .5 Comp., & 2 F.L. [2]	2.0	2.2	1.8	2.4	0.9	0.6	5.6	0.1
4 Eng., 3 S.S., 3 Sci., 3 Math, & .5 Comp. [3]	2.9	3.6	2.3	3.4	1.3	0.9	6.6	0.1
4 Eng., 3 S.S., 3 Sci., 3 Math, & 2 F.L.	9.2	8.8	9.6	10.5	5.3	3.7	17.1	5.7
4 Eng., 3 S.S., 3 Sci., 3 Math	14.0	14.8	13.3	15.5	11.6	6.5	21.3	6.5
4 Eng., 3 S.S., 2 Sci., 2 Math	31.5	31.6	31.5	32.5	31.7	25.2	34.3	35.7
1987 graduates								
4 Eng., 3 S.S., 3 Sci., 3 Math, .5 Comp., & 2 F.L. [2]	12.1	13.0	11.4	12.8	7.8	6.4	25.6	2.8
4 Eng., 3 S.S., 3 Sci., 3 Math, & .5 Comp. [3]	16.6	18.1	15.1	17.6	11.3	9.0	28.8	15.2
4 Eng., 3 S.S., 3 Sci., 3 Math, & 2 F.L.	20.6	20.2	20.9	21.4	15.0	12.9	42.6	5.8
4 Eng., 3 S.S., 3 Sci., 3 Math	27.9	28.8	27.1	29.2	22.0	17.6	48.8	26.6
4 Eng., 3 S.S., 2 Sci., 2 Math	54.0	53.5	54.7	53.4	56.0	51.6	68.9	66.7
1990 graduates								
4 Eng., 3 S.S., 3 Sci., 3 Math, .5 Comp., & 2 F.L. [2]	18.3	18.1	18.4	18.9	15.5	18.2	23.9	7.8
4 Eng., 3 S.S., 3 Sci., 3 Math, & .5 Comp. [3]	23.3	23.9	22.8	23.5	25.3	20.5	27.2	14.6
4 Eng., 3 S.S., 3 Sci., 3 Math, & 2 F.L.	30.3	29.2	31.3	32.0	23.3	25.8	43.7	9.9
4 Eng., 3 S.S., 3 Sci., 3 Math	38.8	39.2	38.4	39.8	39.5	30.3	48.8	20.9
4 Eng., 3 S.S., 2 Sci., 2 Math	66.5	65.9	67.1	65.8	73.3	64.6	70.6	47.9
1994 graduates								
4 Eng., 3 S.S., 3 Sci., 3 Math, .5 Comp., & 2 F.L. [2]	25.3	23.5	26.9	26.5	19.5	27.7	36.3	12.9
4 Eng., 3 S.S., 3 Sci., 3 Math, & .5 Comp. [3]	32.0	31.1	32.9	33.5	28.2	31.1	40.2	25.5
4 Eng., 3 S.S., 3 Sci., 3 Math, & 2 F.L.	39.1	35.1	42.9	41.6	30.2	36.3	51.2	22.5
4 Eng., 3 S.S., 3 Sci., 3 Math	49.8	47.5	51.9	52.7	45.0	41.2	56.1	46.0
4 Eng., 3 S.S., 2 Sci., 2 Math	74.6	72.2	76.9	75.5	76.7	77.5	73.1	77.0

[1] Eng. = English; S.S. = social studies; Sci. = science; Comp. = computer science; and F.L. = foreign language.
[2] The National Commission on Excellence in Education recommended that all college-bound high school students take these courses as a minimum.
[3] The National Commission on Excellence in Education recommended that all high school students take these courses as a minimum.

SOURCE: U.S. Department of Education, National Center for Education Statistics, *The 1994 High School Transcript Study Tabulations: Comparative Data on Credits Earned and Demographics for 1994, 1990, 1987, and 1982 High School Graduates, 1996.* (This table was prepared October 1996.)

Table 137.—Reasons given by twelfth graders for taking current mathematics and science classes, by selected student and school characteristics: 1992

Class subject and opinion	All 12th graders	Sex		Race/ethnicity					Socioeconomic status quartile [1]				Control of school attended		
		Male	Female	White	Black	His-panic	Asian	Amer-ican In-dian	Lowest	Second	Third	Highest	Public	Catholic	Other private
1	2	3	4	5	6	7	8	9	10	11	12	13	14	15	16
Mathematics class															
I am interested in mathematics	74.5	77.4	71.3	72.9	74.6	80.4	81.9	87.7	78.0	74.6	73.1	74.2	73.8	78.4	81.7
I do well in mathematics	77.1	80.2	73.7	76.4	76.1	79.7	83.6	76.8	79.5	77.8	76.3	76.1	76.7	78.4	82.1
I need it for college or trade school	87.2	86.6	87.8	86.5	89.8	86.5	90.8	90.5	83.3	85.4	88.9	88.6	87.1	87.9	87.5
I need it for a job after high school	64.7	65.9	63.4	62.5	69.7	70.9	66.3	83.9	71.2	68.5	65.5	57.8	65.9	58.1	51.9
I need it for advanced placement	53.6	53.3	54.0	49.6	58.4	62.5	72.6	56.9	59.8	46.7	52.2	55.7	54.1	47.2	53.9
Advised to take class by:															
Teacher	65.9	63.3	68.8	63.6	74.8	71.1	66.7	70.6	69.2	65.1	66.3	64.7	65.7	66.2	70.0
Guidance counselor	64.8	62.9	66.8	60.7	77.8	76.2	64.2	83.0	76.4	67.5	62.6	58.6	65.8	55.1	59.6
Parent	71.6	69.1	74.2	70.5	74.6	74.4	73.3	79.8	66.3	67.2	70.3	76.6	71.8	68.4	71.4
Friend	42.2	41.4	43.2	39.8	51.2	43.7	50.8	56.2	46.1	43.2	41.7	40.7	42.5	40.6	39.1
Sibling	30.9	29.5	32.5	26.3	37.2	43.1	46.2	51.5	40.4	29.7	27.7	29.4	31.8	21.9	28.9
Science class															
I am interested in science	78.8	82.7	74.4	78.5	77.4	78.9	83.6	74.9	74.5	76.7	76.9	82.7	77.9	81.1	89.9
I do well in science	80.6	83.9	77.0	80.1	76.7	86.1	84.2	86.6	78.1	80.1	77.1	84.0	80.1	79.8	90.2
I need it for college or trade school	83.3	81.7	85.0	82.4	86.4	83.5	88.4	88.8	78.5	81.9	84.6	84.8	83.3	85.3	80.7
I need it for a job after high school	47.0	47.9	45.9	44.5	53.2	57.6	51.3	55.9	53.4	47.6	50.4	41.6	47.8	45.7	35.7
I need it for advanced placement	50.2	49.7	50.9	47.1	51.6	59.0	66.8	59.6	48.9	47.9	46.8	53.9	49.2	53.5	60.3
Advised to take class by:															
Teacher	58.9	56.2	61.9	57.6	61.7	63.7	61.0	67.2	61.3	57.7	58.3	59.0	57.8	60.3	74.1
Guidance counselor	59.4	57.8	61.2	56.2	71.4	70.9	59.7	57.9	74.0	59.5	55.8	55.5	60.3	44.1	67.3
Parent	66.3	63.4	69.4	65.7	69.1	70.5	64.1	73.8	61.9	59.9	66.4	70.6	67.0	58.7	67.4
Friend	43.5	43.4	43.6	42.9	40.9	44.6	49.7	62.9	45.6	41.6	41.0	45.0	43.6	36.6	52.5
Sibling	28.7	26.8	31.0	25.3	35.0	35.5	44.3	57.6	36.1	25.2	25.2	29.6	29.4	21.0	30.5

[1] Socioeconomic status was measured by a composite score on parental education and occupations, and family income.

SOURCE: U.S. Department of Education, National Center for Education Statistics, "National Education Longitudinal Study of 1988," Second Followup survey. (This table was prepared February 1994.)

Table 138.—Expected occupations of 8th, 10th, and 12th graders at age 30, by selected student and school characteristics: 1988, 1990, and 1992

[Percentage distribution]

Expected occupation at age 30	8th graders in 1988	10th graders in 1990	12th graders in 1992													
			Total	Sex		Race/ethnicity					Socioeconomic status [1]			Control of school attended		
				Male	Female	White	Black	His-panic	Asian	Amer-ican Indian	Low	Middle	High	Public	Catholic	Other private
1	2	3	4	5	6	7	8	9	10	11	12	13	14	15	16	17
Total	100.0	100.0	100.0	100.0	100.0	100.0	100.0	100.0	100.0	100.0	100.0	100.0	100.0	100.0	100.0	100.0
Craftsperson or operator	4.2	5.6	3.5	6.6	0.5	3.7	3.4	2.7	2.4	2.7	6.8	3.9	0.7	3.9	0.9	0.3
Farmer or farm manager	1.0	1.1	0.9	1.4	0.3	1.0	0.6	0.7	0.1	(2)	1.4	1.0	0.5	0.9	0.6	0.6
Housewife/homemaker	2.3	2.0	1.0	0.1	2.0	1.2	0.4	0.7	0.8	(2)	0.9	1.1	1.2	1.1	0.7	1.5
Laborer or farm worker	0.6	0.8	0.7	1.3	0.1	0.7	0.3	0.6	1.2	1.9	1.2	0.8	0.2	0.7	0.4	0.8
Military, police, or security officer	9.6	5.7	6.6	11.2	2.0	6.4	7.7	7.4	5.1	10.0	9.3	7.4	3.6	7.0	3.3	1.7
Professional, business, or managerial	34.5	45.7	50.8	45.9	55.7	50.0	55.1	47.1	61.3	43.3	38.7	48.1	63.0	49.4	66.3	59.2
Teacher	(3)	4.1	7.5	4.1	10.8	8.4	3.7	6.7	3.4	4.8	6.2	7.6	8.2	7.3	8.1	11.1
Business owner	6.2	5.3	6.0	7.8	4.3	5.6	6.8	7.7	7.0	6.4	6.7	6.4	4.9	6.3	3.8	3.3
Technical	6.2	4.7	5.4	7.5	3.4	5.0	5.5	7.5	6.0	8.2	7.1	5.9	3.5	5.7	2.4	3.6
Salesperson, clerical, or office worker	2.8	4.9	4.8	3.1	6.5	4.6	5.3	6.4	4.1	5.2	8.0	4.7	3.1	4.9	2.6	5.8
Service worker	4.9	1.8	2.4	0.5	4.2	2.3	3.1	2.5	0.6	5.8	4.6	2.3	0.9	2.5	1.5	0.8
Other employment	17.0	7.7	10.2	10.3	10.2	10.8	8.0	9.6	8.0	10.6	8.8	10.8	10.2	10.3	9.6	11.3
Don't know or no plans	10.5	10.5	0.2	0.2	0.2	0.2	0.2	0.5	0.2	1.0	0.4	0.2	0.1	0.2	(2)	0.1

[1] Socioeconomic status was measured by a composite score on parental education and occupations, and family income. The "Low" SES group is the lowest quartile; the "Middle" SES group is the middle two quartiles; and the "High" SES group is the upper quartile.

[2] Less than .05 percent.

[3] Included under "Professional, business, or managerial."

SOURCE: U.S. Department of Education, National Center for Education Statistics, "National Education Longitudinal Study of 1988," First and Second Followup surveys. (This table was prepared March 1994.)

Table 139.—Eighth, tenth, and twelfth graders' attitudes about school climate, by student and school characteristics: 1988, 1990, and 1992

Statements about school climate	Eight grad-ers in 1988	Tenth graders in 1990	Percent who strongly agree or agree with statement														
			Twelfth graders in 1992														
			Total	Sex		Race/ethnicity					Socioeconomic status quartile [1]				Control of school attended		
				Male	Fe-male	White	Black	His-panic	Asian	Amer-ican Indian	Low-est	Sec-ond	Third	High-est	Public	Catholic	Other private
1	2	3	4	5	6	7	8	9	10	11	12	13	14	15	16	17	18
There is real school spirit	68.6	70.4	71.4	72.9	69.8	72.1	67.4	71.0	70.7	62.0	73.4	71.3	72.0	69.5	70.4	82.2	76.0
Discipline is fair	69.1	70.2	68.0	67.0	69.0	68.0	58.6	74.7	75.6	73.0	66.3	66.2	68.1	69.7	67.3	69.9	77.0
Teaching is good	80.2	81.9	85.4	84.8	86.0	85.1	84.1	88.5	85.5	88.3	85.6	84.2	84.3	87.2	84.7	90.4	93.7
Teachers are interested in stu-dents	75.2	76.0	81.6	81.5	81.8	81.9	78.4	83.7	80.1	83.0	80.3	80.5	80.1	84.8	80.4	91.1	95.4
I don't feel safe at this school	11.8	8.0	10.4	10.8	10.1	8.6	16.1	14.7	15.8	13.0	13.1	11.2	10.5	7.5	11.1	4.9	3.5
Disruptions by other students interfere with my learning	39.6	39.9	33.1	31.6	34.7	30.8	38.1	39.8	41.4	40.5	37.0	35.9	34.6	26.3	34.2	25.4	21.8
Fights often occur between dif-ferent racial/ethnic groups	—	—	22.7	22.2	23.2	20.9	22.2	31.9	30.5	29.9	25.1	23.9	23.5	18.6	24.5	8.3	3.0
There are many gangs in school	—	—	16.3	16.4	16.2	12.5	17.5	36.4	27.2	23.2	21.9	15.8	16.7	12.1	17.7	4.5	1.5
Students are graded fairly	—	—	78.3	78.6	78.0	79.5	71.6	77.6	77.3	74.7	74.8	76.3	78.3	82.4	77.3	84.1	91.8
There is a lot of cheating on tests and assignments	—	—	58.8	56.0	61.7	59.7	57.1	53.8	63.5	59.8	55.8	59.1	61.8	58.6	60.2	56.9	32.6
Some teachers ignore cheating when they see it	—	—	30.9	29.3	32.6	32.7	25.4	26.0	30.7	24.8	26.9	31.4	32.7	31.9	31.9	26.5	16.9

[1] Socioeconomic status was measured by a composite score on parental education and occupations, and family income.

SOURCE: U.S. Department of Education, National Center for Education Statistics, "National Education Longitudinal Study of 1988," Base Year and First and Second Fol-lowup surveys. (This table was prepared February 1994.)

Table 140.—Home activities of 3- to 8-year-olds, by grade of student: 1991

Home activities	Total	Not en-rolled in school	Grade of student enrollment					
			Nursery school [1]	Kinder-garten [2]	First grade	Second grade	Third grade or higher	Ungraded
1	2	3	4	5	6	7	8	9
Number of children	22,294	4,853	3,571	4,023	3,993	3,554	2,270	29
	Percent of children who are read to							
Total	100	100	100	100	100	100	100	—
Never or several times per year	7	4	2	4	5	11	24	—
Several times per month or per week	58	54	51	56	62	67	62	—
Every day	35	42	47	40	33	22	14	—
	Percent of children who were read to in the previous week							
Total	100	100	100	100	100	100	100	—
Never	12	7	5	5	10	20	35	—
One or two times	27	24	20	24	30	36	34	—
Three or more times	61	69	76	71	60	44	31	—
	Average hours of television watched daily and percentage of families with television-related rules							
Average hours of TV daily [3]	2.5	3.1	2.6	2.5	2.2	2.2	2.3	—
Percentage with TV-related rules [4]								
What shows child may watch	85	82	87	85	86	87	86	—
How early or late child may watch	89	80	87	90	94	94	93	—
Hours child may watch overall	56	50	55	56	59	60	61	—
Hours child may watch on weekdays	60	47	55	61	66	67	68	—

[1] Includes children enrolled in nursery school, prekindergarten, and Head Start.
[2] Includes children enrolled in kindergarten and in transitional grades between kinder-garten and first grade, such as transitional kindergarten or prefirst grade.
[3] Includes hours watching television shows and video tapes.
[4] Includes children whose parents reported viewing hours.
—Unweighted number of cases is less than 30.

SOURCE: U.S. Department of Education, National Center for Education Statistics, Home Activities of 3- to 8-year-olds. (This table was prepared April 1992.)

Table 141.—Participation of 10th and 12th graders in extracurricular activities, by selected student characteristics: 1990 and 1992

Extracurricular activities	Total 1990 10th graders	Percent who participated in school activities													
		1992 12th graders													
		Total	Sex		Race/ethnicity					Socioeconomic status [1]			Control of school attended		
			Male	Female	White	Black	Hispanic	Asian	American Indian	Low	Middle	High	Public	Catholic	Other private
1	2	3	4	5	6	7	8	9	10	11	12	13	14	15	16
Athletics															
Interscholastic team sport .	—	30.4	41.2	19.7	30.8	32.3	25.8	28.3	30.4	25.3	30.1	34.4	29.6	31.2	48.9
Interscholastic individual sport	—	20.3	26.8	13.9	20.9	21.2	14.9	21.6	20.7	13.6	18.7	27.7	20.0	24.6	21.8
Intramural team sport	—	22.7	31.8	13.8	22.3	25.8	20.8	24.9	27.9	20.4	22.9	24.1	22.0	29.7	29.6
Intramural individual sport .	—	13.3	16.7	10.0	12.5	16.7	14.0	14.7	18.2	10.8	12.5	15.9	13.5	13.3	10.7
Performing arts															
Cheerleading	5.9	7.6	2.0	13.0	7.4	10.6	6.7	5.1	11.9	6.5	7.9	7.8	7.6	8.3	5.9
School band or orchestra ..	20.9	19.8	15.1	24.5	19.6	24.4	16.9	17.7	16.8	17.6	19.6	22.0	19.8	12.0	31.3
School play or musical	11.0	15.4	14.1	16.7	16.1	15.9	10.6	13.7	14.0	11.4	14.8	19.4	15.0	14.2	26.2
School government/clubs															
Student government	7.3	15.4	13.1	17.7	15.4	16.7	14.7	14.6	14.3	11.0	14.7	19.8	15.0	14.5	27.9
Academic honor society	7.7	18.5	14.4	22.7	19.6	14.0	12.5	27.2	13.6	9.6	15.9	29.5	17.7	28.0	22.9
School yearbook/newspaper	8.8	18.8	14.0	23.5	19.7	14.3	16.8	18.9	21.2	14.3	16.9	25.1	17.0	28.0	46.7
School service clubs	11.5	13.9	10.3	17.4	13.6	13.6	14.4	19.3	11.6	8.4	12.5	19.6	13.6	17.3	15.4
School academic clubs	30.7	25.1	22.9	27.4	25.8	20.7	22.6	32.3	17.7	18.8	24.1	31.1	25.1	26.4	24.5
School hobby clubs	7.3	7.7	8.1	7.4	7.4	6.6	9.1	11.3	10.8	6.7	7.0	9.3	7.4	9.8	11.0
School FTA, FHA, and FFA	11.7	17.7	14.7	20.7	17.6	22.5	16.4	8.8	22.1	24.8	19.7	9.9	19.4	2.4	2.9

[1] Socioeconomic status was measured by a composite score on parental education and occupations, and family income. The "Low" SES group is the lowest quartile; the "Middle" SES group is the middle two quartiles; and the "High" SES group is the upper quartile.

SOURCE: U.S. Department of Education, National Center for Education Statistics, "National Education Longitudinal Study of 1988," First and Second Followup surveys. (This table was prepared March 1994.)

Table 142.—Percent of high school seniors who plan to go to college after graduation, by student characteristics: 1982 and 1992

Student characteristics	No college		Right after high school		After a year		After more than a year		Don't know	
	1982	1992	1982	1992	1982	1992	1982	1992	1982	1992
1	2	3	4	5	6	7	8	9	10	11
All seniors	**18.3**	**4.0**	**58.3**	**76.6**	**7.1**	**10.7**	**3.9**	**4.1**	**12.3**	**4.6**
Male	22.8	5.7	53.4	73.0	6.6	10.2	4.0	5.6	13.1	5.5
Female	14.0	2.3	63.0	80.1	7.6	11.1	3.8	2.7	11.6	3.8
Race/ethnicity										
White	18.2	3.9	60.2	76.6	7.0	10.6	3.4	4.4	11.3	4.5
Black	14.6	5.4	57.5	75.2	8.2	11.2	5.7	3.2	14.1	5.2
Hispanic	24.1	3.5	45.6	75.4	7.5	11.6	5.8	3.6	17.0	5.9
Asian	5.6	2.6	81.7	83.4	5.6	8.6	2.1	2.4	5.1	3.1
American Indian	22.2	5.8	48.5	65.7	9.0	15.5	3.3	5.3	17.1	7.7
Test performance quartile										
Lowest test quartile	32.3	11.4	32.8	59.3	9.1	15.1	4.5	3.4	21.3	10.9
Second test quartile	26.5	3.9	45.2	71.2	7.8	14.3	4.8	4.4	15.8	6.3
Third test quartile	15.6	2.0	61.9	81.2	7.9	9.9	3.8	4.1	10.8	2.8
Highest test quartile	3.8	0.6	85.4	90.9	4.7	4.8	2.4	2.6	3.8	1.2
Socioeconomic status [1]										
Low quartile	29.1	8.1	38.3	60.3	7.6	16.5	5.8	5.8	19.2	9.4
Middle 2 quartiles	18.3	4.1	56.6	74.6	8.1	11.8	4.1	4.7	12.9	4.8
High quartile	6.6	1.1	82.8	91.1	5.0	4.6	1.5	1.7	4.1	1.5
Control of school										
Public	19.4	4.4	56.0	74.8	7.3	11.4	4.1	4.5	13.1	4.9
Catholic	8.2	0.5	80.0	93.0	5.1	4.3	1.4	0.7	5.4	1.6
Other private	9.9	0.7	77.3	92.0	6.4	3.0	2.5	0.6	3.9	3.7
Location of school										
Urban	16.6	3.0	59.3	79.5	8.2	10.1	4.0	3.0	11.8	4.4
Suburban	15.5	3.3	62.3	78.6	6.8	9.7	4.1	4.4	11.3	4.0
Rural/nonmetropolitan area	24.0	5.9	51.4	71.2	6.9	12.3	3.6	4.9	14.2	5.8

[1] Socioeconomic status was measured by a composite score on parental education and occupations, and family income. The "Low" SES group is the lowest quartile; the "Middle" SES group is the middle two quartiles; and the "High" SES group is the upper quartile.

SOURCE: U.S. Department of Education, National Center for Education Statistics, "High School and Beyond," First Followup survey; and "National Education Longitudinal Study of 1988," Second Followup Student survey. (This table was prepared April 1995.)

Table 143.—Percent of high school seniors who say they engage in various activities, by student characteristics: 1982 and 1992

Activity	Total	Sex		Race/ethncity					Socioeconomic status [1]			Control of school attended		
		Male	Female	White	Black	Hispanic	Asian	American Indian	Low	Middle	High	Public	Catholic	Other private
1	2	3	4	5	6	7	8	9	10	11	12	13	14	15
Percent of 12th graders, 1982														
At least once a week														
Talking with friends	92.7	92.5	93.0	94.2	89.1	88.9	86.7	91.3	88.6	93.7	95.6	92.3	96.4	97.2
Reading for pleasure	50.4	43.4	57.1	51.0	53.9	43.1	56.4	50.3	45.2	50.1	56.8	50.1	51.4	56.2
Going on dates	61.3	60.6	62.0	63.9	51.9	58.1	40.3	54.5	55.8	63.4	62.8	61.4	60.7	60.7
Driving or riding around	62.4	65.9	59.1	65.2	48.9	60.7	42.4	62.3	56.2	65.0	65.1	62.6	64.6	55.0
Thinking or daydreaming	68.5	61.8	74.8	71.1	64.6	58.0	62.4	53.9	63.3	67.5	75.9	67.7	75.2	76.5
Talking with parents	83.9	79.9	87.6	85.6	80.1	78.0	79.8	76.0	78.5	84.7	87.8	83.4	87.7	87.9
Reading front page of newspaper	69.1	70.8	67.5	69.7	71.9	63.3	73.5	61.8	61.5	69.1	77.0	68.5	75.7	72.0
Five or more hours on weekdays														
Watches television	11.5	11.9	11.2	9.4	22.2	13.8	8.1	20.9	16.5	11.5	6.4	12.1	8.0	3.9
Percent of 12th graders, 1992														
At least once a week														
Use personal computer	23.7	28.1	19.3	23.9	23.6	20.9	27.0	23.8	18.9	23.3	27.7	23.4	25.2	28.0
Work on hobbies	40.9	44.4	37.4	42.0	34.8	39.9	37.8	49.8	36.3	41.1	43.5	40.6	43.4	43.2
Attend religious activities	31.0	28.1	33.8	31.4	33.7	26.9	30.4	14.6	22.2	29.4	39.9	29.4	38.8	54.9
Attend youth groups	22.4	24.6	20.1	22.5	23.3	18.5	26.4	22.1	16.6	21.3	28.1	21.8	22.9	33.3
Perform community service	11.3	10.7	11.9	11.1	12.1	10.9	14.0	9.2	7.7	9.5	16.7	9.7	22.3	31.2
Driving or riding around	73.3	74.3	72.3	75.7	67.8	66.2	66.7	71.0	69.6	75.3	72.4	73.4	77.8	63.0
Do things with friends	88.1	88.2	88.0	90.7	79.8	82.4	85.9	77.2	80.8	88.1	93.2	87.5	94.5	91.9
Do things with parent	66.7	61.2	72.1	68.2	62.0	63.8	63.4	61.2	59.6	66.3	71.7	66.0	73.6	72.8
Talk with other adult	47.7	45.4	49.9	48.8	44.3	46.2	43.0	44.0	47.6	49.0	45.0	47.3	46.4	58.8
Take music, art, or dance class	10.1	7.9	12.2	9.9	9.7	9.8	14.0	10.6	7.1	8.8	14.0	9.7	13.4	12.4
Take sports lessons	7.3	9.7	5.0	7.0	7.4	8.2	9.4	11.6	5.6	6.6	9.5	7.1	11.1	7.8
Play ball or other sport	26.3	38.8	14.0	27.1	22.9	23.6	28.7	29.4	20.7	24.5	33.1	25.6	34.0	31.4
More than an hour a day														
Reading for pleasure	55.4	53.1	57.7	56.3	51.0	53.5	54.4	59.3	51.6	55.0	58.6	55.0	56.0	62.9
Plays video games	13.0	19.2	6.8	11.7	19.9	13.0	13.5	21.1	16.9	13.7	9.4	13.3	10.4	8.9
Five or more hours on weekdays														
Watches television	8.4	8.5	8.4	6.4	21.3	9.3	6.4	12.7	12.0	9.4	4.1	8.7	7.9	4.1

[1] Socioeconomic status was measured by a composite score on parental education and occupations, and family income. The "Low" SES group is the lowest quartile; the "Middle" SES group is the middle two quartiles; and the "High" SES group is the upper quartile.

SOURCE: U.S. Department of Education, National Center for Education Statistics, "National Education Longitudinal Study of 1988," Second Followup survey, and "High School and Beyond," First Followup survey. (This table was prepared March 1994.)

Table 144.—Percent of high school seniors who participate in selected school-sponsored extracurricular activities, by student characteristics: 1980 and 1992

Student characteristics	Academic clubs		Athletics		Cheerleading and drill team		Newspaper or yearbook		Music, drama, debate		Vocational clubs	
	1980	1992	1980	1992	1980	1992	1980	1992	1980	1992	1980	1992
1	2	3	4	5	6	7	8	9	10	11	12	13
All seniors	**25.6**	**25.1**	**51.8**	**42.9**	**15.1**	**7.5**	**19.9**	**18.8**	**36.5**	**27.9**	**23.1**	**17.7**
Male	20.3	22.8	64.0	55.3	4.5	2.0	15.4	14.0	28.4	23.0	19.1	14.7
Female	30.9	27.4	40.6	30.3	24.8	13.0	24.0	23.5	44.0	32.7	26.7	20.6
Race/ethnicity												
White	25.0	25.8	51.6	44.1	14.9	7.4	20.1	19.7	35.8	28.1	22.3	17.6
Black	33.1	20.6	54.4	41.4	17.6	10.6	17.8	14.3	43.2	32.2	30.1	22.5
Hispanic	24.2	22.6	49.4	35.3	12.3	6.6	15.8	16.8	31.1	22.3	27.3	16.4
Asian	26.6	32.3	48.8	45.2	14.6	5.1	21.4	18.9	36.6	25.8	9.6	8.8
Test performance quartile												
Lowest test quartile	24.6	18.1	46.3	40.3	15.0	8.5	14.6	12.0	31.8	23.3	33.0	25.0
Middle 2 test quartiles	24.3	23.3	49.4	42.3	16.0	7.6	18.7	17.1	35.6	26.5	24.2	20.0
Highest test quartile	29.0	37.1	54.0	49.0	13.5	7.9	27.1	27.9	43.4	35.2	12.4	11.4
Socioeconomic status [1]												
Low quartile	24.6	19.4	43.2	33.9	13.0	6.7	15.7	14.2	31.0	24.1	30.6	24.8
Middle 2 quartiles	24.3	24.5	52.1	41.7	15.9	8.0	19.2	17.5	35.8	27.8	24.1	18.5
High quartile	29.0	31.7	61.7	53.9	15.6	7.7	25.3	25.5	43.8	31.6	13.4	9.3
Region												
Northwest	19.6	23.1	54.5	48.6	11.5	6.9	24.6	28.3	34.5	28.4	10.6	8.1
Midwest	21.4	25.4	52.8	45.8	15.3	8.0	18.4	18.2	37.1	32.0	20.0	18.4
South	30.8	28.2	48.2	38.8	18.0	8.5	18.8	15.0	37.9	25.6	40.0	27.2
West	21.9	21.6	52.9	40.6	14.0	6.0	16.8	16.5	35.2	25.6	15.8	10.0
High School Program [2]												
General	19.6	18.3	49.9	37.8	14.0	7.1	16.7	14.6	34.5	26.3	22.6	16.7
Academic	28.7	34.2	60.1	50.8	17.2	8.8	26.9	24.9	44.1	32.8	13.1	12.6
Vocational	23.1	14.7	42.4	30.1	13.3	4.9	13.2	11.2	27.7	16.2	39.3	41.2

[1] Socioeconomic status was measured by a composite score on parental education and occupations, and family income. The "low" SES group is the lowest quartile; the middle SES group is the middle two quartiles; and the "high" SES group is the upper quartile.

[2] Program as reported by student.

SOURCE: U.S. Department of Education, National Center for Education Statistics, "High School and Beyond," Senior Cohort; and "National Education Longitudinal Study of 1988," Second Followup survey. (This table was prepared February 1996.)

Table 145.—Percent of high school students who reported experience with drugs and violence on school property, by race/ethnicity, grade, and sex: 1993

Type of violence	Race/ethnicity			Grade				Type of drug-related behavior	Race/ethnicity			Grade			
	White	Black	His-panic	9	10	11	12		White	Black	His-panic	9	10	11	12
1	2	3	4	5	6	7	8	1	2	3	4	5	6	7	8
Felt too unsafe to go to school [1]								Cigarette use on school property [1]							
Total	3.0	7.1	10.1	6.1	5.2	3.3	3.0	Total	14.6	5.9	11.1	11.3	12.3	13.9	15.0
Male	2.9	7.0	10.4	5.8	5.1	3.2	3.3	Male	14.7	7.3	10.6	11.4	12.8	12.9	16.5
Female	3.1	7.3	9.8	6.4	5.4	3.5	2.7	Female	14.5	4.5	11.6	11.3	11.8	14.9	13.3
Carried a weapon on school property [1,2]								Smokeless tobacco use on school property [4]							
Total	10.9	15.0	13.3	12.6	11.5	11.9	10.8	Total	8.7	1.4	2.3	5.6	6.3	7.3	7.7
Male	17.7	18.2	20.2	19.1	17.0	18.2	17.2	Male	16.0	2.8	4.4	10.8	11.3	12.9	14.5
Female	3.4	11.9	6.6	5.6	5.6	5.0	4.1	Female	0.9	0.1	0.2	0.2	1.0	1.1	0.7
Threatened or injured with a weapon on school property [3]								Alcohol use on school property [1]							
Total	6.3	11.2	8.6	9.4	7.3	7.3	5.5	Total	4.6	6.9	6.8	5.2	4.7	5.2	5.5
Male	8.1	12.6	10.7	10.6	9.1	9.5	7.6	Male	5.5	8.7	7.3	5.5	4.8	6.3	7.5
Female	4.4	9.8	6.4	8.1	5.4	4.8	3.3	Female	3.6	5.1	6.2	4.8	4.7	3.9	3.5
In a physical fight on school property [3]								Marijuana use on school property [1]							
Total	15.0	22.0	17.9	23.1	17.2	13.8	11.4	Total	5.0	7.3	7.5	4.4	6.5	6.5	5.1
Male	22.5	28.6	24.1	33.2	25.0	20.0	16.5	Male	7.1	10.1	10.0	5.9	9.2	8.7	7.3
Female	6.8	15.5	11.7	12.7	8.8	7.0	6.1	Female	2.8	4.5	4.9	2.8	3.6	4.0	2.7
Property stolen or deliberately damaged on school property [3]								Offered, sold, or given an illegal drug on school property [3]							
Total	32.0	35.5	32.2	37.2	32.8	32.3	28.9	Total	24.1	17.5	34.1	21.8	23.7	27.5	23.0
Male	35.9	39.2	36.7	41.3	37.5	36.4	33.2	Male	28.8	20.3	41.5	24.6	27.9	32.9	28.2
Female	27.7	31.8	27.6	33.0	27.6	27.9	24.2	Female	18.9	14.8	26.8	18.4	19.2	21.7	17.5

[1] On one or more of the 30 days preceding the survey.
[2] Such as a gun, knife, or club.
[3] One or more times during the 12 months preceding the survey.
[4] Used chewing tobacco or snuff during the 30 days preceding the survey.

SOURCE: U.S. Department of Health and Human Services, Centers for Disease Control and Prevention, National Center for Chronic Disease, Prevention and Health Promotion, Division of Adolescent and School Health, *The Youth Risk Behavior Surveillance System: 1993*. (This table was prepared June 1995.)

Table 146.—Percent of 12- to 17-year olds reporting drug use during the past 30 days and the past year: 1972 to 1994

Type of drug and frequency of use	1972	1974	1976	1977	1979	1982	1985	1988	1990	1991	1992	1993	1994[1]
1	2	3	4	5	6	7	8	9	10	11	12	13	14
					Percent reporting drug use during past 30 days								
Any illicit use	—	—	—	—	17.6	12.7	14.9	9.2	8.1	6.8	6.1	6.6	8.2
Marijuana	7.0	12.0	12.3	16.6	16.7	11.5	11.9	6.4	5.2	4.3	4.0	4.9	6.0
Hallucinogens	1.4	1.3	0.9	1.6	2.2	1.4	1.2	0.8	0.9	0.8	0.6	0.5	1.1
Cocaine	0.6	1.0	1.0	0.8	1.4	1.6	1.4	1.1	0.6	0.4	0.3	0.4	0.3
Heroin	—	—	—	—	—	—	0.1	0.1	0.0	0.1	0.1	0.0	0.2
Nonmedical use of:													
Stimulants	—	1.0	1.2	1.3	1.2	2.6	1.6	1.2	1.0	0.5	0.2	0.5	0.5
Sedatives	—	1.0	—	0.8	1.1	1.3	1.0	0.6	0.9	0.5	0.4	0.2	0.1
Tranquilizers	—	1.0	1.1	0.7	0.6	0.9	0.6	0.2	0.5	0.4	0.2	0.2	0.2
Analgesics	—	—	—	—	0.6	0.7	1.7	0.9	1.4	1.1	0.8	0.7	1.3
Alcohol	—	34.0	32.4	31.2	37.2	30.2	31.0	25.2	24.5	20.3	15.7	18.0	21.6
Cigarettes	—	25.0	23.4	22.3	12.1	14.7	15.3	11.8	11.6	10.8	9.6	9.6	18.9
					Percent reporting drug use during past year								
Any illicit use	—	—	—	—	26.0	22.0	23.3	16.8	15.9	14.8	11.7	13.6	15.5
Marijuana	—	18.5	18.4	22.3	24.1	20.6	19.4	12.6	11.3	10.1	8.1	10.1	11.4
Hallucinogens	3.6	4.3	2.8	3.1	4.7	3.6	2.6	2.8	2.4	2.1	1.9	2.1	2.7
Cocaine	1.5	2.7	2.3	2.6	4.2	4.1	3.9	2.9	2.2	1.5	1.1	0.8	1.1
Heroin	—	—	—	0.6	—	—	0.3	0.4	0.6	0.2	0.1	0.1	0.3
Nonmedical use of:													
Stimulants	—	3.0	2.2	3.7	2.9	5.6	4.1	2.8	3.0	1.9	1.3	1.6	1.2
Sedatives	—	2.0	1.2	2.0	2.2	3.7	2.8	1.7	2.2	1.3	1.0	0.8	0.5
Tranquilizers	—	2.0	1.8	2.9	2.7	3.3	3.4	1.5	1.5	1.3	1.0	0.7	0.9
Analgesics	—	—	—	—	2.2	3.7	4.0	3.0	4.8	3.3	2.4	2.2	2.8
Alcohol	—	51.0	49.3	47.5	53.6	52.4	51.6	44.5	41.0	40.3	32.6	35.2	36.2
Cigarettes	—	—	—	—	—	24.8	25.5	22.8	22.2	20.1	18.2	19.1	24.5

[1] Due to changes in the survey instrument and administration, 1994 estimates are not comparable to previous years.

—Data not available, or low precision; no estimate reported.

SOURCE: U.S. Department of Health and Human Services, Substance Abuse and Mental Health Services Administration, "National Household Survey on Drug Abuse: Population Estimates 1994," 1995. (This table was prepared April 1996.)

Table 147.—Percent of high school seniors reporting drug use, by type of drug and frequency of use: 1975 to 1995

Type of drug and frequency of use	Class of 1975	Class of 1979	Class of 1980	Class of 1981	Class of 1982	Class of 1983	Class of 1984	Class of 1985	Class of 1986	Class of 1987	Class of 1988	Class of 1989	Class of 1990	Class of 1991	Class of 1992	Class of 1993	Class of 1994	Class of 1995
1	2	3	4	5	6	7	8	9	10	11	12	13	14	15	16	17	18	19
Percent reporting having ever used drugs																		
Alcohol[1]	90.4	93.0	93.2	92.6	92.8	92.6	92.6	92.2	91.3	92.2	92.0	90.7	89.5	88.0	87.5	80.0	80.4	80.7
Any illicit drug abuse	55.2	65.1	65.4	65.6	64.4	62.9	61.6	60.6	57.6	56.6	53.9	50.9	47.9	44.1	40.7	42.9	45.6	48.4
Marijuana only	19.0	27.7	26.7	22.8	23.3	22.5	21.3	20.9	19.9	20.8	21.4	19.5	18.5	17.2	15.6	16.2	18.0	20.3
Any illicit drug other than marijuana[2]	36.2	37.4	38.7	42.8	41.1	40.4	40.3	39.7	37.7	35.8	32.5	31.4	29.4	26.9	25.1	26.7	27.6	28.1
Use of selected drugs																		
Cocaine	9.0	15.4	15.7	16.5	16.0	16.2	16.1	17.3	16.9	15.2	12.1	10.3	9.4	7.8	6.1	6.1	5.9	6.0
Heroin	2.2	1.1	1.1	1.1	1.2	1.2	1.3	1.2	1.1	1.2	1.1	1.3	1.3	0.9	1.2	1.1	1.2	1.6
LSD	11.3	9.5	9.3	9.8	9.6	8.9	8.0	7.5	7.2	8.4	7.7	8.3	8.7	8.8	8.6	10.3	10.5	11.7
Marijuana/hashish	47.3	60.4	60.3	59.5	58.7	57.0	54.9	54.2	50.9	50.2	47.2	43.7	40.7	36.7	32.6	35.3	38.2	41.7
PCP	—	12.8	9.6	7.8	6.0	5.6	5.0	4.9	4.8	3.0	2.9	3.9	2.8	2.9	2.4	2.9	2.8	2.7
Percent reporting use of drugs in the past 12 months																		
Alcohol[1]	84.8	88.1	87.9	87.0	86.8	87.3	86.0	85.6	84.5	85.7	85.3	82.7	80.6	77.7	76.8	72.7	73.0	73.7
Any illicit drug abuse	45.0	54.2	53.1	52.1	49.4	47.4	45.8	46.3	44.3	41.7	38.5	35.4	32.5	29.4	27.1	31.0	35.8	39.0
Marijuana only	18.8	26.0	22.7	18.1	19.3	19.0	17.8	18.9	18.4	17.6	17.4	15.4	14.6	13.2	12.2	13.9	17.8	19.6
Any illicit drug other than marijuana[2]	26.2	28.2	30.4	34.0	30.1	28.4	28.0	27.4	25.9	24.1	21.1	20.0	17.9	16.2	14.9	17.1	18.0	19.4
Use of selected drugs																		
Cocaine	5.6	12.0	12.3	12.4	11.5	11.4	11.6	13.1	12.7	10.3	7.9	6.5	5.3	3.5	3.1	3.3	3.6	4.0
Heroin	1.0	0.5	0.5	0.5	0.6	0.6	0.5	0.6	0.5	0.5	0.5	0.6	0.5	0.4	0.6	0.5	0.6	1.1
LSD	7.2	6.6	6.5	6.5	6.1	5.4	4.7	4.4	4.5	5.2	4.8	4.9	5.4	5.2	5.6	6.8	6.9	8.4
Marijuana/hashish	40.0	50.8	48.8	46.1	44.3	42.3	40.0	40.6	38.8	36.3	33.1	29.6	27.0	23.9	21.9	26.0	30.7	34.7
PCP	—	7.0	4.4	3.2	2.2	2.6	2.3	2.9	2.4	1.3	1.2	2.4	1.2	1.4	1.4	1.4	1.6	1.8
Percent reporting use of drugs in the past 30 days																		
Alcohol[1]	68.2	71.8	72.0	70.7	69.7	69.4	67.2	65.9	65.3	66.4	63.9	60.0	57.1	54.0	51.3	48.6	50.1	51.3
Any illicit drug abuse	30.7	38.9	37.2	36.9	32.5	30.5	29.2	29.7	27.1	24.7	21.3	19.7	17.2	16.4	14.4	18.3	21.9	23.8
Marijuana only	15.3	22.2	18.8	15.2	15.5	15.1	14.1	14.8	13.9	13.1	11.3	10.6	9.2	9.3	8.1	10.4	13.1	13.8
Any illicit drug other than marijuana[2]	15.4	16.8	18.4	21.7	17.0	15.4	15.1	14.9	13.2	11.6	10.0	9.1	8.0	7.1	6.3	7.9	8.8	10.0
Use of selected drugs																		
Cocaine	1.9	5.7	5.2	5.8	5.0	4.9	5.8	6.7	6.2	4.3	3.4	2.8	1.9	1.4	1.3	1.3	1.5	1.8
Heroin	0.4	0.2	0.2	0.2	0.2	0.2	0.3	0.3	0.2	0.2	0.2	0.3	0.2	0.2	0.3	0.2	0.3	0.6
LSD	2.3	2.4	2.3	2.5	2.4	1.9	1.5	1.6	1.7	1.8	1.8	1.8	1.9	1.9	2.0	2.4	2.6	4.0
Marijuana/hashish	27.1	36.5	33.7	31.6	28.5	27.0	25.2	25.7	23.4	21.0	18.0	16.7	14.0	13.8	11.9	15.5	19.0	21.2
PCP	—	2.4	1.4	1.4	1.0	1.3	1.0	1.6	1.3	0.6	0.3	1.4	0.4	0.5	0.6	1.0	0.7	0.6

[1] Survey question changed in 1993; data are not comparable to figures for earlier years.
[2] Other illicit drugs include any use of hallucinogens, cocaine, and heroin, or any use of other opiates, stimulants, sedatives, or tranquilizers not under a doctor's orders.
—Data not available.

NOTE.—A revised questionnaire was used in 1982 and later years to reduce the inappropriate reporting of nonprescription stimulants. This slightly reduced the positive responses for some types of drug abuse.

SOURCE: U.S. Department of Health and Human Services, Alcohol, Drug Abuse, and Mental Health Administration, *Drug Use Among American High School Students and Other Young Adults, National Trends Through 1988;* and press releases dated January 1992, April 1993, and January 1994; and University of Michigan, Institute for Social Research, *Monitoring the Future,* unpublished data. (This table was prepared April 1996.)

Table 148.—Percent of teachers (grades 7 to 12) who feel that certain problems are serious or somewhat serious: 1995

Teacher and student characteristics	Drinking	Lack basic skills	Drug use	Teen pregnancy	Dropouts	Violence in and around school	Carrying handguns, knives, and weapons	Teenage suicides
1	2	3	4	5	6	7	8	9
All teachers	**76**	**74**	**63**	**59**	**43**	**41**	**25**	**15**
Location								
Inner city	61	87	73	81	69	72	46	18
Other urban	69	79	73	71	52	54	31	21
Suburb	77	68	59	43	29	41	20	15
Small town	80	72	67	58	40	28	18	10
Rural	80	74	55	62	47	30	24	13
Region								
East	79	70	68	51	36	42	22	14
Midwest	80	66	62	58	37	37	19	16
South	68	78	56	67	49	45	31	11
West	79	82	75	57	54	38	28	17
School level								
Junior high	63	74	58	46	30	43	27	14
High school	87	72	69	69	54	38	23	16
Teaching experience								
Fewer than 10 years	83	71	75	58	43	49	34	18
10 to 19 years	70	72	57	55	40	35	21	12
20 years or more	76	76	62	63	47	40	23	14

SOURCE: Metropolitan Life/Louis Harris Associates, Inc., *The Metropolitan Life Survey of The American Teacher, 1984–1995.* (This table was prepared April 1996.)

Table 149.—Ages for compulsory school attendance, special education services for students, policies for kindergarten programs, and year-round schools, by state: 1995 and 1996

State	Compulsory attendance, 1996	Compulsory special education services, 1996[1]	Year-round schools, 1995		Provision of kindergarten education, 1995				
			Has policy on year-round schools	Has districts with year-round schools	School districts required to offer		Attendance required	
					Half day	Full day	Half day	Full day
1	2	3	4	5	6	7	8	9
Alabama	7 to 16	3 to 20		X		X		
Alaska	[2]7 to 16	3 to 21		X				
Arizona	[3]6 to 16	3 to 21	X	X	X		X	
Arkansas	5 to 17	3 to 21	X	X		X		X
California	6 to 18	3 to 21	X	X	X			
Colorado	7 to 16	[4]3 to 20		X				
Connecticut	7 to 16	3 to 20			X			
Delaware	5 to 16	3 to 20			X			
District of Columbia	7 to 17	[4,5]3 to 21				X		X
Florida	6 to 16	3 to 20	X	X		X		X
Georgia	7 to 16	[4]3 to 21		X		X		
Hawaii	[6]6 to 16	[4]3 to 20		X				
Idaho	7 to 16	3 to 20	X	X				
Illinois	7 to 16	3 to 20	X	X	X			
Indiana	[7]7 to 16	3 to 21		X	X			
Iowa	6 to 16	Birth to 20						
Kansas	5 to 16	3 to 20						
Kentucky	[8]6 to 16	[4]3 to 20		X	X			
Louisiana	7 to 17	3 to 21	—	—	—	—	—	—
Maine	7 to 17	3 to 19						
Maryland	5 to 16	Birth to 20			X			
Massachusetts	6 to 16	3 to 21			X			
Michigan	6 to 16	Birth to 25						
Minnesota	[9]7 to 16	Birth to 20	X	X	X			
Mississippi	6 to 16	[4]3 to 20		X			X	
Missouri	7 to 16	[4]3 to 20		X	X		X	
Montana	[10]7 to 16	3 to 18			X			
Nebraska	7 to 16	Birth to 20	X					
Nevada	7 to 17	[4]3 to 21		X	X			
New Hampshire	6 to 16	3 to 20						
New Jersey	6 to 16	3 to 21						
New Mexico	5 to 16	3 to 21		X	X		X	
New York	[11]6 to 16	3 to 21	X	X	X			
North Carolina	7 to 16	3 to 20	X	X				
North Dakota	5 to 16	3 to 20			X	X	X	X
Ohio	6 to 18	[4]3 to 21		X	X		X	
Oklahoma	5 to 18	3 to 21	X	X	X			
Oregon	7 to 18	3 to 21	X	X	X			
Pennsylvania	8 to 17	3 to 20			X			
Rhode Island	6 to 16	[4]3 to 20			X		X	
South Carolina	[12]5 to 17	[4]3 to 20		X	X		X	
South Dakota	[10]6 to 16	3 to 21	X		X	X		
Tennessee	7 to 18	[4]3 to 21		X	X		X	
Texas	6 to 17	3 to 21	X	X	X	X		
Utah	6 to 18	3 to 21	X	X	X			
Vermont	7 to 16	[4]3 to 21						
Virginia	5 to 18	2 to 21		X	X	X	X	X
Washington	[13]8 to 18	3 to 20		X				
West Virginia	6 to 16	3 to 20	X		X			
Wisconsin	[14]6 to 18	[4]3 to 20			X			
Wyoming	7 to 16	[4]3 to 20			X			

[1] Most states have an upper age limit whereby education is provided up to a certain age or completion of secondary school, whichever comes first.
[2] Ages 7 to 16 or high school graduation.
[3] Ages 6 to 16 or tenth grade completion.
[4] Upper age limit for eligibility has been updated for 1996.
[5] State has established two points in the program year by which children must be 3 years of age to be eligible for services.
[6] Students over the age of 16 may withdraw with the approval of a principal and student's guardians.
[7] From age 7 until student (1) graduates; (2) between age 16–18 and meets requirements for exit interview before graduation; or (3) reaches 18. Withdrawal before 18 requires parent/guardian and principal written permission.
[8] Must have parental signature for leaving school between ages of 16 and 18.
[9] Age 18 takes effect in 2000.
[10] Age 16 or completion of eighth grade.
[11] Ages 6 to 17 for New York City and Buffalo.
[12] Permits parental waiver of kindergarten at age 5.

[13] Or can exit if age 15 and has completed grade 8, has a useful occupation, has met graduation requirements or has certificate of education competency.
[14] Ages 6 to 18 or high school graduation.
—Data not available.

NOTE.—The Education of the Handicapped Act (EHA) Amendments of 1986 make it mandatory for all states receiving EHA funds to serve all 3- to 18-year-old disabled children.

SOURCE: U.S. Department of Education, Office of Special Education and Rehabilitative Services, The Seventeenth Annual Report to Congress on the Implementation of The Individuals with Disabilities Education Act, 1995; National Association of State Directors of Special Education, Inc., unpublished data; Education Commission of the States, "Clearinghouse Notes," April 1996; and Council of Chief State School Officers, State Education Policies on Student Attendance and Use of Time: 1995. (This table was prepared May 1996.)

Table 150.—Tenth and twelfth graders' attendance patterns, by selected student and school characteristics: 1990 and 1992

Attendance pattern	All stu-dents	Sex		Race/ethnicity					Socioeconomic status [1]			Control of school attended		
		Male	Fe-male	White	Black	Hispanic	Asian	American Indian	Low	Middle	High	Public	Catho-lic	Other private
1	2	3	4	5	6	7	8	9	10	11	12	13	14	15
Percent of 10th graders in 1990														
Number of days missed first half of current school year														
None	14.3	17.1	11.6	13.0	21.2	12.5	23.1	12.0	13.1	15.0	14.9	14.0	18.3	15.1
1 or 2 days	23.2	24.9	21.5	22.8	27.2	20.6	28.6	12.5	20.0	23.0	26.6	22.6	26.4	33.6
3 or 4 days	27.7	27.1	28.3	28.8	24.5	25.0	23.9	33.7	25.3	27.6	29.5	27.9	26.6	27.7
5 or more days	34.8	30.9	38.7	35.4	27.1	41.9	24.4	41.9	41.6	34.3	29.0	35.4	28.8	23.5
Number of times late first half of current school year														
None	25.2	25.4	24.9	27.8	17.8	17.8	22.0	18.6	23.9	25.7	26.6	25.3	27.7	17.9
1 or 2 days	38.2	38.1	38.3	38.0	41.1	36.7	39.7	31.3	37.4	38.6	38.2	37.8	39.8	44.6
3 or more days	36.7	36.6	36.8	34.2	41.1	45.5	38.3	50.1	38.7	35.7	35.2	36.9	32.4	37.5
Cut classes														
Never or almost never	84.8	83.5	86.2	85.8	86.5	75.8	87.1	81.4	82.3	84.5	89.0	84.0	95.2	90.9
At least sometimes	15.2	16.5	13.8	14.2	13.5	24.2	12.9	18.6	17.7	15.5	11.0	16.0	4.8	9.1
Percent of 12th graders in 1992														
Number of days missed first half of current school year														
None	8.7	10.5	6.9	7.4	15.8	6.9	15.6	11.3	8.7	8.6	8.8	8.6	10.2	9.1
1 or 2 days	30.3	30.8	29.9	29.9	31.0	31.6	34.3	22.4	27.5	30.8	31.7	30.2	31.2	32.7
3 to 6 days	35.0	35.0	35.1	36.2	31.2	34.4	27.4	37.8	34.0	34.0	37.7	34.8	37.5	37.8
7 or more days	25.9	23.7	28.2	26.5	22.1	27.1	22.7	28.6	29.8	26.6	21.8	26.4	21.1	20.5
Number of times late first half of current school year														
None	19.0	17.7	20.3	20.6	14.0	14.7	16.2	19.1	19.7	19.0	18.7	19.2	19.5	12.3
1 or 2 days	33.5	32.4	34.5	34.4	32.1	28.7	33.8	25.3	32.8	34.2	33.1	33.0	36.4	37.6
3 or more days	47.6	49.9	45.2	45.0	53.9	56.6	50.0	55.6	47.5	46.8	48.2	47.8	44.1	50.1
Cut classes														
Never or almost never	75.6	72.8	78.4	76.5	77.7	67.9	72.7	73.7	76.2	75.6	75.4	74.3	87.1	86.3
At least sometimes	24.4	27.2	21.6	23.5	22.3	32.1	27.3	26.3	23.8	24.4	24.6	25.7	12.9	13.7

[1] Socioeconomic status was measured by a composite score on parental education and occupations, and family income. The "Low" SES group is the lowest quartile; the "Middle" SES group is the middle two quartiles; and the "High" SES group is the upper quartile.

SOURCE: U.S. Department of Education, National Center for Education Statistics, "National Education Longitudinal Study of 1988," First and Second Followup surveys. (This table was prepared March 1994.)

Table 151.—Tenth graders who agree or strongly agree with statements on why they go to school: 1990

Reason for going to school	Percent of 10th graders													
	All 10th grad-ers	Sex		Race/ethnicity					Socioeconomic status [1]			Control of school attended		
		Male	Fe-male	White	Black	Hispanic	Asian	American Indian	Low	Middle	High	Public	Catho-lic	Other private
1	2	3	4	5	6	7	8	9	10	11	12	13	14	15
Think subjects are interesting	71.0	70.1	71.9	68.8	79.1	74.5	77.3	81.2	72.8	68.7	74.9	70.7	75.5	71.4
Get a feeling of satisfaction	76.9	74.2	79.6	74.8	85.8	81.3	79.6	81.6	78.2	75.3	79.1	76.3	81.7	81.3
Nothing else to do	30.3	33.4	27.3	30.1	29.0	31.1	32.4	31.3	33.2	30.8	26.5	30.8	24.2	28.4
Need education to get a job	96.6	95.3	97.8	96.5	96.7	96.8	97.1	93.4	95.4	96.5	97.7	96.4	97.8	98.2
To meet friends	82.7	83.0	82.4	85.5	66.1	80.1	84.9	80.8	76.8	82.5	87.4	82.8	83.5	78.6
Play on a team or belong to a club	53.6	58.4	49.0	55.3	49.3	45.3	56.3	46.2	40.4	54.3	64.1	53.1	59.1	58.8
Teachers care and expect student to succeed	74.0	72.6	75.4	72.4	81.6	76.0	74.6	79.4	75.2	72.8	75.5	73.2	80.6	79.6

[1] Socioeconomic status was measured by a composite score on parental education and occupations, and family income. The "Low" SES group is the lowest quartile; the "Middle" SES group is the middle two quartiles; and the "High" SES group is the upper quartile.

SOURCE: U.S. Department of Education, National Center for Education Statistics, "National Education Longitudinal Study of 1988," First Followup survey. (This table was prepared February 1993.)

Table 152.—State requirements for high school graduation, in Carnegie units: 1980 and 1993

State	1980 All courses	1993 All courses	English/language arts	Social studies	Mathematics	Science	Physical education/health	Electives	Other courses	First graduating class to which these requirements apply	Notes
1	2	3	4	5	6	7	8	9	10	11	12
Alabama Standard	20	22	4	3	2	2	1.5	9.5		1989	Must become computer literate through related coursework. Minimum competency test is required for graduation.
Advanced	—	22	4	4	3	3	1.5	4	2 foreign languages, .5 home/personal management	—	
Alaska	19	21	4	3	2	2	1	9		1991	Minimum competency test is required for graduation.
Arizona	16	20	4	2.5	2	2	—	9	.5 free enterprise	—	
Arkansas	16	20	4	3	3	2	1	6.5	.5 fine arts	1988	Social studies options: 2 or 3 units social studies and 1 practical arts.
California Standard	(1)	13	3	3	2	2	2	—	1 fine arts or foreign language	—	The state board has published "Model Graduation Requirements" to be used as a guide by local districts. These include specifics in core subjects plus computer studies and foreign language. Test and cut-off standards for early exit, with parental approval. Minimum competency test is required for graduation.
Advanced	—	16	3	3	3	2	2	—	2 in same foreign language, 1 fine arts	—	
Colorado	—	(2)	(2)	(2)	(2)	(2)	(2)	(2)		—	State has constitutional prohibition against state requirements. School accreditation requirements total 30 units covering language arts, social studies, math, foreign language, fine/vocational/practical arts, health/safety, and physical education.
Connecticut	(2)	20	4	3	3	2	1	6	1 arts or vocational education	1988	Minimum competency test is required for graduation.
Delaware	18	19	4	3	2	2	1.5	6.5		1987	Electives must include life skills seminar or passage of a test. D.C. requires 100 hours of community service without credit.
District of Columbia	18	23.5	4	3.5	3	3	1.5	3.5	2 foreign languages; 1 life skills; 1 career/vocational; .5 fine arts; .5 music	1996	
Florida Standard	(2)	24	4	3	3	3	0.5	9	.5 practical/exploratory vocational education; .5 performing arts or speech and debate; .5 life management skills	1989	2 of science units must include labs. Students must have 1.5 GPA to graduate. Junior and senior students may receive dual credits for college coursework. Vocational students may substitute certain vocational courses to satisfy up to 2 required vocational credits in each of the areas of English, math, and science. Minimum competency test is required for graduation.
Academic scholars	—	26	4	3	4	4	1	7	2 of same foreign language; 1 fine arts	—	
Georgia Standard	20	21	4	3	3	3	1	6	1 computer technology and/or fine arts and/or vocational education and/or ROTC	1997	Students who completed 4 units of vocational education receive a state seal of endorsement from the State Board of Education. Algebra is required. Minimum competency is required for graduation.
Advanced	—	21	4	3	3	3	1	4	2 foreign languages; 1 fine arts, vocational education, computer technology, or ROTC	1988	
Hawaii	20	22	4	4	3	3	1.5	6	.5 guidance	1997	

Table 152.—State requirements for high school graduation, in Carnegie units: 1980 and 1993—Continued

State	1980 All courses	1993 All courses	English/language arts	Social studies	Mathematics	Science	Physical education/health	Electives	Other courses	First graduating class to which these requirements apply	Notes
1	2	3	4	5	6	7	8	9	10	11	12
Idaho	18	21	4	2	2	2	1.5	6	.5 each: reading, speech, and consumer education; 2 humanities	1989	Practical arts may substitute for 1 unit of humanities. State requires a C average, demonstrated competency in core curriculum on a junior class competency test, or adherence to local district's achievement plan for graduation. State level minimum competency test is an option for the local districts. If passed, students receive special proficiency endorsement on their diploma.
Illinois	16	16	3	2	2	1	4.5	2.25	.25 consumer education; 1 art, foreign language, music, or vocational education	1988	1 year of math may be computer technology. 1 year of social studies must be U.S. history or half U.S. history and half American government. Beginning 1985–86, the school boards were allowed to excuse 11–12th grades from physical education to: 1)participate in interscholastic athletics or 2)enroll in academic class required for college admission or to graduate from high school. 9–12th grade pupils may elect to take a consumer education proficiency test; if passed, they are excused from requirement.
Indiana Standard	16	19.5	4	2	2	2	1.5	8	3 or 4 in foreign language (3 in 1 or 2 years each in 2)	1989	State does not use standard Carnegie units.
Academic honors	—	24	4	3	4	4	1	4 or		1990	
Iowa	—	—	—	—	—	—	1	—		1989	Legislative requirements in effect for many years. Local districts determine remaining requirements. State allows junior and senior students to receive dual credits for college coursework.
Kansas	17	21	4	3	2	2	1	9		1989	
Kentucky Standard	18	20	4	2	3	2	1	7	1 additional math, science, social studies, or vocational education	1987	
Commonwealth	—	22	5	2	—	—	—	1	1 foreign language in advance placement and 6 units in math and science	1986	
Louisiana Standard	20	23	4	3	3	3	2	7.5	.5 computer literacy	1989	Students with ACT score of 29 or above, 3.5 GPA with no semester grade lower than a B, no unexcused absences, and no suspensions receive a Scholar Program seal on their diploma. Algebra is required. Minimum competency test is required for graduation.
Scholar program	—	23	4	3	3	3	2	7.5	.5 computer literacy	1987	
Regents' scholar	—	24	4	3.5	3	3	2	4.5	3 foreign languages, 1 fine arts	1983	American history is required. All students must pass computer proficiency standards. 1 of the science units must include a lab.
Maine	(3)	16	4	2	2	2	1.5	3.5	1 fine arts	1989	
Maryland	20	21	4	3	3	2	1	5	1 fine arts; 1 industrial arts/technology education, home economics, vocational education, or computer studies; and 1 community service	1997	After grade 11, 4 credits must be earned. Students can earn statewide certificate of merit with fulfillment of additional requirements. Special education certificates are available for students unable to meet requirements but who complete a special education program. Minimum competency test, writing test, and passage of quiz on citizenship are required for graduation.
Massachusetts	—	—	—	1	—	—	4	—	—	—	American history is required. Local boards determine additional requirements.

Table 152.—State requirements for high school graduation, in Carnegie units: 1980 and 1993—Continued

State	All courses 1980	All courses 1993	English/ language arts	Social studies	Mathematics	Science	Physical education/ health	Electives	Other courses	First graduating class to which these requirements apply	Notes
1	2	3	4	5	6	7	8	9	10	11	12
Michigan Standard[4]	—	—	4	3	3	2	1	—	2 foreign languages, fine or performing arts, or vocational education; .5 computer education	—	
College preparatory[4]	—	—	4	3	3	2	1	—	At least 2 years foreign language		
Minnesota	15	20	4	3	1	1	1.5	9.5		1982	Junior and senior students may receive dual credits for college coursework.
Mississippi	16	18	4	2	2	2	—	8		1989	At least 1 science unit must include a lab. Minimum competency test is required for graduation.
Missouri Standard	20	22	3	2	2	2	1	10	1 practical arts; 1 fine arts	1988	
College preparatory	20	24	4	3	3	3	1	8	1 practical arts; 1 fine arts	1988	College preparation diploma became available to qualifying graduates. For college preparation, specific core subjects must be taken.
Montana	16	20	4	2	2	2	1	7	1 fine arts; 1 vocational education; 1 practical arts	1992	
Nebraska	—	—	—	—	—	—	—	—		1991	200 credit hours are required for graduation, with at least 80 percent in core curriculum courses.
Nevada	19	22.5	4	2	2	2	2.5	8.5	1 arts/humanities; .5 computer literacy	1992	Computer literacy may be waived by demonstration of competency. Minimum competency test is required for graduation.
New Hampshire	16	19.75	4	2.5	2	2	1.25	4	.5 arts; .5 computer science; 3 units from 2 of the following: arts, foreign language, practical arts, or vocational education	1989	Minimum competency test for high school graduation is an option of the local districts.
New Jersey	—	21.5	4	3	3	2	4	4	1 fine, practical, or performing arts; .5 career exploration	1990	92 credit hours are required for graduation. State does not use standard Carnegie units. Minimum competency test is required for graduation.
New Mexico	20	23	4	3	3	2	1	9	1 communication skills	1990	State board requires student computer literacy prior to graduation. Languages other than English can satisfy communication skills requirement, emphasizing writing and speaking. Students preparing for college have an advanced curriculum. State level minimum competency test is an option of the local districts; passing students receive a special proficiency endorsement on their diploma.
New York Local diploma	16	18.5	4	4	2	2	.5	(5)	1 art and/or music; .5 health; 2 noncredit units of physical education beyond the total	1989	3–5 units from a sequence of specific courses must be chosen by the Regents' diploma students. Minimum competency test is required for graduation.
Regents' diploma	18	18.5	4	4	2	2	.5	(5)		1989	For a Regents' diploma, comprehensive exams are required in most subjects.
North Carolina Standard	16	20	4	2	2	2	1	9		1987	1 science class must include a lab. Minimum competency test is required for graduation.
Scholars program	—	22	4	3	3	3	1	4	2 foreign languages; 2 additional: English, math, social science, or foreign language	1994	
North Dakota	17	17	4	3	2	2	1	5	Social studies must include 1 unit of world history, and 1 unit of U.S. history, each with a strong geography component	1994	1 unit of higher level foreign language may be substituted for the 4th unit of English; 1 unit math may be business math. Although 17 units are required, the local education agencies are urged to require a minimum of 20 units.
Ohio	17	18	3	2	2	1	1	9		1988	Minimum competency test is required for graduation.

Table 152.—State requirements for high school graduation, in Carnegie units: 1980 and 1993—Continued

State	1980 All courses	1993 All courses	Subject areas 1993							First graduating class to which these requirements apply	Notes
			English/language arts	Social studies	Mathematics	Science	Physical education/health	Electives	Other courses		
1	2	3	4	5	6	7	8	9	10	11	12
Oklahoma											
Standard	18	20	4	2	2	2	—	10		1987	
College preparatory	10.5	15	4	2	3	2	—	—	4 from: math, history, computer science, economics, English, geography, government, foreign language, sociology, science, speech, and psychology	1988	If foreign language is elected, 2 years in the same language is required. Total hour requirement is less, but more rigorous and restrictive for college preparatory path.
Oregon	21	22	3	3.5	2	2	2	8	.5 career development; 1 applied arts, fine arts, or foreign language	1988	Minimum competency test is required for graduation. 3.5 GPA students receive an honors seal on their diploma.
Pennsylvania	13	21	4	3	3	3	1	5	2 arts/humanities	1989	Computer science can be an option instead of arts and humanities. State has prescribed learning objectives and curriculum guidelines for 12 goals of quality education.
Rhode Island											
Standard	16	16	4	2	2	2	—	6		1989	
College preparatory	16	18	4	2	3	2	—	4	2 foreign languages; .5 arts; .5 computer literacy	1989	
South Carolina											
Standard	18	20	4	3	3	2	1	7		1987	If approved, 1 unit of computer science can count for a math requirement. 1 unit of science and 6 or more in a specific occupational service area can fulfill the science requirement. Junior and senior students may receive dual credits for college coursework. Minimum competency test is required for graduation.
Academic achievement honors	—	22	4	3	3	2	1	7	2 foreign languages	1986	
South Dakota	16	20	4	3	2	3	—	7	.5 computer studies; .5 fine arts	1989	Requirements include 3 science courses and 7 electives.
Tennessee											
Standard	18	20	4	1	2	2	1.5	9	.5 economics	1989	Economics requirement may include: 1 semester in economics, out-of-school experiences through Junior Achievement, or marketing education. Minimum competency test is required for graduation.
Honors, general education	—	20.5	4	3	3	3	1.5	2	2 in same foreign language; 2 fine visual or performing arts	1988	
Honors, vocational education	—	20.5	4	3	3	3	1.5	2	4 in same vocational education program	1989	
Texas											
Standard	18	21	4	2.5	3	2	1.5/.5	7	.5 economics/free enterprise	1988	1.5 units of physical education and .5 of health are required for either program. Minimum competency test is required for graduation. Junior and senior students can receive dual credits for college coursework.
College preparatory	18	22	4	2.5	3	3	1.5/.5	3	.5 economics/free enterprise; 2 foreign languages; 1 computer science; 1 fine arts	1988	
Utah	15	24	3	3	2	2	2	9.5	1.5 arts; 1 vocational education; optional .5 computer science	1988	State board makes specific course recommendations for college entry, vocational, etc.

Table 152.—State requirements for high school graduation, in Carnegie units: 1980 and 1993—Continued

State	1980 All courses	1993 All courses	English/language arts	Social studies	Mathematics	Science	Physical education/health	Electives	Other courses	First graduating class to which these requirements apply	Notes
1	2	3	4	5	6	7	8	9	10	11	12
Vermont	—	14.5	4	3	0 to 5	0 to 5	1.5	—	1 arts; 5 units in math and science	1989	To allow more flexibility to both vocational education students and smaller or more rural districts, the previous math and science requirement of 3 units in each was modified to a combination of 5 units which may be 2 of one and 3 of the other.
Virginia Standard	18	21	4	3	2	2	2	6	1 additional math or science; 1 fine or practical arts	1989	An appropriate vocational education class or ROTC may satisfy math or science. B average or better earns a state seal on the diploma. Junior and senior students can receive dual credits for college coursework. Minimum competency test is required for graduation.
Advanced studies	18	23	4	3	3	3	2	4	3 foreign languages; 1 fine or practical arts	1989	
Washington	—	19	3	2.5	2	2	2	5.5	1 occupational education; 1 fine/visual or performing arts	1991	State has approved, but not implemented, an advanced studies certificate.
West Virginia	18	21	4	3	2	2	2	7	1 applied arts, fine or performing arts, or foreign language	1989	
Wisconsin	(²)	13	4	3	2	2	2	—		1989	Electives and passage of a minimum competency test as a requirement for graduation are options of local districts. State recommends that districts require a total of 22 units.
Wyoming	18	18	(²)	1	(²)	(²)	(²)	(²)	Local board determines remaining requirements	—	Accreditation standards indicate 4 units of English/language arts, 3 social studies courses, 2 math courses, and 2 science courses.

¹ State permits local board to set minimum academic standards.
² Local boards determine requirements.
³ State requires four credits in English/language arts.
⁴ Legislative requirements in effect for many years. Local boards determine remaining requirements.
⁴ Legislative requirements in effect for many years. Local boards determine additional requirements. The state board, in January 1984, published graduation requirement guidelines which local districts are urged to incorporate. Included in the recommendations are a minimum of 15.5 units, which includes an option of 2 units picked from a foreign language/fine or performing arts/vocational education and .5 computer education. Recommendations include modified academic course work for students who are college bound.

⁵ Electives vary for the local (regular) and the Regents' (college-bound) diploma.
—Data not available or not applicable.

NOTE.—Local school districts frequently have other graduation requirements in addition to state requirements.

SOURCE: Education Commission of the States, *Clearinghouse Notes*, "Minimum High School Graduation Requirements: Standard Diplomas," 1980 and August 1993. (This table was prepared August 1994.)

Table 153.—States using minimum-competency testing, by government level setting standards, grade levels assessed, and expected uses of standards: 1993, 1994, and 1995

State	Grade levels assessed [1]	Expected uses									
		Kindergarten readiness [2]	Grade promotion [1]	High school graduation [1]	Early exit	Student diagnosis/placement [1]	Remediation [2]	Improvement of instruction [2]	Program evaluation [1]	School performance reporting [1]	Other [1]
1	2	3	4	5	6	7	8	9	10	11	12
Alabama	3–11			X		X		X	X	X	
Alaska	4–6,8,10					X		X	X	X	
Arizona	4,7,10					X		X	X	X	
Arkansas	4,7,10					X		X	X		
California	9–12				X			X	X		(3)
Colorado [4]											
Connecticut [5]	4,6,8,10					X		X	X	X	(3,6)
Delaware	3,5,8,10							X			
Florida	4,8,10,11			X	X			X	X	X	(3)
Georgia	K,3,5,8,11	X		X		X		X	X	X	(7)
Hawaii	3,6,8,10			X		X		X	X	X	
Idaho [8]	4,8,11							X		X	
Illinois	3,4,6–8,10,11									X	(9)
Indiana	2,3,6,8,9		X			X	X	X	X	X	(7,9)
Iowa [10]											
Kansas	3–5,7,8,10,11							X	X	X	(9)
Kentucky	4,5,8,11,12							X	X		(7)
Louisiana	K,3–7,10,11	X	X	X		X		X	X	X	(3,6)
Maine	4,8,11							X	X	X	(3)
Maryland	3,5,7,8			X		X		X	X	X	(7,6,9)
Massachusetts [11]								X	X	X	(3,7,9,12)
Michigan	4,5,7,8,10,11							X	X		
Minnesota	4–6,8,9,11			X		X		X	X		(9)
Mississippi	4–9,11					X		X	X		(3,9)
Missouri	3,5,6,8,10,11							X	X		
Montana	4,8,11							X	X		
Nebraska											
Nevada	4,8,11			X		X		X		X	(6)
New Hampshire [13]	3			X				X		X	
New Jersey	8,11			X		X	X	X	X	X	(9)
New Mexico	1–6,8,10	X	X	X		X		X	X	X	(6)
New York	3–6,8–12			X		X	X	X	X	X	(12,14)
North Carolina	3–11			X		X		X	X	X	(9)
North Dakota	3,6,8,11					X		X	X		(3,9)
Ohio [15]	4,6,8,9,12			X				X	X	X	(15)
Oklahoma [15]	3,5,7,8,11					X		X	X	X	
Oregon	3,5,8,11							X	X	X	
Pennsylvania	5,6,8,9,11							X	X	X	
Rhode Island	4,8,10					X		X	X	X	
South Carolina	3–11	X	X	X		X		X	X	X	(7,6)
South Dakota	4,8,9,11							X			(7,12,14)
Tennessee	2–11			X		X		X	X	X	(3,7,6,9)
Texas	3–8,10			X		X		X	X	X	(3)
Utah	1–12							X	X	X	
Vermont	4,5,8							X	X	X	
Virginia [16]	4,6–11	X		X		X		X	X	X	(3)
Washington	4,8,11					X		X	X	X	
West Virginia	1–11							X	X	X	(6,9)
Wisconsin [17]	3,4,8,10					X	X	X	X	X	
Wyoming											

[1] Based on information for the 1994–95 school year.

[2] Based on information for the 1993–94 school year.

[3] Student awards, recognition.

[4] The Colorado Student Assessment Program was suspended for the 1993–94, 1994–95 and 1995–96 school years. A new program will be developed for grades 4, 8, and 10, beginning with the 1996–97 school year.

[5] The Connecticut Academic Performance Test (CAPT) was administered for the first time in the spring of 1994 to all grade 10 students. A certification of mastery is awarded to each student passing each section of the test.

[6] High school skills guarantee.

[7] School awards, recognition.

[8] New performance mathematics assessment for grades 4 and 8 and interdisciplinary assessments for grades 9 through 12 are optional at this time.

[9] School accreditation.

[10] Iowa does not have a mandated state assessment program. All districts must include student achievement goals in their plans and develop an assessment system to monitor progress toward those goals, but the selection of the instruments and the schedule of administration are determined locally. Approximately 99 percent of all districts participate in the Iowa Testing Program on a voluntary basis.

[11] Although first class assessed graduated in 1987, the first class required to pass for graduation was the class of 1989.

[12] Endorsed diploma

[13] By May 1996, all public school third-grade students will be tested in English/language arts and mathematics; sixth and tenth graders will be assessed in English/language arts, mathematics, science, and social studies.

[14] Honors diploma.

[15] Developing U.S. history and government tests for grades 5, 8 and 11.

[16] Standards-based assessments are in development with statewide field testing scheduled for Spring 1997.

[17] The implementation of performance assessments and local option portfolio assessments await legislative fiscal support.

NOTE.—Some states have dates for assessing the first high school graduating class but do not expect to use the results to determine whether students will graduate.

SOURCE: Council of Chief State School Officers/North Central Regional Educational Laboratory, "State Student Assessment Programs Database: May 1996." (This table was prepared June 1996.)

Table 154.—States requiring testing for initial certification of teachers, by authorization, year enacted, year effective, and test used: 1987, 1990, and 1996

State	1987				Assessment for certification 1990				Assessment for certification 1996		
	Authority [1]	Enacted	Effective	Test used [2]	Basic skills	Professional skills	Content knowledge	In-class observation	Basic skills	Other exam(s)	In-class observation
1	2	3	4	5	6	7	8	9	10	11	12
Alabama	St. Bd.	1980	1981	State					X	[3]X	X
Alaska	—	—	—	—							
Arizona	Leg.	1980	1980	State	X	X			X		
Arkansas	Leg.	1979	1983	NTE		X	X		X	[4]X	X
California	Leg.	1981	1982	State	X		X		X	[5]X	X
Colorado	Leg.	1981	1983	California Achievement	X			X	X	X	X
Connecticut	St. Bd.	1982	1985	State	X		X	X	X		X
Delaware	St. Bd.	1982	1983	P-P.S.T	X				X		X
District of Columbia	—	—	—	—	X		X		X	[6]X	X
Florida	Leg.	1978	1980	State		X	X	X	X	X	
Georgia	St. Bd.	1975	1980	State			X	X		[7]X	X
Hawaii	St. Bd.	1986	1986	NTE	X	X	X		X	[4,6]X	X
Idaho	Leg.	1987	1988	NTE		X	X				X
Illinois	Leg.	1985	1988	State		X	X		X	[7]X	X
Indiana	Leg.	1984	1985	NTE	X	X	X		X	[4]X	
Iowa	—	—	—	—	X	X	X	X			X
Kansas	Leg.	1984	1986	To be determined	X	X			X		X
Kentucky	Leg.	1984	1985	NTE				X	X	[4,6]X	X
Louisiana	Leg.	1977	1978	NTE	X	X	X			[4]X	X
Maine	Leg.	1984	1988	NTE	X	X	X	X		[8,9]X	
Maryland	St. Bd.	1986	1986	NTE	X	X	X			[4]X	
Massachusetts	Leg.	1985	([10])	To be determined	([11])				X	[11]X	X
Michigan	Leg.	1986	1991	To be determined [12]					X	X	X
Minnesota	—	—	—	—	X				X		X
Mississippi	Leg.	1975	1977	NTE		X	X	X	X	[4]X	X
Missouri	Leg.	1985	1988	To be determined			X		X	[4]X	X
Montana	B.P.E.	1985	1986	NTE	X	X			X	[4]X	X
Nebraska	Leg.	1984	1989	To be determined [12]	X				X		X
Nevada	St. Bd.	1984	([10])	To be determined	X	X	X		X		X
New Hampshire	St. Bd.	1984	1985	NTE	X				X		X
New Jersey	St. Bd.	1984	1985	NTE			X			X	X
New Mexico	St. Bd.	1981	1983	NTE	X	X		X	X	X	X
New York	St. Bd.	1980	1984	NTE	X	X				X	X
North Carolina	St. Bd.	1964	1964	NTE				X	X	[4]X	X
North Dakota	—	—	—	—					X		X
Ohio [13]	St. Bd.	1986	1987	NTE		X	X		X	[4]X	X
Oklahoma	Leg.	1980	1982	State				X	X	[5]X	X
Oregon	O.T.S.P.C.	1984	1985	C.B.E.S.T.	X	X	X	X	X	[5,9]X	X
Pennsylvania	St. Bd.	1985	1987	State	X	X			X	[5]X	
Rhode Island	St. Bd.	1985	1986	NTE	X	X		X	X		X
South Carolina	Leg.	1979	1982	NTE and State		X		X	X	[5,9]X	X
South Dakota	St. Bd.	1985	1986	NTE					X		X
Tennessee	St. Bd.	1980	1981	NTE				X	X	[4]X	X
Texas	Leg.	1981	1986	State		X	X		X	X	X
Utah	—	—	—	—			X				X
Vermont	—	—	—	—							X
Virginia	Leg.	1979	1980	NTE	X	X	X	X	X	[4]X	X
Washington	St. Bd.	1984	([10])	To be determined [7]			X		X		X
West Virginia [14]	St. Bd.	1982	1985	State	X		X	X	X	[5]X	X
Wisconsin	S.P.I.	1986	1990	To be determined	X				X		X
Wyoming	—	—	—	—							X

[1] St. Bd. = State Board of Education; Leg. = Legislature; B.P.E. = Board of Public Education; O.T.S.P.C. = Oregon Teacher Standards and Practice Commission; S.P.I. = Superintendent of Public Instruction.

[2] NTE = National Teacher Examination; State = State developed test; C.B.E.S.T. = California Basic Education Skills Test; P-P.S.T. = Preprofessional Skills Test (Praxis).

[3] Institution's Exit Exam.

[4] NTE.

[5] Speciality area exams.

[6] Praxis.

[7] State and undetermined tests will be used.

[8] General knowledge.

[9] Pedagogical exams.

[10] Effective year is yet to be determined.

[11] Test required for foreign language, bilingual, and English as a Second Language.

[12] For basic skills and subject-matter competencies.

[13] Test requirements set by local school districts.

[14] Required for individuals entering West Virginia-approved education programs as of fall 1985.

—Data not available or not applicable.

SOURCE: Education Commission of the States, Clearinghouse Notes, "States Requiring Testing for Initial Certification of Teachers, April 1987;" "State Education Leader, Winter 1989;" "State Education Indicators, 1990;" and National Association of State Directors of Teacher Education and Certification, "The NASDTEC Manual, 1996–1997: Manual on Certification & Preparation of Educational Personnel in the United States & Canada." (This table was prepared May 1996.)

Table 155.—Revenues for public elementary and secondary schools, by source of funds: 1919–20 to 1993–94

School year	In thousands				Percentage distribution			
	Total	Federal	State	Local (including intermediate) [1]	Total	Federal	State	Local (including intermediate) [1]
1	2	3	4	5	6	7	8	9
1919–20	$970,121	$2,475	$160,085	$807,561	100.0	0.3	16.5	83.2
1929–30	2,088,557	7,334	353,670	1,727,553	100.0	0.4	16.9	82.7
1939–40	2,260,527	39,810	684,354	1,536,363	100.0	1.8	30.3	68.0
1941–42	2,416,580	34,305	759,993	1,622,281	100.0	1.4	31.4	67.1
1943–44	2,604,322	35,886	859,183	1,709,253	100.0	1.4	33.0	65.6
1945–46	3,059,845	41,378	1,062,057	1,956,409	100.0	1.4	34.7	63.9
1947–48	4,311,534	120,270	1,676,362	2,514,902	100.0	2.8	38.9	58.3
1949–50	5,437,044	155,848	2,165,689	3,115,507	100.0	2.9	39.8	57.3
1951–52	6,423,816	227,711	2,478,596	3,717,507	100.0	3.5	38.6	57.9
1953–54	7,866,852	355,237	2,944,103	4,567,512	100.0	4.5	37.4	58.1
1955–56	9,686,677	441,442	3,828,886	5,416,350	100.0	4.6	39.5	55.9
1957–58	12,181,513	486,484	4,800,368	6,894,661	100.0	4.0	39.4	56.6
1959–60	14,746,618	651,639	5,768,047	8,326,932	100.0	4.4	39.1	56.5
1961–62	17,527,707	760,975	6,789,190	9,977,542	100.0	4.3	38.7	56.9
1963–64	20,544,182	896,956	8,078,014	11,569,213	100.0	4.4	39.3	56.3
1965–66	25,356,858	1,996,954	9,920,219	13,439,686	100.0	7.9	39.1	53.0
1967–68	31,903,064	2,806,469	12,275,536	16,821,063	100.0	8.8	38.5	52.7
1969–70	40,266,923	3,219,557	16,062,776	20,984,589	100.0	8.0	39.9	52.1
1970–71	44,511,292	3,753,461	17,409,086	23,348,745	100.0	8.4	39.1	52.5
1971–72	50,003,645	4,467,969	19,133,256	26,402,420	100.0	8.9	38.3	52.8
1972–73 [2]	52,117,930	4,525,000	20,699,752	26,893,180	100.0	8.7	39.7	51.6
1973–74	58,230,892	4,930,351	24,113,409	29,187,132	100.0	8.5	41.4	50.1
1974–75 [2]	64,445,239	5,811,595	27,060,563	31,573,079	100.0	9.0	42.0	49.0
1975–76 [2]	71,206,073	6,318,345	31,602,885	33,284,840	100.0	8.9	44.4	46.7
1976–77	75,322,532	6,629,498	32,526,018	36,137,018	100.0	8.8	43.2	48.0
1977–78	81,443,160	7,694,194	35,013,266	38,735,700	100.0	9.4	43.0	47.6
1978–79	87,994,143	8,600,116	40,132,136	39,261,891	100.0	9.8	45.6	44.6
1979–80	96,881,165	9,503,537	45,348,814	42,028,813	100.0	9.8	46.8	43.4
1980–81	105,949,087	9,768,262	50,182,659	45,998,166	100.0	9.2	47.4	43.4
1981–82	110,191,257	8,186,466	52,436,435	49,568,356	100.0	7.4	47.6	45.0
1982–83	117,497,502	8,339,990	56,282,157	52,875,354	100.0	7.1	47.9	45.0
1983–84	126,055,419	8,576,547	60,232,981	57,245,892	100.0	6.8	47.8	45.4
1984–85	137,294,678	9,105,569	67,168,684	61,020,425	100.0	6.6	48.9	44.4
1985–86	149,127,779	9,975,622	73,619,575	65,532,582	100.0	6.7	49.4	43.9
1986–87	158,523,693	10,146,013	78,830,437	69,547,243	100.0	6.4	49.7	43.9
1987–88	169,561,974	10,716,687	84,004,415	74,840,873	100.0	6.3	49.5	44.1
1988–89	192,016,374	11,902,001	91,768,911	88,345,462	100.0	6.2	47.8	46.0
1989–90	208,547,573	12,700,784	98,238,633	97,608,157	100.0	6.1	47.1	46.8
1990–91	223,340,537	13,776,066	105,324,533	104,239,939	100.0	6.2	47.2	46.7
1991–92	234,588,732	15,493,330	108,783,449	110,311,953	100.0	6.6	46.4	47.0
1992–93 [2]	247,626,168	17,261,252	113,403,436	116,961,481	100.0	7.0	45.8	47.2
1993–94	260,142,087	18,335,803	117,462,492	124,343,791	100.0	7.0	45.2	47.8

[1] Includes a relatively small amount from nongovernmental private sources (gifts and tuition and transportation fees from patrons). These sources accounted for 2.7 percent of total revenues in 1993–94.

[2] Revised from previously published figures.

NOTE.—Beginning in 1980–81, revenues for state education agencies are excluded. Beginning in 1988–89, data reflect new survey collection procedures and may not be en-tirely comparable with figures for earlier years. Because of rounding, details may not add to totals.

SOURCE: U.S. Department of Education, National Center for Education Statistics, *Statistics of State School Systems; Revenues and Expenditures for Public Elementary and Secondary Education;* and Common Core of Data surveys. (This table was prepared May 1996.)

Table 156.—Revenues for public elementary and secondary schools, by source and state: 1993–94

[Amounts in thousands of dollars]

State or other area	Total	Federal		State		Local and intermediate		Private [1]	
		Amount	Percent of total	Amount	Percent of total	Amount	Percent of total	Amount	Percent of total
1	2	3	4	5	6	7	8	9	10
United States	**$260,142,087**	**$18,335,803**	**7.0**	**$117,462,492**	**45.2**	**$117,424,123**	**45.1**	**$6,919,668**	**2.7**
Alabama	3,121,320	346,246	11.1	1,850,898	59.3	667,382	21.4	256,794	8.2
Alaska	1,159,259	138,061	11.9	777,478	67.1	217,973	18.8	25,747	2.2
Arizona	3,550,177	332,091	9.4	1,474,316	41.5	1,661,537	46.8	82,232	2.3
Arkansas	2,014,900	176,931	8.8	1,164,432	57.8	577,017	28.6	96,521	4.8
California	29,050,409	2,572,258	8.9	16,324,953	56.2	9,824,487	33.8	328,711	1.1
Colorado	3,368,596	185,835	5.5	1,466,584	43.5	1,599,758	47.5	116,419	3.5
Connecticut	4,103,218	163,091	4.0	1,653,755	40.3	2,176,137	53.0	110,234	2.7
Delaware	684,411	53,531	7.8	441,043	64.4	178,558	26.1	11,278	1.6
District of Columbia	735,722	79,433	10.8	—	—	652,754	88.7	3,535	0.5
Florida	11,927,112	921,140	7.7	5,945,110	49.8	4,610,243	38.7	450,619	3.8
Georgia	6,630,693	518,047	7.8	3,360,515	50.7	2,617,848	39.5	134,283	2.0
Hawaii	1,128,456	84,217	7.5	1,014,096	89.9	8,862	0.8	21,281	1.9
Idaho	955,081	80,589	8.4	576,967	60.4	279,049	29.2	18,476	1.9
Illinois	11,322,719	743,760	6.6	3,196,325	28.2	7,116,481	62.9	266,153	2.4
Indiana	5,918,601	299,738	5.1	3,097,205	52.3	2,337,103	39.5	184,554	3.1
Iowa	2,782,621	147,123	5.3	1,339,923	48.2	1,141,428	41.0	154,147	5.5
Kansas	2,695,033	148,303	5.5	1,558,260	57.8	920,280	34.1	68,191	2.5
Kentucky	3,194,404	329,830	10.3	2,105,658	65.9	733,116	23.0	25,800	0.8
Louisiana	3,608,436	439,492	12.2	1,912,880	53.0	1,160,708	32.2	95,356	2.6
Maine	1,327,946	78,641	5.9	641,322	48.3	592,856	44.6	15,127	1.1
Maryland	5,145,236	268,305	5.2	2,002,376	38.9	2,715,108	52.8	159,447	3.1
Massachusetts	6,227,191	334,600	5.4	2,125,314	34.1	3,652,395	58.7	114,882	1.8
Michigan	11,134,083	714,960	6.4	3,200,682	28.7	7,007,174	62.9	211,267	1.9
Minnesota	5,160,259	236,773	4.6	2,840,930	55.1	1,887,199	36.6	195,358	3.8
Mississippi	1,879,377	307,241	16.3	1,024,792	54.5	478,941	25.5	68,404	3.6
Missouri	4,526,828	297,101	6.6	1,733,542	38.3	2,307,866	51.0	188,319	4.2
Montana	877,807	84,632	9.6	451,223	51.4	306,411	34.9	35,542	4.0
Nebraska	1,674,836	106,686	6.4	547,921	32.7	917,262	54.8	102,966	6.1
Nevada	1,268,826	58,523	4.6	416,469	32.8	746,914	58.9	46,920	3.7
New Hampshire	1,097,159	35,284	3.2	89,552	8.2	945,881	86.2	26,442	2.4
New Jersey	11,301,907	406,261	3.6	4,564,512	40.4	6,048,629	53.5	282,505	2.5
New Mexico	1,562,447	188,548	12.1	1,153,974	73.9	184,483	11.8	35,441	2.3
New York	23,775,186	1,472,573	6.2	9,090,191	38.2	12,979,174	54.6	233,248	1.0
North Carolina	5,560,314	454,606	8.2	3,559,792	64.0	1,320,661	23.8	225,257	4.1
North Dakota	563,352	67,042	11.9	240,860	42.8	225,514	40.0	29,936	5.3
Ohio	10,499,236	668,428	6.4	4,280,781	40.8	5,121,069	48.8	428,958	4.1
Oklahoma	3,077,911	263,440	8.6	1,811,319	58.8	870,556	28.3	132,595	4.3
Oregon	3,074,679	212,437	6.9	1,215,454	39.5	1,550,028	50.4	96,760	3.1
Pennsylvania	12,601,361	724,185	5.7	5,075,591	40.3	6,558,357	52.0	243,228	1.9
Rhode Island	1,022,861	60,415	5.9	399,395	39.0	552,150	54.0	10,901	1.1
South Carolina	3,200,412	294,566	9.2	1,478,065	46.2	1,285,545	40.2	142,237	4.4
South Dakota	647,026	69,536	10.7	168,964	26.1	390,003	60.3	18,523	2.9
Tennessee	3,649,630	347,887	9.5	1,707,740	46.8	1,344,658	36.8	249,345	6.8
Texas	18,744,302	1,516,708	8.1	7,542,112	40.2	9,174,217	48.9	511,265	2.7
Utah	1,785,758	126,294	7.1	981,014	54.9	581,418	32.6	97,032	5.4
Vermont	703,939	35,655	5.1	220,614	31.3	432,877	61.5	14,793	2.1
Virginia	6,162,835	370,560	6.0	1,895,429	30.8	3,671,851	59.6	224,995	3.7
Washington	5,723,616	334,306	5.8	3,988,235	69.7	1,224,521	21.4	176,554	3.1
West Virginia	1,879,452	151,207	8.0	1,214,154	64.6	486,196	25.9	27,895	1.5
Wisconsin	5,661,241	249,844	4.4	2,188,298	38.7	3,110,476	54.9	112,622	2.0
Wyoming	673,906	38,846	5.8	351,479	52.2	273,010	40.5	10,571	1.6
Outlying areas									
American Samoa	41,683	34,722	83.3	6,699	16.1	99	0.2	164	0.4
Guam	168,461	16,765	10.0	—	—	150,067	89.1	1,629	1.0
Northern Marianas	41,406	11,042	26.7	30,215	73.0	64	0.2	85	0.2
Puerto Rico	1,510,847	473,394	31.3	1,036,657	68.6	387	(2)	408	(2)
Virgin Islands	132,711	25,169	19.0	—	—	107,467	81.0	75	0.1

[1] Includes revenues from gifts, and tuition and fees from patrons.
[2] Less than .05 percent.
—Data not available or not applicable.

NOTE.—Excludes revenues for state education agencies. Because of rounding, details may not add to totals.

SOURCE: U.S. Department of Education, National Center for Education Statistics, Common Core of Data survey. (This table was prepared May 1996.)

Table 157.—Revenues for public elementary and secondary schools, by source and state: 1992–93

[Amounts in thousands of dollars]

State or other area	Total	Federal		State		Local and intermediate		Private [1]	
		Amount	Percent of total	Amount	Percent of total	Amount	Percent of total	Amount	Percent of total
1	2	3	4	5	6	7	8	9	10
United States	$247,626,168	$17,261,252	7.0	$113,403,436	45.8	$110,260,522	44.5	$6,700,958	2.7
Alabama	2,982,753	347,381	11.6	1,732,506	58.1	661,483	22.2	241,384	8.1
Alaska	1,182,527	173,239	14.6	767,809	64.9	215,825	18.3	25,654	2.2
Arizona	3,402,888	299,926	8.8	1,411,844	41.5	1,614,522	47.4	76,596	2.3
Arkansas	1,933,846	184,934	9.6	1,104,347	57.1	552,744	28.6	91,822	4.7
California	28,039,018	2,256,461	8.0	17,439,021	62.2	8,014,478	28.6	329,058	1.2
Colorado	3,337,266	164,527	4.9	1,403,076	42.0	1,657,801	49.7	111,862	3.4
Connecticut	3,973,498	137,383	3.5	1,544,471	38.9	2,180,356	54.9	111,287	2.8
Delaware	632,150	43,448	6.9	417,965	66.1	160,103	25.3	10,634	1.7
District of Columbia	722,230	74,961	10.4	—	—	643,603	89.1	3,666	0.5
Florida	11,369,988	947,311	8.3	5,511,186	48.5	4,449,712	39.1	461,779	4.1
Georgia	5,997,559	463,476	7.7	3,019,826	50.4	2,391,963	39.9	122,294	2.0
Hawaii	1,067,810	81,518	7.6	962,375	90.1	6,628	0.6	17,288	1.6
Idaho	896,846	75,605	8.4	548,181	61.1	255,240	28.5	17,821	2.0
Illinois	10,575,035	747,825	7.1	3,013,710	28.5	6,559,072	62.0	254,428	2.4
Indiana	5,625,542	293,928	5.2	2,933,242	52.1	2,223,837	39.5	174,534	3.1
Iowa	2,694,532	144,390	5.4	1,299,696	48.2	1,091,553	40.5	158,893	5.9
Kansas	2,373,507	129,930	5.5	1,178,800	49.7	998,030	42.0	66,747	2.8
Kentucky	3,071,172	309,365	10.1	2,058,542	67.0	679,447	22.1	23,819	0.8
Louisiana	3,490,078	410,067	11.7	1,876,960	53.8	1,113,956	31.9	89,095	2.6
Maine	1,337,730	82,713	6.2	678,159	50.7	562,223	42.0	14,636	1.1
Maryland	4,923,313	264,767	5.4	1,940,701	39.4	2,564,887	52.1	152,958	3.1
Massachusetts	5,881,254	331,480	5.6	1,925,405	32.7	3,506,202	59.6	118,167	2.0
Michigan	10,766,136	664,798	6.2	3,295,411	30.6	6,606,216	61.4	199,711	1.9
Minnesota	4,698,237	225,048	4.8	2,261,916	48.1	2,030,657	43.2	180,617	3.8
Mississippi	1,777,016	303,590	17.1	951,723	53.6	454,341	25.6	67,362	3.8
Missouri	4,260,954	274,161	6.4	1,632,185	38.3	2,178,370	51.1	176,238	4.1
Montana	834,660	77,552	9.3	454,922	54.5	268,602	32.2	33,585	4.0
Nebraska	1,597,612	100,340	6.3	529,662	33.2	868,644	54.4	98,966	6.2
Nevada	1,176,376	54,833	4.7	402,727	34.2	676,163	57.5	42,654	3.6
New Hampshire	1,062,532	32,794	3.1	84,340	7.9	920,676	86.6	24,723	2.3
New Jersey	10,995,533	461,806	4.2	4,553,681	41.4	5,724,831	52.1	255,215	2.3
New Mexico	1,429,383	179,606	12.6	1,052,830	73.7	161,003	11.3	35,944	2.5
New York	22,574,304	1,352,381	6.0	8,848,907	39.2	12,032,177	53.3	340,840	1.5
North Carolina	5,357,036	433,593	8.1	3,388,467	63.3	1,321,306	24.7	213,669	4.0
North Dakota	551,527	65,639	11.9	237,908	43.1	218,531	39.6	29,449	5.3
Ohio	10,091,511	628,327	6.2	4,162,431	41.2	4,883,999	48.4	416,754	4.1
Oklahoma	2,771,015	197,037	7.1	1,663,413	60.0	782,957	28.3	127,607	4.6
Oregon	3,135,734	196,684	6.3	1,183,893	37.8	1,664,634	53.1	90,523	2.9
Pennsylvania	12,060,334	736,599	6.1	4,826,383	40.0	6,252,064	51.8	245,287	2.0
Rhode Island	968,667	57,892	6.0	392,841	40.6	510,745	52.7	7,189	0.7
South Carolina	3,061,004	286,136	9.3	1,439,690	47.0	1,199,057	39.2	136,122	4.4
South Dakota	603,085	69,969	11.6	164,040	27.2	350,490	58.1	18,587	3.1
Tennessee	3,394,425	351,089	10.3	1,546,611	45.6	1,255,944	37.0	240,782	7.1
Texas	17,446,887	1,305,976	7.5	6,983,217	40.0	8,654,014	49.6	503,680	2.9
Utah	1,657,433	117,788	7.1	961,278	58.0	521,167	31.4	57,201	3.5
Vermont	673,965	35,222	5.2	220,179	32.7	406,301	60.3	12,264	1.8
Virginia	5,867,968	365,225	6.2	1,886,029	32.1	3,451,606	58.8	165,108	2.8
Washington	5,499,862	307,058	5.6	3,920,527	71.3	1,107,007	20.1	165,270	3.0
West Virginia	1,841,575	142,379	7.7	1,234,018	67.0	438,001	23.8	27,176	1.5
Wisconsin	5,346,988	237,669	4.4	2,047,701	38.3	2,957,776	55.3	103,843	1.9
Wyoming	613,864	35,428	5.8	308,687	50.3	259,578	42.3	10,171	1.7
Outlying areas									
American Samoa	35,031	24,957	71.2	9,810	28.0	77	0.2	187	0.5
Guam	208,767	20,160	9.7	—	—	186,977	89.6	1,631	0.8
Northern Marianas	41,015	11,576	28.2	29,285	71.4	116	0.3	38	0.1
Puerto Rico	1,433,524	485,326	33.9	946,249	66.0	358	([2])	1,590	0.1
Virgin Islands	143,438	27,912	19.5	—	—	115,459	80.5	68	([2])

[1] Includes revenues from gifts, and tuition and fees from patrons.
[2] Less than .05 percent.
—Data not available or not applicable.

NOTE.—Excludes revenues for state education agencies. Some data have been revised from previously published figures. Because of rounding, details may not add to totals.

SOURCE: U.S. Department of Education, National Center for Education Statistics, Common Core of Data survey. (This table was prepared May 1996.)

Table 158.—Funds and staff for state education agencies,[1] by source of funding and state: 1992–93

State	Funds retained for state administration, by source, in thousands				Total state administration funds per student	State education agency (FTE) staff, by source of funds for position			Students per state FTE staff
	Total	Federal (core activities)[2]	Percent federal	State and local		Total FTE staff	Federally supported (core activities)[2]	State and local supported	
1	2	3	4	5	6	7	8	9	10
United States[3]	$1,966,453	$526,847	26.8	$1,439,606	$46	28,626	7,054	21,572	1,496
Alabama	52,111	13,007	25.0	39,103	71	1,006	127	879	727
Alaska	38,461	5,046	13.1	33,414	314	503	44	460	244
Arizona	19,315	7,460	38.6	11,856	29	362	175	187	1,862
Arkansas	17,561	4,204	23.9	13,356	40	290	74	216	1,522
California	148,989	52,316	35.1	96,673	28	1,898	419	1,479	2,768
Colorado	21,361	5,991	28.0	15,370	35	223	90	133	2,750
Connecticut	139,733	11,433	8.2	128,300	286	2,005	196	1,809	244
Delaware	10,949	2,578	23.5	8,371	105	128	44	84	817
District of Columbia	—	—	—	—	—	—	—	—	—
Florida	56,310	25,470	45.2	30,840	28	688	323		2,878
Georgia	58,632	9,918	16.9	48,714	49	935	147	788	1,291
Hawaii	—	—	—	—	—	—	—	—	—
Idaho	7,346	2,938	40.0	4,408	32	104	45	59	2,224
Illinois	42,854	22,092	51.6	20,762	23	746	317	429	2,511
Indiana	29,220	7,339	25.1	21,880	30	309	132	177	3,109
Iowa	20,589	9,582	46.5	11,007	42	226	106	120	2,192
Kansas	12,701	5,422	42.7	7,279	28	199	83	116	2,269
Kentucky	49,745	6,202	12.5	43,542	76	859	105	754	763
Louisiana	35,978	13,015	36.2	22,963	45	573	254	320	1,393
Maine[4]	17,356	4,248	24.5	13,109	80	207	90	117	1,046
Maryland	42,343	8,737	20.6	33,606	56	556	126	430	1,351
Massachusetts	30,191	13,557	44.9	16,633	35	368	173	195	2,337
Michigan	53,743	15,656	29.1	38,088	34	844	256	588	1,899
Minnesota	23,730	9,072	38.2	14,658	30	416	129	287	1,908
Mississippi	40,892	5,703	13.9	35,190	81	724	144	580	700
Missouri	42,860	8,708	20.3	34,152	50	1,448	132	1,317	593
Montana	8,070	3,490	43.2	4,581	50	137	52	85	1,168
Nebraska	20,624	5,018	24.3	15,607	73	398	75	323	710
Nevada	5,305	2,643	49.8	2,662	24	90	47	42	2,491
New Hampshire	7,889	2,662	33.7	5,226	44	157	60	97	1,154
New Jersey	65,111	25,857	39.7	39,254	58	1,001	326	675	1,129
New Mexico	10,398	3,753	36.1	6,645	33	216	67	149	1,461
New York	181,649	47,866	26.4	133,783	68	2,565	567	1,998	1,049
North Carolina	49,298	13,990	28.4	35,308	44	796	144	652	1,399
North Dakota	5,683	3,187	56.1	2,496	48	93	52	41	1,277
Ohio	32,879	14,741	44.8	18,139	18	511	242	269	3,513
Oklahoma	32,178	8,347	25.9	23,831	54	499	98	401	1,196
Oregon	61,178	15,822	25.9	45,357	120	418	58	360	1,221
Pennsylvania	72,979	19,746	27.1	53,233	42	1,134	237	897	1,515
Rhode Island	13,705	4,347	31.7	9,358	95	152	59	93	948
South Carolina	87,109	9,130	10.5	77,979	136	946	105	841	677
South Dakota	7,419	3,988	53.8	3,430	55	102	42	60	1,324
Tennessee	36,778	10,525	28.6	26,253	43	456	100	356	1,876
Texas	59,560	18,321	30.8	41,238	17	1,013	358	654	3,498
Utah	25,763	6,092	23.6	19,671	56	364	62	302	1,273
Vermont	7,348	2,672	36.4	4,675	75	143	65	78	689
Virginia	29,236	9,830	33.6	19,406	28	371	102	270	2,781
Washington	19,472	6,843	35.1	12,629	22	253	88	165	3,542
West Virginia	21,188	5,069	23.9	16,119	67	403	113	289	790
Wisconsin	87,883	11,377	12.9	76,506	106	692	179	512	1,199
Wyoming	4,782	1,837	38.4	2,945	48	100	25	75	1,003

[1] Excludes funds for schools and school districts.
[2] Core education activities include: Chapter 1; Chapter 2; Special Education; Child Nutrition; Vocational Education; Adult Education; AIDS Education; Civil Rights Act; and Homeless Education Programs.
[3] Excludes District of Columbia and Hawaii.
[4] Excludes State Teacher Retirement Program.

—Data not available.

NOTE.—Because of rounding, details may not add to totals. FTE=full-time equivalent.

SOURCE: U.S. Department of Education, National Center for Education Statistics, Common Core of Data survey. (This table was prepared September 1996.)

Table 159.—Summary of expenditures for public elementary and secondary education, by purpose: 1919–20 to 1993–94

Purpose of expenditures	1919–20	1929–30	1939–40	1949–50	1959–60	1969–70	1979–80	1989–90	1992–93[1]	1993–94
1	2	3	4	5	6	7	8	9	10	11
	Amounts in thousands of dollars									
Total expenditures, all schools ...	$1,036,151	$2,316,790	$2,344,049	$5,837,643	$15,613,255	$40,683,429	$95,961,561	$212,473,108	$252,934,872	$265,285,370
Current expenditures, all schools	864,396	1,853,377	1,955,166	4,722,887	12,461,955	34,853,578	87,581,727	190,915,446	225,326,558	236,203,299
Public elementary and secondary schools	861,120	1,843,552	1,941,799	4,687,274	12,329,389	34,217,773	86,984,142	187,932,903	220,948,052	231,521,500
Administration	36,752	78,680	91,571	220,050	528,408	1,606,646	4,263,757	—	—	—
Instruction	632,556	1,317,727	1,403,285	3,112,340	8,350,738	23,270,158	53,257,937	—	—	—
Plant operation	115,707	216,072	194,365	427,587	1,085,036	2,537,257	[2]9,744,785	—	—	—
Plant maintenance	30,432	78,810	73,321	214,164	422,586	974,941	[2]	—	—	—
Fixed charges	9,286	50,270	50,116	261,469	909,323	3,266,920	11,793,934	—	—	—
Other school services[3]	36,387	101,993	129,141	451,663	1,033,297	2,561,856	7,923,729	—	—	—
Other current expenditures										
Summer schools	[4]	[4]	[4]	[4]	13,263	106,481	24,753	2,982,543	4,378,506	4,681,799
Adult education[4]	3,277	9,825	13,367	35,614	26,858	128,778	—	[5]	[5]	[5]
Community colleges	[4]	[4]	[4]	[4]	34,492	138,813	—	[5]	[5]	[5]
Community services	[3]	[3]	[3]	[3]	57,953	261,731	572,832	[5]	[5]	[5]
Capital outlay[6]	153,543	370,878	257,974	1,014,176	2,661,786	4,659,072	6,506,167	17,781,342	22,171,768	23,747,022
Interest on school debt	18,212	92,536	130,909	100,578	489,514	1,170,782	1,873,666	3,776,321	5,436,547	5,335,049
	Percentage distribution									
Total expenditures, all schools	100.0	100.0	100.0	100.0	100.0	100.0	100.0	100.0	100.0	100.0
Current expenditures, all schools	83.4	80.0	83.4	80.9	79.8	85.7	91.2	89.9	89.1	89.0
Public elementary and secondary schools	83.1	79.6	82.8	80.3	79.0	84.1	90.6	88.5	87.4	87.3
Administration	3.5	3.4	3.9	3.8	3.4	3.9	4.4	—	—	—
Instruction	61.0	56.9	59.9	53.3	53.5	57.2	55.5	—	—	—
Plant operation	11.2	9.3	8.3	7.3	6.9	6.2	[2]10.2	—	—	—
Plant maintenance	2.9	3.4	3.1	3.7	2.7	2.4	[2]	—	—	—
Fixed charges	0.9	2.2	2.1	4.5	5.8	8.0	12.3	—	—	—
Other school services[3]	3.5	4.4	5.5	7.7	6.6	6.3	8.3	—	—	—
Other current expenditures										
Summer schools	[4]	[4]	[4]	[4]	0.1	0.3	[7]	1.4	1.7	1.8
Adult education[4]	0.3	0.4	0.6	0.6	0.2	0.3	—	[5]	[5]	[5]
Community colleges	[4]	[4]	[4]	[4]	0.2	0.3	—	[5]	[5]	[5]
Community services	[3]	[3]	[3]	[3]	0.4	0.6	0.6	[5]	[5]	[5]
Capital outlay[6]	14.8	16.0	11.0	17.4	17.0	11.5	6.8	8.4	8.8	9.0
Interest on school debt	1.8	4.0	5.6	1.7	3.1	2.9	2.0	1.8	2.1	2.0

[1] Revised from previously published data.
[2] Plant operation also includes plant maintenance.
[3] Prior to 1959–60, items included under "other school services" were listed under "auxiliary services," a more comprehensive classification that also included community services.
[4] Prior to 1959–60, data shown for adult education represent combined expenditures for adult education, summer schools, and community colleges.
[5] Included under summer schools.
[6] Prior to 1969–70, excludes capital outlay by state and local schoolhousing authorities.
[7] Less than 0.05 percent.

—Data not available.

NOTE.—Beginning in 1959–60, includes Alaska and Hawaii. Beginning in 1980–81, state administration expenditures were excluded from both "total" and "current" expenditures. Beginning in 1988–89, extensive changes were made in the data collection procedures. Because of rounding, details may not add to totals.

SOURCE: U.S. Department of Education, National Center for Education Statistics, Statistics of State School Systems; and Common Core of Data surveys. (This table was prepared May 1996.)

Table 160.—Total expenditures for public elementary and secondary education, by function and subfunction: 1989–90 to 1993–94

Items	Expenditures (in thousands)					Percentage distribution				
	1989–90	1990–91	1991–92	1992–93	1993–94	1989–90	1990–91	1991–92	1992–93	1993–94
1	2	3	4	5	6	7	8	9	10	11
Total expenditures	$212,473,108	$229,429,715	$241,062,373	$252,934,872	$265,285,370	—	—	—	—	—
Current expenditures	187,932,903	202,037,752	211,221,254	220,948,052	231,521,500	100.00	100.00	100.00	100.00	100.00
Salaries	[1]123,371,072	[1]132,729,751	138,220,586	144,276,674	150,545,503	65.65	65.70	65.44	65.30	65.02
Employee benefits	[1]31,376,416	[1]33,934,301	36,031,004	39,267,087	41,182,096	16.70	16.80	17.06	17.77	17.79
Purchased services	[1]15,443,358	[1]16,376,134	17,844,459	17,933,497	19,232,753	8.22	8.11	8.45	8.12	8.31
Tuition	[1]1,012,623	[1]1,192,505	939,291	967,884	1,231,076	0.54	0.59	0.44	0.44	0.53
Supplies	[1]14,007,262	[1]14,829,909	14,995,849	16,370,100	17,228,278	7.45	7.34	7.10	7.41	7.44
Other	[1]2,722,172	[1]2,975,152	3,190,064	2,132,810	2,101,794	1.45	1.47	1.51	0.97	0.91
Instruction	113,550,405	122,223,362	128,418,502	134,971,088	141,598,786	60.42	60.50	60.80	61.09	61.16
Salaries	84,350,068	90,742,284	94,973,704	99,089,718	103,506,260	44.88	44.91	44.96	44.85	44.71
Employee benefits	20,702,032	22,347,524	23,675,941	26,075,726	27,456,160	11.02	11.06	11.21	11.80	11.86
Purchased services	2,558,153	2,722,639	3,343,852	3,357,323	3,421,363	1.36	1.35	1.58	1.52	1.48
Tuition	1,012,623	1,192,505	939,291	967,884	1,231,076	0.54	0.59	0.44	0.44	0.53
Supplies	4,275,002	4,584,754	4,702,106	5,052,972	5,486,107	2.27	2.27	2.23	2.29	2.37
Other	652,526	633,656	783,608	427,468	497,820	0.35	0.31	0.37	0.19	0.22
Students [2]	8,265,657	8,926,010	9,226,186	9,760,087	10,946,239	4.40	4.42	4.37	4.42	4.73
Salaries	6,073,265	6,565,965	6,787,605	7,134,434	7,998,239	3.23	3.25	3.21	3.23	3.45
Employee benefits	1,528,864	1,660,082	1,750,887	1,904,341	2,110,018	0.81	0.82	0.83	0.86	0.91
Purchased services	431,976	455,996	444,443	489,215	593,526	0.23	0.23	0.21	0.22	0.26
Supplies	173,526	191,482	181,565	195,240	206,354	0.09	0.09	0.09	0.09	0.09
Other	58,025	52,485	61,686	36,857	38,102	0.03	0.03	0.03	0.02	0.02
Instructional services [3]	7,806,238	8,467,142	8,829,364	9,241,929	9,236,617	4.15	4.19	4.18	4.18	3.99
Salaries	5,123,186	5,560,129	5,805,242	6,014,671	5,933,829	2.73	2.75	2.75	2.72	2.56
Employee benefits	1,266,016	1,408,217	1,463,142	1,601,713	1,583,600	0.67	0.70	0.69	0.72	0.68
Purchased services	547,862	622,487	687,650	741,983	785,843	0.29	0.31	0.33	0.34	0.34
Supplies	759,207	776,863	774,059	820,919	860,228	0.40	0.38	0.37	0.37	0.37
Other	109,965	99,445	99,271	62,644	73,117	0.06	0.05	0.05	0.03	0.03
General administration	5,455,371	5,791,253	6,045,783	5,851,983	5,909,737	2.90	2.87	2.86	2.65	2.55
Salaries	2,486,406	2,603,562	2,687,020	2,787,145	2,688,508	1.32	1.29	1.27	1.26	1.16
Employee benefits	770,967	777,381	815,037	846,638	888,215	0.41	0.38	0.39	0.38	0.38
Purchased services	1,393,617	1,482,427	1,547,143	1,592,937	1,856,070	0.74	0.73	0.73	0.72	0.80
Supplies	166,495	172,898	158,845	211,727	168,786	0.09	0.09	0.08	0.10	0.07
Other	637,886	754,985	837,737	413,535	308,158	0.34	0.37	0.40	0.19	0.13
School administration	10,891,620	11,695,344	12,274,916	12,777,815	13,492,581	5.80	5.79	5.81	5.78	5.83
Salaries	8,310,370	8,935,903	9,290,692	9,593,613	10,144,778	4.42	4.42	4.40	4.34	4.38
Employee benefits	2,089,463	2,257,783	2,409,835	2,615,351	2,738,224	1.11	1.12	1.14	1.18	1.18
Purchased services	241,248	247,750	278,807	300,288	320,443	0.13	0.12	0.13	0.14	0.14
Supplies	188,393	189,711	196,804	207,078	223,812	0.10	0.09	0.09	0.09	0.10
Other	62,146	64,197	98,778	61,485	65,323	0.03	0.03	0.05	0.03	0.03
Operation and maintenance	20,261,415	21,290,655	21,917,957	22,823,758	23,875,985	10.78	10.54	10.38	10.33	10.31
Salaries	8,395,005	8,849,559	9,139,268	9,384,209	9,768,822	4.47	4.38	4.33	4.25	4.22
Employee benefits	2,423,326	2,633,075	2,787,333	2,970,466	3,048,622	1.29	1.30	1.32	1.34	1.32
Purchased services	5,554,610	5,721,125	5,857,816	6,013,075	6,451,754	2.96	2.83	2.77	2.72	2.79
Supplies	3,579,084	3,761,738	3,820,651	4,262,006	4,399,101	1.90	1.86	1.81	1.93	1.90
Other	309,391	325,157	312,888	194,002	207,686	0.16	0.16	0.15	0.09	0.09
Transportation	8,030,990	8,678,954	8,789,770	9,252,300	9,627,190	4.27	4.30	4.16	4.19	4.16
Salaries	3,045,942	3,285,127	3,267,418	3,407,602	3,567,576	1.62	1.63	1.55	1.54	1.54
Employee benefits	808,635	892,985	965,750	1,063,064	1,107,881	0.43	0.44	0.46	0.48	0.48
Purchased services	3,094,099	3,345,232	3,564,856	3,758,313	3,946,939	1.65	1.66	1.69	1.70	1.70
Supplies	897,799	961,447	817,908	877,077	854,947	0.48	0.48	0.39	0.40	0.37
Other	184,516	194,163	173,838	146,243	149,846	0.10	0.10	0.08	0.07	0.06
Other student services	4,989,078	5,587,837	6,094,512	6,207,775	6,318,335	2.65	2.77	2.89	2.81	2.73
Salaries	2,533,744	2,900,394	2,890,670	3,192,790	3,164,503	1.35	1.44	1.37	1.45	1.37
Employee benefits	868,792	980,859	1,152,949	1,088,011	1,109,767	0.46	0.49	0.55	0.49	0.48
Purchased services	786,814	798,922	1,154,831	1,045,655	1,141,647	0.42	0.40	0.55	0.47	0.49
Supplies	295,241	294,527	308,445	327,377	362,840	0.16	0.15	0.15	0.15	0.16
Other	504,488	613,135	587,617	553,942	539,578	0.27	0.30	0.28	0.25	0.23
Food services	8,116,277	8,430,490	8,826,600	9,263,181	9,774,315	4.32	4.17	4.18	4.19	4.22
Salaries	—	—	3,122,197	3,398,599	3,532,188	—	—	1.48	1.54	1.53
Employee benefits	—	—	960,079	1,042,743	1,095,682	—	—	0.45	0.47	0.47
Purchased services	—	—	715,611	497,100	556,254	—	—	0.34	0.22	0.24
Supplies	—	—	3,853,699	4,186,945	4,445,896	—	—	1.82	1.89	1.92
Other	—	—	175,014	137,793	144,296	—	—	0.08	0.06	0.06
Enterprise operations [4]	565,852	946,705	797,663	798,136	741,715	0.30	0.47	0.38	0.36	0.32
Salaries	—	—	256,767	273,893	240,800	—	—	0.12	0.12	0.10
Employee benefits	—	—	50,050	59,038	43,927	—	—	0.02	0.03	0.02
Purchased services	—	—	249,450	137,608	158,914	—	—	0.12	0.06	0.07
Supplies	—	—	181,768	228,758	220,206	—	—	0.09	0.10	0.10
Other	—	—	59,628	98,840	77,869	—	—	0.03	0.04	0.03
Other current expenditures	2,982,543	3,295,717	4,392,378	4,378,506	4,681,799	—	—	—	—	—
Community services	872,531	964,370	1,176,422	1,331,004	1,485,671	—	—	—	—	—
Nonpublic school programs	493,252	527,609	652,403	644,150	689,888	—	—	—	—	—
Adult education	1,229,456	1,365,523	1,498,962	1,484,057	1,489,405	—	—	—	—	—
Community colleges	11,555	5,356	5,136	5,454	7,432	—	—	—	—	—
Other	375,750	432,858	1,059,455	913,841	1,009,402	—	—	—	—	—
Capital outlay [5]	17,781,342	19,771,478	20,282,891	22,171,768	23,747,022	—	—	—	—	—
Interest on school debt	3,776,321	4,324,768	5,165,850	5,436,547	5,335,049	—	—	—	—	—

[1] Includes estimated data for subfunctions of food services and enterprise operations.

[2] Includes expenditures for health, attendance, and speech pathology services.

[3] Includes expenditures for curriculum development, staff training, libraries, and media and computer centers.

[4] Includes expenditures for operations funded by sales of products or services (e.g., school bookstore or computer time).

[5] Includes expenditures for property, and for buildings and alterations completed by school district staff or contractors.

— Data not available or not applicable.

NOTE.—Excludes expenditures for state education agencies. Some data have been revised from previously published figures. Because of rounding, details may not add to totals.

SOURCE: U.S. Department of Education, National Center for Education Statistics, Common Core of Data survey. (This table was prepared June 1996.)

Table 161.—Expenditures for instruction in public elementary and secondary schools, by subfunction and state: 1992–93 and 1993–94

[In thousands of dollars]

State or other area	1992–93						1993–94 [1]					
	Total	Salaries	Employee benefits	Purchased services [2]	Supplies	Tuition and other	Total	Salaries	Employee benefits	Purchased services [2]	Supplies	Tuition and other
1	2	3	4	5	6	7	8	9	10	11	12	13
United States	$134,971,088	$99,089,718	$26,075,723	$3,357,323	$5,052,972	$1,395,352	$141,598,786	$103,506,260	$27,456,160	$3,421,363	$5,486,107	$1,728,895
Alabama	1,623,693	1,220,956	299,686	5,253	81,135	16,663	1,757,077	1,329,103	317,861	5,505	87,994	16,613
Alaska	495,869	353,602	80,329	19,469	21,389	21,080	517,200	370,381	84,893	20,562	21,311	20,053
Arizona	1,608,982	1,328,278	216,456	13,243	29,130	21,875	1,680,405	1,404,486	207,938	13,704	28,531	25,745
Arkansas	1,069,642	831,953	180,166	16,610	32,636	8,275	1,116,796	862,527	194,647	17,569	32,663	9,390
California	14,515,129	10,314,041	3,127,651	367,576	453,964	251,897	15,028,418	10,535,742	3,275,864	417,732	534,495	264,585
Colorado	1,791,024	1,386,469	276,573	55,063	66,802	6,117	1,815,426	1,403,567	280,586	54,564	69,799	6,909
Connecticut	2,368,777	1,847,591	408,145	36,677	61,827	14,536	2,501,019	1,949,504	435,277	37,744	64,920	13,574
Delaware	375,684	266,006	86,933	5,778	14,588	2,179	399,147	279,411	94,677	6,374	14,897	3,788
District of Columbia	339,266	245,876	72,417	5,415	2,534	13,024	351,028	251,437	73,230	7,967	5,558	12,835
Florida	5,600,755	3,749,838	1,249,289	361,158	188,728	60,742	5,970,755	4,016,237	1,336,262	361,131	196,670	60,455
Georgia	3,324,729	2,439,241	733,270	26,215	122,002	4,001	3,473,765	2,571,602	712,847	33,534	151,782	4,000
Hawaii	580,597	434,573	97,597	18,778	28,332	1,317	615,270	443,179	123,385	19,218	27,938	1,551
Idaho	504,461	368,810	102,409	8,612	24,199	431	543,377	389,041	120,933	8,960	23,999	444
Illinois	5,886,997	4,610,529	841,002	100,960	216,235	118,272	6,064,603	4,697,555	905,583	105,297	235,412	120,755
Indiana	2,984,096	2,224,815	620,270	32,815	99,938	6,258	3,121,188	2,309,246	673,493	32,707	100,174	5,569
Iowa	1,529,933	1,093,206	255,436	72,230	99,755	9,307	1,558,177	1,115,162	263,334	62,452	107,452	9,777
Kansas	1,304,668	1,025,667	194,625	9,999	67,798	6,578	1,345,121	1,069,472	187,192	11,579	71,444	5,434
Kentucky	1,713,287	1,378,010	272,907	76	62,282	12	1,768,253	1,427,161	269,831	88	71,153	20
Louisiana	1,906,733	1,428,493	384,409	11,134	78,137	4,561	1,967,293	1,459,276	403,272	16,167	84,227	4,352
Maine	807,161	535,747	181,816	20,846	26,217	42,535	808,608	550,050	166,324	22,399	26,660	43,175
Maryland	2,772,443	1,926,293	629,165	67,309	78,095	71,581	2,890,971	1,992,724	658,203	73,927	80,822	85,294
Massachusetts	3,239,997	2,348,009	360,063	267,342	90,522	174,061	3,398,730	2,461,875	385,677	267,298	98,610	185,269
Michigan	5,535,516	4,001,460	1,247,306	70,841	196,417	19,491	5,691,574	4,139,256	1,259,843	77,832	193,110	21,533
Minnesota	2,646,040	1,962,920	506,526	65,704	93,979	16,910	2,757,594	2,033,003	538,195	68,805	98,115	19,476
Mississippi	997,074	768,952	139,823	18,913	64,694	4,691	1,066,080	821,115	166,575	16,477	56,697	5,215
Missouri	2,253,749	1,725,911	298,765	42,674	179,470	6,929	2,415,629	1,840,689	329,085	43,996	191,915	9,944
Montana	487,327	351,786	91,149	10,588	29,921	3,884	514,036	369,489	97,938	13,156	31,205	2,247
Nebraska	885,848	652,273	157,657	20,111	34,670	21,137	941,383	700,528	159,734	21,827	37,875	21,419
Nevada	612,677	463,075	122,885	3,342	22,181	1,194	654,369	491,250	132,187	4,662	25,270	1,000
New Hampshire	623,564	450,309	96,505	13,621	20,261	42,868	646,681	467,975	100,808	13,691	21,158	43,050
New Jersey	5,851,174	4,320,192	1,213,042	58,256	206,702	52,989	6,260,952	4,527,397	1,183,042	45,473	212,716	292,324
New Mexico	727,371	539,987	139,341	5,708	38,193	4,141	775,050	570,209	148,257	7,981	43,549	5,054
New York	14,035,286	10,333,111	3,058,003	312,409	329,471	2,292	14,884,460	10,895,343	3,302,335	340,172	344,180	2,429
North Carolina	3,037,814	2,281,597	565,384	46,057	142,129	2,646	3,161,009	2,383,123	588,767	45,782	140,203	3,134
North Dakota	312,211	229,288	56,720	8,496	15,745	1,962	320,294	234,827	58,894	8,274	15,493	2,806
Ohio	5,438,553	3,978,860	1,096,231	84,980	208,569	69,913	5,717,214	4,170,324	1,158,036	94,873	224,924	69,057
Oklahoma	1,440,157	1,113,925	253,374	15,875	55,578	1,405	1,551,744	1,200,477	269,527	19,727	60,372	1,641
Oregon	1,701,141	1,115,174	426,688	56,660	93,322	9,296	1,708,679	1,133,552	427,436	50,290	88,577	8,823
Pennsylvania	6,956,917	4,594,521	1,617,909	467,682	202,715	74,090	7,144,739	4,753,300	1,609,574	479,975	212,470	89,420
Rhode Island	626,154	438,409	137,202	16,267	13,398	20,877	659,748	461,270	147,798	16,235	13,146	21,300
South Carolina	1,594,927	1,215,329	294,545	19,625	63,436	1,992	1,651,858	1,251,017	312,363	22,422	64,858	1,197
South Dakota	339,207	246,661	52,636	9,626	21,197	9,088	360,621	262,590	57,153	10,549	20,787	9,542
Tennessee	1,907,690	1,465,522	208,744	154,825	72,349	6,251	2,125,274	1,635,375	372,014	39,428	72,376	6,080
Texas	8,890,632	7,055,521	1,114,660	119,715	566,819	33,917	9,602,153	7,492,386	1,197,000	156,463	719,546	36,758
Utah	910,053	624,019	215,723	15,134	40,748	14,428	1,013,630	662,696	230,024	14,387	47,072	59,451
Vermont	400,053	282,529	74,541	14,224	12,489	16,269	419,909	295,898	79,058	14,198	12,934	17,822
Virginia	3,121,272	2,352,245	595,672	39,849	105,942	27,564	3,275,030	2,487,274	621,527	43,510	117,838	4,881
Washington	2,800,233	2,005,997	591,742	76,485	105,406	20,603	2,921,122	2,066,990	639,335	85,052	109,654	20,091
West Virginia	1,007,685	713,453	247,803	8,270	36,601	1,559	1,034,956	723,919	262,282	10,065	38,524	166
Wisconsin	3,143,002	2,208,288	720,016	47,589	116,900	50,209	3,285,249	2,300,226	768,388	49,266	115,175	52,194
Wyoming	334,840	240,201	64,524	11,238	17,425	1,453	345,120	246,023	67,675	10,316	19,854	1,252
Outlying areas												
American Samoa	10,792	8,654	1,342	202	444	150	11,582	8,612	1,336	316	1,090	229
Guam	69,877	58,419	10,119	606	483	251	86,713	72,705	13,292	75	385	255
Northern Marianas	28,814	19,775	4,501	2,094	2,381	63	29,959	19,199	4,620	2,234	3,660	247
Puerto Rico	895,535	743,954	108,074	8,861	6,761	27,886	972,817	798,483	114,161	9,683	20,961	29,529
Virgin Islands	68,564	55,151	10,791	516	596	1,510	68,548	55,140	10,763	525	604	1,515

[1] Preliminary data.
[2] Includes purchased professional services for teachers or others who provide instruction to students and travel for instructional staff.

NOTE.—Excludes expenditures for state education agencies. Because of rounding, details may not add to totals. Some 1992–93 data have been revised from previously published figures.

SOURCE: U.S. Department of Education, National Center for Education Statistics, Common Core of Data surveys. (This table was prepared May 1996.)

Table 162.—Current expenditures for public elementary and secondary education, by state: 1959–60 to 1995–96

[In thousands of dollars]

State or other area	1959–60	1969–70	1979–80	1980–81	1984–85	1985–86	1986–87	1987–88
1	2	3	4	5	6	7	8	9
United States	$12,329,389	$34,217,773	$86,984,142	$94,321,093	$126,337,491	$137,164,965	$146,364,922	$157,097,951
Alabama	171,130	422,730	1,146,713	1,393,137	1,590,856	1,761,154	1,775,997	1,873,390
Alaska	20,641	81,374	377,947	476,368	754,967	818,219	769,015	756,577
Arizona	104,054	281,941	949,753	1,075,362	1,436,844	1,649,832	1,836,908	2,002,395
Arkansas	83,896	235,083	666,949	709,394	1,005,347	1,085,943	1,118,904	1,211,156
California	6 1,481,908	3,831,595	9,172,158	9,936,642	13,477,768	15,040,898	16,512,668	17,402,063
Colorado	136,760	369,218	1,243,049	1,369,883	1,868,058	2,018,579	2,129,964	2,172,563
Connecticut	185,336	588,710	1,227,892	1,440,881	2,117,798	2,144,094	2,414,708	2,748,567
Delaware	33,425	108,747	269,108	270,439	353,191	391,558	418,116	440,631
District of Columbia	45,617	141,138	298,448	295,155	387,918	406,910	441,135	489,357
Florida	276,506	961,273	2,766,468	3,336,657	4,589,068	5,092,668	5,650,083	6,288,977
Georgia	208,096	599,371	1,608,028	1,688,714	2,629,681	2,979,980	3,254,786	3,549,038
Hawaii	42,499	141,324	351,889	395,038	521,692	575,456	576,749	608,264
Idaho	42,719	103,107	313,927	352,912	467,532	492,092	513,011	532,274
Illinois	663,849	1,896,067	4,579,355	4,773,179	5,662,354	6,066,390	6,463,564	6,923,298
Indiana	318,073	809,105	1,851,292	1,898,194	2,696,072	2,851,080	3,106,616	3,330,525
Iowa	197,768	527,086	1,186,659	1,337,504	1,599,674	1,644,359	1,708,440	1,859,173
Kansas	153,346	362,593	830,133	958,281	1,315,469	1,423,225	1,486,814	1,568,041
Kentucky	132,068	353,265	1,054,459	1,096,472	1,384,722	1,434,962	1,583,158	1,741,799
Louisiana	230,402	503,217	1,303,902	1,767,692	2,191,478	2,333,748	2,260,393	2,289,241
Maine	51,465	155,907	385,492	401,355	599,189	688,673	760,446	839,860
Maryland	209,606	721,794	1,783,056	1,937,159	2,446,771	2,634,209	2,845,404	3,128,165
Massachusetts	324,408	907,341	2,638,734	2,794,762	3,139,486	3,403,505	3,744,131	4,098,062
Michigan	605,048	1,799,945	4,642,847	5,196,249	5,735,303	6,184,767	6,427,556	6,913,261
Minnesota	267,376	781,243	1,786,768	1,900,322	2,461,571	2,637,722	2,818,390	2,981,209
Mississippi	100,020	262,760	756,018	716,878	1,023,720	1,058,301	1,112,535	1,221,560
Missouri	242,447	642,030	1,504,988	1,643,258	2,106,539	2,277,576	2,515,846	2,747,234
Montana	54,079	127,176	358,118	380,092	538,245	567,901	583,861	590,226
Nebraska	87,692	231,612	581,615	629,017	870,019	911,983	948,149	995,235
Nevada	23,770	87,273	281,901	287,752	397,254	495,147	513,014	555,272
New Hampshire	33,185	101,370	295,400	340,518	473,151	522,604	589,850	677,507
New Jersey	459,413	1,343,564	3,638,533	3,648,914	4,697,534	5,735,895	6,099,473	6,621,860
New Mexico	73,396	183,736	515,451	560,213	784,442	808,036	865,789	916,305
New York	1,383,706	4,111,839	8,760,500	9,259,948	12,681,301	13,686,039	14,724,687	16,073,392
North Carolina	238,059	676,193	1,880,862	2,112,417	2,674,774	2,991,747	3,193,337	3,424,194
North Dakota	46,254	97,895	228,483	254,197	365,341	379,470	374,941	385,427
Ohio	632,932	1,639,805	3,836,576	4,149,858	5,504,161	5,856,999	6,114,426	6,446,903
Oklahoma	151,181	339,105	1,055,844	1,193,373	1,575,467	1,740,981	1,707,396	1,692,283
Oregon	154,691	403,844	1,126,812	1,292,624	1,560,242	1,662,372	1,747,125	1,944,657
Pennsylvania	732,486	1,912,644	4,584,320	4,955,115	6,660,369	6,750,520	7,176,886	7,679,986
Rhode Island	48,686	145,443	362,046	395,389	525,824	569,935	608,318	663,800
South Carolina	116,939	367,689	997,984	1,006,088	1,556,552	1,708,603	1,814,160	1,932,502
South Dakota	47,899	109,375	238,332	242,215	338,800	360,832	368,266	389,436
Tennessee	175,152	473,226	1,319,303	1,429,938	1,836,012	1,990,889	2,167,026	2,352,183
Texas	605,577	1,518,181	4,997,689	5,310,181	8,996,476	9,642,812	10,152,521	10,791,854
Utah	69,755	179,981	518,251	587,648	813,817	906,484	932,740	974,666
Vermont	24,132	78,921	189,811	224,901	313,026	346,164	378,264	456,992
Virginia	207,399	704,677	1,881,519	2,045,412	2,845,540	3,183,707	3,444,952	3,793,475
Washington	239,069	699,984	1,825,782	1,791,477	2,565,957	2,702,652	2,808,636	3,005,980
West Virginia	108,673	249,404	678,386	754,889	1,090,514	1,164,882	1,229,069	1,231,966
Wisconsin	254,626	777,288	1,908,523	2,035,879	2,655,729	2,893,797	3,086,878	3,318,247
Wyoming	32,175	69,584	226,067	271,153	453,874	488,616	489,825	466,921
Outlying areas								
American Samoa	308	—	—	—	13,348	14,997	19,497	20,186
Guam	3,020	16,652	—	—	58,815	78,545	78,278	76,359
Northern Marianas	—	—	—	—	9,394	12,556	15,714	19,694
Puerto Rico	54,375	—	—	713,000	856,743	842,827	872,050	935,392
Virgin Islands	1,662	—	—	—	—	76,751	97,585	89,217

Table 162.—Current expenditures for public elementary and secondary education, by state: 1959–60 to 1995–96—Continued

[In thousands of dollars]

State or other area	1988–89	1989–90	1990–91	1991–92	1992–93 [1]	1993–94	Estimated 1994–95 [2]	Estimated 1995–96 [2]
1	10	11	12	13	14	15	16	17
United States	**$173,098,906**	**$187,932,903**	**$202,037,752**	**$211,221,254**	**$220,948,052**	**$231,521,500**	**[3] $243,868,127**	**[3] $256,277,029**
Alabama	2,188,020	2,275,233	2,475,216	2,465,523	2,610,514	2,809,713	3,033,517	3,162,102
Alaska	739,020	828,051	854,499	931,869	967,765	1,002,515	1,138,698	1,172,859
Arizona	2,143,148	2,258,653	2,469,543	2,599,587	2,753,504	2,911,304	[4] 3,113,562	[4] 3,393,612
Arkansas	1,319,370	1,404,621	1,510,092	1,656,201	1,703,621	1,782,645	[5] 1,428,006	1,496,991
California	19,417,178	21,485,782	22,748,218	23,696,863	24,219,792	25,140,639	25,385,376	26,841,563
Colorado	2,324,625	2,451,831	2,642,850	2,754,087	2,919,916	2,954,793	3,267,129	3,337,590
Connecticut	2,984,542	3,404,429	3,540,411	3,667,337	3,739,497	3,943,894	3,944,000	4,094,000
Delaware	479,327	520,953	543,933	572,180	600,161	643,915	[5] 708,587	753,140
District of Columbia	584,035	632,458	647,901	677,429	670,677	713,427	[5] 600,000	503,270
Florida	7,245,515	8,228,531	9,045,710	9,314,079	9,661,012	10,331,896	11,017,448	11,766,634
Georgia	4,006,069	4,505,964	4,804,225	4,856,583	5,273,143	5,643,843	[5] 5,839,532	6,271,020
Hawaii	643,319	700,012	827,579	884,591	946,074	998,143	807,600	807,600
Idaho	570,013	627,794	708,045	760,440	804,231	859,088	[5] 975,377	1,030,852
Illinois	7,655,153	8,125,493	8,932,538	9,244,655	9,942,737	10,076,889	10,115,618	10,419,087
Indiana	3,779,468	4,024,098	4,379,142	4,544,829	4,797,946	5,064,685	5,369,000	5,670,000
Iowa	1,925,623	2,004,742	2,136,561	2,356,196	2,459,141	2,527,434	2,608,312	2,728,295
Kansas	1,712,260	1,848,302	1,938,012	2,028,440	2,224,080	2,325,247	[5] 2,464,762	2,588,000
Kentucky	1,918,741	2,134,011	2,480,363	2,709,623	2,823,134	2,952,119	3,507,422	3,682,793
Louisiana	2,468,307	2,802,793	3,023,690	3,189,111	3,199,919	3,309,020	[5] 3,396,986	3,498,896
Maine	921,931	1,048,195	1,070,965	1,121,360	1,217,418	1,208,411	1,244,663	1,282,003
Maryland	3,505,018	3,845,123	4,240,862	4,362,679	4,556,266	4,783,023	4,841,587	5,238,478
Massachusetts	4,516,604	4,760,390	4,906,828	5,035,973	5,281,067	5,637,337	[5] 5,902,161	[6] 6,301,849
Michigan	7,492,267	8,025,621	8,545,805	9,156,501	9,532,994	9,816,830	[5] 9,858,879	10,139,857
Minnesota	3,282,296	3,474,398	3,740,820	3,936,695	4,135,284	4,328,093	5,674,605	5,788,097
Mississippi	1,365,846	1,472,710	1,510,552	1,536,295	1,600,752	1,725,386	[5] 1,918,704	2,014,640
Missouri	3,096,666	3,288,738	3,487,786	3,611,613	3,710,426	3,981,614	[5] 3,859,820	3,878,740
Montana	592,454	641,345	719,963	751,710	785,159	822,015	892,000	909,000
Nebraska	1,105,009	1,233,622	1,297,643	1,381,290	1,430,039	1,513,971	1,440,613	1,498,238
Nevada	628,657	712,898	864,379	962,800	1,035,623	1,099,058	1,155,284	1,247,498
New Hampshire	733,240	821,671	890,116	927,625	972,963	1,007,129	1,130,509	1,195,272
New Jersey	7,309,147	8,119,069	8,897,612	9,664,774	9,915,482	10,448,096	[4] 10,958,706	[4] 11,719,887
New Mexico	975,552	1,020,148	1,134,156	1,212,189	1,240,310	1,323,459	[5] 1,695,385	2,064,854
New York	17,127,596	18,090,978	19,514,583	19,781,384	20,898,267	22,059,949	23,295,441	24,599,986
North Carolina	3,892,971	4,288,474	4,605,384	4,661,685	4,930,823	5,145,420	6,015,627	6,113,959
North Dakota	431,814	459,391	460,581	491,293	511,095	522,377	[5] 540,858	551,675
Ohio	7,484,434	7,994,379	8,407,428	9,124,731	9,173,393	9,612,678	[5] 9,865,665	10,260,291
Oklahoma	1,833,743	1,905,332	2,107,513	2,269,776	2,442,320	2,659,460	[5] 2,330,640	2,330,640
Oregon	2,123,241	2,297,944	2,453,934	2,626,803	2,849,009	2,852,723	2,878,000	3,028,000
Pennsylvania	8,579,546	9,496,788	10,087,322	10,371,796	10,944,392	11,236,417	12,071,000	12,916,000
Rhode Island	747,852	801,908	823,655	865,898	934,815	990,094	[5] 1,036,310	1,098,489
South Carolina	2,118,732	2,322,432	2,494,254	2,564,949	2,690,009	2,790,878	2,855,665	2,969,891
South Dakota	428,014	447,068	481,304	518,156	553,005	584,894	[5] 618,003	658,049
Tennessee	2,668,341	2,790,808	2,903,209	2,859,755	3,139,223	3,305,579	3,613,357	3,763,490
Texas	11,761,447	12,764,500	13,695,327	14,709,628	15,121,655	16,193,722	[5] 18,372,926	19,329,702
Utah	1,043,759	1,130,135	1,235,916	1,296,723	1,376,319	1,511,205	[5] 1,623,404	1,738,206
Vermont	485,226	546,901	599,018	606,410	616,212	643,828	[5] 663,683	682,266
Virginia	4,151,050	4,561,874	4,958,213	4,995,270	5,228,326	5,441,388	[4] 5,598,800	5,957,049
Washington	3,209,992	3,550,672	3,906,471	4,259,021	4,679,698	4,892,690	[5] 5,368,469	5,584,535
West Virginia	1,202,486	1,316,637	1,473,640	1,503,977	1,626,005	1,663,868	[5] 1,783,129	1,863,370
Wisconsin	3,688,311	3,929,920	4,292,434	4,597,004	4,954,900	5,170,343	5,460,916	5,754,714
Wyoming	491,930	509,084	521,549	545,870	547,938	558,353	[5] 582,386	580,000
Outlying areas								
American Samoa	22,314	21,838	24,946	26,972	23,636	25,161	[4] 25,801	[4] 26,983
Guam	94,368	106,033	116,406	132,494	161,477	164,187	[4] 175,729	[4] 191,809
Northern Marianas	16,118	20,476	26,822	32,498	38,784	39,675	[5] 41,125	[5] 41,125
Puerto Rico	1,030,387	1,045,407	1,142,863	1,207,235	1,295,452	1,420,580	1,679,009	1,679,009
Virgin Islands	111,750	128,065	119,950	121,660	120,510	120,617	120,617	141,706

[1] Data revised from previously published figures.

[2] Data estimated by state education agencies.

[3] U.S. total includes National Center for Education Statistics estimates for nonreporting states.

[4] Estimated by the National Center for Education Statistics.

[5] Actual count.

[6] Includes an estimated $144,942,000 for summer schools, adult education, and community colleges.

NOTE.—Beginning in 1980–81, expenditures for state administration are excluded. Because of rounding, details may not add to totals.

SOURCE: U.S. Department of Education, National Center for Education Statistics, *Statistics of State School Systems;* and Common Core of Data surveys. (This table was prepared June 1996.)

Table 163.—Total expenditures for public elementary and secondary education, by function and state: 1993–94

[In thousands]

State or other area	Total expenditures							
	Total	Current expenditures for elementary and secondary programs						
		Current expenditures for public schools	Instruction	Student services				
				Total	Students [2]	Instructional [3]	General administration	School administration
1	2	3	4	5	6	7	8	9
United States	**$265,285,370**	**$231,521,500**	**$141,598,786**	**$79,406,683**	**$10,946,239**	**$9,236,617**	**$5,909,737**	**$13,492,581**
Alabama	3,140,345	2,809,713	1,757,077	830,470	92,628	93,780	63,555	163,638
Alaska	1,136,211	1,002,515	517,200	454,317	102,311	54,248	58,091	60,274
Arizona	3,820,218	2,911,304	1,680,405	1,040,554	125,023	96,949	117,957	157,368
Arkansas	1,990,699	1,782,645	1,116,796	544,702	71,860	69,270	56,068	101,813
California	28,680,918	25,140,639	15,028,418	9,061,351	1,313,791	1,119,247	153,833	1,955,639
Colorado	3,648,423	2,954,793	1,815,426	1,028,399	129,829	96,792	92,901	196,540
Connecticut	4,224,273	3,943,894	2,501,019	1,253,016	198,821	116,173	80,424	211,033
Delaware	725,346	643,915	399,147	217,672	31,874	9,269	7,770	37,608
District of Columbia	748,228	713,427	351,028	332,951	66,083	35,503	29,120	37,893
Florida	12,724,793	10,331,896	5,970,755	3,856,344	458,470	579,523	116,306	704,821
Georgia	6,685,598	5,643,843	3,473,765	1,823,252	209,112	287,043	89,073	356,813
Hawaii	1,174,178	998,143	615,270	322,735	56,024	46,622	8,321	59,276
Idaho	977,726	859,088	543,377	273,726	40,615	25,725	20,973	50,263
Illinois	11,116,627	10,076,889	6,064,603	3,670,213	554,917	390,663	327,040	536,535
Indiana	6,010,771	5,064,685	3,121,188	1,721,595	208,933	144,927	95,039	276,985
Iowa	2,768,958	2,527,434	1,558,177	855,845	81,997	196,920	92,303	129,257
Kansas	2,553,527	2,325,247	1,345,121	865,968	116,836	91,872	90,459	154,565
Kentucky	3,189,586	2,952,119	1,768,253	1,029,693	112,570	93,476	113,005	189,674
Louisiana	3,610,627	3,309,020	1,967,293	1,044,538	119,028	128,684	75,256	181,027
Maine	1,327,718	1,208,411	808,608	355,651	34,478	33,285	23,648	67,802
Maryland	5,240,357	4,783,023	2,890,971	1,649,605	179,302	207,282	27,162	359,987
Massachusetts	5,822,837	5,637,337	3,398,730	2,042,430	252,617	173,536	451,396	243,151
Michigan	11,410,269	9,816,830	5,691,574	3,839,812	641,895	435,048	207,455	622,566
Minnesota	5,352,068	4,328,093	2,757,594	1,395,507	131,930	202,263	104,434	201,957
Mississippi	1,928,072	1,725,386	1,066,080	521,331	60,017	63,291	59,269	93,119
Missouri	4,601,996	3,981,614	2,415,629	1,389,998	158,051	160,103	126,432	233,880
Montana	898,790	822,015	514,036	273,001	35,340	26,517	28,945	43,460
Nebraska	1,709,853	1,513,971	941,383	443,860	57,153	49,708	56,920	76,189
Nevada	1,345,394	1,099,058	654,369	407,307	39,699	34,083	18,682	78,997
New Hampshire	1,071,273	1,007,129	646,681	324,847	53,290	28,760	36,194	57,490
New Jersey	11,324,207	10,448,096	6,260,952	3,852,523	681,251	344,008	321,334	603,959
New Mexico	1,515,025	1,323,459	775,050	471,933	93,399	64,781	34,966	47,405
New York	24,980,871	22,059,949	14,884,460	6,549,494	875,668	477,834	518,700	929,531
North Carolina	5,844,299	5,145,420	3,161,009	1,592,366	244,921	196,158	104,393	336,188
North Dakota	585,115	522,377	320,294	157,071	15,435	10,396	26,899	23,781
Ohio	11,067,854	9,612,678	5,717,214	3,540,689	461,622	451,671	273,479	574,627
Oklahoma	2,874,700	2,659,460	1,551,744	884,472	119,030	79,164	110,220	149,531
Oregon	3,160,049	2,852,723	1,708,679	1,047,136	143,722	137,178	61,734	185,260
Pennsylvania	12,679,566	11,236,417	7,144,739	3,664,768	500,757	345,105	313,539	522,116
Rhode Island	1,028,196	990,094	659,748	304,999	56,472	36,676	21,883	48,212
South Carolina	3,182,916	2,790,878	1,651,858	963,310	187,650	150,825	51,899	177,589
South Dakota	665,531	584,894	360,621	191,974	23,651	19,941	17,913	33,804
Tennessee	3,686,856	3,305,579	2,125,274	998,576	94,205	166,326	79,312	183,930
Texas	19,918,597	16,193,722	9,602,153	5,620,902	765,429	769,606	706,820	929,964
Utah	1,848,240	1,511,205	1,013,630	405,340	41,501	55,714	15,212	84,626
Vermont	717,553	643,828	419,909	202,607	37,508	19,656	19,195	42,195
Virginia	6,276,207	5,441,388	3,275,030	1,883,594	263,523	281,134	67,118	330,525
Washington	5,960,965	4,892,690	2,921,122	1,745,781	303,844	235,649	131,373	245,833
West Virginia	1,864,725	1,663,868	1,034,956	534,640	52,898	45,415	43,133	98,841
Wisconsin	5,848,843	5,170,343	3,285,249	1,730,242	217,354	242,137	150,022	270,778
Wyoming	619,376	558,353	345,120	193,577	31,903	16,681	12,561	34,263
Outlying areas								
American Samoa	31,145	25,161	11,582	10,792	3,416	2,084	440	1,523
Guam	165,099	164,187	86,713	65,406	14,999	4,509	2,494	7,453
Northern Marianas	41,513	39,675	29,959	6,851	0	0	0	0
Puerto Rico	1,456,393	1,420,580	972,817	263,873	26,763	0	88,311	12,653
Virgin Islands	147,011	120,617	68,548	45,795	6,143	7,653	9,204	6,797

Table 163.—Total expenditures for public elementary and secondary education, by function and state: 1993–94—Continued

[In thousands]

State or other area	Total expenditures							
	Current expenditures for elementary and secondary programs					Other current expenditures [1]	Capital outlay	Interest on school debt
	Student services			Food services	Enterprise operations [4]			
	Operation and maintenance	Student transportation	Other support services					
1	10	11	12	13	14	15	16	17
United States	$23,875,985	$9,627,190	$6,318,335	$9,774,315	$741,715	$4,681,799	$23,747,022	$5,335,049
Alabama	247,788	113,563	55,519	222,166	0	49,200	239,011	42,422
Alaska	143,230	33,915	2,247	26,588	4,409	5,572	97,445	30,679
Arizona	333,866	114,757	94,633	156,046	34,299	19,447	710,338	179,130
Arkansas	156,121	67,042	22,529	108,229	12,917	10,176	155,652	42,226
California	2,658,782	727,000	1,133,059	1,047,490	3,380	476,340	2,978,644	85,294
Colorado	275,311	87,611	149,415	106,200	4,769	10,271	383,288	300,070
Connecticut	385,815	173,332	87,419	108,541	81,318	122,649	60,726	97,004
Delaware	61,115	38,241	31,796	27,095	0	18,496	55,794	7,140
District of Columbia ...	122,422	15,810	26,120	27,735	1,713	6,045	22,589	6,167
Florida	1,239,701	427,224	330,297	504,797	0	381,405	1,775,752	235,740
Georgia	514,002	217,646	149,563	343,116	3,710	234,256	722,879	84,621
Hawaii	107,415	20,557	24,521	60,138	0	33,528	114,779	27,728
Idaho	81,687	41,006	13,457	41,985	0	1,489	99,974	17,174
Illinois	1,116,712	464,380	279,965	342,073	0	93,801	692,578	253,360
Indiana	568,362	284,551	142,797	221,901	0	38,286	563,058	344,742
Iowa	226,133	80,523	48,712	105,535	7,877	14,607	195,171	31,746
Kansas	271,427	96,045	44,764	114,158	0	3,117	181,352	43,811
Kentucky	307,320	174,751	38,896	154,173	0	6,761	170,264	60,442
Louisiana	295,414	191,596	53,533	253,175	44,014	20,720	197,619	83,268
Maine	116,695	58,810	20,933	44,101	51	13,973	72,127	33,207
Maryland	524,649	258,431	92,792	161,420	81,028	26,751	382,831	47,752
Massachusetts	569,361	237,490	114,879	181,654	14,523	45,279	42,055	98,166
Michigan	1,099,403	429,437	404,009	285,444	0	402,149	865,393	325,897
Minnesota	360,097	232,303	162,521	174,993	0	187,876	699,746	136,353
Mississippi	150,559	69,814	25,261	137,010	966	10,673	161,552	30,461
Missouri	388,138	243,243	80,151	175,987	0	65,905	444,127	110,349
Montana	85,088	36,323	17,328	34,687	291	4,026	59,778	12,972
Nebraska	134,511	44,734	24,645	57,910	70,818	2,381	165,295	28,207
Nevada	117,104	46,788	71,954	37,382	0	7,653	184,464	54,219
New Hampshire	92,694	47,086	9,334	35,601	0	5,016	34,262	24,865
New Jersey	1,177,387	508,433	216,150	301,037	33,584	153,411	604,357	118,343
New Mexico	145,044	69,160	17,179	68,610	7,865	6,045	165,597	19,925
New York	2,053,189	1,186,347	508,224	625,996	0	861,366	1,598,019	461,537
North Carolina	438,048	183,532	89,125	332,545	59,500	30,251	535,061	133,566
North Dakota	46,234	23,862	10,464	27,015	17,997	2,638	51,684	8,416
Ohio	958,447	255,039	565,803	352,451	2,326	642,813	662,350	150,013
Oklahoma	282,874	88,957	54,695	141,204	82,040	7,353	189,791	18,095
Oregon	274,914	115,801	128,527	94,822	2,087	9,189	243,419	54,719
Pennsylvania	1,185,990	519,714	277,546	421,528	5,382	268,369	941,072	233,708
Rhode Island	86,555	43,882	11,319	25,346	0	6,324	15,285	16,493
South Carolina	251,875	82,780	60,692	167,239	8,471	51,268	258,683	82,086
South Dakota	58,480	24,295	13,889	31,071	1,228	1,134	64,254	15,249
Tennessee	316,043	122,434	36,324	181,729	0	13,993	287,270	80,015
Texas	1,841,570	480,076	127,437	967,578	3,088	65,937	3,123,644	535,294
Utah	139,647	42,932	25,707	88,117	4,117	44,324	247,982	44,729
Vermont	53,629	20,491	9,932	18,734	2,578	3,515	61,388	8,823
Virginia	597,978	239,101	104,216	207,043	75,721	100,079	606,991	127,749
Washington	510,994	200,251	117,836	156,434	69,353	22,535	844,008	201,731
West Virginia	167,345	105,943	21,064	93,977	294	26,439	160,754	13,664
Wisconsin	476,128	218,358	155,466	154,852	0	45,467	508,229	124,803
Wyoming	62,690	21,791	13,687	19,655	0	1,501	48,644	10,878
Outlying areas								
American Samoa	1,405	849	1,075	2,787	0	2,362	3,622	0
Guam	16,935	10,903	8,113	8,677	3,390	912	0	0
Northern Marianas	0	0	6,851	2,865	0	498	1,340	0
Puerto Rico	39,147	36,582	60,417	183,890	0	15,744	20,069	0
Virgin Islands	7,014	3,209	5,774	6,213	61	1,481	24,914	0

[1] Includes expenditures for adult education, community colleges, private school programs funded by local and state education agencies, and community services.

[2] Includes expenditures for health, attendance, and speech pathology services.

[3] Includes expenditures for curriculum development, staff training, libraries, and media and computer centers.

[4] Includes expenditures for operations funded by sales of products or services (e.g., school bookstore or computer time).

NOTE.—Excludes expenditures for state education agencies. Because of rounding, details may not add to totals.

SOURCE: U.S. Department of Education, National Center for Education Statistics, Common Core of Data survey. (This table was prepared May 1996.)

Table 164.—Total expenditures for public elementary and secondary education, by function and state: 1992–93

[In thousands]

State or other area	Total expenditures							
		Current expenditures for elementary and secondary programs						
	Total	Current expenditures for public schools	Instruction	Student services				
				Total	Students [2]	Instructional [3]	General administration	School administration
1	2	3	4	5	6	7	8	9
United States	$252,934,872	$220,948,052	$134,971,088	$75,915,646	$9,760,087	$9,241,929	$5,851,983	$12,777,815
Alabama	2,915,655	2,610,514	1,623,693	773,464	87,366	86,788	63,036	150,602
Alaska	1,097,909	967,765	495,869	441,461	97,054	50,492	59,142	58,432
Arizona	3,632,089	2,753,504	1,608,982	989,791	114,073	95,555	116,680	149,824
Arkansas	1,898,548	1,703,621	1,069,642	519,521	67,792	67,346	52,761	97,407
California	26,990,569	24,219,792	14,515,129	8,693,446	1,246,422	1,059,248	147,393	1,866,020
Colorado	3,543,846	2,919,916	1,791,024	1,022,879	121,356	101,198	100,691	193,386
Connecticut	3,997,733	3,739,497	2,368,777	1,220,894	207,399	111,435	77,976	204,851
Delaware	670,147	600,161	375,684	202,360	27,924	8,643	7,773	34,812
District of Columbia ...	727,525	670,677	339,266	302,282	58,319	30,681	30,872	34,057
Florida	11,694,573	9,661,012	5,609,755	3,566,770	428,607	528,175	130,282	664,988
Georgia	6,108,216	5,273,143	3,324,729	1,630,161	182,533	251,044	83,256	321,169
Hawaii	1,087,683	946,074	580,597	304,362	54,159	40,745	8,119	54,350
Idaho	903,040	804,231	504,461	260,672	37,051	24,502	22,950	47,873
Illinois	10,976,188	9,942,737	5,886,997	3,695,515	534,742	356,710	290,981	515,804
Indiana	5,613,875	4,797,946	2,984,096	1,598,786	197,079	136,164	88,408	264,241
Iowa	2,692,069	2,459,141	1,529,933	820,898	76,892	187,886	86,256	122,337
Kansas	2,468,279	2,224,080	1,304,668	816,085	109,169	86,060	86,501	141,011
Kentucky	3,060,263	2,823,134	1,713,287	968,536	100,677	89,808	105,104	180,566
Louisiana	3,497,435	3,199,919	1,906,733	1,007,563	112,580	121,832	81,771	174,447
Maine	1,316,834	1,217,418	807,161	366,169	34,012	32,775	23,547	67,907
Maryland	4,948,882	4,556,266	2,772,443	1,561,968	167,925	200,624	24,240	324,479
Massachusetts	5,472,560	5,281,067	3,239,997	1,868,806	225,205	161,142	348,585	227,194
Michigan	11,273,173	9,532,994	5,535,516	3,722,486	622,004	420,455	212,200	604,814
Minnesota	5,057,306	4,135,284	2,646,040	1,323,114	125,533	193,236	101,170	196,051
Mississippi	1,771,848	1,600,752	997,074	472,867	53,349	58,424	55,473	84,704
Missouri	4,289,248	3,710,426	2,253,749	1,292,890	144,207	140,200	120,647	219,033
Montana	860,640	785,159	487,327	265,132	32,541	25,378	28,631	42,077
Nebraska	1,586,049	1,430,039	885,848	422,808	52,843	46,547	55,328	74,644
Nevada	1,294,227	1,035,623	612,677	388,280	45,650	32,403	17,753	74,922
New Hampshire	1,043,934	972,963	623,564	315,593	51,365	29,374	35,723	55,426
New Jersey	10,710,608	9,915,482	5,851,174	3,797,394	165,405	752,012	562,957	469,618
New Mexico	1,429,889	1,240,310	727,371	451,556	65,160	105,523	49,054	40,666
New York	23,709,998	20,898,267	14,035,286	6,254,766	812,349	446,333	526,690	878,872
North Carolina	5,779,932	4,930,823	3,037,814	1,509,934	226,610	184,281	100,909	321,316
North Dakota	564,658	511,095	312,211	155,299	14,170	10,346	28,062	23,624
Ohio	10,534,857	9,173,393	5,438,553	3,384,226	431,447	436,528	240,383	557,312
Oklahoma	2,632,696	2,442,320	1,440,157	787,220	105,748	73,492	103,492	143,072
Oregon	3,121,655	2,849,009	1,701,141	1,053,453	136,031	148,805	61,951	183,725
Pennsylvania	12,435,568	10,944,392	6,956,917	3,577,579	498,476	342,764	300,886	518,519
Rhode Island	968,852	934,815	626,154	287,742	51,909	31,741	21,538	44,888
South Carolina	3,052,790	2,690,009	1,594,927	857,238	112,147	147,015	48,326	171,864
South Dakota	619,106	553,005	339,207	182,691	21,840	18,640	17,541	31,775
Tennessee	3,505,845	3,139,223	1,907,690	1,071,652	116,863	150,075	46,978	211,161
Texas	19,192,686	15,121,655	8,890,632	5,248,579	687,962	741,977	654,200	868,640
Utah	1,650,709	1,376,319	910,053	380,212	35,647	51,494	15,596	79,651
Vermont	666,377	616,212	400,053	196,964	35,690	19,224	18,606	40,634
Virginia	5,958,753	5,228,326	3,121,272	1,837,789	253,424	278,275	70,548	319,930
Washington	5,848,627	4,679,698	2,800,233	1,665,971	284,730	232,036	125,951	236,376
West Virginia	1,844,445	1,626,005	1,007,685	523,330	50,505	45,094	38,997	98,899
Wisconsin	5,606,762	4,954,900	3,143,002	1,662,810	205,869	234,106	144,330	255,899
Wyoming	609,717	547,938	334,840	193,622	32,544	17,298	11,738	33,947
Outlying areas								
American Samoa	27,503	23,636	10,792	8,916	2,554	1,386	467	1,610
Guam	186,295	161,477	69,877	76,036	19,263	4,684	6,322	8,571
Northern Marianas	42,774	38,784	28,814	6,777	0	0	0	0
Puerto Rico	1,320,621	1,295,452	895,535	253,659	39,094	0	92,015	5,837
Virgin Islands	139,591	120,510	68,564	45,905	6,140	7,744	9,253	6,858

Table 164.—Total expenditures for public elementary and secondary education, by function and state: 1992–93—Continued

[In thousands]

State or other area	Total expenditures							
	Current expenditures for elementary and secondary programs					Other current expenditures [1]	Capital outlay	Interest on school debt
	Student services			Food services	Enterprise operations [4]			
	Operation and maintenance	Student transportation	Other support services					
1	10	11	12	13	14	15	16	17
United States	$22,823,758	$9,252,300	$6,207,775	$9,263,181	$798,136	$4,378,506	$22,171,768	$5,436,547
Alabama	227,077	106,954	51,641	213,357	0	42,606	207,608	54,926
Alaska	141,442	32,691	2,208	26,281	4,154	5,978	81,731	42,435
Arizona	316,070	107,007	90,582	125,821	28,910	18,532	691,724	168,329
Arkansas	144,125	65,081	25,009	101,443	13,015	9,145	144,012	41,770
California	2,551,495	709,647	1,113,221	1,008,592	2,625	463,528	2,238,315	68,933
Colorado	273,658	90,639	141,950	102,912	3,102	9,397	372,398	242,134
Connecticut	374,490	165,839	78,903	71,702	78,124	118,680	50,886	88,670
Delaware	56,674	36,582	29,951	22,116	0	14,615	49,529	5,842
District of Columbia ...	114,036	13,510	20,806	27,492	1,637	5,645	40,189	11,014
Florida	1,124,811	385,346	304,562	484,487	0	344,125	1,430,981	258,454
Georgia	467,770	197,853	126,536	312,905	5,349	153,162	597,124	84,787
Hawaii	103,341	20,243	23,404	61,115	0	34,614	82,431	24,564
Idaho	79,020	38,753	10,524	39,097	0	1,222	81,511	16,076
Illinois	1,088,552	455,744	453,043	360,165	0	90,978	692,343	250,130
Indiana	539,048	264,354	109,493	215,063	0	37,128	483,802	295,000
Iowa	219,193	84,155	44,179	100,980	7,330	6,333	196,176	30,419
Kansas	261,228	92,880	39,236	103,327	0	2,974	205,927	35,298
Kentucky	288,307	168,348	35,726	141,311	0	5,600	172,938	58,591
Louisiana	282,204	184,084	50,645	243,342	42,281	20,752	173,163	103,600
Maine	123,820	61,252	22,856	44,025	63	13,126	54,515	31,775
Maryland	503,218	249,855	91,627	152,962	68,894	21,205	327,484	43,926
Massachusetts	559,329	224,114	123,238	157,011	15,253	43,596	59,431	88,466
Michigan	1,071,120	422,081	369,811	274,991	0	436,190	933,898	370,092
Minnesota	345,918	223,099	138,108	166,129	0	175,651	622,251	124,120
Mississippi	133,013	64,764	23,140	130,177	634	10,968	130,628	29,501
Missouri	360,106	230,153	78,543	163,786	0	61,384	400,361	117,078
Montana	84,533	35,544	16,427	32,283	417	2,535	61,811	11,135
Nebraska	128,978	42,492	21,976	54,372	67,012	1,601	133,084	21,325
Nevada	109,902	40,236	67,413	34,667	0	7,297	195,957	55,350
New Hampshire	87,858	46,660	9,187	33,806	0	3,076	42,168	25,727
New Jersey	1,165,546	483,412	198,445	266,915	0	138,362	552,556	104,208
New Mexico	121,201	67,891	2,061	60,478	905	4,020	159,550	26,009
New York	1,955,478	1,135,189	499,855	608,215	0	775,817	1,609,676	426,238
North Carolina	421,859	171,475	83,485	318,264	64,811	27,121	495,852	326,136
North Dakota	45,117	23,469	10,511	26,266	17,318	3,048	42,782	7,734
Ohio	919,933	258,123	540,500	349,971	644	614,756	594,693	152,014
Oklahoma	225,144	86,775	49,767	136,038	78,905	3,663	169,870	16,842
Oregon	279,163	109,660	134,117	93,264	1,152	8,465	217,462	46,719
Pennsylvania	1,140,962	499,729	276,243	404,262	5,634	263,227	971,889	256,060
Rhode Island	83,909	42,727	11,031	20,919	0	5,807	13,027	15,203
South Carolina	242,373	79,885	55,628	157,634	80,210	46,498	229,028	87,255
South Dakota	56,727	23,174	12,994	29,835	1,273	1,270	55,483	9,348
Tennessee	326,979	138,584	81,012	159,881	0	25,086	248,900	92,636
Texas	1,738,440	447,197	110,161	919,133	63,311	68,034	3,429,724	573,273
Utah	133,967	40,020	23,836	82,207	3,848	41,872	197,818	34,701
Vermont	51,977	20,848	9,985	17,321	1,874	3,987	38,106	8,072
Virginia	583,456	232,667	99,489	196,231	73,034	95,924	506,710	127,793
Washington	486,465	191,578	108,835	147,298	66,196	18,650	952,030	198,249
West Virginia	164,401	103,030	22,404	94,767	223	25,464	179,865	13,111
Wisconsin	460,073	214,069	148,465	149,088	0	44,220	504,295	103,347
Wyoming	60,249	22,840	15,006	19,476	0	1,573	48,076	12,130
Outlying areas								
American Samoa	1,408	602	888	3,929	0	1,538	2,329	0
Guam	20,048	11,234	5,915	10,007	5,557	943	23,875	0
Northern Marianas	0	0	6,777	3,193	0	168	3,821	0
Puerto Rico	35,179	30,240	51,295	146,258	0	15,029	10,140	0
Virgin Islands	6,994	3,147	5,769	6,010	30	1,550	17,531	0

[1] Includes expenditures for adult education, community colleges, private school programs funded by local and state education agencies, and community services.

[2] Includes expenditures for health, attendance, and speech pathology services.

[3] Includes expenditures for curriculum development, staff training, libraries, and media and computer centers.

[4] Includes expenditures for operations funded by sales of products or services (e.g., school bookstore or computer time).

NOTE.—Some data revised from previously published figures. Excludes expenditures for state education agencies. Because of rounding, details may not add to totals.

SOURCE: U.S. Department of Education, National Center for Education Statistics, Common Core of Data survey. (This table was prepared May 1996.)

Table 165.—Current expenditure per pupil in average daily attendance in public elementary and secondary schools, by state: 1959–60 to 1993–94

State or other area	Unadjusted dollars												
	1959–60	1969–70	1979–80	1980–81	1985–86	1986–87	1987–88	1988–89	1989–90	1990–91	1991–92	1992–93	1993–94
1	2	3	4	5	6	7	8	9	10	11	12	13	14
United States	**$375**	**$816**	**$2,272**	**$2,502**	**$3,756**	**$3,970**	**$4,240**	**$4,645**	**$4,972**	**$5,258**	**$5,421**	**$5,584**	**$5,767**
Alabama	241	544	1,612	1,985	2,565	2,573	2,718	3,197	3,327	3,627	3,616	3,761	4,037
Alaska	546	1,123	4,728	5,688	8,304	8,010	7,971	7,716	8,431	8,330	8,450	8,735	8,882
Arizona	404	720	1,971	2,258	3,336	3,544	3,744	3,902	4,053	4,309	4,381	4,510	4,611
Arkansas	225	568	1,574	1,701	2,658	2,733	2,989	3,273	3,485	3,700	4,031	4,124	4,280
California	[2]424	867	2,268	2,475	3,543	3,728	3,840	4,135	4,391	4,491	4,746	4,780	4,921
Colorado	396	738	2,421	2,693	3,975	4,147	4,220	4,521	4,720	5,064	5,172	5,139	5,097
Connecticut	436	951	2,420	2,876	4,743	5,435	6,230	6,857	7,746	7,853	8,016	7,973	8,473
Delaware	456	900	2,861	3,018	4,610	4,825	5,017	5,422	5,799	5,974	6,093	6,274	6,621
District of Columbia	431	1,018	3,259	3,441	5,337	5,742	6,132	7,850	8,850	9,377	9,549	9,419	10,180
Florida	318	732	1,889	2,401	3,529	3,794	4,092	4,563	4,997	5,276	5,243	5,314	5,516
Georgia	253	588	1,625	1,708	2,966	3,181	3,434	3,852	4,275	4,466	4,419	4,686	4,915
Hawaii	325	841	2,322	2,604	3,807	3,787	3,919	4,121	4,448	5,166	5,420	5,704	5,879
Idaho	290	603	1,659	1,856	2,484	2,585	2,667	2,833	3,078	3,386	3,556	3,690	3,844
Illinois	438	909	2,587	2,704	3,781	4,106	4,369	4,906	5,118	5,520	5,670	5,898	5,893
Indiana	369	728	1,882	2,010	3,275	3,556	3,794	4,284	4,549	4,930	5,074	5,344	5,630
Iowa	368	844	2,326	2,668	3,619	3,770	4,124	4,285	4,453	4,679	5,096	5,257	5,288
Kansas	348	771	2,173	2,559	3,829	3,933	4,076	4,443	4,752	4,874	5,007	5,442	5,659
Kentucky	233	545	1,701	1,784	2,486	2,733	3,011	3,347	3,745	4,354	4,719	4,872	5,107
Louisiana	372	648	1,792	2,469	3,187	3,069	3,138	3,317	3,855	4,196	4,354	4,428	4,519
Maine	283	692	1,824	1,934	3,472	3,850	4,258	4,744	5,373	5,458	5,652	6,073	6,069
Maryland	393	918	2,598	2,914	4,447	4,777	5,201	5,758	6,196	6,654	6,679	6,813	6,958
Massachusetts	409	859	2,819	2,940	4,562	5,145	5,471	5,972	6,237	6,366	6,408	6,627	6,959
Michigan	415	904	2,640	3,037	4,176	4,353	4,692	5,150	5,546	5,883	6,268	6,494	6,658
Minnesota	425	904	2,387	2,673	3,941	4,180	4,386	4,755	4,971	5,239	5,409	5,554	5,720
Mississippi	206	501	1,664	1,605	2,362	2,350	2,548	2,861	3,094	3,187	3,245	3,382	3,660
Missouri	344	709	1,936	2,172	3,189	3,472	3,786	4,263	4,507	4,754	4,830	4,885	5,114
Montana	411	782	2,476	2,683	4,091	4,194	4,246	4,293	4,736	5,204	5,319	5,425	5,598
Nebraska	337	736	2,150	2,384	3,634	3,756	3,943	4,360	4,842	5,038	5,263	5,336	5,651
Nevada	430	769	2,088	2,078	3,440	3,440	3,623	3,871	4,117	4,653	4,926	5,066	5,049
New Hampshire	347	723	1,916	2,265	3,542	3,933	4,457	4,807	5,304	5,685	5,790	5,644	5,723
New Jersey	388	1,016	3,191	3,254	5,570	5,953	6,564	7,549	8,139	8,756	9,321	9,415	9,677
New Mexico	363	707	2,034	2,329	3,195	3,558	3,691	3,473	3,515	3,895	3,765	4,071	4,261
New York	562	1,327	3,462	3,741	6,011	6,497	7,151	7,663	8,062	8,565	8,527	8,902	9,175
North Carolina	237	612	1,754	2,001	2,948	3,129	3,368	3,874	4,236	4,548	4,556	4,763	4,894
North Dakota	367	690	1,920	2,275	3,483	3,437	3,519	3,952	4,189	4,199	4,441	4,597	4,674
Ohio	365	730	2,075	2,303	3,527	3,673	3,998	4,686	5,045	5,245	5,694	5,754	5,971
Oklahoma	311	604	1,926	2,199	3,146	3,099	3,093	3,379	3,508	3,843	4,078	4,355	4,697
Oregon	448	925	2,692	3,100	4,141	4,337	4,789	5,182	5,474	5,683	5,913	6,296	6,263
Pennsylvania	409	882	2,535	2,824	4,325	4,616	4,989	5,597	6,228	6,541	6,613	6,890	6,983
Rhode Island	413	891	2,601	2,927	4,667	4,985	5,329	6,064	6,368	6,343	6,546	6,938	7,333
South Carolina	220	613	1,752	1,734	3,058	3,214	3,408	3,736	4,081	4,352	4,436	4,624	4,761
South Dakota	347	690	1,908	1,991	3,051	3,097	3,249	3,585	3,731	3,965	4,173	4,357	4,586
Tennessee	238	566	1,635	1,794	2,612	2,827	3,068	3,491	3,664	3,782	3,692	3,993	4,149
Texas	332	624	1,916	2,006	3,298	3,409	3,608	3,877	4,151	4,438	4,632	4,670	4,898
Utah	322	626	1,657	1,819	2,390	2,415	2,454	2,588	2,764	2,960	3,040	3,180	3,439
Vermont	344	807	1,997	2,475	4,031	4,399	5,207	5,481	6,227	6,738	6,671	6,411	6,600
Virginia	274	708	1,970	2,179	3,520	3,780	4,149	4,539	4,612	4,902	4,880	4,980	5,109
Washington	420	915	2,568	2,542	3,881	3,964	4,164	4,359	4,702	5,000	5,270	5,614	5,751
West Virginia	258	670	1,920	2,146	3,528	3,784	3,858	3,883	4,360	4,911	5,078	5,527	5,713
Wisconsin	413	883	2,477	2,738	4,168	4,523	4,747	5,266	5,524	5,871	6,139	6,475	6,717
Wyoming	450	856	2,527	2,967	5,114	5,201	5,051	5,375	5,577	5,638	5,812	5,822	5,899
Outlying areas													
American Samoa	—	—	—	—	1,387	1,846	1,908	1,988	1,908	2,033	2,085	1,670	1,785
Guam	236	820	—	—	3,383	3,344	3,295	4,067	4,440	4,596	5,231	5,309	5,178
Northern Marianas	—	—	—	—	2,552	3,099	3,366	2,414	3,007	4,425	5,247	5,288	5,451
Puerto Rico	106	—	—	—	1,325	1,384	1,504	1,692	1,750	1,913	2,162	2,364	2,414
Virgin Islands	271	—	—	—	3,223	4,277	4,036	5,281	6,767	6,002	5,935	5,843	5,918

Table 165.—Current expenditure per pupil in average daily attendance in public elementary and secondary schools, by state: 1959–60 to 1993–94—Continued

State or other area	Constant 1993–94 dollars [1]												
	1959–60	1969–70	1979–80	1980–81	1985–86	1986–87	1987–88	1988–89	1989–90	1990–91	1991–92	1992–93	1993–94
1	15	16	17	18	19	20	21	22	23	24	25	26	27
United States	$1,867	$3,158	$4,279	$4,223	$5,046	$5,219	$5,352	$5,604	$5,725	$5,741	$5,736	$5,728	$5,767
Alabama	1,200	2,106	3,036	3,350	3,446	3,382	3,430	3,857	3,831	3,960	3,826	3,859	4,037
Alaska	2,719	4,345	8,904	9,601	11,158	10,530	10,061	9,309	9,709	9,095	8,940	8,961	8,882
Arizona	2,008	2,787	3,712	3,812	4,483	4,659	4,726	4,708	4,667	4,705	4,635	4,627	4,611
Arkansas	1,121	2,197	2,965	2,871	3,571	3,593	3,773	3,949	4,013	4,040	4,264	4,231	4,280
California	[2]2,110	3,357	4,271	4,178	4,761	4,900	4,847	4,989	5,056	4,903	5,021	4,904	4,921
Colorado	1,971	2,856	4,560	4,545	5,341	5,452	5,326	5,454	5,436	5,529	5,471	5,272	5,097
Connecticut	2,170	3,682	4,558	4,854	6,373	7,144	7,864	8,273	8,920	8,575	8,481	8,180	8,473
Delaware	2,268	3,484	5,389	5,094	6,194	6,343	6,333	6,542	6,678	6,523	6,446	6,436	6,621
District of Columbia	2,146	3,942	6,138	5,808	7,172	7,548	7,740	9,471	10,191	10,239	10,103	9,663	10,180
Florida	1,581	2,835	3,558	4,053	4,742	4,987	5,165	5,505	5,755	5,761	5,547	5,452	5,516
Georgia	1,261	2,276	3,061	2,883	3,985	4,182	4,335	4,647	4,923	4,876	4,675	4,807	4,915
Hawaii	1,615	3,253	4,373	4,395	5,115	4,978	4,946	4,972	5,123	5,641	5,734	5,852	5,879
Idaho	1,442	2,335	3,125	3,133	3,337	3,398	3,367	3,418	3,544	3,697	3,762	3,786	3,844
Illinois	2,182	3,520	4,872	4,564	5,081	5,398	5,514	5,919	5,893	6,027	5,998	6,051	5,893
Indiana	1,835	2,818	3,545	3,393	4,401	4,674	4,788	5,169	5,239	5,383	5,368	5,483	5,630
Iowa	1,830	3,267	4,382	4,503	4,863	4,956	5,205	5,169	5,128	5,109	5,391	5,393	5,288
Kansas	1,730	2,984	4,093	4,320	5,146	5,169	5,145	5,361	5,472	5,322	5,298	5,583	5,659
Kentucky	1,160	2,110	3,204	3,011	3,341	3,593	3,800	4,038	4,313	4,754	4,992	4,998	5,107
Louisiana	1,851	2,508	3,375	4,168	4,283	4,035	3,961	4,002	4,439	4,582	4,606	4,543	4,519
Maine	1,407	2,680	3,434	3,264	4,665	5,060	5,375	5,723	6,187	5,959	5,979	6,230	6,069
Maryland	1,954	3,555	4,893	4,918	5,975	6,280	6,565	6,947	7,135	7,265	7,066	6,989	6,958
Massachusetts	2,035	3,325	5,310	4,962	6,130	6,764	6,906	7,205	7,182	6,951	6,780	6,799	6,959
Michigan	2,066	3,499	4,973	5,126	5,611	5,722	5,922	6,213	6,387	6,423	6,631	6,663	6,658
Minnesota	2,116	3,498	4,495	4,512	5,295	5,495	5,536	5,737	5,724	5,720	5,722	5,698	5,720
Mississippi	1,025	1,939	3,134	2,710	3,173	3,089	3,216	3,451	3,562	3,479	3,433	3,470	3,660
Missouri	1,712	2,743	3,647	3,666	4,285	4,563	4,779	5,143	5,190	5,190	5,110	5,012	5,114
Montana	2,044	3,026	4,664	4,530	5,497	5,514	5,359	5,179	5,454	5,682	5,628	5,566	5,598
Nebraska	1,677	2,850	4,049	4,025	4,883	4,937	4,977	5,261	5,576	5,500	5,568	5,475	5,651
Nevada	2,142	2,978	3,933	3,507	4,622	4,522	4,573	4,670	4,741	5,081	5,211	5,197	5,049
New Hampshire	1,728	2,799	3,608	3,824	4,759	5,170	5,626	5,800	6,108	6,207	6,126	5,791	5,723
New Jersey	1,928	3,934	6,011	5,493	7,484	7,825	8,286	9,108	9,372	9,560	9,861	9,659	9,677
New Mexico	1,805	2,737	3,830	3,932	4,293	4,677	4,659	4,190	4,047	4,252	3,983	4,177	4,261
New York	2,795	5,135	6,521	6,315	8,077	8,541	9,027	9,246	9,283	9,351	9,022	9,133	9,175
North Carolina	1,181	2,370	3,304	3,378	3,961	4,113	4,251	4,674	4,878	4,966	4,820	4,886	4,894
North Dakota	1,825	2,669	3,617	3,839	4,680	4,519	4,442	4,768	4,824	4,585	4,698	4,716	4,674
Ohio	1,817	2,826	3,907	3,887	4,739	4,828	5,046	5,654	5,809	5,726	6,024	5,903	5,971
Oklahoma	1,549	2,340	3,628	3,711	4,227	4,074	3,904	4,077	4,039	4,196	4,314	4,468	4,697
Oregon	2,231	3,579	5,070	5,232	5,564	5,701	6,045	6,252	6,304	6,205	6,255	6,459	6,263
Pennsylvania	2,037	3,413	4,774	4,766	5,812	6,068	6,297	6,753	7,172	7,142	6,997	7,068	6,983
Rhode Island	2,057	3,449	4,899	4,940	6,272	6,553	6,727	7,316	7,333	6,925	6,925	7,118	7,333
South Carolina	1,095	2,371	3,300	2,927	4,109	4,224	4,301	4,507	4,700	4,752	4,693	4,744	4,761
South Dakota	1,726	2,670	3,593	3,360	4,100	4,071	4,101	4,325	4,296	4,329	4,415	4,470	4,586
Tennessee	1,185	2,191	3,080	3,028	3,510	3,716	3,873	4,212	4,219	4,129	3,906	4,097	4,149
Texas	1,654	2,416	3,608	3,386	4,432	4,482	4,554	4,678	4,780	4,846	4,846	4,791	4,898
Utah	1,605	2,424	3,120	3,070	3,212	3,174	3,097	3,123	3,183	3,231	3,217	3,263	3,439
Vermont	1,711	3,124	3,761	4,177	5,416	5,783	6,573	6,613	7,170	7,357	7,057	6,577	6,600
Virginia	1,365	2,740	3,710	3,678	4,730	4,969	5,237	5,477	5,311	5,352	5,162	5,109	5,109
Washington	2,092	3,543	4,837	4,291	5,215	5,210	5,255	5,260	5,415	5,459	5,576	5,759	5,751
West Virginia	1,286	2,593	3,617	3,622	4,741	4,974	4,870	4,685	5,021	5,362	5,372	5,670	5,713
Wisconsin	2,055	3,417	4,665	4,622	5,600	5,945	5,992	6,353	6,361	6,411	6,495	6,643	6,717
Wyoming	2,241	3,313	4,759	5,009	6,872	6,837	6,376	6,485	6,423	6,156	6,148	5,973	5,899
Outlying areas													
American Samoa	—	—	—	—	1,863	2,427	2,408	2,399	2,197	2,219	2,206	1,714	1,785
Guam	1,176	3,173	—	—	4,545	4,396	4,159	4,907	5,112	5,018	5,534	5,446	5,178
Northern Marianas	—	—	—	—	3,429	4,073	4,248	—	3,463	4,831	5,551	5,425	5,451
Puerto Rico	529	—	—	—	1,780	1,820	1,899	2,041	2,015	2,089	2,287	2,425	2,414
Virgin Islands	1,347	—	—	—	4,331	5,623	5,095	6,372	7,793	6,554	6,279	5,995	5,918

[1] Based on the Consumer Price Index, prepared by the Bureau of Labor Statistics, U.S. Department of Labor, adjusted to a school-year basis. These data do not reflect differences in inflation rates from state to state.

[2] Estimated by the National Center for Education Statistics.

—Data not available or not applicable.

NOTE.—Beginning in 1980–81, state administration expenditures are excluded. Beginning in 1988–89, extensive changes were made in the data collection procedures. Some data have been revised from previously published figures.

SOURCE: U.S. Department of Education, National Center for Education Statistics, *Statistics of State School Systems;* and Common Core of Data surveys. (This table was prepared June 1996.)

Table 166.—Total and current expenditure per pupil in public elementary and secondary schools: 1919–20 to 1995–96

School year	Expenditure per pupil in average daily attendance				Expenditure per pupil in fall enrollment [1]			
	Unadjusted dollars		Constant 1995–96 [2] dollars		Unadjusted dollars		Constant 1995–96 dollars [2]	
	Total expenditure	Current expenditure	Total expenditure	Current expenditure	Total expenditure	Current expenditure	Total expenditure	Current expenditure
1	2	3	4	5	6	7	8	9
1919–20	$64	$53	$519	$433	$48	$40	$389	$324
1929–30	108	87	981	784	90	72	812	649
1931–32	97	81	1,040	870	82	69	880	737
1933–34	76	67	891	789	65	57	757	670
1935–36	88	74	990	837	74	63	838	708
1937–38	100	84	1,077	906	86	72	925	778
1939–40	106	88	1,171	976	92	76	1,015	846
1941–42	110	98	1,092	976	94	84	935	836
1943–44	125	117	1,107	1,039	105	99	933	875
1945–46	146	136	1,238	1,157	124	116	1,054	986
1947–48	205	181	1,361	1,205	179	158	1,188	1,053
1949–50	260	210	1,701	1,375	231	187	1,510	1,220
1951–52	314	246	1,852	1,449	275	215	1,621	1,268
1953–54	351	265	2,020	1,524	312	236	1,796	1,355
1955–56	387	294	2,228	1,694	354	269	2,037	1,548
1957–58	447	341	2,425	1,849	408	311	2,211	1,686
1959–60	471	375	2,481	1,976	440	350	2,318	1,846
1961–62	517	419	2,663	2,157	485	393	2,498	2,024
1963–64	559	460	2,803	2,310	520	428	2,609	2,150
1965–66	654	538	3,171	2,608	607	499	2,944	2,421
1967–68	786	658	3,579	2,996	732	612	3,329	2,787
1969–70	955	816	3,913	3,343	878	750	3,597	3,073
1970–71	1,049	911	4,089	3,550	970	842	3,779	3,280
1971–72	1,128	990	4,242	3,722	1,034	907	3,889	3,413
1972–73	1,211	1,077	4,377	3,893	1,116	993	4,036	3,590
1973–74	1,364	1,207	4,527	4,007	1,244	1,101	4,129	3,655
1974–75	1,545	1,365	4,616	4,077	1,424	1,258	4,254	3,758
1975–76	1,697	1,504	4,737	4,196	1,564	1,385	4,364	3,866
1976–77	1,816	1,638	4,789	4,318	1,673	1,509	4,413	3,978
1977–78	2,002	1,823	4,948	4,504	1,842	1,677	4,551	4,143
1978–79	2,210	2,020	4,993	4,565	2,029	1,855	4,585	4,192
1979–80	2,491	2,272	4,965	4,529	2,290	2,089	4,565	4,164
1980–81	[3]2,742	2,502	[3]4,899	4,469	[3]2,529	2,307	[3]4,519	4,122
1981–82	[3]2,973	2,726	[3]4,890	4,483	[3]2,754	2,525	[3]4,530	4,152
1982–83	[3]3,203	2,955	[3]5,051	4,660	[3]2,966	2,736	[3]4,677	4,315
1983–84	[3]3,471	3,173	[3]5,278	4,825	[3]3,216	2,940	[3]4,890	4,470
1984–85	[3]3,722	3,470	[3]5,446	5,078	[3]3,456	3,222	[3]5,057	4,715
1985–86	[3]4,020	3,756	[3]5,717	5,341	[3]3,724	3,479	[3]5,297	4,949
1986–87	[3]4,308	3,970	[3]5,994	5,524	[3]3,995	3,682	[3]5,558	5,123
1987–88	[3]4,654	4,240	[3]6,218	5,665	[3]4,310	3,927	[3]5,758	5,246
1988–89	5,109	4,645	6,525	5,931	4,738	4,307	6,051	5,500
1989–90	5,542	4,972	6,755	6,060	5,167	4,635	6,298	5,650
1990–91	5,885	5,258	6,801	6,076	5,486	4,902	6,341	5,665
1991–92	6,075	5,421	6,802	6,071	5,629	5,023	6,303	5,625
1992–93	6,281	5,584	6,821	6,063	5,805	5,160	6,304	5,604
1993–94	6,491	5,767	6,871	6,104	5,996	5,327	6,346	5,638
1994–95 [3]	6,738	5,986	6,933	6,159	6,223	5,529	6,404	5,689
1995–96 [3]	6,993	6,213	6,993	6,213	6,459	5,738	6,459	5,738

[1] Data for 1919–20 to 1953–54 are based on school-year enrollment.

[2] Based on the Consumer Price Index, prepared by the Bureau of Labor Statistics, U.S. Department of Labor, adjusted to a school-year basis.

[3] Estimated.

NOTE.—Beginning in 1980–81, state administration expenditures are excluded from both "total" and "current" expenditures. Beginning in 1988–89, extensive changes were made in the data collection procedures. Some data have been revised from previously published figures.

SOURCE: U.S. Department of Education, National Center for Education Statistics, *Statistics of State School Systems; Revenues and Expenditures for Public Elementary and Secondary Education;* and Common Core of Data surveys. (This table was prepared June 1996.)

CHAPTER 3
Postsecondary Education

Postsecondary education includes an array of diverse educational experiences, including a wide range of programs offered by American colleges and universities. For example, a community college may offer vocational training or the first 2 years of training at the college level. A university typically offers a full undergraduate course of study leading to a bachelor's degree as well as first-professional and graduate programs leading to advanced degrees. Vocational and technical institutions offer training programs which are designed to prepare students for specific careers. Other types of educational opportunities for adults include community groups, churches, libraries, and businesses.

In recent decades, postsecondary education has become more accessible to all segments of the population. The growth of community colleges and low-cost institutions means that the student's cost to attend can be held to a minimum. Federal student financial aid and other aid programs also have attracted many students who otherwise would have found it difficult to finance a college education.

This chapter provides an overview of the latest statistics on postsecondary education, which includes academic, vocational and continuing professional education programs after high school. However, to maintain comparability over time, most of the data in the *Digest* are for higher education institutions, which include 2- and 4-year colleges and universities and exclude most vocational and continuing education programs. This chapter highlights historical data that enable the reader to observe long-range trends in American higher education.

Other chapters provide related information on postsecondary education. Data on price indexes and on the number of degrees held by the general population are in chapter 1. Chapter 4 contains tabulations on federal funding for postsecondary education. Information on employment outcomes for college graduates is in chapter 5. Chapter 7 contains data on college libraries and use of computers by young adults. Further information on survey methodologies is in the "Guide to Sources" in the appendix and in the publications cited in the source notes.

Enrollment

Higher education enrollment increased by 20 percent between 1974 and 1984. Between 1984 and 1994, enrollment increased at nearly the same rate (17 percent), from 12.2 million to 14.3 million, though it declined slightly after 1992. Much of this growth was in part-time and female enrollment. Between 1984 and 1994, the number of men enrolled rose 9 percent, while the number of women increased by 24 percent (table 169). In addition to the enrollment in 2-year colleges, 4-year colleges, and universities, over half a million students attended postsecondary less-than-2-year institutions (table 167).

The number of older students has been growing more rapidly than the number of younger students. Between 1980 and 1990, the enrollment of students under age 25 increased by 3 percent. During the same period, enrollment of persons 25 and over rose by 34 percent. From 1990 to 2000, NCES projects a rise of 14 percent in enrollments of persons under 25 and an increase of 10 percent in the number over 25 (table 171).

Enrollment trends have differed at the undergraduate, graduate, and first-professional levels. Undergraduate enrollment generally increased during the 1970s, but dipped between 1983 and 1985. From 1985 to 1992, undergraduate enrollment has increased each year, rising 18 percent before declining slightly in 1993 and 1994. Graduate enrollment had been steady at about 1.3 million in the late 1970s and early 1980s, but rose about 28 percent between 1984 and 1994. After rising very rapidly during the 1970s, enrollment in first-professional programs stabilized in the 1980s. There was an 8 percent increase in first-professional enrollment between 1990 and 1994 (tables 183, 184, and 185).

Since 1984, the number of women in graduate schools has exceeded the number of men. Between 1984 and 1994, the number of male full-time graduate students increased by 25 percent, compared to 62 percent for full-time women. Among part-time graduate students, the number of men increased by 8 percent compared to a 30 percent increase for women (table 184).

The proportion of American college students who are minorities has been increasing. In 1976, 15.7 percent were minorities, compared with 24.6 percent in 1994. Much of the change can be attributed to rising numbers of Hispanic and Asian students. The proportion of black students has fluctuated over the past 15 years, before rising to 10.5 percent in 1994. These percentages exclude foreign students enrolled in U.S. colleges and universities (table 203).

Despite the sizable numbers of small colleges, most students attend the larger colleges and universities. In fall 1994, 37 percent of higher education campuses had fewer than 1,000 students; however, these campuses enrolled only 4 percent of college students. While 11 percent of the campuses enrolled 10,000 or more students, they accounted for 50 percent of total college enrollment (table 210).

Faculty, Staff, and Salaries

The student-staff ratio at colleges and universities dropped from 5.4 in 1976 to 4.9 in 1993. During the same time period, the student-faculty ratio dropped from 16.6 to 15.5. The proportion of administrative staff and other non-teaching professional staff rose from 15 percent in 1976 to 22 percent in 1993, while the proportion of nonprofessional staff declined from 42 percent to 35 percent (table 216).

Approximately 2.6 million people were employed in colleges and universities in the fall of 1993, including 1.7 million professional and .9 million nonprofessional staff. About 43 percent of the staff were faculty or teaching assistants, 6 percent were managerial, 16 percent were other non-teaching professionals, and 35 percent were nonprofessional staff (table 218).

Colleges differ widely in their practices of employing part-time and full-time staff. In fall 1993, 51 percent of the employees at public 2-year colleges were employed full-time compared with 72 percent at public 4-year colleges and 73 percent at private 4-year colleges. A higher proportion of the faculty at public 4-year colleges were employed full-time (76 percent) than at private 4-year colleges (62 percent) or public 2-year colleges (35 percent) (table 218).

Full-time and part-time faculty and instructional staff also differ by the number and types of students that they teach. Sixty-seven percent of full-time faculty teach 50 students or more, while only 30 percent of part-time faculty teach that many students. Part-time faculty also teach fewer hours per week. About 46 percent of full-time faculty taught for 10 or more hours per week, compared to 18 percent of part-time faculty. Of the full-time faculty teaching only undergraduate students, 61 percent teach three or more classes (tables 223 and 224).

The proportion of time that full-time faculty spent teaching was 54 percent in 1992. For the remaining faculty time, research and scholarship accounted for 18 percent of the time; professional growth, 5 percent; administration, 13 percent; outside consulting, 3 percent; service and non-teaching activities, 7 percent (table 223).

About 12 percent of U.S. faculty in colleges and universities were minorities in 1993. Five percent of the faculty were black; 4 percent, Asian/Pacific Islanders; 3 percent, Hispanic; and .4 percent, American Indian. The majority of college faculty in fall 1993 were white and male. Fifty-four percent of faculty fell in this category, while 34 percent were white and female. About 14 percent of executive, managerial, and administrative staff were minorities in 1993, compared to about 29 percent of the nonprofessional staff. The distribution of minority staff was similar at public and private institutions. About 19 percent of all staff at public institutions were minorities compared to 20 percent at private institutions (table 217).

College faculty generally suffered losses in the purchasing power of their salaries from 1972–73 to 1980–81, when average salaries fell 17 percent after adjustment for inflation. During the 1980s, average salaries rose and recouped most of the losses. Since 1989–90, faculty salaries have been relatively stable. Average salaries for men in 1994–95 ($51,228) were considerably higher than the average for women ($41,369) and have increased at a slightly faster rate since 1980–81 (table 229).

The proportion of faculty with tenure has remained relatively stable in recent years. About 64 percent of full-time faculty had tenure in 1994–95, but a large difference existed between the proportion of men and women with tenure. Seventy-one percent of men compared with 50 percent of women had tenure in 1994–95. About 67 percent of the faculty at public institutions had tenure, compared with 57 percent of faculty at private institutions (table 235).

The age distribution of full-time faculty is concentrated in the middle age brackets. Faculty under the age of thirty compose one percent of the total, but 36 percent are ages 30 to 44, and 36 percent are 45 to 54 years old. Thirteen percent are 55 to 59; 8 percent, 60 to 64; and 5 percent, 65 or older (table 226).

Degrees

During the 1994–95 academic year, 9,962 institutions offered postsecondary education. This included 2,244 4-year colleges, 1,462 2-year colleges, and 6,256 vocational and technical institutions (tables 236 and 353). Institutions awarding various higher education degrees in 1993–94 numbered 2,182 for associate's degrees, 1,847 for bachelor's degrees, 1,342 for master's degrees, and 472 for doctor degrees (tables 252).

More people are completing college. Between 1983–84 and 1993–94, the number of associate, bachelor's, master's, and doctor's degrees rose. Associate degrees increased 20 percent, bachelor's degrees increased 20 percent, master's degrees increased 36 percent, and doctor's degrees increased 30 percent during this period. The number of first-professional degrees was slightly higher in 1993–94 than it was in 1983–84. The number of first-professional degrees declined in the mid 1980s before increasing in the early 1990s (table 239).

The total number of bachelor's degrees increased slowly during the early 1980s and more rapidly towards the end of that decade, especially for women. Between 1983–84 and 1993–94, the number of bachelor's degrees awarded to men increased by 10 percent, while those awarded to women rose by 29 percent (table 239).

Of the 1,169,000 bachelor's degrees conferred in 1993–94, the largest numbers of degrees were conferred in the fields of business management and administrative services (247,000), social sciences (134,000), and education (108,000). At the master's degree level, the largest fields were education (99,000) and business management and administrative services (93,000). The largest fields at the doctor's degree level were education (7,000), engineering and engineering technology (6,000), and physical sciences (5,000) (tables 246, 247, and 248).

The pattern of bachelor's degrees by field of study has shifted significantly in recent years. Declines are significant in male majority fields such as engineering and computer and information sciences. Engineering and engineering technologies declined 10 percent between 1983–84 and 1988–89, and then posted a further 8 percent decline between 1988–89 and 1993–94. Computer and information sciences grew rapidly during the 1970s and mid 1980s, but dropped 21 percent between 1988–89 and 1993–94, falling well below the 1983–84 levels.

In contrast, some fields that had been growing, such as social sciences and psychology, began to increase more rapidly. For example, the number of bachelor's degrees conferred in social sciences and history increased by 16 percent between 1983–84 and 1988–89, but rose 24 percent between 1988–89 and 1993–94. Psychology increased 22 percent between 1983–84 and 1988–89 and then rose a further 42 percent between 1988–89 and 1993–94. In 1987–88, the number of degrees conferred in education rose for the first time since 1972–73. The number of

education degrees rose a total of 11 percent between 1988–89 and 1993–94. To some extent, these shifts during the 1988–89 and 1993–94 period highlight the increasing female majority on college campuses by reflecting significant increases in degrees in some predominantly female fields and decreases in many predominantly male fields (tables 246, 277, 278, 279, 288, and 290).

Less than half (46 percent) of the bachelor's degree seeking students who enrolled in college in 1989–90 had completed their degree by spring 1994. About 8 percent of students had completed an associate degree or other certificate below the bachelor's degree, 18 percent of the students were still enrolled in college, and 28 percent had left college (table 307).

Finances

For the 1995–96 academic year, annual undergraduate charges for tuition, room, and board were estimated to be $6,252 at public colleges and $17,207 at private colleges. Between 1985–86 and 1995–96, charges at public colleges have risen by 23 percent, and charges at private colleges have increased by 36 percent, after adjustment for inflation (tables 37 and 309).

Trend data show increases in the expenditures per student at institutions of higher education through the late 1980s and relatively small increases thereafter. After an adjustment for inflation at colleges and universities, current-fund expenditures per student rose about 16 percent between 1983–84 and 1988–89, but increased only 4 percent between 1988–89 and 1993–94 (table 331).

Scholarships and fellowships have been rising more rapidly than most other types of college expenditures in recent years. At public universities, between 1983–84 and 1993–94, inflation adjusted scholarships and fellowships expenditures per full-time-equivalent student rose 88 percent compared with 12 percent for instruction expenditures per student. At private universities during the same period, scholarships and fellowships costs per student rose 80 percent, and the instruction costs rose by 38 percent (tables 338 and 341). Another rapidly rising expenditure for public colleges during the decade was research, which rose by 43 percent per student at public universities, and by 53 percent at other public 4-year colleges (tables 338 and 339).

Figure 13.-Enrollment, degrees conferred, and expenditures in institutions of higher education: 1960–61 to 1995–96

Enrollment, in millions

Degrees, in millions

Expenditures in billions of constant 1995-96 dollars

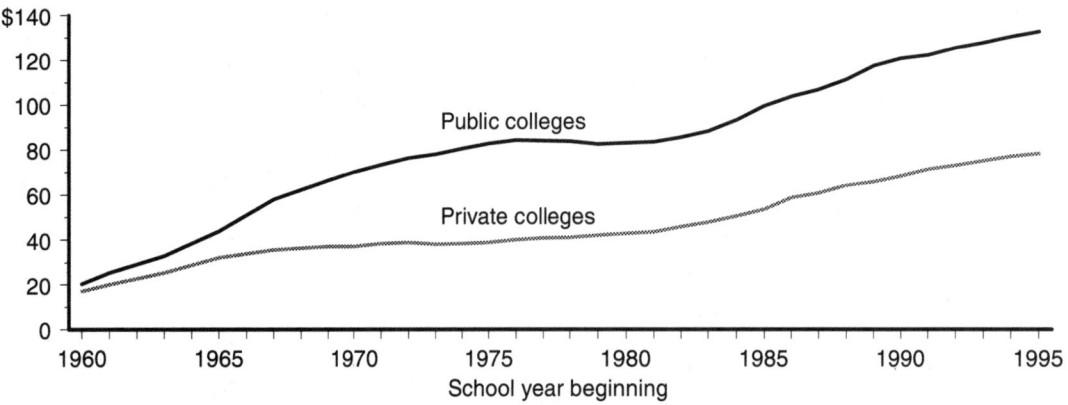

NOTE: Enrollment, degree, and finance data for 1994–95 and 1995-96 are estimated.

SOURCE: U.S. Department of Education, National Center for Education Statistics, HEGIS, "Fall Enrollment in Institutions of Higher Education," "Degrees and Other Formal Awards Conferred," and "Financial Statistics of Institutions of Higher Education" surveys; and Integrated Postsecondary Education Data System (IPEDS), "Fall Enrollment," "Completions," and "Finance" surveys.

Figure 14.–Percentage change in total enrollment of institutions of higher education, by state: Fall 1990 to fall 1994

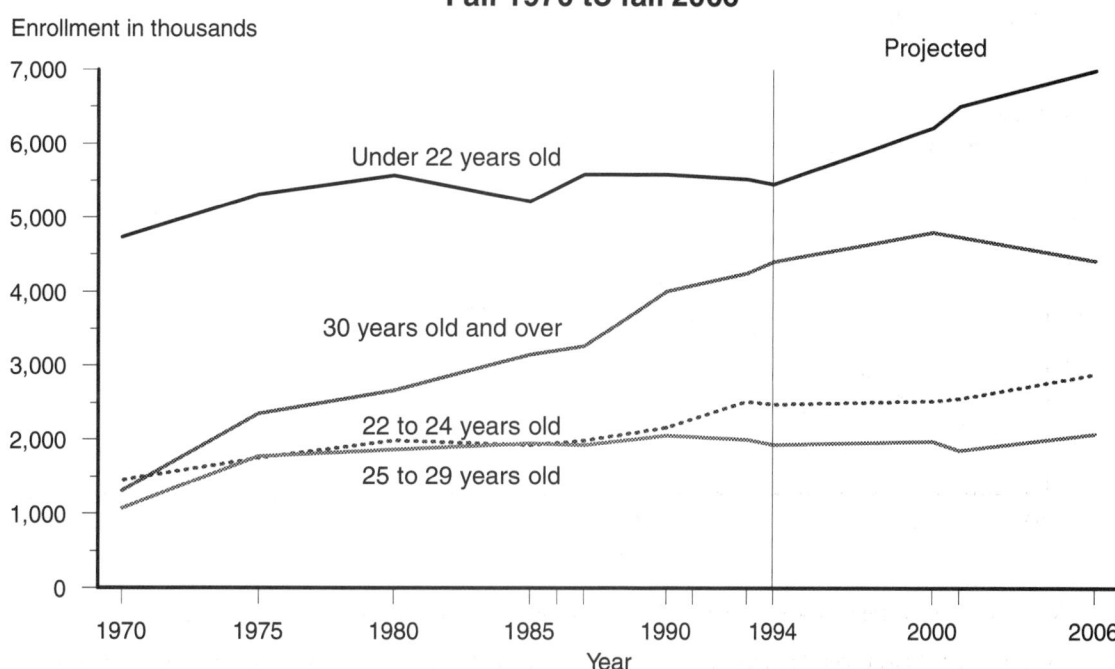

Percent change

	Increase of 20% or more		Increase of at least 10% but less than 20%
	Increase of less than 10%		Decrease or no change

SOURCE: U.S. Department of Education, National Center for Education Statistics, Integrated Postsecondary Education Data System (IPEDS), "Fall Enrollment" surveys.

Figure 15.–Enrollment in institutions of higher education, by age: Fall 1970 to fall 2006

Enrollment in thousands

Projected

Under 22 years old

30 years old and over

22 to 24 years old

25 to 29 years old

Year

SOURCE: U.S. Department of Education, National Center for Education Statistics, "Fall Enrollment in Institutions of Higher Education" surveys; Integrated Postsecondary Education Data System (IPEDS), "Fall Enrollment" surveys; Projections of Education Statistics to 2006; and U.S. Department of Commerce, Bureau of the Census, Current Population Reports, Series P-20, "Social and Economic Characteristics of Students," various years.

Figure 16.-Full-time–equivalent students per staff member in public and private institutions of higher education: 1976, 1991, and 1993

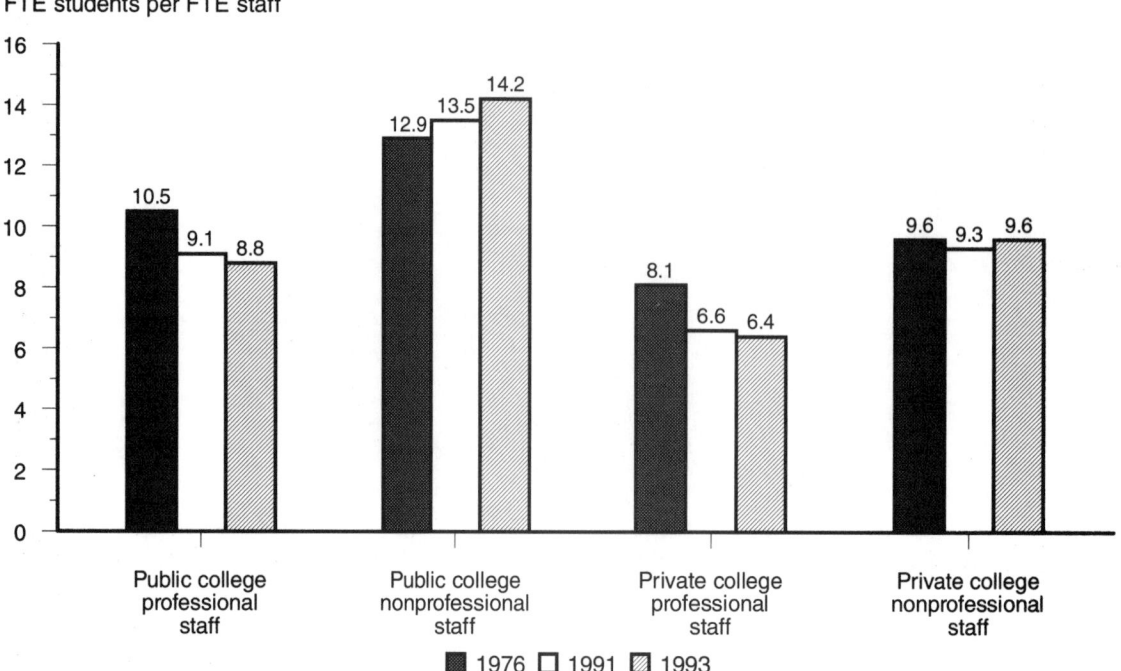

FTE students per FTE staff

SOURCE: U.S. Department of Education, National Center for Education Statistics, Higher Education General Information Survey (HEGIS), "Staff, 1976" survey, and Integrated Postsecondary Education Data System (IPEDS), "Staff" surveys.

Figure 17.-Trends in bachelor's degrees conferred in selected fields of study: 1983-84, 1988-89, and 1993-94

Fields of study

SOURCE: U.S. Department of Education, National Center for Education Statistics, Higher Education General Information Survey (HEGIS), "Degrees and Other Formal Awards Conferred" survey, and Integrated Postsecondary Education Data System (IPEDS), "Completions" surveys.

Figure 18.-Sources of current-fund revenue for public institutions of higher education: 1993–94

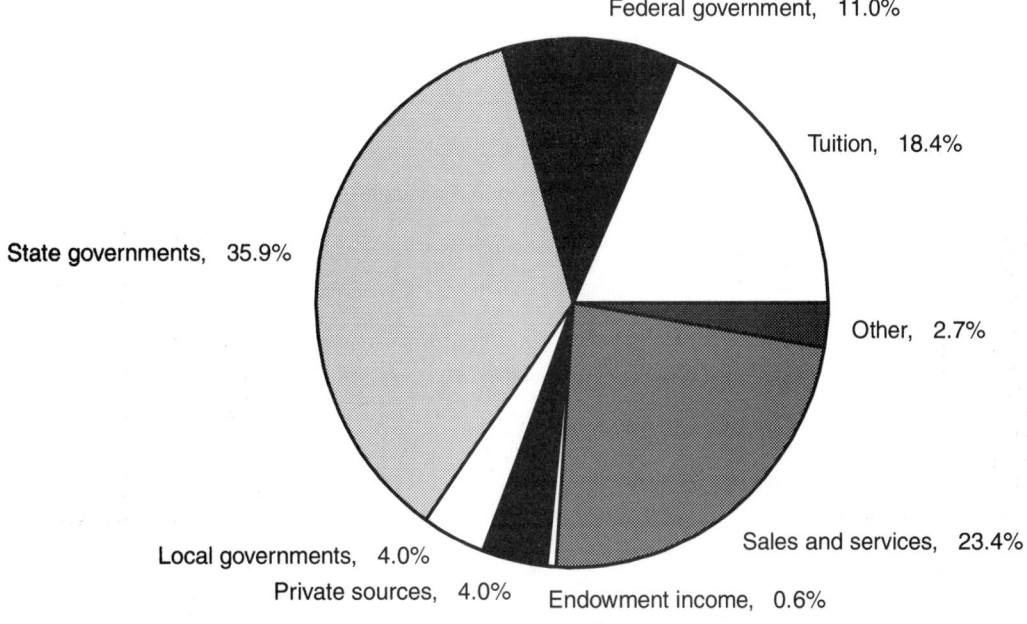

Federal government, 11.0%

Tuition, 18.4%

State governments, 35.9%

Other, 2.7%

Sales and services, 23.4%

Local governments, 4.0%

Private sources, 4.0%   Endowment income, 0.6%

Total revenues = $113.0 billion

SOURCE: U.S. Department of Education, National Center for Education Statistics, Integrated Postsecondary Education Data System (IPEDS), "Finance, FY94" survey.

Figure 19.-Sources of current-fund revenue for private institutions of higher education: 1993–94

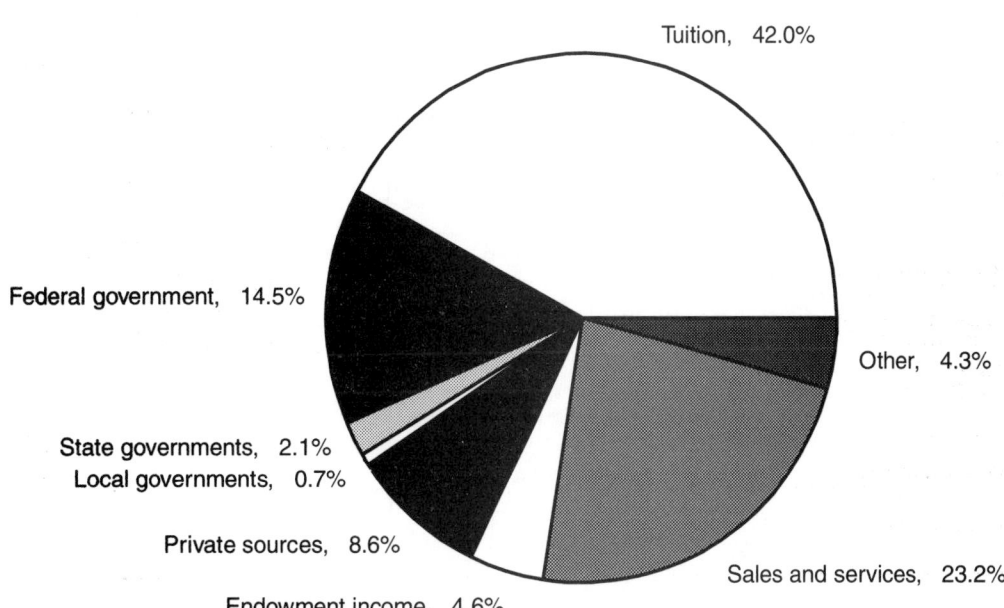

Tuition, 42.0%

Federal government, 14.5%

Other, 4.3%

State governments, 2.1%
Local governments, 0.7%

Private sources, 8.6%

Sales and services, 23.2%

Endowment income, 4.6%

Total revenues = $66.3 billion

SOURCE: U.S. Department of Education, National Center for Education Statistics, Integrated Postsecondary Education Data System (IPEDS), "Finance, FY94" survey.

Table 167.—Enrollment and staff in, and degrees conferred by, institutions of higher education and noncollegiate postsecondary institutions: 1993–94 and fall 1993 and 1994

Level of institution, type of degree, and sex of student	All post-secondary	Institutions of higher education						Noncollegiate postsecondary institutions				
		Total	Public	Private				Total	Public	Private		
				Total	Nonprofit	Proprietary				Total	Nonprofit	Proprietary
1	2	3	4	5	6	7		8	9	10	11	12

					Enrollment, fall 1994							
Total	15,160,426	14,278,790	11,133,680	3,145,110	2,910,107	235,003		881,636	314,924	566,712	173,425	393,287
4-year institutions [1]	8,854,892	8,749,080	5,825,213	2,923,867	2,824,500	99,367		105,812	427	105,385	88,316	17,069
Men	4,115,579	4,048,695	2,703,415	1,345,280	1,287,138	58,142		66,884	188	66,696	57,318	9,378
Women	4,700,863	4,700,385	3,121,798	1,578,587	1,537,362	41,225		478	239	239	30,998	7,691
2-year institutions [1]	5,797,246	5,502,081	5,308,467	193,614	85,351	108,263		295,165	155,556	139,609	38,108	101,501
Men	2,434,214	2,310,607	2,226,653	83,954	32,392	51,562		123,607	75,004	48,603	12,788	35,815
Women	3,363,032	3,191,474	3,081,814	109,660	52,959	56,701		171,558	80,552	91,006	25,320	65,686
Less than 2-year	508,288	27,629	—	27,629	256	27,373		480,659	158,941	321,718	47,001	274,717
Men	186,377	12,596	—	12,596	186	12,410		173,781	70,891	102,890	20,743	82,147
Women	321,911	15,033	—	15,033	70	14,963		306,878	88,050	218,828	26,258	192,570

					Staff, fall 1993							
Total	2,727,504	2,602,612	1,812,513	790,099	766,723	23,376		124,892	31,554	93,338	34,348	58,990
Professional staff	1,777,843	1,687,287	1,193,284	494,003	476,257	17,746		90,556	23,076	67,480	22,408	45,072
Administrative	160,638	143,675	81,209	62,466	59,867	2,599		16,963	1,652	15,311	4,041	11,270
Faculty	973,289	915,474	650,434	265,040	254,130	10,910		57,815	18,142	39,673	12,485	27,188
Faculty assistants	203,049	202,819	173,678	29,141	28,065	1,076		230	22	208	189	19
Other professionals	440,867	425,319	287,963	137,356	134,195	3,161		15,548	3,260	12,288	5,693	6,595
Nonprofessional staff	949,661	915,325	619,229	296,096	290,466	5,630		34,336	8,478	25,858	11,940	13,918
Student/staff ratio	5.6	5.5	6.2	3.9	3.7	9.9		7.4	9.0	6.9	4.5	8.3

					Degrees conferred, 1993–94							
Less than 1-year awards and 1- to 4-year awards	763,428	224,597	165,490	59,107	13,671	45,436		538,831	166,820	372,011	46,964	325,047
4-year institutions	25,539	18,834	8,805	10,029	8,268	1,761		6,705	—	6,705	6,531	174
Men	13,366	8,578	4,394	4,184	3,276	908		4,788	—	4,788	4,754	34
Women	12,173	10,256	4,411	5,845	4,992	853		1,917	—	1,917	1,777	140
2-year institutions	318,136	176,219	156,685	19,534	5,077	14,457		141,917	77,377	64,540	14,448	50,092
Men	138,446	76,234	67,707	8,527	2,142	6,385		62,212	37,034	25,178	4,767	20,411
Women	179,690	99,985	88,978	11,007	2,935	8,072		79,705	40,343	39,362	9,681	29,681
Less than 2-year	419,753	29,544	—	29,544	326	29,218		390,209	89,443	300,766	25,985	274,781
Men	160,783	13,806	—	13,806	242	13,564		146,977	42,785	104,192	12,198	91,994
Women	258,970	15,738	—	15,738	84	15,654		243,232	46,658	196,574	13,787	182,787
Associate [1]	562,993	542,449	456,190	86,259	48,493	37,766		20,544	3,097	17,447	3,034	14,413
4-year	78,991	77,396	38,520	38,876	29,939	8,937		1,595	—	1,595	920	675
Men	34,270	33,503	15,840	17,663	11,799	5,864		767	—	767	471	296
Women	44,721	43,893	22,680	21,213	18,140	3,073		828	—	828	449	379
2-year	483,902	465,053	417,670	47,383	18,554	28,829		18,849	3,097	15,752	2,088	13,664
Men	195,844	187,487	166,538	20,949	7,248	13,701		8,357	1,573	6,784	1,377	5,407
Women	288,058	277,566	251,132	26,434	11,306	15,128		10,492	1,524	8,968	711	8,257
Less than 2-year	100	—	—	—	—	—		100	—	100	26	74
Men	43	—	—	—	—	—		43	—	43	17	26
Women	57	—	—	—	—	—		57	—	57	9	48
Bachelor's [1]	1,177,157	1,169,275	789,148	380,127	371,561	8,566		7,882	6	7,876	6,487	1,389
Men	536,357	532,422	360,796	171,626	166,729	4,897		3,935	3	3,932	3,082	850
Women	640,800	636,853	428,352	208,501	204,832	3,669		3,947	3	3,944	3,405	539
Master's [1]	390,415	387,070	221,428	165,642	162,751	2,891		3,345	7	3,338	2,116	1,222
Men	178,026	176,085	97,139	78,946	77,288	1,658		1,941	1	1,940	1,175	765
Women	212,389	210,985	124,289	86,696	85,463	1,233		1,404	6	1,398	941	457
Doctor's [1]	43,863	43,185	28,524	14,661	14,418	243		678	—	678	278	400
Men	27,059	26,552	17,689	8,863	8,765	98		507	—	507	228	279
Women	16,804	16,633	10,835	5,798	5,653	145		171	—	171	50	121
First-professional [1]	77,131	75,418	29,842	45,576	45,051	525		1,713	82	1,631	1,384	247
Men	45,841	44,707	17,040	27,667	27,364	303		1,134	50	1,084	915	169
Women	31,290	30,711	12,802	17,909	17,687	222		579	32	547	469	78

[1] Includes noncollegiate institutions that offer non-accredited degree programs.
—Not applicable.

NOTE.—Enrollment data are preliminary.

SOURCE: U.S. Department of Education, National Center for Education Statistics, Integrated Postsecondary Education Data System (IPEDS), "Fall Enrollment," "Staff," and "Completions" surveys. (This table was prepared July 1996.)

Table 168.—Historical summary of faculty, students, degrees, and finances in institutions of higher education: 1869–70 to 1993–94

Item	1869–70	1879–80	1889–90	1899–1900	1909–10	1919–20	1929–30	1939–40	1949–50	1959–60	1969–70	1979–80	1989–90	1992–93	1993–94
1	2	3	4	5	6	7	8	9	10	11	12	13	14	15	16
Total institutions[1]	563	811	998	977	951	1,041	1,409	1,708	1,851	2,008	2,525	3,152	3,535	3,638	3,632
Total faculty[2]	[3]5,553	[3]11,522	[3]15,809	23,868	36,480	48,615	82,386	146,929	246,722	380,554	[4]450,000	[4]675,000	[5]824,220	[5]877,000	915,474
Men	[3]4,887	[3]7,328	[3]12,704	19,151	29,132	35,807	60,017	106,328	186,189	296,773	[4]346,000	[4]479,000	[5]577,298	—	561,123
Women	[3]666	[3]4,194	[3]3,105	4,717	7,348	12,808	22,369	40,601	60,533	83,781	[4]104,000	[4]196,000	[5]246,922	—	354,351
Total fall enrollment[6]	[3]52,286	[3]115,817	[3]156,756	237,592	[3]355,213	597,880	1,100,737	1,494,203	2,659,021	3,639,847	8,004,660	11,569,899	13,538,560	14,487,359	14,304,803
Men	[3]41,160	[3]77,972	[3]100,453	152,254	[3]214,648	314,938	619,935	893,250	1,853,068	2,332,617	4,746,201	5,682,877	6,190,015	6,523,989	6,427,450
Women	[3]11,126	[3]37,845	[3]56,303	85,338	[3]140,565	282,942	480,802	600,953	805,953	1,307,230	3,258,459	5,887,022	7,348,545	7,963,370	7,877,353
Earned degrees conferred															
Associate, total	—	—	—					—	—	—	206,023	400,910	455,102	514,756	[7]542,449
Men	—	—	—					—	—	—	117,432	183,737	191,195	211,964	[7]220,990
Women	—	—	—					—	—	—	88,591	217,173	263,907	302,792	[7]321,459
Bachelor's,[8] total	9,371	12,896	15,539	27,410	37,199	48,622	122,484	186,500	432,058	392,440	792,656	929,417	1,051,344	1,165,178	[7]1,169,275
Men	7,993	10,411	12,857	22,173	28,762	31,980	73,615	109,546	328,841	254,063	451,380	473,611	491,696	532,881	[7]532,422
Women	1,378	2,485	2,682	5,237	8,437	16,642	48,869	76,954	103,217	138,377	341,276	455,806	559,648	632,297	[7]636,853
Master's,[9] total	0	879	1,015	1,583	2,113	4,279	14,969	26,731	58,183	74,435	208,291	298,081	324,301	369,585	[7]387,070
Men	0	868	821	1,280	1,555	2,985	8,925	16,508	41,220	50,898	125,624	150,749	153,653	169,258	[7]176,085
Women	0	11	194	303	558	1,294	6,044	10,223	16,963	23,537	82,667	147,332	170,648	200,327	[7]210,985
First-professional,[8] total	(8)	(8)	(8)	(8)	(8)	(8)	(8)	(8)	(8)	(8)	34,578	70,131	70,988	75,387	[7]75,418
Men	(8)	(8)	(8)	(8)	(8)	(8)	(8)	(8)	(8)	(8)	32,794	52,716	43,961	45,153	[7]44,707
Women	(8)	(8)	(8)	(8)	(8)	(8)	(8)	(8)	(8)	(8)	1,784	17,415	27,027	30,234	[7]30,711
Doctor's, total	1	54	149	382	443	615	2,299	3,290	6,420	9,829	29,866	32,615	38,371	42,132	43,185
Men	1	51	147	359	399	522	1,946	2,861	5,804	8,801	25,890	22,943	24,401	26,073	[7]26,552
Women	0	3	2	23	44	93	353	429	616	1,028	3,976	9,672	13,970	16,059	[7]16,633
Finances, in thousands															
Current-fund revenue	—	—	$21,464	$35,084	$76,883	$199,922	$554,511	$715,211	$2,374,645	$5,785,537	$21,515,242	$58,519,982	$139,635,477	$170,880,503	[7]$179,226,601
Educational and general income	—	—	—	—	67,917	172,929	483,065	571,288	1,833,845	4,688,352	16,486,177	—	—	—	—
Current-fund expenditures	—	—	—	—	—	—	507,142	674,688	2,245,661	5,601,376	21,043,113	56,913,588	134,655,571	165,241,040	[7]173,350,617
Educational and general expenditures	—	—	—	—	—	—	377,903	521,990	1,706,444	4,685,258	16,845,210	44,542,843	105,585,076	128,977,968	[7]136,024,350
Value of physical property	—	—	95,426	253,599	457,594	747,333	2,065,049	[10]2,753,780	4,799,964	13,548,548	42,093,580	83,733,387	164,635,000	192,760,817	199,463,715
Market value of endowment funds	—	—	[11]78,788	[11]194,998	[11]323,661	[11]569,071	[11]1,372,068	[11]1,686,283	[11]2,601,223	[11]5,322,080	11,206,632	20,743,045	67,978,726	92,239,311	96,012,591

[1] Prior to 1979–80, excludes branch campuses.

[2] Total number of different individuals (not reduced to full-time equivalent). Beginning in 1959–60, data are for the first term of the academic year. Beginning in 1969–70, data include only instructional faculty with the rank of instructor or above.

[3] Estimated.

[4] Estimated number of senior instructional staff. Excludes graduate assistants.

[5] Because of revised survey procedures, data may not be directly comparable with figures prior to 1989–90.

[6] Data for 1869–70 to 1949–50 are for resident degree-credit students who enrolled at any time during the academic year.

[7] Preliminary data.

[8] From 1869–70 to 1959–60, first-professional degrees included under bachelor's degrees.

[9] Figures for years prior to 1969–70 are not precisely comparable with later data.

[10] Includes unexpended plant funds.

[11] Book value. Includes other nonexpendable funds.

—Data not available.

NOTE.—Some data have been revised from previously published figures.

SOURCE: U.S. Department of Education, National Center for Education Statistics, *Biennial Survey of Education in the United States; Education Directory, Colleges and Universities; Faculty and Other Professional Staff in Institutions of Higher Education; Fall Enrollment in Colleges and Universities; Earned Degrees Conferred; Financial Statistics of Institutions of Higher Education*; and "Fall Enrollment in Institutions of Higher Education," "Degrees and Other Formal Awards Conferred," and "Financial Statistics of Institutions of Higher Education" surveys; and Integrated Postsecondary Education Data System (IPEDS), "Fall Enrollment," "Completions," and "Finance" surveys. (This table was prepared July 1996.)

Table 169.—Total fall enrollment in institutions of higher education, by attendance status, sex of student, and control of institution: 1947 to 1994

Year	Total enrollment	Attendance status		Sex of student		Control of institution			
		Full-time	Part-time	Men	Women	Public	Private		
							Total	Nonprofit	Proprietary
1	2	3	4	5	6	7	8	9	10
1947 [1]	2,338,226	—	—	1,659,249	678,977	1,152,377	1,185,849	—	—
1948 [1]	2,403,396	—	—	1,709,367	694,029	1,185,588	1,217,808	—	—
1949 [1]	2,444,900	—	—	1,721,572	723,328	1,207,151	1,237,749	—	—
1950 [1]	2,281,298	—	—	1,560,392	720,906	1,139,699	1,141,599	—	—
1951 [1]	2,101,962	—	—	1,390,740	711,222	1,037,938	1,064,024	—	—
1952 [1]	2,134,242	—	—	1,380,357	753,885	1,101,240	1,033,002	—	—
1953 [1]	2,231,054	—	—	1,422,598	808,456	1,185,876	1,045,178	—	—
1954 [1]	2,446,693	—	—	1,563,382	883,311	1,353,531	1,093,162	—	—
1955 [1]	2,653,034	—	—	1,733,184	919,850	1,476,282	1,176,752	—	—
1956 [1]	2,918,212	—	—	1,911,458	1,006,754	1,656,402	1,261,810	—	—
1957	3,323,783	—	—	2,170,765	1,153,018	1,972,673	1,351,110	—	—
1959	3,639,847	2,421,016	[2] 1,218,831	2,332,617	1,307,230	2,180,982	1,458,865	—	—
1961	4,145,065	2,785,133	[2] 1,359,932	2,585,821	1,559,244	2,561,447	1,583,618	—	—
1963	4,779,609	3,183,833	[2] 1,595,776	2,961,540	1,818,069	3,081,279	1,698,330	—	—
1964	5,280,020	3,573,238	[2] 1,706,782	3,248,713	2,031,307	3,467,708	1,812,312	—	—
1965	5,920,864	4,095,728	[2] 1,825,136	3,630,020	2,290,844	3,969,596	1,951,268	—	—
1966	6,389,872	4,438,606	[2] 1,951,266	3,856,216	2,533,656	4,348,917	2,040,955	—	—
1967	6,911,748	4,793,128	[2][2] 2,118,620	4,132,800	2,778,948	4,816,028	2,095,720	—	—
1968	7,513,091	5,210,155	2,302,936	4,477,649	3,035,442	5,430,652	2,082,439	—	—
1969	8,004,660	5,498,883	2,505,777	4,746,201	3,258,459	5,896,868	2,107,792	—	—
1970	8,580,887	5,816,290	2,764,597	5,043,642	3,537,245	6,428,134	2,152,753	—	—
1971	8,948,644	6,077,232	2,871,412	5,207,004	3,741,640	6,804,309	2,144,335	—	—
1972	9,214,820	6,072,389	3,142,471	5,238,757	3,976,103	7,070,635	2,144,185	—	—
1973	9,602,123	6,189,493	3,412,630	5,371,052	4,231,071	7,419,516	2,182,607	—	—
1974	10,223,729	6,370,273	3,853,456	5,622,429	4,601,300	7,988,500	2,235,229	—	—
1975	11,184,859	6,841,334	4,343,525	6,148,997	5,035,862	8,834,508	2,350,351	—	—
1976	11,012,137	6,717,058	4,295,079	5,810,828	5,201,309	8,653,477	2,358,660	2,314,298	44,362
1977	11,285,787	6,792,925	4,492,862	5,789,016	5,496,771	8,846,993	2,438,794	2,386,652	52,142
1978	11,260,092	6,667,657	4,592,435	5,640,998	5,619,094	8,785,893	2,474,199	2,408,331	65,868
1979	11,569,899	6,794,039	4,775,860	5,682,877	5,887,022	9,036,822	2,533,077	2,461,773	71,304
1980	12,096,895	7,097,958	4,998,937	5,874,374	6,222,521	9,457,394	2,639,501	2,527,787	[3] 111,714
1981	12,371,672	7,181,250	5,190,422	5,975,056	6,396,616	9,647,032	2,724,640	2,572,405	[3] 152,235
1982	12,425,780	7,220,618	5,205,162	6,031,384	6,394,396	9,696,087	2,729,693	2,552,739	[3] 176,954
1983	12,464,661	7,261,050	5,203,611	6,023,725	6,440,936	9,682,734	2,781,927	2,589,187	192,740
1984	12,241,940	7,098,388	5,143,552	5,863,574	6,378,366	9,477,370	2,764,570	2,574,419	190,151
1985	12,247,055	7,075,221	5,171,834	5,818,450	6,428,605	9,479,273	2,767,782	2,571,791	195,991
1986	12,503,511	7,119,550	5,383,961	5,884,515	6,618,996	9,713,893	2,789,618	2,572,479	[4] 217,139
1987	12,766,642	7,231,085	5,535,557	5,932,056	6,834,586	9,973,254	2,793,388	2,602,350	[4] 191,038
1988	13,055,337	7,436,768	5,618,569	6,001,896	7,053,441	10,161,388	2,893,949	2,673,567	220,382
1989	13,538,560	7,660,950	5,877,610	6,190,015	7,348,545	10,577,963	2,960,597	2,731,174	229,423
1990	13,818,637	7,820,985	5,997,652	6,283,909	7,534,728	10,844,717	2,973,920	2,760,227	213,693
1991	14,358,953	8,115,329	6,243,624	6,501,844	7,857,109	11,309,563	3,049,390	2,819,041	230,349
1992	14,487,359	8,162,118	6,325,241	6,523,989	7,963,370	11,384,567	3,102,792	2,872,523	230,269
1993 [5]	14,304,803	8,127,618	6,177,185	6,427,450	7,877,353	11,189,088	3,115,715	2,888,897	226,818
1994 [6]	14,278,790	8,137,776	6,141,014	6,371,898	7,906,892	11,133,680	3,145,110	2,910,107	235,003

[1] Degree-credit enrollment only.

[2] Includes part-time resident students and all extension students.

[3] Large increases are due to the addition of schools accredited by the Accrediting Commission of Career Schools and Colleges of Technology.

[4] Because of imputation techniques, data are not consistent with figures for other years.

[5] Revised from previously published data.

[6] Preliminary data.

—Data not available.

SOURCE: U.S. Department of Education, National Center for Education Statistics, "Fall Enrollment in Colleges and Universities;" and Integrated Postsecondary Education Data System (IPEDS), "Fall Enrollment" surveys. (This table was prepared December 1995.)

Table 170.—Total fall enrollment in institutions of higher education, by control and type of institution: 1963 to 1994

Year	All institutions					Public institutions					Private institutions				
	Total	4-year Total	University	Other 4-year	2-year	Total	4-year Total	University	Other 4-year	2-year	Total	4-year Total	University	Other 4-year	2-year
1	2	3	4	5	6	7	8	9	10	11	12	13	14	15	16
1963[1]	4,779,609	3,929,248	—	—	850,361	3,081,279	2,341,468	—	—	739,811	1,698,330	1,587,780	—	—	110,550
1964[1]	5,280,020	4,291,094	—	—	988,926	3,467,708	2,592,929	—	—	874,779	1,812,312	1,698,165	—	—	114,147
1965[1]	5,920,864	4,747,912	—	—	1,172,952	3,969,596	2,928,332	—	—	1,041,264	1,951,268	1,819,580	—	—	131,688
1966[1]	6,389,872	5,063,902	—	—	1,325,970	4,348,917	3,159,748	—	—	1,189,169	2,040,955	1,904,154	—	—	136,801
1967[1]	6,911,748	5,398,986	—	—	1,512,762	4,816,028	3,443,975	—	—	1,372,053	2,095,720	1,955,011	—	—	140,709
1968[1]	7,513,091	5,720,795	—	—	1,792,296	5,430,652	3,784,178	—	—	1,646,474	2,082,439	1,936,617	—	—	145,822
1969	8,004,660	5,937,127	—	—	2,067,533	5,896,868	3,962,522	—	—	1,934,346	2,107,792	1,974,605	—	—	133,187
1970	8,580,887	6,261,502	—	—	2,319,385	6,428,134	4,232,722	—	—	2,195,412	2,152,753	2,028,780	—	—	123,973
1971	8,948,644	6,369,355	—	—	2,579,289	6,804,309	4,346,990	—	—	2,457,319	2,144,335	2,022,365	—	—	121,970
1972	9,214,820	6,458,634	—	—	2,756,186	7,070,635	4,429,696	—	—	2,640,939	2,144,185	2,028,938	—	—	115,247
1973	9,602,123	6,590,023	—	—	3,012,100	7,419,516	4,529,895	—	—	2,889,621	2,182,607	2,060,128	—	—	122,479
1974	10,223,729	6,819,735	—	—	3,403,994	7,988,500	4,703,018	—	—	3,285,482	2,235,229	2,116,717	—	—	118,512
1975	11,184,859	7,214,740	2,838,266	4,376,474	3,970,119	8,834,508	4,998,142	2,124,221	2,873,921	3,836,366	2,350,351	2,216,598	714,045	1,502,553	133,753
1976	11,012,137	7,128,816	2,780,289	4,348,527	3,883,321	8,653,477	4,901,691	2,079,929	2,821,762	3,751,786	2,358,660	2,227,125	700,360	1,526,765	131,535
1977	11,285,787	7,242,845	2,793,418	4,449,427	4,042,942	8,846,993	4,945,224	2,070,032	2,875,192	3,901,769	2,438,794	2,297,621	723,386	1,574,235	141,173
1978	11,260,092	7,231,625	2,780,729	4,451,222	4,028,467	8,785,893	4,912,203	2,062,295	2,849,908	3,873,690	2,474,199	2,319,422	718,434	1,601,314	154,777
1979	11,569,899	7,353,233	2,839,582	4,513,651	4,216,666	9,036,822	4,980,012	2,099,525	2,880,487	4,056,810	2,533,077	2,373,221	740,057	1,633,164	159,856
1980	12,096,895	7,570,608	2,902,014	4,668,594	4,526,287	9,457,394	5,128,612	2,154,283	2,974,329	4,328,782	2,639,501	2,441,996	747,731	1,694,265	197,505[2]
1981	12,371,672	7,655,461	2,901,344	4,754,117	4,716,211	9,647,032	5,166,324	2,152,474	3,013,850	4,480,708	2,724,640	2,489,137	748,870	1,740,267	235,503[2]
1982	12,425,780	7,654,074	2,883,735	4,770,339	4,771,706	9,696,087	5,176,434	2,152,547	3,023,887	4,519,653	2,729,693	2,477,640	731,188	1,746,452	252,053
1983	12,464,661	7,741,195	2,888,813	4,852,382	4,723,466	9,682,734	5,223,404	2,154,790	3,068,614	4,459,330	2,781,927	2,517,791	734,023	1,783,768	264,136
1984	12,241,940	7,711,167	2,870,329	4,840,838	4,530,773	9,477,370	5,198,273	2,138,621	3,059,652	4,279,097	2,764,570	2,512,894	731,708	1,781,186	251,676
1985	12,247,055	7,715,978	2,870,692	4,845,286	4,531,077	9,479,273	5,209,540	2,141,112	3,068,428	4,269,733	2,767,782	2,506,438	729,580	1,776,858	261,344
1986	12,503,511	7,823,963	2,897,207	4,926,756	4,679,548	9,713,893	5,300,202	2,160,646	3,139,556	4,413,691	2,789,618	2,523,761	736,561	1,787,200	265,857[3]
1987	12,766,642	7,990,420	2,929,327	5,061,093	4,776,222	9,973,254	5,432,200	2,188,008	3,244,192	4,541,054	2,793,388	2,558,220	741,319	1,816,901	235,168[3]
1988	13,055,337	8,180,182	2,978,593	5,201,589	4,875,155	10,161,388	5,545,901	2,229,868	3,316,033	4,615,487	2,893,949	2,634,281	748,725	1,885,556	259,668
1989	13,538,560	8,387,671	3,019,115	5,368,556	5,150,889	10,577,963	5,694,303	2,266,056	3,428,247	4,883,660	2,960,597	2,693,368	753,059	1,940,309	267,229
1990	13,818,637	8,578,554	3,044,670	5,533,884	5,240,083	10,844,717	5,848,242	2,290,464	3,557,778	4,996,475	2,973,920	2,730,312	754,206	1,976,106	243,608
1991	14,358,953	8,707,053	3,065,429	5,641,624	5,651,900	11,309,563	5,904,748	2,301,222	3,603,526	5,404,815	3,049,390	2,802,305	764,207	2,038,098	247,085
1992	14,487,359	8,764,969	3,050,345	5,714,624	5,722,390	11,384,567	5,900,012	2,283,834	3,616,178	5,484,555	3,102,792	2,864,957	766,511	2,098,446	237,835
1993[4]	14,304,803	8,738,936	3,022,728	5,716,208	5,565,867	11,189,088	5,851,760	2,259,692	3,592,068	5,337,328	3,115,715	2,887,176	763,036	2,124,140	228,539
1994[5]	14,278,790	8,749,080	3,009,072	5,740,008	5,529,710	11,133,680	5,825,213	2,244,636	3,580,577	5,308,467	3,145,110	2,923,867	764,436	2,159,431	221,243

[1] Data for 2-year branch campuses of 4-year institutions are included with the 4-year institutions.
[2] Large increases are due to the addition of schools accredited by the Accrediting Commission of Career Schools and Colleges of Technology.
[3] Because of imputation techniques, data are not consistent with figures for other years.
[4] Revised from previously published data.
[5] Preliminary data.

—Data not available.

SOURCE: U.S. Department of Education, National Center for Education Statistics, "Fall Enrollment in Colleges and Universities," and Integrated Postsecondary Education Data System (IPEDS), "Fall Enrollment" surveys. (This table was prepared January 1996.)

Table 171.—Total fall enrollment in institutions of higher education, by attendance status, sex, and age: Fall 1970 to fall 2006

[In thousands]

Sex and age	1970	1975	1980	1985	1986	1987	1990	1991	1993	1994	Projected 2000	Projected 2001	Projected 2006
1	2	3	4	5	6	7	8	9	10	11	12	13	14
Men and women, total	**8,581**	**11,185**	**12,097**	**12,247**	**12,504**	**12,767**	**13,819**	**14,359**	**14,305**	**14,279**	**15,497**	**15,671**	**16,389**
14 to 17 years old	259	278	247	235	200	237	167	120	176	163	188	183	201
18 and 19 years old	2,600	2,786	2,901	2,600	2,727	2,847	2,800	2,714	2,640	2,756	3,279	3,346	3,574
20 and 21 years old	1,880	2,243	2,423	2,383	2,206	2,504	2,619	2,769	2,708	2,538	2,906	2,982	3,221
22 to 24 years old	1,457	1,754	1,989	1,933	2,100	1,989	2,166	2,287	2,523	2,483	2,469	2,559	2,890
25 to 29 years old	1,074	1,774	1,871	1,953	1,941	1,930	2,063	2,134	2,008	1,935	1,905	1,861	2,082
30 to 34 years old	487	967	1,243	1,261	1,301	1,266	1,360	1,467	1,472	1,409	1,278	1,289	1,181
35 years old and over	823	1,383	1,422	1,885	2,030	1,993	2,644	2,867	2,779	2,995	3,472	3,452	3,241
Men	**5,044**	**6,149**	**5,874**	**5,818**	**5,885**	**5,932**	**6,284**	**6,502**	**6,427**	**6,372**	**6,985**	**7,079**	**7,375**
14 to 17 years old	130	126	99	121	84	114	82	46	83	66	82	81	91
18 and 19 years old	1,349	1,397	1,375	1,230	1,312	1,363	1,351	1,217	1,224	1,251	1,512	1,544	1,638
20 and 21 years old	1,095	1,245	1,259	1,216	1,090	1,258	1,304	1,306	1,294	1,185	1,382	1,424	1,520
22 to 24 years old	964	1,047	1,064	1,048	1,085	1,003	1,107	1,214	1,260	1,280	1,247	1,291	1,432
25 to 29 years old	783	1,122	993	991	1,026	964	976	1,082	950	890	837	813	901
30 to 34 years old	308	557	576	574	605	541	564	664	661	608	546	555	511
35 years old and over	415	654	507	639	683	690	901	972	955	1,092	1,378	1,370	1,282
Women	**3,537**	**5,036**	**6,223**	**6,429**	**6,619**	**6,835**	**7,535**	**7,857**	**7,877**	**7,907**	**8,512**	**8,592**	**9,014**
14 to 17 years old	129	152	148	113	116	123	85	75	93	96	105	101	110
18 and 19 years old	1,250	1,389	1,526	1,370	1,415	1,484	1,450	1,497	1,416	1,504	1,767	1,802	1,936
20 and 21 years old	786	998	1,165	1,166	1,115	1,246	1,315	1,463	1,414	1,353	1,524	1,558	1,701
22 to 24 years old	493	706	925	885	1,014	986	1,059	1,072	1,263	1,204	1,223	1,268	1,458
25 to 29 years old	291	652	878	962	916	966	1,087	1,053	1,058	1,045	1,068	1,048	1,181
30 to 34 years old	179	410	667	687	696	725	796	803	811	801	732	734	669
35 years old and over	409	729	914	1,246	1,347	1,303	1,743	1,895	1,824	1,903	2,093	2,081	1,960
Full-time	**5,816**	**6,841**	**7,098**	**7,075**	**7,120**	**7,231**	**7,821**	**8,115**	**8,128**	**8,138**	**9,171**	**9,318**	**9,943**
14 to 17 years old	242	242	216	203	182	142	141	114	159	140	163	158	174
18 and 19 years old	2,406	2,510	2,580	2,322	2,415	2,488	2,479	2,407	2,330	2,418	2,849	2,908	3,120
20 and 21 years old	1,647	1,854	2,060	1,975	1,813	2,024	2,121	2,299	2,219	2,086	2,375	2,434	2,626
22 to 24 years old	881	1,008	1,174	1,227	1,323	1,223	1,387	1,497	1,639	1,597	1,625	1,685	1,903
25 to 29 years old	407	692	610	695	699	693	802	868	755	782	767	745	820
30 to 34 years old	100	279	264	310	333	293	403	401	413	426	406	407	379
35 years old and over	134	256	193	345	355	367	487	528	613	689	986	980	920
Men	**3,505**	**3,926**	**3,689**	**3,608**	**3,599**	**3,611**	**3,808**	**3,929**	**3,891**	**3,855**	**4,458**	**4,537**	**4,825**
14 to 17 years old	124	109	84	102	78	69	70	39	72	53	68	67	75
18 and 19 years old	1,265	1,269	1,229	1,108	1,181	1,190	1,198	1,096	1,086	1,098	1,336	1,363	1,451
20 and 21 years old	990	1,053	1,104	1,027	923	1,029	1,055	1,077	1,084	964	1,136	1,171	1,256
22 to 24 years old	650	686	687	730	720	669	757	836	868	867	859	890	991
25 to 29 years old	327	474	379	395	410	371	413	494	386	406	383	372	418
30 to 34 years old	72	184	129	149	167	146	162	190	177	178	166	166	159
35 years old and over	75	152	77	97	121	138	154	197	216	290	511	508	475
Women	**2,311**	**2,915**	**3,409**	**3,468**	**3,521**	**3,620**	**4,013**	**4,186**	**4,237**	**4,283**	**4,713**	**4,781**	**5,117**
14 to 17 years old	117	133	132	101	104	73	71	75	87	88	95	91	99
18 and 19 years old	1,140	1,241	1,352	1,214	1,234	1,298	1,281	1,311	1,244	1,319	1,513	1,545	1,669
20 and 21 years old	657	800	955	948	890	995	1,067	1,223	1,135	1,123	1,240	1,264	1,371
22 to 24 years old	231	322	487	497	604	554	630	661	770	731	767	794	911
25 to 29 years old	80	218	232	299	289	323	389	374	369	375	384	373	402
30 to 34 years old	28	95	135	161	166	147	242	211	236	248	241	241	220
35 years old and over	59	105	115	248	233	229	333	331	397	399	474	472	444
Part-time	**2,765**	**4,344**	**4,999**	**5,172**	**5,384**	**5,536**	**5,998**	**6,244**	**6,177**	**6,141**	**6,325**	**6,353**	**6,446**
14 to 17 years old	17	36	31	32	18	95	26	6	16	22	25	24	27
18 and 19 years old	194	276	320	278	312	359	321	307	310	338	430	438	454
20 and 21 years old	233	390	364	408	392	480	498	470	488	452	531	547	594
22 to 24 years old	576	746	815	705	777	766	779	790	885	886	844	874	987
25 to 29 years old	668	1,082	1,261	1,258	1,242	1,237	1,261	1,266	1,253	1,153	1,138	1,115	1,262
30 to 34 years old	388	687	979	951	968	972	957	1,066	1,059	983	871	882	802
35 years old and over	689	1,127	1,229	1,540	1,675	1,626	2,157	2,339	2,167	2,307	2,486	2,472	2,322
Men	**1,540**	**2,222**	**2,185**	**2,211**	**2,285**	**2,321**	**2,476**	**2,572**	**2,537**	**2,517**	**2,526**	**2,541**	**2,549**
14 to 17 years old	5	17	15	19	6	46	12	6	10	13	14	14	15
18 and 19 years old	84	128	146	122	131	173	153	121	138	153	176	181	187
20 and 21 years old	105	192	154	189	167	229	250	230	209	221	247	253	264
22 to 24 years old	314	362	377	318	366	334	350	378	392	413	388	401	440
25 to 29 years old	456	649	615	596	616	593	563	587	564	483	454	441	483
30 to 34 years old	236	373	447	424	438	395	402	475	484	430	380	390	353
35 years old and over	340	502	430	542	562	552	747	775	739	803	867	862	806
Women	**1,225**	**2,120**	**2,814**	**2,961**	**3,098**	**3,214**	**3,521**	**3,671**	**3,640**	**3,624**	**3,799**	**3,812**	**3,897**
14 to 17 years old	12	19	17	12	12	50	13	0	6	9	10	10	11
18 and 19 years old	110	147	174	156	181	186	168	186	172	185	254	258	267
20 and 21 years old	128	198	209	218	225	251	248	240	279	231	284	295	330
22 to 24 years old	262	384	438	388	411	432	429	411	493	473	456	474	547
25 to 29 years old	212	433	646	662	626	643	699	679	689	670	684	674	778
30 to 34 years old	151	315	531	527	530	578	555	591	575	553	491	492	449
35 years old and over	349	625	799	998	1,114	1,074	1,410	1,563	1,427	1,504	1,619	1,610	1,516

NOTE.—Distributions by age are estimates based on samples of the civilian noninstitutional population. Because of rounding, details may not add to totals.

SOURCE: U.S. Department of Education, National Center for Education Statistics, "Fall Enrollment in Institutions of Higher Education" surveys; Integrated Postsecondary Education Data System (IPEDS), "Fall Enrollment" surveys; *Projections of Education Statistics to 2006;* and U.S. Department of Commerce, Bureau of the Census, Current Population Reports, *Social and Economic Characteristics of Students,* various years. (This table was prepared July 1996.)

Table 172.—Total fall enrollment in institutions of higher education, by level, sex, age, and attendance status of student: 1993

Attendance status and age of student	All levels			Undergraduate			First-professional			Graduate		
	Total	Men	Women	Total	Men	Women	Total	Men	Women	Total	Men	Women
1	2	3	4	5	6	7	8	9	10	11	12	13
All students	14,304,803	6,427,450	7,877,353	12,323,959	5,483,682	6,840,277	292,431	172,788	119,643	1,688,413	770,980	917,433
Under 18	245,920	98,896	147,024	245,286	98,647	146,639	56	27	29	578	222	356
18 and 19	2,722,131	1,237,569	1,484,562	2,720,798	1,237,102	1,483,696	156	84	72	1,177	383	794
20 and 21	2,607,019	1,228,707	1,378,312	2,589,995	1,221,262	1,368,733	6,782	3,167	3,615	10,242	4,278	5,964
22 to 24	2,492,269	1,252,571	1,239,698	2,124,328	1,077,790	1,046,538	107,913	60,625	47,288	260,028	114,156	145,872
25 to 29	2,025,972	980,118	1,045,854	1,446,230	674,123	772,107	99,848	62,727	37,121	479,894	243,268	236,626
30 to 34	1,338,069	579,400	758,669	1,008,988	401,347	607,641	33,117	21,020	12,097	295,964	157,033	138,931
35 to 39	1,019,588	388,960	630,628	787,287	280,941	506,346	17,890	10,650	7,240	214,411	97,369	117,042
40 to 49	1,181,248	399,544	781,704	872,239	287,473	584,766	14,724	7,749	6,975	294,285	104,322	189,963
50 to 64	339,497	113,834	225,663	260,447	87,359	173,088	3,638	1,702	1,936	75,412	24,773	50,639
65 and over	78,375	30,997	47,378	72,877	28,554	44,323	258	146	112	5,240	2,297	2,943
Age unknown	254,715	116,854	137,861	195,484	89,084	106,400	8,049	4,891	3,158	51,182	22,879	28,303
Full-time	8,127,618	3,890,571	4,237,047	7,179,482	3,381,997	3,797,485	259,764	153,873	105,891	688,372	354,701	333,671
Under 18	111,151	44,204	66,947	110,937	44,117	66,820	45	20	25	169	67	102
18 and 19	2,324,860	1,057,170	1,267,690	2,323,726	1,056,782	1,266,944	153	82	71	981	306	675
20 and 21	2,070,480	983,843	1,086,637	2,055,691	977,319	1,078,372	6,707	3,128	3,579	8,082	3,396	4,686
22 to 24	1,583,062	840,071	742,991	1,304,599	700,230	604,369	104,670	58,865	45,805	173,793	80,976	92,817
25 to 29	884,787	472,116	412,671	564,648	285,851	278,797	89,976	56,723	33,253	230,163	129,542	100,621
30 to 34	433,467	200,114	233,353	295,838	117,483	178,355	26,414	16,825	9,589	111,215	65,806	45,409
35 to 39	276,170	111,100	165,070	199,982	71,005	128,977	13,077	7,772	5,305	63,111	32,323	30,788
40 to 49	268,390	103,182	165,208	190,408	69,746	120,662	9,685	5,201	4,484	68,297	28,235	40,062
50 to 64	57,723	21,942	35,781	40,268	15,138	25,130	2,121	1,033	1,088	15,334	5,771	9,563
65 and over	9,359	4,356	5,003	8,271	3,806	4,465	170	105	65	918	445	473
Age unknown	108,169	52,473	55,696	85,114	40,520	44,594	6,746	4,119	2,627	16,309	7,834	8,475
Part-time	6,177,185	2,536,879	3,640,306	5,144,477	2,101,685	3,042,792	32,667	18,915	13,752	1,000,041	416,279	583,762
Under 18	134,769	54,692	80,077	134,349	54,530	79,819	11	7	4	409	155	254
18 and 19	397,271	180,399	216,872	397,072	180,320	216,752	3	2	1	196	77	119
20 and 21	536,539	244,864	291,675	534,304	243,943	290,361	75	39	36	2,160	882	1,278
22 to 24	909,207	412,500	496,707	819,729	377,560	442,169	3,243	1,760	1,483	86,235	33,180	53,055
25 to 29	1,141,185	508,002	633,183	881,582	388,272	493,310	9,872	6,004	3,868	249,731	113,726	136,005
30 to 34	904,602	379,286	525,316	713,150	283,864	429,286	6,703	4,195	2,508	184,749	91,227	93,522
35 to 39	743,418	277,860	465,558	587,305	209,936	377,369	4,813	2,878	1,935	151,300	65,046	86,254
40 to 49	912,858	296,362	616,496	681,831	217,727	464,104	5,039	2,548	2,491	225,988	76,087	149,901
50 to 64	281,774	91,892	189,882	220,179	72,221	147,958	1,517	669	848	60,078	19,002	41,076
65 and over	69,016	26,641	42,375	64,606	24,748	39,858	88	41	47	4,322	1,852	2,470
Age unknown	146,546	64,381	82,165	110,370	48,564	61,806	1,303	772	531	34,873	15,045	19,828
Percentage distribution												
All students	100.0	100.0	100.0	100.0	100.0	100.0	100.0	100.0	100.0	100.0	100.0	100.0
Under 18	1.7	1.5	1.9	2.0	1.8	2.1	(¹)	(¹)	(¹)	(¹)	(¹)	(¹)
18 and 19	19.0	19.3	18.8	22.1	22.6	21.7	0.1	(¹)	0.1	0.1	(¹)	0.1
20 and 21	18.2	19.1	17.5	21.0	22.3	20.0	2.3	1.8	3.0	0.6	0.6	0.7
22 to 24	17.4	19.5	15.7	17.2	19.7	15.3	36.9	35.1	39.5	15.4	14.8	15.9
25 to 29	14.2	15.2	13.3	11.7	12.3	11.3	34.1	36.3	31.0	28.4	31.6	25.8
30 to 34	9.4	9.0	9.6	8.2	7.3	8.9	11.3	12.2	10.1	17.5	20.4	15.1
35 to 39	7.1	6.1	8.0	6.4	5.1	7.4	6.1	6.2	6.1	12.7	12.6	12.8
40 to 49	8.3	6.2	9.9	7.1	5.2	8.5	5.0	4.5	5.8	17.4	13.5	20.7
50 to 64	2.4	1.8	2.9	2.1	1.6	2.5	1.2	1.0	1.6	4.5	3.2	5.5
65 and over	0.5	0.5	0.6	0.6	0.5	0.6	0.1	0.1	0.1	0.3	0.3	0.3
Age unknown	1.8	1.8	1.8	1.6	1.6	1.6	2.8	2.8	2.6	3.0	3.0	3.1
Full-time	100.0	100.0	100.0	100.0	100.0	100.0	100.0	100.0	100.0	100.0	100.0	100.0
Under 18	1.4	1.1	1.6	1.5	1.3	1.8	(¹)	(¹)	(¹)	(¹)	(¹)	0.2
18 and 19	28.6	27.2	29.9	32.4	31.2	33.4	0.1	0.1	0.1	0.1	0.1	0.2
20 and 21	25.5	25.3	25.6	28.6	28.9	28.4	2.6	2.0	3.4	1.2	1.0	1.4
22 to 24	19.5	21.6	17.5	18.2	20.7	15.9	40.3	38.3	43.3	25.2	22.8	27.8
25 to 29	10.9	12.1	9.7	7.9	8.5	7.3	34.6	36.9	31.4	33.4	36.5	30.2
30 to 34	5.3	5.1	5.5	4.1	3.5	4.7	10.2	10.9	9.1	16.2	18.6	13.6
35 to 39	3.4	2.9	3.9	2.8	2.1	3.4	5.0	5.1	5.0	9.2	9.1	9.2
40 to 49	3.3	2.7	3.9	2.7	2.1	3.2	3.7	3.4	4.2	9.9	8.0	12.0
50 to 64	0.7	0.6	0.8	0.6	0.4	0.7	0.8	0.7	1.0	2.2	1.6	2.9
65 and over	0.1	0.1	0.1	0.1	0.1	0.1	0.1	0.1	0.1	0.1	0.1	0.1
Age unknown	1.3	1.3	1.3	1.2	1.2	1.2	2.6	2.7	2.5	2.4	2.2	2.5
Part-time	100.0	100.0	100.0	100.0	100.0	100.0	100.0	100.0	100.0	100.0	100.0	100.0
Under 18	2.2	2.2	2.2	2.6	2.6	2.6	(¹)	(¹)	(¹)	(¹)	(¹)	(¹)
18 and 19	6.4	7.1	6.0	7.7	8.6	7.1	(¹)	(¹)	(¹)	(¹)	(¹)	(¹)
20 and 21	8.7	9.7	8.0	10.4	11.6	9.5	0.2	0.2	0.3	0.2	0.2	0.2
22 to 24	14.7	16.3	13.6	15.9	18.0	14.5	9.9	9.3	10.8	8.6	8.0	9.1
25 to 29	18.5	20.0	17.4	17.1	18.5	16.2	30.2	31.7	28.1	25.0	27.3	23.3
30 to 34	14.6	15.0	14.4	13.9	13.5	14.1	20.5	22.2	18.2	18.5	21.9	16.0
35 to 39	12.0	11.0	12.8	11.4	10.0	12.4	14.7	15.2	14.1	15.1	15.6	14.8
40 to 49	14.8	11.7	16.9	13.3	10.4	15.3	15.4	13.5	18.1	22.6	18.3	25.7
50 to 64	4.6	3.6	5.2	4.3	3.4	4.9	4.6	3.5	6.2	6.0	4.6	7.0
65 and over	1.1	1.1	1.2	1.3	1.2	1.3	0.3	0.2	0.3	0.4	0.4	0.4
Age unknown	2.4	2.5	2.3	2.1	2.3	2.0	4.0	4.1	3.9	3.5	3.6	3.4

¹ Less than .05 percent.

NOTE.—Because of rounding, details may not add to 100.0 percent.

SOURCE: U.S. Department of Education, National Center for Education Statistics, Integrated Postsecondary Education Data System, "Fall Enrollment, 1993" survey. (This table was prepared June 1996.)

Table 173.—Total fall enrollment in institutions of higher education, by type and control of institution, and age and attendance status of student: 1993

Attendance status and age of student	All institutions			Public institutions			Private institutions		
	Total	4-year	2-year	Total	4-year	2-year	Total	4-year	2-year
1	2	3	4	5	6	7	8	9	10
All students	**14,304,803**	**8,738,936**	**5,565,867**	**11,189,088**	**5,851,760**	**5,337,328**	**3,115,715**	**2,887,176**	**228,539**
Under 18	245,920	112,217	133,703	196,178	66,397	129,781	49,742	45,820	3,922
18 and 19	2,722,131	1,703,521	1,018,610	2,109,469	1,140,149	969,320	612,662	563,372	49,290
20 and 21	2,607,019	1,789,498	817,521	2,023,501	1,239,368	784,133	583,518	550,130	33,388
22 to 24	2,492,269	1,707,290	784,979	2,024,090	1,270,865	753,225	468,179	436,425	31,754
25 to 29	2,025,972	1,233,292	792,680	1,582,751	821,872	760,879	443,221	411,420	31,801
30 to 34	1,338,069	706,440	631,629	1,064,932	456,191	608,741	273,137	250,249	22,888
35 to 39	1,019,588	519,311	500,277	819,190	335,086	484,104	200,398	184,225	16,173
40 to 49	1,181,248	612,919	568,329	942,905	389,907	552,998	238,343	223,012	15,331
50 to 64	339,497	151,039	188,458	276,864	92,736	184,128	62,633	58,303	4,330
65 and over	78,375	22,079	56,296	69,019	13,865	55,154	9,356	8,214	1,142
Age unknown	254,715	181,330	73,385	80,189	25,324	54,865	174,526	156,006	18,520
Full-time	**8,127,618**	**6,084,299**	**2,043,319**	**5,962,562**	**4,074,055**	**1,888,507**	**2,165,056**	**2,010,244**	**154,812**
Under 18	111,151	75,070	36,081	75,580	42,712	32,868	35,571	32,358	3,213
18 and 19	2,324,860	1,625,439	699,421	1,729,060	1,075,406	653,654	595,800	550,033	45,767
20 and 21	2,070,480	1,644,331	426,149	1,520,282	1,120,894	399,388	550,198	523,437	26,761
22 to 24	1,583,062	1,303,527	279,535	1,217,718	959,668	258,050	365,344	343,859	21,485
25 to 29	884,787	672,135	212,652	636,950	442,260	194,690	247,837	229,875	17,962
30 to 34	433,467	291,480	141,987	318,994	188,274	130,720	114,473	103,206	11,267
35 to 39	276,170	177,314	98,856	203,559	111,990	91,569	72,611	65,324	7,287
40 to 49	268,390	172,244	96,146	193,412	103,577	89,835	74,978	68,667	6,311
50 to 64	57,723	35,556	22,167	37,945	17,883	20,062	19,778	17,673	2,105
65 and over	9,359	5,355	4,004	4,544	1,477	3,067	4,815	3,878	937
Age unknown	108,169	81,848	26,321	24,518	9,914	14,604	83,651	71,934	11,717
Part-time	**6,177,185**	**2,654,637**	**3,522,548**	**5,226,526**	**1,777,705**	**3,448,821**	**950,659**	**876,932**	**73,727**
Under 18	134,769	37,147	97,622	120,598	23,685	96,913	14,171	13,462	709
18 and 19	397,271	78,082	319,189	380,409	64,743	315,666	16,862	13,339	3,523
20 and 21	536,539	145,167	391,372	503,219	118,474	384,745	33,320	26,693	6,627
22 to 24	909,207	403,763	505,444	806,372	311,197	495,175	102,835	92,566	10,269
25 to 29	1,141,185	561,157	580,028	945,801	379,612	566,189	195,384	181,545	13,839
30 to 34	904,602	414,960	489,642	745,938	267,917	478,021	158,664	147,043	11,621
35 to 39	743,418	341,997	401,421	615,631	223,096	392,535	127,787	118,901	8,886
40 to 49	912,858	440,675	472,183	749,493	286,330	463,163	163,365	154,345	9,020
50 to 64	281,774	115,483	166,291	238,919	74,853	164,066	42,855	40,630	2,225
65 and over	69,016	16,724	52,292	64,475	12,388	52,087	4,541	4,336	205
Age unknown	146,546	99,482	47,064	55,671	15,410	40,261	90,875	84,072	6,803
	Percentage distribution								
All students	**100.0**	**100.0**	**100.0**	**100.0**	**100.0**	**100.0**	**100.0**	**100.0**	**100.0**
Under 18	1.7	1.3	2.4	1.8	1.1	2.4	1.6	1.6	1.7
18 and 19	19.0	19.5	18.3	18.9	19.5	18.2	19.7	19.5	21.6
20 and 21	18.2	20.5	14.7	18.1	21.2	14.7	18.7	19.1	14.6
22 to 24	17.4	19.5	14.1	18.1	21.7	14.1	15.0	15.1	13.9
25 to 29	14.2	14.1	14.2	14.1	14.0	14.3	14.2	14.2	13.9
30 to 34	9.4	8.1	11.3	9.5	7.8	11.4	8.8	8.7	10.0
35 to 39	7.1	5.9	9.0	7.3	5.7	9.1	6.4	6.4	7.1
40 to 49	8.3	7.0	10.2	8.4	6.7	10.4	7.6	7.7	6.7
50 to 64	2.4	1.7	3.4	2.5	1.6	3.4	2.0	2.0	1.9
65 and over	0.5	0.3	1.0	0.6	0.2	1.0	0.3	0.3	0.5
Age unknown	1.8	2.1	1.3	0.7	0.4	1.0	5.6	5.4	8.1
Full-time	**100.0**	**100.0**	**100.0**	**100.0**	**100.0**	**100.0**	**100.0**	**100.0**	**100.0**
Under 18	1.4	1.2	1.8	1.3	1.0	1.7	1.6	1.6	2.1
18 and 19	28.6	26.7	34.2	29.0	26.4	34.6	27.5	27.4	29.6
20 and 21	25.5	27.0	20.9	25.5	27.5	21.1	25.4	26.0	17.3
22 to 24	19.5	21.4	13.7	20.4	23.6	13.7	16.9	17.1	13.9
25 to 29	10.9	11.0	10.4	10.7	10.9	10.3	11.4	11.4	11.6
30 to 34	5.3	4.8	6.9	5.3	4.6	6.9	5.3	5.1	7.3
35 to 39	3.4	2.9	4.8	3.4	2.7	4.8	3.4	3.2	4.7
40 to 49	3.3	2.8	4.7	3.2	2.5	4.8	3.5	3.4	4.1
50 to 64	0.7	0.6	1.1	0.6	0.4	1.1	0.9	0.9	1.4
65 and over	0.1	0.1	0.2	0.1	0.0	0.2	0.2	0.2	0.2
Age unknown	1.3	1.3	1.3	0.4	0.2	0.8	3.9	3.6	7.6
Part-time	**100.0**	**100.0**	**100.0**	**100.0**	**100.0**	**100.0**	**100.0**	**100.0**	**100.0**
Under 18	2.2	1.4	2.8	2.3	1.3	2.8	1.5	1.5	1.0
18 and 19	6.4	2.9	9.1	7.3	3.6	9.2	1.8	1.5	4.8
20 and 21	8.7	5.5	11.1	9.6	6.7	11.2	3.5	3.0	9.0
22 to 24	14.7	15.2	14.3	15.4	17.5	14.4	10.8	10.6	13.9
25 to 29	18.5	21.1	16.5	18.1	21.4	16.4	20.6	20.7	18.8
30 to 34	14.6	15.6	13.9	14.3	15.1	13.9	16.7	16.8	15.8
35 to 39	12.0	12.9	11.4	11.8	12.5	11.4	13.4	13.6	12.1
40 to 49	14.8	16.6	13.4	14.3	16.1	13.4	17.2	17.6	12.2
50 to 64	4.6	4.4	4.7	4.6	4.2	4.8	4.5	4.6	3.0
65 and over	1.1	0.6	1.5	1.2	0.7	1.5	0.5	0.5	0.3
Age unknown	2.4	3.7	1.3	1.1	0.9	1.2	9.6	9.6	9.2

NOTE.—Because of rounding, details may not add to 100.0 percent.

SOURCE: U.S. Department of Education, National Center for Education Statistics, Integrated Postsecondary Education Data System, "Fall Enrollment, 1993" survey. (This table was prepared June 1996.)

Table 174.—Total fall enrollment in institutions of higher education, by level of enrollment, sex, attendance status, and type and control of institution: 1993 and 1994

Attendance status, and type and control of institution	Total			Undergraduate			First-professional			Graduate		
	Total	Men	Women	Total	Men	Women	Total	Men	Women	Total	Men	Women
1	2	3	4	5	6	7	8	9	10	11	12	13
	1993[1]											
Total	14,304,803	6,427,450	7,877,353	12,323,959	5,483,682	6,840,277	292,431	172,788	119,643	1,688,413	770,980	917,433
Full-time	8,127,618	3,890,571	4,237,047	7,179,482	3,381,997	3,797,485	259,764	153,873	105,891	688,372	354,701	333,671
Part-time	6,177,185	2,536,879	3,640,306	5,144,477	2,101,685	3,042,792	32,667	18,915	13,752	1,000,041	416,279	583,762
Total 4-year	8,738,936	4,081,991	4,656,945	6,758,398	3,138,286	3,620,112	292,431	172,788	119,643	1,688,107	770,917	917,190
Full-time	6,084,299	2,962,355	3,121,944	5,136,163	2,453,781	2,682,382	259,764	153,873	105,891	688,372	354,701	333,671
Part-time	2,654,637	1,119,636	1,535,001	1,622,235	684,505	937,730	32,667	18,915	13,752	999,735	416,216	583,519
Total 2-year	5,565,867	2,345,459	3,220,408	5,565,561	2,345,396	3,220,165	—	—	—	306	63	243
Full-time	2,043,319	928,216	1,115,103	2,043,319	928,216	1,115,103	—	—	—	—	—	—
Part-time	3,522,548	1,417,243	2,105,305	3,522,242	1,417,180	2,105,062	—	—	—	306	63	243
Public, total	11,189,088	4,984,511	6,204,577	10,011,787	4,447,266	5,564,521	113,654	63,973	49,681	1,063,647	473,272	590,375
Full-time	5,962,562	2,848,010	3,114,552	5,425,772	2,565,659	2,860,113	108,088	61,023	47,065	428,702	221,328	207,374
Part-time	5,226,526	2,136,501	3,090,025	4,586,015	1,881,607	2,704,408	5,566	2,950	2,616	634,945	251,944	383,001
Public 4-year	5,851,760	2,739,819	3,111,941	4,674,765	2,202,637	2,472,128	113,654	63,973	49,681	1,063,341	473,209	590,132
Full-time	4,074,055	1,989,410	2,084,645	3,537,265	1,707,059	1,830,206	108,088	61,023	47,065	428,702	221,328	207,374
Part-time	1,777,705	750,409	1,027,296	1,137,500	495,578	641,922	5,566	2,950	2,616	634,639	251,881	382,758
Public 2-year	5,337,328	2,244,692	3,092,636	5,337,022	2,244,629	3,092,393	—	—	—	306	63	243
Full-time	1,888,507	858,600	1,029,907	1,888,507	858,600	1,029,907	—	—	—	—	—	—
Part-time	3,448,821	1,386,092	2,062,729	3,448,515	1,386,029	2,062,486	—	—	—	306	63	243
Private, total	3,115,715	1,442,939	1,672,776	2,312,172	1,036,416	1,275,756	178,777	108,815	69,962	624,766	297,708	327,058
Full-time	2,165,056	1,042,561	1,122,495	1,753,710	816,338	937,372	151,676	92,850	58,826	259,670	133,373	126,297
Part-time	950,659	400,378	550,281	558,462	220,078	338,384	27,101	15,965	11,136	365,096	164,335	200,761
Private 4-year	2,887,176	1,342,172	1,545,004	2,083,633	935,649	1,147,984	178,777	108,815	69,962	624,766	297,708	327,058
Full-time	2,010,244	972,945	1,037,299	1,598,898	746,722	852,176	151,676	92,850	58,826	259,670	133,373	126,297
Part-time	876,932	369,227	507,705	484,735	188,927	295,808	27,101	15,965	11,136	365,096	164,335	200,761
Private 2-year	228,539	100,767	127,772	228,539	100,767	127,772	—	—	—	—	—	—
Full-time	154,812	69,616	85,196	154,812	69,616	85,196	—	—	—	—	—	—
Part-time	73,727	31,151	42,576	73,727	31,151	42,576	—	—	—	—	—	—
	1994[2]											
Total	14,278,790	6,371,898	7,906,892	12,262,608	5,422,113	6,840,495	294,713	173,956	120,757	1,721,469	775,829	945,640
Full-time	8,137,776	3,855,183	4,282,593	7,168,706	3,341,591	3,827,115	263,311	155,018	108,293	705,759	358,574	347,185
Part-time	6,141,014	2,516,715	3,624,299	5,093,902	2,080,522	3,013,380	31,402	18,938	12,464	1,015,710	417,255	598,455
Total 4-year	8,749,080	4,048,695	4,700,385	6,732,999	3,098,952	3,634,047	294,711	173,955	120,756	1,721,370	775,788	945,582
Full-time	6,106,062	2,943,593	3,162,469	5,136,993	2,430,002	2,706,991	263,311	155,018	108,293	705,758	358,573	347,185
Part-time	2,643,018	1,105,102	1,537,916	1,596,006	668,950	927,056	31,400	18,937	12,463	1,015,612	417,215	598,397
Total 2-year	5,529,710	2,323,203	3,206,507	5,529,609	2,323,161	3,206,448	2	1	1	99	41	58
Full-time	2,031,714	911,590	1,120,124	2,031,713	911,589	1,120,124	—	—	—	1	1	—
Part-time	3,497,996	1,411,613	2,086,383	3,497,896	1,411,572	2,086,324	2	1	1	98	40	58
Public, total	11,133,680	4,930,068	6,203,612	9,945,128	4,394,309	5,550,819	113,997	63,844	50,153	1,074,555	471,915	602,640
Full-time	5,950,820	2,813,226	3,137,594	5,406,741	2,531,506	2,875,235	109,245	61,225	48,020	434,834	220,495	214,339
Part-time	5,182,860	2,116,842	3,066,018	4,538,387	1,862,803	2,675,584	4,752	2,619	2,133	639,721	251,420	388,301
Public 4-year	5,825,213	2,703,415	3,121,798	4,636,762	2,167,698	2,469,064	113,995	63,843	50,152	1,074,456	471,874	602,582
Full-time	4,065,067	1,965,524	2,099,543	3,520,989	1,683,805	1,837,184	109,245	61,225	48,020	434,833	220,494	214,339
Part-time	1,760,146	737,891	1,022,255	1,115,773	483,893	631,880	4,750	2,618	2,132	639,623	251,380	388,243
Public 2-year	5,308,467	2,226,653	3,081,814	5,308,366	2,226,611	3,081,755	2	1	1	99	41	58
Full-time	1,885,753	847,702	1,038,051	1,885,752	847,701	1,038,051	—	—	—	1	1	—
Part-time	3,422,714	1,378,951	2,043,763	3,422,614	1,378,910	2,043,704	2	1	1	98	40	58
Private, total	3,145,110	1,441,830	1,703,280	2,317,480	1,027,804	1,289,676	180,716	110,112	70,604	646,914	303,914	343,000
Full-time	2,186,956	1,041,957	1,144,999	1,761,965	810,085	951,880	154,066	93,793	60,273	270,925	138,079	132,846
Part-time	958,154	399,873	558,281	555,515	217,719	337,796	26,650	16,319	10,331	375,989	165,835	210,154
Private 4-year	2,923,867	1,345,280	1,578,587	2,096,237	931,254	1,164,983	180,716	110,112	70,604	646,914	303,914	343,000
Full-time	2,040,995	978,069	1,062,926	1,616,004	746,197	869,807	154,066	93,793	60,273	270,925	138,079	132,846
Part-time	882,872	367,211	515,661	480,233	185,057	295,176	26,650	16,319	10,331	375,989	165,835	210,154
Private 2-year	221,243	96,550	124,693	221,243	96,550	124,693	—	—	—	—	—	—
Full-time	145,961	63,888	82,073	145,961	63,888	82,073	—	—	—	—	—	—
Part-time	75,282	32,662	42,620	75,282	32,662	42,620	—	—	—	—	—	—

[1] Revised from previously published data.
[2] Preliminary data.
—Not applicable.

SOURCE: U.S. Department of Education, National Center for Education Statistics, Integrated Postsecondary Education Data System (IPEDS), "Fall Enrollment" surveys. (This table was prepared December 1995.)

Table 175.—Total fall enrollment in institutions of higher education, by type and control of institution, attendance status, and sex of student: 1970 to 1994

Type and control of institution, sex and attendance status of student	1970	1975	1980	1985	1988	1989	1990	1991	1992 [1]	1993 [1]	1994 [2]
1	2	3	4	5	6	7	8	9	10	11	12
Total	**8,580,887**	**11,184,859**	**12,096,895**	**12,247,055**	**13,055,337**	**13,538,560**	**13,818,637**	**14,358,953**	**14,487,359**	**14,304,803**	**14,278,790**
Full-time	5,816,290	6,841,334	7,097,958	7,075,221	7,436,768	7,660,950	7,820,985	8,115,329	8,162,118	8,127,618	8,137,776
Men	3,504,095	3,926,753	3,689,244	3,607,720	3,661,779	3,740,243	3,807,752	3,929,375	3,926,905	3,890,571	3,855,183
Women	2,312,195	2,914,581	3,408,714	3,467,501	3,774,989	3,920,707	4,013,233	4,185,954	4,235,213	4,237,047	4,282,593
Part-time	2,764,597	4,343,525	4,998,937	5,171,834	5,618,569	5,877,610	5,997,652	6,243,624	6,325,241	6,177,185	6,141,014
Men	1,539,547	2,222,244	2,185,130	2,210,730	2,340,117	2,449,772	2,476,157	2,572,469	2,597,084	2,536,879	2,516,715
Women	1,225,050	2,121,281	2,813,807	2,961,104	3,278,452	3,427,838	3,521,495	3,671,155	3,728,157	3,640,306	3,624,299
4-year, total	6,261,502	7,214,740	7,570,608	7,715,978	8,180,182	8,387,671	8,578,554	8,707,053	8,764,969	8,738,936	8,749,080
Full-time	4,587,379	5,080,256	5,344,163	5,384,614	5,693,176	5,805,249	5,937,023	6,040,799	6,082,112	6,084,299	6,106,062
Men	2,732,796	2,891,192	2,809,528	2,781,412	2,843,186	2,870,555	2,926,360	2,967,978	2,975,089	2,962,355	2,943,593
Women	1,854,583	2,189,064	2,534,635	2,603,202	2,849,990	2,934,694	3,010,663	3,072,821	3,107,023	3,121,944	3,162,469
Part-time	1,674,123	2,134,484	2,226,445	2,331,364	2,487,006	2,582,422	2,641,531	2,666,254	2,682,857	2,654,637	2,643,018
Men	936,189	1,092,461	1,017,813	1,034,804	1,069,021	1,102,660	1,124,780	1,131,956	1,135,624	1,119,636	1,105,102
Women	737,934	1,042,023	1,208,632	1,296,560	1,417,985	1,479,762	1,516,751	1,534,298	1,547,233	1,535,001	1,537,916
Public 4-year	4,232,722	4,998,142	5,128,612	5,209,540	5,545,901	5,694,303	5,848,242	5,904,748	5,900,012	5,851,760	5,825,213
Full-time	3,086,491	3,469,821	3,592,193	3,623,341	3,842,375	3,934,437	4,033,654	4,088,970	4,095,310	4,074,055	4,065,067
Men	1,813,584	1,947,823	1,873,397	1,863,689	1,910,326	1,937,888	1,982,369	2,005,941	2,005,043	1,989,410	1,965,524
Women	1,272,907	1,521,998	1,718,796	1,759,652	1,932,049	1,996,549	2,051,285	2,083,029	2,090,267	2,084,645	2,099,543
Part-time	1,146,231	1,528,321	1,536,419	1,586,199	1,703,526	1,759,866	1,814,588	1,815,778	1,804,702	1,777,705	1,760,146
Men	609,422	760,469	685,051	693,115	721,832	743,137	764,248	764,969	760,186	750,409	737,891
Women	536,809	767,852	851,368	893,084	981,694	1,016,729	1,050,340	1,050,809	1,044,516	1,027,296	1,022,255
Private 4-year	2,028,780	2,216,598	2,441,996	2,506,438	2,634,281	2,693,368	2,730,312	2,802,305	2,864,957	2,887,176	2,923,867
Full-time	1,500,888	1,610,435	1,751,970	1,761,273	1,850,801	1,870,812	1,903,369	1,951,829	1,986,802	2,010,244	2,040,995
Men	919,212	943,369	936,131	917,723	932,860	932,667	943,991	962,037	970,046	972,945	978,069
Women	581,676	667,066	815,839	843,550	917,941	938,145	959,378	989,792	1,016,756	1,037,299	1,062,926
Part-time	527,892	606,163	690,026	745,165	783,480	822,556	826,943	850,476	878,155	876,932	882,872
Men	326,767	331,992	332,762	341,689	347,189	359,523	360,532	366,987	375,438	369,227	367,211
Women	201,125	274,171	357,264	403,476	436,291	463,033	466,411	483,489	502,717	507,705	515,661
2-year, total	2,319,385	3,970,119	4,526,287	4,531,077	4,875,155	5,150,889	5,240,083	5,651,900	5,722,390	5,565,867	5,529,710
Full-time	1,228,911	1,761,078	1,753,795	1,690,607	1,743,592	1,855,701	1,883,962	2,074,530	2,080,006	2,043,319	2,031,714
Men	771,299	1,035,561	879,716	826,308	818,593	869,688	881,392	961,397	951,816	928,216	911,590
Women	457,612	725,517	874,079	864,299	924,999	986,013	1,002,570	1,113,133	1,128,190	1,115,103	1,120,124
Part-time	1,090,474	2,209,041	2,772,492	2,840,470	3,131,563	3,295,188	3,356,121	3,577,370	3,642,384	3,522,548	3,497,996
Men	603,358	1,129,783	1,167,317	1,175,926	1,271,096	1,347,112	1,351,377	1,440,513	1,461,460	1,417,243	1,411,613
Women	487,116	1,079,258	1,605,175	1,664,544	1,860,467	1,948,076	2,004,744	2,136,857	2,180,924	2,105,305	2,086,383
Public 2-year	2,195,412	3,836,366	4,328,782	4,269,733	4,615,487	4,883,660	4,996,475	5,404,815	5,484,555	5,337,328	5,308,467
Full-time	1,129,165	1,662,621	1,595,493	1,496,905	1,567,973	1,674,249	1,716,843	1,885,607	1,915,565	1,888,507	1,885,753
Men	720,440	988,701	811,871	742,673	745,912	793,251	810,664	881,576	878,076	858,600	847,702
Women	408,725	673,920	783,622	754,232	822,061	880,998	906,179	1,004,031	1,037,489	1,029,907	1,038,051
Part-time	1,066,247	2,173,745	2,733,289	2,772,828	3,047,514	3,209,411	3,279,632	3,519,208	3,568,990	3,448,821	3,422,714
Men	589,439	1,107,680	1,152,268	1,138,011	1,230,888	1,302,074	1,317,730	1,413,870	1,431,091	1,386,092	1,378,951
Women	476,808	1,066,065	1,581,021	1,634,817	1,816,626	1,907,337	1,961,902	2,105,338	2,137,899	2,062,729	2,043,763
Private 2-year	123,973	133,753	[3] 197,505	261,344	259,668	267,229	243,608	247,085	237,835	228,539	221,243
Full-time	99,746	98,457	[3] 158,302	193,702	175,619	181,452	167,119	188,923	164,441	154,812	145,961
Men	50,859	46,860	[3] 67,845	83,635	72,681	76,437	70,728	79,821	73,740	69,616	63,888
Women	48,887	51,597	[3] 90,457	110,067	102,938	105,015	96,391	109,102	90,701	85,196	82,073
Part-time	24,227	35,296	[3] 39,203	67,642	84,049	85,777	76,489	58,162	73,394	73,727	75,282
Men	13,919	22,103	[3] 15,049	37,915	40,208	45,038	33,647	26,643	30,369	31,151	32,662
Women	10,308	13,193	[3] 24,154	29,727	43,841	40,739	42,842	31,519	43,025	42,576	42,620

[1] Data revised from previously published figures.
[2] Preliminary data.
[3] Large increase is due to the addition of schools accredited by the Accrediting Commission of Career Schools and Colleges of Technology.

SOURCE: U.S. Department of Education, National Center for Education Statistics, Fall Enrollment in Colleges and Universities, and Integrated Postsecondary Education Data Systems (IPEDS), "Fall Enrollment" surveys. (This table was prepared December 1995.)

Table 176.—Fall enrollment and number of institutions of higher education, by affiliation[1] of institution: 1980 to 1994

Affiliation	Total, fall 1980	Total, fall 1990	Total, fall 1993	Enrollment Fall 1994[3] Total	Full-time Men	Full-time Women	Part-time Men	Part-time Women	Number of institutions[2] Fall 1980	Number of institutions[2] Fall 1994
1	2	3	4	5	6	7	8	9	10	11
All institutions	**12,096,895**	**13,818,637**	**14,304,803**	**14,278,790**	**3,855,183**	**4,282,593**	**2,516,715**	**3,624,299**	**3,226**	**3,561**
Public institutions	9,457,394	10,844,717	11,189,088	11,133,680	2,813,226	3,137,594	2,116,842	3,066,018	1,493	1,595
Private institutions	2,639,501	2,973,920	3,115,715	3,145,110	1,041,957	1,144,999	399,873	558,281	1,733	1,966
Independent nonprofit	1,521,614	1,471,446	1,496,888	1,506,879	515,731	527,373	200,989	262,786	795	719
Proprietary	111,714	213,693	226,818	235,003	85,309	79,875	36,805	33,014	164	314
Religiously affiliated	1,006,173	1,288,781	1,392,009	1,403,228	440,917	537,751	162,079	262,481	774	933
Advent Christian Church	143	—	—	—	—	—	—	—	1	—
African Methodist Episcopal Zion Church	1,091	88	—	—	—	—	—	—	3	—
African Methodist Episcopal	4,541	3,220	3,643	3,799	1,572	1,960	111	156	6	6
American Baptist	6,131	10,800	11,767	12,221	2,821	3,576	1,895	3,929	11	12
American Evangelical Lutheran Church			819	814	434	263	46	71	—	1
American Lutheran and Lutheran Church in America	3,092	—	1,324	1,335	343	481	231	280	3	1
American Lutheran	21,608	—	10,138	10,163	3,727	4,530	433	1,473	13	9
Assemblies of God Church	7,814	8,307	9,045	9,493	4,236	4,172	558	527	10	13
Baptist	38,231	99,314	102,041	100,991	35,282	42,267	10,429	13,013	33	64
Brethren Church	3,925	958	1,463	1,447	581	615	144	107	3	3
Brethren in Christ Church	1,301	2,239	2,330	2,344	921	1,376	20	27	1	1
Christian and Missionary Alliance Church	1,705	2,519	3,139	3,386	1,367	1,565	165	289	3	4
Christian Church (Disciples of Christ)	14,913	30,397	31,360	32,629	6,537	9,925	6,860	9,307	12	16
Christian Churches and Churches of Christ	1,342	2,263	3,016	3,394	1,463	1,328	323	280	7	11
Christian Methodist Episcopal	2,486	2,174	2,240	2,456	963	1,259	104	130	4	3
Christian Reformed Church	5,408	4,488	3,956	4,075	1,755	1,990	184	146	3	2
Church of Christ (Scientist)	2,773	2,557	4,043	4,222	1,770	1,851	345	256	6	5
Church of God of Prophecy		249								
Church of God	6,082	5,627	6,441	4,534	1,668	1,964	442	460	9	7
Church of New Jerusalem	170	—							1	—
Church of the Brethren	8,482	4,463	2,852	2,870	1,014	1,481	154	221	6	3
Church of the Nazarene	11,716	10,779	13,852	14,450	5,117	6,291	1,212	1,830	10	10
Churches of Christ	9,343	14,331	22,157	22,495	7,824	8,390	2,951	3,330	9	14
Cumberland Presbyterian	594	746	734	715	299	226	84	106	2	2
Evangelical Congregational Church	80	88	98	95	18	2	57	18	1	1
Evangelical Convent Church of America	1,401	1,035	1,417	1,650	484	622	219	325	1	1
Evangelical Free Church of America	833	2,355	3,743	3,840	1,394	1,096	925	425	1	4
Evangelical Lutheran Church	743	49,210	36,755	38,218	13,888	18,360	2,194	3,776	3	26
Free Methodist	5,543	5,902	8,269	8,375	2,919	3,878	634	944	5	5
Free Will Baptist Church	1,132	1,177	1,197	1,312	395	419	276	222	4	2
Friends United Meeting	1,109	—	—	—	—	—	—	—	1	—
Friends	5,157	5,844	6,529	6,586	2,486	3,164	410	526	5	6
General Conference Mennonite Church	820	1,243	841	899	358	462	34	45	2	1
Greek Orthodox	204	148	171	197	147	34	10	6	1	1
Interdenominational	1,254	11,103	5,244	6,342	2,958	2,476	529	379	4	10

Table 176.—Fall enrollment and number of institutions of higher education, by affiliation [1] of institution: 1980 to 1994—Continued

Affiliation	Enrollment			Fall 1994 [3]					Number of institutions [2]	
	Total, fall 1980	Total, fall 1990	Total, fall 1993	Total	Full-time		Part-time		Fall 1980	Fall 1994
					Men	Women	Men	Women		
1	2	3	4	5	6	7	8	9	10	11
Jewish	5,738	15,628	19,942	13,153	10,440	1,752	683	278	24	62
Latter-Day Saints	39,172	42,274	40,725	40,296	17,501	19,200	1,716	1,879	4	3
Lutheran Church—Missouri Synod	11,727	13,827	9,925	10,614	3,786	4,598	845	1,385	15	8
Lutheran Church in America	23,877	5,796	7,416	4,338	1,661	2,200	142	335	20	3
Mennonite Brethren Church	1,344	1,864	2,115	2,161	606	713	258	584	3	3
Mennonite Church	4,008	2,859	3,486	3,462	1,344	1,561	203	354	6	5
Missionary Church Inc.	487	699	1,158	1,201	341	418	142	300	1	1
Moravian Church	2,434	2,511	2,727	2,741	623	1,222	307	589	2	2
Multiple Protestant Denominations	5,526	211	189	167	30	37	39	61	8	1
North American Baptist	155	—	173	170	70	39	37	24	1	1
Pentecostal Holiness Church	767	566	916	968	347	357	122	142	3	3
Presbyterian U.S. and United Presbyterian	47,144	76,625	72,123	69,790	26,342	31,377	4,716	7,355	57	64
Presbyterian Church in America	—	1,877	3,643	3,745	1,636	1,660	267	182	—	3
Protestant Episcopal	5,396	4,559	4,640	4,514	1,850	2,181	172	311	12	11
Protestant, other	4,072	38,136	62,238	59,870	21,109	24,494	6,687	7,580	11	67
Reformed Church in America	2,713	5,525	5,345	5,419	2,228	2,837	146	208	4	4
Reformed Episcopal Church	67	—	—	—	—	—	—	—	1	—
Reformed Presbyterian Church	2,014	1,556	1,693	1,767	673	722	223	149	4	2
Reorganized Latter-Day Saints Church	4,274	4,793	9,922	10,508	2,628	1,755	2,203	3,922	2	2
Roman Catholic	422,842	530,742	585,722	592,119	152,121	204,746	81,816	153,436	229	252
Russian Orthodox	47	—	30	24	20	—	4	—	1	1
Seventh-Day Adventists	19,168	15,771	16,572	17,110	6,164	7,320	1,327	2,299	11	11
Southern Baptist	85,281	49,493	43,148	45,165	14,067	15,696	7,540	7,862	54	30
Undenominational	—	1,714	10,760	12,304	3,874	4,847	1,844	1,739	—	11
Unitarian Universalist	87	82	93	106	30	56	7	13	2	2
United Brethren Church	545	601	565	635	267	273	68	27	1	1
United Church of Christ	14,169	19,219	23,282	24,305	6,858	10,110	2,504	4,833	16	21
United Methodist	127,099	148,851	142,031	146,935	50,413	60,966	14,143	21,413	91	90
Wesleyan Church	3,583	5,311	6,846	7,497	2,763	3,888	345	501	5	3
Wisconsin Evangelical Lutheran Synod	808	931	1,078	1,142	532	565	18	27	1	3
Other religiously affiliated	462	13,136	12,882	15,655	5,852	6,138	1,576	2,089	1	19

[1] Religious affiliation as reported by institutions of higher education.
[2] Because data are derived from the "Fall Enrollment" survey, counts of institutions may differ from counts on other tables.
[3] Preliminary data.
—Data not applicable or not reported.

SOURCE: U.S. Department of Education, National Center for Education Statistics, "Fall Enrollment in Institutions of Higher Education" surveys; and Integrated Postsecondary Education Data System (IPEDS), "Fall Enrollment" surveys. (This table was prepared March 1996).

Table 177.—Total first-time freshmen enrolled in institutions of higher education, by sex of student, attendance status, and type and control of institution: Fall 1955 to fall 1994

[In thousands]

Year	Total, all freshmen	Men			Women			Type of institution, by control			
								4-year		2-year	
		Total	Full-time	Part-time	Total	Full-time	Part-time	Public	Private	Public	Private
1	2	3	4	5	6	7	8	9	10	11	12
1955[1]	670	416	—	—	254	—	—	[2]283	[2]247	[2]117	[2]23
1956[1]	718	443	—	—	275	—	—	[2]293	[2]262	[2]137	[2]25
1957[1]	724	442	—	—	282	—	—	[2]294	[2]263	[2]141	[2]27
1958[1]	775	465	—	—	310	—	—	[2]328	[2]272	[2]146	[2]29
1959[1]	822	488	—	—	334	—	—	[2]348	[2]292	[2]153	[2]28
1960[1]	923	540	—	—	384	—	—	[2]396	[2]313	[2]182	[2]32
1961[1]	1,018	592	—	—	426	—	—	[2]438	[2]336	[2]210	[2]34
1962[1]	1,031	598	—	—	432	—	—	[2]445	[2]325	[2]225	[2]36
1963[1]	1,046	604	—	—	442	—	—	—	—	—	—
1964[1]	1,225	702	—	—	523	—	—	[2]539	[2]363	[2]275	[2]47
1965[1]	1,442	829	—	—	613	—	—	[2]642	[2]399	[2]348	[2]53
1966	1,554	890	—	—	665	—	—	[2]626	[2]383	[2]478	[2]67
1967	1,641	931	761	170	710	574	136	[2]645	[2]368	[2]561	[2]67
1968	1,893	1,082	847	235	810	624	187	[2]725	[2]378	[2]718	[2]72
1969	1,967	1,118	876	242	849	649	200	[2]737	[2]393	[2]776	[2]61
1970	2,063	1,152	896	256	911	691	221	[2]754	[2]397	[2]854	[2]58
1971	2,119	1,171	896	275	949	710	238	[2]738	[2]386	[2]937	[2]58
1972	2,153	1,158	858	299	995	716	279	680	381	1,037	55
1973	2,226	1,182	867	315	1,044	740	304	699	379	1,089	59
1974	2,366	1,244	896	348	1,122	777	345	746	386	1,176	58
1975	2,515	1,328	942	386	1,187	821	366	772	395	1,284	64
1976	2,347	1,170	855	316	1,177	808	369	717	414	1,153	63
1977	2,394	1,156	840	316	1,239	841	398	737	405	1,186	67
1978	2,390	1,142	817	324	1,248	834	414	737	407	1,174	73
1979	2,503	1,180	840	340	1,323	866	457	760	415	1,254	74
1980	2,588	1,219	862	357	1,369	887	481	765	418	1,314	91
1981	2,595	1,218	852	366	1,378	886	492	754	419	1,318	104
1982	2,505	1,199	837	362	1,306	851	455	731	404	1,254	116
1983	2,444	1,159	825	334	1,285	853	431	728	404	1,190	122
1984	2,357	1,112	786	326	1,245	827	418	714	403	1,130	110
1985	2,292	1,076	775	301	1,216	827	389	717	399	1,060	116
1986	2,219	1,047	769	278	1,173	821	352	720	392	991	[3]117
1987	2,246	1,047	779	267	1,200	847	352	758	405	980	[3]104
1988	2,379	1,100	807	293	1,279	892	387	783	426	1,049	121
1989	2,341	1,095	791	303	1,246	865	381	762	414	1,049	116
1990	2,257	1,045	771	274	1,211	846	366	727	400	1,041	[4]88
1991	2,278	1,068	798	270	1,209	855	355	718	393	1,070	[4]97
1992[5]	2,184	1,013	760	253	1,171	843	328	697	408	993	[4]85
1993[5]	2,161	1,008	762	245	1,153	846	307	702	411	974	[4]74
1994[6]	2,133	985	751	233	1,149	852	297	709	406	952	[4]66

[1] Excludes first-time freshmen in occupational programs not creditable towards a bachelor's degree.

[2] Data for 2-year branches of 4-year college systems are aggregated with the 4-year institutions.

[3] Because of imputation techniques, data are not consistent with figures for other years.

[4] Data not comparable with pre-1990 figures because of a change in reporting procedures.

[5] Revised.

[6] Preliminary data.

—Data not available.

NOTE.—Alaska and Hawaii are included in all years. Because of rounding, details may not add to totals.

SOURCE: U.S. Department of Education, National Center for Education Statistics, *Fall Enrollment in Higher Education,* various years; "Fall Enrollment in Colleges and Universities" survey; and Integrated Postsecondary Education Data System (IPEDS), "Fall Enrollment" surveys. (This table was prepared April 1996.)

Table 178.—Total first-time freshmen enrolled in institutions of higher education, by attendance status, sex, control of institution, and state: Fall 1991 to fall 1994

State or other area	Fall 1991	Fall 1992[1]	Fall 1993[1]	Fall 1994[2]								
				Total	Full-time			Part-time			Public institutions	Private institutions
					Total	Men	Women	Total	Men	Women		
1	2	3	4	5	6	7	8	9	10	11	12	13
United States	2,277,920	2,184,113	2,160,710	2,133,205	1,603,106	751,081	852,025	530,099	233,477	296,622	1,661,510	471,695
Alabama	42,271	42,604	41,812	41,542	33,166	14,736	18,430	8,376	3,487	4,889	36,979	4,563
Alaska	2,378	2,584	2,700	1,835	1,563	774	789	272	114	158	1,660	175
Arizona	57,927	31,358	36,671	32,753	21,314	10,435	10,879	11,439	5,163	6,276	30,106	2,647
Arkansas	18,214	18,680	17,406	16,378	14,496	6,533	7,963	1,882	826	1,056	13,637	2,741
California	293,739	252,762	250,810	258,687	139,089	66,018	73,071	119,598	56,767	62,831	231,426	27,261
Colorado	32,089	33,359	31,353	31,001	22,767	11,224	11,543	8,234	3,893	4,341	27,083	3,918
Connecticut	22,222	22,490	21,489	21,259	16,398	7,762	8,636	4,861	1,790	3,071	12,928	8,331
Delaware	7,955	7,227	7,361	6,921	5,500	2,397	3,103	1,421	565	856	6,105	816
District of Columbia	7,655	8,427	8,954	9,706	7,494	3,094	4,400	2,212	833	1,379	2,502	7,204
Florida	73,751	72,311	71,351	71,318	51,584	24,164	27,420	19,734	8,692	11,042	56,106	15,212
Georgia	55,090	56,389	59,784	58,991	45,170	20,228	24,942	13,821	5,804	8,017	46,371	12,620
Hawaii	8,525	9,461	9,752	10,309	6,784	3,093	3,691	3,525	1,724	1,801	7,793	2,516
Idaho	10,408	10,960	11,069	10,646	9,077	4,292	4,785	1,569	677	892	7,449	3,197
Illinois	120,988	116,967	112,542	111,309	72,809	34,857	37,952	38,500	16,779	21,721	87,963	23,346
Indiana	50,761	50,147	49,111	48,059	40,420	19,775	20,645	7,639	2,987	4,652	33,648	14,411
Iowa	32,644	36,730	35,922	35,229	28,502	13,702	14,800	6,727	2,606	4,121	27,088	8,141
Kansas	26,182	25,453	25,304	24,641	17,941	9,113	8,828	6,700	3,050	3,650	22,056	2,585
Kentucky	31,713	29,738	31,334	28,983	25,520	11,263	14,257	3,463	1,392	2,071	22,440	6,543
Louisiana	30,323	31,810	30,160	30,951	27,377	11,879	15,498	3,574	1,406	2,168	26,428	4,523
Maine	9,088	8,765	8,751	8,149	7,265	3,538	3,727	884	282	602	5,367	2,782
Maryland	31,912	32,133	31,675	31,647	22,441	10,307	12,134	9,206	3,511	5,695	27,040	4,607
Massachusetts	63,968	64,751	68,316	65,768	55,466	25,162	30,304	10,302	3,756	6,546	31,881	33,887
Michigan	83,483	88,744	87,025	83,697	56,984	25,962	31,022	26,713	11,479	15,234	68,554	15,143
Minnesota	43,702	50,869	43,794	43,783	33,153	15,792	17,361	10,630	4,391	6,239	34,495	9,288
Mississippi	27,648	25,960	26,223	25,862	22,153	10,190	11,963	3,709	1,404	2,305	23,891	1,971
Missouri	39,441	39,886	40,868	38,544	32,193	14,605	17,588	6,351	2,738	3,613	26,176	12,368
Montana	6,146	6,413	6,950	6,819	6,114	3,068	3,046	705	270	435	5,934	885
Nebraska	15,842	17,362	15,943	16,616	13,184	6,404	6,780	3,432	1,407	2,025	13,539	3,077
Nevada	5,968	4,620	5,367	6,939	3,589	1,742	1,847	3,350	1,487	1,863	6,834	105
New Hampshire	11,484	11,316	11,659	11,373	9,551	4,314	5,237	1,822	619	1,203	5,982	5,391
New Jersey	43,950	44,932	44,971	43,063	35,597	16,574	19,023	7,466	3,151	4,315	34,590	8,473
New Mexico	12,708	11,818	13,358	13,864	8,433	4,010	4,423	5,431	2,392	3,039	13,020	844
New York	157,449	158,380	157,350	155,922	138,071	63,337	74,734	17,851	7,372	10,479	97,078	58,844
North Carolina	54,851	55,075	52,857	51,346	45,148	20,147	25,001	6,198	2,724	3,474	38,303	13,043
North Dakota	7,923	8,813	8,322	8,122	7,219	3,830	3,389	903	387	516	7,308	814
Ohio	94,645	92,902	90,190	88,585	70,846	33,065	37,781	17,739	8,336	9,403	64,539	24,046
Oklahoma	30,115	30,296	30,252	29,627	20,972	10,031	10,941	8,655	3,530	5,125	26,162	3,465
Oregon	23,088	22,930	23,293	23,321	16,634	8,106	8,528	6,687	3,145	3,542	19,177	4,144
Pennsylvania	111,285	113,070	100,372	98,488	83,752	39,785	43,967	14,736	6,016	8,720	58,381	40,107
Rhode Island	12,717	12,813	13,106	12,645	11,147	5,509	5,638	1,498	569	929	5,546	7,099
South Carolina	33,471	30,185	30,070	28,577	23,926	10,706	13,220	4,651	1,974	2,677	22,913	5,664
South Dakota	6,288	6,513	6,691	6,607	5,967	2,774	3,193	640	231	409	5,287	1,320
Tennessee	36,882	35,721	35,341	34,180	30,019	13,722	16,297	4,161	1,722	2,439	24,136	10,044
Texas	129,666	127,584	129,921	127,586	91,388	44,128	47,260	36,198	16,554	19,644	109,689	17,897
Utah	26,125	23,536	24,465	24,383	18,494	8,476	10,018	5,889	2,973	2,916	18,841	5,542
Vermont	6,242	6,274	6,347	6,132	5,306	2,611	2,695	826	290	536	3,655	2,477
Virginia	45,006	45,011	43,820	45,272	38,655	17,568	21,087	6,617	3,045	3,572	33,946	11,326
Washington	70,043	68,649	70,476	68,613	41,629	19,941	21,688	26,984	12,318	14,666	63,536	5,077
West Virginia	17,447	17,029	15,727	15,928	13,946	6,703	7,243	1,982	696	1,286	13,316	2,612
Wisconsin	50,511	47,271	47,351	46,479	35,623	16,735	18,888	10,856	4,669	6,187	38,060	8,419
Wyoming	5,675	4,686	4,858	4,814	3,949	1,974	1,975	865	357	508	4,630	184
U.S. Service Schools	38,316	10,349	10,116	9,936	7,321	4,926	2,395	2,615	1,127	1,488	9,936	—
Outlying areas	35,320	35,409	41,759	30,573	27,613	11,261	16,352	2,960	1,544	1,416	14,030	16,543
American Samoa	979	989	967	948	702	361	341	246	136	110	948	—
Federated States of Micronesia	158	409	235	410	392	196	196	18	14	4	410	—
Guam	726	709	1,490	956	680	281	399	276	127	149	956	—
Marshall Islands	139	139	166	22	16	8	8	6	5	1	22	—
Northern Marianas	262	173	455	440	80	34	46	360	221	139	440	—
Palau	10	24	24	13	13	4	9	—	—	—	13	—
Puerto Rico	32,480	32,664	38,057	27,408	25,405	10,297	15,108	2,003	1,027	976	10,865	16,543
Virgin Islands	705	302	365	376	325	80	245	51	14	37	376	—

[1] Revised from previously published data.
[2] Preliminary data.
—Data not available or not applicable.

SOURCE: U.S. Department of Education, National Center for Education Statistics, Integrated Postsecondary Education Data System, "Fall Enrollment" surveys. (This table was prepared April 1996.)

Table 179.—College enrollment rates of high school graduates, by race/ethnicity: 1960 to 1995

[Numbers in thousands]

Year	High school graduates [1]				Enrolled in college [2]								
	Total	White [3]	Black [3,4]	His-panic [4]	Total		White [3]		Black [3,4]		Hispanic [4]		
												Percent	
					Number	Percent	Number	Percent	Number	Percent	Number	Annual	3-year moving average
1	2	3	4	5	6	7	8	9	10	11	12	13	14
1960	1,679	1,565	—	—	758	45.1	717	45.8	—	—	—	—	—
1961	1,763	1,612	—	—	847	48.0	798	49.5	—	—	—	—	—
1962	1,838	1,660	—	—	900	49.0	840	50.6	—	—	—	—	—
1963	1,741	1,615	—	—	784	45.0	736	45.6	—	—	—	—	—
1964	2,145	1,964	—	—	1,037	48.3	967	49.2	—	—	—	—	—
1965	2,659	2,417	—	—	1,354	50.9	1,249	51.7	—	—	—	—	—
1966	2,612	2,403	—	—	1,309	50.1	1,243	51.7	—	—	—	—	—
1967	2,525	2,267	—	—	1,311	51.9	1,202	53.0	—	—	—	—	—
1968	2,606	2,303	—	—	1,444	55.4	1,304	56.6	—	—	—	—	—
1969	2,842	2,538	—	—	1,516	53.3	1,402	55.2	—	—	—	—	—
1970	2,757	2,461	—	—	1,427	51.8	1,280	52.0	—	—	—	—	—
1971	2,872	2,596	—	—	1,535	53.4	1,402	54.0	—	—	—	—	—
1972	2,961	2,614	—	—	1,457	49.2	1,292	49.4	—	—	—	—	—
1973	3,059	2,707	—	—	1,425	46.6	1,302	48.1	—	—	—	—	—
1974	3,101	2,736	—	—	1,474	47.5	1,288	47.1	—	—	—	—	—
1975	3,186	2,825	—	—	1,615	50.7	1,446	51.2	—	—	—	—	—
1976	2,987	2,640	320	152	1,458	48.8	1,291	48.9	134	41.9	80	52.6	—
1977	3,140	2,768	335	156	1,590	50.6	1,403	50.7	166	49.6	80	51.3	48.9
1978	3,161	2,750	352	133	1,584	50.1	1,378	50.1	161	45.7	57	42.9	46.3
1979	3,160	2,776	324	154	1,559	49.3	1,376	49.6	147	45.4	69	44.8	46.8
1980	3,089	2,682	361	129	1,524	49.3	1,339	49.9	151	41.8	68	52.7	49.9
1981	3,053	2,626	359	146	1,646	53.9	1,434	54.6	154	42.9	76	52.1	49.3
1982	3,100	2,644	384	174	1,568	50.6	1,376	52.0	140	36.5	75	43.1	49.8
1983	2,964	2,496	392	138	1,562	52.7	1,372	55.0	151	38.5	75	54.3	47.3
1984	3,012	2,514	438	185	1,662	55.2	1,455	57.9	176	40.2	82	44.3	49.9
1985	2,666	2,241	333	141	1,539	57.7	1,332	59.4	141	42.3	72	51.1	46.6
1986	2,786	2,307	386	169	1,499	53.8	1,292	56.0	141	36.5	75	44.4	43.0
1987	2,647	2,207	337	176	1,503	56.8	1,249	56.6	175	51.9	59	33.5	45.0
1988	2,673	2,187	382	179	1,575	58.9	1,328	60.7	172	45.0	102	57.0	48.6
1989	2,454	2,051	337	168	1,463	59.6	1,238	60.4	178	52.8	93	55.4	53.2
1990	2,355	1,921	341	112	1,410	59.9	1,182	61.5	158	46.3	53	47.3	53.3
1991	2,276	1,867	320	154	1,420	62.4	1,207	64.6	146	45.6	88	57.1	53.1
1992	2,398	1,900	353	199	1,479	61.7	1,204	63.4	169	47.9	109	54.8	58.1
1993	2,338	1,910	302	200	1,464	62.6	1,200	62.8	168	55.6	125	62.5	55.4
1994	2,517	2,065	318	178	1,559	61.9	1,313	63.6	162	50.9	87	48.9	55.1
1995	2,599	2,088	356	288	1,610	61.9	1,308	62.6	183	51.4	155	53.8	—

[1] Individuals age 16 to 24 who graduated from high school during the preceding 12 months.

[2] Enrollment in college as of October of each year for individuals age 16 to 24 who graduated from high school during the preceding 12 months.

[3] Includes persons of Hispanic origin.

[4] Due to the small sample size, data are subject to relatively large sampling errors.

—Data not available.

NOTE.—Data are based upon sample surveys of the civilian population. High school graduate data in this table differ from figures appearing in other tables because of varying survey procedures and coverage. High school graduates include GED recipients.

SOURCE: American College Testing Program, unpublished tabulations, 1987, derived from statistics collected by the U.S. Bureau of the Census; and U.S. Department of Labor, *College Enrollment of High School Graduates*, various years. (This table was prepared May 1996.)

Table 180.—College enrollment rates of high school graduates, by sex: 1960 to 1995

[Numbers in thousands]

Year	Total high school graduates [1]			Enrolled in college [2]					
	Total	Males	Females	Total		Males		Females	
				Number	Percent	Number	Percent	Number	Percent
1	2	3	4	5	6	7	8	9	10
1960	1,679	756	923	758	45.1	408	54.0	350	37.9
1961	1,763	790	973	847	48.0	445	56.3	402	41.3
1962	1,838	872	966	900	49.0	480	55.0	420	43.5
1963	1,741	794	947	784	45.0	415	52.3	369	39.0
1964	2,145	997	1,148	1,037	48.3	570	57.2	467	40.7
1965	2,659	1,254	1,405	1,354	50.9	718	57.3	636	45.3
1966	2,612	1,207	1,405	1,309	50.1	709	58.7	600	42.7
1967	2,525	1,142	1,383	1,311	51.9	658	57.6	653	47.2
1968	2,606	1,184	1,422	1,444	55.4	748	63.2	696	48.9
1969	2,842	1,352	1,490	1,516	53.3	812	60.1	704	47.2
1970	2,757	1,343	1,414	1,427	51.8	741	55.2	686	48.5
1971	2,872	1,369	1,503	1,535	53.4	788	57.6	747	49.7
1972	2,961	1,420	1,541	1,457	49.2	749	52.7	708	45.9
1973	3,059	1,458	1,601	1,425	46.6	730	50.1	695	43.4
1974	3,101	1,491	1,610	1,474	47.5	736	49.4	738	45.8
1975	3,186	1,513	1,673	1,615	50.7	796	52.6	819	49.0
1976	2,987	1,450	1,537	1,458	48.8	685	47.2	773	50.3
1977	3,140	1,482	1,658	1,590	50.6	773	52.2	817	49.3
1978	3,161	1,485	1,676	1,584	50.1	758	51.0	826	49.3
1979	3,160	1,474	1,686	1,559	49.3	743	50.4	816	48.4
1980	3,089	1,500	1,589	1,524	49.3	701	46.7	823	51.8
1981	3,053	1,490	1,563	1,646	53.9	816	54.8	830	53.1
1982	3,100	1,508	1,592	1,568	50.6	739	49.0	829	52.1
1983	2,964	1,390	1,574	1,562	52.7	721	51.9	841	53.4
1984	3,012	1,429	1,583	1,662	55.2	800	56.0	862	54.5
1985	2,666	1,286	1,380	1,539	57.7	754	58.6	785	56.9
1986	2,786	1,331	1,455	1,499	53.8	744	55.9	755	51.9
1987	2,647	1,278	1,369	1,503	56.8	746	58.4	757	55.3
1988	2,673	1,334	1,339	1,575	58.9	761	57.0	814	60.8
1989	2,454	1,208	1,245	1,463	59.6	696	57.6	767	61.6
1990	2,355	1,169	1,185	1,410	59.9	676	57.8	735	62.0
1991	2,276	1,139	1,137	1,420	62.4	656	57.6	763	67.1
1992	2,398	1,216	1,182	1,479	61.7	725	59.6	754	63.8
1993	2,338	1,118	1,219	1,464	62.6	668	59.7	797	65.4
1994	2,517	1,244	1,273	1,559	61.9	754	60.6	805	63.2
1995	2,599	1,238	1,361	1,610	61.9	775	62.6	835	61.4

[1] Individuals age 16 to 24 who graduated from high school during the preceding 12 months.

[2] Enrollment in college as of October of each year for individuals age 16 to 24 who graduated from high school during the preceding 12 months.

NOTE.—Data are based upon sample surveys of the civilian population. High school graduate data in this table differ from figures appearing in other tables because of varying survey procedures and coverage. High school graduates include GED recipients.

SOURCE: American College Testing Program, unpublished tabulations, 1987, derived from statistics collected by the U.S. Bureau of the Census; and U.S. Department of Labor, *College Enrollment of High School Graduates*, various years. (This table was prepared May 1996.)

Table 181.—Graduation, college preparation, and college application rates of high school students, by selected school characteristics: 1993–94

Selected school characteristics	Public schools			Private schools		
	Number of schools with 12th graders	1993 graduation rate of fall 1992 12th graders	Average college application rate of 12th graders	Number of schools with 12th graders	1993 graduation rate of fall 1992 12th graders	Average college application rate of 12th graders
1	2	3	4	5	6	7
Total	**17,838**	**92.6**	**57.4**	**7,875**	**98.2**	**87.5**
Percent minority students						
Less than 5%	6,843	94.1	56.4	2,926	98.9	84.8
5% to 19%	3,784	93.7	60.2	2,735	98.5	90.0
20% to 49%	3,850	92.1	58.5	1,439	97.7	90.2
50% or more	3,360	90.1	54.2	775	96.5	79.9
Community type						
Central city	2,949	89.7	56.5	2,808	98.3	89.0
Suburban/large town	3,798	92.5	61.6	2,486	98.4	88.1
Small town/rural	11,091	94.6	54.3	2,581	97.6	81.5

NOTE.—Data are based upon a sample survey and may not be strictly comparable with data reported elsewhere. Only includes schools with students enrolled in 12th grade. Some data have been revised from previously published figures. Because of rounding, details may not add to totals.

SOURCE: U.S. Department of Education, National Center for Education Statistics, "Schools and Staffing Survey, 1993–94." (This table was prepared September 1996.)

Table 182.—Enrollment rates of 18- to 24-year-olds in institutions of higher education, by race/ethnicity: 1967 to 1995

| Year | Total | | White, non-Hispanic | | Black, non-Hispanic | | Hispanic origin | |
	Enrollment as a percent of 18- to 24-year-olds	Enrollment as a percent of high school graduates	Enrollment as a percent of 18- to 24-year-olds	Enrollment as a percent of high school graduates	Enrollment as a percent of 18- to 24-year-olds	Enrollment as a percent of high school graduates	Enrollment as a percent of 18- to 24-year-olds	Enrollment as a percent of high school graduates
1	2	3	4	5	6	7	8	9
1967[1]	25.5	33.7	26.9	34.5	13.0	23.3	—	—
1968[1]	26.0	34.2	27.5	34.9	14.5	25.2	—	—
1969[1]	27.3	35.0	28.7	35.6	16.0	27.2	—	—
1970[1]	25.7	32.7	27.1	33.2	15.5	26.0	—	—
1971[1]	26.2	33.2	27.2	33.5	18.2	29.2	—	—
1972	25.5	31.1	27.2	31.9	18.3	25.2	13.4	24.1
1973	24.0	28.9	25.5	29.5	15.9	22.5	16.1	27.6
1974	24.6	29.8	25.8	29.9	17.6	24.6	18.0	30.7
1975	26.3	31.4	27.4	31.3	20.4	30.1	20.4	33.0
1976	26.7	32.3	27.6	32.1	22.5	32.1	20.0	34.7
1977	26.1	31.4	27.2	31.3	21.1	29.1	17.2	30.5
1978	25.3	30.0	26.5	30.1	20.1	27.9	15.2	25.9
1979	25.0	29.9	26.3	30.2	19.8	27.5	16.7	27.8
1980	25.7	30.5	27.3	31.0	19.4	26.0	16.1	27.6
1981	26.2	31.3	27.7	31.6	19.9	26.6	16.6	28.5
1982	26.6	31.6	28.1	32.0	19.9	26.5	16.8	27.6
1983	26.2	31.3	28.0	31.8	19.2	25.3	17.3	29.9
1984	27.1	31.8	28.9	32.6	20.3	25.6	17.9	28.8
1985	27.8	32.5	30.0	33.9	19.6	24.5	16.9	25.0
1986	27.9	32.7	29.7	33.3	21.9	26.9	17.6	28.3
1987	29.7	35.4	31.9	36.6	23.0	28.2	17.7	26.6
1988	30.2	36.0	33.1	37.4	21.1	26.8	17.1	29.1
1989	30.9	36.5	34.2	38.3	23.4	28.5	16.0	26.6
1990	32.1	37.7	35.2	39.2	25.3	30.4	16.2	26.8
1991	33.3	39.3	36.8	41.0	23.4	28.2	17.8	31.4
1992	34.4	42.0	37.3	42.8	25.2	33.9	21.3	37.5
1993	34.0	41.6	36.8	42.6	24.5	32.8	21.7	36.1
1994	34.6	42.3	38.1	43.7	27.7	35.6	18.8	33.1
1995	34.3	42.3	37.9	44.0	27.5	35.4	20.7	35.2

[1] Data for white and black enrollment include persons of Hispanic origin.
—Data not available.

NOTE.—Data are based upon sample surveys of the civilian noninstitutional population. Percents based on 18- to 24-year-old high school graduates for 1992 and later years, use a slightly different definition of graduation and may not be directly comparable with figures for other years. All college students are counted as high school graduates.

SOURCE: U.S. Department of Commerce, Bureau of the Census, Current Population Survey, unpublished data. (This table was prepared July 1996.)

Table 183.—Total undergraduate fall enrollment[1] in institutions of higher education, by sex of student, attendance status, and control of institution: 1969 to 1994

[In thousands]

Year	Total	Full-time	Part-time	Men	Women	Men Full-time	Men Part-time	Women Full-time	Women Part-time	Men Public	Men Private	Women Public	Women Private
1	2	3	4	5	6	7	8	9	10	11	12	13	14
1969	6,884	4,991	1,893	4,008	2,876	2,952	1,056	2,039	837	2,997	1,011	2,162	714
1970	7,376	5,280	2,096	4,254	3,122	3,097	1,157	2,183	939	3,241	1,013	2,387	735
1971	7,743	5,512	2,231	4,418	3,325	3,201	1,217	2,311	1,014	3,427	991	2,580	745
1972	7,941	5,488	2,453	4,429	3,512	3,121	1,308	2,367	1,145	3,467	962	2,756	756
1973	8,261	5,580	2,681	4,538	3,723	3,135	1,403	2,445	1,278	3,579	959	2,943	780
1974	8,798	5,726	3,072	4,765	4,033	3,191	1,574	2,535	1,498	3,799	966	3,232	801
1975	9,679	6,169	3,510	5,257	4,422	3,459	1,798	2,710	1,712	4,245	1,012	3,581	841
1976	9,429	6,030	3,399	4,902	4,527	3,242	1,660	2,788	1,739	3,949	953	3,668	859
1977	9,717	6,094	3,623	4,897	4,820	3,188	1,709	2,906	1,914	3,937	960	3,906	914
1978	9,691	5,967	3,724	4,766	4,925	3,072	1,694	2,895	2,030	3,812	954	3,974	951
1979	9,998	6,080	3,919	4,821	5,178	3,087	1,734	2,993	2,185	3,865	956	4,181	995
1980	10,475	6,362	4,113	5,000	5,475	3,227	1,773	3,135	2,340	4,014	985	4,427	1,048
1981	10,755	6,449	4,306	5,109	5,646	3,261	1,848	3,188	2,458	4,090	1,018	4,558	1,088
1982	10,825	6,484	4,341	5,170	5,655	3,299	1,871	3,184	2,470	4,140	1,031	4,573	1,081
1983	10,846	6,514	4,332	5,158	5,688	3,304	1,854	3,210	2,478	4,117	1,042	4,580	1,107
1984	10,618	6,348	4,270	5,007	5,611	3,195	1,812	3,153	2,459	3,990	1,017	4,504	1,107
1985	10,597	6,320	4,277	4,962	5,635	3,156	1,806	3,163	2,471	3,953	1,010	4,525	1,110
1986	10,798	6,352	4,446	5,018	5,780	3,146	1,871	3,206	2,575	4,002	1,015	4,658	1,122
1987	11,046	6,463	4,584	5,068	5,978	3,164	1,905	3,299	2,679	4,076	992	4,842	1,136
1988	11,317	6,642	4,674	5,138	6,179	3,206	1,931	3,436	2,743	4,113	1,024	4,990	1,189
1989	11,743	6,841	4,902	5,311	6,432	3,279	2,032	3,562	2,869	4,272	1,039	5,216	1,216
1990	11,959	6,976	4,983	5,380	6,579	3,337	2,043	3,639	2,940	4,353	1,027	5,357	1,223
1991	12,439	7,221	5,218	5,571	6,868	3,436	2,135	3,786	3,082	4,531	1,040	5,617	1,251
1992	12,538	7,244	5,293	5,583	6,955	3,425	2,158	3,820	3,135	4,537	1,046	5,679	1,275
1993	12,324	7,179	5,144	5,484	6,840	3,382	2,102	3,797	3,043	4,447	1,036	5,565	1,276
1994[2]	12,263	7,169	5,094	5,422	6,840	3,342	2,081	3,827	3,013	4,394	1,028	5,551	1,290

[1] Includes unclassified undergraduate students.
[2] Preliminary data.

NOTE.—Because of rounding, details may not add to totals.

SOURCE: U.S. Department of Education, National Center for Education Statistics, "Fall Enrollment in Colleges and Universities;" and Integrated Postsecondary Education Data System, "Fall Enrollment" survey. (This table was prepared December 1995.)

Table 184.—Total graduate fall enrollment [1] in institutions of higher education, by attendance status, sex of student, and control of institution: 1969 to 1994

[In thousands]

Year	Total	Full-time	Part-time	Men	Women	Men Full-time	Men Part-time	Women Full-time	Women Part-time	Men Public	Men Private	Women Public	Women Private
1	2	3	4	5	6	7	8	9	10	11	12	13	14
1969	955	363	593	590	366	252	338	111	255	393	197	273	93
1970	1,031	379	651	630	400	264	366	115	285	423	207	301	99
1971	1,012	388	621	615	394	269	346	119	275	415	200	296	100
1972	1,066	394	671	626	439	268	358	126	313	427	199	330	109
1973	1,123	410	715	648	477	273	375	137	340	442	206	358	119
1974	1,190	427	762	663	526	276	387	151	375	454	209	398	128
1975	1,263	453	810	700	563	290	410	163	400	481	219	425	138
1976	1,333	463	870	714	619	287	427	176	443	477	237	454	165
1977	1,319	473	845	700	617	289	411	184	434	458	243	443	174
1978	1,312	468	844	682	630	280	402	188	442	441	241	453	177
1979	1,309	476	833	669	640	280	389	196	444	427	242	457	182
1980	1,343	485	860	675	670	281	394	204	466	426	247	474	195
1981	1,343	484	859	674	669	277	397	207	462	419	255	468	201
1982	1,322	485	838	670	653	280	390	205	447	417	253	453	200
1983	1,340	497	843	677	663	286	391	211	452	418	259	454	209
1984	1,345	501	844	672	673	286	386	215	459	411	261	459	215
1985	1,376	509	867	677	700	289	388	220	479	414	263	477	223
1986	1,435	522	913	693	742	294	399	228	514	433	260	508	234
1987	1,452	527	925	693	759	294	400	233	525	429	264	516	243
1988	1,472	553	919	697	774	304	393	249	526	429	268	520	254
1989	1,522	572	949	710	811	309	401	263	548	437	273	541	271
1990	1,586	599	987	737	849	321	416	278	571	456	281	567	282
1991	1,639	642	997	761	878	341	419	300	578	471	290	580	299
1992	1,669	666	1,003	772	896	351	421	314	582	474	298	584	313
1993 [2]	1,688	688	1,000	771	917	355	416	334	584	473	298	590	327
1994 [3]	1,721	706	1,016	776	946	359	417	347	598	472	304	603	343

[1] Includes unclassified postbaccalaureate students.
[2] Revised from previously published data.
[3] Preliminary data.

NOTE.—Because of rounding, details may not add to totals.

SOURCE: U.S. Department of Education, National Center for Education Statistics, "Fall Enrollment in Colleges and Universities;" and Integrated Postsecondary Education Data System (IPEDS), "Fall Enrollment" survey. (This table was prepared December 1995.)

Table 185.—Total first-professional fall enrollment in institutions of higher education, by attendance status, sex of student, and control of institution: 1969 to 1994

Year	Total	Full-time	Part-time	Men	Women	Men Full-time	Men Part-time	Women Full-time	Women Part-time	Men Public	Men Private	Women Public	Women Private
1	2	3	4	5	6	7	8	9	10	11	12	13	14
1969	164,737	143,081	21,656	148,926	15,811	131,368	17,558	11,713	4,098	64,241	84,685	8,354	7,457
1970	173,411	157,384	16,027	158,649	14,762	144,270	14,379	13,114	1,648	68,956	89,693	6,501	8,261
1971	192,668	176,224	16,444	174,058	18,610	159,386	14,672	16,838	1,772	98,233	75,825	9,430	9,180
1972	206,659	190,039	16,620	183,443	23,216	168,990	14,453	21,049	2,167	79,723	103,720	10,842	12,374
1973	218,990	201,663	17,327	186,297	32,693	171,731	14,566	29,932	2,761	81,811	104,486	16,138	16,555
1974	235,452	216,329	19,123	194,079	41,373	178,926	15,153	37,403	3,970	84,271	109,808	20,085	21,288
1975	242,267	219,886	22,381	192,100	50,167	177,117	14,983	42,769	7,398	79,240	112,860	23,557	26,610
1976	244,292	220,124	24,168	189,810	54,482	171,967	17,843	48,157	6,325	77,873	111,937	23,468	31,014
1977	251,357	226,318	25,039	191,451	59,906	173,165	18,286	53,153	6,753	78,189	113,262	24,901	35,005
1978	256,904	232,540	24,364	192,221	64,683	174,906	17,315	57,634	7,049	77,748	114,473	26,839	37,844
1979	263,404	238,949	24,455	193,363	70,041	176,394	16,969	62,555	7,486	77,122	116,241	29,026	41,015
1980	277,767	251,359	26,408	199,344	78,423	181,448	17,896	69,911	8,512	81,022	118,322	33,415	45,008
1981	274,595	248,328	26,267	192,936	81,659	175,414	17,522	72,914	8,745	77,562	115,374	34,177	47,482
1982	278,425	252,108	26,317	191,200	87,225	173,941	17,259	78,167	9,058	76,273	114,927	37,183	50,042
1983	278,529	249,636	28,893	188,096	90,433	169,071	19,025	80,565	9,868	74,938	113,158	38,484	51,949
1984	278,598	249,708	28,890	184,949	93,649	166,286	18,663	83,422	10,227	73,722	111,227	40,186	53,463
1985	274,200	246,619	27,581	179,792	94,408	162,368	17,424	84,251	10,157	71,373	108,419	40,435	53,973
1986	270,401	245,647	24,754	173,851	96,550	158,557	15,294	87,090	9,460	70,326	103,525	41,699	54,851
1987	268,332	241,807	26,525	170,129	98,203	153,668	16,461	88,139	10,064	68,089	102,040	41,947	56,256
1988	267,109	241,228	25,881	166,912	100,197	151,045	15,867	90,183	10,014	66,196	100,716	42,743	57,454
1989	274,451	247,812	26,639	168,773	105,678	152,511	16,262	95,301	10,377	67,548	101,225	45,090	60,588
1990	273,366	245,854	27,512	166,798	106,568	149,805	16,993	96,049	10,519	66,071	100,727	45,674	60,894
1991	280,531	252,012	28,519	169,875	110,656	152,356	17,519	99,656	11,000	64,821	105,054	46,661	63,995
1992	280,922	252,138	28,784	168,620	112,302	151,025	17,595	101,113	11,189	63,511	105,109	47,178	65,124
1993	292,431	259,764	32,667	172,788	119,643	153,873	18,915	105,891	13,752	63,973	108,815	49,681	69,962
1994 [1]	294,713	263,311	31,402	173,956	120,757	155,018	18,938	108,293	12,464	63,844	110,112	50,153	70,604

[1] Preliminary data.

SOURCE: U.S. Department of Education, National Center for Education Statistics, "Fall Enrollment in Colleges and Universities;" and Integrated Postsecondary Education Data System (IPEDS), "Fall Enrollment" survey. (This table was prepared December 1995.)

Table 186.—Total fall enrollment in institutions of higher education, by state: 1970 to 1994

State or other area	Fall 1970	Fall 1975	Fall 1980	Fall 1985	Fall 1990	Fall 1991	Fall 1992	Fall 1993[1]	Fall 1994[2]	Percent change, 1990 to 1994
1	2	3	4	5	6	7	8	9	10	11
United States	8,580,887	11,184,859	12,096,895	12,247,055	13,818,637	14,358,953	14,487,359	14,304,803	14,278,790	3.3
Alabama	103,936	164,700	164,306	179,343	218,589	224,331	230,537	233,525	229,511	5.0
Alaska	9,471	13,998	21,296	27,479	29,833	30,793	30,902	30,638	28,798	−3.5
Arizona	109,619	173,542	202,716	216,854	264,148	272,971	274,671	272,300	274,932	4.1
Arkansas	52,039	65,547	77,607	77,958	90,425	94,340	97,578	99,262	96,294	6.5
California	1,257,245	1,787,932	1,790,993	1,650,439	1,808,740	2,024,274	1,978,003	1,836,349	1,835,791	1.5
Colorado	123,395	149,814	162,916	161,314	227,131	235,108	241,352	239,805	241,295	6.2
Connecticut	124,700	148,491	159,632	159,348	168,604	165,824	165,874	162,300	159,990	−5.1
Delaware	25,260	32,389	32,939	31,883	42,004	42,988	42,763	43,528	44,197	5.2
District of Columbia	77,158	84,190	86,675	78,868	80,156	77,964	81,909	81,916	77,705	−3.1
Florida	235,525	344,267	411,891	451,392	588,086	611,781	618,285	623,403	634,237	7.8
Georgia	126,511	173,585	184,159	196,826	251,786	277,023	293,606	302,844	308,587	22.6
Hawaii	36,562	46,671	47,181	49,937	56,436	57,302	61,162	62,871	64,322	14.0
Idaho	34,567	39,075	43,018	42,668	51,881	55,397	57,798	58,768	60,393	16.4
Illinois	452,146	584,089	644,245	678,689	729,246	753,297	748,805	734,089	731,420	0.3
Indiana	192,668	213,820	247,253	250,567	284,832	290,301	296,912	294,685	292,276	2.6
Iowa	108,902	121,678	140,449	152,897	170,515	171,024	172,805	172,797	172,450	1.1
Kansas	102,485	120,833	136,605	141,359	163,733	167,699	169,419	170,135	170,603	4.2
Kentucky	98,591	125,253	143,066	141,724	177,852	187,958	188,322	187,332	182,577	2.7
Louisiana	120,728	153,213	160,058	177,176	186,840	197,438	204,379	201,987	203,567	9.0
Maine	34,134	40,443	43,264	52,201	57,186	57,178	57,977	56,294	56,724	−0.8
Maryland	149,607	205,570	225,526	231,649	259,700	267,931	268,399	268,005	266,214	2.5
Massachusetts	303,809	384,485	418,415	421,175	417,833	419,381	422,976	420,127	416,505	−0.3
Michigan	392,726	496,405	520,131	507,293	569,803	568,491	560,773	568,210	551,307	−3.2
Minnesota	160,788	184,756	206,691	221,162	253,789	255,054	272,920	268,118	289,300	14.0
Mississippi	73,967	99,962	102,364	101,180	122,883	125,350	123,754	122,408	120,884	−1.6
Missouri	183,930	223,115	234,421	241,146	289,899	297,154	296,617	297,062	293,810	1.3
Montana	30,062	30,843	35,177	35,958	35,876	37,821	39,644	39,557	40,095	11.8
Nebraska	66,915	74,705	89,488	97,769	112,831	113,648	122,603	115,523	116,000	2.8
Nevada	13,669	30,187	40,455	43,656	61,728	62,664	63,877	63,947	64,085	3.8
New Hampshire	29,400	41,030	46,794	52,283	59,510	63,718	63,924	64,043	62,847	5.6
New Jersey	216,121	297,114	321,610	297,658	324,286	334,641	343,232	343,029	335,480	3.5
New Mexico	44,461	51,944	58,283	68,295	85,500	93,507	99,276	101,460	101,881	19.2
New York	806,479	1,005,063	992,237	1,000,098	1,048,286	1,056,487	1,064,822	1,062,924	1,057,841	0.9
North Carolina	171,925	251,786	287,537	327,288	352,138	371,968	383,453	371,280	369,386	4.9
North Dakota	31,495	29,743	34,069	37,939	37,878	38,739	40,470	40,316	40,184	6.1
Ohio	376,267	436,052	489,145	514,745	557,690	569,326	573,183	562,402	549,304	−1.5
Oklahoma	110,155	146,613	160,295	169,173	173,221	183,536	187,846	183,342	185,174	6.9
Oregon	122,177	145,281	157,458	137,967	165,741	167,107	167,415	165,834	164,447	−0.8
Pennsylvania	411,044	470,536	507,716	533,198	604,060	620,036	626,904	621,228	611,174	1.2
Rhode Island	45,898	64,479	66,869	69,927	78,273	79,112	79,165	77,407	74,718	−4.5
South Carolina	69,518	133,023	132,476	131,902	159,302	164,907	171,443	174,302	173,070	8.6
South Dakota	30,639	30,260	32,761	32,772	34,208	36,332	37,596	38,166	37,764	10.4
Tennessee	135,103	181,435	204,581	194,845	226,238	238,042	242,970	244,936	242,966	7.4
Texas	442,225	624,390	701,391	769,692	901,437	917,443	938,526	942,178	954,495	5.9
Utah	81,687	87,323	93,987	103,994	121,303	130,419	133,083	138,139	146,196	20.5
Vermont	22,209	29,095	30,628	31,416	36,398	37,436	37,377	36,415	35,409	−2.7
Virginia	151,915	244,671	280,504	292,416	353,442	356,325	354,172	348,535	354,149	0.2
Washington	183,544	227,168	303,603	231,553	263,384	274,760	275,556	279,845	284,662	8.1
West Virginia	63,153	78,619	81,973	76,659	84,790	88,602	90,252	88,852	87,741	3.5
Wisconsin	202,058	240,701	269,086	275,069	299,774	308,986	307,902	309,036	303,861	1.4
Wyoming	15,220	18,078	21,147	24,204	31,326	32,118	31,548	30,702	30,682	−2.1
U.S. Service Schools	17,079	36,897	49,808	54,052	48,087	52,921	52,622	52,647	51,490	7.1
Outlying areas	67,237	104,270	137,749	164,890	164,618	168,771	169,759	172,989	170,686	3.7
American Samoa	—	689	976	758	1,219	1,267	1,295	1,264	1,249	2.5
Federated States of Micronesia	—	—	—	—	975	837	1,028	1,148	1,374	40.9
Guam	2,719	3,800	3,217	4,601	4,741	5,016	4,845	5,843	6,449	36.0
Marshall Islands	—	—	—	—	—	—	374	386	424	
Northern Marianas	—	—	—	318	661	847	796	1,261	1,253	89.6
Palau	—	—	—	—	491	355	445	436	403	−17.9
Puerto Rico	63,073	97,517	131,184	155,917	154,065	157,733	158,120	159,709	156,439	1.5
Trust Territory of the Pacific	—	185	224	724	—	—	—	—	—	
Virgin Islands	1,445	2,079	2,148	2,572	2,466	2,716	2,856	2,942	3,095	25.5

[1] Revised from previously published data.

[2] Preliminary data.

—Data not reported or not applicable.

SOURCE: U.S. Department of Education, National Center for Education Statistics, "Fall Enrollment in Colleges and Universities;" and Integrated Postsecondary Education Data System (IPEDS), "Fall Enrollment" survey. (This table was prepared January 1996.)

Table 187.—Total fall enrollment in public institutions of higher education, by state: 1970 to 1994

State or other area	Fall 1970	Fall 1975	Fall 1980	Fall 1985	Fall 1990	Fall 1991	Fall 1992	Fall 1993	Fall 1994 [1]	Percent change, 1990 to 1994
1	2	3	4	5	6	7	8	9	10	11
United States	**6,428,134**	**8,834,508**	**9,457,394**	**9,479,273**	**10,844,717**	**11,309,563**	**11,384,567**	**11,189,088**	**11,133,680**	**2.7**
Alabama	87,884	145,698	143,674	158,688	195,939	202,311	206,287	210,094	206,546	5.4
Alaska	8,563	13,218	20,561	26,510	27,792	29,019	29,037	28,708	27,631	–0.6
Arizona	107,315	168,666	194,034	202,036	248,213	253,631	255,907	246,754	252,184	1.6
Arkansas	43,599	56,127	66,068	66,123	78,645	82,152	85,829	87,942	85,601	8.8
California	1,123,529	1,617,558	1,599,838	1,444,207	1,594,710	1,804,654	1,748,649	1,604,158	1,582,837	–0.7
Colorado	108,562	136,370	145,598	142,031	200,653	206,645	212,427	209,932	209,717	4.5
Connecticut	73,391	93,567	97,788	98,616	109,556	107,321	107,786	105,446	102,450	–6.5
Delaware	21,151	27,082	28,325	27,933	34,252	35,311	35,313	35,771	36,322	6.0
District of Columbia	12,194	15,159	13,900	12,747	12,595	12,033	12,285	10,959	11,048	–12.3
Florida	189,450	287,745	334,349	362,241	489,081	506,342	511,226	518,480	528,024	8.0
Georgia	101,900	142,593	140,158	148,956	196,413	218,924	233,078	239,755	243,855	24.2
Hawaii	32,963	43,278	43,269	43,246	45,728	45,682	49,605	50,618	51,646	12.9
Idaho	27,072	31,298	34,491	33,666	41,315	44,149	46,607	47,524	48,994	18.6
Illinois	315,634	444,458	491,274	520,224	551,333	571,249	566,614	549,745	545,958	–1.0
Indiana	136,739	159,453	189,224	193,833	223,953	228,378	234,624	231,259	228,270	1.9
Iowa	68,390	83,572	97,454	109,765	117,834	120,360	122,841	122,267	122,017	3.5
Kansas	88,215	107,761	121,987	127,220	149,117	152,349	153,399	154,016	152,798	2.5
Kentucky	77,240	105,265	114,884	110,836	147,095	155,773	157,838	156,160	151,575	3.0
Louisiana	101,127	132,054	136,703	153,173	158,290	168,822	177,373	173,950	175,112	10.6
Maine	25,405	31,092	31,878	33,188	41,500	40,928	40,846	39,819	39,188	–5.6
Maryland	118,988	176,544	195,051	198,992	220,783	228,638	227,987	226,666	223,692	1.3
Massachusetts	116,127	173,564	183,765	185,602	186,035	180,559	183,119	181,461	179,799	–3.4
Michigan	339,625	436,655	454,147	434,270	487,359	486,301	473,322	483,145	466,758	–4.2
Minnesota	130,567	148,630	162,379	173,984	199,211	199,753	212,158	207,131	227,015	14.0
Mississippi	64,968	89,919	90,661	90,704	109,038	111,386	109,911	109,373	108,398	–0.6
Missouri	132,540	158,196	165,179	168,829	200,093	203,125	198,610	197,821	191,859	–4.1
Montana	27,287	27,798	31,178	32,032	31,865	33,453	33,765	34,326	34,927	9.6
Nebraska	51,454	61,240	73,509	81,202	94,614	94,692	103,196	95,782	95,877	1.3
Nevada	13,576	30,010	40,280	43,368	61,242	61,985	63,192	63,229	63,271	3.3
New Hampshire	15,979	24,205	24,119	26,669	32,163	34,518	35,255	35,571	34,988	8.8
New Jersey	145,373	227,764	247,028	237,297	261,601	270,728	278,385	278,361	272,420	4.1
New Mexico	40,795	47,605	55,077	66,059	83,403	89,853	94,901	98,093	97,073	16.4
New York	449,437	613,842	563,250	563,251	616,884	605,898	606,308	604,989	604,433	–2.0
North Carolina	123,761	201,288	228,154	267,044	285,405	305,473	315,518	303,556	303,649	6.4
North Dakota	30,192	27,954	31,709	34,802	34,690	35,218	36,783	36,644	36,639	5.6
Ohio	281,099	336,931	381,765	379,164	427,613	436,292	437,027	429,756	417,566	–2.3
Oklahoma	91,438	124,372	137,188	146,827	151,073	160,166	164,728	160,901	161,748	7.1
Oregon	108,483	129,785	140,102	119,612	144,427	144,451	144,902	143,352	141,027	–2.4
Pennsylvania	232,982	287,436	292,499	300,523	343,478	354,435	359,856	351,747	342,565	–0.3
Rhode Island	25,527	32,311	35,052	35,389	42,350	42,503	43,264	40,833	39,376	–7.0
South Carolina	47,101	107,690	107,683	105,854	131,134	137,012	145,580	148,933	148,514	13.3
South Dakota	23,936	21,925	24,328	23,339	26,596	28,888	30,346	31,427	30,980	16.5
Tennessee	98,897	139,526	156,835	147,951	175,049	186,441	192,302	194,225	191,425	9.4
Texas	365,522	542,212	613,552	677,192	802,314	816,554	832,438	834,696	843,002	5.1
Utah	49,588	56,536	59,598	69,426	86,108	94,802	96,958	100,271	108,593	26.1
Vermont	12,536	17,145	17,984	18,844	20,910	21,485	21,397	21,001	20,505	–1.9
Virginia	123,279	215,253	246,500	250,754	291,286	298,107	297,522	293,810	293,165	0.6
Washington	162,718	202,531	276,028	201,532	227,632	238,345	238,763	241,813	244,772	7.5
West Virginia	51,363	68,117	71,228	66,531	74,108	78,215	79,284	77,500	76,120	2.7
Wisconsin	170,374	210,535	235,179	238,735	253,529	260,082	256,890	256,669	250,246	–1.3
Wyoming	15,220	18,078	21,121	24,204	30,623	31,251	30,687	30,002	30,015	–2.0
U.S. Service Schools	17,079	36,897	49,808	54,052	48,087	52,921	52,622	52,647	51,490	7.1
Outlying areas	46,680	59,923	60,692	65,411	66,244	66,074	66,702	69,115	70,917	7.1
American Samoa	—	689	976	758	1,219	1,267	1,295	1,264	1,249	2.5
Federated States of Micronesia	—	—	—	—	975	837	1,028	1,148	1,374	40.9
Guam	2,719	3,800	3,217	4,601	4,741	5,016	4,845	5,843	6,449	36.0
Marshall Islands	—	—	—	—	—	—	374	386	424	—
Northern Marianas	—	—	—	318	661	847	796	1,261	1,253	89.6
Palau	—	—	—	—	491	355	445	436	403	–17.9
Puerto Rico	42,516	53,170	54,127	56,438	55,691	55,036	55,063	55,835	56,670	1.8
Trust Territory of the Pacific	—	185	224	724	—	—	—	—	—	—
Virgin Islands	1,445	2,079	2,148	2,572	2,466	2,716	2,856	2,942	3,095	25.5

[1] Preliminary data.

—Data not reported or not applicable.

SOURCE: U.S. Department of Education, National Center for Education Statistics, "Fall Enrollment in Colleges and Universities;" and Integrated Postsecondary Education Data System (IPEDS), "Fall Enrollment" survey. (This table was prepared November 1995).

Table 188.—Total fall enrollment in private institutions of higher education, by state: 1970 to 1994

State or other area	Fall 1970	Fall 1975	Fall 1980	Fall 1985	Fall 1990	Fall 1991	Fall 1992	Fall 1993 [1]	Fall 1994 [2]	Percent change, 1990 to 1994
1	2	3	4	5	6	7	8	9	10	11
United States	**2,152,753**	**2,350,351**	**2,639,501**	**2,767,782**	**2,973,920**	**3,049,390**	**3,102,792**	**3,115,715**	**3,145,110**	**5.8**
Alabama	16,052	19,002	20,632	20,655	22,650	22,020	24,250	23,431	22,965	1.4
Alaska	908	780	735	969	2,041	1,774	1,865	1,930	1,167	−42.8
Arizona	2,304	4,876	8,682	14,818	15,935	19,340	18,764	25,546	22,748	42.8
Arkansas	8,440	9,420	11,539	11,835	11,780	12,188	11,749	11,320	10,693	−9.2
California	133,716	170,374	191,155	206,232	214,030	219,620	229,354	232,191	252,954	18.2
Colorado	14,833	13,444	17,318	19,283	26,478	28,463	28,925	29,873	31,578	19.3
Connecticut	51,309	54,924	61,844	60,732	59,048	58,503	58,088	56,854	57,540	−2.6
Delaware	4,109	5,307	4,614	3,950	7,752	7,677	7,450	7,757	7,875	1.6
District of Columbia	64,964	69,031	72,775	66,121	67,561	65,931	69,624	70,957	66,657	−1.3
Florida	46,075	56,522	77,542	89,151	99,005	105,439	107,059	104,923	106,213	7.3
Georgia	24,611	30,992	44,001	47,870	55,373	58,099	60,528	63,089	64,732	16.9
Hawaii	3,599	3,393	3,912	6,691	10,708	11,620	11,557	12,253	12,676	18.4
Idaho	7,495	7,777	8,527	9,002	10,566	11,248	11,191	11,244	11,399	7.9
Illinois	136,512	139,631	152,971	158,465	177,913	182,048	182,191	184,344	185,462	4.2
Indiana	55,929	54,367	58,029	56,734	60,879	61,923	62,288	63,426	64,006	5.1
Iowa	40,512	38,106	42,995	43,132	52,681	50,664	49,964	50,530	50,433	−4.3
Kansas	14,270	13,072	14,618	14,139	14,616	15,350	16,020	16,119	17,805	21.8
Kentucky	21,351	19,988	28,182	30,888	30,757	32,185	30,484	31,172	31,002	0.8
Louisiana	19,601	21,159	23,355	24,003	28,550	28,616	27,006	28,037	28,455	−0.3
Maine	8,729	9,351	11,386	19,013	15,686	16,250	17,131	16,475	17,536	11.8
Maryland	30,619	29,026	30,475	32,657	38,917	39,293	40,412	41,339	42,522	9.3
Massachusetts	187,682	210,921	234,650	235,573	231,798	238,822	239,857	238,666	236,706	2.1
Michigan	53,101	59,750	65,984	73,023	82,444	82,190	87,451	85,065	84,549	2.6
Minnesota	30,221	36,126	44,312	47,178	54,578	55,301	60,762	60,987	62,285	14.1
Mississippi	8,999	10,043	11,703	10,476	13,845	13,964	13,843	13,035	12,486	−9.8
Missouri	51,390	64,919	69,242	72,317	89,806	94,029	98,007	99,241	101,951	13.5
Montana	2,775	3,045	3,999	3,926	4,011	4,368	5,879	5,231	5,168	28.8
Nebraska	15,461	13,465	15,979	16,567	18,217	18,956	19,407	19,741	20,123	10.5
Nevada	93	177	175	288	486	679	685	718	814	67.5
New Hampshire	13,421	16,825	22,675	25,614	27,347	29,200	28,669	28,472	27,859	1.9
New Jersey	70,748	69,350	74,582	60,361	62,685	63,913	64,847	64,668	63,060	0.6
New Mexico	3,666	4,339	3,206	2,236	2,097	3,654	4,375	3,367	4,808	129.3
New York	357,042	391,221	428,986	436,847	431,402	450,589	458,514	457,935	453,408	5.1
North Carolina	48,164	50,498	59,383	60,244	66,733	66,495	67,935	67,724	65,737	−1.5
North Dakota	1,303	1,789	2,360	3,137	3,188	3,521	3,687	3,672	3,545	11.2
Ohio	95,168	99,121	107,380	135,581	130,077	133,034	136,156	132,646	131,738	1.3
Oklahoma	18,717	22,241	23,107	22,346	22,148	23,370	23,118	22,441	23,426	5.8
Oregon	13,694	15,496	17,356	18,355	21,314	22,656	22,513	22,482	23,420	9.9
Pennsylvania	178,062	183,100	215,217	232,675	260,582	265,601	267,048	269,481	268,609	3.1
Rhode Island	20,371	32,168	31,817	34,538	35,923	36,609	35,901	36,574	35,342	−1.6
South Carolina	22,417	25,333	24,793	26,048	28,168	27,895	25,863	25,369	24,556	−12.8
South Dakota	6,703	8,335	8,433	9,433	7,612	7,444	7,250	6,739	6,784	−10.9
Tennessee	36,206	41,909	47,746	46,894	51,189	51,601	50,668	50,711	51,541	0.7
Texas	76,703	82,178	87,839	92,500	99,123	100,889	106,068	107,482	111,493	12.5
Utah	32,099	30,787	34,389	34,568	35,195	35,617	36,125	37,868	37,603	6.8
Vermont	9,673	11,950	12,644	12,572	15,488	15,951	15,980	15,414	14,904	−3.8
Virginia	28,636	29,418	34,004	41,662	62,156	58,218	56,650	54,725	60,984	−1.9
Washington	20,826	24,637	27,575	30,021	35,752	36,415	36,793	38,032	39,890	11.6
West Virginia	11,790	10,502	10,745	10,128	10,682	10,387	10,968	11,352	11,621	8.8
Wisconsin	31,684	30,166	33,907	36,334	46,245	48,904	51,012	52,367	53,615	15.9
Wyoming	—	—	26	—	703	867	861	700	667	−5.1
Outlying areas	20,557	44,347	77,057	99,479	98,374	102,697	103,057	103,874	99,769	1.4
American Samoa	—	—	—	—	—	—	—	—	—	—
Federated States of Micronesia	—	—	—	—	—	—	—	—	—	—
Guam	—	—	—	—	—	—	—	—	—	—
Marshall Islands	—	—	—	—	—	—	—	—	—	—
Northern Marianas	—	—	—	—	—	—	—	—	—	—
Palau	—	—	—	—	—	—	—	—	—	—
Puerto Rico	20,557	44,347	77,057	99,479	98,374	102,697	103,057	103,874	99,769	1.4
Trust Territory of the Pacific	—	—	—	—	—	—	—	—	—	—
Virgin Islands	—	—	—	—	—	—	—	—	—	—

[1] Revised from previously published data.
[2] Preliminary data.
—Data not reported or not applicable.

SOURCE: U.S. Department of Education, National Center for Education Statistics, "Fall Enrollment in Colleges and Universities;" and Integrated Postsecondary Education Data System (IPEDS), "Fall Enrollment" survey. (This table was prepared November 1995.)

Table 189.—Total fall enrollment in all institutions of higher education, by attendance status, sex, and state: 1993 and 1994

State or other area	Fall 1993 [1]					Fall 1994 [2]				
	Total	Full-time		Part-time		Total	Full-time		Part-time	
		Men	Women	Men	Women		Men	Women	Men	Women
1	2	3	4	5	6	7	8	9	10	11
United States	14,304,803	3,890,571	4,237,047	2,536,879	3,640,306	14,278,790	3,855,183	4,282,593	2,516,715	3,624,299
Alabama	233,525	71,148	82,841	33,714	45,822	229,511	69,230	82,660	33,045	44,576
Alaska	30,638	5,566	6,651	6,784	11,637	28,798	5,668	6,788	6,161	10,181
Arizona	272,300	64,181	64,053	59,430	84,636	274,932	63,697	64,013	60,773	86,449
Arkansas	99,262	31,427	37,720	11,376	18,739	96,294	30,261	36,712	11,093	18,228
California	1,836,349	406,101	435,586	432,747	561,915	1,835,791	412,716	450,914	421,148	551,013
Colorado	239,805	63,284	63,610	48,383	64,528	241,295	63,265	65,091	48,463	64,476
Connecticut	162,300	39,634	42,464	31,570	48,632	159,990	39,144	42,766	30,283	47,797
Delaware	43,528	11,497	14,338	7,258	10,435	44,197	11,521	14,411	7,533	10,732
District of Columbia	81,916	23,544	26,983	14,146	17,243	77,705	22,605	26,641	12,868	15,591
Florida	623,403	141,429	155,591	135,506	190,877	634,237	142,547	159,592	136,851	195,247
Georgia	302,844	92,115	107,003	41,417	62,309	308,587	92,709	110,110	42,371	63,397
Hawaii	62,871	15,898	18,564	12,539	15,870	64,322	16,061	19,169	12,871	16,221
Idaho	58,768	19,469	20,463	7,674	11,162	60,393	19,255	21,103	7,908	12,127
Illinois	734,089	181,736	191,806	146,735	213,812	731,420	178,957	193,474	145,279	213,710
Indiana	294,685	94,283	97,858	41,745	60,799	292,276	92,089	97,935	41,063	61,189
Iowa	172,797	60,629	61,612	18,549	32,007	172,450	58,901	61,720	19,478	32,351
Kansas	170,135	48,178	49,373	27,220	45,364	170,603	48,013	49,915	28,114	44,561
Kentucky	187,332	54,597	66,751	23,505	42,479	182,577	53,533	65,836	22,407	40,801
Louisiana	201,987	64,588	77,444	22,422	37,533	203,567	64,832	79,536	21,798	37,401
Maine	56,294	15,523	17,008	8,097	15,666	56,724	15,014	17,035	8,032	16,643
Maryland	268,005	57,985	65,487	56,519	88,014	266,214	57,746	66,913	54,678	86,877
Massachusetts	420,127	124,561	138,201	63,123	94,242	416,505	123,189	138,072	60,797	94,447
Michigan	568,210	136,177	150,788	117,085	164,160	551,307	130,298	148,247	112,668	160,094
Minnesota	268,118	75,511	80,410	44,827	67,370	289,300	77,477	84,168	53,571	74,084
Mississippi	122,408	42,717	50,496	10,916	18,279	120,884	40,937	49,527	11,282	19,138
Missouri	297,062	81,671	87,341	51,166	76,884	293,810	79,571	87,509	50,435	76,295
Montana	39,557	14,922	15,290	3,813	5,532	40,095	15,246	15,508	3,798	5,543
Nebraska	115,523	31,939	34,103	20,687	28,794	116,000	32,353	34,308	19,706	29,633
Nevada	63,947	9,734	10,460	18,437	25,316	64,085	10,186	11,011	18,044	24,844
New Hampshire	64,043	18,880	21,145	9,229	14,789	62,847	18,376	21,513	8,470	14,488
New Jersey	343,029	83,378	90,846	67,955	100,850	335,480	81,351	91,263	65,599	97,267
New Mexico	101,460	24,215	27,078	19,887	30,280	101,881	23,684	27,696	20,075	30,426
New York	1,062,924	317,192	362,324	147,140	236,268	1,057,841	311,858	363,375	144,142	238,466
North Carolina	371,280	107,253	128,415	54,978	80,634	369,386	104,943	130,290	54,140	80,013
North Dakota	40,316	16,722	15,417	3,550	4,627	40,184	16,426	15,439	3,585	4,734
Ohio	562,402	164,434	182,990	91,593	123,385	549,304	160,869	181,175	87,286	119,974
Oklahoma	183,342	52,795	56,202	30,484	43,861	185,174	52,979	57,218	30,890	44,087
Oregon	165,834	46,585	46,506	31,818	40,925	164,447	45,748	46,680	31,295	40,724
Pennsylvania	621,228	190,522	198,637	92,270	139,799	611,174	186,827	199,592	91,629	133,126
Rhode Island	77,407	23,936	24,740	11,007	17,724	74,718	22,796	24,221	10,770	16,931
South Carolina	174,302	49,955	58,119	24,544	41,684	173,070	49,154	58,332	24,356	41,228
South Dakota	38,166	13,243	14,545	3,742	6,636	37,764	12,950	14,538	3,717	6,559
Tennessee	244,936	73,381	82,828	36,459	52,268	242,966	72,240	83,777	35,384	51,565
Texas	942,178	251,344	259,172	185,881	245,781	954,495	250,851	263,609	192,609	247,426
Utah	138,139	47,405	46,397	21,967	22,370	146,196	48,699	47,148	24,669	25,680
Vermont	36,415	11,834	12,477	3,787	8,317	35,409	11,434	12,461	3,684	7,830
Virginia	348,535	91,543	105,504	62,481	89,007	354,149	92,054	107,374	63,443	91,278
Washington	279,845	78,096	86,050	47,007	68,692	284,662	81,419	90,980	45,744	66,519
West Virginia	88,852	29,701	30,733	9,733	18,685	87,741	29,373	31,215	9,381	17,772
Wisconsin	309,036	88,106	98,766	49,879	72,285	303,861	85,012	95,951	49,305	73,593
Wyoming	30,702	8,715	8,724	4,688	8,575	30,682	8,669	8,886	4,793	8,334
U.S. Service Schools	52,647	21,292	9,137	9,410	12,808	51,490	20,450	9,176	9,231	12,633
Outlying areas	172,989	51,176	78,522	17,829	25,462	170,686	49,427	76,346	19,016	25,897
American Samoa	1,264	438	439	227	160	1,249	433	438	222	156
Federated States of Micronesia	1,148	279	260	288	321	1,374	449	422	316	187
Guam	5,843	1,051	1,626	1,546	1,620	6,449	1,174	1,770	1,645	1,860
Marshall Islands	386	222	146	10	8	424	92	76	147	109
Northern Marianas	1,261	147	198	433	483	1,253	148	202	425	478
Palau	436	221	126	26	63	403	198	136	34	35
Puerto Rico	159,709	48,467	74,841	14,879	21,522	156,439	46,580	72,315	15,769	21,775
Virgin Islands	2,942	351	886	420	1,285	3,095	353	987	458	1,297

[1] Revised from previously published data.
[2] Preliminary data.

SOURCE: U.S. Department of Education, National Center for Education Statistics, Integrated Postsecondary Education Data System (IPEDS), "Fall Enrollment" survey. (This table was prepared November 1995.)

Table 190.—Total fall enrollment in public institutions of higher education, by attendance status, sex, and state: 1993 and 1994

State or other area	Fall 1993					Fall 1994 [1]				
	Total	Full-time		Part-time		Total	Full-time		Part-time	
		Men	Women	Men	Women		Men	Women	Men	Women
1	2	3	4	5	6	7	8	9	10	11
United States	11,189,088	2,848,010	3,114,552	2,136,501	3,090,025	11,133,680	2,813,226	3,137,594	2,116,842	3,066,018
Alabama	210,094	62,613	72,000	32,005	43,476	206,546	60,804	71,839	31,510	42,393
Alaska	28,708	5,282	6,133	6,484	10,809	27,631	5,367	6,318	5,995	9,951
Arizona	246,754	53,172	53,337	57,886	82,359	252,184	53,487	55,865	58,995	83,837
Arkansas	87,942	26,779	32,315	10,854	17,994	85,601	25,767	31,632	10,681	17,521
California	1,604,158	324,690	352,169	400,062	527,237	1,582,837	323,244	356,573	388,424	514,596
Colorado	209,932	53,942	54,658	42,375	58,957	209,717	52,922	55,323	42,777	58,695
Connecticut	105,446	22,376	24,620	22,313	36,137	102,450	21,556	24,035	21,546	35,313
Delaware	35,771	9,924	12,497	5,608	7,742	36,322	9,961	12,534	5,874	7,953
District of Columbia	10,959	1,928	2,163	2,912	3,956	11,048	1,786	2,124	3,026	4,112
Florida	518,480	104,745	121,237	118,013	174,485	528,024	105,949	124,501	119,118	178,456
Georgia	239,755	67,997	79,748	36,051	55,959	243,855	68,164	81,927	36,659	57,105
Hawaii	50,618	12,346	14,736	9,706	13,830	51,646	12,600	15,202	9,809	14,035
Idaho	47,524	14,916	14,720	7,349	10,539	48,994	14,930	15,440	7,481	11,143
Illinois	549,745	122,920	130,253	119,228	177,344	545,958	120,292	130,610	117,878	177,178
Indiana	231,259	68,190	72,858	37,895	52,316	228,270	66,120	72,001	37,294	52,855
Iowa	122,267	43,007	41,796	14,245	23,219	122,017	41,780	42,084	14,724	23,429
Kansas	154,016	42,670	43,110	25,695	42,541	152,798	41,950	42,874	26,354	41,620
Kentucky	156,160	43,561	53,741	21,143	37,715	151,575	42,852	52,976	19,789	35,958
Louisiana	173,950	55,168	66,119	18,931	33,732	175,112	55,288	67,727	18,522	33,575
Maine	39,819	11,112	10,570	6,862	11,275	39,188	10,588	10,479	6,748	11,373
Maryland	226,666	47,709	53,821	48,933	76,203	223,692	47,252	54,760	47,011	74,669
Massachusetts	181,461	45,369	51,706	33,337	51,049	179,799	44,675	50,704	32,804	51,616
Michigan	483,145	114,628	122,296	102,934	143,287	466,758	109,531	120,876	98,338	138,013
Minnesota	207,131	56,178	56,801	38,221	55,931	227,015	58,482	59,576	46,968	61,989
Mississippi	109,373	38,628	44,850	9,756	16,139	108,398	37,258	44,200	10,041	16,899
Missouri	197,821	52,284	57,610	33,396	54,531	191,859	49,912	56,907	32,007	53,033
Montana	34,326	13,583	13,218	3,156	4,369	34,927	13,835	13,378	3,191	4,523
Nebraska	95,782	25,186	26,070	19,111	25,415	95,877	25,633	26,008	18,119	26,117
Nevada	63,229	9,492	10,204	18,362	25,171	63,271	9,938	10,756	17,939	24,638
New Hampshire	35,571	10,485	11,710	5,285	8,091	34,988	10,169	12,204	4,715	7,900
New Jersey	278,361	63,949	72,117	57,214	85,081	272,420	62,691	72,201	55,501	82,027
New Mexico	98,093	23,047	25,848	19,589	29,609	97,073	21,890	25,679	19,779	29,725
New York	604,989	165,661	197,828	91,197	150,303	604,433	165,600	200,641	88,732	149,460
North Carolina	303,556	80,772	98,924	50,387	73,473	303,649	79,562	101,016	50,051	73,020
North Dakota	36,644	15,396	13,586	3,389	4,273	36,639	15,137	13,620	3,447	4,435
Ohio	429,756	121,237	137,989	70,349	100,181	417,566	117,887	135,467	67,350	96,862
Oklahoma	160,901	43,734	47,496	28,190	41,481	161,748	43,443	47,988	28,561	41,756
Oregon	143,352	38,227	37,309	29,747	38,069	141,027	37,290	37,211	29,039	37,487
Pennsylvania	351,747	107,370	112,558	51,541	80,278	342,565	104,923	112,304	49,492	75,846
Rhode Island	40,833	8,758	11,366	7,324	13,385	39,376	8,302	11,100	7,127	12,847
South Carolina	148,933	40,317	46,554	22,871	39,191	148,514	39,912	46,905	22,928	38,769
South Dakota	31,427	11,449	11,705	3,054	5,219	30,980	11,139	11,643	3,045	5,153
Tennessee	194,225	52,269	61,038	33,502	47,416	191,425	51,302	61,486	32,341	46,296
Texas	834,696	209,912	219,895	172,992	231,897	843,002	208,779	223,409	178,286	232,528
Utah	100,271	30,967	29,554	19,864	19,886	108,593	32,052	30,885	22,471	23,185
Vermont	21,001	6,434	6,589	2,528	5,450	20,505	6,216	6,614	2,478	5,197
Virginia	293,810	74,443	82,672	56,022	80,673	293,165	73,308	82,383	55,892	81,582
Washington	241,813	65,719	71,245	42,459	62,390	244,772	68,791	75,747	40,628	59,606
West Virginia	77,500	25,883	25,741	8,878	16,998	76,120	25,514	25,794	8,620	16,192
Wisconsin	256,669	72,273	79,617	43,198	61,581	250,246	68,941	76,009	42,713	62,583
Wyoming	30,002	8,021	8,718	4,688	8,575	30,015	8,005	8,883	4,793	8,334
U.S. Service Schools	52,647	21,292	9,137	9,410	12,808	51,490	20,450	9,176	9,231	12,633
Outlying areas	69,115	19,946	31,182	7,010	10,977	70,917	20,386	32,001	7,297	11,233
American Samoa	1,264	438	439	227	160	1,249	433	438	222	156
Federated States of Micronesia	1,148	279	260	288	321	1,374	449	422	316	187
Guam	5,843	1,051	1,626	1,546	1,620	6,449	1,174	1,770	1,645	1,860
Marshall Islands	386	222	146	10	8	424	92	76	147	109
Northern Marianas	1,261	147	198	433	483	1,253	148	202	425	478
Palau	436	221	126	26	63	403	198	136	34	35
Puerto Rico	55,835	17,237	27,501	4,060	7,037	56,670	17,539	27,970	4,050	7,111
Virgin Islands	2,942	351	886	420	1,285	3,095	353	987	458	1,297

[1] Preliminary data.

SOURCE: U.S. Department of Education, National Center for Education Statistics, Integrated Postsecondary Education Data System (IPEDS), "Fall Enrollment" surveys. (This table was prepared November 1995.)

Table 191.—Total fall enrollment in private institutions of higher education, by attendance status, sex, and state: 1993 and 1994

State or other area	Fall 1993[1]					Fall 1994[2]				
	Total	Full-time		Part-time		Total	Full-time		Part-time	
		Men	Women	Men	Women		Men	Women	Men	Women
1	2	3	4	5	6	7	8	9	10	11
United States	3,115,715	1,042,561	1,122,495	400,378	550,281	3,145,110	1,041,957	1,144,999	399,873	558,281
Alabama	23,431	8,535	10,841	1,709	2,346	22,965	8,426	10,821	1,535	2,183
Alaska	1,930	284	518	300	828	1,167	301	470	166	230
Arizona	25,546	11,009	10,716	1,544	2,277	22,748	10,210	8,148	1,778	2,612
Arkansas	11,320	4,648	5,405	522	745	10,693	4,494	5,080	412	707
California	232,191	81,411	83,417	32,685	34,678	252,954	89,472	94,341	32,724	36,417
Colorado	29,873	9,342	8,952	6,008	5,571	31,578	10,343	9,768	5,686	5,781
Connecticut	56,854	17,258	17,844	9,257	12,495	57,540	17,588	18,731	8,737	12,484
Delaware	7,757	1,573	1,841	1,650	2,693	7,875	1,560	1,877	1,659	2,779
District of Columbia	70,957	21,616	24,820	11,234	13,287	66,657	20,819	24,517	9,842	11,479
Florida	104,923	36,684	34,354	17,493	16,392	106,213	36,598	35,091	17,733	16,791
Georgia	63,089	24,118	27,255	5,366	6,350	64,732	24,545	28,183	5,712	6,292
Hawaii	12,253	3,552	3,828	2,833	2,040	12,676	3,461	3,967	3,062	2,186
Idaho	11,244	4,553	5,743	325	623	11,399	4,325	5,663	427	984
Illinois	184,344	58,816	61,553	27,507	36,468	185,462	58,665	62,864	27,401	36,532
Indiana	63,426	26,093	25,000	3,850	8,483	64,006	25,969	25,934	3,769	8,334
Iowa	50,530	17,622	19,816	4,304	8,788	50,433	17,121	19,636	4,754	8,922
Kansas	16,119	5,508	6,263	1,525	2,823	17,805	6,063	7,041	1,760	2,941
Kentucky	31,172	11,036	13,010	2,362	4,764	31,002	10,681	12,860	2,618	4,843
Louisiana	28,037	9,420	11,325	3,491	3,801	28,455	9,544	11,809	3,276	3,826
Maine	16,475	4,411	6,438	1,235	4,391	17,536	4,426	6,556	1,284	5,270
Maryland	41,339	10,276	11,666	7,586	11,811	42,522	10,494	12,153	7,667	12,208
Massachusetts	238,666	79,192	86,495	29,786	43,193	236,706	78,514	87,368	27,993	42,831
Michigan	85,065	21,549	28,492	14,151	20,873	84,549	20,767	27,371	14,330	22,081
Minnesota	60,987	19,333	23,609	6,606	11,439	62,285	18,995	24,592	6,603	12,095
Mississippi	13,035	4,089	5,646	1,160	2,140	12,486	3,679	5,327	1,241	2,239
Missouri	99,241	29,387	29,731	17,770	22,353	101,951	29,659	30,602	18,428	23,262
Montana	5,231	1,339	2,072	657	1,163	5,168	1,411	2,130	607	1,020
Nebraska	19,741	6,753	8,033	1,576	3,379	20,123	6,720	8,300	1,587	3,516
Nevada	718	242	256	75	145	814	248	255	105	206
New Hampshire	28,472	8,395	9,435	3,944	6,698	27,859	8,207	9,309	3,755	6,588
New Jersey	64,668	19,429	18,729	10,741	15,769	63,060	18,660	19,062	10,098	15,240
New Mexico	3,367	1,168	1,230	298	671	4,808	1,794	2,017	296	701
New York	457,935	151,531	164,496	55,943	85,965	453,408	146,258	162,734	55,410	89,006
North Carolina	67,724	26,481	29,491	4,591	7,161	65,737	25,381	29,274	4,089	6,993
North Dakota	3,672	1,326	1,831	161	354	3,545	1,289	1,819	138	299
Ohio	132,646	43,197	45,001	21,244	23,204	131,738	42,982	45,708	19,936	23,112
Oklahoma	22,441	9,061	8,706	2,294	2,380	23,426	9,536	9,230	2,329	2,331
Oregon	22,482	8,358	9,197	2,071	2,856	23,420	8,458	9,469	2,256	3,237
Pennsylvania	269,481	83,152	86,079	40,729	59,521	268,609	81,904	87,288	42,137	57,280
Rhode Island	36,574	15,178	13,374	3,683	4,339	35,342	14,494	13,121	3,643	4,084
South Carolina	25,369	9,638	11,565	1,673	2,493	24,556	9,242	11,427	1,428	2,459
South Dakota	6,739	1,794	2,840	688	1,417	6,784	1,811	2,895	672	1,406
Tennessee	50,711	21,112	21,790	2,957	4,852	51,541	20,938	22,291	3,043	5,269
Texas	107,482	41,432	39,277	12,889	13,884	111,493	42,072	40,200	14,323	14,898
Utah	37,868	16,438	16,843	2,103	2,484	37,603	16,647	16,263	2,198	2,495
Vermont	15,414	5,400	5,888	1,259	2,867	14,904	5,218	5,847	1,206	2,633
Virginia	54,725	17,100	22,832	6,459	8,334	60,984	18,746	24,991	7,551	9,696
Washington	38,032	12,377	14,805	4,548	6,302	39,890	12,628	15,233	5,116	6,913
West Virginia	11,352	3,818	4,992	855	1,687	11,621	3,859	5,421	761	1,580
Wisconsin	52,367	15,833	19,149	6,681	10,704	53,615	16,071	19,942	6,592	11,010
Wyoming	700	694	6	—	—	667	664	3	—	—
Outlying areas	103,874	31,230	47,340	10,819	14,485	99,769	29,041	44,345	11,719	14,664
American Samoa	—	—	—	—	—	—	—	—	—	—
Federated States of Micronesia	—	—	—	—	—	—	—	—	—	—
Guam	—	—	—	—	—	—	—	—	—	—
Marshall Islands	—	—	—	—	—	—	—	—	—	—
Northern Marianas	—	—	—	—	—	—	—	—	—	—
Palau	—	—	—	—	—	—	—	—	—	—
Puerto Rico	103,874	31,230	47,340	10,819	14,485	99,769	29,041	44,345	11,719	14,664
Virgin Islands	—	—	—	—	—	—	—	—	—	—

[1] Revised from previously published data.
[2] Preliminary data.
—Data not reported or not applicable.

SOURCE: U.S. Department of Education, National Center for Education Statistics, Integrated Postsecondary Education Data System (IPEDS), "Fall Enrollment" surveys. (This table was prepared November 1995.)

Table 192.—Total fall enrollment in institutions of higher education, by control, type of institution, and state: 1993 and 1994

State or other area	Fall 1993 [1]				Fall 1994 [2]			
	Public 4-year	Public 2-year	Private 4-year	Private 2-year	Public 4-year	Public 2-year	Private 4-year	Private 2-year
1	2	3	4	5	6	7	8	9
United States	**5,851,760**	**5,337,328**	**2,887,176**	**228,539**	**5,825,213**	**5,308,467**	**2,923,867**	**221,243**
Alabama	128,350	81,744	21,399	2,032	126,079	80,467	21,609	1,356
Alaska	28,108	600	1,682	248	27,037	594	828	339
Arizona	95,346	151,408	24,469	1,077	101,418	150,766	21,819	929
Arkansas	65,966	21,976	10,288	1,032	64,540	21,061	10,347	346
California	490,479	1,113,679	217,520	14,671	483,332	1,099,505	239,288	13,666
Colorado	132,113	77,819	25,981	3,892	132,748	76,969	28,224	3,354
Connecticut	59,904	45,542	55,223	1,631	57,867	44,583	55,767	1,773
Delaware	25,036	10,735	7,757	—	24,966	11,356	7,875	—
District of Columbia	10,959	—	70,957	—	11,048	—	66,657	—
Florida	191,457	327,023	100,368	4,555	201,242	326,782	101,233	4,980
Georgia	155,834	83,921	56,569	6,520	157,391	86,464	58,559	6,173
Hawaii	23,911	26,707	12,253	—	23,741	27,905	12,676	—
Idaho	40,434	7,090	2,574	8,670	41,629	7,365	2,988	8,411
Illinois	197,377	352,368	177,790	6,554	194,489	351,469	179,359	6,103
Indiana	191,356	39,903	59,837	3,589	186,586	41,684	60,357	3,649
Iowa	66,115	56,152	48,372	2,158	65,617	56,400	49,042	1,391
Kansas	89,296	64,720	15,161	958	86,285	66,513	16,888	917
Kentucky	107,945	48,215	26,221	4,951	106,259	45,316	26,496	4,506
Louisiana	146,158	27,792	27,435	602	147,110	28,002	27,251	1,204
Maine	32,395	7,424	14,767	1,708	31,899	7,289	15,664	1,872
Maryland	112,298	114,368	40,287	1,052	112,250	111,442	41,381	1,141
Massachusetts	101,732	79,729	223,667	14,999	101,796	78,003	222,237	14,469
Michigan	263,279	219,866	82,364	2,701	258,107	208,651	82,086	2,463
Minnesota	121,591	85,540	56,355	4,632	119,233	107,782	57,897	4,388
Mississippi	57,665	51,708	11,816	1,219	57,507	50,891	11,431	1,055
Missouri	119,116	78,705	93,515	5,726	117,361	74,498	96,085	5,866
Montana	30,396	3,930	4,375	856	30,604	4,323	4,395	773
Nebraska	59,515	36,267	19,149	592	58,007	37,870	19,698	425
Nevada	30,536	32,693	693	25	31,333	31,938	787	27
New Hampshire	26,137	9,434	24,496	3,976	26,315	8,673	24,011	3,848
New Jersey	138,391	139,970	60,506	4,162	136,654	135,766	59,079	3,981
New Mexico	52,238	45,855	2,801	566	50,800	46,273	4,157	651
New York	341,772	263,217	427,752	30,183	345,202	259,231	424,708	28,700
North Carolina	155,661	147,895	64,906	2,818	156,445	147,204	63,203	2,534
North Dakota	28,521	8,123	3,404	268	28,301	8,338	3,299	246
Ohio	274,583	155,173	116,587	16,059	267,719	149,847	117,273	14,465
Oklahoma	96,417	64,484	20,193	2,248	97,271	64,477	20,768	2,658
Oregon	63,113	80,239	22,296	186	62,651	78,376	23,252	168
Pennsylvania	234,187	117,560	221,793	47,688	231,347	111,218	220,321	48,288
Rhode Island	24,434	16,399	34,462	2,112	23,375	16,001	33,211	2,131
South Carolina	88,293	60,640	23,465	1,904	87,374	61,140	23,070	1,486
South Dakota	31,216	211	6,528	211	30,783	197	6,573	211
Tennessee	115,774	78,451	47,498	3,213	114,151	77,274	48,722	2,819
Texas	422,811	411,885	102,486	4,996	423,647	419,355	105,376	6,117
Utah	74,011	26,260	36,669	1,199	79,554	29,039	36,405	1,198
Vermont	15,532	5,469	15,240	174	15,873	4,632	14,717	187
Virginia	162,567	131,243	50,424	4,301	162,432	130,733	56,440	4,544
Washington	84,695	157,118	35,957	2,075	85,523	159,249	37,781	2,109
West Virginia	70,340	7,160	10,395	957	68,912	7,208	10,768	853
Wisconsin	145,188	111,481	50,474	1,893	142,998	107,248	51,809	1,806
Wyoming	12,012	17,990	—	700	12,022	17,993	—	667
U.S. Service Schools	19,200	33,447	—	—	18,383	33,107	—	—
Outlying areas	56,824	12,291	90,886	12,988	57,588	13,329	87,311	12,458
American Samoa	—	1,264	—	—	—	1,249	—	—
Federated States of Micronesia	—	1,148	—	—	—	1,374	—	—
Guam	3,697	2,146	—	—	4,064	2,385	—	—
Marshall Islands	—	386	—	—	—	424	—	—
Northern Marianas	—	1,261	—	—	—	1,253	—	—
Palau	—	436	—	—	—	403	—	—
Puerto Rico	50,185	5,650	90,886	12,988	50,429	6,241	87,311	12,458
Virgin Islands	2,942	—	—	—	3,095	—	—	—

[1] Revised from previously published data.
[2] Preliminary data.
—Data not reported or not applicable.

SOURCE: U.S. Department of Education, National Center for Education Statistics, Integrated Postsecondary Education Data System (IPEDS), "Fall Enrollment" surveys. (This table was prepared November 1995.)

Table 193.—Total fall enrollment in institutions of higher education, by level of enrollment and state: 1992 to 1994

State or other area	Fall 1992			Fall 1993 [1]				Fall 1994 [2]			
	Under-graduate [1]	First-profes-sional	Graduate	Total	Under-graduate	First-profes-sional	Graduate	Total	Under-graduate	First-profes-sional	Graduate
1	2	3	4	5	6	7	8	9	10	11	12
United States	12,537,700	280,922	1,668,737	14,304,803	12,323,959	292,431	1,688,413	14,278,790	12,262,608	294,713	1,721,469
Alabama	206,607	3,389	20,541	233,525	208,019	3,520	21,986	229,511	202,408	3,834	23,269
Alaska	29,349	—	1,553	30,638	29,047	—	1,591	28,798	27,189	—	1,609
Arizona	244,028	1,564	29,079	272,300	239,657	2,720	29,923	274,932	241,290	1,549	32,093
Arkansas	88,536	1,712	7,330	99,262	90,123	1,705	7,434	96,294	87,197	1,705	7,392
California	1,765,630	31,291	181,082	1,836,349	1,628,210	35,331	172,808	1,835,791	1,624,924	35,340	175,527
Colorado	202,777	3,137	35,438	239,805	200,368	3,183	36,254	241,295	201,110	3,206	36,979
Connecticut	131,462	3,202	31,210	162,300	128,063	3,309	30,928	159,990	125,939	3,394	30,657
Delaware	37,538	1,370	3,855	43,528	37,913	1,403	4,212	44,197	38,296	1,333	4,568
District of Columbia	48,815	8,450	24,644	81,916	47,701	8,732	25,483	77,705	43,667	8,819	25,219
Florida	552,553	8,684	57,048	623,403	554,662	8,693	60,048	634,237	562,961	8,653	62,623
Georgia	251,697	8,974	32,935	302,844	259,718	8,970	34,156	308,587	263,604	9,595	35,388
Hawaii	53,012	450	7,700	62,871	54,512	516	7,843	64,322	55,850	495	7,977
Idaho	50,003	580	7,215	58,768	51,651	509	6,608	60,393	51,783	559	8,051
Illinois	638,139	16,712	93,954	734,089	621,576	16,817	95,696	731,420	617,549	17,173	96,698
Indiana	258,714	5,458	32,740	294,685	255,747	5,470	33,468	292,276	252,801	5,513	33,962
Iowa	150,046	6,313	16,446	172,797	149,762	6,580	16,455	172,450	149,331	6,650	16,469
Kansas	147,725	2,160	19,534	170,135	148,164	2,129	19,842	170,603	148,046	2,075	20,482
Kentucky	164,790	4,995	18,537	187,332	163,460	4,946	18,926	182,577	158,177	4,512	19,888
Louisiana	173,861	5,919	24,599	201,987	171,195	6,071	24,721	203,567	172,561	6,102	24,904
Maine	52,059	630	5,288	56,294	50,391	663	5,240	56,724	50,274	667	5,783
Maryland	224,927	3,849	39,623	268,005	223,272	3,900	40,833	266,214	220,535	4,173	41,506
Massachusetts	334,873	13,132	74,971	420,127	329,593	13,421	77,113	416,505	323,868	13,283	79,354
Michigan	490,058	9,708	61,007	568,210	490,372	11,361	66,477	551,307	474,357	10,681	66,269
Minnesota	237,535	6,896	28,489	268,118	231,090	7,082	29,946	289,300	251,649	5,838	31,813
Mississippi	111,510	1,800	10,444	122,408	109,959	1,779	10,670	120,884	108,003	1,895	10,986
Missouri	252,028	8,397	36,192	297,062	251,661	10,050	35,351	293,810	247,484	10,208	36,118
Montana	36,198	222	3,224	39,557	35,945	223	3,389	40,095	36,414	235	3,446
Nebraska	107,851	2,844	11,908	115,523	101,048	3,159	11,316	116,000	100,482	3,219	12,299
Nevada	57,512	205	6,160	63,947	57,227	202	6,518	64,085	57,103	218	6,764
New Hampshire	54,534	304	9,086	64,043	54,884	484	8,675	62,847	53,154	724	8,969
New Jersey	293,190	6,394	43,648	343,029	293,162	6,512	43,355	335,480	286,020	6,588	42,872
New Mexico	85,622	630	13,024	101,460	88,301	649	12,510	101,881	88,643	625	12,613
New York	865,839	27,006	171,977	1,062,924	865,052	27,393	170,479	1,057,841	856,719	27,707	173,415
North Carolina	345,470	6,088	31,895	371,280	331,937	6,196	33,147	369,386	327,812	6,525	35,049
North Dakota	37,307	505	2,658	40,316	37,226	497	2,593	40,184	37,016	483	2,685
Ohio	495,892	12,260	65,031	562,402	484,422	12,304	65,676	549,304	471,266	12,321	65,717
Oklahoma	161,499	3,575	22,772	183,342	157,413	3,349	22,580	185,174	159,288	3,582	22,304
Oregon	146,778	3,770	16,867	165,834	146,370	4,013	15,451	164,447	144,583	3,559	16,305
Pennsylvania	530,713	15,177	81,014	621,228	524,312	15,190	81,726	611,174	513,257	15,462	82,455
Rhode Island	69,364	312	9,489	77,407	67,598	324	9,485	74,718	64,743	655	9,320
South Carolina	148,044	2,425	20,974	174,302	149,183	2,470	22,649	173,070	148,120	2,369	22,581
South Dakota	32,788	502	4,306	38,166	33,573	516	4,077	37,764	33,281	512	3,971
Tennessee	213,672	5,548	23,750	244,936	214,249	5,451	25,236	242,966	211,374	5,766	25,826
Texas	820,888	16,990	100,669	942,178	822,359	17,017	102,802	954,495	832,145	19,194	103,156
Utah	122,208	1,263	9,612	138,139	125,984	1,247	10,908	146,196	132,211	1,250	12,735
Vermont	32,113	881	4,383	36,415	31,228	885	4,302	35,409	30,459	898	4,052
Virginia	302,927	6,308	44,937	348,535	296,858	6,396	45,281	354,149	300,598	6,419	47,132
Washington	251,058	3,244	21,254	279,845	254,630	3,285	21,930	284,662	257,746	3,307	23,609
West Virginia	76,817	1,359	12,076	88,852	75,138	1,413	12,301	87,741	74,844	1,384	11,513
Wisconsin	273,254	3,471	31,177	309,036	274,280	3,509	31,247	303,861	269,548	3,568	30,745
Wyoming	28,791	222	2,535	30,702	27,713	224	2,765	30,682	27,771	232	2,679
U.S. Service Schools	49,099	666	2,857	52,647	47,981	663	4,003	51,490	47,158	659	3,673
Outlying areas	156,078	2,774	10,907	172,989	158,854	3,256	10,879	170,686	155,093	2,691	12,902
American Samoa	1,295	—	—	1,264	1,264	—	—	1,249	1,249	—	—
Federated States of Micronesia	1,028	—	—	1,148	1,148	—	—	1,374	1,374	—	—
Guam	4,581	—	264	5,843	5,522	—	321	6,449	6,052	—	397
Marshall Islands	374	—	—	386	386	—	—	424	424	—	—
Northern Marianas	796	—	—	1,261	1,261	—	—	1,253	1,253	—	—
Palau	445	—	—	436	436	—	—	403	403	—	—
Puerto Rico	144,975	2,774	10,371	159,709	146,164	3,256	10,289	156,439	141,543	2,691	12,205
Virgin Islands	2,584	—	272	2,942	2,673	—	269	3,095	2,795	—	300

[1] Revised from previously published data.
[2] Preliminary data.
—Data not reported or not applicable.

SOURCE: U.S. Department of Education, National Center for Education Statistics, Integrated Postsecondary Education Data System (IPEDS), "Fall Enrollment" survey. (This table was prepared November 1995.)

Table 194.—Total fall enrollment in institutions of higher education, by control, level of enrollment, and state: 1994 [1]

State or other area	Public					Private				
	Undergraduate			First-pro-fessional	Graduate	Undergraduate			First-pro-fessional	Graduate
	Total	4-year	2-year			Total	4-year	2-year		
1	2	3	4	5	6	7	8	9	10	11
United States	9,945,128	4,636,762	5,308,366	113,997	1,074,555	2,317,480	2,096,237	221,243	180,716	646,914
Alabama	182,503	102,036	80,467	2,315	21,728	19,905	18,549	1,356	1,519	1,541
Alaska	26,239	25,645	594	—	1,392	950	611	339	—	217
Arizona	225,991	75,225	150,766	1,549	24,644	15,299	14,370	929	—	7,449
Arkansas	76,743	55,682	21,061	1,705	7,153	10,454	10,108	346	—	239
California	1,480,506	381,001	1,099,505	7,879	94,452	144,418	130,752	13,666	27,461	81,075
Colorado	180,120	103,151	76,969	1,773	27,824	20,990	17,636	3,354	1,433	9,155
Connecticut	86,884	42,301	44,583	1,172	14,394	39,055	37,282	1,773	2,222	16,263
Delaware	32,839	21,483	11,356	—	3,483	5,457	5,457	—	1,333	1,085
District of Columbia	10,048	10,048	—	—	1,000	33,619	33,619	—	8,819	24,219
Florida	484,380	157,598	326,782	3,296	40,348	78,581	73,601	4,980	5,357	22,275
Georgia	213,503	127,041	86,462	3,029	27,323	50,101	43,928	6,173	6,566	8,065
Hawaii	44,678	16,773	27,905	450	6,518	11,172	11,172	—	45	1,459
Idaho	41,484	34,119	7,365	559	6,951	10,299	1,888	8,411	—	1,100
Illinois	495,208	143,739	351,469	4,364	46,386	122,341	116,238	6,103	12,809	50,312
Indiana	196,811	155,127	41,684	3,530	27,929	55,990	52,341	3,649	1,983	6,033
Iowa	106,200	49,800	56,400	2,808	13,009	43,131	41,740	1,391	3,842	3,460
Kansas	132,289	65,776	66,513	2,023	18,486	15,757	14,840	917	52	1,996
Kentucky	131,985	86,669	45,316	2,852	16,738	26,192	21,686	4,506	1,660	3,150
Louisiana	152,312	124,310	28,002	2,645	20,155	20,249	19,045	1,204	3,457	4,749
Maine	35,102	27,813	7,289	268	3,818	15,172	13,300	1,872	399	1,965
Maryland	196,203	84,761	111,442	3,355	24,134	24,332	23,191	1,141	818	17,372
Massachusetts	160,901	82,898	78,003	422	18,476	162,967	148,498	14,469	12,861	60,878
Michigan	401,826	193,175	208,651	6,608	58,324	72,531	70,068	2,463	4,073	7,945
Minnesota	207,720	99,938	107,782	2,520	16,775	43,929	39,541	4,388	3,318	15,038
Mississippi	97,507	46,616	50,891	1,200	9,691	10,496	9,441	1,055	695	1,295
Missouri	172,048	97,550	74,498	2,466	17,345	75,436	69,570	5,866	7,742	18,773
Montana	31,361	27,038	4,323	235	3,331	5,053	4,280	773	—	115
Nebraska	83,460	45,590	37,870	1,421	10,996	17,022	16,597	425	1,798	1,303
Nevada	56,459	24,521	31,938	218	6,594	644	617	27	—	170
New Hampshire	31,486	22,813	8,673	—	3,502	21,668	17,820	3,848	724	5,467
New Jersey	241,849	106,083	135,766	3,536	27,035	44,171	40,190	3,981	3,052	15,837
New Mexico	84,582	38,309	46,273	625	11,866	4,061	3,410	651	—	747
New York	538,260	279,029	259,231	4,733	61,440	318,459	289,759	28,700	22,974	111,975
North Carolina	273,034	125,830	147,204	2,645	27,970	54,778	52,244	2,534	3,880	7,079
North Dakota	33,576	25,238	8,338	483	2,580	3,440	3,194	246	—	105
Ohio	363,892	214,144	149,748	7,554	46,120	107,374	92,909	14,465	4,767	19,597
Oklahoma	140,615	76,138	64,477	2,118	19,015	18,673	16,015	2,658	1,464	3,289
Oregon	127,125	48,749	78,376	1,135	12,767	17,458	17,290	168	2,424	3,538
Pennsylvania	300,209	188,991	111,218	4,449	37,907	213,048	164,760	48,288	11,013	44,548
Rhode Island	34,077	18,076	16,001	5	5,294	30,666	28,535	2,131	650	4,026
South Carolina	125,742	64,602	61,140	1,888	20,884	22,378	20,892	1,486	481	1,697
South Dakota	26,849	26,652	197	418	3,713	6,432	6,221	211	94	258
Tennessee	168,981	91,707	77,274	2,888	19,556	42,393	39,574	2,819	2,878	6,270
Texas	749,620	330,265	419,355	9,800	83,582	82,525	76,408	6,117	9,394	19,574
Utah	99,180	70,141	29,039	762	8,651	33,031	31,833	1,198	488	4,084
Vermont	18,529	13,897	4,632	374	1,602	11,930	11,743	187	524	2,450
Virginia	250,242	119,509	130,733	4,227	38,696	50,356	45,812	4,544	2,192	8,436
Washington	230,132	70,883	159,249	1,632	13,008	27,614	25,505	2,109	1,675	10,601
West Virginia	63,636	56,428	7,208	1,384	11,100	11,208	10,355	853	—	413
Wisconsin	225,940	118,692	107,248	1,788	22,518	43,608	41,802	1,806	1,780	8,227
Wyoming	27,104	9,111	17,993	232	2,679	667	—	667	—	—
U.S. Service Schools	47,158	14,051	33,107	659	3,673	—	—	—	—	—
Outlying areas	64,849	51,520	13,329	1,124	4,944	90,244	77,786	12,458	1,567	7,958
American Samoa	1,249	—	1,249	—	—	—	—	—	—	—
Federated States of Micronesia	1,374	—	1,374	—	—	—	—	—	—	—
Guam	6,052	3,667	2,385	—	397	—	—	—	—	—
Marshall Islands	424	—	424	—	—	—	—	—	—	—
Northern Marianas	1,253	—	1,253	—	—	—	—	—	—	—
Palau	403	—	403	—	—	—	—	—	—	—
Puerto Rico	51,299	45,058	6,241	1,124	4,247	90,244	77,786	12,458	1,567	7,958
Virgin Islands	2,795	2,795	—	—	300	—	—	—	—	—

[1] Preliminary data.
—Data not reported or not applicable.

SOURCE: U.S. Department of Education, National Center for Education Statistics, Integrated Postsecondary Education Data System (IPEDS), "Fall Enrollment, 1994" survey. (This table was prepared November 1995.)

Table 195.—Total fall enrollment in institutions of higher education, by control, level of enrollment, and state: 1993

State or other area	Public					Private				
	Undergraduate			First-pro-fessional	Graduate	Undergraduate			First-pro-fessional	Graduate [1]
	Total	4-year	2-year			Total	4-year	2-year		
1	2	3	4	5	6	7	8	9	10	11
United States	10,011,787	4,674,765	5,337,022	113,654	1,063,647	2,312,172	2,083,633	228,539	178,777	624,766
Alabama	187,261	105,517	81,744	2,247	20,586	20,758	18,726	2,032	1,273	1,400
Alaska	27,351	26,751	600	—	1,357	1,696	1,448	248	—	234
Arizona	222,075	70,667	151,408	1,556	23,123	17,582	16,505	1,077	1,164	6,800
Arkansas	78,986	57,010	21,976	1,705	7,251	11,137	10,105	1,032	—	183
California	1,498,921	385,242	1,113,679	7,888	97,349	129,289	114,618	14,671	27,443	75,459
Colorado	180,466	102,647	77,819	1,739	27,727	19,902	16,010	3,892	1,444	8,527
Connecticut	89,799	44,257	45,542	1,144	14,503	38,264	36,633	1,631	2,165	16,425
Delaware	32,438	21,703	10,735	—	3,333	5,475	5,475	—	1,403	879
District of Columbia	10,020	10,020	—	—	939	37,681	37,681	—	8,732	24,544
Florida	476,985	149,962	327,023	3,231	38,264	77,677	73,122	4,555	5,462	21,784
Georgia	210,177	126,256	83,921	2,997	26,581	49,541	43,021	6,520	5,973	7,575
Hawaii	43,707	17,000	26,707	459	6,452	10,805	10,805	—	57	1,391
Idaho	40,988	33,898	7,090	509	6,027	10,663	1,993	8,670	—	581
Illinois	499,601	147,233	352,368	4,279	45,865	121,975	115,421	6,554	12,538	49,831
Indiana	200,110	160,207	39,903	3,462	27,687	55,637	52,048	3,589	2,008	5,781
Iowa	106,567	50,415	56,152	2,678	13,022	43,195	41,037	2,158	3,902	3,433
Kansas	133,249	68,529	64,720	2,045	18,722	14,915	13,957	958	84	1,120
Kentucky	136,974	88,759	48,215	2,851	16,335	26,486	21,535	4,951	2,095	2,591
Louisiana	151,259	123,467	27,792	2,660	20,031	19,936	19,334	602	3,411	4,690
Maine	35,883	28,459	7,424	270	3,666	14,508	12,800	1,708	393	1,574
Maryland	199,277	84,909	114,368	3,080	24,309	23,995	22,943	1,052	820	16,524
Massachusetts	164,351	84,622	79,729	415	16,695	165,242	150,243	14,999	13,006	60,418
Michigan	416,853	196,987	219,866	7,302	58,990	73,519	70,818	2,701	4,059	7,487
Minnesota	187,982	102,442	85,540	2,548	16,601	43,108	38,476	4,632	4,534	13,345
Mississippi	99,137	47,429	51,708	1,196	9,040	10,822	9,603	1,219	583	1,630
Missouri	178,119	99,414	78,705	2,455	17,247	73,542	67,816	5,726	7,595	18,104
Montana	30,840	26,910	3,930	223	3,263	5,105	4,249	856	—	126
Nebraska	84,103	47,836	36,267	1,426	10,253	16,945	16,353	592	1,733	1,063
Nevada	56,633	23,940	32,693	202	6,394	594	569	25	—	124
New Hampshire	32,339	22,905	9,434	—	3,232	22,545	18,569	3,976	484	5,443
New Jersey	247,862	107,892	139,970	3,416	27,083	45,300	41,138	4,162	3,096	16,272
New Mexico	85,323	39,468	45,855	649	12,121	2,978	2,412	566	—	389
New York	539,634	276,417	263,217	4,746	60,609	325,418	295,235	30,183	22,647	109,870
North Carolina	274,413	126,518	147,895	2,580	26,563	57,524	54,706	2,818	3,616	6,584
North Dakota	33,689	25,566	8,123	497	2,458	3,537	3,269	268	—	135
Ohio	375,756	220,889	154,867	7,594	46,406	108,666	92,607	16,059	4,710	19,270
Oklahoma	139,847	75,363	64,484	1,899	19,155	17,566	15,318	2,248	1,450	3,425
Oregon	129,352	49,113	80,239	1,594	12,406	17,018	16,832	186	2,419	3,045
Pennsylvania	309,249	191,689	117,560	4,454	38,044	215,063	167,375	47,688	10,736	43,682
Rhode Island	35,337	18,938	16,399	13	5,483	32,261	30,149	2,112	311	4,002
South Carolina	125,911	65,271	60,640	1,846	21,176	23,272	21,368	1,904	624	1,473
South Dakota	27,192	26,981	211	420	3,815	6,381	6,170	211	96	262
Tennessee	172,087	93,636	78,451	2,633	19,505	42,162	38,949	3,213	2,818	5,731
Texas	742,236	330,351	411,885	9,760	82,700	80,123	75,127	4,996	7,257	20,102
Utah	92,357	66,097	26,260	779	7,135	33,627	32,428	1,199	468	3,773
Vermont	18,976	13,507	5,469	375	1,650	12,252	12,078	174	510	2,652
Virginia	251,723	120,480	131,243	4,191	37,896	45,135	40,834	4,301	2,205	7,385
Washington	227,411	70,293	157,118	1,584	12,818	27,219	25,144	2,075	1,701	9,112
West Virginia	64,131	56,971	7,160	1,413	11,956	11,007	10,050	957	—	345
Wisconsin	231,856	120,375	111,481	1,757	23,056	42,424	40,531	1,893	1,752	8,191
Wyoming	27,013	9,023	17,990	224	2,765	700	—	700	—	—
U.S. Service Schools	47,981	14,534	33,447	663	4,003	—	—	—	—	—
Outlying areas	62,550	50,259	12,291	1,527	5,038	96,304	83,316	12,988	1,729	5,841
American Samoa	1,264	—	1,264	—	—	—	—	—	—	—
Federated States of Micronesia	1,148	—	1,148	—	—	—	—	—	—	—
Guam	5,522	3,376	2,146	—	321	—	—	—	—	—
Marshall Islands	386	—	386	—	—	—	—	—	—	—
Northern Marianas	1,261	—	1,261	—	—	—	—	—	—	—
Palau	436	—	436	—	—	—	—	—	—	—
Puerto Rico	49,860	44,210	5,650	1,527	4,448	96,304	83,316	12,988	1,729	5,841
Virgin Islands	2,673	2,673	—	—	269	—	—	—	—	—

[1] Revised from previously published data.
—Data not reported or not applicable.

SOURCE: U.S. Department of Education, National Center for Education Statistics, Integrated Postsecondary Education Data System (IPEDS), "Fall Enrollment, 1993" survey. (This table was prepared November 1995.)

Table 196.—Full-time-equivalent fall enrollment in institutions of higher education, by control and type of institution: 1969 to 1994

Year	All institutions			Public institutions			Private institutions		
	Total	4-year	2-year	Total	4-year	2-year	Total	4-year	2-year
1	2	3	4	5	6	7	8	9	10
1969	6,334,139	4,899,526	1,434,612	4,577,985	3,259,676	1,318,309	1,756,153	1,639,850	116,303
1970	6,737,817	5,145,410	1,592,404	4,953,149	3,468,572	1,484,577	1,784,665	1,676,838	107,827
1971	7,148,575	5,357,708	1,790,867	5,344,356	3,660,624	1,683,732	1,804,219	1,697,084	107,135
1972	7,253,712	5,406,792	1,846,921	5,452,851	3,706,238	1,746,613	1,800,862	1,700,554	100,308
1973	7,453,467	5,439,226	2,014,241	5,629,568	3,721,035	1,908,533	1,823,899	1,718,191	105,708
1974	7,805,454	5,606,248	2,199,206	5,944,799	3,847,542	2,097,257	1,860,655	1,758,706	101,949
1975	8,479,688	5,900,403	2,579,285	6,522,310	4,056,500	2,465,810	1,957,378	1,843,903	113,475
1976	8,312,502	5,848,001	2,464,501	6,349,903	3,998,450	2,351,453	1,962,599	1,849,551	113,048
1977	8,415,339	5,935,076	2,480,263	6,396,476	4,039,071	2,357,405	2,018,863	1,896,005	122,858
1978	8,348,482	5,932,357	2,416,125	6,279,199	3,996,126	2,283,073	2,069,283	1,936,231	133,052
1979	8,487,317	6,016,072	2,471,245	6,392,617	4,059,304	2,333,313	2,094,700	1,956,768	137,932
1980	8,819,013	6,161,372	2,657,641	6,642,294	4,158,267	2,484,027	2,176,719	2,003,105	[1] 173,614
1981	9,014,521	6,249,847	2,764,674	6,781,300	4,208,506	2,572,794	2,233,221	2,041,341	[1] 191,880
1982	9,091,648	6,248,923	2,842,725	6,850,589	4,220,648	2,629,941	2,241,059	2,028,275	212,784
1983	9,166,398	6,325,222	2,841,176	6,881,479	4,265,807	2,615,672	2,284,919	2,059,415	225,504
1984	8,951,695	6,292,711	2,658,984	6,684,664	4,237,895	2,446,769	2,267,031	2,054,816	212,215
1985	8,943,433	6,294,339	2,649,094	6,667,781	4,239,622	2,428,159	2,275,652	2,054,717	220,935
1986	9,064,165	6,360,325	2,703,842	6,778,045	4,295,494	2,482,551	2,286,122	2,064,831	[2] 221,291
1987	9,229,736	6,486,504	2,743,230	6,937,690	4,395,728	2,541,961	2,292,045	2,090,776	201,269
1988	9,464,271	6,664,146	2,800,125	7,096,905	4,505,774	2,591,131	2,367,366	2,158,372	208,994
1989	9,780,881	6,813,602	2,967,279	7,371,590	4,619,828	2,751,762	2,409,291	2,193,774	215,517
1990	9,983,436	6,968,008	3,015,428	7,557,982	4,740,049	2,817,933	2,425,454	2,227,959	197,495
1991	10,360,606	7,081,454	3,279,152	7,862,845	4,795,704	3,067,141	2,497,761	2,285,750	212,011
1992	10,436,776	7,129,379	3,307,397	7,911,701	4,797,884	3,113,817	2,525,075	2,331,495	193,580
1993 [3]	10,351,415	7,120,921	3,230,494	7,812,394	4,765,983	3,046,411	2,539,021	2,354,938	184,083
1994 [4]	10,348,072	7,137,341	3,210,731	7,784,396	4,749,524	3,034,872	2,563,676	2,387,817	175,859

[1] Large increases are due to the addition of schools accredited by the Accrediting Commission of Career Schools and Colleges of Technology in 1980 and 1981.
[2] Because of imputation techniques, data are not consistent with figures for other years.
[3] Revised from previously published data.
[4] Preliminary data.

NOTE.—Because of a revision in data compilation procedures, figures for 1986 and later years are not directly comparable with data for earlier years.

SOURCE: U.S. Department of Education, National Center for Education Statistics, "Fall Enrollment in Colleges and Universities;" and Integrated Postsecondary Education Data System (IPEDS), "Fall Enrollment" surveys. (This table was prepared April 1996.)

Table 197.—Full-time-equivalent fall enrollment in institutions of higher education, by control, type of institution, and state: 1992 to 1994

State or other area	Public 4-year			Public 2-year			Private 4-year			Private 2-year		
	1992	1993	1994[1]	1992	1993	1994[1]	1992[2]	1993[2]	1994[1]	1992	1993	1994[1]
1	2	3	4	5	6	7	8	9	10	11	12	13
United States	**4,797,884**	**4,765,983**	**4,749,524**	**3,113,817**	**3,046,411**	**3,034,872**	**2,331,495**	**2,354,938**	**2,387,817**	**193,580**	**184,083**	**175,859**
Alabama	105,069	105,089	103,200	55,679	56,950	56,255	18,830	19,224	19,485	2,950	1,750	1,231
Alaska	18,039	18,072	17,810	235	253	244	974	1,004	622	359	238	303
Arizona	79,429	78,324	82,558	79,433	76,627	76,262	15,853	22,320	19,129	1,005	1,077	929
Arkansas	56,106	55,685	54,540	12,376	14,074	13,281	9,446	9,599	9,666	1,526	951	346
California	433,625	417,202	413,527	626,990	577,405	575,613	175,364	178,651	199,213	12,568	13,271	12,344
Colorado	104,438	104,399	104,474	41,449	40,444	40,104	17,934	18,942	21,477	4,011	3,867	3,121
Connecticut	46,388	45,083	43,582	23,073	22,805	22,303	42,727	42,414	43,398	1,212	1,163	1,188
Delaware	20,281	20,946	20,982	6,629	6,349	6,529	5,072	5,182	5,232	—	—	—
District of Columbia	7,405	6,839	6,763	—	—	—	55,456	56,151	53,802	—	—	—
Florida	142,906	147,729	155,232	182,004	180,327	179,177	80,717	79,769	80,234	5,815	4,454	4,884
Georgia	125,076	126,594	128,563	52,110	54,825	55,739	46,568	50,329	52,189	7,298	5,685	5,319
Hawaii	18,660	19,311	19,437	15,729	16,025	16,692	9,116	9,287	9,485			
Idaho	30,993	31,449	32,237	4,630	5,007	5,218	2,279	2,141	2,252	8,056	8,522	8,280
Illinois	165,247	163,884	161,500	197,756	191,411	190,946	137,704	139,625	141,160	6,182	5,819	5,421
Indiana	153,190	151,282	147,844	25,216	23,954	24,279	52,037	53,004	53,673	2,829	2,953	2,997
Iowa	58,773	58,156	57,556	39,895	39,833	39,735	40,369	40,644	40,905	1,913	1,930	1,212
Kansas	73,356	73,783	71,257	36,435	36,132	37,568	12,411	12,663	14,166	868	819	784
Kentucky	89,506	88,286	87,211	30,134	30,565	29,039	22,079	22,256	22,331	4,280	4,618	4,153
Louisiana	126,708	123,798	124,883	16,916	17,155	17,595	22,376	23,050	23,195	680	602	985
Maine	24,626	24,035	23,461	4,594	4,593	4,549	11,657	11,545	11,945	1,373	1,506	1,602
Maryland	86,358	85,869	86,578	60,510	59,917	58,471	28,175	28,575	29,393	836	870	937
Massachusetts	81,357	79,000	78,686	48,116	48,436	47,035	185,982	184,779	184,199	9,735	9,592	9,506
Michigan	206,325	209,703	205,800	114,237	114,289	108,182	63,802	62,076	61,100	2,279	1,971	1,614
Minnesota	94,668	91,811	89,990	56,709	55,659	67,471	45,596	46,201	47,395	4,804	3,833	3,521
Mississippi	52,038	51,147	50,417	40,955	41,568	40,669	9,589	9,928	9,425	2,044	1,107	960
Missouri	99,726	97,160	95,401	42,758	44,231	41,935	69,008	69,802	71,773	4,367	5,150	4,934
Montana	26,088	26,678	26,857	3,039	2,992	3,294	2,807	3,556	3,652	1,591	571	529
Nebraska	48,846	48,511	47,248	23,029	18,634	20,129	15,823	16,285	16,682	428	443	338
Nevada	21,696	21,318	21,963	13,998	13,807	13,855	575	559	598	25	25	27
New Hampshire	21,630	21,763	21,962	5,368	5,316	5,025	19,216	18,876	18,603	3,048	3,108	2,952
New Jersey	104,568	103,462	102,204	81,494	83,472	81,903	45,071	45,114	44,368	3,439	3,435	3,295
New Mexico	40,008	41,227	39,973	23,693	25,099	25,126	2,705	2,214	3,550	762	566	651
New York	268,332	268,270	272,066	179,438	182,769	180,543	342,511	343,641	339,369	28,056	27,827	26,016
North Carolina	131,736	131,718	132,091	95,541	91,489	91,727	58,312	58,064	56,789	2,947	2,538	2,241
North Dakota	25,105	25,257	25,055	6,567	6,592	6,642	3,107	3,094	3,038	234	264	242
Ohio	234,763	228,303	223,580	91,025	92,358	88,888	94,134	95,266	95,994	14,318	10,381	9,586
Oklahoma	78,795	77,877	78,501	43,586	38,250	38,063	17,292	17,652	18,138	2,776	1,948	2,459
Oregon	53,812	52,787	52,916	46,742	46,522	44,748	19,172	19,345	19,949	299	182	163
Pennsylvania	204,341	200,053	198,056	68,492	67,024	64,045	179,575	179,371	179,269	29,184	28,926	28,926
Rhode Island	19,476	18,836	18,015	9,693	8,696	8,524	30,937	29,658	28,720	—	2,025	1,930
South Carolina	72,719	71,698	71,132	36,394	37,219	37,571	20,969	21,103	20,849	2,117	1,748	1,343
South Dakota	24,707	26,215	25,822	141	171	158	5,651	5,336	5,384	116	128	143
Tennessee	94,401	94,910	93,976	47,696	47,353	46,958	42,201	43,144	44,083	3,586	2,846	2,425
Texas	338,888	339,313	339,801	234,411	233,900	237,787	85,507	86,388	87,907	4,802	4,875	5,987
Utah	49,252	58,244	61,636	23,857	17,260	18,453	32,383	33,985	33,661	969	1,085	1,079
Vermont	13,646	13,415	13,765	2,530	2,479	1,834	13,295	12,729	12,390	163	161	163
Virginia	137,313	136,339	136,115	69,624	68,650	67,688	43,721	42,023	46,742	3,430	3,698	3,744
Washington	75,079	76,501	77,461	94,077	96,444	101,499	27,593	29,432	30,620	2,372	1,988	1,938
West Virginia	57,750	56,628	55,841	4,947	4,840	4,930	8,575	8,860	9,349	861	944	846
Wisconsin	126,240	123,700	122,297	62,623	65,297	59,860	39,242	40,082	41,269	1,581	1,665	1,598
Wyoming	10,180	9,976	10,116	11,298	11,364	11,318	—	—	—	754	700	667
U.S. Service Schools	18,220	18,348	17,586	19,946	19,575	19,413	—	—	—	—	—	—
Outlying areas	48,186	48,931	49,518	7,654	9,021	9,886	78,952	77,146	73,595	10,745	11,393	10,161
American Samoa	—	—	—	1,029	1,007	998	—	—	—	—	—	—
Federated States of Micronesia	—	—	—	690	743	1,040	—	—	—	—	—	—
Guam	2,418	2,908	3,159	689	912	1,049	—	—	—	—	—	—
Marshall Islands	—	—	—	—	374	254	—	—	—	—	—	—
Northern Marianas	—	—	—	476	653	653	—	—	—	—	—	—
Palau	—	—	—	382	377	357	—	—	—	—	—	—
Puerto Rico	43,962	44,107	44,321	4,388	4,955	5,535	78,952	77,146	73,595	10,745	11,393	10,161
Virgin Islands	1,806	1,916	2,038	—	—	—	—	—	—	—	—	—

[1] Preliminary data.
[2] Revised from previously published data.
—Data not reported or not applicable.

SOURCE: U.S. Department of Education, National Center for Education Statistics, Integrated Postsecondary Education Data System (IPEDS), "Fall Enrollment" surveys. (This table was prepared November 1995.)

Table 198.—Full-time-equivalent fall enrollment in institutions of higher education, by control and state: 1980 to 1994

State or other area	Total					Public			Private		
	1980	1985	1990	1993[1]	1994[2]	1990	1993[1]	1994[2]	1990	1993[1]	1994[2]
1	2	3	4	5	6	7	8	9	10	11	12
United States	8,819,013	8,943,433	9,983,436	10,351,415	10,348,072	7,557,982	7,812,394	7,784,396	2,425,454	2,539,021	2,563,676
Alabama	138,910	149,895	174,610	183,013	180,171	154,343	162,039	159,455	20,267	20,974	20,716
Alaska	10,073	14,098	18,496	19,567	18,979	17,087	18,325	18,054	1,409	1,242	925
Arizona	127,114	134,954	167,617	178,348	178,878	153,500	154,951	158,820	14,117	23,397	20,058
Arkansas	64,307	63,230	74,449	80,309	77,833	63,472	69,759	67,821	10,977	10,550	10,012
California	1,099,559	1,062,439	1,156,288	1,186,529	1,200,697	979,663	994,607	989,140	176,625	191,922	211,557
Colorado	123,589	121,804	159,032	167,652	169,176	138,350	144,843	144,578	20,682	22,809	24,598
Connecticut	112,612	107,803	115,791	111,465	110,471	70,870	67,888	65,885	44,921	43,577	44,586
Delaware	26,284	25,750	31,612	32,477	32,743	26,059	27,295	27,511	5,553	5,182	5,232
District of Columbia	62,126	59,198	61,845	62,990	60,565	7,590	6,839	6,763	54,255	56,151	53,802
Florida	290,647	308,315	383,385	412,279	419,527	302,579	328,056	334,409	80,806	84,223	85,118
Georgia	152,369	161,952	198,549	237,433	241,810	149,115	181,419	184,302	49,434	56,014	57,508
Hawaii	35,859	36,986	41,097	44,623	45,614	32,496	35,336	36,129	8,601	9,287	9,485
Idaho	33,938	32,649	41,275	47,119	47,987	31,408	36,456	37,455	9,867	10,663	10,532
Illinois	432,365	450,504	493,364	500,739	499,027	353,247	355,295	352,446	140,117	145,444	146,581
Indiana	193,445	195,630	222,835	231,193	228,793	168,984	175,236	172,123	53,851	55,957	56,670
Iowa	120,083	128,492	138,565	140,563	139,408	95,772	97,989	97,291	42,793	42,574	42,117
Kansas	101,147	100,807	118,969	123,397	123,775	106,570	109,915	108,825	12,399	13,482	14,950
Kentucky	113,709	110,539	137,651	145,725	142,734	111,858	118,851	116,250	25,793	26,874	26,484
Louisiana	132,780	148,983	154,132	164,605	166,658	129,357	140,953	142,478	24,775	23,652	24,180
Maine	34,471	37,993	42,021	41,679	41,557	29,876	28,628	28,010	12,145	13,051	13,547
Maryland	149,202	148,091	169,972	175,231	175,379	141,950	145,786	145,049	28,022	29,445	30,330
Massachusetts	315,937	321,022	320,299	321,807	319,426	130,962	127,436	125,721	189,337	194,371	193,705
Michigan	366,058	354,690	389,814	388,039	376,696	326,952	323,992	313,982	62,862	64,047	62,714
Minnesota	162,559	170,958	190,608	197,504	208,377	143,424	147,470	157,461	47,184	50,034	50,916
Mississippi	85,621	86,846	103,957	103,750	101,471	92,269	92,715	91,086	11,688	11,035	10,385
Missouri	180,156	178,090	210,104	216,343	214,043	142,953	141,391	137,336	67,151	74,952	76,707
Montana	29,428	29,992	29,905	33,797	34,332	26,835	29,670	30,151	3,070	4,127	4,181
Nebraska	68,505	70,778	80,989	83,873	84,397	65,739	67,145	67,377	15,250	16,728	17,020
Nevada	22,467	23,093	33,814	35,709	36,443	33,392	35,125	35,818	422	584	625
New Hampshire	39,456	41,733	45,762	49,063	48,542	24,948	27,079	26,987	20,814	21,984	21,555
New Jersey	218,838	201,270	221,468	235,483	231,770	174,324	186,934	184,107	47,144	48,549	47,663
New Mexico	43,722	47,169	59,517	69,106	69,300	57,870	66,326	65,099	1,647	2,780	4,201
New York	760,305	763,596	798,696	822,507	817,994	446,379	451,039	452,609	352,317	371,468	365,385
North Carolina	235,266	249,901	269,025	283,809	282,848	208,321	223,207	223,818	60,704	60,602	59,030
North Dakota	30,188	32,456	33,118	35,207	34,977	30,276	31,849	31,697	2,842	3,358	3,280
Ohio	369,342	383,898	420,499	426,308	418,048	317,837	320,661	312,468	102,662	105,647	105,580
Oklahoma	115,701	126,691	128,203	135,727	137,161	108,933	116,127	116,564	19,270	19,600	20,597
Oregon	110,649	102,247	120,176	118,836	117,776	101,424	99,309	97,664	18,752	19,527	20,112
Pennsylvania	404,192	422,349	464,179	475,632	470,296	261,305	267,077	262,101	202,874	208,555	208,195
Rhode Island	50,628	53,016	60,168	59,215	57,189	28,804	27,532	26,539	31,364	31,683	30,650
South Carolina	109,346	109,303	127,225	131,768	130,895	101,918	108,917	108,703	25,307	22,851	22,192
South Dakota	27,873	26,988	28,256	31,850	31,507	22,128	26,386	25,980	6,128	5,464	5,527
Tennessee	161,058	152,967	175,961	188,253	187,442	130,184	142,263	140,934	45,777	45,990	46,508
Texas	527,724	566,736	637,742	664,476	671,482	553,436	573,213	577,588	84,306	91,263	93,894
Utah	78,199	84,095	94,012	110,574	114,829	63,495	75,504	80,089	30,517	35,070	34,740
Vermont	25,572	25,649	29,072	28,784	28,152	16,048	15,894	15,599	13,024	12,890	12,553
Virginia	199,549	204,928	251,708	250,710	254,289	202,285	204,989	203,803	49,423	45,721	50,486
Washington	194,440	171,668	189,521	204,370	211,518	160,889	172,950	178,960	28,632	31,420	32,558
West Virginia	60,394	58,438	68,235	71,272	70,966	59,229	61,468	60,771	9,006	9,804	10,195
Wisconsin	206,790	211,749	229,975	230,744	225,024	192,107	188,997	182,157	37,868	41,747	42,867
Wyoming	14,725	17,037	21,888	22,040	22,101	21,185	21,340	21,434	703	700	667
U.S. Service Schools	49,736	53,968	47,985	37,923	36,999	47,985	37,923	36,999	—	—	—
Outlying areas	117,637	145,530	140,954	146,491	143,160	55,908	57,952	59,404	85,046	88,539	83,756
American Samoa	824	497	952	1,007	998	952	1,007	998	—	—	—
Federated States of Micronesia	—	—	549	743	1,040	549	743	1,040	—	—	—
Guam	2,115	3,049	2,956	3,820	4,208	2,956	3,820	4,208	—	—	—
Marshall Islands	—	—	—	374	254	—	374	254	—	—	—
Northern Marianas	—	183	376	653	653	376	653	653	—	—	—
Palau	—	—	423	377	357	423	377	357	—	—	—
Puerto Rico	113,285	139,627	134,193	137,601	133,612	49,147	49,062	49,856	85,046	88,539	83,756
Trust Territory of the Pacific	195	680	—	—	—	—	—	—	—	—	—
Virgin Islands	1,218	1,494	1,505	1,916	2,038	1,505	1,916	2,038	—	—	—

[1] Revised from previously published data.
[2] Preliminary data.
—Data not reported or not applicable.

SOURCE: U.S. Department of Education, National Center for Education Statistics, Integrated Postsecondary Education Data System (IPEDS), "Fall Enrollment" surveys. (This table was prepared November 1995.)

Table 199.—Residence and migration of all freshmen students [1] in institutions of higher education, by state: Fall 1994

State or other area	Students enrolled in institutions located in the state [2]	Student residents of state		Ratio of students remaining to—		Migration of students		
		Attending college in any state [3]	Attending college in home state [4]	Students enrolled (col.4 ÷ col.2)	Student residents (col.4 ÷ col.3)	Out of (col.3 – col.4)	Into (col.2 – col.4)	Net (col.8 – col.7)
1	2	3	4	5	6	7	8	9
United States	2,111,310	2,074,864	1,745,994	0.83	0.84	328,870	365,316	[5] 36,446
Alabama	41,542	36,857	34,230	0.82	0.93	2,627	7,312	4,685
Alaska	1,761	2,988	1,487	0.84	0.50	1,501	274	−1,227
Arizona	32,753	28,930	26,320	0.80	0.91	2,610	6,433	3,823
Arkansas	16,178	15,728	13,454	0.83	0.86	2,274	2,724	450
California	255,308	254,425	235,856	0.92	0.93	18,569	19,452	883
Colorado	32,113	29,362	24,109	0.75	0.82	5,253	8,004	2,751
Connecticut	21,524	25,661	14,699	0.68	0.57	10,962	6,825	−4,137
Delaware	6,921	5,745	4,074	0.59	0.71	1,671	2,847	1,176
District of Columbia	9,706	3,877	2,339	0.24	0.60	1,538	7,367	5,829
Florida	70,212	67,821	57,316	0.82	0.85	10,505	12,896	2,391
Georgia	58,991	56,834	49,857	0.85	0.88	6,977	9,134	2,157
Hawaii	10,279	10,314	8,320	0.81	0.81	1,994	1,959	−35
Idaho	10,646	9,770	7,738	0.73	0.79	2,032	2,908	876
Illinois	110,396	120,047	102,114	0.92	0.85	17,933	8,282	−9,651
Indiana	48,059	42,528	37,023	0.77	0.87	5,505	11,036	5,531
Iowa	35,229	31,423	27,737	0.79	0.88	3,686	7,492	3,806
Kansas	24,641	22,762	20,340	0.83	0.89	2,422	4,301	1,879
Kentucky	28,604	27,210	24,091	0.84	0.89	3,119	4,513	1,394
Louisiana	30,897	29,129	25,413	0.82	0.87	3,716	5,484	1,768
Maine	8,102	9,283	5,893	0.73	0.63	3,390	2,209	−1,181
Maryland	32,734	35,472	24,962	0.76	0.70	10,510	7,772	−2,738
Massachusetts	65,768	55,720	42,892	0.65	0.77	12,828	22,876	10,048
Michigan	83,446	84,406	76,823	0.92	0.91	7,583	6,623	−960
Minnesota	37,991	38,095	29,384	0.77	0.77	8,711	8,607	−104
Mississippi	25,862	24,512	22,349	0.86	0.91	2,163	3,513	1,350
Missouri	38,302	35,660	29,961	0.78	0.84	5,699	8,341	2,642
Montana	6,819	7,219	5,225	0.77	0.72	1,994	1,594	−400
Nebraska	16,616	16,498	13,883	0.84	0.84	2,615	2,733	118
Nevada	6,939	6,404	4,746	0.68	0.74	1,658	2,193	535
New Hampshire	11,373	9,275	5,569	0.49	0.60	3,706	5,804	2,098
New Jersey	43,063	63,528	39,376	0.91	0.62	24,152	3,687	−20,465
New Mexico	13,864	15,170	12,059	0.87	0.79	3,111	1,805	−1,306
New York	155,799	156,987	130,998	0.84	0.83	25,989	24,801	−1,188
North Carolina	51,346	42,658	39,256	0.76	0.92	3,402	12,090	8,688
North Dakota	8,122	7,048	5,544	0.68	0.79	1,504	2,578	1,074
Ohio	88,460	86,809	75,746	0.86	0.87	11,063	12,714	1,651
Oklahoma	29,345	28,797	26,032	0.89	0.90	2,765	3,313	548
Oregon	23,321	21,992	18,209	0.78	0.83	3,783	5,112	1,329
Pennsylvania	97,982	91,568	76,826	0.78	0.84	14,742	21,156	6,414
Rhode Island	12,645	7,958	5,524	0.44	0.69	2,434	7,121	4,687
South Carolina	28,532	26,626	23,547	0.83	0.88	3,079	4,985	1,906
South Dakota	6,600	6,038	4,543	0.69	0.75	1,495	2,057	562
Tennessee	33,870	31,499	26,715	0.79	0.85	4,784	7,155	2,371
Texas	127,166	124,773	114,927	0.90	0.92	9,846	12,239	2,393
Utah	24,383	19,397	18,096	0.74	0.93	1,301	6,287	4,986
Vermont	6,132	4,616	2,603	0.42	0.56	2,013	3,529	1,516
Virginia	45,272	41,233	33,012	0.73	0.80	8,221	12,260	4,039
Washington	68,604	65,505	60,346	0.88	0.92	5,159	8,258	3,099
West Virginia	15,799	13,818	11,725	0.74	0.85	2,093	4,074	1,981
Wisconsin	46,479	45,339	39,109	0.84	0.86	6,230	7,370	1,140
Wyoming	4,814	4,646	3,597	0.75	0.77	1,049	1,217	168
State unknown [6]	—	24,904	—	—	—	24,904	—	−24,904
Outlying areas	29,061	29,608	28,047	0.97	0.95	1,561	1,014	−547
American Samoa	—	53	—	—	—	53	—	−53
Federated States of Micronesia	410	1,322	409	1.00	0.31	913	1	−912
Guam	956	191	14	0.01	0.07	177	942	765
Marshall Islands	22	34	18	0.82	0.53	16	4	−12
Northern Marianas	440	450	440	1.00	0.98	10	—	−10
Palau	13	19	13	1.00	0.68	6	—	−6
Puerto Rico	27,276	28,121	27,221	1.00	0.97	900	55	−845
Virgin Islands	376	774	359	0.95	0.46	415	17	−398
Foreign countries	—	34,975	—	—	—	34,975	—	−34,975

[1] Students who are enrolled at the reporting institution for the first time.

[2] All of the new students reported by the institutions in that state; i.e., all in-migrants and "remaining" students.

[3] All students living in a particular state when admitted to an institution in any state. Students may be enrolled in any state.

[4] Students who attend institutions in their home state.

[5] Includes students coming to U.S. colleges from foreign countries and the outlying areas.

[6] Students are reported in "state unknown" when an institution is unable to determine the student's home state.

—Data not available or not applicable.

NOTE.—Data for U.S. Service Schools are included in state totals.

SOURCE: U.S. Department of Education, National Center for Education Statistics, Integrated Postsecondary Education Data System (IPEDS), "Residence of First-Time Students" survey, 1994. (This table was prepared February 1996.)

Table 200.—Residence and migration of all freshmen students [1] in institutions of higher education graduating from high school in the past 12 months, by state: Fall 1994

State or other area	Students enrolled in institutions located in the state [2]	Student residents of state		Ratio of students remaining to—		Migration of students		
		Attending college in any state [3]	Attending college in home state [4]	Students enrolled (col.4 ÷ col.2)	Student residents (col.4 ÷ col.3)	Out of (col.3 − col.4)	Into (col.2 − col.4)	Net (col.8 − col.7)
1	2	3	4	5	6	7	8	9
United States	1,441,705	1,418,338	1,145,571	0.79	0.81	272,767	296,134	[5] 23,367
Alabama	28,927	24,757	22,554	0.78	0.91	2,203	6,373	4,170
Alaska	1,198	2,227	997	0.83	0.45	1,230	201	−1,029
Arizona	17,850	15,160	13,002	0.73	0.86	2,158	4,848	2,690
Arkansas	12,734	12,535	10,689	0.84	0.85	1,846	2,045	199
California	167,374	168,803	153,097	0.91	0.91	15,706	14,277	−1,429
Colorado	18,410	17,435	12,773	0.69	0.73	4,662	5,637	975
Connecticut	15,055	19,120	9,011	0.60	0.47	10,109	6,044	−4,065
Delaware	5,504	4,343	2,818	0.51	0.65	1,525	2,686	1,161
District of Columbia	8,476	3,039	1,758	0.21	0.58	1,281	6,718	5,437
Florida	48,583	48,192	39,134	0.81	0.81	9,058	9,449	391
Georgia	38,246	36,797	30,746	0.80	0.84	6,051	7,500	1,449
Hawaii	5,944	6,943	5,188	0.87	0.75	1,755	756	−999
Idaho	7,316	6,545	4,860	0.66	0.74	1,685	2,456	771
Illinois	64,861	74,362	58,504	0.90	0.79	15,858	6,357	−9,501
Indiana	37,514	32,316	27,758	0.74	0.86	4,558	9,756	5,198
Iowa	24,063	20,978	17,769	0.74	0.85	3,209	6,294	3,085
Kansas	16,910	15,429	13,397	0.79	0.87	2,032	3,513	1,481
Kentucky	21,823	20,454	17,985	0.82	0.88	2,469	3,838	1,369
Louisiana	24,550	22,766	19,584	0.80	0.86	3,182	4,966	1,784
Maine	5,913	6,831	3,863	0.65	0.57	2,968	2,050	−918
Maryland	21,803	24,700	15,285	0.70	0.62	9,415	6,518	−2,897
Massachusetts	46,209	37,740	26,154	0.57	0.69	11,586	20,055	8,469
Michigan	54,817	55,492	49,170	0.90	0.89	6,322	5,647	−675
Minnesota	25,651	26,790	19,359	0.75	0.72	7,431	6,292	−1,139
Mississippi	19,922	18,713	16,821	0.84	0.90	1,892	3,101	1,209
Missouri	28,430	26,645	21,875	0.77	0.82	4,770	6,555	1,785
Montana	5,031	5,399	3,707	0.74	0.69	1,692	1,324	−368
Nebraska	11,532	11,463	9,234	0.80	0.81	2,229	2,298	69
Nevada	3,282	3,807	2,425	0.74	0.64	1,382	857	−525
New Hampshire	8,148	6,481	3,464	0.43	0.53	3,017	4,684	1,667
New Jersey	30,524	49,681	27,486	0.90	0.55	22,195	3,038	−19,157
New Mexico	7,693	8,522	6,379	0.83	0.75	2,143	1,314	−829
New York	106,847	110,750	87,169	0.82	0.79	23,581	19,678	−3,903
North Carolina	39,418	30,960	28,285	0.72	0.91	2,675	11,133	8,458
North Dakota	6,609	5,353	4,309	0.65	0.80	1,044	2,300	1,256
Ohio	61,777	61,673	51,983	0.84	0.84	9,690	9,794	104
Oklahoma	16,516	16,482	14,221	0.86	0.86	2,261	2,295	34
Oregon	16,487	16,103	12,766	0.77	0.79	3,337	3,721	384
Pennsylvania	74,938	68,581	55,543	0.74	0.81	13,038	19,395	6,357
Rhode Island	10,344	5,795	3,644	0.35	0.63	2,151	6,700	4,549
South Carolina	20,994	19,271	16,594	0.79	0.86	2,677	4,400	1,723
South Dakota	4,786	4,342	3,067	0.64	0.71	1,275	1,719	444
Tennessee	26,527	24,407	20,227	0.76	0.83	4,180	6,300	2,120
Texas	86,748	86,586	78,262	0.90	0.90	8,324	8,486	162
Utah	19,420	15,072	13,994	0.72	0.93	1,078	5,426	4,348
Vermont	4,802	3,306	1,573	0.33	0.48	1,733	3,229	1,496
Virginia	35,769	32,385	25,141	0.70	0.78	7,244	10,628	3,384
Washington	28,578	28,617	24,425	0.85	0.85	4,192	4,153	−39
West Virginia	12,162	10,183	8,561	0.70	0.84	1,622	3,601	1,979
Wisconsin	31,404	32,013	26,627	0.85	0.83	5,386	4,777	−609
Wyoming	3,286	3,173	2,334	0.71	0.74	839	952	113
State unknown [6]	—	8,821	—	—	—	8,821	—	−8,821
Outlying areas	25,868	26,897	25,652	0.99	0.95	1,245	216	−1,029
American Samoa	—	38	—	—	—	38	—	−38
Federated States of Micronesia	212	462	212	1.00	0.46	250	—	−250
Guam	177	166	7	0.04	0.04	159	170	11
Marshall Islands	11	22	9	0.82	0.41	13	2	−11
Northern Marianas	440	445	440	1.00	0.99	5	—	−5
Palau	13	17	13	1.00	0.76	4	—	−4
Puerto Rico	24,956	25,677	24,916	1.00	0.97	761	40	−721
Virgin Islands	282	554	276	0.98	0.50	278	6	−272
Foreign countries	—	22,077	—	—	—	22,077	—	−22,077

[1] Students who are enrolled at the reporting institution for the first time.

[2] All of the new students reported by the institutions in that state; i.e., all inmigrants and "remaining" students.

[3] All students living in a particular state when first admitted to an institution in any state. Students may be enrolled in any state.

[4] Students who attend institutions in their home state.

[5] Includes students coming to U.S. colleges from foreign countries and the outlying areas.

[6] Students are reported in "state unknown" when an institution is unable to determine the student's home state.

—Data not available or not applicable.

NOTE.—Data for U.S. Service Schools are included in state totals.

SOURCE: U.S. Department of Education, National Center for Education Statistics, Integrated Postsecondary Education Data System (IPEDS), "Residence of First-Time Students" survey, 1994. (This table was prepared February 1996.)

Table 201.—Residence and migration of all freshmen students [1] in 4-year colleges graduating from high school in the past 12 months, by state: Fall 1994

State or other area	Students enrolled in institutions located in the state [2]	Student residents of state		Ratio of students remaining to—		Migration of students		
		Attending college in any state [3]	Attending college in home state [4]	Students enrolled (col.4 ÷ col.2)	Student residents (col.4 ÷ col.3)	Out of (col.3 − col.4)	Into (col.2 − col.4)	Net (col.8 − col.7)
1	2	3	4	5	6	7	8	9
United States	963,335	937,904	691,211	0.72	0.74	251,024	272,124	[5]21,100
Alabama	16,883	13,016	11,044	0.65	0.85	1,972	5,839	3,867
Alaska	1,193	2,117	992	0.83	0.47	1,125	201	−924
Arizona	10,937	8,563	6,668	0.61	0.78	1,895	4,269	2,374
Arkansas	10,423	9,957	8,570	0.82	0.86	1,387	1,853	466
California	63,217	67,244	52,260	0.83	0.78	14,984	10,957	−4,027
Colorado	15,068	14,207	9,943	0.66	0.70	4,264	5,125	861
Connecticut	12,193	15,982	6,286	0.52	0.39	9,696	5,907	−3,789
Delaware	4,581	3,446	1,961	0.43	0.57	1,485	2,620	1,135
District of Columbia	8,476	2,983	1,758	0.21	0.59	1,225	6,718	5,493
Florida	26,950	27,521	19,007	0.71	0.69	8,514	7,943	−571
Georgia	26,954	25,559	19,945	0.74	0.78	5,614	7,009	1,395
Hawaii	2,877	3,792	2,177	0.76	0.57	1,615	700	−915
Idaho	3,747	4,440	2,971	0.79	0.67	1,469	776	−693
Illinois	35,655	44,598	29,500	0.83	0.66	15,098	6,155	−8,943
Indiana	33,419	28,060	24,061	0.72	0.86	3,999	9,358	5,359
Iowa	15,336	12,578	9,576	0.62	0.76	3,002	5,760	2,758
Kansas	10,997	10,278	8,359	0.76	0.81	1,919	2,638	719
Kentucky	15,811	14,411	12,222	0.77	0.85	2,189	3,589	1,400
Louisiana	21,760	19,651	16,828	0.77	0.86	2,823	4,932	2,109
Maine	5,003	5,806	3,004	0.60	0.52	2,802	1,999	−803
Maryland	14,022	17,144	7,937	0.57	0.46	9,207	6,085	−3,122
Massachusetts	36,548	28,639	17,493	0.48	0.61	11,146	19,055	7,909
Michigan	37,214	37,656	31,792	0.85	0.84	5,864	5,422	−442
Minnesota	18,162	19,542	12,517	0.69	0.64	7,025	5,645	−1,380
Mississippi	8,416	7,545	5,789	0.69	0.77	1,756	2,627	871
Missouri	22,449	20,591	16,264	0.72	0.79	4,327	6,185	1,858
Montana	4,402	4,343	3,116	0.71	0.72	1,227	1,286	59
Nebraska	9,035	8,897	6,900	0.76	0.78	1,997	2,135	138
Nevada	2,552	2,928	1,811	0.71	0.62	1,117	741	−376
New Hampshire	6,713	5,175	2,440	0.36	0.47	2,735	4,273	1,538
New Jersey	17,446	36,312	14,695	0.84	0.40	21,617	2,751	−18,866
New Mexico	4,520	5,451	3,596	0.80	0.66	1,855	924	−931
New York	75,455	79,504	56,654	0.75	0.71	22,850	18,801	−4,049
North Carolina	32,053	23,765	21,358	0.67	0.90	2,407	10,695	8,288
North Dakota	4,588	3,628	2,669	0.58	0.74	959	1,919	960
Ohio	48,165	48,105	38,967	0.81	0.81	9,138	9,198	60
Oklahoma	10,638	10,517	8,679	0.82	0.83	1,838	1,959	121
Oregon	9,892	9,594	6,509	0.66	0.68	3,085	3,383	298
Pennsylvania	61,040	54,695	42,322	0.69	0.77	12,373	18,718	6,345
Rhode Island	8,598	4,135	2,138	0.25	0.52	1,997	6,460	4,463
South Carolina	14,733	12,981	10,514	0.71	0.81	2,467	4,219	1,752
South Dakota	4,773	4,145	3,056	0.64	0.74	1,089	1,717	628
Tennessee	18,803	16,587	12,709	0.68	0.77	3,878	6,094	2,216
Texas	55,610	56,430	48,543	0.87	0.86	7,887	7,067	−820
Utah	14,476	9,966	9,390	0.65	0.94	576	5,086	4,510
Vermont	4,688	3,064	1,484	0.32	0.48	1,580	3,204	1,624
Virginia	28,864	25,412	18,525	0.64	0.73	6,887	10,339	3,452
Washington	13,371	13,787	10,031	0.75	0.73	3,756	3,340	−416
West Virginia	11,040	9,003	7,642	0.69	0.85	1,361	3,398	2,037
Wisconsin	22,343	22,676	17,770	0.80	0.78	4,906	4,573	−333
Wyoming	1,246	1,478	769	0.62	0.52	709	477	−232
State unknown [6]	—	4,331	—	—	—	4,331	—	−4,331
Outlying areas	20,456	21,396	20,241	0.99	0.95	1,155	215	−940
American Samoa	—	30	—	—	—	30	—	−30
Federated States of Micronesia	—	109	—	—	—	109	—	−109
Guam	169	146	—	—	—	146	169	23
Marshall Islands	—	10	—	—	—	10	—	−10
Northern Marianas	—	3	—	—	—	3	—	−3
Palau	—	2	—	—	—	2	—	−2
Puerto Rico	20,005	20,682	19,965	1.00	0.97	717	40	−677
Virgin Islands	282	533	276	0.98	0.52	257	6	−251
Foreign countries	—	20,041	—	—	—	20,041	—	−20,041

[1] Students who are enrolled at the reporting institution for the first time.

[2] All of the new students reported by the institutions in that state; i.e., all inmigrants and "remaining" students.

[3] All students living in a particular state when first admitted to an institution in any state. Students may be enrolled in any state.

[4] Students who attend institutions in their home state.

[5] Includes students coming to U.S. colleges from foreign countries and the outlying areas.

[6] Students are reported in "state unknown" when an institution is unable to determine the student's home state.

—Data not available or not applicable.

NOTE.—Data for U.S. Service Schools are included in state totals.

SOURCE: U.S. Department of Education, National Center for Education Statistics, Integrated Postsecondary Education Data System (IPEDS), "Residence of First-Time Students" survey, 1994. (This table was prepared February 1996.)

Table 202.—Total fall enrollment in institutions of higher education, by type and control of institution and race/ethnicity of student: 1976 to 1994

Type and control of institution and race/ethnicity of student	Number, in thousands									Percentage distribution by type and control [1]						
	1976	1980	1984	1988	1990	1991	1992 [2]	1993 [2]	1994 [3]	1976	1980	1988	1990	1992 [2]	1993 [2]	1994 [3]
1	2	3	4	5	6	7	8	9	10	11	12	13	14	15	16	17
All students																
Total	10,985.6	12,086.8	12,233.0	13,043.1	13,818.6	14,359.0	14,487.4	14,304.8	14,278.8	100.0	100.0	100.0	100.0	100.0	100.0	100.0
White, non-Hispanic	9,076.1	9,833.0	9,814.7	10,283.2	10,722.5	10,989.8	10,875.4	10,600.0	10,427.0	84.3	83.5	81.1	79.9	77.5	76.5	75.4
Total minority	1,690.8	1,948.8	2,083.8	2,398.8	2,704.7	2,952.8	3,164.2	3,247.7	3,395.9	15.7	16.5	18.9	20.1	22.5	23.5	24.6
Black, non-Hispanic	1,033.0	1,106.8	1,075.8	1,129.6	1,247.0	1,335.4	1,392.9	1,412.8	1,448.6	9.6	9.4	8.9	9.3	9.9	10.2	10.5
Hispanic	383.8	471.7	534.9	680.0	782.4	866.6	955.0	988.8	1,045.6	3.6	4.0	5.4	5.8	6.8	7.1	7.6
Asian or Pacific Islander	197.9	286.4	389.5	496.7	572.4	637.2	697.0	724.4	774.3	1.8	2.4	3.9	4.3	5.0	5.2	5.6
American Indian/Alaskan Native	76.1	83.9	83.6	92.5	102.8	113.7	119.3	121.7	127.4	0.7	0.7	0.7	0.8	0.8	0.9	0.9
Nonresident alien	218.7	305.0	334.6	361.2	391.5	416.4	447.7	457.1	455.9	—	—	—	—	—	—	—
4-year																
Total	7,106.5	7,565.4	7,706.1	8,175.0	8,578.6	8,707.1	8,765.0	8,738.9	8,749.1	100.0	100.0	100.0	100.0	100.0	100.0	100.0
White, non-Hispanic	5,999.0	6,274.5	6,300.4	6,581.6	6,768.1	6,791.0	6,744.3	6,639.5	6,565.3	86.6	85.7	83.6	82.0	80.2	79.3	78.3
Total minority	931.0	1,049.9	1,123.6	1,291.8	1,486.1	1,573.3	1,663.7	1,733.6	1,819.2	13.4	14.3	16.4	18.0	19.8	20.7	21.7
Black, non-Hispanic	603.7	634.3	617.0	656.3	722.8	757.8	791.2	813.7	833.6	8.7	8.7	8.3	8.8	9.4	9.7	9.9
Hispanic	173.6	216.6	246.1	296.0	358.2	382.9	410.0	432.0	462.7	2.5	3.0	3.8	4.3	4.9	5.2	5.5
Asian or Pacific Islander	118.7	162.1	222.4	297.4	357.2	381.5	407.5	429.4	461.8	1.7	2.2	3.8	4.3	4.8	5.1	5.5
American Indian/Alaskan Native	35.0	36.9	38.1	42.1	47.9	51.1	54.9	58.5	61.2	0.5	0.5	0.5	0.6	0.7	0.7	0.7
Nonresident alien	176.5	240.9	282.1	301.5	324.3	342.8	357.0	365.9	364.5	—	—	—	—	—	—	—
Public	4,892.9	5,127.6	5,196.0	5,544.0	5,848.2	5,904.7	5,900.0	5,851.8	5,825.2	69.1	68.0	68.1	68.5	67.6	67.3	66.9
White, non-Hispanic	4,120.2	4,243.0	4,229.9	4,454.8	4,605.6	4,597.4	4,531.6	4,432.9	4,355.0	59.5	57.9	56.6	55.8	53.9	52.9	51.9
Total minority	666.7	740.8	795.9	907.7	1,046.2	1,101.7	1,155.8	1,202.1	1,256.7	9.6	10.1	11.5	12.7	13.7	14.4	15.0
Black, non-Hispanic	421.8	438.2	426.7	448.5	495.1	516.2	535.5	548.2	561.4	6.1	6.0	5.7	6.0	6.4	6.5	6.7
Hispanic	129.3	156.4	178.8	215.8	262.5	278.7	295.2	311.5	332.6	1.9	2.1	2.7	3.2	3.5	3.7	4.0
Asian or Pacific Islander	87.5	117.2	160.3	210.2	250.6	266.2	281.9	296.6	315.3	1.3	1.6	2.7	3.0	3.4	3.5	3.8
American Indian/Alaskan Native	28.2	29.0	30.1	33.3	38.0	40.6	43.0	45.9	47.5	0.4	0.4	0.4	0.5	0.5	0.5	0.6
Nonresident alien	106.0	143.8	170.1	181.4	196.4	205.6	212.6	216.7	213.4	—	—	—	—	—	—	—
Private	2,213.6	2,437.8	2,510.2	2,631.0	2,730.3	2,802.3	2,865.0	2,887.2	2,923.9	30.9	32.0	31.9	31.5	32.4	32.7	33.1
White, non-Hispanic	1,878.8	2,031.5	2,070.5	2,126.8	2,162.5	2,193.5	2,212.6	2,206.6	2,210.3	27.1	27.7	27.0	26.2	26.3	26.4	26.4
Total minority	264.3	309.2	327.7	384.1	439.8	471.5	507.9	531.5	562.5	3.8	4.2	4.9	5.3	6.0	6.3	6.7
Black, non-Hispanic	182.0	196.1	190.4	207.8	227.7	241.5	255.7	265.6	272.2	2.6	2.7	2.6	2.8	3.0	3.2	3.2
Hispanic	44.3	60.2	67.3	80.2	95.7	104.2	114.8	120.4	130.1	0.6	0.8	1.0	1.2	1.4	1.4	1.6
Asian or Pacific Islander	31.2	44.9	62.1	87.2	106.6	115.3	125.6	132.8	146.5	0.5	0.6	1.1	1.3	1.5	1.6	1.7
American Indian/Alaskan Native	6.8	7.9	7.9	8.8	9.9	10.6	11.8	12.6	13.6	0.1	0.1	0.1	0.1	0.1	0.2	0.2
Nonresident alien	70.5	97.1	112.0	120.1	127.9	137.2	144.4	149.1	151.1	—	—	—	—	—	—	—
2-year																
Total	3,879.1	4,521.4	4,526.9	4,868.1	5,240.1	5,651.9	5,722.4	5,565.9	5,529.7	100.0	100.0	100.0	100.0	100.0	100.0	100.0
White, non-Hispanic	3,077.1	3,558.5	3,514.3	3,701.5	3,954.3	4,198.8	4,131.2	3,960.6	3,861.7	80.2	79.8	77.0	76.4	73.4	72.3	71.0
Total minority	759.8	898.9	960.1	1,106.9	1,218.6	1,379.6	1,500.6	1,514.1	1,576.6	19.8	20.2	23.0	23.6	26.6	27.7	29.0
Black, non-Hispanic	429.3	472.5	458.7	473.3	524.3	577.6	601.6	599.0	615.0	11.2	10.6	9.8	10.1	10.7	10.9	11.3
Hispanic	210.2	255.1	288.8	383.9	424.2	483.7	545.0	556.8	582.9	5.5	5.7	8.0	8.2	9.7	10.2	10.7
Asian or Pacific Islander	79.2	124.3	167.1	199.3	215.2	255.7	289.5	295.0	312.5	2.1	2.8	4.1	4.2	5.1	5.4	5.7
American Indian/Alaskan Native	41.2	47.0	45.5	50.4	54.9	62.6	64.4	63.2	66.2	1.1	1.1	1.0	1.1	1.1	1.2	1.2
Nonresident alien	42.2	64.1	52.5	59.6	67.1	73.5	90.6	91.2	91.4	—	—	—	—	—	—	—
Public	3,748.1	4,328.8	4,260.4	4,612.4	4,996.5	5,404.8	5,484.6	5,337.3	5,308.5	96.7	95.8	94.7	95.4	95.8	95.9	96.0
White, non-Hispanic	2,974.3	3,413.1	3,312.5	3,509.0	3,779.8	4,024.8	3,961.2	3,793.7	3,701.3	77.5	76.6	73.0	73.1	70.3	69.3	68.1
Total minority	734.5	855.4	899.0	1,047.0	1,153.0	1,310.3	1,436.4	1,456.0	1,519.3	19.1	19.2	21.8	22.3	25.5	26.6	27.9
Black, non-Hispanic	409.5	437.9	417.3	432.6	481.4	537.2	565.0	566.1	583.2	10.7	9.8	9.0	9.3	10.0	10.3	10.7
Hispanic	207.5	249.8	277.3	371.1	408.9	463.4	527.1	539.8	566.1	5.4	5.6	7.7	7.9	9.4	9.9	10.4
Asian or Pacific Islander	78.2	122.5	162.4	195.5	210.3	250.1	284.0	289.7	306.8	2.0	2.7	4.1	4.1	5.0	5.3	5.6
American Indian/Alaskan Native	39.3	45.2	42.0	47.8	52.4	59.6	60.3	60.5	63.2	1.0	1.0	1.0	1.0	1.1	1.1	1.2
Nonresident alien	39.2	60.3	48.9	56.4	63.6	69.7	86.9	87.6	87.8	—	—	—	—	—	—	—
Private	131.0	192.6	266.4	255.7	243.6	247.1	237.8	228.5	221.2	3.3	4.2	5.3	4.6	4.2	4.1	4.0
White, non-Hispanic	102.8	145.4	201.8	192.6	174.5	174.0	170.0	166.9	160.3	2.7	3.3	4.0	3.4	3.0	3.0	2.9
Total minority	25.3	43.5	61.2	60.0	65.6	69.3	64.1	58.1	57.3	0.7	1.0	1.2	1.3	1.1	1.1	1.1
Black, non-Hispanic	19.8	34.6	41.4	40.7	42.9	40.4	36.6	32.9	31.9	0.5	0.8	0.8	0.8	0.7	0.6	0.6
Hispanic	2.6	5.3	11.6	12.9	15.3	20.3	17.9	17.1	16.7	0.1	0.1	0.3	0.3	0.3	0.3	0.3
Asian or Pacific Islander	0.9	1.8	4.7	3.8	4.9	5.6	5.5	5.4	5.7	(4)	(4)	0.1	0.1	0.1	0.1	0.1
American Indian/Alaskan Native	1.8	1.8	3.5	2.7	2.5	3.0	4.1	2.7	3.0	(4)	(4)	(4)	(4)	0.1	(4)	0.1
Nonresident alien	3.0	3.7	3.5	3.2	3.5	3.8	3.7	3.6	3.6	—	—	—	—	—	—	—

[1] Distribution for U.S. citizens only.
[2] Revised from prevously published data.
[3] Preliminary data.
[4] Less than 0.05 percent.
—Not applicable.

NOTE.—Because of underreporting and nonreporting of racial/ethnic data, some figures are slightly lower than corresponding data in other tables. Because of rounding, details may not add to totals.

SOURCE: U.S. Department of Education, National Center for Education Statistics, "Fall Enrollment in Colleges and Universities;" and Integrated Postsecondary Education Data System (IPEDS), "Fall Enrollment" surveys. (This table was prepared May 1996.)

Table 203.—Total fall enrollment in institutions of higher education, by level of study, sex, and race/ethnicity of student: 1976 to 1994

Level of study, sex, and race/ethnicity of student	Number, in thousands									Percent distribution by level of study [1]						
	1976	1980	1984	1988	1990	1991	1992[2]	1993[2]	1994[3]	1976	1980	1988	1990	1992[2]	1993[2]	1994[3]
1	2	3	4	5	6	7	8	9	10	11	12	13	14	15	16	17
All students																
Total	10,985.6	12,086.8	12,233.0	13,043.1	13,818.6	14,359.0	14,487.4	14,304.8	14,278.8	100.0	100.0	100.0	100.0	100.0	100.0	100.0
White, non-Hispanic	9,076.1	9,833.0	9,814.7	10,283.2	10,722.5	10,989.8	10,875.4	10,600.0	10,427.0	84.3	83.5	81.1	79.9	77.5	76.5	75.4
Total minority	1,690.8	1,948.8	2,083.8	2,398.8	2,704.7	2,952.8	3,164.2	3,247.7	3,395.9	15.7	16.5	18.9	20.1	22.5	23.5	24.6
Black, non-Hispanic	1,033.0	1,106.8	1,075.8	1,129.6	1,247.0	1,335.4	1,392.9	1,412.8	1,448.6	9.6	9.4	8.9	9.3	9.9	10.2	10.5
Hispanic	383.8	471.7	534.9	680.0	782.4	866.6	955.0	988.8	1,045.6	3.6	4.0	5.4	5.8	6.8	7.1	7.6
Asian or Pacific Islander	197.9	286.4	389.5	496.7	572.4	637.2	697.0	724.4	774.3	1.8	2.4	3.9	4.3	5.0	5.2	5.6
American Indian/Alaskan Native	76.1	83.9	83.6	92.5	102.8	113.7	119.3	121.7	127.4	0.7	0.7	0.7	0.8	0.8	0.9	0.9
Nonresident alien	218.7	305.0	334.6	361.2	391.5	416.4	447.7	457.1	455.9	—	—	—	—	—	—	—
Men	5,794.4	5,868.1	5,858.3	5,998.2	6,283.9	6,501.8	6,524.0	6,427.5	6,371.9	52.4	48.0	45.4	45.0	44.5	44.4	44.1
White, non-Hispanic	4,813.7	4,772.9	4,689.9	4,711.6	4,861.0	4,962.2	4,884.6	4,755.0	4,650.7	44.7	40.5	37.2	36.2	34.8	34.3	33.6
Total minority	826.6	884.4	937.9	1,051.3	1,176.6	1,280.3	1,366.3	1,399.1	1,451.7	7.7	7.5	8.3	8.8	9.7	10.1	10.5
Black, non-Hispanic	469.9	463.7	436.8	442.7	484.7	517.0	536.9	543.7	549.7	4.4	3.9	3.5	3.6	3.8	3.9	4.0
Hispanic	209.7	231.6	253.8	310.3	353.9	390.5	427.7	441.2	464.0	1.9	2.0	2.4	2.6	3.0	3.2	3.4
Asian or Pacific Islander	108.4	151.3	210.0	259.2	294.9	325.1	351.5	363.1	385.0	1.0	1.3	2.0	2.2	2.5	2.6	2.8
American Indian/Alaskan Native	38.5	37.8	37.4	39.1	43.1	47.6	50.2	51.2	53.0	0.4	0.3	0.3	0.3	0.4	0.4	0.4
Nonresident alien	154.1	210.8	230.4	235.3	246.3	259.4	273.1	273.4	269.5	—	—	—	—	—	—	—
Women	5,191.2	6,218.7	6,374.7	7,044.9	7,534.7	7,857.1	7,963.4	7,877.4	7,906.9	47.6	52.0	54.6	55.0	55.5	55.6	55.9
White, non-Hispanic	4,262.4	5,060.1	5,124.7	5,571.6	5,861.5	6,027.6	5,990.8	5,845.1	5,776.3	39.6	42.9	43.9	43.7	42.7	42.2	41.8
Total minority	864.2	1,064.4	1,145.8	1,347.4	1,528.1	1,672.5	1,797.9	1,848.6	1,944.2	8.0	9.0	10.6	11.4	12.8	13.3	14.1
Black, non-Hispanic	563.1	643.0	639.0	686.9	762.3	818.4	856.0	869.1	898.9	5.2	5.5	5.4	5.7	6.1	6.3	6.5
Hispanic	174.1	240.1	281.2	369.6	428.5	476.0	527.3	547.6	581.6	1.6	2.0	2.9	3.2	3.8	4.0	4.2
Asian or Pacific Islander	89.4	135.2	179.5	237.5	277.5	312.0	345.6	361.3	389.3	0.8	1.1	1.9	2.1	2.5	2.6	2.8
American Indian/Alaskan Native	37.6	46.1	46.1	53.4	59.7	66.1	69.1	70.5	74.4	0.3	0.4	0.4	0.4	0.5	0.5	0.5
Nonresident alien	64.6	94.2	104.1	125.9	145.2	157.0	174.6	183.7	186.4	—	—	—	—	—	—	—
Undergraduate																
Total	9,419.0	10,469.1	10,610.8	11,304.2	11,959.1	12,439.3	12,537.7	12,324.0	12,262.6	100.0	100.0	100.0	100.0	100.0	100.0	100.0
White, non-Hispanic	7,740.5	8,480.7	8,484.0	8,906.7	9,272.6	9,507.7	9,387.6	9,100.4	8,916.0	83.4	82.7	80.2	79.0	76.4	75.5	74.3
Total minority	1,535.3	1,778.5	1,911.0	2,192.4	2,467.7	2,697.9	2,892.2	2,955.4	3,077.2	16.6	17.3	19.8	21.0	23.6	24.5	25.7
Black, non-Hispanic	943.4	1,018.6	994.9	1,038.8	1,147.2	1,229.3	1,280.6	1,290.4	1,317.3	10.2	9.9	9.4	9.8	10.4	10.7	11.0
Hispanic	352.9	433.1	495.2	631.2	724.6	804.2	887.8	918.1	968.3	3.8	4.2	5.7	6.2	7.2	7.6	8.1
Asian or Pacific Islander	169.3	248.7	343.0	436.6	500.5	558.7	613.0	634.2	674.1	1.8	2.4	3.9	4.3	5.0	5.3	5.6
American Indian/Alaskan Native	69.7	77.9	77.8	85.9	95.5	105.8	110.9	112.7	117.4	0.8	0.8	0.8	0.8	0.9	0.9	1.0
Nonresident alien	143.2	209.9	215.8	205.0	218.7	233.6	257.9	268.2	269.4	—	—	—	—	—	—	—
Men	4,896.8	4,997.4	5,002.4	5,133.7	5,379.8	5,571.0	5,582.9	5,483.7	5,422.1	51.8	47.3	45.1	44.7	44.3	44.3	44.0
White, non-Hispanic	4,052.2	4,054.9	4,005.1	4,053.8	4,184.4	4,273.0	4,195.5	4,067.0	3,963.1	43.7	39.5	36.5	35.6	34.2	33.7	33.0
Total minority	748.2	802.7	855.0	956.0	1,069.3	1,165.2	1,244.2	1,270.1	1,312.4	8.1	7.8	8.6	9.1	10.1	10.5	10.9
Black, non-Hispanic	430.7	428.2	404.8	408.2	448.0	478.1	495.6	499.6	502.9	4.6	4.2	3.7	3.8	4.0	4.1	4.2
Hispanic	191.7	211.2	233.9	287.2	326.9	361.4	397.1	409.2	429.4	2.1	2.1	2.6	2.8	3.2	3.4	3.6
Asian or Pacific Islander	91.1	128.5	181.7	224.4	254.5	281.5	305.0	314.1	331.4	1.0	1.3	2.0	2.2	2.5	2.6	2.8
American Indian/Alaskan Native	34.8	34.8	34.6	36.2	39.9	44.2	46.6	47.2	48.6	0.4	0.3	0.3	0.3	0.4	0.4	0.4
Nonresident alien	96.4	139.8	142.3	124.0	126.1	132.8	143.3	146.6	146.6	—	—	—	—	—	—	—
Women	4,522.1	5,471.7	5,608.4	6,170.4	6,579.3	6,868.3	6,954.8	6,840.3	6,840.5	48.2	52.7	54.9	55.3	55.7	55.7	56.0
White, non-Hispanic	3,688.3	4,425.8	4,478.9	4,852.9	5,088.2	5,234.8	5,192.1	5,033.4	4,953.0	39.8	43.1	43.7	43.3	42.3	41.8	41.3
Total minority	787.0	975.8	1,056.0	1,236.5	1,398.5	1,532.7	1,648.0	1,685.2	1,764.8	8.5	9.5	11.1	11.9	13.4	14.0	14.7
Black, non-Hispanic	512.7	590.6	590.2	630.6	699.2	751.1	785.0	790.8	814.4	5.5	5.8	5.7	6.0	6.4	6.6	6.8
Hispanic	161.2	221.8	261.3	344.0	397.6	442.7	490.7	508.9	538.9	1.7	2.2	3.1	3.4	4.0	4.2	4.5
Asian or Pacific Islander	78.2	120.2	161.4	212.2	246.0	277.2	308.0	320.0	342.7	0.8	1.2	1.9	2.1	2.5	2.7	2.9
American Indian/Alaskan Native	34.9	43.1	43.2	49.7	55.5	61.6	64.3	65.5	68.8	0.4	0.4	0.4	0.5	0.5	0.5	0.6
Nonresident alien	46.8	70.1	73.5	81.1	92.6	100.8	114.6	121.7	122.8	—	—	—	—	—	—	—
Graduate																
Total	1,322.5	1,340.9	1,343.7	1,471.9	1,586.2	1,639.1	1,668.7	1,688.4	1,721.5	100.0	100.0	100.0	100.0	100.0	100.0	100.0
White, non-Hispanic	1,115.6	1,104.7	1087.3	1153.2	1228.4	1258.0	1,267.2	1,273.8	1,286.8	89.2	88.5	87.3	86.6	85.3	84.6	83.5
Total minority	134.5	144.0	141.1	167.2	190.5	204.1	217.9	232.7	255.2	10.8	11.5	12.7	13.4	14.7	15.4	16.5
Black, non-Hispanic	78.5	75.1	67.4	76.5	83.9	88.9	94.1	102.2	110.6	6.3	6.0	5.8	5.9	6.3	6.8	7.2
Hispanic	26.4	32.1	31.7	39.5	47.2	50.9	55.3	57.9	63.9	2.1	2.6	3.0	3.3	3.7	3.8	4.1
Asian or Pacific Islander	24.5	31.6	37.1	45.7	53.2	57.6	61.5	65.2	72.6	2.0	2.5	3.5	3.8	4.1	4.3	4.7
American Indian/Alaskan Native	5.1	5.2	4.8	5.6	6.2	6.6	7.0	7.3	8.1	0.4	0.4	0.4	0.4	0.5	0.5	0.5
Nonresident alien	72.4	92.2	115.3	151.4	167.3	177.0	183.6	182.0	179.5	—	—	—	—	—	—	—
Men	707.9	672.2	671.0	697.8	737.4	761.0	772.4	771.0	775.8	52.2	48.3	44.7	43.8	43.6	43.1	42.7
White, non-Hispanic	589.1	538.5	521.3	516.5	538.8	550.7	553.7	550.9	551.4	47.1	43.1	39.1	38.0	37.3	36.6	35.8
Total minority	63.7	65.0	64.2	73.3	82.1	87.3	93.3	98.1	106.3	5.1	5.2	5.6	5.8	6.3	6.5	6.9
Black, non-Hispanic	32.0	28.2	24.9	27.4	29.3	31.0	33.1	35.3	37.7	2.6	2.3	2.1	2.1	2.2	2.3	2.4
Hispanic	14.6	15.7	14.7	17.4	20.6	22.4	23.6	24.8	27.0	1.2	1.3	1.3	1.5	1.6	1.6	1.8
Asian or Pacific Islander	14.4	18.6	22.4	26.2	29.7	31.8	33.8	35.1	38.3	1.2	1.5	2.0	2.1	2.3	2.3	2.5
American Indian/Alaskan Native	2.7	2.5	2.2	2.3	2.6	2.7	2.9	3.0	3.3	0.2	0.2	0.2	0.2	0.2	0.2	0.2
Nonresident alien	55.1	68.7	85.6	108.0	116.4	122.4	125.4	122.0	118.1	—	—	—	—	—	—	—
Women	614.6	668.7	672.6	774.1	848.8	878.2	896.3	917.4	945.6	47.8	51.7	55.3	56.2	56.4	56.9	57.3
White, non-Hispanic	526.5	566.2	566.0	636.8	689.5	707.3	713.6	722.9	735.4	42.1	45.3	48.2	48.6	48.0	48.0	47.7
Total minority	70.8	79.0	76.9	93.9	108.3	116.3	124.6	134.6	148.9	5.7	6.3	7.1	7.6	8.4	8.9	9.7
Black, non-Hispanic	46.5	46.9	42.5	49.1	54.6	57.9	61.0	66.9	72.9	3.7	3.8	3.7	3.8	4.1	4.4	4.7
Hispanic	11.8	16.4	17.1	22.0	26.6	28.6	31.7	33.1	36.9	0.9	1.3	1.7	1.9	2.1	2.2	2.4
Asian or Pacific Islander	10.1	13.0	14.7	19.5	23.6	25.9	27.8	30.2	34.3	0.8	1.0	1.5	1.7	1.9	2.0	2.2
American Indian/Alaskan Native	2.4	2.7	2.6	3.3	3.6	3.9	4.1	4.3	4.8	0.2	0.2	0.2	0.3	0.3	0.3	0.3
Nonresident alien	17.3	23.5	29.7	43.4	50.9	54.6	58.2	59.9	61.4	—	—	—	—	—	—	—

Table 203.—Total fall enrollment in institutions of higher education, by level of study, sex, and race/ethnicity of student: 1976 to 1994—Continued

Level of study, sex, and race/ethnicity of student	Number, in thousands									Percent distribution by level of study [1]						
	1976	1980	1984	1988	1990	1991	1992 [2]	1993 [2]	1994 [3]	1976	1980	1988	1990	1992 [2]	1993 [2]	1994 [3]
1	2	3	4	5	6	7	8	9	10	11	12	13	14	15	16	17
First-professional																
Total	244.1	276.8	278.5	267.1	273.4	280.5	280.9	292.4	294.7	100.0	100.0	100.0	100.0	100.0	100.0	100.0
White, non-Hispanic	220.0	247.7	243.4	223.2	221.5	224.0	220.6	225.9	224.2	91.3	90.4	85.1	82.6	80.3	79.1	77.9
Total minority	21.1	26.3	31.7	39.1	46.5	50.8	54.1	59.6	63.5	8.7	9.6	14.9	17.4	19.7	20.9	22.1
Black, non-Hispanic	11.2	12.8	13.4	14.3	15.9	17.2	18.2	20.2	20.7	4.6	4.7	5.5	5.9	6.6	7.1	7.2
Hispanic	4.5	6.5	8.0	9.3	10.7	11.4	12.0	12.8	13.4	1.9	2.4	3.6	4.0	4.4	4.5	4.7
Asian or Pacific Islander	4.1	6.1	9.3	14.4	18.7	20.8	22.5	25.0	27.6	1.7	2.2	5.5	7.0	8.2	8.8	9.6
American Indian/Alaskan Native	1.3	0.8	1.0	1.1	1.1	1.3	1.5	1.7	1.8	0.5	0.3	0.4	0.4	0.5	0.6	0.6
Nonresident alien	3.1	2.9	3.4	4.7	5.4	5.8	6.2	6.9	7.0	—	—	—	—	—	—	—
Men	189.6	198.5	184.9	166.7	166.8	169.9	168.6	172.8	174.0	77.6	71.6	62.3	60.8	59.8	58.8	58.8
White, non-Hispanic	172.4	179.5	163.6	141.3	137.8	138.6	135.5	137.2	136.2	71.5	65.5	53.8	51.4	49.3	48.0	47.3
Total minority	14.7	16.7	18.8	22.1	25.3	27.2	28.8	30.9	33.0	6.1	6.1	8.4	9.4	10.5	10.8	11.5
Black, non-Hispanic	7.2	7.4	7.1	7.1	7.4	7.9	8.2	8.8	9.1	3.0	2.7	2.7	2.8	3.0	3.1	3.2
Hispanic	3.5	4.6	5.2	5.7	6.4	6.7	7.0	7.2	7.5	1.5	1.7	2.2	2.4	2.6	2.5	2.6
Asian or Pacific Islander	2.9	4.1	5.9	8.6	10.8	11.9	12.7	13.9	15.3	1.2	1.5	3.3	4.0	4.6	4.9	5.3
American Indian/Alaskan Native	1.0	0.5	0.6	0.6	0.6	0.7	0.8	0.9	1.0	0.4	0.2	0.2	0.2	0.3	0.3	0.4
Nonresident alien	2.5	2.3	2.5	3.4	3.8	4.1	4.4	4.8	4.8	—	—	—	—	—	—	—
Women	54.5	78.4	93.6	100.4	106.6	110.7	112.3	119.6	120.8	22.4	28.4	37.7	39.2	40.2	41.2	41.2
White, non-Hispanic	47.6	68.1	79.8	82.0	83.7	85.4	85.1	88.8	88.0	19.7	24.9	31.2	31.2	31.0	31.1	30.6
Total minority	6.4	9.6	12.9	17.1	21.3	23.5	25.3	28.8	30.5	2.6	3.5	6.5	7.9	9.2	10.1	10.6
Black, non-Hispanic	3.9	5.5	6.3	7.2	8.5	9.3	10.0	11.4	11.5	1.6	2.0	2.7	3.2	3.6	4.0	4.0
Hispanic	1.0	1.9	2.8	3.6	4.3	4.7	4.9	5.5	5.9	0.4	0.7	1.4	1.6	1.8	1.9	2.0
Asian or Pacific Islander	1.1	2.0	3.5	5.8	7.9	8.9	9.8	11.1	12.3	0.5	0.7	2.2	3.0	3.6	3.9	4.3
American Indian/Alaskan Native	0.2	0.3	0.4	0.5	0.5	0.6	0.7	0.7	0.8	0.1	0.1	0.2	0.2	0.2	0.3	0.3
Nonresident alien	0.5	0.6	0.9	1.4	1.6	1.7	1.8	2.1	2.3	—	—	—	—	—	—	—

[1] Distribution for U.S. citizens only.
[2] Revised from previously published data.
[3] Preliminary data.
—Not applicable.

NOTE.—Because of underreporting and nonreporting of racial/ethnic data, some figures are slightly lower than corresponding data in other tables. Because of rounding, details may not add to totals.

SOURCE: U.S. Department of Education, National Center for Education Statistics, "Fall Enrollment in Colleges and Universities;" and Integrated Postsecondary Education Data System (IPEDS), "Fall Enrollment" survey. (This table was prepared May 1996.)

Table 204.—Total number of institutions and fall enrollment in institutions of higher education, by percentage minority enrollment: 1994[1]

Minority percentage of U.S. citizen enrollment	Total enrollment	Public institutions					Private institutions				
		Total	4-year institutions			2-year	Total	4-year institutions			2-year
			Total	University	Other 4-year			Total	University	Other 4-year	
1	2	3	4	5	6	7	8	9	10	11	12
All institutions											
Number of institutions	3,561	1,595	599	94	505	996	1,966	1,565	62	1,503	401
Total enrollment	14,278,790	11,133,680	5,825,213	2,244,636	3,580,577	5,308,467	3,145,110	2,923,867	764,436	2,159,431	221,243
U.S. citizens	13,822,855	10,832,425	5,611,790	2,123,285	3,488,505	5,220,635	2,990,430	2,772,767	696,586	2,076,181	217,663
Minority	3,395,861	2,776,074	1,256,743	363,492	893,251	1,519,331	619,787	562,473	163,286	399,187	57,314
90.0 percent or more minority enrollment											
Number of institutions	123	48	23	0	23	25	75	62	1	61	13
Total enrollment	316,189	232,689	118,094	0	118,094	114,595	83,500	75,846	10,115	65,731	7,654
U.S. citizens	306,690	225,497	114,603	0	114,603	110,894	81,193	73,639	9,414	64,225	7,554
Minority	292,835	213,907	109,072	0	109,072	104,835	78,928	71,771	9,240	62,531	7,157
75.0 to 89.9 percent minority enrollment											
Number of institutions	80	53	20	0	20	33	27	11	0	11	16
Total enrollment	417,454	402,109	133,168	0	133,168	268,941	15,345	6,947	0	6,947	8,398
U.S. citizens	401,698	387,064	128,691	0	128,691	258,373	14,634	6,306	0	6,306	8,328
Minority	328,721	316,752	107,596	0	107,596	209,156	11,969	5,152	0	5,152	6,817
50.0 to 74.9 percent minority enrollment											
Number of institutions	181	99	27	3	24	72	82	43	0	43	39
Total enrollment	1,071,517	975,608	373,478	84,754	288,724	602,130	95,909	79,346	0	79,346	16,563
U.S. citizens	1,028,504	937,633	356,702	79,282	277,420	580,931	90,871	74,848	0	74,848	16,023
Minority	621,060	566,220	216,070	47,706	168,364	350,150	54,840	45,243	0	45,243	9,597
25.0 to 49.9 percent minority enrollment											
Number of institutions	620	299	79	10	69	220	321	222	18	204	99
Total enrollment	2,993,948	2,343,456	918,043	318,212	599,831	1,425,413	650,492	601,810	252,237	349,573	48,682
U.S. citizens	2,874,717	2,274,307	879,005	298,125	580,880	1,395,302	600,410	552,851	224,130	328,721	47,559
Minority	984,802	784,995	301,390	91,434	209,956	483,605	199,807	183,109	74,563	108,546	16,698
10.0 to 24.9 percent minority enrollment											
Number of institutions	1,208	544	226	46	180	318	664	570	39	531	94
Total enrollment	5,787,384	4,413,997	2,587,016	1,165,955	1,421,061	1,826,981	1,373,387	1,295,845	444,896	850,949	77,542
U.S. citizens	5,600,055	4,298,897	2,488,632	1,103,074	1,385,558	1,810,265	1,301,158	1,224,426	408,219	816,207	76,732
Minority	940,250	720,363	411,183	175,352	235,831	309,180	219,887	206,124	76,312	129,812	13,763
Less than 10.0 percent minority enrollment											
Number of institutions	1,349	552	224	35	189	328	797	657	4	653	140
Total enrollment	3,692,298	2,765,821	1,695,414	675,715	1,019,699	1,070,407	926,477	864,073	57,188	806,885	62,404
U.S. citizens	3,611,191	2,709,027	1,644,157	642,804	1,001,353	1,064,870	902,164	840,697	54,823	785,874	61,467
Minority	228,193	173,837	111,432	49,000	62,432	62,405	54,356	51,074	3,171	47,903	3,282

[1] Preliminary data. Minority includes black, Hispanic, Asian or Pacific Islander, and American Indian/Alaskan Native students.

NOTE.-Some institutions do not report separate enrollment data for each branch campus. For this reason, counts of institutions in this table are somewhat lower than figures appearing in other tables.

SOURCE: U.S. Department of Education, National Center for Education Statistics, Integrated Postsecondary Education Data System (IPEDS), "Fall Enrollment" survey. (This table was prepared June 1996.)

Table 205.—Total fall enrollment in institutions of higher education, by race/ethnicity of student and by state: 1992, 1993, and 1994

State or other area	1994 [1]								Percent minority [2]		
	Total	White, non-His-panic	Minority enrollment, by race/ethnicity					Nonresident alien	1992 [3]	1993 [3]	1994
			Total	Black, non-His-panic	Hispanic	Asian/ Pacific Islander	American Indian/ Alaskan Native				
1	2	3	4	5	6	7	8	9	10	11	12
United States	14,278,790	10,426,994	3,395,861	1,448,630	1,045,564	774,295	127,372	455,935	22.5	23.5	24.6
Alabama	229,511	167,605	57,306	52,178	1,645	2,278	1,205	4,600	23.7	24.8	25.5
Alaska	28,798	22,932	5,280	1,087	706	852	2,635	586	18.3	18.6	18.7
Arizona	274,932	203,407	64,127	8,629	36,904	8,287	10,307	7,398	22.2	23.8	24.0
Arkansas	96,294	77,862	16,021	13,660	633	1,006	722	2,411	16.8	17.2	17.1
California	1,835,791	941,020	810,022	137,663	343,408	308,002	20,949	84,749	40.5	44.0	46.3
Colorado	241,295	195,440	39,853	7,907	21,414	7,671	2,861	6,002	15.8	16.4	16.9
Connecticut	159,990	129,491	25,140	11,850	7,573	5,245	472	5,359	14.2	15.1	16.3
Delaware	44,197	35,440	7,761	5,898	753	924	186	996	16.0	16.9	18.0
District of Columbia	77,705	37,961	31,319	24,207	2,775	4,129	208	8,425	43.7	43.9	45.2
Florida	634,237	433,610	181,838	80,268	80,880	17,969	2,721	18,789	27.5	28.4	29.5
Georgia	308,587	213,678	87,378	74,549	4,495	7,527	807	7,531	26.4	27.9	29.0
Hawaii	64,322	17,278	41,505	1,596	1,552	38,066	291	5,539	69.6	69.9	70.6
Idaho	60,393	55,313	3,601	390	1,541	810	860	1,479	5.5	6.1	6.1
Illinois	731,420	521,706	191,917	92,735	56,979	39,739	2,464	17,797	25.6	26.1	26.9
Indiana	292,276	253,840	29,920	17,695	5,941	5,173	1,111	8,516	9.8	10.2	10.5
Iowa	172,450	153,316	11,896	4,992	2,691	3,562	651	7,238	6.2	6.6	7.2
Kansas	170,603	145,173	18,957	8,251	4,859	3,493	2,354	6,473	10.7	11.0	11.5
Kentucky	182,577	163,477	16,060	12,449	1,096	1,934	581	3,040	8.2	8.6	8.9
Louisiana	203,567	135,983	62,251	52,338	4,747	4,093	1,073	5,333	29.7	30.2	31.4
Maine	56,724	54,088	2,071	481	295	716	579	565	4.4	3.3	3.7
Maryland	266,214	180,290	77,136	55,824	5,886	14,413	1,013	8,788	27.3	28.5	30.0
Massachusetts	416,505	327,256	64,824	22,968	16,920	23,321	1,615	24,425	14.4	15.2	16.5
Michigan	551,307	445,421	89,766	59,369	11,301	14,706	4,390	16,120	15.3	16.2	16.8
Minnesota	289,458	260,458	22,758	6,998	3,771	9,022	2,967	6,084	6.8	7.5	8.0
Mississippi	120,884	81,926	37,145	35,159	598	969	419	1,813	29.8	30.6	31.2
Missouri	293,810	248,108	37,833	25,782	4,527	6,072	1,452	7,869	12.6	12.9	13.2
Montana	40,095	34,481	4,479	140	457	313	3,569	1,135	12.9	11.5	11.5
Nebraska	116,000	105,064	8,338	3,351	2,230	1,816	941	2,598	7.2	7.0	7.4
Nevada	64,085	50,026	12,084	3,240	4,338	3,486	1,020	1,975	18.7	18.0	19.5
New Hampshire	62,847	58,878	2,839	809	776	973	281	1,130	5.4	4.9	4.6
New Jersey	335,480	235,453	88,866	39,174	29,385	19,427	880	11,161	24.8	25.6	27.4
New Mexico	101,881	58,219	41,834	2,530	30,661	1,577	7,066	1,828	39.8	40.9	41.8
New York	1,057,841	712,802	302,999	137,364	97,011	65,071	3,553	42,040	26.9	28.1	29.8
North Carolina	369,386	276,236	87,720	73,276	4,034	6,847	3,563	5,430	22.6	23.2	24.1
North Dakota	40,184	35,474	3,003	324	228	341	2,110	1,707	7.3	7.5	7.8
Ohio	549,304	463,369	70,194	50,117	7,527	10,626	1,924	15,741	12.1	12.7	13.2
Oklahoma	185,174	141,608	35,183	13,546	4,014	4,030	13,593	8,383	17.7	18.7	19.9
Oregon	164,447	138,508	19,259	2,675	5,225	8,959	2,400	6,680	10.6	11.6	12.2
Pennsylvania	611,174	515,192	78,649	46,656	10,744	19,697	1,552	17,333	12.5	12.5	13.2
Rhode Island	74,718	64,054	8,258	3,060	2,405	2,540	253	2,406	10.2	11.0	11.4
South Carolina	173,070	128,002	41,975	37,755	1,454	2,165	601	3,093	23.7	23.8	24.7
South Dakota	37,764	33,726	3,154	290	176	299	2,389	884	7.5	6.8	8.6
Tennessee	242,966	196,134	42,321	35,917	2,237	3,462	705	4,511	17.1	17.3	17.7
Texas	954,495	602,088	325,512	93,741	186,206	41,169	4,396	26,895	32.4	33.4	35.1
Utah	146,196	131,617	9,079	857	3,667	3,055	1,500	5,500	5.9	6.6	6.5
Vermont	35,409	32,971	1,678	407	428	641	202	760	4.0	3.9	4.8
Virginia	354,149	264,939	81,949	56,728	7,346	16,674	1,201	7,261	21.3	22.4	23.6
Washington	284,662	228,671	46,533	10,264	9,709	21,385	5,175	9,458	14.8	15.7	16.9
West Virginia	87,741	80,910	5,030	3,452	455	941	182	1,801	5.4	5.6	5.9
Wisconsin	303,861	268,900	27,969	12,946	6,077	6,457	2,489	6,992	8.7	9.1	9.4
Wyoming	30,682	28,074	2,084	258	1,134	245	447	524	7.3	6.7	6.9
U.S. Service Schools	51,490	39,519	11,187	4,830	3,750	2,120	487	784	21.2	21.7	22.1
Outlying areas	170,686	918	168,776	2,587	156,502	9,666	21	992	99.5	99.4	99.5
American Samoa	1,249	0	1,249	0	0	1,249	0	0	100.0	100.0	100.0
Federated States of Micronesia	1,374	0	1,374	0	0	1,374	0	0	100.0	100.0	100.0
Guam	6,449	592	5,305	35	50	5,204	16	552	89.5	89.3	90.0
Marshall Islands	424	0	413	0	0	413	0	11	100.0	99.7	100.0
Northern Marianas	1,253	82	981	2	2	976	1	190	89.5	92.1	92.3
Palau	403	0	403	0	0	403	0	0	100.0	100.0	100.0
Puerto Rico	156,439	23	156,337	4	156,319	14	0	79	91.3	99.9	100.0
Virgin Islands	3,095	221	2,714	2,546	131	33	4	160	91.3	91.7	92.5

[1] Preliminary data.
[2] Percent minority based on U.S. citizen enrollment (total enrollment less enrollment of nonresident aliens).
[3] Revised from previously published data.

NOTE.—Because of adjustments to underreported and nonreported racial/ethnic data, figures are slightly different from corresponding data in other tables.

SOURCE: U.S. Department of Education, National Center for Education Statistics, Integrated Postsecondary Education Data System (IPEDS), "Fall Enrollment" surveys. (This table was prepared May 1996.)

Table 206.—Percent of students enrolled in postsecondary institutions, by disability status and selected student characteristics: 1992–93

Selected student characteristics	Undergraduate			Graduate and first-professional [1]		
	All students	Disabled students [2]	Nondisabled students	All students	Disabled students [2]	Nondisabled students
1	2	3	4	5	6	7
Total	100.0	6.3	93.7	100.0	4.0	96.0
Sex	100.0	100.0	100.0	100.0	100.0	100.0
Male	44.5	53.0	44.0	46.4	51.0	46.2
Female	55.5	47.0	56.0	53.6	49.0	53.8
Race/ethnicity	100.0	100.0	100.0	100.0	100.0	100.0
White, non-Hispanic	76.8	80.8	76.6	81.4	85.3	81.3
Black, non-Hispanic	10.3	9.3	10.3	6.4	4.4	6.4
Hispanic	8.0	6.3	8.1	4.0	5.1	3.9
Asian American	4.0	1.7	4.1	7.5	3.8	7.6
American Indian	1.0	1.8	0.9	0.8	1.3	0.7
Age	100.0	100.0	100.0	100.0	100.0	100.0
15 to 23	55.1	37.8	56.1	11.4	6.7	11.6
24 to 29	17.1	15.2	17.2	34.7	20.4	35.2
30 or older	27.7	47.0	26.7	53.9	72.9	53.2
Veteran status	100.0	100.0	100.0	100.0	100.0	100.0
Veteran	7.5	17.5	6.8	6.1	16.4	5.7
Not a veteran	92.5	82.5	93.2	93.9	83.6	94.3
Dependency status	100.0	100.0	100.0	100.0	100.0	100.0
Dependent	47.9	32.9	48.7	8.5	4.9	8.7
Independent	32.9	37.0	32.7	66.2	52.5	66.6
Independent with dependents	19.2	30.1	18.6	25.3	42.6	24.7
Housing status	100.0	100.0	100.0	100.0	100.0	100.0
School-owned	12.8	7.4	13.1	5.9	6.1	5.8
Off-campus, not with parents	58.8	69.7	58.2	84.2	84.1	84.2
With parents	25.9	20.1	26.3	7.5	5.2	7.6
With relatives	2.2	2.7	2.2	2.3	4.3	2.2
Other	0.2	0.2	0.2	0.1	0.3	0.1
Attendance status	100.0	100.0	100.0	100.0	100.0	100.0
Full-time	52.6	46.3	52.9	37.1	33.8	37.2
Part-time	47.4	53.7	47.1	62.9	66.2	62.8
Field of study	100.0	100.0	100.0	100.0	100.0	100.0
Business	22.8	21.9	22.8	16.0	11.5	16.2
Computer science	4.6	6.2	4.5	3.0	2.6	3.0
Education	10.3	9.4	10.3	25.7	33.3	25.5
Engineering	6.9	6.9	6.9	6.5	6.0	6.6
Health	13.4	12.4	13.5	11.5	7.4	11.6
Humanities	11.3	11.9	11.3	8.5	8.8	8.5
Life sciences	5.4	4.8	5.4	5.1	6.6	5.0
Mathematics	0.9	0.6	0.9	1.4	2.4	1.4
Physical sciences	1.1	1.2	1.1	2.6	2.6	2.6
Social sciences	8.0	7.2	8.0	9.1	9.2	9.1
Vocational	5.3	6.4	5.2	0.8	0.7	0.8
Other technical/professional	10.0	11.0	10.0	9.8	8.9	9.8

[1] Includes chiropractic medicine, medicine, dentistry, optometry, osteopathic medicine, pharmacy, podiatry, and veterinary medicine.

[2] Disabled students are those who reported that they had one or more of the following conditions: a specific learning disability, a visual handicap, hard of hearing, deafness, a speech disability, an orthopedic handicap, or a health impairment.

NOTE.—Because of rounding and survey item nonresponse, details may not add to totals.

SOURCE: U.S. Department of Education, National Center for Education Statistics, "The 1992–93 National Postsecondary Student Aid Study." (This table was prepared October 1996.)

Table 207.—Enrollment of persons 14 to 34 years of age [1] in institutions of higher education, by race/ethnicity, sex, and year of college: October 1965 to October 1995

Characteristic	1965	1970	1975	1980	1984[2]	1985	1986	1987	1988	1989	1990	1991	1992	1993	1994[3]	1995[3]
1	2	3	4	5	6	7	8	9	10	11	12	13	14	15	16	17
						Numbers in thousands										
All students	5,675	7,413	9,697	10,181	10,858	10,863	10,605	10,915	10,937	11,066	11,303	11,589	11,671	11,409	12,298	12,406
White, non-Hispanic[4]																
Total	5,317	6,759	8,141	8,453	8,764	8,781	8,284	8,519	8,616	8,786	8,892	8,916	8,883	8,592	9,076	8,973
Men	3,326	4,066	4,566	4,225	4,487	4,361	4,158	4,221	4,155	4,220	4,298	4,323	4,207	4,168	4,313	4,319
Women	1,991	2,693	3,576	4,228	4,277	4,420	4,126	4,299	4,461	4,565	4,594	4,594	4,676	4,424	4,764	4,654
Black, non-Hispanic[4]																
Total	274	522	927	996	1,124	1,036	1,126	1,162	1,096	1,116	1,167	1,190	1,205	1,227	1,469	1,415
Men	126	253	433	431	538	458	484	505	423	425	508	523	467	515	641	579
Women	148	269	494	565	586	578	642	657	674	690	659	667	738	713	828	837
Hispanic origin																
Total	—	—	411	443	524	579	677	667	654	640	617	721	816	867	982	1,014
Men	—	—	219	222	232	280	331	369	313	311	297	310	349	391	443	495
Women	—	—	192	221	292	299	346	298	341	330	321	411	468	475	539	519
Year of college																
First	1,861	2,212	2,886	2,958	3,023	2,956	2,965	2,915	3,131	2,983	3,109	2,995	3,274	3,139	3,357	3,236
Second	1,256	1,739	2,376	2,411	2,454	2,585	2,564	2,745	2,598	2,680	2,798	2,959	3,002	2,964	3,075	3,068
Third	896	1,248	1,491	1,716	1,981	1,931	1,803	2,011	1,979	2,017	1,958	2,009	2,136	2,080	2,244	2,239
Fourth	803	1,074	1,354	1,403	1,599	1,642	1,640	1,556	1,631	1,676	1,817	1,877	1,681	1,692	1,902	1,772
Fifth or higher	859	1,140	1,590	1,692	1,802	1,749	1,633	1,690	1,598	1,711	1,620	1,749	1,578	1,535	1,719	1,731
						Percentage distribution										
All students	100.0	100.0	100.0	100.0	100.0	100.0	100.0	100.0	100.0	100.0	100.0	100.0	100.0	100.0	100.0	100.0
White, non-Hispanic[4]																
Total	93.7	91.2	84.0	83.0	80.7	80.8	78.1	78.0	78.8	79.4	78.7	76.9	76.1	75.3	73.8	74.5
Men	58.6	54.8	47.1	41.5	41.3	40.1	39.2	38.7	38.0	38.1	38.0	37.3	36.0	36.5	35.1	35.9
Women	35.1	36.3	36.9	41.5	39.4	40.7	38.9	39.4	40.8	41.2	40.6	39.6	40.1	38.8	38.7	38.6
Black, non-Hispanic[4]																
Total	4.8	7.0	9.6	9.8	10.4	9.5	10.6	10.6	10.0	10.1	10.3	10.3	10.3	10.8	11.9	11.7
Men	2.2	3.4	4.5	4.2	5.0	4.2	4.6	4.6	3.9	3.8	4.5	4.5	4.0	4.5	5.2	4.8
Women	2.6	3.6	5.1	5.5	5.4	5.3	6.1	6.0	6.2	6.2	5.8	5.8	6.3	6.2	6.7	6.9
Hispanic origin																
Total	—	—	4.2	4.4	4.8	5.3	6.4	6.1	6.0	5.8	5.5	6.2	7.0	7.6	8.0	8.4
Men	—	—	2.3	2.2	2.1	2.6	3.1	3.4	2.9	2.8	2.6	2.7	3.0	3.4	3.6	4.1
Women	—	—	2.0	2.2	2.7	2.8	3.3	2.7	3.1	3.0	2.8	3.5	4.0	4.2	4.4	4.3
Year of college																
First	32.8	29.8	29.8	29.1	27.8	27.2	28.0	26.7	28.6	27.0	27.5	25.8	28.1	27.5	27.3	26.9
Second	22.1	23.5	24.5	23.7	22.6	23.8	24.2	25.1	23.8	24.2	24.8	25.5	25.7	26.0	25.0	25.5
Third	15.8	16.8	15.4	16.9	18.2	17.8	17.0	18.4	18.1	18.2	17.3	17.3	18.3	18.2	18.3	18.6
Fourth	14.1	14.5	14.0	13.8	14.7	15.1	15.5	15.5	14.3	14.9	15.1	16.1	16.2	14.4	14.8	15.5	14.7
Fifth or higher	15.1	15.4	16.4	16.6	16.6	16.1	15.4	15.5	14.6	15.5	14.3	15.1	13.5	13.5	14.0	14.4

[1] Totals differ from those shown in other tables. This table presents data collected in sample surveys of households rather than surveys of institutions. Excludes persons age 35 and over.

[2] Data for 1984 to 1993 are controlled to 1980 census base.

[3] Data are controlled to 1990 census base. Large increase in 1994 is partly due to the change in census base and change in survey form administrative procedures.

[4] Data for 1965 and 1970 include persons of Hispanic origin.

—Data not available.

NOTE.—Data are based upon sample surveys of the civilian noninstitutional population. Because of rounding, details may not add to totals.

SOURCE: U.S. Department of Commerce, Bureau of the Census, *Current Population Reports*, Series P-20, No. 403, and unpublished data. (This table was prepared July 1996.)

Table 208.—Enrollment in postsecondary education, by major field of study, age, and level of student: 1992–93

Field of study	All students				Undergraduate — 2-year institutions				Undergraduate — 4-year institutions				Graduate and first-professional			
	Total, in thousands	Percentage distribution, by age			Total, in thousands	Percentage distribution, by age			Total, in thousands	Percentage distribution, by age			Total, in thousands	Percentage distribution, by age		
		Under 25	25 to 34	Over 35		Under 25	25 to 34	Over 35		Under 25	25 to 34	Over 35		Under 25	25 to 34	Over 35
1	2	3	4	5	6	7	8	9	10	11	12	13	14	15	16	17
Total	**21,096**	**54.1**	**25.0**	**20.9**	**9,881**	**48.5**	**26.9**	**24.6**	**8,558**	**71.7**	**16.7**	**11.7**	**2,657**	**18.6**	**45.0**	**36.4**
Agriculture	299	58.2	23.6	18.2	141	47.0	29.7	23.3	125	82.6	8.4	9.0	32	12.4	56.2	31.4
Architecture	118	62.2	25.4	12.3	40	52.7	28.7	18.6	62	78.2	14.5	7.3	15	21.4	62.0	16.6
Business and management	4,082	51.8	27.1	21.0	1,945	46.8	27.5	25.6	1,766	65.0	20.5	14.6	372	15.3	56.9	27.9
Accounting	897	49.8	28.5	21.7	450	40.1	31.7	28.2	401	63.9	22.5	13.6	47	21.9	48.5	29.6
Business	2,125	51.8	27.5	20.8	870	48.1	26.4	25.5	988	64.9	20.2	14.9	267	15.1	57.8	27.1
Secretary/bookkeeping	973	51.2	26.6	22.2	582	47.8	27.4	24.8	333	64.2	19.7	16.1	58	10.7	59.2	30.1
Marketing	87	80.3	10.8	8.8	43	78.6	8.8	12.7	44	82.0	12.9	5.1	(¹)	(¹)	(¹)	(¹)
Communications/journalism	516	70.6	18.3	11.1	174	60.4	22.5	17.2	296	84.3	11.9	3.8	47	21.3	43.5	35.2
Computer science	927	41.7	30.8	27.5	583	37.1	29.0	34.0	266	59.6	27.4	13.1	78	15.4	56.3	28.3
Cosmetology	271	59.8	24.5	15.7	271	59.8	24.5	15.7	(¹)	(¹)	(¹)	(¹)	(¹)	(¹)	(¹)	(¹)
Consumer/personal services	10	68.9	7.0	24.2	10	68.9	7.0	24.2	(¹)	(¹)	(¹)	(¹)	(¹)	(¹)	(¹)	(¹)
Education	2,325	47.2	24.3	28.6	690	49.0	26.4	24.6	1,005	69.0	16.8	14.2	631	10.4	33.9	55.7
Engineering	1,229	60.9	27.5	11.6	501	49.5	31.7	18.8	564	80.5	15.0	4.6	164	28.6	57.5	13.9
Foreign languages	130	53.2	15.8	31.0	40	29.7	6.6	63.7	72	74.9	13.9	11.2	18	18.7	43.9	37.4
Health	2,809	47.3	30.6	22.2	1,735	44.1	32.4	23.5	766	62.0	20.5	17.4	307	28.2	45.0	26.8
Medical doctor	147	51.1	41.9	7.0	38	51.9	36.0	12.1	27	76.5	17.7	5.9	81	42.1	52.9	5.0
Nursing	1,286	38.8	33.9	27.3	872	35.6	37.6	26.7	355	51.7	23.9	24.4	59	8.1	38.9	53.1
Other	1,375	54.7	26.2	19.0	825	52.7	26.8	20.6	384	70.1	17.9	12.0	167	30.9	41.2	27.9
Home economics	165	58.4	17.4	24.3	133	54.4	19.9	25.7	60	76.8	12.7	10.5	15	9.3	20.3	70.4
Law	293	45.2	33.5	21.2	90	46.8	24.6	28.7	45	53.8	26.2	20.1	115	40.1	46.8	13.2
Letters	301	57.3	24.0	18.6	104	37.0	36.4	26.6	157	80.4	10.3	9.3	40	19.9	45.7	34.4
Liberal arts	636	55.8	23.5	20.6	435	56.6	22.1	21.4	177	59.0	25.3	15.6	24	18.6	37.1	44.3
Library science	15	6.0	25.6	68.5	(¹)	(¹)	(¹)	(¹)	(¹)	(¹)	(¹)	(¹)	15	6.0	25.6	68.5
Life sciences	630	74.2	17.3	8.5	149	66.6	20.0	13.5	401	86.8	9.1	4.1	81	26.0	52.7	21.2
Mathematics	190	54.9	23.9	21.1	66	49.3	21.1	29.6	89	73.0	17.3	9.7	36	19.9	45.9	34.2
Philosophy and theology	144	36.3	27.0	36.7	16	61.3	26.1	12.6	59	63.4	14.4	22.2	69	7.2	38.1	54.7
Physical sciences	254	57.5	30.4	12.1	54	49.7	33.3	17.0	133	78.8	15.5	5.7	67	21.5	57.5	21.0
Protective services	465	65.6	22.9	11.5	285	60.1	26.9	13.0	171	76.6	15.2	8.2	9	30.3	44.3	25.4
Psychology	444	64.8	19.5	15.7	116	58.5	19.4	22.2	279	74.6	15.8	9.6	49	23.9	40.5	35.6
Social work/public administration	234	40.0	27.1	32.9	65	36.6	31.2	32.3	99	58.0	16.6	25.4	70	17.7	38.0	44.3
Social sciences	974	70.0	18.1	11.9	181	60.8	18.8	20.4	677	80.6	12.4	7.0	116	22.4	49.9	27.7
Visual and performing arts	788	59.6	17.3	23.2	318	48.3	18.6	33.1	388	77.2	11.8	11.0	81	19.2	38.0	42.8
Other and not reported	2,847	53.6	22.9	23.4	1,741	48.7	24.6	26.8	901	72.4	15.3	12.3	205	13.5	42.4	44.0

¹ Too few sample cases for a reliable estimate.

NOTE.—Because of different survey editing and processing procedures, enrollment data in this table may differ from those appearing in other tables. Because of rounding, details may not add to totals. Includes students who enrolled at any time during the 1992–93 academic year.

SOURCE: U.S. Department of Education, National Center for Education Statistics, "The 1992–93 National Postsecondary Student Aid Study," unpublished data. (This table was prepared July 1995.)

Table 209.—Graduate enrollment in science and engineering programs in institutions of higher education, by field of study: United States and outlying areas, fall 1981 to fall 1992

Field of engineering or science	1981	1982	1983	1984[1]	1985[1]	1986[1]	1987[1]	1988	1989	1990	1991	1992	Percent change, 1985 to 1992
1	2	3	4	5	6	7	8	9	10	11	12	13	14
Total, all fields	378,104	384,872	392,376	396,449	405,596	416,577	422,585	425,932	436,071	454,065	472,950	495,937	22.3
Engineering, total	80,479	84,581	91,111	92,780	96,214	102,135	104,104	103,137	104,150	107,728	113,300	118,047	22.7
Aerospace	1,883	1,941	2,305	2,340	2,538	2,804	3,015	3,223	3,454	3,866	4,052	4,036	59.0
Agricultural	802	875	969	954	941	1,054	1,063	1,039	1,031	936	978	989	5.1
Biomedical	1,057	1,116	1,244	1,345	1,373	1,549	1,689	1,755	1,919	2,130	2,233	2,479	80.6
Chemical	6,496	7,189	7,563	7,373	7,150	7,012	7,111	6,618	6,460	6,735	7,127	7,415	3.7
Civil	14,515	14,510	14,921	15,203	14,916	14,987	14,718	14,822	14,919	15,553	17,356	19,385	30.0
Electrical	20,193	22,017	25,116	26,198	28,203	29,969	31,399	32,035	33,257	33,722	34,973	36,272	28.6
Engineering science	1,965	2,130	2,261	2,153	2,098	2,362	2,386	2,077	2,020	2,154	2,218		5.7
Industrial	10,026	9,870	9,373	9,535	10,805	11,843	12,416	11,638	11,328	11,505	12,832	13,735	27.1
Mechanical	10,618	11,467	12,911	13,855	14,157	15,713	16,366	16,186	16,212	16,788	17,647	18,768	32.6
Metallurgical/materials	3,125	3,124	3,447	3,657	3,943	4,208	4,366	4,335	4,589	4,946	5,164	5,470	38.7
Mining	462	449	524	502	489	512	513	489	418	437	489	479	−2.0
Nuclear	1,283	1,301	1,203	1,234	1,220	1,265	1,279	1,303	1,323	1,278	1,282	1,286	5.4
Petroleum	521	586	737	744	782	747	818	742	665	670	705	737	−5.8
Other engineering	7,533	8,006	8,537	7,687	7,599	8,110	7,008	6,566	6,498	7,142	6,308	4,778	−37.1
All sciences, total	297,625	300,291	301,265	303,669	309,382	314,442	318,481	322,795	331,921	346,337	359,650	377,890	22.1
Physical sciences, total	27,382	28,199	29,456	30,056	30,981	32,248	32,730	32,962	33,619	34,135	34,799	35,496	14.6
Astronomy	597	632	618	639	671	689	722	731	789	810	829	869	29.5
Chemistry	16,347	17,015	17,796	17,752	18,300	18,737	18,819	18,572	18,812	19,101	19,388	19,904	8.8
Physics	10,150	10,306	10,806	11,331	11,672	12,439	12,807	13,308	13,657	13,868	14,140	14,264	22.2
Other physical sciences	288	246	236	334	338	383	382	351	361	356	442	459	35.8
Earth, atmospheric, and ocean sciences	14,422	15,174	15,590	15,655	15,591	15,210	14,522	14,067	13,830	14,195	14,720	15,609	0.1
Atmospheric sciences	882	889	896	907	964	961	952	940	912	929	968	1,089	13.0
Geosciences	8,808	9,621	10,321	10,370	10,294	9,819	8,998	8,463	8,052	7,694	7,583	7,759	−24.6
Oceanography	2,082	2,091	2,063	2,102	2,081	2,128	2,127	2,033	2,207	2,333	2,386	2,530	21.6
Other environmental sciences	2,650	2,573	2,310	2,276	2,252	2,302	2,445	2,631	2,659	3,239	3,783	4,231	87.9
Mathematical sciences, total	15,915	17,199	17,380	17,459	17,591	17,967	18,524	19,103	19,308	19,801	19,978	20,375	15.8
Mathematics and applied mathematics	—	—	—	—	15,465	15,633	16,031	16,516	16,784	17,123	17,232	17,426	12.7
Statistics					2,126	2,334	2,493	2,587	2,524	2,678	2,746	2,949	38.7
Computer sciences, total	16,437	19,812	23,616	25,810	29,602	31,175	31,901	32,053	32,320	34,349	34,788	36,936	24.8
Life sciences, total	103,124	102,789	102,228	103,767	103,976	106,025	106,498	108,707	112,572	117,134	122,574	129,830	24.9
Agricultural sciences, total	12,100	12,314	12,396	12,181	11,364	11,281	10,942	10,940	10,979	11,125	11,315	11,609	2.2
Biological sciences, total	46,979	46,310	45,771	45,892	46,201	46,873	46,901	47,682	48,970	50,090	51,875	54,437	17.8
Anatomy	1,072	1,074	1,037	1,029	993	973	1,016	1,056	1,078	996	1,051	1,031	3.8
Biochemistry	4,061	4,124	4,205	4,462	4,656	4,875	4,813	4,921	5,082	5,053	5,207	5,386	15.7
Biology	14,203	13,397	13,051	12,890	12,710	12,678	12,331	12,393	12,761	13,035	13,299	13,897	9.3
Biometry/epidemiology	1,182	1,166	1,156	1,004	1,360	1,434	1,556	1,682	1,722	1,871	2,032	2,369	74.2
Biophysics	463	440	450	433	441	547	591	592	655	642	697	751	70.3
Botany	3,498	3,644	3,299	3,251	3,188	3,149	3,005	2,936	2,844	2,720	2,675	2,690	−15.6
Cell biology	1,018	1,143	1,182	1,256	1,429	1,716	1,964	2,078	2,234	2,555	2,809	3,093	116.4
Ecology	1,101	1,051	1,007	1,088	1,028	1,022	963	999	1,084	1,136	1,180	1,301	26.6
Entomology/parasitology	1,664	1,540	1,475	1,438	1,342	1,306	1,244	1,240	1,181	1,173	1,171	1,193	−11.1
Genetics	937	990	1,035	1,059	1,120	1,262	1,314	1,289	1,365	1,408	1,520	1,643	46.7
Microbiology	4,070	4,130	4,262	4,326	4,446	4,372	4,452	4,773	4,827	4,872	4,936	5,008	12.6
Nutrition	4,355	4,359	4,351	4,277	4,314	4,321	4,288	4,228	4,259	4,268	4,251	4,245	−1.6
Pathology	1,444	1,460	1,449	1,454	1,321	1,362	1,397	1,357	1,393	1,386	1,492	1,517	14.8
Pharmacology	2,024	2,084	2,069	2,050	2,107	2,078	2,072	2,124	2,267	2,352	2,432	2,545	20.8
Physiology	2,144	2,058	1,994	2,160	2,211	2,220	2,213	2,220	2,206	2,236	2,332	2,319	4.9
Zoology	2,625	2,503	2,430	2,303	2,135	2,083	2,113	2,034	2,088	2,109	2,196	2,203	3.2
Other biosciences	1,118	1,147	1,319	1,412	1,400	1,475	1,569	1,760	1,924	2,278	2,595	3,246	131.9
Health fields, total	44,045	44,165	44,061	45,694	46,411	47,871	48,655	50,085	52,623	55,919	59,384	63,784	37.4
Medical fields	9,027	8,758	8,565	8,714	9,280	9,227	9,730	10,110	10,243	10,962	11,564	12,470	34.4
Other health fields	35,018	35,407	35,496	36,980	37,131	38,644	38,925	39,975	42,380	44,957	47,820	51,314	38.2
Dentistry	942	836	776	854	833	947	1,062	1,083	1,004	956	1,016	1,067	28.1
Nursing	15,703	16,254	16,945	17,987	17,977	18,424	18,479	18,910	19,733	21,245	22,116	23,333	29.8
Pharmaceutical sciences	2,549	2,519	2,641	2,519	2,553	2,682	2,607	2,613	2,834	2,938	3,011	2,846	11.5
Speech pathology/audiology	8,596	8,592	7,836	7,745	7,986	7,957	7,497	7,668	8,088	8,510	9,121	10,017	25.4
Veterinary sciences	481	471	466	557	637	630	731	752	801	900	894	942	47.9
Other health related	6,747	6,735	6,832	7,318	7,145	8,004	8,549	8,949	9,920	10,408	11,662	13,109	83.5
Psychology, total	40,691	40,082	40,912	40,937	41,173	41,417	42,750	44,127	46,003	48,678	51,791	53,820	30.7
Psychology, general	—	—	—	—	—	—	—	15,479	17,126	18,524	21,230	23,117	—
Clinical psychology	—	—	—	—	—	—	—	20,842	19,726	20,383	19,855	18,738	—
Other psychology	—	—	—	—	—	—	—	7,806	9,151	9,771	10,706	11,965	—
Social sciences, total	79,654	77,036	72,083	69,985	70,468	70,400	71,556	71,776	74,269	78,045	81,000	85,824	21.8
Agricultural economics	2,262	2,267	2,295	2,279	2,268	2,248	2,203	2,259	2,276	2,273	2,364	2,513	10.8
Anthropology	6,118	5,948	5,644	5,590	5,631	5,835	5,835	5,945	6,128	6,494	6,729	7,129	26.6
Economics (except agricultural)	13,344	13,735	13,064	12,507	12,430	12,103	12,020	12,036	12,143	12,306	12,728	13,266	6.7
Geography	3,187	3,166	3,060	3,035	2,936	3,055	3,223	3,208	3,479	3,530	3,760	4,097	39.5
History and philosophy of science	248	256	253	274	272	266	294	288	304	331	337	360	32.4
Linguistics	3,139	2,803	3,022	3,160	3,055	3,109	3,282	3,243	3,285	3,404	3,425	3,288	7.6
Political science	30,791	29,887	28,050	25,921	27,012	27,251	27,601	27,859	29,291	30,595	31,887	33,770	25.0
Sociology	7,816	7,246	6,920	6,740	6,586	5,532	6,986	7,087	7,393	7,784	8,292	8,861	34.5
Sociology/anthropology	1,110	1,133	1,200	1,075	1,034	1,021	982	991	1,022	1,212	1,032	1,123	8.6
Other social sciences	11,639	10,595	8,575	9,404	9,244	9,010	9,130	8,860	8,947	10,116	10,446	11,417	23.5

—Data not available.

[1] Includes estimates for master's degree granting institutions which were surveyed on a sample basis from 1985 through 1987.

NOTE.—Some data have been revised from previously published figures. Because of rounding, details may not add to totals.

SOURCE: National Science Foundation, Division of Science Resources Studies, *Academic Science/Engineering: Graduate Enrollment and Support, Fall 1992.* (This table was prepared April 1994.)

Table 210.—Institutions of higher education and branches, by type, control, and size of enrollment: Fall 1993 and fall 1994 [1]

Control of institution branch and size of total enrollment	All institutions		Universities		All other 4-year institutions		2-year institutions	
	Number[2]	Enrollment	Number[2]	Enrollment	Number[2]	Enrollment	Number[2]	Enrollment
1	2	3	4	5	6	7	8	9
Fall 1993 [3]								
Total	3,546	14,304,803	156	3,022,728	1,994	5,716,208	1,396	5,565,867
Under 200	363	39,145	0	0	252	26,224	111	12,921
200 to 499	457	155,431	0	0	241	83,526	216	71,905
500 to 999	482	354,224	0	0	326	240,474	156	113,750
1,000 to 2,499	849	1,402,827	0	0	564	912,092	285	490,735
2,500 to 4,999	538	1,862,075	5	20,965	270	931,534	263	909,576
5,000 to 9,999	449	3,176,828	27	212,373	205	1,420,813	217	1,543,642
10,000 to 19,999	283	3,887,575	55	772,721	113	1,532,665	115	1,582,189
20,000 to 29,999	95	2,302,829	45	1,117,177	22	534,112	28	651,540
30,000 or more	30	1,123,869	24	899,492	1	34,768	5	189,609
Fall 1994 [1]								
Total	3,561	14,278,790	156	3,009,072	2,008	5,740,008	1,397	5,529,710
Under 200	377	41,590	0	0	252	26,625	125	14,965
200 to 499	417	140,028	0	0	219	74,393	198	65,635
500 to 999	507	371,102	0	0	357	263,286	150	107,816
1,000 to 2,499	864	1,438,335	0	0	567	924,194	297	514,141
2,500 to 4,999	536	1,851,721	4	15,975	272	941,366	260	894,380
5,000 to 9,999	459	3,247,731	26	198,321	208	1,446,400	225	1,603,010
10,000 to 19,999	281	3,889,296	57	793,929	112	1,540,219	112	1,555,148
20,000 to 29,999	92	2,230,957	47	1,163,390	20	487,482	25	580,085
30,000 or more	28	1,068,030	22	837,457	1	36,043	5	194,530
Public institutions	1,595	11,133,680	94	2,244,636	505	3,580,577	996	5,308,467
Under 200	7	1,086	0	0	0	0	7	1,086
200 to 499	31	11,187	0	0	10	4,002	21	7,185
500 to 999	114	87,064	0	0	26	20,036	88	67,028
1,000 to 2,499	344	602,845	0	0	84	142,576	260	460,269
2,500 to 4,999	370	1,289,233	0	0	114	409,917	256	879,316
5,000 to 9,999	373	2,660,188	4	35,403	146	1,036,054	223	1,588,731
10,000 to 19,999	244	3,404,806	28	405,191	104	1,444,467	112	1,555,148
20,000 to 29,999	86	2,076,177	42	1,033,521	20	487,482	24	555,174
30,000 or more	26	1,001,094	20	770,521	1	36,043	5	194,530
Private institutions	1,966	3,145,110	62	764,436	1,503	2,159,431	401	221,243
Under 200	370	40,504	0	0	252	26,625	118	13,879
200 to 499	386	128,841	0	0	209	70,391	177	58,450
500 to 999	393	284,038	0	0	331	243,250	62	40,788
1,000 to 2,499	520	835,490	0	0	483	781,618	37	53,872
2,500 to 4,999	166	562,488	4	15,975	158	531,449	4	15,064
5,000 to 9,999	86	587,543	22	162,918	62	410,346	2	14,279
10,000 to 19,999	37	484,490	29	388,738	8	95,752	0	0
20,000 to 29,999	6	154,780	5	129,869	0	0	1	24,911
30,000 or more	2	66,936	2	66,936	0	0	0	0

[1] These preliminary data represent the institution branches and enrollments reported in the "Fall Enrollment" survey.

[2] Some institutions do not report separate enrollment data for each branch campus. For this reason, counts of institutions in this table are somewhat lower than figures appearing in other tables.

[3] Data revised from previously published figures.

SOURCE: U.S. Department of Education, National Center for Education Statistics, Integrated Postsecondary Education Data System (IPEDS), "Fall Enrollment" surveys. (This table was prepared December 1995.)

Table 211.—Enrollment of the 120 largest college and university campuses: [1] Fall 1994

Institution	State	Rank	Control[2]	Type[3]	Total enrollment, fall 1994	Institution	State	Rank	Control[2]	Type[3]	Total enrollment, fall 1994
1	2	3	4	5	6	1	2	3	4	5	6
University of Minnesota, Twin Cities	Minn.	1	1	1	51,478	University of Kansas, Main Campus	Kans.	61	1	1	25,336
Ohio State University, Main Campus	Ohio	2	1	1	49,542	Austin Community College	Tex.	62	1	2	25,276
University of Texas, Austin	Tex.	3	1	1	47,957	Northeastern University	Mass.	63	2	1	25,086
Miami-Dade Community College	Fla.	4	1	2	47,069	University of Illinois at Chicago	Ill.	64	1	1	25,040
Houston Community College System	Tex.	5	1	2	45,893	Iowa State University	Iowa	65	1	1	24,990
Arizona State University	Ariz.	6	1	1	42,189	SUNY at Buffalo	N.Y.	66	1	1	24,943
Texas A&M University	Tex.	7	1	1	42,018	International Correspondence Schools	Pa.	67	2	2	24,911
Michigan State University	Mich.	8	1	1	40,254	University of Massachusetts at Amherst	Mass.	68	1	1	24,825
University of Wisconsin, Madison	Wisc.	9	1	1	39,361	Harvard University	Mass.	69	2	1	24,806
University of Illinois, Urbana Campus	Ill.	10	1	1	38,545	University of New Mexico, Main Campus	N.Mex.	70	1	1	24,572
Pennsylvania State U., Main Campus	Pa.	11	1	1	38,294	University of North Carolina, Chapel Hill	N.C.	71	1	1	24,565
University of Florida	Fla.	12	1	1	38,277	University of Akron, Main Campus	Ohio	72	1	1	24,488
Northern Virginia Community College	Va.	13	1	2	37,655	California State University, Northridge	Calif.	73	1	1	24,310
University of Michigan, Ann Arbor	Mich.	14	1	1	36,543	Texas Tech University	Tex.	74	1	1	24,083
Purdue University, Main Campus	Ind.	15	1	1	36,172	Cuyahoga Community College District	Ohio	75	1	2	24,079
University of South Florida	Fla.	16	1	1	36,043	University of Nebraska, Lincoln	Nebr.	76	1	1	23,854
Indiana University, Bloomington	Ind.	17	1	1	35,594	Georgia State University	Ga.	77	1	1	23,730
New York University	N.Y.	18	2	1	35,425	University of Kentucky	Ky.	78	1	1	23,622
University of Arizona	Ariz.	19	1	1	35,306	Central Michigan University	Mich.	79	1	1	23,390
University of California, Los Angeles	Calif.	20	1	1	35,110	University of Texas, Arlington	Tex.	80	1	1	23,373
University of Washington	Wash.	21	1	1	33,719	Eastern Michigan University	Mich.	81	1	1	23,321
Rutgers University, New Brunswick	N.J.	22	1	1	33,464	Southern Illinois University, Carbondale	Ill.	82	1	1	23,162
Community College of the Air Force[4]	Ala.	23	1	2	33,107	Portland Community College	Oreg.	83	1	2	23,158
Wayne State University	Mich.	24	1	1	32,906	University of Toledo	Ohio	84	1	1	23,107
U. of Maryland, College Park Campus	Md.	25	1	1	32,493	Milwaukee Area Technical College	Wisc.	85	1	2	23,010
Brigham Young University	Utah	26	2	1	31,511	Northern Illinois University	Ill.	86	1	1	22,881
University of Houston, University Park	Tex.	27	1	1	31,299	Valencia Community College	Fla.	87	1	2	22,727
College of Du Page	Ill.	28	1	2	30,806	California State University, Sacramento	Calif.	88	1	1	22,726
University of California, Berkeley	Calif.	29	1	1	29,634	University of Pennsylvania	Pa.	89	2	1	22,720
Temple University	Pa.	30	1	1	29,616	De Anza College	Calif.	90	1	2	22,634
Florida State University	Fla.	31	1	1	29,527	University of Wisconsin, Milwaukee	Wisc.	91	1	1	22,604
University of Georgia	Ga.	32	1	1	29,469	West Virginia University	W.Va.	92	1	1	22,500
Boston University	Mass.	33	2	1	29,072	University of Connecticut	Conn.	93	1	1	22,466
University of Cincinnati, Main Campus	Ohio	34	1	1	28,758	University of California, Davis	Calif.	94	1	1	22,442
San Diego State University	Calif.	35	1	1	28,372	Mount San Antonio College	Calif.	95	1	2	22,274
North Carolina State Universitiy, Raleigh	N.C.	36	1	1	28,223	University of Missouri, Columbia	Mo.	96	1	1	22,175
University of Southern California	Calif.	37	2	1	28,185	Saint Petersburg Junior College	Fla.	97	1	2	22,112
Pima Community College	Ariz.	38	1	2	27,960	California State University, Fullerton	Calif.	98	1	1	22,097
University of Colorado at Boulder	Colo.	39	1	1	27,862	University of Oklahoma, Norman Campus	Okla.	99	1	1	22,043
University of Iowa	Iowa	40	1	1	27,671	Nassau Community College	N.Y.	100	1	2	21,955
Colorado State University	Colo.	41	1	1	27,130	Florida Community College, Jacksonville	Fla.	101	1	2	21,840
University of Utah	Utah	42	1	1	26,906	Pasadena City College	Calif.	102	1	2	21,787
Indiana U. - Purdue U. at Indianapolis	Ind.	43	1	1	26,766	George Mason University	Va.	103	1	1	21,774
University of South Carolina, Columbia	S.C.	44	1	1	26,754	El Camino College	Calif.	104	1	2	21,763
Florida International University	Fla.	45	1	1	26,547	Orange Coast College	Calif.	105	1	2	21,662
City College of San Francisco	Calif.	46	1	2	26,356	University of Delaware	Del.	106	1	1	21,585
University of Pittsburgh, Main Campus	Pa.	47	1	1	26,328	Virginia Commonwealth University	Va.	107	1	1	21,523
Oakland Community College	Mich.	48	1	2	26,324	University of Virginia, Main Campus	Va.	108	1	1	21,421
San Jose State University	Calif.	49	1	1	26,299	Kent State University, Main Campus	Ohio	109	1	1	21,413
California State University, Long Beach	Calif.	50	1	1	26,277	Auburn University, Main Campus	Ala.	110	1	1	21,226
San Francisco State University	Calif.	51	1	1	26,260	Southwest Texas State University	Tex.	111	1	1	20,889
Tarrant County Junior College District	Tex.	52	1	2	26,257	Rancho Santiago College	Calif.	112	1	2	20,875
Broward Community College	Fla.	53	1	2	26,151	Santa Rosa Junior College	Calif.	113	1	2	20,869
La. St. U. & A&M & Hebert Laws Center	La.	54	1	1	26,010	University of Louisville	Ky.	114	1	1	20,721
University of Tennessee, Knoxville	Tenn.	55	1	1	25,914	Ball State University	Ind.	115	1	1	20,390
Virginia Polytechnic Inst. and State Univ.	Va.	56	1	1	25,842	Utah State University	Utah	116	1	1	20,371
Macomb Community College	Mich.	57	1	2	25,809	Mesa Community College	Ariz.	117	1	2	20,110
Western Michigan University	Mich.	58	1	1	25,673	Santa Monica College	Calif.	118	1	2	20,102
University of North Texas	Tex.	59	1	1	25,605	Hillsborough Community College	Fla.	119	1	2	20,084
University of Central Florida	Fla.	60	1	1	25,592	University of Hawaii at Manoa	Hi.	120	1	1	20,010

[1] College and university campuses ranked by fall 1994 preliminary enrollment data.

[2] Publicly controlled institutions are identified by a "1," privately controlled, by a "2."

[3] The types of institutions are identified as follows: "1" for 4-year institutions and "2" for 2-year institutions.

[4] Estimated.

NOTE.—Excludes nonreporting institutions and also institutions that reported enrollment data with other branch campuses.

SOURCE: U.S. Department of Education, National Center for Education Statistics, Integrated Postsecondary Education Data System (IPEDS), "Fall Enrollment, 1994" survey. (This table was prepared July 1996.)

Table 212.—Selected statistics for college and university campuses enrolling more than 14,600 students in 1994

Line no.	Institution	State	Con-trol[1]	Type[2]	Total enrollment, fall 1987	Total enrollment, fall 1992	Total enrollment, fall 1993	Total enrollment, fall 1994	Enrollment, by sex, fall 1994 Men	Enrollment, by sex, fall 1994 Women	Enrollment, by attendance status, fall 1994 Full-time	Enrollment, by attendance status, fall 1994 Part-time
1	2	3	4	5	6	7	8	9	10	11	12	13
—	United States, all institutions	—	—	—	12,766,642	14,487,359	14,304,803	14,278,790	6,371,898	7,906,892	8,137,776	6,141,014
—	Colleges with enrollment over 14,600	—	—	—	4,766,232	5,215,883	5,100,539	5,086,648	2,388,282	2,698,366	2,989,704	2,096,944
1	Auburn University, Main Campus	Ala.	1	1	19,363	21,551	21,363	21,226	11,478	9,748	17,953	3,273
2	University of Alabama	Ala.	1	1	17,166	19,233	19,480	19,306	9,320	9,986	15,628	3,678
3	University of Alabama at Birmingham	Ala.	1	1	13,479	15,735	15,913	15,362	6,946	8,416	9,606	5,756
4	University of Alaska, Anchorage	Alaska	1	1	4,616	17,257	17,275	16,189	6,461	9,728	6,526	9,663
5	Arizona State University	Ariz.	1	1	42,968	43,628	41,250	42,189	21,229	20,960	29,061	13,128
6	Glendale Community College	Ariz.	1	2	15,826	18,618	17,520	18,033	8,135	9,898	5,325	12,708
7	Mesa Community College	Ariz.	1	2	19,443	20,911	19,508	20,110	9,504	10,606	6,565	13,545
8	Northern Arizona University	Ariz.	1	1	13,396	18,485	18,817	19,242	8,097	11,145	12,970	6,272
9	Pima Community College	Ariz.	1	2	24,866	30,175	28,268	27,960	12,510	15,450	7,256	20,704
10	University of Arizona	Ariz.	1	1	33,009	35,118	35,279	35,306	17,744	17,562	27,186	8,120
11	American River College	Calif.	1	2	19,318	21,416	20,377	19,766	8,639	11,127	4,657	15,109
12	Calif Polytechnic State U., San Luis Obispo	Calif.	1	1	16,049	16,373	15,449	15,440	8,909	6,531	13,701	1,739
13	California State Polytechnic U., Pomona	Calif.	1	1	18,317	18,294	17,050	16,304	9,379	6,925	11,079	5,225
14	California State University, Fresno	Calif.	1	1	18,364	18,902	17,956	17,293	7,924	9,369	13,647	3,646
15	California State University, Fullerton	Calif.	1	1	24,317	24,402	22,565	22,097	9,576	12,521	13,583	8,514
16	California State University, Long Beach	Calif.	1	1	34,926	30,067	27,073	26,277	11,928	14,349	16,749	9,528
17	California State University, Los Angeles	Calif.	1	1	20,977	19,399	17,788	18,224	7,523	10,701	10,743	7,481
18	California State University, Northridge	Calif.	1	1	29,719	29,088	27,282	24,310	10,389	13,921	15,288	9,022
19	California State University, Sacramento	Calif.	1	1	24,128	24,466	23,316	22,726	10,126	12,600	15,394	7,332
20	Cerritos College	Calif.	1	2	18,110	21,471	19,653	19,571	8,548	11,023	4,369	15,202
21	City College of San Francisco	Calif.	1	2	24,641	29,708	26,630	26,356	12,009	14,347	7,304	19,052
22	De Anza College	Calif.	1	2	25,036	24,779	22,701	22,634	10,451	12,183	7,209	15,425
23	Diablo Valley College	Calif.	1	2	20,043	21,200	18,888	18,075	8,199	9,876	6,176	11,899
24	East Los Angeles College	Calif.	1	2	12,446	15,476	14,470	15,257	6,416	8,841	4,395	10,862
25	El Camino College	Calif.	1	2	25,485	24,469	22,953	21,763	9,757	12,006	5,810	15,953
26	Fresno City College	Calif.	1	2	15,177	18,431	16,554	16,962	7,974	8,988	5,477	11,485
27	Fullerton College	Calif.	1	2	17,235	20,432	18,387	18,141	8,715	9,426	5,070	13,071
28	Grossmont College	Calif.	1	2	15,715	16,332	14,789	14,614	6,355	8,259	5,180	9,434
29	Long Beach City College	Calif.	1	2	20,585	19,861	18,745	18,438	8,248	10,190	4,485	13,953
30	Los Angeles City College	Calif.	1	2	14,223	17,017	15,378	15,433	7,107	8,326	5,172	10,261
31	Los Angeles Pierce College	Calif.	1	2	18,316	18,697	15,702	14,629	6,705	7,924	4,163	10,466
32	Los Angeles Valley College	Calif.	1	2	18,139	19,033	16,684	16,290	7,125	9,165	3,895	12,395
33	Mount San Antonio College	Calif.	1	2	19,840	23,073	22,438	22,274	10,276	11,998	6,716	15,558
34	Orange Coast College	Calif.	1	2	24,167	23,822	21,928	21,662	10,793	10,869	6,447	15,215
35	Palomar College	Calif.	1	2	15,404	18,884	18,983	18,659	8,972	9,687	4,974	13,685
36	Pasadena City College	Calif.	1	2	20,178	22,024	22,248	21,787	9,770	12,017	6,528	15,259
37	Rancho Santiago College	Calif.	1	2	20,606	25,660	20,920	20,875	11,421	9,454	5,063	15,812
38	Riverside Community College	Calif.	1	2	15,033	21,902	20,293	19,263	8,027	11,236	4,322	14,941
39	Sacramento City College	Calif.	1	2	13,893	16,968	16,052	16,154	6,806	9,348	5,015	11,139
40	Saddleback College	Calif.	1	2	14,772	17,990	16,649	16,736	6,960	9,776	4,058	12,678
41	San Diego Mesa College	Calif.	1	2	21,336	21,446	20,217	19,284	8,897	10,387	5,337	13,947
42	San Diego State University	Calif.	1	1	36,280	30,887	28,131	28,372	13,087	15,285	19,705	8,667
43	San Francisco State University	Calif.	1	1	26,002	26,528	25,713	26,260	10,948	15,312	16,748	9,512
44	San Joaquin Delta College	Calif.	1	2	14,988	16,210	15,806	14,895	6,422	8,473	5,013	9,882
45	San Jose State University	Calif.	1	1	27,549	29,625	27,057	26,299	12,554	13,745	16,507	9,792
46	Santa Monica College	Calif.	1	2	17,413	23,405	21,768	20,102	8,838	11,264	6,166	13,936
47	Santa Rosa Junior College	Calif.	1	2	21,305	23,390	20,428	20,869	8,817	12,052	6,265	14,604
48	Southwestern College	Calif.	1	2	12,439	16,282	15,384	15,116	7,012	8,104	4,931	10,185
49	Stanford University	Calif.	2	1	14,132	15,674	15,980	16,049	9,616	6,433	12,655	3,394
50	University of California, Berkeley	Calif.	1	1	32,055	30,616	30,341	29,634	15,958	13,676	26,818	2,816
51	University of California, Davis	Calif.	1	1	20,847	22,880	22,476	22,442	11,195	11,247	20,221	2,221
52	University of California, Irvine	Calif.	1	1	15,139	17,181	16,815	17,073	8,553	8,520	15,950	1,123
53	University of California, Los Angeles	Calif.	1	1	35,435	35,403	34,446	35,110	18,202	16,908	32,812	2,298
54	University of California, San Diego	Calif.	1	1	16,589	18,239	17,851	17,774	9,366	8,408	16,843	931
55	University of California, Santa Barbara	Calif.	1	1	17,879	18,651	18,581	17,834	8,831	9,003	17,084	750
56	University of Southern California	Calif.	2	1	30,504	28,586	27,658	28,185	15,526	12,659	21,081	7,104
57	Colorado State University	Colo.	1	1	19,192	27,306	27,384	27,130	13,422	13,708	19,444	7,686
58	Metropolitan State College of Denver	Colo.	1	1	15,710	17,617	17,721	17,624	8,070	9,554	9,396	8,228
59	University of Colorado at Boulder	Colo.	1	1	23,551	28,524	28,352	27,862	14,989	12,873	21,014	6,848
60	University of Connecticut	Conn.	1	1	24,552	24,131	23,182	22,466	11,188	11,278	15,832	6,634
61	University of Delaware	Del.	1	1	19,067	21,136	21,735	21,585	9,745	11,840	15,740	5,845
62	George Washington University	D.C.	2	1	19,500	18,600	18,992	19,298	10,162	9,136	11,016	8,282
63	Broward Community College	Fla.	1	2	21,621	25,348	25,714	26,151	10,191	15,960	7,552	18,599
64	Florida Atlantic University	Fla.	1	1	10,892	14,673	15,769	17,487	7,220	10,267	7,562	9,925
65	Florida Community College, Jacksonville	Fla.	1	2	11,998	21,459	21,228	21,840	9,220	12,620	5,334	16,506
66	Florida International University	Fla.	1	1	16,619	23,093	24,321	26,547	11,382	15,165	12,607	13,940
67	Florida State University	Fla.	1	1	23,826	28,424	28,575	29,527	13,583	15,944	23,653	5,874
68	Hillsborough Community College	Fla.	1	2	14,246	21,275	21,497	20,084	8,531	11,553	4,442	15,642
69	Miami-Dade Community College	Fla.	1	2	42,663	51,768	48,232	47,069	19,419	27,650	15,607	31,462
70	Palm Beach Community College	Fla.	1	2	13,084	18,193	18,586	19,022	7,353	11,669	4,816	14,206
71	Saint Petersburg Junior College	Fla.	1	2	18,764	22,297	22,799	22,112	8,563	13,549	6,813	15,299
72	University of Central Florida	Fla.	1	1	17,527	21,873	23,692	25,592	12,187	13,405	14,468	11,124
73	University of Florida	Fla.	1	1	33,568	36,447	37,324	38,277	20,533	17,744	32,334	5,943
74	University of South Florida	Fla.	1	1	29,069	34,145	34,768	36,043	15,290	20,753	18,070	17,973
75	Valencia Community College	Fla.	1	2	13,773	22,081	22,593	22,727	9,569	13,158	7,506	15,221

Table 212.—Selected statistics for college and university campuses enrolling more than 14,600 students in 1994—Continued

Enrollment, by level, fall 1994		Earned degrees conferred, 1993–94					Financial statistics, 1993–94, in thousands			Full-time-equivalent enrollment, fall 1993	Full-time-equivalent enrollment, fall 1994	Line no.
Undergraduate	Postbaccalaureate	Associate	Bachelor's	Master's	Doctor's	First professional	Current-fund revenues	Current-fund expenditures	Educational and general expenditures			
14	15	16	17	18	19	20	21	22	23	24	25	26
12,262,608	2,016,182	542,449	1,169,275	387,070	43,185	75,418	$179,226,601	$173,350,617	$136,024,350	10,351,415	10,348,072	—
4,167,712	918,936	122,809	497,869	177,943	28,873	26,999	³74,461,986	³71,799,241	³55,370,200	3,723,621	3,749,845	—
17,727	3,499	—	3,990	656	153	88	331,312	324,438	283,686	19,386	19,206	1
14,995	4,311	—	3,043	963	176	172	275,220	260,680	214,393	17,393	17,034	2
10,805	4,557	—	1,582	859	107	238	890,942	832,736	410,837	12,183	11,865	3
15,660	529	645	723	173	—	—	111,266	111,787	103,991	10,769	10,411	4
31,198	10,991	—	5,766	1,877	258	165	461,740	441,322	385,268	33,067	34,128	5
18,033	—	606	—	—	—	—	38,487	34,693	31,686	9,454	9,593	6
20,110	—	853	—	—	—	—	50,753	43,877	39,315	10,691	11,114	7
14,018	5,224	—	2,693	1,149	54	—	176,664	165,163	144,408	14,927	15,343	8
27,960	—	1,119	—	—	—	—	68,005	67,287	66,456	14,438	14,210	9
26,468	8,838	—	4,749	1,354	442	297	753,784	732,007	609,444	30,331	30,328	10
19,766	—	963	—	—	—	—	59,683	51,469	50,132	9,911	9,732	11
14,292	1,148	—	3,411	303	—	—	149,632	147,169	133,092	14,333	14,385	12
14,660	1,644	—	2,650	323	—	—	131,167	127,465	124,671	13,800	13,140	13
14,291	3,002	—	3,090	626	—	—	145,845	138,896	132,817	15,551	15,055	14
18,346	3,751	—	4,193	770	—	—	136,281	135,326	128,848	16,968	16,918	15
21,094	5,183	—	4,593	1,090	—	—	181,631	179,604	169,913	20,810	20,455	16
13,882	4,342	—	2,272	782	1	—	128,994	126,187	121,769	13,082	13,639	17
19,393	4,917	—	4,219	824	—	—	218,062	208,533	200,839	20,893	18,800	18
18,397	4,329	—	4,327	912	—	—	161,225	160,346	154,892	18,826	18,258	19
19,571	—	1,072	—	—	—	—	55,922	53,437	48,632	9,850	9,475	20
26,356	—	1,388	—	—	—	—	121,139	116,018	111,910	13,818	13,703	21
22,634	—	1,407	—	—	—	—	—	—	—	12,327	12,390	22
18,075	—	761	—	—	—	—	49,736	49,148	44,369	10,588	10,173	23
15,257	—	569	—	—	—	—	38,887	38,027	38,027	7,347	8,043	24
21,763	—	1,230	—	—	—	—	66,030	69,370	64,084	11,701	11,168	25
16,962	—	1,234	—	—	—	—	47,562	47,598	40,569	8,662	9,335	26
18,141	—	1,022	—	—	—	—	—	—	—	9,798	9,460	27
14,614	—	881	—	—	—	—	37,947	35,397	35,397	8,353	8,349	28
18,438	—	818	—	—	—	—	58,210	56,969	56,450	9,255	9,172	29
15,433	—	364	—	—	—	—	44,159	42,469	42,469	8,405	8,618	30
14,629	—	668	—	—	—	—	44,450	43,400	43,400	8,236	7,678	31
16,290	—	472	—	—	—	—	41,929	40,592	40,592	8,042	8,058	32
22,274	—	1,047	—	—	—	—	74,293	68,679	67,960	12,095	11,942	33
21,662	—	878	—	—	—	—	75,850	75,353	69,210	11,947	11,557	34
18,659	—	827	—	—	—	—	64,268	63,064	57,665	9,807	9,571	35
21,787	—	766	—	—	—	—	63,710	64,393	64,393	11,621	11,653	36
20,875	—	990	—	—	—	—	77,795	66,259	62,127	10,281	10,374	37
19,263	—	1,090	—	—	—	—	59,736	52,529	46,984	10,279	9,340	38
16,154	—	773	—	—	—	—	51,460	44,378	43,225	8,753	8,756	39
16,736	—	857	—	—	—	—	86,388	80,976	78,276	8,355	8,316	40
19,284	—	226	—	—	—	—	45,878	37,333	31,543	9,989	10,022	41
22,590	5,782	—	5,034	1,400	25	—	216,393	206,429	194,614	22,627	23,069	42
19,902	6,358	—	3,692	1,295	11	—	189,048	180,692	172,373	19,890	20,449	43
14,895	—	772	—	—	—	—	50,695	50,421	45,722	8,776	8,332	44
20,608	5,691	—	4,271	1,308	—	—	187,408	183,834	174,348	20,652	20,316	45
20,102	—	1,036	—	—	—	—	78,698	68,314	58,369	11,529	10,847	46
20,869	—	872	—	—	—	—	63,414	66,446	62,684	11,021	11,170	47
15,116	—	753	—	—	—	—	40,950	44,981	39,865	8,362	8,352	48
7,075	8,974	—	1,747	1,972	560	264	1,654,658	1,624,321	1,058,331	13,940	13,978	49
21,005	8,629	—	5,740	1,826	896	295	841,464	842,014	779,260	28,388	27,909	50
17,300	5,142	—	4,304	622	323	367	1,081,464	1,025,957	607,398	21,157	21,105	51
13,455	3,618	—	3,090	599	172	90	630,673	604,958	404,890	16,159	16,390	52
23,619	11,491	—	5,622	2,061	620	565	1,709,295	1,677,695	1,085,413	33,100	33,699	53
14,325	3,449	—	3,500	459	285	140	1,037,397	1,000,423	659,138	17,353	17,213	54
15,525	2,309	—	4,364	437	222	—	331,861	315,034	268,663	17,944	17,379	55
15,082	13,103	—	3,194	2,589	415	637	955,220	927,951	725,475	23,337	23,820	56
20,502	6,628	—	3,288	791	175	127	361,253	353,261	300,946	22,435	22,385	57
17,624	—	—	1,954	—	—	—	66,412	66,337	64,244	12,843	12,716	58
21,534	6,328	—	4,429	1,126	306	151	453,569	434,635	377,070	24,038	23,607	59
14,719	7,747	—	3,082	1,258	246	204	353,546	352,160	296,216	19,019	18,379	60
18,375	3,210	15	3,056	585	121	—	364,240	344,729	295,969	18,139	18,036	61
7,205	12,093	24	1,255	2,304	152	601	712,243	693,494	331,137	13,664	14,246	62
26,151	—	1,902	—	—	—	—	72,872	75,295	68,725	13,663	13,799	63
13,962	3,525	29	2,203	565	38	—	135,087	129,915	115,227	10,328	11,452	64
21,840	—	1,833	—	—	—	—	83,145	82,136	79,877	10,630	10,878	65
21,138	5,409	—	3,331	775	26	—	171,192	170,914	153,496	16,638	18,071	66
23,069	6,458	666	5,368	1,398	274	122	383,935	379,057	314,338	25,036	25,914	67
20,084	—	1,920	—	—	—	—	54,108	51,217	47,073	10,385	9,696	68
47,069	—	4,533	—	—	—	—	209,280	213,941	201,626	27,351	26,174	69
19,022	—	1,670	—	—	—	—	45,458	44,692	43,413	9,454	9,588	70
22,112	—	2,591	—	—	—	—	57,545	57,713	57,478	12,357	11,952	71
20,860	4,732	215	4,302	842	46	—	170,507	165,573	144,006	17,276	18,801	72
28,479	9,798	1,045	5,651	1,735	442	702	849,746	857,973	779,049	33,603	34,618	73
26,445	9,598	297	5,296	1,596	121	91	392,313	388,347	354,979	24,177	25,044	74
22,727	—	2,431	—	—	—	—	60,836	59,820	53,690	12,322	12,618	75

Table 212.—Selected statistics for college and university campuses enrolling more than 14,600 students in 1994—Continued

Line no.	Institution	State	Con-trol[1]	Type[2]	Total enrollment, fall 1987	Total enrollment, fall 1992	Total enrollment, fall 1993	Total enrollment, fall 1994	Enrollment, by sex, fall 1994 Men	Enrollment, by sex, fall 1994 Women	Enrollment, by attendance status, fall 1994 Full-time	Enrollment, by attendance status, fall 1994 Part-time
1	2	3	4	5	6	7	8	9	10	11	12	13
76	DeKalb College	Ga.	1	2	9,116	15,532	16,349	16,099	6,372	9,727	5,706	10,393
77	Georgia State University	Ga.	1	1	22,070	24,050	23,605	23,730	9,867	13,863	11,581	12,149
78	University of Georgia	Ga.	1	1	26,547	28,493	28,753	29,469	13,656	15,813	25,129	4,340
79	University of Hawaii at Manoa	Hi.	1	1	18,382	19,799	20,061	20,010	9,088	10,922	14,333	5,677
80	Boise State University	Iowa	1	1	11,319	14,526	14,886	14,675	6,190	8,485	8,225	6,450
81	City Colleges of Chicago-Harry S Truman College	Ill.	1	2	14,258	14,547	15,566	15,405	7,145	8,260	4,314	11,091
82	College of Du Page	Ill.	1	2	24,474	31,621	31,132	30,806	13,150	17,656	8,587	22,219
83	De Paul University	Ill.	2	1	13,688	16,489	16,479	16,747	7,703	9,044	9,270	7,477
84	Illinois State University	Ill.	1	1	23,141	21,761	20,610	19,595	8,617	10,978	16,003	3,592
85	Northern Illinois University	Ill.	1	1	25,455	24,052	23,177	22,881	10,341	12,540	16,686	6,195
86	Northwestern University	Ill.	2	1	16,437	17,285	17,551	17,781	9,344	8,437	14,024	3,757
87	Southern Illinois University, Carbondale	Ill.	1	1	24,160	24,761	23,881	23,162	13,366	9,796	18,808	4,354
88	Triton College	Ill.	1	2	18,022	16,804	15,308	15,150	6,707	8,443	3,715	11,435
89	University of Illinois at Chicago	Ill.	1	1	23,924	24,610	25,445	25,040	11,823	13,217	18,786	6,254
90	University of Illinois, Urbana Campus	Ill.	1	1	38,970	38,396	38,912	38,545	21,216	17,329	33,542	5,003
91	William Rainey Harper College	Ill.	1	2	16,034	17,610	16,212	16,051	6,637	9,414	4,736	11,315
92	Ball State University	Ind.	1	1	19,080	21,235	21,626	20,390	9,436	10,954	16,464	3,926
93	Indiana University, Bloomington	Ind.	1	1	33,421	36,071	35,551	35,594	16,677	18,917	29,695	5,899
94	Indiana U. - Purdue U. at Indianapolis	Ind.	1	1	23,618	28,342	27,552	26,766	11,194	15,572	12,051	14,715
95	Purdue University, Main Campus	Ind.	1	1	34,069	37,746	37,094	36,172	21,217	14,955	30,373	5,799
96	Iowa State University	Iowa	1	1	26,600	25,695	25,413	24,990	14,465	10,525	21,231	3,759
97	University of Iowa	Iowa	1	1	29,995	28,145	27,688	27,671	13,618	14,053	20,914	6,757
98	Johnson County Community College	Kans.	1	2	10,065	15,494	15,353	15,035	6,698	8,337	4,678	10,357
99	Kansas State U. of Agr. and App. Sci.	Kans.	1	1	18,049	20,451	20,050	19,883	10,528	9,355	16,109	3,774
100	University of Kansas, Main Campus	Kans.	1	1	26,306	26,457	26,127	25,336	12,563	12,773	19,681	5,655
101	Eastern Kentucky University	Ky.	1	1	13,083	16,811	16,343	16,038	6,660	9,378	11,942	4,096
102	University of Kentucky	Ky.	1	1	21,869	23,699	23,670	23,622	11,629	11,993	18,418	5,204
103	University of Louisville	Ky.	1	1	20,497	21,987	21,172	20,721	9,713	11,008	12,583	8,138
104	Western Kentucky University	Ky.	1	1	13,466	15,653	15,271	14,728	5,918	8,810	10,475	4,253
105	Delgado Community College	La.	1	2	7,054	15,112	14,932	14,845	5,573	9,272	6,305	8,540
106	La. St. U. & A&M & Hebert Laws Center	La.	1	1	28,011	27,358	26,085	26,010	13,172	12,838	20,379	5,631
107	University of New Orleans	La.	1	1	16,109	16,308	15,570	15,239	6,711	8,528	9,060	6,179
108	University of Southwestern Louisiana	La.	1	1	15,419	16,648	16,573	16,789	7,487	9,302	12,556	4,233
109	Johns Hopkins University	Md.	2	1	12,052	14,506	15,074	15,548	8,195	7,353	7,292	8,256
110	U. of Maryland, College Park Campus	Md.	1	1	38,058	32,916	32,441	32,493	16,993	15,500	24,479	8,014
111	Boston College	Mass.	2	1	14,318	14,450	14,586	14,713	6,719	7,994	11,551	3,162
112	Boston University	Mass.	2	1	28,308	28,375	28,653	29,072	13,706	15,366	22,659	6,413
113	Harvard University	Mass.	2	1	23,691	25,012	26,007	24,806	13,036	11,770	18,285	6,521
114	Northeastern University	Mass.	2	1	33,042	27,586	26,554	25,086	13,102	11,984	13,576	11,510
115	University of Massachusetts at Amherst	Mass.	1	1	28,118	24,185	24,234	24,825	12,654	12,171	19,182	5,643
116	Central Michigan University	Mich.	1	1	19,141	17,268	23,998	23,390	10,419	12,971	14,338	9,052
117	Eastern Michigan University	Mich.	1	1	22,375	24,096	24,600	23,321	9,551	13,770	12,862	10,459
118	Lansing Community College	Mich.	1	2	21,153	21,204	18,419	16,816	7,353	9,463	4,466	12,350
119	Macomb Community College	Mich.	1	2	32,141	26,498	27,391	25,809	12,483	13,326	5,993	19,816
120	Michigan State University	Mich.	1	1	43,960	39,138	39,743	40,254	19,419	20,835	32,396	7,858
121	Oakland Community College	Mich.	1	2	26,251	26,088	28,232	26,324	10,510	15,814	5,454	20,870
122	University of Michigan, Ann Arbor	Mich.	1	1	35,623	35,476	36,845	36,543	19,723	16,820	32,937	3,606
123	Wayne State University	Mich.	1	1	30,377	34,945	34,280	32,906	14,573	18,333	15,265	17,641
124	Western Michigan University	Mich.	1	1	23,336	27,281	26,555	25,673	11,831	13,842	16,560	9,113
125	Saint Cloud State University	Minn.	1	1	15,520	16,042	15,118	14,673	6,978	7,695	11,387	3,286
126	University of Minnesota, Twin Cities	Minn.	1	1	62,223	54,671	51,880	51,478	24,939	26,539	22,828	28,650
127	Southwest Missouri State University	Mo.	1	1	16,085	19,002	18,160	17,310	7,851	9,459	12,726	4,584
128	University of Missouri, Columbia	Mo.	1	1	22,958	23,418	22,225	22,175	10,879	11,296	17,969	4,206
129	University of Missouri, Saint Louis	Mo.	1	1	13,162	14,918	15,411	15,588	6,006	9,582	6,428	9,160
130	University of Nebraska, Lincoln	Nebr.	1	1	23,469	24,573	24,491	23,854	12,811	11,043	18,676	5,178
131	University of Nebraska, Omaha	Nebr.	1	1	14,210	16,221	15,897	15,051	6,796	8,255	7,906	7,145
132	Community College of Southern Nevada	Nev.	1	2	10,370	17,745	17,118	16,718	7,257	9,461	2,211	14,507
133	University of Nevada, Las Vegas	Nev.	1	1	13,476	18,694	18,534	18,954	8,765	10,189	8,723	10,231
134	University of New Hampshire, Main Campus	N.H.	1	1	12,747	13,872	13,942	15,394	6,592	8,802	11,705	3,689
135	Rutgers University, New Brunswick	N.J.	1	1	33,157	33,577	33,568	33,464	15,373	18,091	24,070	9,394
136	New Mexico State University, Main Campus	N.Mex.	1	1	14,003	15,500	15,788	15,643	7,847	7,796	11,138	4,505
137	University of New Mexico, Main Campus	N.Mex.	1	1	24,856	24,279	25,663	24,572	10,894	13,678	14,545	10,027
138	Columbia University, New York	N.Y.	2	1	18,066	19,290	19,023	19,051	9,896	9,155	15,180	3,871
139	CUNY, Bernard Baruch College	N.Y.	1	1	16,587	15,346	15,064	15,091	6,529	8,562	9,006	6,085
140	CUNY, Borough of Manhattan Community College	N.Y.	1	2	12,217	15,677	16,702	16,728	5,712	11,016	9,880	6,848
141	CUNY, Brooklyn College	N.Y.	1	1	14,961	15,467	15,580	15,984	6,175	9,809	8,293	7,691
142	CUNY, City College	N.Y.	1	1	12,948	14,783	14,832	14,885	7,537	7,348	8,279	6,606
143	CUNY, Hunter College	N.Y.	1	1	19,657	18,390	18,657	19,663	5,244	14,419	9,755	9,908
144	CUNY, Kingsborough Community College	N.Y.	1	2	11,840	14,331	14,994	15,464	5,761	9,703	7,438	8,026
145	Nassau Community College	N.Y.	1	2	19,692	22,367	22,215	21,955	9,923	12,032	11,041	10,914
146	New York University	N.Y.	2	1	31,691	33,695	33,309	35,425	15,550	19,875	22,278	13,147
147	Queens College	N.Y.	1	1	16,613	17,930	17,753	17,958	6,696	11,262	9,313	8,645
148	Regents College-U. of the State of NY	N.Y.	1	1	14,829	14,463	15,628	17,259	6,541	10,718	—	17,259
149	Saint John's University of New York	N.Y.	2	1	19,234	18,813	18,188	17,820	8,285	9,535	13,070	4,750
150	SUNY at Albany	N.Y.	1	1	16,219	19,001	16,759	16,622	8,098	8,524	12,262	4,360
151	SUNY at Buffalo	N.Y.	1	1	24,449	25,357	25,635	24,943	13,572	11,371	18,375	6,568
152	SUNY at Stony Brook	N.Y.	1	1	14,524	17,125	17,205	17,621	8,464	9,157	13,379	4,242
153	Syracuse University, Main Campus	N.Y.	2	1	21,334	20,496	19,353	18,971	9,024	9,947	13,688	5,283

Table 212.—Selected statistics for college and university campuses enrolling more than 14,600 students in 1994—Continued

Enrollment, by level, fall 1994		Earned degrees conferred, 1993–94					Financial statistics, 1993–94, in thousands			Full-time-equivalent enrollment, fall 1993	Full-time-equivalent enrollment, fall 1994	Line no.
Undergraduate	Postbaccalaureate	Associate	Bachelor's	Master's	Doctor's	First professional	Current-fund revenues	Current-fund expenditures	Educational and general expenditures			
14	15	16	17	18	19	20	21	22	23	24	25	26
16,099	—	891	—	—	—	—	52,447	52,154	48,656	9,260	9,197	76
16,633	7,097	6	2,697	1,608	115	171	188,800	187,078	184,684	16,055	16,372	77
22,832	6,637	—	4,939	1,232	309	293	592,670	583,991	534,094	26,076	26,812	78
13,290	6,720	—	2,519	1,010	159	133	435,976	429,457	386,325	16,375	16,480	79
12,357	2,318	217	1,205	185	—	—	105,005	101,050	78,397	10,738	10,738	80
15,405	—	444	—	—	—	—	43,588	43,069	43,069	8,150	8,039	81
30,806	—	1,658	—	—	—	—	80,868	76,616	70,983	16,218	16,050	82
10,113	6,634	—	1,617	1,392	12	289	165,383	160,563	144,522	12,022	12,228	83
16,525	3,070	—	4,005	655	43	—	182,814	184,040	147,687	18,296	17,374	84
16,423	6,458	—	3,558	1,399	108	86	218,355	222,778	172,294	19,334	19,009	85
9,806	7,975	—	1,872	2,070	305	429	691,741	670,033	634,648	15,350	15,488	86
18,712	4,450	486	4,801	770	174	181	309,030	313,028	280,823	20,402	20,479	87
15,150	—	705	—	—	—	—	46,170	44,880	40,995	7,625	7,556	88
16,214	8,826	—	2,756	1,442	232	508	850,974	826,282	546,214	21,483	21,187	89
27,647	10,898	—	6,026	2,583	666	284	844,912	835,531	731,341	35,708	35,450	90
16,051	—	1,220	—	—	—	—	64,416	67,235	59,643	8,624	8,536	91
17,865	2,525	287	3,553	706	68	—	235,875	229,504	188,897	19,106	17,984	92
27,462	8,132	67	5,206	1,610	348	261	650,742	632,405	460,034	32,011	31,959	93
19,483	7,283	581	1,994	522	28	572	827,928	767,900	390,249	18,250	17,855	94
29,374	6,798	739	5,496	1,243	493	90	669,846	636,328	541,079	33,277	32,624	95
20,039	4,951	—	3,938	793	307	73	551,104	523,417	419,897	23,111	22,666	96
18,356	9,315	—	3,542	1,439	342	435	999,941	999,968	536,526	23,486	23,490	97
15,035	—	902	—	—	—	—	66,224	59,007	53,062	8,426	8,157	98
16,211	3,672	29	3,159	748	154	79	263,237	262,793	243,714	17,748	17,555	99
18,219	7,117	—	3,452	1,200	225	217	336,588	314,343	267,898	22,569	21,793	100
14,131	1,907	268	1,749	368	—	—	118,960	114,855	99,458	13,693	13,535	101
17,406	6,216	—	2,781	961	229	326	738,209	689,875	467,349	20,408	20,415	102
15,427	5,294	143	1,919	814	58	327	313,921	302,585	265,619	15,976	15,765	103
12,672	2,056	303	1,828	498	—	—	108,149	103,958	91,972	12,518	12,127	104
14,845	—	952	—	—	—	—	40,333	39,954	36,659	9,116	9,173	105
19,962	6,048	—	3,154	1,075	218	294	420,122	417,118	348,134	22,574	22,572	106
11,672	3,567	—	1,350	488	33	—	97,263	96,108	85,962	11,605	11,444	107
15,261	1,528	85	1,696	362	31	—	108,462	106,642	90,933	14,013	14,224	108
5,282	10,266	14	1,024	2,188	262	104	1,404,639	1,396,820	937,586	10,104	10,474	109
23,724	8,769	—	5,097	1,524	528	—	562,497	546,589	454,848	26,937	27,522	110
10,389	4,324	—	2,126	990	117	278	310,615	281,047	216,081	12,619	12,774	111
18,404	10,668	4	3,465	2,725	289	722	780,999	756,876	641,498	24,692	25,156	112
10,484	14,322	11	1,857	2,630	538	809	1,376,416	1,390,069	1,262,927	21,477	20,829	113
20,146	4,940	319	2,787	1,296	78	196	288,799	282,488	266,633	18,976	18,099	114
18,692	6,133	99	3,834	829	338	—	465,680	468,351	367,889	20,787	21,305	115
15,783	7,607	—	3,057	2,248	7	—	170,340	160,690	130,956	18,030	17,731	116
18,368	4,953	—	3,277	1,248	1	—	169,116	164,554	138,341	18,006	16,906	117
16,816	—	13,718	—	—	—	—	67,946	60,505	59,649	9,253	8,614	118
25,809	—	2,619	—	—	—	—	80,871	72,345	66,522	13,458	12,649	119
31,056	9,198	—	6,664	1,541	429	375	860,068	823,654	683,119	34,927	35,414	120
26,324	—	1,748	—	—	—	—	83,786	83,104	77,264	13,376	12,464	121
23,238	13,305	—	5,487	2,858	649	725	2,154,525	1,850,197	1,043,776	34,519	34,295	122
19,248	13,658	—	2,654	2,250	263	433	435,807	417,171	404,126	22,874	22,070	123
19,499	6,174	—	4,054	1,600	56	—	245,366	237,120	186,261	20,600	20,029	124
13,260	1,413	119	2,602	304	—	—	95,823	95,438	81,110	13,096	12,667	125
37,754	13,724	12	5,209	2,225	707	634	1,472,157	1,450,696	1,048,522	34,089	34,093	126
15,577	1,733	12	2,540	293	—	—	118,536	112,549	96,096	15,322	14,522	127
16,439	5,736	—	3,805	1,098	253	293	693,681	629,290	388,180	19,678	19,565	128
12,736	2,852	—	1,690	556	16	39	87,467	85,836	78,536	9,783	10,060	129
18,700	5,154	23	3,073	806	227	153	377,990	371,360	297,078	21,191	20,661	130
12,218	2,833	—	1,501	547	—	—	89,427	88,439	81,250	11,392	10,695	131
16,718	—	571	—	—	—	—	30,445	29,432	29,223	7,014	7,084	132
15,371	3,583	—	1,942	496	11	—	142,767	147,850	133,495	12,408	12,728	133
12,912	2,482	260	2,306	469	59	—	242,277	231,998	187,152	12,297	13,129	134
24,900	8,564	—	5,225	1,284	400	17	—	—	—	27,698	27,627	135
13,097	2,546	216	1,848	691	66	—	240,615	233,913	199,319	13,049	12,915	136
16,564	8,008	65	2,557	1,068	165	192	644,814	620,881	349,695	19,326	18,392	137
6,776	12,275	—	1,299	4,385	644	562	1,171,744	1,139,474	1,086,977	16,633	16,684	138
12,787	2,304	—	1,934	709	—	—	103,656	104,148	103,862	11,300	11,392	139
16,728	—	1,515	—	—	—	—	75,221	76,591	75,861	11,940	12,180	140
11,478	4,506	—	1,519	847	—	—	109,845	109,472	108,968	10,912	11,221	141
11,570	3,315	—	1,301	894	—	—	129,470	132,168	131,876	10,931	10,821	142
14,935	4,728	—	1,580	1,061	—	—	133,477	135,010	133,517	12,692	13,592	143
15,464	—	1,616	—	—	—	—	70,562	71,100	70,360	9,862	10,134	144
21,955	—	3,027	—	—	—	—	110,458	110,458	110,458	14,892	14,707	145
15,854	19,571	354	3,135	4,553	391	812	1,416,493	1,397,680	912,756	25,706	27,357	146
14,541	3,417	—	1,939	841	—	—	124,185	124,320	120,751	12,487	12,672	147
17,259	—	1,807	2,634	—	—	—	11,785	11,282	11,282	6,176	6,821	148
12,708	5,112	432	2,632	970	31	401	197,253	187,592	180,533	15,228	14,957	149
11,352	5,270	—	2,667	1,367	131	—	229,443	222,636	196,525	13,954	13,892	150
16,411	8,532	43	3,227	1,477	345	472	462,229	465,493	429,522	21,349	20,873	151
11,309	6,312	—	2,101	1,146	268	128	760,857	691,263	377,053	14,649	14,970	152
12,122	6,849	1	2,713	1,691	179	266	402,396	388,220	320,090	16,141	15,733	153

Table 212.—Selected statistics for college and university campuses enrolling more than 14,600 students in 1994—Continued

Line no.	Institution	State	Con-trol [1]	Type [2]	Total enrollment, fall 1987	Total enrollment, fall 1992	Total enrollment, fall 1993	Total enrollment, fall 1994	Enrollment, by sex, fall 1994		Enrollment, by attendance status, fall 1994	
									Men	Women	Full-time	Part-time
1	2	3	4	5	6	7	8	9	10	11	12	13
154	Central Piedmont Community College	N.C.	1	2	16,186	26,428	16,575	16,056	6,910	9,146	4,887	11,169
155	East Carolina University	N.C.	1	1	15,901	19,264	18,186	18,076	7,561	10,515	14,352	3,724
156	North Carolina State Universitiy, Raleigh	N.C.	1	1	24,349	27,766	27,810	28,223	16,859	11,364	18,660	9,563
157	University of North Carolina, Chapel Hill	N.C.	1	1	22,958	23,977	24,334	24,565	10,409	14,156	19,737	4,828
158	University of North Carolina, Charlotte	N.C.	1	1	12,385	15,781	15,942	15,648	7,623	8,025	10,276	5,372
159	Bowling Green State U., Main Campus	Ohio	1	1	17,960	18,173	17,767	17,669	7,489	10,180	15,065	2,604
160	Cleveland State University	Ohio	1	1	17,714	17,813	16,881	16,377	7,935	8,442	9,127	7,250
161	Columbus State Community College	Ohio	1	2	8,601	16,507	17,042	16,795	7,134	9,661	6,105	10,690
162	Cuyahoga Community College District	Ohio	1	2	22,825	24,832	25,913	24,079	8,424	15,655	8,126	15,953
163	Kent State University, Main Campus	Ohio	1	1	21,521	24,098	22,700	21,413	8,891	12,522	15,672	5,741
164	Miami University, Oxford Campus	Ohio	1	1	15,980	16,098	16,281	15,624	7,090	8,534	14,315	1,309
165	Ohio State University, Main Campus	Ohio	1	1	53,115	52,179	50,623	49,542	25,809	23,733	39,511	10,031
166	Ohio University, Main Campus	Ohio	1	1	16,693	18,862	19,086	19,461	9,330	10,131	17,564	1,897
167	Sinclair Community College	Ohio	1	2	16,344	18,922	18,751	17,783	6,805	10,978	6,130	11,653
168	University of Akron, Main Campus	Ohio	1	1	27,069	27,063	26,032	24,488	11,782	12,706	13,983	10,505
169	University of Cincinnati, Main Campus	Ohio	1	1	31,233	28,779	28,662	28,758	14,991	13,767	19,862	8,896
170	University of Toledo	Ohio	1	1	21,740	24,539	24,188	23,107	11,161	11,946	16,200	6,907
171	Wright State University, Main Campus	Ohio	1	1	16,123	16,749	16,460	16,029	7,268	8,761	10,521	5,508
172	Oklahoma State University, Main Campus	Okla.	1	1	21,082	19,602	19,153	18,807	10,309	8,498	14,233	4,574
173	Tulsa Junior College	Okla.	1	2	16,011	19,583	19,098	18,604	7,376	11,228	4,872	13,732
174	University of Central Oklahoma	Okla.	1	1	13,921	15,167	15,043	16,076	6,674	9,402	8,919	7,157
175	University of Oklahoma, Norman Campus	Okla.	1	1	22,352	21,724	21,696	22,043	11,873	10,170	15,213	6,830
176	Portland Community College	Oreg.	1	2	20,492	22,803	22,527	23,158	10,738	12,420	7,073	16,085
177	Portland State University	Oreg.	1	1	17,316	17,357	16,243	15,818	7,136	8,682	7,987	7,831
178	University of Oregon	Oreg.	1	1	18,195	17,285	16,877	16,962	8,304	8,658	14,634	2,328
179	Community College of Allegheny County	Pa.	1	2	17,255	21,743	20,721	18,859	7,720	11,139	7,730	11,129
180	Community College of Philadelphia	Pa.	1	2	13,866	19,476	19,786	18,305	6,365	11,940	5,539	12,766
181	International Correspondence Schools	Pa.	2	2	—	18,728	23,552	24,911	11,444	13,467	—	24,911
182	Pennsylvania State U., Main Campus	Pa.	1	1	36,271	38,446	37,658	38,294	21,481	16,813	33,654	4,640
183	Temple University	Pa.	1	1	30,431	30,229	30,040	29,616	14,079	15,537	19,116	10,500
184	University of Pennsylvania	Pa.	2	1	21,875	22,418	22,469	22,720	11,864	10,856	18,419	4,301
185	University of Pittsburgh, Main Campus	Pa.	1	1	28,364	27,852	27,528	26,328	13,108	13,220	18,797	7,531
186	Community College of Rhode Island	R.I.	1	2	13,107	17,986	16,399	16,001	5,991	10,010	4,745	11,256
187	Clemson University	S.C.	1	1	13,865	17,666	16,609	16,290	8,882	7,408	13,344	2,946
188	University of South Carolina, Columbia	S.C.	1	1	25,504	26,471	26,710	26,754	11,688	15,066	16,789	9,965
189	Middle Tennessee State University	Tenn.	1	1	11,977	16,787	17,383	17,120	7,795	9,325	12,347	4,773
190	University of Memphis	Tenn.	1	1	20,470	20,578	20,373	19,849	8,847	11,002	12,677	7,172
191	University of Tennessee, Knoxville	Tenn.	1	1	25,986	26,579	26,397	25,914	13,224	12,690	19,853	6,061
192	Austin Community College	Tex.	1	2	19,905	25,186	24,564	25,276	11,537	13,739	6,593	18,683
193	El Paso Community College	Tex.	1	2	14,878	18,479	18,843	18,656	7,248	11,408	8,437	10,219
194	Houston Community College System	Tex.	1	2	27,196	37,410	39,321	45,893	20,393	25,500	11,438	34,455
195	North Harris-Montgomery Community College	Tex.	1	2	—	17,537	17,587	17,850	7,061	10,789	6,333	11,517
196	San Antonio College	Tex.	1	2	21,816	20,051	18,944	18,558	8,010	10,548	6,596	11,962
197	Southwest Texas State University	Tex.	1	1	20,039	21,302	20,879	20,889	9,603	11,286	14,829	6,060
198	Tarrant County Junior College District	Tex.	1	2	24,490	28,516	27,353	26,257	11,462	14,795	7,709	18,548
199	Texas A&M University	Tex.	1	1	39,079	41,710	42,524	42,018	23,905	18,113	37,235	4,783
200	Texas Tech University	Tex.	1	1	23,564	24,154	24,007	24,083	13,142	10,941	19,819	4,264
201	University of Texas, Arlington	Tex.	1	1	22,760	24,729	23,763	23,373	12,129	11,244	12,766	10,607
202	University of Texas, Austin	Tex.	1	1	47,743	49,253	48,555	47,957	25,454	22,503	41,316	6,641
203	University of Texas, El Paso	Tex.	1	1	14,056	17,223	17,006	17,196	7,984	9,212	10,406	6,790
204	University of Texas, San Antonio	Tex.	1	1	12,879	16,767	17,097	17,579	8,176	9,403	10,099	7,480
205	University of Texas, Pan American	Tex.	1	1	9,625	13,293	13,701	15,104	7,049	8,055	7,877	7,227
206	University of Houston, University Park	Tex.	1	1	28,907	33,022	32,124	31,299	15,545	15,754	18,824	12,475
207	University of North Texas	Tex.	1	1	22,379	26,433	25,759	25,605	12,332	13,273	16,605	9,000
208	Brigham Young University	Utah	2	1	29,674	32,289	31,706	31,511	15,684	15,827	28,331	3,180
209	Salt Lake Community College	Utah	1	2	9,436	17,024	17,437	18,534	9,456	9,078	7,043	11,491
210	University of Utah	Utah	1	1	24,124	26,795	27,113	26,906	14,418	12,488	17,652	9,254
211	Utah State University	Utah	1	1	13,582	16,513	17,556	20,371	9,638	10,733	11,945	8,426
212	George Mason University	Va.	1	1	18,112	20,829	21,300	21,774	10,087	11,687	11,392	10,382
213	Northern Virginia Community College	Va.	1	2	34,884	38,343	37,477	37,655	16,934	20,721	9,240	28,415
214	Old Dominion University	Va.	1	1	15,640	16,507	15,974	16,490	7,845	8,645	9,741	6,749
215	Tidewater Community College	Va.	1	2	16,818	16,944	17,511	17,749	7,661	10,088	4,643	13,106
216	University of Virginia, Main Campus	Va.	1	1	21,268	21,535	21,394	21,421	9,943	11,478	17,051	4,370
217	Virginia Commonwealth University	Va.	1	1	20,485	21,939	21,854	21,523	8,729	12,794	13,371	8,152
218	Virginia Polytechnic Inst. and State Univ.	Va.	1	1	24,977	26,003	26,030	25,842	15,195	10,647	22,505	3,337
219	University of Washington	Wash.	1	1	33,302	34,597	34,000	33,719	16,924	16,795	27,682	6,037
220	Washington State University	Wash.	1	1	16,484	17,871	18,822	19,314	10,188	9,126	16,894	2,420
221	West Virginia University	W.Va.	1	1	17,270	22,712	23,080	22,500	11,130	11,370	17,720	4,780
222	Milwaukee Area Technical College	Wisc.	1	2	20,781	23,170	24,072	23,010	9,622	13,388	5,729	17,281
223	University of Wisconsin, Madison	Wisc.	1	1	43,368	41,824	39,999	39,361	19,858	19,503	33,435	5,926
224	University of Wisconsin, Milwaukee	Wisc.	1	1	25,210	24,991	23,806	22,604	10,244	12,360	12,632	9,972
225	Community College of the Air Force	Ala.	1	2	40,310	33,447	13,895	33,107	13,694	19,413	12,492	20,615

Table 212.—Selected statistics for college and university campuses enrolling more than 14,600 students in 1994—Continued

Enrollment, by level, fall 1994		Earned degrees conferred, 1993–94					Financial statistics, 1993–94, in thousands			Full-time-equivalent enrollment, fall 1993	Full-time-equivalent enrollment, fall 1994	Line no.
Undergraduate	Postbaccalaureate	Associate	Bachelor's	Master's	Doctor's	First professional	Current-fund revenues	Current-fund expenditures	Educational and general expenditures			
14	15	16	17	18	19	20	21	22	23	24	25	26
16,056	—	983	—	—	—	—	51,578	51,988	46,077	8,461	8,638	154
14,531	3,545	—	2,532	693	11	72	269,987	254,133	216,968	15,918	15,766	155
21,653	6,570	129	3,992	929	300	71	540,236	531,783	463,100	22,065	22,327	156
15,849	8,716	—	3,610	1,512	373	464	874,162	855,072	653,261	21,325	21,534	157
13,029	2,619	—	2,490	480	—	—	133,440	129,286	101,657	12,679	12,356	158
14,800	2,869	6	3,245	686	78	—	199,740	197,232	150,714	16,138	16,057	159
11,215	5,162	—	1,787	1,015	27	273	136,524	136,460	126,645	12,253	11,949	160
16,795	—	1,358	—	—	—	—	54,383	48,311	44,141	9,917	9,696	161
24,079	—	1,456	—	—	—	—	121,130	108,389	101,383	14,302	13,484	162
16,620	4,793	—	3,206	1,006	140	—	214,898	208,981	164,245	18,934	17,868	163
13,996	1,628	226	3,577	554	39	—	208,242	203,302	150,828	15,268	14,820	164
36,166	13,376	278	7,182	2,408	710	711	1,425,676	1,311,555	841,425	43,594	43,380	165
16,536	2,925	152	3,392	932	102	99	243,835	238,159	193,632	18,020	18,309	166
17,783	—	1,029	—	—	—	—	71,755	62,984	57,158	10,443	10,044	167
20,275	4,213	676	2,548	809	110	182	198,125	200,297	175,792	19,153	18,139	168
21,215	7,543	623	3,041	1,130	273	282	783,242	733,163	403,198	23,091	23,330	169
19,854	3,253	588	2,475	641	75	186	199,544	195,428	160,980	19,840	18,920	170
12,058	3,971	—	1,804	795	31	91	165,636	162,405	149,927	13,074	12,637	171
14,195	4,612	—	2,762	763	203	69	306,231	287,422	234,501	16,356	15,957	172
18,604	—	1,471	—	—	—	—	49,305	45,912	40,731	9,676	9,484	173
12,397	3,679	—	2,015	653	—	—	60,849	60,959	52,240	11,057	11,702	174
14,992	7,051	—	2,286	1,263	148	210	261,230	256,159	202,754	17,501	17,785	175
23,158	—	1,217	—	—	—	—	88,483	83,806	76,582	12,136	12,476	176
10,796	5,022	—	1,750	808	31	—	115,151	110,683	97,338	10,967	11,001	177
13,316	3,646	—	2,923	760	227	116	232,886	235,520	187,440	15,255	15,535	178
18,859	—	2,001	—	—	—	—	91,057	87,623	82,783	12,412	11,468	179
18,305	—	1,102	—	—	—	—	65,631	67,365	66,711	10,486	9,827	180
24,911	—	—	—	—	—	—	46,087	36,668	36,668	9,645	10,201	181
31,496	6,798	69	8,040	1,252	507	—	798,212	775,455	681,155	34,868	35,423	182
19,121	10,495	20	3,305	1,553	287	606	811,958	783,262	405,253	23,437	23,158	183
11,300	11,420	17	2,539	2,230	488	592	1,668,062	1,492,514	819,562	19,909	20,096	184
16,721	9,607	—	3,170	2,161	334	451	685,181	643,718	596,864	22,495	21,682	185
16,001	—	1,546	—	—	—	—	53,312	52,917	49,260	8,698	8,526	186
12,290	4,000	—	2,715	1,113	115	—	318,547	313,760	254,361	14,821	14,444	187
16,028	10,726	21	3,182	1,894	288	318	350,909	335,911	300,172	20,620	20,549	188
15,108	2,012	5	2,070	385	18	—	104,968	103,890	92,589	14,558	14,200	189
15,087	4,762	—	1,973	901	113	109	170,212	167,482	148,308	15,756	15,467	190
18,620	7,294	—	3,442	1,562	226	207	482,953	471,108	399,625	22,267	22,168	191
25,276	—	806	—	—	—	—	71,299	69,469	68,772	12,472	12,868	192
18,656	—	666	—	—	—	—	72,438	69,604	69,292	11,980	11,869	193
45,893	—	1,103	—	—	—	—	126,713	122,186	122,133	19,723	23,011	194
17,850	—	757	—	—	—	—	55,695	54,885	52,675	10,072	10,201	195
18,558	—	659	—	—	—	—	56,131	56,050	55,803	11,006	10,614	196
17,928	2,961	28	3,109	499	—	—	147,878	145,542	109,180	17,096	17,191	197
26,257	—	1,469	—	—	—	—	78,928	78,159	72,143	14,553	13,939	198
34,278	7,740	—	6,933	1,472	579	157	807,691	792,567	710,376	.	39,084	199
19,652	4,431	—	3,324	770	163	193	255,888	228,506	186,585	21,285	21,473	200
19,012	4,361	—	2,948	1,043	76	—	159,262	153,803	129,566	17,221	16,947	201
34,746	13,211	—	7,497	2,619	714	529	873,412	818,533	720,931	44,419	43,930	202
14,746	2,450	—	1,541	388	4	—	124,359	119,916	97,455	12,975	13,076	203
14,775	2,804	—	1,985	502	—	—	95,595	91,904	83,757	12,797	13,029	204
13,554	1,550	97	935	158	—	—	63,004	50,365	43,243	9,723	10,756	205
24,051	7,248	—	3,582	1,491	202	434	306,047	298,840	263,267	24,018	23,752	206
19,018	6,587	—	3,587	1,149	176	—	194,662	184,625	151,537	20,196	20,075	207
28,576	2,935	17	6,249	1,056	72	144	495,285	431,537	291,172	29,663	29,576	208
18,534	—	1,286	—	—	—	—	69,457	67,162	58,884	10,444	10,903	209
21,958	4,948	—	3,375	775	205	223	781,642	742,307	462,360	21,325	21,343	210
16,032	4,339	66	1,954	655	61	—	236,036	232,625	207,557	13,604	15,201	211
13,331	8,443	—	2,784	1,346	79	187	192,655	185,750	145,397	15,081	15,350	212
37,655	—	2,438	—	—	—	—	81,800	81,072	80,280	18,716	18,784	213
10,909	5,581	—	2,044	1,033	60	—	132,511	128,441	106,957	12,021	12,296	214
17,749	—	1,198	—	—	—	—	40,710	39,956	39,282	8,949	9,045	215
12,568	8,853	—	2,808	1,421	294	510	877,178	848,747	438,126	18,661	18,682	216
14,929	6,594	19	2,489	1,267	120	240	709,424	726,729	299,215	16,640	16,521	217
19,229	6,613	38	3,939	1,416	379	75	490,102	494,208	415,165	23,791	23,737	218
24,592	9,127	—	6,103	1,967	455	365	1,310,872	1,267,468	895,221	30,188	30,062	219
16,123	3,191	—	3,607	575	202	90	392,512	381,392	326,085	17,383	17,827	220
15,383	7,117	—	3,304	1,154	126	251	352,468	346,355	306,923	19,753	19,499	221
23,010	—	1,461	—	—	—	—	115,570	112,121	103,671	11,977	11,533	222
27,544	11,817	—	5,827	2,066	783	517	1,446,621	1,382,723	1,042,616	36,252	35,751	223
17,841	4,763	—	2,644	1,151	97	—	230,220	228,865	210,367	17,316	16,524	224
33,107	—	11,010	—	—	—	—	—	—	—	19,578	19,416	225

[1] Publicly controlled institutions are identified by a "1;" and privately controlled, by a "2."

[2] The types of institutions are identified as follows: "1" 4-year institutions; "2" 2-year institutions.

[3] Excludes data for nonreporting institutions.

—Data not available or not applicable.

SOURCE: U.S. Department of Education, National Center for Education Statistics, "Fall Enrollment in Institutions of Higher Education" survey; and Integrated Postsecondary Education Data System (IPEDS), "Completions," "Finance," and "Fall Enrollment" surveys. (This table was prepared July 1996.)

Table 213.—Fall enrollment, degrees conferred, and expenditures in historically black colleges and universities, by institution: 1994

Institution	Type and control[1]	Enrollment, 1994		Degrees conferred, 1993–94					Expenditures, 1993–94 (In thousands)	
		Total	Black	Associate	Bachelor's	Master's	Doctor's	First-professional	Current-fund expenditures	Educational and general expenditures
1	2	3	4	5	6	7	8	9	10	11
Total	—	280,071	230,162	2,830	27,425	4,986	213	1,013	$3,437,221	$2,828,784
** Alabama A&M University, AL	1	5,543	4,245	—	507	276	2	—	58,299	52,427
Alabama State University, AL	1	5,037	4,872	4	360	96	—	—	43,541	36,451
Bishop State Community College, AL[2]	2	4,511	2,370	339	—	—	—	—	21,024	19,607
C.A. Fredd State Technical College, AL	2	190	166	23	—	—	—	—	1,979	1,979
Concordia College, AL	4	435	418	45	—	—	—	—	3,200	2,861
J.F. Drake Technical College, AL	2	768	335	48	—	—	—	—	4,424	4,296
Lawson State Community College, AL	2	1,920	1,853	141	—	—	—	—	9,693	9,313
Miles College, AL	3	1,068	1,065	—	72	—	—	—	8,044	7,364
Oakwood College, AL	3	1,534	1,335	34	207	—	—	—	18,373	14,296
Selma University, AL	3	206	205	13	21	—	—	—	5,519	4,918
Stillman College, AL	3	913	895	—	164	—	—	—	11,142	9,555
Talladega College, AL	3	976	940	—	93	—	—	—	12,732	10,967
Trenholm State Technical College, AL	2	785	610	62	—	—	—	—	6,351	6,119
** Tuskegee University, AL	3	3,322	3,047	—	491	58	—	46	73,861	66,968
Arkansas Baptist College, AR	3	225	222	—	21	—	—	—	1,926	1,823
Philander Smith College, AR	3	841	780	—	128	—	—	—	5,523	5,069
Shorter College, AR	4	282	207	20	—	—	—	—	712	652
** University of Arkansas, Pine Bluff, AR	1	3,823	3,271	3	361	12	—	—	32,453	28,549
** Delaware State College, DE	1	3,381	2,243	—	322	83	—	—	41,700	36,370
Howard University, DC	3	10,115	8,922	—	1,333	369	79	304	[2]548,011	[2]316,601
** University of the District of Columbia, DC	1	10,599	8,991	193	555	130	—	—	97,072	95,824
Bethune-Cookman College, FL	3	2,345	2,221	—	295	—	—	—	27,604	23,629
Edward Waters College, FL	3	782	740	—	53	—	—	—	[2]7,973	[2]7,357
** Florida A&M University, FL	1	10,084	8,923	29	1,210	193	3	27	117,855	105,886
Florida Memorial College, FL	3	1,320	1,148	—	182	—	—	—	14,203	13,002
Albany State College, GA	1	3,062	2,708	—	307	73	—	—	25,612	21,169
Clark Atlanta University, GA	3	5,193	4,990	—	528	337	33	—	106,681	102,674
** Fort Valley State College, GA	1	2,823	2,630	3	251	86	—	—	30,018	26,209
Interdenominational Theological Center, GA .	3	398	369	—	—	12	2	69	6,164	6,114
Morehouse College, GA	3	2,992	2,972	—	496	—	—	—	45,198	39,378
Morehouse School of Medicine, GA	3	164	136	—	—	—	—	24	47,509	47,509
Morris Brown College, GA	3	1,894	1,852	—	179	—	—	—	[2]31,416	[2]26,805
Paine College, GA	3	721	705	—	75	—	—	—	9,582	8,453
Savannah State College, GA	1	3,253	2,951	—	278	3	—	—	25,724	21,162
Spelman College, GA	3	1,977	1,927	—	409	—	—	—	35,144	29,329
** Kentucky State University, KY	1	2,563	1,248	80	186	20	—	—	33,370	30,050
Dillard University, LA	3	1,675	1,663	—	194	—	—	—	19,677	17,785
Grambling State University, LA	1	7,610	7,281	80	908	196	10	—	57,632	41,967
** Southern University and A&M College, Baton Rouge, LA	1	9,904	9,315	28	903	191	1	110	84,086	72,906
Southern University, New Orleans, LA	1	4,302	4,016	30	422	80	—	—	20,542	19,322
Southern University, Shreveport-Bossier City Campus, LA	2	1,267	1,178	64	—	—	—	—	7,211	6,954
Xavier University of Louisiana, LA	3	3,463	3,120	—	367	112	—	18	41,686	38,594
Bowie State University, MD	1	4,896	3,519	—	460	373	—	—	28,965	26,250
Coppin State College, MD	1	3,380	3,119	—	274	93	—	—	24,912	22,312
Morgan State University, MD	1	5,766	5,399	—	547	126	9	—	70,626	58,565
** University of Maryland, Eastern Shore, MD ...	1	2,925	2,049	—	277	41	2	—	35,844	31,160
Lewis College of Business, MI	4	245	245	13	—	—	—	—	2,109	2,076
** Alcorn State University, MS	1	2,742	2,556	37	408	69	—	—	34,103	28,881
Coahoma Community College, MS	2	969	948	78	—	—	—	—	7,609	6,937
Hinds Community College, Utica Campus, MS	2	964	901	138	—	—	—	—	—	—
Jackson State University, MS	1	6,224	5,882	—	735	185	10	—	65,688	54,348
Mary Holmes College, MS	4	327	311	64	—	—	—	—	[2]5,394	[2]5,019
Mississippi Valley State University, MS	1	2,182	2,166	—	200	4	—	—	21,347	18,254
Rust College, MS	3	1,055	984	2	172	—	—	—	12,361	10,761
Tougaloo College, MS	3	1,105	1,105	—	120	—	—	—	13,890	12,769
Harris-Stowe State College, MO	1	1,757	1,313	—	118	—	—	—	9,498	9,498
** Lincoln University, MO	1	3,512	931	98	256	50	—	—	27,415	25,415
Barber-Scotia College, NC	3	432	430	—	55	—	—	—	8,323	7,578
Bennett College, NC	3	655	646	—	101	—	—	—	12,018	10,971
Elizabeth City State University, NC	1	2,099	1,555	—	327	—	—	—	27,960	23,683
Fayetteville State University, NC	1	4,109	2,632	22	583	91	—	—	36,136	30,673

Table 213.—Fall enrollment, degrees conferred, and expenditures in historically black colleges and universities, by institution: 1994—Continued

Institution	Type and control [1]	Enrollment, 1994		Degrees conferred, 1993–94					Expenditures, 1993–94 (In thousands)	
		Total	Black	Associate	Bachelor's	Master's	Doctor's	First-professional	Current-fund expenditures	Educational and general expenditures
1	2	3	4	5	6	7	8	9	10	11
Johnson C. Smith University, NC	3	1,413	1,409	—	169	—	—	—	19,760	17,070
Livingstone College, NC	3	836	835	—	55	1	—	5	10,095	8,934
** North Carolina Agricultural and Technical State University, NC	1	8,136	7,047	—	824	204	—	—	95,157	82,863
North Carolina Central University, NC	1	5,692	4,780	—	635	217	—	76	56,431	47,357
St. Augustine's College, NC	3	1,673	1,655	—	146	—	—	—	24,094	20,326
Shaw University, NC	3	2,432	2,317	—	402	—	—	—	23,213	21,599
Winston-Salem State University, NC	1	2,915	2,227	—	468	—	—	—	32,148	27,100
Central State University, OH	1	2,763	2,501	—	341	—	—	—	39,566	32,656
Wilberforce University, OH	3	976	948	—	118	—	—	—	12,785	10,416
** Langston University, OK	1	3,408	1,874	—	459	7	—	—	22,599	19,114
Cheyney University of Pennsylvania, PA	1	1,357	1,289	—	161	73	—	—	24,810	22,211
Lincoln University, PA	1	1,371	1,235	—	220	103	—	—	25,641	22,515
Allen University, SC	3	256	256	—	35	—	—	—	3,968	3,740
Benedict College, SC	3	1,501	1,464	—	180	—	—	—	16,146	14,326
Claflin College, SC	3	1,023	1,005	—	116	—	—	—	10,250	8,452
Clinton Junior College, SC [3]	4	—	—	—	—	—	—	—	—	—
Denmark Technical College, SC	2	840	786	66	—	—	—	—	4,930	4,165
Morris College, SC	3	889	886	—	87	—	—	—	10,497	9,011
** South Carolina State College, SC	1	4,693	4,392	—	605	78	17	—	48,881	39,097
Voorhees College, SC	3	716	701	—	62	—	—	—	7,992	6,594
Fisk University, TN	3	872	869	—	149	9	—	—	12,830	11,225
Knoxville College, TN	3	728	715	9	66	—	—	—	[2]8,188	[2]7,107
Lane College, TN	3	667	667	—	69	—	—	—	7,830	6,184
Le Moyne-Owen College, TN	3	1,436	1,430	—	167	22	—	—	11,618	11,363
Meharry Medical College, TN	3	726	594	—	—	14	8	91	97,859	60,097
** Tennessee State University, TN	1	8,180	5,270	161	493	122	23	—	69,283	64,203
Huston-Tillotson College, TX	3	613	475	—	82	—	—	—	7,844	7,015
Jarvis Christian College, TX	3	382	377	—	66	—	—	—	7,467	6,802
Paul Quinn College, TX	3	667	645	—	70	—	—	—	7,362	7,190
** Prairie View A&M University, TX	1	5,849	5,030	—	586	214	—	—	68,281	54,846
St. Philip's College, TX	2	6,571	1,269	350	—	—	—	—	26,890	26,826
Southwestern Christian College, TX	3	182	159	36	4	—	—	—	3,002	2,579
Texas College, TX	3	262	254	—	57	—	—	—	6,887	6,135
Texas Southern University, TX	1	10,078	8,332	—	520	178	11	207	79,371	73,245
Wiley College, TX	3	584	546	—	107	—	—	—	6,667	6,038
Hampton University, VA	3	5,769	5,052	—	804	91	—	—	73,553	64,468
Norfolk State University, VA	1	8,667	6,922	70	872	165	—	—	65,380	49,932
St. Paul's College, VA	3	763	712	—	118	—	—	—	9,087	7,929
** Virginia State University, VA	1	4,007	3,620	—	578	96	—	—	46,481	37,065
Virginia Union University, VA	3	1,525	1,493	—	150	—	3	36	17,206	14,729
Bluefield State College, WV	1	2,609	202	275	316	—	—	—	11,890	10,965
West Virginia State College, WV	1	4,519	581	135	428	—	—	—	25,132	21,144
** University of the Virgin Islands, St. Thomas Campus, VI	1	1,915	1,565	37	129	33	—	—	33,489	30,743

[1] 1=public 4-year; 2=public 2-year; 3=private 4-year; and 4=private 2-year.
[2] School did not report. Data imputed.
[3] School lost accreditation.
—Data not reported or not applicable.
**Land-grant institution.

SOURCE: U.S. Department of Education, National Center for Education Statistics, Integrated Postsecondary Education Data System (IPEDS), "Fall Enrollment, 1994," "Completions, 1993–94," and "Finance, 1993–94" surveys. (This table was prepared May 1996.)

Table 214.—Selected statistics on historically black colleges and universities: [1] 1980, 1988, and 1994

Item	Total	Public		Private	
		4-year	2-year	4-year	2-year
1	2	3	4	5	6
Number of institutions, fall 1994	**103**	**40**	**10**	**49**	**4**
Total enrollment, fall 1980	233,557	155,085	13,132	62,924	2,416
Men	106,387	70,236	6,758	28,352	1,041
Men, black	81,818	53,654	2,781	24,412	971
Women	127,170	84,849	6,374	34,572	1,375
Women, black	109,171	70,582	4,644	32,589	1,356
Total enrollment, fall 1988	239,755	158,606	15,066	64,644	1,439
Men	100,561	66,097	6,772	27,219	473
Men, black	78,268	50,545	3,192	24,081	450
Women	139,194	92,509	8,294	37,425	966
Women, black	115,883	73,893	5,894	35,145	951
Total enrollment, fall 1994	280,071	187,735	18,785	72,262	1,289
Men	114,006	76,654	7,778	29,108	466
Men, black	91,908	60,931	3,700	26,895	382
Women	166,065	111,081	11,007	43,154	823
Women, black	138,254	89,751	6,716	40,988	799
Full-time enrollment, fall 1994	214,889	138,215	10,493	65,134	1,047
Men	89,707	58,813	4,244	26,230	420
Women	125,182	79,402	6,249	38,904	627
Part-time enrollment, fall 1994	65,182	49,520	8,292	7,128	242
Men	24,299	17,841	3,534	2,878	46
Women	40,883	31,679	4,758	4,250	196
Earned degrees conferred, 1993–94					
Associate	2,830	1,285	1,309	94	142
Men	984	428	475	37	44
Men, black	450	164	215	29	42
Women	1,846	857	834	57	98
Women, black	1,016	327	537	56	96
Bachelor's	27,425	18,390	—	9,035	—
Men	10,249	7,062	—	3,187	—
Men, black	8,475	5,539	—	2,936	—
Women	17,176	11,328	—	5,848	—
Women, black	14,959	9,348	—	5,611	—
Master's	4,986	3,961	—	1,025	—
Men	1,670	1,343	—	327	—
Men, black	939	727	—	212	—
Women	3,316	2,618	—	698	—
Women, black	2,248	1,686	—	562	—
Doctor's	213	88	—	125	—
Men	105	32	—	73	—
Men, black	61	15	—	46	—
Women	108	56	—	52	—
Women, black	69	31	—	38	—
First-professional	1,013	420	—	593	—
Men	522	206	—	316	—
Men, black	320	84	—	236	—
Women	491	214	—	277	—
Women, black	368	156	—	212	—
Financial statistics, 1993–94, in thousands of dollars					
Current-fund revenues	$3,496,796	$1,814,596	$90,843	$1,580,355	$11,002
Tuition and fees	862,615	383,268	16,243	458,507	4,598
Federal government [2]	719,926	272,994	14,872	429,590	2,470
State governments [2]	840,144	747,812	46,715	45,029	587
Local governments [2]	90,103	81,119	7,068	1,657	259
Private gifts, grants, and contracts	189,157	28,503	515	158,759	1,379
Endowment income	28,709	2,812	1	25,758	138
Sales and services	696,758	256,820	4,532	433,951	1,455
Other sources	69,385	41,269	896	27,104	116
Current-fund expenditures	3,437,221	1,794,937	90,109	1,540,760	11,415
Educational and general expenditures	2,828,784	1,552,387	86,195	1,179,594	10,607
Auxiliary enterprises	352,928	242,550	3,914	105,657	808
Hospitals	254,957	0	0	254,957	0
Independent operations	553	0	0	553	0

[1] Historically black colleges and universities are accredited institutions of higher education established prior to 1964 with the principal mission of educating black Americans. Federal regulations, 20 U.S. Code, Section 1061 (2), allow for certain exceptions to the founding date. Most institutions are in the southern and border states and were established prior to 1954.

[2] Includes appropriations, grants, contracts, and independent operations.

—Not applicable.

NOTE.—Because of rounding, details may not add to totals.

SOURCE: U.S. Department of Education, National Center for Education Statistics, "Fall Enrollment in Institutions of Higher Education;" and Integrated Postsecondary Education Data System (IPEDS), "Fall Enrollment," "Completions," and "Finance" surveys. (This table was prepared May 1996.)

Table 215.—Fall enrollment in historically black colleges and universities, by type and control of institution: 1976 to 1994

Year	Total enrollment	Type of institution		Public institutions			Private institutions		
		4-year	2-year	Total	4-year	2-year	Total	4-year	2-year
1	2	3	4	5	6	7	8	9	10
1976	222,613	206,676	15,937	156,836	143,528	13,308	65,777	63,148	2,629
1977	226,062	209,898	16,164	158,823	145,450	13,373	67,239	64,448	2,791
1978	227,797	211,651	16,146	163,237	150,168	13,069	64,560	61,483	3,077
1979	230,124	214,147	15,977	166,315	153,139	13,176	63,809	61,008	2,801
1980	233,557	218,009	15,548	168,217	155,085	13,132	65,340	62,924	2,416
1981	232,460	217,152	15,308	166,991	154,269	12,722	65,469	62,883	2,586
1982	228,371	212,017	16,354	165,871	151,472	14,399	62,500	60,545	1,955
1983	234,446	217,909	16,537	170,051	155,665	14,386	64,395	62,244	2,151
1984	227,519	212,844	14,675	164,116	151,289	12,827	63,403	61,555	1,848
1985	225,801	210,648	15,153	163,677	150,002	13,675	62,124	60,646	1,478
1986	223,275	207,231	16,044	162,048	147,631	14,417	61,227	59,600	1,627
1987	227,994	211,654	16,340	165,486	150,560	14,926	62,508	61,094	1,414
1988	239,755	223,250	16,505	173,672	158,606	15,066	66,083	64,644	1,439
1989	249,096	232,890	16,206	181,151	166,481	14,670	67,945	66,409	1,536
1990	257,152	240,497	16,655	187,046	171,969	15,077	70,106	68,528	1,578
1991	269,335	252,093	17,242	197,847	182,204	15,643	71,488	69,889	1,599
1992	279,541	261,089	18,452	204,966	188,143	16,823	74,575	72,946	1,629
1993	282,856	262,430	20,426	208,197	189,032	19,165	74,659	73,398	1,261
1994 [1]	280,071	259,997	20,074	206,520	187,735	18,785	73,551	72,262	1,289

[1] Preliminary data.

SOURCE: U.S. Department of Education, National Center for Education Statistics, Higher Education General Information Survey (HEGIS), "Fall Enrollment in Colleges and Universities;" and Integrated Postsecondary Education Data System (IPEDS), "Fall Enrollment" survey. (This table was prepared May 1996.)

Table 216.—Employees in institutions of higher education, by primary occupation, employment status, and control of institution: Fall 1976, fall 1991, and fall 1993

Primary occupation and control of institution	Fall 1976					Fall 1991				Fall 1993			
	Total staff		Full-time	Full-time equivalent staff		Total staff		Full-time equivalent staff		Total staff		Full-time equivalent staff	
	Number	Percent	Full-time	Total	FTE students per FTE staff	Number	Percent	Total	FTE students per FTE staff	Number	Percent	Total	FTE students per FTE staff
1	2	3	4	5	6	7	8	9	10	11	12	13	14
Total, all institutions	**1,863,790**	**100.0**	**1,339,911**	**1,541,339**	**5.4**	**2,545,235**	**100.0**	**2,094,628**	**4.9**	**2,602,612**	**100.0**	**2,094,681**	**4.9**
Professional staff	1,073,119	57.6	709,400	845,456	9.8	1,595,460	62.7	1,244,588	8.3	1,687,287	64.8	1,280,382	8.1
Executive/administrative/managerial	101,263	5.4	97,003	98,972	84.0	144,755	5.7	141,718	73.1	143,675	5.5	140,522	73.7
Faculty (instruction and research)	633,210	34.0	434,071	500,533	16.6	826,252	32.5	632,565	16.4	915,474	35.2	668,819	15.5
Instruction and research assistants	160,086	8.6	28,007	82,684	100.5	197,751	7.8	81,467	127.2	202,819	7.8	83,717	123.6
Non-faculty professionals	178,560	9.6	150,319	163,267	50.9	426,702	16.8	388,838	26.6	425,319	16.3	387,323	26.7
Nonprofessional staff	790,671	42.4	630,511	695,883	11.9	949,775	37.3	850,040	12.2	915,325	35.2	814,299	12.7
Public, total	1,329,122	100.0	946,354	1,092,558	5.8	1,783,328	100.0	1,449,398	5.4	1,812,513	100.0	1,434,747	5.4
Professional staff	769,836	57.9	502,325	601,942	10.5	1,133,264	63.5	868,112	9.1	1,193,284	65.8	883,579	8.8
Executive/administrative/managerial	60,733	4.6	58,649	59,579	106.6	84,446	4.7	82,835	94.9	81,209	4.5	79,426	98.4
Faculty (instruction and research)	448,733	33.8	313,367	357,761	17.7	580,908	32.6	446,113	17.6	650,434	35.9	470,537	16.6
Instruction and research assistants	127,925	9.6	19,076	63,420	100.1	173,560	9.7	70,707	111.2	173,678	9.6	70,755	110.4
Non-faculty professionals	132,445	10.0	111,233	121,182	52.4	294,350	16.5	268,458	29.3	287,963	15.9	262,862	29.7
Nonprofessional staff	559,286	42.1	444,029	490,616	12.9	650,064	36.5	581,286	13.5	619,229	34.2	551,168	14.2
Private, total	534,668	100.0	393,557	448,781	4.4	761,907	100.0	645,231	3.9	790,099	100.0	659,934	3.8
Professional staff	303,283	56.7	207,075	243,514	8.1	462,196	60.7	376,476	6.6	494,003	62.5	396,802	6.4
Executive/administrative/managerial	40,530	7.6	38,354	39,393	49.8	60,309	7.9	58,883	42.4	62,466	7.9	61,096	41.6
Faculty (instruction and research)	184,477	34.5	120,704	142,772	13.7	245,344	32.2	186,452	13.4	265,040	33.5	198,282	12.8
Instruction and research assistants	32,161	6.0	8,931	19,264	101.9	24,191	3.2	10,760	232.1	29,141	3.7	12,962	195.9
Non-faculty professionals	46,115	8.6	39,086	42,085	46.6	132,352	17.4	120,380	20.7	137,356	17.4	124,461	20.4
Nonprofessional staff	231,385	43.3	186,482	205,267	9.6	299,711	39.3	268,755	9.3	296,096	37.5	263,131	9.6

NOTE.—Because of rounding, details may not add to totals.

SOURCE: U.S. Department of Education, National Center for Education Statistics, Higher Education General Information Survey (HEGIS), "Staff, 1976" survey; and Integrated Postsecondary Education Data System (IPEDS), "Staff" survey. (This table was prepared January 1996.)

Table 217.—Employees in institutions of higher education by race, primary occupation, control of institution, sex, and employment status: Fall 1993

Primary occupation, control of institution, sex, and employment status	Total	White, non-Hispanic	Black, non-Hispanic	Hispanic	Asian/ Pacific Islander	American Indian/ Alaskan Native	Non-resident alien	Race/ ethnicity unknown
1	2	3	4	5	6	7	8	9
Total, all institutions	**2,602,612**	**2,021,998**	**274,555**	**100,990**	**95,831**	**12,615**	**70,359**	**26,264**
Professional staff	1,687,287	1,375,939	103,327	44,085	70,518	6,829	64,097	22,492
Executive/administrative/managerial	143,675	123,737	12,619	3,715	2,395	745	279	185
Faculty (instruction and research)	915,474	779,041	45,172	22,312	35,289	3,407	14,878	15,375
Instruction and research assistants	202,819	131,242	7,487	5,245	14,832	677	37,751	5,585
Non-faculty professionals	425,319	341,919	38,049	12,813	18,002	2,000	11,189	1,347
Nonprofessional staff	915,325	646,059	171,228	56,905	25,313	5,786	6,262	3,772
Public, total	1,812,513	1,408,756	183,885	71,862	65,685	10,495	54,921	16,909
Professional staff	1,193,284	966,121	72,658	33,120	49,711	5,679	51,820	14,175
Executive/administrative/managerial	81,209	69,596	7,268	2,206	1,340	559	147	93
Faculty (instruction and research)	650,434	551,205	33,895	17,217	24,308	2,870	11,179	9,760
Instruction and research assistants	173,678	113,600	5,966	4,547	12,616	610	32,966	3,373
Non-faculty professionals	287,963	231,720	25,529	9,150	11,447	1,640	7,528	949
Nonprofessional staff	619,229	442,635	111,227	38,742	15,974	4,816	3,101	2,734
Private, total	790,099	613,242	90,670	29,128	30,146	2,120	15,438	9,355
Professional staff	494,003	409,818	30,669	10,965	20,807	1,150	12,277	8,317
Executive/administrative/managerial	62,466	54,141	5,351	1,509	1,055	186	132	92
Faculty (instruction and research)	265,040	227,836	11,277	5,095	10,981	537	3,699	5,615
Instruction and research assistants	29,141	17,642	1,521	698	2,216	67	4,785	2,212
Non-faculty professionals	137,356	110,199	12,520	3,663	6,555	360	3,661	398
Nonprofessional staff	296,096	203,424	60,001	18,163	9,339	970	3,161	1,038
Men, total	1,256,037	980,640	106,290	46,953	53,029	5,827	48,411	14,887
Professional staff	930,933	758,678	44,270	22,778	43,072	3,534	45,347	13,254
Executive/administrative/managerial	82,748	72,585	6,097	2,026	1,314	421	185	120
Faculty (instruction and research)	561,123	478,654	22,660	12,966	24,695	1,955	11,122	9,071
Instruction and research assistants	120,384	73,979	3,415	2,767	9,627	354	26,836	3,406
Non-faculty professionals	166,678	133,460	12,098	5,019	7,436	804	7,204	657
Nonprofessional staff	325,104	221,962	62,020	24,175	9,957	2,293	3,064	1,633
Women, total	1,346,575	1,041,358	168,265	54,037	42,802	6,788	21,948	11,377
Professional staff	756,354	617,261	59,057	21,307	27,446	3,295	18,750	9,238
Executive/administrative/managerial	60,927	51,152	6,522	1,689	1,081	324	94	65
Faculty (instruction and research)	354,351	300,387	22,512	9,346	10,594	1,452	3,756	6,304
Instruction and research assistants	82,435	57,263	4,072	2,478	5,205	323	10,915	2,179
Non-faculty professionals	258,641	208,459	25,951	7,794	10,566	1,196	3,985	690
Nonprofessional staff	590,221	424,097	109,208	32,730	15,356	3,493	3,198	2,139
Full-time, total	1,783,510	1,392,311	219,074	73,960	62,034	9,229	23,912	2,990
Professional staff	1,039,094	871,647	71,263	26,700	42,946	4,446	20,284	1,808
Executive/administrative/managerial	137,834	118,651	12,232	3,580	2,243	726	246	156
Faculty (instruction and research)	545,706	468,770	25,658	12,076	25,269	1,997	10,829	1,107
Non-faculty professionals	355,554	284,226	33,373	11,044	15,434	1,723	9,209	545
Nonprofessional staff	744,416	520,664	147,811	47,260	19,088	4,783	3,628	1,182
Part-time, total	819,102	629,687	55,481	27,030	33,797	3,386	46,447	23,274
Professional staff	648,193	504,292	32,064	17,385	27,572	2,383	43,813	20,684
Executive/administrative/managerial	5,841	5,086	387	135	152	19	33	29
Faculty (instruction and research)	369,768	310,271	19,514	10,236	10,020	1,410	4,049	14,268
Instruction and research assistants	202,819	131,242	7,487	5,245	14,832	677	37,751	5,585
Non-faculty professionals	69,765	57,693	4,676	1,769	2,568	277	1,980	802
Nonprofessional staff	170,909	125,395	23,417	9,645	6,225	1,003	2,634	2,590

SOURCE: U.S. Department of Education, National Center for Education Statistics, Integrated Postsecondary Education Data System (IPEDS), "Staff" survey. (This table was prepared January 1996.)

Table 218.—Employees in institutions of higher education, by primary occupation, sex, employment status, and by type and control of institution: Fall 1993

Primary occupation and type and control of institution	Full-time and part-time					Full-time				Part-time		
	Total		Men	Women		Total		Men	Women	Total	Men	Women
	Number	Percent		Number	Percent of all employees	Number	Percent of all employees					
1	2	3	4	5	6	7	8	9	10	11	12	13
Total, all employees	2,602,612	100.0	1,256,037	1,346,575	51.7	1,783,510	68.5	854,308	929,202	819,102	401,729	417,373
Professional staff	1,687,287	64.8	930,933	756,354	44.8	1,039,094	61.6	586,228	452,866	648,193	344,705	303,488
Executive/administrative/managerial	143,675	5.5	82,748	60,927	42.4	137,834	95.9	80,098	57,736	5,841	2,650	3,191
Faculty (instruction and research)	915,474	35.2	561,123	354,351	38.7	545,706	59.6	363,430	182,276	369,768	197,693	172,075
Instruction and research assistants	202,819	7.8	120,384	82,435	40.6	—	—	—	—	202,819	120,384	82,435
Non-faculty professionals	425,319	16.3	166,678	258,641	60.8	355,554	83.6	142,700	212,854	69,765	23,978	45,787
Nonprofessional staff	915,325	35.2	325,104	590,221	64.5	744,416	81.3	268,080	476,336	170,909	57,024	113,885
Technical and paraprofessionals	183,987	7.1	73,241	110,746	60.2	142,846	77.6	59,070	83,776	41,141	14,171	26,970
Clerical and secretarial	438,041	16.8	50,898	387,143	88.4	351,962	80.3	32,801	319,161	86,079	18,097	67,982
Skilled crafts	64,065	2.5	59,901	4,164	6.5	60,926	95.1	57,736	3,190	3,139	2,165	974
Service and maintenance	229,232	8.8	141,064	88,168	38.5	188,682	82.3	118,473	70,209	40,550	22,591	17,959
Public 4-year, total	1,333,533	100.0	659,112	674,421	50.6	964,028	72.3	472,776	491,252	369,505	186,336	183,169
Professional staff	855,913	64.2	487,132	368,781	43.1	555,457	64.9	322,992	232,465	300,456	164,140	136,316
Executive/administrative/managerial	59,678	4.5	37,238	22,440	37.6	57,847	96.9	36,332	21,515	1,831	906	925
Faculty (instruction and research)	374,021	28.0	248,397	125,624	33.6	285,457	76.3	199,899	85,558	88,564	48,498	40,066
Instruction and research assistants	170,916	12.8	101,836	69,080	40.4	—	—	—	—	170,916	101,836	69,080
Non-faculty professionals	251,298	18.8	99,661	151,637	60.3	212,153	84.4	86,761	125,392	39,145	12,900	26,245
Nonprofessional staff	477,620	35.8	171,980	305,640	64.0	408,571	85.5	149,784	258,787	69,049	22,196	46,853
Technical and paraprofessionals	99,950	7.5	39,707	60,243	60.3	80,053	80.1	33,099	46,954	19,897	6,608	13,289
Clerical and secretarial	217,581	16.3	23,465	194,116	89.2	185,414	85.2	17,061	168,353	32,167	6,404	25,763
Skilled crafts	40,299	3.0	37,989	2,310	5.7	38,865	96.4	36,917	1,948	1,434	1,072	362
Service and maintenance	119,790	9.0	70,819	48,971	40.9	104,239	87.0	62,707	41,532	15,551	8,112	7,439
Public 2-year, total	478,980	100.0	219,672	259,308	54.1	242,392	50.6	109,938	132,454	236,588	109,734	126,854
Professional staff	337,371	70.4	171,764	165,607	49.1	145,969	43.3	76,762	69,207	191,402	95,002	96,400
Executive/administrative/managerial	21,531	4.5	12,813	8,718	40.5	20,142	93.5	12,174	7,968	1,389	639	750
Faculty (instruction and research)	276,413	57.7	143,650	132,763	48.0	97,291	35.2	53,288	44,003	179,122	90,362	88,760
Instruction and research assistants	2,762	0.6	1,145	1,617	58.5	—	—	—	—	2,762	1,145	1,617
Non-faculty professionals	36,665	7.7	14,156	22,509	61.4	28,536	77.8	11,300	17,236	8,129	2,856	5,273
Nonprofessional staff	141,609	29.6	47,908	93,701	66.2	96,423	68.1	33,176	63,247	45,186	14,732	30,454
Technical and paraprofessionals	31,701	6.6	11,939	19,762	62.3	19,536	61.6	7,752	11,784	12,165	4,187	7,978
Clerical and secretarial	72,571	15.2	8,160	64,411	88.8	48,176	66.4	2,903	45,273	24,395	5,257	19,138
Skilled crafts	6,363	1.3	5,589	774	12.2	5,635	88.6	5,173	462	728	416	312
Service and maintenance	30,974	6.5	22,220	8,754	28.3	23,076	74.5	17,348	5,728	7,898	4,872	3,026
Private 4-year, total	762,034	100.0	364,978	397,056	52.1	558,179	73.2	263,311	294,868	203,855	101,667	102,188
Professional staff	473,372	62.1	262,106	211,266	44.6	324,189	68.5	179,871	144,318	149,183	82,235	66,948
Executive/administrative/managerial	59,230	7.8	30,988	28,242	47.7	56,701	95.7	29,919	26,782	2,529	1,069	1,460
Faculty (instruction and research)	251,948	33.1	162,287	89,661	35.6	156,039	61.9	106,428	49,611	95,909	55,859	40,050
Instruction and research assistants	28,880	3.8	17,254	11,626	40.3	—	—	—	—	28,880	17,254	11,626
Non-faculty professionals	133,314	17.5	51,577	81,737	61.3	111,449	83.6	43,524	67,925	21,865	8,053	13,812
Nonprofessional staff	288,662	37.9	102,872	185,790	64.4	233,990	81.1	83,440	150,550	54,672	19,432	35,240
Technical and paraprofessionals	51,111	6.7	21,211	29,900	58.5	42,367	82.9	17,915	24,452	8,744	3,296	5,448
Clerical and secretarial	144,047	18.9	18,943	125,104	86.8	115,493	80.2	12,654	102,839	28,554	6,289	22,265
Skilled crafts	17,072	2.2	16,071	1,001	5.9	16,158	94.6	15,415	743	914	656	258
Service and maintenance	76,432	10.0	46,647	29,785	39.0	59,972	78.5	37,456	22,516	16,460	9,191	7,269
Private 2-year, total	28,065	100.0	12,275	15,790	56.3	18,911	67.4	8,283	10,628	9,154	3,992	5,162
Professional staff	20,631	73.5	9,931	10,700	51.9	13,479	65.3	6,603	6,876	7,152	3,328	3,824
Executive/administrative/managerial	3,236	11.5	1,709	1,527	47.2	3,144	97.2	1,673	1,471	92	36	56
Faculty (instruction and research)	13,092	46.6	6,789	6,303	48.1	6,919	52.8	3,815	3,104	6,173	2,974	3,199
Instruction and research assistants	261	0.9	149	112	42.9	—	—	—	—	261	149	112
Non-faculty professionals	4,042	14.4	1,284	2,758	68.2	3,416	84.5	1,115	2,301	626	169	457
Nonprofessional staff	7,434	26.5	2,344	5,090	68.5	5,432	73.1	1,680	3,752	2,002	664	1,338
Technical and paraprofessionals	1,225	4.4	384	841	68.7	890	72.7	304	586	335	80	255
Clerical and secretarial	3,842	13.7	330	3,512	91.4	2,879	74.9	183	2,696	963	147	816
Skilled crafts	331	1.2	252	79	23.9	268	81.0	231	37	63	21	42
Service and maintenance	2,036	7.3	1,378	658	32.3	1,395	68.5	962	433	641	416	225

—Not applicable.

NOTE.—Because of rounding, details may not add to totals.

SOURCE: U.S. Department of Education, National Center for Education Statistics, Integrated Postsecondary Education Data System (IPEDS), "Staff" survey. (This table was prepared December 1995.)

Table 219.—Staff and student/staff ratios in institutions of higher education, by type and control of institution and by state: Fall 1993

State or other area	Full-time-equivalent staff				Full-time-equivalent faculty				Full-time-equivalent students per FTE staff				Full-time-equivalent students per FTE faculty				Full-time-equivalent faculty as a percent of FTE staff			
	Public		Private		Public		Private		Public		Private		Public		Private		Public		Private	
	4-year	2-year	4-year	2-year	4-year	2-year	4-year	2-year	4-year	2-year	4-year	2-year	4-year	2-year	4-year	2-year	4-year	2-year	4-year	2-year
1	2	3	4	5	6	7	8	9	10	11	12	13	14	15	16	17	18	19	20	21
United States	1,109,789	324,958	637,622	22,312	314,502	156,035	189,227	9,055	4.3	9.4	3.7	8.3	15.2	19.5	12.4	20.3	28.3	48.0	29.7	40.6
Alabama	32,656	5,338	3,947	267	6,878	2,856	1,377	105	3.2	10.7	4.9	6.5	15.3	19.9	14.0	16.7	21.1	53.5	34.9	39.3
Alaska	3,122	29	209	31	991	9	77	11	5.8	—	4.8	7.8	18.2	—	13.1	20.8	31.7	—	36.7	37.5
Arizona	17,912	6,376	1,540	128	4,352	2,820	703	48	4.4	12.0	14.5	8.4	18.0	27.2	31.7	22.3	24.3	44.2	45.7	37.7
Arkansas	14,197	1,520	1,886	70	3,791	717	635	36	3.9	9.3	5.1	13.6	14.7	19.6	15.1	26.4	26.7	47.1	33.7	51.5
California	91,480	46,908	44,282	1,983	29,363	23,003	13,960	731	4.6	12.3	4.0	6.7	14.2	25.1	12.8	18.1	32.1	49.0	31.5	36.9
Colorado	20,415	4,260	3,720	406	7,633	2,184	1,326	176	5.1	9.5	5.1	9.5	13.7	18.5	14.3	22.0	37.4	51.3	35.6	43.2
Connecticut	10,598	2,723	14,722	238	3,092	1,482	4,920	89	4.3	8.4	2.9	4.9	14.6	15.4	8.6	13.1	29.2	54.4	33.4	37.3
Delaware	4,340	786	609	—	992	297	236	—	4.8	8.1	8.5	—	21.1	21.3	21.9	—	22.9	37.9	38.8	—
District of Columbia ..	1,509	—	26,456	—	601	—	5,605	—	4.5	—	2.1	—	11.4	—	10.0	—	39.8	—	21.2	—
Florida	31,694	22,487	18,174	712	9,067	9,602	5,811	334	4.7	8.0	4.4	6.3	16.3	18.8	13.7	13.3	28.6	42.7	32.0	46.9
Georgia	30,490	7,542	14,352	673	7,593	3,735	4,103	300	4.2	7.3	3.5	8.5	16.7	14.7	12.3	19.0	24.9	49.5	28.6	44.6
Hawaii	4,903	1,505	1,216	—	1,787	771	489	—	3.9	10.6	7.6	—	10.8	20.8	19.0	—	36.5	51.2	40.3	—
Idaho	5,681	640	374	874	2,082	281	171	372	5.5	7.8	5.7	9.7	15.1	17.8	12.5	22.9	36.7	44.0	45.8	42.5
Illinois	43,829	19,673	38,784	703	11,200	9,219	11,439	316	3.7	9.7	3.6	8.3	14.6	20.8	12.2	18.4	25.6	46.9	29.5	44.9
Indiana	33,476	3,711	12,212	240	9,940	1,828	3,749	102	4.5	6.5	4.3	12.3	15.2	13.1	14.1	29.0	29.7	49.3	30.7	42.4
Iowa	16,981	4,645	7,852	270	3,926	1,995	2,772	88	3.4	8.6	5.2	7.2	14.8	20.0	14.7	21.9	23.1	42.9	35.3	32.7
Kansas	15,759	4,739	2,407	185	4,705	2,198	955	73	4.7	7.6	5.3	4.4	15.7	16.4	13.3	11.2	29.9	46.4	39.7	39.6
Kentucky	20,157	2,677	4,457	413	5,833	1,570	1,598	161	4.4	11.4	5.0	11.2	15.1	19.5	13.9	28.7	28.9	58.7	35.8	39.0
Louisiana	16,702	1,509	6,259	66	5,674	853	1,906	31	7.4	11.4	3.7	9.1	21.8	20.1	12.1	19.3	34.0	56.5	30.5	47.1
Maine	5,097	600	2,860	113	1,475	296	822	58	4.7	7.7	4.0	13.3	16.3	15.5	14.1	26.2	28.9	49.4	28.7	51.0
Maryland	19,968	7,671	12,572	155	6,678	3,305	3,524	52	4.3	7.8	2.3	5.6	12.9	18.1	8.1	16.7	33.4	43.1	28.0	33.6
Massachusetts	18,285	5,486	55,034	1,247	5,165	2,617	14,103	495	4.3	8.8	3.4	7.7	15.3	18.5	13.1	19.4	28.2	47.7	25.6	39.7
Michigan	50,871	10,844	10,245	316	13,805	5,212	3,593	118	4.1	10.5	6.1	6.2	15.2	21.9	17.3	16.7	27.1	48.1	35.1	37.4
Minnesota	22,409	5,474	8,693	410	5,527	3,089	3,247	203	4.1	10.2	5.3	9.3	16.6	18.0	14.2	18.9	24.7	56.4	37.4	49.4
Mississippi	14,675	4,682	1,525	168	3,389	2,461	533	60	3.5	8.9	6.5	6.6	15.1	16.9	18.6	18.4	23.1	52.6	35.0	35.8
Missouri	22,494	4,723	18,095	721	7,531	2,211	5,588	321	4.3	9.4	3.9	7.1	12.9	20.0	12.5	16.0	33.5	46.8	30.9	44.5
Montana	4,790	444	668	92	1,550	201	227	33	5.6	6.7	5.3	6.2	17.2	14.9	15.7	17.3	32.4	45.2	34.0	36.0
Nebraska	12,424	2,158	3,904	139	3,291	887	1,421	45	3.9	8.6	4.2	3.2	14.7	21.0	11.5	9.8	26.5	41.1	36.4	32.7
Nevada	3,999	1,598	74	13	1,329	973	21	5	5.3	8.6	7.6	1.9	16.0	14.2	27.3	5.0	33.2	60.9	27.8	38.8
New Hampshire	3,879	834	5,145	265	1,233	548	1,530	102	5.6	6.4	3.7	11.7	17.6	9.7	12.3	30.5	31.8	65.7	29.7	38.4
New Jersey	27,779	8,188	11,854	371	6,914	3,373	3,442	139	3.7	10.2	3.8	9.3	15.0	24.7	13.1	24.6	24.9	41.2	29.0	37.6
New Mexico	12,122	2,992	405	43	2,817	1,309	166	20	3.4	8.4	5.5	13.0	14.6	19.2	13.3	27.7	23.2	43.7	41.0	47.0
New York	53,411	20,521	112,837	2,741	17,549	9,667	30,835	1,142	5.0	8.9	3.0	10.2	15.3	18.9	11.2	24.4	32.9	47.1	27.3	41.7
North Carolina	32,803	14,468	26,042	510	8,428	7,983	5,292	211	4.0	6.3	2.2	5.0	15.6	11.5	11.0	12.0	25.7	55.2	20.3	41.4
North Dakota	5,752	916	373	175	1,911	395	172	36	4.4	7.2	8.3	1.5	13.2	16.7	18.0	7.3	33.2	43.1	46.1	20.6
Ohio	49,726	9,961	19,099	889	13,916	4,847	6,978	432	4.6	9.3	5.0	11.7	16.4	19.1	13.7	24.0	28.0	48.7	36.5	48.6
Oklahoma	15,388	4,367	3,491	635	4,619	1,757	1,260	168	5.1	8.8	5.1	3.1	16.9	21.8	14.0	11.3	30.0	40.2	36.1	26.5
Oregon	15,169	6,836	3,909	23	4,894	3,098	1,533	8	3.5	6.8	4.9	7.9	10.8	15.0	12.6	22.8	32.3	45.3	39.2	34.6
Pennsylvania	51,345	7,583	51,886	3,207	15,180	4,034	16,216	1,131	3.9	8.8	3.5	9.1	13.2	16.6	11.1	25.8	29.6	53.2	31.3	35.3
Rhode Island	3,522	666	7,078	197	1,091	285	1,970	100	5.3	13.0	4.2	—	17.3	30.5	15.1	—	31.0	42.8	27.8	—
South Carolina	19,962	4,985	4,103	217	5,369	2,278	1,362	80	3.6	7.5	5.1	8.1	13.4	16.3	15.5	21.8	26.9	45.7	33.2	37.0
South Dakota	4,181	30	997	24	1,482	13	382	14	6.3	5.8	5.3	5.2	17.7	13.5	14.0	8.9	35.4	42.6	38.3	59.1
Tennessee	22,325	4,728	17,842	348	6,428	2,240	4,330	166	4.3	10.0	2.4	8.2	14.8	21.1	10.0	17.2	28.8	47.4	24.3	47.5
Texas	80,362	28,794	21,879	535	19,876	13,895	6,801	234	4.2	8.1	3.9	9.1	17.1	16.8	12.7	20.8	24.7	48.3	31.1	43.7
Utah	11,894	1,506	4,351	131	3,343	556	1,647	69	4.9	11.5	7.8	8.3	17.4	31.0	20.6	15.7	28.1	36.9	37.9	52.9
Vermont	3,437	459	3,069	151	1,131	235	954	99	3.9	5.4	4.1	1.1	11.9	10.5	13.3	1.6	32.9	51.3	31.1	65.0
Virginia	35,868	4,759	10,123	664	9,025	2,015	3,347	322	3.8	14.4	4.2	5.6	15.1	34.1	12.6	11.5	25.2	42.3	33.1	48.5
Washington	24,149	8,823	5,645	215	6,066	4,074	2,374	95	3.2	10.9	5.2	9.2	12.6	23.7	12.4	20.9	25.1	46.2	42.0	44.3
West Virginia	10,454	530	1,623	56	3,744	233	576	17	5.4	9.1	5.5	16.8	15.1	20.8	15.4	54.4	35.8	43.9	35.5	30.8
Wisconsin	26,118	10,643	8,744	130	7,798	5,826	3,153	62	4.7	6.1	4.6	12.8	15.9	11.2	12.7	26.8	29.9	54.7	36.1	48.0
Wyoming	2,848	1,533	—	150	805	700	—	43	3.5	7.4	—	4.7	12.4	16.2	—	16.3	28.3	45.7	—	28.7
U.S. Service Schools	6,383	88	—	—	1,643	—	—	—	2.9	222.4	—	—	11.2	—	—	—	25.7	—	—	—
Outlying areas	11,297	1,680	6,926	1,206	3,740	684	2,711	438	4.3	5.1	11.1	9.5	13.1	12.6	28.5	26.0	33.1	40.7	39.1	36.3
American Samoa	—	180	—	—	—	98	—	—	—	5.6	—	—	—	10.3	—	—	—	54.4	—	—
Federated States of Micronesia	—	83	—	—	—	42	—	—	—	9.0	—	—	—	17.7	—	—	—	50.6	—	—
Guam	591	325	—	—	222	152	—	—	4.9	2.8	—	—	13.1	6.0	—	37.6	46.8	—	—
Marshall Islands	—	31	—	—	—	8	—	—	—	—	—	—	—	—	—	—	—	25.7	—	—
Northern Marianas	—	181	—	—	—	73	—	—	—	3.6	—	—	—	8.9	—	—	—	40.4	—	—
Palau	—	116	—	—	—	43	—	—	—	3.2	—	—	—	8.7	—	—	—	37.2	—	—
Puerto Rico	10,222	764	6,926	1,206	3,397	268	2,711	438	4.3	6.5	11.1	9.5	13.0	18.5	28.5	26.0	33.2	35.0	39.1	36.3
Virgin Islands	484	—	—	—	121	—	—	—	4.0	—	—	—	15.8	—	—	—	25.0	—	—	—

—Data not reported or not applicable.

NOTE.—Data include imputations for nonrespondent institutions.

SOURCE: U.S. Department of Education, National Center for Education Statistics, Integrated Postsecondary Education Data System (IPEDS), "Staff, 1993" and "Fall Enrollment" surveys. (This table was prepared January 1996.)

Table 220.—Full-time and part-time senior instructional faculty [1] in institutions of higher education, by employment status, control, and type of institution: Fall 1970 to fall 1993

[In thousands]

Year	Total	Employment status		Control		Type	
		Full-time	Part-time	Public	Private	4-year	2-year
1	2	3	4	5	6	7	8
1970	474	369	104	314	160	382	92
1971[2]	492	379	113	333	159	387	105
1972	500	380	120	343	157	384	116
1973[2]	527	389	138	365	162	401	126
1974[2]	567	406	161	397	170	427	140
1975[2]	628	440	188	443	185	467	161
1976	633	434	199	449	184	467	166
1977	678	448	230	492	186	485	193
1979[2]	675	445	230	488	187	494	182
1980[2]	686	450	236	495	191	494	192
1981	705	461	244	509	196	493	212
1982[2]	710	462	248	506	204	493	217
1983	724	471	254	512	212	504	220
1984[2]	717	462	255	505	212	504	213
1985[2]	715	459	256	503	212	504	211
1986[2]	722	459	263	510	212	506	216
1987[3]	793	523	270	553	240	548	246
1989[3]	824	524	300	577	247	584	241
1991[3]	826	536	291	581	245	591	235
1993[3]	915	546	370	650	265	626	290

[1] Includes faculty members with the title of professor, associate professor, assistant professor, instructor, lecturer, assisting professor, adjunct professor, or interim professor (or the equivalent). Excluded are graduate students with titles such as graduate or teaching fellow who assist senior faculty.

[2] Estimated on the basis of enrollment.

[3] Because of revised survey methods, data are not directly comparable with figures for years prior to 1987.

NOTE.—Data exclude faculty employed by system offices. Some data have been revised from previously published figures. For methodological details on estimates, see *Projections of Education Statistics to 2000.* Because of rounding, details may not add to totals.

SOURCE: U.S. Department of Education, National Center for Education Statistics, Employees in Institutions of Higher Education, various years; *Projections of Education Statistics to 2000;* Integrated Postsecondary Education Data System (IPEDS), "Staff" survey; and U.S. Equal Employment Opportunity Commission, Higher Education Staff Information Report File, 1977, 1981, and 1983. (This table was prepared April 1996.)

Table 221.—Full-time instructional faculty in institutions of higher education, by race/ethnicity, academic rank, and sex: Fall 1993

Academic rank and sex	Total	Race/ethnicity						
		White, non-Hispanic	Black, non-Hispanic	Hispanic	Asian or Pacific Islander	American Indian/ Alaskan Native	Nonresident alien	Race/ ethnicity unknown
1	2	3	4	5	6	7	8	9
Men and women, all ranks	**545,706**	**468,770**	**25,658**	**12,076**	**25,269**	**1,997**	**10,829**	**1,107**
Professors	157,253	141,848	4,526	2,387	7,033	352	942	165
Associate professors	120,696	106,017	5,326	2,291	5,471	283	1,139	169
Assistant professors	129,159	105,091	7,686	3,387	7,586	431	4,602	376
Instructors	67,700	56,900	4,712	2,260	2,143	610	852	223
Lecturers	13,714	11,292	839	418	557	56	527	25
Other faculty	57,184	47,622	2,569	1,333	2,479	265	2,767	149
Men, all ranks	**363,430**	**313,278**	**13,385**	**7,459**	**18,943**	**1,237**	**8,355**	**773**
Professors	130,574	118,308	2,982	1,776	6,245	283	848	132
Associate professors	84,506	74,191	3,089	1,590	4,367	193	942	134
Assistant professors	74,822	59,709	3,801	1,951	5,277	208	3,628	248
Instructors	34,343	28,768	2,094	1,214	1,136	394	582	155
Lecturers	6,689	5,503	377	190	254	29	321	15
Other faculty	32,496	26,799	1,042	738	1,664	130	2,034	89
Women, all ranks	**182,276**	**155,492**	**12,273**	**4,617**	**6,326**	**760**	**2,474**	**334**
Professors	26,679	23,540	1,544	611	788	69	94	33
Associate professors	36,190	31,826	2,237	701	1,104	90	197	35
Assistant professors	54,337	45,382	3,885	1,436	2,309	223	974	128
Instructors	33,357	28,132	2,618	1,046	1,007	216	270	68
Lecturers	7,025	5,789	462	228	303	27	206	10
Other faculty	24,688	20,823	1,527	595	815	135	733	60

NOTE.—Data exclude faculty employed by system offices. Totals may differ from figures reported in other tables because of varying survey methodologies.

SOURCE: U.S. Department of Education, National Center for Education Statistics, Integrated Postsecondary Education Data System (IPEDS), "Staff" survey. (This table was prepared June 1996.)

Table 222.—Full-time and part-time instructional faculty and staff in institutions of higher education, by selected characteristics and type and control of institution: Fall 1992

Selected characteristics	Number in thousands	Percent total	Public research	Private research	Public doctoral	Private doctoral	Public comprehensive	Private comprehensive	Private liberal arts	Public 2-year	Other
1	2	3	4	5	6	7	8	9	10	11	12
Full-time instructional faculty											
Total (in thousands)	528	—	107	32	53	29	94	39	38	110	26
Percent	—	100.0	20.3	6.1	10.0	5.4	17.9	7.3	7.2	20.8	5.0
Percentage distribution											
Total	—	100.0	100.0	100.0	100.0	100.0	100.0	100.0	100.0	100.0	100.0
Sex											
Male	353	66.8	76.7	69.1	69.9	76.4	66.1	64.9	61.1	54.7	70.5
Female	176	33.2	23.3	30.9	30.1	23.6	33.9	35.2	38.9	45.3	29.5
Race											
White, non-Hispanic	457	86.5	88.0	83.7	87.5	84.1	82.7	91.3	90.0	85.5	89.2
Black, non-Hispanic	27	5.2	2.8	5.0	3.1	4.9	9.1	3.5	5.4	6.2	3.7
Hispanic	14	2.6	2.2	2.1	2.5	3.7	2.6	1.6	1.3	4.1	1.4
Asian/Pacific Islander	28	5.2	6.9	9.0	6.1	7.1	5.1	3.3	2.8	3.3	5.2
American Indian/Alaskan Native	3	0.5	0.1	0.2	0.8	0.2	0.5	0.2	0.5	1.0	0.5
Age											
29 or younger	8	1.4	1.0	1.8	1.2	0.6	1.5	1.4	2.1	1.7	2.0
30 to 34	35	6.7	7.2	7.8	8.4	9.2	5.9	7.0	7.0	5.3	5.1
35 to 39	67	12.6	14.3	20.4	14.4	15.4	10.6	10.4	13.9	9.8	10.8
40 to 44	90	17.1	18.1	19.9	17.4	17.9	15.1	16.4	17.4	16.8	16.5
45 to 49	98	18.5	17.0	15.3	16.8	19.7	18.8	18.9	17.4	20.8	17.8
50 to 54	95	18.0	15.9	11.5	17.4	12.8	21.5	16.7	14.7	21.9	18.2
55 to 59	67	12.7	12.8	9.1	11.7	10.0	14.4	12.8	11.9	13.5	14.4
60 to 64	45	8.4	8.9	8.3	8.2	8.0	8.2	11.3	8.5	7.1	9.6
65 or older	24	4.5	4.8	5.9	4.5	6.5	3.9	5.1	4.8	3.2	5.8
Highest degree											
Doctoral	284	54.0	70.8	63.7	62.6	58.2	68.1	60.8	58.4	16.6	40.7
Professional	58	11.1	17.0	24.9	20.1	29.4	4.3	7.7	3.2	2.3	9.7
Master's	156	29.7	10.6	10.2	16.0	10.5	26.4	29.3	35.3	63.9	42.1
Bachelor's	21	4.0	1.6	1.1	1.3	1.9	1.1	2.1	3.1	11.9	6.6
Less than bachelor's	6	1.2	0.1	0.1	(1)	(1)	0.2	0.1	(1)	5.4	0.9
Academic rank											
Full professor	161	30.4	39.8	33.3	31.3	30.5	34.3	26.8	28.7	19.1	27.8
Associate professor	124	23.4	26.4	22.7	26.3	26.8	26.9	29.0	25.3	12.9	23.4
Assistant professor	124	23.5	22.7	27.0	31.2	29.1	26.1	31.9	29.9	11.3	21.8
Instructor	74	14.0	4.0	4.6	7.6	9.1	8.6	8.0	9.2	39.7	12.5
Lecturer	12	2.2	3.9	6.7	1.7	1.8	2.6	1.2	1.6	0.4	0.7
Other	17	3.2	3.2	4.8	1.8	2.6	1.4	1.9	3.7	5.7	2.9
No rank	17	3.2	0.2	1.0	0.2	0.1	0.2	1.3	1.7	11.0	10.9
Base salary											
Under $10,000	14	2.6	2.0	3.0	2.1	2.7	2.1	2.7	2.5	3.5	3.6
$10,000 to 24,999	29	5.6	3.6	5.1	4.7	2.8	5.5	5.3	10.0	6.2	10.7
$25,000 to 39,999	182	34.4	19.5	14.4	29.0	24.5	37.1	44.0	53.5	47.2	36.9
$40,000 to 54,999	164	31.0	29.4	28.5	29.8	24.9	34.0	32.1	24.6	33.8	35.5
$55,000 to 69,999	77	14.5	22.7	15.7	17.0	19.8	16.9	10.0	6.0	8.0	6.5
$70,000 to 84,999	32	6.1	12.1	13.0	9.0	9.9	3.3	3.6	2.2	0.8	4.0
$85,000 to 99,999	11	2.1	4.4	3.7	2.3	7.7	0.7	1.0	0.6	0.1	1.6
$100,000 or more	20	3.7	6.5	16.6	6.2	7.7	0.4	1.4	0.5	0.4	1.2

Table 222.—Full-time and part-time instructional faculty and staff in institutions of higher education, by selected characteristics and type and control of institution: Fall 1992—Continued

Selected characteristics	Number in thousands	Percent total	Public research	Private research	Public doctoral	Private doctoral	Public comprehensive	Private comprehensive	Private liberal arts	Public 2-year	Other
1	2	3	4	5	6	7	8	9	10	11	12
Part-time instructional faculty											
Total (in thousands)	377	—	25	17	21	18	47	37	21	166	24
Percent	—	100.0	6.7	4.6	5.5	4.8	12.5	9.7	5.6	44.2	6.5
Percentage distribution											
Total	—	100.0	100.0	100.0	100.0	100.0	100.0	100.0	100.0	100.0	100.0
Sex											
Male	209	55.4	56.8	58.7	55.4	63.1	49.1	56.4	46.6	56.6	56.1
Female	168	44.6	43.3	41.3	44.6	36.9	51.0	43.7	53.4	43.4	44.0
Race											
White, non-Hispanic	333	88.3	87.8	89.5	91.4	87.7	85.0	90.8	89.6	87.9	90.8
Black, non-Hispanic	18	4.8	2.5	4.4	3.3	7.1	7.2	5.0	5.9	4.0	3.2
Hispanic	11	3.0	3.2	2.7	1.6	1.5	3.0	1.1	2.9	4.0	1.1
Asian/Pacific Islander	12	3.2	6.6	3.0	3.3	3.5	4.1	2.5	1.6	2.7	3.8
American Indian/Alaskan Native	2	0.6	(¹)	0.4	0.4	0.2	0.7	0.5	0.1	0.8	1.1
Age											
29 or younger	20	5.4	4.0	2.7	8.3	1.9	7.7	4.0	2.7	6.1	5.0
30 to 34	36	9.5	6.5	18.5	6.5	7.4	10.1	6.9	8.0	10.0	11.7
35 to 39	59	15.6	15.7	13.8	16.8	27.3	15.0	14.6	19.3	14.6	14.5
40 to 44	70	18.6	20.1	11.8	19.4	16.0	17.9	18.4	21.4	19.5	16.1
45 to 49	68	18.0	19.0	19.0	17.1	18.9	16.1	20.9	21.8	17.5	16.7
50 to 54	45	12.0	12.9	12.1	10.5	9.9	11.0	11.8	9.3	12.7	13.4
55 to 59	29	7.6	8.1	11.1	6.2	3.8	10.0	9.3	6.1	7.2	6.3
60 to 64	23	6.1	5.0	8.1	5.4	6.5	5.9	6.5	4.2	6.5	4.9
65 or older	27	7.1	8.9	2.8	10.0	8.4	6.4	7.6	7.2	6.1	11.6
Highest degree											
Doctoral	59	16.0	30.4	26.3	17.5	26.0	19.0	21.5	21.8	8.1	17.6
Professional	40	10.7	18.5	23.7	29.2	34.4	5.2	10.5	3.2	5.1	15.0
Master's	190	51.6	39.1	43.2	41.4	31.5	61.1	58.4	58.7	53.0	50.3
Bachelor's	63	17.0	12.1	6.8	11.7	7.9	14.0	9.3	15.7	24.0	13.3
Less than bachelor's	17	4.7	(¹)	(¹)	0.2	0.2	0.7	0.2	0.6	9.8	3.8
Academic rank											
Full professor	32	8.6	11.6	18.6	9.5	14.0	6.6	15.2	11.5	4.1	15.1
Associate professor	23	6.0	17.3	15.5	13.5	11.6	3.2	6.4	4.7	2.4	7.0
Assistant professor	24	6.4	14.2	12.6	11.6	19.9	4.1	7.5	11.3	2.4	5.8
Instructor	215	57.2	24.7	27.8	40.1	27.4	51.3	43.5	53.6	76.4	52.7
Lecturer	45	12.0	24.2	18.1	12.9	18.9	23.1	17.6	10.4	5.2	7.4
Other	28	7.3	7.8	5.9	10.9	7.3	11.0	7.9	7.8	5.7	7.7
No rank	9	2.5	0.3	1.6	1.4	0.8	0.8	1.9	0.7	3.8	4.3
Base salary											
Under $10,000	281	74.5	51.8	70.9	65.1	66.3	69.2	79.4	70.0	81.7	72.2
$10,000 to 24,999	68	18.1	30.8	19.3	21.8	23.3	23.0	16.4	23.1	13.2	19.3
$25,000 to 39,999	16	4.2	8.8	5.0	8.1	4.2	5.1	2.9	4.4	2.9	4.7
$40,000 to 54,999	5	1.4	2.6	1.9	2.8	2.2	1.0	0.7	1.1	1.1	2.1
$55,000 to 69,999	2	0.6	3.5	0.9	0.5	0.5	0.3	0.5	0.1	0.3	(¹)
$70,000 to 84,999	1	0.3	0.2	(¹)	0.6	1.4	0.2	(¹)	0.1	0.2	0.9
$85,000 to 99,999	1	0.3	1.7	1.6	0.1	0.2	(¹)	(¹)	0.1	0.1	(¹)
$100,000 or more	3	0.7	0.6	0.4	1.0	1.9	1.1	0.1	1.1	0.5	0.9

¹ Less than 0.05 percent.
—Data not applicable.

NOTE.—Data may not add to totals because of rounding or missing data. Data have been revised from previously published figures.

SOURCE: U.S. Department of Education, National Center for Education Statistics, National Study of Postsecondary Faculty (NSOPF), 1993. (This table was prepared September 1996.)

Table 223.—Full-time instructional faculty and staff in institutions of higher education, by instruction activities and type and control of institution: Fall 1992

Instruction activities	All institutions	Public research	Private research	Public doctoral	Private doctoral	Public comprehensive	Private comprehensive	Private liberal arts	Public 2-year	Other
1	2	3	4	5	6	7	8	9	10	11
Number of full-time instructional and staff (in thousands)	**528**	**107**	**32**	**53**	**29**	**94**	**39**	**38**	**110**	**26**
Percentage distribution	**100.0**	**20.3**	**6.1**	**10.0**	**5.4**	**17.9**	**7.3**	**7.2**	**20.8**	**5.0**
Hours worked per week										
Average hours worked per week	52.5	56.4	57.6	55.1	53.4	52.4	51.8	52.5	46.9	49.0
Paid activities within institution	42.6	48.0	48.6	46.2	44.6	41.3	40.9	42.4	36.0	39.5
Unpaid activities within institution	5.1	4.3	4.1	4.3	3.4	5.9	5.8	5.8	6.0	5.1
Outside paid activities	2.8	2.4	2.6	2.5	3.6	2.8	3.0	2.6	3.1	2.8
Unpaid activities outside institution	2.0	1.8	2.2	2.1	1.8	2.3	2.1	1.6	1.9	1.7
Work time distribution (percent)										
Total	100.0	100.0	100.0	100.0	100.0	100.0	100.0	100.0	100.0	100.0
Teaching	54.5	40.4	34.7	46.9	44.5	60.3	59.7	63.7	68.8	60.8
Research/scholarship	17.7	31.6	35.5	23.8	21.7	14.0	11.8	9.7	4.5	10.7
Professional growth	4.6	3.7	3.3	4.1	4.3	5.0	4.9	4.7	5.8	5.1
Administration	13.0	12.9	12.9	13.2	15.7	12.0	14.6	14.7	12.0	14.9
Outside consulting	2.7	2.5	3.0	2.5	2.8	2.7	3.1	2.3	2.7	2.8
Service/non-teaching	7.4	8.9	10.6	9.6	11.0	6.1	5.9	4.9	6.1	5.6
Preferred work time distribution (percent)										
Total	100.0	100.0	100.0	100.0	100.0	100.0	100.0	100.0	100.0	100.0
Teaching	49.0	36.6	33.2	41.8	39.4	52.4	52.9	56.1	64.1	54.1
Research/scholarship	24.7	38.5	41.7	31.1	30.1	22.4	19.8	18.8	9.2	17.6
Professional growth	8.1	6.5	6.2	7.2	6.9	8.5	8.6	8.8	9.8	9.3
Administration	8.2	7.8	7.1	8.0	10.2	7.7	9.2	8.6	8.1	9.6
Outside consulting	3.3	3.1	3.4	3.3	3.6	3.5	3.9	2.9	3.1	3.7
Service/non-teaching	6.6	7.4	8.4	8.6	9.9	5.6	5.7	4.8	5.7	5.6
Distribution of hours taught per week (percent)										
Total	100.0	100.0	100.0	100.0	100.0	100.0	100.0	100.0	100.0	100.0
Less than 4.0	15.0	30.4	36.7	18.9	21.5	8.2	8.2	6.3	6.2	10.5
4.0 to 5.9	8.0	15.0	18.9	10.4	9.1	4.9	5.2	5.8	3.3	5.9
6.0 to 7.9	15.9	26.5	21.0	21.2	24.9	12.6	14.7	13.1	6.0	14.6
8.0 to 9.9	14.6	11.9	7.0	19.0	18.9	19.9	21.9	22.2	6.5	12.3
10.0 to 14.9	22.5	8.9	8.4	16.9	15.1	36.5	34.6	34.1	19.8	28.6
15.0 or more	23.9	7.3	8.1	13.6	10.6	17.9	15.4	18.5	58.2	28.0
Distribution of number of students taught (percent)										
Total	100.0	100.0	100.0	100.0	100.0	100.0	100.0	100.0	100.0	100.0
Less than 25	13.1	21.7	33.3	15.9	18.5	7.3	8.3	11.7	5.9	13.2
25 to 49	19.9	23.1	24.3	22.2	22.4	15.1	20.4	29.8	14.3	23.0
50 to 74	19.5	18.7	11.6	16.7	13.0	20.2	27.8	26.7	17.4	24.7
75 to 99	15.8	11.0	8.9	13.7	11.1	19.4	21.2	15.8	18.8	15.1
100 to 149	18.9	10.9	10.2	15.5	17.6	25.1	17.4	12.0	27.6	16.3
150 or more	12.8	14.7	11.7	16.1	17.5	13.0	5.0	4.0	16.0	7.7
Distribution of student classroom contact hours/week [1] (percent)										
Total	100.0	100.0	100.0	100.0	100.0	100.0	100.0	100.0	100.0	100.0
Less than 50	8.4	16.6	25.7	10.3	13.2	3.3	4.6	6.1	2.4	6.6
50 to 99	10.6	16.2	18.2	13.5	12.7	7.6	9.9	11.8	4.6	12.1
100 to 199	21.9	25.8	21.9	22.5	25.3	20.0	27.6	34.8	11.8	25.7
200 to 349	27.6	20.1	18.4	25.9	18.1	34.0	38.4	30.2	28.2	28.7
350 to 499	15.7	8.3	4.8	11.3	13.6	20.4	11.8	10.4	26.5	14.8
500 or more	15.8	13.0	11.0	16.6	17.1	14.8	7.8	6.9	26.6	12.1
Distribution of total classroom credit hours (percent)										
Total	100.0	100.0	100.0	100.0	100.0	100.0	100.0	100.0	100.0	100.0
Less than 4.0	14.1	26.2	28.6	15.4	19.4	8.0	8.5	11.8	7.2	12.1
4.0 to 5.9	8.6	14.7	14.8	12.5	10.8	5.8	6.0	5.9	4.2	7.8
6.0 to 7.9	18.3	31.0	25.0	26.0	26.5	15.0	13.6	13.2	8.0	15.3
8.0 to 9.9	18.6	15.0	16.1	22.6	18.8	23.6	28.2	24.4	10.7	18.8
10.0 to 14.9	24.9	9.5	7.4	17.9	17.0	37.3	34.6	34.9	28.4	29.1
15.0 or more	15.5	3.7	8.0	5.6	7.5	10.3	9.2	9.9	41.5	17.0
Number of classes taught for credit										
Faculty with undergraduate classes only (percent)										
Total	100.0	100.0	100.0	100.0	100.0	100.0	100.0	100.0	100.0	100.0
1	16.0	34.4	40.9	20.6	22.1	11.5	11.3	9.9	12.3	13.1
2	23.2	42.9	37.2	34.0	40.8	20.8	21.2	21.6	13.9	19.6
3	23.6	14.5	7.9	27.6	25.0	31.9	31.2	35.0	15.3	27.1
4	20.0	6.1	7.4	13.3	6.5	26.7	26.1	20.7	21.9	25.4
5 or more	17.2	2.1	6.5	4.5	5.5	9.2	10.2	12.9	36.6	14.8
Faculty with graduate classes only (percent)										
Total	100.0	100.0	100.0	100.0	100.0	100.0	100.0	—	—	100.0
1	47.9	57.1	53.2	45.4	46.4	30.3	21.0	—	—	32.6
2	33.4	33.7	38.4	35.0	31.3	23.0	36.3	—	—	36.0
3	12.6	6.8	4.7	13.4	17.4	28.2	30.1	—	—	18.1
4	4.1	1.9	1.6	3.5	3.5	13.3	9.9	—	—	9.3
5 or more	2.0	0.6	2.1	2.7	1.4	5.2	2.8	—	—	4.1
Faculty with both undergraduate and graduate classes (percent)										
Total	100.0	100.0	100.0	100.0	100.0	100.0	100.0	100.0	—	—
2	42.3	58.9	67.6	48.3	40.5	25.0	17.6	22.1	—	—
3	32.2	29.9	22.8	31.3	36.6	34.0	45.7	21.7	—	—
4	16.1	5.5	7.4	14.6	12.1	25.7	27.6	37.0	—	—
5 or more	9.5	5.7	2.2	5.8	10.8	15.3	9.1	19.3	—	—

[1] Hours that faculty and instructional staff spend each week with students during classroom instruction multiplied by the number of students taught.

[2] Less than .05 percent.

—Data not available or not applicable.

NOTE.—Because of rounding, details may not add to totals. Data have been revised from previously published figures.

SOURCE: U.S. Department of Education, National Center for Education Statistics, National Survey of Postsecondary Faculty (NSOPF), 1993. (This table was prepared September 1996.)

Table 224.—Part-time instructional faculty and staff in institutions of higher education, by instruction activities and type and control of institution: Fall 1992

Instruction activities	All institutions	Public research	Private research	Public doctoral	Private doctoral	Public comprehensive	Private comprehensive	Private liberal arts	Public 2-year	Other
1	2	3	4	5	6	7	8	9	10	11
Number of part-time instructional faculty and staff (in thousands)	**377**	**25**	**17**	**21**	**18**	**47**	**37**	**21**	**166**	**24**
Percentage distribution	**100.0**	**6.7**	**4.6**	**5.5**	**4.8**	**12.5**	**9.7**	**5.6**	**44.2**	**6.5**
Hours worked per week										
Average hours worked per week	33.8	38.9	40.3	34.6	37.0	34.7	35.6	33.4	31.5	32.6
Paid activities within institution	11.7	19.9	11.6	14.3	10.7	13.5	10.3	12.8	10.1	10.4
Unpaid activities within institution	3.2	4.2	4.3	3.9	3.6	3.5	2.3	2.5	3.1	2.8
Outside paid activities	16.9	12.5	22.7	14.5	20.6	15.5	20.9	16.2	16.5	17.1
Unpaid activities outside institution	1.9	2.3	1.7	2.0	2.0	2.2	2.1	1.9	1.8	2.3
Work time distribution (percent)										
Total	100.0	100.0	100.0	100.0	100.0	100.0	100.0	100.0	100.0	100.0
Teaching	59.8	52.1	38.7	60.7	42.7	61.6	56.6	61.4	64.9	59.3
Research/scholarship	7.1	15.7	17.7	8.7	8.9	8.2	5.9	6.6	4.4	7.0
Professional growth	5.8	5.2	8.2	7.5	5.8	6.0	5.8	6.1	5.5	5.1
Administration	5.8	5.4	12.7	5.1	4.6	6.2	6.3	7.0	5.0	5.2
Outside consulting	10.4	10.4	11.0	8.6	17.0	8.2	12.4	10.6	9.9	11.0
Service/non-teaching	11.1	11.2	11.6	9.2	21.0	9.7	12.9	8.3	10.3	12.5
Preferred work time distribution (percent)										
Total	100.0	100.0	100.0	100.0	100.0	100.0	100.0	100.0	100.0	100.0
Teaching	57.7	51.9	37.5	58.2	40.6	57.0	56.2	58.8	63.1	56.4
Research/scholarship	11.2	18.8	21.2	13.2	12.6	13.3	10.1	11.4	8.1	11.4
Professional growth	9.0	7.6	9.4	9.7	8.6	9.3	8.4	9.0	9.1	8.6
Administration	4.3	3.8	9.6	3.2	4.0	5.0	5.1	4.8	3.6	3.8
Outside consulting	8.6	7.6	9.9	7.2	16.8	7.2	9.4	8.8	8.0	9.2
Service/non-teaching	9.3	10.3	12.3	8.5	17.4	8.3	10.8	7.3	8.0	10.6
Distribution of hours taught per week (percent)										
Total	100.0	100.0	100.0	100.0	100.0	100.0	100.0	100.0	100.0	100.0
Less than 4.0	34.6	44.3	60.5	36.2	52.5	36.0	42.0	36.7	26.7	37.2
4.0 to 5.9	15.3	11.1	14.8	15.3	16.4	15.7	13.2	16.7	15.9	16.1
6.0 to 7.9	20.0	15.7	14.5	19.5	13.8	20.9	18.0	20.2	22.9	12.9
8.0 to 9.9	12.4	13.0	4.6	14.9	6.9	11.6	9.7	8.8	14.6	12.8
10.0 to 14.9	9.7	5.7	3.4	8.5	4.0	9.7	8.5	9.2	11.6	10.9
15.0 or more	7.9	10.2	2.2	5.8	6.4	6.2	8.6	8.5	8.4	10.2
Distribution of number of students taught (percent)										
Total hours taught per week	100.0	100.0	100.0	100.0	100.0	100.0	100.0	100.0	100.0	100.0
Less than 25	36.5	36.0	57.4	27.1	48.2	26.2	47.2	50.1	31.8	49.2
25 to 49	33.5	22.9	25.5	29.4	31.8	33.7	28.9	32.7	38.7	23.4
50 to 74	16.2	15.6	11.1	20.2	9.9	21.1	13.2	10.1	16.9	15.7
75 to 99	6.2	5.9	3.1	8.7	2.4	8.0	5.4	3.5	6.7	5.3
100 to 149	5.1	8.5	2.7	8.3	0.5	8.4	4.0	3.1	4.4	5.7
150 or more	2.5	11.1	0.2	6.2	7.2	2.7	1.4	0.6	1.5	0.7
Distribution of student classroom contact hours per week [1] (percent)										
Total students taught	100.0	100.0	100.0	100.0	100.0	100.0	100.0	100.0	100.0	100.0
Less than 50	18.6	23.8	45.3	13.2	35.4	12.4	27.6	27.2	11.6	30.3
50 to 99	26.8	18.9	34.6	21.8	28.5	24.0	30.0	33.3	27.8	20.2
100 to 199	30.3	25.0	9.5	35.7	22.1	36.9	25.5	25.6	33.6	24.7
200 to 349	15.4	14.4	7.7	17.6	4.5	14.8	9.6	8.9	18.8	18.0
350 to 499	4.6	6.7	2.7	5.0	2.1	6.7	2.7	4.0	4.6	4.5
500 or more	4.4	11.1	0.2	6.6	7.5	5.2	4.7	1.1	3.7	2.3
Distribution of total classroom credit hours (percent)										
Total contact hours	100.0	100.0	100.0	100.0	100.0	100.0	100.0	100.0	100.0	100.0
Less than 4.0	40.3	48.7	51.5	36.9	54.6	39.9	48.5	47.8	35.1	37.3
4.0 to 5.9	15.7	12.8	27.8	17.2	10.9	13.7	9.6	14.2	16.4	21.9
6.0 to 7.9	21.5	16.8	8.9	21.6	16.8	24.9	20.9	18.8	23.8	17.2
8.0 to 9.9	12.4	16.9	5.5	9.3	11.5	13.9	8.9	9.5	13.4	13.7
10.0 to 14.9	6.9	3.2	6.3	8.1	4.3	5.4	7.9	7.3	8.0	5.2
15.0 or more	3.2	1.6	(2)	7.0	2.0	2.3	4.4	2.5	3.3	4.7
Number of classes taught for credit										
Faculty with undergraduate classes only (percent)										
Total undergraduate credit courses	100.0	100.0	100.0	100.0	100.0	100.0	100.0	100.0	100.0	100.0
1	50.2	49.4	69.1	48.6	61.6	49.6	54.5	50.7	48.1	52.4
2	32.0	26.7	26.1	34.8	27.0	32.6	28.0	30.8	33.8	28.3
3	11.2	12.8	0.8	11.0	8.5	12.5	10.7	9.3	11.6	12.1
4	4.0	6.6	4.0	4.6	1.5	3.6	4.0	4.1	3.8	5.6
5 or more	2.6	4.5	(2)	1.1	1.5	1.7	3.0	5.2	2.8	1.6
Faculty with graduate classes only (percent)										
Total graduate credit courses	100.0	100.0	100.0	100.0	100.0	100.0	100.0	—	—	100.0
1	72.4	70.5	77.6	62.7	72.9	57.6	74.5	—	—	84.1
2	18.0	13.1	14.5	33.0	16.1	33.2	18.9	—	—	6.3
3	7.1	12.8	5.9	4.1	8.7	8.1	3.1	—	—	5.7
4	1.3	0.9	2.0	(2)	1.4	1.0	1.4	—	—	1.8
5 or more	1.2	2.7	(2)	0.2	1.0	(2)	2.1	—	—	2.2
Faculty with both undergraduate and graduate classes (percent)										
Total graduate and undergraduate courses	100.0	—	—	—	—	—	—	—	—	—
2	48.0	—	—	—	—	—	—	—	—	—
3	35.7	—	—	—	—	—	—	—	—	—
4	10.6	—	—	—	—	—	—	—	—	—
5 or more	5.7	—	—	—	—	—	—	—	—	—

[1] Hours that faculty and instructional staff spend each week with students during classroom instruction multiplied by the number of students taught.

[2] Less than .05 percent.

—Data not available or not applicable.

NOTE.—Because of rounding, details may not add to totals. Data have been revised from previously published figures.

SOURCE: U.S. Department of Education, National Center for Education Statistics, National Study of Postsecondary Faculty (NSOPF), 1993. (This table was prepared September 1996.)

Table 225.—Full-time and part-time instructional faculty and staff in institutions of higher education, by type and control, academic rank, age, salary, race/ethnicity, and sex: Fall 1992

Selected characteristics	Number	Percent	White, non-Hispanic		Black, non-Hispanic		Hispanic		Asian/Pacific Islander		American Indian/Alaskan Native	
			Male	Female	Male	Female	Male	Female	Male	Female	Male	Female
1	2	3	4	5	6	7	8	9	10	11	12	13
Full-time instructional faculty and staff												
All institutions	528,260	—	306,477	150,265	14,457	12,941	9,289	4,564	20,858	6,851	1,638	920
Percentage distribution	—	100.0	58.0	28.4	2.7	2.4	1.8	0.9	3.9	1.3	0.3	0.2
Type and control												
Public research	107,358	100.0	67.8	20.2	1.5	1.2	1.6	0.6	5.6	1.3	0.1	0.1
Private research	32,164	100.0	58.0	25.7	3.0	2.0	1.3	0.8	6.6	2.4	0.2	—
Public doctoral	52,808	100.0	61.0	26.5	1.7	1.4	1.8	0.7	4.7	1.4	0.6	0.2
Private doctoral	28,684	100.0	64.8	19.4	3.4	1.5	2.6	1.1	5.6	1.6	0.1	0.1
Public comprehensive	94,477	100.0	55.0	27.7	5.0	4.1	1.8	0.8	4.1	1.0	0.2	0.3
Private comprehensive	38,561	100.0	59.7	31.6	1.7	1.9	1.0	0.6	2.5	0.9	(1)	0.1
Private liberal arts	38,052	100.0	54.4	35.6	3.7	1.7	0.8	0.5	1.9	0.9	0.3	0.2
Public 2-year	109,957	100.0	47.2	38.3	2.5	3.7	2.5	1.6	1.9	1.4	0.7	0.3
Other	26,200	100.0	63.6	25.5	1.7	2.1	1.1	0.4	3.8	1.4	0.3	0.2
Academic rank												
Full professor	160,559	100.0	75.0	14.7	2.2	1.1	1.5	0.4	4.4	0.4	0.2	0.1
Associate professor	123,708	100.0	62.3	25.2	2.9	2.3	1.5	0.8	3.6	1.0	0.3	0.1
Assistant professor	124,293	100.0	46.8	36.3	2.9	3.2	2.1	1.2	4.9	2.2	0.2	0.2
Instructor	73,897	100.0	43.2	41.3	3.2	4.0	2.2	1.1	2.4	1.8	0.6	0.3
Lecturer	11,869	100.0	28.7	54.5	2.6	3.7	2.0	1.2	3.8	2.5	—	1.1
Other	17,072	100.0	40.3	40.6	4.2	4.8	2.2	1.8	4.1	1.7	0.2	0.1
No rank	16,862	100.0	50.9	39.0	1.3	1.3	1.8	0.9	1.9	1.7	0.9	0.3
Age												
Under 30	7,636	100.0	39.5	39.5	2.4	5.3	2.0	1.9	6.1	3.0	0.3	0.1
30 to 34	35,418	100.0	45.6	33.3	4.1	3.6	3.1	1.2	6.4	2.4	0.2	—
35 to 39	66,757	100.0	49.9	33.9	2.7	2.5	1.8	1.0	5.5	2.1	0.4	0.2
40 to 44	90,175	100.0	51.1	33.3	2.5	3.1	2.1	1.5	4.2	1.6	0.2	0.5
45 to 49	97,705	100.0	56.2	31.5	2.5	2.9	2.0	0.9	2.7	1.2	0.3	0.1
50 to 54	94,852	100.0	63.3	26.2	2.5	1.9	1.3	0.6	3.1	0.8	0.3	0.2
55 to 59	67,332	100.0	67.2	21.2	2.8	1.7	1.3	0.3	4.0	0.8	0.7	0.1
60 to 64	44,609	100.0	70.2	18.2	2.8	1.8	1.3	0.5	4.2	0.8	0.2	0.1
65 or older	23,778	100.0	69.5	20.0	3.9	1.1	1.6	0.7	2.3	0.5	0.1	0.3
Base salary												
Under $10,000	13,771	100.0	53.2	30.4	7.1	4.9	0.9	0.3	1.9	1.0	0.3	0.1
10,000 to 24,999	29,384	100.0	35.7	50.6	1.8	3.9	1.3	1.3	2.5	2.3	0.1	0.6
25,000 to 39,999	181,830	100.0	45.4	40.7	2.8	3.4	1.8	1.2	2.5	1.6	0.4	0.2
40,000 to 54,999	163,774	100.0	61.8	23.7	2.8	2.1	1.9	1.0	5.1	1.2	0.3	0.1
55,000 to 69,999	76,716	100.0	73.3	15.2	2.4	1.3	2.3	0.4	4.0	0.9	0.2	0.1
70,000 to 84,999	32,096	100.0	78.9	11.2	2.1	0.9	1.7	(1)	4.5	0.6	0.2	—
85,000 to 99,999	11,068	100.0	71.2	12.7	4.7	0.4	0.7	—	9.6	0.8	—	—
100,000 or more	19,622	100.0	78.5	9.4	1.4	0.6	0.7	0.1	7.1	1.5	0.6	0.2
Total income												
Under $10,000	6,825	100.0	47.4	39.1	3.0	4.9	0.6	0.5	2.3	1.9	—	0.3
10,000 to 24,999	17,522	100.0	32.5	50.3	3.4	4.6	1.6	1.5	2.8	1.8	0.4	1.0
25,000 to 39,999	129,649	100.0	40.2	46.2	2.6	3.6	1.1	1.3	2.7	1.8	0.2	0.3
40,000 to 54,999	158,575	100.0	55.1	30.2	3.0	2.7	2.2	1.1	3.9	1.3	0.4	0.1
55,000 to 69,999	94,903	100.0	69.6	17.6	2.7	1.9	1.7	0.7	4.4	0.9	0.4	0.2
70,000 to 84,999	49,484	100.0	75.3	13.0	2.1	1.4	1.8	0.4	4.7	1.0	0.3	(1)
85,000 to 99,999	23,811	100.0	76.4	11.1	4.0	0.6	1.8	0.1	5.3	0.4	0.3	—
100,000 or more	47,490	100.0	77.1	10.9	1.9	0.7	2.3	0.1	5.8	1.0	0.2	0.1

Table 225.—Full-time and part-time instructional faculty and staff in institutions of higher education, by type and control, academic rank, age, salary, race/ethnicity, and sex: Fall 1992—Continued

Selected characteristics	Number	Percent	White, non-Hispanic		Black, non-Hispanic		Hispanic		Asian/Pacific Islander		American Indian/Alaskan Native	
			Male	Female	Male	Female	Male	Female	Male	Female	Male	Female
1	2	3	4	5	6	7	8	9	10	11	12	13
Part-time instructional faculty and staff												
All institutions	**376,675**	**—**	**182,976**	**149,814**	**10,274**	**7,987**	**6,965**	**4,232**	**7,016**	**5,135**	**1,478**	**797**
Percentage distribution	**—**	**100.0**	**48.6**	**39.8**	**2.7**	**2.1**	**1.8**	**1.1**	**1.9**	**1.4**	**0.4**	**0.2**
Type and control												
Public research	25,360	100.0	49.0	38.7	0.8	1.7	2.1	1.1	4.8	1.7	—	—
Private research	17,259	100.0	50.6	39.0	3.3	1.2	2.7	—	1.8	1.2	0.4	—
Public doctoral	20,761	100.0	50.6	40.8	1.7	1.6	1.0	0.5	1.8	1.5	0.2	0.3
Private doctoral	18,014	100.0	54.6	33.1	6.0	1.2	1.3	0.2	1.0	2.5	0.2	—
Public comprehensive	47,056	100.0	40.4	44.6	4.3	2.9	1.1	1.9	2.7	1.4	0.5	0.2
Private comprehensive	36,525	100.0	51.4	39.5	2.1	2.8	0.8	0.3	1.6	0.9	0.4	0.1
Private liberal arts	20,909	100.0	40.5	49.1	3.9	2.0	1.4	1.5	0.8	0.8	0.1	—
Public 2-year	166,335	100.0	49.6	38.3	2.6	2.0	2.6	1.4	1.5	1.2	0.4	0.3
Other	24,454	100.0	52.4	38.4	0.7	2.5	0.6	0.5	1.6	2.2	0.8	0.3
Academic rank												
Full professor	32,269	100.0	63.2	25.0	3.5	1.7	1.7	0.4	2.9	0.7	0.8	0.2
Associate professor	22,518	100.0	59.4	30.1	1.6	1.2	1.5	0.4	3.7	1.3	0.4	0.4
Assistant professor	24,237	100.0	49.1	37.4	5.7	2.5	0.6	0.4	2.4	1.9	—	0.1
Instructor	215,442	100.0	46.1	42.4	2.5	2.2	2.4	1.2	1.4	1.2	0.5	0.2
Lecturer	45,328	100.0	48.5	39.8	2.1	2.0	1.3	1.6	2.5	1.8	0.2	0.2
Other	27,553	100.0	43.7	44.8	3.6	2.3	0.8	1.2	1.2	2.0	—	0.5
No rank	9,328	100.0	42.4	45.9	2.1	2.8	—	2.0	2.9	1.3	0.6	—
Age												
Under 30	20,483	100.0	41.2	46.3	2.1	2.1	1.5	1.9	1.5	2.5	0.3	0.5
30 to 34	35,908	100.0	41.6	44.6	2.0	2.1	2.6	1.5	2.1	2.7	0.5	0.2
35 to 39	58,923	100.0	42.8	43.8	4.1	2.2	2.1	1.0	2.0	1.1	0.6	0.2
40 to 44	70,025	100.0	47.5	41.8	2.2	1.9	1.8	1.4	1.6	1.5	0.2	0.2
45 to 49	67,969	100.0	48.2	41.8	2.1	1.7	1.5	1.3	2.2	1.0	(1)	0.3
50 to 54	45,093	100.0	49.2	36.5	3.6	2.8	2.2	0.6	2.3	1.6	0.9	0.3
55 to 59	28,764	100.0	55.3	34.6	3.3	1.6	1.4	0.6	2.0	1.0	0.2	—
60 to 64	22,943	100.0	56.2	33.6	2.1	2.3	2.2	0.5	1.2	0.9	1.1	0.1
65 or older	26,565	100.0	65.6	25.4	2.4	2.8	1.1	0.9	1.3	0.4	—	—
Base salary												
Under $10,000	280,526	100.0	49.6	39.1	2.7	2.3	1.7	1.1	1.6	1.3	0.3	0.2
10,000 to 24,999	68,117	100.0	43.1	44.9	2.2	1.4	2.8	1.3	2.5	1.5	0.3	0.2
25,000 to 39,999	15,840	100.0	49.4	38.1	4.1	2.0	1.6	0.3	2.5	1.2	0.8	—
40,000 to 54,999	5,307	100.0	55.2	32.8	2.1	1.9	1.5	2.7	0.1	1.8	1.9	—
55,000 to 69,999	2,157	—	—	—	3.5	—	0.6	—	22.0	8.6	—	—
70,000 to 84,999	1,127	—	—	—	7.7	4.2	—	—	2.7	—	8.0	—
85,000 to 99,999	942	—	—	—	—	—	—	—	—	—	—	—
100,000 or more	2,657	100.0	46.9	39.0	10.5	0.5	1.2	—	—	2.0	—	—
Total income												
Under $10,000	70,693	100.0	35.4	52.6	2.3	2.9	1.9	1.3	1.6	1.6	(1)	0.4
10,000 to 24,999	84,803	100.0	33.2	57.1	1.3	1.8	1.3	1.7	1.3	1.9	0.4	0.1
25,000 to 39,999	74,809	100.0	48.5	39.6	2.5	2.9	2.0	1.2	1.6	1.4	0.2	0.3
40,000 to 54,999	58,057	100.0	55.8	32.1	3.4	1.9	1.5	1.2	1.8	0.7	1.3	0.4
55,000 to 69,999	32,386	100.0	69.3	17.5	3.4	1.6	3.2	0.5	3.0	1.2	0.3	—
70,000 to 84,999	17,199	100.0	69.4	17.8	4.7	0.7	2.9	0.7	2.8	0.5	0.5	—
85,000 to 99,999	8,231	100.0	70.2	18.1	4.7	0.8	4.7	—	1.4	—	—	—
100,000 or more	30,497	100.0	68.9	19.0	4.7	1.5	1.0	—	3.3	1.6	0.1	—

[1] Less than 0.05 percent.

—Data not available or applicable.

NOTE.—Data have been revised from previously published figures. Because of rounding, details may not add to totals.

SOURCE: U.S. Department of Education, National Center for Education Statistics, National Study of Postsecondary Faculty (NSOPF), 1993. (This table was prepared September 1996.)

Table 226.—Full-time and part-time instructional faculty and staff in institutions of higher education, by faculty characteristics and field: Fall 1992

Faculty characteristics	Number in thou-sands	All fields	Agriculture and home economics	Busi-ness	Edu-cation	Engineering	Fine arts	Health	Human-ities	Natural sciences	Social sciences	Other and not reported
1	2	3	4	5	6	7	8	9	10	11	12	13
Full-time instructional faculty and staff												
Full-time, in thousands	528	—	11	40	37	24	32	79	74	102	58	62
Percent	—	100.0	2.2	7.7	7.1	4.7	6.1	15.3	14.2	19.5	11.2	11.9
Percentage distribution of full-time faculty												
Total	528	100.0	100.0	100.0	100.0	100.0	100.0	100.0	100.0	100.0	100.0	100.0
Sex												
Male	353	66.8	75.3	68.9	48.9	93.9	67.0	49.9	58.6	79.9	72.5	69.6
Female	176	33.2	24.7	31.2	51.1	6.1	33.0	50.1	41.4	20.1	27.5	30.4
Race/ethnicity												
White, non-Hispanic	457	86.5	90.8	88.5	84.7	76.6	88.6	85.9	88.1	85.8	87.3	88.1
Black, non-Hispanic	27	5.2	3.9	4.1	9.4	2.8	5.8	5.6	4.2	3.6	6.2	6.0
Hispanic	14	2.6	1.8	1.6	3.3	3.1	2.5	2.3	4.1	1.9	2.8	2.5
Asian	28	5.2	2.9	4.8	1.6	16.8	2.7	6.0	3.2	8.3	3.3	2.9
American Indian	3	0.5	0.7	1.0	1.0	0.7	0.5	0.2	0.5	0.3	0.5	0.4
Age												
Under 30	8	1.4	0.4	1.2	1.1	1.3	1.3	1.1	1.7	1.5	0.8	2.4
30 to 34	35	6.7	7.3	6.3	3.5	11.0	6.2	8.4	4.7	6.7	7.3	6.8
35 to 39	67	12.6	9.1	13.5	7.7	13.1	13.1	16.2	9.6	13.9	13.0	12.3
40 to 44	90	17.1	15.7	16.6	17.6	16.9	17.7	21.8	13.4	15.8	16.4	17.9
45 to 49	98	18.5	17.7	20.9	19.7	14.8	18.5	19.2	19.9	17.2	17.9	17.7
50 to 54	95	18.0	18.4	16.2	21.1	12.2	17.2	13.3	21.4	19.3	19.2	18.4
55 to 59	67	12.7	14.4	11.7	14.1	15.0	14.1	9.6	14.7	13.5	12.2	12.4
60 to 64	45	8.4	11.4	7.9	10.5	10.6	7.9	7.6	9.9	7.4	9.2	7.3
65 or older	24	4.5	5.7	5.7	4.7	5.0	4.1	2.8	4.8	4.7	4.1	5.0
Degree												
Less than bachelor's	6	1.2	0.2	0.5	0.3	2.0	0.7	1.2	(¹)	0.2	0.1	6.2
Bachelor's	21	4.0	5.7	4.5	2.9	5.2	5.4	5.8	1.3	2.8	0.7	8.2
Master's	156	29.7	22.0	38.4	30.8	18.7	56.2	30.1	31.7	22.2	19.3	33.6
Professional	58	11.1	4.4	4.5	2.9	2.3	4.3	42.9	2.4	4.5	3.5	17.1
Doctoral	284	54.0	67.8	52.0	63.2	71.8	33.4	20.0	64.6	70.3	76.4	35.0
Rank												
Full professor	161	30.4	41.4	24.7	24.3	36.8	32.0	21.2	33.1	37.0	36.8	26.9
Associate professor	124	23.4	22.6	25.5	29.5	28.0	25.4	23.0	22.4	22.5	24.8	19.3
Assistant professor	124	23.5	19.3	25.6	22.9	22.5	21.4	32.9	19.3	20.7	24.3	23.0
Instructor	74	14.0	10.8	16.7	13.2	10.4	10.3	16.9	14.9	11.7	7.9	21.7
Lecturer	12	2.2	1.0	1.3	2.5	0.9	2.8	2.3	3.9	1.7	1.7	2.7
Other	17	3.2	3.2	2.2	5.5	0.5	3.3	2.5	1.9	2.4	2.0	3.6
No rank	17	3.2	1.7	4.0	1.9	1.0	4.8	1.4	4.7	3.9	2.5	3.0

Table 226.—Full-time and part-time instructional faculty and staff in institutions of higher education, by faculty characteristics and field: Fall 1992—Continued

Faculty characteristics	Number in thou- sands	All fields	Agriculture and home economics	Busi- ness	Edu- cation	Engineering	Fine arts	Health	Human- ities	Natural sciences	Social sciences	Other and not reported
1	2	3	4	5	6	7	8	9	10	11	12	13
Part-time instructional faculty and staff												
Part-time, in thousands	377	—	3	35	31	12	33	45	60	60	34	60
Percent	—	100.0	0.7	9.3	8.3	3.1	8.8	12.0	16.2	16.2	9.1	16.2
Percentage distribution of part-time faculty												
Total	377	100.0	100.0	100.0	100.0	100.0	100.0	100.0	100.0	100.0	100.0	100.0
Sex												
Male	209	55.4	48.0	70.0	32.7	92.0	51.7	43.5	41.0	67.8	56.9	63.9
Female	168	44.6	52.0	30.0	67.3	8.0	48.3	56.5	59.0	32.2	43.2	36.1
Race/ethnicity												
White, non-Hispanic	333	88.3	98.9	89.6	87.7	86.5	89.3	88.2	87.4	87.5	87.2	90.2
Black, non-Hispanic	18	4.8	0.0	5.1	8.0	1.9	5.1	5.7	3.3	4.1	6.6	4.6
Hispanic	11	3.0	1.1	2.7	2.0	2.0	2.6	1.6	5.8	2.5	2.7	2.9
Asian	12	3.2	(¹)	2.1	1.5	7.6	2.3	4.0	2.8	5.2	3.1	2.3
American Indian	2	0.6	(¹)	0.6	0.9	1.9	0.6	0.5	0.8	0.7	0.5	0.1
Age												
Under 30	20	5.4	8.4	2.2	2.4	7.9	4.3	4.6	6.6	6.8	7.6	5.4
30 to 34	36	9.5	5.9	7.3	3.6	8.9	11.1	11.1	10.6	11.2	8.3	9.7
35 to 39	59	15.6	18.9	13.3	7.3	21.9	18.6	22.8	11.5	13.1	16.2	19.8
40 to 44	70	18.6	22.1	17.1	26.7	16.0	21.0	20.4	15.6	15.2	16.7	21.1
45 to 49	68	18.0	16.2	23.1	18.8	12.8	14.3	14.1	20.6	16.8	16.6	19.8
50 to 54	45	12.0	6.9	15.4	13.3	9.2	10.2	11.1	13.5	13.0	12.8	9.4
55 to 59	29	7.6	7.5	7.7	8.6	6.3	8.7	4.9	8.9	8.4	8.8	6.5
60 to 64	23	6.1	10.0	6.0	8.6	7.2	5.7	2.9	6.1	8.7	6.7	4.1
65 or older	27	7.1	4.2	7.8	10.7	9.9	6.2	8.1	6.7	6.7	6.4	4.3
Degree												
Less than bachelor's	17	4.7	1.8	2.2	0.7	13.4	3.6	9.6	0.3	1.9	0.1	13.0
Bachelor's	63	17.0	30.2	21.3	14.0	27.5	21.8	17.5	7.3	22.2	6.0	21.4
Master's	190	51.6	52.8	59.6	61.3	32.5	66.3	26.4	71.9	53.0	53.3	34.1
Professional	40	10.7	8.6	8.1	0.7	(¹)	1.6	38.2	2.0	4.7	6.2	21.5
Doctoral	59	16.0	6.6	8.8	23.4	26.6	6.7	8.4	18.5	18.2	34.3	9.9
Rank												
Full professor	32	8.6	8.8	8.5	7.4	15.7	9.8	6.7	6.9	6.7	8.5	12.0
Associate professor	23	6.0	11.6	4.6	5.2	5.4	4.2	17.4	3.2	4.3	6.3	4.2
Assistant professor	24	6.4	(¹)	6.4	4.9	7.4	6.9	16.9	3.5	4.3	8.8	3.4
Instructor	215	57.2	55.1	60.2	57.4	50.4	56.3	45.6	60.0	62.5	51.9	61.8
Lecturer	45	12.0	19.9	11.3	10.8	13.0	12.3	6.5	17.5	10.6	16.4	10.0
Other	28	7.3	4.5	6.3	10.8	7.2	6.8	6.0	5.8	8.2	6.7	7.1
No rank	9	2.5	(¹)	2.8	3.6	0.8	3.9	0.9	3.0	3.5	1.4	1.5

¹ Less than 0.05 percent.
—Not applicable.

NOTE.—Because of rounding and survey item nonresponse, details may not add to totals. Data have been revised from previously published figures.

SOURCE: U.S. Department of Education, National Center for Education Statistics, National Study of Postsecondary Faculty (NSOPF), 1993. (This table was prepared September 1996.)

Table 227.—Percentage distribution of full-time and part-time instructional faculty and staff in institutions of higher education, by program area, race/ethnicity, and sex: Fall 1992

Program area	Number	Percent	White, non-Hispanic		Black, non-Hispanic		Hispanic		Asian/Pacific Islander		American Indian/Alaskan Native	
			Male	Female	Male	Female	Male	Female	Male	Female	Male	Female
1	2	3	4	5	6	7	8	9	10	11	12	13
				Full-time instructional faculty and staff								
Total	528,260	100.0	58.0	28.4	2.7	2.4	1.8	0.9	3.9	1.3	0.3	0.2
Agriculture and home economics	11,366	100.0	70.4	20.3	2.3	1.6	1.6	0.2	1.0	1.9	—	0.7
Business	39,928	100.0	61.3	27.2	2.0	2.2	1.0	0.6	3.9	0.8	0.6	0.3
Communications	10,296	100.0	55.9	30.4	2.9	2.7	1.5	—	4.3	1.2	0.8	0.3
Education	37,066	100.0	42.8	41.9	4.0	5.4	1.0	2.4	0.5	1.1	0.7	0.3
Teacher education	12,490	100.0	39.8	50.3	2.1	4.9	0.1	0.7	0.3	1.0	0.5	0.2
Other education	24,576	100.0	44.4	37.6	4.9	5.7	1.4	3.3	0.6	1.1	0.8	0.3
Engineering	24,431	100.0	72.7	3.9	2.1	0.7	2.9	0.2	15.5	1.3	0.7	—
Fine arts	31,659	100.0	59.6	29.0	3.8	1.9	2.1	0.3	1.2	1.5	0.3	0.2
Health sciences	79,422	100.0	42.1	43.8	2.3	3.4	1.5	0.7	3.9	2.2	0.1	0.1
First-professional	36,867	100.0	63.3	19.0	3.6	1.0	2.8	0.9	7.2	2.1	0.2	—
Nursing	21,776	100.0	0.9	87.5	0.5	7.1	—	0.9	0.1	2.9	—	0.2
Other health sciences	20,779	100.0	47.5	42.0	1.8	3.7	0.9	0.3	2.0	1.5	0.2	0.2
Humanities	73,923	100.0	52.8	35.2	2.1	2.1	2.1	2.0	1.2	1.9	0.3	0.1
English and literature	37,432	100.0	44.5	45.5	2.2	2.9	1.3	1.0	0.8	1.2	0.5	0.1
Foreign languages	13,722	100.0	39.5	36.8	1.2	0.6	5.7	7.5	1.8	6.4	—	0.4
History	14,574	100.0	70.2	20.2	3.0	2.3	1.3	0.4	1.7	0.4	0.3	—
Philosophy	8,195	100.0	82.1	12.5	1.7	0.2	1.2	0.3	1.5	0.2	0.2	—
Law	8,524	100.0	57.6	30.1	5.4	3.0	1.2	1.0	0.2	1.4	—	—
Natural sciences	101,505	100.0	68.2	17.6	2.6	1.0	1.6	0.4	7.3	1.0	0.2	0.1
Biological sciences	34,289	100.0	67.1	20.8	3.2	1.5	1.1	0.5	4.5	0.9	0.3	0.1
Physical sciences	28,313	100.0	76.7	10.2	2.2	0.3	2.0	0.1	7.7	0.9	—	—
Mathematics	25,325	100.0	61.3	21.6	2.7	1.0	1.7	0.6	9.1	1.2	0.5	0.4
Computer sciences	13,578	100.0	65.8	17.8	2.1	1.3	1.7	0.1	10.3	0.8	—	—
Social sciences	58,232	100.0	64.6	22.7	3.1	3.1	1.9	0.8	2.6	0.7	0.3	0.2
Economics	9,778	100.0	69.8	12.3	3.9	0.3	3.0	1.1	7.8	1.7	—	—
Political science	9,324	100.0	75.0	14.8	3.6	1.9	2.7	0.5	1.1	0.2	0.1	—
Psychology	17,784	100.0	56.9	32.3	2.3	4.3	1.5	0.8	1.1	0.3	0.1	0.2
Sociology	9,511	100.0	67.4	20.6	2.7	3.3	2.3	0.5	1.3	0.8	0.9	—
Other social sciences	11,835	100.0	61.3	25.0	3.4	4.3	0.8	1.1	2.7	0.6	0.3	0.6
Occupationally specific programs	15,268	100.0	75.7	13.8	3.6	0.9	2.9	0.3	1.9	0.2	0.5	0.2
All other programs	27,717	100.0	57.4	30.7	2.8	3.4	2.0	0.6	2.2	0.6	—	0.1
				Part-time instructional faculty and staff								
Total	376,675	100.0	48.6	39.8	2.7	2.1	1.8	1.1	1.9	1.4	0.4	0.2
Agriculture and home economics	2,758	100.0	46.9	52.0	—	—	1.1	—	—	—	—	—
Business	34,679	100.0	63.6	25.9	3.3	1.9	2.0	0.7	1.0	1.1	0.2	0.4
Communications	10,307	100.0	43.2	49.9	4.0	0.9	—	0.6	0.5	0.3	0.3	0.1
Education	30,758	100.0	28.9	58.8	2.5	5.5	0.7	1.3	0.4	1.1	0.3	0.6
Teacher education	12,390	100.0	20.0	68.5	2.3	6.6	0.6	0.8	0.5	0.8	—	—
Other education	18,368	100.0	34.9	52.2	2.7	4.8	0.7	1.6	0.3	1.3	0.5	1.0
Engineering	11,632	100.0	79.3	7.2	1.9	—	2.0	—	6.8	0.8	1.9	—
Fine arts	32,814	100.0	46.2	43.1	3.4	1.8	1.3	1.3	0.4	1.9	0.5	0.2
Health sciences	44,763	100.0	36.8	51.4	3.0	2.6	1.0	0.7	2.3	1.7	0.4	0.1
First-professional	17,710	100.0	57.6	27.7	6.1	1.1	0.6	0.3	4.9	1.8	—	—
Nursing	10,498	100.0	5.4	84.0	—	6.6	—	0.9	—	2.4	—	0.6
Other health sciences	16,555	100.0	34.5	56.0	1.7	1.8	2.0	0.9	0.9	1.2	1.1	—
Humanities	60,041	100.0	35.8	51.5	1.1	2.2	2.7	3.1	1.1	1.7	0.3	0.5
English and literature	37,395	100.0	29.4	60.9	0.6	2.9	2.0	1.5	0.6	1.2	0.4	0.6
Foreign languages	10,566	100.0	27.0	44.7	1.1	1.7	5.9	12.1	2.2	4.9	—	0.5
History	7,812	100.0	61.9	30.7	2.9	0.7	1.7	0.2	1.5	—	0.3	—
Philosophy	4,268	100.0	66.3	24.6	2.6	0.3	2.7	—	2.3	1.2	—	—
Law	13,552	100.0	68.2	23.6	3.7	2.7	0.3	0.2	1.3	—	—	—
Natural sciences	60,242	100.0	58.3	29.2	3.1	1.0	2.1	0.4	3.6	1.6	0.7	(¹)
Biological sciences	11,747	100.0	50.3	37.4	3.2	1.1	2.1	0.6	1.8	3.5	—	—
Physical sciences	10,626	100.0	67.6	21.2	1.5	0.4	1.1	0.9	5.5	1.9	—	—
Mathematics	24,559	100.0	52.8	34.5	4.6	0.9	2.4	0.2	3.4	0.7	0.4	0.1
Computer sciences	13,310	100.0	68.2	18.4	1.7	1.4	2.3	0.3	4.0	1.2	2.4	—
Social sciences	33,854	100.0	48.8	38.3	3.7	2.9	1.8	0.9	2.2	0.9	0.4	0.1
Economics	3,038	100.0	69.0	13.8	1.7	1.0	2.7	—	9.1	2.5	—	—
Political science	3,055	100.0	72.4	18.6	4.6	0.4	3.4	0.5	—	—	—	—
Psychology	15,617	100.0	45.6	45.7	2.5	1.5	1.5	0.5	2.0	0.3	0.2	0.3
Sociology	4,384	100.0	33.2	52.5	6.3	4.0	1.2	0.2	1.5	1.0	—	—
Other social sciences	7,760	100.0	47.0	32.8	4.9	7.0	1.7	2.4	1.0	1.9	1.2	—
Occupationally specific programs	16,490	100.0	71.2	18.0	3.5	0.8	5.1	—	1.3	—	0.1	—
All other programs	19,769	100.0	44.7	43.5	1.9	1.5	2.3	1.6	2.4	2.1	—	—

¹ Less than 0.05 percent.
—Data not available or not applicable.

NOTE.—Because of rounding and nonresponse to program area question, details may not add to totals. Data have been revised from previously published figures.

SOURCE: U.S. Department of Education, National Center for Education Statistics, National Study of Postsecondary Faculty (NSOPF), 1993. (This table was prepared September 1996.)

Table 228.—Average base salaries of full-time instructional faculty and staff in institutions of higher education, by type and control of institution and by field of instruction: 1987–88 and 1992–93

Field of instruction	All institutions	Total public	Total private	Public research	Private research	Public doctoral	Private doctoral	Public comprehensive	Private comprehensive	Private liberal arts	Public 2-year	Other
1	2	3	4	5	6	7	8	9	10	11	12	13
1987–88 salaries in 1992–93 dollars												
Instructional faculty, in thousands	515	356	159	102	42	56	25	97	37	38	96	22
All fields	$48,381	$48,826	$47,386	$58,118	$63,669	$54,028	$57,215	$45,342	$39,564	$35,462	$39,847	$37,698
Agriculture and home economics	48,452	48,713	—	54,431	—	43,501	—	46,934	—	—	—	—
Business	45,243	45,785	44,078	58,218	—	49,161	—	43,413	45,319	29,400	40,707	35,292
Education	40,498	42,517	33,529	45,861	—	43,315	—	41,766	33,499	—	41,133	—
Engineering	52,213	51,412	55,095	61,363	—	53,133	—	50,316	51,481	—	36,794	—
Fine arts	37,840	39,547	34,368	40,297	—	38,155	—	39,367	33,170	34,484	40,216	—
Health	64,860	64,447	65,689	73,454	77,144	71,065	67,278	57,124	47,683	—	37,017	—
Humanities	42,420	44,092	39,867	46,326	48,988	39,327	46,313	44,601	37,089	38,127	43,461	34,783
Natural sciences	47,811	48,399	46,495	57,947	61,731	49,917	46,912	46,684	38,763	37,760	39,692	37,499
Social sciences	46,234	46,506	45,730	52,842	61,043	47,938	—	44,933	38,613	35,728	41,052	—
Other	44,712	44,239	45,834	52,646	—	45,427	—	41,853	35,733	—	37,762	44,331
1992–93												
Instructional faculty, in thousands	478	339	140	89	25	46	23	91	37	37	105	25
All fields	$46,833	$46,767	$46,993	$56,443	$63,967	$51,497	$56,011	$43,487	$43,255	$37,623	$39,351	$40,458
Agriculture and home economics	47,809	48,488	—	54,735	—	44,480	—	43,377	—	—	39,788	—
Business	49,223	49,955	47,318	65,209	—	58,808	54,369	47,739	53,786	32,322	42,017	33,587
Education	42,046	43,259	37,618	49,822	—	42,202	49,254	41,456	37,961	32,419	41,224	—
Engineering	55,569	55,923	54,190	66,781	61,084	53,577	55,040	48,703	45,855	—	38,648	56,036
Fine arts	40,574	39,285	42,526	41,337	86,221	39,379	37,874	39,144	35,812	37,764	37,524	34,100
Health	55,624	54,097	59,720	73,467	73,080	63,839	66,120	38,311	45,678	42,363	35,790	41,900
Humanities	40,972	41,601	39,634	44,018	44,695	39,661	42,928	40,735	41,043	37,667	41,183	36,547
Natural sciences	48,192	47,500	49,933	55,432	67,170	51,691	56,665	45,922	46,666	37,534	39,651	42,143
Social sciences	45,960	46,103	45,667	53,139	59,296	48,709	49,505	43,686	39,838	40,492	40,312	44,389
Other	44,594	43,431	47,030	51,007	65,685	43,777	61,854	45,357	41,722	36,436	37,668	39,199

—Too few sample cases (fewer than 30) for a reliable estimate.

NOTE.—Data for 1992–93 differ from other tables because of adjustments to maintain consistency with the 1987–88 data. Data have been revised from previously published figures. Because of rounding, details may not add to totals.

SOURCE: U.S. Department of Education, National Center for Education Statistics, National Study of Postsecondary Faculty (NSOPF), 1987–88 and 1992–93. (This table was prepared September 1996.)

Table 229.—Average salary of full-time instructional faculty on 9-month contracts in institutions of higher education, by academic rank, sex, and control and type of institution: 1970–71 to 1994–95

Academic year and sex	All faculty	Academic rank						Public institutions			Private institutions		
		Professor	Associate professor	Assistant professor	Instructor	Lecturer	No rank	Total	4-year	2-year	Total	4-year	2-year
1	2	3	4	5	6	7	8	9	10	11	12	13	14

Current dollars

Academic year and sex	All faculty	Professor	Associate professor	Assistant professor	Instructor	Lecturer	No rank	Public Total	Public 4-year	Public 2-year	Private Total	Private 4-year	Private 2-year
Total													
1970–71	$12,710	$17,958	$13,563	$11,176	$9,360	$11,196	$12,333	$12,953	$13,121	$12,644	$11,619	$11,824	$8,664
1972–73	13,856	19,191	14,580	12,032	10,737	11,637	12,676	14,016	14,417	12,919	13,452	13,622	9,288
1974–75	15,622	21,277	16,146	13,295	12,691	12,575	13,532	15,879	16,271	14,897	14,912	15,092	10,242
1975–76	16,659	22,649	17,065	13,986	13,672	12,906	15,196	16,942	17,400	15,820	15,921	16,116	10,901
1976–77	17,560	23,792	17,905	14,662	11,835	13,431	16,634	17,845	18,313	16,685	16,787	16,977	11,637
1977–78	18,709	25,133	18,987	15,530	12,504	14,528	17,831	19,045	19,517	17,895	17,773	17,966	12,191
1978–79	19,820	26,470	20,047	16,374	13,193	15,281	18,725	20,179	20,722	18,844	18,807	19,010	12,496
1979–80	21,348	28,388	21,451	17,465	14,023	16,122	20,262	21,798	22,349	20,429	20,105	20,318	13,250
1980–81	23,302	30,753	23,214	18,901	15,178	17,301	22,334	23,745	24,373	22,177	22,093	22,325	15,065
1981–82	25,449	33,437	25,278	20,608	16,450	18,756	24,331	25,886	26,591	24,193	24,255	24,509	15,926
1982–83	27,196	35,540	26,921	22,056	17,601	20,072	25,557	27,488	28,293	25,567	26,393	26,691	16,595
1984–85	30,447	39,743	29,945	24,668	20,230	22,334	27,683	30,646	31,764	27,864	29,910	30,247	18,510
1985–86	32,392	42,268	31,787	26,277	20,918	23,770	29,088	32,750	34,033	29,590	31,402	31,732	19,436
1987–88	35,897	47,040	35,231	29,110	22,728	25,977	31,532	36,231	37,840	32,209	35,049	35,346	21,867
1989–90	40,133	52,810	39,392	32,689	25,030	28,990	34,559	40,416	42,365	35,516	39,464	39,817	24,601
1990–91	42,165	55,540	41,414	34,434	26,332	30,097	36,395	42,317	44,510	37,055	41,788	42,224	24,088
1991–92	43,851	57,433	42,929	35,745	30,916	30,456	37,783	43,641	45,638	38,959	44,376	44,793	25,673
1992–93	44,714	58,788	43,945	36,625	28,499	30,543	37,771	44,197	46,515	38,935	45,985	46,427	26,105
1993–94	46,364	60,649	45,278	37,630	28,828	32,729	40,584	45,920	48,019	41,040	47,465	47,880	28,435
1994–95[1]	47,811	62,709	46,713	38,756	29,665	33,198	41,227	47,432	49,738	42,101	48,741	49,379	25,613
Men													
1972–73	14,422	19,414	14,723	12,193	11,147	12,106	13,047	14,545	14,944	13,268	14,116	14,253	9,571
1974–75	16,303	21,532	16,282	13,458	13,350	13,232	14,008	16,522	16,918	15,350	15,709	15,852	10,633
1975–76	17,414	22,902	17,209	14,174	14,430	13,579	15,761	17,661	18,121	16,339	16,784	16,946	11,378
1976–77	18,378	24,029	18,055	14,851	12,085	14,147	17,253	18,620	19,091	17,235	17,736	17,891	12,193
1977–78	19,575	25,370	19,133	15,726	12,729	15,181	18,459	19,867	20,347	18,479	18,783	18,935	12,759
1978–79	20,777	26,727	20,221	16,602	13,441	15,927	19,400	21,080	21,628	19,475	19,935	20,086	13,048
1979–80	22,394	28,672	21,651	17,720	14,323	16,932	20,901	22,789	23,350	21,131	21,317	21,472	13,938
1980–81	24,499	31,082	23,451	19,227	15,545	18,281	23,170	24,873	25,509	22,965	23,493	23,669	16,075
1981–82	26,796	33,799	25,553	21,025	16,906	19,721	25,276	27,149	27,864	25,085	25,849	26,037	16,834
1982–83	28,664	35,956	27,262	22,586	18,160	21,225	26,541	28,851	29,661	26,524	28,159	28,380	17,346
1984–85	32,182	40,269	30,392	25,330	21,159	23,557	28,670	32,240	33,344	28,891	32,028	32,278	19,460
1985–86	34,294	42,833	32,273	27,094	21,693	25,238	30,267	34,528	35,786	30,758	33,656	33,900	20,412
1987–88	38,112	47,735	35,823	30,086	23,645	27,652	32,747	38,314	39,898	33,477	37,603	37,817	22,641
1989–90	42,763	53,650	40,131	33,781	25,933	31,162	35,980	42,959	44,834	37,081	42,312	42,595	25,218
1990–91	45,065	56,549	42,239	35,636	27,388	32,398	38,036	45,084	47,168	38,787	45,019	45,319	25,937
1991–92	46,848	58,494	43,814	36,969	33,359	32,843	39,422	46,483	48,401	40,811	47,733	48,042	26,825
1992–93	47,866	59,972	44,855	37,842	29,583	32,512	39,365	47,175	49,392	40,725	49,518	49,837	27,402
1993–94	49,579	61,857	46,229	38,794	29,815	34,796	42,251	48,956	50,989	42,938	51,076	51,397	30,783
1994–95[1]	51,228	64,046	47,705	39,923	30,528	35,082	43,103	50,629	52,874	44,020	52,653	53,036	29,639
Women													
1972–73	11,925	17,123	13,827	11,510	10,098	10,775	11,913	12,250	12,300	12,165	11,044	11,219	8,888
1974–75	13,471	19,012	15,481	12,858	11,740	11,543	12,619	13,892	13,831	13,987	12,233	12,423	9,735
1975–76	14,308	20,308	16,364	13,522	12,572	11,901	14,094	14,762	14,758	14,769	13,030	13,231	10,201
1976–77	15,100	21,536	17,189	14,225	11,589	12,397	15,467	15,573	15,539	15,628	13,709	13,899	10,850
1977–78	16,159	22,943	18,325	15,109	12,288	13,688	16,637	16,684	16,619	16,785	14,597	14,799	11,470
1978–79	17,080	24,143	19,300	15,914	12,966	14,465	17,482	17,646	17,627	17,676	15,388	15,611	11,898
1979–80	18,396	25,910	20,642	16,974	13,750	15,142	19,069	19,042	18,985	19,134	16,539	16,787	12,541
1980–81	19,996	27,959	22,295	18,302	14,854	16,168	20,843	20,673	20,608	20,778	18,073	18,326	13,892
1981–82	21,802	30,438	24,271	19,866	16,054	17,676	22,672	22,524	22,454	22,632	19,743	20,024	14,984
1982–83	23,261	32,221	25,738	21,130	17,102	18,830	23,855	23,892	23,876	23,917	21,451	21,785	15,845
1984–85	25,941	35,824	28,517	23,575	19,362	21,004	26,050	26,566	26,813	26,172	24,186	24,560	17,575
1985–86	27,576	38,252	30,300	24,966	20,237	22,273	27,171	28,299	28,680	27,693	25,523	25,889	18,504
1987–88	30,499	42,371	33,528	27,600	21,962	24,370	29,605	31,215	31,820	30,228	28,621	28,946	21,215
1989–90	34,183	47,663	37,469	31,090	24,320	26,995	32,528	34,796	35,704	33,307	32,650	33,010	24,002
1990–91	35,881	49,728	39,329	32,724	25,534	28,111	34,179	36,459	37,573	34,720	34,359	34,898	22,585
1991–92	37,534	51,621	40,766	34,063	28,873	28,550	35,622	37,800	38,634	36,517	36,828	37,309	24,683
1992–93	38,385	52,755	41,861	35,032	27,700	28,922	35,792	38,356	39,470	36,710	38,460	38,987	25,068
1993–94	40,058	54,746	43,178	36,169	28,136	31,048	38,474	40,118	41,031	38,707	39,902	40,378	26,142
1994–95[1]	41,369	56,555	44,626	37,352	29,072	31,677	38,967	41,548	42,663	39,812	40,908	41,815	22,851

Table 229.—Average salary of full-time instructional faculty on 9-month contracts in institutions of higher education, by academic rank, sex, and control and type of institution: 1970–71 to 1994–95—Continued

Academic year and sex	All faculty	Academic rank						Public institutions			Private institutions		
		Professor	Associate professor	Assistant professor	Instructor	Lecturer	No rank	Total	4-year	2-year	Total	4-year	2-year
1	2	3	4	5	6	7	8	9	10	11	12	13	14
Constant 1994–95 dollars[2]													
Total													
1970–71	48,121	67,991	51,354	42,315	35,438	42,391	46,696	49,044	49,681	47,873	43,990	44,769	32,804
1972–73	48,684	67,427	51,228	42,274	37,724	40,886	44,537	49,245	50,654	45,390	47,264	47,861	32,635
1974–75	45,367	61,790	46,890	38,609	36,854	36,520	39,298	46,113	47,253	43,263	43,304	43,828	29,743
1975–76	45,180	61,427	46,283	37,932	37,081	35,002	41,213	45,949	47,191	42,905	43,179	43,709	29,564
1976–77	45,002	60,971	45,884	37,575	30,329	34,420	42,627	45,730	46,931	42,758	43,019	43,505	29,822
1977–78	44,927	60,356	45,596	37,295	30,027	34,887	42,820	45,735	46,869	42,973	42,681	43,143	29,275
1978–79	43,520	58,122	44,019	35,954	28,968	33,552	41,115	44,308	45,500	41,376	41,296	41,740	27,438
1979–80	41,360	55,000	41,559	33,837	27,168	31,234	39,255	42,233	43,299	39,580	38,951	39,364	25,671
1980–81	40,460	53,397	40,307	32,818	26,354	30,040	38,779	41,229	42,319	38,506	38,360	38,763	26,158
1981–82	40,674	53,441	40,401	32,937	26,291	29,977	38,887	41,372	42,499	38,666	38,766	39,172	25,453
1982–83	41,676	54,463	41,255	33,799	26,972	30,759	39,164	42,123	43,357	39,180	40,445	40,902	25,431
1984–85	43,298	56,517	42,584	35,080	28,768	31,760	39,367	43,581	45,171	39,625	42,534	43,013	26,323
1985–86	44,773	58,423	43,936	36,320	28,913	32,855	40,206	45,267	47,041	40,900	43,404	43,860	26,865
1987–88	46,608	61,076	45,744	37,796	29,509	33,728	40,941	47,042	49,131	41,820	45,507	45,893	28,392
1989–90	47,540	62,555	46,662	38,722	29,649	34,340	40,936	47,875	50,183	42,071	46,747	47,166	29,141
1990–91	47,358	62,379	46,513	38,675	29,574	33,804	40,877	47,528	49,991	41,618	46,934	47,424	27,054
1991–92	47,722	62,503	46,718	38,901	33,645	33,144	41,119	47,493	49,666	42,398	48,293	48,747	27,939
1992–93	47,187	62,039	46,375	38,650	30,076	32,232	39,860	46,641	49,088	41,088	48,528	48,955	27,549
1993–94	47,693	62,387	46,575	38,709	29,654	33,667	41,747	47,236	49,396	42,216	48,826	49,252	29,250
1994–95[1]	47,811	62,709	46,713	38,756	29,665	33,198	41,227	47,432	49,738	42,101	48,741	49,379	25,613
Men													
1972–73	50,673	68,213	51,731	42,841	39,166	42,533	45,842	51,106	52,506	46,618	49,597	50,079	33,628
1974–75	47,344	62,530	47,283	39,084	38,769	38,426	40,680	47,981	49,131	44,578	45,621	46,034	30,879
1975–76	47,228	62,112	46,672	38,442	39,135	36,827	42,745	47,899	49,145	44,314	45,521	45,959	30,857
1976–77	47,096	61,578	46,270	38,059	30,971	36,253	44,215	47,716	48,924	44,167	45,450	45,849	31,247
1977–78	47,008	60,924	45,947	37,765	30,568	36,455	44,327	47,708	48,861	44,376	45,106	45,470	30,639
1978–79	45,620	58,686	44,399	36,453	29,512	34,972	42,596	46,287	47,490	42,762	43,771	44,103	28,650
1979–80	43,386	55,550	41,947	34,331	27,750	32,804	40,494	44,152	45,239	40,939	41,301	41,600	27,004
1980–81	42,538	53,968	40,718	33,384	26,991	31,742	40,230	43,187	44,292	39,874	40,791	41,097	27,911
1981–82	42,827	54,019	40,840	33,603	27,020	31,519	40,397	43,390	44,533	40,092	41,313	41,613	26,905
1982–83	43,926	55,100	41,777	34,611	27,829	32,526	40,672	44,212	45,453	40,646	43,152	43,490	26,582
1984–85	45,765	57,265	43,220	36,021	30,090	33,500	40,771	45,848	47,417	41,085	45,546	45,902	27,673
1985–86	47,402	59,204	44,608	37,450	29,984	34,884	41,835	47,725	49,464	42,514	46,520	46,857	28,214
1987–88	49,484	61,978	46,512	39,064	30,700	35,903	42,518	49,746	51,803	43,466	48,823	49,101	29,397
1989–90	50,655	63,551	47,537	40,015	30,718	36,913	42,620	50,887	53,108	43,925	50,121	50,455	29,872
1990–91	50,615	63,513	47,440	40,024	30,761	36,387	42,720	50,636	52,976	43,563	50,563	50,900	29,131
1991–92	50,983	63,657	47,682	40,232	36,304	35,743	42,902	50,586	52,674	44,414	51,946	52,283	29,193
1992–93	50,513	63,289	47,336	39,935	31,219	34,310	41,542	49,784	52,124	42,977	52,257	52,594	28,917
1993–94	51,000	63,630	47,554	39,906	30,670	35,793	43,462	50,359	52,450	44,168	52,540	52,870	31,666
1994–95[1]	51,228	64,046	47,705	39,923	30,528	35,082	43,103	50,629	52,874	44,020	52,653	53,036	29,639
Women													
1972–73	41,898	60,161	48,581	40,440	35,481	37,857	41,858	43,042	43,217	42,741	38,804	39,418	31,227
1974–75	39,120	55,212	44,959	37,340	34,095	33,521	36,645	40,342	40,166	40,619	35,526	36,077	28,271
1975–76	38,804	55,077	44,380	36,673	34,096	32,275	38,224	40,037	40,027	40,055	35,340	35,883	27,665
1976–77	38,695	55,189	44,050	36,455	29,698	31,769	39,636	39,908	39,820	40,048	35,131	35,619	27,804
1977–78	38,804	55,096	44,006	36,283	29,508	32,871	39,954	40,065	39,910	40,308	35,053	35,540	27,545
1978–79	37,503	53,011	42,378	34,942	28,470	31,761	38,387	38,746	38,705	38,811	33,788	34,278	26,124
1979–80	35,641	50,200	39,992	32,885	26,640	29,337	36,946	36,892	36,782	37,072	32,043	32,524	24,296
1980–81	34,719	48,546	38,711	31,778	25,791	28,073	36,190	35,895	35,782	36,077	31,380	31,820	24,121
1981–82	34,845	48,647	38,791	31,751	25,658	28,251	36,235	35,998	35,887	36,172	31,554	32,003	23,948
1982–83	35,646	49,376	39,442	32,380	26,208	28,856	36,556	36,613	36,588	36,651	32,872	33,384	24,281
1984–85	36,890	50,944	40,553	33,525	27,534	29,869	37,045	37,779	38,130	37,218	34,394	34,926	24,993
1985–86	38,116	52,872	41,881	34,508	27,972	30,786	37,556	39,115	39,642	37,556	35,278	35,784	25,576
1987–88	39,600	55,014	43,532	35,836	28,515	31,642	38,439	40,529	41,315	39,248	37,161	37,583	27,545
1989–90	40,491	56,459	44,384	36,827	28,808	31,977	38,531	41,218	42,294	39,453	38,675	39,102	28,432
1990–91	40,299	55,852	44,173	36,754	28,678	31,573	38,387	40,949	42,200	38,996	38,590	39,195	25,367
1991–92	40,847	56,178	44,364	37,070	31,422	31,070	38,767	41,137	42,044	38,741	40,079	40,602	26,862
1992–93	40,508	55,673	44,176	36,970	29,233	30,522	37,771	40,477	41,653	38,741	40,587	41,143	26,454
1993–94	41,207	56,315	44,415	37,206	28,943	31,938	39,577	41,268	42,207	39,816	41,046	41,535	26,891
1994–95[1]	41,369	56,555	44,626	37,352	29,072	31,677	38,967	41,548	42,663	39,812	40,908	41,815	22,851

[1] Preliminary data.
[2] Data adjusted by the Consumer Price Index prepared by the Bureau of Labor Statistics, averaged on an academic year time frame.

NOTE.—Data for 1987–88 to 1994–95 include imputations for nonrespondent institutions.

SOURCE: U.S. Department of Education, National Center for Education Statistics, *Faculty Salaries, Tenure, and Fringe Benefits;* and Integrated Postsecondary Education Data System (IPEDS), "Salaries, Tenure, and Fringe Benefits of Full-Time Instructional Faculty" surveys. (This table was prepared November 1995.)

Table 230.—Average salary of full-time instructional faculty on 9-month contracts in institutions of higher education, by academic rank, sex, and by type and control of institution: 1980–81, 1990–91, 1993–94, and 1994–95

Academic year, control, and type of institution	All faculty	Academic rank						Sex	
		Professor	Associate professor	Assistant professor	Instructor	Lecturer	No academic rank	Men	Women
1	2	3	4	5	6	7	8	9	10
1980–81									
All institutions	$23,302	$30,753	$23,214	$18,901	$15,178	$17,301	$22,334	$24,499	$19,996
4-year	23,693	31,016	23,265	18,867	15,056	17,375	17,380	24,909	19,809
University	25,949	33,622	24,392	19,684	15,530	17,327	17,856	27,206	20,736
Other 4-year	22,230	28,798	22,558	18,398	14,887	17,425	17,334	23,271	19,372
2-year	21,898	26,528	22,750	19,166	15,621	16,222	22,615	22,736	20,434
Public institutions	23,745	31,077	23,772	19,431	15,613	17,620	22,820	24,873	20,673
4-year	24,373	31,442	23,898	19,442	15,486	17,712	19,240	25,509	20,608
University	25,571	32,945	24,268	19,637	15,305	17,426	17,358	26,788	20,564
Other 4-year	23,500	30,097	23,639	19,315	15,567	17,997	19,798	24,499	20,633
2-year	22,177	26,880	22,947	19,370	15,928	16,458	22,875	22,965	20,778
Private institutions	22,093	29,994	21,833	17,767	14,192	15,899	15,946	23,493	18,073
4-year	22,325	30,089	21,887	17,816	14,316	15,971	16,706	23,669	18,326
University	26,897	35,227	24,730	19,792	16,197	16,956	18,933	28,251	21,176
Other 4-year	19,996	26,173	20,502	16,939	13,905	14,741	16,617	21,040	17,342
2-year	15,065	18,645	17,685	14,663	12,155	12,441	14,993	16,075	13,892
1990–91									
All institutions	42,165	55,540	41,414	34,434	26,332	30,097	36,395	45,065	35,881
4-year	43,693	56,485	41,811	34,657	25,772	30,209	31,494	46,519	36,574
University	49,430	63,437	44,877	37,838	27,105	31,748	31,533	52,426	39,788
Other 4-year	40,313	51,467	39,994	33,020	25,370	29,009	31,488	42,660	35,135
2-year	36,642	44,916	37,650	32,253	27,933	28,048	36,752	38,465	34,224
Public institutions	42,317	55,371	42,101	35,137	26,907	29,881	36,990	45,084	36,459
4-year	44,510	56,668	42,742	35,520	26,134	29,956	32,349	47,168	37,573
University	47,499	60,536	43,851	36,889	25,647	30,429	30,412	50,405	38,363
Other 4-year	42,499	53,704	41,969	34,680	26,316	29,664	33,507	44,804	37,147
2-year	37,055	45,411	38,051	32,673	28,389	28,780	37,096	38,787	34,720
Private institutions	41,788	55,911	39,983	33,116	24,928	30,864	28,523	45,019	34,359
4-year	42,224	56,127	40,122	33,235	25,159	31,053	31,122	45,319	34,898
University	53,875	69,732	47,405	40,013	31,239	34,444	36,211	56,989	43,273
Other 4-year	36,888	47,405	36,965	30,688	23,973	25,416	30,915	39,162	32,251
2-year	24,088	29,520	26,353	24,587	20,911	—	23,187	25,937	22,585
1993–94									
All institutions	46,364	60,649	45,278	37,630	28,828	32,729	40,584	49,579	40,058
4-year	47,969	61,824	45,656	37,901	28,226	32,620	34,099	51,133	40,785
University	54,357	69,644	48,856	41,367	29,114	34,077	34,196	57,799	44,410
Other 4-year	44,235	56,170	43,759	36,208	27,935	31,496	34,084	46,786	39,154
2-year	40,689	49,173	41,534	35,117	30,279	34,542	41,040	42,634	38,314
Public institutions	45,920	59,354	45,375	37,913	29,003	31,887	41,229	48,956	40,118
4-year	48,019	60,869	45,903	38,323	28,039	31,652	34,733	50,989	41,031
University	51,493	65,327	47,089	39,979	27,503	32,455	32,219	54,734	42,322
Other 4-year	45,677	57,406	45,064	37,344	28,247	31,174	35,772	48,232	40,328
2-year	41,040	49,435	41,922	35,448	30,531	34,943	41,372	42,938	38,707
Private institutions	47,465	63,503	45,080	37,100	28,356	35,472	31,854	51,076	39,902
4-year	47,880	63,661	45,219	37,214	28,550	35,572	33,820	51,397	40,378
University	60,962	79,043	53,219	44,628	34,299	37,014	38,163	64,745	49,484
Other 4-year	42,028	53,993	41,829	34,649	27,474	33,147	33,524	44,477	37,501
2-year	28,435	35,540	30,200	27,901	23,813	19,933	27,978	30,783	26,142
1994–95[1]									
All institutions	47,811	62,709	46,713	38,756	29,665	33,198	41,227	51,228	41,369
4-year	49,608	64,027	47,141	39,048	29,193	33,104	35,324	52,932	42,343
University	56,455	72,476	50,560	42,634	30,277	34,722	36,104	60,104	46,342
Other 4-year	45,674	57,989	45,154	37,350	28,857	31,899	35,208	48,330	40,563
2-year	41,523	50,412	42,531	36,080	30,815	35,298	41,635	43,640	39,046
Public institutions	47,432	61,366	46,955	39,147	29,877	32,761	42,186	50,629	41,548
4-year	49,738	63,091	47,581	39,605	29,058	32,606	35,523	52,874	42,663
University	53,444	67,853	48,855	41,219	28,632	33,328	32,627	56,881	44,153
Other 4-year	47,294	59,451	46,696	38,681	29,222	32,206	36,563	49,988	41,863
2-year	42,101	50,656	42,925	36,434	31,211	35,339	42,334	44,020	39,812
Private institutions	48,741	65,633	46,228	38,025	29,089	34,597	30,095	52,653	40,908
4-year	49,379	65,791	46,369	38,146	29,433	34,605	35,235	53,036	41,815
University	63,280	82,279	54,734	45,941	35,254	37,085	42,030	67,250	51,617
Other 4-year	43,196	55,446	42,892	35,516	28,302	30,261	34,726	45,690	38,722
2-year	25,613	37,096	30,861	28,315	22,140	21,132	23,473	29,639	22,851

[1] Preliminary data.
—Data not available.

NOTE.—Data for 1990–91 through 1994–95 include imputations for nonrespondent institutions.

SOURCE: U.S. Department of Education, National Center for Education Statistics, *Faculty Salaries, Tenure, and Fringe Benefits, 1980–81;* and Integrated Postsecondary Education Data System (IPEDS), "Salaries, Tenure, and Fringe Benefits of Full-Time Instructional Faculty" surveys. (This table was prepared November 1995.)

Table 231.—Average salary of full-time instructional faculty on 9-month contracts in institutions of higher education, by type and control of institution and by state: 1994–95 [1]

State or other area	All institutions	Public institutions					Private institutions				
		Total	4-year institutions			2-year	Total	4-year institutions			2-year
			Total	University	Other 4-year			Total	University	Other 4-year	
1	2	3	4	5	6	7	8	9	10	11	12
United States	$47,811	$47,432	$49,738	$53,444	$47,294	$42,101	$48,741	$49,379	$63,280	$43,196	$25,613
Alabama	40,576	41,681	43,457	47,655	40,731	37,442	34,517	34,685	—	34,685	22,073
Alaska	49,023	49,601	49,554	50,160	49,150	53,813	37,514	37,514	—	37,514	—
Arizona	48,863	49,089	51,903	54,269	44,433	43,935	42,552	42,552	—	42,552	—
Arkansas	37,655	38,262	40,073	45,026	38,541	30,003	34,907	35,939	—	35,939	10,730
California	55,247	54,814	58,335	65,800	56,978	50,541	57,006	57,249	72,275	50,026	35,504
Colorado	46,350	46,290	49,137	55,186	44,131	33,320	46,757	46,757	51,759	41,755	—
Connecticut	56,559	55,421	58,443	64,088	52,883	46,344	57,914	58,711	73,973	52,239	29,119
Delaware	52,773	52,741	54,684	57,443	40,198	41,883	53,041	53,041	—	53,041	—
District of Columbia	54,560	50,764	50,764	—	50,764	—	55,078	55,078	56,708	42,353	—
Florida	43,078	42,837	48,581	52,611	45,957	36,463	44,045	44,106	55,494	40,263	22,510
Georgia	42,852	42,848	44,833	49,712	43,660	34,010	42,861	43,434	65,210	37,493	28,538
Hawaii	51,978	52,545	57,481	58,714	49,137	44,501	45,581	45,581	—	45,581	—
Idaho	40,248	40,670	41,418	45,199	39,685	35,349	38,655	34,275	—	34,275	39,771
Illinois	49,511	47,960	48,312	51,818	45,157	47,391	52,289	52,627	68,938	41,972	29,281
Indiana	45,395	45,140	47,206	49,624	42,304	33,648	45,953	46,140	66,026	40,515	29,320
Iowa	44,571	47,658	53,226	55,522	46,385	34,634	39,299	39,343	48,205	38,107	33,420
Kansas	40,538	42,292	45,166	47,224	40,033	35,848	29,763	30,063	—	30,063	24,757
Kentucky	40,463	42,080	44,860	50,737	41,424	32,157	34,652	34,821	—	34,821	25,968
Louisiana	39,725	38,105	39,029	46,090	37,181	30,406	47,775	47,775	55,151	35,816	—
Maine	41,499	40,293	42,268	44,564	40,712	32,483	44,756	45,383	—	45,383	28,987
Maryland	48,051	47,428	49,333	55,476	46,410	44,174	50,292	50,350	66,638	42,373	23,500
Massachusetts	55,110	48,814	52,787	60,658	49,688	39,945	58,669	59,076	67,018	50,342	33,712
Michigan	50,804	53,038	53,641	59,084	49,086	51,134	39,929	40,488	43,039	40,161	26,727
Minnesota	46,147	47,716	50,685	60,309	45,887	42,743	42,366	42,619	—	42,619	34,277
Mississippi	37,250	37,641	41,109	41,505	40,850	33,359	34,340	35,202	—	35,202	21,442
Missouri	43,280	43,639	45,199	52,406	43,796	38,175	42,579	43,032	57,276	35,653	30,849
Montana	36,728	37,436	38,522	39,784	35,796	29,390	31,986	32,081	—	32,081	30,943
Nebraska	42,293	43,598	46,341	52,393	42,002	32,167	38,278	38,278	44,885	34,675	—
Nevada	46,820	47,042	48,957	52,147	46,928	41,863	29,877	31,773	—	31,773	21,658
New Hampshire	47,424	46,402	49,267	53,432	42,944	34,543	48,747	49,433	—	49,433	22,709
New Jersey	59,200	60,174	64,540	73,731	61,189	50,457	56,822	56,952	69,320	47,640	24,900
New Mexico	41,898	42,129	45,575	48,154	38,232	31,153	37,362	37,362	—	37,362	—
New York	53,915	54,815	57,273	60,991	56,709	50,274	52,980	55,295	64,679	48,539	16,233
North Carolina	44,472	45,525	47,844	55,701	44,593	30,454	42,053	42,600	60,048	34,841	29,536
North Dakota	35,213	36,001	37,229	37,923	35,714	31,311	29,413	30,866	—	30,866	20,917
Ohio	47,164	48,768	51,520	52,924	46,614	39,750	43,484	43,714	62,449	41,655	19,224
Oklahoma	39,686	39,677	41,622	46,235	37,849	33,648	39,723	40,545	50,579	35,385	25,693
Oregon	42,639	42,490	44,533	46,776	41,794	40,213	43,193	43,193	—	43,193	—
Pennsylvania	52,303	53,446	54,748	59,074	52,288	46,963	50,920	51,528	67,414	46,261	28,248
Rhode Island	51,818	51,032	54,102	57,853	47,610	41,758	52,440	52,440	—	52,440	—
South Carolina	39,333	40,182	44,821	50,699	38,961	30,336	35,696	35,825	—	35,825	30,217
South Dakota	35,269	36,298	36,324	37,170	35,090	27,514	31,386	31,386	—	31,386	—
Tennessee	43,721	44,595	47,601	54,417	45,244	34,736	41,730	42,132	64,035	34,009	28,159
Texas	43,892	43,202	45,785	52,241	41,442	38,624	46,952	47,108	56,044	40,056	23,613
Utah	43,744	42,037	44,454	48,611	38,008	32,854	47,542	47,822	48,675	37,074	31,537
Vermont	42,053	43,336	43,336	46,851	34,877	—	40,804	41,730	—	41,730	20,729
Virginia	45,710	46,557	49,811	54,497	46,596	36,766	42,797	43,081	—	43,081	26,726
Washington	44,107	44,044	49,086	52,271	43,796	37,453	44,353	44,353	—	44,353	—
West Virginia	37,812	38,644	39,226	44,861	36,513	30,492	33,101	33,341	—	33,341	24,538
Wisconsin	47,633	48,955	51,171	61,756	47,271	45,511	41,455	41,455	53,411	37,682	—
Wyoming	39,291	39,291	46,418	46,418	—	31,622	—	—	—	—	—
U.S. Service Schools	56,032	56,032	56,032	—	56,032	—	—	—	—	—	—
Outlying areas	32,230	33,696	33,886	31,962	33,886	32,519	19,796	19,796	—	19,796	—
American Samoa	33,334	33,334	—	—	—	33,334	—	—	—	—	—
Federated States of Micronesia	18,681	18,681	—	—	—	18,681	—	—	—	—	—
Guam	46,839	46,839	50,586	—	50,586	42,171	—	—	—	—	—
Marshall Islands	16,032	16,032	—	—	—	16,032	—	—	—	—	—
Northern Marianas	33,706	33,706	—	—	—	33,706	—	—	—	—	—
Palau	15,143	15,143	—	—	—	15,143	—	—	—	—	—
Puerto Rico	30,626	32,232	32,175	31,962	32,392	33,641	19,796	19,796	—	19,796	—
Virgin Islands	42,821	42,821	42,821	—	42,821	—	—	—	—	—	—

[1] Preliminary data.

—Data not reported or not applicable.

NOTE.—Data include imputations for nonrespondent institutions.

SOURCE: U.S. Department of Education, National Center for Education Statistics, Integrated Postsecondary Education Data System (IPEDS), "Salaries, Tenure, and Fringe Benefits of Full-Time Instructional Faculty, 1994–95" survey. (This table was prepared November 1995.)

Table 232.—Average salary of full-time instructional faculty on 9-month contracts in institutions of higher education, by type and control of institution and by state: 1993–94

State or other area	All institutions	Public institutions					Private institutions				
		Total	4-year institutions			2-year	Total	4-year institutions			2-year
			Total	University	Other 4-year			Total	University	Other 4-year	
1	2	3	4	5	6	7	8	9	10	11	12
United States	$46,364	$45,920	$48,019	$51,493	$45,677	$41,040	$47,465	$47,880	$60,962	$42,028	$28,435
Alabama	38,418	39,268	41,248	44,780	38,941	34,037	33,942	34,129	—	34,129	28,181
Alaska	47,917	48,585	48,556	48,470	48,613	51,052	37,705	37,705	—	37,705	—
Arizona	46,825	47,076	49,225	51,258	40,646	43,395	39,994	41,724	—	41,724	24,121
Arkansas	37,222	37,720	39,498	44,127	38,066	29,506	34,794	35,241	—	35,241	13,109
California	54,259	53,999	57,051	65,132	55,493	50,368	55,418	56,089	68,310	48,937	30,608
Colorado	44,008	43,590	46,709	52,388	42,183	31,598	47,060	47,060	50,592	43,466	—
Connecticut	55,483	55,243	58,001	62,965	53,374	46,813	55,757	56,572	71,857	50,236	26,857
Delaware	49,780	49,728	51,371	54,289	36,012	40,011	50,219	50,219	—	50,219	—
District of Columbia	52,586	49,114	49,114	—	49,114	—	53,046	53,046	54,640	40,297	—
Florida	41,543	41,129	45,865	49,280	43,619	35,795	43,131	43,204	52,248	40,176	29,530
Georgia	40,707	40,525	42,401	47,035	41,272	32,096	41,229	41,687	61,822	35,941	27,568
Hawaii	49,958	50,531	55,155	56,327	46,341	42,967	43,631	43,631	—	43,631	—
Idaho	38,813	39,015	39,680	43,464	37,993	33,977	38,066	34,194	—	34,194	39,034
Illinois	47,435	45,766	46,076	49,697	42,769	45,283	50,458	50,700	66,146	40,698	29,700
Indiana	44,921	45,024	45,902	48,205	41,216	34,211	44,710	44,870	63,709	39,546	29,172
Iowa	43,491	46,686	51,711	54,011	44,717	34,329	38,124	38,326	47,950	36,907	30,160
Kansas	38,481	40,160	42,973	44,837	38,309	33,478	28,236	28,687	—	28,687	22,054
Kentucky	39,393	40,934	43,646	49,500	40,181	31,339	33,591	33,756	—	33,756	25,846
Louisiana	39,304	37,787	38,643	46,409	36,596	30,464	46,497	46,497	53,436	34,892	—
Maine	41,232	40,509	42,521	45,096	40,753	32,514	43,257	43,663	—	43,663	24,047
Maryland	46,212	45,642	47,376	52,906	44,639	42,617	48,177	48,225	65,478	40,466	25,839
Massachusetts	54,233	49,015	52,946	60,961	49,899	39,721	57,133	57,561	64,905	49,318	31,709
Michigan	49,152	51,188	51,919	56,910	47,692	48,882	38,783	39,293	42,240	38,941	26,828
Minnesota	44,617	46,077	48,805	57,010	44,766	41,376	40,980	41,221	—	41,221	32,702
Mississippi	35,214	35,575	39,433	43,214	37,213	30,636	32,569	33,570	—	33,570	21,406
Missouri	41,786	41,874	43,187	49,124	42,027	37,318	41,608	42,306	55,217	34,796	28,468
Montana	36,549	37,365	38,357	39,587	35,662	27,701	30,054	30,417	—	30,417	23,373
Nebraska	41,663	43,172	45,931	52,303	41,371	30,879	37,079	37,079	43,672	33,629	—
Nevada	45,505	45,620	47,239	50,984	44,966	40,736	33,359	37,401	—	37,401	21,233
New Hampshire	45,173	43,148	45,409	48,114	41,276	33,682	47,730	48,338	—	48,338	22,760
New Jersey	55,629	55,678	59,045	67,727	55,879	48,185	55,507	55,713	68,492	45,964	17,098
New Mexico	40,008	40,089	43,306	45,297	37,461	30,270	38,308	38,308	—	38,308	—
New York	52,498	52,636	55,176	59,195	54,560	48,027	52,348	52,819	61,520	47,194	22,617
North Carolina	42,202	42,818	45,208	52,389	42,183	27,454	40,817	41,403	59,302	33,633	28,460
North Dakota	34,379	35,205	36,618	37,926	33,880	29,874	28,559	30,261	—	30,261	20,426
Ohio	45,830	47,276	49,841	51,080	45,484	38,902	42,449	42,590	59,605	40,681	19,744
Oklahoma	39,255	38,859	40,796	44,922	37,472	32,769	41,001	41,668	51,340	36,420	22,867
Oregon	42,161	41,800	44,890	46,806	42,473	38,321	43,796	43,796	—	43,796	—
Pennsylvania	50,390	51,461	52,646	56,677	50,378	45,218	49,116	49,629	64,430	44,656	27,109
Rhode Island	49,560	48,469	51,037	54,472	45,257	40,398	50,429	50,429	—	50,429	—
South Carolina	37,101	37,697	42,078	47,035	37,019	28,085	34,530	34,640	—	34,640	29,494
South Dakota	34,877	35,818	35,929	36,310	35,347	24,780	31,222	31,243	—	31,243	28,500
Tennessee	41,382	41,716	44,485	49,563	42,688	32,652	40,622	41,014	62,247	33,234	24,810
Texas	43,158	42,461	45,110	50,632	40,248	37,760	46,119	46,294	54,490	40,155	22,681
Utah	42,111	40,120	42,330	46,380	36,177	31,244	46,533	46,664	47,568	35,403	33,209
Vermont	40,842	42,792	43,599	45,743	35,972	33,087	39,036	39,953	—	39,953	19,700
Virginia	44,226	45,154	48,313	52,696	45,345	35,503	41,028	41,257	—	41,257	26,573
Washington	43,782	44,231	49,187	52,251	43,953	37,607	41,930	41,930	—	41,930	—
West Virginia	36,486	37,247	37,806	43,704	34,959	29,378	32,173	32,173	—	32,173	—
Wisconsin	45,306	46,306	48,040	58,260	44,231	43,548	40,524	40,524	51,882	36,766	—
Wyoming	37,422	37,422	44,923	44,923	—	30,162	—	—	—	—	—
U.S. Service Schools	56,789	56,789	56,789	—	56,789	—	—	—	—	—	—
Outlying areas	24,793	32,683	32,075	29,952	35,466	35,715	8,238	9,062	—	9,062	6,413
American Samoa	37,530	37,530	—	—	—	37,530	—	—	—	—	—
Federated States of Micronesia	20,001	20,001	—	—	—	20,001	—	—	—	—	—
Guam	46,374	46,374	50,001	—	50,001	41,877	—	—	—	—	—
Northern Marianas	30,005	30,005	—	—	—	30,005	—	—	—	—	—
Palau	36,360	36,360	—	—	—	36,360	—	—	—	—	—
Puerto Rico	21,222	29,523	29,279	29,952	27,489	33,783	8,238	9,062	—	9,062	6,413
Virgin Islands	43,801	43,801	43,801	—	43,801	—	—	—	—	—	—

—Data not reported or not applicable.

NOTE.—Data include imputations for nonrespondent institutions.

SOURCE: U.S. Department of Education, National Center for Education Statistics, Integrated Postsecondary Education Data System (IPEDS), "Salaries, Tenure, and Fringe Benefits of Full-Time Instructional Faculty, 1993–94" survey. (This table was prepared November 1995.)

Table 233.—Average salary of full-time instructional faculty on 9-month contracts in 4-year institutions of higher education, by type and control of institution and rank of faculty and by state: 1994–95 [1]

State or other area	Public university			Public other 4-year			Private university			Private other 4-year		
	Professor	Associate professor	Assistant professor	Professor	Associate professor	Assistant professor	Professor	Associate professor	Assistant professor	Professor	Associate professor	Assistant professor
1	2	3	4	5	6	7	8	9	10	11	12	13
United States	$67,853	$48,855	$41,219	$59,451	$46,696	$38,681	$82,279	$54,734	$45,941	$55,446	$42,892	$35,516
Alabama	62,540	46,441	39,699	52,368	42,775	36,478	—	—	—	45,677	35,456	30,448
Alaska	64,525	55,389	44,724	61,380	50,783	40,956	—	—	—	43,902	44,831	34,143
Arizona	66,703	48,332	42,454	57,867	46,968	39,287	—	—	—	47,370	52,471	29,441
Arkansas	57,623	45,635	39,789	49,959	40,278	34,625	—	—	—	42,414	36,160	30,352
California	79,866	53,573	45,808	64,815	50,052	41,566	90,140	60,209	50,580	63,724	47,687	39,186
Colorado	66,061	49,869	42,991	54,041	43,755	37,459	64,122	49,224	44,356	55,084	40,814	32,995
Connecticut	78,326	58,895	46,685	64,742	51,848	39,817	96,821	54,891	46,489	64,872	49,086	41,781
Delaware	75,506	55,059	43,639	53,035	44,171	37,381	—	—	—	62,256	56,355	39,203
District of Columbia	—	—	—	59,630	47,628	38,645	75,358	52,147	42,549	58,903	43,501	37,036
Florida	63,138	44,275	41,079	57,320	44,624	39,903	73,275	51,445	42,657	51,332	39,957	34,121
Georgia	65,381	47,086	39,590	56,441	45,138	37,681	84,710	55,042	47,675	46,615	38,596	33,145
Hawaii	73,450	55,002	47,472	58,359	48,120	43,375	—	—	—	54,179	45,446	40,613
Idaho	52,388	43,004	39,357	46,858	39,135	35,099	—	—	—	30,559		33,000
Illinois	67,068	48,004	40,283	55,782	44,733	38,428	88,131	58,382	48,988	52,221	42,641	35,998
Indiana	64,414	46,766	39,160	57,392	44,596	37,659	82,747	58,258	48,250	49,470	40,086	34,273
Iowa	71,033	50,892	42,389	60,088	47,642	40,464	60,759	44,986	40,338	47,272	37,883	33,027
Kansas	59,503	44,079	37,821	50,340	40,148	34,886	—	—	—	35,110	31,183	27,462
Kentucky	63,819	46,364	39,875	51,655	42,217	35,577	—	—	—	43,521	34,892	30,951
Louisiana	61,197	44,139	38,230	48,008	38,855	33,929	69,891	50,247	42,618	45,068	36,356	33,083
Maine	56,652	43,363	36,143	50,518	40,398	33,152	—	—	—	62,332	45,123	35,672
Maryland	71,645	50,090	43,312	60,306	48,017	40,345	82,202	55,415	46,644	53,065	42,853	35,663
Massachusetts	70,551	53,505	44,080	56,898	48,101	39,441	87,864	55,904	48,648	65,493	47,649	39,926
Michigan	73,515	54,845	45,950	59,353	48,067	40,508	53,982	43,961	36,430	48,520	39,532	34,773
Minnesota	71,786	50,028	44,136	54,387	44,452	37,443	—	—	—	54,852	41,997	34,881
Mississippi	52,972	41,639	37,685	52,287	42,827	36,959	—	—	—	44,232	34,682	31,042
Missouri	64,582	48,262	42,597	55,177	44,523	37,374	74,667	50,369	44,576	44,234	36,449	32,402
Montana	47,208	38,688	34,265	43,388	35,920	30,700	—	—	—	38,745	34,016	29,073
Nebraska	68,242	47,898	41,750	51,522	43,602	36,993	67,860	47,072	34,420	42,264	35,479	30,773
Nevada	66,395	49,162	39,915	61,642	49,365	40,879	—	—	—	41,910	35,685	25,166
New Hampshire	65,286	49,609	40,680	52,849	42,436	35,150	—	—	—	66,783	44,158	37,607
New Jersey	92,907	65,637	51,099	77,490	61,168	47,585	93,741	57,396	43,567	58,284	47,485	39,030
New Mexico	60,566	46,084	39,017	49,834	39,316	32,976	—	—	—	35,229	35,598	28,858
New York	77,256	54,667	43,508	70,357	54,093	43,273	81,561	56,321	46,700	62,143	48,247	38,869
North Carolina	71,748	50,951	43,676	56,675	45,737	39,595	76,174	53,636	44,645	43,945	35,475	30,831
North Dakota	47,360	39,905	35,483	44,507	37,224	34,254	—	—	—	39,746	33,463	30,245
Ohio	67,041	49,016	40,581	61,206	46,156	38,387	78,434	54,957	48,710	53,079	41,331	34,379
Oklahoma	57,936	43,599	37,520	46,647	39,700	35,975	68,621	49,807	38,992	46,127	36,877	31,438
Oregon	58,766	45,315	38,860	50,637	40,143	34,646	—	—	—	54,656	41,096	34,987
Pennsylvania	76,390	55,337	44,463	68,726	53,966	42,837	85,880	58,021	48,499	59,152	45,996	37,860
Rhode Island	66,974	50,053	44,619	54,208	46,341	39,600	—	—	—	70,527	48,844	41,572
South Carolina	63,596	46,740	40,733	48,678	40,692	34,114	—	—	—	46,147	36,105	30,180
South Dakota	46,861	37,730	34,298	45,999	37,878	32,040	—	—	—	40,943	33,823	29,077
Tennessee	64,114	49,245	43,373	55,842	45,000	37,303	83,129	54,647	44,451	42,161	35,027	30,416
Texas	68,359	45,910	40,232	53,265	42,791	36,098	73,682	51,097	44,475	49,986	40,575	33,058
Utah	61,493	44,315	38,788	46,511	37,526	34,040	61,136	46,634	38,932	45,760	38,127	33,352
Vermont	60,942	46,076	37,216	42,544	34,612	29,550	—	—	—	54,825	40,165	35,429
Virginia	69,653	49,472	42,481	59,680	46,390	38,086	—	—	—	55,538	42,286	34,464
Washington	65,346	46,514	40,845	50,193	41,866	35,651	—	—	—	56,015	43,474	36,952
West Virginia	54,984	44,217	37,145	45,616	36,460	30,526	—	—	—	41,156	35,379	29,616
Wisconsin	70,553	52,223	46,433	56,142	45,887	39,514	69,974	51,928	42,844	46,613	38,534	32,479
Wyoming	57,025	44,608	40,052	—	—	—	—	—	—	—	—	—
U.S. Service Schools	—	—	—	67,164	53,236	44,774	—	—	—	—	—	—
Outlying areas	39,392	32,646	27,406	41,364	35,082	29,623	—	—	—	16,282	26,029	22,141
American Samoa	—	—	—	—	—	—	—	—	—	—	—	—
Federated States of Micronesia	—	—	—	—	—	—	—	—	—	—	—	—
Guam	—	—	—	69,087	54,807	43,628	—	—	—	—	—	—
Northern Marianas	—	—	—	—	—	—	—	—	—	—	—	—
Palau	—	—	—	—	—	—	—	—	—	—	—	—
Puerto Rico	39,392	32,646	27,406	40,570	32,895	27,771	—	—	—	16,282	26,029	22,141
Virgin Islands	—	—	—	53,747	44,580	37,691	—	—	—	—	—	—

[1] Preliminary data.

—Data not reported or not applicable.

NOTE.—Data include imputations for nonrespondent institutions.

SOURCE: U.S. Department of Education, National Center for Education Statistics, Integrated Postsecondary Education Data System (IPEDS), "Salaries, Tenure, and Fringe Benefits of Full-Time Instructional Faculty, 1994–95" survey. (This table was prepared November 1995.)

Table 234.—Average salary of full-time instructional faculty on 9-month contracts in 4-year institutions of higher education, by type and control of institution and rank of faculty and by state: 1993–94

State or other area	Public university			Public other 4-year			Private university			Private other 4-year		
	Professor	Associate professor	Assistant professor	Professor	Associate professor	Assistant professor	Professor	Associate professor	Assistant professor	Professor	Associate professor	Assistant professor
1	2	3	4	5	6	7	8	9	10	11	12	13
United States	$65,327	$47,089	$39,979	$57,406	$45,064	$37,344	$79,043	$53,219	$44,628	$53,993	$41,829	$34,649
Alabama	59,077	43,852	37,457	50,627	40,890	34,712	—	—	—	44,521	34,605	30,165
Alaska	64,546	55,213	43,409	60,461	50,407	40,480	—	—	—	45,495	40,620	33,878
Arizona	62,975	45,610	40,888	50,652	42,069	35,879	—	—	—	49,241	46,583	31,267
Arkansas	56,376	44,331	38,641	49,716	39,780	34,153	—	—	—	40,839	35,320	30,543
California	78,006	52,343	44,316	63,097	48,507	40,196	83,693	57,491	48,334	61,627	46,476	38,490
Colorado	62,386	47,597	41,466	50,666	42,123	36,049	62,487	47,522	43,239	56,219	44,442	33,532
Connecticut	75,702	57,316	46,848	65,663	52,586	39,818	93,045	52,638	44,852	62,839	47,413	40,039
Delaware	71,397	53,332	42,254	52,482	41,568	34,501	—	—	—	59,579	53,164	40,318
District of Columbia	—	—	—	55,909	47,596	39,006	72,384	50,476	41,412	57,389	43,947	35,365
Florida	59,590	40,881	38,660	54,753	41,546	37,623	70,338	51,015	42,251	54,444	39,755	33,869
Georgia	61,765	44,702	37,255	53,265	42,805	35,687	80,171	54,375	45,421	45,899	37,111	30,908
Hawaii	70,790	52,743	45,802	56,030	45,164	41,975	—	—	—	53,081	43,069	40,098
Idaho	50,767	41,122	38,239	44,770	37,490	33,612	—	—	—	36,615	30,598	—
Illinois	63,915	46,246	38,932	52,301	42,322	36,956	85,031	56,547	47,430	50,643	41,369	34,974
Indiana	62,435	45,706	37,946	56,181	43,093	37,051	79,751	56,189	46,958	48,402	38,924	33,417
Iowa	69,191	50,189	41,325	58,595	46,905	38,948	59,938	45,936	40,069	45,834	37,079	31,919
Kansas	56,144	41,678	36,284	47,921	39,014	33,114	—	—	—	33,801	30,157	25,542
Kentucky	61,932	45,157	39,763	49,852	41,077	34,744	—	—	—	42,415	34,402	29,584
Louisiana	61,831	44,225	38,465	47,418	38,561	33,355	67,736	49,054	41,206	44,579	35,622	32,304
Maine	57,428	43,726	36,612	50,387	40,361	32,664	—	—	—	60,495	43,785	34,564
Maryland	69,306	48,268	40,677	57,316	45,548	38,906	80,605	55,537	45,475	51,040	41,282	35,431
Massachusetts	70,492	53,782	44,135	56,923	48,387	40,052	84,963	54,840	46,438	64,164	47,017	38,781
Michigan	70,682	52,894	44,471	57,635	47,220	39,696	52,729	42,785	35,623	47,369	38,484	33,676
Minnesota	67,802	47,181	42,305	54,730	42,598	35,903	—	—	—	52,926	40,546	34,364
Mississippi	53,665	42,346	38,673	47,854	39,898	33,800	—	—	—	41,324	34,747	29,295
Missouri	60,636	44,861	40,838	53,017	43,036	36,472	71,532	49,388	43,278	42,920	36,491	31,192
Montana	46,327	38,625	33,565	43,496	35,792	30,313	—	—	—	36,640	30,681	27,199
Nebraska	66,907	47,162	42,189	51,169	43,190	36,646	64,553	45,408	33,618	40,667	34,356	30,145
Nevada	64,850	48,276	39,386	59,828	47,758	39,246	—	—	—	62,191	30,484	28,306
New Hampshire	59,173	45,419	37,435	50,525	40,793	34,502	—	—	—	66,038	43,203	35,990
New Jersey	86,228	61,194	48,353	70,270	55,286	43,519	91,961	56,417	42,778	56,206	45,681	37,303
New Mexico	56,630	43,273	37,243	48,147	38,404	32,550	—	—	—	39,039	33,610	28,387
New York	74,644	53,322	42,016	67,718	51,794	41,590	77,729	54,211	44,968	60,798	47,132	38,262
North Carolina	67,498	47,791	40,812	53,642	43,318	37,609	74,895	53,254	44,528	42,043	34,611	29,902
North Dakota	46,554	39,102	34,626	43,210	37,132	31,898	—	—	—	39,091	33,087	29,707
Ohio	64,742	47,593	39,392	59,583	44,713	37,475	75,846	51,757	47,831	51,208	40,332	33,770
Oklahoma	55,935	42,396	37,217	46,104	39,472	35,490	68,645	49,995	40,423	46,371	37,685	27,983
Oregon	59,039	45,658	38,801	50,028	40,499	35,496	—	—	—	55,096	39,644	34,825
Pennsylvania	73,358	53,087	43,210	66,108	51,990	41,496	81,900	56,501	47,248	57,222	44,331	36,645
Rhode Island	63,458	47,921	42,242	51,746	44,194	38,116	—	—	—	69,010	47,366	39,712
South Carolina	59,098	43,598	38,271	45,903	38,847	32,118	—	—	—	45,176	35,069	29,315
South Dakota	45,479	36,471	33,481	44,218	36,552	31,155	—	—	—	40,775	32,683	29,177
Tennessee	58,944	45,440	40,307	52,578	42,486	35,420	80,778	52,279	44,095	41,294	33,883	29,468
Texas	66,476	45,013	39,529	51,168	42,022	35,654	70,894	49,814	44,175	51,118	40,170	32,784
Utah	58,325	41,988	37,594	44,947	36,320	32,597	59,276	45,197	38,079	44,249	36,680	32,330
Vermont	60,339	44,704	36,916	43,263	36,073	29,975	—	—	—	52,382	39,116	34,254
Virginia	68,022	47,715	40,888	57,150	45,441	37,046	—	—	—	52,849	40,432	33,454
Washington	65,675	46,837	40,825	50,395	41,920	35,225	—	—	—	51,723	41,889	35,502
West Virginia	54,422	43,124	36,269	43,582	35,369	29,418	—	—	—	39,428	34,017	29,212
Wisconsin	67,082	49,677	44,196	52,760	43,073	37,679	69,536	51,141	41,485	45,438	37,507	31,359
Wyoming	54,441	41,744	37,655	—	—	—	—	—	—	—	—	—
U.S. Service Schools	—	—	—	67,502	53,576	44,480	—	—	—	—	—	—
Outlying areas	36,996	30,384	25,469	45,814	37,485	32,176	—	—	—	30,552	26,452	22,858
American Samoa	—	—	—	—	—	—	—	—	—	—	—	—
Federated States of Micronesia	—	—	—	—	—	—	—	—	—	—	—	—
Guam	—	—	—	68,717	54,827	43,464	—	—	—	—	—	—
Northern Marianas	—	—	—	—	—	—	—	—	—	—	—	—
Palau	—	—	—	—	—	—	—	—	—	—	—	—
Puerto Rico	36,996	30,384	25,469	36,042	29,218	24,719	—	—	—	30,552	26,452	22,858
Virgin Islands	—	—	—	55,512	45,173	38,194	—	—	—	—	—	—

—Data not reported or not applicable.

NOTE.—Data include imputations for nonrespondent institutions.

SOURCE: U.S. Department of Education, National Center for Education Statistics, Integrated Postsecondary Education Data System (IPEDS), "Salaries, Tenure, and Fringe Benefits of Full-Time Instructional Faculty, 1993–94" survey. (This table was prepared November 1995.)

Table 235.—Full-time instructional faculty with tenure for institutions reporting tenure status, by academic rank, sex, and type and control of institution: 1980–81, 1990–91, 1993–94, and 1994–95

Academic year, type, and control of institution	Percent with tenure, by rank							Percent with tenure, by sex	
	All ranks	Professor	Associate professor	Assistant professor	Instructor	Lecturer	No academic rank	Men	Women
1	2	3	4	5	6	7	8	9	10
1980–81									
All institutions	64.8	95.8	82.9	27.9	9.2	11.9	77.4	70.0	49.7
4-year	62.7	95.8	82.2	24.1	6.6	10.7	24.7	68.3	44.0
University	64.5	96.7	83.7	15.3	5.4	4.3	3.5	70.0	41.0
Other 4-year	61.3	94.9	81.2	29.7	7.1	17.8	32.4	67.0	45.5
2-year	74.5	95.6	89.2	58.9	19.8	34.8	81.1	78.8	66.6
Public institutions	68.0	96.6	85.9	32.5	11.8	14.3	79.4	72.8	54.0
4-year	65.7	96.6	85.3	27.6	8.7	12.8	12.2	71.1	47.5
University	66.0	96.9	86.5	16.8	6.1	4.9	4.5	71.3	42.8
Other 4-year	65.5	96.3	84.4	35.5	10.0	21.4	17.2	70.9	50.2
2-year	75.2	95.9	89.5	59.5	20.3	35.8	81.8	79.3	67.5
Private institutions	55.9	93.8	75.2	17.5	3.0	1.5	43.4	62.2	37.2
4-year	56.0	93.8	75.2	17.4	2.8	1.5	37.5	62.2	37.2
University	60.4	96.3	75.8	11.5	3.5	1.8	0.6	66.3	36.5
Other 4-year	53.6	92.0	74.9	20.2	2.6	1.2	43.4	59.8	37.4
2-year	49.5	84.7	77.3	35.2	8.8	—	52.2	57.3	39.5
1990–91									
All institutions	61.2	95.6	80.8	18.6	6.8	6.9	36.3	67.8	45.3
4-year	61.7	95.7	80.4	15.8	4.1	6.0	19.1	68.6	43.9
University	65.2	97.2	85.4	9.0	3.5	2.1	1.4	71.6	43.6
Other 4-year	59.4	94.6	77.1	19.7	4.3	9.2	30.2	66.3	44.0
2-year	57.1	93.7	85.3	50.7	16.3	26.6	39.8	60.9	51.9
Public institutions	62.9	96.3	83.7	21.7	8.6	8.4	36.6	69.4	47.4
4-year	64.0	96.5	83.5	18.0	5.3	7.3	11.3	70.8	45.9
University	66.3	97.3	88.3	9.7	4.2	2.4	0.4	72.8	44.5
Other 4-year	62.3	95.9	79.9	23.4	5.7	10.6	23.5	69.1	46.7
2-year	57.3	93.7	85.6	51.4	16.7	26.7	39.7	61.0	52.2
Private institutions	56.7	93.9	73.8	11.8	1.5	1.0	33.3	63.7	39.8
4-year	56.8	93.9	73.8	11.6	1.4	1.0	31.2	63.7	39.8
University	62.2	96.9	77.4	7.3	1.4	1.4	6.5	68.5	41.3
Other 4-year	53.9	91.9	72.0	13.5	1.5	0.5	36.3	60.9	39.2
2-year	45.7	90.2	70.9	29.0	4.3	—	49.7	53.1	39.3
1993–94									
All institutions	64.2	96.0	81.8	17.0	7.0	2.2	76.2	71.0	49.9
4-year	62.3	96.3	81.6	14.2	4.0	1.8	22.8	69.8	44.8
University	66.4	97.6	86.5	7.9	2.6	1.8	3.8	73.5	45.2
Other 4-year	59.7	95.3	78.4	17.6	4.5	1.9	30.7	67.1	44.6
2-year	72.9	92.6	84.1	46.9	15.9	8.4	80.4	78.1	66.2
Public institutions	67.0	96.9	85.5	20.2	8.9	2.4	78.0	73.7	53.3
4-year	65.1	97.4	85.7	16.3	5.2	2.0	13.6	72.5	47.1
University	68.2	98.0	90.0	8.6	3.2	1.9	2.0	75.3	46.7
Other 4-year	62.8	96.9	82.4	21.1	6.1	2.0	20.0	70.2	47.3
2-year	73.2	93.0	84.4	47.8	16.2	8.4	80.6	78.4	66.6
Private institutions	57.0	93.9	73.7	10.6	1.6	1.4	52.8	64.4	40.9
4-year	56.9	94.0	73.8	10.6	1.6	1.4	32.5	64.4	40.7
University	61.9	96.4	77.4	6.2	0.8	1.5	6.8	68.9	41.6
Other 4-year	54.5	92.5	72.1	12.3	1.8	1.1	40.0	61.8	40.4
2-year	61.9	66.7	67.3	19.2	1.8	—	73.6	70.2	49.8
1994–95 [1]									
All institutions	64.3	96.0	82.2	16.8	7.4	1.5	75.9	71.3	50.3
4-year	62.5	96.2	82.1	13.9	3.9	1.5	22.8	70.2	45.3
University	66.6	97.4	87.0	7.5	2.7	1.3	3.7	74.0	45.7
Other 4-year	59.9	95.3	78.9	17.2	4.2	1.7	31.2	67.5	45.1
2-year	73.3	93.4	84.0	48.5	18.4	0.3	79.9	78.2	67.1
Public institutions	67.2	97.0	86.1	20.0	9.3	1.6	77.1	74.0	53.6
4-year	65.3	97.4	86.3	15.9	5.0	1.6	13.0	73.0	47.4
University	68.7	98.1	90.7	8.5	3.4	1.5	1.3	76.0	47.6
Other 4-year	62.8	96.9	83.0	20.3	5.6	1.7	19.2	70.6	47.3
2-year	73.4	93.4	84.3	49.1	18.1	0.3	79.9	78.2	67.3
Private institutions	57.3	93.7	73.8	10.6	2.2	1.2	56.1	64.8	41.7
4-year	57.2	93.7	73.8	10.5	1.7	1.2	34.9	64.6	41.4
University	61.6	95.9	77.1	5.4	0.9	0.7	7.6	68.9	41.3
Other 4-year	55.0	92.3	72.3	12.5	1.9	2.0	44.4	62.2	41.5
2-year	68.2	89.7	66.4	27.2	29.9	—	80.4	75.8	57.3

[1] Preliminary data.

—Data not available or not applicable.

SOURCE: U.S. Department of Education, National Center for Education Statistics, *Faculty Salaries, Tenure, and Fringe Benefits;* and Integrated Postsecondary Education Data System (IPEDS), "Salaries, Tenure, and Fringe Benefits of Full-Time Instructional Faculty" surveys. (This table was prepared November 1995.)

Table 236.—Institutions of higher education, by control and type of institution: 1949–50 to 1995–96

Year	All institutions			Public			Private		
	Total	4-year	2-year	Total	4-year	2-year	Total	4-year	2-year
1	2	3	4	5	6	7	8	9	10
Excluding branch campuses									
1949–50	1,851	1,327	524	641	344	297	1,210	983	227
1950–51	1,852	1,312	540	636	341	295	1,216	971	245
1951–52	1,832	1,326	506	641	350	291	1,191	976	215
1952–53	1,882	1,355	527	639	349	290	1,243	1,006	237
1953–54	1,863	1,345	518	662	369	293	1,201	976	225
1954–55	1,849	1,333	516	648	353	295	1,201	980	221
1955–56	1,850	1,347	503	650	360	290	1,200	987	213
1956–57	1,878	1,355	523	656	359	297	1,222	996	226
1957–58	1,930	1,390	540	666	366	300	1,264	1,024	240
1958–59	1,947	1,394	553	673	366	307	1,274	1,028	246
1959–60	2,004	1,422	582	695	367	328	1,309	1,055	254
1960–61	2,021	1,431	590	700	368	332	1,321	1,063	258
1961–62	2,033	1,443	590	718	374	344	1,315	1,069	246
1962–63	2,093	1,468	625	740	376	364	1,353	1,092	261
1963–64	2,132	1,499	633	760	386	374	1,372	1,113	259
1964–65	2,175	1,521	654	799	393	406	1,376	1,128	248
1965–66	2,230	1,551	679	821	401	420	1,409	1,150	259
1966–67	2,329	1,577	752	880	403	477	1,449	1,174	275
1967–68	2,374	1,588	786	934	414	520	1,440	1,174	266
1968–69	2,483	1,619	864	1,011	417	594	1,472	1,202	270
1969–70	2,525	1,639	886	1,060	426	634	1,465	1,213	252
1970–71	2,556	1,665	891	1,089	435	654	1,467	1,230	237
1971–72	2,606	1,675	931	1,137	440	697	1,469	1,235	234
1972–73	2,665	1,701	964	1,182	449	733	1,483	1,252	231
1973–74	2,720	1,717	1,003	1,200	440	760	1,520	1,277	243
1974–75	2,747	1,744	1,003	1,214	447	767	1,533	1,297	236
1975–76	2,765	1,767	998	1,219	447	772	1,546	1,320	226
1976–77	2,785	1,783	1,002	1,231	452	779	1,554	1,331	223
1977–78	2,826	1,808	1,018	1,241	454	787	1,585	1,354	231
1978–79	2,954	1,843	1,111	1,308	463	845	1,646	1,380	266
1979–80	2,975	1,863	1,112	1,310	464	846	1,665	1,399	266
1980–81	3,056	1,861	1,195	1,334	465	869	1,722	1,396	[1]326
1981–82	3,083	1,883	1,200	1,340	471	869	1,743	1,412	[1]331
1982–83	3,111	1,887	1,224	1,336	472	864	1,775	1,415	[1]360
1983–84	3,117	1,914	1,203	1,325	474	851	1,792	1,440	352
1984–85	3,146	1,911	1,235	1,329	461	868	1,817	1,450	367
1985–86	3,155	1,915	1,240	1,326	461	865	1,829	1,454	375
Including branch campuses									
1974–75	3,004	1,866	1,138	1,433	537	896	1,571	1,329	242
1975–76	3,026	1,898	1,128	1,442	545	897	1,584	1,353	231
1976–77	3,046	1,913	1,133	1,455	550	905	1,591	1,363	228
1977–78	3,095	1,938	1,157	1,473	552	921	1,622	1,386	236
1978–79	3,134	1,941	1,193	1,474	550	924	1,660	1,391	269
1979–80	3,152	1,957	1,195	1,475	549	926	1,677	1,408	269
1980–81	3,231	1,957	1,274	1,497	552	945	1,734	1,405	[1]329
1981–82	3,253	1,979	1,274	1,498	558	940	1,755	1,421	[1]334
1982–83	3,280	1,984	1,296	1,493	560	933	1,787	1,424	[1]363
1983–84	3,284	2,013	1,271	1,481	565	916	1,803	1,448	355
1984–85	3,331	2,025	1,306	1,501	566	935	1,830	1,459	371
1985–86	3,340	2,029	1,311	1,498	566	932	1,842	1,463	379
1986–87 [2]	3,406	2,070	1,336	1,533	573	960	1,873	1,497	376
1987–88 [2]	3,587	2,135	1,452	1,591	599	992	1,996	1,536	460
1988–89 [2]	3,565	2,129	1,436	1,582	598	984	1,983	1,531	452
1989–90 [2]	3,535	2,127	1,408	1,563	595	968	1,972	1,532	440
1990–91 [2]	3,559	2,141	1,418	1,567	595	972	1,992	1,546	446
1991–92 [2]	3,601	2,157	1,444	1,598	599	999	2,003	1,558	445
1992–93 [2]	3,638	2,169	1,469	1,624	600	1,024	2,014	1,569	445
1993–94 [2]	3,632	2,190	1,442	1,625	604	1,021	2,007	1,586	421
1994–95 [2]	3,688	2,215	1,473	1,641	605	1,036	2,047	1,610	437
1995–96 [2]	3,706	2,244	1,462	1,655	608	1,047	2,051	1,636	415

[1] Large increases are due to the addition of schools accredited by the Accrediting Commission of Career Schools and Colleges of Technology.

[2] Because of revised survey procedures, data are not entirely comparable with figures for earlier years. The number of branch campuses reporting separately has increased since 1986–87.

NOTE.—Includes those colleges designated as institutions of higher education by the Integrated Postsecondary Education Data System, even if they have a less than 2-year program.

SOURCE: U.S. Department of Education, National Center for Education Statistics, *Education Directory, Colleges and Universities;* "Fall Enrollment in Higher Education" and "Institutional Characteristics of Colleges and Universities" surveys; and Integrated Postsecondary Education Data System (IPEDS), "Institutional Characteristics" surveys. (This table was prepared September 1996.)

Table 237.—Institutions of higher education and branches, by type, control of institution, and state: 1995–96

State or other area	Total	All institutions Public	All institutions Private	4-year All 4-year Total	4-year All 4-year Public	4-year All 4-year Private	Universities Public	Universities Private	Other 4-year Public	Other 4-year Private	2-year Total	2-year Public	2-year Private
1	2	3	4	5	6	7	8	9	10	11	12	13	14
United States	3,706	1,655	2,051	2,244	608	1,636	94	62	514	1,574	1,462	1,047	415
Alabama	82	53	29	36	18	18	2	0	16	18	46	35	11
Alaska	9	4	5	6	3	3	1	0	2	3	3	1	2
Arizona	45	23	22	23	5	18	2	0	3	18	22	18	4
Arkansas	38	26	12	20	10	10	1	0	9	10	18	16	2
California	348	138	210	199	31	168	2	4	29	164	149	107	42
Colorado	59	30	29	34	14	20	2	1	12	19	25	16	9
Connecticut	42	19	23	26	7	19	1	1	6	18	16	12	4
Delaware	9	5	4	6	2	4	1	0	1	4	3	3	0
District of Columbia	19	2	17	19	2	17	0	5	2	12	0	0	0
Florida	114	38	76	68	9	59	2	1	7	58	46	29	17
Georgia	120	73	47	56	19	37	1	1	18	36	64	54	10
Hawaii	17	10	7	10	3	7	1	0	2	7	7	7	0
Idaho	12	6	6	8	4	4	1	0	3	4	4	2	2
Illinois	169	61	108	107	12	95	3	4	9	91	62	49	13
Indiana	78	28	50	54	14	40	4	1	10	39	24	14	10
Iowa	59	20	39	39	3	36	2	1	1	35	20	17	3
Kansas	54	31	23	31	10	21	3	0	7	21	23	21	2
Kentucky	61	22	39	37	8	29	2	0	6	29	24	14	10
Louisiana	36	20	16	27	14	13	1	2	13	11	9	6	3
Maine	33	14	19	21	8	13	1	0	7	13	12	6	6
Maryland	57	33	24	34	13	21	1	1	12	20	23	20	3
Massachusetts	118	32	86	90	15	75	1	7	14	68	28	17	11
Michigan	109	45	64	71	15	56	3	1	12	55	38	30	8
Minnesota	107	62	45	48	11	37	1	0	10	37	59	51	8
Mississippi	46	31	15	21	9	12	2	0	7	12	25	22	3
Missouri	101	30	71	70	13	57	1	2	12	55	31	17	14
Montana	26	19	7	11	6	5	2	0	4	5	15	13	2
Nebraska	35	18	17	22	7	15	1	1	6	14	13	11	2
Nevada	10	6	4	5	2	3	1	0	1	3	5	4	1
New Hampshire	30	12	18	19	5	14	1	0	4	14	11	7	4
New Jersey	61	33	28	35	14	21	1	2	13	19	26	19	7
New Mexico	35	24	11	15	6	9	2	0	4	9	20	18	2
New York	311	89	222	212	42	170	2	12	40	158	99	47	52
North Carolina	121	74	47	58	16	42	2	2	14	40	63	58	5
North Dakota	20	15	5	10	6	4	2	0	4	4	10	9	1
Ohio	156	61	95	92	24	68	8	1	16	67	64	37	27
Oklahoma	45	29	16	25	14	11	2	1	12	10	20	15	5
Oregon	45	22	23	30	8	22	2	0	6	22	15	14	1
Pennsylvania	217	65	152	146	45	101	3	4	42	97	71	20	51
Rhode Island	12	3	9	10	2	8	1	0	1	8	2	1	1
South Carolina	59	33	26	34	12	22	2	0	10	22	25	21	4
South Dakota	21	9	12	18	8	10	2	0	6	10	3	1	2
Tennessee	76	24	52	52	10	42	1	1	9	41	24	14	10
Texas	179	107	72	98	40	58	6	4	34	54	81	67	14
Utah	17	10	7	9	5	4	2	1	3	3	8	5	3
Vermont	22	6	16	19	5	14	1	0	4	14	3	1	2
Virginia	89	39	50	54	15	39	3	0	12	39	35	24	11
Washington	64	37	27	32	8	24	2	0	6	24	32	29	3
West Virginia	28	16	12	23	13	10	1	0	12	10	5	3	2
Wisconsin	66	30	36	44	13	31	1	1	12	30	22	17	5
Wyoming	9	8	1	1	1	0	1	0	0	0	8	7	1
U.S. Service Schools	10	10	0	9	9	0	0	0	9	0	1	1	0
Outlying areas	74	27	47	50	13	37	1	0	12	37	24	14	10
American Samoa	1	1	0	0	0	0	0	0	0	0	1	1	0
Guam	2	2	0	1	1	0	0	0	1	0	1	1	0
Marshall Islands	1	1	0	0	0	0	0	0	0	0	1	1	0
Micronesia	5	5	0	0	0	0	0	0	0	0	5	5	0
Northern Marianas	1	1	0	0	0	0	0	0	0	0	1	1	0
Palau	1	1	0	0	0	0	0	0	0	0	1	1	0
Puerto Rico	61	14	47	47	10	37	1	0	9	37	14	4	10
Virgin Islands	2	2	0	2	2	0	0	0	2	0	0	0	0

NOTE.—Because of revised survey procedures, data are not entirely comparable with figures for years prior to 1986–87. The number of branch campuses reporting separately has increased since 1986–87.

SOURCE: U.S. Department of Education, National Center for Education Statistics, Integrated Postsecondary Education Data System (IPEDS), "Institutional Characteristics, 1995–96" survey. (This table was prepared September 1996.)

Table 238.—Institutions of higher education that have closed their doors, by control and type of institution: 1960–61 to 1994–95

Year	All institutions			Public			Private		
	Total	4-year	2-year	Total	4-year	2-year	Total	4-year	2-year
1	2	3	4	5	6	7	8	9	10
Excluding branch campuses:									
Total, 1960–61 to 1991–92	**364**	**185**	**179**	**38**	**1**	**37**	**326**	**184**	**142**
1960–61	8	1	7	1	—	1	7	1	6
1961–62	2	1	1	—	—	—	2	1	1
1962–63	—	—	—	—	—	—	—	—	—
1963–64	7	1	6	1	—	1	6	1	5
1964–65	8	1	7	4	—	4	4	1	3
1965–66	8	2	6	4	—	4	4	2	2
1966–67	9	2	7	3	—	3	6	2	4
1967–68	14	6	8	—	—	—	14	6	8
1968–69	21	11	10	1	—	1	20	11	9
1969–70	18	8	10	3	—	3	15	8	7
1970–71	32	9	23	9	—	9	23	9	14
1971–72	12	3	9	3	—	3	9	3	6
1972–73	19	12	7	2	—	2	17	12	5
1973–74	18	11	7	—	—	—	18	11	7
1974–75	17	13	4	3	—	3	14	13	1
1975–76	8	6	2	2	1	1	6	5	1
1976–77	8	5	3	—	—	—	8	5	3
1977–78	12	9	3	—	—	—	12	9	3
1978–79	9	4	5	—	—	—	9	4	5
1979–80	6	5	1	—	—	—	6	5	1
1980–81	4	3	1	—	—	—	4	3	1
1981–82	7	6	1	—	—	—	7	6	1
1982–83	7	4	3	—	—	—	7	4	3
1983–84	4	4	—	—	—	—	4	4	—
1984–85	4	4	—	—	—	—	4	4	—
1985–86	10	6	4	1	—	1	9	6	3
1986–87 and 1987–88	25	19	6	1	—	1	24	19	5
1988–89	14	6	8	—	—	—	14	6	8
1989–90	12	6	6	—	—	—	12	6	6
1990–91	10	4	6	—	—	—	10	4	6
1991–92	10	7	3	—	—	—	10	7	3
Including branch campuses:									
Total, 1969–70 to 1994–95	**346**	**178**	**168**	**34**	**4**	**30**	**312**	**174**	**138**
1969–70	24	10	14	5	1	4	19	9	10
1970–71	35	10	25	11	—	11	24	10	14
1971–72	14	5	9	3	—	3	11	5	6
1972–73	21	12	9	4	—	4	17	12	5
1973–74	20	12	8	1	—	1	19	12	7
1974–75	18	13	5	4	—	4	14	13	1
1975–76	9	7	2	2	1	1	7	6	1
1976–77	9	6	3	—	—	—	9	6	3
1977–78	12	9	3	—	—	—	12	9	3
1978–79	9	4	5	—	—	—	9	4	5
1979–80	6	5	1	—	—	—	6	5	1
1980–81	4	3	1	—	—	—	4	3	1
1981–82	7	6	1	—	—	—	7	6	1
1982–83	7	4	3	—	—	—	7	4	3
1983–84	5	5	—	1	1	—	4	4	—
1984–85	4	4	—	—	—	—	4	4	—
1985–86	12	8	4	1	1	—	11	7	4
1986–87 and 1987–88	26	19	7	1	—	1	25	19	6
1988–89	14	6	8	—	—	—	14	6	8
1989–90	19	8	11	—	—	—	19	8	11
1990–91	18	6	12	—	—	—	18	6	12
1991–92	26	8	18	1	—	1	25	8	17
1992–93	24	6	18	—	—	—	24	6	18
1993–94	38	11	27	1	—	1	37	11	26
1994–95	16	8	8	2	—	2	14	8	6

—Data not applicable or not available.

NOTE.—This table indicates the year in which the institution closed.

SOURCE: U.S. Department of Education, National Center for Education Statistics, *Education Directory, Higher Education*, 1960–61 to 1974–75; *Education Directory, Colleges and Universities*, 1975–76 to 1983–84; *1982–83 Supplement to the Education Directory, Colleges and Universities*; and Integrated Postsecondary Education Data System, "Institutional Characteristics" surveys, unpublished data. (This table was prepared August 1996.)

Table 239.—Earned degrees conferred by institutions of higher education, by level of degree and sex of student: 1869–70 to 2005–06

Year	Associate degrees			Bachelor's degrees			Master's degrees			First-professional degrees			Doctor's degrees		
	Total	Men	Women	Total	Men	Women	Total	Men	Women	Total	Men	Women	Total	Men	Women
1	2	3	4	5	6	7	8	9	10	11	12	13	14	15	16
1869–70	—	—	—	[1]9,371	[1]7,993	[1]1,378	0	0	0	[2]	[2]	[2]	1	1	0
1879–80	—	—	—	[1]12,896	[1]10,411	[1]2,485	879	868	11	[2]	[2]	[2]	54	51	3
1889–90	—	—	—	[1]15,539	[1]12,857	[1]2,682	1,015	821	194	[2]	[2]	[2]	149	147	2
1899–1900	—	—	—	[1]27,410	[1]22,173	[1]5,237	1,583	1,280	303	[2]	[2]	[2]	382	359	23
1909–10	—	—	—	[1]37,199	[1]28,762	[1]8,437	2,113	1,555	558	[2]	[2]	[2]	443	399	44
1919–20	—	—	—	[1]48,622	[1]31,980	[1]16,642	4,279	2,985	1,294	[2]	[2]	[2]	615	522	93
1929–30	—	—	—	[1]122,484	[1]73,615	[1]48,869	14,969	8,925	6,044	[2]	[2]	[2]	2,299	1,946	353
1939–40	—	—	—	[1]186,500	[1]109,546	[1]76,954	26,731	16,508	10,223	[2]	[2]	[2]	3,290	2,861	429
1949–50	—	—	—	[1]432,058	[1]328,841	[1]103,217	58,183	41,220	16,963	[2]	[2]	[2]	6,420	5,804	616
1959–60	—	—	—	[1]392,440	[1]254,063	[1]138,377	74,435	50,898	23,537	[2]	[2]	[2]	9,829	8,801	1,028
1960–61	—	—	—	365,174	224,538	140,636	84,609	57,830	26,779	25,253	24,577	676	10,575	9,463	1,112
1961–62	—	—	—	383,961	230,456	153,505	91,418	62,603	28,815	25,607	24,836	771	11,622	10,377	1,245
1962–63	—	—	—	411,420	241,309	170,111	98,684	67,302	31,382	26,590	25,753	837	12,822	11,448	1,374
1963–64	—	—	—	461,266	265,349	195,917	109,183	73,850	35,333	27,209	26,357	852	14,490	12,955	1,535
1964–65	—	—	—	493,757	282,173	211,584	121,167	81,319	39,848	28,290	27,283	1,007	16,467	14,692	1,775
1965–66	111,607	63,779	47,828	520,115	299,287	220,828	140,602	93,081	47,521	30,124	28,982	1,142	18,237	16,121	2,116
1966–67	139,183	78,356	60,827	558,534	322,711	235,823	157,726	103,109	54,617	31,695	30,401	1,294	20,617	18,163	2,454
1967–68	159,441	90,317	69,124	632,289	357,682	274,607	176,749	113,552	63,197	33,939	32,402	1,537	23,089	20,183	2,906
1968–69	183,279	105,661	77,618	728,845	410,595	318,250	193,756	121,531	72,225	35,114	33,595	1,519	26,158	22,722	3,436
1969–70	206,023	117,432	88,591	792,316	451,097	341,219	208,291	125,624	82,667	34,918	33,077	1,841	29,866	25,890	3,976
1970–71	252,311	144,144	108,167	839,730	475,594	364,136	230,509	138,146	92,363	37,946	35,544	2,402	32,107	27,530	4,577
1971–72	292,014	166,227	125,787	887,273	500,590	386,683	251,633	149,550	102,083	43,411	40,723	2,688	33,363	28,090	5,273
1972–73	316,174	175,413	140,761	922,362	518,191	404,171	263,371	154,468	108,903	50,018	46,489	3,529	34,777	28,571	6,206
1973–74	343,924	188,591	155,333	945,776	527,313	418,463	277,033	157,842	119,191	53,816	48,530	5,286	33,816	27,365	6,451
1974–75	360,171	191,017	169,154	922,933	504,841	418,092	292,450	161,570	130,880	55,916	48,956	6,960	34,083	26,817	7,266
1975–76	391,454	209,996	181,458	925,746	504,925	420,821	311,771	167,248	144,523	62,649	52,892	9,757	34,064	26,267	7,797
1976–77	406,377	210,842	195,535	919,549	495,545	424,004	317,164	167,783	149,381	64,359	52,374	11,985	33,232	25,142	8,090
1977–78	412,246	204,718	207,528	921,204	487,347	433,857	311,620	161,212	150,408	66,581	52,270	14,311	32,131	23,658	8,473
1978–79	402,702	192,091	210,611	921,390	477,344	444,046	301,079	153,370	147,709	68,848	52,652	16,196	32,730	23,541	9,189
1979–80	400,910	183,737	217,173	929,417	473,611	455,806	298,081	150,749	147,332	70,131	52,716	17,415	32,615	22,943	9,672
1980–81	416,377	188,638	227,739	935,140	469,883	465,257	295,739	147,043	148,696	71,956	52,792	19,164	32,958	22,711	10,247
1981–82	434,526	196,944	237,582	952,998	473,364	479,634	295,546	145,532	150,014	72,032	52,223	19,809	32,707	22,224	10,483
1982–83	449,620	203,991	245,629	969,510	479,140	490,370	289,921	144,697	145,224	73,054	51,250	21,804	32,775	21,902	10,873
1983–84	452,240	202,704	249,536	974,309	482,319	491,990	284,263	143,595	140,668	74,468	51,378	23,090	33,209	22,064	11,145
1984–85	454,712	202,932	251,780	979,477	482,528	496,949	286,251	143,390	142,861	75,063	50,455	24,608	32,943	21,700	11,243
1985–86	446,047	196,166	249,881	987,823	485,923	501,900	288,567	143,508	145,059	73,910	49,261	24,649	33,653	21,819	11,834
1986–87	436,304	190,839	245,465	991,264	480,782	510,482	289,349	141,269	148,080	71,617	46,523	25,094	34,041	22,061	11,980
1987–88	435,085	190,047	245,038	994,829	477,203	517,626	299,317	145,163	154,154	70,735	45,484	25,251	34,870	22,615	12,255
1988–89	436,764	186,316	250,448	1,018,755	483,346	535,409	310,621	149,354	161,267	70,856	45,046	25,810	35,720	22,648	13,072
1989–90	455,102	191,195	263,907	1,051,344	491,696	559,648	324,301	153,653	170,648	70,988	43,961	27,027	38,371	24,401	13,970
1990–91	481,720	198,634	283,086	1,094,538	504,045	590,493	337,168	156,482	180,686	71,948	43,846	28,102	39,294	24,756	14,538
1991–92	504,231	207,481	296,750	1,136,553	520,811	615,742	352,838	161,842	190,996	74,146	45,071	29,075	40,659	25,557	15,102
1992–93	514,756	211,964	302,792	1,165,178	532,881	632,297	369,585	169,258	200,327	75,387	45,153	30,234	42,132	26,073	16,059
1993–94	542,449	220,990	321,459	1,169,275	532,422	636,853	387,070	176,085	210,985	75,418	44,707	30,711	43,185	26,552	16,633
1994–95[3]	530,000	216,000	314,000	1,192,000	535,000	657,000	405,000	195,000	210,000	77,100	45,400	31,700	43,000	26,700	16,300
1995–96[3]	534,000	212,000	323,000	1,195,000	533,000	663,000	409,000	199,000	210,000	78,000	45,900	32,100	43,300	26,500	16,800
1996–97[3]	519,000	208,000	311,000	1,188,000	526,000	663,000	421,000	206,000	215,000	80,900	48,700	32,200	44,000	26,800	17,200
1997–98[3]	523,000	209,000	315,000	1,173,000	529,000	644,000	421,000	206,000	215,000	81,600	48,900	32,600	44,300	26,600	17,700
1998–99[3]	531,000	211,000	320,000	1,180,000	534,000	646,000	428,000	208,000	220,000	83,000	49,900	33,100	45,000	26,800	18,100
1999–2000[3]	538,000	212,000	326,000	1,191,000	539,000	652,000	428,000	208,000	220,000	84,100	50,400	33,700	46,200	27,600	18,600
2000–01[3]	549,000	215,000	334,000	1,211,000	550,000	661,000	435,000	210,000	225,000	86,100	51,600	34,500	46,200	27,100	19,100
2001–02[3]	561,000	219,000	343,000	1,237,000	561,000	675,000	440,000	210,000	230,000	88,900	53,700	35,200	45,600	26,000	19,500
2002–03[3]	571,000	221,000	350,000	1,264,000	572,000	692,000	445,000	210,000	235,000	89,700	54,400	35,400	45,100	25,100	20,000
2003–04[3]	576,000	222,000	354,000	1,288,000	580,000	708,000	452,000	212,000	240,000	90,200	54,500	35,700	44,400	23,900	20,500
2004–05[3]	579,000	223,000	356,000	1,302,000	585,000	717,000	457,000	212,000	245,000	91,100	55,000	36,100	43,900	23,000	20,900
2005–06[3]	584,000	224,000	360,000	1,316,000	591,000	725,000	462,000	212,000	250,000	91,700	55,200	36,500	43,200	21,800	21,400

[1] Includes first-professional degrees.
[2] First-professional degrees are included with bachelor's degrees.
[3] Projected.
—Data not available.

NOTE.—Some data have been revised from previously published figures. Because of rounding, details may not add to totals.

SOURCE: U.S. Department of Education, National Center for Education Statistics, Earned Degrees Conferred; Projections of Education Statistics to 2006; and Integrated Postsecondary Education Data System (IPEDS), "Completions" surveys. (This table was prepared February 1996.)

Table 240.—Earned degrees conferred by institutions of higher education, by level of degree and by state: 1992–93 and 1993–94

State or other area	1992–93					1993–94				
	Associate degrees	Bachelor's degrees	First-pro-fessional degrees [1]	Master's degrees	Doctor's degrees (Ph.D., Ed.D., etc.)	Associate degrees	Bachelor's degrees	First-pro-fessional degrees [1]	Master's degrees	Doctor's degrees (Ph.D., Ed.D., etc.)
1	2	3	4	5	6	7	8	9	10	11
United States	514,756	1,165,178	75,387	369,585	42,132	542,449	1,169,275	75,418	387,070	43,185
Alabama	7,484	20,525	866	5,636	406	7,781	21,150	908	5,763	476
Alaska	940	1,260	—	363	10	1,002	1,396	—	422	24
Arizona	6,928	15,807	436	5,694	690	6,796	16,093	462	6,399	754
Arkansas	2,618	8,449	449	1,836	120	2,808	8,549	441	1,995	146
California	54,688	111,010	9,195	37,046	4,987	56,417	111,848	9,228	38,708	5,034
Colorado	6,294	18,925	813	6,391	768	6,746	18,954	809	6,859	765
Connecticut	5,094	14,931	679	6,590	630	5,081	13,929	769	6,649	646
Delaware	1,313	4,119	550	954	144	1,191	4,187	461	955	121
District of Columbia	435	8,095	2,321	6,059	562	305	7,184	2,420	6,311	489
Florida	39,405	43,212	2,322	13,145	1,661	40,620	44,075	2,382	14,056	1,644
Georgia	8,316	25,390	1,949	7,958	899	9,419	26,283	2,015	8,326	813
Hawaii	2,515	4,186	176	1,383	168	2,391	4,314	172	1,369	175
Idaho	3,544	3,923	146	1,005	65	4,068	4,203	148	1,017	88
Illinois	27,620	51,482	4,410	22,440	2,601	27,022	52,330	4,321	23,689	2,592
Indiana	9,236	31,453	1,496	6,874	1,107	9,589	30,769	1,454	6,962	1,103
Iowa	8,344	17,598	1,534	3,517	683	8,314	17,846	1,442	3,488	689
Kansas	6,312	14,282	601	3,920	387	6,716	14,599	619	4,618	415
Kentucky	6,546	14,396	985	4,195	328	6,416	14,629	1,118	4,028	401
Louisiana	2,865	17,825	1,502	4,723	428	3,303	17,787	1,582	5,205	447
Maine	2,433	5,976	168	917	40	2,463	5,953	173	896	53
Maryland	8,425	20,427	1,050	8,006	963	8,292	20,720	972	8,182	934
Massachusetts	13,354	42,747	3,677	19,215	2,276	13,084	42,351	3,771	20,745	2,228
Michigan	24,231	45,711	2,581	14,944	1,513	36,032	44,925	2,746	15,474	1,483
Minnesota	9,766	24,762	1,854	5,217	674	9,708	24,746	1,536	5,678	917
Mississippi	5,575	10,673	466	2,672	303	5,538	10,524	478	2,630	352
Missouri	8,023	26,954	2,171	9,303	711	8,424	27,494	2,206	10,130	778
Montana	801	4,194	68	756	57	1,031	4,357	70	803	57
Nebraska	2,494	9,522	806	2,007	238	3,189	10,087	811	2,201	244
Nevada	1,311	3,029	54	845	39	1,295	3,276	39	922	52
New Hampshire	3,343	7,524	195	2,267	118	3,350	7,546	182	2,228	136
New Jersey	12,299	25,185	1,679	8,110	965	12,625	25,234	1,709	8,274	1,032
New Mexico	3,007	5,667	178	2,142	243	3,065	6,118	192	2,348	243
New York	53,393	97,104	7,476	42,539	4,045	53,784	93,134	7,442	42,903	4,025
North Carolina	12,164	31,852	1,709	6,864	980	13,621	32,730	1,673	7,276	988
North Dakota	1,696	4,555	142	649	74	1,718	4,558	189	675	74
Ohio	19,881	51,487	3,225	14,613	1,973	20,117	50,982	3,251	14,992	2,127
Oklahoma	6,304	15,002	928	4,457	416	6,689	15,734	846	4,954	387
Oregon	5,676	13,139	988	3,650	535	5,986	13,272	946	3,617	531
Pennsylvania	20,091	65,073	3,774	17,649	2,267	21,172	64,326	3,745	18,906	2,247
Rhode Island	4,156	9,341	81	2,070	269	3,941	9,145	87	2,019	255
South Carolina	5,953	15,254	604	4,245	408	6,218	15,318	627	4,452	459
South Dakota	848	4,252	130	913	52	873	4,164	141	1,038	60
Tennessee	6,801	20,371	1,341	5,016	721	6,894	19,992	1,296	5,740	672
Texas	24,804	67,598	4,882	20,887	2,546	25,787	69,298	4,768	21,838	2,732
Utah	4,839	12,901	388	2,868	376	5,318	14,191	367	2,837	338
Vermont	1,264	4,707	96	1,103	53	1,268	4,671	93	1,174	62
Virginia	10,232	30,858	1,811	9,325	998	11,339	31,226	1,839	9,980	1,006
Washington	16,619	20,829	920	6,745	618	18,365	21,321	918	7,268	696
West Virginia	2,919	8,606	320	1,916	99	3,012	9,045	367	2,032	127
Wisconsin	9,481	27,709	971	6,340	851	9,394	27,484	966	6,267	956
Wyoming	1,850	1,856	69	342	50	1,862	1,794	66	457	73
U.S. Service Schools	10,226	3,445	155	1,264	17	11,010	3,434	155	1,315	39
Outlying areas	4,342	14,100	681	1,388	74	4,125	13,866	582	1,938	76
American Samoa	43	—	—	—	—	44	—	—	—	—
Federated States of Micronesia	56	—	—	—	—	105	—	—	—	—
Guam	36	178	—	15	—	25	208	—	26	—
Marshall Islands	35	—	—	—	—	40	—	—	—	—
Northern Marianas	87	—	—	—	—	69	—	—	—	—
Palau	4	—	—	—	—	13	—	—	—	—
Puerto Rico	4,017	13,746	681	1,330	74	3,769	13,486	582	1,858	76
Virgin Islands	64	176	—	43	—	60	172	—	54	—

[1] Includes degrees which require at least 6 years of college work for completion (including at least 2 years of preprofessional training).

—Data not available or not applicable.

SOURCE: U.S. Department of Education, National Center for Education Statistics, Integrated Postsecondary Education Data System (IPEDS), "Completions" surveys. (This table was prepared May 1996.)

Table 241.—Associate degrees conferred by institutions of higher education, by sex and field of study: 1987–88 to 1991–92

Field of study	Total					Women				
	1987–88	1988–89	1989–90	1990–91	1991–92	1987–88	1988–89	1989–90	1990–91	1991–92
1	2	3	4	5	6	7	8	9	10	11
Total	435,085	436,764	455,102	481,720	504,231	245,038	250,448	263,907	283,086	296,750
Agriculture and natural resources, total	5,029	4,725	4,832	4,910	5,251	1,658	1,655	1,600	1,588	1,675
Agricultural business and production	3,003	2,884	2,894	2,905	3,046	960	969	930	962	1,011
Agricultural sciences	1,015	963	925	879	951	543	543	507	444	432
Conservation and renewable natural resources	1,011	878	1,013	1,126	1,254	155	143	163	182	232
Architecture and related programs	1,809	1,815	2,013	2,031	443	1,591	1,559	1,745	1,741	337
Area, ethnic, and cultural studies	18	16	68	19	29	14	8	56	13	20
Biological/life sciences	854	982	1,023	1,119	1,361	506	568	593	667	797
Business management and administrative services	110,064	106,819	106,405	102,250	102,227	75,412	73,706	73,992	71,619	71,953
Accounting	14,221	14,266	14,858	14,577	15,687	10,615	10,690	11,275	11,111	11,888
Business, general	12,458	11,929	11,878	11,618	11,823	7,295	6,940	7,095	7,188	7,293
Business administration and management	26,791	27,252	28,292	26,625	31,185	15,392	15,782	16,753	15,863	18,902
Business and management, other	11,936	11,162	11,691	11,663	11,089	6,399	6,130	6,480	6,655	6,769
Business data processing	10,544	9,831	8,532	8,182	6,394	5,861	5,501	4,733	4,775	3,679
Secretarial and related programs	19,059	18,041	17,139	16,872	17,584	18,732	17,660	16,827	16,517	16,928
Marketing and distribution	15,055	14,338	14,015	12,713	8,465	11,118	11,003	10,829	9,510	6,494
Communications	1,919	1,777	1,657	1,847	1,886	915	955	910	966	996
Communications technologies	1,507	1,993	2,027	2,032	1,794	592	681	678	681	649
Computer and information sciences	8,628	7,900	7,574	7,677	9,290	4,154	3,908	3,768	3,770	4,725
Construction trades	2,020	1,731	1,765	1,793	1,560	64	75	68	78	69
Consumer and personal services	2,542	2,815	2,121	2,494	4,420	985	1,028	843	887	1,519
Education	7,219	7,445	8,061	7,842	10,267	4,904	5,285	5,731	5,640	6,559
Engineering	3,850	2,676	2,345	2,451	2,685	413	310	279	268	344
Engineering-related technologies	44,019	42,593	40,033	37,890	35,861	4,265	4,237	4,006	3,724	3,757
English language and literature/letters	484	468	527	426	1,019	321	330	358	302	671
Foreign languages and literatures	418	324	329	327	433	193	214	251	210	305
Health professions and related sciences	59,692	59,535	64,113	70,833	79,453	52,759	52,495	56,125	61,495	68,648
Dental assisting	3,675	3,650	3,697	3,810	4,013	3,425	3,427	3,502	3,612	3,822
Emergency medical technician-ambulance and paramedic	356	354	332	371	378	110	99	100	116	114
Medical lab technician	1,839	1,724	1,627	1,731	1,874	1,436	1,339	1,284	1,311	1,425
Medical assisting	1,701	1,786	1,404	1,496	1,960	1,659	1,695	1,375	1,451	1,741
Nursing assisting	8	12	0	5	19	6	11	0	4	13
Practical nursing	561	591	589	797	795	522	539	535	692	742
Nursing, R.N. and other	36,945	36,475	40,212	45,317	51,193	34,338	33,904	36,915	41,261	46,217
Health sciences, other	14,607	14,943	16,252	17,306	19,221	11,263	11,481	12,414	13,048	14,574
Home economics and vocational home economics	7,043	7,559	7,798	8,067	6,436	5,369	5,745	6,080	6,243	5,749
Law and legal studies	3,139	3,742	4,552	5,484	7,053	2,770	3,271	3,967	4,892	6,146
Liberal/general studies and humanities	116,411	121,988	133,466	142,722	154,594	67,172	71,588	78,768	84,977	91,777
Library science	67	101	107	111	103	61	90	95	102	85
Mathematics	765	654	756	670	744	295	239	270	264	280
Mechanics and repairers	10,473	7,769	7,704	7,640	10,264	588	427	431	445	671
Multi/interdisciplinary studies	7,477	7,737	8,176	7,454	7,841	3,719	3,888	4,156	3,998	4,059
Parks, recreation, leisure, and fitness studies	647	641	485	425	620	350	329	200	177	251
Philosophy and religion	94	81	93	89	60	30	23	34	28	17
Physical sciences	1,856	1,838	2,021	2,091	2,066	774	806	811	901	861
Physical sciences, other	1,176	1,090	1,279	1,281	1,228	480	487	539	562	522
Science technologies	680	748	742	810	838	294	319	272	339	339
Precision production trades	7,734	7,414	8,616	9,093	9,005	1,720	1,584	1,898	1,975	1,872
Protective services	11,829	11,682	12,855	13,564	15,117	3,157	3,292	3,402	3,599	3,876
Criminal justice and corrections	9,901	9,663	10,658	11,358	12,649	2,949	3,079	3,137	3,367	3,628
Fire control and safety	1,397	1,493	1,621	1,634	1,989	53	78	91	92	116
Protective services, other	531	526	576	572	479	155	135	174	140	132
Psychology	1,000	1,090	1,115	997	1,209	701	811	829	740	871
Public administration and services	2,317	2,493	2,613	2,779	3,162	1,823	1,959	2,076	2,243	2,523
R.O.T.C. and military technologies	138	164	129	85	172	20	31	15	8	16
Social sciences and history	2,709	2,741	2,872	2,505	3,160	1,556	1,544	1,611	1,494	1,760
Theological studies/religious vocations	627	568	653	578	496	239	248	264	243	216
Transportation and material moving	1,327	2,090	2,619	2,609	2,418	202	340	395	469	440
Visual and performing arts	8,998	8,178	8,740	9,126	11,888	5,495	4,952	5,327	5,362	7,085
Fine arts, general	1,123	1,091	1,150	1,166	1,159	742	719	729	766	767
Design and music	5,677	5,340	5,900	5,986	9,142	3,510	3,218	3,588	3,499	5,536
Visual and performing arts, other	2,198	1,747	1,690	1,974	1,587	1,243	1,015	1,010	1,097	782
Not classified by field of study	362	4,620	4,839	19,690	9,844	251	2,267	2,275	11,277	5,171

SOURCE: U.S. Department of Education, National Center for Education Statistics, Integrated Postsecondary Education Data System (IPEDS), "Completions" surveys. (This table was prepared November 1995.)

Table 242.—Associate degrees and other subbaccalaureate awards conferred by institutions of higher education, by length of curriculum, sex of student, and field of study: 1993–94

Field of study	Less than 1-year awards			1- to less than 4-year awards			Associate degrees		
	Total	Men	Women	Total	Men	Women	Total	Men	Women
1	2	3	4	5	6	7	8	9	10
Total	71,748	34,732	37,016	152,849	63,886	88,963	542,449	220,990	321,459
Agriculture and natural resources, total	1,459	1,128	331	4,157	2,290	1,867	5,720	3,869	1,851
Agricultural business and production	1,233	949	284	1,339	920	419	3,518	2,400	1,118
Agricultural sciences	155	116	39	1,596	430	1,166	871	483	388
Conservation and renewable natural resources	71	63	8	1,222	940	282	1,331	986	345
Architecture and related programs	10	0	10	44	16	28	353	115	238
Area, ethnic, and cultural studies	133	32	101	505	141	364	92	34	58
Biological/life sciences	43	34	9	93	45	48	1,852	744	1,108
Business management and administrative services	12,535	3,541	8,994	30,908	5,931	24,977	103,098	30,569	72,529
Accounting	1,088	217	871	4,356	813	3,543	15,963	3,652	12,311
Business, general	245	104	141	1,463	463	1,000	11,452	4,215	7,237
Business administration and management	1,914	796	1,118	2,218	789	1,429	31,031	12,134	18,897
Business and management, other	2,125	1,025	1,100	4,206	1,716	2,490	12,561	5,243	7,318
Business data processing	901	361	540	2,297	803	1,494	6,883	3,030	3,853
Secretarial and related programs	4,222	326	3,896	14,097	784	13,313	18,313	535	17,778
Marketing and distribution	2,040	712	1,328	2,271	563	1,708	6,895	1,760	5,135
Communications	426	246	180	350	135	215	2,110	984	1,126
Communications technologies	82	53	29	331	192	139	2,789	1,807	982
Computer and information sciences	1,793	878	915	3,938	1,965	1,973	9,456	4,740	4,716
Construction trades	1,495	1,393	102	4,557	4,311	246	1,724	1,644	80
Consumer and personal services	1,229	296	933	6,109	1,462	4,647	5,212	3,499	1,713
Education	499	135	364	1,294	133	1,161	10,021	3,149	6,872
Engineering	228	204	24	104	84	20	2,799	2,447	352
Engineering-related technologies	2,351	2,027	324	9,011	8,024	987	36,877	32,784	4,093
English language and literature/letters	92	28	64	120	39	81	1,354	493	861
Foreign languages and literatures	324	132	192	77	35	42	517	151	366
Health professions and related sciences	24,909	7,140	17,769	42,569	6,805	35,764	95,832	15,476	80,356
Dental assisting	283	16	267	2,552	126	2,426	4,325	284	4,041
Emergency medical technician-ambulance and paramedic	6,551	4,293	2,258	1,863	1,327	536	514	357	157
Medical lab technician	39	5	34	207	91	116	2,570	665	1,905
Medical assisting	1,707	205	1,502	3,410	105	3,305	2,785	113	2,672
Nursing assisting	8,046	1,010	7,036	295	35	260	6	1	5
Practical nursing	519	63	456	19,431	2,124	17,307	740	68	672
Nursing, R.N. and other	2,355	280	2,075	3,529	384	3,145	57,531	6,679	50,852
Health sciences, other	5,409	1,268	4,141	11,282	2,613	8,669	27,361	7,309	20,052
Home economics and vocational home economics	3,428	974	2,454	8,570	1,792	6,778	7,562	643	6,919
Law and legal studies	962	167	795	2,104	378	1,726	9,008	1,103	7,905
Liberal/general studies and humanities	149	57	92	631	270	361	164,575	65,879	98,696
Library science	97	4	93	57	5	52	118	16	102
Mathematics	17	11	6	0	0	0	765	436	329
Mechanics and repairers	3,505	3,373	132	20,526	19,007	1,519	11,618	10,873	745
Multi/interdisciplinary studies	379	128	251	119	47	72	8,461	4,059	4,402
Parks, recreation, leisure, and fitness studies	47	34	13	129	53	76	767	465	302
Philosophy and religion	53	22	31	514	212	302	94	55	39
Physical sciences	38	22	16	57	33	24	2,622	1,527	1,095
Physical sciences, other	17	9	8	18	12	6	1,639	945	694
Science technologies	21	13	8	39	21	18	983	582	401
Precision production trades	2,374	1,996	378	7,662	6,372	1,290	9,661	7,779	1,882
Protective services	6,683	5,403	1,280	2,398	1,667	731	19,416	13,956	5,460
Criminal justice and corrections	5,657	4,484	1,173	1,916	1,262	654	16,350	11,206	5,144
Fire control and safety	939	842	97	375	342	33	2,372	2,232	140
Protective services, other	87	77	10	107	63	44	694	518	176
Psychology	30	7	23	6	1	5	1,756	433	1,323
Public administration and services	249	72	177	500	143	357	3,720	762	2,958
R.O.T.C. and military technologies	0	0	0	0	0	0	265	245	20
Social sciences and history	40	32	8	93	25	68	4,100	1,631	2,469
Theological studies/religious vocations	126	69	57	590	288	302	642	343	299
Transportation and material moving	5,591	4,958	633	500	418	82	1,988	1,654	334
Visual and performing arts	329	121	208	3,913	1,443	2,470	13,979	5,827	8,152
Fine arts, general	7	4	3	646	259	387	1,667	643	1,024
Design and music	311	112	199	2,422	765	1,657	10,595	4,341	6,254
Visual and performing arts, other	11	5	6	845	419	426	1,717	843	874
Not classified by field of study	43	15	28	313	124	189	1,526	799	727

SOURCE: U.S. Department of Education, National Center for Education Statistics, Integrated Postsecondary Education Data System (IPEDS), "Completions" survey. (This table was prepared May 1996.)

Table 243.—Associate degrees and other subbaccalaureate awards conferred by institutions of higher education, by length of curriculum, sex of student, and field of study: 1992–93

Field of study	Less than 1-year awards			1- to less than 4-year awards			Associate degrees		
	Total	Men	Women	Total	Men	Women	Total	Men	Women
1	2	3	4	5	6	7	8	9	10
Total	70,922	34,981	35,941	146,859	60,828	86,031	514,756	211,964	302,792
Agriculture and natural resources, total	1,778	1,369	409	4,741	2,214	2,527	5,398	3,750	1,648
Agricultural business and production	1,523	1,152	371	1,348	964	384	3,222	2,204	1,018
Agricultural sciences	194	160	34	2,138	348	1,790	837	465	372
Conservation and renewable natural resources	61	57	4	1,255	902	353	1,339	1,081	258
Architecture and related programs	2	0	2	56	8	48	372	119	253
Area, ethnic, and cultural studies	105	29	76	414	138	276	33	10	23
Biological/life sciences	116	85	31	20	9	11	1,435	588	847
Business management and administrative services	13,373	3,620	9,753	29,291	5,058	24,233	99,164	30,154	69,010
Accounting	1,246	275	971	4,081	687	3,394	15,115	3,528	11,587
Business, general	445	209	236	1,432	422	1,010	11,190	4,144	7,046
Business administration and management	1,590	622	968	2,017	738	1,279	29,556	11,624	17,932
Business and management, other	1,589	799	790	3,136	1,200	1,936	12,285	5,640	6,645
Business data processing	973	330	643	2,460	797	1,663	6,405	2,712	3,693
Secretarial and related programs	4,609	358	4,251	14,111	720	13,391	17,168	707	16,461
Marketing and distribution	2,921	1,027	1,894	2,054	494	1,560	7,445	1,799	5,646
Communications	398	230	168	391	137	254	1,904	945	959
Communications technologies	118	82	36	291	160	131	1,828	1,196	632
Computer and information sciences	1,859	940	919	4,594	2,065	2,529	9,196	4,541	4,655
Construction trades	1,497	1,407	90	4,062	3,859	203	1,653	1,581	72
Consumer and personal services	855	237	618	5,591	1,315	4,276	4,692	3,120	1,572
Education	510	131	379	954	106	848	9,315	3,031	6,284
Engineering	261	237	24	93	76	17	2,478	2,169	309
Engineering-related technologies	2,070	1,768	302	8,514	7,659	855	36,321	32,631	3,690
English language and literature/letters	165	74	91	53	5	48	1,320	469	851
Foreign languages and literatures	339	121	218	27	4	23	511	153	358
Health professions and related sciences	23,278	6,640	16,638	38,933	6,041	32,892	86,237	12,971	73,266
Dental assisting	246	17	229	2,522	134	2,388	4,165	236	3,929
Emergency medical technician-ambulance and paramedic	5,819	3,919	1,900	1,868	1,336	532	442	303	139
Medical lab technician	81	14	67	191	68	123	2,172	571	1,601
Medical assisting	1,407	77	1,330	2,664	76	2,588	2,130	223	1,907
Nursing assisting	7,649	1,003	6,646	151	11	140	86	16	70
Practical nursing	587	85	502	18,153	1,835	16,318	890	86	804
Nursing, R.N. and other	2,175	295	1,880	3,050	330	2,720	54,085	5,796	48,289
Health sciences, other	5,314	1,230	4,084	10,334	2,251	8,083	22,267	5,740	16,527
Home economics and vocational home economics	3,214	1,118	2,096	7,512	1,019	6,493	6,914	655	6,259
Law and legal studies	866	142	724	2,447	473	1,974	8,028	959	7,069
Liberal/general studies and humanities	132	40	92	808	324	484	158,040	63,867	94,173
Library science	97	6	91	53	4	49	85	9	76
Mathematics	0	0	0	15	9	6	743	428	315
Mechanics and repairers	3,613	3,488	125	18,417	17,243	1,174	10,966	10,280	686
Multi/interdisciplinary studies	246	119	127	133	57	76	8,486	4,075	4,411
Parks, recreation, leisure, and fitness studies	29	8	21	126	59	67	717	429	288
Philosophy and religion	6	3	3	668	274	394	111	76	35
Physical sciences	30	15	15	81	56	25	2,241	1,296	945
Physical sciences, other	13	4	9	3	0	3	1,390	792	598
Science technologies	17	11	6	78	56	22	851	504	347
Precision production trades	2,552	2,155	397	7,408	6,333	1,075	9,204	7,393	1,811
Protective services	6,664	5,498	1,166	4,330	3,512	818	16,834	12,289	4,545
Criminal justice and corrections	5,633	4,537	1,096	2,382	1,724	658	14,295	10,030	4,265
Fire control and safety	1,031	961	70	380	351	29	2,020	1,883	137
Protective services, other	0	0	0	1,568	1,437	131	519	376	143
Psychology	33	10	23	47	9	38	1,237	282	955
Public administration and services	235	66	169	589	214	375	3,301	648	2,653
R.O.T.C. and military technologies	0	0	0	0	0	0	52	44	8
Social sciences and history	22	8	14	117	45	72	3,930	1,678	2,252
Theological studies/religious vocations	88	27	61	582	245	337	508	281	227
Transportation and material moving	5,525	4,927	598	437	367	70	2,210	1,850	360
Visual and performing arts	279	104	175	3,913	1,232	2,681	12,690	5,084	7,606
Fine arts, general	17	3	14	725	241	484	1,346	460	886
Design and music	255	98	157	2,402	639	1,763	9,699	3,833	5,866
Visual and performing arts, other	7	3	4	786	352	434	1,645	791	854
Not classified by field of study	567	277	290	1,151	499	652	6,602	2,913	3,689

SOURCE: U.S. Department of Education, National Center for Education Statistics, Integrated Postsecondary Education Data System (IPEDS), "Completions" survey. (This table was prepared February 1995.)

Table 244.—Bachelor's, master's, and doctor's degrees conferred by institutions of higher education, by sex of student and field of study: 1993–94

Field of study	Bachelor's degrees requiring 4 or 5 years			Master's degrees			Doctor's degrees (Ph.D., Ed.D., etc.)		
	Total	Men	Women	Total	Men	Women	Total	Men	Women
1	2	3	4	5	6	7	8	9	10
All fields	1,169,275	532,422	636,853	387,070	176,085	210,985	43,185	26,552	16,633
Agriculture and natural resources, total	18,070	11,748	6,322	4,119	2,515	1,604	1,278	982	296
Agricultural business and production, total	4,959	3,611	1,348	703	487	216	206	170	36
Agricultural business and management, total	3,370	2,505	865	543	376	167	166	143	23
Agricultural business and management, general	816	556	260	54	35	19	0	0	0
Agricultural business/agribusiness operations	1,005	779	226	21	11	10	0	0	0
Agricultural economics	1,368	1,018	350	454	321	133	166	143	23
Agricultural business and management, other	181	152	29	14	9	5	0	0	0
Agricultural mechanization	244	229	15	9	7	2	1	1	0
Agricultural production workers and managers	140	106	34	59	51	8	12	8	4
Horticulture service operations and management	466	335	131	23	10	13	16	12	4
International agriculture	18	11	7	19	7	12	0	0	0
Agricultural business and production, other	721	425	296	50	36	14	13	6	5
Agricultural sciences, total	6,432	3,750	2,682	1,595	951	644	789	594	195
Agriculture/agricultural sciences, general	936	696	240	151	108	43	2	0	2
Animal sciences, total	3,165	1,511	1,654	441	268	173	226	168	58
Animal sciences, general	2,641	1,251	1,390	339	203	136	159	118	41
Agricultural animal breeding and genetics	32	12	20	10	7	3	15	14	1
Agricultural animal health	14	4	10	4	2	2	0	0	0
Agricultural animal nutrition	0	0	0	9	6	3	10	8	2
Dairy science	109	71	38	22	13	9	3	2	1
Poultry science	121	92	29	20	15	5	17	14	3
Animal sciences, other	248	81	167	37	22	15	22	12	10
Food sciences and technology	448	187	261	329	122	207	148	81	67
Plant sciences, total	1,557	1,158	399	519	355	164	344	289	55
Plant sciences, general	242	180	62	61	42	19	34	29	5
Agronomy and crop science	526	458	68	234	167	67	195	171	24
Horticulture science	552	347	205	129	77	52	62	49	13
Plant breeding and genetics	0	0	0	10	7	3	8	7	1
Agricultural plant pathology	0	0	0	2	0	2	8	6	2
Plant protection (pest management)	16	13	3	16	12	4	1	1	0
Range science and management	162	116	46	49	38	11	20	12	8
Plant sciences, other	59	44	15	18	12	6	16	14	2
Soil sciences	129	95	34	71	47	24	57	48	9
Agriculture/agricultural sciences, other	197	103	94	84	51	33	12	8	4
Conservation and renewable natural resources, total	6,679	4,387	2,292	1,821	1,077	744	283	218	65
Natural resources conservation, general	3,333	1,955	1,378	925	514	411	80	57	23
Natural resources management and policy	375	256	119	89	54	35	1	1	0
Fishing and fisheries sciences and management	215	171	44	90	53	37	27	22	5
Forest harvesting and production technology/technician	218	163	55	25	21	4	15	14	1
Forestry, general	1,187	955	232	522	326	196	123	97	26
Wildlife and wildlands management	957	654	303	123	86	37	18	14	4
Conservation and renewable natural resources, other	394	233	161	47	23	24	19	13	6
Architecture and related programs, total	8,975	5,764	3,211	3,943	2,428	1,515	161	111	50
Architecture	5,141	3,617	1,524	2,031	1,376	655	53	42	11
City/urban, community, and regional planning	567	402	165	1,240	710	530	86	55	31
Architectural environmental design	717	458	259	49	17	32	2	2	0
Interior architecture	902	129	773	11	2	9	0	0	0
Landscape architecture	1,045	748	297	378	181	197	2	2	0
Architectural urban design and planning	29	18	11	62	43	19	3	1	2
Architecture and related programs, other	574	392	182	172	99	73	15	9	6
Area, ethnic, and cultural studies, total	5,573	1,958	3,615	1,633	768	865	155	75	80
Area studies, total	3,931	1,513	2,418	1,207	565	642	123	60	63
African studies	24	5	19	14	4	10	2	1	1
American studies/civilization	1,587	569	1,018	244	95	149	76	35	41
Latin American studies	406	153	253	252	116	136	7	1	6
Middle Eastern studies	96	40	56	94	51	43	18	10	8
Russian and Slavic studies	264	107	157	119	58	61	0	0	0
Asian studies	842	388	454	292	149	143	11	9	2
European studies	266	86	180	80	35	45	3	0	3
Area studies, other	446	165	281	112	57	55	6	4	2
Ethnic and cultural studies, total	1,435	369	1,066	264	96	168	26	13	13
Afro-American (black) studies	492	175	317	79	36	43	6	3	3
Hispanic-American studies	128	42	86	12	3	9	0	0	0
Women's studies	479	11	468	52	0	52	5	0	5
Ethnic studies, other	336	141	195	121	57	64	15	10	5
Area, ethnic and cultural studies, other	207	76	131	162	107	55	6	2	4
Biological sciences/life sciences, total	51,383	25,050	26,333	5,196	2,465	2,731	4,534	2,690	1,844
Biology, general	38,103	18,252	19,851	2,178	1,033	1,145	665	392	273

Table 244.—Bachelor's, master's, and doctor's degrees conferred by institutions of higher education, by sex of student and field of study: 1993–94—Continued

Field of study	Bachelor's degrees requiring 4 or 5 years			Master's degrees			Doctor's degrees (Ph.D., Ed.D., etc.)		
	Total	Men	Women	Total	Men	Women	Total	Men	Women
1	2	3	4	5	6	7	8	9	10
Biochemistry and biophysics	2,570	1,420	1,150	276	147	129	659	392	267
Botany, total	303	138	165	220	122	98	264	173	91
Botany, general	283	128	155	129	69	60	136	85	51
Plant pathology	6	3	3	73	46	27	80	56	24
Botany, other	14	7	7	18	7	11	48	32	16
Cell and molecular biology, total	1,574	839	735	170	72	98	444	250	194
Cell biology	170	77	93	60	23	37	127	68	59
Molecular biology	544	296	248	64	30	34	205	113	92
Cell and molecular biology, other	860	466	394	46	19	27	112	69	43
Microbiology/bacteriology	1,841	916	925	332	139	193	478	273	205
Miscellaneous biological specializations, total	2,444	1,143	1,301	1,149	473	676	1,036	586	450
Anatomy	20	13	7	72	34	38	111	59	52
Ecology	659	354	305	185	102	83	90	57	33
Marine/aquatic biology	613	289	324	89	50	39	41	30	11
Neurosciences	139	69	70	72	37	35	167	101	66
Nutritional sciences	346	75	271	266	32	234	111	40	71
Toxicology	63	35	28	64	33	31	67	32	35
Genetics, plant and animal	203	99	104	136	54	82	241	153	88
Biometrics	18	10	8	25	14	11	19	13	6
Miscellaneous specialized areas, other	383	199	184	240	117	123	189	101	88
Zoology, total	3,207	1,688	1,519	749	420	329	805	515	290
Zoology, general	2,592	1,354	1,238	278	158	120	156	109	47
Entomology	83	59	24	135	82	53	123	95	28
Pathology, human and animal	15	2	13	36	15	21	93	55	38
Pharmacology, human and animal	44	24	20	59	30	29	211	116	95
Physiology, human and animal	465	244	221	241	135	106	222	140	82
Zoology, other	8	5	3	0	0	0	0	0	0
Biological sciences/life sciences, other	1,341	654	687	122	59	63	183	109	74
Business management, administrative services and marketing operations/marketing and distribution, total	246,654	129,161	117,493	93,437	59,335	34,102	1,364	980	384
Business management and administrative services, total	240,864	126,891	113,973	92,759	58,950	33,809	1,356	979	377
Business, general	25,572	13,746	11,826	13,191	8,594	4,597	232	174	58
Business administration and management, total	87,395	46,166	41,229	51,833	33,574	18,259	714	535	179
Office supervision and management	1,040	122	918	0	0	0	0	0	0
Operations management and supervision	1,993	1,428	565	506	370	136	16	11	5
Business administration and management, other	84,362	44,616	39,746	51,327	33,204	18,123	698	524	174
Accounting	47,804	21,446	26,358	4,162	2,258	1,904	63	34	29
Secretarial and related programs	594	152	442	1	0	1	0	0	0
Business/managerial economics	3,454	2,274	1,180	251	159	92	47	34	13
Small business management and ownership	399	258	141	57	40	17	0	0	0
Finance, general and banking and financial support services	21,465	14,593	6,872	4,903	3,470	1,433	64	53	11
Actuarial sciences	371	227	144	82	53	29	0	0	0
Insurance and risk management	600	382	218	66	41	25	7	4	3
Investments and securities and financial planning	353	212	141	260	198	62	0	0	0
Hospitality services management	5,910	2,662	3,248	421	211	210	2	1	1
Human resources management	4,960	1,953	3,007	2,195	980	1,215	29	17	12
Labor/personnel relations and studies	1,061	544	517	810	333	477	23	14	9
Organizational behavior studies	989	464	525	302	116	186	29	12	17
International business	2,875	1,325	1,550	3,000	1,878	1,122	21	18	3
Business information systems, total	5,839	3,474	2,365	2,140	1,429	711	13	7	6
Management information systems and data processing, general	5,434	3,221	2,213	1,877	1,239	638	13	7	6
Business information systems, other	405	253	152	263	190	73	0	0	0
Quantitative methods and management science, total	1,846	1,031	815	990	634	356	36	31	5
Business statistics	51	23	28	30	15	15	5	4	1
Management science, other	1,795	1,008	787	960	619	341	31	27	4
Marketing management and research	24,692	13,312	11,380	1,891	1,026	865	38	17	21
Real estate	558	416	142	317	261	56	1	1	0
Taxation	0	0	0	1,396	873	523	0	0	0
Consumer and personal services	155	98	57	0	0	0	0	0	0
Business management and administrative services, other	3,972	2,156	1,816	4,491	2,822	1,669	37	27	10
Marketing operations/marketing and distribution, total	5,790	2,270	3,520	678	385	293	8	1	7
Apparel and accessories marketing operations	1,383	59	1,324	0	1	2	6	0	6
Business and personal services marketing operations	456	247	209	9	2	7	0	0	0
General/retailing and wholesaling operations and skills	3,132	1,506	1,626	440	226	214	2	1	1
Transportation and travel marketing	173	44	129	12	3	9	0	0	0
Marketing and distribution, other	646	414	232	214	153	61	0	0	0
Communications and communications technologies, total	51,827	21,359	30,468	5,419	2,098	3,321	345	174	171
Communications, total	51,164	21,023	30,141	5,005	1,870	3,135	337	172	165
Communications, general	24,496	9,783	14,713	1,822	636	1,186	215	108	107
Advertising	2,773	1,095	1,678	256	90	166	4	2	2
Journalism	10,214	3,718	6,496	1,432	517	915	28	19	9
Broadcast journalism	630	258	372	16	7	9	0	0	0

Table 244.—Bachelor's, master's, and doctor's degrees conferred by institutions of higher education, by sex of student and field of study: 1993–94—Continued

Field of study	Bachelor's degrees requiring 4 or 5 years			Master's degrees			Doctor's degrees (Ph.D., Ed.D., etc.)		
	Total	Men	Women	Total	Men	Women	Total	Men	Women
1	2	3	4	5	6	7	8	9	10
Public relations and organizational communications	2,393	779	1,614	240	58	182	0	0	0
Radio and television broadcasting	5,883	3,246	2,637	383	183	200	10	6	4
Communications, other	4,775	2,144	2,631	856	379	477	80	37	43
Communications technologies, total	663	336	327	414	228	186	8	2	6
Photographic technology	11	5	6	0	0	0	0	0	0
Radio and television technology	575	292	283	317	165	152	8	2	6
Communications technologies, other	77	39	38	97	63	34	0	0	0
Computer and information sciences, total	24,200	17,317	6,883	10,416	7,724	2,692	810	685	125
Computer and information sciences, general	15,411	11,302	4,109	7,533	5,687	1,846	652	555	97
Computer programming	175	122	53	23	19	4	0	0	0
Data processing technology/technician	222	139	83	0	0	0	1	1	0
Information science and systems	3,947	2,500	1,447	1,305	832	473	23	13	10
Computer systems analysis	301	206	95	51	43	8	12	10	2
Computer and information sciences, other	4,144	3,048	1,096	1,504	1,143	361	122	106	16
Education, total	107,600	24,450	83,150	98,938	23,008	75,930	6,908	2,706	4,202
Education, general	1,617	266	1,351	10,553	2,537	8,016	1,232	440	792
Bilingual/bicultural education	54	6	48	264	46	218	13	2	11
Curriculum and instruction	7	2	5	8,246	1,552	6,694	775	253	522
Education administration and supervision, total	9	3	6	10,892	4,290	6,602	2,187	988	1,199
Education administration and supervision, general	2	0	2	7,339	2,947	4,392	1,562	733	829
Administration of special education	0	0	0	5	1	4	8	0	8
Adult and continuing education administration	3	1	2	133	32	101	72	29	43
Educational supervision	0	0	0	683	200	483	30	6	24
Elementary, middle, and secondary education administration	3	1	2	1,498	626	872	44	23	21
Higher education administration	1	1	0	544	196	348	340	141	199
Community and junior college education administration	0	0	0	86	38	48	6	4	2
Education administration and supervision, other	0	0	0	604	250	354	125	52	73
Educational/instructional media design	35	20	15	957	261	696	60	26	34
Educational evaluation and research, general	30	8	22	38	11	27	14	4	10
Educational statistics and research methods	2	0	2	54	37	17	28	14	14
Educational assessment, testing and measurement	0	0	0	98	21	77	28	12	16
Social and philosophical foundations of education	3	3	0	262	54	208	131	55	76
Special education, total	9,099	729	8,370	10,497	1,423	9,074	194	34	160
Special education, general	6,085	528	5,557	8,284	1,158	7,126	184	31	153
Education of the deaf and hearing impaired	222	8	214	238	25	213	0	0	0
Education of the gifted and talented	4	0	4	135	14	121	0	0	0
Education of the emotionally handicapped	329	43	286	239	47	192	0	0	0
Education of the mentally handicapped	691	37	654	154	24	130	0	0	0
Education of the multiple handicapped	125	7	118	187	20	167	1	0	1
Education of the physically handicapped	21	2	19	62	5	57	0	0	0
Education of the blind and visually handicapped	32	0	32	40	5	35	0	0	0
Education of the specific learning disabled	649	58	591	602	66	536	3	1	2
Education of the speech impaired	673	19	654	224	4	220	0	0	0
Special education, other	268	27	241	332	55	277	6	2	4
Counselor education/counseling and guidance services	36	7	29	12,217	2,664	9,553	364	129	235
General teacher education, total	61,017	6,699	54,318	22,877	3,808	19,069	402	129	273
Adult and continuing education	89	20	69	880	224	656	134	55	79
Elementary education	48,733	4,642	44,091	12,958	1,444	11,514	91	19	72
Junior high/intermediate/middle school education	1,378	298	1,080	653	98	555	0	0	0
Pre-elementary/early childhood/kindergarten education	6,474	164	6,310	1,996	41	1,955	31	1	30
Secondary education	3,746	1,537	2,209	3,986	1,467	2,519	56	21	35
Teacher education, general programs, other	597	38	559	2,404	534	1,870	90	33	57
Teacher education, academic and vocational programs	34,428	16,229	18,199	16,106	4,935	11,171	832	397	435
Agricultural education (vocational)	470	312	158	222	131	91	50	38	12
Art education	1,535	336	1,199	650	118	532	20	5	15
Business education (vocational)	1,434	360	1,074	456	122	334	11	5	6
Driver and safety education	46	38	8	56	42	14	0	0	0
English education	2,904	609	2,295	683	144	539	15	7	8
Foreign languages education	361	64	297	279	55	224	24	8	16
Health education	1,547	413	1,134	808	151	657	116	42	74
Home economics education (vocational)	318	6	312	112	4	108	8	0	8
Technology/industrial arts education	1,502	1,252	250	493	343	150	30	20	10
Marketing operations/marketing and distribution education	92	32	60	16	6	10	1	0	1
Mathematics education	1,914	741	1,173	846	272	574	31	14	17
Music education	2,771	1,172	1,599	838	322	516	74	31	43
Physical education and coaching	11,888	6,998	4,890	2,994	1,544	1,450	154	92	62
Reading education	161	13	148	3,869	179	3,690	78	12	66
Science education	1,102	469	633	720	289	431	48	27	21
Social science education	850	426	424	132	65	67	1	1	0
Social studies education	2,088	1,229	859	501	282	219	3	1	2
Technical education (vocational)	209	134	75	267	106	161	42	24	18
Trade and industrial education (vocational)	1,014	714	300	391	172	219	74	44	30
Teacher education, academic and vocational programs, other	2,222	911	1,311	1,773	588	1,185	52	26	26

Table 244.—Bachelor's, master's, and doctor's degrees conferred by institutions of higher education, by sex of student and field of study: 1993–94—Continued

Field of study	Bachelor's degrees requiring 4 or 5 years			Master's degrees			Doctor's degrees (Ph.D., Ed.D., etc.)		
	Total	Men	Women	Total	Men	Women	Total	Men	Women
1	2	3	4	5	6	7	8	9	10
Teaching English as a second language/foreign language	45	15	30	1,548	334	1,214	6	1	5
Education, other	1,218	463	755	4,329	1,035	3,294	642	222	420
Engineering and engineering-related technologies, total	78,225	66,597	11,628	29,754	25,154	4,600	5,979	5,315	664
Engineering, total	62,220	52,035	10,185	28,621	24,218	4,403	5,963	5,299	664
Engineering, general	2,015	1,670	345	1,391	1,171	220	233	204	29
Aerospace, aeronautical, and astronautical engineering	2,330	2,035	295	1,038	938	100	220	209	11
Agricultural engineering	519	440	79	150	121	29	87	77	10
Architectural engineering	525	418	107	36	31	5	1	1	0
Bioengineering and biomedical engineering	719	481	238	489	349	140	168	128	40
Ceramic sciences and engineering	240	188	52	92	67	25	57	51	6
Chemical engineering	5,163	3,588	1,575	1,032	785	247	604	510	94
Civil engineering	9,479	7,776	1,703	3,873	3,199	674	651	582	69
Computer engineering	2,237	1,944	293	1,071	893	178	123	109	14
Electrical, electronics, and communications engineering	15,823	13,892	1,931	7,791	6,820	971	1,470	1,331	139
Engineering mechanics	128	111	17	172	155	17	92	87	5
Engineering physics	293	260	33	70	63	7	38	34	4
Engineering science	268	218	50	295	257	38	50	45	5
Environmental/environmental health engineering	434	296	138	985	716	269	46	34	12
Geological engineering	143	100	43	57	45	12	12	11	1
Geophysical engineering	11	7	4	9	7	2	4	4	0
Industrial/manufacturing engineering	3,122	2,207	915	2,096	1,701	395	253	215	38
Material engineering	532	416	116	569	452	117	347	289	58
Mechanical engineering	15,030	13,327	1,703	4,099	3,700	399	887	825	62
Metallurgical engineering	250	209	41	172	139	33	83	73	10
Mining and mineral engineering	118	107	11	57	49	8	21	20	1
Naval architecture and marine engineering	307	287	20	23	22	1	5	5	0
Nuclear engineering	256	228	28	255	220	35	94	84	10
Ocean engineering	127	97	30	125	108	17	31	29	2
Petroleum engineering	316	275	41	167	155	12	45	38	7
Systems engineering	420	336	84	404	328	76	39	33	6
Textile sciences and engineering	72	45	27	32	24	8	1	1	0
Engineering, other	1,343	1,077	266	2,071	1,703	368	301	270	31
Engineering-related technologies, total	16,005	14,562	1,443	1,133	936	197	16	16	0
Architectural engineering technologies	670	603	67	0	0	0	0	0	0
Civil technologies	482	443	39	0	0	0	0	0	0
Electrical and electronic technologies	4,142	3,869	273	77	65	12	0	0	0
Electromechanical instrumentation and maintenance technologies	202	188	14	6	6	0	8	8	0
Environmental control technologies	263	212	51	53	35	18	0	0	0
Industrial production technologies	4,134	3,651	483	304	248	56	5	5	0
Quality control and safety technologies	554	464	90	301	246	55	0	0	0
Mechanical and related technologies	1,750	1,656	94	2	2	0	0	0	0
Mining and petroleum technologies	20	20	0	0	0	0	0	0	0
Surveying	131	118	13	25	22	3	3	3	0
Mechanics and repairers	107	106	1	0	0	0	0	0	0
Construction trades	75	70	5	0	0	0	0	0	0
Engineering and related technologies, other	3,475	3,162	313	365	312	53	0	0	0
English language and literature/letters, total	53,924	18,425	35,499	7,885	2,712	5,173	1,344	568	776
English language and literature, general	40,497	13,426	27,071	5,375	1,842	3,533	946	406	540
Comparative literature	774	211	563	274	92	182	139	56	83
English composition	331	138	193	21	4	17	4	0	4
English creative writing	903	424	479	835	360	475	7	4	3
American literature (United States)	59	18	41	16	6	10	4	2	2
English literature (British and Commonwealth)	1,368	483	885	372	110	262	74	32	42
Speech and rhetorical studies	8,637	3,272	5,365	725	210	515	128	54	74
English technical and business writing	156	52	104	142	44	98	0	0	0
English language and literature/letters, other	1,199	401	798	125	44	81	42	14	28
Foreign languages and literatures, total	14,378	4,304	10,074	3,288	1,087	2,201	886	355	531
Foreign languages and literatures, total	1,463	398	1,065	970	316	654	252	108	144
Foreign languages and literatures, general	852	225	627	321	85	236	63	22	41
Linguistics	611	173	438	649	231	418	189	86	103
East and Southeast Asian languages and literatures, total	546	276	270	138	46	92	32	18	14
Chinese	112	59	53	48	16	32	18	11	7
Japanese	311	149	162	48	10	38	2	0	2
East and Southeast Asian languages, other	123	68	55	42	20	22	12	7	5
East European languages and literatures, total	702	297	405	179	56	123	38	16	22
Russian languages	611	259	352	71	22	49	3	0	3
Slavic languages (other than Russian)	83	36	47	98	30	68	33	15	18
East European languages, other	8	2	6	10	4	6	2	1	1
Germanic languages and literatures, total	1,626	628	998	338	126	212	64	30	34
German	1,580	610	970	298	114	184	61	28	33

Table 244.—Bachelor's, master's, and doctor's degrees conferred by institutions of higher education, by sex of student and field of study: 1993–94—Continued

Field of study	Bachelor's degrees requiring 4 or 5 years			Master's degrees			Doctor's degrees (Ph.D., Ed.D., etc.)		
	Total	Men	Women	Total	Men	Women	Total	Men	Women
1	2	3	4	5	6	7	8	9	10
Scandinavian languages	31	9	22	11	1	10	1	0	1
Germanic languages, other	15	9	6	29	11	18	2	2	0
South Asian languages and literatures	6	2	4	4	1	3	8	6	2
Romance languages and literatures, total	8,981	2,215	6,766	1,307	363	944	358	105	253
French	3,094	587	2,507	479	116	363	104	31	73
Italian	264	67	197	47	13	34	24	10	14
Portuguese	37	18	19	8	3	5	0	0	0
Spanish	5,505	1,516	3,989	691	206	485	160	46	114
Romance languages, other	81	27	54	82	25	57	70	18	52
Middle Eastern languages and literatures, total	72	29	43	56	35	21	15	11	4
Arabic	8	3	5	2	1	1	0	0	0
Hebrew	49	18	31	35	25	10	3	2	1
Middle East languages, other	15	8	7	19	9	10	12	9	3
Classical and ancient Near East languages and literatures, total	756	371	385	193	107	86	77	43	34
Classics	617	298	319	169	98	71	74	40	34
Greek (ancient and medieval)	34	17	17	10	7	3	1	1	0
Latin (ancient and medieval)	105	56	49	14	2	12	2	2	0
Foreign languages, other	226	88	138	103	37	66	42	18	24
Health professions and related sciences, total	74,421	13,062	61,359	28,025	5,814	22,211	1,902	789	1,113
Communication disorders sciences and services	5,405	270	5,135	4,176	211	3,965	94	21	73
Community health liaison	586	120	466	176	41	135	0	0	0
Dentistry	0	0	0	346	251	95	42	32	10
Dental services	915	27	888	42	20	22	0	0	0
Epidemiology	0	0	0	271	106	165	111	43	68
Health services administration, total	3,635	899	2,736	3,525	1,219	2,306	80	30	50
Health services administration	1,815	474	1,341	1,807	683	1,124	47	18	29
Medical records administration	699	93	606	0	0	0	0	0	0
Medical records technology/technician	1	0	1	3	2	1	2	2	0
Health and medical administrative services, other	1,120	332	788	1,715	534	1,181	31	10	21
Health and medical assistants, total	1,015	497	518	178	54	124	0	0	0
Medical assistant	1	0	1	0	0	0	0	0	0
Physician assistant	924	479	445	160	49	111	0	0	0
Health and medical assistants, other	90	18	72	18	5	13	0	0	0
Health and medical diagnostic and treatment services, total	1,459	553	906	95	68	27	2	2	0
Respiratory therapy technology/technician	417	184	233	0	0	0	0	0	0
Health and medical diagnostic and treatment services, other	1,042	369	673	95	68	27	2	2	0
Medical laboratory technologies, total	2,763	856	1,907	481	185	296	80	33	47
Medical technology	2,393	725	1,668	75	26	49	4	3	1
Health and medical laboratory technologies/technicians, other	370	131	239	406	159	247	76	30	46
Pre-dentistry studies	70	46	24	0	0	0	0	0	0
Pre-medicine studies	756	438	318	23	5	18	0	0	0
Pre-pharmacy studies	52	25	27	0	0	0	0	0	0
Pre-veterinary studies	314	101	213	3	1	2	0	0	0
Medical basic sciences	245	94	151	261	136	125	335	201	134
Mental health services, total	546	103	443	384	89	295	31	7	24
Alcohol/drug abuse counseling	69	22	47	62	18	44	1	0	1
Psychiatric/mental health services technician	127	26	101	36	11	25	0	0	0
Clinical and medical social work	119	22	97	103	31	72	30	7	23
Mental health services, other	231	33	198	183	29	154	0	0	0
Nursing	39,076	3,735	35,341	8,991	599	8,392	382	24	358
Optometry	221	95	126	18	4	14	1	1	0
Pharmacy	6,044	2,235	3,809	243	134	109	278	144	134
Rehabilitation/therapeutic services, total	7,169	1,531	5,638	4,433	1,084	3,349	34	15	19
Art therapy	74	1	73	164	9	155	0	0	0
Dance therapy	2	0	2	30	1	29	0	0	0
Music therapy	144	21	123	18	4	14	0	0	0
Occupational therapy	2,652	305	2,347	619	58	561	4	0	4
Orthotics/prosthetics	58	46	12	0	0	0	0	0	0
Physical therapy	3,265	903	2,362	2,583	734	1,849	4	1	3
Recreational therapy	137	28	109	22	2	20	1	0	1
Vocational rehabilitation counseling	155	45	110	640	175	465	8	6	2
Rehabilitative services, other	682	182	500	357	101	256	17	8	9
Veterinary medicine	87	33	54	178	95	83	117	75	42
Miscellaneous health professions	436	205	231	249	122	127	35	23	12
Health professions and related sciences, other	3,627	1,199	2,428	3,952	1,390	2,562	280	138	142
Home economics and vocational home economics, total	15,522	1,933	13,589	2,421	405	2,016	365	93	272
Home economics, total	14,874	1,616	13,258	2,379	401	1,978	361	93	268
Home economics, general	2,801	206	2,595	284	22	262	28	4	24
Home economics business services	155	14	141	1	0	1	0	0	0
Family and community studies	179	23	156	58	10	48	3	1	2
Family and consumer resource management	1,327	437	890	60	5	55	21	3	18
Food and nutrition studies	2,967	391	2,576	519	65	454	55	23	32
Housing studies	583	97	486	18	3	15	2	1	1
Individual and family development studies	5,051	362	4,689	1,295	274	1,021	225	56	169

Table 244.—Bachelor's, master's, and doctor's degrees conferred by institutions of higher education, by sex of student and field of study: 1993–94—Continued

Field of study	Bachelor's degrees requiring 4 or 5 years			Master's degrees			Doctor's degrees (Ph.D., Ed.D., etc.)		
	Total	Men	Women	Total	Men	Women	Total	Men	Women
1	2	3	4	5	6	7	8	9	10
Clothing/apparel and textile studies	1,699	81	1,618	107	19	88	24	4	20
Home economics, other	112	5	107	37	3	34	3	1	2
Vocational home economics, total	648	317	331	42	4	38	4	0	4
Child care and guidance management	148	8	140	40	4	36	3	0	3
Custodial, housekeeping and home services workers and managers	2	1	1	0	0	0	0	0	0
Vocational home economics, other	498	308	190	2	0	2	1	0	1
Law and legal studies, total	2,171	648	1,523	2,432	1,608	824	79	63	16
Pre-law studies	239	120	119	0	0	0	0	0	0
Paralegal/legal assistant	1,028	154	874	97	70	27	36	31	5
Law and legal studies, other	904	374	530	2,335	1,538	797	43	32	11
Liberal arts and sciences, general studies, and humanities, total	33,397	13,117	20,280	2,496	913	1,583	80	46	34
Liberal arts and sciences/liberal studies	20,963	7,597	13,366	1,633	589	1,044	25	12	13
Humanities/humanistic studies	2,796	949	1,847	504	203	301	44	24	20
Liberal arts and sciences, general studies, other	9,638	4,571	5,067	359	121	238	11	10	1
Library science, total	62	5	57	5,116	1,040	4,076	45	14	31
Library science/librarianship	61	5	56	4,995	1,013	3,982	45	14	31
Library science, other	1	0	1	121	27	94	0	0	0
Mathematics, total	14,396	7,735	6,661	4,100	2,536	1,564	1,157	904	253
Mathematics	12,517	6,539	5,978	2,400	1,446	954	818	648	170
Applied mathematics, total	1,012	622	390	770	556	214	147	115	32
Applied mathematics, general and other	787	481	306	352	257	95	115	91	24
Operations research (quantitative methods)	225	141	84	418	299	119	32	24	8
Mathematical statistics	534	343	191	829	480	349	178	131	47
Mathematics, other	333	231	102	101	54	47	14	10	4
Multi/interdisciplinary studies, total	25,167	9,058	16,109	2,464	1,194	1,270	227	151	76
Biological and physical sciences	2,191	1,141	1,050	231	136	95	24	15	9
Systems science and theory	112	72	40	226	150	76	11	10	1
Museology/museum studies	4	1	3	107	21	86	0	0	0
Multi/interdisciplinary studies, other	22,860	7,844	15,016	1,900	887	1,013	192	126	66
Parks, recreation, leisure, and fitness studies, total	11,470	5,823	5,647	1,625	845	780	116	70	46
Parks, recreation and leisure studies	2,197	966	1,231	244	110	134	21	11	10
Parks, recreation and leisure facilities management	2,709	1,287	1,422	234	113	121	18	9	9
Health and physical education/fitness	6,242	3,385	2,857	1,130	612	518	75	48	27
Parks, recreation, leisure and fitness studies, other	322	185	137	17	10	7	2	2	0
Philosophy and religion, total	7,546	4,844	2,702	1,350	837	513	528	383	145
Philosophy	4,691	3,218	1,473	727	508	219	301	217	84
Religion/religious studies	2,486	1,425	1,061	563	315	248	221	162	59
Philosophy and religion, other	369	201	168	60	14	46	6	4	2
Physical sciences and science technologies, total	18,400	12,223	6,177	5,679	4,018	1,661	4,650	3,642	1,008
Physical sciences, total	18,295	12,164	6,131	5,670	4,015	1,655	4,634	3,626	1,008
Physical sciences, general	353	236	117	47	35	12	0	0	0
Astronomy	88	62	26	93	68	25	74	63	11
Astrophysics	75	55	20	36	30	6	26	20	6
Atmospheric science and meteorology	405	329	76	197	150	47	91	74	17
Chemistry, total	9,425	5,591	3,834	1,999	1,173	826	2,353	1,691	662
Chemistry, general	9,138	5,409	3,729	1,850	1,089	761	2,149	1,531	618
Analytical chemistry	0	0	0	26	16	10	14	12	2
Inorganic chemistry	0	0	0	3	3	0	10	8	2
Organic chemistry	8	3	5	17	8	9	16	14	2
Medicinal/pharmaceutical chemistry	8	5	3	31	8	23	55	36	19
Chemistry, other	271	174	97	72	49	23	109	90	19
Geological and related sciences, total	2,677	1,766	911	937	645	292	422	345	77
Geology	2,482	1,639	843	798	549	249	344	283	61
Geochemistry	8	5	3	3	3	0	5	5	0
Geophysics and seismology	50	35	15	62	45	17	53	44	9
Geological and related sciences, other	137	87	50	74	48	26	20	13	7
Miscellaneous physical sciences, total	852	596	256	357	246	111	166	121	45
Metallurgy	2	0	2	7	6	1	1	1	0
Oceanography	197	142	55	148	99	49	77	58	19
Earth and planetary sciences	582	425	157	136	100	36	78	59	19
Miscellaneous physical sciences, other	71	29	42	66	41	25	10	3	7
Physics, total	4,001	3,292	709	1,945	1,650	295	1,465	1,285	180
Physics, general	3,717	3,063	654	1,791	1,518	273	1,321	1,156	165

Table 244.—Bachelor's, master's, and doctor's degrees conferred by institutions of higher education, by sex of student and field of study: 1993–94—Continued

Field of study	Bachelor's degrees requiring 4 or 5 years			Master's degrees			Doctor's degrees (Ph.D., Ed.D., etc.)		
	Total	Men	Women	Total	Men	Women	Total	Men	Women
1	2	3	4	5	6	7	8	9	10
Physics, other	284	229	55	154	132	22	144	129	15
Physical sciences, other	419	237	182	59	18	41	37	27	10
Science technologies, total	105	59	46	9	3	6	16	16	0
Precision production trades, total	420	308	112	2	0	2	0	0	0
Drafting, general	145	125	20	0	0	0	0	0	0
Precision production trades, other	275	183	92	2	0	2	0	0	0
Protective services, total	23,009	14,169	8,840	1,437	902	535	25	14	11
Criminal justice and corrections, total	22,745	13,920	8,825	1,405	871	534	25	14	11
Corrections/correctional administration	705	388	317	50	36	14	0	0	0
Criminal justice/law enforcement administration	7,267	4,490	2,777	539	340	199	0	0	0
Criminal justice studies	11,702	6,959	4,743	678	426	252	25	14	11
Forensic studies	158	96	62	56	30	26	0	0	0
Law enforcement/police science	1,799	1,317	482	53	28	25	0	0	0
Criminal justice, other	1,114	670	444	29	11	18	0	0	0
Fire control and safety	229	221	8	22	21	1	0	0	0
Protective services, other	35	28	7	10	10	0	0	0	0
Psychology, total	69,259	18,642	50,617	12,181	3,401	8,780	3,563	1,346	2,217
Psychology, general	65,559	17,662	47,897	4,644	1,432	3,212	1,618	652	966
Clinical psychology	48	10	38	1,368	366	1,002	1,206	413	793
Counseling psychology	261	58	203	3,560	871	2,689	296	111	185
Developmental and child psychology	755	77	678	116	25	91	56	12	44
Experimental psychology	227	61	166	97	41	56	65	30	35
Industrial and organizational psychology	134	33	101	352	116	236	45	18	27
Physiological psychology/psychobiology	189	70	119	2	0	2	22	6	16
Social psychology	240	54	186	99	31	68	35	15	20
School psychology	0	0	0	702	130	572	87	37	50
Psychology, other	1,846	617	1,229	1,241	389	852	133	52	81
Public administration and services, total	17,815	3,919	13,896	21,833	6,406	15,427	519	238	281
Public administration	2,600	1,335	1,265	6,698	3,421	3,277	148	98	50
Community organization, resources and services	1,339	314	1,025	265	91	174	5	0	5
Public policy analysis	424	211	213	777	402	375	80	51	29
Social work	13,016	1,853	11,163	13,738	2,353	11,385	259	79	180
Public affairs, other	436	206	230	355	139	216	27	10	17
R.O.T.C. and military technologies, total	19	16	3	124	117	7	0	0	0
Social sciences and history, total	133,680	72,006	61,674	14,561	8,152	6,409	3,627	2,317	1,310
Social sciences, general	7,375	3,122	4,253	527	226	301	69	37	32
Anthropology	5,502	2,009	3,493	962	371	591	383	179	204
Archeology	120	43	77	27	8	19	21	8	13
Criminology	2,181	1,272	909	102	61	41	12	8	4
Demography and population studies	2	1	1	34	15	19	12	9	3
Economics	19,496	13,747	5,749	2,521	1,697	824	869	660	209
Geography, total	4,449	3,011	1,438	723	481	242	141	105	36
Geography	4,401	2,971	1,430	720	479	241	141	105	36
Cartography	48	40	8	3	2	1	0	0	0
History	27,503	17,260	10,243	3,009	1,824	1,185	752	472	280
International relations and affairs	5,860	2,547	3,313	1,995	1,089	906	85	67	18
Political science and government, general	36,097	20,741	15,356	2,147	1,348	799	616	438	178
Sociology	22,368	7,114	15,254	1,639	636	1,003	530	261	269
Urban affairs/studies	709	366	343	377	183	194	58	30	28
Social sciences and history, other	2,018	773	1,245	498	213	285	79	43	36
Theological studies/religious vocations, total	5,434	4,125	1,309	4,956	3,034	1,922	1,448	1,235	213
Biblical and other theological languages and literatures	57	53	4	50	20	30	8	7	1
Bible/biblical studies	1,390	1,086	304	285	239	46	34	31	3
Missions/missionary studies and misology	323	190	133	189	126	63	37	37	0
Religious education	923	546	377	964	550	414	52	36	16
Religious/sacred music	156	88	68	138	88	50	9	7	2
Theology/theological studies	2,121	1,826	295	2,396	1,521	875	921	797	124
Pastoral counseling and specialized ministries	163	124	39	560	236	324	205	172	33
Theological studies and religious vocations, other	301	212	89	374	254	120	182	148	34
Transportation and material moving, total	3,923	3,500	423	664	610	54	0	0	0
Water transportation workers	305	278	27	0	0	0	0	0	0
Transportation and material moving, other	3,618	3,222	396	664	610	54	0	0	0
Visual and performing arts, total	49,053	19,538	29,515	9,925	4,229	5,696	1,054	585	469

Table 244.—Bachelor's, master's, and doctor's degrees conferred by institutions of higher education, by sex of student and field of study: 1993–94—Continued

Field of study	Bachelor's degrees requiring 4 or 5 years			Master's degrees			Doctor's degrees (Ph.D., Ed.D., etc.)		
	Total	Men	Women	Total	Men	Women	Total	Men	Women
1	2	3	4	5	6	7	8	9	10
Visual and performing arts, general	1,571	676	895	114	45	69	9	5	4
Crafts, folk art, and artisanry	108	32	76	8	5	3	0	0	0
Dance	813	75	738	184	24	160	14	2	12
Design and applied art	8,077	3,148	4,929	462	188	274	1	0	1
Dramatic/theater arts and stagecraft	6,117	2,452	3,665	1,283	607	676	104	55	49
Film/video and photographic arts, total	2,652	1,641	1,011	583	331	252	12	8	4
Film-video making/cinematography and production	918	634	284	244	133	111	4	2	2
Photography	961	495	466	151	86	65	1	1	0
Film arts, other	773	512	261	188	112	76	7	5	2
Fine arts and art studies, total	20,865	7,136	13,729	3,363	1,240	2,123	177	67	110
Art, general	11,422	4,152	7,270	1,020	429	591	27	11	16
Art history, criticism and conservation	3,006	609	2,397	645	138	507	141	55	86
Arts management	117	23	94	119	26	93	0	0	0
Painting	811	335	476	202	93	109	0	0	0
Ceramic arts and ceramics	181	69	112	48	25	23	0	0	0
Fiber, textile and weaving arts	109	8	101	34	3	31	1	0	1
Metal and jewelry arts	84	14	70	25	9	16	0	0	0
Fine arts and art studies, other	5,135	1,926	3,209	1,270	517	753	8	1	7
Music, total	8,268	4,151	4,117	3,619	1,697	1,922	708	438	270
Music, general	4,149	2,003	2,146	1,209	585	624	308	191	117
Music history and literature	70	32	38	41	16	25	26	14	12
Music, general performance	2,728	1,282	1,446	1,849	850	999	232	135	97
Music theory and composition	244	190	54	161	105	56	71	52	19
Music, other	1,077	644	433	359	141	218	71	46	25
Visual and performing arts, other	582	227	355	309	92	217	29	10	19
Not classified by field of study	3,302	1,618	1,684	1,651	730	921	36	21	15

NOTE.—Aggregations by field of study derived from the Classification of Instructional Programs developed by the National Center for Education Statistics.

SOURCE: U.S. Department of Education, National Center for Education Statistics, Integrated Postsecondary Education Data System (IPEDS), "Completions" survey. (This table was prepared February 1996.)

Table 245.—Bachelor's, master's, and doctor's degrees conferred by institutions of higher education, by sex of student and field of study: 1992–93

Field of study	Bachelor's degrees requiring 4 or 5 years			Master's degrees			Doctor's degrees (Ph.D., Ed.D., etc.)		
	Total	Men	Women	Total	Men	Women	Total	Men	Women
1	2	3	4	5	6	7	8	9	10
All fields	**1,165,178**	**532,881**	**632,297**	**369,585**	**169,258**	**200,327**	**42,132**	**26,073**	**16,059**
Agriculture and natural resources, total	16,778	11,080	5,698	3,965	2,477	1,488	1,173	879	294
Agricultural business and production, total	4,995	3,661	1,334	679	460	219	195	149	46
Agricultural business and management, total	3,368	2,532	836	512	355	157	146	112	34
Agricultural business and management, general	789	562	227	48	32	16	0	0	0
Agricultural business/agribusiness operations	865	688	177	31	26	5	2	2	0
Agricultural economics	1,566	1,159	407	425	291	134	144	110	34
Agricultural business and management, other	148	123	25	8	6	2	0	0	0
Agricultural mechanization	242	220	22	5	5	0	1	1	0
Agricultural production workers and managers	114	89	25	65	47	18	9	8	1
Horticulture service operations and management	479	329	150	35	21	14	19	15	4
International agriculture	19	12	7	18	9	9	0	0	0
Agricultural business and production, other	773	479	294	44	23	21	13	13	7
Agricultural sciences, total	5,918	3,457	2,461	1,583	985	598	708	522	186
Agriculture/agricultural sciences, general	953	670	283	174	129	45	5	5	0
Animal sciences, total	2,811	1,369	1,442	422	286	136	193	144	49
Animal sciences, general	2,359	1,112	1,247	331	219	112	139	106	33
Agricultural animal breeding and genetics	22	7	15	13	10	3	5	3	2
Agricultural animal health	7	3	4	8	5	3	0	0	0
Agricultural animal nutrition	0	0	0	2	2	0	12	11	1
Dairy science	99	65	34	19	16	3	6	5	1
Poultry science	107	89	18	24	18	6	12	7	5
Animal sciences, other	217	93	124	25	16	9	19	12	7
Food sciences and technology	449	197	252	317	134	183	138	75	63
Plant sciences, total	1,447	1,066	381	513	345	168	299	237	62
Plant sciences, general	216	161	55	75	48	27	48	38	10
Agronomy and crop science	539	458	81	228	175	53	154	127	27
Horticulture science	508	322	186	125	68	57	53	37	16
Plant breeding and genetics	0	0	0	16	12	4	7	6	1
Agricultural plant pathology	0	0	0	4	2	2	8	6	2
Plant protection (pest management)	18	12	6	22	11	11	1	0	1
Range science and management	112	78	34	30	18	12	22	17	5
Plant sciences, other	54	35	19	13	11	2	6	6	0
Soil sciences	92	69	23	86	54	32	60	53	7
Agriculture/agricultural sciences, other	166	86	80	71	37	34	13	8	5
Conservation and renewable natural resources, total	5,865	3,962	1,903	1,703	1,032	671	270	208	62
Natural resources conservation, general	2,789	1,700	1,089	768	431	337	79	51	28
Natural resources management and policy	341	236	105	96	58	38	1	1	0
Fishing and fisheries sciences and management	207	169	38	98	66	32	24	22	2
Forest harvesting and production technology/technician	195	149	46	27	22	5	12	10	2
Forestry, general	1,082	887	195	493	314	179	124	104	20
Wildlife and wildlands management	912	606	306	166	112	54	17	11	6
Conservation and renewable natural resources, other	339	215	124	55	29	26	13	9	4
Architecture and related programs, total	9,167	5,940	3,227	3,808	2,376	1,432	148	105	43
Architecture	5,267	3,765	1,502	1,950	1,326	624	48	37	11
City/urban, community, and regional planning	487	349	138	1,272	739	533	79	52	27
Architectural environmental design	722	479	243	36	14	22	6	5	1
Interior architecture	995	144	851	21	4	17	0	0	0
Landscape architecture	1,033	716	317	327	163	164	2	1	1
Architectural urban design and planning	30	18	12	69	47	22	1	1	0
Architecture and related programs, other	633	469	164	133	83	50	12	9	3
Area, ethnic, and cultural studies, total	5,481	1,977	3,504	1,523	732	791	178	90	88
Area studies, total	3,978	1,564	2,414	1,164	568	596	154	77	77
African studies	41	16	25	15	9	6	3	2	1
American studies/civilization	1,558	580	978	251	100	151	87	36	51
Latin American studies	389	122	267	219	114	105	8	6	2
Middle Eastern studies	89	40	49	95	45	50	18	10	8
Russian and Slavic studies	292	124	168	126	60	66	2	2	0
Asian studies	934	444	490	311	155	156	24	14	10
European studies	246	88	158	64	34	30	8	4	4
Area studies, other	429	150	279	83	51	32	4	3	1
Ethnic and cultural studies, total	1,263	332	931	214	58	156	18	10	8
Afro-American (black) studies	433	159	274	68	21	47	8	4	4
Hispanic-American studies	133	38	95	28	3	25	0	0	0
Women's studies	411	11	400	33	0	33	0	0	0
Ethnic studies, other	286	124	162	85	34	51	10	6	4
Area, ethnic and cultural studies, other	240	81	159	145	106	39	6	3	3
Biological sciences/life sciences, total	47,038	22,842	24,196	4,756	2,343	2,413	4,435	2,664	1,771
Biology, general	34,932	16,500	18,432	2,000	1,001	999	671	398	273

Table 245.—Bachelor's, master's, and doctor's degrees conferred by institutions of higher education, by sex of student and field of study: 1992–93—Continued

Field of study	Bachelor's degrees requiring 4 or 5 years			Master's degrees			Doctor's degrees (Ph.D., Ed.D., etc.)		
	Total	Men	Women	Total	Men	Women	Total	Men	Women
1	2	3	4	5	6	7	8	9	10
Biochemistry and biophysics	2,327	1,370	957	207	108	99	692	448	244
Botany, total	263	135	128	224	111	113	223	140	83
Botany, general	249	128	121	137	68	69	119	66	53
Plant pathology	11	5	6	76	36	40	78	55	23
Botany, other	3	2	1	11	7	4	26	19	7
Cell and molecular biology, total	1,222	688	534	160	72	88	405	235	170
Cell biology	157	87	70	64	28	36	138	74	64
Molecular biology	424	244	180	76	37	39	188	111	77
Cell and molecular biology, other	641	357	284	20	7	13	79	50	29
Microbiology/bacteriology	1,769	872	897	328	153	175	520	290	230
Miscellaneous biological specializations, total	2,098	1,045	1,053	1,086	472	614	945	551	394
Anatomy	102	62	40	43	21	22	107	55	52
Ecology	485	286	199	240	144	96	83	55	28
Marine/aquatic biology	513	257	256	96	56	40	30	20	10
Neurosciences	141	75	66	52	35	17	154	99	55
Nutritional sciences	254	57	197	234	27	207	100	36	64
Toxicology	45	20	25	61	30	31	53	30	23
Genetics, plant and animal	160	78	82	123	47	76	219	135	84
Biometrics	18	8	10	31	15	16	24	20	4
Miscellaneous specialized areas, other	380	202	178	206	97	109	175	101	74
Zoology, total	3,071	1,563	1,508	637	372	265	786	494	292
Zoology, general	2,552	1,268	1,284	208	118	90	134	87	47
Entomology	70	54	16	122	86	36	116	86	30
Pathology, human and animal	11	3	8	29	16	13	110	72	38
Pharmacology, human and animal	33	21	12	51	25	26	215	116	99
Physiology, human and animal	404	217	187	226	127	99	211	133	78
Zoology, other	1	0	1	1	0	1	0	0	0
Biological sciences/life sciences, other	1,356	669	687	114	54	60	193	108	85
Business management, administrative services and marketing operations/marketing and distribution, total	256,842	135,573	121,269	89,615	57,651	31,964	1,346	969	377
Business management and administrative services, total	249,871	132,674	117,197	89,064	57,327	31,737	1,339	968	371
Business, general	26,786	14,655	12,131	12,517	8,373	4,144	271	190	81
Business administration and management, total	89,390	47,741	41,649	48,695	31,831	16,864	662	488	174
Office supervision and management	854	109	745	41	23	18	0	0	0
Operations management and supervision	1,855	1,390	465	565	434	131	0	0	0
Business administration and management, other	86,681	46,242	40,439	48,089	31,374	16,715	662	488	174
Accounting	48,853	22,371	26,482	3,887	2,111	1,776	69	45	24
Secretarial and related programs	443	65	378	1	0	1	0	0	0
Business/managerial economics	3,740	2,452	1,288	209	146	63	42	33	9
Small business management and ownership	434	288	146	53	37	16	0	0	0
Finance, general and banking and financial support services	22,903	15,602	7,301	4,942	3,573	1,369	53	45	8
Actuarial sciences	393	243	150	62	38	24	0	0	0
Insurance and risk management	658	403	255	108	79	29	4	3	1
Investments and securities and financial planning	324	197	127	217	152	65	0	0	0
Hospitality services management	5,945	2,737	3,208	533	277	256	4	3	1
Human resources management	5,139	1,972	3,167	2,023	916	1,107	19	10	9
Labor/personnel relations and studies	1,180	579	601	816	325	491	16	8	8
Organizational behavior studies	902	389	513	813	460	353	19	6	13
International business	2,584	1,236	1,348	2,787	1,713	1,074	12	10	2
Business information systems, total	5,570	3,258	2,312	1,800	1,269	531	7	5	2
Management information systems and data processing, general	5,174	3,014	2,160	1,592	1,110	482	7	5	2
Business information systems, other	396	244	152	208	159	49	0	0	0
Quantitative methods and management science, total	2,090	1,206	884	921	651	270	32	24	8
Business statistics	38	22	16	29	18	11	8	5	3
Management science, other	2,052	1,184	868	892	633	259	24	19	5
Marketing management and research	27,437	14,424	13,013	2,131	1,161	970	39	29	10
Real estate	660	482	178	348	286	62	1	1	0
Taxation	2	1	1	1,559	934	625	0	0	0
Consumer and personal services	160	113	47	0	0	0	0	0	0
Business management and administrative services, other	4,278	2,260	2,018	4,642	2,995	1,647	89	68	21
Marketing operations/marketing and distribution, total	6,971	2,899	4,072	551	324	227	7	1	6
Apparel and accessories marketing operations	1,624	71	1,553	0	0	0	5	0	5
Business and personal services marketing operations	561	331	230	7	3	4	0	0	0
General/retailing and wholesaling operations and skills	3,728	1,885	1,843	393	218	175	2	1	1
Transportation and travel marketing	284	87	197	20	6	14	0	0	0
Marketing and distribution, other	774	525	249	131	97	34	0	0	0
Communications and communications technologies, total	54,706	22,028	32,678	5,209	1,980	3,229	301	146	155
Communications, total	53,874	21,601	32,273	4,754	1,725	3,029	293	143	150
Communications, general	25,308	9,876	15,432	1,565	569	996	184	81	103
Advertising	3,109	1,244	1,865	239	83	156	0	0	0
Journalism	11,443	4,128	7,315	1,528	518	1,010	26	13	13
Broadcast journalism	495	203	292	12	6	6	0	0	0

Table 245.—Bachelor's, master's, and doctor's degrees conferred by institutions of higher education, by sex of student and field of study: 1992–93—Continued

Field of study	Bachelor's degrees requiring 4 or 5 years			Master's degrees			Doctor's degrees (Ph.D., Ed.D., etc.)		
	Total	Men	Women	Total	Men	Women	Total	Men	Women
1	2	3	4	5	6	7	8	9	10
Public relations and organizational communications	2,255	695	1,560	231	49	182	0	0	0
Radio and television broadcasting	6,469	3,374	3,095	365	188	177	14	8	6
Communications, other	4,795	2,081	2,714	814	312	502	69	41	28
Communications technologies, total	832	427	405	455	255	200	8	3	5
Photographic technology	23	10	13	0	0	0	0	0	0
Radio and television technology	725	370	355	327	177	150	8	3	5
Communications technologies, other	84	47	37	128	78	50	0	0	0
Computer and information sciences, total	24,200	17,403	6,797	10,163	7,410	2,753	805	689	116
Computer and information sciences, general	15,997	11,914	4,083	7,438	5,554	1,884	686	587	99
Computer programming	145	107	38	15	13	2	0	0	0
Data processing technology/technician	225	127	98	62	44	18	0	0	0
Information science and systems	3,644	2,184	1,460	1,301	790	511	15	11	4
Computer systems analysis	231	156	75	78	60	18	8	7	1
Computer and information sciences, other	3,958	2,915	1,043	1,269	949	320	96	84	12
Education, total	107,781	23,233	84,548	96,028	22,197	73,831	7,030	2,867	4,163
Education, general	2,009	287	1,722	10,127	2,379	7,748	1,196	455	741
Bilingual/bicultural education	56	5	51	227	38	189	11	6	5
Curriculum and instruction	9	4	5	7,694	1,430	6,264	785	269	516
Education administration and supervision, total	6	1	5	10,638	4,142	6,496	2,248	1,046	1,202
Education administration and supervision, general	4	0	4	7,030	2,776	4,254	1,620	772	848
Administration of special education	0	0	0	10	2	8	11	0	11
Adult and continuing education administration	0	0	0	217	49	168	61	21	40
Educational supervision	0	0	0	724	203	521	24	5	19
Elementary, middle, and secondary education administration	0	0	0	1,644	721	923	41	23	18
Higher education administration	1	0	1	406	147	259	391	176	215
Community and junior college education administration	0	0	0	71	31	40	7	4	3
Education administration and supervision, other	1	1	0	536	213	323	93	45	48
Educational/instructional media design	27	12	15	939	279	660	62	32	30
Educational evaluation and research, general	18	7	11	31	7	24	26	10	16
Educational statistics and research methods	1	0	1	35	13	22	41	23	18
Educational assessment, testing and measurement	0	0	0	89	18	71	23	13	10
Social and philosophical foundations of education	24	7	17	250	69	181	102	46	56
Special education, total	8,657	674	7,983	9,765	1,324	8,441	249	67	182
Special education, general	5,835	460	5,375	7,545	1,059	6,486	233	62	171
Education of the deaf and hearing impaired	203	11	192	235	25	210	0	0	0
Education of the gifted and talented	1	0	1	171	20	151	0	0	0
Education of the emotionally handicapped	297	41	256	218	52	166	2	0	2
Education of the mentally handicapped	627	46	581	147	25	122	0	0	0
Education of the multiple handicapped	113	5	108	99	3	96	0	0	0
Education of the physically handicapped	28	3	25	63	11	52	0	0	0
Education of the blind and visually handicapped	27	0	27	28	5	23	0	0	0
Education of the specific learning disabled	573	48	525	659	50	609	9	3	6
Education of the speech impaired	672	21	651	295	22	273	0	0	0
Special education, other	281	39	242	305	52	253	5	2	3
Counselor education/counseling and guidance services	76	18	58	11,555	2,502	9,053	375	135	240
General teacher education, total	61,244	5,860	55,384	22,127	3,470	18,657	433	144	289
Adult and continuing education	24	10	14	927	259	668	148	58	90
Elementary education	49,485	3,881	45,604	13,234	1,250	11,984	76	17	59
Junior high/intermediate/middle school education	1,308	254	1,054	563	86	477	0	0	0
Pre-elementary/early childhood/kindergarten education	6,154	163	5,991	1,893	43	1,850	45	2	43
Secondary education	3,773	1,522	2,251	3,707	1,387	2,320	76	32	44
Teacher education, general programs, other	500	30	470	1,803	445	1,358	88	35	53
Teacher education, academic and vocational programs	34,742	16,059	18,683	16,467	5,124	11,343	821	381	440
Agricultural education (vocational)	427	312	115	234	164	70	48	37	11
Art education	1,804	310	1,494	656	94	562	27	8	19
Business education (vocational)	1,572	371	1,201	525	133	392	16	6	10
Driver and safety education	35	29	6	60	42	18	1	1	0
English education	2,895	596	2,299	739	161	578	21	5	16
Foreign languages education	399	79	320	242	39	203	9	1	8
Health education	1,540	432	1,108	841	181	660	87	24	63
Home economics education (vocational)	340	8	332	177	6	171	10	0	10
Technology/industrial arts education	1,506	1,307	199	495	361	134	22	19	3
Marketing operations/marketing and distribution education	99	43	56	17	3	14	2	1	1
Mathematics education	1,953	710	1,243	912	282	630	35	11	24
Music education	2,821	1,175	1,646	896	375	521	74	35	39
Physical education and coaching	11,553	6,578	4,975	3,044	1,594	1,450	174	96	78
Reading education	152	15	137	3,935	183	3,752	71	11	60
Science education	1,138	468	670	720	313	407	36	22	14
Social science education	855	460	395	118	60	58	6	1	5
Social studies education	2,402	1,416	986	453	260	193	5	4	1
Technical education (vocational)	223	148	75	275	113	162	42	16	26
Trade and industrial education (vocational)	1,100	777	323	458	222	236	75	51	24
Teacher education, academic and vocational programs, other	1,928	825	1,103	1,670	538	1,132	60	32	28

Table 245.—Bachelor's, master's, and doctor's degrees conferred by institutions of higher education, by sex of student and field of study: 1992–93—Continued

Field of study	Bachelor's degrees requiring 4 or 5 years			Master's degrees			Doctor's degrees (Ph.D., Ed.D., etc.)		
	Total	Men	Women	Total	Men	Women	Total	Men	Women
1	2	3	4	5	6	7	8	9	10
Teaching English as a second language/foreign language	39	14	25	1,544	365	1,179	2	2	0
Education, other	873	285	588	4,540	1,037	3,503	656	238	418
Engineering and engineering-related technologies, total	78,051	66,836	11,215	28,726	24,454	4,272	5,843	5,283	560
Engineering, total	61,973	52,185	9,788	27,626	23,537	4,089	5,823	5,265	558
Engineering, general	2,128	1,802	326	1,338	1,142	196	274	249	25
Aerospace, aeronautical, and astronautical engineering	2,735	2,419	316	1,047	941	106	203	197	6
Agricultural engineering	512	432	80	150	122	28	80	73	7
Architectural engineering	497	400	97	29	23	6	0	0	0
Bioengineering and biomedical engineering	706	480	226	469	322	147	150	121	29
Ceramic sciences and engineering	287	234	53	92	69	23	60	52	8
Chemical engineering	4,459	2,995	1,464	990	792	198	595	516	79
Civil engineering	8,868	7,291	1,577	3,610	3,003	607	577	527	50
Computer engineering	2,138	1,888	250	955	817	138	123	108	15
Electrical, electronics, and communications engineering	17,281	15,314	1,967	7,870	6,957	913	1,413	1,295	118
Engineering mechanics	134	116	18	186	170	16	98	90	8
Engineering physics	295	253	42	68	65	3	50	46	4
Engineering science	286	215	71	357	285	72	49	41	8
Environmental/environmental health engineering	262	180	82	783	566	217	40	37	3
Geological engineering	104	71	33	46	40	6	11	10	1
Geophysical engineering	8	5	3	10	9	1	1	1	0
Industrial/manufacturing engineering	3,300	2,354	946	2,058	1,622	436	267	235	32
Material engineering	588	447	141	537	434	103	336	275	61
Mechanical engineering	14,464	12,863	1,601	3,982	3,598	384	871	823	48
Metallurgical engineering	298	241	57	171	139	32	93	86	7
Mining and mineral engineering	111	100	11	66	61	5	25	25	0
Naval architecture and marine engineering	275	259	16	31	27	4	6	5	1
Nuclear engineering	234	207	27	269	236	33	115	108	7
Ocean engineering	99	78	21	94	81	13	29	28	1
Petroleum engineering	256	226	30	139	128	11	50	44	6
Systems engineering	411	342	69	403	318	85	31	25	6
Textile sciences and engineering	34	21	13	19	12	7	1	1	0
Engineering, other	1,203	952	251	1,857	1,558	299	275	247	28
Engineering-related technologies, total	16,078	14,651	1,427	1,100	917	183	20	18	2
Architectural engineering technologies	600	530	70	1	1	0	0	0	0
Civil technologies	435	387	48	0	0	0	0	0	0
Electrical and electronic technologies	3,986	3,705	281	37	34	3	0	0	0
Electromechanical instrumentation and maintenance technologies	316	303	13	10	9	1	3	2	1
Environmental control technologies	253	199	54	58	38	20	1	1	0
Industrial production technologies	4,377	3,905	472	295	258	37	5	5	0
Quality control and safety technologies	395	310	85	265	202	63	4	4	0
Mechanical and related technologies	1,836	1,715	121	0	0	0	0	0	0
Mining and petroleum technologies	24	24	0	0	0	0	0	0	0
Surveying	125	115	10	26	19	7	7	6	1
Mechanics and repairers	69	64	5	0	0	0	0	0	0
Construction trades	105	102	3	0	0	0	0	0	0
Engineering and related technologies, other	3,557	3,292	265	408	356	52	0	0	0
English language and literature/letters, total	56,133	19,247	36,886	7,790	2,667	5,123	1,341	550	791
English language and literature, general	41,564	13,822	27,742	5,287	1,812	3,475	949	388	561
Comparative literature	844	240	604	253	97	156	140	55	85
English composition	307	145	162	12	4	8	7	2	5
English creative writing	872	363	509	749	305	444	7	5	2
American literature (United States)	135	48	87	23	5	18	12	3	9
English literature (British and Commonwealth)	1,493	535	958	332	104	228	69	28	41
Speech and rhetorical studies	9,605	3,630	5,975	833	261	572	108	53	55
English technical and business writing	106	44	62	158	45	113	0	0	0
English language and literature/letters, other	1,207	420	787	143	34	109	49	16	33
Foreign languages and literatures, total	14,387	4,158	10,229	3,198	1,062	2,136	830	355	475
Foreign languages and literatures, total	1,481	411	1,070	926	310	616	235	103	132
Foreign languages and literatures, general	928	252	676	318	93	225	53	19	34
Linguistics	553	159	394	608	217	391	182	84	98
East and Southeast Asian languages and literatures, total	585	294	291	142	57	85	20	13	7
Chinese	129	67	62	54	26	28	8	7	1
Japanese	327	151	176	57	13	44	2	1	1
East and Southeast Asian languages, other	129	76	53	31	18	13	10	5	5
East European languages and literatures, total	693	266	427	166	62	104	28	14	14
Russian languages	612	231	381	68	20	48	4	0	4
Slavic languages (other than Russian)	77	33	44	93	39	54	24	14	10
East European languages, other	4	2	2	5	3	2	0	0	0
Germanic languages and literatures, total	1,611	640	971	346	133	213	97	42	55
German	1,572	629	943	317	123	194	86	37	49

Table 245.—Bachelor's, master's, and doctor's degrees conferred by institutions of higher education, by sex of student and field of study: 1992–93—Continued

Field of study	Bachelor's degrees requiring 4 or 5 years			Master's degrees			Doctor's degrees (Ph.D., Ed.D., etc.)		
	Total	Men	Women	Total	Men	Women	Total	Men	Women
1	2	3	4	5	6	7	8	9	10
Scandinavian languages	20	5	15	8	2	6	1	1	0
Germanic languages, other	19	6	13	21	8	13	10	4	6
South Asian languages and literatures	4	2	2	1	0	1	5	3	2
Romance languages and literatures, total	8,916	2,047	6,869	1,329	364	965	312	107	205
French	3,280	634	2,646	513	125	388	98	34	64
Italian	274	62	212	50	18	32	13	5	8
Portuguese	41	27	14	9	3	6	1	1	0
Spanish	5,233	1,309	3,924	667	194	473	145	47	98
Romance languages, other	88	15	73	90	24	66	55	20	35
Middle Eastern languages and literatures, total	82	36	46	51	35	16	20	12	8
Arabic	8	3	5	3	2	1	2	1	1
Hebrew	54	22	32	33	26	7	7	6	1
Middle East languages, other	20	11	9	15	7	8	11	5	6
Classical and ancient Near East languages and literatures, total	741	371	370	144	77	67	60	34	26
Classics	598	300	298	128	69	59	58	33	25
Greek (ancient and medieval)	35	18	17	3	1	2	1	0	1
Latin (ancient and medieval)	108	53	55	13	7	6	1	1	0
Foreign languages, other	274	91	183	93	24	69	53	27	26
Health professions and related sciences, total	67,089	11,347	55,742	25,718	5,227	20,491	1,767	753	1,014
Communication disorders sciences and services	4,814	252	4,562	4,002	171	3,831	102	23	79
Community health liaison	460	86	374	121	37	84	2	2	0
Dentistry	0	0	0	352	221	131	27	21	6
Dental services	927	25	902	48	27	21	0	0	0
Epidemiology	0	0	0	239	96	143	82	34	48
Health services administration, total	3,341	821	2,520	3,303	1,155	2,148	51	26	25
Health services administration	1,681	456	1,225	1,774	655	1,119	30	11	19
Medical records administration	635	49	586	0	0	0	0	0	0
Medical records technology/technician	3	0	3	5	3	2	6	5	1
Health and medical administrative services, other	1,022	316	706	1,524	497	1,027	15	10	5
Health and medical assistants, total	967	468	499	184	48	136	0	0	0
Medical assistant	2	0	2	0	0	0	0	0	0
Physician assistant	858	441	417	171	44	127	0	0	0
Health and medical assistants, other	107	27	80	13	4	9	0	0	0
Health and medical diagnostic and treatment services, total	1,255	467	788	56	30	26	0	0	0
Respiratory therapy technology/technician	322	112	210	0	0	0	0	0	0
Health and medical diagnostic and treatment services, other	933	355	578	56	30	26	0	0	0
Medical laboratory technologies, total	2,458	700	1,758	380	159	221	111	52	59
Medical technology	2,135	593	1,542	61	21	40	3	2	1
Health and medical laboratory technologies/technicians, other	323	107	216	319	138	181	108	50	58
Pre-dentistry studies	176	102	74	3	2	1	0	0	0
Pre-medicine studies	690	382	308	0	0	0	0	0	0
Pre-pharmacy studies	400	161	239	0	0	0	0	0	0
Pre-veterinary studies	265	103	162	2	1	1	0	0	0
Medical basic sciences	216	84	132	249	116	133	313	192	121
Mental health services, total	537	86	451	383	90	293	6	2	4
Alcohol/drug abuse counseling	88	29	59	52	15	37	0	0	0
Psychiatric/mental health services technician	153	26	127	48	21	27	0	0	0
Clinical and medical social work	82	9	73	97	24	73	6	2	4
Mental health services, other	214	22	192	186	30	156	0	0	0
Nursing	34,792	2,934	31,858	8,151	527	7,624	396	20	376
Optometry	183	81	102	7	2	5	1	1	0
Pharmacy	5,489	2,071	3,418	257	115	142	203	124	79
Rehabilitation/therapeutic services, total	6,625	1,276	5,349	3,889	902	2,987	37	13	24
Art therapy	58	3	55	202	12	190	0	0	0
Dance therapy	1	0	1	34	0	34	0	0	0
Music therapy	155	19	136	16	4	12	0	0	0
Occupational therapy	2,500	241	2,259	521	51	470	3	1	2
Orthotics/prosthetics	34	25	9	0	0	0	0	0	0
Physical therapy	2,928	792	2,136	2,202	586	1,616	9	5	4
Recreational therapy	125	24	101	3	1	2	5	0	5
Vocational rehabilitation counseling	178	46	132	578	155	423	5	2	3
Rehabilitative services, other	646	126	520	333	93	240	15	5	10
Veterinary medicine	126	53	73	153	87	66	132	87	45
Miscellaneous health professions	297	160	137	201	92	109	28	24	4
Health professions and related sciences, other	3,071	1,035	2,036	3,738	1,349	2,389	276	132	144
Home economics and vocational home economics, total	15,100	1,638	13,462	2,479	422	2,057	345	97	248
Home economics, total	14,444	1,382	13,062	2,440	417	2,023	335	95	240
Home economics, general	2,974	201	2,773	300	23	277	42	14	28
Home economics business services	156	10	146	2	0	2	0	0	0
Family and community studies	185	24	161	65	16	49	2	2	0
Family and consumer resource management	1,285	368	917	60	9	51	22	2	20
Food and nutrition studies	2,735	343	2,392	534	61	473	60	13	47
Housing studies	576	65	511	51	19	32	1	0	1
Individual and family development studies	4,422	279	4,143	1,287	276	1,011	190	58	132

Table 245.—Bachelor's, master's, and doctor's degrees conferred by institutions of higher education, by sex of student and field of study: 1992–93—Continued

Field of study	Bachelor's degrees requiring 4 or 5 years			Master's degrees			Doctor's degrees (Ph.D., Ed.D., etc.)		
	Total	Men	Women	Total	Men	Women	Total	Men	Women
1	2	3	4	5	6	7	8	9	10
Clothing/apparel and textile studies	1,960	77	1,883	110	12	98	14	5	9
Home economics, other	151	15	136	31	1	30	4	1	3
Vocational home economics, total	656	256	400	39	5	34	10	2	8
Child care and guidance management	180	0	180	34	1	33	4	0	4
Custodial, housekeeping and home services workers and managers	5	3	2	4	4	0	0	0	0
Vocational home economics, other	471	253	218	1	0	1	6	2	4
Law and legal studies, total	2,056	667	1,389	2,197	1,481	716	86	65	21
Pre-law studies	262	140	122	12	4	8	0	0	0
Paralegal/legal assistant	913	143	770	13	5	8	0	0	0
Law and legal studies, other	881	384	497	2,172	1,472	700	86	65	21
Liberal arts and sciences, general studies, and humanities, total	33,456	13,275	20,181	2,416	840	1,576	81	38	43
Liberal arts and sciences/liberal studies	21,044	7,655	13,389	1,630	548	1,082	18	9	9
Humanities/humanistic studies	2,898	1,011	1,887	491	188	303	32	17	15
Liberal arts and sciences, general studies, other	9,514	4,609	4,905	295	104	191	31	12	19
Library science, total	83	9	74	4,871	961	3,910	77	26	51
Library science/librarianship	81	9	72	4,767	950	3,817	72	22	50
Library science, other	2	0	2	104	11	93	5	4	1
Mathematics, total	14,812	7,827	6,985	4,067	2,455	1,612	1,189	906	283
Mathematics	12,635	6,522	6,113	2,423	1,449	974	808	623	185
Applied mathematics, total	1,285	758	527	822	553	269	159	116	43
Applied mathematics, general and other	857	497	360	399	249	150	108	77	31
Operations research (quantitative methods)	428	261	167	423	304	119	51	39	12
Mathematical statistics	520	296	224	763	420	343	214	160	54
Mathematics, other	372	251	121	59	33	26	8	7	1
Multi/interdisciplinary studies, total	23,955	8,917	15,038	2,498	1,221	1,277	196	115	81
Biological and physical sciences	2,007	1,115	892	163	92	71	24	14	10
Systems science and theory	121	70	51	276	163	113	12	11	1
Museology/museum studies	2	1	1	103	24	79	0	0	0
Multi/interdisciplinary studies, other	21,825	7,731	14,094	1,956	942	1,014	160	90	70
Parks, recreation, leisure, and fitness studies, total	9,859	4,885	4,974	1,434	714	720	108	75	33
Parks, recreation and leisure studies	2,040	871	1,169	222	107	115	23	16	7
Parks, recreation and leisure facilities management	2,455	1,095	1,360	249	107	142	10	6	4
Health and physical education/fitness	5,230	2,832	2,398	940	493	447	73	52	21
Parks, recreation, leisure and fitness studies, other	134	87	47	23	7	16	2	1	1
Philosophy and religion, total	7,781	4,938	2,843	1,425	988	437	448	323	125
Philosophy	4,842	3,310	1,532	707	519	188	266	199	67
Religion/religious studies	2,569	1,415	1,154	680	459	221	177	120	57
Philosophy and religion, other	370	213	157	38	10	28	5	4	1
Physical sciences and science technologies, total	17,545	11,825	5,720	5,366	3,808	1,558	4,393	3,432	961
Physical sciences, total	17,462	11,773	5,689	5,347	3,793	1,554	4,376	3,419	957
Physical sciences, general	380	270	110	68	52	16	0	0	0
Astronomy	116	89	27	89	66	23	82	68	14
Astrophysics	51	31	20	46	40	6	16	13	3
Atmospheric science and meteorology	369	305	64	202	161	41	65	55	10
Chemistry, total	8,914	5,288	3,626	1,842	1,105	737	2,261	1,623	638
Chemistry, general	8,674	5,148	3,526	1,713	1,040	673	2,081	1,494	587
Analytical chemistry	0	0	0	19	8	11	22	16	6
Inorganic chemistry	0	0	0	0	0	0	7	6	1
Organic chemistry	11	2	9	11	3	8	14	9	5
Medicinal/pharmaceutical chemistry	11	6	5	20	5	15	45	28	17
Chemistry, other	218	132	86	79	49	30	92	70	22
Geological and related sciences, total	2,299	1,554	745	925	670	255	406	334	72
Geology	2,136	1,446	690	793	565	228	314	254	60
Geochemistry	6	3	3	5	3	2	10	8	2
Geophysics and seismology	45	32	13	69	59	10	53	48	5
Geological and related sciences, other	112	73	39	58	43	15	29	24	5
Miscellaneous physical sciences, total	924	639	285	335	213	122	233	187	46
Metallurgy	0	0	0	3	3	0	0	0	0
Oceanography	233	170	63	143	89	54	112	85	27
Earth and planetary sciences	591	415	176	127	86	41	108	90	18
Miscellaneous physical sciences, other	100	54	46	62	35	27	13	12	1
Physics, total	4,063	3,390	673	1,777	1,460	317	1,277	1,107	170
Physics, general	3,892	3,249	643	1,643	1,356	287	1,210	1,051	159

Table 245.—Bachelor's, master's, and doctor's degrees conferred by institutions of higher education, by sex of student and field of study: 1992–93—Continued

Field of study	Bachelor's degrees requiring 4 or 5 years			Master's degrees			Doctor's degrees (Ph.D., Ed.D., etc.)		
	Total	Men	Women	Total	Men	Women	Total	Men	Women
1	2	3	4	5	6	7	8	9	10
Physics, other	171	141	30	134	104	30	67	56	11
Physical sciences, other	346	207	139	63	26	37	36	32	4
Science technologies, total	83	52	31	19	15	4	17	13	4
Precision production trades, total	388	281	107	2	2	0	0	0	0
Drafting, general	149	127	22	0	0	0	0	0	0
Precision production trades, other	239	154	85	2	2	0	0	0	0
Protective services, total	20,902	13,020	7,882	1,357	837	520	32	23	9
Criminal justice and corrections, total	20,623	12,774	7,849	1,323	806	517	32	23	9
Corrections/correctional administration	666	363	303	56	42	14	0	0	0
Criminal justice/law enforcement administration	6,642	4,178	2,464	472	288	184	6	4	2
Criminal justice studies	10,436	6,277	4,159	683	416	267	26	19	7
Forensic studies	163	91	72	38	20	18	0	0	0
Law enforcement/police science	1,712	1,287	425	47	24	23	0	0	0
Criminal justice, other	1,004	578	426	27	16	11	0	0	0
Fire control and safety	230	218	12	25	23	2	0	0	0
Protective services, other	49	28	21	9	8	1	0	0	0
Psychology, total	66,728	17,908	48,820	10,957	3,029	7,928	3,651	1,415	2,236
Psychology, general	63,247	17,021	46,226	4,265	1,323	2,942	1,575	659	916
Clinical psychology	64	14	50	1,319	345	974	1,205	426	779
Counseling psychology	261	57	204	3,117	761	2,356	236	88	148
Developmental and child psychology	732	79	653	115	26	89	57	15	42
Experimental psychology	251	57	194	82	29	53	90	38	52
Industrial and organizational psychology	156	62	94	309	124	185	63	28	35
Physiological psychology/psychobiology	172	75	97	7	4	3	26	12	14
Social psychology	195	40	155	110	19	91	34	11	23
School psychology	0	0	0	609	114	495	108	30	78
Psychology, other	1,650	503	1,147	1,024	284	740	257	108	149
Public administration and services, total	16,775	3,801	12,974	20,634	6,105	14,529	459	215	244
Public administration	2,607	1,384	1,223	6,347	3,340	3,007	120	82	38
Community organization, resources and services	1,241	312	929	210	72	138	4	1	3
Public policy analysis	382	210	172	670	330	340	70	42	28
Social work	12,090	1,663	10,427	13,032	2,223	10,809	233	81	152
Public affairs, other	455	232	223	375	140	235	32	9	23
R.O.T.C. and military technologies, total	11	11	0	108	100	8	0	0	0
Social sciences and history, total	135,703	73,589	62,114	13,471	7,671	5,800	3,460	2,203	1,257
Social sciences, general	7,390	3,188	4,202	473	213	260	70	39	31
Anthropology	5,098	1,819	3,279	913	388	525	359	138	221
Archeology	95	41	54	14	5	9	11	5	6
Criminology	1,772	1,005	767	83	48	35	8	2	6
Demography and population studies	0	0	0	38	13	25	13	8	5
Economics	21,321	14,965	6,356	2,292	1,611	681	879	674	205
Geography, total	4,151	2,752	1,399	646	423	223	150	105	45
Geography	4,116	2,724	1,392	643	421	222	150	105	45
Cartography	35	28	7	3	2	1	0	0	0
History	27,774	17,212	10,562	2,952	1,812	1,140	690	451	239
International relations and affairs	6,361	2,721	3,640	1,859	994	865	79	55	24
Political science and government, general	37,931	22,052	15,879	1,943	1,239	704	529	389	140
Sociology	20,896	6,605	14,291	1,521	591	930	536	272	264
Urban affairs/studies	699	370	329	291	148	143	74	43	31
Social sciences and history, other	2,215	859	1,356	446	186	260	62	22	40
Theological studies/religious vocations, total	5,433	4,168	1,265	4,985	2,989	1,996	1,417	1,219	198
Biblical and other theological languages and literatures	52	37	15	62	23	39	7	7	0
Bible/biblical studies	1,439	1,112	327	275	221	54	11	11	0
Missions/missionary studies and misology	312	185	127	195	111	84	45	41	4
Religious education	832	507	325	788	391	397	55	48	7
Religious/sacred music	173	90	83	102	52	50	17	15	2
Theology/theological studies	2,131	1,883	248	2,546	1,682	864	922	812	110
Pastoral counseling and specialized ministries	101	75	26	680	298	382	198	155	43
Theological studies and religious vocations, other	393	279	114	337	211	126	162	130	32
Transportation and materials moving workers, total	3,930	3,508	422	495	456	39	0	0	0
Water transportation workers	286	264	22	0	0	0	0	0	0
Transportation and material moving, other	3,644	3,244	400	495	456	39	0	0	0
Visual and performing arts, total	47,761	18,610	29,151	9,440	4,099	5,341	882	478	404

Table 245.—Bachelor's, master's, and doctor's degrees conferred by institutions of higher education, by sex of student and field of study: 1992–93—Continued

Field of study	Bachelor's degrees requiring 4 or 5 years			Master's degrees			Doctor's degrees (Ph.D., Ed.D., etc.)		
	Total	Men	Women	Total	Men	Women	Total	Men	Women
1	2	3	4	5	6	7	8	9	10
Visual and performing arts, general	1,477	559	918	120	45	75	9	7	2
Crafts, folk art, and artisanry	99	37	62	7	2	5	0	0	0
Dance	812	79	733	204	38	166	3	0	3
Design and applied art	7,914	2,929	4,985	431	185	246	1	0	1
Dramatic/theater arts and stagecraft	5,891	2,357	3,534	1,290	626	664	76	47	29
Film/video and photographic arts, total	2,681	1,664	1,017	566	347	219	14	9	5
Film-video making/cinematography and production	868	575	293	284	182	102	5	2	3
Photography	987	527	460	150	83	67	1	1	0
Film arts, other	826	562	264	132	82	50	8	6	2
Fine arts and art studies, total	20,526	6,825	13,701	3,090	1,143	1,947	137	49	88
Art, general	11,347	4,039	7,308	980	384	596	39	14	25
Art history, criticism and conservation	4,192	998	3,194	798	232	566	97	34	63
Arts management	119	27	92	111	25	86	0	0	0
Painting	846	316	530	214	97	117	0	0	0
Ceramic arts and ceramics	212	73	139	44	21	23	0	0	0
Fiber, textile and weaving arts	118	9	109	37	7	30	1	1	0
Metal and jewelry arts	75	23	52	20	5	15	0	0	0
Fine arts and art studies, other	3,617	1,340	2,277	886	372	514	0	0	0
Music, total	7,853	3,962	3,891	3,488	1,629	1,859	609	357	252
Music, general	3,836	1,856	1,980	1,090	511	579	238	136	102
Music history and literature	58	18	40	37	18	19	33	21	12
Music, general performance	2,683	1,271	1,412	1,862	826	1,036	219	125	94
Music theory and composition	209	161	48	151	111	40	62	44	18
Music, other	1,067	656	411	348	163	185	57	31	26
Visual and performing arts, other	508	198	310	244	84	160	33	9	24
Not classified by field of study	5,247	2,340	2,907	884	504	380	111	93	18

NOTE.—Aggregations by field of study derived from the *Classification of Instructional Programs* developed by the National Center for Education Statistics.

SOURCE: U.S. Department of Education, National Center for Education Statistics, Integrated Postsecondary Education Data System (IPEDS), "Completions" survey. (This table was prepared January 1995.)

Table 246.—Bachelor's degrees conferred by institutions of higher education, by discipline division: 1970-71 to 1993-94

Discipline division	1970-71	1975-76	1980-81	1981-82	1982-83	1983-84	1984-85	1985-86	1986-87	1987-88	1988-89	1989-90	1990-91	1991-92	1992-93	1993-94
1	2	3	4	5	6	7	8	9	10	11	12	13	14	15	16	17
Total	**839,730**	**925,746**	**935,140**	**952,998**	**969,510**	**974,309**	**979,477**	**987,823**	**991,264**	**994,829**	**1,018,755**	**1,051,344**	**1,094,538**	**1,136,553**	**1,165,178**	**1,169,275**
Agriculture and natural resources	12,672	19,402	21,886	21,029	20,909	19,317	18,107	16,823	14,991	14,222	13,492	12,900	13,124	15,124	16,778	18,070
Architecture and related programs	5,570	9,146	9,455	9,728	9,823	9,186	9,325	9,119	8,950	8,603	9,150	9,364	9,781	8,753	9,167	8,975
Area, ethnic and cultural studies	2,582	3,577	2,887	2,862	3,068	3,005	2,985	3,178	3,427	3,601	4,102	4,613	4,884	5,342	5,481	5,573
Biological sciences/life sciences	35,743	54,275	43,216	41,639	39,982	38,640	38,445	38,524	38,121	36,755	36,059	37,204	39,530	42,941	47,038	51,383
Business management and administrative services	114,729	142,034	198,983	213,374	226,627	229,478	232,636	237,319	240,546	243,021	246,399	248,698	249,311	256,603	256,842	246,654
Communications	10,324	20,045	29,428	32,428	36,954	38,586	40,358	41,666	43,953	45,410	47,405	50,114	51,650	54,257	53,874	51,164
Communications technologies	478	1,237	1,854	1,794	1,613	1,527	1,644	1,410	1,384	1,239	1,204	1,194	1,123	720	832	663
Computer and information sciences	2,388	5,652	15,121	20,267	24,510	32,172	38,878	41,889	39,589	34,523	30,454	27,257	25,083	24,557	24,200	24,200
Education	176,307	154,437	108,074	100,932	97,895	92,299	88,072	87,114	86,936	91,112	96,913	105,112	110,807	108,006	107,781	107,600
Engineering	44,898	38,388	63,287	67,021	72,163	75,638	77,066	76,225	73,747	69,380	66,099	63,609	61,531	61,206	61,973	62,220
Engineering-related technologies	5,148	7,943	11,713	12,984	16,855	18,547	18,762	19,435	19,069	19,126	18,903	17,713	17,119	16,335	16,078	16,005
English language and literature/letters	64,342	42,006	32,254	33,419	31,829	32,834	33,218	34,552	36,284	38,661	42,470	47,519	51,841	54,951	56,133	53,924
Foreign languages and literatures	20,536	16,484	11,273	10,756	10,599	10,384	10,827	10,984	11,034	10,926	11,693	12,386	13,133	13,903	14,387	14,378
Health professions and related sciences	25,226	53,958	63,649	63,653	64,685	64,288	64,422	64,396	63,103	60,644	59,005	58,302	59,070	61,720	67,089	74,421
Home economics and vocational home economics	11,167	17,409	18,370	17,872	16,296	15,948	15,157	14,889	14,417	14,320	14,160	14,491	14,892	14,898	15,100	15,522
Law and legal studies	545	531	776	846	1,099	1,272	1,157	1,197	1,178	1,303	1,976	1,592	1,758	2,144	2,056	2,171
Liberal arts and sciences, general studies, and humanities	7,481	18,855	21,643	21,089	21,603	21,479	21,818	21,336	23,717	24,274	26,388	27,985	30,526	32,174	33,456	33,397
Library science	1,013	843	375	307	254	252	197	155	136	119	121	77	90	97	83	62
Mathematics	24,937	16,329	11,433	12,226	12,719	13,764	15,861	17,147	16,999	16,608	15,994	15,176	15,310	14,783	14,812	14,396
Multi/interdisciplinary studies	6,286	13,588	12,848	14,707	14,107	13,940	12,978	13,489	13,933	14,723	15,168	16,267	17,561	20,647	23,955	25,167
Parks, recreation, leisure and fitness studies	1,621	5,182	5,729	5,335	5,214	4,850	4,725	4,620	4,264	4,235	4,376	4,582	4,315	8,446	9,859	11,470
Philosophy and religion	8,146	8,447	6,776	6,309	6,483	6,435	6,400	6,239	5,984	5,963	6,425	6,868	7,315	7,526	7,781	7,546
Physical sciences and science technologies	21,412	21,465	23,952	24,052	23,381	23,651	23,704	21,717	20,070	17,806	17,186	16,066	16,344	16,960	17,545	18,400
Precision production trades	0	0	0	0	384	371	553	400	455	481	482	528	460	378	388	420
Protective services	2,045	12,507	13,707	12,438	12,579	12,654	12,510	12,704	12,930	13,367	14,698	15,354	16,806	18,855	20,902	23,009
Psychology	38,187	50,278	41,068	41,212	40,460	39,955	39,900	40,628	42,994	45,187	48,910	53,952	58,655	63,513	66,728	69,259
Public administration and services	5,466	15,440	16,707	16,495	14,414	12,570	11,754	11,887	12,328	12,385	13,162	13,908	14,350	15,987	16,775	17,815
R.O.T.C. and military technologies	357	952	42	55	267	195	299	256	384	82	198	196	183	184	11	19
Social sciences and history	155,324	126,396	100,513	99,705	95,228	93,323	91,570	93,840	96,342	100,460	108,151	118,083	125,107	133,974	135,703	133,680
Theological studies/religious vocations	3,744	5,520	5,841	5,998	6,054	5,920	6,047	5,607	5,730	5,565	5,318	5,200	4,813	4,729	5,433	5,434
Transportation and material moving	662	1,282	1,801	2,044	1,662	1,698	1,962	1,837	1,654	1,983	2,062	2,387	2,622	3,598	3,930	3,923
Visual and performing arts	30,394	42,138	40,479	40,422	39,794	40,131	38,140	37,241	36,615	36,944	38,227	39,934	42,186	46,522	47,761	49,053
Not classified by field of study	0	0	0	0	0	0	0	0	0	1,801	2,405	2,713	13,258	6,720	5,247	3,302

NOTE.—The new Classification of Instructional Programs was initiated in 1991–92. The figures for earlier years have been reclassified when necessary to make them conform to the new taxonomy. To facilitate trend comparisons, certain aggregations have been made of the degree fields as reported in the IPEDS "Completions" survey: "Agriculture and natural resources" includes Agribusiness and agriculture production, Agricultural sciences, and Conservation and renewable natural resources; "Business management and administrative services" includes Business and management; Business (administrative support), Marketing and distribution, and Consumer, personal, and miscellaneous services; and "Engineering-related technologies" includes Engineering-related technologies, Mechanics and repairers, and Construction trades.

SOURCE: U.S. Department of Education, National Center for Education Statistics, "Degrees and Other Formal Awards Conferred" surveys, and Integrated Postsecondary Education Data System (IPEDS), "Completions" surveys. (This table was prepared February 1996.)

Table 247.—Master's degrees conferred by institutions of higher education, by discipline division: 1970–71 to 1993–94

Discipline division	1970–71	1975–76	1980–81	1981–82	1982–83	1983–84	1984–85	1985–86	1986–87	1987–88	1988–89	1989–90	1990–91	1991–92	1992–93	1993–94
1	2	3	4	5	6	7	8	9	10	11	12	13	14	15	16	17
Total	**230,509**	**311,771**	**295,739**	**295,546**	**289,921**	**284,263**	**286,251**	**288,567**	**289,349**	**299,317**	**310,621**	**324,301**	**337,168**	**352,838**	**369,585**	**387,070**
Agriculture and natural resources	2,457	3,340	4,003	4,163	4,254	4,178	3,928	3,801	3,522	3,479	3,245	3,382	3,295	3,735	3,965	4,119
Architecture and related programs	1,705	3,215	3,153	3,327	3,357	3,223	3,275	3,260	3,163	3,159	3,383	3,499	3,490	3,640	3,808	3,943
Area, ethnic, and cultural studies	1,032	995	804	809	845	897	904	945	864	911	1,016	1,212	1,263	1,385	1,523	1,633
Biological sciences/life sciences	5,728	6,582	5,978	5,874	5,696	5,406	5,059	5,013	4,952	4,784	4,961	4,869	4,765	4,785	4,756	5,196
Business management and administrative services	25,977	42,054	57,391	60,763	64,758	66,150	66,996	66,689	67,093	69,230	73,065	76,676	78,255	84,642	89,615	93,437
Communications	1,770	2,961	2,896	3,104	3,502	3,513	3,460	3,500	3,622	3,678	3,940	4,063	4,123	4,180	4,754	5,005
Communications technologies	86	165	209	223	102	143	209	323	271	247	317	299	213	284	455	414
Computer and information sciences	1,588	2,603	4,218	4,935	5,321	6,190	7,101	8,070	8,481	9,197	9,414	9,677	9,324	9,530	10,163	10,416
Education	87,666	126,061	96,713	91,601	83,250	75,664	74,654	74,801	74,045	76,566	81,174	84,881	87,343	92,668	96,028	98,938
Engineering	16,309	16,014	16,386	17,526	18,807	20,078	20,905	21,040	22,015	22,627	23,740	23,863	23,962	24,983	27,626	28,621
Engineering-related technologies	134	328	323	413	537	577	650	617	639	758	828	909	996	994	1,100	1,133
English language and literature/letters	10,686	8,809	5,929	5,772	5,048	5,010	5,187	5,518	5,483	5,562	5,950	6,567	7,026	7,450	7,790	7,885
Foreign languages and literatures	5,217	4,190	2,690	2,657	2,478	2,581	2,471	2,494	2,379	2,469	2,595	2,760	2,800	2,926	3,198	3,288
Health professions and related sciences	5,749	12,556	16,515	16,503	17,047	17,411	17,385	18,573	18,394	18,657	19,268	20,321	21,200	23,065	25,718	28,025
Home economics and vocational home economics	1,452	2,179	2,570	2,355	2,385	2,416	2,375	2,294	2,064	2,047	2,164	2,100	2,019	2,412	2,479	2,421
Law and legal studies	955	1,442	1,832	1,893	2,091	1,802	1,796	1,924	1,943	1,880	2,013	1,888	2,057	2,369	2,197	2,432
Liberal arts and sciences, general studies, and humanities	885	2,633	2,375	2,425	1,286	1,796	1,696	1,586	1,581	1,814	1,850	1,999	2,213	2,394	2,416	2,496
Library science	7,001	8,037	4,859	4,506	3,904	3,782	3,870	3,564	3,783	3,674	3,906	4,341	4,763	4,893	4,871	5,116
Mathematics	5,695	4,315	3,074	3,263	3,398	3,244	3,413	3,607	3,730	3,867	3,903	4,146	4,041	4,011	4,067	4,100
Multi/interdisciplinary studies	821	1,158	2,144	2,553	2,499	2,431	2,583	2,625	2,482	2,575	2,762	2,834	1,796	2,126	2,498	2,464
Parks, recreation, leisure and fitness studies	218	571	643	526	608	603	596	570	560	544	535	529	483	1,358	1,434	1,625
Philosophy and religion	1,326	1,356	1,229	1,152	1,091	1,153	1,167	1,163	1,109	1,099	1,280	1,306	1,441	1,146	1,425	1,350
Physical sciences and science technologies	6,367	5,466	5,284	5,514	5,290	5,576	5,796	5,902	5,629	5,733	5,723	5,449	5,309	5,374	5,366	5,679
Precision production trades	0	0	0	0	0	0	4	0	0	4	3	0	0	0	2	2
Protective services	194	1,197	1,538	1,336	1,300	1,219	1,235	1,074	1,019	1,024	1,047	1,151	1,108	1,249	1,357	1,437
Psychology	5,717	10,167	10,223	9,947	9,981	9,525	9,891	9,845	9,562	9,180	9,940	10,730	11,349	10,215	10,957	12,181
Public administration and services	7,785	15,209	17,803	17,416	16,046	15,060	15,575	15,692	16,432	16,424	17,020	17,399	17,905	19,243	20,634	21,833
R.O.T.C. and military technologies	2	0	43	49	110	127	119	83	119	49	0	0	0	0	108	124
Social sciences and history	16,539	15,953	11,945	12,002	11,205	10,577	10,503	10,564	10,506	10,412	11,023	11,634	12,233	12,702	13,471	14,561
Theological studies/religious vocations	2,710	3,290	4,220	4,064	4,871	5,211	4,435	4,556	4,966	4,905	4,749	4,959	4,810	5,185	4,985	4,956
Transportation and material moving	63	108	120	129	91	194	295	454	433	679	692	538	406	385	495	664
Visual and performing arts	6,675	8,817	8,629	8,746	8,763	8,526	8,718	8,420	8,508	7,939	8,267	8,481	8,657	9,353	9,440	9,925
Not classified by field of study	0	0	0	0	0	0	0	0	0	4,144	851	1,836	8,523	4,156	884	1,651

NOTE.—The new Classification of Instructional Programs was initiated in 1991–92. To facilitate trend comparisons, certain aggregations have been made of the degree fields as reported in the IPEDS "Completions" survey: "Agriculture and natural resources" includes Agribusiness and agriculture production, Agricultural sciences, and Conservation and renewable natural resources; "Business management and administrative services" includes Business and management, Business (administrative support), Marketing and distribution, and Consumer, personal, and miscellaneous services;

and "Engineering-related technologies" includes Mechanics and repairers, Construction trades, and Engineering-related technologies.

SOURCE: U.S. Department of Education, National Center for Education Statistics, "Degrees and Other Formal Awards Conferred" surveys, and Integrated Postsecondary Education Data System (IPEDS), "Completions" surveys. (This table was prepared February 1996.)

Table 248.—Doctor's degrees conferred by institutions of higher education, by discipline division: 1970-71 to 1993-94

Discipline division	1970-71	1975-76	1980-81	1981-82	1982-83	1983-84	1984-85	1985-86	1986-87	1987-88	1988-89	1989-90	1990-91	1991-92	1992-93	1993-94
1	2	3	4	5	6	7	8	9	10	11	12	13	14	15	16	17
Total	32,107	34,064	32,958	32,707	32,775	33,209	32,943	33,653	34,041	34,870	35,720	38,371	39,294	40,659	42,132	43,185
Agriculture and natural resources	1,086	928	1,067	1,079	1,149	1,172	1,213	1,158	1,049	1,142	1,183	1,295	1,185	1,214	1,173	1,278
Architecture and related programs	36	82	93	80	97	84	89	73	92	98	86	103	135	132	148	161
Area, ethnic, and cultural studies	144	188	162	102	155	141	140	159	134	142	114	131	167	155	178	155
Biological sciences/life sciences	3,645	3,392	3,718	3,743	3,341	3,437	3,432	3,358	3,419	3,629	3,520	3,844	4,093	4,243	4,435	4,534
Business management and administrative services	757	900	795	815	776	929	831	934	1,062	1,063	1,100	1,093	1,185	1,242	1,346	1,364
Communications	145	196	171	182	205	215	228	212	273	230	247	267	259	252	293	337
Communications technologies	0	8	11	18	9	4	6	11	2	4	6	6	15	3	8	8
Computer and information sciences	128	244	252	251	262	251	248	344	374	428	551	627	676	772	805	810
Education	6,041	7,202	7,279	6,999	7,057	6,911	6,612	6,605	6,407	6,060	6,337	6,502	6,187	6,864	7,030	6,908
Engineering	3,637	2,819	2,551	2,621	2,818	2,979	3,221	3,398	3,801	4,174	4,506	4,967	5,258	5,488	5,823	5,963
Engineering-related technologies	1	2	10	15	13	2	9	12	17	17	17	14	14	11	20	16
English language and literature/letters	1,650	1,672	1,164	1,101	991	1,018	1,041	991	961	981	1,022	1,078	1,184	1,273	1,341	1,344
Foreign languages and literatures	988	1,076	804	748	673	659	635	672	661	602	632	724	758	850	830	886
Health professions and related sciences	466	577	842	925	1,155	1,164	1,199	1,241	1,213	1,261	1,437	1,536	1,613	1,661	1,767	1,902
Home economics and vocational home economics	123	178	247	247	255	277	273	311	296	307	264	301	253	293	345	365
Law and legal studies	20	76	60	22	72	121	105	54	120	89	76	111	90	68	86	79
Liberal arts and sciences, general studies, and humanities	32	162	121	155	215	173	112	90	56	66	72	63	70	67	81	80
Library science	39	71	71	84	52	74	87	62	57	46	61	42	56	50	77	45
Mathematics	1,249	909	775	721	731	743	734	777	759	796	915	966	1,036	1,082	1,189	1,157
Multi/interdisciplinary studies	59	111	158	238	225	249	219	263	247	224	212	272	220	231	196	227
Parks, recreation, leisure, and fitness studies	2	15	42	33	33	27	36	39	32	29	35	35	28	61	108	116
Philosophy and religion	554	554	410	364	404	442	468	477	421	405	465	439	456	475	448	528
Physical sciences and science technologies	4,390	3,431	3,141	3,286	3,269	3,306	3,403	3,551	3,673	3,809	3,858	4,164	4,290	4,391	4,393	4,650
Precision production trades	0	0	0	0	0	0	0	0	0	0	0	0	0	0	0	0
Protective services	1	9	21	24	38	31	33	21	18	32	26	38	28	24	32	25
Psychology	2,144	3,157	3,576	3,461	3,602	3,535	3,447	3,593	3,560	3,480	3,685	3,811	3,932	3,373	3,651	3,563
Public administration and services	174	292	362	372	347	420	431	382	398	470	428	508	430	432	459	519
R.O.T.C. and military technologies	0	0	0	0	0	0	0	0	0	0	0	0	0	0	0	0
Social sciences and history	3,660	4,157	3,122	3,061	2,931	2,911	2,851	2,955	2,916	2,781	2,885	3,010	3,012	3,218	3,460	3,627
Theological studies/religious vocations	312	1,033	1,276	1,288	1,208	1,204	1,144	1,185	1,230	1,199	1,166	1,317	1,079	1,259	1,417	1,448
Transportation and material moving	3	3	3	2	0	0	0	3	0	0	0	0	0	0	0	0
Visual and performing arts	621	620	654	670	692	730	696	722	793	727	753	849	838	906	882	1,054
Not classified by field of study	0	0	0	0	0	0	0	0	0	579	61	258	747	569	111	36

NOTE.—The new Classification of Instructional Programs was initiated in 1991-92. The figures for earlier years have been reclassified when necessary to make them conform to the new taxonomy. To facilitate trend comparisons, certain aggregations have been made of the degree fields as reported in the IPEDS "Completions" survey: "Agriculture and natural resources" includes Agribusiness and agriculture production, Agricultural sciences, and Conservation and renewable natural resources; "Business management and administrative services" includes Business and management, Business (administrative support), Marketing and distribution, and Consumer, personal, and miscellaneous services;

and "Engineering-related technologies" includes Engineering-related technologies, Mechanics and repairers, and Construction trades.

SOURCE: U.S. Department of Education, National Center for Education Statistics, "Degrees and Other Formal Awards Conferred" surveys, and Integrated Postsecondary Education Data System (IPEDS), "Completions" surveys. (This table was prepared February 1996.)

Table 249.—Degrees conferred by institutions of higher education, by control of institution: 1969–70 to 1993–94

Year	Public institutions					Private institutions				
	Associate	Bachelor's	Master's	Doctor's	First-profes-sional [1]	Associate	Bachelor's	Master's	Doctor's	First-profes-sional [1]
1	2	3	4	5	6	7	8	9	10	11
1969–70	170,966	519,550	134,545	19,183	14,542	35,057	272,766	73,746	10,683	20,376
1970–71	215,645	557,996	151,603	20,788	16,139	36,666	281,734	78,906	11,319	21,807
1971–72	255,218	599,615	167,075	21,776	18,521	36,796	287,658	84,558	11,587	24,890
1972–73	278,132	630,899	174,405	22,357	21,872	38,042	291,463	88,966	12,420	28,146
1973–74	303,188	651,544	184,632	21,810	23,208	40,736	294,232	92,401	12,006	30,608
1974–75	318,474	634,785	193,804	22,176	23,612	41,697	288,148	98,646	11,907	32,304
1975–76	345,006	635,161	206,298	21,751	25,766	46,448	290,585	105,473	12,313	36,883
1976–77	355,650	630,463	208,901	21,229	26,344	50,727	289,086	108,263	12,003	38,015
1977–78	358,874	627,903	202,099	20,456	27,097	53,372	293,301	109,521	11,675	39,484
1978–79	346,808	621,666	192,016	20,817	27,785	55,894	299,724	109,063	11,913	41,063
1979–80	344,536	624,084	187,499	20,608	27,942	56,374	305,333	110,582	12,007	42,189
1980–81	352,391	626,452	184,384	20,895	29,128	63,986	308,688	111,355	12,063	42,828
1981–82	[2]366,732	636,475	182,295	20,889	29,611	[2]67,794	316,523	113,251	11,818	42,421
1982–83	377,817	646,317	176,246	21,186	29,757	71,803	323,193	113,675	11,589	43,297
1983–84	[2]379,249	646,013	170,693	21,141	29,586	[2]72,991	328,296	113,570	12,068	44,882
1984–85	377,625	652,246	170,000	21,337	30,152	77,087	327,231	116,251	11,606	44,911
1985–86	369,052	658,586	169,903	21,433	29,568	76,995	329,237	118,664	12,220	44,342
1986–87	358,811	659,260	167,797	21,870	29,346	77,493	332,004	121,552	12,171	42,271
1987–88	354,180	658,491	173,778	22,488	29,153	80,905	336,338	125,539	12,382	41,582
1988–89	357,001	675,675	179,109	22,970	28,993	79,763	343,080	131,512	12,750	41,863
1989–90	375,635	700,015	186,104	24,641	28,810	79,467	351,329	138,197	13,730	42,178
1990–91	398,055	724,062	193,057	25,681	29,554	83,665	370,476	144,111	13,613	42,394
1991–92	420,265	759,475	203,398	26,820	29,366	83,966	377,078	149,440	13,839	44,780
1992–93	430,321	785,112	213,843	27,392	29,628	84,435	380,066	155,742	14,740	45,759
1993–94	456,190	789,148	221,428	28,524	29,842	86,259	380,127	165,642	14,661	45,576

[1] Includes degrees which require at least 6 years of college work for completion (including at least 2 years of preprofessional training).

[2] Data are approximations.

SOURCE: U.S. Department of Education, National Center for Education Statistics, "Degrees and Other Formal Awards Conferred" surveys, and Integrated Postsecondary Education Data System (IPEDS), "Completions" surveys. (This table was prepared May 1996.)

Table 250.—Degrees conferred by institutions of higher education, by control of institution, level of degree, and discipline division: 1993–94

Discipline division	Public institutions				Private institutions			
	Associate degrees	Bachelor's degrees	Master's degrees	Doctor's degrees	Associate degrees	Bachelor's degrees	Master's degrees	Doctor's degrees
1	2	3	4	5	6	7	8	9
Total	**456,190**	**789,148**	**221,428**	**28,524**	**86,259**	**380,127**	**165,642**	**14,661**
Agriculture and natural resources [1]	5,385	17,080	3,745	1,255	335	990	374	23
Architecture and related programs	314	6,585	2,711	97	39	2,390	1,232	64
Area, ethnic, and cultural studies	65	2,956	1,007	79	27	2,617	626	76
Biological sciences/life sciences	1,771	33,747	3,847	3,240	81	17,636	1,349	1,294
Business management and administrative services [2]	81,118	153,288	37,578	987	27,192	93,366	55,859	377
Communications	1,490	36,024	2,827	297	620	15,140	2,178	40
Communications technologies	2,392	438	61	0	397	225	353	8
Computer and information sciences	7,081	15,231	5,748	553	2,375	8,969	4,668	257
Construction trades	1,322	34	0	0	402	41	0	0
Education	8,817	81,577	64,753	5,112	1,204	26,023	34,185	1,796
Engineering	2,351	46,690	19,297	4,156	448	15,530	9,324	1,807
Engineering-related technologies	24,833	11,641	1,017	16	12,044	4,182	116	0
English language and literature/letters	1,296	36,379	5,905	981	58	17,545	1,980	363
Foreign languages and literatures	328	9,181	2,419	529	189	5,197	869	357
Health professions and related sciences	83,889	50,641	17,009	1,356	11,943	23,780	11,016	546
Home economics and vocational home economics	7,128	13,457	1,410	245	434	2,065	1,011	120
Law and legal studies	6,284	1,429	546	6	2,724	742	1,886	73
Liberal/general studies and humanities	153,616	21,298	1,182	26	10,959	12,099	1,314	54
Library science	109	52	4,298	43	9	10	818	2
Mathematics	746	9,394	3,159	819	19	5,002	941	338
Mechanics and repairers	10,051	45	0	0	1,567	62	0	0
Multi/interdisciplinary studies	8,369	19,392	1,588	176	92	5,775	876	51
Parks, recreation, leisure, and fitness studies	652	9,246	1,313	110	115	2,224	312	6
Philosophy and religion	47	3,009	540	207	47	4,537	810	321
Physical sciences and science technologies	2,549	12,133	4,271	3,344	73	6,267	1,408	1,306
Precision production trades	6,867	364	0	0	2,794	56	2	0
Protective services	18,777	18,693	964	24	639	4,316	473	1
Psychology	1,608	47,005	5,554	1,727	148	22,254	6,627	1,836
Public administration and services	3,294	12,824	13,403	310	426	4,991	8,430	209
R.O.T.C. and military technologies	253	3	124	0	12	16	0	0
Social sciences and history	3,709	88,111	9,479	2,172	391	45,569	5,082	1,455
Theological studies/religious vocations	1	1	0	0	641	5,433	4,956	1,448
Transportation and material moving	1,710	1,826	70	0	278	2,097	594	0
Visual and performing arts	7,531	28,906	5,526	657	6,448	20,147	4,399	397
Not classified by field of study	437	468	77	0	1,089	2,834	1,574	36

[1] Includes "Agricultural business and production," "Agricultural sciences," and "Conservation and renewable natural resources."

[2] Includes "Marketing operations/marketing and distribution" and "Consumer and personal services."

SOURCE: U.S. Department of Education, National Center for Education Statistics, Integrated Postsecondary Education Data System, "Completions" survey, 1993–94 and "Consolidated" survey 1994. (This table was prepared May 1996.)

Table 251.—Degrees conferred by institutions of higher education, by control of institution, level of degree, and discipline division: 1992–93

Discipline division	Public institutions				Private institutions			
	Associate degrees	Bachelor's degrees	Master's degrees	Doctor's degrees	Associate degrees	Bachelor's degrees	Master's degrees	Doctor's degrees
1	2	3	4	5	6	7	8	9
Total	**430,321**	**785,112**	**213,843**	**27,392**	**84,435**	**380,066**	**155,742**	**14,740**
Agriculture and natural resources [1]	5,080	15,977	3,668	1,148	318	801	297	25
Architecture and related programs	322	6,771	2,667	88	50	2,396	1,141	60
Area, ethnic, and cultural studies	23	2,745	908	83	10	2,736	615	95
Biological sciences/life sciences	1,356	30,531	3,525	3,073	79	16,507	1,231	1,362
Business management and administrative services [2]	76,317	160,944	36,624	941	27,539	95,898	52,991	405
Communications	1,413	37,791	2,716	249	491	16,083	2,038	44
Communications technologies	1,386	510	86	0	442	322	369	8
Computer and information sciences	6,821	15,371	5,467	540	2,375	8,829	4,696	265
Construction trades	1,351	24	0	0	302	45	0	0
Education	8,137	82,202	63,805	5,122	1,178	25,579	32,223	1,908
Engineering	2,079	46,118	18,671	4,021	399	15,855	8,955	1,802
Engineering-related technologies	23,830	11,891	965	20	12,491	4,013	135	0
English language and literature/letters	1,264	37,406	5,839	959	56	18,727	1,951	382
Foreign languages and literatures	331	9,123	2,344	483	180	5,264	854	347
Health professions and related sciences	76,461	46,331	15,580	1,328	9,776	20,758	10,138	439
Home economics and vocational home economics	6,464	13,166	1,453	259	450	1,934	1,026	86
Law and legal studies	5,422	1,347	420	8	2,606	709	1,777	78
Liberal/general studies and humanities	147,375	21,637	1,220	28	10,665	11,819	1,196	53
Library science	74	72	4,090	65	11	11	781	12
Mathematics	716	9,737	3,118	855	27	5,075	949	334
Mechanics and repairers	9,426	14	0	0	1,540	91	0	0
Multi/interdisciplinary studies	8,402	18,210	1,653	142	84	5,745	845	54
Parks, recreation, leisure, and fitness studies	635	7,998	1,130	102	82	1,871	304	6
Philosophy and religion	36	3,003	479	164	75	4,778	946	284
Physical sciences and science technologies	2,144	11,372	3,930	3,039	97	6,173	1,436	1,354
Precision production trades	6,585	351	0	0	2,619	37	2	0
Protective services	16,350	16,983	894	31	484	3,919	463	1
Psychology	1,151	44,958	5,220	1,751	86	21,770	5,737	1,900
Public administration and services	2,895	12,173	12,909	240	406	4,602	7,725	219
R.O.T.C. and military technologies	42	0	108	0	10	11	0	0
Social sciences and history	3,560	87,508	8,653	2,101	370	48,195	4,818	1,359
Theological studies/religious vocations	0	0	0	0	508	5,433	4,985	1,417
Transportation and material moving	1,970	1,821	60	0	240	2,109	435	0
Visual and performing arts	6,467	28,055	5,441	552	6,223	19,706	3,999	330
Not classified by field of study	4,436	2,982	200	0	2,166	2,265	684	111

[1] Includes "Agricultural business and production," "Agricultural sciences," and "Conservation and renewable natural resources."

[2] Includes "Marketing operations/marketing and distribution" and "Consumer and personal services."

SOURCE: U.S. Department of Education, National Center for Education Statistics, Integrated Postsecondary Education Data System, "Completions" survey, 1992–93 and "Consolidated" survey 1993. (This table was prepared January 1995.)

Table 252.—Number of institutions of higher education conferring degrees, by level of degree and discipline division: 1993–94

Discipline division	Total number of institutions awarding degrees				Number of public institutions awarding degrees				Number of private institutions awarding degrees			
	Associate degrees	Bachelor's degrees	Master's degrees	Doctor's degrees	Associate degrees	Bachelor's degrees	Master's degrees	Doctor's degrees	Associate degrees	Bachelor's degrees	Master's degrees	Doctor's degrees
1	2	3	4	5	6	7	8	9	10	11	12	13
Total	2,182	1,847	1,342	472	1,242	552	487	214	940	1,295	855	258
Agricultural business and production ..	305	127	63	33	294	99	60	32	11	28	3	1
Agricultural sciences	94	133	76	51	86	115	73	50	8	18	3	1
Architecture and related programs	42	171	120	24	36	109	92	16	6	62	28	8
Area, ethnic, and cultural studies	23	348	106	34	21	164	65	20	2	184	41	14
Biological sciences/life sciences	176	1,230	418	223	164	471	303	148	12	759	115	75
Business management and administrative services	1,584	1,369	714	113	1,094	491	353	79	490	878	361	34
Communications	239	886	223	47	195	362	156	38	44	524	67	9
Communications technologies	161	30	10	2	140	14	1	0	21	16	9	2
Computer and information sciences ...	709	1,042	325	117	514	432	208	81	195	610	117	36
Conservation and renewable natural resources	111	208	96	43	100	129	85	38	11	79	11	5
Consumer and personal services	198	8	0	0	169	5	0	0	29	3	0	0
Construction trades	172	4	0	0	161	2	0	0	11	2	0	0
Education	379	1,146	829	207	288	428	414	141	91	718	415	66
Engineering	269	390	268	167	240	214	174	119	29	176	94	48
Engineering-related technologies	980	315	62	3	809	219	52	3	171	96	10	0
English language and literature/letters	136	1,248	414	134	123	478	290	91	13	770	124	43
Foreign languages and literatures	78	833	198	86	73	364	142	54	5	469	56	32
Health professions and related sciences	1,224	929	520	151	954	419	291	111	270	510	229	40
Home economics	85	327	177	38	66	212	119	29	19	115	58	9
Law and legal studies	401	121	60	14	277	41	26	2	124	80	34	12
Liberal/general studies and humanities	1,284	711	146	17	983	291	69	6	301	420	77	11
Library science	35	13	73	14	33	11	61	12	2	2	12	2
Marketing operations/marketing and distribution	501	190	21	3	391	67	4	2	110	123	17	1
Mathematics	133	1,147	338	151	127	473	254	106	6	674	84	45
Mechanics and repairers	522	10	0	0	489	4	0	0	33	6	0	0
Multi/interdisciplinary studies	158	602	177	53	143	265	118	38	15	337	59	15
Parks, recreation, leisure, and fitness studies	119	461	110	25	108	231	92	23	11	230	18	2
Philosophy and religion	29	845	186	92	20	284	88	49	9	561	98	43
Physical sciences	142	1,057	334	200	132	456	238	133	10	601	96	67
Precision production trades	613	32	1	0	540	23	0	0	73	9	1	0
Protective services	781	429	105	7	721	242	79	6	60	187	26	1
Psychology	150	1,228	517	225	127	457	301	127	23	771	216	98
Public administration and services	256	627	337	72	219	292	227	43	37	335	110	29
R.O.T.C. and military technologies	6	4	1	0	5	3	1	0	1	1	0	0
Science technologies	111	16	3	2	104	8	2	2	7	8	1	0
Social sciences and history	222	1,289	425	171	182	485	297	114	40	804	128	57
Theological studies/religious vocations	87	343	271	107	1	1	0	0	86	342	271	107
Transportation and material moving ...	121	58	5	0	107	31	2	0	14	27	3	0
Visual and performing arts	547	1,194	376	98	404	434	238	63	143	760	138	35
Vocational home economics	512	38	7	2	480	21	5	1	32	17	2	1
Not classified by field of study	15	20	18	4	1	1	1	0	14	19	17	4

NOTE.—Data represent programs, not organizational units within institutions.

SOURCE: U.S. Department of Education, National Center for Education Statistics, Integrated Postsecondary Education Data System, "Completions" survey, 1993–94 and "Consolidated" survey, 1994. (This table was prepared May 1996.)

Table 253.—Number of institutions of higher education conferring degrees, by level of degree and discipline division: 1992–93

Discipline division	Total number of institutions awarding degrees				Number of public institutions awarding degrees				Number of private institutions awarding degrees			
	Associate degrees	Bachelor's degrees	Master's degrees	Doctor's degrees	Associate degrees	Bachelor's degrees	Master's degrees	Doctor's degrees	Associate degrees	Bachelor's degrees	Master's degrees	Doctor's degrees
1	2	3	4	5	6	7	8	9	10	11	12	13
Total	2,145	1,813	1,310	473	1,229	550	482	209	916	1,263	828	264
Agricultural business and production ..	297	125	65	34	283	99	61	33	14	26	4	1
Agricultural sciences	101	131	77	51	93	114	74	51	8	17	3	0
Architecture and related programs	57	167	119	25	48	105	88	18	9	62	31	7
Area, ethnic, and cultural studies	16	355	105	35	13	159	62	19	3	196	43	16
Biological sciences/life sciences	166	1,217	422	217	153	463	301	144	13	754	121	73
Business management and administrative services	1,557	1,331	691	111	1,077	483	347	75	480	848	344	36
Communications	225	868	220	44	186	355	153	35	39	513	67	9
Communications technologies	169	42	11	2	145	17	1	0	24	25	10	2
Computer and information sciences ...	697	1,039	316	112	512	429	208	76	185	610	108	36
Conservation and renewable natural resources	115	187	92	43	103	123	84	39	12	64	8	4
Construction trades	178	5	0	0	165	2	0	0	13	3	0	0
Consumer and personal services	191	10	0	0	163	6	0	0	28	4	0	0
Education	383	1,137	805	201	291	423	409	136	92	714	396	65
Engineering	272	398	264	165	245	214	172	117	27	184	92	48
Engineering-related technologies	961	311	67	6	799	218	57	6	162	93	10	0
English language and literature/letters	125	1,242	405	137	112	470	288	93	13	772	117	44
Foreign languages and literatures	71	837	196	84	67	367	142	55	4	470	54	29
Health professions and related sciences	1,170	903	506	138	925	412	281	101	245	491	225	37
Home economics	77	335	172	37	59	216	115	28	18	119	57	9
Law and legal studies	385	114	61	14	267	41	26	4	118	73	35	10
Liberal/general studies and humanities	1,268	697	141	17	968	291	68	8	300	406	73	9
Library science	29	18	73	18	26	16	62	15	3	2	11	3
Marketing operations/marketing and distribution	527	195	18	1	406	68	2	0	121	127	16	1
Mathematics	134	1,121	333	147	126	463	250	102	8	658	83	45
Mechanics and repairers	509	10	0	0	480	3	0	0	29	7	0	0
Multi/interdisciplinary studies	177	591	170	51	159	259	116	39	18	332	54	12
Parks, recreation, leisure, and fitness studies	113	428	108	23	102	223	92	20	11	205	16	3
Philosophy and religion	29	834	183	88	18	280	82	45	11	554	101	43
Physical sciences	140	1,050	336	204	130	449	243	135	10	601	93	69
Precision production trades	600	26	1	0	532	20	0	0	68	6	1	0
Protective services	739	407	106	8	689	240	80	7	50	167	26	1
Psychology	143	1,222	510	225	128	453	299	124	15	769	211	101
Public administration and services	230	625	337	74	190	288	226	43	40	337	111	31
R.O.T.C. and military technologies	2	2	1	0	1	0	1	0	1	2	0	0
Science technologies	106	16	3	3	97	7	2	3	9	9	1	0
Social sciences and history	213	1,280	404	168	177	481	289	111	36	799	115	57
Theological studies/religious vocations	84	335	268	113	0	0	0	0	84	335	268	113
Transportation and material moving ...	117	57	6	0	105	28	2	0	12	29	4	0
Visual and performing arts	524	1,177	366	94	389	434	232	60	135	743	134	34
Vocational home economics	490	38	6	3	464	22	4	2	26	16	2	1
Not classified by field of study	34	27	15	4	10	5	3	0	24	22	12	4

NOTE.—Data represent programs, not organizational units within institutions.

SOURCE: U.S. Department of Education, National Center for Education Statistics, Integrated Postsecondary Education Data System, "Completions" survey, 1992–93 and "Consolidated" survey, 1993. (This table was prepared January 1995.)

Table 254.—First-professional degrees conferred by institutions of higher education in dentistry, medicine, and law, by sex, and number of institutions conferring degrees: 1949–50 to 1993–94

Year	Dentistry (D.D.S. or D.M.D.)				Medicine (M.D.)				Law (LL.B. or J.D.)			
	Number of institutions conferring degrees	Degrees conferred			Number of institutions conferring degrees	Degrees conferred			Number of institutions conferring degrees	Degrees conferred		
		Total	Men	Women		Total	Men	Women		Total	Men	Women
1	2	3	4	5	6	7	8	9	10	11	12	13
1949–50	40	2,579	2,561	18	72	5,612	5,028	584	(1)	(1)	(1)	(1)
1951–52	41	2,918	2,895	23	72	6,201	5,871	330	(1)	(1)	(1)	(1)
1953–54	42	3,102	3,063	39	73	6,712	6,377	335	(1)	(1)	(1)	(1)
1955–56	42	3,009	2,975	34	73	6,810	6,464	346	131	8,262	7,974	288
1957–58	43	3,065	3,031	34	75	6,816	6,469	347	131	9,394	9,122	272
1959–60	45	3,247	3,221	26	79	7,032	6,645	387	134	9,240	9,010	230
1961–62	46	3,183	3,166	17	81	7,138	6,749	389	134	9,364	9,091	273
1963–64	46	3,180	3,168	12	82	7,303	6,878	425	133	10,679	10,372	307
1965–66	47	3,178	3,146	32	84	7,673	7,170	503	136	13,246	12,776	470
1967–68	48	3,422	3,375	47	85	7,944	7,318	626	138	16,454	15,805	649
1969–70	48	3,718	3,684	34	86	8,314	7,615	699	145	14,916	14,115	801
1970–71	48	3,745	3,703	42	89	8,919	8,110	809	147	17,421	16,181	1,240
1971–72	48	3,862	3,819	43	92	9,253	8,423	830	147	21,764	20,266	1,498
1972–73	51	4,047	3,992	55	97	10,307	9,388	919	152	27,205	25,037	2,168
1973–74	52	4,440	4,355	85	99	11,356	10,093	1,263	151	29,326	25,986	3,340
1974–75	52	4,773	4,627	146	104	12,447	10,818	1,629	154	29,296	24,881	4,415
1975–76	56	5,425	5,187	238	107	13,426	11,252	2,174	166	32,293	26,085	6,208
1976–77	57	5,138	4,764	374	109	13,461	10,891	2,570	169	34,104	26,447	7,657
1977–78	57	5,189	4,623	566	109	14,279	11,210	3,069	169	34,402	25,457	8,945
1978–79	58	5,434	4,794	640	109	14,786	11,381	3,405	175	35,206	25,180	10,026
1979–80	58	5,258	4,558	700	112	14,902	11,416	3,486	179	35,647	24,893	10,754
1980–81	58	5,460	4,672	788	116	15,505	11,672	3,833	176	36,331	24,563	11,768
1981–82	59	5,282	4,467	815	119	15,814	11,867	3,947	180	35,991	23,965	12,026
1982–83	59	5,585	4,631	954	118	15,484	11,350	4,134	177	36,853	23,550	13,303
1983–84	60	5,353	4,302	1,051	119	15,813	11,359	4,454	179	37,012	23,382	13,630
1984–85	59	5,339	4,233	1,106	120	16,041	11,167	4,874	181	37,491	23,070	14,421
1985–86	59	5,046	3,907	1,139	120	15,938	11,022	4,916	181	35,844	21,874	13,970
1986–87	58	4,741	3,603	1,138	121	15,428	10,431	4,997	179	36,056	21,561	14,495
1987–88	57	4,477	3,300	1,177	122	15,358	10,278	5,080	180	35,397	21,067	14,330
1988–89	58	4,265	3,124	1,141	124	15,460	10,310	5,150	182	35,634	21,069	14,565
1989–90	57	4,100	2,834	1,266	124	15,075	9,923	5,152	182	36,485	21,079	15,406
1990–91	55	3,699	2,510	1,189	121	15,043	9,629	5,414	179	37,945	21,643	16,302
1991–92	52	3,593	2,431	1,162	120	15,243	9,796	5,447	177	38,848	22,260	16,588
1992–93	55	3,605	2,383	1,222	122	15,531	9,679	5,852	184	40,302	23,182	17,120
1993–94	53	3,787	2,330	1,457	121	15,368	9,544	5,824	185	40,044	22,826	17,218

[1] Data prior to 1955–56 are not shown because they lack comparability with the figures for subsequent years.

SOURCE: U.S. Department of Education, National Center for Education Statistics, "Degrees and Other Formal Awards Conferred" surveys, and Integrated Postsecondary Education Data System (IPEDS), "Completions" surveys. (This table was prepared November 1995.)

Table 255.—First-professional degrees [1] conferred by institutions of higher education, by sex of student, control of institution, and field of study: 1982–83 to 1993–94

Control of institution and field of study	1982-83 Total	1983-84 Total	1984-85 Total	1985-86 Total	1986-87 Total	1987-88 Total	1988-89 Total	1989-90 Total	1990-91 Total	1991-92 Total	1991-92 Men	1991-92 Women	1992-93 Total	1992-93 Men	1992-93 Women	1993-94 Total	1993-94 Men	1993-94 Women
	2	3	4	5	6	7	8	9	10	11	12	13	14	15	16	17	18	19
Total, all institutions	**73,136**	**74,407**	**75,063**	**73,910**	**71,617**	**70,735**	**70,856**	**70,988**	**71,948**	**74,146**	**45,071**	**29,075**	**75,387**	**45,153**	**30,234**	**75,418**	**44,707**	**30,711**
Dentistry (D.D.S. or D.M.D.)	5,585	5,353	5,339	5,046	4,741	4,477	4,265	4,100	3,699	3,593	2,431	1,162	3,605	2,383	1,222	3,787	2,330	1,457
Medicine (M.D.)	15,484	15,813	16,041	15,938	15,428	15,358	15,460	15,075	15,043	15,243	9,796	5,447	15,531	9,679	5,852	15,368	9,544	5,824
Optometry (O.D.)	1,116	1,086	1,115	1,029	1,082	1,023	1,093	1,072	1,115	1,232	676	556	1,148	584	564	1,103	554	549
Osteopathic medicine (D.O.)	1,319	1,515	1,489	1,547	1,618	1,544	1,635	1,555	1,459	1,326	887	439	1,627	1,091	536	1,798	1,165	633
Pharmacy (Pharm.D.)	705	709	861	903	861	962	1,074	1,199	1,244	1,339	493	846	1,904	673	1,231	1,936	643	1,293
Podiatry (Pod.D. or D.P.) or podiatric medicine (D.P.M.)	631	607	582	612	590	645	636	675	589	504	359	145	476	350	126	465	330	135
Veterinary medicine (D.V.M.)	2,060	2,269	2,178	2,270	2,230	2,235	2,157	2,151	2,032	2,044	850	1,194	2,057	766	1,291	2,089	798	1,291
Chiropractic (D.C. or D.C.M.)	2,889	3,105	2,661	3,395	2,493	2,628	2,890	2,581	2,640	2,694	2,012	682	2,799	1,991	808	2,806	2,010	796
Law (LL.B. or J.D.)	36,853	37,012	37,491	35,844	36,056	35,397	35,634	36,485	37,945	38,848	22,260	16,588	40,302	23,182	17,120	40,044	22,826	17,218
Theology (M. Div., M.H.L., B.D., or Ord. and M.H.L./Rav.)	6,494	6,878	7,221	7,283	6,518	6,466	6,012	5,851	5,695	5,251	4,025	1,226	5,447	4,096	1,351	5,967	4,486	1,481
Other	0	60	85	43	0	0	0	244	487	2,072	1,282	790	491	358	133	55	21	34
Total, public institutions	**29,757**	**29,586**	**30,152**	**29,568**	**29,346**	**29,153**	**28,993**	**28,810**	**29,554**	**29,366**	**17,338**	**12,028**	**29,628**	**17,126**	**12,502**	**29,842**	**17,040**	**12,802**
Dentistry (D.D.S. or D.M.D.)	3,438	3,174	3,051	2,827	2,655	2,524	2,512	2,353	2,308	2,200	1,505	695	2,167	1,462	705	2,189	1,377	812
Medicine (M.D.)	9,569	9,674	10,071	9,991	9,711	9,557	9,491	9,108	9,364	9,259	5,908	3,351	9,370	5,843	3,527	9,506	5,977	3,529
Optometry (O.D.)	427	384	456	441	454	429	451	444	477	595	309	286	460	221	239	471	219	252
Osteopathic medicine (D.O.)	386	537	455	486	480	434	500	458	493	416	290	126	490	336	154	531	349	182
Pharmacy (Pharm.D.)	366	356	416	473	475	615	679	727	808	852	316	536	1,171	405	766	1,185	390	795
Podiatry (Pod.D. or D.P.) or podiatric medicine (D.P.M.)	0	0	0	0	0	0	0	0	0	0	0	0	0	0	0	0	0	0
Veterinary medicine (D.V.M.)	1,828	2,060	1,963	1,931	2,003	2,014	1,943	1,943	1,814	1,831	782	1,049	1,840	701	1,139	1,895	744	1,151
Chiropractic (D.C. or D.C.M.)	0	0	0	0	0	0	0	0	0	0	0	0	0	0	0	0	0	0
Law (LL.B. or J.D.)	13,743	13,380	13,695	13,419	13,568	13,580	13,417	13,585	14,290	14,097	8,160	5,937	14,130	8,158	5,972	14,065	7,984	6,081
Theology (M. Div., M.H.L., B.D., or Ord. and M.H.L./Rav.)	0	0	2	0	0	0	0	0	0	0	0	0	0	0	0	0	0	0
Other	0	21	43	0	0	0	0	192	0	116	68	48	0	0	0	0	0	0
Total, private institutions	**43,379**	**44,821**	**44,911**	**44,342**	**42,271**	**41,582**	**41,863**	**42,178**	**42,394**	**44,780**	**27,733**	**17,047**	**45,759**	**28,027**	**17,732**	**45,576**	**27,667**	**17,909**
Dentistry (D.D.S. or D.M.D.)	2,147	2,179	2,288	2,219	2,086	1,953	1,753	1,747	1,391	1,393	926	467	1,438	921	517	1,598	953	645
Medicine (M.D.)	5,915	6,139	5,970	5,947	5,717	5,801	5,969	5,967	5,679	5,984	3,888	2,096	6,161	3,836	2,325	5,862	3,567	2,295
Optometry (O.D.)	689	702	659	588	628	594	642	628	638	637	367	270	688	363	325	632	335	297
Osteopathic medicine (D.O.)	933	978	1,034	1,061	1,138	1,110	1,135	1,097	966	910	597	313	1,137	755	382	1,267	816	451
Pharmacy (Pharm.D.)	339	353	445	430	386	347	395	472	436	487	177	310	733	268	465	751	253	498
Podiatry (Pod.D. or D.P.) or podiatric medicine (D.P.M.)	631	607	582	612.0	590	645	636	675	589	504	359	145	476	350	126	465	330	135
Veterinary medicine (D.V.M.)	232	209	215	339	227	221	214	208	218	213	68	145	217	65	152	194	54	140
Chiropractic (D.C. or D.C.M.)	2,889	3,105	2,661	3,395	2,493	2,628	2,890	2,581	2,640	2,694	2,012	682	2,799	1,991	808	2,806	2,010	796
Law (LL.B. or J.D.)	23,110	23,632	23,796	22,425	22,488	21,817	22,217	22,900	23,655	24,751	14,100	10,651	26,172	15,024	11,148	25,979	14,842	11,137
Theology (M. Div., M.H.L., B.D., or Ord. and M.H.L./Rav.)	6,494	6,878	7,219	7,283	6,518	6,466	6,012	5,851	5,695	5,251	4,025	1,226	5,447	4,096	1,351	5,967	4,486	1,481
Other	0	39	42	43	0	0	0	52	487	1,956	1,214	742	491	358	133	55	21	34

[1] Includes degrees which require at least 6 years of college work for completion (including at least 2 years of preprofessional training).

SOURCE: U.S. Department of Education, National Center for Education Statistics, "Degrees and Other Formal Awards Conferred" surveys, and Integrated Postsecondary Education Data System (IPEDS), "Completions" survey. (This table was prepared November 1995.)

Table 256.—Associate degrees conferred by institutions of higher education, by racial/ethnic group and sex of student: 1976–77 to 1993–94

Year and sex of student	Total	White, non-Hispanic	Black, non-Hispanic	Hispanic	Asian or Pacific Islander	American Indian/Alaskan Native	Nonresident alien
1	2	3	4	5	6	7	8
	Number of degrees conferred						
1976–77, total [1]	404,956	342,290	33,159	16,636	7,044	2,498	3,329
Men	209,672	178,236	15,330	9,105	3,630	1,216	2,155
Women	195,284	164,054	17,829	7,531	3,414	1,282	1,174
1978–79, total [2]	396,745	331,092	34,979	16,269	7,518	2,336	4,551
Men	187,284	156,671	14,425	8,135	4,058	1,069	2,926
Women	209,461	174,421	20,554	8,134	3,460	1,267	1,625
1980–81, total [3]	410,174	339,167	35,330	17,800	8,650	2,584	6,643
Men	183,819	151,242	14,290	8,327	4,557	1,108	4,295
Women	226,355	187,925	21,040	9,473	4,093	1,476	2,348
1984–85, total [4]	429,815	355,343	35,791	19,407	9,914	2,953	6,407
Men	190,409	157,278	14,184	8,561	5,492	1,198	3,696
Women	239,406	198,065	21,607	10,846	4,422	1,755	2,711
1986–87, total [5]	436,304	361,861	35,447	19,334	11,779	3,195	4,688
Men	190,839	158,132	13,959	8,760	6,169	1,263	2,556
Women	245,465	203,729	21,488	10,574	5,610	1,932	2,132
1988–89, total [6,7]	432,144	354,865	34,664	20,384	12,519	3,331	6,381
Men	183,963	150,978	12,884	9,217	6,366	1,323	3,195
Women	248,181	203,887	21,780	11,167	6,153	2,008	3,186
1989–90, total [6,8]	450,263	369,580	35,327	22,195	13,482	3,530	6,149
Men	188,631	154,748	13,147	9,859	6,477	1,433	2,967
Women	261,632	214,832	22,180	12,336	7,005	2,097	3,182
1990–91, total [6,9]	462,030	376,081	37,657	24,251	13,725	3,672	6,644
Men	190,221	155,330	13,718	10,210	6,440	1,373	3,150
Women	271,809	220,751	23,939	14,041	7,285	2,299	3,494
1991–92, total [6,10]	494,387	400,530	39,411	26,905	15,596	4,008	7,937
Men	202,808	164,799	14,294	11,536	7,254	1,531	3,394
Women	291,579	235,731	25,117	15,369	8,342	2,477	4,543
1992–93, total [6,11]	508,154	405,883	42,340	29,991	16,632	4,379	8,929
Men	209,051	167,312	15,497	12,924	7,877	1,663	3,778
Women	299,103	238,571	26,843	17,067	8,755	2,716	5,151
1993–94, total [6,12]	540,923	428,273	46,451	32,438	18,659	4,975	10,127
Men	220,191	174,947	17,379	13,395	8,403	1,895	4,172
Women	320,732	253,326	29,072	19,043	10,256	3,080	5,955
	Percentage distribution of degrees conferred						
1976–77, total [1]	100.0	84.5	8.2	4.1	1.7	0.6	0.8
Men	100.0	85.0	7.3	4.3	1.7	0.6	1.0
Women	100.0	84.0	9.1	3.9	1.7	0.7	0.6
1978–79, total [2]	100.0	83.5	8.8	4.1	1.9	0.6	1.1
Men	100.0	83.7	7.7	4.3	2.2	0.6	1.6
Women	100.0	83.3	9.8	3.9	1.7	0.6	0.8
1980–81, total [3]	100.0	82.7	8.6	4.3	2.1	0.6	1.6
Men	100.0	82.3	7.8	4.5	2.5	0.6	2.3
Women	100.0	83.0	9.3	4.2	1.8	0.7	1.0
1984–85, total [4]	100.0	82.7	8.3	4.5	2.3	0.7	1.5
Men	100.0	82.6	7.4	4.5	2.9	0.6	1.9
Women	100.0	82.7	9.0	4.5	1.8	0.7	1.1
1986–87, total [5]	100.0	82.9	8.1	4.4	2.7	0.7	1.1
Men	100.0	82.9	7.3	4.6	3.2	0.7	1.3
Women	100.0	83.0	8.8	4.3	2.3	0.8	0.9
1988–89, total [6,7]	100.0	82.1	8.0	4.7	2.9	0.8	1.5
Men	100.0	82.1	7.0	5.0	3.5	0.7	1.7
Women	100.0	82.2	8.8	4.5	2.5	0.8	1.3
1989–90, total [6,8]	100.0	82.1	7.8	4.9	3.0	0.8	1.4
Men	100.0	82.0	7.0	5.2	3.4	0.8	1.6
Women	100.0	82.1	8.5	4.7	2.7	0.8	1.2
1990–91, total [6,9]	100.0	81.4	8.2	5.2	3.0	0.8	1.4
Men	100.0	81.7	7.2	5.4	3.4	0.7	1.7
Women	100.0	81.2	8.8	5.2	2.7	0.8	1.3
1991–92, total [6,10]	100.0	81.0	8.0	5.4	3.2	0.8	1.6
Men	100.0	81.3	7.0	5.7	3.6	0.8	1.7
Women	100.0	80.8	8.6	5.3	2.9	0.8	1.6
1992–93, total [6,11]	100.0	79.9	8.3	5.9	3.3	0.9	1.8
Men	100.0	80.0	7.4	6.2	3.8	0.8	1.8
Women	100.0	79.8	9.0	5.7	2.9	0.9	1.7
1993–94, total [6,12]	100.0	79.2	8.6	6.0	3.4	0.9	1.9
Men	100.0	79.5	7.9	6.1	3.8	0.9	1.9
Women	100.0	79.0	9.1	5.9	3.2	1.0	1.9

[1] Excludes 1,170 men and 251 women whose racial/ethnic group was not available.
[2] Excludes 4,807 men and 1,150 women whose racial/ethnic group was not available.
[3] Excludes 4,819 men and 1,384 women whose racial/ethnic group was not available.
[4] Racial/ethnic data were imputed for approximately 45,400 men and 55,400 women. This tabulation excludes 11,490 men and 10,862 women whose racial/ethnic group could not be imputed. In addition, data for 1,033 men and 1,512 women were not available by field of study and were not imputed by race.
[5] Excludes 3 men and 1 woman whose racial/ethnic group was not available.
[6] Reported racial/ethnic distributions of students by level of degree, field of degree, and sex were used to estimate race/ethnicity for students whose race/ethnicity was not reported.
[7] Excludes 2,353 men and 2,267 women whose racial/ethnic group and field of study were not available.
[8] Excludes 2,564 men and 2,275 women whose racial/ethnic group and field of study were not available.

[9] Excludes 8,413 men and 11,277 women whose racial/ethnic group and field of study were not available.
[10] Excludes 4,673 men and 5,171 women whose racial/ethnic group and field of study were not available.
[11] Excludes 2,913 men and 3,689 women whose racial/ethnic group and field of study were not available.
[12] Excludes 799 men and 727 women whose racial/ethnic group and field of study were not available.

SOURCE: U.S. Department of Education, National Center for Education Statistics, "Degrees and Other Formal Awards Conferred" surveys, and Integrated Postsecondary Education Data System (IPEDS), "Completions" surveys. (This table was prepared May 1996.)

Table 257.—Associate degrees conferred by institutions of higher education, by racial/ethnic group, major field of study, and sex of student: 1993–94

Major field of study	Total							Men							Women						
	Total	White, non-His-panic	Black, non-His-panic	His-panic	Asian/ Pacific Islander	Amer-ican Indian/ Alas-kan Native	Non-resi-dent alien	Total	White, non-His-panic	Black, non-His-panic	His-panic	Asian/ Pacific Is-lander	Amer-ican Indian/ Alas-kan Native	Non-resi-dent alien	Total	White, non-His-panic	Black, non-His-panic	His-panic	Asian/ Pacific Is-lander	Amer-ican Indian/ Alas-kan Native	Non-resi-dent alien
1	2	3	4	5	6	7	8	9	10	11	12	13	14	15	16	17	18	19	20	21	22
All fields, total [1]	540,923	428,273	46,451	32,438	18,659	4,975	10,127	220,191	174,947	17,379	13,395	8,403	1,895	4,172	320,732	253,326	29,072	19,043	10,256	3,080	5,955
Agriculture and natural resources	5,720	5,363	54	108	33	87	75	3,869	3,627	35	74	26	59	48	1,851	1,736	19	34	7	28	27
Architecture and related programs	353	260	8	42	31	0	12	115	66	6	26	12	0	5	238	194	2	16	19	0	7
Area, ethnic, and cultural studies	92	20	13	11	0	20	28	34	9	8	3	0	11	3	58	11	5	8	0	9	25
Biological sciences/life sciences	1,852	1,334	99	152	175	36	56	744	528	31	68	78	17	22	1,108	806	68	84	97	19	34
Business management and administrative services	108,310	81,952	11,895	6,763	4,047	892	2,761	34,068	26,006	3,500	1,984	1,366	226	986	74,242	55,946	8,395	4,779	2,681	666	1,775
Communications	2,110	1,696	180	104	54	16	60	984	823	66	48	16	7	24	1,126	873	114	56	38	9	36
Communications technologies	2,789	2,252	343	110	35	10	39	1,807	1,474	223	71	24	4	11	982	778	120	39	11	6	28
Computer and information sciences	9,456	6,801	1,108	697	499	108	243	4,740	3,503	432	353	280	36	136	4,716	3,298	676	344	219	72	107
Construction trades	1,724	1,447	90	63	74	38	12	1,644	1,383	82	62	72	35	10	80	64	8	1	2	3	2
Education	10,021	8,064	897	672	105	196	87	3,149	2,552	339	153	25	56	24	6,872	5,512	558	519	80	140	63
Engineering	2,799	2,195	184	122	189	19	90	2,447	1,949	152	100	152	17	77	352	246	32	22	37	2	13
Engineering-related technologies	36,877	29,875	2,922	2,199	1,247	259	375	32,784	26,671	2,470	1,987	1,122	221	313	4,093	3,204	452	212	125	38	62
English language and literature/letters	1,354	794	70	173	92	12	213	493	275	26	69	27	4	92	861	519	44	104	65	8	121
Foreign languages and literatures	517	367	5	62	27	8	45	151	105	3	21	11	2	9	366	262	2	41	16	6	36
Health professions and related sciences	95,832	81,747	6,758	3,469	2,293	761	804	15,476	12,616	1,140	826	571	153	170	80,356	69,131	5,618	2,643	1,722	608	634
Home economics and vocational home economics	7,562	5,634	885	553	257	79	154	643	476	55	31	58	12	11	6,919	5,158	830	522	199	67	143
Law and legal studies	9,008	7,190	962	590	127	86	53	1,103	788	165	91	31	17	11	7,905	6,402	797	499	96	69	42
Liberal arts and sciences, general studies, and humanities	164,575	127,907	13,699	11,384	6,487	1,502	3,596	65,879	51,217	5,239	4,426	2,844	534	1,619	98,696	76,690	8,460	6,958	3,643	968	1,977
Library science	118	103	8	3	4	0	0	16	11	0	1	3	1	0	102	92	7	7	1	0	0
Mathematics	765	509	40	87	79	11	39	436	278	29	46	50	7	26	329	231	11	41	29	4	13
Mechanics and repairers	11,618	9,579	808	558	453	103	117	10,873	9,024	725	505	413	96	110	745	555	83	53	40	7	7
Multi/interdisciplinary studies	8,461	6,883	729	396	352	47	54	4,059	3,281	360	192	179	25	22	4,402	3,602	369	204	173	22	32
Parks, recreation, leisure and fitness studies	767	614	74	39	38	11	11	465	359	56	23	13	9	5	302	255	18	16	5	0	6
Philosophy and religion	94	78	5	7	4	0	0	55	45	5	2	0	0	0	39	33	0	5	5	0	0
Physical sciences and science technologies	2,622	2,067	185	123	161	26	60	1,527	1,242	76	69	94	13	33	1,095	825	109	54	67	13	27
Precision production trades	9,661	7,972	384	704	434	84	83	7,779	6,453	293	588	318	70	57	1,882	1,519	91	116	116	14	26
Protective services	19,416	16,030	1,677	1,156	264	172	117	13,956	11,930	872	776	197	115	66	5,460	4,100	805	380	67	57	51
Psychology	1,756	1,347	152	156	38	39	24	433	318	49	40	10	10	6	1,323	1,029	103	116	28	29	18
Public administration and services	3,720	2,457	724	331	78	79	51	762	480	151	69	27	17	18	2,958	1,977	573	262	51	62	33
R.O.T.C. and military technologies	265	221	40	4	0	0	0	245	207	35	3	0	0	0	20	14	5	1	0	0	0
Social sciences and history	4,100	2,780	412	479	196	106	127	1,631	1,137	160	160	83	33	58	2,469	1,643	252	319	113	73	69
Theological studies/religious vocations	642	511	71	18	19	5	18	343	268	39	12	16	2	6	299	243	32	6	3	2	12
Transportation and material moving	1,988	1,663	143	74	38	15	55	1,654	1,397	124	66	30	11	26	334	266	19	8	8	4	29
Visual and performing arts	13,979	10,561	824	1,029	749	148	668	5,827	4,449	432	450	252	76	168	8,152	6,112	392	579	497	72	500

[1] Reported racial/ethnic distributions of students by level of degree, field of degree, and sex were used to estimate race/ethnicity for students whose race/ethnicity was not reported. Excludes 799 men and 727 women whose racial/ethnic group and field of study were not available.

NOTE.—To facilitate trend comparisons, certain aggregations have been made of the degree fields as reported in the IPEDS "Completions" survey: "Agriculture and natural resources" includes Agribusiness and agriculture production,

Agricultural sciences, and Conservation and renewable natural resources; and "Business management and administrative services" includes Business and management, Business and office, Marketing and distribution, and Consumer and personal services.

SOURCE: U.S. Department of Education, National Center for Education Statistics, Integrated Postsecondary Education Data System (IPEDS), "Completions" survey. (This table was prepared May 1996.)

Table 258.—Associate degrees conferred by institutions of higher education, by racial/ethnic group, major field of study, and sex of student: 1992–93

Major field of study	Total							Men							Women						
	Total	White, non-His-panic	Black, non-His-panic	His-panic	Asian/ Pacific Islander	Amer-ican Indian/ Alas-kan Native	Non-resi-dent alien	Total	White, non-His-panic	Black, non-His-panic	His-panic	Asian/ Pacific Is-lander	Amer-ican Indian/ Alas-kan Native	Non-resi-dent alien	Total	White, non-His-panic	Black, non-His-panic	His-panic	Asian/ Pacific Is-lander	Amer-ican Indian/ Alas-kan Native	Non-resi-dent alien
1	2	3	4	5	6	7	8	9	10	11	12	13	14	15	16	17	18	19	20	21	22
All fields, total [1]	508,154	405,883	42,340	29,991	16,632	4,379	8,929	209,051	167,312	15,497	12,924	7,877	1,663	3,778	299,103	238,571	26,843	17,067	8,755	2,716	5,151
Agriculture and natural resources	5,398	5,130	47	75	18	58	70	3,750	3,569	40	46	11	37	47	1,648	1,561	7	29	7	21	23
Architecture and related programs	372	300	12	23	24	1	12	119	83	8	11	12	0	5	253	217	4	12	12	1	7
Area, ethnic, and cultural studies	33	5	10	5	7	7		10	7	7			2		23		3	2	7	5	2
Biological sciences/life sciences	1,435	1,000	96	131	145	25	38	588	406	31	62	68	7	14	847	594	65	69	77	18	24
Business management and administrative services	103,856	79,407	11,088	6,595	3,629	848	2,289	33,274	25,629	3,084	2,127	1,332	210	892	70,582	53,778	8,004	4,468	2,297	638	1,397
Communications	1,904	1,564	144	79	53	10	54	945	805	68	27	26	4	15	959	759	76	52	27	6	39
Communications technologies	1,828	1,468	178	98	42	7	35	1,196	975	101	65	29	4	22	632	493	77	33	13	3	13
Computer and information sciences	9,196	6,528	1,056	792	480	109	231	4,541	3,322	418	388	248	36	129	4,655	3,206	638	404	232	73	102
Construction trades	1,653	1,399	76	47	86	40	5	1,581	1,339	73	46	79	39	5	72	60	3	1	7	1	0
Education	9,315	7,313	867	732	140	198	65	3,031	2,356	300	221	59	72	23	6,284	4,957	567	511	81	126	42
Engineering	2,478	1,936	207	109	139	8	79	2,169	1,699	178	86	127	7	72	309	237	29	23	12	1	7
Engineering-related technologies	36,321	29,417	2,750	2,157	1,431	221	345	32,631	26,531	2,306	1,989	1,317	188	300	3,690	2,886	444	168	114	33	45
English language and literature/letters	1,320	758	104	138	59	19	242	469	243	57	49	20	9	91	851	515	47	89	39	10	151
Foreign languages and literatures	511	373	9	83	12	4	30	153	116	2	24	5	1	5	358	257	7	59	7	3	25
Health professions and related sciences	86,237	73,795	6,187	3,032	1,915	662	646	12,971	10,613	869	706	524	115	144	73,266	63,182	5,318	2,326	1,391	547	502
Home economics and vocational home economics	6,914	5,329	767	417	248	47	106	655	485	66	32	62	2	8	6,259	4,844	701	385	186	45	98
Law and legal studies	8,028	6,617	751	506	91	45	18	959	719	127	83	21	5	4	7,069	5,898	624	423	70	40	14
Liberal arts and sciences, general studies, and humanities	158,040	124,989	12,593	10,359	5,441	1,287	3,371	63,867	50,543	4,860	4,156	2,369	477	1,462	94,173	74,446	7,733	6,203	3,072	810	1,909
Library science	85	79	2	3	1	0	0	9	9	0	0	0	0	0	76	70	2	3	1	0	0
Mathematics	743	516	26	69	70	15	47	428	295	10	40	46	12	25	315	221	16	29	24	3	22
Mechanics and repairers	10,966	8,878	670	634	548	119	117	10,280	8,380	595	596	493	109	107	686	498	75	38	55	10	10
Multi/interdisciplinary studies	8,486	7,089	621	361	302	39	74	4,075	3,430	273	169	145	20	38	4,411	3,659	348	192	157	19	36
Parks, recreation, leisure and fitness studies	717	549	98	37	19	6	8	429	309	71	27	15	4	3	288	240	10	10	10	2	5
Philosophy and religion	111	95	6	8	2	0	0	76	68	3	3	2	0	0	35	27	3	5	0	0	0
Physical sciences and science technologies	2,241	1,784	143	100	123	12	79	1,296	1,072	62	55	59	7	41	945	712	81	45	64	5	38
Precision production trades	9,204	7,654	411	642	349	86	62	7,393	6,174	326	533	254	66	40	1,811	1,480	85	109	95	20	22
Protective services	16,834	14,077	1,382	952	215	163	45	12,289	10,593	724	666	173	101	32	4,545	3,484	658	286	42	62	13
Psychology	1,237	913	111	144	34	18	17	282	197	33	38	7	6	1	955	716	78	106	27	12	16
Public administration and services	3,301	2,240	635	296	47	69	14	648	446	115	55	17	11	4	2,653	1,794	520	241	30	58	10
R.O.T.C. and military technologies	52	52	21	1	2	0	0	44	25	17	1	1	0	0	8	3	4	0	0	1	0
Social sciences and history	3,930	2,555	507	458	192	100	118	1,678	1,086	255	174	82	33	48	2,252	1,469	252	284	110	67	70
Theological studies/religious vocations	508	438	33	12	5	5	15	281	237	20	12	2	3	7	227	201	13	0	3	2	8
Transportation and material moving	2,210	1,927	68	98	60	18	39	1,850	1,633	56	84	42	12	23	360	294	12	14	18	6	16
Visual and performing arts	12,690	9,733	664	801	703	133	656	5,084	3,924	342	353	230	64	171	7,606	5,809	322	448	473	69	485

[1] Reported racial/ethnic distributions of students by level of degree, field of degree, and sex were used to estimate race/ethnicity for students whose race/ethnicity was not reported. Excludes 2,913 men and 3,689 women whose racial/ethnic group and field of study were not available.

NOTE.—To facilitate trend comparisons, certain aggregations have been made of the degree fields as reported in the IPEDS "Completions" survey. "Agriculture and natural resources" includes Agribusiness and agriculture production, Agricultural sciences, and Conservation and renewable natural resources; and "Business management and administrative services" includes Business and management, Business and office, Marketing and distribution, and Consumer and personal services.

SOURCE: U.S. Department of Education, National Center for Education Statistics, Integrated Postsecondary Education Data System (IPEDS), "Completions" survey. (This table was prepared January 1995.)

Table 259.—Bachelor's degrees conferred by institutions of higher education, by racial/ethnic group and sex of student: 1976–77 to 1993–94

Year and sex of student	Total	White, non-Hispanic	Black, non-Hispanic	Hispanic	Asian or Pacific Islander	American Indian/Alaskan Native	Nonresident alien
1	2	3	4	5	6	7	8
Number of degrees conferred							
1976–77, total [1]	917,900	807,688	58,636	18,743	13,793	3,326	15,714
Men	494,424	438,161	25,147	10,318	7,638	1,804	11,356
Women	423,476	369,527	33,489	8,425	6,155	1,522	4,358
1978–79, total [2]	919,540	802,542	60,246	20,096	15,407	3,410	17,839
Men	476,065	418,215	24,659	10,418	8,261	1,736	12,776
Women	443,475	384,327	35,587	9,678	7,146	1,674	5,063
1980–81, total [3]	934,800	807,319	60,673	21,832	18,794	3,593	22,589
Men	469,625	406,173	24,511	10,810	10,107	1,700	16,324
Women	465,175	401,146	36,162	11,022	8,687	1,893	6,265
1984–85, total [4]	968,311	826,106	57,473	25,874	25,395	4,246	29,217
Men	476,148	405,085	23,018	12,402	13,554	1,998	20,091
Women	492,163	421,021	34,455	13,472	11,841	2,248	9,126
1986–87, total [5]	991,264	841,818	56,560	26,988	32,624	3,968	29,306
Men	480,782	406,749	22,501	12,865	17,253	1,817	19,597
Women	510,482	435,069	34,059	14,123	15,371	2,151	9,709
1988–89, total [5,6]	1,016,350	859,703	58,078	29,918	37,674	3,951	27,026
Men	481,946	407,154	22,370	13,950	19,260	1,730	17,482
Women	534,404	452,549	35,708	15,968	18,414	2,221	9,544
1989–90, total [5,7]	1,048,631	884,376	61,063	32,844	39,248	4,392	26,708
Men	490,317	413,573	23,262	14,941	19,721	1,859	16,961
Women	558,314	470,803	37,801	17,903	19,527	2,533	9,747
1990–91, total [5,8]	1,081,280	904,062	65,341	36,612	41,618	4,513	29,134
Men	496,424	415,505	24,328	16,158	20,678	1,901	17,854
Women	584,856	488,557	41,013	20,454	20,940	2,612	11,280
1991–92, total [5,9]	1,129,833	936,771	72,326	40,761	46,720	5,176	28,079
Men	516,976	429,842	26,956	17,976	23,248	2,182	16,772
Women	612,857	506,929	45,370	22,785	23,472	2,994	11,307
1992–93, total [5,10]	1,159,931	947,309	77,872	45,376	51,463	5,671	32,240
Men	530,541	435,084	28,883	19,865	25,293	2,449	18,967
Women	629,390	512,225	48,989	25,511	26,170	3,222	13,273
1993–94, total [5,11]	1,165,973	936,227	83,576	50,241	55,660	6,189	34,080
Men	530,804	429,121	30,648	21,807	26,938	2,616	19,674
Women	635,169	507,106	52,928	28,434	28,722	3,573	14,406
Percentage distribution of degrees conferred							
1976–77, total[1]	100.0	88.0	6.4	2.0	1.5	0.4	1.7
Men	100.0	88.6	5.1	2.1	1.5	0.4	2.3
Women	100.0	87.3	7.9	2.0	1.5	0.4	1.0
1978–79, total[2]	100.0	87.3	6.6	2.2	1.7	0.4	1.9
Men	100.0	87.8	5.2	2.2	1.7	0.4	2.7
Women	100.0	86.7	8.0	2.2	1.6	0.4	1.1
1980–81, total[3]	100.0	86.4	6.5	2.3	2.0	0.4	2.4
Men	100.0	86.5	5.2	2.3	2.2	0.4	3.5
Women	100.0	86.2	7.8	2.4	1.9	0.4	1.3
1984–85, total[4]	100.0	85.3	5.9	2.7	2.6	0.4	3.0
Men	100.0	85.1	4.8	2.6	2.8	0.4	4.2
Women	100.0	85.5	7.0	2.7	2.4	0.5	1.9
1986–87, total[5]	100.0	84.9	5.7	2.7	3.3	0.4	3.0
Men	100.0	84.6	4.7	2.7	3.6	0.4	4.1
Women	100.0	85.2	6.7	2.8	3.0	0.4	1.9
1988–89, total[5,6]	100.0	84.6	5.7	2.9	3.7	0.4	2.7
Men	100.0	84.5	4.6	2.9	4.0	0.4	3.6
Women	100.0	84.7	6.7	3.0	3.4	0.4	1.8
1989–90, total[5,7]	100.0	84.3	5.8	3.1	3.7	0.4	2.5
Men	100.0	84.3	4.7	3.0	4.0	0.4	3.5
Women	100.0	84.3	6.8	3.2	3.5	0.5	1.7
1990–91, total[5,8]	100.0	83.6	6.0	3.4	3.8	0.4	2.7
Men	100.0	83.7	4.9	3.3	4.2	0.4	3.6
Women	100.0	83.5	7.0	3.5	3.6	0.4	1.9
1991–92, total[5,9]	100.0	82.9	6.4	3.6	4.1	0.5	2.5
Men	100.0	83.1	5.2	3.5	4.5	0.4	3.2
Women	100.0	82.7	7.4	3.7	3.8	0.5	1.8
1992–93, total[5,10]	100.0	81.7	6.7	3.9	4.4	0.5	2.8
Men	100.0	82.0	5.4	3.7	4.8	0.5	3.6
Women	100.0	81.4	7.8	4.1	4.2	0.5	2.1
1993–94, total[5,11]	100.0	80.3	7.2	4.3	4.8	0.5	2.9
Men	100.0	80.8	5.8	4.1	5.1	0.5	3.7
Women	100.0	79.8	8.3	4.5	4.5	0.6	2.3

[1] Excludes 1,121 men and 528 women whose racial/ethnic group was not available.
[2] Excludes 1,279 men and 571 women whose racial/ethnic group was not available.
[3] Excludes 258 men and 82 women whose racial/ethnic group was not available.
[4] Excludes 6,380 men and 4,786 women whose racial/ethnic group was not available.
[5] Reported racial/ethnic distributions of students by level of degree, field of degree, and sex were used to estimate race/ethnicity for students whose race/ethnicity was not reported.
[6] Excludes 1,400 men and 1,005 women whose racial/ethnic group was not available.
[7] Excludes 1,379 men and 1,334 women whose racial/ethnic group was not available.

[8] Excludes 7,621 men and 5,637 women whose racial/ethnic group was not available.
[9] Excludes 3,835 men and 2,885 women whose racial/ethnic group was not available.
[10] Excludes 2,340 men and 2,907 women whose racial/ethnic group was not available.
[11] Excludes 1,618 men and 1,684 women whose racial/ethnic group was not available.

SOURCE: U.S. Department of Education, National Center for Education Statistics, "Degrees and Other Formal Awards Conferred" surveys, and Integrated Postsecondary Education Data System (IPEDS), "Completions" surveys. (This table was prepared February 1996.)

Table 260.—Bachelor's degrees conferred by institutions of higher education, by racial/ethnic group, major field of study, and sex of student: 1993–94

Major field of study	Total							Men							Women						
	Total	White, non-Hispanic	Black, non-Hispanic	Hispanic	Asian/Pacific Islander	American Indian/Alaskan Native	Nonresident alien	Total	White, non-Hispanic	Black, non-Hispanic	Hispanic	Asian/Pacific Islander	American Indian/Alaskan Native	Nonresident alien	Total	White, non-Hispanic	Black, non-Hispanic	Hispanic	Asian/Pacific Islander	American Indian/Alaskan Native	Nonresident alien
1	2	3	4	5	6	7	8	9	10	11	12	13	14	15	16	17	18	19	20	21	22
All fields, total [1]	1,165,973	936,227	83,576	50,241	55,660	6,189	34,080	530,804	429,121	30,648	21,807	26,938	2,616	19,674	635,169	507,106	52,928	28,434	28,722	3,573	14,406
Agriculture and natural resources	18,070	16,404	502	386	309	128	341	11,748	10,801	266	223	148	78	232	6,322	5,603	236	163	161	50	109
Architecture and related programs	8,975	6,961	348	479	717	36	434	5,764	4,495	233	305	424	22	285	3,211	2,466	115	174	293	14	149
Area, ethnic, and cultural studies	5,573	3,737	636	484	479	53	184	1,958	1,318	215	161	148	19	97	3,615	2,419	421	323	331	34	87
Biological/life sciences	51,383	38,736	3,022	2,137	6,083	252	1,153	25,050	19,298	944	1,063	3,057	115	573	26,333	19,438	2,078	1,074	3,026	137	580
Business management and administrative services	246,654	191,111	20,366	10,264	12,486	1,036	11,391	129,161	103,573	7,966	4,997	5,619	474	6,532	117,493	87,538	12,400	5,267	6,867	562	4,859
Communications	51,164	42,453	4,122	1,942	1,301	223	1,123	21,023	17,854	1,427	765	450	95	432	30,141	24,599	2,695	1,177	851	128	691
Communications technologies	663	535	88	10	11	2	17	336	284	32	6	4	0	10	327	251	56	7	7	2	7
Computer and information sciences	24,200	16,191	2,455	899	2,301	79	2,275	17,317	12,305	1,188	584	1,511	60	1,669	6,883	3,886	1,267	315	790	19	606
Construction trades	75	57	11	1	0	1	5	70	55	8	1	1	1	3	5	2	3	0	0	0	0
Education	107,600	95,482	6,316	3,295	1,122	739	646	24,450	21,549	1,477	746	270	199	209	83,150	73,933	4,839	2,549	852	540	437
Engineering	62,220	45,639	2,712	2,452	6,652	223	4,542	52,035	38,677	1,824	2,005	5,352	183	3,994	10,185	6,962	888	447	1,300	40	548
Engineering-related technologies	15,823	12,682	1,190	651	726	98	476	14,386	11,693	950	582	652	85	424	1,437	989	240	69	74	13	52
English language and literature/letters	53,924	46,166	3,250	1,980	1,738	262	528	18,425	16,150	829	639	548	93	166	35,499	30,016	2,421	1,341	1,190	169	362
Foreign languages and literatures	14,378	10,963	510	1,798	588	55	464	4,304	3,374	113	515	162	18	122	10,074	7,589	397	1,283	426	37	342
Health professions and related sciences	74,421	62,756	4,896	2,274	3,070	398	1,027	13,062	10,861	674	469	709	82	267	61,359	51,895	4,222	1,805	2,361	316	760
Home economics and vocational home economics	15,522	13,369	959	394	476	87	237	1,933	1,618	148	53	64	11	39	13,589	11,751	811	341	412	76	198
Law and legal studies	2,171	1,735	208	121	87	14	6	648	503	52	46	37	8	2	1,523	1,232	156	75	50	6	4
Liberal arts and sciences, general studies, and humanities	33,397	26,450	2,968	2,084	1,072	302	521	13,117	10,715	995	671	396	105	235	20,280	15,735	1,973	1,413	676	197	286
Library science	62	54	4	0	0	0	4	5	5	0	0	0	0	0	57	50	4	0	0	0	3
Mathematics	14,396	11,300	1,004	526	944	61	561	7,735	6,051	465	291	535	30	363	6,661	5,249	539	235	409	31	198
Mechanics and repairers	107	88	3	2	1	2	11	106	88	3	2	0	2	11	1	0	0	0	1	0	0
Multi/interdisciplinary studies	25,167	19,778	1,687	1,884	1,340	141	337	9,058	7,264	557	451	561	57	168	16,109	12,514	1,130	1,433	779	84	169
Parks, recreation, leisure and fitness studies	11,470	10,190	556	424	118	75	107	5,823	5,085	320	257	66	32	63	5,647	5,105	236	167	52	43	44
Philosophy and religion	7,546	6,416	319	305	336	35	135	4,844	4,136	207	202	200	20	79	2,702	2,280	112	103	136	15	56
Physical sciences and science technologies	18,400	15,007	946	523	1,126	85	713	12,223	10,220	475	342	666	53	467	6,177	4,787	471	181	460	32	246
Precision production trades	420	355	41	6	9	1	8	308	264	31	3	5	0	5	112	91	10	3	4	1	3
Protective services	23,009	17,393	3,482	1,412	403	160	159	14,169	11,254	1,634	798	280	96	107	8,840	6,139	1,848	614	123	64	52
Psychology	69,259	56,220	5,359	3,581	2,841	404	854	18,642	15,307	1,266	917	829	116	207	50,617	40,913	4,093	2,664	2,012	288	647
Public administration and services	17,815	13,253	2,717	1,067	396	188	194	3,919	2,879	593	258	115	35	39	13,896	10,374	2,124	809	281	153	155
R.O.T.C. and military sciences	19	18	0	0	1	0	0	16	15	0	0	1	0	0	3	3	0	0	0	0	0
Social sciences and history	133,680	105,776	10,460	6,851	6,408	783	3,402	72,006	58,555	4,543	3,453	3,133	385	1,937	61,674	47,221	5,917	3,398	3,275	398	1,465
Theological studies/religious vocations	5,434	4,770	188	121	159	20	176	4,125	3,649	144	85	99	16	132	1,309	1,121	44	36	60	4	44
Transportation and material moving	3,923	3,425	183	134	79	18	84	3,500	3,057	156	119	71	16	81	423	368	27	15	8	2	3
Visual and performing arts	49,053	40,757	2,068	1,754	2,279	228	1,967	19,538	16,170	913	798	824	110	723	29,515	24,587	1,155	956	1,455	118	1,244

[1] Reported racial/ethnic distributions of students by level of degree, field of degree, and sex were used to estimate race/ethnicity for students whose race/ethnicity was not reported. Excludes 1,618 men and 1,684 women whose racial/ethnic group and field of study were not available.

NOTE.—To facilitate trend comparisons, certain aggregations have been made of the degree fields as reported in the IPEDS "Completions" survey: "Agriculture and natural resources" includes Agribusiness and agriculture production, Agricultural sciences, and Conservation and renewable natural resources; and "Business management and administrative services" includes Business and management, Business and office, Marketing and distribution, and Consumer and personal services.

SOURCE: U.S. Department of Education, National Center for Education Statistics, Integrated Postsecondary Education Data System (IPEDS), "Completions" survey. (This table was prepared February 1996.)

Table 261.—Bachelor's degrees conferred by institutions of higher education, by racial/ethnic group, major field of study, and sex of student: 1992–93

Major field of study	Total							Men							Women						
	Total	White, non-His-panic	Black, non-His-panic	His-panic	Asian/ Pacific Islander	American Indian/ Alaskan Native	Non-resi-dent alien	Total	White, non-His-panic	Black, non-His-panic	His-panic	Asian/ Pacific Is-lander	American Indian/ Alas-kan Native	Non-resi-dent alien	Total	White, non-His-panic	Black, non-His-panic	His-panic	Asian/ Pacific Is-lander	American Indian/ Alas-kan Native	Non-resi-dent alien
1	2	3	4	5	6	7	8	9	10	11	12	13	14	15	16	17	18	19	20	21	22
All fields, total [1]	1,159,931	947,309	77,872	45,376	51,463	5,671	32,240	530,541	435,084	28,883	19,865	25,293	2,449	18,967	629,390	512,225	48,989	25,511	26,170	3,222	13,273
Agriculture and natural resources	16,778	15,152	435	325	318	90	458	11,080	10,101	233	210	168	63	305	5,698	5,051	202	115	150	27	153
Architecture and related programs	9,167	7,289	293	461	667	35	422	5,940	4,762	200	313	373	23	269	3,227	2,527	93	148	294	12	153
Area, ethnic, and cultural studies	5,481	3,864	530	437	463	51	136	1,977	1,430	191	140	150	17	49	3,504	2,434	339	297	313	34	87
Biological/life sciences	47,038	35,766	2,784	1,855	5,203	215	1,215	22,842	17,673	898	909	2,690	105	1,215	24,196	18,093	1,886	946	2,513	110	648
Business management and administrative services	256,842	205,083	19,187	9,588	11,780	1,051	10,153	135,573	111,478	7,644	4,711	5,249	530	5,961	121,269	93,605	11,543	4,877	6,531	521	4,192
Communications	53,874	45,480	4,164	1,883	1,178	201	968	21,601	18,621	1,435	706	399	86	354	32,273	26,859	2,729	1,177	779	115	614
Communications technologies	832	666	93	26	12	10	25	427	359	35	12	4	3	14	405	307	58	14	8	7	11
Computer and information sciences	24,200	16,502	2,261	860	2,294	83	2,200	17,403	12,591	1,071	565	1,524	54	1,598	6,797	3,911	1,190	295	770	29	602
Construction trades	69	58	7	1	2	1	0	64	53	7	1	2	1	0	5	5	0	0	0	0	0
Education	107,781	96,857	5,590	2,973	1,100	644	617	23,233	20,538	1,380	657	288	154	216	84,548	76,319	4,210	2,316	812	490	401
Engineering	61,973	45,803	2,630	2,312	6,542	180	4,506	52,185	39,071	1,802	1,884	5,241	145	4,042	9,788	6,732	828	428	1,301	35	464
Engineering-related technologies	15,904	12,929	1,068	622	765	103	417	14,485	11,878	882	553	692	91	389	1,419	1,051	186	69	73	12	28
English language and literature/letters	56,133	48,957	3,065	1,756	1,583	235	537	19,247	17,129	751	605	492	94	176	36,886	31,828	2,314	1,151	1,091	141	361
Foreign languages and literatures	14,387	11,240	477	1,647	526	53	444	4,158	3,315	123	417	148	21	134	10,229	7,925	354	1,230	378	32	310
Health professions and related sciences	67,089	56,464	4,744	2,009	2,513	348	1,011	11,347	9,282	688	457	573	69	278	55,742	47,182	4,056	1,552	1,940	279	733
Home economics and vocational home economics	15,100	13,019	945	400	475	59	202	1,638	1,371	137	43	53	6	28	13,462	11,648	808	357	422	53	174
Law and legal studies	2,056	1,678	192	100	71	12	3	667	520	54	52	37	4	0	1,389	1,158	138	48	34	8	3
Liberal arts and sciences, general studies, and humanities	33,456	26,965	2,725	1,892	1,004	258	612	13,275	10,916	992	639	361	94	273	20,181	16,049	1,733	1,253	643	164	339
Library science	83	74	4	2	0	1	2	9	8	0	0	0	0	1	74	66	4	2	0	1	1
Mathematics	14,812	11,867	978	437	929	56	545	7,827	6,244	450	254	510	27	342	6,985	5,623	528	183	419	29	203
Mechanics and repairers	105	76	6	5	14	0	4	102	74	5	5	14	0	4	3	2	1	0	0	0	0
Multi/interdisciplinary studies	23,955	19,207	1,495	1,556	1,188	117	392	8,917	7,140	551	411	561	54	200	15,038	12,067	944	1,145	627	63	192
Parks, recreation, leisure and fitness studies	9,859	8,885	447	285	103	36	103	4,885	4,317	258	183	53	15	59	4,974	4,568	189	102	50	21	44
Philosophy and religion	7,781	6,693	333	244	314	46	151	4,938	4,259	197	168	173	29	112	2,843	2,434	136	76	141	17	39
Physical sciences and science technologies	17,545	14,275	850	438	1,124	93	765	11,825	9,865	379	300	695	62	524	5,720	4,410	471	138	429	31	241
Precision production trades	388	331	34	4	4	2	13	281	240	23	3	3	1	11	107	91	11	1	3	1	2
Protective services	20,902	15,952	3,099	1,265	325	130	131	13,020	10,478	1,448	724	223	71	76	7,882	5,474	1,651	541	102	59	55
Psychology	66,728	55,057	4,727	3,175	2,596	344	829	17,908	14,876	1,127	833	756	96	220	48,820	40,181	3,600	2,342	1,840	248	609
Public administration and services	16,775	12,716	2,506	886	327	187	153	3,801	2,819	547	229	109	46	51	12,974	9,897	1,959	657	218	141	102
R.O.T.C. and military sciences	11	11	0	0	0	0	0	11	11	0	0	0	0	0	0	0	0	0	0	0	0
Social sciences and history	135,703	109,942	9,964	6,067	5,712	772	3,246	73,589	61,332	4,277	2,992	2,802	372	1,814	62,114	48,610	5,687	3,075	2,910	400	1,432
Theological studies/religious vocations	5,433	4,841	151	111	128	27	175	4,168	3,734	117	82	88	18	129	1,265	1,107	34	29	40	9	46
Transportation and material moving	3,930	3,482	163	136	73	18	58	3,508	3,121	131	120	66	15	55	422	361	32	16	7	3	3
Visual and performing arts	47,761	40,128	1,925	1,618	2,130	213	1,747	18,610	15,478	850	687	796	83	716	29,151	24,650	1,075	931	1,334	130	1,031

[1] Reported racial/ethnic distributions of students by level of degree, field of degree, and sex were used to estimate race/ethnicity for students whose race/ethnicity was not reported. Excludes 2,340 men and 2,907 women whose racial/ethnic group and field of study were not available.

NOTE.—To facilitate trend comparisons, certain aggregations have been made of the degree fields as reported in the IPEDS "Completions" survey. "Agriculture and natural resources" includes Agribusiness and agriculture production, Agricultural sciences, and Conservation and renewable natural resources; and "Business management and administrative services" includes Business and management; Business and office, Marketing and distribution, and Consumer and personal services.

SOURCE: U.S. Department of Education, National Center for Education Statistics, Integrated Postsecondary Education Data System (IPEDS), "Completions" survey. (This table was prepared January 1995.)

Table 262.—Master's degrees conferred by institutions of higher education, by racial/ethnic group and sex of student: 1976–77 to 1993–94

Year and sex of student	Total	White, non-Hispanic	Black, non-Hispanic	Hispanic	Asian or Pacific Islander	American Indian/Alaskan Native	Nonresident alien
1	2	3	4	5	6	7	8
			Number of degrees conferred				
1976–77, total[1]	316,602	266,061	21,037	6,071	5,122	967	17,344
Men	167,396	139,210	7,781	3,268	3,123	521	13,493
Women	149,206	126,851	13,256	2,803	1,999	446	3,851
1978–79, total[2]	300,255	249,360	19,418	5,555	5,496	999	19,427
Men	152,637	124,058	7,070	2,786	3,325	495	14,903
Women	147,618	125,302	12,348	2,769	2,171	504	4,524
1980–81, total[3]	294,183	241,216	17,133	6,461	6,282	1,034	22,057
Men	145,666	115,562	6,158	3,085	3,773	501	16,587
Women	148,517	125,654	10,975	3,376	2,509	533	5,470
1984–85, total[4]	280,421	223,628	13,939	6,864	7,782	1,256	26,952
Men	139,417	106,059	5,200	3,059	4,842	583	19,674
Women	141,004	117,569	8,739	3,805	2,940	673	7,278
1986–87, total[5]	289,349	228,874	13,873	7,044	8,559	1,103	29,896
Men	141,269	105,572	5,153	3,331	5,239	518	21,456
Women	148,080	123,302	8,720	3,713	3,320	585	8,440
1988–89, total[5,6]	309,770	242,764	14,095	7,277	10,335	1,086	34,213
Men	148,872	109,715	5,175	3,325	6,048	476	24,133
Women	160,898	133,049	8,920	3,952	4,287	610	10,080
1989–90, total[5,7]	322,465	251,690	15,446	7,950	10,577	1,101	35,701
Men	152,926	112,877	5,539	3,586	6,002	463	24,459
Women	169,539	138,813	9,907	4,364	4,575	638	11,242
1990–91, total[5,8]	328,645	255,281	16,139	8,386	11,180	1,136	36,523
Men	151,796	111,224	5,709	3,670	6,319	459	24,415
Women	176,849	144,057	10,430	4,716	4,861	677	12,108
1991–92, total[5,9]	348,682	268,371	18,116	9,358	12,658	1,273	38,906
Men	159,543	116,096	6,054	4,132	7,062	523	25,676
Women	189,139	152,275	12,062	5,226	5,596	750	13,230
1992–93, total[5,10]	368,701	278,829	19,780	10,665	13,866	1,407	44,154
Men	168,754	120,225	6,821	4,735	7,544	586	28,843
Women	199,947	158,604	12,959	5,930	6,322	821	15,311
1993–94, total[5,11]	385,419	288,288	21,937	11,913	15,267	1,697	46,317
Men	175,355	123,854	7,413	5,113	8,225	691	30,059
Women	210,064	164,434	14,524	6,800	7,042	1,006	16,258
			Percentage distribution of degrees conferred				
1976–77, total[1]	100.0	84.0	6.6	1.9	1.6	0.3	5.5
Men	100.0	83.2	4.6	2.0	1.9	0.3	8.1
Women	100.0	85.0	8.9	1.9	1.3	0.3	2.6
1978–79, total[2]	100.0	83.0	6.5	1.9	1.8	0.3	6.5
Men	100.0	81.3	4.6	1.8	2.2	0.3	9.8
Women	100.0	84.9	8.4	1.9	1.5	0.3	3.1
1980–81, total[3]	100.0	82.0	5.8	2.2	2.1	0.4	7.5
Men	100.0	79.3	4.2	2.1	2.6	0.3	11.4
Women	100.0	84.6	7.4	2.3	1.7	0.4	3.7
1984–85, total[4]	100.0	79.7	5.0	2.4	2.8	0.4	9.6
Men	100.0	76.1	3.7	2.2	3.5	0.4	14.1
Women	100.0	83.4	6.2	2.7	2.1	0.5	5.2
1986–87, total[5]	100.0	79.1	4.8	2.4	3.0	0.4	10.3
Men	100.0	74.7	3.6	2.4	3.7	0.4	15.2
Women	100.0	83.3	5.9	2.5	2.2	0.4	5.7
1988–89, total[5,6]	100.0	78.4	4.6	2.3	3.3	0.4	11.0
Men	100.0	73.7	3.5	2.2	4.1	0.3	16.2
Women	100.0	82.7	5.5	2.5	2.7	0.4	6.3
1989–90, total[5,7]	100.0	78.1	4.8	2.5	3.3	0.3	11.1
Men	100.0	73.8	3.6	2.3	3.9	0.3	16.0
Women	100.0	81.9	5.8	2.6	2.7	0.4	6.6
1990–91, total[5,8]	100.0	77.7	4.9	2.6	3.4	0.3	11.1
Men	100.0	73.3	3.8	2.4	4.2	0.3	16.1
Women	100.0	81.5	5.9	2.7	2.7	0.4	6.8
1991–92, total[5,9]	100.0	77.0	5.2	2.7	3.6	0.4	11.2
Men	100.0	72.8	3.8	2.6	4.4	0.3	16.1
Women	100.0	80.5	6.4	2.8	3.0	0.4	7.0
1992–93, total[5,10]	100.0	75.6	5.4	2.9	3.8	0.4	12.0
Men	100.0	71.2	4.0	2.8	4.5	0.3	17.1
Women	100.0	79.3	6.5	3.0	3.2	0.4	7.7
1993–94, total[5,11]	100.0	74.8	5.7	3.1	4.0	0.4	12.0
Men	100.0	70.6	4.2	2.9	4.7	0.4	17.1
Women	100.0	78.3	6.9	3.2	3.4	0.5	7.7

[1] Excludes 387 men and 175 women whose racial/ethnic group was not available.
[2] Excludes 733 men and 91 women whose racial/ethnic group was not available.
[3] Excludes 1,377 men and 179 women whose racial/ethnic group was not available.
[4] Excludes 3,973 men and 1,857 women whose racial/ethnic group was not available.
[5] Reported racial/ethnic distributions of students by level of degree, field of degree, and sex were used to estimate race/ethnicity for students whose race/ethnicity was not reported.
[6] Excludes 482 men and 369 women whose racial/ethnic group was not available.
[7] Excludes 727 men and 1,109 women whose racial/ethnic group was not available.

[8] Excludes 4,686 men and 3,837 women whose racial/ethnic group was not available.
[9] Excludes 2,299 men and 1,857 women whose racial/ethnic group was not available.
[10] Excludes 504 men and 380 women whose racial/ethnic group was not available.
[11] Excludes 730 men and 921 women whose racial/ethnic group was not available.

SOURCE: U.S. Department of Education, National Center for Education Statistics, "Degrees and Other Formal Awards Conferred" surveys, and Integrated Postsecondary Education Data System (IPEDS), "Completions" surveys. (This table was prepared February 1996.)

Table 263.—Master's degrees conferred by institutions of higher education, by racial/ethnic group, major field of study, and sex of student: 1993–94

Major field of study	Total							Men							Women						
	Total	White, non-Hispanic	Black, non-Hispanic	Hispanic	Asian/ Pacific Islander	American Indian/ Alaskan Native	Nonresident alien	Total	White, non-Hispanic	Black, non-Hispanic	Hispanic	Asian/ Pacific Islander	American Indian/ Alaskan Native	Nonresident alien	Total	White, non-Hispanic	Black, non-Hispanic	Hispanic	Asian/ Pacific Islander	American Indian/ Alaskan Native	Nonresident alien
1	2	3	4	5	6	7	8	9	10	11	12	13	14	15	16	17	18	19	20	21	22
All fields, total [1]	385,419	288,288	21,937	11,913	15,267	1,697	46,317	175,355	123,854	7,413	5,113	8,225	691	30,059	210,064	164,434	14,524	6,800	7,042	1,006	16,258
Agriculture and natural resources	4,119	2,767	116	190	96	12	938	2,515	1,670	72	109	43	9	612	1,604	1,097	44	81	53	3	326
Architecture and related programs	3,943	2,676	144	135	221	12	755	2,428	1,640	87	78	115	6	502	1,515	1,036	57	57	106	6	253
Area, ethnic, and cultural studies	1,633	1,129	113	96	103	17	175	768	542	46	48	50	9	73	865	587	67	48	53	8	102
Biological sciences/life sciences	5,196	3,621	149	126	347	18	935	2,465	1,722	50	60	157	13	463	2,731	1,899	99	66	190	5	472
Business management and administrative services	93,437	67,669	5,213	2,568	4,625	299	13,063	59,335	43,591	2,519	1,590	2,752	175	8,708	34,102	24,078	2,694	978	1,873	124	4,355
Communications	5,005	3,609	343	107	136	21	789	1,870	1,378	92	35	41	18	306	3,135	2,231	251	72	95	3	483
Communications technologies	414	263	21	10	13		105	228	158	9	4	4	15	54	186	105	12	7	9	2	51
Computer and information sciences	10,416	4,605	391	176	1,317	19	3,908	7,724	3,570	221	126	847	13	2,947	2,692	1,035	170	50	470	6	961
Education	98,938	83,065	7,199	3,601	1,534	605	2,934	23,008	19,031	1,574	918	405	166	914	75,930	64,034	5,625	2,683	1,129	439	2,020
Engineering	28,621	15,327	623	670	2,586	64	9,351	24,218	12,980	448	545	2,050	51	8,144	4,403	2,347	175	125	536	13	1,207
Engineering-related technologies	1,133	820	59	30	37	1	186	936	671	45	27	32	0	161	197	149	14	3	5	1	25
English language and literature/letters	7,885	6,781	248	195	202	39	420	2,712	2,369	53	70	64	15	141	5,173	4,412	195	125	138	24	279
Foreign languages and literatures	3,288	2,158	49	307	137	9	628	1,087	737	16	99	34	7	194	2,201	1,421	33	208	103	2	434
Health professions and related sciences	28,025	23,175	1,496	710	1,007	137	1,500	5,814	4,446	232	200	311	27	598	22,211	18,729	1,264	510	696	110	902
Home economics and vocational home economics	2,421	1,928	139	56	70	7	221	405	308	20	10	11	3	53	2,016	1,620	119	46	59	4	168
Law and legal studies	2,432	1,218	47	76	61	7	1,023	1,608	787	24	52	43	5	697	824	431	23	24	18	2	326
Liberal arts and sciences, general studies, and humanities	2,496	2,125	125	48	34	14	150	913	767	44	14	15	7	66	1,583	1,358	81	34	19	7	84
Library science	5,116	4,409	244	92	150	14	207	1,040	871	53	26	32	2	56	4,076	3,538	191	66	118	12	151
Mathematics	4,100	2,559	118	71	250	14	1,096	2,536	1,546	68	42	137	5	738	1,564	1,013	50	29	113	1	358
Multi/interdisciplinary studies	2,464	2,024	111	95	62	14	158	1,194	968	39	46	40	3	98	1,270	1,056	72	49	22	11	60
Parks, recreation, leisure and fitness studies	1,625	1,361	78	22	28	8	128	845	696	38	14	17	2	78	780	665	40	8	11	6	50
Philosophy and religion	1,350	1,102	38	53	38	3	116	837	683	19	28	24	3	80	513	419	19	25	14	0	36
Physical sciences and science technologies	5,679	3,354	136	102	301	17	1,769	4,018	2,419	80	70	195	14	1,240	1,661	935	56	32	106	3	529
Precision production trades	2	0	0	0	0	0		2							0	0					
Protective services	1,437	1,092	220	48	23	7	47	902	706	110	33	16	3	34	535	386	110	15	7	4	13
Psychology	12,181	10,333	659	483	280	65	361	3,401	2,877	167	130	77	20	130	8,780	7,456	492	353	203	45	231
Public administration and services	21,833	16,891	2,506	990	495	143	808	6,406	4,848	612	300	161	42	443	15,427	12,043	1,894	690	334	101	365
R.O.T.C. and military technologies	124	111	0	4	4	1	0	117	106	0	3	4	1	0	7	5	0	1	0	0	0
Social sciences and history	14,561	10,247	737	459	481	71	2,566	8,152	5,712	336	237	246	38	1,583	6,409	4,535	401	222	235	33	983
Theological studies/religious vocations	4,956	3,773	259	125	226	10	563	3,034	2,256	182	63	150	4	379	1,922	1,517	77	62	76	6	184
Transportation and material moving	664	598	25	15	15	4	7	610	551	21	15	13	4	6	54	47	4	0	2	0	1
Visual and performing arts	9,925	7,496	327	253	388	51	1,410	4,229	3,248	133	122	139	26	561	5,696	4,248	194	131	249	25	849

[1] Reported racial/ethnic distributions of students by level of degree, field of degree, and sex were used to estimate race/ethnicity for students whose race/ethnicity was not reported. Excludes 730 men and 921 women whose racial/ethnic group and field of study were not available.

NOTE.—To facilitate trend comparisons, certain aggregations have been made of the degree fields as reported in the IPEDS "Completions" survey. "Agriculture and natural resources" includes Agribusiness and agriculture production, Agricultural sciences, and Conservation and renewable natural resources; and "Business management and administrative services" includes Business management, Business and office, Marketing and distribution, and Consumer and personal services.

SOURCE: U.S. Department of Education, National Center for Education Statistics, Integrated Postsecondary Education Data System (IPEDS), "Completions" survey. (This table was prepared February 1996.)

Table 264.—Master's degrees conferred by institutions of higher education, by racial/ethnic group, major field of study, and sex of student: 1992–93

Major field of study	Total							Men							Women						
	Total	White, non-His-panic	Black, non-His-panic	His-panic	Asian/ Pacific Islander	Amer-ican Indian/ Alas-kan Native	Non-resi-dent alien	Total	White, non-His-panic	Black, non-His-panic	His-panic	Asian/ Pacific Is-lander	Amer-ican Indian/ Alas-kan Native	Non-resi-dent alien	Total	White, non-His-panic	Black, non-His-panic	His-panic	Asian/ Pacific Is-lander	Amer-ican Indian/ Alas-kan Native	Non-resi-dent alien
1	2	3	4	5	6	7	8	9	10	11	12	13	14	15	16	17	18	19	20	21	22
All fields, total [1]	368,701	278,829	19,780	10,665	13,866	1,407	44,154	168,754	120,225	6,821	4,735	7,544	586	28,843	199,947	158,604	12,959	5,930	6,322	821	15,311
Agriculture and natural resources	3,965	2,743	93	85	80	10	954	2,477	1,655	56	44	40	7	675	1,488	1,088	37	41	40	3	279
Architecture and related programs	3,808	2,586	145	148	206	12	711	2,376	1,604	80	95	124	7	466	1,432	982	65	53	82	5	245
Area, ethnic, and cultural studies	1,523	1,040	131	77	86	10	179	732	531	38	38	30	5	90	791	509	93	39	56	5	89
Biological sciences/life sciences	4,756	3,281	141	140	317	27	850	2,343	1,663	49	74	141	9	407	2,413	1,618	92	66	176	18	443
Business management and administrative services	89,615	66,535	4,474	2,241	4,304	269	11,792	57,651	43,235	2,184	1,432	2,627	158	8,015	31,964	23,300	2,290	809	1,677	111	3,777
Communications	4,754	3,461	273	122	151	10	737	1,725	1,284	80	42	56	5	258	3,029	2,177	193	80	95	5	479
Communications technologies	455	307	25	10	7	1	105	255	176	11	5	4	1	58	200	131	14	5	3	0	47
Computer and information sciences	10,163	4,700	324	167	1,163	15	3,794	7,410	3,513	204	109	750	12	2,822	2,753	1,187	120	58	413	3	972
Education	96,028	81,290	6,725	3,181	1,391	459	2,982	22,197	18,341	1,523	835	369	142	987	73,831	62,949	5,202	2,346	1,022	317	1,995
Engineering	27,626	14,827	600	618	2,405	53	9,123	23,537	12,580	435	512	1,943	39	8,028	4,089	2,247	165	106	462	14	1,095
Engineering-related technologies	1,100	824	40	17	36	8	175	917	690	24	15	27	7	154	183	134	16	2	9	1	21
English language and literature/letters	7,790	6,732	269	174	158	37	420	2,667	2,341	66	67	46	17	130	5,123	4,391	203	107	112	20	290
Foreign languages and literatures	3,198	2,060	44	262	108	6	718	1,062	718	9	82	26	2	225	2,136	1,342	35	180	82	4	493
Health professions and related sciences	25,718	21,328	1,301	638	864	120	1,467	5,227	3,987	217	158	233	21	611	20,491	17,341	1,084	480	631	99	856
Home economics and vocational home economics	2,479	1,935	153	105	52	9	225	422	310	27	27	6	2	50	2,057	1,625	126	78	46	7	175
Law and legal studies	2,197	1,188	41	84	66	5	813	1,481	814	22	45	37	3	560	716	374	19	39	29	2	253
Liberal arts and sciences, general studies, and humanities	2,416	2,076	106	50	34	7	143	840	709	35	21	13	3	59	1,576	1,367	71	29	21	4	84
Library science	4,871	4,154	187	118	118	16	278	961	807	30	23	20	3	78	3,910	3,347	157	95	98	13	200
Mathematics	4,067	2,530	105	69	212	8	1,143	2,455	1,467	53	43	133	4	755	1,612	1,063	52	26	79	4	388
Multi/interdisciplinary studies	2,498	2,100	96	65	63	14	160	1,221	1,018	39	31	34	4	95	1,277	1,082	57	34	29	10	65
Parks, recreation, leisure and fitness studies	1,434	1,227	80	25	14	4	84	714	603	38	14	10	2	47	720	624	42	11	4	2	37
Philosophy and religion	1,425	1,170	57	26	50	5	117	988	802	37	16	37	3	92	437	368	20	10	13	1	25
Physical sciences and science technologies	5,366	3,262	112	107	262	13	1,610	3,808	2,379	63	74	159	9	1,124	1,558	883	49	33	103	4	486
Precision production trades	2	2	0	0	0	0	0	2	2	0	0	0	0	0	0	0	0	0	0	0	0
Protective services	1,357	1,024	214	45	17	6	51	837	663	99	26	13	3	33	520	361	115	19	4	3	18
Psychology	10,957	9,357	578	425	203	61	333	3,029	2,583	123	148	53	11	111	7,928	6,774	455	277	150	50	222
Public administration and services	20,634	16,130	2,271	890	466	92	785	6,105	4,536	633	294	143	31	468	14,529	11,594	1,638	596	323	61	317
R.O.T.C. and military technologies	108	93	6	3	5	1	0	100	86	5	3	5	1	0	8	7	1	0	0	0	0
Social sciences and history	13,471	9,474	645	396	422	72	2,462	7,671	5,276	330	247	205	43	1,570	5,800	4,198	315	149	217	29	892
Theological studies/religious vocations	4,985	3,836	227	123	207	9	583	2,989	2,274	143	74	133	5	360	1,996	1,562	84	49	74	4	223
Transportation and material moving	495	439	22	19	6	1	8	456	401	22	18	6	1	8	39	38	0	1	0	0	0
Visual and performing arts	9,440	7,118	295	235	393	47	1,352	4,099	3,177	146	123	121	25	507	5,341	3,941	149	112	272	22	845

[1] Reported racial/ethnic distributions of students by level of degree, field of degree, and sex were used to estimate race/ethnicity for students whose race/ethnicity was not reported. Excludes 504 men and 380 women whose racial/ethnic group and field of study were not available.

NOTE.—To facilitate trend comparisons, certain aggregations have been made of the degree fields as reported in the IPEDS "Completions" survey. "Agriculture and natural resources" includes Agribusiness and agriculture production,

Agricultural sciences, and Conservation and renewable natural resources; and "Business management and administrative services" includes Business and management, Business and office, Marketing and distribution, and Consumer and personal services.

SOURCE: U.S. Department of Education, National Center for Education Statistics, Integrated Postsecondary Education Data System (IPEDS), "Completions" survey. (This table was prepared February 1996.)

Table 265.—Doctor's degrees [1] conferred by institutions of higher education, by racial/ethnic group and sex of student: 1976–77 to 1993–94

Year and sex of student	Total	White, non-Hispanic	Black, non-Hispanic	Hispanic	Asian or Pacific Islander	American Indian/Alaskan Native	Nonresident alien
1	2	3	4	5	6	7	8
Number of degrees conferred							
1976–77, total [2]	33,126	26,851	1,253	522	658	95	3,747
Men	25,036	20,032	766	383	540	67	3,248
Women	8,090	6,819	487	139	118	28	499
1978–79, total [3]	32,675	26,138	1,268	439	811	104	3,915
Men	23,488	18,433	734	294	646	69	3,312
Women	9,187	7,705	534	145	165	35	603
1980–81, total [4]	32,839	25,908	1,265	456	877	130	4,203
Men	22,595	17,310	694	277	655	95	3,564
Women	10,244	8,598	571	179	222	35	639
1984–85, total [5]	32,307	23,934	1,154	677	1,106	119	5,317
Men	21,296	15,017	561	431	802	64	4,421
Women	11,011	8,917	593	246	304	55	896
1986–87, total [6]	34,041	24,434	1,057	751	1,098	105	6,596
Men	22,061	14,812	485	441	794	57	5,472
Women	11,980	9,622	572	310	304	48	1,124
1988–89, total [6,7]	35,659	24,884	1,066	629	1,323	85	7,672
Men	22,597	14,541	491	350	945	50	6,220
Women	13,062	10,343	575	279	378	35	1,452
1989–90, total [6,8]	38,113	25,880	1,153	788	1,235	99	8,958
Men	24,248	15,105	533	423	871	49	7,267
Women	13,865	10,775	620	365	364	50	1,691
1990–91, total [6,9]	38,547	25,328	1,211	732	1,459	102	9,715
Men	24,333	14,565	581	387	987	58	7,755
Women	14,214	10,763	630	345	472	44	1,960
1991–92, total [6,10]	40,090	25,813	1,223	811	1,559	118	10,566
Men	25,168	14,674	576	458	1,062	65	8,333
Women	14,922	11,139	647	353	497	53	2,233
1992–93, total [6,11]	42,021	26,700	1,352	827	1,582	106	11,454
Men	25,980	14,902	615	439	1,041	51	8,932
Women	16,041	11,798	737	388	541	55	2,522
1993–94, total [6,12]	43,149	27,156	1,393	903	2,025	134	11,538
Men	26,531	15,126	631	465	1,373	66	8,870
Women	16,618	12,030	762	438	652	68	2,668
Percentage distribution of degrees conferred							
1976–77, total [2]	100.0	81.1	3.8	1.6	2.0	0.3	11.3
Men	100.0	80.0	3.1	1.5	2.2	0.3	13.0
Women	100.0	84.3	6.0	1.7	1.5	0.3	6.2
1978–79, total [3]	100.0	80.0	3.9	1.3	2.5	0.3	12.0
Men	100.0	78.5	3.1	1.3	2.8	0.3	14.1
Women	100.0	83.9	5.8	1.6	1.8	0.4	6.6
1980–81, total [4]	100.0	78.9	3.9	1.4	2.7	0.4	12.8
Men	100.0	76.6	3.1	1.2	2.9	0.4	15.8
Women	100.0	83.9	5.6	1.7	2.2	0.3	6.2
1984–85, total [5]	100.0	74.1	3.6	2.1	3.4	0.4	16.5
Men	100.0	70.5	2.6	2.0	3.8	0.3	20.8
Women	100.0	81.0	5.4	2.2	2.8	0.5	8.1
1986–87, total [6]	100.0	71.8	3.1	2.2	3.2	0.3	19.4
Men	100.0	67.1	2.2	2.0	3.6	0.3	24.8
Women	100.0	80.3	4.8	2.6	2.5	0.4	9.4
1988–89, total [6,7]	100.0	69.8	3.0	1.8	3.7	0.2	21.5
Men	100.0	64.3	2.2	1.5	4.2	0.2	27.5
Women	100.0	79.2	4.4	2.1	2.9	0.3	11.1
1989–90, total [6,8]	100.0	67.9	3.0	2.1	3.2	0.3	23.5
Men	100.0	62.3	2.2	1.7	3.6	0.2	30.0
Women	100.0	77.7	4.5	2.6	2.6	0.4	12.2
1990–91, total [6,9]	100.0	65.7	3.1	1.9	3.8	0.3	25.2
Men	100.0	59.9	2.4	1.6	4.1	0.2	31.9
Women	100.0	75.7	4.4	2.4	3.3	0.3	13.8
1991–92, total [6,10]	100.0	64.4	3.1	2.0	3.9	0.3	26.4
Men	100.0	58.3	2.3	1.8	4.2	0.3	33.1
Women	100.0	74.6	4.3	2.4	3.3	0.4	15.0
1992–93, total [6,11]	100.0	63.5	3.2	2.0	3.8	0.3	27.3
Men	100.0	57.4	2.4	1.7	4.0	0.2	34.4
Women	100.0	73.5	4.6	2.4	3.4	0.3	15.7
1993–94, total [6,12]	100.0	62.9	3.2	2.1	4.7	0.3	26.7
Men	100.0	57.0	2.4	1.8	5.2	0.2	33.4
Women	100.0	72.4	4.6	2.6	3.9	0.4	16.1

[1] Includes Ph.D., Ed.D, and comparable degrees at the doctoral level. Excludes first-professional degrees.
[2] Excludes 106 men whose racial/ethnic group was not available.
[3] Excludes 53 men and 2 women whose racial/ethnic group was not available.
[4] Excludes 116 men and 3 women whose racial/ethnic group was not available.
[5] Excludes 404 men and 232 women whose racial/ethnic group was not available.
[6] Reported racial/ethnic distributions of students by level of degree, field of degree, and sex were used to estimate race/ethnicity for students whose race/ethnicity was not reported.
[7] Excludes 51 men and 10 women whose racial/ethnic group was not available.

[8] Excludes 153 men and 105 women whose racial/ethnic group was not available.
[9] Excludes 423 men and 324 women whose racial/ethnic group was not available.
[10] Excludes 389 men and 180 women whose racial/ethnic group was not available.
[11] Excludes 93 men and 18 women whose racial/ethnic group was not available.
[12] Excludes 21 men and 15 women whose racial/ethnic group was not available.

SOURCE: U.S. Department of Education, National Center for Education Statistics, "Degrees and Other Formal Awards Conferred" surveys, and Integrated Postsecondary Education Data System (IPEDS), "Completions" surveys. (This table was prepared February 1996.)

Table 266.—Doctor's degrees conferred by institutions of higher education, by racial/ethnic group, major field of study, and sex of student: 1993–94

Major field of study	Total							Men							Women						
	Total	White, non-His-panic	Black, non-His-panic	His-panic	Asian/Pacific Islander	Amer-ican Indian/Alas-kan Native	Non-resi-dent alien	Total	White, non-His-panic	Black, non-His-panic	His-panic	Asian/Pacific Is-lander	Amer-ican Indian/Alas-kan Native	Non-resi-dent alien	Total	White, non-His-panic	Black, non-His-panic	His-panic	Asian/Pacific Is-lander	Amer-ican Indian/Alas-kan Native	Non-resi-dent alien
1	2	3	4	5	6	7	8	9	10	11	12	13	14	15	16	17	18	19	20	21	22
All fields, total [1]	43,149	27,156	1,393	903	2,025	134	11,538	26,531	15,126	631	465	1,373	66	8,870	16,618	12,030	762	438	652	68	2,668
Agriculture and natural resources	1,278	596	16	18	34	2	612	982	429	13	13	25	1	501	296	167	3	5	9	1	111
Architecture and related programs	161	65	4	0	6	1	85	111	44	1	0	4	0	62	50	21	3	0	2	1	23
Area, ethnic, and cultural studies	155	99	16	2	8	4	26	75	43	8	0	4	4	16	80	56	8	2	4	0	10
Biological sciences/life sciences	4,534	2,828	64	96	291	9	1,246	2,690	1,625	31	51	172	5	806	1,844	1,203	33	45	119	4	440
Business management and administrative services	1,364	847	38	13	66	7	393	980	561	22	10	52	5	330	384	286	16	3	14	2	63
Communications	337	221	23	7	6	2	78	172	110	9	3	3	1	46	165	111	14	4	3	1	32
Communications technologies	8	4	0	0	0	1	3	2	1	0	0	0	0	1	6	3	0	0	0	1	2
Computer and information sciences	810	366	11	5	64	1	363	685	295	9	5	56	0	320	125	71	2	0	8	1	43
Education	6,908	5,393	523	201	152	42	597	2,706	2,101	160	69	67	16	293	4,202	3,292	363	132	85	26	304
Engineering	5,963	2,209	60	51	461	5	3,177	5,299	1,886	45	44	403	4	2,917	664	323	15	7	58	1	260
Engineering-related technologies	16	1	0	1	3	0	11	16	1	0	1	3	0	11	0	0	0	0	0	0	0
English language and literature/letters	1,344	1,088	32	26	24	9	165	568	448	6	16	7	2	89	776	640	26	10	17	7	76
Foreign languages and literatures	886	514	8	73	24	0	267	355	198	5	23	12	0	117	531	316	3	50	12	0	150
Health professions and related sciences	1,902	1,282	59	26	104	7	424	789	465	14	10	58	1	241	1,113	817	45	16	46	6	183
Home economics and vocational home economics	365	279	10	5	9	1	61	93	70	2	1	1	1	18	272	209	8	4	8	0	43
Law and legal studies	79	16	1	7	3	0	52	63	12	1	7	3	0	40	16	4	0	0	0	0	12
Liberal arts and sciences, general studies, and humanities	80	59	7	2	5	0	7	46	34	2	2	2	0	6	34	25	5	0	3	0	1
Library science	45	31	3	1	2	0	8	14	9	1	1	0	0	3	31	22	2	0	2	0	5
Mathematics	1,157	494	7	11	83	1	561	904	373	6	9	61	1	454	253	121	1	2	22	0	107
Multi/interdisciplinary studies	227	140	10	6	5	4	62	151	83	5	3	3	2	55	76	57	5	3	2	2	7
Parks, recreation, leisure and fitness studies	116	78	3	1	2	1	31	70	43	0	1	1	1	24	46	35	3	0	1	0	7
Philosophy and religion	528	417	22	5	16	0	68	383	296	17	4	13	0	53	145	121	5	1	3	0	15
Physical sciences and science technologies	4,650	2,536	46	83	323	6	1,656	3,642	2,006	35	63	225	6	1,307	1,008	530	11	20	98	0	349
Precision production trades	0	0	0	0	0	0	0	0	0	0	0	0	0	0	0	0	0	0	0	0	0
Protective services	25	19	2	1	0	0	3	14	10	1	1	0	0	2	11	9	1	0	0	0	1
Psychology	3,563	3,027	126	140	93	11	166	1,346	1,137	46	49	33	5	76	2,217	1,890	80	91	60	6	90
Public administration and services	519	356	44	14	14	4	87	238	135	19	11	9	2	62	281	221	25	3	5	2	25
R.O.T.C. and military technologies	0	0	0	0	0	0	0	0	0	0	0	0	0	0	0	0	0	0	0	0	0
Social sciences and history	3,627	2,318	123	73	130	12	971	2,317	1,362	68	41	84	6	756	1,310	956	55	32	46	6	215
Theological studies/religious vocations	1,448	1,058	113	17	66	2	192	1,235	892	89	13	64	2	175	213	166	24	4	2	0	17
Transportation and material moving	0	0	0	0	0	0	0	0	0	0	0	0	0	0	0	0	0	0	0	0	0
Visual and performing arts	1,054	815	22	18	31	2	166	585	457	15	14	8	2	89	469	358	7	4	23	0	77

[1] Reported racial/ethnic distributions of students by level of degree, field of degree, and sex were used to estimate race/ethnicity for students whose race/ethnicity was not reported. Excludes 21 men and 15 women whose racial/ethnic group and field of study were not available.

NOTE.—To facilitate trend comparisons, certain aggregations have been made of the degree fields as reported in the IPEDS "Completions" survey: "Agriculture and natural resources" includes Agribusiness and agriculture production, Agricultural sciences, and Conservation and renewable natural resources; and "Business management and administrative services" includes Business and management, Business and office, Marketing and distribution, and Consumer and personal services.

SOURCE: U.S. Department of Education, National Center for Education Statistics, Integrated Postsecondary Education Data System (IPEDS), "Completions" survey. (This table was prepared February 1996.)

Table 267.—Doctor's degrees conferred by institutions of higher education, by racial/ethnic group, major field of study, and sex of student: 1992–93

Major field of study	Total							Men							Women						
	Total	White, non-Hispanic	Black, non-Hispanic	Hispanic	Asian/ Pacific Islander	American Indian/ Alaskan Native	Nonresident alien	Total	White, non-Hispanic	Black, non-Hispanic	Hispanic	Asian/ Pacific Islander	American Indian/ Alaskan Native	Nonresident alien	Total	White, non-Hispanic	Black, non-Hispanic	Hispanic	Asian/ Pacific Islander	American Indian/ Alaskan Native	Nonresident alien
1	2	3	4	5	6	7	8	9	10	11	12	13	14	15	16	17	18	19	20	21	22
All fields, total [1]	**42,021**	**26,700**	**1,352**	**827**	**1,582**	**106**	**11,454**	**25,980**	**14,902**	**615**	**439**	**1,041**	**51**	**8,932**	**16,041**	**11,798**	**737**	**388**	**541**	**55**	**2,522**
Agriculture and natural resources	1,173	564	13	20	23	0	553	879	416	10	14	15	0	424	294	148	3	6	8	0	129
Architecture and related programs	148	61	11	5	5	0	66	105	36	8	5	4	0	52	43	25	3	0	1	0	14
Area, ethnic, and cultural studies	178	114	11	5	13	1	34	90	54	3	3	6	1	24	88	60	8	2	7	0	10
Biological sciences/life sciences	4,435	2,810	63	84	265	5	1,208	2,664	1,652	37	50	136	3	786	1,771	1,158	26	34	129	2	422
Business management and administrative services	1,346	815	29	10	45	3	444	969	521	17	7	34	2	388	377	294	12	3	11	1	56
Communications	293	196	21	8	12	3	53	143	87	6	2	7	2	39	150	109	15	6	5	1	14
Communications technologies	8	5	0	0	0	0	3	3	2	0	0	0	0	1	5	3	0	0	0	0	2
Computer and information sciences	805	383	6	7	56	1	352	689	309	3	7	44	1	325	116	74	3	0	12	0	27
Education	7,030	5,497	552	185	123	35	638	2,867	2,175	193	86	53	16	344	4,163	3,322	359	99	70	19	294
Engineering	5,823	2,210	42	51	379	2	3,139	5,265	1,932	31	39	343	1	2,919	558	278	11	12	36	1	220
Engineering-related technologies	20	9	1	1	1	0	8	18	8	1	1	1	0	7	2	1	0	0	0	0	1
English language and literature/letters	1,341	1,094	32	22	23	7	163	550	432	14	12	7	3	82	791	662	18	10	16	4	81
Foreign languages and literatures	830	488	8	65	26	3	240	355	200	6	19	5	3	125	475	288	2	46	21	0	115
Health professions and related sciences	1,767	1,205	66	26	64	4	402	753	432	18	6	32	1	264	1,014	773	48	20	32	3	138
Home economics and vocational home economics	345	255	16	3	6	0	65	97	69	5	0	3	0	20	248	186	11	3	3	0	45
Law and legal studies	86	11	1	0	1	0	73	65	8	0	0	1	0	56	21	3	1	0	0	0	17
Liberal arts and sciences, general studies, and humanities	81	65	9	1	0	1	5	38	32	3	0	0	0	3	43	33	6	1	0	1	2
Library science	77	46	6	2	2	0	21	26	17	0	0	2	0	7	51	29	6	2	0	0	14
Mathematics	1,189	484	8	8	57	0	632	906	353	6	7	39	0	501	283	131	2	1	18	0	131
Multi/interdisciplinary studies	196	140	1	4	2	0	49	115	72	0	3	2	0	38	81	68	1	1	0	0	11
Parks, recreation, leisure and fitness studies	108	77	3	0	2	0	26	75	48	3	0	2	0	22	33	29	0	0	0	0	4
Philosophy and religion	448	340	17	5	12	0	74	323	233	14	3	10	0	63	125	107	3	2	2	0	11
Physical sciences and science technologies	4,393	2,405	37	68	215	4	1,664	3,432	1,874	29	49	154	2	1,324	961	531	8	19	61	2	340
Precision production trades	0	0	0	0	0	0	0	0	0	0	0	0	0	0	0	0	0	0	0	0	0
Protective services	32	22	2	0	0	0	8	23	16	1	0	0	0	6	9	6	1	0	0	0	2
Psychology	3,651	3,125	134	125	63	22	182	1,415	1,214	44	45	23	9	80	2,236	1,911	90	80	40	13	102
Public administration and services	459	318	47	9	10	2	73	215	135	15	3	6	2	54	244	183	32	6	4	0	19
R.O.T.C. and military technologies	0	0	0	0	0	0	0	0	0	0	0	0	0	0	0	0	0	0	0	0	0
Social sciences and history	3,460	2,201	91	85	111	7	965	2,203	1,284	46	55	73	3	742	1,257	917	45	30	38	4	223
Theological studies/religious vocations	1,417	1,065	102	12	38	4	196	1,219	905	88	10	28	4	184	198	160	14	2	10	0	12
Transportation and material moving	0	0	0	0	0	0	0	0	0	0	0	0	0	0	0	0	0	0	0	0	0
Visual and performing arts	882	695	23	16	28	1	119	478	386	14	13	11	1	53	404	309	9	3	17	0	66

[1] Reported racial/ethnic distributions of students by level of degree, field of degree, and sex were used to estimate race/ethnicity for students whose race/ethnicity was not reported. Excludes 93 men and 18 women whose race/ethnic group and field of study were not available.

Agricultural sciences, and Conservation and renewable natural resources; and "Business management and administrative services" includes Business and management, Business and office, Marketing and distribution, and Consumer and personal services.

NOTE—To facilitate trend comparisons, certain aggregations have been made of the degree fields as reported in the IPEDS "Completions" survey. "Agriculture and natural resources" includes Agribusiness and agriculture production,

SOURCE: U.S. Department of Education, National Center for Education Statistics, Integrated Postsecondary Education Data System (IPEDS), "Completions" survey. (This table was prepared January 1995.)

Table 268.—First-professional degrees conferred by institutions of higher education, by racial/ethnic group and sex of student: 1976–77 to 1993–94

Year and sex of student	Total	White, non-Hispanic	Black, non-Hispanic	Hispanic	Asian or Pacific Islander	American Indian/Alaskan Native	Nonresident alien
1	2	3	4	5	6	7	8
			Number of degrees conferred				
1976–77, total [1]	63,953	58,422	2,537	1,076	1,021	196	701
Men	51,980	47,777	1,761	893	776	159	614
Women	11,973	10,645	776	183	245	37	87
1978–79, total [2]	68,611	62,430	2,836	1,283	1,205	216	641
Men	52,425	48,123	1,783	989	860	150	520
Women	16,186	14,307	1,053	294	345	66	121
1980–81, total [3]	71,340	64,551	2,931	1,541	1,456	192	669
Men	52,194	47,629	1,772	1,131	991	134	537
Women	19,146	16,922	1,159	410	465	58	132
1984–85, total [4]	71,057	63,219	3,029	1,884	1,816	248	861
Men	47,501	42,630	1,623	1,239	1,152	176	681
Women	23,556	20,589	1,406	645	664	72	180
1986–87, total	71,617	62,688	3,420	2,051	2,270	304	884
Men	46,523	41,149	1,835	1,303	1,420	183	633
Women	25,094	21,539	1,585	748	850	121	251
1988–89, total	70,856	61,214	3,148	2,269	2,976	264	985
Men	45,046	39,399	1,618	1,374	1,819	148	688
Women	25,810	21,815	1,530	895	1,157	116	297
1989–90, total [5]	70,744	60,240	3,410	2,427	3,362	257	1,048
Men	43,778	37,850	1,672	1,450	1,963	135	708
Women	26,966	22,390	1,738	977	1,399	122	340
1990–91, total [6]	71,515	60,327	3,575	2,527	3,755	261	1,070
Men	43,601	37,348	1,672	1,506	2,178	144	753
Women	27,914	22,979	1,903	1,021	1,577	117	317
1991–92, total [7]	72,129	59,800	3,560	2,766	4,455	296	1,252
Men	43,812	36,939	1,603	1,635	2,593	157	885
Women	28,317	22,861	1,957	1,131	1,862	139	367
1992–93, total [8]	74,960	60,830	4,100	2,984	5,160	368	1,518
Men	44,821	37,157	1,777	1,762	2,858	190	1,077
Women	30,139	23,673	2,323	1,222	2,302	178	441
1993–94, total	75,418	60,140	4,444	3,134	5,892	371	1,437
Men	44,707	36,573	1,902	1,781	3,214	222	1,015
Women	30,711	23,567	2,542	1,353	2,678	149	422
			Percentage distribution of degrees conferred				
1976–77, total [1]	100.0	91.4	4.0	1.7	1.6	0.3	1.1
Men	100.0	91.9	3.4	1.7	1.5	0.3	1.2
Women	100.0	88.9	6.5	1.5	2.0	0.3	0.7
1978–79, total [2]	100.0	91.0	4.1	1.9	1.8	0.3	0.9
Men	100.0	91.8	3.4	1.9	1.6	0.3	1.0
Women	100.0	88.4	6.5	1.8	2.1	0.4	0.7
1980–81, total [3]	100.0	90.5	4.1	2.2	2.0	0.3	0.9
Men	100.0	91.3	3.4	2.2	1.9	0.3	1.0
Women	100.0	88.4	6.1	2.1	2.4	0.3	0.7
1984–85, total [4]	100.0	89.0	4.3	2.7	2.6	0.3	1.2
Men	100.0	89.7	3.4	2.6	2.4	0.4	1.4
Women	100.0	87.4	6.0	2.7	2.8	0.3	0.8
1986–87, total	100.0	87.5	4.8	2.9	3.2	0.4	1.2
Men	100.0	88.4	3.9	2.8	3.1	0.4	1.4
Women	100.0	85.8	6.3	3.0	3.4	0.5	1.0
1988–89, total	100.0	86.4	4.4	3.2	4.2	0.4	1.4
Men	100.0	87.5	3.6	3.1	4.0	0.3	1.5
Women	100.0	84.5	5.9	3.5	4.5	0.4	1.2
1989–90, total [5]	100.0	85.2	4.8	3.4	4.8	0.4	1.5
Men	100.0	86.5	3.8	3.3	4.5	0.3	1.6
Women	100.0	83.0	6.4	3.6	5.2	0.5	1.3
1990–91, total [6]	100.0	84.4	5.0	3.5	5.3	0.4	1.5
Men	100.0	85.7	3.8	3.5	5.0	0.3	1.7
Women	100.0	82.3	6.8	3.7	5.6	0.4	1.1
1991–92, total [7]	100.0	82.9	4.9	3.8	6.2	0.4	1.7
Men	100.0	84.3	3.7	3.7	5.9	0.4	2.0
Women	100.0	80.7	6.9	4.0	6.6	0.5	1.3
1992–93, total [8]	100.0	81.1	5.5	4.0	6.9	0.5	2.0
Men	100.0	82.9	4.0	3.9	6.4	0.4	2.4
Women	100.0	78.5	7.7	4.1	7.6	0.6	1.5
1993–94, total	100.0	79.7	5.9	4.2	7.8	0.5	1.9
Men	100.0	81.8	4.3	4.0	7.2	0.5	2.3
Women	100.0	76.7	8.3	4.4	8.7	0.5	1.4

[1] Excludes 394 men and 12 women whose racial/ethnic group was not available.
[2] Excludes 227 men and 10 women whose racial/ethnic group was not available.
[3] Excludes 598 men and 18 women whose racial/ethnic group was not available.
[4] Excludes 2,954 men and 1,052 women whose racial/ethnic group was not available.
[5] Excludes 183 men and 61 women whose racial/ethnic group was not available.
[6] Excludes 245 men and 188 women whose racial/ethnic group was not available.
[7] Excludes 1,259 men and 758 women whose racial/ethnic group was not available.
[8] Excludes 332 men and 95 women whose racial/ethnic group was not available.

NOTE.—For years 1984–85 to 1993–94, reported racial/ethnic distributions of students by level of degree, field of degree, and sex were used to estimate race/ethnicity for students whose race/ethnicity was not reported.

SOURCE: U.S. Department of Education, National Center for Education Statistics, "Degrees and Other Formal Awards Conferred" surveys, and Integrated Postsecondary Education Data System (IPEDS), "Completions" surveys. (This table was prepared November 1995.)

Table 269.—First-professional degrees conferred by institutions of higher education, by racial/ethnic group, major field of study, and sex of student: 1993–94

Major field of study	Total							Men							Women						
	Total	White, non-His-panic	Black, non-His-panic	His-panic	Asian/ Pacific Is-lander	Amer-ican Indian/ Alas-kan Native	Non-resi-dent alien	Total	White, non-His-panic	Black, non-His-panic	His-panic	Asian/ Pacific Is-lander	Amer-ican Indian/ Alas-kan Native	Non-resi-dent alien	Total	White, non-His-panic	Black, non-His-panic	His-panic	Asian/ Pacific Is-lander	Amer-ican Indian/ Alas-kan Native	Non-resi-dent alien
1	2	3	4	5	6	7	8	9	10	11	12	13	14	15	16	17	18	19	20	21	22
All fields [1]	75,418	60,140	4,444	3,134	5,892	371	1,437	44,707	36,573	1,902	1,781	3,214	222	1,015	30,711	23,567	2,542	1,353	2,678	149	422
Dentistry (D.D.S. or D.M.D.)	3,787	2,559	171	218	538	17	284	2,330	1,672	73	117	272	10	186	1,457	887	98	101	266	7	98
Medicine (M.D.)	15,368	11,287	937	613	2,282	68	181	9,544	7,223	398	363	1,398	41	121	5,824	4,064	539	250	884	27	60
Optometry (O.D.)	1,103	818	36	38	153	3	55	554	448	9	14	51	7	31	549	370	27	24	102	2	24
Osteopathic medicine (D.O.)	1,798	1,478	48	70	182	8	12	1,165	975	29	41	104	1	9	633	503	19	29	78	1	3
Pharmacy (Pharm.D.)	1,936	1,297	155	54	347	1	82	643	464	39	30	74	0	36	1,293	833	116	24	273	1	46
Podiatry (Pod.D. or D.P.) or podiatric medicine (D.P.M.)	465	339	32	41	43	2	8	330	248	13	33	26	2	8	135	91	19	8	17	0	0
Veterinary medicine (D.V.M.)	2,089	1,923	39	66	40	14	7	798	740	11	30	8	6	3	1,291	1,183	28	36	32	8	4
Chiropractic medicine (D.C. or D.C.M.)	2,806	2,370	40	80	115	19	182	2,010	1,710	21	55	77	16	131	796	660	19	25	38	3	51
Law (LL.B. or J.D.)	40,044	33,420	2,472	1,842	1,816	223	271	22,826	19,624	988	1,002	890	130	192	17,218	13,796	1,484	840	926	93	79
Theology (M.Div., M.H.L., B.D., or Ord.)	5,967	4,607	513	109	375	16	347	4,486	3,455	321	95	314	9	292	1,481	1,152	192	14	61	7	55
Other	55	42	1	3	1	0	8	21	14	1	1	0	0	6	34	28	0	2	1	0	2

[1] Reported racial/ethnic distributions of students by level of degree, field of degree, and sex were used to estimate race/ethnicity for students whose race/ethnicity was not reported.

SOURCE: U.S. Department of Education, National Center for Education Statistics, Integrated Postsecondary Education Data System (IPEDS), "Completions" survey. (This table was prepared November 1995.)

Table 270.—First-professional degrees conferred by institutions of higher education, by racial/ethnic group, major field of study, and sex of student: 1992–93

Major field of study	Total							Men							Women						
	Total	White, non-His-panic	Black, non-His-panic	His-panic	Asian/ Pacific Is-lander	Amer-ican Indian/ Alas-kan Native	Non-resi-dent alien	Total	White, non-His-panic	Black, non-His-panic	His-panic	Asian/ Pacific Is-lander	Amer-ican Indian/ Alas-kan Native	Non-resi-dent alien	Total	White, non-His-panic	Black, non-His-panic	His-panic	Asian/ Pacific Is-lander	Amer-ican Indian/ Alas-kan Native	Non-resi-dent alien
1	2	3	4	5	6	7	8	9	10	11	12	13	14	15	16	17	18	19	20	21	22
All fields [1]	74,960	60,830	4,100	2,984	5,160	368	1,518	44,821	37,157	1,777	1,762	2,858	190	1,077	30,139	23,673	2,323	1,222	2,302	178	441
Dentistry (D.D.S. or D.M.D.)	3,605	2,451	159	212	532	10	241	2,383	1,705	74	131	305	7	161	1,222	746	85	81	227	3	80
Medicine (M.D.)	15,531	11,729	900	610	2,001	73	218	9,679	7,512	378	372	1,226	34	157	5,852	4,217	522	238	775	39	61
Optometry (O.D.)	1,148	903	24	31	139	3	48	584	492	5	20	38	3	26	564	411	19	11	101	0	22
Osteopathic medicine (D.O.)	1,627	1,359	45	69	132	9	13	1,091	924	21	47	85	6	8	536	435	24	22	47	1	6
Pharmacy (Pharm.D.)	1,904	1,263	109	56	369	7	100	673	461	28	24	110	4	46	1,231	802	81	32	259	3	54
Podiatry (Pod.D. or D.P.) or podiatric medicine (D.P.M.)	476	350	42	30	35	1	18	350	266	20	21	26	1	16	126	84	22	9	9	0	2
Veterinary medicine (D.V.M.)	2,057	1,888	51	60	39	12	7	766	710	14	25	11	3	3	1,291	1,178	37	35	28	9	4
Chiropractic medicine (D.C. or D.C.M.)	2,799	2,383	38	113	115	23	127	1,991	1,709	23	69	86	16	88	808	674	15	44	29	7	39
Law (LL.B. or J.D.)	40,302	34,267	2,284	1,665	1,550	213	323	23,182	20,263	914	935	756	104	210	17,120	14,004	1,370	730	794	109	357
Theology (M.Div., M.H.L., B.D. or Ord.)	5,447	4,189	447	137	246	15	413	4,096	3,097	299	118	215	10	357	1,351	1,092	148	19	31	5	113
Other	64	48	1	1	2	2	10	26	18	1	0	0	2	5	38	30	0	1	2	0	5

[1] Reported racial/ethnic distributions of students by level of degree, field of degree, and sex were used to estimate race/ethnicity for students whose race/ethnicity was not reported. Excludes 332 men and 95 women whose racial/ethnic group and field of study were not available.

SOURCE: U.S. Department of Education, National Center for Education Statistics, Integrated Postsecondary Education Data System (IPEDS), "Completions" survey. (This table was prepared January 1995.)

Table 271.—Earned degrees in agriculture and natural resources [1] conferred by institutions of higher education, by level of degree and sex of student: 1970–71 to 1993–94

Year	Bachelor's degrees			Master's degrees			Doctor's degrees		
	Total	Men	Women	Total	Men	Women	Total	Men	Women
1	2	3	4	5	6	7	8	9	10
1970–71	12,672	12,136	536	2,457	2,313	144	1,086	1,055	31
1971–72	13,516	12,779	737	2,680	2,490	190	971	945	26
1972–73	14,756	13,661	1,095	2,807	2,588	219	1,059	1,031	28
1973–74	16,253	14,684	1,569	2,928	2,640	288	930	897	33
1974–75	17,528	15,061	2,467	3,067	2,703	364	991	958	33
1975–76	19,402	15,845	3,557	3,340	2,862	478	928	867	61
1976–77	21,467	16,690	4,777	3,724	3,177	547	893	831	62
1977–78	22,650	17,069	5,581	4,023	3,268	755	971	909	62
1978–79	23,134	16,854	6,280	3,994	3,187	807	950	877	73
1979–80	22,802	16,045	6,757	3,976	3,082	894	991	879	112
1980–81	21,886	15,154	6,732	4,003	3,061	942	1,067	940	127
1981–82	21,029	14,443	6,586	4,163	3,114	1,049	1,079	925	154
1982–83	20,909	14,085	6,824	4,254	3,129	1,125	1,149	1,004	145
1983–84	19,317	13,206	6,111	4,178	2,989	1,189	1,172	1,001	171
1984–85	18,107	12,477	5,630	3,928	2,846	1,082	1,213	1,036	177
1985–86	16,823	11,544	5,279	3,801	2,701	1,100	1,158	966	192
1986–87	14,991	10,314	4,677	3,522	2,460	1,062	1,049	871	178
1987–88	14,222	9,744	4,478	3,479	2,427	1,052	1,142	926	216
1988–89	13,492	9,298	4,194	3,245	2,231	1,014	1,183	950	233
1989–90	12,900	8,822	4,078	3,382	2,239	1,143	1,295	1,038	257
1990–91	13,124	8,832	4,292	3,295	2,160	1,135	1,185	953	232
1991–92	15,124	9,869	5,255	3,735	2,413	1,322	1,214	963	251
1992–93	16,778	11,080	5,698	3,965	2,477	1,488	1,173	879	294
1993–94	18,070	11,748	6,322	4,119	2,515	1,604	1,278	982	296

[1] Includes degrees in agricultural business and production; agricultural sciences; and conservation and renewable natural resources.

SOURCE: U.S. Department of Education, National Center for Education Statistics, "Degrees and Other Formal Awards Conferred" surveys, and Integrated Postsecondary Education Data System (IPEDS), "Completions" surveys. (This table was prepared November 1995.)

Table 272.—Earned degrees in architecture and related programs [1] conferred by institutions of higher education, by level of degree and sex of student: 1949–50 to 1993–94

Year	Bachelor's degrees			Master's degrees			Doctor's degrees		
	Total	Men	Women	Total	Men	Women	Total	Men	Women
1	2	3	4	5	6	7	8	9	10
1949–50	2,563	2,441	122	166	159	7	1	1	0
1959–60	1,801	1,744	57	319	305	14	17	17	0
1967–68	3,057	2,931	126	1,021	953	68	15	15	0
1969–70	4,105	3,888	217	1,427	1,260	167	35	33	2
1970–71	5,570	4,906	664	1,705	1,469	236	36	33	3
1971–72	6,440	5,667	773	1,899	1,626	273	50	43	7
1972–73	6,962	6,042	920	2,307	1,943	364	58	54	4
1973–74	7,822	6,665	1,157	2,702	2,208	494	69	65	4
1974–75	8,226	6,791	1,435	2,938	2,343	595	69	58	11
1975–76	9,146	7,396	1,750	3,215	2,545	670	82	69	13
1976–77	9,222	7,249	1,973	3,213	2,489	724	73	62	11
1977–78	9,250	7,054	2,196	3,115	2,304	811	73	57	16
1978–79	9,273	6,876	2,397	3,113	2,226	887	96	74	22
1979–80	9,132	6,596	2,536	3,139	2,245	894	79	66	13
1980–81	9,455	6,800	2,655	3,153	2,234	919	93	73	20
1981–82	9,728	6,825	2,903	3,327	2,242	1,085	80	58	22
1982–83	9,823	6,403	3,420	3,357	2,224	1,133	97	74	23
1983–84	9,186	5,895	3,291	3,223	2,197	1,026	84	62	22
1984–85	9,325	6,019	3,306	3,275	2,148	1,127	89	66	23
1985–86	9,119	5,824	3,295	3,260	2,129	1,131	73	56	17
1986–87	8,950	5,617	3,333	3,163	2,086	1,077	92	66	26
1987–88	8,603	5,271	3,332	3,159	2,042	1,117	98	66	32
1988–89	9,150	5,545	3,605	3,383	2,192	1,191	86	63	23
1989–90	9,364	5,703	3,661	3,499	2,228	1,271	103	73	30
1990–91	9,781	5,788	3,993	3,490	2,244	1,246	135	101	34
1991–92	8,753	5,805	2,948	3,640	2,271	1,369	132	93	39
1992–93	9,167	5,940	3,227	3,808	2,376	1,432	148	105	43
1993–94	8,975	5,764	3,211	3,943	2,428	1,515	161	111	50

[1] Prior to 1967–68, includes degrees in architecture. From 1967–68, includes degrees in architecture; city/urban, community, and regional planning; architectural environmental design; interior architecture; landscape architecture; architectural urban design and planning; and architecture and related programs, other.

SOURCE: U.S. Department of Education, National Center for Education Statistics, "Degrees and Other Formal Awards Conferred" surveys, and Integrated Postsecondary Education Data System (IPEDS), "Completions" surveys. (This table was prepared November 1995.)

Table 273.—Earned degrees in the biological/life sciences [1] conferred by institutions of higher education, by level of degree and sex of student: 1951–52 to 1993–94

Year	Bachelor's degrees			Master's degrees			Doctor's degrees		
	Total	Men	Women	Total	Men	Women	Total	Men	Women
1	2	3	4	5	6	7	8	9	10
1951–52	11,094	8,212	2,882	2,307	1,908	399	764	680	84
1953–54	9,279	6,710	2,569	1,610	1,287	323	1,077	977	100
1955–56	12,423	9,515	2,908	1,759	1,379	380	1,025	908	117
1957–58	14,308	11,159	3,149	1,852	1,448	404	1,125	987	138
1959–60	15,576	11,654	3,922	2,154	1,668	486	1,205	1,086	119
1961–62	16,915	12,136	4,779	2,642	1,982	660	1,338	1,179	159
1963–64	22,723	16,321	6,402	3,296	2,348	948	1,625	1,432	193
1965–66	26,916	19,368	7,548	4,232	3,085	1,147	2,097	1,792	305
1967–68	31,826	22,986	8,840	5,506	3,959	1,547	2,784	2,345	439
1969–70	34,034	23,919	10,115	5,800	3,975	1,825	3,289	2,820	469
1970–71	35,743	25,333	10,410	5,728	3,805	1,923	3,645	3,050	595
1971–72	37,293	26,323	10,970	6,101	4,087	2,014	3,653	3,031	622
1972–73	42,233	29,636	12,597	6,263	4,354	1,909	3,636	2,926	710
1973–74	48,340	33,245	15,095	6,552	4,555	1,997	3,439	2,740	699
1974–75	51,741	34,612	17,129	6,550	4,587	1,963	3,384	2,641	743
1975–76	54,275	35,520	18,755	6,582	4,497	2,085	3,392	2,663	729
1976–77	53,605	34,218	19,387	7,114	4,718	2,396	3,397	2,671	726
1977–78	51,502	31,705	19,797	6,806	4,400	2,406	3,309	2,511	798
1978–79	48,846	29,191	19,655	6,831	4,265	2,566	3,542	2,636	906
1979–80	46,370	26,828	19,542	6,510	4,098	2,412	3,636	2,690	946
1980–81	43,216	24,149	19,067	5,978	3,654	2,324	3,718	2,666	1,052
1981–82	41,639	22,754	18,885	5,874	3,426	2,448	3,743	2,654	1,089
1982–83	39,982	21,564	18,418	5,696	3,214	2,482	3,341	2,266	1,075
1983–84	38,640	20,558	18,082	5,406	2,996	2,410	3,437	2,381	1,056
1984–85	38,445	20,064	18,381	5,059	2,647	2,412	3,432	2,307	1,125
1985–86	38,524	19,993	18,531	5,013	2,616	2,397	3,358	2,229	1,129
1986–87	38,121	19,657	18,464	4,952	2,538	2,414	3,419	2,225	1,194
1987–88	36,755	18,245	18,510	4,784	2,423	2,361	3,629	2,349	1,280
1988–89	36,059	17,953	18,106	4,961	2,492	2,469	3,520	2,234	1,286
1989–90	37,204	18,312	18,892	4,869	2,395	2,474	3,844	2,394	1,450
1990–91	39,530	19,412	20,118	4,765	2,302	2,463	4,093	2,577	1,516
1991–92	42,941	20,798	22,143	4,785	2,301	2,484	4,243	2,620	1,623
1992–93	47,038	22,842	24,196	4,756	2,343	2,413	4,435	2,664	1,771
1993–94	51,383	25,050	26,333	5,196	2,465	2,731	4,534	2,690	1,844

[1] Includes degrees in biology; biochemistry and biophysics; botany; cell and molecular biology; microbiology/bacteriology; zoology; and other biological sciences.

SOURCE: U.S. Department of Education, National Center for Education Statistics, "Degrees and Other Formal Awards Conferred" surveys, and Integrated Postsecondary Education Data System (IPEDS), "Completions" surveys. (This table was prepared November 1995.)

Table 274.—Earned degrees in biology, microbiology, and zoology conferred by institutions of higher education, by level of degree: 1970–71 to 1993–94

Year	Biology, general			Microbiology [1]			Zoology [2]		
	Bachelor's	Master's	Doctor's	Bachelor's	Master's	Doctor's	Bachelor's	Master's	Doctor's
1	2	3	4	5	6	7	8	9	10
1970–71	26,294	2,665	536	1,475	456	365	5,722	1,167	1,107
1971–72	27,473	2,943	580	1,548	470	351	5,522	1,189	1,094
1972–73	31,185	2,959	627	1,940	517	344	5,770	1,191	1,008
1973–74	36,188	3,186	657	2,311	505	384	6,192	1,250	919
1974–75	38,748	3,109	637	2,767	552	345	6,116	1,216	920
1975–76	40,163	3,177	624	2,927	585	364	6,105	1,153	909
1976–77	39,530	3,322	608	2,884	659	325	5,608	1,168	950
1977–78	37,598	3,094	664	2,695	615	353	5,139	1,160	885
1978–79	35,962	3,093	663	2,670	597	395	4,913	1,109	938
1979–80	33,523	2,911	718	2,631	596	376	4,374	1,078	955
1980–81	31,323	2,598	734	2,414	482	370	3,946	1,090	946
1981–82	29,651	2,579	678	2,377	470	350	3,664	1,028	936
1982–83	28,022	2,354	521	2,306	446	331	3,453	918	809
1983–84	27,379	2,313	617	2,329	447	360	3,294	867	826
1984–85	27,593	2,130	658	2,180	413	302	3,128	778	802
1985–86	27,618	2,173	574	2,217	353	336	2,940	723	844
1986–87	27,465	2,022	537	2,098	390	337	2,858	740	787
1987–88	26,838	1,981	576	2,014	357	386	2,580	725	786
1988–89	26,229	2,097	527	1,780	411	356	2,582	736	744
1989–90	27,213	1,998	551	1,814	366	409	2,501	638	810
1990–91	29,285	1,956	632	1,757	324	419	2,673	640	833
1991–92	31,909	1,995	657	1,722	336	454	2,840	620	818
1992–93	34,932	2,000	671	1,769	328	520	3,071	637	786
1993–94	38,103	2,178	665	1,841	332	478	3,207	749	805

[1] Includes bacteriology.

[2] Includes general zoology; entomology; pathology; pharmacology; physiology; and zoology, other.

SOURCE: U.S. Department of Education, National Center for Education Statistics, "Degrees and Other Formal Awards Conferred" surveys, and Integrated Postsecondary Education Data System (IPEDS), "Completions" surveys. (This table was prepared November 1995.)

Table 275.—Earned degrees in business management and administrative services[1] conferred by institutions of higher education, by level of degree and sex of student: 1955–56 to 1993–94

Year	Bachelor's degrees			Master's degrees			Doctor's degrees		
	Total	Men	Women	Total	Men	Women	Total	Men	Women
1	2	3	4	5	6	7	8	9	10
1955–56	42,813	38,706	4,107	3,280	3,118	162	129	127	2
1957–58	51,991	48,063	3,928	4,223	4,072	151	110	105	5
1959–60	51,076	47,262	3,814	4,643	4,476	167	135	133	2
1961–62	49,017	45,184	3,833	7,691	7,484	207	226	221	5
1963–64	55,474	51,056	4,418	9,251	9,008	243	275	268	7
1965–66	62,721	57,516	5,205	12,959	12,628	331	387	370	17
1967–68	79,074	72,126	6,948	17,795	17,186	609	441	427	14
1969–70	105,580	96,346	9,234	21,561	20,792	769	620	610	10
1970–71	114,729	104,275	10,454	25,977	24,967	1,010	757	736	21
1971–72	121,266	109,688	11,578	30,028	28,845	1,183	859	840	19
1972–73	126,144	112,783	13,361	30,638	29,128	1,510	902	850	52
1973–74	131,640	114,729	16,911	32,172	30,044	2,128	919	870	49
1974–75	132,731	111,144	21,587	35,758	32,732	3,026	936	897	39
1975–76	142,034	113,954	28,080	42,054	37,145	4,909	900	851	49
1976–77	150,765	115,353	35,412	46,006	39,400	6,606	827	775	52
1977–78	159,691	116,171	43,520	47,837	39,743	8,094	823	753	70
1978–79	171,241	118,825	52,416	49,855	40,274	9,581	821	724	97
1979–80	184,867	122,508	62,359	54,484	42,288	12,196	753	642	111
1980–81	198,983	125,523	73,460	57,391	42,980	14,411	795	675	120
1981–82	213,374	129,262	84,112	60,763	43,807	16,956	815	668	147
1982–83	226,627	131,538	95,089	64,758	45,999	18,759	776	644	132
1983–84	229,478	129,559	99,919	66,150	46,178	19,972	929	730	199
1984–85	232,636	127,659	104,977	66,996	46,209	20,787	831	688	143
1985–86	237,319	128,780	108,539	66,689	45,938	20,751	934	729	205
1986–87	240,546	128,603	111,943	67,093	44,913	22,180	1,062	808	254
1987–88	243,021	129,552	113,469	69,230	45,980	23,250	1,063	810	253
1988–89	246,399	131,157	115,242	73,065	48,540	24,525	1,100	800	300
1989–90	248,698	132,329	116,369	76,676	50,585	26,091	1,093	818	275
1990–91	249,311	131,624	117,687	78,255	50,883	27,372	1,185	876	309
1991–92	256,603	135,440	121,163	84,642	54,705	29,937	1,242	953	289
1992–93	256,842	135,573	121,269	89,615	57,651	31,964	1,346	969	377
1993–94	246,654	129,161	117,493	93,437	59,335	34,102	1,364	980	384

[1] Includes degrees in business management/administrative services; marketing operations/marketing and distribution; and consumer and personal services.

SOURCE: U.S. Department of Education, National Center for Education Statistics, "Degrees and Other Formal Awards Conferred" surveys, and Integrated Postsecondary Education Data System (IPEDS), "Completions" surveys. (This table was prepared November 1995.)

Table 276.—Earned degrees in communications[1] conferred by institutions of higher education, by level of degree and sex of student: 1970–71 to 1993–94

Year	Bachelor's degrees			Master's degrees			Doctor's degrees		
	Total	Men	Women	Total	Men	Women	Total	Men	Women
1	2	3	4	5	6	7	8	9	10
1970–71	10,802	6,989	3,813	1,856	1,214	642	145	126	19
1971–72	12,340	7,964	4,376	2,200	1,443	757	111	96	15
1972–73	14,317	9,074	5,243	2,406	1,546	860	139	114	25
1973–74	17,096	10,536	6,560	2,640	1,668	972	175	146	29
1974–75	19,248	11,455	7,793	2,794	1,618	1,176	165	119	46
1975–76	21,282	12,458	8,824	3,126	1,818	1,308	204	154	50
1976–77	23,214	12,932	10,282	3,091	1,719	1,372	171	130	41
1977–78	25,400	13,480	11,920	3,296	1,673	1,623	191	138	53
1978–79	26,457	13,266	13,191	2,882	1,483	1,399	192	138	54
1979–80	28,616	13,656	14,960	3,082	1,527	1,555	193	121	72
1980–81	31,282	14,179	17,103	3,105	1,448	1,657	182	107	75
1981–82	34,222	14,917	19,305	3,327	1,578	1,749	200	136	64
1982–83	38,567	16,161	22,406	3,604	1,661	1,943	214	126	88
1983–84	40,113	16,604	23,509	3,656	1,600	2,056	219	131	88
1984–85	42,002	17,175	24,827	3,669	1,576	2,093	234	143	91
1985–86	43,076	17,639	25,437	3,823	1,610	2,213	223	116	107
1986–87	45,337	18,110	27,227	3,893	1,590	2,303	275	158	117
1987–88	46,649	18,527	28,122	3,925	1,568	2,357	234	134	100
1988–89	48,609	19,215	29,394	4,257	1,737	2,520	253	138	115
1989–90	51,308	20,218	31,090	4,362	1,707	2,655	273	145	128
1990–91	52,773	20,645	32,128	4,336	1,711	2,625	274	151	123
1991–92	54,977	21,497	33,480	4,464	1,692	2,772	255	132	123
1992–93	54,706	22,028	32,678	5,209	1,980	3,229	301	146	155
1993–94	51,827	21,359	30,468	5,419	2,098	3,321	345	174	171

[1] Includes degrees in communications, general; advertising; journalism; broadcast journalism; public relations and organizational communications; radio and television broadcasting; other communications; and communications technology.

SOURCE: U.S. Department of Education, National Center for Education Statistics, "Degrees and Other Formal Awards Conferred" surveys, and Integrated Postsecondary Education Data System (IPEDS), "Completions" surveys. (This table was prepared November 1995.)

Table 277.—Earned degrees in computer and information sciences [1] conferred by institutions of higher education, by level of degree and sex of student: 1970–71 to 1993–94

Year	Bachelor's degrees			Master's degrees			Doctor's degrees		
	Total	Men	Women	Total	Men	Women	Total	Men	Women
1	2	3	4	5	6	7	8	9	10
1970–71	2,388	2,064	324	1,588	1,424	164	128	125	3
1971–72	3,402	2,941	461	1,977	1,752	225	167	155	12
1972–73	4,304	3,664	640	2,113	1,888	225	196	181	15
1973–74	4,756	3,976	780	2,276	1,983	293	198	189	9
1974–75	5,033	4,080	953	2,299	1,961	338	213	199	14
1975–76	5,652	4,534	1,118	2,603	2,226	377	244	221	23
1976–77	6,407	4,876	1,531	2,798	2,332	466	216	197	19
1977–78	7,201	5,349	1,852	3,038	2,471	567	196	181	15
1978–79	8,719	6,272	2,447	3,055	2,480	575	236	206	30
1979–80	11,154	7,782	3,372	3,647	2,883	764	240	213	27
1980–81	15,121	10,202	4,919	4,218	3,247	971	252	227	25
1981–82	20,267	13,218	7,049	4,935	3,625	1,310	251	230	21
1982–83	24,510	15,606	8,904	5,321	3,813	1,508	262	228	34
1983–84	32,172	20,246	11,926	6,190	4,379	1,811	251	225	26
1984–85	38,878	24,579	14,299	7,101	5,064	2,037	248	223	25
1985–86	41,889	26,923	14,966	8,070	5,658	2,412	344	299	45
1986–87	39,589	25,865	13,724	8,481	5,985	2,496	374	322	52
1987–88	34,523	23,331	11,192	9,197	6,726	2,471	428	380	48
1988–89	30,454	21,087	9,367	9,414	6,775	2,639	551	466	85
1989–90	27,257	19,117	8,140	9,677	6,960	2,717	627	534	93
1990–91	25,083	17,726	7,357	9,324	6,563	2,761	676	584	92
1991–92	24,557	17,510	7,047	9,530	6,884	2,646	772	669	103
1992–93	24,200	17,403	6,797	10,163	7,410	2,753	805	689	116
1993–94	24,200	17,317	6,883	10,416	7,724	2,692	810	685	125

[1] Includes degrees in computer and information sciences, general; computer programming; data processing technology/technician; information science and systems; computer systems analysis; and other computer and information sciences.

SOURCE: U.S. Department of Education, National Center for Education Statistics, "Degrees and Other Formal Awards Conferred" surveys, and Integrated Postsecondary Education Data System (IPEDS), "Completions" surveys. (This table was prepared November 1995.)

Table 278.—Earned degrees in education conferred by institutions of higher education, by level of degree and sex of student: 1949–50 to 1993–94

Year	Bachelor's degrees			Master's degrees			Doctor's degrees		
	Total	Men	Women	Total	Men	Women	Total	Men	Women
1	2	3	4	5	6	7	8	9	10
1949–50	61,472	31,398	30,074	20,069	12,025	8,044	953	797	156
1959–60	89,002	25,556	63,446	33,433	18,057	15,376	1,591	1,279	312
1967–68	133,965	31,926	102,039	63,399	30,672	32,727	4,078	3,250	828
1969–70	163,964	40,420	123,544	78,020	34,832	43,188	5,588	4,479	1,109
1970–71	176,307	44,896	131,411	87,666	38,365	49,301	6,041	4,771	1,270
1971–72	190,880	49,344	141,536	96,668	41,141	55,527	6,648	5,104	1,544
1972–73	193,984	51,300	142,684	103,777	43,298	60,479	6,857	5,191	1,666
1973–74	184,907	48,997	135,910	110,402	44,112	66,290	6,757	4,974	1,783
1974–75	166,758	44,463	122,295	117,841	44,430	73,411	6,975	4,856	2,119
1975–76	154,437	42,004	112,433	126,061	44,831	81,230	7,202	4,826	2,376
1976–77	143,234	39,867	103,367	124,267	42,308	81,959	7,338	4,832	2,506
1977–78	135,821	37,410	98,411	116,916	37,662	79,254	7,018	4,281	2,737
1978–79	125,873	33,743	92,130	109,866	34,410	75,456	7,170	4,174	2,996
1979–80	118,038	30,901	87,137	101,819	30,300	71,519	7,314	4,100	3,214
1980–81	108,074	27,039	81,035	96,713	27,548	69,165	7,279	3,843	3,436
1981–82	100,932	24,380	76,552	91,601	25,339	66,262	6,999	3,612	3,387
1982–83	97,895	23,644	74,251	83,250	22,823	60,427	7,057	3,547	3,510
1983–84	92,299	22,195	70,104	75,664	21,142	54,522	6,911	3,446	3,465
1984–85	88,072	21,252	66,820	74,654	20,537	54,117	6,612	3,172	3,440
1985–86	87,114	20,959	66,155	74,801	20,295	54,506	6,605	3,088	3,517
1986–87	86,936	20,729	66,207	74,045	19,293	54,752	6,407	2,931	3,476
1987–88	91,112	20,988	70,124	76,566	19,108	57,458	6,060	2,739	3,321
1988–89	96,913	21,662	75,251	81,174	19,956	61,218	6,337	2,704	3,633
1989–90	105,112	23,007	82,105	84,881	20,467	64,414	6,502	2,776	3,726
1990–91	110,807	23,417	87,390	87,343	20,448	66,895	6,187	2,613	3,574
1991–92	108,006	22,686	85,320	92,668	21,244	71,424	6,864	2,783	4,081
1992–93	107,781	23,233	84,548	96,028	22,197	73,831	7,030	2,867	4,163
1993–94	107,600	24,450	83,150	98,938	23,008	75,930	6,908	2,706	4,202

SOURCE: U.S. Department of Education, National Center for Education Statistics, "Degrees and Other Formal Awards Conferred" surveys, and Integrated Postsecondary Education Data System (IPEDS), "Completions" surveys. (This table was prepared November 1995.)

Table 279.—Earned degrees in engineering [1] conferred by institutions of higher education, by level of degree and sex of student: 1949–50 to 1993–94

Year	Bachelor's degrees			Master's degrees			Doctor's degrees		
	Total	Men	Women	Total	Men	Women	Total	Men	Women
1	2	3	4	5	6	7	8	9	10
1949–50	52,246	52,071	175	4,496	4,481	15	417	416	1
1959–60	37,679	37,537	142	7,159	7,133	26	786	783	3
1963–64	35,226	35,067	159	10,827	10,793	34	1,693	1,686	7
1965–66	35,615	35,472	143	13,675	13,599	76	2,304	2,295	9
1967–68	37,368	37,159	209	15,182	15,083	99	2,932	2,920	12
1969–70	44,479	44,149	330	15,593	15,421	172	3,681	3,657	24
1970–71	50,046	49,646	400	16,443	16,258	185	3,638	3,615	23
1971–72	51,164	50,638	526	16,960	16,688	272	3,671	3,649	22
1972–73	51,265	50,652	613	16,619	16,341	278	3,492	3,438	54
1973–74	50,286	49,490	796	15,379	15,023	356	3,312	3,257	55
1974–75	46,852	45,838	1,014	15,348	14,973	375	3,108	3,042	66
1975–76	46,331	44,871	1,460	16,342	15,760	582	2,821	2,755	66
1976–77	49,283	47,065	2,218	16,245	15,525	720	2,586	2,513	73
1977–78	55,654	51,945	3,709	16,398	15,533	865	2,440	2,383	57
1978–79	62,375	57,201	5,174	15,495	14,544	951	2,506	2,423	83
1979–80	68,893	62,488	6,405	16,243	15,101	1,142	2,507	2,412	95
1980–81	75,000	67,301	7,699	16,709	15,347	1,362	2,561	2,457	104
1981–82	80,005	70,899	9,106	17,939	16,311	1,628	2,636	2,496	140
1982–83	89,018	78,096	10,922	19,344	17,548	1,796	2,831	2,706	125
1983–84	94,185	82,092	12,093	20,655	18,500	2,155	2,981	2,816	165
1984–85	95,828	83,232	12,596	21,555	19,247	2,308	3,230	3,022	208
1985–86	95,660	83,117	12,543	21,657	19,165	2,492	3,410	3,181	229
1986–87	92,816	80,104	12,712	22,654	19,804	2,850	3,818	3,555	263
1987–88	88,506	76,372	12,134	23,385	20,476	2,909	4,191	3,898	293
1988–89	85,002	73,436	11,566	24,568	21,374	3,194	4,523	4,123	400
1989–90	81,322	70,071	11,251	24,772	21,357	3,415	4,981	4,536	445
1990–91	78,650	67,738	10,912	24,958	21,430	3,528	5,272	4,787	485
1991–92	77,541	66,716	10,825	25,977	22,143	3,834	5,499	4,972	527
1992–93	78,051	66,836	11,215	28,726	24,454	4,272	5,843	5,283	560
1993–94	78,225	66,597	11,628	29,754	25,154	4,600	5,979	5,315	664

[1] Includes degrees in engineering and engineering-related technologies from 1969–70 through 1993–94.

SOURCE: U.S. Department of Education, National Center for Education Statistics, "Degrees and Other Formal Awards Conferred" surveys, and Integrated Postsecondary Education Data System (IPEDS), "Completions" surveys. (This table was prepared November 1995.)

Table 280.—Earned degrees in chemical, civil, electrical, and mechanical engineering conferred by institutions of higher education, by level of degree: 1970–71 to 1993–94

Year	Chemical engineering			Civil engineering [1]			Electrical engineering			Mechanical engineering		
	Bachelor's	Master's	Doctor's	Bachelor's	Master's	Doctor's	Bachelor's	Master's	Doctor's	Bachelor's	Master's	Doctor's
1	2	3	4	5	6	7	8	9	10	11	12	13
1970–71	3,579	1,100	406	6,526	2,425	446	12,198	4,282	879	8,858	2,237	438
1971–72	3,625	1,154	394	6,803	2,487	415	12,101	4,206	824	8,530	2,282	411
1972–73	3,578	1,051	397	7,390	2,627	397	12,313	3,895	791	8,523	2,141	370
1973–74	3,399	1,044	400	8,017	2,652	368	11,316	3,499	705	7,677	1,843	385
1974–75	3,070	990	346	7,651	2,769	356	10,161	3,469	701	6,890	1,858	340
1975–76	3,140	1,031	308	7,923	2,999	370	9,791	3,774	649	6,800	1,907	305
1976–77	3,524	1,086	291	8,228	2,964	309	9,936	3,788	566	7,703	1,952	283
1977–78	4,569	1,235	259	9,135	2,685	277	11,133	3,740	503	8,875	1,942	279
1978–79	5,568	1,149	304	9,809	2,646	253	12,338	3,591	586	10,107	1,877	271
1979–80	6,320	1,270	284	10,326	2,683	270	13,821	3,836	525	11,808	2,060	281
1980–81	6,527	1,267	300	10,678	2,891	325	14,938	3,901	535	13,329	2,291	276
1981–82	6,740	1,285	311	10,524	2,995	329	16,455	4,462	526	13,922	2,399	333
1982–83	7,185	1,368	319	9,989	3,074	340	18,049	4,531	550	15,675	2,511	299
1983–84	7,475	1,514	330	9,693	3,146	369	19,943	5,078	585	16,629	2,797	319
1984–85	7,146	1,544	418	9,162	3,172	377	21,691	5,153	660	16,794	3,053	409
1985–86	5,877	1,361	446	8,679	2,926	395	23,742	5,534	722	16,194	3,075	426
1986–87	4,991	1,184	497	8,147	2,901	451	24,547	6,183	724	15,450	3,198	528
1987–88	3,917	1,088	579	7,488	2,836	481	23,597	6,688	860	14,900	3,329	596
1988–89	3,663	1,093	602	7,312	2,903	505	21,908	7,028	998	14,843	3,498	633
1989–90	3,430	1,035	562	7,252	2,812	516	20,711	7,225	1,162	14,336	3,424	742
1990–91	3,444	903	611	7,314	2,927	536	19,320	7,095	1,220	13,977	3,516	757
1991–92	3,754	956	590	8,034	3,113	540	17,958	7,360	1,282	14,067	3,653	851
1992–93	4,459	990	595	8,868	3,610	577	17,281	7,870	1,413	14,464	3,982	871
1993–94	5,163	1,032	604	9,479	3,873	651	15,823	7,791	1,470	15,030	4,099	887

[1] From 1970–71 to 1981–82 includes "construction and transportation engineering."

NOTE.—Degrees in engineering-related technologies are not included in this tabulation.

SOURCE: U.S. Department of Education, National Center for Education Statistics, "Degrees and Other Formal Awards Conferred" surveys, and Integrated Postsecondary Education Data System (IPEDS), "Completions" surveys. (This table was prepared November 1995.)

Table 281.—Earned degrees in English language and literature/letters [1] conferred by institutions of higher education, by level of degree and sex of student: 1949–50 to 1993–94

Year	Bachelor's degrees			Master's degrees			Doctor's degrees		
	Total	Men	Women	Total	Men	Women	Total	Men	Women
1	2	3	4	5	6	7	8	9	10
1949–50	17,240	8,221	9,019	2,259	1,320	939	230	181	49
1959–60	20,128	7,580	12,548	2,931	1,458	1,473	397	314	83
1967–68	47,977	15,700	32,277	7,916	3,434	4,482	977	717	260
1969–70	56,410	18,650	37,760	8,517	3,326	5,191	1,213	837	376
1970–71	64,342	22,155	42,187	10,686	4,211	6,475	1,650	1,175	475
1971–72	63,976	22,657	41,319	10,579	4,123	6,456	1,826	1,233	593
1972–73	61,003	22,156	38,847	10,239	4,063	6,176	1,935	1,258	677
1973–74	54,590	20,214	34,376	9,803	3,917	5,886	1,885	1,208	677
1974–75	47,619	17,880	29,739	9,444	3,569	5,875	1,711	1,025	686
1975–76	42,006	16,073	25,933	8,809	3,383	5,426	1,672	967	705
1976–77	37,794	14,295	23,499	8,016	2,985	5,031	1,508	841	667
1977–78	35,328	13,137	22,191	7,655	2,706	4,949	1,400	758	642
1978–79	33,561	12,198	21,363	6,684	2,369	4,315	1,314	708	606
1979–80	32,541	11,380	21,161	6,189	2,233	3,956	1,294	686	608
1980–81	32,254	11,198	21,056	5,929	2,092	3,837	1,164	553	611
1981–82	33,419	11,414	22,005	5,772	1,983	3,789	1,101	511	590
1982–83	31,829	10,859	20,970	5,048	1,710	3,338	991	471	520
1983–84	32,834	11,170	21,664	5,010	1,736	3,274	1,018	459	559
1984–85	33,218	11,334	21,884	5,187	1,786	3,401	1,041	470	571
1985–86	34,552	11,819	22,733	5,518	1,881	3,637	991	428	563
1986–87	36,284	12,353	23,931	5,483	1,891	3,592	961	415	546
1987–88	38,661	12,836	25,825	5,562	1,870	3,692	981	428	553
1988–89	42,470	13,927	28,543	5,950	2,002	3,948	1,022	458	564
1989–90	47,519	15,662	31,857	6,567	2,205	4,362	1,078	480	598
1990–91	51,841	17,146	34,695	7,026	2,296	4,730	1,184	517	667
1991–92	54,951	18,536	36,415	7,450	2,513	4,937	1,273	537	736
1992–93	56,133	19,247	36,886	7,790	2,667	5,123	1,341	550	791
1993–94	53,924	18,425	35,499	7,885	2,712	5,173	1,344	568	776

[1] Includes degrees conferred in English language and literature, general; comparative literature; English composition; English creative writing; American literature; English literature; speech and rhetorical studies; English technical and business writing; and English language and literature/letters, other.

SOURCE: U.S. Department of Education, National Center for Education Statistics, "Degrees and Other Formal Awards Conferred" surveys, and Integrated Postsecondary Education Data System (IPEDS), "Completions" surveys. (This table was prepared November 1995.)

Table 282.—Earned degrees in modern foreign languages and literatures [1] conferred by institutions of higher education, by level of degree and sex of student: 1949–50 to 1993–94

Year	Bachelor's degrees			Master's degrees			Doctor's degrees		
	Total	Men	Women	Total	Men	Women	Total	Men	Women
1	2	3	4	5	6	7	8	9	10
1949–50	4,477	1,746	2,731	919	456	463	168	135	33
1959–60	4,527	1,548	2,979	832	392	440	150	100	50
1967–68	17,499	4,450	13,049	3,911	1,555	2,356	491	336	155
1969–70	19,457	4,921	14,536	4,154	1,476	2,678	590	369	221
1970–71	19,055	4,734	14,321	4,407	1,492	2,915	703	425	278
1971–72	18,137	4,445	13,692	4,277	1,449	2,828	753	466	287
1972–73	18,232	4,347	13,885	3,992	1,407	2,585	889	519	370
1973–74	18,252	4,276	13,976	3,793	1,252	2,541	875	487	388
1974–75	17,115	3,912	13,203	3,672	1,179	2,493	829	442	387
1975–76	15,079	3,495	11,584	3,359	1,095	2,264	830	429	401
1976–77	13,626	3,225	10,401	2,986	886	2,100	728	347	381
1977–78	12,448	2,938	9,510	2,653	768	1,885	626	282	344
1978–79	11,531	2,705	8,826	2,338	685	1,653	625	287	338
1979–80	10,816	2,583	8,233	2,152	628	1,524	522	217	305
1980–81	10,050	2,402	7,648	2,018	657	1,361	556	259	297
1981–82	9,576	2,278	7,298	1,913	571	1,342	495	220	275
1982–83	9,334	2,343	6,991	1,597	528	1,069	451	183	268
1983–84	9,152	2,399	6,753	1,640	512	1,128	424	191	233
1984–85	9,675	2,529	7,146	1,611	503	1,108	387	156	231
1985–86	9,808	2,685	7,123	1,655	482	1,173	426	173	253
1986–87	9,858	2,655	7,203	1,692	491	1,201	403	162	241
1987–88	9,790	2,628	7,162	1,795	564	1,231	380	159	221
1988–89	10,498	2,767	7,731	1,821	552	1,269	389	145	244
1989–90	11,092	2,902	8,190	1,931	584	1,347	475	183	292
1990–91	11,724	3,207	8,517	1,973	595	1,378	477	200	277
1991–92	12,367	3,390	8,977	2,119	652	1,467	537	222	315
1992–93	12,819	3,537	9,282	2,353	744	1,609	535	210	325
1993–94	12,785	3,672	9,113	2,343	712	1,631	578	208	370

[1] Includes degrees conferred in a single language or a combination of modern foreign languages. Excludes degrees in linguistics, Latin, classical Greek, and "other" foreign languages.

SOURCE: U.S. Department of Education, National Center for Education Statistics, "Degrees and Other Formal Awards Conferred" surveys, and Integrated Postsecondary Education Data System (IPEDS), "Completions" surveys. (This table was prepared November 1995.)

Table 283.—Earned degrees in French, German, and Spanish conferred by institutions of higher education, by level of degree: 1949–50 to 1993–94

Year	French			German			Spanish		
	Bachelor's	Master's	Doctor's	Bachelor's	Master's	Doctor's	Bachelor's	Master's	Doctor's
1	2	3	4	5	6	7	8	9	10
1949–50	1,471	299	53	540	121	40	2,122	373	34
1959–60	1,927	316	58	659	126	21	1,610	261	31
1967–68	7,068	1,301	152	2,368	771	117	6,381	1,188	123
1969–70	7,624	1,409	181	2,652	669	118	7,226	1,372	139
1970–71	7,306	1,437	192	2,601	690	144	7,068	1,456	168
1971–72	6,822	1,421	193	2,477	608	167	6,847	1,421	152
1972–73	6,705	1,277	203	2,520	598	176	7,209	1,298	206
1973–74	6,263	1,195	213	2,425	550	149	7,250	1,217	203
1974–75	5,745	1,077	200	2,289	480	147	6,719	1,228	202
1975–76	4,783	914	190	1,983	471	164	5,984	1,080	176
1976–77	4,228	875	177	1,820	394	126	5,359	930	153
1977–78	3,708	692	155	1,647	357	101	4,832	822	113
1978–79	3,558	576	143	1,524	344	106	4,563	720	118
1979–80	3,285	513	128	1,466	309	94	4,331	685	103
1980–81	3,178	460	115	1,286	294	79	3,870	592	131
1981–82	3,054	485	92	1,327	324	76	3,633	568	140
1982–83	2,871	360	106	1,367	281	68	3,349	506	129
1983–84	2,876	418	86	1,292	241	63	3,254	537	102
1984–85	2,991	385	74	1,411	240	58	3,415	505	115
1985–86	3,015	409	86	1,396	249	73	3,385	521	95
1986–87	3,062	421	85	1,366	234	70	3,450	504	104
1987–88	3,082	437	89	1,350	244	71	3,416	553	93
1988–89	3,297	444	83	1,428	263	59	3,748	552	101
1989–90	3,259	478	115	1,437	253	67	4,176	573	108
1990–91	3,355	480	98	1,543	242	58	4,480	609	125
1991–92	3,371	465	112	1,616	273	85	4,768	647	143
1992–93	3,280	513	98	1,572	317	86	5,233	667	145
1993–94	3,094	479	104	1,580	298	61	5,505	691	160

SOURCE: U.S. Department of Education, National Center for Education Statistics, "Degrees and Other Formal Awards Conferred" surveys, and Integrated Postsecondary Education Data System (IPEDS), "Completions" surveys. (This table was prepared November 1995.)

Table 284.—Earned degrees in the health professions and related sciences [1] conferred by institutions of higher education, by level of degree and sex of student: 1970–71 to 1993–94

Year	Bachelor's degrees			Master's degrees			Doctor's degrees		
	Total	Men	Women	Total	Men	Women	Total	Men	Women
1	2	3	4	5	6	7	8	9	10
1970–71	25,226	5,788	19,438	5,749	2,567	3,182	466	389	77
1971–72	28,611	7,005	21,606	7,207	3,141	4,066	442	362	80
1972–73	33,564	7,754	25,810	8,362	3,567	4,795	646	485	161
1973–74	41,459	9,388	32,071	9,599	3,819	5,780	578	447	131
1974–75	49,090	10,930	38,160	10,692	4,092	6,600	618	441	177
1975–76	53,958	11,456	42,502	12,556	4,217	8,339	577	411	166
1976–77	57,328	11,947	45,381	12,951	4,163	8,788	538	366	172
1977–78	59,434	11,593	47,841	14,325	4,265	10,060	654	402	252
1978–79	62,085	11,205	50,880	15,485	4,494	10,991	718	454	264
1979–80	63,920	11,391	52,529	15,704	4,357	11,347	786	435	351
1980–81	63,649	10,519	53,130	16,515	4,316	12,199	842	475	367
1981–82	63,653	10,105	53,548	16,503	4,006	12,497	925	503	422
1982–83	64,685	10,218	54,467	17,047	4,235	12,812	1,155	649	506
1983–84	64,288	10,040	54,248	17,411	4,251	13,160	1,164	574	590
1984–85	64,422	9,741	54,681	17,385	4,119	13,266	1,199	565	634
1985–86	64,396	9,630	54,766	18,573	4,428	14,145	1,241	604	637
1986–87	63,103	9,134	53,969	18,394	3,874	14,520	1,213	564	649
1987–88	60,644	8,929	51,715	18,657	4,047	14,610	1,261	548	713
1988–89	59,005	8,872	50,133	19,268	4,226	15,042	1,437	609	828
1989–90	58,302	9,118	49,184	20,321	4,534	15,787	1,536	704	832
1990–91	59,070	9,596	49,474	21,200	4,444	16,756	1,613	694	919
1991–92	61,720	10,189	51,531	23,065	4,691	18,374	1,661	698	963
1992–93	67,089	11,347	55,742	25,718	5,227	20,491	1,767	753	1,014
1993–94	74,421	13,062	61,359	28,025	5,814	22,211	1,902	789	1,113

[1] Includes degrees in chiropractic; communication disorders sciences; community health liaison; dentistry; dental services; health services administration; health and medical assistants; health and medical diagnostic and treatment services; medical laboratory technologies; predentistry; premedicine; prepharmacy; preveterinary; medical basic sciences; mental health services; nursing; optometry; pharmacy; epidemiology; rehabilitation and therapeutic services; veterinary medicine; and other health professions.

SOURCE: U.S. Department of Education, National Center for Education Statistics, "Degrees and Other Formal Awards Conferred" surveys, and Integrated Postsecondary Education Data System (IPEDS), "Completions" surveys. (This table was prepared November 1995.)

Table 285.—Earned degrees in mathematics [1] conferred by institutions of higher education, by level of degree and sex of student: 1949–50 to 1993–94

Year	Bachelor's degrees			Master's degrees			Doctor's degrees		
	Total	Men	Women	Total	Men	Women	Total	Men	Women
1	2	3	4	5	6	7	8	9	10
1949–50	6,382	4,942	1,440	974	784	190	160	151	9
1959–60	11,399	8,293	3,106	1,757	1,422	335	303	285	18
1967–68	23,513	14,782	8,731	5,527	4,199	1,328	947	895	52
1969–70	27,442	17,177	10,265	5,636	3,966	1,670	1,236	1,140	96
1970–71	24,937	15,498	9,439	5,695	4,149	1,546	1,249	1,154	95
1971–72	23,807	14,542	9,265	5,537	3,976	1,561	1,165	1,075	90
1972–73	23,186	13,910	9,276	5,397	3,878	1,519	1,089	987	102
1973–74	21,761	12,912	8,849	5,306	3,784	1,522	1,093	992	101
1974–75	18,460	10,853	7,607	4,816	3,358	1,458	1,048	936	112
1975–76	16,329	9,788	6,541	4,315	2,961	1,354	909	812	97
1976–77	14,395	8,476	5,919	4,109	2,762	1,347	859	748	111
1977–78	13,065	7,806	5,259	3,862	2,635	1,227	848	722	126
1978–79	12,329	7,301	5,028	3,553	2,412	1,141	769	644	125
1979–80	11,872	6,951	4,921	3,382	2,262	1,120	763	659	104
1980–81	11,433	6,614	4,819	3,074	2,106	968	775	656	119
1981–82	12,226	6,999	5,227	3,263	2,257	1,006	721	623	98
1982–83	12,719	7,175	5,544	3,398	2,316	1,082	731	611	120
1983–84	13,764	7,716	6,048	3,244	2,178	1,066	743	614	129
1984–85	15,861	8,537	7,324	3,413	2,289	1,124	734	620	114
1985–86	17,147	9,216	7,931	3,607	2,397	1,210	777	648	129
1986–87	16,999	9,110	7,889	3,730	2,328	1,402	759	628	131
1987–88	16,608	8,919	7,689	3,867	2,391	1,476	796	668	128
1988–89	15,994	8,662	7,332	3,903	2,418	1,485	915	737	178
1989–90	15,176	8,236	6,940	4,146	2,568	1,578	966	794	172
1990–91	15,310	8,178	7,132	4,041	2,446	1,595	1,036	837	199
1991–92	14,783	7,888	6,895	4,011	2,452	1,559	1,082	851	231
1992–93	14,812	7,827	6,985	4,067	2,455	1,612	1,189	906	283
1993–94	14,396	7,735	6,661	4,100	2,536	1,564	1,157	904	253

[1] Includes degrees conferred in statistics.

SOURCE: U.S. Department of Education, National Center for Education Statistics, "Degrees and Other Formal Awards Conferred" surveys, and Integrated Postsecondary Education Data System (IPEDS), "Completions" surveys. (This table was prepared November 1995.)

Table 286.—Earned degrees in the physical sciences [1] conferred by institutions of higher education, by level of degree and sex of student: 1959–60 to 1993–94

Year	Bachelor's degrees			Master's degrees			Doctor's degrees		
	Total	Men	Women	Total	Men	Women	Total	Men	Women
1	2	3	4	5	6	7	8	9	10
1959–60	16,007	14,013	1,994	3,376	3,049	327	1,838	1,776	62
1967–68	19,380	16,739	2,641	5,499	4,869	630	3,593	3,405	188
1969–70	21,439	18,522	2,917	5,935	5,093	842	4,312	4,077	235
1970–71	21,412	18,459	2,953	6,367	5,521	846	4,390	4,144	246
1971–72	20,745	17,663	3,082	6,287	5,404	883	4,103	3,830	273
1972–73	20,696	17,626	3,070	6,257	5,414	843	4,006	3,738	268
1973–74	21,178	17,674	3,504	6,062	5,186	876	3,626	3,373	253
1974–75	20,778	16,992	3,786	5,807	4,969	838	3,626	3,325	301
1975–76	21,465	17,353	4,112	5,466	4,648	818	3,431	3,132	299
1976–77	22,497	17,996	4,501	5,331	4,450	881	3,341	3,022	319
1977–78	22,986	18,090	4,896	5,561	4,620	941	3,133	2,821	312
1978–79	23,207	17,985	5,222	5,451	4,461	990	3,102	2,752	350
1979–80	23,410	17,864	5,546	5,219	4,248	971	3,089	2,705	384
1980–81	23,952	18,064	5,888	5,284	4,200	1,084	3,141	2,765	376
1981–82	24,052	17,866	6,186	5,514	4,318	1,196	3,286	2,835	451
1982–83	23,381	16,993	6,388	5,290	4,157	1,133	3,269	2,811	458
1983–84	23,651	17,116	6,535	5,576	4,268	1,308	3,306	2,815	491
1984–85	23,704	17,069	6,635	5,796	4,452	1,344	3,403	2,851	552
1985–86	21,717	15,755	5,962	5,902	4,470	1,432	3,551	2,963	588
1986–87	20,070	14,372	5,698	5,629	4,219	1,410	3,673	3,039	634
1987–88	17,806	12,389	5,417	5,733	4,324	1,409	3,809	3,123	686
1988–89	17,186	12,077	5,109	5,723	4,199	1,524	3,858	3,088	770
1989–90	16,066	11,031	5,035	5,449	4,010	1,439	4,164	3,356	808
1990–91	16,344	11,176	5,168	5,309	3,837	1,472	4,290	3,447	843
1991–92	16,960	11,431	5,529	5,374	3,909	1,465	4,391	3,429	962
1992–93	17,545	11,825	5,720	5,366	3,808	1,558	4,393	3,432	961
1993–94	18,400	12,223	6,177	5,679	4,018	1,661	4,650	3,642	1,008

[1] Includes degrees in physical sciences, general; astronomy, astrophysics; atmospheric science and meteorology; chemistry, geology, miscellaneous physical sciences; physics, science technologies, and other physical sciences.

SOURCE: U.S. Department of Education, National Center for Education Statistics, "Degrees and Other Formal Awards Conferred" surveys, and Integrated Postsecondary Education Data System (IPEDS), "Completions" surveys. (This table was prepared November 1995.)

Table 287.—Earned degrees in chemistry, geology, and physics conferred by institutions of higher education, by level of degree: 1970–71 to 1993–94

Year	Chemistry			Geology [1]			Physics		
	Bachelor's	Master's	Doctor's	Bachelor's	Master's	Doctor's	Bachelor's	Master's	Doctor's
1	2	3	4	5	6	7	8	9	10
1970–71	11,063	2,275	2,159	2,414	651	324	5,071	2,188	1,482
1971–72	10,590	2,248	1,971	2,573	841	310	4,634	2,033	1,344
1972–73	10,128	2,225	1,872	2,923	827	305	4,259	1,747	1,338
1973–74	10,438	2,125	1,823	3,253	938	315	3,952	1,655	1,115
1974–75	10,549	1,986	1,822	3,319	932	292	3,706	1,574	1,080
1975–76	11,022	1,783	1,621	3,358	1,003	313	3,544	1,451	997
1976–77	11,215	1,767	1,568	3,879	1,047	325	3,420	1,319	945
1977–78	11,315	1,886	1,521	4,342	1,239	268	3,330	1,294	873
1978–79	11,509	1,757	1,516	4,502	1,300	286	3,337	1,319	918
1979–80	11,232	1,723	1,545	4,597	1,295	313	3,396	1,192	830
1980–81	11,347	1,654	1,622	5,202	1,396	294	3,441	1,294	866
1981–82	11,062	1,751	1,722	5,538	1,540	282	3,472	1,284	873
1982–83	10,796	1,622	1,746	6,102	1,552	295	3,793	1,369	873
1983–84	10,704	1,667	1,744	6,549	1,514	315	3,907	1,532	953
1984–85	10,482	1,719	1,789	6,308	1,692	289	4,097	1,523	951
1985–86	10,116	1,754	1,908	4,974	1,767	271	4,180	1,501	1,010
1986–87	9,670	1,738	1,976	3,665	1,603	280	4,318	1,543	1,074
1987–88	9,052	1,708	1,995	2,551	1,523	350	4,100	1,675	1,093
1988–89	8,625	1,774	2,037	2,252	1,404	358	4,352	1,736	1,112
1989–90	8,132	1,682	2,183	1,767	1,200	414	4,155	1,831	1,192
1990–91	8,321	1,665	2,238	1,784	1,089	446	4,236	1,725	1,209
1991–92	8,641	1,780	2,280	2,078	990	413	4,098	1,834	1,337
1992–93	8,914	1,842	2,261	2,299	925	406	4,063	1,777	1,277
1993–94	9,425	1,999	2,353	2,677	937	422	4,001	1,945	1,465

[1] Includes geology, geochemistry, and geophysics and seismology. Beginning in 1982–83, also includes other geological sciences.

SOURCE: U.S. Department of Education, National Center for Education Statistics, "Degrees and Other Formal Awards Conferred" surveys, and Integrated Postsecondary Education Data System (IPEDS), "Completions" surveys. (This table was prepared November 1995.)

Table 288.—Earned degrees in psychology conferred by institutions of higher education, by level of degree and by sex of student: 1949–50 to 1993–94

Year	Bachelor's degrees			Master's degrees			Doctor's degrees		
	Total	Men	Women	Total	Men	Women	Total	Men	Women
1	2	3	4	5	6	7	8	9	10
1949–50	9,569	6,055	3,514	1,316	948	368	283	241	42
1959–60	8,061	4,773	3,288	1,406	981	425	641	544	97
1967–68	23,819	13,792	10,027	3,479	2,321	1,158	1,268	982	286
1969–70	33,679	19,077	14,602	5,158	2,975	2,183	1,962	1,505	457
1970–71	38,187	21,227	16,960	5,717	3,395	2,322	2,144	1,629	515
1971–72	43,433	23,352	20,081	6,764	3,934	2,830	2,277	1,694	583
1972–73	47,940	25,117	22,823	7,619	4,325	3,294	2,550	1,797	753
1973–74	52,139	25,868	26,271	8,796	4,983	3,813	2,872	1,987	885
1974–75	51,245	24,284	26,961	9,394	5,035	4,359	2,913	1,979	934
1975–76	50,278	22,898	27,380	10,167	5,136	5,031	3,157	2,115	1,042
1976–77	47,861	20,627	27,234	10,859	5,293	5,566	3,386	2,127	1,259
1977–78	44,879	18,422	26,457	10,282	4,670	5,612	3,164	1,974	1,190
1978–79	42,697	16,540	26,157	10,132	4,405	5,727	3,228	1,895	1,333
1979–80	42,093	15,440	26,653	9,938	4,096	5,842	3,395	1,921	1,474
1980–81	41,068	14,332	26,736	10,223	4,066	6,157	3,576	2,002	1,574
1981–82	41,212	13,645	27,567	9,947	3,823	6,124	3,461	1,856	1,605
1982–83	40,460	13,131	27,329	9,981	3,647	6,334	3,602	1,838	1,764
1983–84	39,955	12,812	27,143	9,525	3,400	6,125	3,535	1,774	1,761
1984–85	39,900	12,706	27,194	9,891	3,452	6,439	3,447	1,739	1,708
1985–86	40,628	12,605	28,023	9,845	3,347	6,498	3,593	1,724	1,869
1986–87	42,994	13,362	29,632	9,562	3,172	6,390	3,560	1,615	1,945
1987–88	45,187	13,538	31,649	9,180	2,923	6,257	3,480	1,573	1,907
1988–89	48,910	14,246	34,664	9,940	3,122	6,818	3,685	1,590	2,095
1989–90	53,952	15,336	38,616	10,730	3,377	7,353	3,811	1,566	2,245
1990–91	58,655	16,067	42,588	11,349	3,329	8,020	3,932	1,520	2,412
1991–92	63,513	17,031	46,482	10,215	2,988	7,227	3,373	1,359	2,014
1992–93	66,728	17,908	48,820	10,957	3,029	7,928	3,651	1,415	2,236
1993–94	69,259	18,642	50,617	12,181	3,401	8,780	3,563	1,346	2,217

SOURCE: U.S. Department of Education, National Center for Education Statistics, "Degrees and Other Formal Awards Conferred" surveys, and Integrated Postsecondary Education Data System (IPEDS), "Completions" surveys. (This table was prepared November 1995.)

Table 289.—Earned degrees in public administration and services [1] conferred by institutions of higher education, by level of degree and sex of student: 1970–71 to 1993–94

Year	Bachelor's degrees			Master's degrees			Doctor's degrees		
	Total	Men	Women	Total	Men	Women	Total	Men	Women
1	2	3	4	5	6	7	8	9	10
1970–71	5,466	1,726	3,740	7,785	3,893	3,892	174	132	42
1971–72	7,508	2,588	4,920	8,756	4,537	4,219	193	150	43
1972–73	10,690	3,998	6,692	10,068	5,271	4,797	198	160	38
1973–74	11,966	4,266	7,700	11,415	6,028	5,387	201	154	47
1974–75	13,661	4,630	9,031	13,617	7,200	6,417	257	192	65
1975–76	15,440	5,706	9,734	15,209	7,969	7,240	292	192	100
1976–77	16,136	5,544	10,592	17,026	8,810	8,216	292	197	95
1977–78	16,607	5,096	11,511	17,337	8,513	8,824	357	237	120
1978–79	17,328	4,938	12,390	17,306	8,051	9,255	315	215	100
1979–80	16,644	4,451	12,193	17,560	7,866	9,694	342	216	126
1980–81	16,707	4,248	12,459	17,803	7,460	10,343	362	212	150
1981–82	16,495	4,176	12,319	17,416	6,975	10,441	372	205	167
1982–83	14,414	3,343	11,071	16,046	5,961	10,085	347	184	163
1983–84	12,570	2,998	9,572	15,060	5,634	9,426	420	230	190
1984–85	11,754	2,829	8,925	15,575	5,573	10,002	431	213	218
1985–86	11,887	2,966	8,921	15,692	5,594	10,098	382	171	211
1986–87	12,328	2,993	9,335	16,432	5,673	10,759	398	216	182
1987–88	12,385	2,923	9,462	16,424	5,631	10,793	470	238	232
1988–89	13,162	3,214	9,948	17,020	5,615	11,405	428	210	218
1989–90	13,908	3,334	10,574	17,399	5,634	11,765	508	235	273
1990–91	14,350	3,215	11,135	17,905	5,679	12,226	430	190	240
1991–92	15,987	3,479	12,508	19,243	5,769	13,474	432	204	228
1992–93	16,775	3,801	12,974	20,634	6,105	14,529	459	215	244
1993–94	17,815	3,919	13,896	21,833	6,406	15,427	519	238	281

[1] Includes degrees in public administration; community organization, resources and services; public policy analysis; social work; and public affairs, other.

SOURCE: U.S. Department of Education, National Center for Education Statistics, "Degrees and Other Formal Awards Conferred" surveys, and Integrated Postsecondary Education Data System (IPEDS), "Completions" surveys. (This table was prepared November 1995.)

Table 290.—Earned degrees in the social sciences [1] and history conferred by institutions of higher education, by level of degree and sex of student: 1970–71 to 1993–94

Year	Bachelor's degrees			Master's degrees			Doctor's degrees		
	Total	Men	Women	Total	Men	Women	Total	Men	Women
1	2	3	4	5	6	7	8	9	10
1970–71	155,324	98,173	57,151	16,539	11,833	4,706	3,660	3,153	507
1971–72	158,060	100,895	57,165	17,445	12,540	4,905	4,081	3,483	598
1972–73	155,970	99,735	56,235	17,477	12,605	4,872	4,234	3,573	661
1973–74	150,320	95,650	54,670	17,293	12,321	4,972	4,124	3,383	741
1974–75	135,190	84,826	50,364	16,977	11,875	5,102	4,212	3,334	878
1975–76	126,396	78,691	47,705	15,953	10,918	5,035	4,157	3,262	895
1976–77	117,040	71,128	45,912	15,533	10,413	5,120	3,802	2,957	845
1977–78	112,952	67,217	45,735	14,718	9,845	4,873	3,594	2,722	872
1978–79	108,059	62,852	45,207	12,963	8,395	4,568	3,371	2,501	870
1979–80	103,662	58,511	45,151	12,176	7,794	4,382	3,230	2,357	873
1980–81	100,513	56,131	44,382	11,945	7,457	4,488	3,122	2,274	848
1981–82	99,705	55,196	44,509	12,002	7,468	4,534	3,061	2,237	824
1982–83	95,228	52,771	42,457	11,205	6,974	4,231	2,931	2,042	889
1983–84	93,323	52,154	41,169	10,577	6,551	4,026	2,911	2,030	881
1984–85	91,570	51,226	40,344	10,503	6,475	4,028	2,851	1,933	918
1985–86	93,840	52,724	41,116	10,564	6,419	4,145	2,955	1,970	985
1986–87	96,342	53,949	42,393	10,506	6,373	4,133	2,916	2,026	890
1987–88	100,460	56,377	44,083	10,412	6,310	4,102	2,781	1,849	932
1988–89	108,151	60,121	48,030	11,023	6,599	4,424	2,885	1,949	936
1989–90	118,083	65,887	52,196	11,634	6,898	4,736	3,010	2,019	991
1990–91	125,107	68,701	56,406	12,233	7,016	5,217	3,012	1,956	1,056
1991–92	133,974	73,001	60,973	12,702	7,237	5,465	3,218	2,126	1,092
1992–93	135,703	73,589	62,114	13,471	7,671	5,800	3,460	2,203	1,257
1993–94	133,680	72,006	61,674	14,561	8,152	6,409	3,627	2,317	1,310

[1] Includes degrees in social sciences, general; anthropology; archeology; criminology; demography and population studies; economics; geography; history; international relations and affairs; political science and government; sociology; urban affairs/studies; and social sciences and history, other.

SOURCE: U.S. Department of Education, National Center for Education Statistics, "Degrees and Other Formal Awards Conferred" surveys, and Integrated Postsecondary Education Data System (IPEDS), "Completions" surveys. (This table was prepared November 1995.)

Table 291.—Earned degrees in economics, history, political science and government, and sociology conferred by institutions of higher education, by level of degree: 1949–50 to 1993–94

Year	Economics Bachelor's	Economics Master's	Economics Doctor's	History Bachelor's	History Master's	History Doctor's	Political science and government[1] Bachelor's	Political science and government[1] Master's	Political science and government[1] Doctor's	Sociology Bachelor's	Sociology Master's	Sociology Doctor's
1	2	3	4	5	6	7	8	9	10	11	12	13
1949–50	14,568	921	200	13,542	1,801	275	6,336	710	127	7,870	552	98
1951–52	8,593	695	239	10,187	1,445	317	4,911	525	147	6,648	517	141
1953–54	6,719	609	245	9,363	1,220	355	5,314	534	153	5,692	440	184
1955–56	6,555	581	232	10,510	1,114	259	5,633	509	203	5,878	402	170
1957–58	7,457	669	239	12,840	1,397	297	6,116	665	170	6,568	397	150
1959–60	7,453	708	237	14,737	1,794	342	6,596	722	201	7,147	440	161
1961–62	8,366	853	268	17,340	2,163	343	8,326	839	214	8,120	578	173
1963–64	10,583	1,104	385	23,668	2,705	507	12,126	1,163	263	10,943	646	198
1965–66	11,555	1,522	458	28,612	3,883	599	15,242	1,429	336	15,038	981	244
1967–68	15,193	1,916	600	35,291	4,845	688	20,387	1,937	457	21,710	1,193	367
1969–70	17,197	1,988	794	43,386	5,049	1,038	25,713	2,105	525	30,436	1,813	534
1970–71	15,758	1,995	721	44,663	5,157	991	27,482	2,318	700	33,263	1,808	574
1971–72	15,231	2,224	794	43,695	5,217	1,133	28,135	2,451	758	35,216	1,944	636
1972–73	14,770	2,225	845	40,943	5,030	1,140	30,100	2,398	747	35,436	1,923	583
1973–74	14,285	2,141	788	37,049	4,533	1,114	30,744	2,448	766	35,491	2,196	632
1974–75	14,046	2,127	815	31,470	4,226	1,117	29,126	2,333	680	31,488	2,112	693
1975–76	14,741	2,087	763	28,400	3,658	1,014	28,302	2,191	723	27,634	2,009	729
1976–77	15,296	2,158	758	25,433	3,393	921	26,411	2,222	641	24,713	1,830	714
1977–78	15,661	1,995	706	23,004	3,033	813	26,069	2,069	636	22,750	1,611	599
1978–79	16,409	1,955	712	21,019	2,536	756	25,628	2,037	563	20,285	1,415	612
1979–80	17,863	1,821	677	19,301	2,367	712	25,457	1,938	535	18,881	1,341	583
1980–81	18,753	1,911	727	18,301	2,237	643	24,977	1,875	484	17,272	1,240	610
1981–82	19,876	1,964	677	17,146	2,210	636	25,658	1,954	513	16,042	1,145	558
1982–83	20,517	1,972	734	16,467	2,041	575	25,791	1,829	435	14,105	1,112	522
1983–84	20,719	1,891	729	16,643	1,940	561	25,719	1,769	457	13,145	1,008	520
1984–85	20,711	1,992	749	16,049	1,921	468	25,834	1,500	441	11,968	1,022	480
1985–86	21,602	1,937	789	16,415	1,961	497	26,439	1,704	439	12,271	965	504
1986–87	22,378	1,855	750	16,997	2,021	534	26,817	1,618	435	12,239	950	451
1987–88	22,911	1,847	770	18,207	2,093	517	27,207	1,579	391	13,024	984	452
1988–89	23,454	1,886	827	20,159	2,121	487	30,450	1,598	452	14,435	1,135	451
1989–90	23,923	1,950	806	22,476	2,369	570	33,560	1,580	480	16,035	1,198	432
1990–91	23,488	1,951	802	24,541	2,591	606	35,737	1,772	468	17,550	1,260	465
1991–92	23,423	2,106	866	26,966	2,754	644	37,805	1,908	535	19,568	1,347	501
1992–93	21,321	2,292	879	27,774	2,952	690	37,931	1,943	529	20,896	1,521	536
1993–94	19,496	2,521	869	27,503	3,009	752	36,097	2,147	616	22,368	1,639	530

[1] Excludes degrees in public administration and international relations.

SOURCE: U.S. Department of Education, National Center for Education Statistics, "Degrees and Other Formal Awards Conferred" surveys, and Integrated Postsecondary Education Data System (IPEDS), "Completions" surveys. (This table was prepared November 1995.)

Table 292.—Earned degrees in visual and performing arts[1] conferred by institutions of higher education, by level of degree and sex of student: 1970–71 to 1993–94

Year	Bachelor's degrees Total	Bachelor's degrees Men	Bachelor's degrees Women	Master's degrees Total	Master's degrees Men	Master's degrees Women	Doctor's degrees Total	Doctor's degrees Men	Doctor's degrees Women
1	2	3	4	5	6	7	8	9	10
1970–71	30,394	12,256	18,138	6,675	3,510	3,165	621	483	138
1971–72	33,831	13,580	20,251	7,537	4,049	3,488	572	428	144
1972–73	36,017	14,267	21,750	7,254	4,005	3,249	616	449	167
1973–74	39,730	15,821	23,909	8,001	4,325	3,676	585	440	145
1974–75	40,782	15,532	25,250	8,362	4,448	3,914	649	446	203
1975–76	42,138	16,491	25,647	8,817	4,507	4,310	620	447	173
1976–77	41,793	16,166	25,627	8,636	4,211	4,425	662	447	215
1977–78	40,951	15,572	25,379	9,036	4,327	4,709	708	448	260
1978–79	40,969	15,380	25,589	8,524	3,933	4,591	700	454	246
1979–80	40,892	15,065	25,827	8,708	4,067	4,641	655	413	242
1980–81	40,479	14,798	25,681	8,629	4,056	4,573	654	396	258
1981–82	40,422	14,819	25,603	8,746	3,866	4,880	670	380	290
1982–83	39,794	14,690	25,104	8,763	4,013	4,750	692	404	288
1983–84	40,131	15,089	25,042	8,526	3,897	4,629	730	406	324
1984–85	38,140	14,462	23,678	8,718	3,894	4,824	696	407	289
1985–86	37,241	14,236	23,005	8,420	3,775	4,645	722	396	326
1986–87	36,615	13,751	22,864	8,508	3,756	4,752	793	447	346
1987–88	36,944	14,068	22,876	7,939	3,442	4,497	727	424	303
1988–89	38,227	14,539	23,688	8,267	3,611	4,656	753	446	307
1989–90	38,934	15,189	23,745	8,481	3,706	4,775	849	472	377
1990–91	42,186	15,761	26,425	8,657	3,830	4,827	838	466	372
1991–92	46,522	17,616	28,906	9,353	4,078	5,275	906	504	402
1992–93	47,761	18,610	29,151	9,440	4,099	5,341	882	478	404
1993–94	49,053	19,538	29,515	9,925	4,229	5,696	1,054	585	469

[1] Prior to 1982–83: Includes visual and performing arts, general; crafts, folk art, and artisanry; dance; design and applied art; theatre arts; film and photographic arts; fine arts; graphic arts technology; music; and precision production. From 1982–83: Includes visual and performing arts, general; crafts, folk art, and artisanry; dance; design and applied art; theatre arts and stagecraft; film/video and photographic arts; fine arts and art studies; music; and visual performing arts, other.

SOURCE: U.S. Department of Education, National Center for Education Statistics, "Degrees and Other Formal Awards Conferred" surveys, and Integrated Postsecondary Education Data System (IPEDS), "Completions" surveys. (This table was prepared November 1995.)

Table 293.—Statistical profile of persons receiving doctor's degrees,[1] by field of study: 1993–94

Item	All fields	Education	Engineering	Humanities	Life sciences	Physical sciences[2]		Business and management	Social sciences and psychology	Other professional fields
						Total	Mathematics			
1	2	3	4	5	6	7	8	9	10	11
Doctor's degrees conferred (number)	**41,011**	**6,683**	**5,826**	**4,743**	**7,734**	**6,821**	**1,118**	**1,285**	**6,624**	**1,256**
Sex (percent)										
Men	61.5	39.1	89.1	52.3	58.4	79.7	78.9	71.6	50.6	54.0
Women	38.5	60.9	10.9	47.7	41.6	20.3	21.1	28.4	49.4	46.0
Racial/ethnic group (percent)[3]										
American Indian	0.5	0.6	0.2	0.6	0.4	0.2	0.3	0.8	0.5	0.8
Asian	11.6	2.9	28.8	4.6	15.7	20.8	22.1	9.4	6.1	5.7
Black	4.2	8.6	1.8	2.9	2.6	1.6	1.7	4.1	4.7	7.8
Hispanic	3.4	4.0	2.2	4.4	3.2	2.6	2.0	2.0	3.6	3.3
White	80.4	83.9	67.0	87.5	78.2	74.8	73.8	83.7	85.0	82.4
Citizenship (percent)										
United States	66.1	87.4	38.0	78.3	64.0	53.1	44.4	63.1	75.5	74.5
Non-U.S., permanent visa	9.1	3.0	14.4	6.6	11.3	14.1	13.5	7.3	5.9	5.1
Non-U.S., temporary visa	22.9	8.0	45.6	13.3	23.6	30.6	39.1	28.0	15.8	18.9
Unknown	1.9	1.6	2.1	1.8	1.1	2.2	3.0	1.6	2.8	1.4
Median age at doctorate (years)	34.1	43.6	31.7	35.7	32.7	31.0	31.2	35.5	34.1	39.6
Percent with bachelor's degree in same field as doctorate	55.6	36.9	80.4	57.4	51.0	68.4	74.3	36.0	53.2	26.0
Median time lapse from bachelor's to doctorate (years)										
Total time	10.8	19.7	9.0	12.0	9.5	8.5	8.9	12.2	10.5	15.8
Registered time	7.2	8.1	6.4	8.5	7.0	6.7	6.8	7.2	7.5	8.0
Postdoctoral plans (percent)										
Postdoctoral study plans	27.0	4.6	24.5	8.1	57.6	46.2	26.7	3.7	18.4	5.3
Fellowship	13.7	1.7	8.4	4.4	33.5	20.2	14.1	1.2	12.1	2.1
Research associateship	10.5	1.2	14.4	1.2	18.0	24.4	10.7	1.6	3.6	1.6
Traineeship	0.9	0.5	0.8	0.4	1.7	0.4	0.4	0.3	1.5	0.3
Other	1.8	1.2	0.7	2.0	4.4	1.2	1.3	0.5	1.2	1.2
Postdoctoral employment	65.3	86.5	67.6	84.0	36.0	47.1	65.3	89.6	72.9	86.6
Educational institution[4]	38.8	66.9	19.6	69.8	18.0	19.6	46.2	71.4	39.8	55.8
Industry, business	13.5	5.5	35.9	4.0	7.8	19.9	11.4	11.4	10.4	7.7
Government	5.0	5.3	6.0	1.5	5.1	3.6	2.3	2.9	7.7	6.4
Nonprofit organization	3.5	4.1	1.2	3.7	2.3	0.6	0.5	0.8	7.9	12.7
Other and unknown	4.5	4.6	5.0	4.9	2.9	3.3	4.8	3.1	7.1	4.1
Postdoctoral plans unknown	7.7	8.9	7.9	8.0	6.3	6.8	8.1	6.8	8.7	8.1
Definite postdoctoral study	17.7	2.4	12.2	3.8	42.1	30.6	14.7	1.7	12.0	3.1
Seeking postdoctoral study	9.3	2.2	12.2	4.3	15.5	15.5	12.0	1.9	6.4	2.1
Definite employment	42.6	63.3	38.3	49.9	23.7	28.9	38.9	67.3	47.9	62.3
Seeking employment	22.7	23.2	29.4	34.1	12.3	18.2	26.4	22.3	25.0	24.3
Primary postdoctoral activity (percent)[5]										
Research and development	27.3	5.7	63.7	7.8	41.2	53.9	33.9	27.4	24.5	11.2
Teaching	35.1	34.3	14.9	66.9	26.8	26.4	49.0	50.2	29.5	48.0
Administration	11.5	33.5	2.1	3.5	5.9	2.2	1.3	4.4	5.4	12.0
Professional services	11.2	10.0	7.1	3.7	11.2	5.3	3.7	2.8	26.8	13.2
Other	3.0	2.3	3.2	4.1	3.7	2.2	0.7	2.9	2.9	4.7
Activity unknown	11.9	14.3	8.9	14.0	11.2	10.1	11.5	12.4	11.0	10.9
Region of employment after doctorate (percent)[5]										
New England	5.8	4.7	6.5	7.4	4.8	7.0	6.7	5.1	6.2	2.6
Middle Atlantic	12.5	11.8	10.8	13.0	9.9	14.8	11.3	12.4	14.6	12.0
East North Central	13.3	14.8	11.6	15.3	10.5	14.1	15.4	12.5	12.5	11.7
West North Central	6.5	8.7	3.3	7.2	7.6	5.0	7.6	6.2	5.8	5.7
South Atlantic	15.7	19.0	10.8	15.3	14.3	13.5	13.1	16.2	16.6	17.8
East South Central	4.8	6.3	2.3	5.3	5.6	3.1	4.1	7.4	3.6	7.8
West South Central	7.7	8.9	6.4	7.7	7.4	6.0	6.7	10.4	7.1	9.7
Mountain	5.1	5.3	5.5	4.5	4.2	5.7	4.4	4.7	5.0	5.4
Pacific and insular	10.9	9.2	15.7	10.2	9.8	12.7	9.9	6.4	11.7	8.9
U.S., region unknown	4.1	5.3	3.5	4.4	3.4	3.2	1.6	2.2	4.1	4.2
Foreign	13.5	6.0	23.3	9.6	22.2	14.6	19.1	16.5	12.8	14.0
Region unknown	0.1	0.1	0.3	0.0	0.2	0.2	0.2	0.0	0.1	0.1

[1] Includes Ph.D., Ed.D., and comparable degrees at the doctoral level. Excludes first-professional degrees, such as M.D., D.D.S., and D.V.M.

[2] Includes mathematics, computer science, physics, astronomy, chemistry, and earth, atmospheric, and marine sciences.

[3] Distribution by race/ethnicity based on U.S. citizens and those with permanent visas only.

[4] Includes 2-year, 4-year, and foreign colleges and universities, medical schools, and elementary/secondary schools.

[5] Includes only recipients with definite employment plans.

NOTE.—The above classification of degrees by field differs somewhat from that in most publications of the National Center for Education Statistics (NCES). The major differences are that history is included under humanities rather than social sciences and that psychology is included under social sciences. The number of degrees also differs slightly from that reported in the NCES "Degrees and Other Formal Awards Conferred" survey. The above tabulation excludes some non-research doctorate degrees such as doctor's degrees in theology. Because of rounding, percents may not add to 100.0.

SOURCE: National Academy of Sciences, National Research Council, Office of Scientific and Engineering Personnel, *Summary Report 1994: Doctorate Recipients from United States Universities.* (This table was prepared April 1996.)

Table 294.—Statistical profile of persons receiving doctor's degrees in education: 1979–80 to 1993–94

Item	1979–80	1980–81	1981–82	1982–83	1983–84	1984–85	1985–86	1986–87	1987–88	1988–89	1989–90	1990–91	1991–92	1992–93	1993–94
1	2	3	4	5	6	7	8	9	10	11	12	13	14	15	16
Number of doctorates	**7,576**	**7,489**	**7,226**	**7,147**	**6,780**	**6,717**	**6,602**	**6,447**	**6,349**	**6,265**	**6,484**	**6,397**	**6,622**	**6,647**	**6,683**
Sex (percent)															
Men	55.5	52.8	51.2	49.6	49.0	48.2	45.6	44.9	44.8	42.5	42.4	41.9	40.5	41.3	39.1
Women	44.5	47.2	48.8	50.4	51.0	51.8	54.4	55.1	55.2	57.5	57.6	58.1	59.5	58.7	60.9
Racial/ethnic group (percent) [1]															
American Indian	0.8	0.6	0.5	0.7	0.5	0.7	0.5	0.7	0.6	0.4	0.6	1.0	0.8	0.8	0.6
Asian	1.3	1.9	1.7	1.9	1.5	1.7	1.6	1.7	2.4	1.9	1.8	2.2	2.4	2.4	2.9
Black	9.1	9.1	9.7	8.2	8.7	8.7	8.1	7.4	7.6	8.1	8.2	7.9	8.4	9.4	8.6
Hispanic	2.4	2.5	3.0	2.9	2.6	3.2	3.7	3.6	2.9	3.1	3.3	3.3	3.5	3.7	4.0
White	86.3	85.9	85.1	86.2	86.7	85.6	86.1	86.6	86.4	86.5	86.0	85.6	84.8	83.7	83.9
Citizenship (percent)															
United States	88.7	87.7	86.6	87.1	86.8	85.5	84.7	84.9	83.1	82.9	84.4	84.8	86.8	86.4	87.4
Foreign	8.2	8.8	9.9	9.8	9.8	10.4	9.6	9.2	10.2	9.7	9.7	10.2	10.7	10.8	11.0
Unknown	3.1	3.6	3.5	3.1	3.4	4.1	5.6	6.0	6.7	7.4	5.8	5.0	2.4	2.7	1.6
Median age at doctorate (years)	37.0	37.3	37.4	37.8	38.4	38.7	39.4	39.8	40.5	41.1	41.6	42.1	42.7	43.0	43.6
Percent with bachelor's degree in same field as doctorate	39.0	38.9	39.9	39.5	39.6	38.7	39.0	37.8	36.9	38.5	37.5	39.3	38.7	37.4	36.9
Median time lapse from bachelor's to doctorate (years)															
Total time	13.1	13.5	13.6	14.1	14.6	15.1	15.7	16.2	16.9	17.3	17.9	18.4	18.9	19.2	19.7
Registered time	6.9	7.0	7.2	7.4	7.6	7.6	7.8	7.9	8.1	8.2	8.1	8.1	8.2	8.2	8.1

[1] Longitudinal comparisons by race/ethnicity should be done with extreme care, due to periodic changes in the survey. Distribution by race/ethnicity based on U.S. citizens and those with permanent visas only.

NOTE.—The National Research Council's classification of degrees by field differs somewhat from that in most publications of the National Center for Education Statistics (NCES). The number of degrees also differs slightly from that reported in the NCES "Completions" survey. Because of rounding, percents may not add to 100.0.

SOURCE: National Academy of Sciences, National Research Council, Office of Scientific and Engineering Personnel, *Doctorate Records File.* (This table was prepared April 1996.)

Table 295.—Statistical profile of persons receiving doctor's degrees in engineering: 1979–80 to 1993–94

Item	1979–80	1980–81	1981–82	1982–83	1983–84	1984–85	1985–86	1986–87	1987–88	1988–89	1989–90	1990–91	1991–92	1992–93	1993–94
1	2	3	4	5	6	7	8	9	10	11	12	13	14	15	16
Number of doctorates	**2,479**	**2,528**	**2,644**	**2,780**	**2,915**	**3,165**	**3,376**	**3,716**	**4,190**	**4,536**	**4,892**	**5,212**	**5,437**	**5,696**	**5,826**
Sex (percent)															
Men	96.4	96.1	95.3	95.5	94.8	93.7	93.3	93.5	93.2	91.8	91.5	91.3	90.7	90.9	89.1
Women	3.6	3.9	4.7	4.5	5.2	6.3	6.7	6.6	6.8	8.2	8.5	8.7	9.3	9.1	10.9
Racial/ethnic group (percent) [1]															
American Indian	0.2	0.3	0.2	0.1	0.2	0.1	0.3	0.4	0.2	0.3	0.2	0.3	0.4	0.1	0.2
Asian	18.9	20.0	17.5	17.3	17.1	18.4	15.6	17.7	16.0	16.6	15.3	17.4	18.2	19.7	28.8
Black	1.2	1.4	1.5	2.0	1.0	2.2	1.4	1.3	1.4	1.4	1.8	2.4	1.9	1.9	1.8
Hispanic	1.9	1.0	2.5	2.1	2.4	1.5	2.1	1.8	3.0	2.2	2.4	2.6	3.0	2.4	2.2
White	77.8	77.3	78.3	78.6	79.3	77.8	80.6	78.8	79.4	79.5	80.4	77.4	76.5	75.9	67.0
Citizenship (percent)															
United States	50.6	46.2	44.1	41.8	42.5	40.4	40.8	41.8	42.4	40.9	39.4	37.9	38.7	39.1	38.0
Foreign	46.3	49.1	50.1	53.5	52.9	54.6	50.8	50.7	49.8	50.4	52.5	54.7	57.8	57.1	60.0
Unknown	3.1	4.7	5.9	4.7	4.6	5.0	8.4	7.4	7.7	8.8	8.1	7.3	3.5	3.9	2.1
Median age at doctorate (years)	30.3	30.5	30.7	30.8	30.7	30.9	31.0	31.0	31.0	31.1	31.2	31.4	31.5	31.6	31.7
Percent with bachelor's degree in same field as doctorate	75.2	74.1	72.4	74.0	74.3	74.2	73.0	75.2	76.4	76.2	76.9	79.0	81.8	80.1	80.4
Median time lapse from bachelor's to doctorate (years)															
Total time	7.6	7.9	8.0	8.0	8.0	8.1	8.1	8.1	8.1	8.1	8.2	8.5	8.7	8.8	9.0
Registered time	5.6	5.6	5.8	5.7	5.8	5.8	5.9	5.9	5.9	6.0	6.0	6.1	6.2	6.3	6.4

[1] Longitudinal comparisons by race/ethnicity should be done with extreme care, due to periodic changes in the survey. Distribution by race/ethnicity based on U.S. citizens and those with permanent visas only.

NOTE.—The National Research Council's classification of degrees by field differs somewhat from that in most publications of the National Center for Education Statistics (NCES). The number of degrees also differs slightly from that reported in the NCES "Completions" survey. Because of rounding, percents may not add to 100.0.

SOURCE: National Academy of Sciences, National Research Council, Office of Scientific and Engineering Personnel, *Doctorate Records File.* (This table was prepared April 1996.)

Table 296.—Statistical profile of persons receiving doctor's degrees in the humanities: [1] 1979–80 to 1993–94

Item	1979–80	1980–81	1981–82	1982–83	1983–84	1984–85	1985–86	1986–87	1987–88	1988–89	1989–90	1990–91	1991–92	1992–93	1993–94
1	2	3	4	5	6	7	8	9	10	11	12	13	14	15	16
Number of doctorates	**3,863**	**3,745**	**3,560**	**3,494**	**3,528**	**3,428**	**3,461**	**3,504**	**3,553**	**3,558**	**3,820**	**4,094**	**4,444**	**4,481**	**4,743**
Sex (percent)															
Men	60.4	58.7	57.6	56.2	55.0	56.6	54.8	55.1	55.7	54.5	54.4	53.5	53.7	52.5	52.3
Women	39.6	41.3	42.4	43.8	45.0	43.4	45.2	44.9	44.3	45.5	45.6	46.5	46.3	47.5	47.7
Racial/ethnic group (percent)[2]															
American Indian	0.3	0.4	0.2	0.2	0.2	0.3	0.2	0.4	0.2	0.2	0.3	0.3	0.5	0.3	0.6
Asian	2.0	1.8	1.7	1.5	1.8	2.3	1.8	2.1	2.3	3.0	2.4	2.5	3.0	3.6	4.6
Black	3.0	2.9	3.4	2.6	3.4	2.6	2.9	2.9	3.0	2.9	2.3	3.0	2.7	3.0	2.9
Hispanic	3.0	3.2	4.3	3.7	3.7	3.8	3.5	4.3	3.9	3.8	4.2	4.3	3.9	4.2	4.4
White	91.6	91.7	90.3	92.0	90.9	91.1	91.6	90.3	90.5	90.2	90.9	89.9	89.9	88.9	87.5
Citizenship (percent)															
United States	87.3	85.7	84.7	85.3	83.7	83.1	78.8	78.0	78.4	76.4	78.3	77.0	77.7	78.3	78.3
Foreign	8.8	10.2	10.2	10.7	11.2	12.1	13.7	14.3	14.4	15.5	15.2	18.3	19.2	18.7	19.9
Unknown	3.9	4.1	5.1	4.0	5.2	4.8	7.4	7.7	7.1	8.1	6.5	4.7	3.2	3.0	1.8
Median age at doctorate (years)	33.4	33.5	34.0	34.0	34.5	34.7	35.0	35.0	35.4	35.7	35.7	35.8	35.6	35.6	35.7
Percent with bachelor's degree in same field as doctorate	64.2	61.0	61.1	58.4	60.2	58.8	58.2	58.5	56.7	55.5	57.1	57.7	56.5	56.4	57.4
Median time lapse from bachelor's to doctorate (years).															
Total time	10.6	10.8	11.2	11.1	11.5	11.7	12.1	12.0	12.2	12.5	12.2	12.3	12.0	11.9	12.0
Registered time	7.7	7.7	8.0	8.0	8.2	8.3	8.2	8.4	8.5	8.4	8.3	8.4	8.3	8.3	8.5

[1] Includes American studies, archeology, art history, classics, history, letters, literature, music, philosophy, religion, and theatre.

[2] Longitudinal comparisons by race/ethnicity should be done with extreme care, due to periodic changes in the survey. Distribution by race/ethnicity based on U.S. citizens and those with permanent visas only.

NOTE.—The National Research Council's classification of degrees by field differs somewhat from that in most publications of the National Center for Education Statistics (NCES). The major differences are that history is included under humanities rather than social sciences and that psychology is included under social sciences. The number of degrees also differs slightly from that reported in the NCES "Completions" survey. Because of rounding, percents may not add to 100.0.

SOURCE: National Academy of Sciences, National Research Council, Office of Scientific and Engineering Personnel, *Doctorate Records File*. (This table was prepared May 1996.)

Table 297.—Statistical profile of persons receiving doctor's degrees in the life sciences: [1] 1979–80 to 1993–94

Item	1979–80	1980–81	1981–82	1982–83	1983–84	1984–85	1985–86	1986–87	1987–88	1988–89	1989–90	1990–91	1991–92	1992–93	1993–94
1	2	3	4	5	6	7	8	9	10	11	12	13	14	15	16
Number of doctorates	**5,325**	**5,461**	**5,565**	**5,540**	**5,745**	**5,748**	**5,720**	**5,742**	**6,143**	**6,343**	**6,613**	**6,928**	**7,108**	**7,397**	**7,734**
Sex (percent)															
Men	74.8	73.6	72.3	69.0	68.9	67.7	66.0	64.8	63.2	61.8	62.6	61.4	60.7	58.3	58.4
Women	25.2	26.4	27.7	31.0	31.1	32.3	34.0	35.2	36.8	38.2	37.4	38.6	39.3	41.7	41.6
Racial/ethnic group (percent)[2]															
American Indian	0.2	0.2	0.3	0.2	0.3	0.4	0.5	0.4	0.4	0.3	0.2	0.4	0.4	0.3	0.4
Asian	5.3	4.8	4.6	5.3	4.7	4.7	4.9	5.7	5.0	5.3	5.6	6.6	7.1	8.7	15.7
Black	1.6	1.9	1.5	1.6	2.1	2.1	1.9	2.5	2.2	2.1	1.9	2.4	2.3	2.9	2.6
Hispanic	1.1	1.4	1.5	1.2	1.4	1.9	2.1	2.0	2.3	2.1	2.7	2.6	2.8	3.0	3.2
White	91.8	91.7	92.0	91.6	91.5	90.8	90.5	89.4	90.0	90.1	89.6	88.0	87.3	85.1	78.2
Citizenship (percent)															
United States	80.4	80.3	80.4	79.9	79.4	77.1	75.9	73.5	71.3	71.1	68.0	66.8	65.7	65.3	64.0
Foreign	17.6	17.1	16.6	17.4	17.6	19.3	18.8	20.5	22.2	22.1	26.3	29.1	31.8	32.6	34.9
Unknown	2.0	2.6	3.0	2.6	3.0	3.6	5.3	6.1	6.4	6.9	5.6	4.0	2.5	2.2	1.1
Median age at doctorate (years)	30.0	30.1	30.3	30.6	31.0	31.3	31.6	31.7	31.9	32.2	32.3	32.4	32.7	32.5	32.7
Percent with bachelor's degree in same field as doctorate	40.9	40.7	41.4	56.3	58.1	58.3	57.1	55.6	55.4	53.4	53.8	54.1	53.5	51.9	51.0
Median time lapse from bachelor's to doctorate (years)															
Total time	7.3	7.3	7.6	7.9	8.2	8.4	8.7	8.7	8.9	9.1	9.1	9.1	9.4	9.4	9.5
Registered time	5.8	5.9	6.0	6.1	6.3	6.3	6.4	6.5	6.5	6.5	6.7	6.7	6.7	6.8	7.0

[1] Includes agricultural, biological, and health sciences.

[2] Longitudinal comparisons by race/ethnicity should be done with extreme care, due to periodic changes in the survey. Distribution by race/ethnicity based on U.S. citizens and those with permanent visas only.

NOTE.—The National Research Council's classification of degrees by field differs somewhat from that in most publications of the National Center for Education Statistics (NCES). The number of degrees also differs slightly from that reported in the NCES "Completions" survey. Because of rounding, percents may not add to 100.0.

SOURCE: National Academy of Sciences, National Research Council, Office of Scientific and Engineering Personnel, *Doctorate Records File*. (This table was prepared April 1996.)

Table 298.—Statistical profile of persons receiving doctor's degrees in the physical sciences: [1] 1979–80 to 1993–94

Item	1979–80	1980–81	1981–82	1982–83	1983–84	1984–85	1985–86	1986–87	1987–88	1988–89	1989–90	1990–91	1991–92	1992–93	1993–94
1	2	3	4	5	6	7	8	9	10	11	12	13	14	15	16
Number of doctorates	**3,151**	**3,208**	**3,348**	**3,438**	**3,459**	**3,531**	**3,679**	**3,837**	**4,046**	**3,987**	**4,263**	**4,439**	**4,573**	**4,472**	**4,799**
Sex (percent)															
Men	87.7	88.7	86.3	86.4	85.4	83.7	83.6	83.3	82.6	80.9	81.2	81.0	79.1	78.9	79.0
Women	12.3	11.3	13.7	13.6	14.6	16.3	16.4	16.7	17.4	19.1	18.8	19.0	20.9	21.1	21.0
Racial/ethnic group (percent) [2]															
American Indian	0.2	0.1	0.2	0.3	0.2	0.1	0.2	0.3	0.3	0.6	0.1	0.5	0.5	0.3	0.2
Asian	7.7	6.9	6.2	6.6	6.6	6.9	7.1	7.0	5.7	6.7	6.6	6.6	8.9	10.2	20.8
Black	1.0	1.3	1.1	1.0	1.3	1.2	1.0	1.0	1.3	1.3	1.0	1.2	1.1	1.6	1.6
Hispanic	1.1	1.3	1.2	1.3	2.0	1.7	2.1	2.4	2.6	2.6	3.1	2.9	3.2	3.4	2.6
White	90.0	90.5	91.2	90.7	89.9	90.1	89.5	89.3	90.1	88.8	89.3	88.8	86.4	84.5	74.8
Citizenship (percent)															
United States	75.9	75.4	75.0	74.0	73.6	70.3	66.1	65.1	64.3	62.5	61.0	59.3	57.9	57.1	56.3
Foreign	21.6	21.3	21.9	23.1	23.5	25.5	27.8	28.5	28.8	29.8	32.4	35.9	39.6	39.7	41.7
Unknown	2.4	3.3	3.1	2.9	2.9	4.1	6.1	6.4	6.9	7.8	6.7	4.8	2.5	3.2	2.1
Median age at doctorate (years)	29.1	29.0	29.2	29.3	29.5	29.5	29.9	29.8	30.1	30.0	30.7	30.2	30.3	30.6	30.7
Percent with bachelor's degree in same field as doctorate	76.5	76.6	77.2	75.4	77.7	75.0	73.4	72.6	72.6	72.6	80.0	76.9	74.5	72.9	73.0
Median time lapse from bachelor's to doctorate (years)															
Total time	6.8	6.7	6.8	7.0	7.0	7.1	7.1	7.1	7.2	7.2	7.8	7.5	7.8	8.0	8.2
Registered time	5.7	5.7	5.8	5.9	6.0	6.0	6.0	5.9	6.1	6.0	6.3	6.2	6.4	6.4	6.6

[1] Includes physics, astronomy, chemistry, and earth, atmospheric, and marine sciences. Excludes mathematics and computer science.

[2] Longitudinal comparisons by race/ethnicity should be done with extreme care, due to periodic changes in the survey. Distribution by race/ethnicity based on U.S. citizens and those with permanent visas only.

NOTE.—The National Research Council's classification of degrees by field differs somewhat from that in most publications of the National Center for Education Statistics (NCES). The number of degrees also differs slightly from that reported in the NCES "Completions" survey. Because of rounding, percents may not add to 100.0.

SOURCE: National Academy of Sciences, National Research Council, Office of Scientific and Engineering Personnel, *Doctorate Records File*. (This table was prepared April 1996.)

Table 299.—Statistical profile of persons receiving doctor's degrees in the social sciences: [1] 1979–80 to 1993–94

Item	1979–80	1980–81	1981–82	1982–83	1983–84	1984–85	1985–86	1986–87	1987–88	1988–89	1989–90	1990–91	1991–92	1992–93	1993–94
1	2	3	4	5	6	7	8	9	10	11	12	13	14	15	16
Number of doctorates	**6,253**	**6,505**	**6,250**	**6,055**	**5,895**	**5,720**	**5,841**	**5,718**	**5,769**	**5,955**	**6,076**	**6,127**	**6,205**	**6,545**	**6,624**
Sex (percent)															
Men	65.4	64.4	63.3	60.7	59.2	58.9	57.6	57.2	55.0	54.8	53.7	50.6	52.6	50.7	50.6
Women	34.6	35.6	36.7	39.3	40.8	41.1	42.4	42.8	45.0	45.2	46.3	49.4	47.4	49.3	49.4
Racial/ethnic group (percent) [2]															
American Indian	0.3	0.2	0.4	0.2	0.2	0.4	0.4	0.5	0.3	0.4	0.5	0.4	0.5	0.4	0.5
Asian	2.8	2.5	2.5	2.2	2.5	2.6	2.6	3.2	3.3	3.1	3.0	3.3	3.6	4.0	6.1
Black	4.2	4.0	4.7	3.9	4.6	4.4	4.1	3.8	4.4	4.4	4.4	4.9	4.5	4.7	4.7
Hispanic	2.0	2.3	2.7	3.0	2.8	2.9	3.3	3.6	3.3	3.3	3.9	4.2	3.8	4.1	3.6
White	90.7	91.0	89.8	90.7	90.0	89.8	89.7	89.0	88.8	88.7	88.2	87.2	87.7	86.9	85.0
Citizenship (percent)															
United States	84.7	84.0	81.8	82.9	80.6	79.3	77.9	76.1	74.8	70.4	73.8	73.4	74.3	75.5	75.5
Foreign	11.6	11.9	12.6	12.5	14.1	15.3	15.3	15.7	16.1	17.3	18.0	19.8	21.2	21.3	21.7
Unknown	3.7	4.2	5.6	4.5	5.4	5.4	6.9	8.3	9.1	12.2	8.2	6.8	4.4	3.1	2.8
Median age at doctorate (years)	31.6	32.0	32.3	32.4	32.7	33.0	33.4	33.5	34.1	33.9	34.2	34.1	34.3	34.3	34.1
Percent with bachelor's degree in same field as doctorate	58.6	59.1	57.4	58.9	59.3	58.5	57.0	56.4	54.5	52.3	55.4	54.2	53.1	53.7	53.2
Median time lapse from bachelor's to doctorate (years)															
Total time	8.7	9.0	9.2	9.3	9.7	9.9	10.0	10.3	10.5	10.3	10.6	10.5	10.6	10.4	10.5
Registered time	6.4	6.5	6.7	6.8	7.1	7.1	7.2	7.4	7.4	7.4	7.5	7.5	7.5	7.5	7.5

[1] Includes anthropology, area studies, criminology, economics, geography, political science, public policy, psychology, and sociology.

[2] Longitudinal comparisons by race/ethnicity should be done with extreme care, due to periodic changes in the survey. Distribution by race/ethnicity based on U.S. citizens and those with permanent visas only.

NOTE.—The National Research Council's classification of degrees by field differs somewhat from that in most publications of the National Center for Education Statistics (NCES). The major differences are that history is included under humanities rather than social sciences and that psychology is included under social sciences. The number of degrees also differs slightly from that reported in the NCES "Completions" survey. Because of rounding, percents may not add to 100.0.

SOURCE: National Academy of Sciences, National Research Council, Office of Scientific and Engineering Personnel, *Doctorate Records File*. (This table was prepared April 1996.)

Table 300.—Doctor's degrees [1] conferred by 60 large institutions of higher education: 1984–85 to 1993–94

Institution	Rank order [2]	Total, 1984–85 to 1993–94	1984–85	1985–86	1986–87	1987–88	1988–89	1989–90	1990–91	1991–92	1992–93	1993–94
1	2	3	4	5	6	7	8	9	10	11	12	13
United States, all institutions	—	374,868	32,943	33,653	34,041	34,870	35,720	38,371	39,294	40,659	42,132	43,185
Total, 60 large institutions	—	218,488	19,705	19,733	20,178	20,532	21,116	22,290	22,867	23,479	24,012	24,576
University of California-Berkeley	1	7,853	689	753	727	742	838	800	800	798	810	896
University of Wisconsin-Madison	2	6,862	674	606	667	684	667	717	708	680	676	783
University of Illinois, Urbana Campus	3	6,681	622	560	616	646	647	707	737	775	705	666
Columbia University in the City of New York	4	6,496	625	610	593	567	615	723	802	630	687	644
University of Texas at Austin	5	6,230	474	545	612	588	583	647	710	671	686	714
University of Michigan-Ann Arbor	6	6,108	607	598	589	564	527	583	661	676	654	649
Ohio State University-Main Campus	7	6,089	543	512	570	542	608	604	644	671	685	710
University of Minnesota, Twin Cities	8	5,973	515	556	508	527	543	633	706	651	627	707
Stanford University (Calif.)	9	5,418	497	530	562	560	540	532	487	569	581	560
University of California-Los Angeles	10	5,303	449	433	448	508	459	558	558	613	657	620
Cornell University (N.Y.) [3]	11	5,008	433	456	445	454	481	555	531	540	520	593
Massachusetts Institute of Technology	12	4,912	447	455	458	516	492	509	497	514	516	508
Harvard University (Mass.)	13	4,786	385	452	434	465	461	505	505	501	540	538
University of Maryland, College Park Campus	14	4,323	373	370	378	364	393	468	453	506	490	528
Michigan State University	15	4,303	405	438	464	427	434	432	397	476	401	429
Purdue University-Main Campus (Ind.)	16	4,296	389	379	370	366	420	467	430	478	504	493
Pennsylvania State University-Main Campus	17	4,284	371	350	341	379	417	420	463	541	495	507
Texas A & M University	18	4,226	315	336	369	382	420	411	446	472	496	579
University of Pennsylvania	19	4,176	367	341	307	319	414	462	495	477	506	488
University of Washington	20	4,076	342	345	411	392	403	457	459	396	416	455
New York University	21	3,940	391	377	392	421	376	392	392	404	404	391
University of Southern California	22	3,897	424	363	354	354	429	429	359	355	415	415
University of Pittsburgh-Main Campus	23	3,630	398	390	394	390	367	337	344	343	333	334
Indiana University, Bloomington	24	3,513	397	353	374	319	313	321	342	398	348	348
University of Florida	25	3,475	301	290	313	315	342	366	370	364	372	442
Rutgers University, New Brunswick (N.J.)	26	3,467	343	320	320	311	327	342	326	402	376	400
University of Massachusetts at Amherst	27	3,390	300	290	311	281	329	362	400	409	370	338
University of Arizona	28	3,295	261	260	298	290	326	311	382	352	373	442
Northwestern University (Ill.)	29	3,282	326	312	319	313	358	327	308	351	363	305
University of Chicago (Ill.)	30	3,282	291	329	319	318	310	335	317	322	346	395
University of Georgia	31	3,232	355	309	275	316	340	313	332	331	352	309
University of North Carolina at Chapel Hill	32	3,226	260	283	311	301	299	337	336	338	388	373
Virginia Polytechnic Institute and State University	33	3,207	260	274	295	287	303	342	332	366	369	379
Nova Southeastern University (Fla.)	34	3,201	209	263	271	292	306	316	290	336	433	485
Yale University (Conn.)	35	3,167	276	259	305	290	317	312	344	347	369	348
University of Iowa	36	3,140	284	258	287	312	287	299	360	380	331	342
Iowa State University	37	2,848	245	256	296	309	257	282	297	277	322	307
Boston University (Mass.)	38	2,806	276	307	299	245	304	277	258	280	271	289
Temple University (Pa.)	39	2,744	264	277	290	277	285	249	251	282	282	287
City University of New York Graduate School and University Center	40	2,621	234	232	232	258	225	259	320	257	318	286
State University of New York at Buffalo	41	2,592	194	206	209	240	274	249	265	290	320	345
University of California-Davis	42	2,585	224	245	228	238	221	258	258	284	306	323
Johns Hopkins University (Md.)	43	2,585	254	220	213	267	229	240	285	297	318	262
University of Virginia-Main Campus	44	2,571	221	217	218	229	242	253	291	291	315	294
Florida State University	45	2,531	257	224	226	250	246	249	257	286	262	274
North Carolina State University at Raleigh	46	2,498	204	219	200	239	224	294	256	279	283	300
University of Colorado at Boulder	47	2,442	198	198	229	231	221	248	263	249	299	306
Princeton University (N.J.)	48	2,396	211	216	218	269	227	240	244	255	249	267
University of Missouri-Columbia	49	2,295	230	202	181	227	236	236	212	258	260	253
University of Tennessee-Knoxville	50	2,251	223	233	206	217	209	214	214	260	249	226
Vanderbilt University (Tenn.)	51	2,243	239	259	252	196	218	229	222	220	215	193
University of Kansas-Main Campus	52	2,171	260	211	221	213	224	180	209	235	193	225
University of Nebraska-Lincoln	53	2,131	179	201	203	233	236	217	202	212	221	227
University of South Carolina at Columbia	54	2,127	156	168	169	191	169	215	248	242	281	288
Oklahoma Sate University-Main Campus	55	2,074	220	224	189	184	211	229	206	183	225	203
University of Cincinnati-Main Campus (Ohio)	56	2,073	171	187	182	188	182	213	231	220	226	273
State University of New York at Stony Brook	57	2,057	147	144	156	196	190	200	248	225	283	268
University of Rochester (N.Y.)	58	2,047	168	195	198	167	208	226	194	231	224	236
University of Connecticut	59	2,039	181	174	193	180	198	217	228	206	216	246
University of California, San Diego	60	2,014	151	163	163	186	189	185	185	227	280	285

[1] Includes Ph.D., Ed.D., and comparable degrees at the doctoral level. Excludes first-professional degrees (e.g., M.D., D.D.S., and D.V.M.).

[2] Institutions are ranked by the total number of doctor's degrees conferred during the 10-year period ending June 30, 1994.

[3] Includes degrees conferred by the Endowed and Statutory Colleges.

—Not applicable.

SOURCE: U.S. Department of Education, National Center for Education Statistics, Higher Education General Information Survey (HEGIS), "Degrees and Other Formal Awards Conferred" survey, and Integrated Postsecondary Education Data System (IPEDS), "Completions" survey. (This table was prepared May 1996.)

Table 301.—Percentage distribution of 1980 high school sophomores by the timing of their first postsecondary enrollment, by selected characteristics: 1982 to 1992

Student and institution characteristics	All 1980 sophomores	Never enrolled	Before November 1982	November 1982 to May 1983	June 1983 to May 1984	June 1984 to May 1985	June 1985 to May 1986	June 1986 to May 1987	June 1987 to May 1988	June 1988 to May 1989	June 1989 to May 1990	June 1990 to May 1991	June 1991 or later
1	2	3	4	5	6	7	8	9	10	11	12	13	14
Total	**100.0**	**35.5**	**44.1**	**3.5**	**6.5**	**2.7**	**2.4**	**1.3**	**1.1**	**0.9**	**1.0**	**0.6**	**0.5**
College expectations in sixth grade													
Decided to go	100.0	18.0	64.4	3.4	6.1	2.1	2.3	1.2	0.7	0.8	0.5	0.3	0.2
Planned not to go	100.0	54.4	24.6	3.3	6.4	2.6	2.6	1.4	1.4	0.9	1.0	0.9	0.6
Not sure	100.0	35.9	43.7	4.3	6.5	2.6	2.0	1.5	1.0	0.4	1.3	0.6	0.3
Hadn't thought about it	100.0	30.6	46.3	4.2	6.4	3.7	2.8	1.4	1.1	1.3	1.2	0.5	0.5
Postsecondary expectations in 1982													
None	100.0	75.7	4.7	1.8	4.5	2.5	3.0	1.5	1.6	1.3	1.5	1.0	0.9
Vocational/technical	100.0	43.6	27.1	5.5	8.7	4.2	3.6	1.8	1.6	1.6	1.1	0.7	0.5
Less-than-4–year degree	100.0	23.5	51.8	5.2	8.8	2.9	2.9	1.3	1.0	0.6	1.0	0.4	0.7
Bachelor's degree	100.0	9.0	76.7	3.1	5.0	2.2	1.4	1.3	0.4	0.6	0.3	0.1	0.1
Advanced degree	100.0	7.3	80.4	2.5	5.5	1.5	1.2	0.4	0.4	0.2	0.4	0.2	—
First postsecondary institution type													
Never enrolled	100.0	100.0	—	—	—	—	—	—	—	—	—	—	—
Private for-profit	100.0	—	39.6	10.1	15.8	10.7	7.8	3.6	4.1	1.1	3.9	2.3	1.0
Private not-for-profit less-than-4–year	100.0	—	66.2	3.8	15.0	5.9	2.7	0.3	0.3	2.4	2.7	0.9	—
Public less-than-2–year	100.0	—	48.5	8.3	13.6	8.8	7.2	4.7	2.6	0.7	3.5	1.6	0.4
Public 2–year	100.0	—	58.6	7.7	12.5	4.5	5.2	2.4	2.2	2.5	1.8	1.3	1.2
Public 4–year	100.0	—	84.5	2.2	6.4	2.2	1.3	1.2	0.5	0.8	0.4	0.4	0.2
Private not-for-profit 4–year	100.0	—	86.9	2.3	5.3	1.7	1.2	0.9	0.7	0.3	0.2	0.1	0.5
Number of applications to college in 1982													
Did not apply	100.0	56.3	17.9	3.7	7.8	3.4	3.5	1.8	1.6	1.3	1.3	0.9	0.6
1 college	100.0	9.9	77.0	3.8	4.6	1.6	1.1	0.6	0.3	0.3	0.3	0.3	0.2
2 or 3 colleges	100.0	5.6	82.7	2.8	3.9	2.3	1.0	0.7	0.2	0.5	0.3	—	0.1
4 or more colleges	100.0	5.0	89.9	0.7	3.2	0.3	0.8	—	0.1	—	—	0.1	—
Accepted at 1982 first choice college													
No applications	100.0	62.4	10.2	3.3	7.1	4.0	4.1	2.1	1.9	1.7	1.4	1.1	0.9
Attended first choice	100.0	—	89.7	3.8	5.0	0.8	0.3	0.2	0.1	—	0.1	0.1	—
Accepted, but did not attend first choice	100.0	23.3	51.0	5.3	8.2	4.3	2.3	1.8	1.2	1.0	0.9	0.4	0.3
Was not accepted at first choice	100.0	12.8	73.1	2.7	7.1	1.9	1.0	0.4	0.1	0.4	—	0.5	—

—Data not available or not applicable.

NOTE.—Because of rounding, details may not add to 100.0 percent.

SOURCE: National Center for Education Statistics, *High School and Beyond, Educational Attainment of 1980 High School Sophomores by 1992*. (This table was prepared May 1995.)

Table 302.—Percentage distribution of 1980 high school sophomores, by highest level of education completed through 1992, by selected student characteristics: 1980 to 1992

Student characteristics	All 1980 sopho-mores	Less than high school	High school	Certificate	Associate degree	Bachelor's degree	Master's degree	Professional degree	Doctor's degree
1	2	3	4	5	6	7	8	9	10
Total	100.0	5.8	51.5	11.0	7.9	20.0	2.7	0.9	0.2
Sex									
Male	100.0	6.5	53.5	9.7	6.7	19.5	2.6	1.3	0.2
Female	100.0	5.0	49.5	12.4	9.1	20.5	2.8	0.5	0.1
Race/ethnicity									
White, non-Hispanic	100.0	4.9	49.1	10.1	8.4	23.1	3.2	1.0	0.2
Black, non-Hispanic	100.0	6.9	59.6	16.3	5.2	10.0	1.5	0.5	0.2
Hispanic	100.0	11.9	59.6	11.2	7.3	9.0	0.6	0.3	—
Asian/Pacific Islander	100.0	0.6	40.9	6.9	6.2	32.7	4.7	7.5	0.7
American Indian/Alaskan Native	100.0	17.8	58.2	11.8	5.0	6.7	0.5	—	—
Socioeconomic status (1980)									
Low quartile	100.0	9.0	64.6	12.3	6.9	6.4	0.7	0.1	—
Middle two quartiles	100.0	3.9	53.8	11.5	9.1	19.0	2.0	0.5	0.1
High quartile	100.0	1.4	32.7	7.0	7.6	41.2	6.9	2.7	0.5
Test score composite (1982)									
Low quartile	100.0	15.6	64.0	13.0	4.1	3.0	0.2	—	0.1
Middle two quartiles	100.0	3.1	56.2	12.8	10.1	16.1	1.5	0.3	—
High quartile	100.0	0.1	26.5	4.8	7.2	49.2	8.7	3.0	0.6
Parents' educational attainment in 1980									
No high school diploma	100.0	6.5	59.8	12.8	8.6	10.8	1.2	0.3	0.1
High school graduate	100.0	5.2	59.1	12.4	6.0	16.6	0.3	0.4	—
Vocational/technical	100.0	3.0	49.2	15.4	10.2	19.1	2.4	0.5	0.1
Some college	100.0	2.1	43.7	8.4	8.4	32.0	4.3	1.0	0.2
Bachelor's degree	100.0	1.4	32.6	4.9	8.1	42.4	6.9	3.1	0.5
Advanced degree	100.0	3.5	23.9	8.6	4.9	44.1	10.0	4.3	0.7
High school diploma status									
Regular diploma in 1982	100.0	0.3	51.9	10.8	8.7	23.9	3.2	1.1	0.2
Returned for diploma	100.0	6.8	68.3	14.4	7.0	3.4	0.1	0.1	—
Returned but no diploma	100.0	27.1	47.7	19.9	3.4	1.9	—	—	—
Never returned	100.0	51.5	35.7	9.5	2.1	0.9	0.3	—	—
Postsecondary expectations in 1982									
None	100.0	15.5	71.1	9.3	3.0	1.0	0.1	—	0.1
Vocational/technical	100.0	4.6	61.6	19.8	10.7	3.3	0.1	—	—
Less-than-4-year degree	100.0	1.6	53.2	13.3	15.6	15.0	1.1	0.2	—
Bachelor's degree	100.0	0.9	35.3	6.8	6.3	44.9	5.0	0.8	0.1
Advanced degree	100.0	0.8	28.9	5.2	5.7	45.1	9.0	4.4	0.8
Type of start in postsecondary education									
Fall 1982 full-time 4-year	100.0	—	21.2	3.5	4.6	57.8	9.0	3.4	0.5
Fall 1982 full-time public 2-year	100.0	0.3	36.5	11.9	24.4	24.6	2.1	0.2	—
Fall 1982 part-time 4-year	100.0	—	52.2	6.7	10.0	27.2	3.5	0.1	0.4
Fall 1982 part-time public 2-year	100.0	1.6	59.5	13.4	9.4	14.4	0.9	0.8	—
Fall 1982 other	100.0	0.2	23.0	34.3	24.5	15.7	1.9	0.4	—
Delayed 4-year	100.0	0.4	55.6	8.1	7.4	24.0	3.7	0.4	0.4
Delayed public 2-year	100.0	1.7	63.0	16.9	12.0	6.2	0.2	—	—
Delayed other	100.0	1.9	31.4	48.4	14.4	3.8	0.1	0.1	—
Other enrollment	100.0	—	—	86.5	5.1	6.0	1.1	0.4	0.8
Never enrolled	100.0	16.1	83.9	—	—	—	—	—	—

—Data not applicable or not available.

NOTE.—Because of rounding, details may not add to 100.0 percent.

SOURCE: National Center for Education Statistics, *High School and Beyond, Educational Attainment of High School Sophomores by 1992.* (This table was prepared May 1995.)

Table 303.—Mean number of semester credits completed by bachelor's degree recipients, by major and course area: 1972 to 1976 and 1980 to 1984

Selected college majors	Course areas									
	Total	Business	Computer science	Education	Engineering	Mathe-matics	Biological sciences	Physical sciences	Social sciences	Other
1	2	3	4	5	6	7	8	9	10	11
1972–76 [1]										
Mean, all majors	**124.0**	**7.8**	**1.0**	**9.7**	**2.3**	**7.4**	**7.6**	**9.0**	**30.3**	**48.8**
Business and management	124.4	41.2	2.3	0.5	0.4	10.2	2.5	4.8	30.4	32.0
Computer science	133.3	6.6	33.5	0.4	5.3	22.4	1.9	7.8	20.6	34.8
Education	126.4	0.9	0.3	40.2	—	5.0	5.5	4.3	23.9	46.4
Engineering	134.8	1.6	2.0	0.1	50.0	18.2	1.3	20.5	14.0	27.1
English	117.8	0.5	0.1	7.8	0.1	3.2	3.4	3.4	24.2	75.2
Fine arts	124.9	0.3	0.1	6.6	—	1.3	2.5	2.1	13.6	98.4
Life sciences	122.2	0.4	0.8	1.7	—	8.4	35.6	26.2	17.8	31.3
Physical sciences	122.7	0.8	1.4	0.9	1.9	16.2	9.6	49.5	13.1	29.2
Psychology	119.1	2.0	0.5	5.9	0.3	5.5	6.2	5.9	56.0	36.9
Social sciences	120.6	3.4	0.4	3.3	0.4	5.3	3.2	4.3	60.3	40.1
1980–84 [2]										
Mean, all majors	**123.5**	**12.8**	**3.3**	**6.2**	**4.6**	**8.4**	**5.3**	**8.1**	**27.5**	**47.2**
Business and management	122.8	41.2	4.5	0.6	1.1	8.9	2.2	3.9	27.5	32.7
Computer science	129.3	11.8	27.9	0.3	4.7	21.3	1.8	8.5	19.0	33.9
Education	127.4	0.7	0.3	45.5	0.1	4.4	4.4	3.8	20.8	47.3
Engineering	132.3	1.0	2.3	0.8	52.5	16.2	1.1	20.2	12.3	25.9
English	114.8	1.7	1.5	6.9	—	2.2	2.1	4.7	21.4	74.4
Fine arts	120.5	1.7	0.6	5.1	—	1.7	2.7	1.5	14.1	93.1
Life sciences	121.9	0.7	1.5	1.9	0.2	10.1	33.5	22.6	18.1	33.3
Physical sciences	124.3	0.2	4.9	0.1	2.0	14.1	12.9	48.7	11.6	30.0
Psychology	120.7	3.0	2.7	2.1	—	6.5	5.8	4.2	55.2	41.2
Social sciences	119.2	6.0	1.4	1.0	0.5	5.4	4.4	5.1	52.0	43.3

[1] Sample survey based on 1972 high school seniors who completed bachelor's degrees by 1976.

[2] Sample survey based on 1980 high school seniors who completed bachelor's degrees by 1984.

—Data not available.

NOTE.—Because of rounding, details may not add to totals.

SOURCE: U.S. Department of Education, National Center for Education Statistics, National Longitudinal Study of 1972 and High School and Beyond survey. (This table was prepared April 1986.)

Table 304.—Colleges and universities offering remedial services, by type and control of institution: 1987–88 to 1995–96

Type and control of institution	Percent of colleges offering remedial instruction or tutoring									Change in percentage points	
	1987–88	1988–89	1989–90	1990–91	1991–92	1992–93	1993–94	1994–95	1995–96	1987–88 to 1995–96	1990–91 to 1995–96
1	2	3	4	5	6	7	8	9	10	11	12
Total	**72.7**	**74.9**	**76.6**	**77.7**	**78.6**	**76.6**	**77.1**	**78.0**	**77.8**	**5.1**	**0.1**
All 4-year colleges	66.0	68.2	69.6	70.6	71.4	69.7	70.4	71.9	71.6	5.6	1.0
All 2-year colleges	82.7	84.7	87.2	88.4	89.2	86.6	87.2	87.1	87.4	4.7	1.0
Public institutions											
4-year colleges	80.5	81.8	82.9	83.5	84.5	78.4	78.4	79.4	80.0	0.5	3.6
2-year colleges	96.4	96.6	98.2	98.9	99.6	95.6	95.5	95.5	95.5	0.9	3.4
Private institutions											
4-year colleges	60.3	63.0	64.5	65.6	66.4	66.2	67.2	68.9	68.2	7.9	2.6
2-year colleges	53.0	58.6	63.0	65.5	65.8	65.4	66.7	66.6	66.3	13.2	0.8

SOURCE: U.S. Department of Education, National Center for Education Statistics, Integrated Postsecondary Education Data System (IPEDS), "Institutional Characteristics" surveys. (This table was prepared September 1996.)

Table 305.—Highest level of education attained by 1980 high school seniors, by selected student and school characteristics: Spring 1986

Student and school characteristics	Highest educational attainment of 1980 high school seniors in 1986						
	Total	No high school diploma [1]	High school diploma	License [2]	Associate degree	Bachelor's degree	Graduate/ professional degree
1	2	3	4	5	6	7	8
Total	**100.0**	**0.9**	**61.8**	**11.9**	**6.5**	**18.2**	**0.7**
Sex							
Men	100.0	1.0	64.0	10.5	5.9	17.6	0.9
Women	100.0	0.8	59.6	13.3	7.0	18.8	0.6
Race/ethnicity							
White, non-Hispanic	100.0	0.8	60.0	11.5	6.6	20.2	0.9
Black, non-Hispanic	100.0	1.2	69.4	13.9	5.3	9.9	0.2
Hispanic	100.0	1.7	70.2	13.8	7.3	6.8	0.1
Asian	100.0	([3])	49.6	12.6	8.7	27.3	1.7
American Indian	100.0	([3])	61.3	18.6	9.3	10.8	([3])
Socioeconomic status quartile [4]							
Low	100.0	1.2	74.1	12.3	5.5	6.6	0.2
Low-middle	100.0	0.5	66.7	13.6	8.0	11.1	0.2
High-middle	100.0	0.1	58.4	12.9	7.7	20.4	0.6
High	100.0	([3])	45.7	8.7	6.3	37.1	2.2
High school program [5]							
General	100.0	0.8	69.7	12.6	6.5	10.2	0.2
Academic	100.0	0.1	45.6	8.8	7.2	36.6	1.8
Vocational	100.0	0.6	72.8	16.2	6.9	3.6	0.0
Postsecondary education plans [6]							
No plans	100.0	1.4	83.5	12.7	2.1	0.2	([3])
Attend vocational/technical school	100.0	0.3	72.5	17.7	8.4	1.1	([3])
Attend college less than 4 years .	100.0	0.2	65.5	14.4	13.1	6.8	([3])
Earn bachelor's degree	100.0	([3])	48.3	8.2	6.9	35.8	0.7
Earn advanced degree	100.0	0.1	43.5	7.9	4.9	40.6	3.0
Type of high school							
Public	100.0	1.0	63.2	12.1	6.6	16.4	0.7
Catholic	100.0	([3])	47.4	11.9	6.4	32.8	1.6
Other private	100.0	([3])	52.3	7.0	3.9	36.7	0.1

[1] Seniors who dropped out of high school after spring 1980 survey and had not completed high school by 1986.

[2] Persons who earned a certificate for completing a program of study.

[3] Less than .05 percent.

[4] Socioeconomic status was measured by a composite score on parental education, family income, father's occupation, and household characteristics in 1980.

[5] Students' self-reported high school program.

[6] During their senior year of high school, students were asked about the highest level of education they planned to attain. Students who planned to get less than a high school education or a high school education only were classified as having no postsecondary education plans.

NOTE.—Because of rounding, percents may not add to 100.0.

SOURCE: U.S. Department of Education, National Center for Education Statistics, High School and Beyond survey. (This table was prepared September 1987.)

Table 306.—Highest level of education attained by 1980 high school seniors, by race/ethnicity and October 1980 postsecondary education attendance status: Spring 1986

Race/ethnicity and October 1980 postsecondary education attendance status	Highest educational attainment of 1980 high school seniors in 1986						
	Total	No high school diploma [1]	High school diploma	License [2]	Associate degree	Bachelor's degree	Graduate/ professional degree
1	2	3	4	5	6	7	8
Total							
Part-time 2-year public college	100.0	0.7	66.4	17.7	8.8	6.5	([3])
Part-time 4-year public college	100.0	2.7	57.1	15.4	1.6	22.6	0.6
Full-time 2-year public college	100.0	([3])	49.5	11.7	20.7	17.6	0.5
Full-time 4-year public college	100.0	([3])	41.7	7.6	4.5	44.9	1.3
Full-time 4-year private college	100.0	([3])	31.1	8.8	5.1	51.9	3.0
Not a student	100.0	1.8	78.2	12.8	3.6	3.5	0.2
White, non-Hispanic							
Part-time 2-year public college	100.0	0.8	67.7	17.9	6.9	6.7	([3])
Part-time 4-year public college	100.0	3.4	54.8	14.5	0.3	27.0	([3])
Full-time 2-year public college	100.0	([3])	48.6	10.8	20.7	19.3	0.7
Full-time 4-year public college	100.0	([3])	39.0	6.8	4.8	48.0	1.5
Full-time 4-year private college	100.0	([3])	28.1	7.9	5.1	55.7	3.3
Not a student	100.0	1.6	78.5	12.7	3.5	3.5	0.2
Black, non-Hispanic							
Part-time 2-year public college	100.0	([3])	65.8	22.1	9.8	2.3	([3])
Part-time 4-year public college	100.0	([3])	58.5	25.1	6.0	8.5	1.8
Full-time 2-year public college	100.0	([3])	52.8	19.2	18.9	9.1	([3])
Full-time 4-year public college	100.0	([3])	59.4	11.2	3.4	25.6	0.5
Full-time 4-year private college	100.0	([3])	50.5	15.0	5.5	28.5	0.6
Not a student	100.0	2.2	78.1	13.3	3.6	2.8	([3])
Hispanic							
Part-time 2-year public college	100.0	([3])	57.4	14.9	23.4	4.4	([3])
Part-time 4-year public college	([4])	([4])	([4])	([4])	([4])	([4])	([4])
Full-time 2-year public college	100.0	([3])	53.9	14.9	22.7	8.5	([3])
Full-time 4-year public college	100.0	([3])	51.1	18.4	4.1	25.6	0.9
Full-time 4-year private college	100.0	([3])	46.8	19.4	6.1	26.8	1.0
Not a student	100.0	3.1	83.2	10.3	2.4	0.9	([3])

[1] Seniors who dropped out of high school after spring 1980 survey and had not completed high school by 1986.

[2] Includes persons who earned a certificate for completing a program of study.

[3] Less than .05 percent.

[4] Fewer than 30 cases available for analysis. Estimates are suppressed because they are unreliable.

NOTE.—Because of rounding, percents may not add to 100.0.

SOURCE: U.S. Department of Education, National Center for Education Statistics, High School and Beyond survey. (This table was prepared September 1987.)

Table 307.—Enrollment and completion status of first-time postsecondary students starting during the 1989–90 academic year, by degree objective and other student characteristics: 1994

Student characteristics	2-year college students starting in 1989–90						Students seeking bachelor's degrees in 1989–90					
	Attained by 1994[1]				No degree by 1994		Highest degree completed, not enrolled for bachelor's degree[2]				Still enrolled for bachelor's[3]	No degree, not enrolled[4]
	Total	Certificate	Associate	Bachelor's	Enrolled	Not enrolled	Total, any degree	Certificate	Associate	Bachelor's		
1	2	3	4	5	6	7	8	9	10	11	12	13
Total	**36.7**	**12.9**	**17.5**	**6.3**	**14.7**	**48.6**	**54.3**	**3.3**	**5.1**	**45.8**	**17.5**	**28.3**
Male	33.8	12.7	15.5	5.6	17.1	49.1	48.8	2.7	4.8	41.3	20.3	30.9
Female	39.6	13.2	19.5	7.0	12.4	48.1	59.7	4.0	5.4	50.3	14.6	25.7
Race												
White, non-Hispanic	37.3	12.3	18.4	6.6	13.0	49.7	56.4	3.3	4.9	48.1	16.6	27.0
Black, non-Hispanic	31.8	16.1	12.5	3.1	13.2	55.1	45.2	3.6	7.3	34.3	18.0	36.8
Hispanic	38.0	15.2	15.6	7.2	22.2	39.8	41.3	5.4	3.5	32.4	22.1	36.6
Asian/Pacific Islander	—	—	—	—	—	—	52.8	0.6	5.3	46.8	21.8	25.5
Socioeconomic status in 1989–90												
Low (25 percent)	30.2	17.7	10.6	1.9	10.3	59.5	31.7	3.8	5.7	22.1	16.5	51.8
Middle (50 percent)	34.3	13.7	15.0	5.7	16.4	49.3	47.1	3.5	4.8	38.9	19.4	33.5
High (25 percent)	44.8	8.7	26.1	10.1	14.5	40.7	61.5	3.2	5.3	52.9	16.3	22.3
Dependent student family income in 1989–90												
Less than $20,000	39.4	12.0	21.4	5.9	15.5	45.2	43.2	1.4	4.9	36.9	19.2	37.6
$20,000 to $39,999	43.4	12.8	20.5	10.0	13.8	42.9	52.6	4.1	5.3	43.2	18.2	29.2
$40,000 to $59,999	42.4	11.2	21.9	9.3	13.1	44.6	57.0	4.4	4.1	48.5	16.1	26.9
$60,000 or more	46.9	5.4	31.5	10.0	24.6	28.5	68.1	1.5	6.0	60.6	16.0	15.9
Diploma/delayed entry status[5]												
Diploma, did not delay	45.5	10.6	24.9	10.0	16.3	38.3	58.2	2.9	4.9	50.3	17.0	24.8
Diploma, delayed entry	26.4	16.3	8.6	1.5	14.5	59.1	30.9	6.6	7.1	17.3	21.5	47.6
No diploma	21.8	14.2	5.9	1.7	4.5	73.7	21.0	3.7	2.4	15.0	14.1	64.8
Age (as of 12/31/89)												
18 years or younger	47.4	9.4	26.1	11.9	14.9	37.7	59.2	2.9	4.9	51.4	16.4	24.5
19 years	31.9	12.7	17.1	2.2	20.8	47.3	45.8	3.4	4.2	38.3	21.1	33.0
20 to 29 years	27.3	16.4	8.3	2.5	13.0	59.8	36.3	7.9	9.4	19.0	19.6	44.1
30 years or over	25.7	18.2	6.9	0.6	9.2	65.1	19.1	3.3	6.0	9.8	17.3	63.5
Marital status												
Never married	41.1	11.8	21.1	8.1	16.2	42.7	56.8	3.4	5.3	48.1	17.4	25.8
Married	26.3	15.4	8.7	2.2	9.2	64.5	26.7	4.2	2.4	20.1	17.8	55.5
Divorced, widowed, separated	29.9	25.6	3.3	1.0	8.8	61.2	21.7	0.6	9.5	11.6	18.4	59.9
Expected degree level for 2-year students												
Less than 2 years	23.9	19.8	4.1	0.0	12.3	63.8	—	—	—	—	—	—
2 to 4 years	30.2	18.3	10.5	1.4	11.8	58.0	—	—	—	—	—	—
Bachelor's or higher	40.6	9.9	21.7	9.0	16.1	43.3	—	—	—	—	—	—
Average hours worked per week while enrolled												
None	40.5	21.2	13.8	5.6	11.1	48.4	56.2	2.0	4.4	49.8	17.8	26.0
1 to 20 hours	45.4	12.2	23.7	9.6	14.6	40.0	59.0	2.5	5.2	51.3	16.4	24.5
More than 20 hours	33.3	10.9	16.8	5.6	15.7	51.0	50.3	4.5	5.4	40.4	17.9	31.7
Received financial aid during 1989–90												
Yes	39.9	13.1	17.3	9.6	8.6	51.5	60.4	2.2	3.2	55.1	13.8	25.8
No	35.5	12.9	17.6	5.0	17.0	47.5	48.4	4.5	7.0	36.9	21.0	30.7

[1] Highest degree attained at any institution. Students who have attained may also be enrolled.

[2] Status as of 1994. Includes those students who are no longer working towards a bachelor's degree, but who had completed another type of degree or award.

[3] Status as of 1994. Includes students who had completed another type of degree or award (associate degree: 11.8 percent, certificate: 2.7 percent) but are still working toward a bachelor's degree.

[4] Status as of 1994. Enrollment can be full-time or part-time. Includes students who are still enrolled, but are no longer working toward a bachelor's degree.

[5] Students were considered to have a diploma only if they had a regular high school diploma. Students with a GED or other high school credentials were considered to have no diploma.

—Data not available or not applicable.

NOTE.—Data reflect completion and enrollment status by spring 1994 of first-time postsecondary students starting academic year 1989–90. Some cells in this table have relatively large sampling errors. See sampling error table in appendix.

SOURCE: U.S. Department of Education, National Center for Education Statistics, Beginning Postsecondary Student Longitudinal Survey, 1994. (This table was prepared September 1996.)

Table 308.—Scores on Graduate Record Examination (GRE) and subject matter tests: 1965 to 1995

Academic year ending	Number of GRE takers	GRE takers as a percent of bachelor's degrees	Verbal		Quantitative		Analytical		Biology		Chemistry		Education		Engineering		Literature		Psychology	
			Mean	Standard deviation	Mean	Standard deviation	Mean	Standard deviation	Mean	Standard deviation	Mean	Standard deviation	Mean	Standard deviation	Mean	Standard deviation	Mean	Standard deviation	Mean	Standard deviation
1	2	3	4	5	6	7	8	9	10	11	12	13	14	15	16	17	18	19	20	21
1965	93,792	18.7	530	124	533	137	—	—	617	117	628	114	481	86	618	108	591	95	556	91
1966	123,960	23.8	520	124	528	133	—	—	610	115	618	110	474	87	609	106	588	94	552	91
1967	151,134	27.0	519	125	528	134	—	—	613	114	615	104	476	90	603	104	582	91	553	93
1968	182,432	28.8	520	124	527	135	—	—	614	114	617	104	478	87	601	105	572	91	547	93
1969	206,113	28.3	515	124	524	132	—	—	613	112	613	104	477	88	591	103	569	89	543	89
1970	265,359	33.5	503	123	516	132	—	—	603	111	613	113	462	92	586	110	556	90	532	91
1971	293,600	35.0	497	125	512	134	—	—	603	114	618	117	457	95	587	115	546	91	530	92
1972	293,506	33.1	494	126	508	136	—	—	606	115	624	124	446	93	594	119	544	96	528	92
1973	290,104	31.5	497	125	512	135	—	—	619	110	630	114	459	96	593	114	545	96	529	92
1974	301,070	31.8	492	126	509	137	—	—	624	110	634	115	452	93	591	121	547	99	530	95
1975	298,335	32.3	493	125	508	137	—	—	—	—	—	—	—	—	—	—	—	—	—	—
1976	299,292	32.3	492	127	510	138	—	—	627	112	627	107	454	93	594	119	539	101	531	93
1977	287,715	31.3	490	129	514	139	—	—	625	113	630	109	453	93	592	115	532	101	532	95
1978	286,383	31.1	484	128	518	135	—	—	622	113	624	108	452	91	594	114	530	102	529	97
1979	282,482	30.7	476	130	517	135	—	—	621	117	623	104	451	89	592	115	525	102	530	97
1980	272,281	29.3	474	131	522	136	—	—	619	115	618	105	449	90	590	116	521	105	534	98
1981	262,855	28.1	473	128	523	136	—	—	617	115	615	103	453	90	590	116	520	99	532	97
1982	256,381	26.9	469	130	533	137	498	126	616	114	616	105	456	89	593	115	521	100	532	97
1983	263,674	27.2	473	131	541	138	504	128	623	115	620	105	459	90	599	114	527	98	542	95
1984	265,221	27.2	475	130	541	139	512	129	622	115	619	102	461	90	604	114	530	97	543	96
1985	271,972	27.8	474	126	545	140	516	129	619	114	621	101	459	89	615	120	531	95	541	95
1986	279,428	28.3	475	126	552	140	520	129	612	114	628	106	464	87	616	119	527	96	542	97
1987	293,560	29.6	477	126	550	140	521	128	616	116	629	104	465	86	619	119	526	95	536	95
1988	303,703	30.5	483	123	557	140	528	128	615	114	631	108	467	85	622	120	525	94	537	94
1989	326,096	32.0	484	125	560	142	530	129	612	114	642	117	465	87	626	116	528	91	538	95
1990	344,572	32.8	486	123	562	143	534	128	612	114	662	123	461	84	617	111	523	92	537	95
1991	379,882	34.7	485	122	562	141	536	129	609	113	660	123	457	85	611	111	523	93	535	95
1992	411,528	36.2	483	120	561	140	537	129	605	113	654	128	462	82	610	117	525	92	536	95
1993	400,246	34.4	481	117	557	140	541	129	606	114	662	133	462	80	602	115	516	94	536	97
1994	[1]399,395	34.3	479	116	553	139	545	129	620	116	627	113	[2]493	104	601	115	517	95	538	96
1995	[1]389,539	33.0	477	115	553	140	544	131	622	116	675	138	[2]488	102	596	113	513	96	544	98

[1] Total includes examinees who received no score on one or more General Test measures.

[2] Data reported for 1994 and 1995 are from the revised education test.

— Data not reported or not applicable.

NOTE.—GRE scores for the verbal, quantitative, and analytical sections range from 200 to 800. Subject matter test scores range from 200 to 990.

SOURCE: Graduate Record Examination Board, Examinee and Score Trends for the GRE General Test, various years; and A Summary of Data Collected From Graduate Record Examinations Test-Takers During 1986–87; unpublished data; and U.S. Department of Education, National Center for Education Statistics, "Degrees and Other Formal Awards Conferred" surveys, and Integrated Postsecondary Education Data System (IPEDS), "Completions" surveys. (This table was prepared April 1996.)

Table 309.—Average undergraduate tuition and fees and room and board rates paid by students in institutions of higher education, by type and control of institution: 1964–65 to 1995–96

Year and control of institution	Total tuition, room, and board					Tuition and required fees (in-state)					Dormitory rooms					Board (7-day basis) [1]				
	All insti-tutions	4-year institutions			2-year	All insti-tutions	4-year institutions			2-year	All insti-tutions	4-year institutions			2-year	All insti-tutions	4-year institutions			2-year
		All 4-year	Univer-sities	Other 4-year			All 4-year	Univer-sities	Other 4-year			All 4-year	Univer-sities	Other 4-year			All 4-year	Univer-sities	Other 4-year	
1	2	3	4	5	6	7	8	9	10	11	12	13	14	15	16	17	18	19	20	21
All institutions																				
1976–77	$2,275	$2,577	$2,647	$2,527	$1,598	$924	$1,218	$1,210	$1,223	$346	$603	$611	$649	$584	$503	$748	$748	$788	$719	$750
1977–78	2,411	2,725	2,777	2,685	1,703	984	1,291	1,269	1,305	378	645	654	691	628	525	781	780	818	752	801
1978–79	2,587	2,917	2,967	2,879	1,828	1,073	1,397	1,370	1,413	411	688	696	737	667	575	826	825	860	800	842
1979–80	2,809	3,167	3,223	3,124	1,979	1,163	1,513	1,484	1,530	451	751	759	803	729	628	895	895	936	865	900
1980–81	3,101	3,499	3,535	3,469	2,230	1,289	1,679	1,634	1,705	526	836	846	881	821	705	976	975	1,020	943	1,000
1981–82	3,489	3,951	4,005	3,908	2,476	1,457	1,907	1,860	1,935	590	950	961	1,023	919	793	1,083	1,082	1,121	1,055	1,094
1982–83	3,877	4,406	4,466	4,356	2,713	1,626	2,139	2,081	2,173	675	1,064	1,078	1,150	1,028	873	1,187	1,189	1,235	1,155	1,165
1983–84	4,167	4,747	4,793	4,712	2,854	1,783	2,344	2,300	2,368	730	1,145	1,162	1,211	1,130	916	1,239	1,242	1,282	1,214	1,208
1984–85	4,563	5,160	5,236	5,107	3,179	1,985	2,567	2,539	2,583	821	1,267	1,282	1,343	1,242	1,058	1,310	1,311	1,353	1,282	1,301
1985–86 [2]	4,885	5,504	5,597	5,441	3,367	2,181	2,784	2,770	2,793	888	1,338	1,355	1,424	1,309	1,107	1,365	1,365	1,403	1,339	1,372
1986–87 [3]	5,206	5,964	6,124	5,857	3,295	2,312	3,042	3,042	3,042	897	1,405	1,427	1,501	1,376	1,034	1,489	1,495	1,581	1,439	1,364
1987–88	5,494	6,272	6,339	6,226	3,263	2,458	3,201	3,168	3,220	809	1,488	1,516	1,576	1,478	1,017	1,549	1,555	1,596	1,529	1,437
1988–89	5,869	6,725	6,801	6,673	3,573	2,658	3,472	3,422	3,499	979	1,575	1,609	1,665	1,573	1,085	1,636	1,644	1,715	1,601	1,509
1989–90	6,207	7,212	7,347	7,120	3,705	2,839	3,800	3,765	3,819	978	1,638	1,675	1,732	1,638	1,105	1,730	1,737	1,850	1,663	1,622
1990–91	6,562	7,602	7,709	7,528	3,930	3,016	4,009	3,958	4,036	1,087	1,743	1,782	1,848	1,740	1,182	1,802	1,811	1,903	1,751	1,660
1991–92	7,074	8,252	8,389	8,164	4,089	3,282	4,399	4,366	4,417	1,186	1,874	1,921	1,998	1,874	1,210	1,918	1,931	2,026	1,873	1,692
1992–93	7,452	8,758	8,934	8,648	4,207	3,517	4,752	4,665	4,795	1,276	1,939	1,991	2,104	1,926	1,240	1,996	2,015	2,165	1,927	1,692
1993–94	7,931	9,296	9,495	9,186	4,449	3,827	5,119	5,104	5,127	1,399	2,057	2,111	2,190	2,068	1,332	2,047	2,067	2,201	1,992	1,718
1994–95	8,306	9,728	9,863	9,646	4,633	4,044	5,391	5,287	5,441	1,488	2,145	2,200	2,281	2,155	1,396	2,116	2,138	2,295	2,049	1,750
1995–96 [4]	8,774	10,315	10,551	10,177	4,730	4,312	5,771	5,725	5,794	1,518	2,263	2,317	2,423	2,259	1,476	2,199	2,226	2,404	2,124	1,735
Public institutions																				
1964–65	950	—	1,051	867	638	243	—	298	224	99	271	—	291	241	178	436	—	462	402	361
1965–66	983	—	1,105	904	670	257	—	327	241	109	281	—	304	255	194	445	—	474	408	367
1966–67	1,026	—	1,171	947	710	275	—	360	259	121	294	—	321	271	213	457	—	490	417	376
1967–68	1,064	—	1,199	997	789	283	—	366	268	144	313	—	337	292	243	468	—	496	437	402
1968–69	1,117	—	1,245	1,063	883	295	—	377	281	170	337	—	359	318	278	485	—	509	464	435
1969–70	1,203	—	1,362	1,135	951	323	—	427	306	178	369	—	395	346	308	511	—	540	483	465
1970–71	1,287	—	1,477	1,206	998	351	—	478	332	187	401	—	431	375	338	535	—	568	499	473
1971–72	1,357	—	1,579	1,263	1,073	376	—	526	354	192	430	—	463	400	366	551	—	590	509	515
1972–73	1,458	—	1,668	1,460	1,197	407	—	566	455	233	476	—	500	455	398	575	—	602	550	566
1973–74	1,517	—	1,707	1,506	1,274	438	—	581	463	274	480	—	505	464	409	599	—	621	579	591
1974–75	1,563	—	1,760	1,558	1,339	432	—	599	448	277	506	—	527	497	424	625	—	634	613	638
1975–76	1,666	—	1,935	1,657	1,386	433	—	642	469	245	544	—	573	533	442	689	—	720	655	699
1976–77	1,789	1,935	2,067	1,827	1,491	479	617	689	564	283	582	592	614	572	465	728	727	763	692	742
1977–78	1,888	2,038	2,170	1,931	1,590	512	655	736	596	306	621	631	649	616	486	755	752	785	720	797
1978–79	1,994	2,145	2,289	2,027	1,691	543	688	777	622	327	655	664	689	641	527	796	793	823	764	837
1979–80	2,165	2,327	2,487	2,198	1,822	583	738	840	662	355	715	725	750	703	574	867	865	898	833	893
1980–81	2,373	2,550	2,712	2,421	2,027	635	804	915	722	391	799	811	827	796	642	940	936	969	904	994
1981–82	2,663	2,871	3,079	2,705	2,224	714	909	1,042	813	434	909	925	970	885	703	1,039	1,036	1,067	1,006	1,086
1982–83	2,945	3,196	3,403	3,032	2,390	798	1,031	1,164	936	473	1,010	1,030	1,072	993	755	1,136	1,134	1,167	1,103	1,162
1983–84	3,156	3,433	3,628	3,285	2,534	891	1,148	1,284	1,052	528	1,087	1,110	1,131	1,092	801	1,178	1,175	1,213	1,141	1,205
1984–85	3,408	3,682	3,899	3,518	2,807	971	1,228	1,386	1,117	584	1,196	1,217	1,237	1,200	921	1,241	1,237	1,276	1,201	1,302
1985–86 [2]	3,571	3,859	4,146	3,637	2,981	1,045	1,318	1,536	1,157	641	1,242	1,263	1,290	1,240	960	1,285	1,278	1,320	1,240	1,380
1986–87 [3]	3,805	4,138	4,469	3,891	2,989	1,106	1,414	1,651	1,248	660	1,301	1,323	1,355	1,295	979	1,398	1,401	1,464	1,348	1,349
1987–88	4,050	4,403	4,619	4,250	3,066	1,218	1,537	1,726	1,407	706	1,378	1,410	1,410	1,409	943	1,454	1,456	1,482	1,434	1,417
1988–89	4,274	4,678	4,905	4,526	3,183	1,285	1,646	1,846	1,515	730	1,457	1,496	1,483	1,506	965	1,533	1,536	1,576	1,504	1,488
1989–90	4,504	4,975	5,324	4,723	3,299	1,356	1,780	2,035	1,608	756	1,513	1,557	1,561	1,554	962	1,635	1,638	1,728	1,561	1,581
1990–91	4,757	5,243	5,585	5,004	3,467	1,454	1,888	2,159	1,707	824	1,612	1,657	1,658	1,655	1,050	1,691	1,698	1,767	1,641	1,594
1991–92	5,135	5,695	6,051	5,459	3,623	1,624	2,119	2,410	1,933	937	1,731	1,785	1,789	1,782	1,074	1,780	1,792	1,852	1,745	1,612

Table 309.—Average undergraduate tuition and fees and room and board rates paid by students in institutions of higher education, by type and control of institution: 1964–65 to 1995–96—Continued

Year and control of institution	Total tuition, room, and board					Tuition and required fees (in-state)					Dormitory rooms					Board (7-day basis)[1]				
	All institutions	4-year institutions			2-year	All institutions	4-year institutions			2-year	All institutions	4-year institutions			2-year	All institutions	4-year institutions			2-year
		All 4-year	Universities	Other 4-year			All 4-year	Universities	Other 4-year			All 4-year	Universities	Other 4-year			All 4-year	Universities	Other 4-year	
1	2	3	4	5	6	7	8	9	10	11	12	13	14	15	16	17	18	19	20	21
1992–93	5,379	6,020	6,442	5,740	3,799	1,782	2,349	2,604	2,192	1,025	1,756	1,816	1,856	1,787	1,106	1,841	1,854	1,982	1,761	1,668
1993–94	5,694	6,365	6,710	6,146	3,996	1,942	2,537	2,820	2,360	1,125	1,873	1,934	1,897	1,958	1,190	1,880	1,895	1,993	1,828	1,681
1994–95	5,965	6,670	7,077	6,409	4,137	2,057	2,681	2,977	2,499	1,192	1,959	2,023	1,992	2,044	1,232	1,949	1,967	2,108	1,866	1,712
1995–96[4]	6,252	7,013	7,451	6,727	4,236	2,176	2,848	3,151	2,661	1,245	2,057	2,121	2,107	2,130	1,303	2,019	2,045	2,193	1,936	1,688
Private institutions																				
1964–65	1,907	—	2,202	1,810	1,455	1,088	—	1,297	1,023	702	331	—	390	308	289	488	—	515	479	464
1965–66	2,005	—	2,316	1,899	1,557	1,154	—	1,369	1,086	768	356	—	418	330	316	495	—	529	483	473
1966–67	2,124	—	2,456	2,007	1,679	1,233	—	1,456	1,162	845	385	—	452	355	347	506	—	548	490	487
1967–68	2,205	—	2,545	2,104	1,762	1,297	—	1,534	1,237	892	392	—	455	366	366	516	—	556	501	504
1968–69	2,321	—	2,673	2,237	1,876	1,383	—	1,638	1,335	956	404	—	463	382	391	534	—	572	520	529
1969–70	2,530	—	2,920	2,420	1,993	1,533	—	1,809	1,468	1,034	436	—	503	409	413	561	—	608	543	546
1970–71	2,738	—	3,163	2,599	2,103	1,684	—	1,980	1,603	1,109	468	—	542	434	434	586	—	641	562	560
1971–72	2,917	—	3,375	2,748	2,186	1,820	—	2,133	1,721	1,172	494	—	576	454	449	603	—	666	573	565
1972–73	3,038	—	3,512	2,934	2,273	1,898	—	2,226	1,846	1,221	524	—	622	490	457	616	—	664	598	595
1973–74	3,164	—	3,717	3,040	2,410	1,989	—	2,375	1,925	1,303	533	—	622	502	483	642	—	720	613	624
1974–75	3,403	—	4,076	3,156	2,591	2,117	—	2,614	1,954	1,367	586	—	691	536	564	700	—	771	666	660
1975–76	3,663	—	4,467	3,385	2,711	2,272	—	2,881	2,084	1,427	636	—	753	583	572	755	—	833	718	712
1976–77	3,906	3,977	4,715	3,714	2,971	2,467	2,534	3,051	2,351	1,592	649	651	783	604	607	790	791	882	759	772
1977–78	4,158	4,240	5,033	3,967	3,148	2,624	2,700	3,240	2,520	1,706	698	702	850	648	631	836	838	943	800	811
1978–79	4,514	4,609	5,403	4,327	3,389	2,867	2,958	3,487	2,771	1,831	758	761	916	704	700	889	890	1,000	851	858
1979–80	4,912	5,013	5,891	4,700	3,751	3,130	3,225	3,811	3,020	2,062	827	831	1,001	768	766	955	957	1,078	912	923
1980–81	5,470	5,594	6,569	5,249	4,303	3,498	3,617	4,275	3,390	2,413	918	921	1,086	859	871	1,054	1,056	1,209	1,000	1,019
1981–82	6,166	6,330	7,443	5,947	4,746	3,953	4,113	4,887	3,853	2,605	1,038	1,039	1,229	970	1,022	1,175	1,178	1,327	1,124	1,119
1982–83	6,920	7,126	8,536	6,646	5,364	4,439	4,639	5,583	4,329	3,008	1,181	1,181	1,453	1,083	1,177	1,300	1,306	1,501	1,234	1,179
1983–84	7,508	7,759	9,308	7,244	5,571	4,851	5,093	6,217	4,726	3,099	1,278	1,279	1,531	1,191	1,253	1,380	1,387	1,559	1,327	1,219
1984–85	8,202	8,451	10,243	7,849	6,203	5,315	5,556	6,843	5,135	3,485	1,426	1,426	1,753	1,309	1,424	1,462	1,469	1,647	1,405	1,294
1985–86[2]	8,885	9,228	11,034	8,551	6,512	5,789	6,121	7,374	5,641	3,672	1,553	1,557	1,940	1,420	1,500	1,542	1,551	1,720	1,490	1,340
1986–87[3]	9,676	10,039	12,278	9,276	6,384	6,316	6,658	8,118	6,171	3,684	1,658	1,673	2,097	1,518	1,266	1,702	1,708	2,063	1,587	1,434
1987–88	10,512	10,659	13,075	9,854	7,078	6,988	7,116	8,771	6,574	4,161	1,748	1,760	2,244	1,593	1,380	1,775	1,783	2,060	1,687	1,537
1988–89	11,189	11,474	14,073	10,620	7,967	7,461	7,722	9,451	7,172	4,817	1,849	1,863	2,353	1,686	1,540	1,880	1,889	2,269	1,762	1,609
1989–90	12,018	12,284	15,098	11,374	8,670	8,147	8,396	10,348	7,778	5,196	1,923	1,935	2,411	1,774	1,663	1,948	1,953	2,339	1,823	1,811
1990–91	12,910	13,237	16,503	12,220	8,772	8,772	9,083	11,379	8,389	5,570	2,063	2,077	2,654	1,889	1,744	2,074	2,077	2,470	1,943	1,989
1991–92	13,907	14,273	17,779	13,189	9,631	9,434	9,775	12,192	9,053	5,752	2,221	2,241	2,860	2,038	1,789	2,252	2,257	2,727	2,098	2,090
1992–93	14,634	15,009	18,898	13,882	9,903	9,942	10,294	13,055	9,533	6,059	2,348	2,362	3,018	2,151	1,970	2,344	2,354	2,825	2,197	1,875
1993–94	15,496	15,904	20,097	14,640	10,406	10,572	10,952	13,874	10,100	6,370	2,490	2,506	3,277	2,261	2,067	2,434	2,445	2,946	2,278	1,970
1994–95	16,207	16,602	21,041	15,363	11,170	11,111	11,481	14,537	10,653	6,914	2,587	2,601	3,469	2,347	2,233	2,509	2,520	3,035	2,362	2,023
1995–96[4]	17,207	17,613	22,470	16,203	11,502	11,858	12,239	15,581	11,294	7,039	2,739	2,753	3,672	2,475	2,363	2,610	2,622	3,216	2,434	2,100

[1] Data for 1986–87 and later years reflect 20 meals per week rather than meals 7 days per week.

[2] Room and board data are estimated.

[3] Because of revisions in data collection procedures, figures are not entirely comparable with those for previous years. In particular, data on board rates are somewhat higher than earlier years because they reflect a basis of 20 meals per week rather than meals served 7 days per week. Since many institutions serve fewer than 3 meals each day, the 1986–87 and later data reflect a more accurate accounting of total board costs. Because of their low response rate, data for private 2-year colleges must be interpreted with caution.

[4] Preliminary data based on fall 1994 enrollment weights.

—Data not available.

NOTE.—Data are for the entire academic year and are average charges paid by students. Tuition and fees were weighted by the number of full-time-equivalent undergraduates but were not adjusted to reflect student residency. Room and board were based on full-time students. The data have not been adjusted for changes in the purchasing power of the dollar. Some data have been revised from previously published figures. Because of rounding, details may not add to totals.

SOURCE: U.S. Department of Education, National Center for Education Statistics, "Institutional Characteristics of Colleges and Universities" and "Fall Enrollment in Institutions of Higher Education" surveys; Integrated Postsecondary Education Data System (IPEDS), "Fall Enrollment" and "Institutional Characteristics" surveys. (This table was prepared September 1996.)

Table 310.—Average undergraduate tuition and fees and room and board rates paid by students in institutions of higher education, by control of institution and by state: 1994–95 and 1995–96

State or other area	Public 4-year, 1994–95		Public 4-year, 1995–96 [1]				Private 4-year, 1994–95		Private 4-year, 1995–96 [1]				Public 2-year, tuition only (in-state)	
	Total	Tuition (in-state)	Total	Tuition (in-state)	Room	Board	Total	Tuition	Total	Tuition (in-state)	Room	Board	1994–95	1995–96 [1]
1	2	3	4	5	6	7	8	9	10	11	12	13	14	15
United States	$6,670	$2,681	$7,013	$2,848	$2,121	$2,045	$16,602	$11,481	$17,613	$12,239	$2,753	$2,622	$1,192	$1,245
Alabama	5,429	2,107	5,737	2,240	1,757	1,739	11,208	7,318	11,635	7,580	1,799	2,256	1,132	1,317
Alaska	6,153	2,039	6,665	2,489	2,238	1,937	12,849	8,302	12,917	8,293	1,879	2,745	1,320	2,120
Arizona	5,825	1,894	5,998	1,926	2,257	1,815	10,358	6,225	10,934	6,779	2,012	2,143	735	764
Arkansas	4,912	1,954	5,064	2,028	1,613	1,423	9,615	6,197	10,183	6,574	1,488	2,121	884	903
California	7,924	2,696	8,213	2,666	3,031	2,516	17,696	11,847	20,143	13,977	3,196	2,970	365	362
Colorado	6,524	2,380	7,037	2,473	2,000	2,564	16,262	11,060	17,120	11,796	2,574	2,750	1,282	1,340
Connecticut	8,491	3,737	8,753	3,845	2,609	2,299	21,739	15,521	23,011	16,646	3,621	2,744	1,520	1,646
Delaware	8,118	3,805	8,489	3,981	2,407	2,101	11,349	7,159	11,518	7,373	2,701	1,443	1,266	1,266
District of Columbia	—	1,046	—	1,118	—	—	20,311	14,021	21,337	14,681	3,917	2,740	—	—
Florida	6,201	1,783	6,254	1,767	2,193	2,295	14,329	9,785	15,028	10,364	2,428	2,236	1,113	1,103
Georgia	5,382	1,964	5,691	2,103	1,712	1,877	14,329	9,562	15,194	10,208	2,719	2,267	1,023	1,062
Hawaii	—	1,504	—	1,576	—	—	11,020	5,971	11,632	6,234	3,050	2,347	500	524
Idaho	5,203	1,581	5,321	1,682	1,541	2,098	14,451	11,130	15,307	11,843	1,430	2,035	991	991
Illinois	7,498	3,195	7,829	3,352	2,072	2,405	16,009	11,078	16,678	11,653	2,718	2,306	1,193	1,232
Indiana	6,920	2,862	7,392	3,037	1,931	2,425	15,920	11,842	16,829	12,592	1,987	2,250	1,848	1,937
Iowa	5,701	2,462	5,945	2,565	1,693	1,688	15,184	11,349	15,934	11,932	1,864	2,138	1,700	1,782
Kansas	5,441	2,019	5,691	2,120	1,731	1,841	11,698	8,063	12,400	8,634	1,582	2,183	1,051	1,147
Kentucky	5,327	2,057	5,455	2,161	1,527	1,767	10,679	7,046	11,192	7,497	1,711	1,985	1,088	1,112
Louisiana	5,268	2,212	5,491	2,221	1,464	1,806	16,748	11,768	17,796	12,449	2,906	2,440	1,023	1,031
Maine	7,763	3,303	7,966	3,474	2,235	2,257	20,520	15,058	21,872	16,204	2,758	2,910	2,151	2,381
Maryland	8,300	3,321	8,728	3,572	2,722	2,435	20,120	13,805	21,245	14,700	3,524	3,022	1,843	1,967
Massachusetts	8,562	4,148	8,757	4,253	2,462	2,042	22,330	15,689	23,335	16,403	3,688	3,244	2,437	2,359
Michigan	7,948	3,733	8,195	3,895	2,024	2,276	12,849	8,771	13,331	9,176	1,974	2,182	1,436	1,529
Minnesota	6,203	2,931	6,712	3,216	2,022	1,474	16,339	12,233	17,222	12,897	2,058	2,267	1,965	2,065
Mississippi	5,250	2,446	5,425	2,459	1,399	1,568	9,312	6,384	9,901	6,782	1,582	1,536	938	941
Missouri	6,347	2,797	6,750	3,015	2,022	1,713	14,057	9,577	14,116	9,566	2,162	2,387	1,204	1,255
Montana	6,004	2,109	7,754	2,367	1,778	3,609	10,438	6,999	11,062	7,545	1,388	2,128	1,376	1,382
Nebraska	5,187	2,058	5,497	2,182	1,422	1,892	12,541	8,861	13,234	9,430	1,801	2,003	1,102	1,132
Nevada	6,905	1,601	7,388	1,684	3,090	2,614	—	7,532	—	7,841	3,050	—	843	970
New Hampshire	8,181	4,039	8,729	4,446	2,573	1,710	17,180	12,148	21,071	15,038	3,024	3,009	2,316	2,420
New Jersey	8,727	3,776	9,125	3,972	3,101	2,052	18,949	12,928	19,751	13,566	3,226	2,959	1,754	1,878
New Mexico	5,365	1,836	5,298	1,940	1,504	1,854	13,489	9,104	14,355	9,784	2,289	2,282	675	690
New York	7,926	2,944	8,960	3,714	2,937	2,310	19,663	13,069	20,831	13,852	3,724	3,255	2,151	2,427
North Carolina	4,857	1,502	5,119	1,639	1,742	1,737	14,658	10,493	15,428	10,984	2,128	2,316	582	581
North Dakota	5,514	2,248	5,642	2,248	1,016	2,378	9,520	6,663	9,907	6,998	1,260	1,649	1,689	1,698
Ohio	7,732	3,403	8,169	3,603	2,386	2,181	16,282	11,735	17,139	12,377	2,349	2,414	2,166	2,261
Oklahoma	4,196	1,672	4,287	1,839	837	1,611	11,562	7,781	11,773	7,831	1,803	2,140	1,149	1,260
Oregon	6,930	3,064	7,354	3,233	1,647	2,474	17,592	12,971	18,899	13,892	2,257	2,750	1,322	1,338
Pennsylvania	8,672	4,517	9,124	4,723	2,227	2,174	18,979	13,418	19,876	14,111	2,943	2,822	1,755	1,909
Rhode Island	9,067	3,706	9,446	3,856	3,029	2,561	20,957	14,604	22,075	15,390	3,613	3,072	1,686	1,726
South Carolina	6,756	3,020	6,964	3,094	1,998	1,872	12,651	9,073	13,517	9,741	1,786	1,990	1,048	1,071
South Dakota	5,271	2,509	5,619	2,642	1,247	1,730	12,352	8,536	13,039	9,123	1,541	2,374	3,430	3,430
Tennessee	5,131	1,897	5,372	1,990	1,644	1,737	13,235	9,257	14,068	9,830	2,153	2,085	976	1,022
Texas	5,177	1,606	5,464	1,820	1,885	1,759	12,390	8,386	13,156	8,959	2,000	2,198	689	771
Utah	5,334	1,943	5,414	2,011	1,458	1,945	7,060	2,761	7,384	2,936	1,380	3,068	1,340	1,375
Vermont	10,327	5,682	10,640	5,898	3,072	1,670	20,596	14,960	21,612	15,670	3,375	2,567	2,196	2,370
Virginia	7,958	3,776	8,202	3,907	2,261	2,033	14,166	9,943	15,021	10,596	2,062	2,363	1,384	1,433
Washington	7,068	2,685	7,136	2,791	2,187	2,158	16,988	12,408	18,092	13,276	2,487	2,329	1,313	1,369
West Virginia	5,912	1,961	6,128	2,024	1,970	2,133	13,354	9,460	14,231	10,008	1,853	2,370	1,303	1,312
Wisconsin	5,613	2,468	5,847	2,614	1,706	1,527	14,693	10,761	15,652	11,569	1,812	2,271	1,682	1,840
Wyoming	5,237	1,908	5,429	2,005	1,512	1,912	—	—	—	—	—	—	892	948

[1] Preliminary data based on fall 1994 enrollments.

—Data not reported or not applicable.

NOTE.—Data are for the entire academic year and are average charges. Tuition and fees were weighted by the number of full-time-equivalent undergraduates in 1994, but are not adjusted to reflect student residency. Room and board are based on full-time students.

SOURCE: U.S. Department of Education, National Center for Education Statistics, Integrated Postsecondary Education Data System (IPEDS), "Fall Enrollment" and "Institutional Characteristics" surveys. (This table was prepared September 1996.)

Table 311.—Average graduate and first-professional tuition paid by students in institutions of higher education: 1987–88 to 1995–96

Year	Average full-time graduate tuition	Average full-time first-professional tuition									
		Chiroprac-tic	Dentistry	Medicine	Optometry	Osteo-pathic medicine	Pharmacy	Podiatry	Veterinary medicine	Law	Theology
1	2	3	4	5	6	7	8	9	10	11	12
All institutions											
1987–88	$3,599	$6,996	$9,399	$9,034	$7,926	$10,674	$5,201	$12,736	$4,503	$6,636	$3,572
1988–89	3,728	7,972	9,324	9,439	8,503	11,462	4,952	13,232	4,856	7,099	3,911
1989–90	4,135	8,315	10,515	10,597	9,469	11,888	5,890	14,611	5,470	8,059	4,079
1990–91	4,488	9,108	10,270	10,571	9,512	12,830	5,889	15,143	5,396	8,708	4,569
1991–92	5,116	10,226	12,049	11,646	9,610	13,004	6,731	16,257	6,367	9,469	4,876
1992–93	5,475	11,117	12,710	12,265	10,858	14,297	6,635	17,426	6,771	10,463	5,331
1993–94	5,973	11,503	14,403	13,074	10,385	15,038	7,960	17,621	7,159	11,552	5,253
1994–95 [1]	6,247	12,391	15,059	13,808	10,800	15,688	8,432	18,252	7,708	12,386	5,593
1995–96 [2]	6,732	12,559	16,053	14,619	11,522	16,607	9,001	18,552	8,132	13,237	5,956
Public [3]											
1987–88	1,827	—	4,614	5,245	2,789	5,125	2,462	—	3,523	2,810	—
1988–89	1,913	—	5,286	5,669	3,455	6,269	2,218	—	3,889	2,766	—
1989–90	1,999	—	5,728	6,259	3,569	6,521	2,816	—	4,505	3,196	—
1990–91	2,206	—	5,927	6,437	3,821	7,188	2,697	—	4,840	3,430	—
1991–92	2,524	—	6,595	7,106	4,161	7,699	2,871	—	5,231	3,933	—
1992–93	2,791	—	7,006	7,867	5,106	8,404	2,987	—	5,553	4,261	—
1993–94	3,050	—	7,525	8,329	5,325	8,640	3,567	—	6,107	4,835	—
1994–95 [1]	3,250	—	7,985	8,807	5,676	9,123	3,787	—	6,638	5,300	—
1995–96 [2]	3,459	—	8,602	9,518	6,266	9,498	4,151	—	7,030	5,813	—
Private											
1987–88	6,769	6,996	16,201	14,945	11,635	13,311	8,834	12,736	12,544	9,048	3,572
1988–89	6,945	7,972	16,127	15,610	12,050	13,536	9,692	13,232	13,285	9,892	3,911
1989–90	7,881	8,315	16,800	16,826	13,640	14,117	10,656	14,611	14,184	10,901	4,079
1990–91	8,507	9,108	18,270	17,899	13,767	15,009	11,546	15,143	14,159	12,247	4,569
1991–92	9,592	10,226	20,318	19,225	14,366	16,098	12,937	16,257	15,816	12,946	4,876
1992–93	10,008	11,117	21,309	19,585	14,459	17,098	13,373	17,426	17,103	13,975	5,331
1993–94	10,790	11,503	23,824	20,769	14,156	17,720	14,838	17,621	17,433	15,193	5,253
1994–95 [1]	11,338	12,391	24,749	21,820	14,619	18,440	15,705	18,252	18,163	16,227	5,593
1995–96 [2]	12,170	12,559	26,260	22,958	15,438	19,586	16,595	18,552	18,900	17,260	5,956

[1] Preliminary first-professional figures based on 1993–94 graduates.
[2] Preliminary graduate figures based on fall 1994 data and first-professional figures based on 1993–94 graduates.
[3] Data are based on in-state tuition only.
—Data not available or not applicable.

NOTE.—Average graduate student tuition weighted by fall full-time-equivalent graduate enrollment. Average first-professional tuition weighted by number of degrees conferred during the academic year. Some year-to-year fluctuations in tuition data may reflect non-

reporting by individual institutions. Excludes institutions not reporting degrees conferred and institutions reporting no tuition. Some data have been revised from previously published figures.

SOURCE: U.S. Department of Education, National Center for Education Statistics, Integrated Postsecondary Education Data System (IPEDS), "Institutional Characteristics," "Fall Enrollment," and "Degrees Conferred" surveys. (This table was prepared September 1996.)

Table 312.—Percent of undergraduates enrolled in fall 1992 receiving aid and average amount awarded in 1992–93 per student, by type and source of aid and selected student characteristics

Selected student characteristics	Enrollment of under- graduates,[1] in thousands	Any aid			Grants			Loans			Work study	Other		
		Total[2]	Federal	Non- federal	Total	Federal	Non- federal	Total	Federal	Non- federal	Total[3]	Total	Federal	Non- federal
1	2	3	4	5	6	7	8	9	10	11	12	13	14	15
		Percent of all undergraduates receiving aid												
All undergraduates	**18,478**	**41.4**	**32.1**	**23.6**	**36.6**	**22.6**	**20.9**	**20.4**	**19.9**	**1.4**	**4.8**	**5.8**	**2.7**	**3.3**
Sex														
Men	8,166	39.1	29.5	23.3	31.8	19.2	20.6	19.7	19.1	1.5	4.6	6.9	2.9	4.2
Women	10,188	42.9	33.7	23.7	36.6	25.0	21.1	20.7	20.1	1.4	5.0	4.9	2.6	2.5
Race/ethnicity														
White, non-Hispanic	13,818	39.3	29.2	23.3	32.1	19.2	20.8	20.0	19.4	1.4	4.5	5.6	2.7	3.1
Black, non-Hispanic	1,847	54.1	47.6	24.7	47.2	38.2	20.9	26.8	26.4	1.3	6.8	8.2	3.9	4.7
Hispanic	1,432	43.0	36.3	21.5	38.8	30.7	19.1	15.2	14.5	1.2	4.0	4.9	1.6	3.4
Asian American	718	30.8	25.1	20.1	26.8	18.7	18.2	15.3	15.0	0.9	5.8	2.7	1.1	1.7
American Indian	172	47.8	35.2	28.7	42.6	29.2	25.1	15.4	15.0	0.9	4.4	8.4	1.6	6.7
Age														
23 years old or younger	10,163	45.6	35.5	27.3	37.4	23.1	24.3	24.8	24.0	2.0	7.0	7.3	4.6	2.9
24 to 29 years old	3,159	41.2	35.3	18.7	35.1	27.3	16.5	19.9	19.7	0.7	2.8	5.0	0.5	4.6
30 years old or over	5,116	33.3	23.5	19.1	28.8	18.5	16.9	12.1	11.9	0.7	1.7	3.5	0.3	3.2
Marital status														
Married	4,481	32.4	22.9	17.8	26.8	16.1	15.9	13.3	13.0	0.7	1.5	3.6	0.4	3.3
Not married[4]	12,744	44.5	35.5	25.8	37.1	24.6	22.9	23.4	22.8	1.7	6.1	6.6	3.6	3.2
Separated	322	61.6	56.1	27.8	59.2	52.5	22.9	23.1	23.0	0.7	4.7	5.7	0.2	5.5
Attendance status[5]														
Full-time	6,000	57.9	45.6	37.9	48.1	29.4	34.0	33.6	32.7	2.7	10.2	9.5	5.2	4.6
Part-time	12,293	32.9	25.0	16.5	27.7	18.8	14.5	13.6	13.2	0.8	2.1	4.0	1.4	2.7
Dependency status														
Dependent	8,858	41.7	31.2	26.7	33.5	18.6	23.8	23.0	22.2	2.1	7.1	7.1	5.0	2.3
Independent	9,620	41.2	33.0	20.7	35.7	26.3	18.2	18.0	17.8	0.8	2.7	4.7	0.6	4.2
Housing status														
School-owned	2,369	63.0	47.7	46.0	52.5	26.7	41.6	40.7	39.4	3.5	17.5	12.0	8.3	4.2
Off-campus, not with parents	10,163	39.8	30.6	21.4	33.0	22.1	18.8	18.9	18.6	1.2	3.2	5.1	1.7	3.5
With parents	4,793	35.0	28.1	17.8	29.7	21.4	15.8	14.2	13.7	1.1	2.3	4.5	2.3	2.3
With relatives	406	36.7	30.6	16.9	32.3	24.9	14.3	16.0	15.6	1.0	2.9	4.4	1.6	2.9
Other	38	40.9	28.6	26.4	38.2	24.1	26.3	8.4	7.9	0.4	2.2	1.5	1.3	0.2
		Average 1992–93 award for full-time, full-year undergraduates enrolled in fall 1992 (Award averages are computed for students participating in the designated program.)												
All full-time, full-year undergraduates	**6,000**	**$5,543**	**$4,257**	**$3,347**	**$3,487**	**$2,003**	**$3,201**	**$3,834**	**$3,723**	**$2,639**	**$1,357**	**$2,932**	**$3,340**	**$2,289**
Sex														
Men	2,838	5,759	4,407	3,499	3,616	1,990	3,372	3,944	3,839	2,626	1,372	3,061	3,452	2,539
Women	3,145	5,370	4,137	3,226	3,391	2,016	3,064	3,740	3,625	2,656	1,348	2,793	3,238	1,951
Race/ethnicity														
White, non-Hispanic	4,542	5,495	4,297	3,312	3,438	1,955	3,154	3,879	3,761	2,671	1,362	2,978	3,407	2,304
Black, non-Hispanic	553	5,738	4,329	3,439	3,424	2,094	3,411	3,619	3,538	2,359	1,324	2,809	3,061	2,174
Hispanic	384	4,960	3,666	2,843	3,302	2,079	2,659	3,655	3,597	—	1,301	2,587	3,294	2,090
Asian American	268	6,454	4,111	4,127	4,569	2,067	4,073	3,827	3,667	—	1,542	3,078	—	—
American Indian	48	5,072	4,047	2,752	3,181	2,231	2,368	3,568	3,475	—	—	2,800	—	—
Age														
23 years old or younger	4,785	5,622	4,147	3,629	3,697	1,947	3,470	3,722	3,588	2,744	1,323	3,205	3,379	2,568
24 to 29 years old	606	5,528	4,710	2,337	2,944	2,125	2,191	4,269	4,216	1,976	1,495	2,223	3,029	2,120
30 years old or over	605	5,062	4,383	2,035	2,718	2,107	1,820	4,091	4,050	2,100	1,674	1,802	—	1,712
Marital status														
Married	608	4,872	4,355	2,106	2,537	1,965	1,905	3,797	3,676	2,650	1,341	3,011	3,362	2,294
Not married[4]	4,917	5,706	4,254	3,479	3,631	2,004	3,328	4,147	4,114	2,046	1,409	2,215	—	2,156
Separated	63	4,914	3,981	1,978	2,858	2,275	1,711	3,678	3,548	—	—	—	—	—
Dependency status														
Dependent	4,334	5,676	4,094	3,766	3,819	1,874	3,611	3,716	3,570	2,753	1,319	3,289	3,389	2,658
Independent	1,666	5,298	4,495	2,287	2,906	2,130	2,107	4,046	3,994	2,231	1,491	2,165	2,879	1,999
Housing status														
School-owned	1,643	7,103	4,631	4,723	4,822	2,093	4,540	3,732	3,581	2,906	1,275	3,395	3,412	2,930
Off-campus, not with parents	2,717	5,194	4,413	2,613	2,961	2,035	2,437	3,998	3,902	2,558	1,458	2,689	3,283	2,173
With parents	1,549	4,044	3,369	2,363	2,681	1,836	2,265	3,525	3,455	2,152	1,406	2,640	3,272	1,788
With relatives	85	4,948	4,225	2,279	2,687	2,027	2,043	4,129	4,035	—	1,633	—	—	—
Other	7	—	—	—	—	—	—	—	—	—	—	—	—	—
		Average 1992–93 award for other undergraduates enrolled in fall 1992 (Award averages are computed for students participating in the designated program.)												
All other undergraduates[6] .	**12,293**	**2,976**	**2,916**	**1,521**	**1,711**	**1,435**	**1,407**	**3,256**	**3,219**	**2,017**	**1,353**	**1,942**	**3,094**	**1,274**
Sex														
Men	5,282	3,108	3,067	1,646	1,776	1,438	1,550	3,418	3,371	2,109	1,322	1,959	3,308	1,308
Women	6,958	2,886	2,824	1,428	1,672	1,432	1,302	3,150	3,122	1,924	1,373	1,942	2,909	1,243
Race/ethnicity														
White, non-Hispanic	9,152	3,007	3,040	1,515	1,691	1,412	1,407	3,311	3,268	2,108	1,353	1,968	3,085	1,281
Black, non-Hispanic	1,271	2,928	2,686	1,478	1,753	1,478	1,375	3,052	3,008	1,779	1,192	2,052	3,122	1,387
Hispanic	1,042	2,598	2,479	1,356	1,686	1,518	1,234	3,059	3,187	944	1,805	1,683	3,218	1,199
Asian American	449	3,664	3,159	1,896	2,142	1,590	1,690	3,125	3,131	—	1,282	1,833	—	—
American Indian	123	2,441	2,327	1,514	1,622	1,260	1,488	3,073	2,939	—	—	—	—	—

Table 312.—Percent of undergraduates enrolled in fall 1992 receiving aid and average amount awarded in 1992–93 per student, by type and source of aid and selected student characteristics—Continued

Selected student characteristics	Enrollment of under-graduates,[1] in thousands	Any aid			Grants			Loans			Work study	Other		
		Total[2]	Federal	Non-federal	Total	Federal	Non-federal	Total	Federal	Non-federal	Total[3]	Total	Federal	Non-federal
1	2	3	4	5	6	7	8	9	10	11	12	13	14	15
Age														
23 years old or younger	5,277	3,320	2,989	1,878	1,908	1,435	1,747	3,199	3,154	2,172	1,195	2,385	3,224	1,262
24 to 29 years old	2,523	2,920	2,925	1,189	1,560	1,446	1,075	3,282	3,257	1,766	1,625	1,357	2,207	1,284
30 years old or over	4,465	2,498	2,775	1,249	1,538	1,424	1,175	3,380	3,352	1,552	1,672	1,339	1,712	1,291
Marital status														
Married	3,847	2,484	2,804	1,214	1,447	1,367	1,162	3,256	3,246	1,680	1,477	1,356	2,656	1,222
Not married[4]	7,709	3,181	2,970	1,650	1,817	1,449	1,517	3,273	3,231	2,018	1,343	2,135	3,160	1,293
Separated	257	2,649	2,498	1,046	1,619	1,472	928	2,857	2,846	—	—	1,194	—	1,124
Dependency status														
Dependent	4,440	3,457	3,039	2,097	2,018	1,391	1,961	3,275	3,216	2,318	1,191	2,648	3,217	1,370
Independent	7,854	2,729	2,849	1,216	1,569	1,455	1,126	3,243	3,222	1,632	1,552	1,354	2,344	1,242
Housing status														
School-owned	709	4,811	3,640	3,148	2,881	1,580	2,961	3,443	3,305	3,020	1,007	2,965	3,195	2,049
Off-campus, not with parents	8,040	2,834	2,969	1,316	1,583	1,435	1,212	3,313	3,270	2,006	1,575	1,664	2,989	1,229
With parents	3,195	2,615	2,475	1,333	1,617	1,379	1,232	2,961	2,999	1,445	1,383	2,038	3,155	1,063
With relatives	319	2,894	2,943	1,159	1,648	1,560	1,127	3,151	3,186	—	—	1,717	—	—
Other	31	—	—	—	—	—	—	—	—	—	—	—	—	—

[1] Numbers of undergraduates may not equal figures reported in other tables, since these data are based on a sample survey of students who enrolled at any time during the academic year. Includes all postsecondary institutions.

[2] Includes students who reported they were awarded aid, but did not specify the source or type of aid.

[3] Details on federal and nonfederal Work Study participants are not available.

[4] Includes students who were single, divorced, or widowed.

[5] Excludes persons whose attendance status was not reported.

[6] Enrollment data include persons whose attendance status was not reported.

NOTE.—Because of rounding and/or the fact that some students receive aid from multiple sources, row details may not add to totals. Because of rounding and survey item nonresponse, enrollment data may not add to totals. Data include undergraduates in noncollegiate and collegiate institutions.

SOURCE: U.S. Department of Education, National Center for Education Statistics, National Postsecondary Student Aid Study, 1992–93. (This table was prepared August 1995.)

Table 313.—Undergraduates enrolled full-time and part-time in 1992, by aid status and source of aid during 1992–93, and control and level of institution

Control and level of institution	Number of undergraduates, 1992,[1] in thousands	Aid status, 1992–93, in percents					
		Nonaided	Receiving aid, by source				
			Any aid[2]	Federal	State	Institutional	Other[2]
1	2	3	4	5	6	7	8
		Full-time students[3]					
All institutions	6,000	42.1	57.9	45.6	17.9	23.4	9.7
Public	4,110	48.1	51.9	40.0	16.5	16.2	8.8
4-year doctoral	1,772	46.3	53.7	39.3	14.9	20.8	9.7
Other 4-year	1,087	43.6	56.4	46.1	21.6	16.1	8.1
2-year	1,196	54.1	45.9	36.0	14.6	10.1	8.2
Less than 2-year	55	65.0	35.0	31.6	10.9	0.4	7.7
Private, nonprofit	1,469	30.5	69.5	53.4	24.6	48.5	13.2
4-year doctoral	681	37.3	62.7	44.5	17.9	48.2	13.4
Other 4-year	719	24.5	75.5	60.8	31.0	51.2	13.3
2-year or less	70	26.1	73.9	63.9	23.2	23.8	10.4
Private, proprietary	421	23.9	76.1	72.4	8.1	6.1	6.9
2-year and above	182	19.4	80.6	77.4	14.1	7.5	10.6
Less than 2-year	238	27.3	72.7	68.6	3.5	5.0	4.1
		Part-time students[3]					
All institutions	12,293	67.1	32.9	25.0	6.7	6.6	6.6
Public	9,911	72.9	27.1	19.8	6.2	4.9	6.1
4-year doctoral	1,504	63.5	36.5	27.5	7.6	9.5	6.9
Other 4-year	1,330	64.4	35.6	28.4	10.0	6.7	6.2
2-year	6,850	76.4	23.6	16.5	5.3	3.7	5.9
Less than 2-year	227	80.8	19.2	15.1	1.5	1.0	5.3
Private, nonprofit	1,431	50.6	49.4	35.1	11.6	20.2	11.0
4-year doctoral	391	55.6	44.4	28.3	8.8	23.7	8.9
Other 4-year	818	47.8	52.2	38.1	13.4	19.8	13.3
2-year or less	223	52.4	47.6	35.8	10.0	15.3	6.4
Private, proprietary	951	31.0	69.0	64.4	4.7	3.8	5.0
2-year and above	383	39.6	60.4	54.9	6.4	2.9	6.8
Less than 2-year	568	25.2	74.8	70.8	3.5	4.3	3.8

[1] Numbers of undergraduates may not equal figures reported in other tables, since these data are based on a sample survey. Includes students who enrolled at any time during the academic year.

[2] Includes students who reported that they were awarded aid but did not specify the source of the aid.

[3] Full-time students are students who attend full-time for the entire academic year. All other students, including those who attend full-time for part of the academic year, are counted as part-time students.

NOTE.—Because some students receive aid from multiple sources, percents do not add to totals. Excludes students whose attendance status was not reported. Data have been revised from previously published figures.

SOURCE: U.S. Department of Education, National Center for Education Statistics, National Postsecondary Student Aid Study, 1992–93. (This table was prepared July 1995.)

Table 314.—Undergraduates enrolled full-time and part-time in 1992, by type and source of aid received during 1992–93, and by control and level of institution

Control and level of institution	Number of undergraduates, 1992,[1] in thousands	Percent receiving aid in 1992–93, by type and source													
		Any aid			Grants			Loans			Work-study		Other		
		Total[2]	Federal	Non-federal	Total	Federal	Non-federal	Total	Federal	Non-federal	Total	Federal	Total	Federal	Non-federal
1	2	3	4	5	6	7	8	9	10	11	12	13	14	15	16
Full-time students[4]															
All institutions	6,000	57.9	45.6	37.9	48.1	29.4	34.0	33.6	32.7	2.7	10.2	6.8	9.5	5.2	4.6
Public	4,110	51.9	40.0	33.0	42.3	27.8	29.1	26.9	26.1	2.0	6.8	4.2	7.9	3.7	4.4
4-year doctoral	1,772	53.7	39.3	34.8	41.9	23.8	30.8	33.0	32.2	2.4	7.1	4.3	8.6	5.0	3.9
Other 4-year	1,087	56.4	46.1	37.4	45.5	32.1	32.4	33.7	32.7	2.8	9.5	5.5	7.9	4.2	3.8
2-year	1,196	45.9	36.0	27.0	40.6	29.9	24.3	12.7	12.3	0.7	4.1	3.0	7.0	1.3	5.7
Less than 2-year	55	35.0	31.6	15.7	29.9	26.6	12.8	3.0	3.0	0.6	1.5	1.4	5.1	0.8	4.4
Private, nonprofit	1,469	69.5	53.4	58.0	62.1	27.7	54.1	46.5	44.9	4.9	22.2	15.9	12.1	7.7	5.0
4-year doctoral	681	62.7	44.5	54.8	55.2	17.3	51.8	41.6	39.7	6.1	18.9	13.2	11.6	7.4	4.5
Other 4-year	719	75.5	60.8	62.7	68.7	35.6	58.1	51.7	50.3	4.1	27.0	19.7	12.2	7.9	5.3
2-year or less	70	73.9	63.9	42.0	61.3	47.3	35.4	41.1	39.5	2.5	4.6	3.0	17.2	9.4	7.8
Private, proprietary	421	76.1	72.4	16.4	55.3	50.9	11.4	54.1	53.8	2.1	1.9	0.7	15.6	11.3	4.5
2-year and above	182	80.6	77.4	22.7	49.5	43.4	16.4	65.2	65.2	3.0	3.5	1.4	24.6	18.8	6.5
Less than 2-year	238	72.7	68.6	11.5	59.7	56.7	7.5	45.6	45.1	1.5	0.7	0.2	8.7	5.6	3.1
Part-time students[4]															
All institutions	12,293	32.9	25.0	16.5	27.7	18.8	14.5	13.6	13.2	0.8	2.1	1.2	4.0	1.4	2.7
Public	9,911	27.1	19.8	14.5	23.0	15.3	12.6	9.4	9.1	0.6	1.7	0.9	3.5	1.0	2.6
4-year doctoral	1,504	36.5	27.5	19.5	27.2	17.1	16.6	21.5	21.1	1.1	3.6	2.1	6.2	3.1	3.4
Other 4-year	1,330	35.6	28.4	19.2	29.9	22.0	16.1	16.5	15.9	1.3	3.1	1.6	4.1	1.5	2.6
2-year	6,850	23.6	16.5	12.7	20.9	13.7	11.2	5.6	5.4	0.4	1.1	0.6	2.9	0.4	2.5
Less than 2-year	227	19.2	15.1	6.9	17.3	13.8	6.0	0.6	0.6	0.0	0.6	0.4	1.7	0.3	1.3
Private, nonprofit	1,431	49.4	35.1	33.7	43.1	23.2	31.7	24.0	23.4	1.8	5.9	3.8	5.3	2.6	2.9
4-year doctoral	391	44.4	28.3	33.0	37.3	12.8	31.7	24.3	23.4	2.7	5.4	3.1	4.2	2.9	1.5
Other 4-year	818	52.2	38.1	35.6	46.4	26.8	33.6	24.8	24.2	1.5	7.3	4.8	5.7	2.5	3.4
2-year or less	223	47.6	35.8	28.4	41.4	28.3	24.4	20.7	20.3	1.2	1.2	1.2	5.8	2.2	3.6
Private, proprietary	951	69.0	64.4	11.8	53.2	48.8	8.6	42.0	41.5	1.5	0.9	0.4	6.8	4.4	2.5
2-year and above	383	60.4	54.9	14.3	42.0	35.0	12.1	45.4	45.3	0.9	1.4	0.6	8.0	6.0	2.1
Less than 2-year	568	74.8	70.8	10.2	60.8	58.1	6.3	39.6	39.0	1.8	0.5	0.3	5.9	3.2	2.7

[1] Numbers of undergraduates may not equal figures reported in other tables, since these data are based on a sample survey. Includes students who enrolled at any time during the academic year.

[2] Includes students who reported they were awarded aid but did not specify the source of aid.

[3] Details on nonfederal work study participants are not available.

[4] Full-time students are students who attend full-time for the entire academic year. All other students, including those who attend full-time for part of the academic year, are counted as part-time students.

NOTE.—Excludes students whose attendance status was not reported. Because some students receive multiple types and sources of aid, details may not add to totals.

SOURCE: U.S. Department of Education, National Center for Education Statistics, National Postsecondary Student Aid Study, 1992–93. (This table was prepared July 1995.)

Table 315.—Undergraduates enrolled full-time and part-time in 1992, by federal aid program and by control and level of institution: 1992–93

Control and level of institution	Number of undergraduates, 1992 [1]	Percent receiving federal aid in 1992–93, by type									
		Any federal aid	Selected Title IV programs [2]								Any other federal aid [9]
			Any Title IV aid	Pell	SEOG [3]	CWS [4]	Per-kins [5]	Stafford [6]	Plus [7]	SLS [8]	
1	2	3	4	5	6	7	8	9	10	11	12
		Full-time students [10]									
All institutions	**6,000**	**45.6**	**44.5**	**28.2**	**8.5**	**10.2**	**6.6**	**29.5**	**5.0**	**3.4**	**5.2**
Public	4,110	40.0	38.7	26.8	6.7	6.8	4.4	23.0	3.5	2.1	3.7
4-year doctoral	1,772	39.3	38.5	23.0	6.1	7.1	5.9	28.4	5.0	2.7	5.0
Other 4-year	1,087	46.1	45.3	31.1	8.4	9.5	5.6	28.7	4.2	2.2	4.2
2-year	1,196	36.0	33.4	28.5	6.3	4.1	1.4	10.6	0.8	1.2	1.3
Less than 2-year	55	31.6	27.2	24.9	0.8	1.5	0.1	3.0	0.0	0.9	0.8
Private, nonprofit	1,469	53.4	52.8	26.0	12.4	22.2	13.6	41.6	7.6	4.0	7.7
4-year doctoral	681	44.5	43.8	15.2	8.9	18.9	15.0	36.7	7.4	3.9	7.4
Other 4-year	719	60.8	60.3	34.1	15.7	27.0	13.5	46.6	7.8	4.1	7.9
2-year or less	70	63.9	63.4	46.4	12.0	4.6	0.6	37.6	8.2	3.6	9.4
Private, proprietary	421	72.4	71.9	49.6	12.5	1.9	3.1	51.5	11.3	14.1	11.3
2-year and above	182	77.4	76.7	42.1	14.0	3.5	4.0	62.7	18.8	18.6	18.8
Less than 2-year	238	68.6	68.1	55.3	11.4	0.7	2.3	43.0	5.5	10.6	5.6
		Part-time students [10]									
All institutions	**12,293**	**25.0**	**23.9**	**18.0**	**3.5**	**2.1**	**1.6**	**12.2**	**1.3**	**2.0**	**1.4**
Public	9,911	19.8	18.5	14.5	2.6	1.7	1.1	8.2	0.8	1.0	1.0
4-year doctoral	1,504	27.5	26.4	16.1	3.8	3.6	3.5	19.2	2.9	2.2	3.1
Other 4-year	1,330	28.4	27.5	21.3	3.7	3.1	2.2	14.0	1.4	1.4	1.5
2-year	6,850	16.5	15.2	13.0	2.1	1.1	0.5	4.9	0.3	0.7	0.4
Less than 2-year	227	15.1	13.5	10.8	2.4	0.6	—	0.6	—	0.1	0.3
Private, nonprofit	1,431	35.1	34.3	21.9	5.4	5.9	3.8	21.8	2.5	3.4	2.6
4-year doctoral	391	28.3	27.6	11.1	3.6	5.4	4.5	21.5	2.8	5.0	2.9
Other 4-year	818	38.1	37.2	25.7	6.2	7.3	4.3	22.8	2.5	3.0	2.5
2-year or less	223	35.8	35.4	27.1	5.7	1.2	0.9	19.0	2.0	2.1	2.2
Private, proprietary	951	64.4	64.0	47.8	9.9	0.9	2.5	40.1	4.3	10.8	4.4
2-year and above	383	54.9	54.8	34.2	9.9	1.4	3.7	44.3	6.0	13.6	6.0
Less than 2-year	568	70.8	70.3	56.9	9.9	0.5	1.6	37.4	3.2	8.9	3.2

[1] Numbers of undergraduates may not equal figures reported in other tables, since these data are based on a sample survey. Includes students who enrolled at any time during the academic year.

[2] Title IV of the Higher Education Act.

[3] Supplemental Educational Opportunity Grants.

[4] College Work Study (CWS). Prior to October 17, 1986, private, proprietary institutions were prohibited by law from spending CWS funds for on-campus work. Includes persons who participated in the program, but had no earnings.

[5] Formerly National Direct Student Loans (NDSL).

[6] Formerly Guaranteed Student Loans (GSL).

[7] Parent Loans for Undergraduate Students.

[8] Supplementary Loans for Students.

[9] Includes aid from all federal departments and agencies except Title IV aid.

[10] Full-time students are students who attend full-time for the entire academic year. All other students, including those who attend full-time for part of the academic year, are counted as part-time students.

—Less than .05 percent.

NOTE.—Excludes students whose attendance status was not reported. Because some students receive aid from multiple sources, percents do not add to totals.

SOURCE: U.S. Department of Education, National Center for Education Statistics, National Postsecondary Student Aid Study, 1992–93. (This table was prepared July 1995.)

Table 316.—Postbaccalaureate students enrolled full-time and part-time in 1992, by aid status and source of aid during 1992–93, by level of study and by control and level of institution

Level of degree, control and type of institution	Postbaccalaureate students,[1] 1992, in thousands	Aid status, 1992–93, in percents						
		Nonaided	Receiving aid, by source					
			Any aid[2]	Federal	State	Institutional	Employer	Other[3]
1	2	3	4	5	6	7	8	9
		Full-time students[4]						
All institutions	**673**	**31.9**	**68.1**	**44.4**	**7.0**	**40.6**	**3.3**	**14.6**
Master's degree	281	37.5	62.5	33.8	5.8	42.4	5.1	12.0
Public	163	34.6	65.4	33.9	7.8	44.0	4.8	9.7
4-year doctoral	139	34.3	65.7	32.4	6.7	46.3	4.7	10.1
Other 4-year	24	36.1	63.9	42.5	14.4	30.4	5.3	7.5
Private	118	41.6	58.4	33.7	3.2	40.2	5.6	15.2
4-year doctoral	102	39.3	60.7	34.2	2.9	42.9	5.7	16.4
Other 4-year	16	56.5	43.5	30.5	5.1	22.8	4.7	7.4
Doctor's degree	120	30.4	69.6	28.3	4.4	51.6	2.2	13.2
Public	73	30.3	69.7	22.3	6.5	55.5	3.1	11.7
Private	46	30.4	69.6	37.8	1.1	45.5	0.9	15.7
First-professional	211	23.0	77.0	68.2	10.0	37.0	1.2	20.3
Public	101	20.7	79.3	72.5	13.4	37.7	1.3	15.8
Private	110	25.1	74.9	64.3	6.8	36.4	1.2	24.4
Other graduate	61	39.3	60.7	42.4	6.7	22.9	3.7	9.1
		Part-time students[4]						
All institutions	**1,980**	**71.3**	**28.7**	**10.8**	**1.9**	**12.7**	**7.9**	**9.9**
Master's degree	1,322	71.7	28.3	10.5	1.6	11.1	8.8	10.8
Public	773	73.9	26.1	10.1	2.5	11.7	6.7	8.0
4-year doctoral	489	69.6	30.4	11.9	2.5	15.3	6.7	8.2
Other 4-year	284	81.2	18.8	6.9	2.4	5.5	6.5	7.5
Private	549	68.6	31.4	11.1	0.4	10.3	11.8	14.9
4-year doctoral	357	66.9	33.1	12.1	0.4	12.1	12.1	15.0
Other 4–year	192	71.7	28.3	9.3	0.6	6.9	11.2	14.7
Doctor's degree	149	56.2	43.8	8.6	3.5	33.1	5.4	9.9
Public	97	56.1	43.9	8.5	4.4	33.3	6.4	8.9
Private	51	56.4	43.6	8.9	1.6	32.6	3.7	11.8
First-professional	64	42.6	57.4	44.9	3.3	25.7	3.4	13.9
Public	24	50.8	49.2	42.9	3.6	22.2	2.5	7.5
Private	40	37.8	62.2	46.1	3.2	27.8	3.9	17.6
Other graduate	446	79.7	20.3	7.7	1.7	8.4	6.4	6.5

[1] Numbers of postbaccalaureate students may not equal figures reported in other tables, since these data are based on a sample survey of all postbaccalaureate students. Includes students who enrolled at any time during the academic year.

[2] Includes students who reported they were awarded aid but did not specify the source of aid.

[3] Includes aid provided by corporations, unions, foundations, fraternal organizations, community organizations, etc.

[4] Full-time students are students who attend full-time for the entire academic year. All other students, including those who attend full-time for part of the academic year, are counted as part-time students.

NOTE.—Excludes students whose attendance status was not reported. Because some students receive aid from multiple sources, percents do not add to totals.

SOURCE: U.S. Department of Education, National Center for Education Statistics, National Postsecondary Student Aid Study, 1992–93. (This table was prepared July 1995.)

Table 317.—Postbaccalaureate students enrolled full-time and part-time in 1992, by type of aid received during 1992–93, by level of study and by control and level of institution

Level of degree, control and type of institution	Postbaccalaureate students,[1] 1992, in thousands	Type of aid, 1992–93, in percents					Loans		
		Any aid[2]	Fellowship grants	Tuition waivers	Assistantships[3]	Employer	Any loans	Stafford[4]	SLS[5]
1	2	3	4	5	6	7	8	9	10
Full-time students[6]									
All institutions	**673**	**68.1**	**3.5**	**12.4**	**14.3**	**3.3**	**43.5**	**41.1**	**19.2**
Master's degree	281	62.5	3.5	15.6	18.1	5.1	32.5	30.5	10.0
Public	163	65.4	2.2	20.5	22.4	4.8	32.2	30.8	7.3
4-year doctoral	139	65.7	2.4	23.3	23.5	4.7	30.6	29.6	7.4
Other 4-year	24	63.9	1.0	4.4	15.8	5.3	41.5	38.4	6.8
Private	118	58.4	5.3	8.9	12.1	5.6	32.9	30.0	13.6
4-year doctoral	103	60.7	6.2	9.5	13.6	5.7	33.6	30.8	14.9
Other 4-year	16	43.5	0.0	5.4	3.0	4.7	28.7	24.6	5.6
Doctor's degree	120	69.6	9.3	19.4	27.0	2.2	25.8	23.9	10.0
Public	73	69.7	4.2	23.1	31.6	3.1	20.6	18.9	5.6
Private	46	69.6	17.5	13.6	19.9	0.9	34.1	31.9	17.0
First-professional	211	77.0	0.9	5.6	4.4	1.2	67.8	65.5	38.3
Public	101	79.3	0.4	5.4	4.3	1.3	71.8	69.9	37.5
Private	110	74.9	1.2	5.8	4.5	1.2	64.1	61.6	39.1
Other graduate	61	60.7	1.1	7.5	6.2	3.7	44.4	39.6	14.2
Part-time students[6]									
All institutions	**1,980**	**28.7**	**0.6**	**5.1**	**4.3**	**7.9**	**10.5**	**9.4**	**2.8**
Master's degree	1,322	28.3	0.6	4.6	3.8	8.8	10.3	9.3	2.1
Public	773	26.1	0.9	4.9	5.2	6.7	9.9	9.0	1.7
4-year doctoral	489	30.4	1.4	6.5	6.7	6.7	11.8	10.7	2.3
Other 4-year	284	18.8	0.1	2.3	2.6	6.5	6.0	6.0	0.8
Private	549	31.4	0.2	4.2	1.8	11.8	11.0	9.7	2.6
4-year doctoral	357	33.1	0.3	4.4	2.5	12.1	11.9	10.5	3.3
Other 4-year	192	28.3	0.2	3.8	0.7	11.2	9.3	8.1	1.3
Doctor's degree	149	43.8	2.4	12.7	17.0	5.4	7.3	6.9	1.6
Public	97	43.9	2.1	15.0	17.0	6.4	7.1	6.5	0.6
Private	51	43.6	3.1	8.3	17.0	3.7	7.7	7.5	3.6
First-professional	64	57.4	0.3	5.9	3.1	3.4	45.6	42.0	22.8
Public	24	49.2	0.0	6.8	6.1	2.5	42.4	41.4	19.6
Private	40	62.2	0.5	5.4	1.4	3.9	47.5	42.3	24.8
Other graduate	446	20.3	0.1	3.4	1.6	6.4	7.1	6.0	2.2

[1] Numbers of postbaccalaureate students may not equal figures reported in other tables, since these data are based on a sample survey of all postbaccalaureate students. Includes students who enrolled at any time during the academic year.

[2] Includes students who reported they were awarded aid but did not specify the source of aid.

[3] Includes students who received teaching or research assistantships and/or participated in work-study programs.

[4] Stafford loans, formerly Graduate Student Loans (GSL).

[5] Supplementary Loans for Students.

[6] Full-time students are students who attend full-time for the entire academic year. All other students, including those who attend full-time for part of the academic year, are counted as part-time students.

NOTE.—Excludes students whose attendance status was not reported. Because some students receive aid from multiple sources, percents do not add to totals.

SOURCE: U.S. Department of Education, National Center for Education Statistics, National Postsecondary Student Aid Study, 1992–93. (This table was prepared July 1995.)

Table 318.—Scholarship and fellowship awards [1] of institutions of higher education, by control of institution: 1959–60 to 1993–94

[In thousands]

Year	Total scholarship and fellowship awards			Scholarship and fellowship awards from unrestricted funds			Scholarship and fellowship awards from restricted funds		
	All institutions	Public	Private	All institutions	Public	Private	All institutions	Public	Private
1	2	3	4	5	6	7	8	9	10
1959–60	$172,051	$59,673	$112,377	—	—	—	—	—	—
1961–62	228,765	78,255	150,510	—	—	—	—	—	—
1963–64	300,370	107,767	192,603	—	—	—	—	—	—
1965–66	425,524	153,256	272,269	—	—	—	—	—	—
1966–67	583,390	248,077	335,311	—	—	—	—	—	—
1967–68	712,425	326,915	385,510	—	—	—	—	—	—
1968–69	814,755	367,433	447,322	—	—	—	—	—	—
1969–70	984,594	456,977	527,617	—	—	—	—	—	—
1970–71	1,098,198	528,243	569,955	—	—	—	—	—	—
1971–72	1,241,372	621,387	619,986	—	—	—	—	—	—
1972–73	1,322,411	656,054	666,357	—	—	—	—	—	—
1973–74	1,396,488	705,691	690,797	—	—	—	—	—	—
1974–75	1,449,542	718,780	730,762	$631,801	$267,191	$364,610	$817,741	$451,589	$366,152
1975–76	1,635,859	798,515	837,343	686,604	276,334	410,269	949,255	522,181	427,074
1976–77	1,770,215	859,011	911,204	748,763	291,073	457,690	1,021,451	567,938	453,514
1977–78	1,839,298	840,666	998,632	818,101	305,563	512,537	1,021,197	535,102	486,095
1978–79	1,944,599	861,578	1,083,021	883,213	326,201	557,012	1,061,386	535,377	526,009
1979–80	2,200,468	970,363	1,230,106	904,876	324,224	580,652	1,295,592	646,138	649,454
1980–81	2,504,525	1,064,864	1,439,661	1,080,614	367,476	713,138	1,423,911	697,388	726,523
1981–82	2,684,945	1,088,717	1,596,228	1,236,081	374,632	861,449	1,448,864	714,085	734,779
1982–83	2,922,897	1,188,383	1,734,514	1,478,762	460,291	1,018,470	1,444,136	728,092	716,044
1983–84	3,301,673	1,276,644	2,025,028	1,738,188	518,626	1,219,562	1,563,485	758,018	805,466
1984–85	3,670,355	1,374,803	2,295,551	1,961,597	569,058	1,392,539	1,708,758	805,745	903,012
1985–86	4,160,174	1,575,909	2,584,266	2,285,116	696,973	1,588,143	1,875,059	878,935	996,123
1986–87	4,776,100	1,751,671	3,024,430	2,644,615	750,931	1,893,684	2,131,486	1,000,740	1,130,746
1987–88	5,325,358	1,941,389	3,383,968	2,941,143	830,195	2,110,948	2,384,215	1,111,194	1,273,021
1988–89	5,918,666	2,150,350	3,768,316	3,282,698	944,001	2,338,697	2,635,969	1,206,349	1,429,619
1989–90	6,655,544	2,386,493	4,269,051	3,853,904	1,099,425	2,754,479	2,801,640	1,287,068	1,514,572
1990–91	7,551,184	2,688,532	4,862,651	4,445,106	1,270,158	3,174,947	3,106,078	1,418,374	1,687,704
1991–92	9,060,000	3,255,660	5,804,340	5,205,797	1,523,721	3,682,076	3,854,203	1,731,939	2,122,264
1992–93	10,148,373	3,727,838	6,420,536	5,949,037	1,745,339	4,203,697	4,199,337	1,982,498	2,216,838
1993–94 [2]	11,238,010	4,222,923	7,015,087	6,644,717	1,934,617	4,710,100	4,593,293	2,288,306	2,304,987

[1] Includes Supplemental Educational Opportunity Grants and State Student Incentive Grants, but excludes Pell Grants.

[2] Preliminary data.

—Data not collected.

NOTE.—Because of rounding, details may not add to totals.

SOURCE: U.S. Department of Education, National Center for Education Statistics, "Financial Statistics of Institutions of Higher Education" surveys and Integrated Postsecondary Education Data System (IPEDS), "Finance" surveys. (This table was prepared April 1996.)

Table 319.—Pell Grant revenue of institutions of higher education compared to current-fund revenue and tuition, by type and control of institution: 1985–86 to 1993–94

[Amounts in thousands]

Year and type of control of institution	Total				Public				Private			
	Current-fund revenue	Tuition	Pell Grant revenue	Pell Grants as a percent of current-fund revenue	Current-fund revenue	Tuition	Pell Grant revenue	Pell Grants as a percent of current-fund revenue	Current-fund revenue	Tuition	Pell Grant revenue	Pell Grants as a percent of current-fund revenue
1	2	3	4	5	6	7	8	9	10	11	12	13
1985–86	$100,437,616	$23,116,605	$2,565,048	2.6	$65,004,632	$9,439,177	$1,873,456	2.9	$35,432,985	$13,677,429	$691,592	2.0
4-year	88,144,386	20,498,399	1,770,042	2.0	53,746,503	7,539,717	1,214,303	2.3	34,397,882	12,958,683	555,739	1.6
2-year	12,293,231	2,618,206	795,006	6.5	11,258,128	1,899,460	659,153	5.9	1,035,102	718,746	135,853	13.1
1987–88	117,340,109	27,836,781	2,496,133	2.1	74,771,255	11,184,657	1,876,777	2.5	42,568,854	16,652,124	619,355	1.5
4-year	103,280,070	24,779,364	1,714,118	1.7	61,958,780	9,032,936	1,207,418	1.9	41,321,290	15,746,428	506,700	1.2
2-year	14,060,039	3,057,417	782,015	5.6	12,812,475	2,151,721	669,359	5.2	1,247,564	905,696	112,656	9.0
1989–90	139,635,477	33,926,060	3,348,018	2.4	88,911,433	13,820,240	2,566,209	2.9	50,724,044	20,105,820	781,809	1.5
4-year	122,858,290	30,302,689	2,253,803	1.8	73,415,696	11,090,012	1,591,684	2.2	49,442,595	19,212,677	662,119	1.3
2-year	16,777,187	3,623,371	1,094,215	6.5	15,495,738	2,730,229	974,525	6.3	1,281,449	893,143	119,690	9.3
1990–91	149,766,051	37,434,462	3,510,537	2.3	94,904,506	15,258,024	2,725,357	2.9	54,861,545	22,176,439	785,180	1.4
4-year	131,743,973	33,405,241	2,312,931	1.8	78,272,989	12,188,851	1,647,376	2.1	53,470,984	21,216,389	665,554	1.2
2-year	18,022,078	4,029,222	1,197,606	6.6	16,631,517	3,069,173	1,077,981	6.5	1,390,562	960,049	119,625	8.6
1991–92	161,395,896	41,559,037	4,238,047	2.6	102,202,890	17,460,263	3,312,386	3.2	59,193,006	24,098,774	925,661	1.6
4-year	141,700,893	36,910,390	2,710,510	1.9	83,969,040	13,827,245	1,928,623	2.3	57,731,852	23,083,145	781,887	1.4
2-year	19,695,003	4,648,647	1,527,537	7.8	18,233,850	3,633,018	1,383,763	7.6	1,461,153	1,015,629	143,774	9.8
1992–93	170,880,503	45,346,071	4,701,905	2.8	108,186,484	19,490,221	3,663,529	3.4	62,694,018	25,855,850	1,038,377	1.7
4-year	150,075,119	40,127,624	2,982,999	2.0	88,952,983	15,406,746	2,097,638	2.4	61,122,135	24,720,878	885,360	1.4
2-year	20,805,384	5,218,447	1,718,907	8.3	19,233,501	4,083,475	1,565,890	8.1	1,571,883	1,134,972	153,017	9.7
1993–94 [1]	179,226,601	48,646,538	4,564,790	2.5	112,968,097	20,825,388	3,543,643	3.1	66,258,504	27,821,149	1,021,147	1.5
4-year	157,265,446	43,052,545	2,674,392	1.7	92,747,344	16,457,225	1,860,187	2.0	64,518,102	26,595,320	814,204	1.3
2-year	21,961,155	5,593,993	1,890,399	8.6	20,220,753	4,368,164	1,683,456	8.3	1,740,402	1,225,829	206,942	11.9

[1] Preliminary data.

NOTE.—Pell Grants which are spent on campus for tuition, room, board or other college expenses are included in current-fund revenue. Because of rounding, details may not add to totals.

SOURCE: U.S. Department of Education, National Center for Education Statistics, "Financial Statistics of Institutions of Higher Education" surveys; and Integrated Postsecondary Education Data System (IPEDS), "Finance" surveys. (This table was prepared April 1996.)

Table 320.—State awards for need-based [1] undergraduate scholarship and grant programs, by state: 1983–84 to 1994–95

[In thousands]

State	1983–84	1985–86	1986–87	1987–88	1988–89	1989–90	1990–91	1991–92	1992–93 [2]	1993–94 [2]	1994–95 [2]	Percent change, 1983–84 to 1994–95 [3]
1	2	3	4	5	6	7	8	9	10	11	12	13
United States	$1,024,206	$1,222,112	$1,325,984	$1,377,996	$1,423,743	$1,529,421	$1,658,221	$1,781,820	$1,923,720	$2,195,993	$2,421,952	136.5
Alabama	1,731	2,242	2,120	2,260	2,196	2,984	2,878	2,183	2,271	2,283	2,281	31.8
Alaska	189	241	229	240	234	228	464	475	470	454	444	134.9
Arizona	2,027	2,401	2,437	3,222	3,508	3,420	3,318	2,278	2,437	3,476	3,482	71.8
Arkansas	2,226	4,108	3,800	3,759	3,903	3,946	3,885	4,742	6,319	7,701	8,907	300.1
California	86,031	112,373	112,770	118,819	129,264	153,045	161,642	172,852	151,379	207,969	232,067	169.7
Colorado	7,341	9,282	9,491	9,327	9,395	10,349	11,276	12,380	14,812	16,480	18,252	148.6
Connecticut	9,371	11,095	9,094	14,650	21,149	19,915	20,580	20,595	20,805	20,641	20,690	120.8
Delaware	548	756	875	807	829	956	1,066	906	1,121	1,270	1,033	88.5
District of Columbia	759	1,106	1,059	1,106	1,075	1,069	947	978	1,015	1,022	1,022	34.7
Florida	12,515	14,819	14,151	15,245	16,522	20,134	24,729	29,279	29,628	31,277	36,824	194.2
Georgia	3,683	4,510	4,946	4,599	5,197	4,607	5,070	5,084	4,951	26,853	5,147	39.8
Hawaii	493	604	595	563	598	726	612	632	724	748	732	48.5
Idaho	378	509	487	343	348	346	350	483	580	634	779	106.1
Illinois	104,384	122,300	131,788	135,880	143,373	171,361	183,508	184,753	203,532	214,809	244,352	134.1
Indiana	20,380	26,448	30,512	45,408	35,692	41,874	46,756	[4]50,441	55,814	55,814	67,742	232.4
Iowa	20,263	22,379	22,378	25,960	30,050	32,467	35,586	34,654	34,067	34,718	35,642	75.9
Kansas	4,664	5,609	5,250	5,337	5,540	6,478	6,462	6,587	6,894	9,060	9,802	110.2
Kentucky	7,886	8,758	12,139	12,161	12,522	12,605	19,866	16,996	20,520	20,619	25,517	223.6
Louisiana	1,693	2,003	1,818	1,880	1,947	2,786	3,827	4,446	5,125	6,374	6,429	279.7
Maine	477	809	1,151	1,418	1,408	1,877	4,802	5,002	5,200	5,170	5,787	1,113.2
Maryland	5,459	6,859	7,822	8,737	12,841	14,800	15,607	16,253	20,828	23,713	24,571	350.1
Massachusetts	25,655	43,466	56,995	61,600	62,443	50,844	46,000	23,690	45,989	45,059	61,850	141.1
Michigan	30,753	57,645	66,864	70,099	75,467	70,721	68,918	78,116	75,469	79,735	81,340	164.5
Minnesota	46,600	45,486	65,473	63,300	68,293	58,136	74,656	81,322	83,170	102,920	97,920	110.1
Mississippi	1,015	1,288	1,287	1,230	1,251	1,243	1,136	1,131	1,244	1,255	1,248	23.0
Missouri	8,766	9,645	9,692	8,394	10,234	10,796	11,078	10,142	11,097	11,124	11,913	35.9
Montana	353	440	401	419	420	415	383	414	418	401	419	18.7
Nebraska	860	1,093	1,042	1,094	1,052	1,276	2,192	2,370	2,613	2,686	2,726	217.0
Nevada	327	414	326	352	352	[4]352	321	326	341	342	342	4.6
New Hampshire	536	660	623	810	886	918	770	825	1,253	840	1,425	165.9
New Jersey	47,980	65,173	63,978	70,298	76,204	84,347	87,054	100,220	118,868	135,251	159,683	232.8
New Mexico	695	1,461	1,461	4,107	5,024	5,601	6,479	[4]7,293	8,295	9,266	13,886	1,898.0
New York	327,320	363,949	391,989	372,363	355,192	382,655	428,358	504,195	554,803	618,849	636,704	94.5
North Carolina	3,974	4,440	4,386	4,559	4,489	3,046	2,519	2,908	3,163	14,436	13,774	246.6
North Dakota	635	808	503	490	976	1,242	1,177	1,475	2,162	2,036	1,996	214.3
Ohio	41,974	45,000	47,846	49,200	50,865	53,848	54,600	57,275	66,000	77,940	91,225	117.3
Oklahoma	6,561	8,242	8,630	10,245	9,861	11,591	11,871	12,612	13,286	13,405	13,325	103.1
Oregon	8,546	9,514	9,204	9,959	10,108	10,092	11,809	12,023	12,606	12,903	13,761	61.0
Pennsylvania	83,474	96,800	103,401	110,992	118,986	132,344	142,389	158,092	173,214	188,751	218,604	161.9
Rhode Island	6,745	7,856	8,930	8,138	8,967	9,917	9,522	9,141	9,586	6,500	6,340	6.0
South Carolina	12,588	15,146	16,348	16,346	17,810	18,150	17,901	16,800	17,105	16,795	17,297	37.4
South Dakota	440	624	563	516	506	504	468	480	587	589	589	33.9
Tennessee	6,700	9,434	10,618	12,591	11,977	12,977	13,487	12,793	13,723	16,755	18,313	173.3
Texas	21,438	19,033	20,990	22,705	22,266	24,784	24,135	27,385	27,467	29,102	29,102	35.7
Utah	1,538	1,131	1,080	1,133	1,081	1,091	1,001	1,034	1,115	1,132	1,129	26.6
Vermont	7,039	7,724	8,088	8,414	9,264	11,137	10,184	11,019	11,120	11,167	11,788	67.5
Virginia	4,075	4,415	4,349	4,414	8,062	7,966	7,351	4,892	6,654	6,408	53,885	1,222.3
Washington	7,530	8,827	10,022	12,425	12,858	13,925	21,095	23,527	23,571	46,617	53,369	608.8
West Virginia	4,376	5,167	5,157	5,189	5,204	5,217	5,559	5,781	5,868	5,802	6,761	54.5
Wisconsin	23,011	27,816	30,622	34,653	35,842	38,072	42,365	42,324	44,216	46,592	49,511	115.2
Wyoming	204	204	204	240	212	[4]241	[4]212	216	225	250	225	10.3

[1] In 1987–88, 1988–89, 1989–90, 1990–91, 1991–92, 1992–93, 1993–94, and 1994–95 need-based aid to undergraduates comprised 81.0, 78.2, 76.8, 77.4, 74.7, 75.7, 75.7 and 77.5 percent of all aid, respectively, compared with non-need-based aid or other types of aid to all undergraduate and graduate students. This table excludes loans.

[2] Estimated.

[3] Changes may reflect introduction of new programs or discontinuation of existing programs.

[4] Data are estimated based on prior year's report.

NOTE.-Some data have been revised from previously published figures. Because of rounding, details may not add to totals.

SOURCE: National Association of State Scholarship and Grant Programs, *Annual Survey Report,* various years. (This table was prepared April 1996.)

Table 321.—Current-fund revenue of institutions of higher education, by source: 1980–81 to 1993–94

Source	1980–81	1985–86	1987–88	1988–89	1989–90	1990–91	1991–92	1992–93	1993–94 [1]
1	2	3	4	5	6	7	8	9	10
	In thousands								
Total current-fund revenue	**$65,584,789**	**$100,437,616**	**$117,340,109**	**$128,501,638**	**$139,635,477**	**$149,766,051**	**$161,395,896**	**$170,880,503**	**$179,226,601**
Tuition and fees	13,773,259	23,116,605	27,836,781	30,806,566	33,926,060	37,434,462	41,559,037	45,346,071	48,646,538
Federal government	9,747,586	12,704,750	14,771,954	15,893,978	17,254,874	18,236,082	19,833,317	21,014,564	22,076,385
Appropriations	1,346,835	1,617,510	1,664,054	1,677,430	1,890,046	1,840,694	1,907,403	1,872,840	1,994,279
Unrestricted grants and contracts	1,126,558	1,658,636	1,980,749	2,150,079	2,353,119	2,504,859	2,703,590	2,913,256	3,129,307
Restricted grants and contracts [2]	6,005,317	7,190,345	8,225,129	9,009,709	9,773,266	10,443,977	11,561,444	12,589,727	13,554,435
Independent operations (FFRDC) [3]	1,268,877	2,238,259	2,902,022	3,056,760	3,238,442	3,446,552	3,660,881	3,638,741	3,398,364
State governments	20,106,222	29,911,500	33,517,166	36,031,208	38,349,239	39,480,874	40,586,907	41,247,955	41,910,288
Appropriations	19,266,186	28,402,288	31,298,537	33,287,034	35,223,174	36,255,090	36,884,957	37,314,176	37,824,061
Unrestricted grants and contracts	84,848	154,109	217,208	357,221	411,757	366,206	376,176	382,204	360,852
Restricted grants and contracts	755,188	1,355,102	2,001,421	2,386,953	2,714,309	2,859,577	3,325,774	3,551,575	3,725,375
Local governments	1,790,740	2,544,506	3,006,263	3,363,676	3,639,902	3,931,239	4,159,876	4,444,875	4,998,306
Appropriations	1,482,536	2,153,160	2,470,439	2,758,086	2,919,447	3,177,696	3,336,012	3,599,983	4,023,620
Unrestricted grants and contracts	29,629	56,975	76,638	98,787	122,404	116,982	140,135	139,881	134,491
Restricted grants and contracts	278,575	334,371	459,186	506,803	598,051	636,561	683,729	705,011	840,195
Private gifts, grants, and contracts	3,176,670	5,410,905	6,359,282	7,060,730	7,781,422	8,361,265	8,977,271	9,659,977	10,203,062
Unrestricted	1,210,903	2,111,972	2,235,096	2,429,579	2,634,974	2,720,233	2,921,997	3,229,718	3,400,457
Restricted	1,965,766	3,298,933	4,124,186	4,631,151	5,146,448	5,641,032	6,055,274	6,430,259	6,802,605
Endowment income	1,364,443	2,275,898	2,586,441	2,914,396	3,143,696	3,268,629	3,442,009	3,627,773	3,669,536
Unrestricted	770,358	1,285,194	1,340,788	1,498,703	1,614,088	1,521,940	1,549,930	1,536,511	1,557,733
Restricted	594,085	990,704	1,245,654	1,415,694	1,529,608	1,746,690	1,892,079	2,091,262	2,111,803
Sales and services	13,677,366	21,274,265	25,492,435	28,162,465	30,787,233	34,107,502	37,519,828	39,824,766	41,791,319
Educational activities	1,409,730	2,373,494	2,918,090	3,315,620	3,632,100	4,054,703	4,520,890	5,037,901	5,294,030
Auxiliary enterprises	7,287,290	10,674,136	11,947,778	12,855,580	13,938,469	14,903,127	15,758,599	16,662,850	17,537,514
Hospitals	4,980,346	8,226,635	10,626,566	11,991,265	13,216,664	15,149,672	17,240,338	18,124,015	18,959,776
Other sources	1,948,503	3,199,186	3,769,787	4,268,618	4,753,051	4,945,998	5,317,651	5,714,523	5,931,167
	Percentage distribution								
Total current-fund revenue	**100.0**	**100.0**	**100.0**	**100.0**	**100.0**	**100.0**	**100.0**	**100.0**	**100.0**
Tuition and fees	21.0	23.0	23.7	24.0	24.3	25.0	25.7	26.5	27.1
Federal government	14.9	12.6	12.6	12.4	12.4	12.2	12.3	12.3	12.3
Appropriations	2.1	1.6	1.4	1.3	1.4	1.2	1.2	1.1	1.1
Unrestricted grants and contracts	1.7	1.7	1.7	1.7	1.7	1.7	1.7	1.7	1.7
Restricted grants and contracts [2]	9.2	7.2	7.0	7.0	7.0	7.0	7.2	7.4	7.6
Independent operations (FFRDC) [3]	1.9	2.2	2.5	2.4	2.3	2.3	2.3	2.1	1.9
State governments	30.7	29.8	28.6	28.0	27.5	26.4	25.1	24.1	23.4
Appropriations	29.4	28.3	26.7	25.9	25.2	24.2	22.9	21.8	21.1
Unrestricted grants and contracts	0.1	0.2	0.2	0.3	0.3	0.2	0.2	0.2	0.2
Restricted grants and contracts	1.2	1.3	1.7	1.9	1.9	1.9	2.1	2.1	2.1
Local governments	2.7	2.5	2.6	2.6	2.6	2.6	2.6	2.6	2.8
Appropriations	2.3	2.1	2.1	2.1	2.1	2.1	2.1	2.1	2.2
Unrestricted grants and contracts	(⁴)	0.1	0.1	0.1	0.1	0.1	0.1	0.1	0.1
Restricted grants and contracts	0.4	0.3	0.4	0.4	0.4	0.4	0.4	0.4	0.5
Private gifts, grants, and contracts	4.8	5.4	5.4	5.5	5.6	5.6	5.6	5.7	5.7
Unrestricted	1.8	2.1	1.9	1.9	1.9	1.8	1.8	1.9	1.9
Restricted	3.0	3.3	3.5	3.6	3.7	3.8	3.8	3.8	3.8
Endowment income	2.1	2.3	2.2	2.3	2.3	2.2	2.1	2.1	2.0
Unrestricted	1.2	1.3	1.1	1.2	1.2	1.0	1.0	0.9	0.9
Restricted	0.9	1.0	1.1	1.1	1.1	1.2	1.2	1.2	1.2
Sales and services	20.9	21.2	21.7	21.9	22.0	22.8	23.2	23.3	23.3
Educational activities	2.1	2.4	2.5	2.6	2.6	2.7	2.8	2.9	3.0
Auxiliary enterprises	11.1	10.6	10.2	10.0	10.0	10.0	9.8	9.8	9.8
Hospitals	7.6	8.2	9.1	9.3	9.5	10.1	10.7	10.6	10.6
Other sources	3.0	3.2	3.2	3.3	3.4	3.3	3.3	3.3	3.3

[1] Preliminary data.

[2] Excludes Pell Grants. Federally supported student aid that is received through students is included under tuition and auxiliary enterprises.

[3] Generally includes only those revenues associated with major federally funded research and development centers (FFRDC).

[4] Less than 0.05 percent.

NOTE.—Because of rounding, details may not add to totals.

SOURCE: U.S. Department of Education, National Center for Education Statistics, "Financial Statistics of Institutions of Higher Education" surveys; and Integrated Postsecondary Education Data System (IPEDS), "Finance" surveys. (This table was prepared April 1996.)

Table 322.—Current-fund revenue of public institutions of higher education, by source: 1980–81 to 1993–94

Source	1980–81	1985–86	1987–88	1988–89	1989–90	1990–91	1991–92	1992–93	1993–94 [1]
1	2	3	4	5	6	7	8	9	10
	In thousands								
Total current-fund revenue	$43,195,617	$65,004,632	$74,771,255	$81,927,371	$88,911,433	$94,904,506	$102,202,890	$108,186,484	$112,968,097
Tuition and fees	5,570,404	9,439,177	11,184,657	12,435,763	13,820,240	15,258,024	17,460,263	19,490,221	20,825,388
Federal government	5,540,101	6,852,370	7,714,261	8,412,582	9,171,488	9,763,427	10,783,842	11,655,011	12,465,038
Appropriations	1,128,101	1,401,367	1,434,906	1,443,539	1,636,047	1,604,548	1,662,229	1,658,052	1,781,837
Unrestricted grants and contracts	529,424	816,364	989,781	1,083,575	1,214,836	1,319,035	1,462,372	1,601,201	1,694,596
Restricted grants and contracts [2]	3,812,197	4,481,723	5,095,910	5,656,468	6,106,112	6,629,484	7,426,627	8,155,317	8,776,458
Independent operations (FFRDC) [3]	70,379	152,916	193,664	228,999	214,493	210,360	232,613	240,441	212,148
State governments	19,675,968	29,220,586	32,437,504	34,835,716	37,052,307	38,239,978	39,107,560	39,789,641	40,536,393
Appropriations	19,006,716	28,071,070	30,917,354	32,929,719	34,858,904	35,898,653	36,612,540	37,073,932	37,565,065
Unrestricted grants and contracts	45,390	88,779	113,204	240,028	297,338	250,168	253,184	259,046	271,298
Restricted grants and contracts	623,863	1,060,737	1,406,946	1,665,969	1,896,065	2,091,157	2,241,836	2,456,663	2,700,030
Local governments	1,622,938	2,325,844	2,731,862	3,025,703	3,264,303	3,531,714	3,778,615	4,040,897	4,508,604
Appropriations	1,478,001	2,150,459	2,465,172	2,751,704	2,910,444	3,159,789	3,319,119	3,594,207	4,021,421
Unrestricted grants and contracts	9,915	27,852	41,940	64,455	82,405	73,281	90,257	84,974	71,098
Restricted grants and contracts	135,022	147,533	224,751	209,544	271,453	298,644	369,239	361,717	416,084
Private gifts, grants, and contracts	1,100,084	2,109,782	2,517,422	2,948,827	3,368,635	3,651,107	4,039,212	4,330,112	4,521,452
Unrestricted	110,462	279,381	305,457	362,011	436,028	529,496	650,468	686,214	698,497
Restricted	989,622	1,830,401	2,211,966	2,586,815	2,932,607	3,121,611	3,388,743	3,643,898	3,822,955
Endowment income	214,561	398,603	361,545	422,252	461,701	431,235	593,998	667,711	639,343
Unrestricted	102,888	181,624	127,861	149,650	164,242	147,368	248,770	257,113	259,172
Restricted	111,673	216,979	233,684	272,602	297,459	283,867	345,228	410,598	380,172
Sales and services	8,455,449	12,990,670	15,851,714	17,586,819	19,330,429	21,546,202	23,738,382	25,282,113	26,404,241
Educational activities	943,737	1,596,946	1,948,679	2,186,448	2,423,779	2,700,185	2,960,980	3,236,037	3,329,681
Auxiliary enterprises	4,614,561	6,684,794	7,306,302	7,809,284	8,473,282	9,058,745	9,655,373	10,255,044	10,814,804
Hospitals	2,897,151	4,708,930	6,596,733	7,591,087	8,433,369	9,787,271	11,122,029	11,791,033	12,259,757
Other sources	1,016,110	1,667,600	1,972,290	2,259,709	2,442,330	2,482,819	2,701,019	2,930,778	3,067,638
	Percentage distribution								
Total current-fund revenue	100.0	100.0	100.0	100.0	100.0	100.0	100.0	100.0	100.0
Tuition and fees	12.9	14.5	15.0	15.2	15.5	16.1	17.1	18.0	18.4
Federal government	12.8	10.5	10.3	10.3	10.3	10.3	10.6	10.8	11.0
Appropriations	2.6	2.2	1.9	1.8	1.8	1.7	1.6	1.5	1.6
Unrestricted grants and contracts	1.2	1.3	1.3	1.3	1.4	1.4	1.4	1.5	1.5
Restricted grants and contracts [2]	8.8	6.9	6.8	6.9	6.9	7.0	7.3	7.5	7.8
Independent operations (FFRDC) [3]	0.2	0.2	0.3	0.3	0.2	0.2	0.2	0.2	0.2
State governments	45.6	45.0	43.4	42.5	41.7	40.3	38.3	36.8	35.9
Appropriations	44.0	43.2	41.3	40.2	39.2	37.8	35.8	34.3	33.3
Unrestricted grants and contracts	0.1	0.1	0.2	0.3	0.3	0.3	0.2	0.2	0.2
Restricted grants and contracts	1.4	1.6	1.9	2.0	2.1	2.2	2.2	2.3	2.4
Local governments	3.8	3.6	3.7	3.7	3.7	3.7	3.7	3.7	4.0
Appropriations	3.4	3.3	3.3	3.4	3.3	3.3	3.2	3.3	3.6
Unrestricted grants and contracts	(4)	(4)	0.1	0.1	0.1	0.1	0.1	0.1	0.1
Restricted grants and contracts	0.3	0.2	0.3	0.3	0.3	0.3	0.4	0.3	0.4
Private gifts, grants, and contracts	2.5	3.2	3.4	3.6	3.8	3.8	4.0	4.0	4.0
Unrestricted	0.3	0.4	0.4	0.4	0.5	0.6	0.6	0.6	0.6
Restricted	2.3	2.8	3.0	3.2	3.3	3.3	3.3	3.4	3.4
Endowment income	0.5	0.6	0.5	0.5	0.5	0.5	0.6	0.6	0.6
Unrestricted	0.2	0.3	0.2	0.2	0.2	0.2	0.2	0.2	0.2
Restricted	0.3	0.3	0.3	0.3	0.3	0.3	0.3	0.4	0.3
Sales and services	19.6	20.0	21.2	21.5	21.7	22.7	23.2	23.4	23.4
Educational activities	2.2	2.5	2.6	2.7	2.7	2.8	2.9	3.0	2.9
Auxiliary enterprises	10.7	10.3	9.8	9.5	9.5	9.5	9.4	9.5	9.6
Hospitals	6.7	7.2	8.8	9.3	9.5	10.3	10.9	10.9	10.9
Other sources	2.4	2.6	2.6	2.8	2.7	2.6	2.6	2.7	2.7

[1] Preliminary data.

[2] Excludes Pell Grants. Federally supported student aid that is received through students is included under tuition and auxiliary enterprises.

[3] Generally includes only those revenues associated with major federally funded research and development centers (FFRDC).

[4] Less than 0.05 percent.

NOTE.—Because of rounding, details may not add to totals.

SOURCE: U.S. Department of Education, National Center for Education Statistics, "Financial Statistics of Institutions of Higher Education" surveys; and Integrated Postsecondary Education Data System (IPEDS), "Finance" surveys. (This table was prepared April 1996.)

Table 323.—Current-fund revenue of private institutions of higher education, by source: 1980–81 to 1993–94

Source	1980–81	1985–86	1987–88	1988–89	1989–90	1990–91	1991–92	1992–93	1993–94 [1]
1	2	3	4	5	6	7	8	9	10
	In thousands								
Total current-fund revenue	$22,389,172	$35,432,985	$42,568,854	$46,574,267	$50,724,044	$54,861,545	$59,193,006	$62,694,018	$66,258,504
Tuition and fees	8,202,855	13,677,429	16,652,124	18,370,803	20,105,820	22,176,439	24,098,774	25,855,850	27,821,149
Federal government	4,207,485	5,852,380	7,057,693	7,481,396	8,083,386	8,472,654	9,049,476	9,359,554	9,611,348
Appropriations	218,733	216,143	229,148	233,891	254,000	236,146	245,173	214,788	212,443
Unrestricted grants and contracts	597,134	842,272	990,968	1,066,504	1,138,283	1,185,824	1,241,218	1,312,056	1,434,711
Restricted grants and contracts [2]	2,193,119	2,708,622	3,129,219	3,353,241	3,667,154	3,814,493	4,134,817	4,434,410	4,777,978
Independent operations (FFRDC) [3]	1,198,498	2,085,343	2,708,358	2,827,761	3,023,949	3,236,192	3,428,267	3,398,300	3,186,216
State governments	430,253	690,914	1,079,662	1,195,492	1,296,932	1,240,896	1,479,347	1,458,314	1,373,894
Appropriations	259,470	331,219	381,183	357,315	364,270	356,437	272,417	240,244	258,996
Unrestricted grants and contracts	39,458	65,330	104,004	117,193	114,419	116,038	122,992	123,158	89,554
Restricted grants and contracts	131,326	294,365	594,475	720,984	818,244	768,421	1,083,938	1,094,912	1,025,344
Local governments	167,801	218,662	274,400	337,973	375,599	399,525	381,261	403,977	489,703
Appropriations	4,535	2,701	5,267	6,383	9,003	17,907	16,893	5,776	2,199
Unrestricted grants and contracts	19,714	29,123	34,698	34,332	39,999	43,701	49,878	54,907	63,393
Restricted grants and contracts	143,552	186,838	234,435	297,258	326,598	337,917	314,490	343,294	424,111
Private gifts, grants, and contracts	2,076,585	3,301,124	3,841,860	4,111,904	4,412,787	4,710,158	4,938,060	5,329,865	5,681,610
Unrestricted	1,100,441	1,832,592	1,929,639	2,067,568	2,198,946	2,190,736	2,271,529	2,543,504	2,701,960
Restricted	976,144	1,468,532	1,912,220	2,044,336	2,213,841	2,519,421	2,666,531	2,786,361	2,979,650
Endowment income	1,149,883	1,877,295	2,224,896	2,492,144	2,681,995	2,837,394	2,848,012	2,960,062	3,030,193
Unrestricted	667,471	1,103,570	1,212,926	1,349,053	1,449,846	1,374,572	1,301,160	1,279,398	1,298,562
Restricted	482,412	773,725	1,011,970	1,143,091	1,232,149	1,462,822	1,546,851	1,680,664	1,731,631
Sales and services	5,221,917	8,283,595	9,640,720	10,575,646	11,456,804	12,561,301	13,781,446	14,542,653	15,387,078
Educational activities	465,993	776,548	969,411	1,129,171	1,208,322	1,354,518	1,559,910	1,801,865	1,964,349
Auxiliary enterprises	2,672,729	3,989,342	4,641,476	5,046,296	5,465,187	5,844,382	6,103,226	6,407,806	6,722,710
Hospitals	2,083,195	3,517,705	4,029,833	4,400,178	4,783,295	5,362,401	6,118,309	6,332,982	6,700,019
Other sources	932,392	1,531,586	1,797,498	2,008,909	2,310,720	2,463,178	2,616,632	2,783,744	2,863,529
	Percentage distribution								
Total current-fund revenue	100.0	100.0	100.0	100.0	100.0	100.0	100.0	100.0	100.0
Tuition and fees	36.6	38.6	39.1	39.4	39.6	40.4	40.7	41.2	42.0
Federal government	18.8	16.5	16.6	16.1	15.9	15.4	15.3	14.9	14.5
Appropriations	1.0	0.6	0.5	0.5	0.5	0.4	0.4	0.3	0.3
Unrestricted grants and contracts	2.7	2.4	2.3	2.3	2.2	2.2	2.1	2.1	2.2
Restricted grants and contracts [2]	9.8	7.6	7.4	7.2	7.2	7.0	7.0	7.1	7.2
Independent operations (FFRDC) [3]	5.4	5.9	6.4	6.1	6.0	5.9	5.8	5.4	4.8
State governments	1.9	1.9	2.5	2.6	2.6	2.3	2.5	2.3	2.1
Appropriations	1.2	0.9	0.9	0.8	0.7	0.6	0.5	0.4	0.4
Unrestricted grants and contracts	0.2	0.2	0.2	0.3	0.2	0.2	0.2	0.2	0.1
Restricted grants and contracts	0.6	0.8	1.4	1.5	1.6	1.4	1.8	1.7	1.5
Local governments	0.7	0.6	0.6	0.7	0.7	0.7	0.6	0.6	0.7
Appropriations	(4)	(4)	(4)	(4)	(4)	(4)	(4)	(4)	(4)
Unrestricted grants and contracts	0.1	0.1	0.1	0.1	0.1	0.1	0.1	0.1	0.1
Restricted grants and contracts	0.6	0.5	0.6	0.6	0.6	0.6	0.5	0.5	0.6
Private gifts, grants, and contracts	9.3	9.3	9.0	8.8	8.7	8.6	8.3	8.5	8.6
Unrestricted	4.9	5.2	4.5	4.4	4.3	4.0	3.8	4.1	4.1
Restricted	4.4	4.1	4.5	4.4	4.4	4.6	4.5	4.4	4.5
Endowment income	5.1	5.3	5.2	5.4	5.3	5.2	4.8	4.7	4.6
Unrestricted	3.0	3.1	2.8	2.9	2.9	2.5	2.2	2.0	2.0
Restricted	2.2	2.2	2.4	2.5	2.4	2.7	2.6	2.7	2.6
Sales and services	23.3	23.4	22.6	22.7	22.6	22.9	23.3	23.2	23.2
Educational activities	2.1	2.2	2.3	2.4	2.4	2.5	2.6	2.9	3.0
Auxiliary enterprises	11.9	11.3	10.9	10.8	10.8	10.7	10.3	10.2	10.1
Hospitals	9.3	9.9	9.5	9.4	9.4	9.8	10.3	10.1	10.1
Other sources	4.2	4.3	4.2	4.3	4.6	4.5	4.4	4.4	4.3

[1] Preliminary data.
[2] Excludes Pell Grants. Federally supported student aid that is received through students is included under tuition and auxiliary enterprises.
[3] Generally includes only those revenues associated with major federally funded research and development centers (FFRDC).
[4] Less than 0.05 percent.

NOTE.—Because of rounding, details may not add to totals.

SOURCE: U.S. Department of Education, National Center for Education Statistics, "Financial Statistics of Institutions of Higher Education" surveys; and Integrated Postsecondary Education Data System (IPEDS), "Finance" surveys. (This table was prepared April 1996.)

Table 324.—Revenue of institutions of higher education, by source of funds: 1919–20 to 1993–94 [1]

[In thousands]

Year	Current-fund revenue	Student tuition and fees [1]	Federal government [2]	State governments [3]	Local governments	Endowment earnings	Private gifts and grants [4]	Sales and services of educational activities	Auxiliary enterprises	Hospitals [5]	Other current income
1	2	3	4	5	6	7	8	9	10	11	12
1919–20	$199,922	$42,255	$12,783	$61,690	(6)	$26,482	$7,584	—	$26,993	—	$22,135
1929–30	554,511	144,126	20,658	150,847	(6)	68,605	26,172	—	60,419	—	83,684
1939–40	715,211	200,897	38,860	151,222	$24,392	71,304	40,453	$32,777	143,923	—	11,383
1949–50	2,374,645	394,610	524,319	491,636	61,700	96,341	118,627	111,987	511,265	—	64,160
1959–60	5,785,537	1,157,482	1,036,990	1,374,476	151,715	206,619	382,569	102,525	1,004,283	$187,769	181,110
1969–70	21,515,242	4,419,845	4,130,066	5,873,626	778,162	516,038	1,129,438	612,777	2,900,390	619,578	535,323
1975–76	39,703,166	8,171,942	6,477,178	12,260,885	1,616,975	687,470	1,917,036	645,420	4,547,622	2,494,340	884,298
1976–77	43,436,827	9,024,932	7,169,031	13,285,684	1,626,908	764,788	2,105,070	779,058	4,919,602	2,859,376	902,377
1977–78	47,034,032	9,855,270	6,968,501	14,746,166	1,744,230	832,286	2,320,368	882,715	5,327,821	3,268,956	1,087,719
1978–79	51,837,789	10,704,171	7,851,326	16,363,784	1,573,018	985,242	2,489,366	1,037,130	5,741,309	3,763,453	1,328,991
1979–80	58,519,982	11,930,340	8,902,844	18,378,299	1,587,552	1,176,627	2,808,075	1,239,439	6,481,458	4,373,384	1,641,965
1980–81	65,584,789	13,773,259	9,747,586	20,106,222	1,790,740	1,364,443	3,176,670	1,409,730	7,287,290	4,980,346	1,948,503
1981–82	72,190,856	15,774,038	9,591,805	21,848,791	1,937,669	1,596,813	3,563,558	1,582,922	8,121,611	5,838,565	2,335,084
1982–83	77,595,726	17,776,041	9,631,097	23,065,636	2,031,353	1,720,677	4,052,649	1,723,484	8,769,521	6,531,562	2,293,706
1983–84	84,417,287	19,714,884	10,406,166	24,706,990	2,192,275	1,873,945	4,415,275	1,970,747	9,456,369	7,040,662	2,639,973
1984–85	92,472,694	21,283,329	11,509,125	27,583,011	2,387,212	2,096,298	4,896,325	2,126,927	10,100,410	7,474,575	3,015,483
1985–86	100,437,616	23,116,605	12,704,750	29,911,500	2,544,506	2,275,898	5,410,905	2,373,494	10,674,136	8,226,635	3,199,186
1986–87	108,809,827	25,705,827	13,904,049	31,309,303	2,799,321	2,377,958	5,952,682	2,641,906	11,364,188	9,277,834	3,476,760
1987–88	117,340,109	27,836,781	14,771,954	33,517,166	3,006,263	2,586,441	6,359,282	2,918,090	11,947,778	10,626,566	3,769,787
1988–89	128,501,638	30,806,566	15,893,978	36,031,208	3,363,676	2,914,396	7,060,730	3,315,620	12,855,580	11,991,265	4,268,618
1989–90	139,635,477	33,926,060	17,254,874	38,349,239	3,639,902	3,143,696	7,781,422	3,632,100	13,938,469	13,216,664	4,753,051
1990–91	149,766,051	37,434,462	18,236,082	39,480,874	3,931,239	3,268,629	8,361,265	4,054,703	14,903,127	15,149,672	4,945,998
1991–92	161,395,896	41,559,037	19,833,317	40,586,907	4,159,876	3,442,009	8,977,271	4,520,890	15,758,599	17,240,338	5,317,651
1992–93	170,880,503	45,346,071	21,014,564	41,247,955	4,444,875	3,627,773	9,659,977	5,037,901	16,662,850	18,124,015	5,714,523
1993–94[7]	179,226,601	48,646,538	22,076,385	41,910,288	4,998,306	3,669,536	10,203,062	5,294,030	17,537,514	18,959,776	5,931,167

[1] Tuition and fees received from veterans under Public Law 550 are reported under student fees and are not under income from the federal government.

[2] Federally supported student aid that is received through students is included under tuition and auxiliary enterprises.

[3] Includes federal aid received through state channels and regional compacts, through 1959–60.

[4] Beginning in 1969–70, the private grants represent nongovernmental revenue for sponsored research, student aid, and other sponsored programs.

[5] Prior to 1959–60, data for hospitals are included under sales and services of educational activities.

[6] Income from state and local governments tabulated under "State governments."

[7] Preliminary data.

—Data not available.

NOTE.—Data for years prior to 1969–70 are not entirely comparable with data for later years. Also, some details for 1969–70 are not directly comparable with data for later years. Because of rounding, details may not add to totals.

SOURCE: U.S. Department of Education, National Center for Education Statistics, "Financial Statistics of Institutions of Higher Education" surveys; and Integrated Postsecondary Education Data System (IPEDS), "Finance" surveys. (This table was prepared April 1996.)

Table 325.—Revenue of institutions of higher education, by source of funds and by control and type of institution: 1993-94 [1]

Control and type of institution	Current-fund revenue	Student tuition and fees [2]	Federal government [3]	State governments	Local governments	Private gifts and grants	Endowment earnings	Educational activities	Auxiliary enterprises	Hospitals	Other current income
1	2	3	4	5	6	7	8	9	10	11	12
						In thousands					
Total	$179,226,601	$48,646,538	$22,076,385	$41,910,288	$4,998,306	$10,203,062	$3,669,536	$5,294,030	$17,537,514	$18,959,776	$5,931,167
Public	112,968,097	20,825,388	12,465,038	40,536,393	4,508,604	4,521,452	639,343	3,329,681	10,814,804	12,259,757	3,067,638
Research I universities [4]	42,542,656	6,227,003	6,520,800	12,184,511	201,955	2,544,305	361,316	1,792,147	4,328,652	7,522,139	859,830
Research II universities [4]	6,869,797	1,553,654	825,553	2,759,947	25,625	365,804	48,201	217,399	905,471	0	168,142
Doctoral universities	12,007,740	2,741,686	992,896	4,963,334	97,239	498,518	128,803	258,328	1,412,957	380,614	533,367
Master's	18,024,356	4,823,603	898,919	8,542,788	133,283	352,752	42,088	367,242	2,293,858	216,330	353,493
Baccalaureate	2,296,679	722,143	107,299	1,023,881	24,368	51,001	5,333	30,131	291,187	0	41,337
Associate of arts	20,159,232	4,362,471	1,054,760	8,622,929	3,928,077	177,294	16,789	141,068	1,268,533	0	587,311
Specialized institutions [5]											
Health and medicine	9,332,624	260,774	982,364	2,188,451	67,873	510,611	35,347	519,328	203,575	4,065,775	498,525
Engineering	202,947	46,219	16,839	109,336	1	9,282	25	2,188	16,497	0	2,558
Business	22,513	5,816	820	12,621	0	0	12	1,540	1,515	0	190
Fine arts	111,575	26,808	768	32,993	23,656	1,459	8	87	11,203	0	14,595
Other specialized	1,320,671	47,688	1,013,173	93,487	2,359	5,416	293	164	77,405	74,900	5,784
Tribal colleges [6]	77,306	7,524	50,845	2,116	4,167	5,009	1,129	59	3,953	0	2,505
4-year	15,785	1,831	9,227	88	1,162	1,207	312	51	686	0	1,222
2-year	61,521	5,693	41,619	2,028	3,006	3,802	816	8	3,266	0	1,283
Private	66,258,504	27,821,149	9,611,348	1,373,894	489,703	5,681,610	3,030,193	1,964,349	6,722,710	6,700,019	2,863,529
Research I universities [4]	25,290,229	5,793,915	7,244,215	254,521	223,613	2,436,378	1,370,479	1,349,544	1,791,951	3,937,636	887,977
Research II universities [4]	4,028,867	1,474,693	310,294	46,263	565	397,070	186,124	93,567	531,105	811,420	177,766
Doctoral universities	6,283,514	3,352,183	421,979	155,112	7,186	350,544	204,325	109,788	593,589	719,055	369,752
Master's	9,364,991	6,220,186	441,530	286,994	4,727	558,374	224,246	131,289	1,248,257	9,380	240,009
Baccalaureate	11,830,417	7,003,816	390,636	327,401	2,885	1,033,854	756,521	40,823	1,974,891	0	299,589
Associate of arts	1,729,127	1,224,657	46,500	104,715	4,517	84,162	15,392	11,514	126,705	59,268	51,697
Specialized institutions [5]											
Religion and theology	978,667	315,304	14,987	5,380	1,199	343,217	108,833	6,962	147,035	0	35,748
Health and medicine	4,299,798	646,756	662,434	136,267	242,465	343,704	79,479	187,613	93,289	1,163,261	744,530
Engineering	373,969	227,521	25,685	9,493	0	36,270	30,094	6,445	28,171	0	10,291
Business	898,975	679,753	17,140	23,152	270	21,424	9,571	18,392	111,815	0	17,456
Fine arts	666,526	482,254	12,375	18,870	827	46,401	32,417	2,790	56,431	0	14,161
Other specialized	492,341	397,505	8,073	5,522	1,385	29,188	12,634	5,536	19,064	0	13,437
Tribal colleges [6]	21,084	2,606	15,501	205	64	1,025	77	85	405	0	1,116
4-year	9,808	1,434	6,797	0	0	658	0	85	185	0	650
2-year	11,275	1,171	8,704	205	64	368	77	0	221	0	466
						Percentage distribution					
Total	100.00	27.14	12.32	23.38	2.79	5.69	2.05	2.95	9.79	10.58	3.31
Public	100.00	18.43	11.03	35.88	3.99	4.00	0.57	2.95	9.57	10.85	2.72
Research I universities [4]	100.00	14.64	15.33	28.64	0.47	5.98	0.85	4.21	10.17	17.68	2.02
Research II universities [4]	100.00	22.62	12.02	40.18	0.37	5.32	0.70	3.16	13.18	0.00	2.45
Doctoral universities	100.00	22.83	8.27	41.33	0.81	4.15	1.07	2.15	11.77	3.17	4.44
Master's	100.00	26.76	4.99	47.40	0.74	1.96	0.23	2.04	12.73	1.20	1.96
Baccalaureate	100.00	31.44	4.67	44.58	1.06	2.22	0.23	1.31	12.68	0.00	1.80
Associate of arts	100.00	21.64	5.23	42.77	19.49	0.88	0.08	0.70	6.29	0.00	2.91
Specialized institutions [5]											
Health and medicine	100.00	2.79	10.53	23.45	0.73	5.47	0.38	5.56	2.18	43.57	5.34
Engineering	100.00	22.77	8.30	53.87	0.00	4.57	0.01	1.08	8.13	0.00	1.26
Business	100.00	25.84	3.64	56.06	0.00	0.00	0.05	6.84	6.73	0.00	0.84
Fine arts	100.00	24.03	0.69	29.57	21.20	1.31	0.01	0.08	10.04	0.00	13.08
Other specialized	100.00	3.61	76.72	7.08	0.18	0.41	0.02	0.01	5.86	5.67	0.44
Tribal colleges [6]	100.00	9.73	65.77	2.74	5.39	6.48	1.46	0.08	5.11	0.00	3.24
4-year	100.00	11.60	58.45	0.56	7.36	7.65	1.98	0.32	4.35	0.00	7.74
2-year	100.00	9.25	67.65	3.30	4.89	6.18	1.33	0.01	5.31	0.00	2.09
Private	100.00	41.99	14.51	2.07	0.74	8.57	4.57	2.96	10.15	10.11	4.32
Research I universities [4]	100.00	22.91	28.64	1.01	0.88	9.63	5.42	5.34	7.09	15.57	3.51
Research II universities [4]	100.00	36.60	7.70	1.15	0.01	9.86	4.62	2.32	13.18	20.14	4.41
Doctoral universities	100.00	53.35	6.72	2.47	0.11	5.58	3.25	1.75	9.45	11.44	5.88
Master's	100.00	66.42	4.71	3.06	0.05	5.96	2.39	1.40	13.33	0.10	2.56
Baccalaureate	100.00	59.20	3.30	2.77	0.02	8.74	6.39	0.35	16.69	0.00	2.53
Associate of arts	100.00	70.83	2.69	6.06	0.26	4.87	0.89	0.67	7.33	3.43	2.99
Specialized institutions [5]											
Religion and theology	100.00	32.22	1.53	0.55	0.12	35.07	11.12	0.71	15.02	0.00	3.65
Health and medicine	100.00	15.04	15.41	3.17	5.64	7.99	1.85	4.36	2.17	27.05	17.32
Engineering	100.00	60.84	6.87	2.54	0.00	9.70	8.05	1.72	7.53	0.00	2.75
Business	100.00	75.61	1.91	2.58	0.03	2.38	1.06	2.05	12.44	0.00	1.94
Fine arts	100.00	72.35	1.86	2.83	0.12	6.96	4.86	0.42	8.47	0.00	2.12
Other specialized	100.00	80.74	1.64	1.12	0.28	5.93	2.57	1.12	3.87	0.00	2.73
Tribal colleges [6]	100.00	12.36	73.52	0.97	0.30	4.86	0.36	0.40	1.92	0.00	5.29
4-year	100.00	14.63	69.30	0.00	0.00	6.70	0.00	0.86	1.88	0.00	6.63
2-year	100.00	10.39	77.19	1.82	0.56	3.26	0.68	0.00	1.96	0.00	4.13

[1] Preliminary data.

[2] Includes federally supported aid received through students.

[3] Includes appropriations, grants, contracts, and revenues associated with major federally funded research and development centers (FFRDC). Excludes Pell Grants.

[4] Research institutions are committed to graduate education through the doctorate, and give high priority to research. Research I institutions receive $40 million or more annually in federal support. Research II institutions receive between $15.5 million and $40 million annually.

[5] Specialized institutions award baccalaureate or higher level degrees in specific fields of study.

[6] Tribally controlled colleges are located on reservations and are members of the American Indian Higher Education Consortium.

NOTE.—Because of rounding, details may not add to totals.

SOURCE: U.S. Department of Education, National Center for Education Statistics, Integrated Postsecondary Education Data System (IPEDS), "Finance, 1993-94" survey. (This table was prepared July 1996.)

Table 326.—Current-fund revenue of public institutions of higher education, by state: 1980–81 to 1993–94

[In thousands of dollars]

State	1980–81	1985–86	1987–88	1988–89	1989–90	1990–91	1991–92	1992–93	1993–94[1]	Percent change, 1988–89 to 1993–94
1	2	3	4	5	6	7	8	9	10	11
United States	**$43,195,617**	**$65,004,632**	**$74,771,255**	**$81,927,371**	**$88,911,433**	**$94,904,506**	**$102,202,890**	**$108,186,484**	**$112,968,097**	**37.9**
Alabama	889,121	1,401,693	1,552,128	1,743,168	1,926,148	2,131,005	2,296,665	2,521,938	2,614,224	50.0
Alaska	159,446	221,837	220,393	244,857	270,926	291,826	304,857	323,740	342,624	39.9
Arizona	719,835	1,049,493	1,221,641	1,353,468	1,483,996	1,596,710	1,655,873	1,677,711	1,834,035	35.5
Arkansas	350,597	539,185	652,029	716,105	781,375	818,079	920,699	995,482	1,036,610	44.8
California	5,906,729	8,739,396	9,995,464	11,022,341	11,776,298	12,281,700	13,628,928	14,262,239	13,868,703	25.8
Colorado	747,040	1,085,076	1,247,390	1,371,303	1,390,413	1,483,901	1,594,541	1,714,698	1,803,735	31.5
Connecticut	378,527	578,866	692,830	788,194	833,154	889,831	940,067	976,380	1,020,170	29.4
Delaware	168,522	251,677	294,347	324,853	354,322	388,635	433,186	446,768	471,017	45.0
District of Columbia	66,138	91,842	99,457	109,167	109,254	109,642	121,991	118,865	107,296	-1.7
Florida	1,202,788	1,810,090	2,228,502	2,510,894	2,812,644	2,944,935	3,049,921	3,202,499	3,411,727	35.9
Georgia	765,826	1,267,472	1,528,997	1,648,753	1,794,990	1,953,866	2,042,825	2,268,331	2,494,263	51.3
Hawaii	219,633	316,246	358,754	384,775	433,164	497,495	579,805	594,752	628,043	63.2
Idaho	169,274	235,507	270,133	290,303	320,119	359,710	396,173	416,359	456,107	57.1
Illinois	1,809,981	2,560,241	2,812,875	3,067,687	3,370,011	3,566,406	3,659,328	3,924,599	4,100,967	33.7
Indiana	1,094,560	1,701,421	1,910,144	2,083,416	2,302,583	2,494,029	2,767,477	2,882,592	3,009,908	44.5
Iowa	784,950	1,109,681	1,321,697	1,529,907	1,653,221	1,775,267	1,827,776	1,930,399	2,014,244	31.7
Kansas	594,104	864,119	975,159	1,047,219	1,174,759	1,219,129	1,297,129	1,350,052	1,469,872	40.4
Kentucky	671,414	943,068	1,109,682	1,194,424	1,283,778	1,450,958	1,565,021	1,576,644	1,656,119	38.7
Louisiana	735,374	1,055,941	1,118,919	1,180,464	1,301,127	1,447,772	1,553,258	1,821,190	1,844,187	56.2
Maine	157,370	222,624	278,078	317,636	352,024	373,770	375,512	384,730	398,639	25.5
Maryland	818,850	1,144,230	1,344,947	1,515,369	1,638,822	1,777,841	1,745,479	1,913,029	1,984,038	30.9
Massachusetts	582,873	1,075,348	1,287,595	1,365,350	1,429,770	1,457,142	1,525,943	1,639,854	1,491,921	9.3
Michigan	2,094,394	3,071,172	3,699,398	3,992,084	4,322,956	4,648,488	5,127,892	5,329,224	5,529,883	38.5
Minnesota	894,236	1,373,436	1,631,838	1,880,373	1,916,297	2,080,637	2,261,978	2,363,483	2,494,341	32.7
Mississippi	543,209	734,813	802,055	903,637	956,300	1,005,448	1,054,530	1,150,201	1,215,602	34.5
Missouri	717,626	1,032,685	1,169,613	1,289,742	1,416,556	1,517,071	1,566,480	1,698,594	1,805,266	40.0
Montana	123,933	181,462	196,957	197,605	227,403	258,189	334,243	349,102	362,905	83.7
Nebraska	390,372	554,814	628,140	699,859	787,282	870,289	941,062	989,156	1,033,731	47.7
Nevada	113,298	184,883	221,740	243,208	286,719	336,841	368,245	392,258	412,884	69.8
New Hampshire	131,990	190,462	232,411	255,948	275,121	304,315	324,186	348,839	373,498	45.9
New Jersey	917,143	1,446,098	1,853,740	2,065,233	2,253,830	2,413,530	2,610,949	2,745,100	2,920,767	41.4
New Mexico	334,392	473,716	543,196	786,667	858,989	944,248	1,056,819	1,125,366	1,190,519	51.3
New York	2,519,437	3,830,119	4,553,725	4,772,942	5,014,789	5,424,379	5,616,604	6,117,555	6,574,152	37.7
North Carolina	1,146,931	1,857,124	2,138,818	2,295,295	2,480,396	2,650,124	2,873,684	3,113,193	3,299,213	43.7
North Dakota	196,267	286,550	303,700	327,293	365,089	377,960	411,293	431,464	431,381	31.8
Ohio	1,828,079	2,824,411	3,221,449	3,561,646	3,871,477	4,184,621	4,484,576	4,628,902	4,895,812	37.5
Oklahoma	588,936	873,446	862,152	902,463	997,781	1,072,967	1,190,393	1,209,863	1,257,552	39.3
Oregon	647,391	899,709	1,042,939	1,128,211	1,242,595	1,358,244	1,523,505	1,615,882	1,687,205	49.5
Pennsylvania	1,575,104	2,473,794	2,951,559	3,262,178	3,511,535	3,692,745	4,153,483	4,262,533	4,423,633	35.6
Rhode Island	156,451	213,859	247,606	270,500	291,376	292,404	308,383	325,003	329,277	21.7
South Carolina	630,966	957,771	1,096,800	1,216,468	1,333,941	1,502,709	1,629,876	1,733,468	1,924,747	58.2
South Dakota	127,839	147,699	160,019	169,210	184,954	198,583	219,751	241,536	260,907	54.2
Tennessee	675,770	1,104,118	1,346,786	1,435,262	1,556,416	1,634,491	1,672,605	1,839,384	1,961,312	36.7
Texas	2,858,725	4,558,275	4,814,275	5,204,122	5,777,100	6,015,609	6,664,828	7,126,068	7,688,388	47.7
Utah	431,294	686,817	794,630	870,334	960,027	1,020,836	1,160,882	1,224,127	1,307,681	50.3
Vermont	127,337	191,559	223,950	244,836	267,178	281,526	298,524	305,477	316,905	29.4
Virginia	1,159,453	1,876,151	2,245,676	2,486,637	2,736,307	2,902,939	3,041,850	3,176,437	3,323,028	33.6
Washington	998,146	1,445,849	1,627,937	1,809,540	1,966,838	2,188,366	2,355,445	2,539,934	2,744,035	51.6
West Virginia	318,915	385,170	415,387	447,533	502,436	563,796	608,294	631,619	666,268	48.9
Wisconsin	1,228,414	1,761,927	2,032,154	2,191,795	2,343,203	2,487,501	2,629,388	2,775,635	2,954,564	34.8
Wyoming	140,520	208,595	211,403	224,602	237,093	251,760	271,290	270,515	278,270	23.9
U.S. Service Schools	586,095	913,092	980,041	982,495	1,176,548	1,114,245	1,159,395	1,183,716	1,245,921	26.8
Outlying areas	242,380	451,734	508,034	515,558	573,106	557,655	665,323	704,076	589,470	14.3
American Samoa	1,305	2,413	2,791	3,060	3,585	3,939	4,057	4,428	4,610	50.7
Federated States of Micronesia	—	—	—	1,789	1,842	2,063	2,078	3,453	3,932	119.8
Guam	14,291	31,139	35,943	39,282	50,411	61,667	70,658	74,928	68,198	73.6
Marshall Islands	—	—	—	—	—	—	3,798	1,111	2,176	
Northern Marianas	—	1,350	774	748	791	1,458	1,715	2,462	3,511	369.5
Palau	—	—	—	3,643	4,038	4,100	3,948	5,133	4,762	30.7
Puerto Rico	213,012	392,194	440,382	441,449	487,133	428,768	518,747	581,128	468,739	6.2
Trust Territory of the Pacific	1,669	5,681	4,862	—	—	—	—	—	—	
Virgin Islands	12,103	18,957	23,281	25,587	25,307	55,659	60,322	31,432	33,542	31.1

[1] Preliminary data.

—Data not available or not applicable.

NOTE.—Because of rounding, details may not add to totals.

SOURCE: U.S. Department of Education, National Center for Education Statistics, "Financial Statistics of Institutions of Higher Education" survey; and Integrated Postsecondary Education Data System (IPEDS), "Finance" surveys. (This table was prepared April 1996.)

Table 327.—Current-fund revenue of public institutions of higher education, by source of funds and state: 1993–94 [1]

[In thousands of dollars]

State	Total	Tuition and fees	Federal appropri- ations, grants, and contracts [2]	State appropri- ations, grants, and contracts	Local appropri- ations, grants, and contracts	Private gifts, grants, and contracts	Endow- ment income	Auxiliary enterprises	Hospitals	Educational activities and other
1	2	3	4	5	6	7	8	9	10	11
United States	$112,968,097	$20,825,388	$12,465,038	$40,536,393	$4,508,604	$4,521,452	$639,343	$10,814,804	$12,259,757	$6,397,319
Alabama	2,614,224	388,272	273,092	829,100	11,948	106,613	18,715	190,160	669,006	127,319
Alaska	342,624	42,295	55,652	184,624	1,659	9,001	3,133	19,972	0	26,288
Arizona	1,834,035	390,731	258,662	629,532	187,605	88,315	5,425	207,411	0	66,354
Arkansas	1,036,610	152,610	80,718	411,337	2,672	27,156	1,934	83,431	232,355	44,397
California	13,868,703	1,809,463	1,402,402	5,000,654	1,362,354	408,307	87,813	862,152	1,795,767	1,139,791
Colorado	1,803,735	499,752	332,389	489,353	26,832	89,336	10,685	226,012	26,659	102,717
Connecticut	1,020,170	211,790	72,482	381,843	606	30,601	144	89,640	186,726	46,338
Delaware	471,017	161,016	43,134	134,920	5,031	17,789	17,803	62,988	0	28,336
District of Columbia	107,296	10,383	14,404	0	73,622	509	745	657	0	6,976
Florida	3,411,727	617,023	308,662	1,819,205	17,718	248,458	860	320,238	0	79,562
Georgia	2,494,263	401,204	235,427	1,182,831	23,877	126,363	7,070	217,903	231,317	68,270
Hawaii	628,043	51,201	96,272	400,133	805	13,975	1,580	51,553	0	12,525
Idaho	456,107	75,347	42,389	208,662	9,556	28,052	8,931	51,482	0	31,689
Illinois	4,100,967	744,287	408,123	1,428,289	395,718	126,132	4,286	424,531	247,440	322,160
Indiana	3,009,908	633,318	230,338	990,283	3,361	120,609	9,149	492,688	348,540	181,624
Iowa	2,014,244	292,465	282,191	624,926	26,274	62,873	1,362	193,411	396,835	133,906
Kansas	1,469,872	249,485	137,299	510,409	114,791	32,329	32,100	124,624	183,014	85,821
Kentucky	1,656,119	288,258	126,789	691,122	7,658	28,520	5,309	137,165	229,556	141,743
Louisiana	1,844,187	354,362	109,635	654,322	4,921	47,689	1,342	205,454	274,383	192,079
Maine	398,639	93,104	38,512	176,310	105	13,536	2,151	52,445	0	22,476
Maryland	1,984,038	500,885	232,967	732,941	124,672	77,459	3,453	228,509	0	83,152
Massachusetts	1,491,921	476,225	133,474	601,965	4,622	49,886	1,437	160,165	6,921	57,225
Michigan	5,529,883	1,271,950	547,232	1,497,147	228,446	250,279	27,213	769,203	679,763	258,650
Minnesota	2,494,341	437,237	268,831	905,202	27,232	189,788	11,065	221,159	303,480	130,347
Mississippi	1,215,602	209,811	155,880	439,750	31,046	33,492	867	155,630	140,593	48,532
Missouri	1,805,266	411,254	112,346	614,613	64,336	62,301	10,253	175,447	220,545	134,173
Montana	362,905	71,591	64,366	130,490	5,497	12,208	312	51,737	0	26,704
Nebraska	1,033,731	136,898	83,063	366,341	52,726	52,389	2,796	109,703	191,820	37,996
Nevada	412,884	65,470	49,955	202,052	6,154	23,239	1,223	35,747	0	29,043
New Hampshire	373,498	148,366	38,582	81,998	2,006	18,379	1,717	69,869	0	12,581
New Jersey	2,920,767	602,689	181,856	1,125,800	163,761	89,946	11,668	226,609	373,822	144,616
New Mexico	1,190,519	109,788	210,991	386,814	43,131	62,178	12,737	82,049	218,631	64,202
New York	6,574,152	1,333,795	448,010	2,738,816	417,399	252,651	15,747	379,235	829,597	158,901
North Carolina	3,299,213	376,510	379,945	1,617,885	76,314	154,558	15,603	532,251	0	146,146
North Dakota	431,381	83,589	67,408	136,448	22	18,054	1,539	76,300	12,263	35,756
Ohio	4,895,812	1,274,358	337,922	1,411,337	91,256	192,273	38,321	449,627	896,400	204,320
Oklahoma	1,257,552	199,815	186,065	563,195	15,263	42,492	2,075	200,092	0	48,555
Oregon	1,687,205	280,576	239,159	447,540	120,234	74,423	5,270	160,136	281,470	78,398
Pennsylvania	4,423,633	1,295,220	470,654	1,112,965	82,127	180,238	35,330	445,913	623,567	177,618
Rhode Island	329,277	108,895	41,383	116,257	0	5,892	0	45,347	0	11,502
South Carolina	1,924,747	333,680	151,768	597,477	24,254	80,917	2,536	175,457	496,328	62,331
South Dakota	260,907	61,659	36,279	104,824	1,162	7,915	318	29,002	0	19,748
Tennessee	1,961,312	306,436	178,713	802,243	13,625	87,499	14,193	167,916	311,542	79,145
Texas	7,688,388	1,087,047	783,742	3,362,792	317,947	340,517	139,191	545,820	271,289	840,043
Utah	1,307,681	171,251	171,852	380,812	21,081	36,802	9,296	106,146	240,334	170,105
Vermont	316,905	137,912	39,812	46,882	13	23,863	3,533	36,622	0	28,268
Virginia	3,323,028	709,490	287,967	871,285	14,253	154,498	28,618	447,955	749,019	59,944
Washington	2,744,035	452,847	453,159	1,005,332	15,216	129,010	11,306	319,102	228,172	129,892
West Virginia	666,268	164,577	62,620	314,469	1,465	20,548	0	82,084	0	20,506
Wisconsin	2,954,564	501,808	362,833	948,082	252,331	149,641	8,763	213,932	287,705	229,469
Wyoming	278,270	36,821	37,159	124,785	13,899	15,259	2,425	38,841	0	9,080
U.S. Service Schools	1,245,921	572	1,100,474	0	0	6,693	0	63,284	74,900	0
Outlying areas	589,470	68,487	305,741	154,796	20,036	10,295	679	13,283	0	16,153
American Samoa	4,610	78	2,024	2,509	0	0	0	0	0	0
Federated States of Micronesia	3,932	1,441	336	18	1,361	50	0	533	0	194
Guam	68,198	6,002	5,374	38,858	11,469	1,316	464	3,016	0	1,699
Marshall Islands	2,176	698	935	419	0	11	12	89	0	11
Northern Marianas	3,511	1,276	298	16	1,206	50	0	472	0	194
Palau	4,762	998	2,342	697	0	0	0	597	0	128
Puerto Rico	468,739	54,322	290,572	95,191	2,483	6,788	0	5,733	0	13,650
Virgin Islands	33,542	3,672	3,861	17,087	3,518	2,080	202	2,844	0	277

[1] Preliminary data.
[2] Includes independent operations (federally funded research and development centers).

SOURCE: U.S. Department of Education, National Center for Education Statistics, Integrated Postsecondary Education Data System (IPEDS), "Finance" survey. (This table was prepared April 1996.)

NOTE.—Because of rounding, details may not add to totals.

Table 328.—Current-fund revenue of public institutions of higher education, by source of funds and state: 1992–93

[In thousands of dollars]

State	Total	Tuition and fees	Federal appropriations, grants, and contracts[1]	State appropriations, grants, and contracts	Local appropriations, grants, and contracts	Private gifts, grants, and contracts	Endowment income	Auxiliary enterprises	Hospitals	Educational activities and other
1	2	3	4	5	6	7	8	9	10	11
United States	$108,186,484	$19,490,221	$11,655,011	$39,789,641	$4,040,897	$4,330,112	$667,711	$10,255,044	$11,791,033	$6,166,815
Alabama	2,521,938	364,208	268,543	772,713	10,002	107,008	17,486	181,805	706,423	93,751
Alaska	323,740	37,986	51,315	178,497	1,507	8,326	2,618	18,976	0	24,514
Arizona	1,677,711	347,776	221,936	596,087	173,105	86,518	9,071	190,599	0	52,621
Arkansas	995,482	140,941	71,910	404,957	623	31,953	1,330	90,232	209,169	44,367
California	14,262,239	1,608,616	1,312,300	5,914,065	1,114,074	407,246	90,849	901,061	1,782,484	1,131,545
Colorado	1,714,698	482,504	299,613	476,829	26,995	80,960	8,913	212,062	34,863	91,959
Connecticut	976,380	204,407	70,248	348,823	556	37,220	491	101,017	168,589	45,029
Delaware	446,768	147,230	45,249	130,215	3,867	18,774	21,445	56,700	0	23,289
District of Columbia	118,865	28,859	7,228	0	76,258	308	1,283	603	0	4,327
Florida	3,202,499	592,468	292,452	1,699,701	14,743	189,874	40,253	292,430	0	80,579
Georgia	2,268,331	361,389	228,337	1,030,941	24,620	124,694	4,462	202,427	226,927	64,535
Hawaii	594,752	48,659	92,094	378,384	601	13,503	1,429	49,037	0	11,045
Idaho	416,359	65,232	38,808	197,411	7,794	23,968	8,222	44,483	0	30,441
Illinois	3,924,599	712,345	358,133	1,386,402	379,410	138,448	3,299	407,848	238,786	299,928
Indiana	2,882,592	596,565	218,820	968,430	6,494	137,563	9,197	449,794	341,524	154,206
Iowa	1,930,399	279,291	254,716	590,852	24,503	68,557	1,896	195,320	397,540	117,723
Kansas	1,350,052	231,801	121,960	476,753	105,539	28,060	30,706	118,810	161,835	74,588
Kentucky	1,576,644	261,195	112,124	670,197	7,147	33,926	6,116	131,332	215,173	139,434
Louisiana	1,821,190	319,550	105,079	650,344	2,433	45,836	1,002	197,296	316,185	183,464
Maine	384,730	89,324	33,870	174,502	264	11,598	1,782	52,185	0	21,204
Maryland	1,913,029	468,210	217,724	728,205	113,876	68,669	4,021	233,620	0	78,703
Massachusetts	1,639,854	452,851	135,629	547,420	2,802	51,690	935	140,277	177,105	131,144
Michigan	5,329,224	1,196,982	518,493	1,487,865	197,739	256,593	25,597	771,221	639,010	235,724
Minnesota	2,363,483	404,287	249,881	856,739	9,067	161,832	16,693	204,218	300,179	160,586
Mississippi	1,150,201	203,263	140,205	410,776	30,714	34,923	956	148,437	134,582	46,347
Missouri	1,698,594	386,254	106,934	587,986	61,235	57,598	10,640	168,246	188,077	131,624
Montana	349,102	61,148	56,923	128,445	4,010	9,930	311	64,448	0	23,887
Nebraska	989,156	130,924	78,803	353,186	48,226	50,262	2,873	103,262	187,780	33,840
Nevada	392,258	63,352	50,367	192,460	4,740	22,325	1,393	30,997	0	26,626
New Hampshire	348,839	137,307	37,237	77,595	1,953	14,538	1,794	63,623	0	14,793
New Jersey	2,745,100	567,701	157,525	1,058,237	162,968	90,639	9,769	214,193	358,699	125,369
New Mexico	1,125,366	100,406	217,114	368,785	49,393	58,299	12,954	81,072	176,676	60,667
New York	6,117,555	1,299,154	417,160	2,616,728	387,273	226,438	15,410	359,980	656,593	138,819
North Carolina	3,113,193	350,968	348,575	1,524,786	76,406	152,130	12,222	408,522	0	239,584
North Dakota	431,464	79,459	63,377	151,143	206	17,851	2,023	71,468	11,814	34,122
Ohio	4,628,902	1,222,095	330,888	1,319,208	85,735	182,860	33,532	423,491	835,094	195,999
Oklahoma	1,209,863	183,950	161,067	583,977	14,559	34,727	1,461	192,235	0	37,888
Oregon	1,615,882	249,909	213,499	484,275	128,251	70,106	6,632	146,914	263,063	53,232
Pennsylvania	4,262,533	1,246,946	447,056	1,064,949	75,094	172,137	32,934	449,398	593,632	180,388
Rhode Island	325,003	108,328	39,983	117,062	0	5,902	0	43,184	0	10,544
South Carolina	1,733,468	305,566	138,497	595,843	22,550	71,868	2,147	171,629	372,704	52,665
South Dakota	241,536	56,751	36,104	97,242	22	6,232	16	27,469	0	17,701
Tennessee	1,839,384	290,606	170,501	741,326	11,899	80,643	15,302	158,710	298,253	72,145
Texas	7,126,068	1,009,538	736,402	3,118,048	281,364	328,240	132,436	511,731	240,280	768,030
Utah	1,224,127	154,464	171,830	363,909	21,238	32,778	8,509	99,863	223,361	148,175
Vermont	305,477	132,773	37,559	46,439	78	22,721	3,711	36,338	0	25,857
Virginia	3,176,437	649,903	269,765	836,957	12,796	145,689	28,854	423,486	749,682	59,306
Washington	2,539,934	385,943	433,598	976,065	8,504	123,661	8,788	227,848	240,084	135,442
West Virginia	631,619	154,432	59,574	294,996	1,392	19,258	141	80,510	0	21,316
Wisconsin	2,775,635	480,399	336,220	888,921	233,042	141,567	10,561	201,062	274,329	209,533
Wyoming	270,515	35,419	33,760	123,967	13,234	16,826	3,250	35,850	0	8,209
U.S. Service Schools	1,183,716	584	1,038,028	0	0	6,840	0	67,725	70,539	0
Outlying areas	704,076	65,010	89,042	468,882	22,641	8,121	725	12,066	1,915	35,673
American Samoa	4,428	75	1,944	2,410	0	0	0	0	0	0
Federated States of Micronesia	3,453	1,890	0	0	969	0	0	367	0	227
Guam	74,928	5,358	6,861	41,584	15,366	1,036	519	2,856	0	1,348
Marshall Islands	1,111	695	119	156	0	23	0	113	0	5
Northern Marianas	2,462	1,310	0	0	671	0	0	254	0	227
Palau	5,133	961	2,470	885	0	0	0	726	0	91
Puerto Rico	581,128	51,242	73,969	406,760	2,159	6,321	0	5,344	1,915	33,417
Virgin Islands	31,432	3,480	3,680	17,087	3,475	740	206	2,405	0	359

[1] Includes independent operations (federally funded research and development centers).

NOTE.—Because of rounding, details may not add to totals.

SOURCE: U.S. Department of Education, National Center for Education Statistics, Integrated Postsecondary Education Data System (IPEDS), "Finance" survey. (This table was prepared April 1996.)

Table 329.—Current-fund revenue from state and local governments of institutions of higher education, by state: 1985–86 to 1993–94

[In thousands]

State	Current-fund revenue from state and local governments					Current-fund revenue from state and local governments, 1993–94 [1]					
	1985–86	1989–90	1990–91	1991–92	1992–93	Total	State appropriations for public institutions	Local appropriations for public institutions	State and local appropriations for private institutions	State and local grants and contracts for public institutions	State and local grants and contracts for private institutions
1	2	3	4	5	6	7	8	9	10	11	12
United States [2]	$32,456,006	$41,989,141	$43,412,081	$44,746,783	$45,692,830	$46,908,594	$37,565,065	$4,021,421	$261,195	$3,458,511	$1,602,402
Alabama	656,823	727,543	758,900	762,004	791,758	849,967	793,597	4,464	5,142	42,988	3,777
Alaska	159,781	167,360	175,938	181,358	180,110	186,305	175,337	616	0	10,331	23
Arizona	539,054	714,195	768,654	779,292	769,328	817,274	608,640	178,478	0	30,018	138
Arkansas	266,898	326,399	332,367	371,131	407,115	415,536	377,115	2,513	1	34,382	1,526
California	4,943,659	6,425,599	6,628,037	7,127,388	7,072,896	6,411,115	4,496,412	1,253,614	5	612,982	48,101
Colorado	391,468	474,849	510,649	508,624	508,586	521,088	445,496	24,613	0	46,077	4,903
Connecticut	280,012	400,074	406,306	390,250	379,720	411,711	359,722	0	1,600	22,727	27,662
Delaware	88,661	119,602	124,881	142,638	134,355	140,191	128,382	804	0	10,766	239
District of Columbia	71,761	83,756	84,471	83,808	79,935	77,727	0	66,449	0	7,173	4,104
Florida	1,172,112	1,824,902	1,863,133	1,793,785	1,808,015	1,942,724	1,692,248	4,677	13,754	139,999	92,047
Georgia	689,379	920,901	1,001,889	977,304	1,077,918	1,242,527	1,112,771	18,262	11,651	75,675	24,168
Hawaii	195,375	268,859	321,195	381,118	379,025	400,980	383,957	0	0	16,982	42
Idaho	125,338	167,155	193,188	206,819	205,370	218,399	196,847	9,487	0	11,885	181
Illinois	1,405,622	1,783,123	1,855,023	1,821,597	1,865,744	1,931,481	1,290,028	383,470	18,528	150,509	88,945
Indiana	645,880	914,108	984,176	999,381	1,002,215	1,019,058	933,408	2,290	0	57,945	25,415
Iowa	431,840	545,959	599,407	613,147	635,838	673,738	596,617	25,012	0	29,571	22,538
Kansas	422,278	546,565	556,372	571,270	587,290	630,158	478,847	106,172	0	40,182	4,957
Kentucky	483,027	595,727	665,808	707,859	684,648	705,050	651,533	5,785	0	41,460	6,271
Louisiana	562,205	563,543	634,541	670,183	676,781	683,174	572,390	2,524	2,712	84,329	21,219
Maine	103,724	178,358	189,099	171,887	176,327	178,079	160,727	0	0	15,687	1,664
Maryland	631,471	890,011	943,620	823,075	876,755	898,788	668,941	121,435	27,589	67,236	13,586
Massachusetts	589,876	758,239	545,606	507,248	580,056	639,251	554,484	48	4,775	52,056	27,888
Michigan	1,215,291	1,555,997	1,589,630	1,764,129	1,730,143	1,769,771	1,424,502	215,314	558	85,776	43,620
Minnesota	533,573	760,863	818,117	871,048	893,456	956,836	848,665	21,867	67	61,902	24,335
Mississippi	362,517	421,069	419,177	401,458	441,825	471,136	409,154	28,386	0	33,256	340
Missouri	506,246	636,322	651,819	613,905	655,962	685,610	579,585	63,394	0	35,968	6,662
Montana	97,672	109,282	119,813	139,753	133,037	136,263	124,228	4,019	0	7,739	277
Nebraska	248,544	336,087	374,112	387,688	402,829	419,798	351,988	46,895	0	20,184	731
Nevada	99,841	156,966	173,580	191,292	197,213	208,216	185,186	0	0	23,020	10
New Hampshire	52,393	72,201	79,979	80,343	85,033	90,950	75,189	0	0	8,815	6,946
New Jersey	837,214	1,218,368	1,190,657	1,280,172	1,285,916	1,359,960	986,616	155,788	13,667	147,157	56,731
New Mexico	221,094	362,937	413,558	437,925	419,182	431,098	358,189	38,860	0	32,896	1,153
New York	2,726,150	3,413,434	3,421,222	3,578,508	3,675,680	3,893,354	2,379,089	346,962	42,063	430,165	695,076
North Carolina	1,074,960	1,561,133	1,633,096	1,703,504	1,810,371	1,746,867	1,570,743	73,799	0	49,658	52,668
North Dakota	118,691	130,672	133,796	140,149	151,668	136,744	130,183	9	0	6,279	274
Ohio	1,132,678	1,457,509	1,541,996	1,490,804	1,448,082	1,553,389	1,323,256	81,755	6,308	97,581	44,489
Oklahoma	437,693	485,273	535,024	590,597	601,040	580,522	504,877	14,771	1	58,810	2,063
Oregon	394,899	509,225	544,631	580,442	616,623	571,448	405,006	108,930	0	53,838	3,674
Pennsylvania	961,089	1,259,717	1,276,665	1,334,311	1,298,755	1,379,619	1,028,622	75,014	65,412	91,456	119,115
Rhode Island	107,265	136,654	123,502	116,197	118,844	117,735	109,983	0	1	6,274	1,477
South Carolina	491,802	601,516	618,304	601,894	627,013	631,482	581,835	21,972	0	17,923	9,751
South Dakota	65,151	81,315	86,262	93,150	97,575	106,452	98,378	0	1	7,607	466
Tennessee	528,933	712,775	711,103	681,944	763,246	824,936	765,915	1,935	0	48,018	9,068
Texas	2,521,860	3,051,747	3,069,099	3,315,755	3,496,729	3,783,870	3,188,001	249,579	31,442	243,159	71,688
Utah	256,997	322,123	346,711	369,253	385,953	402,523	361,814	0	0	40,079	630
Vermont	35,334	46,061	48,485	49,405	49,418	49,586	40,881	13	0	6,001	2,691
Virginia	775,474	995,573	961,845	887,077	873,539	914,056	807,866	998	10,345	76,674	18,173
Washington	620,383	817,265	915,462	922,706	985,218	1,023,612	894,859	0	2,275	125,688	790
West Virginia	222,693	263,157	280,199	293,370	297,177	316,565	291,886	615	0	23,433	631
Wisconsin	825,610	986,035	1,053,246	1,094,481	1,134,317	1,213,191	938,775	246,471	3,297	15,167	9,481
Wyoming	127,714	131,040	137,727	144,360	137,201	138,684	122,297	13,363	0	3,024	0

[1] Preliminary data.
[2] Excludes U.S. Service Schools.

NOTE.—Because of rounding, details may not add to totals.

SOURCE: U.S. Department of Education, National Center for Education Statistics, "Financial Statistics of Institutions of Higher Education" surveys; and Integrated Postsecondary Education Data System (IPEDS), "Finance" surveys. (This table was prepared April 1996.)

Table 330.—Current-fund revenue received from the federal government by the 120 institutions of higher education receiving the largest amounts: 1993–94

[In thousands]

Institution	Rank order	Current-fund revenue from the federal government [1]	Institution	Rank order	Current-fund revenue from the federal government [1]
1	2	3	1	2	3
United States (all institutions)	—	**$22,076,385**			
120 institutions receiving the largest amounts	—	16,643,136			
California Institute of Technology	1	1,166,994	Boston University (MA)	61	92,592
Johns Hopkins University (MD)	2	[2] 782,091	University of Utah	62	91,367
University of Chicago (IL)	3	734,186	University of Maryland, College Park Campus	63	91,307
Massachusetts Institute of Technology	4	607,550	University of Colorado, Health Sciences	64	90,452
Stanford University (CA)	5	448,599	Oregon State University	65	88,747
University of Washington	6	345,817	University of Hawaii at Manoa	66	85,912
University of Michigan, Ann Arbor	7	306,682	University of Oklahoma, Health Sciences Center	67	83,459
University of Wisconsin, Madison	8	284,356	North Carolina State University at Raleigh	68	82,939
United States Military Academy (NY)	9	278,256	University of Tennessee, Knoxville	69	79,234
University of Miami (FL)	10	257,895	University of Georgia	70	78,920
United States Air Force Academy (CO)	11	251,860	U. of Texas, Southwestern Medical Center, Dallas	71	78,705
University of Southern California	12	250,823	Yeshiva University (NY)	72	76,326
University of California, San Diego	13	[3] 248,441	Colorado State University	73	74,300
Cornell University Medical Center (NY)	14	241,113	State University of New York at Stony Brook	74	[3] 72,736
University of California, Los Angeles	15	[3] 236,552	New Mexico State University, Main Campus	75	[2] 72,106
Columbia University in the City of New York	16	236,309	University of California, Irvine	76	[3] 71,562
Harvard University (MA)	17	233,424	University of Kentucky	77	71,013
University of Pennsylvania	18	223,429	Cornell University, Statutory Colleges (NY)	78	[3] 69,184
University of California, San Francisco	19	[3] 219,050	University of Cincinnati, Main Campus (OH)	79	68,768
University of Minnesota, Twin Cities	20	218,602	Wake Forest University (NC)	80	68,075
United States Naval Academy (MD)	21	212,291	Virginia Polytechnic Institute and State University	81	67,341
Georgetown University (DC)	22	207,724	Mount Sinai School of Medicine (NY)	82	64,775
Yale University (CT)	23	197,402	U. of Maryland, Baltimore Professional Schools	83	63,617
University of Illinois at Urbana	24	187,803	Utah State University	84	63,518
University of North Carolina, Chapel Hill	25	187,308	Washington State University	85	61,617
Howard University (DC)	26	[4] 187,141	State University of New York at Buffalo	86	[3] 61,168
University of Arizona	27	181,041	U. of Texas, Health Science Center, San Antonio	87	60,684
University of Pittsburgh, Main Campus (PA)	28	178,485	Virginia Commonwealth University	88	60,364
Duke University (NC)	29	175,476	Wayne State University (MI)	89	59,953
University of California, Berkeley	30	[3] 173,642	University of California, Santa Barbara	90	[3] 59,549
Pennsylvania State University, Main Campus	31	173,628	Tulane University of Louisiana	91	58,670
Princeton University (NJ)	32	171,910	Indiana University-Purdue University at Indianapolis	92	57,415
University of Texas at Austin	33	[2] 168,016	Gallaudet University (DC)	93	57,390
Washington University (MO)	34	155,199	Oregon Health Science University	94	55,830
Ohio State University, Main Campus	35	146,322	Mississippi State University	95	54,069
University of Iowa	36	128,192	Tufts University (MA)	96	53,676
Carnegie Mellon University (PA)	37	127,412	University of Medicine and Dentistry of New Jersey	97	53,613
Cornell University, Endowed Colleges (NY)	38	124,760	Indiana University, Bloomington	98	53,249
Iowa State University	39	118,681	Air Force Institute of Technology (OH)	99	[4] 52,828
University of Rochester (NY)	40	118,459	University of Texas Health Science Center	100	51,622
University of Alabama at Birmingham	41	117,655	Clark Atlanta University (GA)	101	51,533
Vanderbilt University (TN)	42	116,404	City University of New York System Office	102	50,764
University of Colorado at Boulder	43	114,764	West Virginia University	103	49,237
University of California, Davis	44	[3] 109,115	University of Massachusetts, Amherst	104	49,144
New York University	45	108,600	Florida State University	105	49,073
Case Western Reserve University (OH)	46	108,010	Dartmouth College (NH)	106	48,222
Baylor College of Medicine (TX)	47	107,302	Rochester Institute of Technology (NY)	107	48,175
Michigan State University	48	106,848	Thomas Jefferson University (PA)	108	47,821
Naval Postgraduate School (CA)	49	106,147	University of Alaska, Fairbanks	109	47,773
University of Florida	50	105,619	University of Nebraska at Lincoln	110	46,205
Texas A & M University	51	101,641	Brown University (RI)	111	45,810
Georgia Institute of Technology, Main Campus	52	101,161	Arizona State University, Main Campus	112	45,367
Northwestern University (IL)	53	100,068	University of Missouri, Columbia	113	44,530
Uniformed Services U. of the Health Sciences (MD)	54	99,701	California State University, Northridge	114	42,935
Purdue University, Main Campus (IN)	55	99,472	University of Dayton (OH)	115	42,908
University of Virginia, Main Campus	56	97,820	State University of New York at Albany	116	[3] 42,826
Emory University (GA)	57	95,937	University of South Carolina at Columbia	117	41,853
University of New Mexico, Main Campus	58	[2] 93,803	United States Coast Guard Academy (CT)	118	41,788
Rutgers University, Central Office (NJ)	59	[2] 93,509	Rockefeller University (NY)	119	40,008
University of Illinois at Chicago	60	[3] 92,687	Oklahoma State University, Main Campus	120	39,327

[1] Includes federal appropriations, unrestricted and restricted federal contracts and grants, and revenue for independent operations. Independent operations generally include only the revenues associated with major federally funded research and development centers. Excludes Pell Grants. Federally supported student aid that is received through students is excluded.

[2] Includes some funds from other branch campuses.

[3] Some funds included with other branch campus reports.

[4] NCES estimate based on prior years' data.

—Not applicable.

SOURCE: U.S. Department of Education, National Center for Education Statistics, Integrated Postsecondary Education Data System (IPEDS), "Finance, 1993–94" survey. (This table was prepared April 1996.)

Table 331.—Current-fund expenditures and expenditures per full-time-equivalent student in institutions of higher education, by type and control of institution: 1970–71 to 1993–94

Control of institution and year	All institutions			4-year institutions			2-year institutions		
	Current-fund expenditures, in millions		Current-fund expenditures per student, in constant 1993–94 dollars[1]	Current-fund expenditures, in millions		Current-fund expenditures per student, in constant 1993–94 dollars[1]	Current-fund expenditures, in millions		Current-fund expenditures per student, in constant 1993–94 dollars[1]
	Unadjusted dollars	Constant 1993–94 dollars[1]		Unadjusted dollars	Constant 1993–94 dollars[1]		Unadjusted dollars	Constant 1993–94 dollars[1]	
1	2	3	4	5	6	7	8	9	10
All institutions									
1970–71	$23,375	$91,703	$13,610	$21,049	$82,575	$16,048	$2,327	$9,128	$5,732
1975–76	38,903	109,655	12,931	33,811	95,302	16,152	5,092	14,352	5,565
1976–77	42,600	112,679	13,555	37,052	98,004	16,758	5,548	14,675	5,955
1977–78	45,971	114,019	13,549	39,899	98,958	16,673	6,072	15,061	6,072
1978–79	50,721	117,247	14,044	44,163	102,088	17,209	6,558	15,159	6,274
1979–80	56,914	119,849	14,121	49,661	104,576	17,383	7,253	15,273	6,180
1980–81	64,053	121,693	13,799	55,840	106,090	17,219	8,212	15,603	5,871
1981–82	70,339	122,121	13,547	61,333	106,485	17,038	9,006	15,636	5,656
1982–83	75,936	123,927	13,631	66,238	108,101	17,299	9,697	15,826	5,567
1983–84	81,993	127,684	13,930	71,680	111,624	17,647	10,314	16,061	5,653
1984–85	89,951	132,611	14,814	78,744	116,089	18,448	11,207	16,523	6,214
1985–86	97,536	136,987	15,317	85,560	120,167	19,091	11,976	16,819	6,349
1986–87	105,764	143,004	15,777	92,985	125,726	19,767	12,779	17,279	6,390
1987–88	113,786	147,381	15,968	100,143	129,709	19,997	13,644	17,672	6,442
1988–89	123,867	152,452	16,108	109,141	134,327	20,157	14,726	18,125	6,473
1989–90	134,656	156,189	15,969	118,578	137,541	20,186	16,077	18,648	6,285
1990–91	146,088	160,983	16,125	128,594	141,705	20,337	17,494	19,277	6,393
1991–92	156,189	166,384	16,059	137,375	146,342	20,666	18,814	20,042	6,112
1992–93	165,241	170,787	16,364	145,300	150,177	21,065	19,941	20,611	6,232
1993–94[2]	173,351	173,351	16,747	152,164	152,164	21,369	21,187	21,187	6,558
Public institutions									
1970–71	14,996	58,831	11,877	12,899	50,603	14,589	2,097	8,227	5,542
1975–76	26,184	73,803	11,316	21,392	60,296	14,864	4,792	13,507	5,478
1976–77	28,635	75,741	11,928	23,411	61,923	15,487	5,224	13,818	5,876
1977–78	30,725	76,206	11,914	25,013	62,039	15,360	5,712	14,167	6,010
1978–79	33,733	77,977	12,418	27,600	63,801	15,966	6,132	14,176	6,209
1979–80	37,768	79,532	12,441	30,979	65,235	16,071	6,789	14,297	6,127
1980–81	42,280	80,327	12,093	34,677	65,883	15,844	7,602	14,444	5,815
1981–82	46,219	80,244	11,833	37,890	65,783	15,631	8,330	14,462	5,621
1982–83	49,573	80,903	11,810	40,616	66,285	15,705	8,957	14,618	5,558
1983–84	53,087	82,669	12,013	43,588	67,877	15,912	9,499	14,792	5,655
1984–85	58,315	85,971	12,861	48,017	70,789	16,704	10,298	15,181	6,205
1985–86	63,194	88,754	13,311	52,184	73,291	17,287	11,010	15,463	6,368
1986–87	67,654	91,476	13,496	56,003	75,722	17,628	11,651	15,754	6,346
1987–88	72,641	94,088	13,562	60,137	77,891	17,720	12,505	16,196	6,372
1988–89	78,946	97,164	13,691	65,349	80,429	17,850	13,597	16,734	6,458
1989–90	85,771	99,486	13,496	70,865	82,197	17,792	14,906	17,289	6,283
1990–91	92,961	102,439	13,554	76,722	84,544	17,836	16,239	17,895	6,350
1991–92	98,847	105,299	13,392	81,334	86,643	18,067	17,513	18,656	6,083
1992–93	104,570	108,080	13,661	86,065	88,954	18,540	18,505	19,126	6,142
1993–94[2]	109,310	109,310	13,992	89,697	89,697	18,820	19,612	19,612	6,438
Private institutions									
1970–71	8,379	32,872	18,419	8,150	31,972	19,067	230	901	8,352
1975–76	12,719	35,851	18,316	12,419	35,006	18,985	300	845	7,449
1976–77	13,965	36,938	18,821	13,641	36,081	19,508	324	857	7,585
1977–78	15,246	37,813	18,730	14,885	36,920	19,472	360	893	7,272
1978–79	16,988	39,270	18,978	16,563	38,286	19,774	425	984	7,392
1979–80	19,146	40,317	19,247	18,682	39,340	20,105	464	977	7,081
1980–81	21,773	41,366	19,004	21,163	40,207	20,073	610	1,159	6,676
1981–82	24,120	41,877	18,752	23,444	40,703	19,939	676	1,174	6,120
1982–83	26,363	43,024	19,198	25,623	41,816	20,617	740	1,208	5,677
1983–84	28,907	45,015	19,701	28,092	43,746	21,242	815	1,269	5,627
1984–85	31,637	46,641	20,573	30,727	45,299	22,045	910	1,341	6,320
1985–86	34,342	48,232	21,195	33,376	46,876	22,814	966	1,357	6,141
1986–87	38,110	51,529	22,540	36,982	50,004	24,217	1,128	1,525	6,891
1987–88	41,145	53,293	23,251	40,006	51,817	24,784	1,139	1,476	7,331
1988–89	44,922	55,288	23,354	43,792	53,898	24,972	1,130	1,390	6,652
1989–90	48,885	56,702	23,535	47,713	55,344	25,228	1,172	1,359	6,305
1990–91	53,127	58,543	24,137	51,872	57,161	25,656	1,255	1,382	7,000
1991–92	57,342	61,085	24,456	56,041	59,699	26,118	1,301	1,386	6,537
1992–93	60,671	62,707	24,834	59,235	61,223	26,259	1,436	1,484	7,666
1993–94[2]	64,041	64,041	25,223	62,466	62,466	26,526	1,575	1,575	8,554

[1] Dollars adjusted by the Higher Education Price Index.
[2] Preliminary data.

NOTE.—Because of rounding, details may not add to totals.

SOURCE: U.S. Department of Education, National Center for Education Statistics, "Financial Statistics of Institutions of Higher Education" and "Fall Enrollment in Colleges and Universities" surveys; and Integrated Postsecondary Education Data System (IPEDS), "Fall Enrollment" and "Finance" surveys. (This table was prepared April 1996.)

Table 332.—Current-fund expenditures and educational and general expenditures of institutions of higher education, by purpose and per student: 1929–30 to 1993–94

[Columns 2 through 17 in thousands]

| Year | Current-fund expenditures | Educational and general expenditures | | | | | | | |
		Total	Administration and general expense	Instruction and departmental research	Organized research	Libraries	Plant operation and maintenance	Organized activities related to instructional departments	Other sponsored programs [1]
1	2	3	4	5	6	7	8	9	10
1929–30	$507,142	$377,903	$42,633	$221,598	[5] $18,007	$9,622	$61,061	(6)	—
1931–32	536,523	420,633	47,232	232,645	[5] 21,978	11,379	56,797	[7] $21,297	—
1933–34	469,329	369,661	43,155	203,332	[5] 17,064	13,387	51,046	[7] 14,155	—
1935–36	541,391	419,883	48,069	225,143	[5] 22,091	15,531	56,802	[7] 20,241	—
1937–38	614,385	475,191	56,406	253,006	[5] 25,213	17,588	62,738	[7] 24,031	—
1939–40	674,688	521,990	62,827	280,248	[5] 27,266	19,487	69,612	[7] 27,225	—
1941–42	738,169	572,465	66,968	298,558	[5] 34,287	19,763	72,594	[7] 37,771	—
1943–44	974,118	753,846	69,668	334,189	[5] 58,456	20,452	81,201	[7] 48,415	[8] $97,044
1945–46	1,088,422	820,326	104,808	375,122	[5] 86,812	26,560	110,947	[7] 60,604	—
1947–48	1,883,269	1,391,594	171,829	657,945	[5] 159,090	44,208	201,996	[7] 85,346	—
1949–50	2,245,661	1,706,444	213,070	780,994	[5] 225,341	56,147	225,110	[7] 119,108	—
1951–52	2,471,008	1,960,481	233,844	823,117	[5] 317,928	60,612	240,446	[7] 147,854	—
1953–54	2,882,864	2,345,331	288,147	960,556	[5] 372,643	72,944	277,874	[7] 186,905	—
1955–56	3,499,463	2,861,858	355,207	1,140,655	[5] 500,793	85,563	324,229	[7] 222,007	—
1957–58	4,509,666	3,734,350	473,945	1,465,603	[5] 727,776	109,715	406,226	[7] 238,455	—
1959–60	5,601,376	4,685,258	583,224	1,793,320	[5] 1,022,353	135,384	469,943	[7] 294,255	—
1961–62	7,154,526	5,997,007	730,429	2,202,443	[5] 1,474,406	177,362	564,225	[7] 375,040	—
1963–64	9,177,677	7,725,433	957,512	2,801,707	[5] 1,973,383	236,718	686,054	[7] 458,507	—
1965–66	12,509,489	10,376,630	1,251,107	3,756,175	[5] 2,448,300	346,248	844,506	[7] 558,170	155,202
1966–67	14,230,341	10,724,974	1,445,074	4,356,413	1,565,102	415,903	969,275	591,848	350,950
1967–68	16,480,786	12,847,350	1,738,946	5,139,179	1,933,473	493,266	1,127,290	350,711	514,294
1968–69	18,481,583	14,718,140	2,277,585	5,941,972	2,034,074	571,572	1,337,903	535,269	668,483
1969–70	21,043,110	16,845,210	2,627,993	6,883,844	2,144,076	652,596	1,541,698	648,089	769,253
1970–71	23,375,197	18,714,642	2,983,911	7,804,410	2,209,338	716,212	1,730,664	693,011	890,507
1971–72	25,559,560	20,441,878	3,344,215	8,443,261	2,265,282	764,481	1,927,553	779,728	1,059,989
1972–73	27,955,624	22,400,379	3,713,068	9,243,641	2,394,261	840,727	2,141,162	791,290	1,284,085
1973–74	30,713,581	24,653,849	4,200,955	10,219,118	2,480,450	939,023	2,494,057	838,170	1,355,027
1974–75	35,057,563	27,547,620	4,495,391	11,797,823	3,132,132	1,001,868	2,786,768	1,253,824	—
1975–76	38,903,177	30,598,685	5,240,066	13,094,943	3,287,364	1,223,723	3,082,959	1,248,670	—
1976–77	42,599,816	33,151,681	5,590,669	14,031,145	3,600,067	1,250,314	3,436,705	1,544,646	—
1977–78	45,970,790	36,256,604	6,177,029	15,336,229	3,919,830	1,348,747	3,795,043	1,781,160	—
1978–79	50,720,984	39,833,116	6,832,004	16,662,820	4,447,760	1,426,614	4,178,574	2,044,386	—
1979–80	56,913,588	44,542,843	7,621,143	18,496,717	5,099,151	1,623,811	4,700,070	2,252,577	—
1980–81	64,052,938	50,073,805	8,681,513	20,733,166	5,657,719	1,759,784	5,350,310	2,513,502	—
1981–82	70,339,448	54,848,752	9,648,069	22,962,527	5,929,894	1,922,416	5,979,281	2,734,038	—
1982–83	75,935,749	58,929,218	10,412,233	24,673,293	6,265,280	2,039,671	6,391,596	3,047,220	—
1983–84	81,993,360	63,741,276	11,561,260	26,436,308	6,723,534	2,231,149	6,729,825	3,300,003	—
1984–85	89,951,263	70,061,324	12,765,452	28,777,183	7,551,892	2,361,793	7,345,482	3,712,460	—
1985–86	97,535,742	76,127,965	13,913,724	31,032,099	8,437,367	2,551,331	7,605,226	4,116,061	—
1986–87	105,763,557	82,955,555	15,060,576	33,711,146	9,352,309	2,441,184	7,819,032	5,134,267	—
1987–88	113,786,476	89,157,430	16,171,015	35,833,563	10,350,931	2,836,498	8,230,986	5,305,083	—
1988–89	123,867,184	96,803,377	17,309,956	38,812,690	11,432,170	3,009,870	8,739,895	5,894,409	—
1989–90	134,655,571	105,585,076	19,062,179	42,145,987	12,505,961	3,254,239	9,458,262	6,183,405	—
1990–91	146,087,836	114,139,901	20,751,966	45,496,117	13,444,040	3,343,892	10,062,581	6,706,881	—
1991–92	156,189,161	121,567,157	21,984,118	47,997,196	14,261,554	3,595,834	10,346,580	6,981,184	—
1992–93	165,241,040	128,977,968	23,414,977	50,340,914	15,291,309	3,684,852	10,783,727	7,388,118	—
1993–94 [10]	173,350,617	136,024,350	24,489,022	52,775,599	16,117,610	3,908,412	11,368,496	7,769,499	—

Table 332.—Current-fund expenditures and educational and general expenditures of institutions of higher education, by purpose and per student: 1929–30 to 1993–94—Continued

[Columns 2 through 17 in thousands]

Year	Educational and general expenditures			Auxiliary enterprises	Independent operations [2]	Hospitals	Other current expenditures	Educational and general expenditures per student in fall enrollment [3]	
	Extension and public service	Scholarships and fellowships	Other general expenditures					Current dollars	Constant 1993–94 dollars [4]
1	11	12	13	14	15	16	17	18	19
1929–30	$24,982	(6)	—	$3,127	(5)	(7)	$126,112	$343	$2,933
1931–32	24,066	(6)	$5,239	90,897	(5)	(7)	24,993	364	3,696
1933–34	20,020	(6)	7,502	78,730	(5)	(7)	20,938	350	3,868
1935–36	29,426	(6)	2,580	95,332	(5)	(7)	26,176	348	3,698
1937–38	34,189	(6)	2,020	115,620	(5)	(7)	23,574	352	3,590
1939–40	35,325	(6)	—	124,184	(5)	(7)	28,514	349	3,655
1941–42	42,525	(6)	—	137,328	(5)	(7)	28,375	408	3,824
1943–44	44,421	(6)	—	199,344	(5)	(7)	20,928	653	5,475
1945–46	55,473	(6)	—	242,028	(5)	(7)	26,068	489	3,921
1947–48	71,180	(6)	—	438,988	(5)	(7)	52,687	595	3,735
1949–50	86,674	(6)	—	476,401	(5)	(7)	62,816	698	4,309
1951–52	97,408	$39,272	—	477,672	(5)	(7)	32,855	933	5,189
1953–54	112,227	74,035	—	537,533	(5)	(7)	—	1,051	5,716
1955–56	137,914	95,490	—	637,605	(5)	(7)	—	1,079	5,867
1957–58	175,256	129,935	7,439	775,316	(5)	(7)	—	1,124	5,752
1959–60	205,595	172,050	9,134	916,117	(5)	(7)	—	1,287	6,405
1961–62	244,337	228,765	—	1,157,517	(5)	(7)	—	1,447	7,038
1963–64	297,350	300,370	13,832	1,452,244	(5)	(7)	—	1,616	7,663
1965–66	438,385	425,524	153,013	1,887,744	(5)	(7)	9 245,115	1,753	8,031
1966–67	226,566	583,390	220,453	2,060,130	$951,668	$253,790	9 239,780	1,678	7,456
1967–68	597,544	712,425	240,222	2,302,419	765,495	290,000	9 275,523	1,859	7,992
1968–69	536,527	814,755	—	2,539,183	697,317	526,943	—	1,959	8,031
1969–70	593,067	984,594	—	2,769,276	757,388	671,236	—	2,104	8,146
1970–71	588,390	1,098,198	—	2,988,407	829,596	842,552	—	2,181	8,028
1971–72	615,997	1,241,372	—	3,178,272	940,825	998,585	—	2,284	8,117
1972–73	669,735	1,322,411	—	3,337,789	1,033,746	1,183,709	—	2,431	8,303
1973–74	730,560	1,396,488	—	3,613,256	1,014,872	1,431,604	—	2,568	8,052
1974–75	1,097,788	1,449,542	532,485	4,073,590	1,085,590	2,350,763	—	2,694	7,607
1975–76	1,238,603	1,635,859	546,498	4,476,841	1,132,016	2,695,635	—	2,736	7,213
1976–77	1,343,404	1,770,214	584,515	4,858,328	1,434,738	3,155,069	—	3,010	7,500
1977–78	1,425,294	1,839,298	633,973	5,261,477	855,054	3,597,655	—	3,213	7,500
1978–79	1,593,097	1,944,599	703,262	5,749,974	1,007,119	4,130,775	—	3,538	7,551
1979–80	1,816,521	2,200,468	732,385	6,485,608	1,127,728	4,757,409	—	3,850	7,251
1980–81	2,057,770	2,504,525	815,516	7,288,089	1,257,934	5,433,111	—	4,139	6,987
1981–82	2,203,726	2,684,945	783,854	7,997,632	1,258,777	6,234,287	—	4,433	6,888
1982–83	2,320,478	2,922,897	856,548	8,614,316	1,406,126	6,986,089	—	4,742	7,065
1983–84	2,499,203	3,301,673	958,321	9,250,196	1,622,233	7,379,654	—	5,114	7,346
1984–85	2,861,095	3,670,355	1,015,613	10,012,248	1,867,550	8,010,141	—	5,723	7,912
1985–86	3,119,533	4,160,174	1,192,449	10,528,303	2,187,361	8,692,113	—	6,216	8,352
1986–87	3,448,453	4,776,100	1,212,488	11,037,333	2,597,655	9,173,014	—	6,635	8,721
1987–88	3,786,362	5,325,358	1,317,633	11,399,953	2,822,632	10,406,461	—	6,984	8,815
1988–89	4,227,323	5,918,666	1,458,397	12,280,063	2,958,962	11,824,782	—	7,415	8,946
1989–90	4,689,758	6,655,544	1,629,742	13,203,984	3,187,224	12,679,286	—	7,799	8,981
1990–91	5,076,177	7,551,184	1,707,063	14,272,247	3,349,824	14,325,865	—	8,259	9,018
1991–92	5,489,298	9,060,000	1,851,393	14,966,100	3,551,592	16,104,313	—	8,466	8,957
1992–93	5,935,095	10,148,373	1,990,603	15,561,508	3,651,891	17,049,672	—	8,903	9,133
1993–94 10	6,242,414	11,238,010	2,115,288	16,429,341	3,387,323	17,509,603	—	9,509	9,509

[1] Includes all separately budgeted programs, other than research, which are supported by sponsors outside the institution. Examples are training programs, workshops, and training and instructional institutes. For years not shown, most expenditures for these programs are included under "Extension and public service."

[2] Generally includes only those expenditures associated with federally funded research and development centers (FFRDCs).

[3] Data for 1929–30 to 1945–46 are based on school year enrollment.

[4] Data adjusted by the consumer price index computed on a school year basis.

[5] Expenditures for federally funded research and development centers are included under "Organized research."

[6] Included under "Other current expenditures."

[7] Expenditures for hospitals included under "Organized activities related to instructional departments."

[8] Expenditures were for federal contract courses.

[9] Includes current expenditures for physical plant assets. In later years, the educational and general expenditures for physical plant assets are included under "Other general expenditures."

[10] Preliminary data.

—Data not available.

NOTE.—The data in this table reflect limitations of data availability and comparability. Major changes in data collection forms in 1965–66 and 1974–75 cause significant data comparability problems among the three mostly consistent time periods, 1929–30 to 1963–64, 1965–66 to 1973–74, and 1974–75 to 1993–94. The largest problems affect Hospitals, Independent operations, Organized research, Other sponsored programs, Extension and public service, and Scholarships and fellowships.

SOURCE: U.S. Department of Education, National Center for Education Statistics, Biennial Survey of Education in the United States; Financial Statistics of Institutions of Higher Education; and Integrated Postsecondary Education Data System, "Finance" surveys. (This table was prepared April 1996.)

Table 333.—Expenditures of institutions of higher education, by purpose and by control and type of institution: 1993–94 [1]

Control and type of institution	Current-fund expenditures	Educational and general expenditures					
		Total	Instruction	Research	Public service	Academic support	
						Total	Libraries only
1	2	3	4	5	6	7	8

			In thousands				
Total	$173,350,617	$136,024,350	$52,775,599	$16,117,610	$6,242,414	$11,677,911	$3,908,412
Public	109,309,541	87,139,226	35,688,497	11,180,363	4,741,719	8,035,556	2,449,109
Research I universities [3]	40,881,271	29,784,336	10,101,605	7,501,237	2,230,129	2,859,360	800,826
Research II universities [3]	6,721,792	5,780,861	2,163,789	1,012,615	476,825	600,545	199,652
Doctoral universities	11,567,016	9,805,025	3,849,611	1,143,404	620,364	991,627	335,475
Master's	17,641,854	15,162,320	6,948,168	472,255	584,625	1,424,429	539,102
Baccalaureate	2,258,261	1,966,615	813,350	22,063	65,132	194,031	65,735
Associate of arts	19,549,440	18,282,508	9,034,177	29,287	430,540	1,504,680	423,085
Specialized institutions [4]							
Health and medicine	8,907,516	4,762,294	2,243,804	919,084	317,860	292,653	56,086
Engineering	200,530	180,729	71,532	21,416	3,524	14,888	5,451
Business	22,353	20,974	10,644	0	1,024	2,252	641
Fine arts	110,009	99,233	41,795	0	1,049	8,384	4,486
Other specialized	1,370,832	1,218,514	386,295	58,653	9,568	132,644	16,965
Tribal colleges [5]	78,667	75,815	23,728	349	1,079	10,063	1,604
4-year	15,861	15,515	4,424	76	174	2,988	185
2-year	62,806	60,300	19,304	273	904	7,075	1,419
Private	64,041,076	48,885,124	17,087,102	4,937,247	1,500,695	3,642,355	1,459,304
Research I universities [3]	24,530,372	16,513,169	6,136,064	3,602,163	535,122	1,136,518	485,288
Research II universities [3]	3,837,329	2,593,286	1,074,228	276,170	18,015	220,911	89,288
Doctoral universities	6,132,884	4,888,993	1,866,743	313,972	83,368	437,998	175,737
Master's	9,049,876	7,971,033	2,818,888	148,885	110,459	611,739	230,805
Baccalaureate	11,494,626	9,871,694	3,076,171	91,280	68,617	708,106	313,033
Associate of arts	1,563,756	1,410,017	420,362	970	3,276	120,700	28,277
Specialized institutions [4]							
Religion and theology	984,726	859,633	255,228	2,896	13,241	87,503	47,378
Health and medicine	4,117,591	2,622,661	722,631	464,693	645,469	117,392	31,296
Engineering	351,599	330,137	113,168	29,032	1,295	20,856	5,137
Business	855,947	769,793	222,978	165	2,371	80,737	15,810
Fine arts	646,220	595,176	211,248	377	6,490	43,981	10,881
Other specialized	455,989	439,774	164,686	6,603	9,763	54,110	26,112
Tribal colleges [5]	20,162	19,759	4,706	40	3,210	1,804	261
4-year	9,336	9,145	2,284	14	3,210	629	115
2-year	10,826	10,615	2,422	25	0	1,175	146

			Percentage distribution of current-fund expenditures				
Total	100.00	78.47	30.44	9.30	3.60	6.74	2.25
Public	100.00	79.72	32.65	10.23	4.34	7.35	2.24
Research I universities [3]	100.00	72.86	24.71	18.35	5.46	6.99	1.96
Research II universities [3]	100.00	86.00	32.19	15.06	7.09	8.93	2.97
Doctoral universities	100.00	84.77	33.28	9.89	5.36	8.57	2.90
Master's	100.00	85.95	39.38	2.68	3.31	8.07	3.06
Baccalaureate	100.00	87.09	36.02	0.98	2.88	8.59	2.91
Associate of arts	100.00	93.52	46.21	0.15	2.20	7.70	2.16
Specialized institutions [4]							
Health and medicine	100.00	53.46	25.19	10.32	3.57	3.29	0.63
Engineering	100.00	90.13	35.67	10.68	1.76	7.42	2.72
Business	100.00	93.83	47.62	0.00	4.58	10.07	2.87
Fine arts	100.00	90.21	37.99	0.00	0.95	7.62	4.08
Other specialized	100.00	88.89	28.18	4.28	0.70	9.68	1.24
Tribal colleges [5]	100.00	96.37	30.16	0.44	1.37	12.79	2.04
4-year	100.00	97.82	27.89	0.48	1.10	18.84	1.16
2-year	100.00	96.01	30.74	0.43	1.44	11.26	2.26
Private	100.00	76.33	26.68	7.71	2.34	5.69	2.28
Research I universities [3]	100.00	67.32	25.01	14.68	2.18	4.63	1.98
Research II universities [3]	100.00	67.58	27.99	7.20	0.47	5.76	2.33
Doctoral universities	100.00	79.72	30.44	5.12	1.36	7.14	2.87
Master's	100.00	88.08	31.15	1.65	1.22	6.76	2.55
Baccalaureate	100.00	85.88	26.76	0.79	0.60	6.16	2.72
Associate of arts	100.00	90.17	26.88	0.06	0.21	7.72	1.81
Specialized institutions [4]							
Religion and theology	100.00	87.30	25.92	0.29	1.34	8.89	4.81
Health and medicine	100.00	63.69	17.55	11.29	15.68	2.85	0.76
Engineering	100.00	93.90	32.19	8.26	0.37	5.93	1.46
Business	100.00	89.93	26.05	0.02	0.28	9.43	1.85
Fine arts	100.00	92.10	32.69	0.06	1.00	6.81	1.68
Other specialized	100.00	96.44	36.12	1.45	2.14	11.87	5.73
Tribal colleges [5]	100.00	98.00	23.34	0.20	15.92	8.95	1.30
4-year	100.00	97.95	24.47	0.15	34.38	6.74	1.24
2-year	100.00	98.05	22.37	0.24	0.00	10.85	1.35

Table 333.—Expenditures of institutions of higher education, by purpose and by control and type of institution: 1993–94 [1]—Continued

Control and type of institution	Educational and general expenditures					Auxiliary enterprises	Hospitals	Independent operations [2]
	Student services	Institutional support	Plant operation	Scholarships and fellowships	Mandatory transfers			
1	9	10	11	12	13	14	15	16

In thousands

Control and type of institution	Student services	Institutional support	Plant operation	Scholarships and fellowships	Mandatory transfers	Auxiliary enterprises	Hospitals	Independent operations
Total	$8,562,783	$15,926,239	$11,368,496	$11,238,010	$2,115,288	$16,429,341	$17,509,603	$3,387,323
Public	5,315,370	9,328,236	7,433,185	4,222,923	1,193,379	10,637,783	11,317,674	214,858
Research I universities [3]	1,015,080	1,930,702	2,018,622	1,606,738	520,864	4,176,227	6,829,039	91,669
Research II universities [3]	262,233	463,509	429,219	297,086	75,040	939,522	0	1,409
Doctoral universities	532,371	1,205,542	761,165	545,718	155,223	1,421,544	337,201	3,247
Master's	1,226,411	1,907,705	1,489,669	874,887	234,171	2,250,575	216,845	12,115
Baccalaureate	184,555	297,476	209,510	141,864	38,635	291,640	0	5
Associate of arts	1,898,211	2,759,631	1,881,180	623,359	121,443	1,241,468	0	25,464
Specialized institutions [4]								
Health and medicine	43,125	493,791	356,515	57,349	38,112	207,563	3,859,615	78,043
Engineering	11,699	22,534	19,041	9,737	6,358	16,899	0	2,902
Business	1,267	2,910	2,190	687	0	1,379	0	0
Fine arts	6,297	24,146	12,411	5,067	85	10,775	0	0
Other specialized	124,415	204,452	245,423	54,377	2,686	77,339	74,975	4
Tribal colleges [5]	9,703	15,837	8,240	6,053	764	2,852	0	0
4-year	1,113	4,653	639	1,448	0	346	0	0
2-year	8,590	11,184	7,600	4,606	764	2,506	0	0
Private	3,247,414	6,598,004	3,935,311	7,015,087	921,908	5,791,558	6,191,929	3,172,465
Research I universities [3]	484,293	1,444,983	1,227,476	1,672,060	274,489	1,638,651	3,550,254	2,828,297
Research II universities [3]	113,498	281,847	185,343	382,488	40,784	460,920	775,984	7,139
Doctoral universities	312,903	707,619	359,879	693,334	113,177	555,645	646,045	42,200
Master's	772,824	1,243,382	621,151	1,451,631	192,073	1,046,918	8,570	23,355
Baccalaureate	1,040,795	1,637,650	890,850	2,175,153	183,073	1,585,965	0	36,967
Associate of arts	187,052	305,906	170,988	192,255	8,508	99,734	53,806	199
Specialized institutions [4]								
Religion and theology	64,890	209,627	103,059	112,118	11,071	119,435	0	5,658
Health and medicine	66,724	338,781	157,501	64,178	45,290	109,500	1,157,268	228,162
Engineering	27,193	61,469	37,474	33,447	6,203	21,462	0	0
Business	95,663	161,142	70,124	110,256	26,356	86,154	0	0
Fine arts	47,795	118,853	66,160	88,363	11,908	50,628	0	415
Other specialized	31,122	83,151	43,496	38,034	8,808	16,143	0	73
Tribal colleges [5]	2,660	3,593	1,811	1,770	166	402	0	0
4-year	538	1,098	265	1,005	101	191	0	0
2-year	2,122	2,495	1,546	765	64	211	0	0

Percentage distribution of current-fund expenditures

Control and type of institution	Student services	Institutional support	Plant operation	Scholarships and fellowships	Mandatory transfers	Auxiliary enterprises	Hospitals	Independent operations
Total	4.94	9.19	6.56	6.48	1.22	9.48	10.10	1.95
Public	4.86	8.53	6.80	3.86	1.09	9.73	10.35	0.20
Research I universities [3]	2.48	4.72	4.94	3.93	1.27	10.22	16.70	0.22
Research II universities [3]	3.90	6.90	6.39	4.42	1.12	13.98	0.00	0.02
Doctoral universities	4.60	10.42	6.58	4.72	1.34	12.29	2.92	0.03
Master's	6.95	10.81	8.44	4.96	1.33	12.76	1.23	0.07
Baccalaureate	8.17	13.17	9.28	6.28	1.71	12.91	0.00	0.00
Associate of arts	9.71	14.12	9.62	3.19	0.62	6.35	0.00	0.13
Specialized institutions [4]								
Health and medicine	0.48	5.54	4.00	0.64	0.43	2.33	43.33	0.88
Engineering	5.83	11.24	9.50	4.86	3.17	8.43	0.00	1.45
Business	5.67	13.02	9.80	3.07	0.00	6.17	0.00	0.00
Fine arts	5.72	21.95	11.28	4.61	0.08	9.79	0.00	0.00
Other specialized	9.08	14.91	17.90	3.97	0.20	5.64	5.47	0.00
Tribal colleges [5]	12.33	20.13	10.47	7.69	0.97	3.63	0.00	0.00
4-year	7.02	29.33	4.03	9.13	0.00	2.18	0.00	0.00
2-year	13.68	17.81	12.10	7.33	1.22	3.99	0.00	0.00
Private	5.07	10.30	6.14	10.95	1.44	9.04	9.67	4.95
Research I universities [3]	1.97	5.89	5.00	6.82	1.12	6.68	14.47	11.53
Research II universities [3]	2.96	7.34	4.83	9.97	1.06	12.01	20.22	0.19
Doctoral universities	5.10	11.54	5.87	11.31	1.85	9.06	10.53	0.69
Master's	8.54	13.74	6.86	16.04	2.12	11.57	0.09	0.26
Baccalaureate	9.05	14.25	7.75	18.92	1.59	13.80	0.00	0.32
Associate of arts	11.96	19.56	10.93	12.29	0.54	6.38	3.44	0.01
Specialized institutions [4]								
Religion and theology	6.59	21.29	10.47	11.39	1.12	12.13	0.00	0.57
Health and medicine	1.62	8.23	3.83	1.56	1.10	2.66	28.11	5.54
Engineering	7.73	17.48	10.66	9.51	1.76	6.10	0.00	0.00
Business	11.18	18.83	8.19	12.88	3.08	10.07	0.00	0.06
Fine arts	7.40	18.39	10.24	13.67	1.84	7.83	0.00	0.02
Other specialized	6.83	18.24	9.54	8.34	1.93	3.54	0.00	0.00
Tribal colleges [5]	13.19	17.82	8.98	8.78	0.82	2.00	0.00	0.00
4-year	5.76	11.76	2.84	10.77	1.09	2.05	0.00	0.00
2-year	19.60	23.05	14.28	7.07	0.59	1.95	0.00	0.00

[1] Preliminary data.

[2] Generally includes only those expenditures associated with major federally funded research and development centers (FFRDC).

[3] Research institutions are committed to graduate education through the doctorate, and give high priority to research. Research I institutions receive $40 million or more annually in federal support. Research II institutions receive between $15.5 million and $40 million annually.

[4] Specialized institutions award baccalaureate or higher level degrees in specific fields of study.

[5] Tribally controlled colleges are located on reservations. They are members of the American Indian Higher Education Consortium.

SOURCE: U.S. Department of Education, National Center for Education Statistics, Integrated Postsecondary Education Data System (IPEDS), "Finance, 1993–94" survey. (This table was prepared July 1996.)

Table 334.—Current-fund expenditures of institutions of higher education, by purpose: 1980–81 to 1993–94

Purpose	1980–81	1985–86	1987–88	1988–89	1989–90	1990–91	1991–92	1992–93	1993–94[1]
1	2	3	4	5	6	7	8	9	10
	In thousands								
Total current-fund expenditures	$64,052,938	$97,535,742	$113,786,476	$123,867,184	$134,655,571	$146,087,836	$156,189,161	$165,241,040	$173,350,617
Educational and general expenditures	50,073,805	76,127,965	89,157,430	96,803,377	105,585,076	114,139,901	121,567,157	128,977,968	136,024,350
Instruction	20,733,166	31,032,099	35,833,563	38,812,690	42,145,987	45,496,117	47,997,196	50,340,914	52,775,599
Research	5,657,719	8,437,367	10,350,931	11,432,170	12,505,961	13,444,040	14,261,554	15,291,309	16,117,610
Public service	2,057,770	3,119,533	3,786,362	4,227,323	4,689,758	5,076,177	5,489,298	5,935,095	6,242,414
Academic support	4,273,286	6,667,392	8,141,581	8,904,279	9,437,644	10,050,773	10,577,018	11,072,970	11,677,911
Libraries	1,759,784	2,551,331	2,836,498	3,009,870	3,254,239	3,343,892	3,595,834	3,684,852	3,908,412
Student services	2,908,998	4,562,938	5,396,520	5,780,837	6,388,148	7,025,482	7,509,094	8,165,079	8,562,783
Institutional support	5,772,515	9,350,786	10,774,495	11,529,119	12,674,031	13,726,484	14,475,023	15,249,898	15,926,239
Operation and maintenance of plant	5,350,310	7,605,226	8,230,986	8,739,895	9,458,262	10,062,581	10,346,580	10,783,727	11,368,496
Scholarships and fellowships	2,504,525	4,160,174	5,325,358	5,918,666	6,655,544	7,551,184	9,060,000	10,148,373	11,238,010
From unrestricted funds	1,080,614	2,285,116	2,941,143	3,282,698	3,853,904	4,445,106	5,205,797	5,949,037	6,644,717
From restricted funds[2]	1,423,911	1,875,059	2,384,215	2,635,969	2,801,640	3,106,078	3,854,203	4,199,337	4,593,294
Mandatory transfers	815,516	1,192,449	1,317,633	1,458,397	1,629,742	1,707,063	1,851,393	1,990,603	2,115,288
Auxiliary enterprises	7,288,089	10,528,303	11,399,953	12,280,063	13,203,984	14,272,247	14,966,100	15,561,508	16,429,341
Mandatory transfers	508,377	617,171	629,369	774,752	836,852	936,876	1,003,299	1,109,549	1,158,848
Hospitals	5,433,111	8,692,113	10,406,461	11,824,782	12,679,286	14,325,865	16,104,313	17,049,672	17,509,603
Mandatory transfers	57,963	128,833	178,472	240,278	222,192	274,452	333,714	308,059	344,665
Independent operations (FFRDC)[3]	1,257,934	2,187,361	2,822,632	2,958,962	3,187,224	3,349,824	3,551,592	3,651,891	3,387,323
Mandatory transfers	643	3,432	4,306	6,987	5,812	5,645	3,396	2,271	2,354
	Percentage distribution								
Total current-fund expenditures	100.0	100.0	100.0	100.0	100.0	100.0	100.0	100.0	100.0
Educational and general expenditures	78.2	78.1	78.4	78.2	78.4	78.1	77.8	78.1	78.5
Instruction	32.4	31.8	31.5	31.3	31.3	31.1	30.7	30.5	30.4
Research	8.8	8.7	9.1	9.2	9.3	9.2	9.1	9.3	9.3
Public service	3.2	3.2	3.3	3.4	3.5	3.5	3.5	3.6	3.6
Academic support	6.7	6.8	7.2	7.2	7.0	6.9	6.8	6.7	6.7
Libraries	2.7	2.6	2.5	2.4	2.4	2.3	2.3	2.2	2.3
Student services	4.5	4.7	4.7	4.7	4.7	4.8	4.8	4.9	4.9
Institutional support	9.0	9.6	9.5	9.3	9.4	9.4	9.3	9.2	9.2
Operation and maintenance of plant	8.4	7.8	7.2	7.1	7.0	6.9	6.6	6.5	6.6
Scholarships and fellowships	3.9	4.3	4.7	4.8	4.9	5.2	5.8	6.1	6.5
From unrestricted funds	1.7	2.3	2.6	2.7	2.9	3.0	3.3	3.6	3.8
From restricted funds[2]	2.2	1.9	2.1	2.1	2.1	2.1	2.5	2.5	2.6
Mandatory transfers	1.3	1.2	1.2	1.2	1.2	1.2	1.2	1.2	1.2
Auxiliary enterprises	11.4	10.8	10.0	9.9	9.8	9.8	9.6	9.4	9.5
Mandatory transfers	0.8	0.6	0.6	0.6	0.6	0.6	0.6	0.7	0.7
Hospitals	8.5	8.9	9.1	9.5	9.4	9.8	10.3	10.3	10.1
Mandatory transfers	0.1	0.1	0.2	0.2	0.2	0.2	0.2	0.2	0.2
Independent operations (FFRDC)[3]	2.0	2.2	2.5	2.4	2.4	2.3	2.3	2.2	2.0
Mandatory transfers	(4)	(4)	(4)	(4)	(4)	(4)	(4)	(4)	(4)

[1] Preliminary data.

[2] Excludes Pell Grants.

[3] Generally includes only those expenditures associated with major federally funded research and development centers (FFRDC).

[4] Less than 0.05 percent.

NOTE.—Because of rounding, details may not add to totals.

SOURCE: U.S. Department of Education, National Center for Education Statistics, "Financial Statistics of Institutions of Higher Education" surveys; and Integrated Postsecondary Education Data System (IPEDS), "Finance" surveys. (This table was prepared April 1996.)

Table 335.—Current-fund expenditures of public institutions of higher education, by purpose: 1980–81 to 1993–94

Purpose	1980–81	1985–86	1987–88	1988–89	1989–90	1990–91	1991–92	1992–93	1993–94[1]
1	2	3	4	5	6	7	8	9	10
	In thousands								
Total current-fund expenditures	$42,279,806	$63,193,853	$72,641,301	$78,945,618	$85,770,530	$92,961,093	$98,847,180	$104,570,101	$109,309,541
Educational and general expenditures	34,173,013	50,872,962	58,639,468	63,444,908	69,163,958	74,395,428	78,554,534	83,210,979	87,139,226
Instruction	14,849,822	21,880,782	24,954,204	26,893,691	29,257,209	31,371,394	32,828,420	34,260,177	35,688,497
Research	3,813,350	5,705,144	6,976,925	7,796,952	8,542,235	9,364,213	9,948,580	10,604,973	11,180,363
Public service	1,718,924	2,515,734	2,986,164	3,351,950	3,688,664	3,990,232	4,285,501	4,563,397	4,741,719
Academic support	3,029,284	4,693,543	5,436,155	5,941,906	6,535,076	6,933,847	7,274,159	7,613,244	8,035,556
Libraries	1,187,116	1,685,052	1,853,410	1,956,497	2,102,672	2,167,161	2,284,520	2,329,625	2,449,109
Student services	1,950,566	2,921,758	3,482,112	3,678,419	4,021,328	4,398,365	4,690,921	5,173,239	5,315,370
Institutional support	3,563,194	5,667,144	6,470,162	6,876,360	7,490,137	8,030,642	8,423,156	9,049,589	9,328,236
Operation and maintenance of plant	3,681,921	5,177,254	5,601,732	5,913,267	6,333,582	6,655,605	6,790,215	7,076,805	7,433,185
Scholarships and fellowships	1,064,864	1,575,909	1,941,389	2,150,350	2,386,493	2,688,532	3,255,660	3,727,838	4,222,923
From unrestricted funds	367,476	696,973	830,195	944,001	1,099,425	1,270,158	1,523,721	1,745,339	1,934,617
From restricted funds[2]	697,388	878,935	1,111,194	1,206,349	1,287,068	1,418,374	1,731,939	1,982,498	2,288,306
Mandatory transfers	501,087	735,695	790,624	842,012	909,234	962,598	1,057,923	1,141,717	1,193,379
Auxiliary enterprises	4,658,140	6,830,235	7,237,866	7,744,725	8,282,332	9,049,935	9,634,131	10,024,352	10,637,783
Mandatory transfers	344,043	410,777	412,006	512,413	551,331	623,146	655,301	758,644	784,115
Hospitals	3,377,972	5,358,699	6,532,905	7,533,912	8,113,989	9,315,902	10,432,773	11,100,602	11,317,674
Mandatory transfers	26,613	75,569	106,181	159,507	156,029	195,961	224,095	223,241	242,216
Independent operations (FFRDC)[3]	70,681	131,956	231,063	222,072	210,252	199,827	225,742	234,168	214,858
Mandatory transfers	322	846	2,063	1,787	2,276	1,201	510	462	474
	Percentage distribution								
Total current-fund expenditures	100.0	100.0	100.0	100.0	100.0	100.0	100.0	100.0	100.0
Educational and general expenditures	80.8	80.5	80.7	80.4	80.6	80.0	79.5	79.6	79.7
Instruction	35.1	34.6	34.4	34.1	34.1	33.7	33.2	32.8	32.6
Research	9.0	9.0	9.6	9.9	10.0	10.1	10.1	10.1	10.2
Public service	4.1	4.0	4.1	4.2	4.3	4.3	4.3	4.4	4.3
Academic support	7.2	7.4	7.5	7.5	7.6	7.5	7.4	7.3	7.4
Libraries	2.8	2.7	2.6	2.5	2.5	2.3	2.3	2.2	2.2
Student services	4.6	4.6	4.8	4.7	4.7	4.7	4.7	4.9	4.9
Institutional support	8.4	9.0	8.9	8.7	8.7	8.6	8.5	8.7	8.5
Operation and maintenance of plant	8.7	8.2	7.7	7.5	7.4	7.2	6.9	6.8	6.8
Scholarships and fellowships	2.5	2.5	2.7	2.7	2.8	2.9	3.3	3.6	3.9
From unrestricted funds	0.9	1.1	1.1	1.2	1.3	1.4	1.5	1.7	1.8
From restricted funds[2]	1.6	1.4	1.5	1.5	1.5	1.5	1.8	1.9	2.1
Mandatory transfers	1.2	1.2	1.1	1.1	1.1	1.0	1.1	1.1	1.1
Auxiliary enterprises	11.0	10.8	10.0	9.8	9.7	9.7	9.7	9.6	9.7
Mandatory transfers	0.8	0.7	0.6	0.6	0.6	0.7	0.7	0.7	0.7
Hospitals	8.0	8.5	9.0	9.5	9.5	10.0	10.6	10.6	10.4
Mandatory transfers	0.1	0.1	0.1	0.2	0.2	0.2	0.2	0.2	0.2
Independent operations (FFRDC)[3]	0.2	0.2	0.3	0.3	0.2	0.2	0.2	0.2	0.2
Mandatory transfers	(4)	(4)	(4)	(4)	(4)	(4)	(4)	(4)	(4)

[1] Preliminary data.

[2] Excludes Pell Grants.

[3] Generally includes only those expenditures associated with major federally funded research and development centers (FFRDC).

[4] Less than 0.05 percent.

NOTE.—Because of rounding, details may not add to totals.

SOURCE: U.S. Department of Education, National Center for Education Statistics, "Financial Statistics of Institutions of Higher Education" surveys; and Integrated Postsecondary Education Data System (IPEDS), "Finance" surveys. (This table was prepared April 1996.)

Table 336.—Current-fund expenditures of private institutions of higher education, by purpose: 1980–81 to 1993–94

Purpose	1980–81	1985–86	1987–88	1988–89	1989–90	1990–91	1991–92	1992–93	1993–94 [1]
1	2	3	4	5	6	7	8	9	10
					In thousands				
Total current-fund expenditures	$21,773,132	$34,341,889	$41,145,174	$44,921,566	$48,885,041	$53,126,743	$57,341,982	$60,670,938	$64,041,076
Educational and general expenditures	15,900,792	25,255,003	30,517,962	33,358,469	36,421,118	39,744,472	43,012,623	45,766,989	48,885,124
Instruction	5,883,343	9,151,318	10,879,358	11,918,999	12,888,779	14,124,723	15,168,776	16,080,736	17,087,102
Research	1,844,369	2,732,222	3,374,006	3,635,218	3,963,726	4,079,827	4,312,973	4,686,336	4,937,247
Public service	338,845	603,799	800,198	875,373	1,001,094	1,085,945	1,203,797	1,371,697	1,500,695
Academic support	1,244,002	1,973,849	2,705,426	2,962,374	2,902,568	3,116,927	3,302,859	3,459,726	3,642,355
Libraries	572,667	866,279	983,087	1,053,372	1,151,567	1,176,731	1,311,314	1,355,227	1,459,304
Student services	958,432	1,641,180	1,914,409	2,102,418	2,366,819	2,627,117	2,818,174	2,991,840	3,247,414
Institutional support	2,209,321	3,683,642	4,304,333	4,652,759	5,183,893	5,695,842	6,051,868	6,200,308	6,598,004
Operation and maintenance of plant	1,668,389	2,427,972	2,629,254	2,826,628	3,124,680	3,406,975	3,556,365	3,706,923	3,935,311
Scholarships and fellowships	1,439,661	2,584,266	3,383,968	3,768,316	4,269,051	4,862,651	5,804,340	6,420,536	7,015,087
From unrestricted funds	713,138	1,588,143	2,110,948	2,338,697	2,754,479	3,174,947	3,682,076	4,203,697	4,710,100
From restricted funds [2]	726,523	996,123	1,273,021	1,429,619	1,514,572	1,687,704	2,122,264	2,216,838	2,304,987
Mandatory transfers	314,429	456,754	527,009	616,385	720,508	744,465	793,471	848,886	921,908
Auxiliary enterprises	2,629,948	3,698,067	4,162,087	4,535,337	4,921,653	5,222,312	5,331,969	5,537,156	5,791,558
Mandatory transfers	164,335	206,394	217,364	262,339	285,521	313,730	347,999	350,905	374,733
Hospitals	2,055,139	3,333,414	3,873,556	4,290,869	4,565,297	5,009,963	5,671,540	5,949,070	6,191,929
Mandatory transfers	31,349	53,264	72,291	80,771	66,164	78,491	109,619	84,818	102,449
Independent operations (FFRDC) [3]	1,187,253	2,055,405	2,591,569	2,736,890	2,976,973	3,149,996	3,325,850	3,417,723	3,172,465
Mandatory transfers	321	2,586	2,244	5,200	3,535	4,444	2,886	1,808	1,880
					Percentage distribution				
Total current-fund expenditures	100.0	100.0	100.0	100.0	100.0	100.0	100.0	100.0	100.0
Educational and general expenditures	73.0	73.5	74.2	74.3	74.5	74.8	75.0	75.4	76.3
Instruction	27.0	26.6	26.4	26.5	26.4	26.6	26.5	26.5	26.7
Research	8.5	8.0	8.2	8.1	8.1	7.7	7.5	7.7	7.7
Public service	1.6	1.8	1.9	1.9	2.0	2.0	2.1	2.3	2.3
Academic support	5.7	5.7	6.6	6.6	5.9	5.9	5.8	5.7	5.7
Libraries	2.6	2.5	2.4	2.3	2.4	2.2	2.3	2.2	2.3
Student services	4.4	4.8	4.7	4.7	4.8	4.9	4.9	4.9	5.1
Institutional support	10.1	10.7	10.5	10.4	10.6	10.7	10.6	10.2	10.3
Operation and maintenance of plant	7.7	7.1	6.4	6.3	6.4	6.4	6.2	6.1	6.1
Scholarships and fellowships	6.6	7.5	8.2	8.4	8.7	9.2	10.1	10.6	11.0
From unrestricted funds	3.3	4.6	5.1	5.2	5.6	6.0	6.4	6.9	7.4
From restricted funds [2]	3.3	2.9	3.1	3.2	3.1	3.2	3.7	3.7	3.6
Mandatory transfers	1.4	1.3	1.3	1.4	1.5	1.4	1.4	1.4	1.4
Auxiliary enterprises	12.1	10.8	10.1	10.1	10.1	9.8	9.3	9.1	9.0
Mandatory transfers	0.8	0.6	0.5	0.6	0.6	0.6	0.6	0.6	0.6
Hospitals	9.4	9.7	9.4	9.6	9.3	9.4	9.9	9.8	9.7
Mandatory transfers	0.1	0.2	0.2	0.2	0.1	0.1	0.2	0.1	0.2
Independent operations (FFRDC) [3]	5.5	6.0	6.3	6.1	6.1	5.9	5.8	5.6	5.0
Mandatory transfers	(4)	(4)	(4)	(4)	(4)	(4)	(4)	(4)	(4)

[1] Preliminary data.
[2] Excludes Pell Grants.
[3] Generally includes only those expenditures associated with major federally funded research and development centers (FFRDC).
[4] Less than 0.05 percent.

NOTE.—Because of rounding, details may not add to totals.

SOURCE: U.S. Department of Education, National Center for Education Statistics, "Financial Statistics of Institutions of Higher Education" surveys; and Integrated Postsecondary Education Data System (IPEDS), "Finance" surveys. (This table was prepared April 1996.)

Table 337.—Voluntary support for institutions of higher education, by source and purpose of support: 1949–50 to 1994–95

[In millions]

Source and purpose of support	1949–50	1959–60	1965–66	1970–71	1975–76	1980–81	1985–86	1989–90	1990–91	1991–92	1992–93	1993–94	1994–95
1	2	3	4	5	6	7	8	9	10	11	12	13	14
Total voluntary support [1]	$240	$815	$1,440	$1,860	$2,410	$4,230	$7,400	$9,800	$10,200	$10,700	$11,200	$12,350	$12,750
Sources													
Alumni	60	191	310	458	588	1,049	1,825	2,540	2,680	2,840	2,980	3,410	3,600
Nonalumni individuals	60	194	350	495	569	1,007	1,781	2,230	2,310	2,500	2,530	2,800	2,940
Corporations	28	130	230	259	379	778	1,702	2,170	2,230	2,260	2,400	2,510	2,560
Foundations	60	163	357	418	549	922	1,363	1,920	2,030	2,090	2,200	2,540	2,460
Religious organizations	16	80	108	104	130	140	211	240	240	240	250	240	250
Other	16	57	85	126	195	334	518	700	710	770	840	850	940
Purpose													
Current operations	101	385	675	1,050	1,480	2,590	4,022	5,440	5,830	6,100	6,300	6,710	7,230
Capital purposes	139	430	765	810	930	1,640	3,378	4,360	4,370	4,600	4,900	5,640	5,520
Voluntary support as a percent of total expenditures [2]	9.0	11.4	9.2	6.8	5.5	6.0	6.9	6.5	6.2	6.2	6.1	6.4	6.3

[1] Data are based on sample surveys of institutions of higher education.
[2] Total expenditures include current-fund expenditures and additions to plant value.

SOURCE: Council for Aid to Education, Research Report, "Contributions to Colleges Drop for First Time Since 1975;" and "Voluntary Support of Education," various years. (This table was prepared June 1996.)

Table 338.—Educational and general expenditures of public universities, by purpose: 1976–77 to 1993–94

Year	Educational and general expenditures									
	Total	Instruction	Administration [1]	Student services	Research	Libraries	Public service	Operation and maintenance of plant	Scholarships and fellowships	Mandatory transfers
1	2	3	4	5	6	7	8	9	10	11
Expenditures, in thousands of current dollars										
1976–77	$9,413,626	$3,670,554	$1,222,410	$346,906	$1,727,807	$331,614	$763,809	$857,677	$377,749	2$115,099
1977–78	10,220,191	4,009,870	1,344,538	388,262	1,896,578	343,198	803,309	938,952	389,682	105,803
1978–79	11,284,191	4,408,025	1,478,568	419,231	2,136,135	363,875	920,726	1,046,740	396,356	114,533
1979–80	12,540,072	4,860,411	1,572,523	473,460	2,444,471	463,642	1,012,376	1,148,942	439,461	124,786
1980–81	13,951,029	5,374,271	1,795,504	525,891	2,743,145	451,978	1,158,512	1,270,339	492,225	139,164
1981–82	15,077,263	5,852,958	1,974,219	566,366	2,903,178	488,939	1,223,417	1,412,557	525,498	130,131
1982–83	16,089,168	6,247,358	2,107,933	604,657	3,086,846	528,470	1,300,353	1,512,947	562,903	137,702
1983–84	17,234,711	6,646,501	2,263,565	643,614	3,295,053	577,136	1,385,191	1,627,702	624,642	171,306
1984–85	18,960,810	7,257,618	2,598,784	701,451	3,682,755	609,365	1,519,324	1,745,825	677,533	168,155
1985–86	20,716,657	7,807,522	2,882,006	762,324	4,076,258	669,253	1,664,917	1,831,618	780,080	242,679
1986–87	22,023,387	8,368,187	3,088,348	819,829	4,399,405	677,531	1,725,613	1,829,880	847,328	267,266
1987–88	23,848,427	8,902,624	3,311,806	889,528	4,911,929	762,858	1,857,008	1,934,489	949,438	328,746
1988–89	26,138,665	9,623,797	3,638,424	975,801	5,476,936	813,888	2,096,267	2,069,744	1,096,447	347,362
1989–90	28,077,757	10,269,007	3,867,818	1,028,463	5,997,942	860,981	2,263,623	2,200,111	1,199,643	390,170
1990–91	30,367,325	11,012,373	4,157,677	1,103,058	6,599,209	906,506	2,479,956	2,305,115	1,367,754	435,676
1991–92	31,565,791	11,373,749	4,198,990	1,161,633	6,937,360	946,098	2,609,520	2,323,220	1,556,868	458,354
1992–93	32,836,061	11,708,500	4,317,605	1,211,143	7,330,922	959,306	2,714,785	2,365,942	1,734,530	493,328
1993–94 2 ..	34,318,548	12,115,695	4,578,770	1,273,008	7,676,832	1,006,301	2,784,869	2,459,895	1,909,173	514,006
Percentage distribution										
1976–77	100.0	39.0	13.0	3.7	18.4	3.5	8.1	9.1	4.0	1.2
1977–78	100.0	39.2	13.2	3.8	18.6	3.4	7.9	9.2	3.8	1.0
1978–79	100.0	39.1	13.1	3.7	18.9	3.2	8.2	9.3	3.5	1.0
1979–80	100.0	38.8	12.5	3.8	19.5	3.7	8.1	9.2	3.5	1.0
1980–81	100.0	38.5	12.9	3.8	19.7	3.2	8.3	9.1	3.5	1.0
1981–82	100.0	38.8	13.1	3.8	19.3	3.2	8.1	9.4	3.5	0.9
1982–83	100.0	38.8	13.1	3.8	19.2	3.3	8.1	9.4	3.5	0.9
1983–84	100.0	38.6	13.1	3.7	19.1	3.3	8.0	9.4	3.6	1.0
1984–85	100.0	38.3	13.7	3.7	19.4	3.2	8.0	9.2	3.6	0.9
1985–86	100.0	37.7	13.9	3.7	19.7	3.2	8.0	8.8	3.8	1.2
1986–87	100.0	38.0	14.0	3.7	20.0	3.1	7.8	8.3	3.8	1.2
1987–88	100.0	37.3	13.9	3.7	20.6	3.2	7.8	8.1	4.0	1.4
1988–89	100.0	36.8	13.9	3.7	21.0	3.1	8.0	7.9	4.2	1.3
1989–90	100.0	36.6	13.8	3.7	21.4	3.1	8.1	7.8	4.3	1.4
1990–91	100.0	36.3	13.7	3.6	21.7	3.0	8.2	7.6	4.5	1.4
1991–92	100.0	36.0	13.3	3.7	22.0	3.0	8.3	7.4	4.9	1.5
1992–93	100.0	35.7	13.1	3.7	22.3	2.9	8.3	7.2	5.3	1.5
1993–94 2 ..	100.0	35.3	13.3	3.7	22.4	2.9	8.1	7.2	5.6	1.5
Expenditure per full-time-equivalent student in constant 1993–94 dollars										
1976–77	$14,232	$5,549	$1,848	$524	$2,612	$501	$1,155	$1,297	$571	$174
1977–78	14,358	5,633	1,889	545	2,664	482	1,129	1,319	547	149
1978–79	14,880	5,813	1,950	553	2,817	480	1,214	1,380	523	151
1979–80	14,722	5,706	1,846	556	2,870	544	1,188	1,349	516	146
1980–81	14,494	5,583	1,865	546	2,850	470	1,204	1,320	511	145
1981–82	14,288	5,547	1,871	537	2,751	463	1,159	1,339	498	123
1982–83	14,257	5,536	1,868	536	2,735	468	1,152	1,341	499	122
1983–84	14,602	5,631	1,918	545	2,792	489	1,174	1,379	529	145
1984–85	15,303	5,858	2,098	566	2,972	492	1,226	1,409	547	136
1985–86	15,898	5,992	2,212	585	3,128	514	1,278	1,406	599	186
1986–87	16,189	6,151	2,270	603	3,234	498	1,268	1,345	623	196
1987–88	16,614	6,202	2,307	620	3,422	531	1,294	1,348	661	229
1988–89	16,940	6,237	2,358	632	3,550	527	1,359	1,341	711	225
1989–90	16,883	6,175	2,326	618	3,607	518	1,361	1,323	721	235
1990–91	17,186	6,232	2,353	624	3,735	513	1,403	1,305	774	247
1991–92	17,110	6,165	2,276	630	3,760	513	1,414	1,259	844	248
1992–93	17,505	6,242	2,302	646	3,908	511	1,447	1,261	925	263
1993–94 2 ..	17,863	6,306	2,383	663	3,996	524	1,450	1,280	994	268

[1] Includes institutional and academic support less libraries.
[2] Preliminary data.

NOTE.—Data in this table may differ slightly from data appearing in other tables. Data for 1976–77 through 1985–86 include only institutions which provided both enrollment and finance data. The Higher Education Price Index was used to convert the per student figures to constant dollars. Because of rounding, details may not add to totals.

SOURCE: U.S. Department of Education, National Center for Education Statistics, "Financial Statistics of Institutions of Higher Education" surveys; Integrated Postsecondary Education Data System (IPEDS), "Finance" surveys; and Research Associates of Washington, unpublished data. (This table was prepared May 1996.)

Table 339.—Educational and general expenditures of public 4-year colleges,[1] by purpose: 1976–77 to 1993–94

Year	Educational and general expenditures									
	Total	Instruction	Administration[2]	Student services	Research	Libraries	Public service	Operation and maintenance of plant	Scholarships and fellowships	Mandatory transfers
1	2	3	4	5	6	7	8	9	10	11
	Expenditures, in thousands of current dollars									
1976–77	$8,682,538	$4,027,051	$1,445,651	$500,832	$607,235	$340,002	$250,152	$1,001,848	$338,432	$171,335
1977–78	9,568,977	4,423,487	1,598,092	572,193	677,414	369,408	274,314	1,118,393	332,899	202,777
1978–79	10,455,134	4,770,598	1,789,534	651,541	786,072	395,299	301,387	1,214,996	337,588	208,119
1979–80	11,750,398	5,271,621	2,029,327	733,557	937,874	448,190	359,467	1,375,308	383,036	212,019
1980–81	13,139,618	5,890,759	2,258,987	807,249	1,043,614	511,817	407,816	1,563,514	412,972	242,890
1981–82	14,321,586	6,537,888	2,518,182	834,225	1,086,146	536,080	440,736	1,738,210	403,069	227,050
1982–83	15,286,145	6,980,269	2,660,360	904,745	1,150,011	559,353	469,841	1,857,151	450,067	254,349
1983–84	16,538,128	7,464,035	3,013,666	1,041,488	1,246,289	622,879	513,732	1,873,628	473,503	288,908
1984–85	18,333,578	8,211,171	3,370,676	1,140,312	1,420,844	669,518	603,018	2,137,225	489,188	291,626
1985–86	19,860,947	8,945,373	3,658,627	1,235,418	1,618,737	712,112	648,178	2,118,522	569,841	354,139
1986–87	21,490,078	9,608,239	4,019,850	1,318,666	1,846,712	695,692	766,865	2,226,599	660,940	346,515
1987–88	23,124,455	10,310,532	4,261,440	1,434,726	2,053,638	774,274	864,347	2,340,495	711,704	373,299
1988–89	24,639,653	10,991,086	4,496,286	1,504,869	2,305,152	813,801	941,434	2,429,103	754,412	403,508
1989–90	27,210,634	12,079,093	5,076,792	1,648,526	2,525,080	888,526	1,088,113	2,607,385	871,944	425,175
1990–91	28,903,790	12,818,677	5,374,417	1,800,723	2,745,613	888,162	1,145,892	2,728,949	963,436	437,921
1991–92	30,720,827	13,270,992	5,805,724	1,868,329	2,986,474	945,097	1,310,700	2,782,200	1,248,220	503,091
1992–93	33,119,294	13,906,211	6,416,859	2,164,309	3,246,542	979,635	1,447,684	2,960,373	1,457,901	539,779
1993–94[3] ..	34,477,869	14,519,321	6,477,847	2,135,560	3,473,971	1,018,304	1,525,406	3,084,509	1,685,785	557,166
	Percentage distribution									
1976–77	100.0	46.4	16.7	5.8	7.0	3.9	2.9	11.5	3.9	2.0
1977–78	100.0	46.2	16.7	6.0	7.1	3.9	2.9	11.7	3.5	2.1
1978–79	100.0	45.6	17.1	6.2	7.5	3.8	2.9	11.6	3.2	2.0
1979–80	100.0	44.9	17.3	6.2	8.0	3.8	3.1	11.7	3.3	1.8
1980–81	100.0	44.8	17.2	6.1	7.9	3.9	3.1	11.9	3.1	1.8
1981–82	100.0	45.7	17.6	5.8	7.6	3.7	3.1	12.1	2.8	1.6
1982–83	100.0	45.7	17.4	5.9	7.5	3.7	3.1	12.1	2.9	1.7
1983–84	100.0	45.1	18.2	6.3	7.5	3.8	3.1	11.3	2.9	1.7
1984–85	100.0	44.8	18.4	6.2	7.7	3.7	3.3	11.7	2.7	1.6
1985–86	100.0	45.0	18.4	6.2	8.2	3.6	3.3	10.7	2.9	1.8
1986–87	100.0	44.7	18.7	6.1	8.6	3.2	3.6	10.4	3.1	1.6
1987–88	100.0	44.6	18.4	6.2	8.9	3.3	3.7	10.1	3.1	1.6
1988–89	100.0	44.6	18.2	6.1	9.4	3.3	3.8	9.9	3.1	1.6
1989–90	100.0	44.4	18.7	6.1	9.3	3.3	4.0	9.6	3.2	1.6
1990–91	100.0	44.3	18.6	6.2	9.5	3.1	4.0	9.4	3.3	1.5
1991–92	100.0	43.2	18.9	6.1	9.7	3.1	4.3	9.1	4.1	1.6
1992–93	100.0	42.0	19.4	6.5	9.8	3.0	4.4	8.9	4.4	1.6
1993–94[3] ..	100.0	42.1	18.8	6.2	10.1	3.0	4.4	8.9	4.9	1.6
	Expenditure per full-time-equivalent student in constant 1993–94 dollars									
1976–77	$10,378	$4,813	$1,728	$599	$726	$406	$299	$1,197	$405	$205
1977–78	10,467	4,839	1,748	626	741	404	300	1,223	364	222
1978–79	10,802	4,929	1,849	673	812	408	311	1,255	349	215
1979–80	10,922	4,900	1,886	682	872	417	334	1,278	356	197
1980–81	10,813	4,848	1,859	664	859	421	336	1,287	340	200
1981–82	10,759	4,911	1,892	627	816	403	331	1,306	303	171
1982–83	10,499	4,794	1,827	621	790	384	323	1,275	309	175
1983–84	10,608	4,788	1,933	668	799	400	330	1,202	304	185
1984–85	11,209	5,020	2,061	697	869	409	369	1,307	299	178
1985–86	11,577	5,214	2,133	720	944	415	378	1,235	332	206
1986–87	11,581	5,178	2,166	711	995	375	413	1,200	356	187
1987–88	11,807	5,264	2,176	733	1,049	395	441	1,195	363	191
1988–89	11,634	5,190	2,123	711	1,088	384	445	1,147	356	191
1989–90	11,730	5,207	2,188	711	1,088	383	469	1,124	376	183
1990–91	11,404	5,058	2,121	710	1,083	350	452	1,077	380	173
1991–92	11,562	4,995	2,185	703	1,124	356	493	1,047	470	189
1992–93	11,973	5,027	2,320	782	1,174	354	523	1,070	527	195
1993–94[3] ..	12,120	5,104	2,277	751	1,221	358	536	1,084	593	196

[1] Excludes universities. See preceding table.

[2] Includes institutional and academic support less libraries.

[3] Preliminary data.

NOTE.—Data in this table may differ slightly from data appearing in other tables. Data for 1976–77 through 1985–86 include only institutions which provided both enrollment and finance data. The Higher Education Price Index was used to convert the per student figures to constant dollars. Because of rounding, details may not add to totals.

SOURCE: U.S. Department of Education, National Center for Education Statistics, "Financial Statistics of Institutions of Higher Education" surveys; Integrated Postsecondary Education Data System (IPEDS), "Finance" surveys; and Research Associates of Washington, unpublished data. (This table was prepared May 1996.)

Table 340.—Educational and general expenditures of public 2-year colleges, by purpose: 1976–77 to 1993–94

Year	Educational and general expenditures									
	Total	Instruction	Administration [1]	Student services	Research	Libraries	Public service	Operation and maintenance of plant	Scholarships and fellowships	Mandatory transfers
1	2	3	4	5	6	7	8	9	10	11
Expenditures, in thousands of current dollars										
1976–77	$4,875,998	$2,490,274	$882,813	$409,217	$15,698	$171,409	$97,635	$547,515	$142,827	$118,610
1977–78	5,336,153	2,700,489	1,035,206	437,060	9,333	188,201	112,944	605,464	117,996	129,458
1978–79	5,734,611	2,877,651	1,119,840	482,323	21,289	193,703	110,918	650,447	127,633	150,807
1979–80	6,334,777	3,185,815	1,204,082	547,457	26,288	202,583	141,000	743,014	147,865	136,672
1980–81	7,063,474	3,575,743	1,347,020	615,869	26,591	222,391	152,597	844,781	159,474	119,008
1981–82	7,757,435	3,947,065	1,473,733	684,650	15,632	262,697	147,385	952,691	160,109	113,473
1982–83	8,292,446	4,218,388	1,620,644	741,179	18,090	248,682	123,722	1,016,267	175,069	130,403
1983–84	8,820,575	4,481,854	1,748,535	775,084	18,189	263,485	150,109	1,076,371	178,500	128,448
1984–85	9,560,507	4,806,050	1,929,968	841,101	15,591	278,363	193,903	1,156,074	207,975	131,482
1985–86	10,252,955	5,116,884	2,122,060	920,299	10,136	295,691	202,440	1,220,646	225,979	138,820
1986–87	10,845,969	5,382,631	2,363,275	1,020,496	12,508	246,131	235,115	1,252,152	243,402	90,258
1987–88	11,666,586	5,741,049	2,479,661	1,157,858	11,358	316,278	264,809	1,326,748	280,247	88,578
1988–89	12,666,590	6,278,809	2,727,058	1,197,748	14,864	328,809	314,250	1,414,420	299,491	91,142
1989–90	13,875,566	6,909,109	2,977,932	1,344,339	19,213	353,165	336,927	1,526,086	314,906	93,889
1990–91	15,124,313	7,540,344	3,265,233	1,494,583	19,390	372,492	364,384	1,621,542	357,343	89,001
1991–92	16,267,915	8,183,678	3,408,080	1,660,958	24,747	393,325	365,281	1,684,796	450,572	96,477
1992–93	17,255,624	8,645,466	3,598,745	1,797,787	27,510	390,684	400,927	1,750,489	535,406	108,610
1993–94 [2]	18,342,808	9,053,480	3,858,066	1,906,802	29,560	424,504	431,444	1,888,780	627,964	122,207
Percentage distribution										
1976–77	100.0	51.1	18.1	8.4	0.3	3.5	2.0	11.2	2.9	2.4
1977–78	100.0	50.6	19.4	8.2	0.2	3.5	2.1	11.3	2.2	2.4
1978–79	100.0	50.2	19.5	8.4	0.4	3.4	1.9	11.3	2.2	2.6
1979–80	100.0	50.3	19.0	8.6	0.4	3.2	2.2	11.7	2.3	2.2
1980–81	100.0	50.6	19.1	8.7	0.4	3.1	2.2	12.0	2.3	1.7
1981–82	100.0	50.9	19.0	8.8	0.2	3.4	1.9	12.3	2.1	1.5
1982–83	100.0	50.9	19.5	8.9	0.2	3.0	1.5	12.3	2.1	1.6
1983–84	100.0	50.8	19.8	8.8	0.2	3.0	1.7	12.2	2.0	1.5
1984–85	100.0	50.3	20.2	8.8	0.2	2.9	2.0	12.1	2.2	1.4
1985–86	100.0	49.9	20.7	9.0	0.1	2.9	2.0	11.9	2.2	1.4
1986–87	100.0	49.6	21.8	9.4	0.1	2.3	2.2	11.5	2.2	0.8
1987–88	100.0	49.2	21.3	9.9	0.1	2.7	2.3	11.4	2.4	0.8
1988–89	100.0	49.6	21.5	9.5	0.1	2.6	2.5	11.2	2.4	0.7
1989–90	100.0	49.8	21.5	9.7	0.1	2.5	2.4	11.0	2.3	0.7
1990–91	100.0	49.9	21.6	9.9	0.1	2.5	2.4	10.7	2.4	0.6
1991–92	100.0	50.3	20.9	10.2	0.2	2.4	2.2	10.4	2.8	0.6
1992–93	100.0	50.1	20.9	10.4	0.2	2.3	2.3	10.1	3.1	0.6
1993–94 [2] ..	100.0	49.4	21.0	10.4	0.2	2.3	2.4	10.3	3.4	0.7
Expenditure per full-time-equivalent student in constant 1993–94 dollars										
1976–77	$5,593	$2,857	$1,013	$469	$18	$197	$112	$628	$164	$136
1977–78	5,623	2,846	1,091	461	10	198	119	638	124	136
1978–79	5,815	2,918	1,135	489	22	196	112	660	129	153
1979–80	5,717	2,875	1,087	494	24	183	127	671	133	123
1980–81	5,479	2,774	1,045	478	21	172	118	655	124	92
1981–82	5,473	2,785	1,040	483	11	185	104	672	113	80
1982–83	5,178	2,634	1,012	463	11	155	77	635	109	81
1983–84	5,251	2,668	1,041	461	11	157	89	641	106	76
1984–85	5,761	2,896	1,163	507	9	168	117	697	125	79
1985–86	5,930	2,960	1,227	532	6	171	117	706	131	80
1986–87	6,031	2,993	1,314	567	7	137	131	696	135	50
1987–88	5,946	2,926	1,264	590	6	161	135	676	143	45
1988–89	6,017	2,982	1,295	569	7	156	149	672	142	43
1989–90	5,849	2,912	1,255	567	8	149	142	643	133	40
1990–91	5,914	2,949	1,277	584	8	146	142	634	140	35
1991–92	5,650	2,842	1,184	577	9	137	127	585	156	34
1992–93	5,728	2,870	1,195	597	9	130	133	581	178	36
1993–94 [2] ..	6,021	2,972	1,266	626	10	139	142	620	206	40

[1] Includes institutional and academic support less libraries.
[2] Preliminary data.

NOTE.—Data in this table may differ slightly from data appearing in other tables. Data for 1976–77 through 1985–86 include only institutions which provided both enrollment and finance data. The Higher Education Price Index was used to convert the per student figures to constant dollars. Because of rounding, details may not add to totals.

SOURCE: U.S. Department of Education, National Center for Education Statistics, "Financial Statistics of Institutions of Higher Education" surveys; Integrated Postsecondary Education Data System (IPEDS), "Finance" surveys; and Research Associates of Washington, unpublished data. (This table was prepared May 1996.)

Table 341.—Educational and general expenditures of private (nonprofit) universities, by purpose: 1976–77 to 1993–94

Year	Educational and general expenditures									
	Total	Instruction	Administration [1]	Student services	Research	Libraries	Public service	Operation and maintenance of plant	Scholarships and fellowships	Mandatory transfers
1	2	3	4	5	6	7	8	9	10	11
	Expenditures, in thousands of current dollars									
1976–77	$4,694,593	$1,784,975	$621,733	$156,457	$988,656	$195,146	$105,011	$411,340	$380,821	$50,453
1977–78	5,120,125	1,943,031	683,988	172,261	1,063,906	215,068	108,201	447,743	427,907	58,019
1978–79	5,675,608	2,120,800	796,751	195,238	1,175,657	221,676	119,082	510,819	460,200	75,385
1979–80	6,408,288	2,426,312	908,580	215,646	1,315,469	236,184	148,028	568,806	507,257	82,006
1980–81	7,249,102	2,763,320	1,009,957	254,872	1,436,318	267,142	149,946	660,152	596,241	111,154
1981–82	7,951,934	3,105,731	1,100,088	289,398	1,505,340	294,523	160,496	752,673	650,285	93,401
1982–83	8,198,167	3,227,925	1,214,617	304,617	1,464,809	295,709	169,382	754,480	670,390	96,238
1983–84	9,491,967	3,660,650	1,445,910	350,096	1,683,020	360,238	187,615	859,065	833,108	112,266
1984–85	10,431,950	3,965,165	1,556,854	393,526	1,892,570	366,356	253,010	930,229	931,027	143,212
1985–86	11,407,571	4,308,432	1,711,155	438,678	2,108,731	397,745	271,271	981,131	1,040,677	149,751
1986–87	13,013,183	4,998,565	1,977,175	502,291	2,399,976	397,460	332,223	1,006,334	1,218,002	181,159
1987–88	13,876,586	5,209,101	2,107,206	529,261	2,597,435	484,987	340,475	1,073,880	1,328,775	205,464
1988–89	15,123,369	5,743,104	2,293,256	565,903	2,786,178	510,820	377,820	1,135,273	1,472,675	238,340
1989–90	16,363,342	6,188,447	2,411,051	607,623	3,048,455	555,752	414,916	1,231,028	1,615,096	290,974
1990–91	17,827,649	6,827,220	2,633,605	669,160	3,170,083	567,800	456,615	1,383,686	1,833,124	286,357
1991–92	19,307,030	7,367,629	2,852,739	711,041	3,364,795	624,416	484,871	1,453,365	2,142,466	305,707
1992–93	20,435,319	7,844,576	2,874,208	719,657	3,648,010	644,005	547,159	1,495,825	2,322,331	339,547
1993–94 [2] ..	21,702,227	8,347,500	3,009,434	772,524	3,831,668	693,223	603,658	1,578,840	2,481,742	383,638
	Percentage distribution									
1976–77	100.0	38.0	13.2	3.3	21.1	4.2	2.2	8.8	8.1	1.1
1977–78	100.0	37.9	13.4	3.4	20.8	4.2	2.1	8.7	8.4	1.1
1978–79	100.0	37.4	14.0	3.4	20.7	3.9	2.1	9.0	8.1	1.3
1979–80	100.0	37.9	14.2	3.4	20.5	3.7	2.3	8.9	7.9	1.3
1980–81	100.0	38.1	13.9	3.5	19.8	3.7	2.1	9.1	8.2	1.5
1981–82	100.0	39.1	13.8	3.6	18.9	3.7	2.0	9.5	8.2	1.2
1982–83	100.0	39.4	14.8	3.7	17.9	3.6	2.1	9.2	8.2	1.2
1983–84	100.0	38.6	15.2	3.7	17.7	3.8	2.0	9.1	8.8	1.2
1984–85	100.0	38.0	14.9	3.8	18.1	3.5	2.4	8.9	8.9	1.4
1985–86	100.0	37.8	15.0	3.8	18.5	3.5	2.4	8.6	9.1	1.3
1986–87	100.0	38.4	15.2	3.9	18.4	3.1	2.6	7.7	9.4	1.4
1987–88	100.0	37.5	15.2	3.8	18.7	3.5	2.5	7.7	9.6	1.5
1988–89	100.0	38.0	15.2	3.7	18.4	3.4	2.5	7.5	9.7	1.6
1989–90	100.0	37.8	14.7	3.7	18.6	3.4	2.5	7.5	9.9	1.8
1990–91	100.0	38.3	14.8	3.8	17.8	3.2	2.6	7.8	10.3	1.6
1991–92	100.0	38.2	14.8	3.7	17.4	3.2	2.5	7.5	11.1	1.6
1992–93	100.0	38.4	14.1	3.5	17.9	3.2	2.7	7.3	11.4	1.7
1993–94 [2] ..	100.0	38.5	13.9	3.6	17.7	3.2	2.8	7.3	11.4	1.8
	Expenditure per full-time-equivalent student in constant 1993–94 dollars									
1976–77	$22,031	$8,377	$2,918	$734	$4,640	$916	$493	$1,930	$1,787	$237
1977–78	21,771	8,262	2,908	732	4,524	914	460	1,904	1,819	247
1978–79	22,047	8,238	3,095	758	4,567	861	463	1,984	1,788	293
1979–80	22,366	8,468	3,171	753	4,591	824	517	1,985	1,770	286
1980–81	22,639	8,630	3,154	796	4,486	834	468	2,062	1,862	347
1981–82	22,551	8,808	3,120	821	4,269	835	455	2,135	1,844	265
1982–83	22,733	8,951	3,368	845	4,062	820	470	2,092	1,859	267
1983–84	24,399	9,410	3,717	900	4,326	926	482	2,208	2,142	289
1984–85	25,416	9,660	3,793	959	4,611	893	616	2,266	2,268	349
1985–86	26,375	9,961	3,956	1,014	4,876	920	627	2,268	2,406	346
1986–87	28,812	11,067	4,378	1,112	5,314	880	736	2,228	2,697	401
1987–88	29,154	10,944	4,427	1,112	5,457	1,019	715	2,256	2,792	432
1988–89	29,812	11,321	4,521	1,116	5,492	1,007	745	2,238	2,903	470
1989–90	30,119	11,391	4,438	1,118	5,611	1,023	764	2,266	2,973	536
1990–91	31,046	11,889	4,586	1,165	5,521	989	795	2,410	3,192	499
1991–92	31,987	12,206	4,726	1,178	5,575	1,035	803	2,408	3,550	506
1992–93	32,838	12,605	4,619	1,156	5,862	1,035	879	2,404	3,732	546
1993–94 [2] ..	33,806	13,003	4,688	1,203	5,969	1,080	940	2,459	3,866	598

[1] Includes institutional and academic support less libraries.
[2] Preliminary data.

NOTE.—Data in this table may differ slightly from data appearing in other tables. Data for 1976–77 through 1985–86 include only institutions which provided both enrollment and finance data. The Higher Education Price Index was used to convert the per student figures to constant dollars. Because of rounding, details may not add to totals.

SOURCE: U.S. Department of Education, National Center for Education Statistics, "Financial Statistics of Institutions of Higher Education" surveys; Integrated Postsecondary Education Data System (IPEDS), "Finance" surveys; and Research Associates of Washington, unpublished data. (This table was prepared May 1996.)

Table 342.—Educational and general expenditures of private (nonprofit) 4-year colleges, [1] by purpose: 1976–77 to 1993–94

Year	Educational and general expenditures									
	Total	Instruction	Administration [2]	Student services	Research	Libraries	Public service	Operation and maintenance of plant	Scholarships and fellowships	Mandatory transfers
1	2	3	4	5	6	7	8	9	10	11
Expenditures, in thousands of current dollars										
1976–77	$5,139,939	$1,919,574	$1,047,932	$381,428	$259,530	$200,844	$123,717	$574,910	$511,907	$120,097
1977–78	5,637,836	2,114,043	1,160,141	428,265	271,637	221,807	123,214	638,330	550,372	130,026
1978–79	6,263,692	2,328,418	1,299,063	483,031	328,042	240,098	136,861	704,180	598,487	145,513
1979–80	7,063,953	2,589,908	1,466,556	549,639	374,520	259,969	153,056	807,943	694,791	167,570
1980–81	8,061,774	2,907,255	1,703,307	639,795	407,622	289,944	186,399	930,075	811,636	185,741
1981–82	9,061,667	3,271,255	1,938,727	727,382	419,283	322,702	228,368	1,036,118	913,999	203,834
1982–83	9,805,459	3,552,387	2,124,446	804,943	437,286	356,768	236,142	1,092,836	983,887	216,764
1983–84	10,845,622	3,900,082	2,347,962	890,707	480,459	388,153	259,932	1,184,788	1,149,813	243,726
1984–85	11,835,351	4,213,485	2,564,844	980,416	539,322	416,539	289,124	1,251,490	1,312,673	267,459
1985–86	12,855,040	4,507,505	2,790,504	1,067,717	623,050	446,766	328,827	1,317,062	1,481,954	291,654
1986–87	14,232,003	4,886,585	3,249,910	1,184,395	693,450	410,013	384,594	1,386,729	1,717,948	318,379
1987–88	15,405,503	5,248,764	3,403,379	1,293,302	776,022	485,517	456,111	1,462,345	1,966,124	313,939
1988–89	16,980,645	5,738,789	3,766,237	1,437,829	848,094	530,032	495,683	1,596,786	2,198,328	368,866
1989–90	18,717,398	6,276,102	4,097,242	1,599,951	909,822	578,520	581,730	1,712,000	2,547,600	414,432
1990–91	20,374,743	6,809,318	4,533,043	1,770,071	901,357	589,052	624,663	1,809,977	2,898,547	438,715
1991–92	22,121,380	7,320,211	4,723,853	1,919,662	942,407	659,416	714,728	1,896,424	3,478,153	466,528
1992–93	23,609,625	7,743,656	4,887,700	2,044,830	1,036,676	680,457	821,381	1,995,164	3,900,807	498,954
1993–94 [3] ..	25,262,199	8,169,221	5,199,838	2,205,411	1,104,561	733,711	893,500	2,112,367	4,316,138	527,451
Percentage distribution										
1976–77	100.0	37.3	20.4	7.4	5.0	3.9	2.4	11.2	10.0	2.3
1977–78	100.0	37.5	20.6	7.6	4.8	3.9	2.2	11.3	9.8	2.3
1978–79	100.0	37.2	20.7	7.7	5.2	3.8	2.2	11.2	9.6	2.3
1979–80	100.0	36.7	20.8	7.8	5.3	3.7	2.2	11.4	9.8	2.4
1980–81	100.0	36.1	21.1	7.9	5.1	3.6	2.3	11.5	10.1	2.3
1981–82	100.0	36.1	21.4	8.0	4.6	3.6	2.5	11.4	10.1	2.2
1982–83	100.0	36.2	21.7	8.2	4.5	3.6	2.4	11.1	10.0	2.2
1983–84	100.0	36.0	21.6	8.2	4.4	3.6	2.4	10.9	10.6	2.2
1984–85	100.0	35.6	21.7	8.3	4.6	3.5	2.4	10.6	11.1	2.3
1985–86	100.0	35.1	21.7	8.3	4.8	3.5	2.6	10.2	11.5	2.3
1986–87	100.0	34.3	22.8	8.3	4.9	2.9	2.7	9.7	12.1	2.2
1987–88	100.0	34.1	22.1	8.4	5.0	3.2	3.0	9.5	12.8	2.0
1988–89	100.0	33.8	22.2	8.5	5.0	3.1	2.9	9.4	12.9	2.2
1989–90	100.0	33.5	21.9	8.5	4.9	3.1	3.1	9.1	13.6	2.2
1990–91	100.0	33.4	22.2	8.7	4.4	2.9	3.1	8.9	14.2	2.2
1991–92	100.0	33.1	21.4	8.7	4.3	3.0	3.2	8.6	15.7	2.1
1992–93	100.0	32.8	20.7	8.7	4.4	2.9	3.5	8.5	16.5	2.1
1993–94 [3] ..	100.0	32.3	20.6	8.7	4.4	2.9	3.5	8.4	17.1	2.1
Expenditure per full-time-equivalent student in constant 1993–94 dollars										
1976–77	$10,861	$4,056	$2,214	$806	$548	$424	$261	$1,215	$1,082	$254
1977–78	10,812	4,054	2,225	821	521	425	236	1,224	1,056	249
1978–79	10,945	4,069	2,270	844	573	420	239	1,231	1,046	254
1979–80	11,132	4,081	2,311	866	590	410	241	1,273	1,095	264
1980–81	11,184	4,033	2,363	888	566	402	259	1,290	1,126	258
1981–82	11,327	4,089	2,423	909	524	403	285	1,295	1,142	255
1982–83	11,564	4,189	2,505	949	516	421	278	1,289	1,160	256
1983–84	11,953	4,298	2,588	982	530	428	286	1,306	1,267	269
1984–85	12,397	4,413	2,687	1,027	565	436	303	1,311	1,375	280
1985–86	12,823	4,496	2,784	1,065	622	446	328	1,314	1,478	291
1986–87	13,592	4,667	3,104	1,131	662	392	367	1,324	1,641	304
1987–88	13,919	4,742	3,075	1,168	701	439	412	1,321	1,776	284
1988–89	14,068	4,754	3,120	1,191	703	439	411	1,323	1,821	306
1989–90	14,293	4,793	3,129	1,222	695	442	444	1,307	1,945	316
1990–91	14,529	4,856	3,232	1,262	643	420	445	1,291	2,067	313
1991–92	14,910	4,934	3,184	1,294	635	444	482	1,278	2,344	314
1992–93	15,034	4,931	3,112	1,302	660	433	523	1,270	2,484	318
1993–94 [3] ..	15,397	4,979	3,169	1,344	673	447	545	1,288	2,631	321

[1] Excludes universities. See preceding table.

[2] Includes institutional and academic support less libraries.

[3] Preliminary data.

NOTE.—Data in this table may differ slightly from data appearing in other tables. Data for 1976–77 through 1985–86 include only institutions which provided both enrollment and finance data. The Higher Education Price Index was used to convert the per student figures to constant dollars. Because of rounding, details may not add to totals.

SOURCE: U.S. Department of Education, National Center for Education Statistics, "Financial Statistics of Institutions of Higher Education" surveys; Integrated Postsecondary Education Data System (IPEDS), "Finance" surveys; and Research Associates of Washington, unpublished data. (This table was prepared May 1996.)

Table 343.—Current-fund expenditures of public institutions of higher education, by state: 1980–81 to 1993–94

[In thousands of dollars]

State	1980–81	1985–86	1987–88	1988–89	1989–90	1990–91	1991–92	1992–93	1993–94 [1]	Percent change, 1988–89 to 1993–94
1	2	3	4	5	6	7	8	9	10	11
United States	**$42,279,806**	**$63,193,853**	**$72,641,301**	**$78,945,618**	**$85,770,530**	**$92,961,093**	**$98,847,180**	**$104,570,101**	**$109,309,541**	**38.5**
Alabama	839,366	1,324,774	1,511,246	1,669,401	1,831,657	2,054,798	2,189,029	2,428,620	2,510,081	50.4
Alaska	158,700	224,042	221,296	240,913	268,057	289,606	306,218	322,620	336,405	39.6
Arizona	691,481	1,017,203	1,193,765	1,317,954	1,446,388	1,586,891	1,620,019	1,621,716	1,754,682	33.1
Arkansas	340,621	528,831	622,442	692,970	751,336	797,291	878,783	976,735	1,002,908	44.7
California	5,775,482	8,515,440	9,493,900	10,182,106	11,230,941	12,023,304	12,910,152	13,537,367	13,244,130	30.1
Colorado	738,363	1,057,558	1,225,193	1,331,091	1,374,188	1,452,137	1,546,642	1,670,921	1,760,679	32.3
Connecticut	367,850	562,696	680,087	774,179	811,282	886,846	957,627	981,286	1,026,593	32.6
Delaware	158,332	229,377	279,084	314,003	342,119	367,012	396,947	416,699	442,488	40.9
District of Columbia	71,791	88,462	96,642	104,637	111,468	111,469	121,488	119,522	104,619	([2])
Florida	1,170,305	1,782,180	2,182,947	2,443,879	2,766,267	2,896,046	2,988,794	3,179,353	3,408,957	39.5
Georgia	754,060	1,255,964	1,507,960	1,622,707	1,769,744	1,929,993	2,015,816	2,227,608	2,453,100	51.2
Hawaii	222,718	312,248	349,791	379,799	424,473	498,307	575,337	602,346	613,356	61.5
Idaho	166,844	238,438	269,697	289,148	314,398	353,561	391,441	409,167	445,463	54.1
Illinois	1,780,403	2,571,409	2,789,932	3,015,395	3,310,763	3,528,967	3,644,740	3,877,243	4,053,858	34.4
Indiana	1,064,395	1,602,203	1,841,317	2,005,740	2,186,604	2,391,173	2,643,997	2,671,055	2,858,990	42.5
Iowa	767,590	1,092,542	1,229,142	1,491,442	1,617,626	1,734,476	1,776,217	1,899,159	1,981,068	32.8
Kansas	579,857	848,602	928,956	1,028,578	1,131,558	1,190,573	1,262,215	1,329,587	1,429,200	38.9
Kentucky	673,775	898,718	1,068,927	1,143,612	1,236,680	1,400,529	1,514,985	1,516,017	1,577,584	37.9
Louisiana	716,702	1,039,177	1,112,935	1,172,325	1,286,648	1,439,415	1,541,126	1,800,188	1,835,151	56.5
Maine	153,658	216,737	271,928	315,700	344,435	355,074	362,905	375,090	387,991	22.9
Maryland	795,100	1,064,430	1,249,730	1,389,900	1,522,145	1,684,341	1,674,918	1,829,812	1,940,403	39.6
Massachusetts	553,019	980,585	1,235,566	1,306,814	1,357,588	1,435,063	1,474,589	1,605,121	1,496,856	14.5
Michigan	2,053,795	2,946,336	3,507,141	3,745,488	4,076,519	4,416,914	4,741,682	4,925,759	5,095,422	36.0
Minnesota	876,632	1,324,691	1,565,491	1,809,757	1,802,133	2,012,225	2,219,016	2,286,336	2,459,437	35.9
Mississippi	539,222	706,380	775,821	864,611	922,574	978,366	1,012,544	1,102,806	1,200,196	38.8
Missouri	687,643	999,869	1,132,628	1,237,603	1,349,451	1,453,608	1,501,166	1,582,746	1,694,484	36.9
Montana	121,894	182,102	192,382	198,475	218,231	254,175	320,876	337,189	350,943	76.8
Nebraska	378,928	537,858	610,064	676,527	762,480	848,778	916,814	968,407	1,004,263	48.4
Nevada	111,347	180,107	217,330	240,711	281,018	330,592	363,306	377,786	415,785	72.7
New Hampshire	134,391	183,959	222,842	247,686	259,157	281,542	307,217	335,575	360,833	45.7
New Jersey	903,169	1,406,490	1,770,521	1,968,859	2,165,562	2,309,968	2,489,088	2,630,533	2,809,931	42.7
New Mexico	325,960	456,600	524,181	751,405	828,157	896,299	1,010,859	1,069,497	1,142,903	52.1
New York	2,519,104	3,802,602	4,494,943	4,732,811	5,058,750	5,605,621	5,681,964	6,096,863	6,481,594	37.0
North Carolina	1,128,383	1,799,173	2,076,493	2,238,155	2,420,825	2,581,156	2,770,977	3,002,915	3,192,215	42.6
North Dakota	192,046	288,214	303,762	319,583	357,832	367,959	408,219	419,268	432,190	35.2
Ohio	1,784,754	2,718,408	3,172,348	3,494,228	3,726,135	4,084,840	4,359,943	4,389,408	4,640,316	32.8
Oklahoma	583,174	844,829	844,428	887,293	973,213	1,057,248	1,158,696	1,177,061	1,214,084	36.8
Oregon	642,411	880,696	1,023,207	1,116,966	1,219,341	1,329,794	1,484,621	1,560,699	1,623,771	45.4
Pennsylvania	1,544,586	2,392,145	2,874,641	3,147,180	3,390,869	3,602,685	3,904,332	4,004,062	4,240,094	34.7
Rhode Island	158,365	213,253	246,258	270,411	287,194	292,199	303,606	330,038	331,359	22.5
South Carolina	617,963	951,848	1,079,002	1,179,216	1,324,647	1,475,074	1,595,552	1,702,419	1,766,671	49.8
South Dakota	124,103	149,092	157,736	169,308	184,153	197,853	217,756	240,061	259,120	53.0
Tennessee	665,885	1,081,052	1,311,921	1,411,226	1,519,680	1,585,614	1,621,202	1,776,066	1,911,953	35.5
Texas	2,736,276	4,375,082	4,771,023	5,166,389	5,604,164	5,959,584	6,370,847	6,982,016	7,414,174	43.5
Utah	405,314	669,714	757,976	835,250	914,771	993,625	1,116,845	1,174,239	1,260,797	50.9
Vermont	122,708	188,112	216,972	241,314	260,371	274,746	294,045	298,626	306,100	26.8
Virginia	1,143,755	1,825,156	2,201,018	2,431,539	2,682,902	2,812,109	2,939,683	3,072,851	3,301,020	35.8
Washington	993,171	1,399,780	1,575,333	1,779,855	1,922,673	2,157,074	2,278,549	2,486,455	2,639,504	48.3
West Virginia	317,482	376,293	406,170	451,503	493,825	548,802	582,453	609,447	650,642	44.1
Wisconsin	1,208,396	1,754,395	2,022,712	2,159,069	2,307,325	2,469,260	2,596,853	2,726,350	2,872,001	33.0
Wyoming	126,082	203,307	208,663	212,813	227,131	240,216	265,048	260,592	271,396	27.5
U.S. Service Schools	592,454	904,695	1,015,815	728,092	793,082	1,136,296	1,219,439	1,246,801	1,301,783	78.8
Outlying areas	268,310	451,370	491,892	494,087	543,925	516,958	574,988	654,292	662,130	34.0
American Samoa	1,609	1,092	1,257	2,642	2,879	3,187	3,228	3,356	3,416	29.3
Federated States of Micronesia	—	—	—	1,789	1,842	3,777	3,765	3,294	3,520	96.8
Guam	16,100	31,310	33,481	38,488	48,954	57,645	67,220	71,917	66,913	73.9
Marshall Islands	—	—	—	—	—	—	3,588	1,298	1,527	—
Northern Marianas	—	1,350	2,292	950	1,003	2,798	3,194	2,505	3,214	238.2
Palau	—	—	—	3,513	3,870	3,837	3,687	4,485	3,476	−1.0
Puerto Rico	237,319	394,046	427,572	424,125	460,897	385,511	434,032	536,917	546,575	28.9
Trust Territory of the Pacific	1,447	5,992	6,455	—	—	—	—	—	—	—
Virgin Islands	11,835	17,580	20,834	22,580	24,480	60,202	56,274	30,520	33,489	48.3

[1] Preliminary data.
[2] Change of less than .05 percent.
—Data not reported or not applicable.

NOTE.—Because of rounding, details may not add to totals.

SOURCE: U.S. Department of Education, National Center for Education Statistics, "Financial Statistics of Institutions of Higher Education" surveys; and Integrated Postsecondary Education Data System (IPEDS), "Finance" surveys. (This table was prepared April 1996.)

Table 344.—Educational and general expenditures of public institutions of higher education, by state: 1980–81 to 1993–94

[In thousands of dollars]

State	1980–81	1985–86	1987–88	1988–89	1989–90	1990–91	1991–92	1992–93	1993–94 [1]	Percent change, 1988–89 to 1993–94
1	2	3	4	5	6	7	8	9	10	11
United States	**$34,173,013**	**$50,872,962**	**$58,639,468**	**$63,444,908**	**$69,163,958**	**$74,395,428**	**$78,554,534**	**$83,210,979**	**$87,139,226**	**37.3**
Alabama	611,409	979,770	1,102,484	1,223,329	1,305,463	1,415,440	1,456,605	1,580,484	1,710,955	39.9
Alaska	150,421	210,894	208,641	227,331	253,392	273,577	288,999	304,137	316,779	39.3
Arizona	554,120	862,816	1,019,287	1,122,890	1,236,696	1,364,060	1,407,819	1,409,122	1,523,655	35.7
Arkansas	266,522	415,800	477,369	530,691	573,923	633,194	604,885	676,378	707,166	33.3
California	4,847,879	7,049,635	7,842,747	8,352,924	9,238,960	9,615,356	10,341,888	11,000,665	10,734,842	28.5
Colorado	561,552	809,621	956,381	1,052,644	1,167,864	1,258,356	1,363,615	1,452,957	1,529,290	45.3
Connecticut	281,581	439,397	527,537	605,228	622,298	673,182	736,202	731,570	771,954	27.5
Delaware	135,164	202,331	247,116	277,543	303,220	325,838	349,369	366,801	387,810	39.7
District of Columbia	71,245	87,620	95,569	103,475	109,795	110,324	120,926	118,282	103,371	–0.1
Florida	1,071,754	1,638,227	2,005,883	2,250,014	2,546,201	2,657,553	2,710,041	2,904,932	3,101,072	37.8
Georgia	628,939	1,046,341	1,265,156	1,364,338	1,482,499	1,617,020	1,665,009	1,834,141	2,037,534	49.3
Hawaii	202,154	282,058	314,832	341,609	384,535	454,880	526,269	546,473	556,567	62.9
Idaho	141,296	202,736	229,094	244,969	268,690	303,224	334,762	346,932	375,289	53.2
Illinois	1,487,123	2,152,955	2,354,360	2,556,337	2,812,244	2,979,768	3,068,891	3,245,802	3,397,183	32.9
Indiana	771,564	1,183,098	1,403,895	1,534,653	1,671,111	1,842,610	1,935,566	2,014,834	2,105,645	37.2
Iowa	512,205	736,894	883,335	987,522	1,077,810	1,172,328	1,184,382	1,267,646	1,354,777	37.2
Kansas	461,979	660,995	720,287	801,774	884,775	928,772	994,560	1,059,683	1,134,392	41.5
Kentucky	527,235	737,101	860,198	916,498	992,403	1,112,190	1,208,448	1,212,211	1,254,859	36.9
Louisiana	557,825	810,479	865,860	908,303	1,005,278	1,135,955	1,215,771	1,275,446	1,339,408	47.5
Maine	127,983	183,349	235,916	271,016	297,782	308,699	316,116	324,515	338,776	25.0
Maryland	604,419	911,562	1,063,956	1,186,989	1,299,110	1,443,669	1,428,072	1,564,259	1,673,163	41.0
Massachusetts	441,068	779,341	1,007,570	1,051,636	1,076,241	1,122,629	1,165,598	1,295,720	1,339,199	27.3
Michigan	1,610,016	2,278,217	2,729,356	2,850,114	3,079,227	3,325,625	3,556,178	3,727,115	3,885,984	36.3
Minnesota	667,119	1,023,324	1,202,304	1,330,114	1,420,124	1,563,054	1,728,356	1,775,640	1,937,650	45.7
Mississippi	409,942	542,022	602,499	674,608	719,821	756,492	772,618	842,603	919,354	36.3
Missouri	553,793	802,936	899,646	995,472	1,083,473	1,155,531	1,184,338	1,260,304	1,339,527	34.6
Montana	99,990	148,099	160,413	161,543	179,510	210,813	262,480	279,323	303,495	87.9
Nebraska	286,122	397,523	437,700	489,501	543,341	600,224	639,475	672,427	706,454	44.3
Nevada	105,177	163,714	198,938	220,033	257,526	301,487	332,246	353,875	379,154	72.3
New Hampshire	104,285	143,191	177,908	195,404	206,207	229,360	252,021	275,138	295,687	51.3
New Jersey	735,097	1,140,310	1,446,642	1,607,786	1,765,002	1,875,481	2,002,975	2,103,355	2,237,339	39.2
New Mexico	278,960	393,151	454,493	561,308	626,386	671,206	724,157	769,646	806,673	43.7
New York	2,249,821	3,238,773	3,820,677	3,961,073	4,252,153	4,680,376	4,768,772	5,113,506	5,398,182	36.3
North Carolina	971,928	1,527,535	1,799,484	1,941,331	2,101,016	2,227,060	2,406,405	2,600,325	2,671,176	37.6
North Dakota	151,372	228,609	238,453	248,612	282,247	292,978	328,738	336,361	344,187	38.4
Ohio	1,327,483	2,019,351	2,385,244	2,630,782	2,799,829	3,046,603	3,214,612	3,185,955	3,362,837	27.8
Oklahoma	404,178	594,561	608,121	688,953	762,034	830,929	906,908	930,102	953,027	38.3
Oregon	497,593	672,175	781,964	839,670	911,812	996,887	1,086,673	1,142,781	1,194,805	42.3
Pennsylvania	1,231,502	1,814,384	2,165,078	2,385,349	2,596,987	2,737,817	2,963,168	3,087,186	3,280,879	37.5
Rhode Island	138,965	185,215	214,627	236,790	250,604	251,992	260,123	284,957	285,742	20.7
South Carolina	481,737	741,740	832,075	903,484	1,012,928	1,065,867	1,100,035	1,172,246	1,244,696	37.8
South Dakota	108,632	130,825	138,428	149,457	162,001	173,396	192,001	211,716	229,080	53.3
Tennessee	515,578	865,946	1,037,718	1,107,583	1,194,378	1,231,619	1,228,340	1,352,125	1,478,085	33.5
Texas	2,278,337	3,674,109	4,038,745	4,394,333	4,816,945	5,105,246	5,439,843	5,961,535	6,352,088	44.6
Utah	320,278	503,557	552,193	602,628	656,772	730,496	826,170	856,933	921,052	52.8
Vermont	101,539	157,266	182,916	204,586	222,470	238,512	258,150	263,475	271,261	32.6
Virginia	796,616	1,241,534	1,500,030	1,647,075	1,807,829	1,852,416	1,892,627	1,991,591	2,124,635	29.0
Washington	837,281	1,143,285	1,270,682	1,450,608	1,564,535	1,757,053	1,837,095	2,007,044	2,074,451	43.0
West Virginia	228,755	310,142	331,806	371,151	411,950	459,984	494,733	522,173	560,380	51.0
Wisconsin	998,862	1,438,918	1,663,132	1,824,067	1,931,561	2,057,786	2,158,188	2,266,312	2,394,285	31.3
Wyoming	111,170	171,335	179,700	181,985	194,506	204,028	225,238	222,188	231,190	27.0
U.S. Service Schools	555,447	798,194	901,023	677,797	740,496	1,016,486	1,088,075	1,110,052	1,162,184	71.5
Outlying areas	253,820	421,500	457,094	457,344	501,855	498,958	555,054	607,730	637,164	39.3
American Samoa	1,609	1,092	1,257	2,642	2,879	3,187	3,228	3,356	3,416	29.3
Federated States of Micronesia	—	—	—	1,474	1,351	3,302	3,286	2,898	3,096	110.1
Guam	15,582	29,916	31,762	36,276	47,380	55,641	64,772	68,550	63,515	75.1
Marshall Islands	—	—	—	—	—	—	3,093	1,220	1,454	—
Northern Marianas	—	1,328	2,009	794	766	2,472	2,803	2,230	2,838	257.3
Palau	—	—	—	2,993	3,297	3,277	3,172	3,808	2,847	–4.9
Puerto Rico	224,988	367,523	397,605	392,814	426,754	378,352	427,021	497,590	529,255	34.7
Trust Territory of the Pacific	1,320	5,992	5,684	—	—	—	—	—	—	—
Virgin Islands	10,322	15,649	18,777	20,351	19,427	52,726	47,679	28,078	30,743	51.1

[1] Preliminary data.

—Data not reported or not applicable.

NOTE.—Because of rounding, details may not add to totals.

SOURCE: U.S. Department of Education, National Center for Education Statistics, "Financial Statistics of Institutions of Higher Education" surveys; and Integrated Postsecondary Education Data System (IPEDS), "Finance" surveys. (This table was prepared April 1996.)

Table 345.—Current-fund expenditures and educational and general expenditures of private institutions of higher education, by state: 1985–86 to 1993–94

[In thousands of dollars]

State	Current-fund expenditures					Educational and general expenditures				
	1985–86	1990–91	1991–92	1992–93	1993–94 [1]	1985–86	1990–91	1991–92	1992–93	1993–94 [1]
1	2	3	4	5	6	7	8	9	10	11
United States	$34,341,889	$53,126,743	$57,341,982	$60,670,938	$64,041,076	$25,255,003	$39,744,472	$43,012,623	$45,766,989	$48,885,124
Alabama	186,596	244,425	263,052	286,584	299,982	164,093	212,538	229,670	252,259	265,046
Alaska	10,171	22,127	18,454	22,693	23,199	9,106	19,375	15,851	18,687	18,140
Arizona	52,887	121,482	94,564	106,478	118,954	48,600	110,015	86,087	100,150	111,414
Arkansas	70,755	114,655	118,373	124,091	130,253	56,492	95,560	98,442	103,347	108,969
California	3,644,031	5,525,201	5,957,016	6,171,590	6,419,322	2,275,958	3,484,709	3,836,270	4,051,762	4,366,131
Colorado	160,193	288,865	305,244	306,824	327,275	142,218	257,003	269,386	279,956	297,087
Connecticut	836,949	1,293,468	1,376,756	1,437,827	1,527,283	733,144	1,143,220	1,224,643	1,280,969	1,363,083
Delaware	29,569	23,875	27,215	29,293	31,836	26,501	21,598	24,741	26,575	29,040
District of Columbia	1,307,377	1,955,110	2,100,279	2,307,943	2,386,469	803,566	1,178,178	1,246,366	1,311,616	1,375,811
Florida	723,270	1,274,196	1,386,602	1,510,855	1,561,498	553,391	1,001,000	1,089,712	1,193,708	1,234,246
Georgia	696,734	1,227,745	1,371,887	1,514,055	1,683,308	429,639	788,200	886,314	981,355	1,122,545
Hawaii	32,553	42,881	41,760	91,016	95,803	25,323	36,528	36,124	72,609	76,909
Idaho	49,768	74,519	82,255	87,532	95,011	37,736	59,252	65,018	72,006	82,923
Illinois	2,729,672	3,955,777	4,366,966	4,694,688	4,778,173	1,495,654	2,349,405	2,544,490	2,698,324	2,936,263
Indiana	530,163	847,885	889,004	941,404	1,000,966	426,813	700,346	736,784	782,734	831,223
Iowa	353,753	533,300	595,007	634,046	676,124	292,291	445,631	501,547	534,220	573,136
Kansas	105,193	144,471	147,336	157,139	171,402	87,719	124,578	126,939	136,036	149,127
Kentucky	194,873	282,937	304,780	315,147	330,341	159,293	236,191	255,870	263,722	275,986
Louisiana	353,433	572,049	629,158	673,080	739,368	221,928	372,431	397,191	439,834	459,780
Maine	133,778	200,149	210,328	223,573	238,196	106,912	167,618	176,530	187,523	199,895
Maryland	896,251	1,461,897	1,550,526	1,622,871	1,729,558	562,773	987,405	1,048,953	1,133,491	1,217,678
Massachusetts	3,544,867	5,339,793	5,580,304	5,850,688	6,116,367	2,817,687	4,278,151	4,600,897	4,874,439	5,122,411
Michigan	447,436	699,193	738,699	789,175	826,746	384,533	618,422	651,408	696,518	730,458
Minnesota	521,441	730,974	776,325	812,893	800,291	443,972	625,497	654,953	678,472	679,001
Mississippi	64,054	101,330	110,325	115,789	123,506	55,252	88,305	96,217	101,895	108,547
Missouri	904,573	1,493,892	1,645,969	1,666,001	1,769,749	713,411	1,186,195	1,306,990	1,347,644	1,453,221
Montana	22,349	33,471	33,238	39,500	44,193	18,565	29,165	28,567	33,873	38,509
Nebraska	161,066	245,142	269,968	287,540	303,472	138,929	219,054	242,660	258,485	271,942
Nevada	2,448	4,507	5,971	5,490	6,768	2,448	4,066	5,127	4,666	5,998
New Hampshire	264,440	407,903	432,080	455,312	487,785	230,657	355,056	374,323	395,395	426,736
New Jersey	714,733	982,070	1,082,717	1,167,222	1,208,726	540,245	789,649	863,322	926,131	980,224
New Mexico	22,196	33,272	46,252	33,162	40,520	19,678	28,754	39,813	28,659	35,079
New York	5,596,257	8,246,193	9,003,453	9,536,982	10,157,945	4,572,405	6,735,931	7,401,300	7,837,705	8,315,046
North Carolina	837,291	1,704,643	1,911,631	2,008,628	2,166,337	592,910	1,123,378	1,255,073	1,313,943	1,417,518
North Dakota	18,853	27,978	34,323	33,758	36,380	15,860	24,033	29,719	28,821	31,776
Ohio	976,303	1,510,387	1,613,085	1,696,377	1,807,756	833,879	1,308,048	1,403,786	1,486,111	1,586,086
Oklahoma	178,905	280,889	256,332	266,152	286,118	149,565	239,088	220,403	230,661	248,299
Oregon	171,604	277,152	287,800	307,280	334,424	149,289	247,671	256,162	275,352	299,529
Pennsylvania	3,155,505	4,914,117	5,452,687	5,667,740	6,008,469	2,033,015	3,242,842	3,521,644	3,802,781	4,115,506
Rhode Island	315,651	518,425	559,922	590,911	636,510	261,616	437,800	476,062	504,274	545,057
South Carolina	196,271	319,782	274,300	293,819	318,200	154,496	258,540	225,437	245,689	268,292
South Dakota	51,675	84,903	71,462	63,406	66,315	44,726	74,859	63,351	56,780	59,358
Tennessee	686,514	1,097,066	1,199,755	1,226,183	1,352,769	440,308	706,976	785,347	827,801	894,506
Texas	993,824	1,528,755	1,633,787	1,716,860	1,833,288	855,445	1,365,275	1,460,510	1,540,238	1,653,269
Utah	183,060	272,883	317,586	454,442	458,878	110,880	223,238	257,271	313,342	317,681
Vermont	150,689	266,539	287,261	300,593	269,666	126,299	229,548	250,999	261,364	232,565
Virginia	387,455	671,912	706,344	748,902	807,849	313,055	581,094	607,724	645,752	702,430
Washington	227,211	368,077	401,261	435,993	475,565	189,575	316,014	345,756	375,031	413,941
West Virginia	73,716	108,334	114,586	129,367	143,742	60,900	93,399	98,830	112,959	126,231
Wisconsin	373,533	645,774	651,420	702,292	775,629	326,254	519,270	585,465	633,564	701,051
Wyoming	—	4,370	6,578	9,752	12,788	—	4,370	6,578	7,752	10,426
Outlying areas	198,653	271,237	284,662	306,098	337,721	189,080	256,576	267,789	290,189	320,304
Puerto Rico	198,653	271,237	284,662	306,098	337,721	189,080	256,576	267,789	290,189	320,304

[1] Preliminary data.

—Data not reported or not applicable.

NOTE.—Because of rounding, details may not add to totals.

SOURCE: U.S. Department of Education, National Center for Education Statistics, "Financial Statistics of Institutions of Higher Education" survey; and Integrated Postsecondary Education Data System (IPEDS), "Finance" surveys. (This table was prepared April 1996.)

Table 346.—Current-fund expenditures per full-time-equivalent student in institutions of higher education, by control and type of institution and purpose of expenditure: 1993–94 [1]

Item	Total				Public				Private		
	All institutions	Univer-sities	Other 4-year	2-year	All institutions	Univer-sities	Other 4-year	2-year	All institu-tions [2]	Univer-sities	Other 4-year
1	2	3	4	5	6	7	8	9	10	11	12
Total current-fund expenditures [3]	$16,747	$29,322	$16,896	$6,558	$13,992	$23,150	$15,896	$6,438	$25,223	$47,794	$18,555
Educational and general expenditures	13,141	21,856	13,217	6,118	11,154	17,863	12,120	6,021	19,254	33,806	15,040
Instruction	5,098	7,984	5,010	2,933	4,568	6,306	5,104	2,972	6,730	13,003	4,855
Research	1,557	4,490	1,005	9	1,431	3,996	1,221	10	1,945	5,969	645
Public service	603	1,322	531	135	607	1,450	536	142	591	940	522
Academic support	1,128	1,887	1,142	506	1,029	1,669	1,166	496	1,435	2,541	1,103
Libraries	378	663	385	140	313	524	358	139	575	1,080	431
Student services	827	798	970	649	680	663	751	626	1,279	1,203	1,334
Institutional support	1,539	1,736	1,842	953	1,194	1,238	1,469	910	2,599	3,226	2,463
Operation and maintenance of plant	1,098	1,576	1,156	638	951	1,280	1,084	620	1,550	2,459	1,275
Scholarships and fellowships	1,086	1,713	1,322	254	541	994	593	206	2,763	3,866	2,534
From unrestricted funds	642	1,083	809	57	248	561	258	40	1,855	2,643	1,723
From restricted funds [4]	444	630	513	197	293	432	334	166	908	1,223	811
Mandatory transfers	204	350	238	40	153	268	196	40	363	598	309

[1] Preliminary data.

[2] Includes private 2-year colleges.

[3] Includes expenditures for auxiliary enterprises, hospitals, and independent operations which are not shown separately.

[4] Excludes Pell Grants.

NOTE.—Data for private 2-year colleges are not shown separately because of low survey response rate. Because of rounding, details may not add to totals.

SOURCE: U.S. Department of Education, National Center for Education Statistics, Integrated Postsecondary Education Data System (IPEDS), "Fall Enrollment" and "Finance" surveys. (This table was prepared June 1996.)

Table 347.—Additions to physical plant value of institutions of higher education, by type of addition and control of institution: 1969–70 to 1993–94

[In millions]

Year	Total, all institutions	Public institutions				Private institutions			
		Total	Land	Buildings	Equipment	Total	Land	Buildings	Equipment
1	2	3	4	5	6	7	8	9	10
1969–70	$4,233	$2,985	$152	$2,185	$648	$1,248	$59	$967	$221
1970–71	4,165	3,032	128	2,241	663	1,134	41	895	198
1971–72	4,163	3,054	112	2,277	665	1,109	53	860	195
1972–73	3,967	2,940	126	2,077	737	1,028	53	750	225
1973–74	4,312	3,206	205	2,188	813	1,106	55	816	235
1974–75	4,761	3,476	263	2,246	967	1,284	67	860	357
1975–76	4,702	3,552	168	2,365	1,019	1,150	58	768	325
1976–77	4,623	3,362	128	2,208	1,026	1,261	58	838	366
1977–78	4,527	3,306	102	2,117	1,087	1,221	45	777	400
1978–79	4,576	3,377	154	1,944	1,279	1,199	52	763	383
1979–80	5,551	3,666	164	2,149	1,354	1,886	98	1,220	568
1980–81	6,471	4,279	146	2,555	1,579	2,192	104	1,398	690
1981–82	6,975	4,594	170	2,679	1,744	2,382	83	1,488	811
1982–83	7,421	4,765	374	2,396	1,994	2,656	106	1,666	884
1983–84	7,604	5,038	196	2,427	2,415	2,566	110	1,507	950
1984–85	8,306	5,390	202	2,455	2,733	2,916	135	1,671	1,110
1985–86	10,149	6,875	237	3,318	3,320	3,274	128	1,922	1,225
1986–87	10,675	6,899	313	3,235	3,351	3,776	160	2,408	1,208
1987–88	11,589	7,218	272	3,520	3,426	4,371	250	2,715	1,406
1988–89	13,638	8,162	562	3,845	3,756	5,477	243	3,401	1,833
1989–90	15,900	10,616	532	5,438	4,647	5,284	408	3,277	1,599
1990–91	17,634	11,472	449	6,168	4,855	6,162	448	3,799	1,914
1991–92 [1]	15,543	9,820	412	5,272	4,136	5,723	380	3,419	1,925
1992–93 [1]	16,494	10,599	336	5,982	4,281	5,895	491	3,458	1,946
1993–94	16,379	10,263	361	5,582	4,320	6,116	259	3,840	2,017

[1] Revised from previously published figures.

NOTE.—Because of rounding, details may not add to totals. Some data have been revised from previously published figures.

SOURCE: U.S. Department of Education, National Center for Education Statistics, "Financial Statistics of Institutions of Higher Education" surveys; and Integrated Postsecondary Education Data System (IPEDS), "Finance" surveys. (This table was prepared July 1996.)

Table 348.—Value of property and liabilities of institutions of higher education: 1899–1900 to 1993–94

[In thousands]

Academic year	Property value at end of year						Endowment (end of year market value) [1]	Liabilities of plant funds
	Total	Physical plant value				Endowment (book value) [1]		
		Total	Land	Buildings	Equipment			
1	2	3	4	5	6	7	8	9
1899–1900	$448,597	$253,599	—	—	—	[2] $194,998	—	—
1909–10	781,255	457,594	$92,359	$297,153	$68,082	[2] 323,661	—	—
1919–20	1,316,404	747,333	128,922	495,920	122,491	[2] 569,071	—	—
1929–30	3,437,117	2,065,049	304,114	1,490,014	270,921	[2] 1,372,068	—	—
1935–36	3,913,028	2,359,418	334,085	1,636,722	388,611	[2] 1,553,610	—	—
1937–38	4,208,695	2,556,075	313,665	1,811,309	431,101	1,652,620	—	—
1939–40	4,440,063	2,753,780	—	—	—	1,686,283	—	—
1941–42	4,525,925	2,759,261	—	—	—	[2] 1,766,664	—	—
1947–48	6,076,212	3,691,725	—	—	—	2,384,487	—	—
1949–50	7,401,187	4,799,964	—	—	—	[2] 2,601,223	—	—
1951–52	9,241,725	6,373,195	—	—	—	2,868,530	—	—
1953–54	10,717,082	7,523,193	—	—	—	3,193,889	—	—
1955–56	12,561,046	8,858,907	624,467	[3] 6,697,648	1,536,792	3,702,139	—	$894,383
1957–58	15,770,197	11,124,489	733,182	[3] 8,540,429	1,850,878	4,645,708	—	1,444,602
1959–60	18,870,628	13,548,548	842,664	[3] 10,472,478	2,233,407	5,322,080	—	1,964,306
1961–62	22,761,193	16,681,844	1,009,294	[3] 12,900,093	2,772,457	6,079,349	—	2,806,868
1963–64	28,232,362	21,279,346	1,292,691	[3] 16,460,867	3,525,788	6,953,016	—	4,190,189
1965–66	35,274,597	26,851,273	1,758,901	[3] 20,653,028	4,439,344	8,423,324	$11,126,831	6,071,750
1967–68	—	34,506,348	2,062,545	[3] 26,673,826	5,769,977	—	—	—
1969–70	52,930,923	42,093,580	3,076,751	31,865,179	7,151,649	10,837,343	11,206,632	9,384,731
1970–71	57,394,951	46,053,585	3,117,895	35,042,590	7,893,100	11,341,366	13,714,330	9,786,240
1971–72	62,136,459	50,153,251	3,287,326	38,131,339	8,734,586	11,983,208	15,180,934	10,291,095
1972–73	66,814,103	53,814,596	3,492,611	40,808,481	9,513,503	12,999,507	15,099,840	10,823,595
1973–74	71,305,817	58,002,777	3,888,372	43,701,491	10,412,914	13,303,040	13,168,076	11,400,916
1974–75	75,585,674	62,183,078	4,210,901	46,453,642	11,518,536	13,402,596	14,364,545	12,413,420
1975–76	80,300,595	66,348,304	4,345,232	49,349,224	12,653,847	13,952,291	15,488,265	12,687,015
1976–77	85,486,550	70,739,427	4,444,927	52,384,393	13,910,107	14,747,123	16,304,553	13,068,341
1977–78	90,337,044	74,770,804	4,621,071	55,188,603	14,961,131	15,566,240	16,840,129	13,437,861
1978–79	95,442,468	78,637,991	4,824,250	57,563,005	16,250,737	16,804,477	18,158,634	13,712,648
1979–80	102,294,859	83,733,387	5,037,172	60,847,097	17,849,119	18,561,472	20,743,045	14,181,991
1980–81	109,701,242	88,760,567	5,212,453	64,158,017	19,390,097	20,940,675	23,465,001	14,794,669
1981–82	117,601,954	94,516,512	5,402,339	67,794,877	21,319,297	23,085,442	24,415,245	15,487,618
1982–83	127,345,302	100,992,841	5,889,080	71,519,718	23,584,042	26,352,461	32,691,133	16,749,900
1983–84	137,141,741	107,640,113	6,109,746	75,220,765	26,309,602	29,501,629	32,975,610	18,277,315
1984–85	148,163,096	114,763,986	6,236,159	79,133,998	29,393,829	33,399,110	39,916,361	22,105,712
1985–86	160,959,517	122,261,355	6,573,923	82,886,012	32,801,419	38,698,162	50,280,775	25,699,408
1986–87	—	126,426,171	7,165,445	84,838,657	34,422,069	—	56,585,153	—
1987–88	—	139,456,342	8,307,789	92,428,615	38,719,937	—	57,391,814	—
1988–89	—	158,693,085	9,462,095	104,743,145	44,487,845	—	64,155,247	—
1989–90	—	164,635,000	9,968,000	108,609,000	46,058,000	—	67,978,726	—
1990–91	—	178,084,000	10,028,000	117,683,000	50,373,000	—	72,048,579	—
1991–92 [4]	—	184,813,238	10,528,395	122,422,566	51,862,277	—	82,534,026	—
1992–93 [4]	—	192,760,817	11,006,451	128,436,599	53,317,767	—	92,239,311	—
1993–94	—	199,463,715	11,197,662	133,124,680	55,141,373	—	96,012,591	—

[1] Includes funds functioning as endowment.

[2] Includes annuity funds.

[3] Includes improvements to land and equipment. These funds are included under appropriate categories after 1967–68.

[4] Revised from previously published data.

—Data not available.

NOTE.—Because of rounding, details may not add to totals. Some data have been revised from previously published figures.

SOURCE: U.S. Department of Education, National Center for Education Statistics, "Financial Statistics of Institutions of Higher Education" surveys; and Integrated Postsecondary Education Data System (IPEDS), "Finance" surveys. (This table was prepared July 1996.)

Table 349.—Endowment funds of the 120 institutions of higher education with the largest amounts: Fiscal year 1994

Institution	Rank order [1]	Market value of endowment, in thousands of dollars (end of fiscal year)	Institution	Rank order [1]	Market value of endowment, in thousands of dollars (end of fiscal year)
1	2	3	1	2	3
United States (all institutions)	—	**$96,012,591**			
120 institutions receiving the largest amounts	—	68,927,999			
Harvard University (MA)	1	6,201,220	Middlebury College (VT)	61	323,363
University of Texas at Austin	2	[2]3,626,536	Wesleyan University (CT)	62	319,454
Yale University (CT)	3	3,537,232	Baylor University (TX)	63	318,355
Stanford University (CA)	4	2,954,121	Vassar College (NY)	64	316,269
Princeton University (NJ)	5	2,648,130	Pennsylvania State University, Main Campus	65	312,281
Columbia University (NY)	6	2,028,021	Washington And Lee University (VA)	66	308,289
Massachusetts Institute of Technology	7	1,777,777	Lafayette College (PA)	67	285,234
University of California System	8	[2]1,771,552	Saint Louis University, Main Campus (MO)	68	285,178
Washington University (MO)	9	1,715,490	Tulane University of Louisiana	69	284,033
Emory University (GA)	10	1,634,629	Yeshiva University (NY)	70	277,206
University of Pennsylvania	11	1,464,455	Oberlin College (OH)	71	267,844
Rice University (TX)	12	1,278,524	Rensselaer Polytechnic Institute (NY)	72	265,166
Northwestern University (IL)	13	1,268,708	Mount Sinai School of Medicine (NY)	73	243,084
University of Chicago (IL)	14	1,186,600	The Juilliard School (NY)	74	241,140
University of Michigan, Ann Arbor	15	1,009,840	University of Miami (FL)	75	239,692
Cornell University-Endowed Colleges (NY)	16	897,941	Syracuse University, Main Campus (NY)	76	232,464
University of Notre Dame (IN)	17	878,927	Purdue University, Main Campus (IN)	77	225,414
Dartmouth College (NH)	18	869,925	Bryn Mawr College (PA)	78	222,914
Vanderbilt University (TN)	19	859,947	Mount Holyoke College (MA)	79	222,899
University of Southern California	20	791,355	Rochester Institute of Technology (NY)	80	221,662
Johns Hopkins University (MD)	21	[2]746,777	Carleton College (MN)	81	218,577
New York University	22	710,379	Tufts University (MA)	82	217,298
Duke University (NC)	23	699,002	Northeastern University (MA)	83	217,278
University of Rochester (NY)	24	662,578	Thomas Jefferson University (PA)	84	214,325
University of Virginia, Main Campus	25	634,774	Cornell University Medical College (NY)	85	212,411
Brown University (RI)	26	607,699	University of Texas, Southwest Medical Ctr.	86	207,659
Rockefeller University (NY)	27	597,069	Brigham Young University (UT)	87	201,893
California Institute of Technology	28	591,885	Colgate University (NY)	88	199,233
Case Western Reserve University (OH)	29	557,145	Loyola University in New Orleans (LA)	89	198,266
Princeton Theological Seminary (NJ)	30	487,424	Brandeis University (MA)	90	194,306
Wellesley College (MA)	31	484,126	Bowdoin College (ME)	91	193,962
Ohio State University, Main Campus	32	479,281	Agnes Scott College (GA)	92	193,560
Macalester College (MN)	33	470,938	Rush University (IL)	93	193,031
Loyola University of Chicago (IL)	34	463,556	Claremont McKenna College (CA)	94	189,749
Swarthmore College (PA)	35	458,053	Trinity College (CT)	95	183,995
Southern Methodist University (TX)	36	450,690	Virginia Polytechnic Institute and State U.	96	167,222
Boston College (MA)	37	449,685	Hamilton College (NY)	97	166,598
Smith College (MA)	38	442,071	Rutgers, The State U., Central Office (NJ)	98	[2]165,170
Texas Christian University	39	440,470	University of Tennessee (Central office)	99	164,861
University of Washington	40	440,290	Regent University (VA)	100	161,688
Grinnell College (IA)	41	417,409	Academy of the New Church (PA)	101	161,053
Williams College (MA)	42	416,959	Colorado College	102	159,240
Carnegie Mellon University (PA)	43	414,700	Santa Clara University (CA)	103	154,371
University of Delaware	44	408,487	University of Alabama	104	153,365
University of Richmond (VA)	45	404,157	University of New Mexico, Main Campus	105	[2]153,285
Baylor College of Medicine (TX)	46	403,262	North Carolina State University at Raleigh	106	152,568
Pomona College (CA)	47	388,539	College of the Holy Cross (MA)	107	152,449
University of Pittsburgh, Main Campus (PA)	48	373,498	Earlham College (IN)	108	151,874
Wake Forest University (NC)	49	368,434	Denison University (OH)	109	149,613
George Washington University (DC)	50	366,546	Wabash College (IN)	110	148,798
University of Tulsa (OK)	51	361,825	State University of New York at Buffalo	111	[3]147,848
Berea College (KY)	52	352,704	University of the South (TN)	112	147,516
University of Cincinnati, Main Campus (OH)	53	352,160	Cornell University, Statutory Colleges (NY)	113	[3]147,314
Lehigh University (PA)	54	344,400	Southwestern University (TX)	114	146,074
Trinity University (TX)	55	343,490	Occidental College (CA)	115	145,345
Georgetown University (DC)	56	343,166	University of Louisville (KY)	116	145,313
University of Minnesota, Twin Cities	57	340,382	University of Wisconsin, Madison	117	144,299
Boston University (MA)	58	337,170	Texas A & M University	118	142,864
Amherst College (MA)	59	331,637	Franklin And Marshall College (PA)	119	140,100
University of North Carolina at Chapel Hill	60	327,956	Union College (NY)	120	139,987

[1] Institutions ranked by size of endowment. Excludes institutions which have not reported data for 1993–94.

[2] Includes some funds from other branch campuses.

[3] Some funds included with other branch campus reports.

—Not applicable.

SOURCE: U.S. Department of Education, National Center for Education Statistics, Integrated Postsecondary Education Data System (IPEDS), "Finance, 1993–94" survey. (This table was prepared October 1996.)

Table 350.—Participants in adult education 17 years old and older, by selected characteristics of participants: 1991

[Numbers in thousands]

Characteristics of participants	Number of adults in population [1]	Ever a participant in adult education [2]		Participated in adult education [2] in past 3 years		Participated in adult education [2] in past year	
		Number	Percent of population	Number	Percent of population	Number	Percent of population
1	2	3	4	5	6	7	8
Total	181,800	97,397	54	69,361	38	57,391	32
Age							
17 to 24 years	21,688	9,240	43	8,756	40	7,125	33
25 to 34 years	47,244	27,325	58	22,773	48	17,530	37
35 to 44 years	38,565	25,043	65	19,581	51	17,083	44
45 to 54 years	25,375	14,755	58	9,351	37	8,107	32
55 to 64 years	19,967	10,101	51	5,150	26	4,516	23
65 years and over	28,960	10,934	38	3,750	13	3,031	10
Sex							
Men	82,154	42,163	51	29,945	36	25,923	32
Women	99,646	55,234	55	39,415	40	31,469	32
Racial/ethnic group							
White, non-Hispanic	143,144	80,099	56	56,715	40	47,401	33
Black, non-Hispanic	20,141	8,213	41	5,552	28	4,586	23
Hispanic	13,804	6,905	50	5,396	39	4,032	29
Other races, non-Hispanic	4,711	2,180	46	1,698	36	1,371	29
Highest level of education completed							
Less than high school diploma	28,306	7,337	26	4,127	15	3,437	12
High school diploma	110,384	58,135	53	39,403	36	31,602	29
Associate degree	5,034	3,949	78	3,191	63	2,461	49
Bachelor's degree or higher	38,076	27,976	73	22,640	59	19,891	52
Labor force status							
In labor force	125,440	73,513	59	58,078	46	49,242	39
Employed	115,620	69,421	60	55,093	48	47,143	41
Unemployed	9,820	4,092	42	2,985	30	2,099	21
Not in labor force	56,361	23,884	42	11,283	20	8,149	14
Annual family income							
$10,000 or less	27,504	10,706	39	5,766	21	3,843	14
$10,001 to $15,000	15,465	7,014	45	4,426	29	3,178	21
$15,001 to $20,000	16,117	6,335	39	4,183	26	3,308	21
$20,001 to $25,000	16,092	7,666	48	5,343	33	4,063	25
$25,001 to $30,000	17,973	9,309	52	6,570	37	5,445	30
$30,001 to $40,000	26,110	14,922	57	10,313	39	9,043	35
$40,001 to $50,000	21,303	13,270	62	10,526	49	9,313	44
$50,001 to $75,000	24,540	16,629	68	12,971	53	11,235	46
More than $75,000	16,695	11,546	69	9,263	55	7,963	48

[1] Persons 17 years of age and over on the date of the survey.

[2] Adult education is defined as all non-full-time education activities such as part-time college attendance, classes or seminars given by employers, and classes taken for adult literacy purposes, or for recreation and enjoyment.

NOTE.—Data are based upon a sample survey of the civilian noninstitutional population. Because of rounding and survey item nonresponse, details may not add to totals.

SOURCE: U.S. Department of Education, National Center for Education Statistics, "Participation in Adult Education," unpublished data. (This table was prepared July 1991.)

Table 351.—Type of employer involvement and number of courses taken by adult education participants [1] 17 years old and older, by selected characteristics of participants: 1991

Characteristics of participants	Adult education participants in the past year, in thousands	Type of employer involvement (percent of adult education participants)						Percentage distribution of the number of adult education courses taken in the past year		
		Any type	Given at place of work	Employer paid some portion	Employer provided course	Employer required course	Employer provided time off	One	Two or three	Four or more
1	2	3	4	5	6	7	8	9	10	11
Total	57,391	64	32	51	38	30	48	43	34	21
Age										
17 to 24 years	7,125	54	28	39	36	26	39	46	30	22
25 to 34 years	17,530	68	31	55	40	36	50	43	34	20
35 to 44 years	17,083	70	35	56	40	30	53	38	36	23
45 to 54 years	8,107	71	39	59	44	32	55	41	36	22
55 to 64 years	4,516	64	30	48	36	27	45	50	32	16
65 years and over	3,031	18	8	12	9	9	12	60	27	9
Sex										
Men	25,923	73	35	58	42	34	56	42	37	19
Women	31,469	57	29	46	35	27	41	44	31	22
Racial/ethnic group										
White, non-Hispanic	47,401	65	32	53	39	30	49	42	35	21
Black, non-Hispanic	4,586	59	36	48	41	38	44	41	31	24
Hispanic	4,032	58	30	39	33	31	43	56	27	14
Other races, non-Hispanic	1,371	56	28	36	30	20	40	39	27	28
Highest level of education completed										
Less than high school diploma	3,437	35	17	21	19	21	19	72	17	8
High school diploma	31,602	62	31	50	36	31	45	47	32	18
Associate degree	2,461	76	47	66	51	39	63	32	40	25
Bachelor's degree or higher	19,891	71	34	57	44	30	56	33	39	26
Labor force status										
In labor force	49,242	72	36	58	43	34	54	41	35	22
Employed	47,143	74	37	60	44	35	56	40	36	22
Unemployed	2,099	35	12	13	12	19	18	56	23	16
Not in labor force	8,149	16	7	11	9	8	10	60	26	12
Annual family income										
$10,000 or less	3,843	39	18	25	24	23	29	59	20	15
$10,001 to $15,000	3,178	52	27	37	24	27	37	53	32	13
$15,001 to $20,000	3,308	57	28	42	35	29	39	46	37	15
$20,001 to $25,000	4,063	67	34	46	37	34	48	48	32	17
$25,001 to $30,000	5,445	58	30	48	38	29	39	44	34	19
$30,001 to $40,000	9,043	68	35	57	43	35	50	42	32	24
$40,001 to $50,000	9,313	67	34	55	42	33	50	45	32	20
$50,001 to $75,000	11,235	72	35	61	43	32	58	39	37	22
More than $75,000	7,963	68	30	54	37	24	53	32	41	26

[1] Adult education is defined as all non-full-time education activities such as part-time college attendance, classes or seminars given by employers, and classes taken for adult literacy purposes, or for recreation and enjoyment.

NOTE.—Data are based upon a sample survey of the civilian noninstitutional population. Because of rounding and survey item nonresponse, details may not add to totals.

SOURCE: U.S. Department of Education, National Center for Education Statistics, "Participation in Adult Education," unpublished data. (This table was prepared July 1991.)

Table 352.—Participants in adult basic and secondary education programs, by level of enrollment and state: Fiscal years 1980, 1990, and 1991

State or other area	1980				1990			1991		
	Total	Level of enrollment			Total	Level of enrollment		Total	Level of enrollment	
		Adult basic education	Adult secondary education	Ungraded		Adult basic education [1]	Adult secondary education		Adult basic education [1]	Adult secondary education
1	2	3	4	5	6	7	8	9	10	11
United States	2,018,906	915,936	531,663	571,307	3,535,970	2,435,649	1,100,321	3,694,217	2,513,371	1,180,846
Alabama	51,599	36,726	12,372	2,501	40,177	32,984	7,193	45,700	36,319	9,381
Alaska	5,667	2,200	2,188	1,279	5,067	4,267	800	5,399	4,488	911
Arizona	9,996	9,968	22	6	33,805	24,915	8,890	36,717	26,709	10,008
Arkansas	8,583	7,308	1,275	—	29,065	17,103	11,962	30,845	17,437	13,408
California	267,625	60,385	—	207,240	1,021,227	753,282	267,945	1,022,583	761,637	260,946
Colorado	9,381	4,295	2,644	2,442	12,183	9,877	2,306	13,742	10,764	2,978
Connecticut	21,889	8,882	4,805	8,202	46,434	25,560	20,874	57,188	32,117	25,071
Delaware	1,797	1,110	503	184	2,662	2,348	314	2,567	2,167	400
District of Columbia	25,214	4,928	6,502	13,784	19,586	12,631	6,955	20,309	13,207	7,102
Florida	467,162	100,958	184,568	181,636	419,429	249,339	170,090	436,766	260,761	176,005
Georgia	50,820	26,734	17,008	7,078	69,580	49,622	19,958	80,119	59,107	21,012
Hawaii	16,457	16,457	—	—	52,012	31,766	20,246	53,051	29,816	23,235
Idaho	12,851	8,915	3,010	926	11,171	9,180	1,991	10,215	8,407	1,808
Illinois	76,456	59,314	17,142	—	87,121	69,770	17,351	91,383	72,997	18,386
Indiana	20,882	18,127	2,660	95	44,166	27,138	17,028	50,483	31,101	19,382
Iowa	25,851	16,928	5,153	3,770	41,507	30,470	11,037	38,998	28,009	10,989
Kansas	14,405	3,687	7,436	3,282	10,274	9,191	1,083	11,179	8,877	2,302
Kentucky	27,800	6,147	4,735	16,918	28,090	20,406	7,684	23,248	16,683	6,565
Louisiana	16,046	12,608	2,485	953	40,039	20,941	19,098	43,349	22,254	21,095
Maine	5,327	3,029	942	1,356	14,964	6,620	8,344	16,573	7,505	9,068
Maryland	34,572	23,421	6,043	5,108	41,230	36,244	4,986	53,505	49,804	3,701
Massachusetts	20,420	10,241	5,044	5,135	34,220	28,140	6,080	23,218	18,289	4,929
Michigan	40,973	29,945	—	11,028	194,178	80,206	113,972	205,545	75,897	129,648
Minnesota	10,826	8,627	877	1,322	45,648	33,190	12,458	48,853	31,964	16,889
Mississippi	14,317	10,340	2,918	1,059	18,957	15,834	3,123	20,015	17,269	2,746
Missouri	33,292	27,206	3,732	2,354	31,815	27,274	4,541	33,060	28,211	4,849
Montana	3,525	1,795	978	752	6,071	3,962	2,109	5,942	3,665	2,277
Nebraska	7,514	5,152	2,362	—	6,158	5,349	809	6,597	5,786	811
Nevada	3,063	845	82	2,136	17,262	7,270	9,992	19,682	6,329	13,353
New Hampshire	4,844	2,657	1,625	562	7,198	5,073	2,125	7,137	4,282	2,855
New Jersey	35,770	17,152	6,790	11,828	64,080	46,526	17,554	65,379	43,162	22,217
New Mexico	13,102	3,590	5,147	4,365	30,236	18,069	12,167	30,287	17,154	13,133
New York	94,574	57,217	20,002	17,355	156,611	125,893	30,718	182,879	146,265	36,614
North Carolina	84,252	33,854	46,679	3,719	109,740	71,698	38,042	120,347	79,641	40,706
North Dakota	2,810	1,963	538	309	3,587	2,500	1,087	3,853	2,725	1,128
Ohio	50,056	42,421	7,635	—	95,476	79,527	15,949	108,753	88,302	20,451
Oklahoma	14,701	6,983	5,697	2,021	24,307	19,131	5,176	26,707	20,473	6,234
Oregon	27,645	10,690	12,594	4,361	37,075	24,915	12,160	40,285	24,791	15,494
Pennsylvania	29,477	19,246	6,436	3,795	52,444	40,108	12,336	48,590	38,054	10,536
Rhode Island	5,844	2,266	1,357	2,221	7,347	5,874	1,473	7,264	5,431	1,833
South Carolina	69,659	27,959	35,165	6,535	81,200	37,117	44,083	86,776	35,911	50,865
South Dakota	4,067	2,080	1,109	878	3,184	2,458	726	3,079	2,349	730
Tennessee	26,268	17,079	3,244	5,945	41,721	39,604	2,117	49,556	40,702	8,854
Texas	157,349	94,245	51,126	11,978	218,747	145,067	73,680	220,027	150,322	69,705
Utah	18,541	3,756	14,785	—	24,841	6,003	18,838	24,028	6,788	17,240
Vermont	4,583	3,990	—	593	4,808	4,452	356	5,330	4,862	468
Virginia	21,525	10,480	3,804	7,241	31,649	30,005	1,644	25,456	14,450	11,006
Washington	16,286	7,245	3,894	5,147	31,776	25,336	6,440	34,401	27,752	6,649
West Virginia	14,628	9,743	3,672	1,213	21,186	14,227	[2] 6,959	23,077	16,903	6,174
Wisconsin	16,158	14,185	1,973	—	61,081	45,116	15,965	70,838	53,524	17,314
Wyoming	2,457	857	905	695	3,578	2,071	[2] 1,507	3,337	1,952	1,385
Outlying areas										
American Samoa	313	252	61	—	—	—	—	—	—	—
Northern Marianas	—	—	—	—	—	—	—	290	270	20
Guam	1,346	612	471	263	1,311	414	[2] 897	1,466	478	988
Puerto Rico	30,164	17,844	9,010	3,310	28,436	28,436	—	26,845	26,845	—
Trust Territory of the Pacific	3,753	2,138	699	916	1,653	1,215	438	—	—	—
Virgin Islands	3,500	1,002	859	1,639	—	—	—	—	—	—

[1] Includes English as a second language.
[2] Estimated.
—Data not available or not applicable.

SOURCE: U.S. Department of Education, National Center for Education Statistics, "Women and Minority Groups Make Up Largest Segment of Adult Basic and Secondary Education Programs;" and Office of Vocational and Adult Education, "Adult Education Program Facts, Program Year 1990–1991." (This table was prepared June 1993).

Table 353.—Number of noncollegiate institutions offering postsecondary education, by control and state: 1993–94, 1994–95, and 1995–96

State or other area	1993–94			1994–95					1995–96				
	Total	Public	Private	Total	Public	Private			Total	Public	Private		
						Total	Nonprofit	Proprietary			Total	Nonprofit	Proprietary
1	2	3	4	5	6	7	8	9	10	11	12	13	14
United States	6,737	527	6,210	6,558	538	6,020	1,214	4,806	6,256	534	5,722	1,171	4,551
Alabama	76	10	66	71	8	63	8	55	63	7	56	7	49
Alaska	32	3	29	31	3	28	5	23	31	3	28	5	23
Arizona	125	4	121	124	4	120	16	104	113	4	109	16	93
Arkansas	82	20	62	76	19	57	9	48	69	16	53	8	45
California	1,126	32	1,094	1,041	35	1,006	230	776	997	35	962	225	737
Colorado	138	8	130	146	8	138	21	117	143	6	137	22	115
Connecticut	100	1	99	105	1	104	21	83	97	2	95	20	75
Delaware	15	1	14	14	1	13	2	11	12	1	11	2	9
District of Columbia	24	1	23	21	1	20	9	11	19	1	18	8	10
Florida	341	40	301	339	40	299	56	243	333	39	294	54	240
Georgia	102	4	98	104	4	100	15	85	101	5	96	16	80
Hawaii	29	1	28	26	1	25	4	21	22	1	21	3	18
Idaho	26	1	25	25	1	24	1	23	24	1	23	1	22
Illinois	304	12	292	285	11	274	56	218	264	10	254	56	198
Indiana	117	8	109	114	7	107	13	94	108	8	100	14	86
Iowa	72	0	72	66	0	66	17	49	62	0	62	16	46
Kansas	62	14	48	62	13	49	11	38	53	10	43	7	36
Kentucky	112	21	91	113	22	91	7	84	105	23	82	6	76
Louisiana	165	49	116	150	49	101	9	92	141	51	90	9	81
Maine	21	0	21	23	0	23	8	15	24	1	23	8	15
Maryland	135	0	135	122	0	122	21	101	112	0	112	20	92
Massachusetts	159	13	146	162	12	150	44	106	160	12	148	42	106
Michigan	247	6	241	282	6	276	44	232	264	6	258	43	215
Minnesota	89	14	75	88	5	83	18	65	79	4	75	16	59
Mississippi	52	0	52	49	0	49	4	45	38	0	38	3	35
Missouri	168	30	138	170	31	139	25	114	159	31	128	24	104
Montana	45	5	40	43	4	39	9	30	36	0	36	8	28
Nebraska	50	0	50	51	0	51	8	43	50	0	50	8	42
Nevada	46	0	46	47	0	47	1	46	57	0	57	1	56
New Hampshire	25	0	25	22	0	22	2	20	18	0	18	2	16
New Jersey	176	10	166	166	10	156	37	119	161	12	149	33	116
New Mexico	46	3	43	45	4	41	6	35	38	3	35	6	29
New York	353	15	338	337	26	311	118	193	343	31	312	115	197
North Carolina	81	4	77	81	4	77	8	69	74	4	70	7	63
North Dakota	19	0	19	19	0	19	6	13	17	0	17	5	12
Ohio	312	52	260	303	54	249	60	189	290	55	235	56	179
Oklahoma	95	34	61	111	33	78	5	73	108	33	75	4	71
Oregon	109	0	109	99	0	99	9	90	94	1	93	11	82
Pennsylvania	347	19	328	352	30	322	100	222	345	31	314	103	211
Rhode Island	28	0	28	28	0	28	9	19	29	0	29	9	20
South Carolina	60	2	58	56	2	54	11	43	57	1	56	11	45
South Dakota	17	5	12	17	5	12	5	7	16	5	11	4	7
Tennessee	143	30	113	139	29	110	20	90	135	29	106	17	89
Texas	382	6	376	360	7	353	37	316	350	6	344	38	306
Utah	43	6	37	42	6	36	2	34	39	5	34	2	32
Vermont	13	3	10	13	3	10	4	6	10	0	10	4	6
Virginia	148	11	137	144	11	133	32	101	139	12	127	31	96
Washington	111	5	106	107	5	102	13	89	104	5	99	12	87
West Virginia	70	19	51	73	18	55	14	41	71	19	52	13	39
Wisconsin	90	4	86	86	5	81	24	57	74	5	69	20	49
Wyoming	9	1	8	8	0	8	0	8	8	0	8	0	8
Outlying areas	95	5	90	84	6	78	16	62	84	6	78	14	64
American Samoa	0	0	0	0	0	0	0	0	0	0	0	0	0
Guam	1	0	1	0	0	0	0	0	0	0	0	0	0
Northern Marianas	0	0	0	0	0	0	0	0	0	0	0	0	0
Palau	0	0	0	0	0	0	0	0	0	0	0	0	0
Puerto Rico	94	5	89	84	6	78	16	62	84	6	78	14	64
Virgin Islands	0	0	0	0	0	0	0	0	0	0	0	0	0

SOURCE: U.S. Department of Education, National Center for Education Statistics, Integrated Postsecondary Education Data System (IPEDS), "Institutional Characteristics" surveys. (This table was prepared September 1996.)

CHAPTER 4
Federal Programs for Education and Related Activities

This chapter provides a summary of federal funds for education to help describe the magnitude of the federal fiscal effort and give some indication of the scope and variety of the education programs. Data in this chapter reflect outlays and obligations of federal agencies. These tabulations differ from federal receipts reported in other chapters because of numerous variations in the data collection systems. Federal dollars are not necessarily spent by recipient institutions in the same year they are appropriated. In some cases, institutions cannot identify the source of federal revenues because they flow through state agencies. Some types of revenues, such as tuition and fees, are reported as revenues from students even though they may be supported by federal student aid programs. Some institutions that receive federal education funds are not included in regular surveys conducted by the National Center for Education Statistics. Thus, the revenue data tabulated in this chapter are not comparable with figures reported in other chapters. Readers should be careful about comparing data on obligations shown in some tables with data on outlays and appropriations appearing in others.

Federal funding for education showed sizable growth between fiscal years (FYs) 1965 and 1996, after adjustment for inflation. Particularly large increases occurred between 1965 and 1975. After a period of small increases between 1975 and 1980, federal funding for education, excluding estimated federal tax expenditures for education, declined approximately 9 percent between 1980 and 1985 after adjustment for inflation. From 1985 to 1996, federal funding for education increased by 42 percent (table 354).

During the 1965 to 1975 period, after adjustment for inflation, federal funds for elementary and secondary education rose by 204 percent, postsecondary education by 256 percent, other education by 139 percent, and by 5 percent for research at educational institutions. Between 1975 and 1980, federal funding for elementary and secondary education rose by 1 percent and research by 14 percent, but postsecondary education fell slightly by 3 percent and other education fell by 35 percent. After declining 21 percent between 1980 and 1985, federal funding for elementary and secondary education programs rose

by 47 percent between 1985 and 1996. Postsecondary education fell by 24 percent between 1980 and 1985 then fell 7 percent between 1985 and 1996. Between 1985 and 1996, other education rose by 65 percent, and research by 27 percent, after adjustment for inflation (table 354).

According to FY 1996 estimates, $30.4 billion or about 43 percent of the $70.9 billion spent by the federal government on education came from the U.S. Department of Education. Large amounts of money also came from the U.S. Department of Health and Human Services ($12.8 billion), the U.S. Department of Agriculture ($9.1 billion), the U.S. Department of Labor ($4.1 billion), the U.S. Department of Defense ($3.7 billion), and the U.S. Department of Energy ($2.7 billion) (table 355).

Fiscal year 1996 estimates call for federal program funds for elementary and secondary education to be $35.2 billion; for higher education, $14.8 billion; for research at universities and related institutions, $15.9 billion; and for other programs, $4.9 billion (table 356).

Over 58 percent of total federal education support, excluding estimated federal tax expenditures, went to educational institutions in FY 96. Another 19 percent was used for student support. Banks and other lending agencies received 8 percent, and all other recipients, including libraries, museums, and federal institutions, received 14 percent (table 357).

Between FYs 1990 and 1996, U.S. Department of Education obligations rose 57 percent, after adjustment for inflation. Funds for student financial assistance increased to $30.0 billion in 1996, a rise of 127 percent since 1990. Funds for elementary and secondary education stood at an estimated $7.3 billion in 1996, a decline of 15 percent since 1990, after adjustment for inflation. Funds for the handicapped increased by about 42 percent, to $5.9 billion, and funds for vocational and adult education declined 10 percent, after adjustment for inflation (table 358).

Of the $30.4 billion spent by the U.S. Department of Education in FY 1996, about $11.7 billion went to school districts, $5.0 billion to institutions of higher education, $5.3 billion to college students, and $4.0 billion to state education agencies. A portion of the remaining $4.5 billion went to banks to subsidize student loans (table 359).

Thirty-three percent of public elementary and secondary school students in the United States received publicly funded free or reduced-price lunches in 1993–94. At public elementary schools, the participation rate was 39 percent compared with 22 percent for public secondary schools (table 368).

About 13 percent of all elementary and secondary school children received Title I services in 1993–94. Federally sponsored Title I programs are designed to break the link between family poverty and low student achievement, particularly for children in schools with high concentrations of poverty. Children in rural areas (13 percent) and central cities (17 percent) were more likely to receive services than those in suburban areas (9 percent) (table 369).

Federal Education Legislation

A capsule view of the history of federal education activities is provided in the following list of selected legislation:

1787 *Northwest Ordinance* authorized land grants for the establishment of educational institutions.

1802 *An Act Fixing the Military Peace Establishment of the United States* established the U.S. Military Academy. (The U.S. Naval Academy was established in 1845 by the Secretary of the Navy.)

1862 *First Morrill Act* authorized public land grants to the states for the establishment and maintenance of agricultural and mechanical colleges.

1867 *Department of Education Act* authorized the establishment of the U.S. Department of Education.*

1876 *Appropriation Act,* U.S. Department of the Treasury, established the U.S. Coast Guard Academy.

1890 *Second Morrill Act* provided for money grants for support of instruction in the agricultural and mechanical colleges.

1911 *State Marine School Act* authorized federal funds to be used for the benefit of any nautical school in any of 11 specified state seaport cities.

1917 *Smith-Hughes Act* provided for grants to states for support of vocational education.

---

*The U.S. Department of Education as established in 1867 was later known as the Office of Education. In 1980, under Public Law 96–88, it became a cabinet-level department. Therefore, for purposes of consistency, it is referred to as the "U.S. Department of Education" even in those tables covering years when it was officially the Office of Education.

1918 *Vocational Rehabilitation Act* provided for grants for rehabilitation through training of World War I veterans.

1919 *An Act to Provide for Further Educational Facilities* authorized the sale by the federal government of surplus machine tools to educational institutions at 15 percent of acquisition cost.

1920 *Smith-Bankhead Act* authorized grants to states for vocational rehabilitation programs.

1935 *Bankhead-Jones Act* (Public Law 74–182) authorized grants to states for agricultural experiment stations.

Agricultural Adjustment Act (Public Law 74–320) authorized 30 percent of the annual customs receipts to be used to encourage the exportation and domestic consumption of agricultural commodities. Commodities purchased under this authorization began to be used in school lunch programs in 1936. The National School Lunch Act of 1946 continued and expanded this assistance.

1936 *An Act to Further the Development and Maintenance of an Adequate and Well-Balanced American Merchant Marine* (Public Law 84–415) established the U.S. Merchant Marine Academy.

1937 *National Cancer Institute Act* established the Public Health Service fellowship program.

1941 *Amendment to Lanham Act of 1940* authorized federal aid for construction, maintenance, and operation of schools in federally impacted areas. Such assistance was continued under Public Law 815 and Public Law 874, 81st Congress, in 1950.

1943 *Vocational Rehabilitation Act* (Public Law 78–16) provided assistance to disabled veterans.

School Lunch Indemnity Plan (Public Law 78–129) provided funds for local lunch food purchases.

1944 *Servicemen's Readjustment Act* (Public Law 78–346) known as the GI Bill, provided assistance for the education of veterans.

Surplus Property Act (Public Law 78–457) authorized transfer of surplus property to educational institutions.

1946 *National School Lunch Act* (Public Law 79–396) authorized assistance through grants-in-aid and other means to states to assist in providing adequate foods and facilities for the establishment, maintenance, operation, and expansion of nonprofit school lunch programs.

George-Barden Act (Public Law 80–402) expanded federal support of vocational education.

1948 *United States Information and Educational Exchange Act* (Public Law 80–402) provided for the interchange of persons, knowledge, and skills between the United States and other countries.

1949 *Federal Property and Administrative Services Act* (Public Law 81–152) provided for donation of surplus property to educational institutions and for other public purposes.

1950 *Financial Assistance for Local Educational Agencies Affected by Federal Activities* (Public Law 81–815 and Public Law 81–874) provided assistance for construction (Public Law 815) and operation (Public Law 874) of schools in federally affected areas.

Housing Act (Public Law 81–475) authorized loans for construction of college housing facilities.

1954 *An Act for the Establishment of the United States Air Force Academy and Other Purposes* (Public Law 83–325) established the U.S. Air Force Academy.

Educational Research Act (Public Law 83–531) authorized cooperative arrangements with universities, colleges, and state educational agencies for educational research.

National Advisory Committee on Education Act (Public Law 83–532) established a National Advisory Committee on Education to recommend needed studies of national concern in the field of education and to propose appropriate action indicated by such studies.

School Milk Program Act (Public Law 83–597) provided funds for purchase of milk for school lunch programs.

1956 *Library Services Act* (Public Law 84–597) provided grants to states for extension and improvement of rural public library services.

1957 *Practical Nurse Training Act* (Public Law 84–911) provided grants to states for practical nurse training.

1958 *National Defense Education Act* (Public Law 85–864) provided assistance to state and local school systems for strengthening instruction in science, mathematics, modern foreign languages, and other critical subjects; improvement of state statistical services; guidance, counseling, and testing services and training institutes; higher education student loans and fellowships; foreign language study and training provided by colleges and universities; experimentation and dissemination of information on more effective utilization of television, motion pictures, and related media for educational purposes; and vocational education for technical occupations necessary to the national defense.

Education of Mentally Retarded Children Act (Public Law 85–926) authorized federal assistance for training teachers of the handicapped.

Captioned Films for the Deaf Act (Public Law 85–905) authorized a loan service of captioned films for the deaf.

1961 *Area Redevelopment Act* (Public Law 87–27) included provisions for training or retraining of persons in redevelopment areas.

1962 *Manpower Development and Training Act* (Public Law 87–415) provided training in new and improved skills for the unemployed and underemployed.

Communications Act of 1934, Amendment (Public Law 87–447) provided grants for the construction of educational television broadcasting facilities.

Migration and Refugee Assistance Act of 1962 (Public Law 87–510) authorized loans, advances, and grants for education and training of refugees.

1963 *Health Professions Educational Assistance Act of 1963* (Public Law 88–129) provided funds to expand teaching facilities and for loans to students in the health professions.

Vocational Education Act of 1963 (Part of Public Law 88–210) increased federal support of vocational education schools; vocational work-study programs; and research, training, and demonstrations in vocational education.

Higher Education Facilities Act of 1963 (Public Law 88–204) authorized grants and loans for classrooms, libraries, and laboratories in public community colleges and technical institutes, as well as undergraduate and graduate facilities in other institutions of higher education.

1964 *Civil Rights Act of 1964* (Public Law 88–352) authorized the Commissioner of Education to arrange for support for institutions of higher education and school districts to provide in-service programs for assisting instructional staff in dealing with problems caused by desegregation.

Economic Opportunity Act of 1964 (Public Law 88–452) authorized grants for college work-study programs for students from low-income families; established a Job Corps program and authorized support for work-training programs to provide education and vocational training and work experience opportunities in welfare programs; authorized support of education and training activities and of community action programs, including Head Start, Follow Through, and Upward Bound; and authorized the establishment of Volunteers in Service to America (VISTA).

1965 *Elementary and Secondary Education Act of 1965* (Public Law 89–10) authorized grants for elementary and secondary school programs for children of low-income families; school library resources, textbooks, and other instructional materials for school children; supplementary educational centers and services; strengthening state education agencies; and educational research and research training.

Health Professions Educational Assistance Amendments of 1965 (Public Law 89–290) authorized scholarships to aid needy students in the health professions.

Higher Education Act of 1965 (Public Law 89–329) provided grants for university community service programs, college library assistance, library training and research, strengthening developing institutions, teacher training programs, and undergraduate instructional equipment. Authorized insured student loans, established a National Teacher Corps, and provided for graduate teacher training fellowships.

Medical Library Assistance Act (Public Law 89–291) provided assistance for construction and improvement of health sciences libraries.

National Foundation on the Arts and the Humanities Act (Public Law 89–209) authorized grants and loans for projects in the creative and performing arts and for research, training, and scholarly publications in the humanities.

National Technical Institute for the Deaf Act (Public Law 89–36) provided for the establishment, construction, equipping, and operation of a residential school for postsecondary education and technical training of the deaf.

National Vocational Student Loan Insurance Act of 1965 (Public Law 89–287) encouraged state and nonprofit private institutions and organizations to establish adequate loan insurance programs to assist students to attend postsecondary business, trade, technical, and other vocational schools.

School Assistance in Disaster Areas Act (Public Law 89–313) provided for assistance to local education agencies to help meet exceptional costs resulting from a major disaster.

1966 *International Education Act* (Public Law 89–698) provided grants to institutions of higher education for the establishment, strengthening, and operation of centers for research and training in international studies and the international aspects of other fields of study.

National Sea Grant College and Program Act (Public Law 89–688) authorized the establishment and operation of Sea Grant Colleges and programs by initiating and supporting programs of education and research in the various fields relating to the development of marine resources.

Adult Education Act (Public Law 89–750) authorized grants to states for the encouragement and expansion of educational programs for adults, including training of teachers of adults and demonstrations in adult education (previously part of Economic Opportunity Act of 1964).

Model Secondary School for the Deaf Act (Public Law 89–694) authorized the establishment and operation, by Gallaudet College, of a model secondary school for the deaf.

Elementary and Secondary Education Amendments of 1966 (Public Law 89–750) in addition to modifying existing programs, authorized grants to assist states in the initiation, expansion, and improvement of programs and projects for the education of handicapped children.

1967 *Education Professions Development Act* (Public Law 90–35) amended the Higher Education Act of 1965 for the purpose of improving the quality of teaching and to help meet critical shortages of adequately trained educational personnel.

Public Broadcasting Act of 1967 (Public Law 90–129) established a Corporation for Public Broadcasting to assume major responsibility in channeling federal funds to noncommercial radio and television stations, program production groups, and ETV networks; conduct research, demonstration, or training in matters related to noncommercial broadcasting; and award grants for construction of educational radio and television facilities.

1968 *Elementary and Secondary Education Amendments of 1968* (Public Law 90–247) modified existing programs, authorized support of regional centers for education of handicapped children, model centers and services for deaf-blind children, recruitment of personnel and dissemination of information on education of the handicapped; technical assistance in education to rural areas; support of dropout prevention projects; and support of bilingual education programs.

Handicapped Children's Early Education Assistance Act (Public Law 90–538) authorized preschool and early education programs for handicapped children.

Vocational Education Amendments of 1968 (Public Law 90–576) modified existing programs and provided for a National Advisory Council on Vocational Education and collection and dissemination of information for programs administered by the Commissioner of Education.

Higher Education Amendments of 1968 (Public Law 90–575) authorized new programs to assist disadvantaged college students through special counseling and summer tutorial programs and programs to assist colleges to combine resources of cooperative programs and to expand programs which provide clinical experiences to law students.

1970 *Elementary and Secondary Education Assistance Programs, Extension* (Public Law 91–230) authorized comprehensive planning and evaluation grants to state and local education agencies; provided for the establishment of a National Commission on School Finance.

National Commission on Libraries and Information Services Act (Public Law 91–345) established a National Commission on Libraries and Information Science to effectively utilize the nation's educational resources.

Office of Education Appropriation Act (Public Law 91–380) provided emergency school assistance to desegregating local education agencies.

Environmental Education Act (Public Law 91–516) established an Office of Environmental Education to develop curriculum and initiate and maintain environmental education programs at the elementary-secondary levels; disseminate information; provide training programs for teachers and other educational, public, community, labor, and industrial leaders and employees; provide community education programs; and distribute material dealing with environment and ecology.

Drug Abuse Education Act of 1970 (Public Law 91–527) provided for development, demonstration, and evaluation of curriculums on the problems of drug abuse.

1971 *Comprehensive Health Manpower Training Act of 1971* (Public Law 92–257) amended Title VII of the Public Health Service Act, increasing and expanding provisions for health manpower training and training facilities.

Nurse Training Act of 1971 (Public Law 92–158) amended Title VIII, Nurse Training, of the Public Health Service Act, increasing and expanding provisions for nurse training facilities.

1972 *Drug Abuse Office and Treatment Act of 1972* (Public Law 92–255) established a Special Action Office for Drug Abuse Prevention to provide overall planning and policy for all federal drug-abuse prevention functions; a National Advisory Council for Drug Abuse Prevention; community assistance grants for community mental health center for treatment and rehabilitation of persons with drug-abuse problems, and, in December 1974, a National Institute on Drug Abuse.

Education Amendments of 1972 (Public Law 92–318) established the Education Division in the U.S. Department of Health, Education, and Welfare and the National Institute of Education; general aid for institutions of higher education; federal matching grants for state Student Incentive Grants; a National Commission on Financing Postsecondary Education; State Advisory Councils on Community Colleges; a Bureau of Occupational and Adult Education and State Grants for the design, establishment, and conduct of postsecondary occupational education; and a bureau-level Office of Indian Education. Amended current Office of Education programs to increase their effectiveness and better meet special needs. Prohibited sex bias in admission to vocational, professional, and graduate schools, and public institutions of undergraduate higher education.

1973 *Older Americans Comprehensive Services Amendment of 1973* (Public Law 93–29) made available to older citizens comprehensive programs of health, education, and social services.

Comprehensive Employment and Training Act of 1973 (Public Law 93–203) provided for opportunities for employment and training to unemployed and underemployed persons. Extended and expanded provisions in the Manpower Development and Training Act of 1962, Title I of the Economic Opportunity Act of 1962, Title I of the Economic Opportunity Act of 1964, and the Emergency Employment Act of 1971 as in effect prior to June 30, 1973.

1974 *Education Amendments of 1974* (Public Law 93–380) provided for the consolidation of certain programs; and established a National Center for Education Statistics.

Juvenile Justice and Delinquency Prevention Act of 1974 (Public Law 93–415) provided for technical assistance, staff training, centralized research, and resources to develop and implement programs to keep students in elementary and secondary schools; and established, in the U.S. Department of Justice, a National Institute for Juvenile Justice and Delinquency Prevention.

1975 *Indian Self-Determination and Education Assistance Act* (Public Law 93–638) provided for increased participation of Indians in the establishment and conduct of their education programs and services.

Harry S Truman Memorial Scholarship Act (Public Law 93–642) established the Harry S Truman Scholarship Foundation and created a perpetual education scholarship fund for young Americans to prepare and pursue careers in public service.

Indochina Migration and Refugee Assistance Act of 1975 (Public Law 94–23) authorized funds to be used for education and training of aliens who have fled from Cambodia or Vietnam.

Education for All Handicapped Childen Act (Public Law 94–142) provided that all handicapped children have available to them a free appropriate education designed to meet their unique needs.

1976 *Educational Broadcasting Facilities and Telecommunications Demonstration Act of 1976* (Public Law 94–309) established a telecommunications demonstration program to promote the development of nonbroadcast telecommunications facilities and services for the transmission, distribution, and delivery of health, education, and public or social service information.

Education Amendments of 1976 (Public Law 94–482) extended and revised federal programs for education assistance for higher education, vocational education, and a variety of other programs.

1977 *Youth Employment and Demonstration Projects Act of 1977* (Public Law 95–93) established a youth employment training program that includes, among other activities, promoting education-to-work transition, literacy training and bilingual training, and attainment of certificates of high school equivalency.

Career Education Incentive Act (Public Law 95–207) authorized the establishment of a career education program for elementary and secondary schools.

1978 *Tribally Controlled Community College Assistance Act of 1978* (Public Law 95–471) provided federal funds for the operation and improvement of tribally controlled community colleges for Indian students.

Education Amendments of 1978 (Public Law 95–561) established a comprehensive basic skills program aimed at improving pupil achievement (replaced the existing National Reading Improvement program); and established a community schools program to provide for the use of public buildings.

Middle Income Student Assistance Act (Public Law 95–566) modified the provisions for student financial assistance programs to allow middle-income as well as low-income students attending college or other postsecondary institutions to qualify for federal education assistance.

1979 *Department of Education Organization Act* (Public Law 96–88) established a U.S. Department of Education containing functions from the Education Division of the U.S. Department of Health, Education, and Welfare along with other selected education programs from HEW, the U.S. Department of Justice, U.S. Department of Labor, and the National Science Foundation.

1980 *Asbestos School Hazard Detection and Control Act of 1980* (Public Law 96–270) established a program for inspection of schools for detection of hazardous asbestos materials and provided loans to assist educational agencies to contain or remove and replace such materials.

1981 *Education Consolidation and Improvement Act of 1981* (Part of Public Law 97–35) consolidated 42 programs into 7 programs to be funded under the elementary and secondary block grant authority.

1983 *Student Loan Consolidation and Technical Amendments Act of 1983* (Public Law 98–79) established 8 percent interest rate for Guaranteed Student Loans and extended Family Contribution Schedule.

Challenge Grant Amendments of 1983 (Public Law 98–95) amended Title III, Higher Education Act, and added authorization of Challenge Grant program. The Challenge Grant program provides funds to eligible institutions on a matching basis as incentive to seek alternative sources of funding.

Education of the Handicapped Act Amendments of 1983 (Public Law 98–199) added Architectural Barrier amendment and clarified participation of handicapped children in private schools.

1984 *Education for Economic Security Act* (Public Law 98–377) added new science and mathematics programs for elementary, secondary, and postsecondary education. The new programs include magnet schools, excellence in education, and equal access.

Carl D. Perkins Vocational Education Act (Public Law 98–524) continues federal assistance for vocational education through FY 1989. The act replaces the Vocational Education Act of 1963. It provides aid to the states to make vocational education programs accessible to all persons, including handicapped and disadvantaged, single parents and homemakers, and the incarcerated.

Human Services Reauthorization Act (Public Law 98–558) reauthorized the Head Start and Follow Through programs through FY 1986. It also created a Carl D. Perkins scholarship program, a National Talented Teachers Fellowship program, a Federal Merit Scholarships program, and a Leadership in Educational Administration program.

1985 *Montgomery GI Bill—Active Duty* (Public Law 98–525), brought about a new GI Bill for individuals who initially entered active military duty on or after July 1, 1985.

Montgomery GI Bill—Selected Reserve (Public Law 98–525), is an education program for members of the Selected Reserve (which includes the National Guard) who enlist, reenlist, or extend an enlistment after June 30, 1985, for a 6-year period.

1986 *Handicapped Children's Protection Act of 1986* (Public Law 99–372) allows parents of handicapped children to collect attorneys' fees in cases brought under the Education of the Handicapped Act and provides that the Education of the Handicapped Act does not preempt other laws, such as Section 504 of the Rehabilitation Act.

Drug-Free Schools and Communities Act of 1986 (Part of Public Law 99–570), part of the Anti-Drug Abuse Act of 1986, authorizes funding for FYs 1987–89. Establishes programs for drug abuse education and prevention, coordinated with related community efforts and resources, through the use of federal financial assistance.

1987 *Higher Education Act Amendments of 1987* (Public Law 100–50) makes technical corrections, clarifications, or conforming amendments related to the enactment of the Higher Education Amendments of 1986.

1988 *Augustus F. Hawkins-Robert T. Stafford Elementary and Secondary School Improvement Amendments of 1988* (Public Law 100–297) reauthorizes through 1993 major elementary and secondary education programs including: Chapter 1, Chapter 2, Bilingual Education, Math-Science Education, Magnet Schools, Impact Aid, Indian Education, Adult Education, and other smaller education programs.

Technology-Related Assistance for Individuals with Disabilities Act of 1988 (Public Law 100–407) provides financial assistance to states to develop and implement consumer-responsive statewide programs of technology-related assistance for persons of all ages with disabilities.

Omnibus Trade and Competitiveness Act of 1988 (Public Law 100–418) authorizes new and expanded education programs. Title VI of the Act, Education and Training for American Competitiveness, authorizes new programs in literacy, math-science, foreign language, vocational training, international education, technology training, and technology transfer.

The Omnibus Drug Abuse Prevention Act of 1988 (Public Law 100–690) authorizes a new teacher training program under the Drug-Free Schools and Communities Act, an early childhood education program to be administered jointly by the U.S. Departments of Health and Human Services and Education, and a pilot program for the children of alcoholics.

Stewart B. McKinney Homeless Assistance Amendments Act of 1988 (Public Law 100–628) extends for 2 additional years programs providing assistance to the homeless, including literacy training for homeless adults and education for homeless youths.

Tax Reform Technical Amendments (Public Law 100–647) authorizes an Education Savings Bond for the purpose of postsecondary educational expenses. The bill grants tax exclusion for interest earned on regular series EE savings bonds.

1989 *Children with Disabilities Temporary Care Reauthorization Act of 1989* (Public Law 101–127) revises and extends the programs established in the Temporary Child Care for Handicapped Children and Crises Nurseries Act of 1986.

Drug-Free Schools and Communities Act Amendments of 1989 (Public Law 101–226) amends the Drug-Free Schools and Communities Act of 1986 to revise certain requirements relating to the provision of drug abuse education and prevention programs in elementary and secondary schools.

Childhood Education and Development Act of 1989 (Part of Public Law 101–239) authorizes the appropriations to expand Head Start Programs and programs carried out under the Elementary and Secondary Education Act of 1965 to include child care services.

1990 *Excellence in Mathematics, Science and Engineering Education Act of 1990* (Public Law 101–589) promotes excellence in American mathematics, science, and engineering education by creating a national mathematics and science clearinghouse; establishing regional mathematics and science education consortia; establishing three new mathematics, science, and engineering scholarships programs; and creating several other mathematics, science, and engineering education programs.

Student Right-To-Know and Campus Security Act (Public Law 101–542) requires institutions of higher education receiving federal financial assistance to provide certain information with respect to the graduation rates of student-athletes at such institutions. The act also requires the institution to certify that it has a campus security policy and will annually submit a uniform crime report to the Federal Bureau of Investigation (FBI).

Children's Television Act of 1990 (Public Law 101–437) requires the Federal Communications Commission to reinstate restrictions on advertising during children's television and enforces the obligation of broadcasters to meet the educational and informational needs of the child audience.

Americans with Disabilities Act of 1990 (Public Law 101–336) prohibits discrimination against persons with disabilities.

Stewart B. McKinney Homeless Assistance Amendments Act of 1990 (Public Law 101–645) reauthorized the Stewart B. McKinney Homeless Assistance Act programs of grants to state and local education agencies for the provision of support services to homeless children and youth.

National Assessment of Chapter 1 Act (Public Law 101–305) requires the Secretary of Education to conduct a comprehensive national assessment of programs carried out with assistance under Chapter 1 of Title I of the Elementary and Secondary Education Act of 1965.

Augustus F. Hawkins Human Services Reauthorization Act of 1990 (Public Law 101–501) authorized appropriations for FYs 1991–1994 to carry out the Head Start Act, the Follow Through Act, the Community Services Block Grant Act, and the Low-Income Home Energy Assistance Act of 1981.

National and Community Service Act of 1990 (Public Law 101–610) increased school and college-based community service opportunities and authorized the President's Points of Light Foundation.

School Dropout Prevention and Basic Skills Improvement Act of 1990 (Public Law 101–600) improves secondary school programs for basic skills improvements and dropout reduction.

Medical Residents Student Loan Amendments Act of 1989 (Enacted in Public Law 101–239, the Omnibus Budget Reconciliation Act of 1989) amended the Higher Education Act of 1965 to eliminate student loan deferments for medical students serving in internships or residency programs.

Asbestos School Hazard Abatement Reauthorization Act of 1990 (Public Law 101–637) reauthorized the Asbestos School Hazard Abatement Act of 1984, which provided financial support to elementary and secondary schools to inspect for asbestos and to develop and implement an asbestos management plan. In addition, the act provides for programs of information, technical, and scientific assistance and training.

Eisenhower Exchange Fellowship Act of 1990 (Public Law 101–454) provided a permanent endowment for the Eisenhower Exchange Fellowship Program.

Tribally Controlled Community College Reauthorization Act (Public Law 101–477) reauthorized the Tribally Controlled Community College Assistance Act and the Navajo Community College Act.

National Environmental Education Act (Public Law 101–619) promotes environmental education by the establishment of an Office of Environmental Education in the Environmental Protection Agency and the creation of several environmental education programs.

Anti-Drug Education Act of 1990 and the Drug Abuse Resistance Education (DARE) Act of 1990 (Both bills were enacted as part of Public Law 101–647, the Comprehensive Crime Control Act of 1990.) amends the Drug-Free Schools and Communities Act and raises funding levels for school personnel training, funds the replication of successful drug education programs, helps local education agencies to cooperate with law enforcement agencies, and allows funds to be used for after-school programs. The Drug Abuse Resistance Education Act establishes a program of grants to HHS for Drug Abuse Resistance Education (DARE) programs.

Public Service Assistance Education Act (Enacted as part of Department of Defense Authorization Act, Public Law 101–510) gives federal agencies authority to provide new educational benefits to employees by paying for an employee to obtain an academic degree for which there is an agency shortage of qualified personnel, and by repaying up to $6,000 per year of the student loan of a qualified employee in exchange for a 3-year commitment.

Omnibus Budget Reconciliation Act of 1990 (Public Law 101–508) included a set of student aid provisions that were estimated to yield a savings of $2 billion over 5 years. These provisions included delayed Guaranteed Student Loan disbursements, tightened ability-to-benefit eligibility, and expanded pro rata refund policy and the elimination of student aid eligibility at high default schools.

1991 *Veterans' Education and Employment Programs Amendments. A bill to amend title 38, United States Code, with respect to veterans education and employment programs, and for other purposes* (Public Law 102–16) revises and extends eligibility for veterans' education and employment programs.

National Literacy Act of 1991 (Public Law 102–73) established the National Institute for Literacy, the National Institute Board, and the Interagency Task Force on Literacy. Amends various federal laws to establish and extend various literacy programs.

Dire Emergency Supplemental Appropriations for Consequences of Operation Desert Shield/Desert Storm, Food Stamps, Unemployment Compensation Administration, Veterans Compensation and Pensions, and Other Urgent Needs Act of 1991 (Public Law 102–27) makes dire emergency supplemental appropriations for FY 1991 for the additional costs of Operation Desert Shield/Operation Desert Storm and other programs.

Higher Education Technical Amendments of 1991 (Public Law 102–26) amends the Higher Education Act of 1965 to resolve legal and technical issues relating to federal postsecondary student assistance programs and to prevent undue burdens on participants in Operation Desert Storm, and for other purposes.

Intelligence Authorization Act, Fiscal Year 1992 (Public Law 102–183) provides for the establishment of a National Security Education Board and a National Security Education Trust Fund within the Treasury.

National Defense Authorization Act for Fiscal Years 1992 and 1993 (Public Law 102–190) authorizes appropriations for military functions of the U.S. Department of Defense. Includes Defense Manufacturing Education Program and planning for science, mathematics, and engineering education.

Rehabilitation Act Amendments of 1991 (Public Law 102–52) amends the Rehabilitation Act of 1973 to reauthorize funding for various programs, including vocational rehabilitation services, research and training, supplementary services and facilities, the National Council on Disability, the Architectural and Transportation Barriers Compliance Board, employment opportunities for individuals with handicaps, and comprehensive services for independent living. Reauthorizes funding for the Helen Keller National Center for Deaf-Blind Youths and Adults (under the Helen Keller National Center Act) and for the President's Committee on Employment of People with Disabilities.

Education Acts, Amendments. Amends the School Dropout Demonstration Assistance Act of 1988 to extend authorization of appropriations through FY 1993 and for other purposes (Public Law 102–103) revises and reauthorizes programs under: (1) the School Dropout Demonstration Assistance Act of 1988; and (2) the Star Schools Program Assistance Act. Revises the functional literacy program and adds a life skills program for state and local prisoners under the National Literacy Act of 1991.

A bill making appropriations for the U.S. Department of the Interior and related agencies for the FY ending September 30, 1992, and for other purposes (Public Law 102–154) amends the Anti-Drug Abuse Act of 1988 to extend the authorization of appropriations for drug abuse education and prevention programs relating to youth gangs and for runaway and homeless youth. Directs the Secretary of Health and Human Services to report annually on the program of drug education and prevention relating to youth gangs.

Federal Supplemental Compensation Act of 1991 (Public Law 102–164) revises procedures for student loan debt collection.

25th Anniversary of the Adult Education Act Joint Resolution. A joint resolution to declare it to be the policy of the United States that there should be a renewed and sustained commitment by the federal government and the American people to the importance of adult education (Public Law 102–74) declares it to be the policy of the United States that: (1) the 25th anniversary of federal aid to improve the basic and literacy skills of adults through the Adult Education Act (AEA) should be recognized and observed; and (2) there should be a continued commitment to federal aid for educating adults through AEA to increase adult literacy and assure a productive work force and a competitive United States in the 21st century.

National Commission on Time and Learning Act (Public Law 102–62) establishes the National Education Commission on Time and Learning. Directs the Secretary of Education to: (1) make grants for research in the teaching of writing; and (2) carry out a program to educate students about the history and principles of the Constitution, including the Bill of Rights. Amends the Elementary and Secondary Education Act of 1965 to revise requirements for law-related education program grant and contract applications, review, and award periods. Establishes the National Council on Education Standards and Testing.

High-Performance Computing Act of 1991 (Public Law 102–194) directs the President to implement a National High-Performance Computing Program. Provides for: (1) establishment of a National Research and Education Network; (2) standards and guidelines for high performance networks; and (3) the responsibility of certain federal departments and agencies with regard to the Network.

National and Community Service Technical Amendments Act of 1991 (Public Law 102–10) amends the National and Community Service Act to make various technical amendments.

Persian Gulf Conflict Supplemental Authorization Personnel Benefits Act of 1991 (Public Law 102–25) authorizes supplemental appropriations: (1) to the U.S. Department of Defense in connection with Operation Desert Storm; and (2) for certain national security programs. Revises various military personnel benefits provisions, especially with respect to those personnel serving on active duty in connection with Operation Desert Storm.

Veterans' Educational Assistance Amendments of 1991 (Public Law 102–127) restores certain educational benefits available to reserve and active-duty personnel under the Montgomery GI Bill to students whose course studies under such programs were interrupted by being called to active duty or given increased work in connection with the Persian Gulf War.

Individuals with Disabilities Education Act Amendments of 1991 (Public Law 102–119) amends the Individuals with Disabilities Education Act (IDEA) to extend the authorization of appropriations and revise various features of the early intervention program of services for infants and toddlers with disabilities.

National Sea Grant College Program Authorization Act of 1991 (Public Law 102–186) amends the National Sea Grant College Program Act to: (1) authorize appropriations; and (2) repeal provisions authorizing grants relating to marine affairs and resource management.

National Commission on Libraries and Information Science Act Amendments of 1991 (Public Law 102–95) amends the National Commission on Libraries and Information Science Act to revise provisions and authorize appropriations for the National Commission on Libraries and Information Science.

Civil Rights Act of 1991 (Public Law 102–166) amends the Civil Rights Act of 1964, the Age Discrimination in Employment Act of 1967, and the Americans with Disabilities Act of 1990, with regard to employment discrimination, employment related tests, mixed motives, judgment finality, foreign discrimination, seniority systems, fees, and time limits. Establishes the Technical Assistance Training Institute.

Dropout Prevention Technical Correction Amendment of 1991 (Public Law 102–159) amends federal law relating to impact aid to restore provisions for the Secretary of Education to make certain preliminary payments to local education agencies.

1992 *Higher Education Amendments of 1992* (Public Law 102–325) amends the Higher Education Act of 1965 to revise and reauthorize funding for its various programs.

Ready-To-Learn Act (Public Law 102–545) amends the General Education Provisions Act to establish Ready-To-Learn Television programs to support educational programming and support materials for preschool and elementary school children and their parents, child care providers, and educators.

Job Training Reform Amendments of 1992 (Public Law 102–367), a bill to amend the Job Training Partnerships Act, the Carl Perkins Vocational Education Act, and the Adult Education Act.

National Commission on Time and Learning, Extension (Public Law 102–359) amends the National Education Commission on Time and Learning Act to extend the authorization of appropriations for such Commission, amends the Elementary and Secondary Education Act of 1965 to revise provisions for (1) a specified civic education program; (2) schoolwide projects for educationally disadvantaged children, and provides for additional Assistant Secretaries of Education.

1993 *Student Loan Reform Act* (Public Law 103–66) reforms the student aid process by phasing in a system of direct lending designed to provide savings for taxpayers and students. Students will be able to choose among a variety of repayment options, including income contingency.

National Service Trust Act (Public Law 103–82) amends the National and Community Service Act of 1990 to establish a Corporation for National Service and enhance opportunities for national service. In addition, the Act provides education grants up to $4,725 per year for 2 years to people age 17 years or older who perform community service before, during, or after postsecondary education.

Higher Education Technical Amendments Act (Public Law 103–208) amends the Higher Education Act to make technical changes and conforming amendments.

NAEP Assessment Authorization (Public Law 103–33) authorizes the use of NAEP for state-by-state comparisons.

Migrant Student Record Transfer System Extension (Public Law 103–59) extends the operation of the migrant student record transfer system.

1994 *Goals 2000: Educate America Act* (Public Law 103–227) establishes a new federal partnership through a system of grants to states and local communities to reform the nation's education system. The Act formalizes the national education goals and establishes the National Education Goals Panel. It also creates a National Education Standards and Improvement Council (NESIC) to provide voluntary national certification of state and local education standards and assessments and establishes the National Skill Standards Board to develop voluntary national skill standards.

School-To-Work Opportunities Act of 1994 (Public Law 103–239) establishes a national framework within which states and communities can develop School-To-Work Opportunities systems to prepare young people for first jobs and continuing education. The Act also provides money to states and communities to develop a system of programs that include work-based learning, school-based learning, and connecting activities components. School-To-Work programs will provide students with a high school diploma (or its equivalent), a nationally recognized skill certificate, an associate degree (if appropriate) and may lead to a first job or further education.

Safe Schools Act of 1994 (Part of Public Law 103–227) authorizes the award of competitive grants to local educational agencies with serious crime to implement violence prevention activities such as conflict resolution and peer mediation.

Educational Research, Development, Dissemination, and Improvement Act of 1994 (Part of Public Law 103–227) authorizes the educational research and dissemination activities of the Office of Educational Research and Improvement. The regional educational laboratories and university-based research and development centers are authorized.

Student Loan Default Exemption Extension (Public Law 103–235) amends the Higher Education Act of 1965 to extend until July 1, 1998 the effective date for cohort default rate extension for Historically Black Colleges and Universities, tribally controlled community colleges, and Navajo community colleges.

Technology-Related Assistance for Individuals with Disabilities Amendments of 1993 (Public Law 103–218) amends the Technology-Related Assistance for Individuals with Disabilities Act of 1988 to authorize appropriations for each of the FYs 1994–98.

Improving America's Schools Act (Public Law 103–382) reauthorizes and revamps the Elementary and Secondary Education Act. The legislation includes Title I, the federal government's largest program providing educational assistance to disadvantaged children; professional development and technical assistance programs; safe and drug-free schools and communities provision; and provisions promoting school equity.

1995 *A Bill to Make Emergency Supplemental Appropriations* (Public Law 104–19) provides emergency supplemental appropriations for additional disaster assistance, for antiterrorism initiatives, for assistance at Oklahoma City, and making recissions for the fiscal year ending September 30, 1995, and for other purposes.

Unfunded Mandate Reform Act of 1995 (Public Law 104–4) curbs the practice of imposing unfunded federal mandates on states and local governments; to strengthen the partnership between the federal government and state, local and tribal governments, and for other purposes.

Paperwork Reduction Act of 1995 (Public Law 104–13) furthers the goals of the Paperwork Reduction Act to have federal agencies become more responsible and publicly accountable for reducing the burden of federal paperwork on the public, and for other purposes.

Amendment to the Elementary and Secondary Education Act of 1965 (Public Law 104–5) amends a provision of Part A of title IX of the Elementary and Secondary Education Act of 1965, relating to Indian education, to provide a technical amendment, and for other purposes.

Figure 20.-Federal funds for education, by agency: Fiscal Year 1996

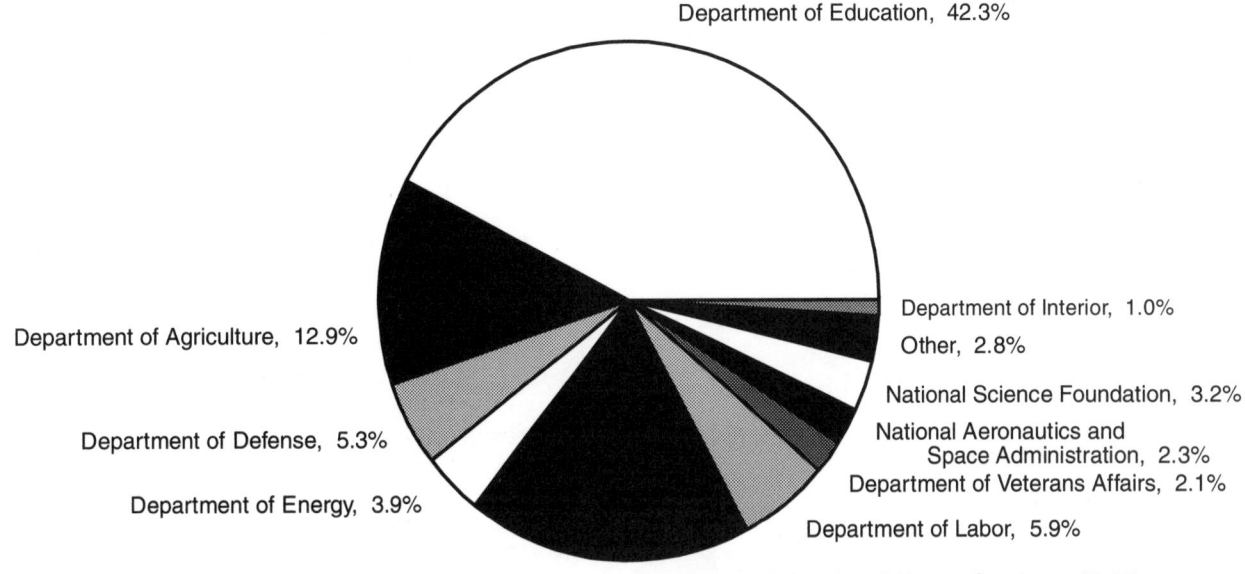

Department of Education, 42.3%

Department of Interior, 1.0%

Other, 2.8%

National Science Foundation, 3.2%

National Aeronautics and
    Space Administration, 2.3%

Department of Veterans Affairs, 2.1%

Department of Labor, 5.9%

Department of Health and Human Services, 18.3%

Department of Energy, 3.9%

Department of Defense, 5.3%

Department of Agriculture, 12.9%

Total = $70.1 billion

SOURCE: U.S. Office of Management and Budget, *Budget of the U.S. Government, Fiscal Year 1997;* and National Science Foundation, *Federal Funds for Research and Development, Fiscal Years 1994, 1995, and 1996.*

Figure 21.-Federal on-budget funds for education, by level or other educational purpose: 1965 to 1996

[In constant FY 1996 dollars]

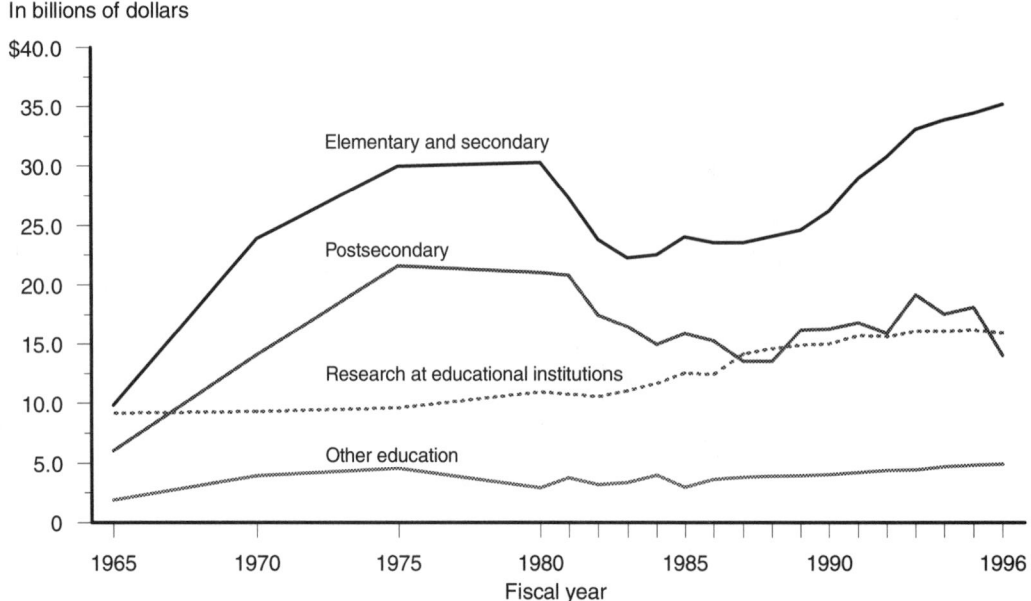

SOURCE: U.S. Office of Management and Budget, *Budget of the U.S. Government*, fiscal years 1967 to 1997; National Science Foundation, *Federal Funds for Research and Development,* fiscal years 1967 to 1996; and unpublished data.

Figure 22.-U.S. Department of Education outlays, by type of recipient: Fiscal Year 1996

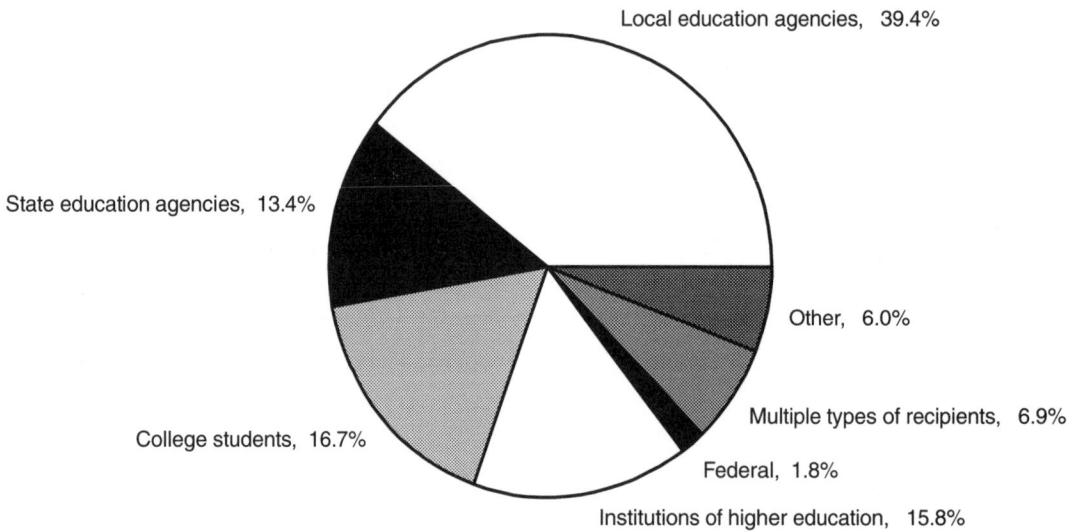

Total outlays = $29.6 billion

SOURCE: U.S. Office of Management and Budget, *Budget of the U.S. Government, Fiscal Year 1997; Catalog of Federal Domestic Assistance;* National Science Foundation, *Federal Funds for Research and Development, Fiscal Years, 1994, 1995, and 1996*; and unpublished data obtained from various federal agencies.

Table 354.—Federal education support and estimated federal tax expenditures for education, by category: Fiscal years 1965 to 1996

[In millions of dollars]

(1) Fiscal year	(2) Total on-budget support, off-budget support, and nonfederal funds generated by federal programs	(3) On-budget support[1] Total	(4) Elementary and secondary	(5) Post-secondary	(6) Other education	(7) Research at educational institutions	(8) Total	(9) Off-budget Federal Direct Student Loan[2]	(10) Federal Family Education Loan Program[3]	(11) Perkins Loans[4]	(12) Income Contingent Loans[5]	(13) Nonfederal State Student Incentive Grants[6]	(14) Supplemental Educational Opportunity Grants[7]	(15) Work-Study aid[8]	(16) Estimated federal tax expenditures for education[9]
Current dollars															
1965	$5,354.7	$5,331.0	$1,942.6	$1,197.5	$374.7	$1,816.3	$23.7	—	—	$16.1	—	—	—	$7.6	—
1970	13,359.1	12,526.5	5,830.4	3,447.7	964.7	2,283.6	832.6	—	$770.0	21.0	—	$20.0	—	41.6	$8,605.0
1975	24,691.5	23,288.1	10,617.2	7,644.0	1,608.5	3,418.4	1,403.4	—	1,233.0	35.7	—	76.5	—	114.7	13,320.0
1980	39,349.2	34,493.5	16,027.7	11,115.9	1,548.7	5,801.2	4,855.7	—	4,598.0	31.8	—	76.5	—	149.4	16,380.0
1981	44,121.5	36,446.2	15,903.7	12,084.8	2,182.2	6,275.5	7,675.4	—	7,433.0	20.7	—	72.0	—	145.2	16,180.0
1982	40,142.2	34,304.7	14,839.2	10,872.8	1,995.1	6,597.4	5,837.5	—	5,597.0	19.8	—	60.0	—	148.7	16,725.0
1983	41,544.8	34,719.2	14,527.8	10,753.4	2,204.1	7,233.8	6,825.5	—	6,582.0	19.8	—	76.0	—	163.7	17,090.0
1984	43,875.9	36,104.5	15,292.4	10,163.2	2,710.4	7,938.6	7,771.4	—	7,520.0	17.9	—	72.7	—	157.5	18,035.0
1985	47,753.4	39,027.9	16,901.3	11,174.4	2,107.6	8,844.6	8,725.5	—	8,467.0	21.4	—	76.0	—	161.1	19,460.0
1986	48,139.4	39,745.0	17,049.9	11,065.6	2,620.0	9,009.4	8,394.4	—	8,142.0	20.2	$0.6	76.0	—	159.5	19,590.0
1987	50,502.0	40,972.2	17,535.7	10,077.5	2,820.4	10,538.6	9,529.8	—	9,272.0	20.9	0.5	73.0	—	160.4	16,190.0
1988	53,840.5	43,216.0	18,564.9	10,419.1	2,981.6	11,250.5	10,624.5	—	10,380.0	20.6	0.5	71.9	$22.0	150.4	18,140.0
1989	59,281.9	48,014.0	19,809.5	13,014.3	3,180.3	12,009.0	11,267.8	—	10,938.0	20.4	0.5	59.2	48.8	215.0	—
1990	62,811.5	51,624.3	21,984.4	13,650.9	3,383.0	12,606.0	11,187.2	—	10,826.0	15.0	0.5	63.5	87.7	237.7	—
1991	70,371.7	57,595.7	25,418.0	14,703.6	3,698.6	13,775.4	12,776.1	—	12,372.0	17.3	—	72.0	97.2	235.0	—
1992	74,477.9	60,479.8	27,926.9	14,384.1	3,992.0	14,176.9	13,998.0	—	13,568.0	29.3	—	72.4	184.6	242.9	—
1993	84,741.5	67,740.6	30,834.3	17,844.0	4,107.2	14,955.1	17,000.0	—	16,524.0	52.7	—	72.4	184.6	190.5	—
1994	93,338.8	68,811.5	32,304.4	16,734.4	4,483.7	15,289.1	24,527.3	$813.0	23,214.0	52.7	—	72.4	184.6	190.5	—
1995	95,890.0	71,718.8	33,623.8	17,623.9	4,721.7	15,749.4	24,171.2	5,161.0	18,519.0	63.4	—	52.7	184.6	190.5	—
1996[10]	96,445.6	70,857.0	35,202.8	14,802.3	4,941.4	15,910.6	25,588.6	10,391.0	14,760.0	31.1	—	31.4	184.6	190.5	—
Constant fiscal year 1996 dollars[11]															
1965	$27,145.4	$27,025.2	$9,847.8	$6,070.7	$1,899.4	$9,207.5	$120.2	—	—	$81.7	—	—	—	$38.5	—
1970	54,681.8	51,273.9	23,865.4	14,112.2	3,948.8	9,347.5	3,407.9	—	$3,151.8	85.9	—	$56.5	—	170.3	$24,295.8
1975	69,715.3	65,753.0	29,977.2	21,582.6	4,541.5	9,651.7	3,962.3	—	3,481.3	100.7	—	144.7	—	323.9	25,195.8
1980	74,432.1	65,247.2	30,317.6	21,026.6	2,929.5	10,973.4	9,184.9	—	8,697.5	60.1	—	131.5	—	282.6	28,150.0
1981	75,825.6	62,635.0	27,331.5	20,768.6	3,750.2	10,784.8	13,190.6	—	12,774.1	35.5	—	115.6	—	249.5	25,602.1
1982	64,436.6	55,066.2	23,820.1	17,453.2	3,202.6	10,590.2	9,370.5	—	8,984.4	31.8	—	91.8	—	238.7	25,972.3
1983	63,595.3	53,147.0	22,238.7	16,461.0	3,374.0	11,073.3	10,448.3	—	10,075.5	30.4	—	111.9	—	250.6	25,602.1
1984	64,595.0	53,153.8	22,513.8	14,962.4	3,990.3	11,687.3	11,441.2	—	11,071.1	26.3	—	108.0	—	231.9	25,160.2
1985	67,871.2	55,469.8	24,021.6	15,892.0	2,995.5	12,570.7	12,401.4	—	12,034.0	30.4	—	108.0	—	229.0	25,632.9
1986	66,430.8	54,846.8	23,528.4	15,270.3	3,615.5	12,432.6	11,584.0	—	12,456.0	27.9	—	100.3	—	220.1	26,854.2
1987	67,844.4	55,042.0	23,557.5	13,509.3	3,788.0	14,157.6	12,802.4	—	13,458.6	28.1	$0.7	102.1	$27.3	215.5	26,317.2
1988	69,809.2	56,033.6	24,071.1	13,538.1	3,865.9	14,587.3	13,775.7	—	13,589.3	26.8	0.6	94.7	58.1	195.0	20,991.8
1989	73,651.4	59,652.3	24,611.2	16,168.9	3,951.2	14,920.9	13,999.1	—	12,891.0	25.3	0.6	89.3	100.0	267.1	20,984.0
1990	74,792.6	61,471.5	26,177.8	16,254.8	4,028.3	15,010.6	13,321.1	—	12,891.0	17.9	0.6	70.5	107.2	283.0	21,600.1
1991	80,232.0	65,665.8	28,959.5	15,861.2	4,216.0	15,705.6	14,566.2	—	14,105.5	19.8	—	79.4	198.2	267.9	—
1992	82,125.6	66,690.2	30,794.5	15,157.4	4,401.9	15,632.6	15,435.4	—	14,961.2	31.4	—	77.8	193.6	267.9	—
1993	90,978.7	72,726.6	33,103.8	17,545.4	4,409.5	16,055.8	18,252.2	—	17,740.2	55.2	—	75.9	189.3	204.6	—
1994	97,862.6	72,146.6	33,870.0	16,146.0	4,701.0	16,030.1	25,716.0	$852.4	24,339.1	55.2	—	65.0	184.6	199.8	—
1995	98,304.8	73,524.9	34,470.6	14,802.3	4,840.6	16,146.0	24,779.9	5,291.0	18,985.4	54.0	—	65.0	184.6	195.3	—
1996[10]	96,445.6	70,857.0	35,202.8	14,802.3	4,941.4	15,910.6	25,588.6	10,391.0	14,760.0	31.1	—	31.4	184.6	190.5	—

[1] On-budget support includes federal funds for education programs tied to appropriations.

[2] The Federal Direct Student Loan program (FDSL) program, recently renamed the William D. Ford Direct Loan program, will provide students with the same benefits they are currently eligible to receive under the Federal Family Education Loan (FFEL) program but will provide loans to students through federal capital rather than through private lenders. The FDSL program will replace the FFEL program and will gradually be phased in, beginning with the 1994–95 academic year. This program will be an off-budget support program.

[3] Formerly the Guaranteed Student Loan program. New student loans guaranteed by the federal government and disbursed to borrowers.

[4] Student loans created from institutional matching funds (1/3 of the federal contribution). Excludes repayments of outstanding loans.

[5] Student loans created from institutional matching funds (1/9 of the federal contribution). This was a demonstration project that involved only 10 institutions and had unsubsidized interest rates.

[6] Required state matching contributions.

[7] Institutions award grants to undergraduate students, and the federal share of such grants may not exceed 75 percent of the total grant.

[8] Employer contributions to student earnings.

[9] Losses of tax revenue attributable to provisions of the federal income tax laws that allow a special exclusion, exemption, or deduction from gross income or provide a special credit, preferential rate of tax, or a deferral of tax liability affecting individual or corporate income tax liabilities.

[10] Estimated.

[11] Data adjusted by the federal funds composite deflator prepared by the U.S. Office of Management and Budget.

—Data not available or not applicable.

NOTE.—To the extent possible, federal education funds data represent outlays rather than obligations. Because of rounding, details may not add to totals. Data have been revised from previously published figures.

SOURCE: U.S. Department of Education, National Center for Education Statistics, compiled from data appearing in U.S. Office of Management and Budget, Budget of the U.S. Government, Appendix, fiscal years 1967 to 1997; National Science Foundation, Federal Funds for Research and Development, fiscal years 1965 to 1996; "Federal Tax Expenditures, FY 1980 to FY 1984," "Federal Tax Expenditures, FY 1984 to FY 1988," and "Federal Tax Expenditures, FY 1970 to FY 1990" by Stephen M. Barro, prepared for the National Center for Education Statistics; and unpublished data obtained from various federal agencies. (This table was prepared June 1996.)

Table 355.—Federal on-budget funds for education, by agency: Fiscal years 1965 to 1996

[In thousands of dollars]

Agency	1965	1970	1975	1980	1981	1982	1983	1984	1985	1986
1	2	3	4	5	6	7	8	9	10	11
Total	$5,331,016	$12,526,499	$23,288,120	$34,493,502	$36,446,159	$34,304,660	$34,719,246	$36,104,549	$39,027,876	$39,744,958
Department of Education	1,000,567	4,625,224	7,350,355	13,137,785	15,081,802	14,109,272	14,585,825	15,534,737	16,701,065	17,740,051
Department of Agriculture	768,927	960,910	2,219,352	4,562,467	4,552,071	4,107,473	4,340,869	4,616,372	4,782,274	5,041,317
Department of Commerce	9,347	13,990	38,967	135,561	61,869	60,150	55,090	55,160	55,114	64,613
Department of Defense	587,412	821,388	1,009,229	1,560,301	1,795,042	2,097,256	2,487,597	2,625,146	3,119,213	3,354,588
Department of Energy	442,434	551,527	764,676	1,605,558	1,796,314	1,751,803	1,933,068	2,042,881	2,247,822	2,181,391
Department of Health and Human Services ...	1,027,537	1,796,854	3,675,225	5,613,930	5,979,973	5,453,996	4,804,004	4,735,554	5,322,356	5,098,910
Department of Housing and Urban Development	221,256	114,709	−52,768	5,314	4,808	969	2,158	2,000	438	342
Department of the Interior	170,088	190,975	300,191	440,547	424,588	476,030	484,314	576,779	549,479	454,273
Department of Justice	10,252	15,728	61,542	60,721	59,310	57,890	68,700	62,282	66,802	72,191
Department of Labor	230,041	424,494	1,103,935	1,862,738	2,129,864	1,799,315	1,833,392	1,755,839	1,948,685	1,976,960
Department of State	64,200	59,742	89,433	25,188	27,239	21,181	23,813	23,086	23,820	23,401
Department of Transportation	—	27,534	52,290	54,712	80,928	75,404	82,139	83,931	82,035	66,214
Department of the Treasury	8,240	18	1,118,840	1,247,463	287,468	286,980	287,300	287,905	290,276	41,257
Department of Veterans Affairs	97,237	1,032,918	4,402,212	2,351,233	2,308,895	1,978,872	1,672,348	1,445,049	1,289,849	1,055,948
Other agencies and programs:										
ACTION	—	—	7,081	2,833	2,752	1,720	1,830	4,975	1,761	1,368
Agency for International Development	63,329	88,034	78,896	176,770	155,542	205,177	173,629	236,983	198,807	198,929
Appalachian Regional Commission	—	37,838	45,786	19,032	15,639	7,626	2,899	4,919	4,745	6,582
Barry Goldwater Scholarship and Excellence in Education Foundation	—	—	—	—	—	—	—	—	—	—
Corporation for National and Community Service	—	—	—	—	—	—	—	—	—	—
Environmental Protection Agency	—	19,446	33,875	41,083	52,210	67,798	43,557	43,700	60,521	69,718
Estimated education share of Federal aid to the District of Columbia	11,350	33,019	55,487	81,847	82,073	91,615	97,516	97,385	107,340	101,844
Federal Emergency Management Agency	—	290	290	1,946	2,151	2,625	1,195	351	1,828	290
General Services Administration	4,013	14,775	22,532	34,800	38,400	37,300	44,200	50,894	—	—
Harry S Truman Scholarship fund	—	—	—	−1,895	699	1,667	1,795	1,929	1,332	2,441
Institute of American Indian and Alaskan Native Culture and Arts Development	—	—	—	—	—	—	—	—	—	—
James Madison Memorial Fellowship Foundation	—	—	—	—	—	—	—	—	—	—
Japanese-United States Friendship Commission	—	—	—	2,294	−44	1,807	2,364	1,611	2,236	235
Library of Congress	15,111	29,478	63,766	151,871	144,131	144,911	154,198	164,080	169,310	166,130
National Aeronautics and Space Administration	208,788	258,366	197,901	255,511	251,184	369,105	367,763	354,528	487,624	490,948
National Archives and Records Administration	—	—	—	—	—	—	—	—	52,118	55,252
National Commission on Libraries and Information Science	—	—	449	2,090	741	638	681	733	723	781
National Endowment for the Arts	—	340	4,754	5,220	5,302	4,823	4,701	5,197	5,536	5,188
National Endowment for the Humanities	—	8,459	63,955	142,586	144,366	115,818	123,315	127,571	125,671	121,125
National Science Foundation	181,216	295,628	535,294	808,392	839,554	854,665	907,917	1,035,746	1,147,115	1,147,273
Nuclear Regulatory Commission	—	—	7,093	32,590	41,309	38,150	37,987	36,400	30,261	27,472
Office of Economic Opportunity	189,871	1,092,410	16,619	—	—	—	—	—	—	—
Smithsonian Institution	2,233	2,461	5,509	5,153	4,853	5,215	6,073	5,758	7,886	6,191
United States Arms Control Agency	—	100	—	661	367	184	157	—	395	276
United States Information Agency	7,512	8,423	9,405	66,210	73,020	77,185	86,556	83,768	143,007	170,514
United States Institute of Peace	—	—	—	—	—	—	—	—	—	230
Other agencies	10,055	1,421	5,949	990	1,739	40	296	1,300	432	715

Table 355.—Federal on-budget funds for education, by agency: Fiscal years 1965 to 1996—Continued

[In thousands of dollars]

Agency	1987	1988	1989	1990	1991	1992	1993	1994 [1]	1995 [1]	1996 [2]
1	12	13	14	15	16	17	18	19	20	21
Total	$40,972,176	$43,215,993	$48,014,017	$51,624,342	$57,595,664	$60,479,844	$67,740,618	$68,811,518	$71,718,752	$70,856,978
Department of Education	16,879,827	18,326,916	21,671,232	23,198,575	25,391,310	26,116,013	30,478,215	30,274,020	31,414,000	30,405,000
Department of Agriculture	5,189,779	5,481,976	5,793,616	6,260,843	6,875,216	7,586,729	8,067,050	8,494,772	9,089,671	9,073,183
Department of Commerce	38,896	38,553	47,586	53,835	67,204	80,510	74,354	85,423	98,902	97,128
Department of Defense	3,695,617	3,461,345	3,746,031	3,605,509	3,707,276	3,948,471	3,958,746	3,899,582	3,947,147	3,722,349
Department of Energy	2,256,799	2,385,966	2,563,978	2,561,950	2,738,862	2,917,137	2,787,423	2,671,660	2,729,138	2,720,316
Department of Health and Human Services ...	5,882,270	6,266,998	6,697,437	7,956,011	9,470,027	9,362,010	10,885,245	11,921,727	12,564,661	12,823,802
Department of Housing and Urban Development	463	51	186	118	48	203	401	856	933	834
Department of the Interior	485,922	528,409	542,466	630,537	844,830	715,382	723,448	696,649	714,208	672,012
Department of Justice	79,815	83,405	88,129	99,775	114,653	134,235	148,381	150,398	170,250	195,298
Department of Labor	2,258,631	2,272,228	2,277,556	2,511,380	3,214,695	3,709,531	4,241,590	4,015,434	3,967,884	4,105,453
Department of State	24,288	38,671	45,848	51,225	49,086	53,343	69,051	54,414	54,663	53,206
Department of Transportation	75,360	65,134	90,840	76,186	69,887	91,485	115,925	119,806	125,078	106,671
Department of the Treasury	19,279	32,768	39,511	41,715	60,356	51,779	56,912	63,301	49,915	50,334
Department of Veterans Affairs	1,002,109	966,549	896,435	757,476	783,789	1,047,579	1,145,108	1,381,925	1,324,632	1,445,153
Other agencies and programs:										
ACTION	3,368	4,110	4,800	8,472	11,321	8,600	—	—	—	—
Agency for International Development	240,827	242,650	227,864	249,786	209,018	245,199	242,907	266,582	281,210	262,477
Appalachian Regional Commission	5,445	6,377	6,145	93	3,907	7,608	7,974	10,242	10,623	9,700
Barry Goldwater Scholarship and Excellence in Education Foundation	—	—	753	1,033	1,941	2,900	3,023	2,789	3,000	3,000
Corporation for National and Community Service	—	—	—	—	—	—	8,500	93,250	214,600	221,800
Environmental Protection Agency	67,465	58,053	64,517	87,481	62,753	152,012	124,500	98,241	97,428	112,723
Estimated education share of Federal aid to the District of Columbia	126,942	122,366	103,764	104,940	125,835	130,371	139,755	97,752	78,796	88,643
Federal Emergency Management Agency	290	290	77	215	33	261	76,467	85,200	170,400	70,600
General Services Administration	—	—	—	—	—	—	—	—	—	—
Harry S Truman Scholarship fund	2,717	2,815	2,851	2,883	2,968	2,401	2,894	2,323	3,000	4,000
Institute of American Indian and Alaskan Native Culture and Arts Development	—	—	3,094	4,305	5,447	6,612	7,462	12,213	13,000	11,000
James Madison Memorial Fellowship Foundation	—	13,200	10,005	191	531	885	1,298	1,464	2,000	2,000
Japanese-United States Friendship Commission	3,225	2,274	3,004	2,299	1,377	1,610	1,503	1,585	2,000	2,000
Library of Congress	160,835	160,505	177,954	189,827	279,745	296,044	311,453	312,724	241,000	243,000
National Aeronautics and Space Administration	787,391	899,897	978,778	1,093,303	1,275,970	1,383,422	1,374,042	1,418,765	1,642,049	1,622,671
National Archives and Records Administration	59,521	65,153	86,266	77,397	81,462	99,412	106,975	110,411	105,172	106,145
National Commission on Libraries and Information Science	512	522	839	3,281	3,447	1,437	867	724	1,000	1,000
National Endowment for the Arts	5,394	5,550	5,655	5,577	6,498	8,286	7,784	7,221	9,421	4,761
National Endowment for the Humanities	124,407	125,230	137,076	141,048	149,832	159,103	160,275	157,468	151,727	91,629
National Science Foundation	1,270,415	1,329,520	1,472,835	1,588,891	1,738,471	1,875,072	2,080,154	2,031,024	2,106,363	2,244,599
Nuclear Regulatory Commission	29,176	25,676	25,690	42,328	23,860	27,418	22,934	20,227	17,619	15,471
Office of Economic Opportunity	—	—	—	—	—	—	—	—	—	—
Smithsonian Institution	6,545	5,393	5,880	5,779	5,906	6,578	7,828	10,059	9,961	11,870
United States Arms Control Agency	3,244	2,633	1,619	25	69	100	25	—	—	—
United States Information Agency	179,653	189,464	185,521	201,547	208,181	237,226	288,059	230,493	294,800	246,200
United States Institute of Peace	4,083	3,476	7,232	7,621	8,238	11,350	10,468	10,794	12,000	10,000
Other agencies	1,666	1,870	947	885	1,616	1,532	1,622	—	500	950

[1] Data revised from previously published figures.

[2] Estimated.

—Data not available or not applicable.

NOTE.—To the extent possible, amounts reported represent outlays, rather than obligations.

SOURCE: U.S. Department of Education, National Center for Education Statistics, compiled from data appearing in U.S. Office of Management and Budget, *Budget of the U.S. Government, Appendix,* fiscal years 1982 to 1997; National Science Foundation, *Federal Funds for Research and Development,* fiscal years 1965 to 1996; and unpublished data obtained from various Federal agencies. (This table was prepared May 1996.)

Table 356.—Federal on-budget funds for education, by level or other educational purpose, by agency and program: Fiscal years 1965 to 1996

[In thousands of dollars]

Level or educational purpose, by agency and program	1965	1970	1975	1980	1981	1982	1983	1984	1985	1986
1	2	3	4	5	6	7	8	9	10	11
Total, all programs	$5,331,016	$12,526,499	$23,288,120	$34,493,502	$36,446,159	$34,304,660	$34,719,246	$36,104,549	$39,027,876	$39,744,958
Elementary/secondary education programs	$1,942,577	$5,830,442	$10,617,195	$16,027,686	$15,903,707	$14,839,241	$14,527,848	$15,292,409	$16,901,334	$17,049,940
Department of Education [8]	567,343	2,719,204	4,132,742	6,629,095	6,835,006	6,456,322	5,986,633	6,220,820	7,296,702	7,551,973
Grants for the disadvantaged	—	1,339,014	1,874,353	3,204,664	3,353,595	2,954,438	2,645,688	3,077,304	4,206,754	3,404,687
Impact aid program [9]	349,671	656,372	618,711	690,170	753,057	546,299	548,205	577,676	647,402	684,311
School improvement programs	72,298	288,304	700,470	788,918	735,321	751,130	552,590	631,537	526,401	618,850
Indian education	—	—	40,036	93,365	56,419	78,353	69,603	71,588	82,328	62,067
Bilingual education	—	21,250	92,693	169,540	172,833	167,114	163,268	167,400	157,539	119,601
Education for the handicapped	13,849	79,090	151,244	821,777	1,035,353	1,141,444	1,289,710	952,778	1,017,964	1,627,894
Vocational and adult education	131,525	335,174	655,235	860,661	728,428	817,544	717,569	742,537	658,314	1,034,563
Education Reform - Goals 2000 [10]	—	—	—	—	—	—	—	—	—	—
Department of Agriculture	623,014	760,477	1,884,345	4,064,497	4,008,962	3,528,208	3,727,171	3,992,808	4,134,906	4,428,143
Child nutrition programs [11]	178,580	299,131	1,452,267	3,377,056	3,438,238	3,019,724	3,278,133	3,536,378	3,664,561	3,819,734
Agricultural Marketing Service—commodities [12]	340,073	341,597	248,839	388,000	345,731	363,883	362,297	338,764	336,502	344,350
Special milk program [11]	86,609	83,800	122,858	159,293	104,384	22,884	14,912	16,000	15,993	15,267
Estimated education share of Forest Service permanent appropriations	17,752	35,949	60,381	140,148	120,609	121,717	71,829	101,666	117,850	248,792
Department of Commerce	—	—	—	54,816	12,788	5,399	1,348	337	—	—
Local public works program—school facilities [13]	—	—	—	54,816	12,788	5,399	1,348	337	—	—
Department of Defense	73,000	143,100	264,500	370,846	414,630	514,993	564,885	694,946	831,625	903,493
Junior R.O.T.C.	—	12,100	12,500	32,000	32,200	42,300	50,400	44,300	55,600	58,600
Overseas dependents schools	73,000	131,000	252,000	338,846	382,430	386,693	414,485	546,072	613,437	691,437
Section VI schools [9]	—	—	—	—	—	86,000	100,000	104,574	162,588	153,456
Department of Energy [14]	100	200	300	77,633	55,063	19,985	40,798	22,469	23,031	21,385
Energy conservation for school buildings [15]	—	—	—	77,240	54,634	19,765	40,634	22,269	22,731	21,000
Pre-engineering program	100	200	300	393	429	220	164	200	300	385
Department of Health and Human Services [16]	79,999	167,333	683,885	1,077,000	1,257,700	1,385,700	1,265,000	1,472,750	1,531,059	1,455,315
Head Start [17]	—	—	403,900	735,000	818,700	911,700	912,000	995,750	1,075,059	1,040,315
Payments to states for AFDC work programs [18]										
Social Security student benefits [19]	79,999	167,333	279,985	342,000	439,000	474,000	353,000	477,000	456,000	415,000
Department of the Interior	130,096	140,705	220,392	318,170	297,420	328,584	346,242	393,529	389,810	308,089
Mineral Leasing Act and other funds: Payments to states—estimated education share	11,075	12,294	27,389	62,636	77,408	124,480	123,670	170,645	127,369	98,606
Payments to counties—estimated education share	10,731	16,359	29,494	48,953	49,561	49,108	20,220	24,221	59,016	5,615
Indian Education: Bureau of Indian Affairs schools	92,603	95,850	141,056	178,112	142,837	114,093	176,878	173,141	177,265	181,235
Johnson-O'Malley assistance [20]	15,534	16,080	22,251	28,081	27,276	40,497	25,077	25,029	25,675	22,053
Education expenses for children of employees, Yellowstone National Park	153	122	202	388	338	406	397	493	485	580
Department of Justice	6,402	8,237	9,822	23,890	25,664	25,620	30,462	31,759	36,117	39,684
Vocational training expenses for prisoners in federal prisons	1,466	2,720	3,039	4,966	5,016	5,066	8,230	7,377	8,292	8,744
Inmate programs [21]	4,936	5,517	6,783	18,924	20,648	20,554	22,232	24,382	27,825	30,940
Department of Labor	230,041	420,927	1,097,811	1,849,800	2,120,100	1,790,400	1,827,000	1,751,039	1,945,268	1,976,619
Job Corps [22]	—	—	175,000	469,800	540,000	570,000	563,000	595,772	604,748	632,619
Training programs—estimated funds for education programs [23]	230,041	420,927	922,811	1,380,000	1,580,100	1,220,400	1,264,000	1,155,267	1,340,520	1,344,000
Department of Transportation [24]	—	45	50	60	62	57	65	105	60	60
Tuition assistance for educational accreditation—Coast Guard personnel [25]	—	45	50	60	62	57	65	105	60	60
Department of the Treasury	32	—	847,139	935,903	273,923	273,728	273,728	273,278	273,728	25,085
Estimated education share of general revenue sharing: [26] State [27]	—	—	475,224	525,019	—	—	—	—	—	—
Local	—	—	371,915	410,884	273,923	273,728	273,728	273,278	273,728	25,085
Tuition assistance for educational accreditation—Coast Guard personnel [25]	32	—	—	—	—	—	—	—	—	—
Department of Veterans Affairs [28]	41,250	338,910	1,371,500	545,786	524,953	427,065	378,663	351,940	344,758	251,782
Noncollegiate and job training programs [29]	14,550	281,640	1,249,410	439,993	391,421	291,818	244,060	227,991	224,035	137,805
Vocational rehabilitation for disabled veterans [30]	17,400	41,700	73,100	87,980	113,876	116,285	117,598	110,187	107,480	103,159
Dependents' education [31]	9,300	15,570	48,990	17,813	19,656	18,962	17,005	13,762	13,243	10,818
Service members occupational conversion and training act of 1992 [32]	—	—	—	—	—	—	—	—	—	—
Other agencies Appalachian Regional Commission [33]	—	33,161	41,667	9,157	7,636	4,936	2,801	4,589	4,632	4,632
National Endowment for the Arts [34]	—	—	3,686	4,989	4,402	4,099	4,069	4,378	4,399	4,060
Arts in education	—	—	3,686	4,989	4,402	4,099	4,069	4,378	4,399	4,060
National Endowment for the Humanities [35]	—	20	149	330	600	418	510	462	321	460

Table 356.—Federal on-budget funds for education, by level or other educational purpose, by agency and program: Fiscal years 1965 to 1996—Continued

[In thousands of dollars]

Level or educational purpose, by agency and program	1987	1988	1989	1990[1]	1991[2]	1992[3]	1993[4]	1994[5]	1995[6]	1996[7]
1	12	13	14	15	16	17	18	19	20	21
Total, all programs	$40,972,176	$43,215,993	$48,014,017	$51,624,342	$57,595,664	$60,479,844	$67,740,618	$68,811,518	$71,718,752	$70,856,978
Elementary/secondary education programs	$17,535,707	$18,564,859	$19,809,528	$21,984,361	$25,418,031	$27,926,888	$30,834,326	$32,304,357	$33,623,809	$35,202,773
Department of Education [8]	7,554,487	8,098,436	8,869,300	9,681,313	10,865,336	12,057,746	13,058,974	13,769,196	14,029,000	15,416,000
Grants for the disadvantaged	3,209,923	4,027,559	4,185,357	4,494,111	5,218,749	6,158,813	6,615,047	6,845,651	6,808,000	7,113,000
Impact aid program [9]	704,197	707,539	755,477	816,366	753,530	794,794	432,153	829,952	808,000	830,000
School improvement programs	889,478	443,468	975,237	1,189,158	1,375,910	1,514,892	2,032,552	1,469,963	1,397,000	1,594,000
Indian education	39,638	18,339	65,683	69,451	65,639	68,523	99,925	79,095	71,000	78,000
Bilingual education	141,483	159,746	164,759	188,919	186,748	198,332	124,778	221,681	225,000	239,000
Education for the handicapped	1,339,241	1,465,985	1,880,751	1,616,623	2,174,358	2,243,338	2,564,070	2,980,328	3,177,000	3,511,000
Vocational and adult education	1,230,527	1,275,800	842,036	1,306,685	1,090,402	1,079,054	1,190,449	1,340,763	1,482,000	1,513,000
Education Reform - Goals 2000 [10]	—	—	—	—	—	—	—	1,763	61,000	538,000
Department of Agriculture	4,562,093	4,806,766	5,104,502	5,528,950	6,074,735	6,714,082	7,154,483	7,604,447	8,201,294	8,192,615
Child nutrition programs [11]	4,044,830	4,286,242	4,555,581	4,977,075	5,536,966	6,126,983	6,596,588	7,043,699	7,644,789	7,644,789
Agricultural Marketing Service—commodities [12]	350,118	349,670	342,071	350,441	350,859	400,000	389,900	400,000	400,000	400,000
Special milk program [11]	15,446	18,342	18,544	18,707	19,900	19,178	15,535	(11)	(11)	(11)
Estimated education share of Forest Service permanent appropriations	151,699	152,512	188,306	182,727	167,010	167,921	152,460	160,748	156,505	147,826
Department of Commerce	—	—	—	—	—	—	—	—	—	—
Local public works program—school facilities [13]	—	—	—	—	—	—	—	—	—	—
Department of Defense	861,393	988,265	1,059,259	1,097,876	1,253,105	1,197,318	1,259,374	1,210,168	1,295,547	1,322,278
Junior R.O.T.C.	57,440	45,300	53,930	39,300	53,174	54,746	84,100	95,500	155,600	172,800
Overseas dependents schools	664,941	773,810	821,365	864,958	960,293	912,916	895,674	849,649	855,772	816,648
Section VI schools [9]	139,012	169,155	183,964	193,618	239,638	229,656	279,600	265,019	284,175	332,830
Department of Energy [14]	12,061	12,931	12,851	15,563	15,676	15,236	6,254	11,615	12,646	7,700
Energy conservation for school buildings [15]	11,761	12,611	12,442	15,213	14,206	12,586	5,054	10,535	10,746	7,200
Pre-engineering program	300	320	409	350	1,470	2,650	1,200	1,080	1,900	500
Department of Health and Human Services [16]	1,555,542	1,651,324	1,789,026	2,396,793	2,997,194	3,310,200	4,114,498	4,669,181	5,116,559	5,119,289
Head Start [17]	1,130,542	1,206,324	1,234,869	1,447,758	1,951,775	2,201,800	2,776,286	3,215,946	3,534,000	3,534,000
Payments to states for AFDC work programs [18]	—	—	85,511	459,221	545,700	594,184	736,474	838,981	953,000	959,000
Social Security student benefits [19]	425,000	445,000	468,646	489,814	499,719	514,216	601,738	614,254	629,559	626,289
Department of the Interior	344,183	379,645	379,381	445,267	644,770	517,666	536,483	485,758	493,124	461,797
Mineral Leasing Act and other funds: Payments to states—estimated education share	87,437	92,227	114,414	123,811	131,683	122,045	108,924	21,693	18,750	9,090
Payments to counties—estimated education share	36,455	34,922	54,804	102,522	35,038	45,805	34,903	39,819	37,490	18,170
Indian Education: Bureau of Indian Affairs schools	195,994	231,512	186,643	192,841	452,521	325,582	368,817	399,234	411,524	410,922
Johnson-O'Malley assistance [20]	22,824	20,400	23,000	25,556	24,931	23,590	22,980	24,326	24,359	22,615
Education expenses for children of employees, Yellowstone National Park	1,473	584	520	538	597	644	859	686	1,000	1,000
Department of Justice	44,531	50,679	58,523	65,997	78,050	94,724	107,857	112,447	128,850	151,600
Vocational training expenses for prisoners in federal prisons	8,744	8,679	6,933	2,066	1,748	1,944	1,725	1,240	3,000	4,000
Inmate programs [21]	35,787	42,000	51,590	63,931	76,302	92,780	106,132	111,207	125,850	147,600
Department of Labor	2,258,199	2,266,700	2,271,966	2,505,487	3,209,147	3,708,362	4,240,990	4,011,184	3,957,800	4,096,000
Job Corps [22]	678,599	712,218	771,966	739,376	805,270	925,826	949,287	964,234	1,029,000	1,096,000
Training programs—estimated funds for education programs [23]	1,579,600	1,554,482	1,500,000	1,766,111	2,403,877	2,782,536	3,291,703	3,046,950	2,928,800	3,000,000
Department of Transportation [24]	55	50	40	46	31	60	60	60	62	62
Tuition assistance for educational accreditation—Coast Guard personnel [25]	55	50	40	46	31	60	60	60	62	62
Department of the Treasury	—	—	—	—	—	—	—	—	—	—
Estimated education share of general revenue sharing: [26] State [27]	—	—	—	—	—	—	—	—	—	—
Local	—	—	—	—	—	—	—	—	—	—
Tuition assistance for educational accreditation—Coast Guard personnel [25]	—	—	—	—	—	—	—	—	—	—
Department of Veterans Affairs [28]	235,297	196,159	168,865	155,351	167,040	190,608	222,567	335,866	311,768	354,181
Noncollegiate and job training programs [29]	119,702	76,367	43,696	12,848	—	—	—	—	—	—
Vocational rehabilitation for disabled veterans [30]	105,947	112,058	118,749	136,780	161,096	184,500	216,276	265,597	298,132	348,810
Dependents' education [31]	9,648	7,734	6,420	5,723	5,944	6,108	5,840	5,740	5,961	5,371
Service members occupational conversion and training act of 1992 [32]	—	—	—	—	—	—	451	64,529	7,675	—
Other agencies Appalachian Regional Commission [33]	5,323	5,327	5,145	93	3,790	5,182	5,382	2,529	2,173	2,000
National Endowment for the Arts [34]	4,099	4,350	4,462	4,641	4,870	5,000	5,000	5,000	7,117	2,850
Arts in education	4,099	4,350	4,462	4,641	4,870	5,000	5,000	5,000	7,117	2,850
National Endowment for the Humanities [35]	352	826	698	404	590	809	1,645	278	997	615

Table 356.—Federal on-budget funds for education, by level or other educational purpose, by agency and program: Fiscal years 1965 to 1996—Continued

[In thousands of dollars]

Level or educational purpose, by agency and program	1965	1970	1975	1980	1981	1982	1983	1984	1985	1986
1	2	3	4	5	6	7	8	9	10	11
Office of Economic Opportunity [36]	182,793	1,072,375	16,619	—	—	—	—	—	—	—
Head Start [37]	96,400	325,700	—	—	—	—	—	—	—	—
Other elementary and secondary programs [38]	20,000	42,809	16,612	—	—	—	—	—	—	—
Job Corps [39]	34,000	144,000	—	—	—	—	—	—	—	—
Youth Corps and other training programs [40]	31,000	553,368	7	—	—	—	—	—	—	—
Volunteers in Service to America (VISTA) [41]	1,393	6,498	—	—	—	—	—	—	—	—
Other programs										
Estimated education share of federal aid to the District of Columbia	8,507	25,748	42,588	65,714	64,798	73,727	78,473	77,200	84,918	79,160
Postsecondary education programs	**$1,197,511**	**$3,447,697**	**$7,644,037**	**$11,115,882**	**$12,084,842**	**$10,872,849**	**$10,753,445**	**$10,163,188**	**$11,174,379**	**$11,065,646**
Department of Education [8]	237,955	1,187,962	2,089,184	5,682,242	6,824,959	6,418,740	7,213,341	7,341,239	8,202,499	8,444,924
Student financial assistance [42]	—	—	—	3,682,789	3,906,285	2,732,467	4,043,597	3,743,262	4,162,695	4,585,210
Federal Direct Student Loan Program [43]	—	—	—	—	—	—	—	—	—	—
Federal Family Education Loan Program [44]	—	2,323	111,087	1,407,977	2,258,723	3,023,463	2,555,539	3,245,226	3,534,795	3,322,734
Higher education	218,264	1,029,131	1,838,066	399,787	419,561	379,281	364,422	419,200	404,511	402,035
Facilities—loans and insurance [45]	3,588	114,199	16,292	−19,031	13,262	25,201	21,148	−945	5,307	1,920
College housing loans [45,46]	—	—	—	14,082	18,106	36,531	−16,510	−238,818	−164,061	−73,992
Educational activities overseas [45]	129	774	1,881	3,561	2,797	1,322	1,243	1,259	1,838	−1,413
Historically Black Colleges and Universities Capital Financing, Program Account [47]	—	—	—	—	—	—	—	—	—	—
Gallaudet College and Howard University	15,974	38,559	111,971	176,829	184,888	196,748	216,782	148,600	229,938	171,729
National Technical Institute for the Deaf [48]	—	2,976	9,887	16,248	21,337	23,727	27,120	23,455	27,476	36,701
Department of Agriculture	—	—	6,450	10,453	11,250	12,241	16,241	17,241	17,741	16,877
Agriculture Extension Service, Second Morrill Act payments to agricultural and mechanical colleges and Tuskegee Institute [49]	—	—	6,450	10,453	11,250	12,241	16,241	17,241	17,741	16,877
Department of Commerce	5,081	8,277	14,973	29,971	2,412	2,533	2,282	2,223	2,163	2,207
Sea Grant Program [50]	—	—	1,886	3,123	2,412	2,533	2,282	2,223	2,163	2,207
Merchant Marine Academy [51]	3,570	6,160	10,152	14,809	—	—	—	—	—	—
State marine schools [51]	1,511	2,117	2,935	12,039	—	—	—	—	—	—
Department of Defense [52]	77,500	322,100	379,800	545,000	621,700	692,400	810,500	857,700	1,041,700	1,068,300
Tuition assistance for military personnel	—	57,500	86,800	(53)	43,500	50,800	61,300	68,900	77,100	89,700
Service academies [54]	77,500	78,700	86,200	106,100	128,100	142,500	151,900	160,700	196,400	214,500
Senior R.O.T.C.	—	108,100	116,500	(53)	290,900	304,500	345,700	395,100	354,000	362,000
Professional development education [55]	—	77,800	90,300	(53)	159,200	194,600	251,600	233,000	414,200	402,100
Department of Energy [14]	3,000	3,000	3,000	57,701	40,877	16,039	31,158	19,012	19,475	18,051
University laboratory cooperative program	3,000	3,000	3,000	2,800	3,500	3,600	4,284	3,467	6,500	5,714
Teacher development projects [56]	—	—	—	1,400	1,700	1,200	—	—	—	—
Graduate traineeship programs [57]	—	—	—	—	—	1,000	—	—	—	52
Energy conservation for buildings—higher education [15]	—	—	—	53,501	35,677	10,239	26,874	15,395	12,705	11,815
Minority honors vocational training [58]	—	—	—	—	—	—	—	150	150	230
Honors research program [58]	—	—	—	—	—	—	—	—	120	240
Students and teachers [59]	—	—	—	—	—	—	—	—	—	—
Department of Health and Human Services [16]	469,223	981,483	1,686,650	2,412,058	2,475,874	1,826,949	1,045,206	463,228	516,088	274,581
Health professions training programs [60]	139,795	353,029	599,350	460,736	255,928	174,887	172,004	180,715	212,200	198,004
Indian health manpower [61]	—	—	—	7,187	3,350	5,676	5,692	5,471	5,577	4,750
National Health Service Corps scholarships	—	—	1,206	70,667	88,207	59,767	32,016	14,526	2,268	2,130
National Institutes of Health training grants [62]	—	—	154,875	176,388				—	217,927	—
National Institute of Occupational Safety and Health training grants	4,327	8,088	7,182	12,899	7,602	5,760	5,760	8,760	8,760	8,383
Alcohol, drug abuse, and mental health training programs [63]	85,101	118,366	83,727	122,103	115,747	100,676	59,380	27,607	43,617	46,216
Health teaching facilities	—	—	353	3,078	4,040	4,183	40,354	6,149	739	15,098
Social Security postsecondary students' benefits [64]	240,000	502,000	839,957	1,559,000	2,001,000	1,476,000	730,000	220,000	25,000	—
Department of Housing and Urban Development [45]	220,744	114,199	−55,418	—	—	—	—	—	—	—
College housing loans [45,46]	220,744	114,199	−55,418	—	—	—	—	—	—	—
Department of the Interior	30,153	31,749	50,844	80,202	86,182	113,275	109,456	146,750	125,247	109,744
Shared revenues, Mineral Leasing Act and other receipts—estimated education share	6,260	6,949	15,480	35,403	43,752	70,358	69,900	96,451	71,991	55,733
Indian programs:										
Continuing education [65]	8,993	9,380	13,311	16,909	15,140	16,636	14,951	25,299	24,338	24,167
Higher education scholarships	14,900	15,420	22,053	27,890	27,290	26,281	24,605	25,000	28,918	29,844
Department of State	53,420	30,850	50,347	—	—	—	—	—	—	—
Educational exchange [66]										
Mutual educational and cultural exchange activities	47,025	30,454	50,300	—	—	—	—	—	—	—
International educational exchange activities	6,395	396	47	—	—	—	—	—	—	—
Russian, Eurasian, and East European Research and Training [67]	—	—	—	—	—	—	—	—	—	—

Table 356.—Federal on-budget funds for education, by level or other educational purpose, by agency and program: Fiscal years 1965 to 1996—Continued

[In thousands of dollars]

Level or educational purpose, by agency and program	1987	1988	1989	1990[1]	1991[2]	1992[3]	1993[4]	1994[5]	1995[6]	1996[7]
1	12	13	14	15	16	17	18	19	20	21
Office of Economic Opportunity[36]	—	—	—	—	—	—	—	—	—	—
Head Start[37]	—	—	—	—	—	—	—	—	—	—
Other elementary and secondary programs[38]	—	—	—	—	—	—	—	—	—	—
Job Corps[39]	—	—	—	—	—	—	—	—	—	—
Youth Corps and other training programs[40]	—	—	—	—	—	—	—	—	—	—
Volunteers in Service to America (VISTA)[41]	—	—	—	—	—	—	—	—	—	—
Other programs										
Estimated education share of federal aid to the District of Columbia	98,092	103,400	85,510	86,579	103,697	109,894	120,759	86,627	66,871	75,786
Postsecondary education programs	**$10,077,456**	**$10,419,100**	**$13,014,330**	**$13,650,915**	**$14,703,594**	**$14,384,138**	**$17,844,015**	**$16,734,359**	**$17,623,937**	**$14,802,259**
Department of Education[8]	7,438,674	8,247,103	10,640,044	11,175,978	12,002,766	11,323,584	14,660,704	13,431,998	14,243,000	11,419,000
Student financial assistance[42]	4,779,817	5,219,916	5,859,774	5,920,328	6,333,839	7,071,440	7,678,293	7,118,034	7,047,000	7,395,000
Federal Direct Student Loan Program[43]	—	—	—	—	—	—	10,000	148,247	840,000	477,000
Federal Family Education Loan Program[44]	2,548,179	2,779,304	3,899,387	4,372,446	4,781,918	3,253,648	5,554,920	5,070,304	5,190,000	2,371,000
Higher education	419,105	411,775	606,849	659,492	615,372	718,406	1,041,583	796,278	871,000	898,000
Facilities—loans and insurance[45]	−84,866	−43,282	10,182	19,219	34,805	25,984	−2,976	16,002	−3,000	4,000
College housing loans[45,46]	−558,178	−372,778	−31,299	−57,167	−33,249	−39,907	−28,355	−40,041	−42,000	−39,000
Educational activities overseas[45]	−8	233	374	82	−47	—	—	—	—	—
Historically Black Colleges and Universities Capital Financing, Program Account[47]	—	—	—	—	—	—	—	129	2,000	3,000
Gallaudet College and Howard University	299,085	224,781	258,519	230,327	233,209	263,497	353,390	280,945	292,000	269,000
National Technical Institute for the Deaf[48]	35,540	27,154	36,258	31,251	36,919	30,516	53,849	42,100	46,000	41,000
Department of Agriculture	16,877	27,799	27,799	31,273	32,302	34,238	32,730	25,472	33,373	32,872
Agriculture Extension Service, Second Morill Act payments to agricultural and mechanical colleges and Tuskegee Institute[49]	16,877	27,799	27,799	31,273	32,302	34,238	32,730	25,472	33,373	32,872
Department of Commerce	2,061	2,420	2,765	3,312	4,334	3,270	3,549	4,000	3,487	3,487
Sea Grant Program[50]	2,061	2,420	2,765	3,312	4,334	3,270	3,549	4,000	3,487	3,487
Merchant Marine Academy[51]	—	—	—	—	—	—	—	—	—	—
State marine schools[51]	—	—	—	—	—	—	—	—	—	—
Department of Defense[52]	1,079,768	573,400	746,464	635,769	665,059	680,194	696,800	679,000	729,500	746,000
Tuition assistance for military personnel	111,368	134,500	236,089	95,300	92,800	102,400	123,400	130,200	127,000	131,000
Service academies[54]	223,700	109,100	115,150	120,613	132,487	125,146	128,000	141,500	163,300	174,900
Senior R.O.T.C.	382,440	179,200	198,325	193,056	198,072	193,348	184,100	195,300	219,400	236,700
Professional development education[55]	362,260	150,600	196,900	226,800	241,700	259,300	261,300	212,000	219,800	203,400
Department of Energy[14]	19,225	22,609	15,062	25,502	30,851	34,373	17,654	17,951	28,027	14,997
University laboratory cooperative program	9,859	13,571	5,929	9,402	19,330	19,100	4,000	3,600	8,552	5,672
Teacher development projects[56]	—	—	—	—	—	—	—	—	—	—
Graduate traineeship programs[57]	−4	−26	—	—	—	—	—	—	—	—
Energy conservation for buildings—higher education[15]	8,500	7,746	6,493	7,459	7,411	9,573	6,654	8,051	7,381	4,945
Minority honors vocational training[58]	390	598	720	—	—	—	—	—	—	—
Honors research program[58]	480	720	820	6,472	1,000	1,000	1,000	900	2,221	892
Students and teachers[59]	—	—	1,100	2,169	3,110	4,700	6,000	5,400	9,873	3,488
Department of Health and Human Services[16]	283,551	271,497	287,238	578,542	697,385	743,456	720,911	795,914	796,035	783,422
Health professions training programs[60]	202,710	210,404	223,811	230,600	271,937	305,829	299,785	305,549	298,302	276,570
Indian health manpower[61]	7,018	5,998	5,972	9,508	13,379	19,460	26,100	26,398	27,000	26,000
National Health Service Corps scholarships	2,277	4,100	6,531	4,759	48,795	58,706	33,323	79,250	78,206	78,000
National Institutes of Health training grants[62]	—	—	—	241,356	268,492	348,034	350,804	372,698	380,502	390,890
National Institute of Occupational Safety and Health training grants	9,900	9,718	10,095	10,461	10,472	10,972	10,472	11,622	11,660	11,600
Alcohol, drug abuse, and mental health training programs[63]	61,075	40,726	40,301	81,353	83,829	—	—	—	—	—
Health teaching facilities	571	551	528	505	481	455	427	397	365	362
Social Security postsecondary students' benefits[64]	—	—	—	—	—	—	—	—	—	—
Department of Housing and Urban Development[45]	—	—	—	—	—	—	—	—	—	—
College housing loans[45,46]	—	—	—	—	—	—	—	—	—	—
Department of the Interior	108,386	113,661	123,529	135,480	141,523	140,266	132,916	156,734	159,054	151,035
Shared revenues, Mineral Leasing Act and other receipts—estimated education share	49,421	52,117	64,669	69,980	74,430	68,982	61,566	79,815	82,810	76,310
Indian programs:										
Continuing education[66]	25,986	30,822	28,424	34,911	36,875	38,970	39,840	43,184	43,907	44,215
Higher education scholarships	32,979	30,722	30,436	30,589	30,218	32,315	31,510	33,735	32,337	30,510
Department of State	—	4,120	4,422	2,167	6,396	9,057	10,211	7,842	3,000	2,000
Educational exchange[66]										
Mutual educational and cultural exchange activities	—	—	—	—	—	—	—	—	—	—
International educational exchange activities	—	—	—	—	—	—	—	—	—	—
Russian, Eurasian, and East European Research and Training[67]	—	4,120	4,422	2,167	6,396	9,057	10,211	7,842	3,000	2,000

Table 356.—Federal on-budget funds for education, by level or other educational purpose, by agency and program: Fiscal years 1965 to 1996—Continued

[In thousands of dollars]

Level or educational purpose, by agency and program	1965	1970	1975	1980	1981	1982	1983	1984	1985	1986
1	2	3	4	5	6	7	8	9	10	11
Department of Transportation [24]	—	11,197	11,885	12,530	40,114	46,709	46,177	57,245	55,569	44,074
Merchant Marine Academy [51]	—	—	—	—	17,094	21,507	23,211	18,739	19,898	19,505
State marine schools [68]	—	—	—	—	10,374	12,351	9,383	23,733	19,777	8,363
Coast Guard Academy [25]	—	9,342	9,780	10,000	10,100	10,200	10,329	11,364	11,857	11,845
Postgraduate training for Coast Guard officers [69]	—	1,655	1,855	2,230	2,242	2,360	2,891	2,959	3,499	3,807
Tuition assistance to Coast Guard military personnel [25]	—	200	250	300	304	291	363	450	538	554
Department of the Treasury	8,208	—	268,605	296,750	—	—	—	—	—	—
General revenue sharing—estimated state share to higher education [26,27]	—	—	268,605	296,750	—	—	—	—	—	—
Coast Guard Academy [25]	6,815	—	—	—	—	—	—	—	—	—
Postgraduate training for Coast Guard officers [69]	1,293	—	—	—	—	—	—	—	—	—
Tuition assistance to Coast Guard military personnel [25]	100	—	—	—	—	—	—	—	—	—
Department of Veterans Affairs [28]	55,650	693,490	3,029,600	1,803,847	1,781,845	1,550,161	1,292,885	1,092,609	944,091	803,166
Vietnam-era veterans: [70]	33,950	638,260	2,840,600	1,579,974	1,548,502	1,319,081	1,077,391	861,310	694,217	514,476
College student support	—	—	—	1,560,081	1,524,783	1,294,698	1,052,859	839,135	679,953	504,290
Work-study	—	—	—	19,893	23,719	24,383	24,532	22,175	14,264	10,186
Service persons college support [71]	—	18,900	74,690	46,617	43,617	38,978	36,054	38,896	35,630	30,707
Post-Vietnam veterans [72]	—	—	—	922	4,603	14,438	24,871	52,241	82,554	121,929
All-volunteer-force educational assistance: [73]	—	—	—	—	—	—	—	—	196	24,171
Veterans [74]	—	—	—	—	—	—	—	—	—	2
Reservists [75]	—	—	—	—	—	—	—	—	196	24,169
Veteran dependents' education [76]	21,700	36,330	114,310	176,334	185,123	177,664	154,569	140,162	131,494	111,883
Payments to state education agencies [77]	—	—	—	—	—	—	—	—	—	—
Other agencies										
Appalachian Regional Commission [33]	—	4,105	2,545	1,751	293	1,039	—	—	—	1,950
National Endowment for the Humanities [35]	—	3,349	25,320	56,451	59,463	46,979	48,457	52,359	49,098	42,346
National Science Foundation	27,170	42,000	60,283	64,583	66,246	67,637	50,126	29,746	60,069	74,151
Science and engineering education programs [50]	27,170	37,000	60,283	64,583	66,246	67,637	50,126	29,746	60,069	74,151
Sea Grant Program [50]	—	5,000	—	—	—	—	—	—	—	—
United States Information Agency [78]	7,512	8,423	9,405	51,095	58,649	60,933	69,298	64,394	124,041	148,483
Educational and cultural affairs [66]	—	—	—	49,546	56,995	59,966	68,041	17,414	21,079	23,008
Educational and cultural exchange programs [79]	—	—	—	—	—	—	—	45,570	101,529	125,246
Educational exchange activities, international	—	—	—	1,549	1,654	967	1,257	1,410	1,433	229
Information center and library activities [80]	7,512	8,423	9,405	—	—	—	—	—	—	—
Other programs										
Barry Goldwater Scholarship and Excellence in Education Foundation [81]	—	—	—	—	—	—	—	—	—	—
Estimated education share of federal aid to the District of Columbia	1,895	5,513	10,564	13,143	14,279	15,547	16,523	17,513	15,266	14,351
Harry S Truman Scholarship fund [45,82]	—	—	—	−1,895	699	1,667	1,795	1,929	1,332	2,441
Institute of American Indian and Alaskan Native Culture and Arts Development [83]	—	—	—	—	—	—	—	—	—	—
James Madison Memorial Fellowship Foundation [84]	—	—	—	—	—	—	—	—	—	—
Other education programs	**$374,652**	**$964,719**	**$1,608,478**	**$1,548,730**	**$2,182,155**	**$1,995,147**	**$2,204,147**	**$2,710,402**	**$2,107,588**	**$2,620,021**
Department of Education [8]	182,021	630,235	1,045,659	747,706	1,361,357	1,152,009	1,326,271	1,813,128	1,173,055	1,674,171
Administration	17,732	47,456	108,372	187,317	247,214	265,726	247,966	307,447	284,900	263,216
Libraries	26,111	108,284	225,810	129,127	80,492	101,437	124,451	87,059	85,650	96,406
Rehabilitative services and disability research	137,313	473,091	709,483	426,886	1,028,999	779,699	948,650	1,414,396	798,298	1,311,485
American Printing House for the Blind	865	1,404	1,994	4,349	4,747	5,000	5,174	4,054	4,230	3,031
Trust funds [45]	—	—	—	27	−95	147	30	172	−23	33
Department of Agriculture	87,551	135,637	220,395	271,112	289,142	311,949	322,430	327,123	336,375	322,599
Extension Service	85,924	131,734	215,523	263,584	281,019	303,461	312,413	317,099	325,986	311,132
National Agricultural Library	1,627	3,903	4,872	7,528	8,123	8,488	10,017	10,024	10,389	11,467
Department of Commerce	251	1,226	2,317	2,479	—	—	—	—	—	—
Maritime Administration: Training for private sector employees [51]	251	1,226	2,317	2,479	—	—	—	—	—	—
Department of Health and Human Services [16]	3,953	24,273	31,653	37,819	46,478	46,640	44,899	48,876	47,195	59,306
National Library of Medicine	3,953	24,273	31,653	37,819	46,478	46,640	44,899	48,876	47,195	59,306
Department of Housing and Urban Development	512	—	—	—	—	—	—	—	—	—
Urban mass transportation—managerial training grants [85]	512	—	—	—	—	—	—	—	—	—
Department of Justice	3,850	5,546	42,818	27,642	24,828	26,304	31,082	23,723	25,517	27,412
F.B.I. National Academy	1,850	2,066	5,100	7,234	3,569	4,843	8,832	4,285	4,189	3,946
F.B.I. Field Police Academy	1,450	2,500	5,254	7,715	7,916	8,332	8,792	8,069	10,220	9,756
Narcotics and dangerous drug training	550	980	1,152	2,416	2,317	1,684	1,740	63	83	68
National Institute of Corrections [86]	—	—	31,312	10,277	11,026	11,445	11,718	11,306	11,025	13,642
Department of State	10,780	20,672	28,113	25,000	27,184	21,174	23,784	23,086	23,791	23,371
Foreign Service Institute	6,395	15,857	20,750	25,000	27,184	21,174	23,784	23,086	23,791	23,371
Center for Cultural and Technical Interchange [66]	4,385	4,815	7,363	—	—	—	—	—	—	—

Table 356.—Federal on-budget funds for education, by level or other educational purpose, by agency and program: Fiscal years 1965 to 1996—Continued

[In thousands of dollars]

Level or educational purpose, by agency and program	1987	1988	1989	1990[1]	1991[2]	1992[3]	1993[4]	1994[5]	1995[6]	1996[7]
1	12	13	14	15	16	17	18	19	20	21
Department of Transportation [24]	47,226	44,998	63,559	46,025	46,647	53,991	57,576	56,640	56,057	56,057
Merchant Marine Academy [51]	20,476	20,579	20,611	20,926	22,855	27,007	26,788	30,241	30,850	30,850
State marine schools [68]	12,073	7,961	26,062	8,269	8,829	11,072	10,320	10,270	8,980	8,980
Coast Guard Academy [25]	10,086	10,810	11,740	12,074	12,074	13,071	13,602	13,103	13,500	13,500
Postgraduate training for Coast Guard officers [69]	3,978	5,084	4,621	4,173	2,248	2,540	6,306	2,726	2,313	2,313
Tuition assistance to Coast Guard military personnel [25]	613	564	525	582	641	301	560	300	414	414
Department of the Treasury	—	—	—	—	—	—	—	—	—	—
General revenue sharing—estimated state share to higher education [26,27]	—	—	—	—	—	—	—	—	—	—
Coast Guard Academy [25]	—	—	—	—	—	—	—	—	—	—
Postgraduate training for Coast Guard officers [69]	—	—	—	—	—	—	—	—	—	—
Tuition assistance to Coast Guard military personnel [25]	—	—	—	—	—	—	—	—	—	—
Department of Veterans Affairs [28]	764,561	768,090	725,270	599,825	614,449	854,480	919,991	1,043,709	1,010,114	1,088,972
Vietnam-era veterans: [70]	411,967	345,242	264,702	46,998	—	—	—	—	—	—
College student support	403,527	337,568	258,982	39,458	—	—	—	—	—	—
Work-study	8,440	7,674	5,720	7,540	—	—	—	—	—	—
Service persons college support [71]	28,410	33,472	34,399	8,911	—	—	—	—	—	—
Post-Vietnam veterans [72]	171,752	203,262	195,142	161,475	118,139	88,500	65,894	48,114	33,596	24,947
All-volunteer-force educational assistance: [73]	45,688	73,731	122,222	269,947	380,720	650,540	745,786	886,951	868,394	957,378
Veterans [74]	107	8,386	43,423	183,765	303,861	530,820	626,669	769,481	760,390	843,907
Reservists [75]	45,581	65,345	78,799	86,182	76,859	119,720	119,117	117,470	108,004	113,471
Veteran dependents' education [76]	106,744	100,883	96,805	100,494	103,590	103,440	96,311	96,644	95,124	93,647
Payments to state education agencies [77]	—	11,500	12,000	12,000	12,000	12,000	12,000	12,000	13,000	13,000
Other agencies										
Appalachian Regional Commission [33]	30	1,050	825	—	92	1,487	1,587	3,413	2,741	2,200
National Endowment for the Humanities [35]	48,679	47,601	51,449	50,938	55,861	58,512	57,804	58,404	56,481	34,006
National Science Foundation	85,494	97,466	130,187	161,884	191,661	210,375	246,591	225,168	211,800	206,400
Science and engineering education programs	85,494	97,466	130,187	161,884	191,661	210,375	246,591	225,168	211,800	206,400
Sea Grant Program [50]	—	—	—	—	—	—	—	—	—	—
United States Information Agency [78]	162,897	166,705	164,807	181,172	185,905	207,676	256,068	200,429	260,800	231,200
Educational and cultural affairs [66]	24,313	29,724	21,596	35,862	35,714	38,858	44,183	28,927	13,600	12,800
Educational and cultural exchange programs [79]	138,039	136,646	143,194	145,307	150,183	168,818	211,885	171,502	247,200	218,400
Educational exchange activities, international	545	335	17	3	8	—	—	—	—	—
Information center and library activities [80]	—	—	—	—	—	—	—	—	—	—
Other programs										
Barry Goldwater Scholarship and Excellence in Education Foundation [81]	—	—	753	1,033	1,941	2,900	3,023	2,789	3,000	3,000
Estimated education share of federal aid to the District of Columbia	17,310	14,566	14,207	14,637	17,477	16,382	14,247	8,896	9,468	10,611
Harry S Truman Scholarship fund [45,82]	2,717	2,815	2,851	2,883	2,968	2,401	2,894	2,323	3,000	4,000
Institute of American Indian and Alaskan Native Culture and Arts Development [83]	—	—	3,094	4,305	5,447	6,612	7,462	12,213	13,000	11,000
James Madison Memorial Fellowship Foundation [84]	—	13,200	10,005	191	531	885	1,298	1,464	2,000	2,000
Other education programs	**$2,820,407**	**$2,981,571**	**$3,180,334**	**$3,383,031**	**$3,698,617**	**$3,991,955**	**$4,107,193**	**$4,483,708**	**$4,721,655**	**$4,941,351**
Department of Education [8]	1,825,754	1,938,998	2,071,574	2,251,801	2,419,277	2,579,883	2,526,372	2,795,988	2,863,000	3,234,000
Administration	285,296	295,615	301,260	328,293	365,681	368,420	353,545	403,877	405,000	464,000
Libraries	129,062	101,202	140,398	137,264	142,596	214,928	181,219	142,223	117,000	169,000
Rehabilitative services and disability research	1,405,357	1,536,905	1,623,255	1,780,360	1,902,338	1,991,875	1,983,848	2,244,226	2,334,000	2,594,000
American Printing House for the Blind	5,989	5,234	6,645	5,736	8,242	4,587	7,774	5,636	7,000	7,000
Trust funds [45]	50	42	16	148	420	73	−14	26	—	—
Department of Agriculture	330,866	342,523	347,021	352,511	382,343	400,442	443,650	426,316	422,878	413,512
Extension Service	322,095	330,164	333,571	337,907	366,176	385,087	424,928	409,110	405,371	394,878
National Agricultural Library	8,771	12,359	13,450	14,604	16,167	15,355	18,722	17,206	17,507	18,634
Department of Commerce										
Maritime Administration:										
Training for private sector employees [51]	—	—	—	—	—	—	—	—	—	—
Department of Health and Human Services [16]	59,770	62,060	71,912	77,962	89,094	97,643	96,860	107,896	138,000	153,000
National Library of Medicine	59,770	62,060	71,912	77,962	89,094	97,643	96,860	107,896	138,000	153,000
Department of Housing and Urban Development	—	—	—	—	—	—	—	—	—	—
Urban mass transportation—managerial training grants [85]	—	—	—	—	—	—	—	—	—	—
Department of Justice	26,293	26,361	23,906	26,920	30,543	34,525	37,028	34,065	36,296	39,148
F.B.I. National Academy	4,408	5,385	5,513	6,028	6,368	10,631	14,388	10,311	12,831	13,708
F.B.I. Field Police Academy	8,984	9,995	7,673	10,548	12,700	12,578	10,563	11,790	11,140	9,008
Narcotics and dangerous drug training	0	142	824	850	1,180	695	230	275	325	432
National Institute of Corrections [86]	12,901	10,839	9,896	9,494	10,295	10,621	11,847	11,689	12,000	16,000
Department of State	23,856	33,308	40,157	47,539	41,790	44,086	58,840	46,557	51,648	51,161
Foreign Service Institute	23,856	33,308	40,157	47,539	41,790	44,086	58,840	46,557	51,648	51,161
Center for Cultural and Technical Interchange [66]	—	—	—	—	—	—	—	—	—	—

Table 356.—Federal on-budget funds for education, by level or other educational purpose, by agency and program: Fiscal years 1965 to 1996—Continued

[In thousands of dollars]

Level or educational purpose, by agency and program	1965	1970	1975	1980	1981	1982	1983	1984	1985	1986
1	2	3	4	5	6	7	8	9	10	11
Department of Transportation [24]	—	3,964	11,877	10,212	8,261	6,030	6,175	4,781	3,785	1,865
Highways training and education grants [87]	—	2,418	3,250	3,412	3,734	3,545	3,527	2,050	1,500	—
Maritime Administration:										
Training for private sector employees [51]	—	—	—	—	2,118	1,305	1,448	1,381	1,135	1,143
Urban mass transportation—managerial training grants [85]	—	1,546	2,627	500	1,000	1,100	1,200	1,350	1,150	722
Federal Aviation Administration [88]										
Air traffic controllers second career program [89]	—	—	6,000	6,300	1,409	80	—	—	—	—
Department of the Treasury	—	18	3,096	14,584	13,506	13,247	13,334	14,327	16,160	15,982
Federal Law Enforcement Training Center [90]	—	18	3,096	14,584	13,506	13,247	13,334	14,327	16,160	15,982
Other agencies										
ACTION [91]	—	—	7,045	2,833	2,752	1,720	1,830	4,975	1,761	1,368
Estimated education funds [92]	—	—	7,045	2,833	2,752	1,720	1,830	4,975	1,761	1,368
Agency for International Development	63,329	88,034	78,896	99,707	109,180	135,580	130,257	127,383	141,847	154,627
Education and human resources	53,968	61,570	58,349	80,518	96,873	105,405	109,624	101,408	115,104	126,132
American schools and hospitals abroad	9,361	26,464	20,547	19,189	12,307	30,175	20,633	25,975	26,743	28,495
Appalachian Regional Commission [33]	—	572	1,574	8,124	7,710	1,651	98	330	113	0
Corporation for National and Community Service [91]	—	—	—	—	—	—	—	—	—	—
Estimated education funds [92]	—	—	—	—	—	—	—	—	—	—
Federal Emergency Management Agency [93]	—	290	290	281	238	278	390	351	405	290
Estimated architect/engineer student development program [94]	—	40	40	31	38	98	90	71	155	40
Estimated other training programs [95]	—	250	250	250	200	180	300	280	250	250
Estimated disaster relief [96]	—	—	—	—	—	—	—	—	—	—
General Services Administration [97]										
Libraries and other archival activities	4,013	14,775	22,532	34,800	38,400	37,300	44,200	50,894	—	—
Japanese-United States Friendship Commission [98]	—	—	—	2,294	−44	1,807	2,364	1,611	2,236	235
Library of Congress	15,111	29,478	63,766	151,871	144,131	144,911	154,198	164,080	169,310	166,130
Salaries and expenses	11,421	20,700	48,798	102,364	103,469	109,235	122,823	127,935	130,354	126,747
Books for the blind and the physically handicapped	2,317	6,195	11,908	31,436	31,523	29,592	26,116	30,739	32,954	35,460
Special foreign currency program	1,187	2,273	2,333	3,492	2,798	3,364	3,578	3,745	4,621	2,372
Furniture and furnishings	186	310	727	14,579	6,341	2,720	1,681	1,661	1,381	1,551
National Aeronautics and Space Administration										
Aerospace education services project	100	350	600	882	868	956	1,323	1,628	1,800	1,900
National Archives and Records Administration [99]										
Libraries and other archival activities	—	—	—	—	—	—	—	—	52,118	55,252
National Commission on Libraries and Information Science [100]	—	—	449	2,090	741	638	681	733	723	781
National Endowment for the Arts [34]	—	340	1,068	231	900	724	632	819	1,137	1,128
National Endowment for the Humanities [35]	—	5,090	38,486	85,805	84,303	68,421	74,348	74,750	76,252	78,319
Smithsonian Institution	2,233	2,461	5,509	5,153	4,853	5,215	6,073	5,758	7,886	6,191
Museum programs and related research	2,133	2,261	4,203	3,254	2,596	2,788	3,365	2,642	4,665	2,341
National Gallery of Art extension service	100	200	300	426	526	524	617	692	675	662
Woodrow Wilson International Center for Scholars	—	—	1,006	1,473	1,731	1,903	2,091	2,424	2,546	3,188
U.S. Information Agency—Center for Cultural and Technical Interchange [66]	—	—	—	15,115	14,371	16,252	17,258	19,374	18,966	20,531
U.S. Institute of Peace [101]	—	—	—	—	—	—	—	—	—	230
Other programs:										
Estimated education share of federal aid to the District of Columbia	948	1,758	2,335	2,990	2,996	2,341	2,520	2,672	7,156	8,333
Research programs at universities and related institutions [102]	**$1,816,276**	**$2,283,641**	**$3,418,410**	**$5,801,204**	**$6,275,455**	**$6,597,423**	**$7,233,806**	**$7,938,550**	**$8,844,575**	**$9,009,351**
Department of Education [103]	13,248	87,823	82,770	78,742	60,480	82,201	59,580	159,550	28,809	68,983
Department of Agriculture	58,362	64,796	108,162	216,405	242,717	255,075	275,027	279,200	293,252	273,698
Department of Commerce	4,015	4,487	21,677	48,295	46,669	52,218	51,460	52,600	52,951	62,406
Department of Defense	436,912	356,188	364,929	644,455	758,712	889,863	1,112,212	1,072,500	1,245,888	1,382,795
Department of Energy	439,334	548,327	761,376	1,470,224	1,700,374	1,715,779	1,861,112	2,001,400	2,205,316	2,141,955
Department of Health and Human Services	474,362	623,765	1,273,037	2,087,053	2,199,921	2,194,707	2,448,899	2,750,700	3,228,014	3,309,708
Department of Housing and Urban Development	—	510	2,650	5,314	4,808	969	2,158	2,000	438	342
Department of the Interior	9,839	18,521	28,955	42,175	40,986	34,171	28,616	36,500	34,422	36,440
Department of Justice	—	1,945	8,902	9,189	8,818	5,966	7,156	6,800	5,168	5,095
Department of Labor	—	3,567	6,124	12,938	9,764	8,915	6,392	4,800	3,417	341
Department of State	—	8,220	10,973	188	55	7	29	—	29	30
Department of Transportation	—	12,328	28,478	31,910	32,491	22,608	29,722	21,800	22,621	20,215
Department of the Treasury	—	—	—	226	39	5	238	300	388	190
Department of Veterans Affairs	337	518	1,112	1,600	2,097	1,646	800	500	1,000	1,000
ACTION	—	—	36	—	—	—	—	—	—	—
Agency for International Development	—	—	—	77,063	46,362	69,597	43,372	109,600	56,960	44,302

Table 356.—Federal on-budget funds for education, by level or other educational purpose, by agency and program: Fiscal years 1965 to 1996—Continued

[In thousands of dollars]

Level or educational purpose, by agency and program	1987	1988	1989	1990 [1]	1991 [2]	1992 [3]	1993 [4]	1994 [5]	1995 [6]	1996 [7]
1	12	13	14	15	16	17	18	19	20	21
Department of Transportation [24]	2,895	3,153	4,415	1,507	2,022	2,419	500	500	650	600
Highways training and education grants [87]	1,000	1,416	1,416	—	1,371	1,945	—	—	—	—
Maritime Administration: Training for private sector employees [51]	1,291	1,517	1,499	1,507	651	474	500	500	650	600
Urban mass transportation—managerial training grants [85]	604	220	1,500	—	—	—	—	—	—	—
Federal Aviation Administration [88] Air traffic controllers second career program [89]	—	—	—	—	—	—	—	—	—	—
Department of the Treasury	19,110	32,768	39,100	41,488	60,127	51,694	56,779	61,992	48,000	49,000
Federal Law Enforcement Training Center [90]	19,110	32,768	39,100	41,488	60,127	51,694	56,779	61,992	48,000	49,000
Other agencies ACTION [91]	3,368	4,110	4,800	8,472	11,321	8,600	—	—	—	—
Estimated education funds [92]	3,368	4,110	4,800	8,472	11,321	8,600	—	—	—	—
Agency for International Development	186,175	193,115	182,839	170,371	154,021	212,220	215,248	241,948	260,408	247,202
Education and human resources	152,332	160,051	146,915	142,801	122,231	195,570	190,020	221,988	248,408	238,202
American schools and hospitals abroad	33,843	33,064	35,924	27,570	31,790	16,650	25,228	19,960	12,000	9,000
Appalachian Regional Commission [33]	92	—	175	—	25	938	1,005	4,299	5,709	5,500
Corporation for National and Community Service [91]	—	—	—	—	—	—	8,500	93,250	214,600	221,800
Estimated education funds [92]	—	—	—	—	—	—	8,500	93,250	214,600	221,800
Federal Emergency Management Agency [93]	290	290	77	215	33	261	76,467	85,200	170,400	42,800
Estimated architect/engineer student development program [94]	40	40	50	200	28	250	375	—	—	—
Estimated other training programs [95]	250	250	27	15	5	11	92	—	—	—
Estimated disaster relief [96]	—	—	—	—	—	—	76,000	85,200	170,400	70,600
General Services Administration [97] Libraries and other archival activities	—	—	—	—	—	—	—	—	—	—
Japanese-United States Friendship Commission [98]	3,225	2,274	3,004	2,299	1,377	1,610	1,503	1,585	2,000	2,000
Library of Congress	160,835	160,505	177,954	189,827	279,745	296,044	311,453	312,724	241,000	243,000
Salaries and expenses	124,878	122,356	137,637	148,985	239,429	252,623	260,918	261,814	198,000	192,000
Books for the blind and the physically handicapped	33,813	36,245	38,233	37,473	36,878	38,688	45,261	46,600	39,000	46,000
Special foreign currency program	809	405	99	10	10	10	30	—	—	—
Furniture and furnishings	1,335	1,499	1,985	3,359	3,428	4,723	5,244	4,310	4,000	5,000
National Aeronautics and Space Administration Aerospace education services project	2,250	2,400	2,300	3,300	5,900	6,100	6,500	6,100	5,923	5,648
National Archives and Records Administration [99] Libraries and other archival activities	59,521	65,153	86,266	77,397	81,462	99,412	106,975	110,411	105,172	106,145
National Commission on Libraries and Information Science [100]	512	522	839	3,281	3,447	1,437	867	724	1,000	1,000
National Endowment for the Arts [34]	1,295	1,200	1,193	936	1,628	3,286	2,784	2,221	2,304	1,911
National Endowment for the Humanities [35]	75,376	76,803	84,929	89,706	93,381	99,782	100,826	98,786	94,249	57,008
Smithsonian Institution	6,545	5,393	5,880	5,779	5,906	6,578	7,828	10,059	9,961	11,870
Museum programs and related research	2,506	1,223	870	690	440	93	1,165	3,060	3,190	3,080
National Gallery of Art extension service	731	656	650	474	641	793	763	816	771	790
Woodrow Wilson International Center for Scholars	3,308	3,514	4,360	4,615	4,825	5,692	5,900	6,183	6,000	8,000
U.S. Information Agency—Center for Cultural and Technical Interchange [66]	16,756	22,759	20,714	20,375	22,276	29,550	31,991	30,064	34,000	15,000
U.S. Institute of Peace [101]	4,083	3,476	7,232	7,621	8,238	11,350	10,468	10,794	12,000	10,000
Other programs: Estimated education share of federal aid to the District of Columbia	11,540	4,400	4,047	3,724	4,661	4,095	4,749	2,229	2,457	2,246
Research programs at universities and related institutions [102]	**$10,538,606**	**$11,250,464**	**$12,009,825**	**$12,606,035**	**$13,775,422**	**$14,176,863**	**$14,955,083**	**$15,289,094**	**$15,749,351**	**$15,910,595**
Department of Education [103]	60,912	42,379	90,314	89,483	103,931	154,800	232,165	276,838	279,000	336,000
Department of Agriculture	279,943	304,888	314,294	348,109	385,836	437,967	436,187	438,537	432,126	434,184
Department of Commerce	36,835	36,133	44,821	50,523	62,870	77,240	70,805	81,423	95,415	93,641
Department of Defense	1,754,456	1,899,680	1,940,308	1,871,864	1,789,112	2,070,959	2,002,572	2,010,414	1,922,100	1,654,071
Department of Energy	2,225,513	2,350,426	2,536,065	2,520,885	2,692,335	2,867,528	2,763,515	2,642,094	2,688,465	2,697,619
Department of Health and Human Services	3,983,407	4,282,117	4,549,261	4,902,714	5,686,354	5,210,711	5,952,976	6,348,736	6,514,067	6,768,091
Department of Housing and Urban Development	463	51	186	118	48	203	401	856	933	834
Department of the Interior	33,353	35,103	39,556	49,790	58,537	57,449	54,049	54,157	62,030	59,180
Department of Justice	8,991	6,365	5,700	6,858	6,060	4,986	3,496	3,886	5,104	4,550
Department of Labor	432	5,528	5,590	5,893	5,548	1,169	600	4,250	10,084	9,453
Department of State	432	1,243	1,269	1,519	900	200	—	15	15	45
Department of Transportation	25,184	16,933	22,826	28,608	21,187	35,015	57,789	62,606	68,309	49,952
Department of the Treasury	169	—	411	227	229	85	133	1,309	1,915	1,334
Department of Veterans Affairs	2,251	2,300	2,300	2,300	2,300	2,491	2,550	2,350	2,750	2,000
ACTION	—	—	—	—	—	—	—	—	—	—
Agency for International Development	54,652	49,535	45,025	79,415	54,997	32,979	27,659	24,634	20,802	15,275

Table 356.—Federal on-budget funds for education, by level or other educational purpose, by agency and program: Fiscal years 1965 to 1996—Continued

[In thousands of dollars]

Level or educational purpose, by agency and program	1965	1970	1975	1980	1981	1982	1983	1984	1985	1986
1	2	3	4	5	6	7	8	9	10	11
Corporation for National and Community Service	—	—	—	—	—	—	—	—	—	—
Environmental Protection Agency	—	19,446	33,875	41,083	52,210	67,798	43,557	43,700	60,521	69,718
Federal Emergency Management Agency	—	—	—	1,665	1,913	2,347	805	—	1,423	—
National Aeronautics and Space Administration	208,688	258,016	197,301	254,629	250,316	368,149	366,440	352,900	485,824	489,048
National Science Foundation	154,046	253,628	475,011	743,809	773,308	787,028	857,791	1,006,000	1,087,046	1,073,122
Nuclear Regulatory Commission	—	—	7,093	32,590	41,309	38,150	37,987	36,400	30,261	27,472
Office of Economic Opportunity	7,078	20,035	—	—	—	—	—	—	—	—
U.S. Arms Control and Disarmament Agency	—	100	—	661	367	184	157	—	395	276
U.S. Information Agency	—	—	—	—	—	—	—	—	—	1,500
Other agencies	10,055	1,421	5,949	990	1,739	40	296	1,300	432	715

Footnotes

[1] Excludes $4,440,000,000 for federal support for medical education benefits under Medicare in the U.S. Department of Health and Human Services. Is not included in the total because data before fiscal year 1990 are not available. This program has existed since Medicare began, but was not available as a separate budget item until FY 90.

[2] Excludes $4,900,000,000 for federal support for medical education benefits under Medicare in the U.S. Department of Health and Human Services. Is not included in the total because data before fiscal year 1990 are not available. This program has existed since Medicare began, but was not available as a separate budget item until FY 90.

[3] Excludes $5,350,000,000 for federal support for medical education benefits under Medicare in the U.S. Department of Health and Human Services. Is not included in the total because data before fiscal year 1990 are not available. This program has existed since Medicare began, but was not available as a separate budget item until FY 90.

[4] Excludes $5,710,000,000 for federal support for medical education benefits under Medicare in the U.S. Department of Health and Human Services. Is not included in the total because data before fiscal year 1990 are not available. This program has existed since Medicare began, but was not available as a separate budget item until FY 90.

[5] Excludes $6,150,000,000 for federal support for medical education benefits under Medicare in the U.S. Department of Health and Human Services. Is not included in the total because data before fiscal year 1990 are not available. This program has existed since Medicare began, but was not available as a separate budget item until FY 90.

[6] Excludes $6,650,000,000 for federal support for medical education benefits under Medicare in the U.S. Department of Health and Human Services. Is not included in the total because data before fiscal year 1990 are not available. This program has existed since Medicare began, but was not available as a separate budget item until FY 90.

[7] Estimated. Excludes $6,780,000,000 for federal support for medical education benefits under Medicare in the U.S. Department of Health and Human Services. Is not included in the total because data before fiscal year 1990 are not available. This program has existed since Medicare began, but was not available as a separate budget item until FY 90.

[8] The U.S. Department of Education was created in May 1980. It formerly was the Office of Education in the U.S. Department of Health, Education, and Welfare.

[9] This program was funded by the U.S. Department of Education in FYs 65–81 in the Impact Aid program. This program provides for the education of dependents of federal employees residing on federal property in cases where free public education is unavailable in the nearby community.

[10] This program creates a national framework for education reform and meeting the National Education Goals. This program includes the School-To-Work Opportunities program which will initiate a national system to be administered jointly by the U.S. Departments of Education and Labor. Both departments are to establish a national framework within which all states can create statewide systems to help youth acquire the knowledge, skills, abilities, and labor market information they need to make an effective transition from school to work or to further their education or training.

[11] Starting in FY 94, the Special Milk program was included in the Child Nutrition program.

[12] These commodities are purchased under Section 32 of the Act of August 24, 1935, for use in the child nutrition programs.

[13] This program assisted in the construction of public facilities, such as vocational schools, through grants or loans. No funds have been appropriated for this account since FY 77, and it was completely phased out in FY 84 after the monitoring of closeouts of projects was completed. Data are not available for previous years.

[14] The U.S. Department of Energy was created in 1977. It formerly was the Energy Research and Development Administration and before that the Atomic Energy Commission.

[15] This program was established in 1979. Funds were first appropriated for this program in FY 80.

[16] The U.S. Department of Health and Human Services was part of the U.S. Department of Health, Education, and Welfare until May 1980.

[17] The Head Start program was formerly in the Office of Economic Opportunity, and funds were appropriated to the U.S. Department of Health, Education, and Welfare, Office of Child Development, beginning in 1972.

[18] This program was created by the Family Support Act of 1988. It provides funds for the Job Opportunities and Basic Skills Training program.

[19] After age 18, benefits terminate at the end of the school term or in 3 months, whichever is less.

[20] This program provides funding for supplemental programs for eligible Indian students in public schools.

[21] This program finances the cost of academic, social, and occupational education courses for inmates in federal prisons.

[22] The Job Corps program was formerly in the Office of Economic Opportunity, and funds were appropriated to the U.S. Department of Labor beginning in 1971 and 1972.

[23] Some of the work and training programs included in this program were in the Office of Economic Opportunity and were transferred to the U.S. Department of Labor in 1971 and 1972. Beginning in FY 94, the School-to-Work Opportunities program is included. This program is administered jointly by the U.S. Departments of Education and Labor.

[24] The U.S. Department of Transportation was created in 1967.

[25] This program was transferred from the U.S. Department of the Treasury to the U.S. Department of Transportation in 1967.

[26] This program was established in FY 72 and closed in FY 86.

[27] The states' share of revenue-sharing funds could not be spent on education in FYs 81–86.

[28] The U.S. Department of Veterans Affairs, formerly the Veterans Administration, was created in March 1989.

Table 356.—Federal on-budget funds for education, by level or other educational purpose, by agency and program: Fiscal years 1965 to 1996—Continued

[In thousands of dollars]

Level or educational purpose, by agency and program	1987	1988	1989	1990[1]	1991[2]	1992[3]	1993[4]	1994[5]	1995[6]	1996[7]
1	12	13	14	15	16	17	18	19	20	21
Corporation for National and Community Service	—	—	—	—	—	—	—	—	—	—
Environmental Protection Agency	67,465	58,053	64,517	87,481	62,753	152,012	124,500	98,241	97,428	112,723
Federal Emergency Management Agency	—	—	—	—	—	—	—	—	—	—
National Aeronautics and Space Administration	785,141	897,497	976,478	1,090,003	1,270,070	1,377,322	1,367,542	1,412,665	1,636,126	1,617,023
National Science Foundation	1,184,921	1,232,054	1,342,648	1,427,007	1,546,810	1,664,697	1,833,563	1,805,856	1,894,563	2,038,199
Nuclear Regulatory Commission	29,176	25,676	25,690	42,328	23,860	27,418	22,934	20,227	17,619	15,471
Office of Economic Opportunity	—	—	—	—	—	—	—	—	—	—
U.S. Arms Control and Disarmament Agency	3,244	2,633	1,619	25	69	100	25	—	—	—
U.S. Information Agency	—	—	—	—	—	—	—	—	—	—
Other agencies	1,666	1,870	947	885	1,616	1,532	1,622	—	500	950

Footnotes—Continued

[29] This program provides educational assistance allowances in order to restore lost educational opportunities to those individuals whose careers were interrupted or impeded by reason of active military service between January 31, 1955, and January 1, 1977. Includes "Readjustment Benefits," Chapter 34, for education other than college and also includes the Veterans Job Training program for service persons and veterans. The Chapter 34 program closed December 31, 1989. The Veterans Job Training program was put in the program Payments to State Education Agencies. Veterans who were still eligible to receive benefits under Chapter 34 were covered by Chapter 30 (The All-Volunteer-Force Educational Assistance program).

[30] This program is in "Readjustment Benefits" program, Chapter 31, and covers the costs of subsistence, tuition, books, supplies, and equipment for disabled veterans requiring vocational rehabilitation.

[31] This program is in the "Readjustment Benefits" program, Chapter 35, and provides benefits to children and spouses of veterans.

[32] The purpose of this program is to provide stable and permanent employment to those men and women who have served on active duty on or after August 2, 1990, and are unemployed.

[33] This agency was established March 9, 1965. First year of appropriations was 1966. The outlays were larger in the years 1970 and 1975 for elementary and secondary education because of the construction of facilities for vocational schools.

[34] This agency was established in 1965. In 1970, $900,000 was appropriated through the Office of Education, U.S. Department of Health, Education, and Welfare, for the National Endowment for the Arts, Arts in Education program.

[35] This agency was established in 1965. First year of appropriations was 1966.

[36] The Economic Opportunity Act of 1964 authorized 10 major action programs, including Job Corps, Neighborhood Youth Corps, Adult Literacy, Work Experience, College Work-Study, and Community Action programs, including Head Start, Follow Through, and Upward Bound, and authorized the establishment of Volunteers in Service to America (VISTA). These programs were transferred to the U.S. Department of Health, Education, and Welfare, U.S. Department of Labor, and the Action Agency in the 1970s. An act on January 4, 1975 established the Community Services Administration as the successor agency to the Office of Economic Opportunity.

[37] Head Start program funds were transferred to the U.S. Department of Health, Education, and Welfare, Office of Child Development, in 1972.

[38] Most of these programs were transferred to the U.S. Department of Health, Education, and Welfare, Office of Education, in 1972.

[39] The Job Corps programs were transferred to the U.S. Department of Labor in 1971 and 1972.

[40] These programs were transferred to the U.S. Department of Labor in 1971 and 1972.

[41] These programs were transferred to the Action Agency in 1972.

[42] Similar programs were included in the "higher education" program in 1965 through 1975.

[43] The Student Loan Reform Act of 1993 authorized a new Federal Direct Student Loan (FDSL) program, recently renamed the William D. Ford Direct Loan program. This program is a new streamlined lending system that will simplify the process of obtaining and repaying loans for student and parent borrowers and will provide borrowers with greater choice in repayment plans. The FDSL program will replace the FFEL program and be phased in beginning with the 1994–95 academic year.

[44] Similar programs were included in the "higher education" program in 1965 through 1975, formerly called the "Guaranteed Student Loan" program. The large drop in FY 94 reflects a $4.79 billion loan prepayment from the Student Loan Marketing Association of its outstanding debt to the Treasury Department.

[45] Negative amounts occur when program receipts exceed outlays.

[46] This program was transferred from the U.S. Department of Housing and Urban Development to the U.S. Department of Health, Education, and Welfare, Office of Education, in FY 79.

[47] The Historically Black Colleges and Universities (HBCUs) Capital Financing program was authorized by the Higher Education Act Amendments of 1992 to provide HBCUs with private funds for projects such as repairs, renovation and construction of classrooms, libraries, laboratories, dormitories, instructional equipment, and research instruments.

[48] First year of appropriations for this program was 1967.

[49] Program funds were first appropriated for Tuskegee Institute in 1972.

[50] The Sea Grant College Program Act of 1966 established a matching fund grant program that provides for the establishment of a network of programs in fields related to development and preservation of the nation's coastal and marine resources. This program was transferred from the National Science Foundation to the U.S. Department of Commerce, October 1970. Appropriations began in 1968.

[51] This program was transferred to the U.S. Department of Transportation in FY 81 by Public Law 97–31, from the U.S. Department of Commerce.

[52] The U.S. Department of Defense funds for FYs 90 to 96 exclude military pay and reserve accounts which were included in previous years. FY 65 data are not available except for service academies.

[53] Included in total above.

[54] Instructional costs only are included. These include academics, audiovisual, academic computing center, faculty training, military training, physical education, and libraries.

[55] Includes special education programs (military and civilian); legal education program; flight training; advanced degree program; college degree program (officers); and "Armed Forces Health Professions Scholarship" program.

Footnotes—Continued

[56] No funds have been appropriated for this program since FY 82.

[57] This program receives funds periodically.

[58] Appropriations began in FY 84.

[59] Appropriations began in FY 89.

[60] Does not include higher education assistance loans.

[61] Appropriations began in FY 78.

[62] Alcohol, drug abuse, and mental health training programs are included starting in fiscal year 1992.

[63] Beginning in fiscal year 1992, data were included in the National Institutes of Health training grants program.

[64] Postsecondary student benefits were ended by the Omnibus Budget Reconciliation Act of 1981 (Public Law 97–35) and were completely phased out by August 1985.

[65] Includes adult education, tribally-controlled community colleges, postsecondary instruction, and other education.

[66] This program was transferred from the U.S. Department of State to the International Communication Agency (I.C.A.) in the Reorganization Plan No. 2 of 1977, which consolidated the functions of the U.S. Information Agency (U.S.I.A.) and the U.S. Department of State's Bureau of Educational and Cultural Affairs. In FY 82 the I.C.A. became the U.S.I.A.

[67] This program provides funds for advanced study and research projects of the Russian, Eurasian, and Eastern European countries by American institutions of higher education and private research firms. Appropriations began in FY 88.

[68] This program was transferred to the U.S. Department of Transportation in FY 81 by Public Law 97–31 from the U.S. Department of Commerce.

[69] Includes flight training. This program was in the U.S. Department of the Treasury in 1965 and was transferred to the U.S. Department of Transportation in 1967.

[70] Includes benefits for Vietnam-era veterans under Chapter 34 (GI Bill) of the "Readjustment Benefits" education and training program. This program provides educational assistance allowances, primarily on a monthly basis, in order to restore lost educational opportunities to those individuals whose careers were interrupted or impeded by reason of active military service between January 31, 1955, and January 1, 1977. This program closed December 31, 1989. Some veterans who were still eligible were put in Chapter 30 (the All-Volunteer-Force Educational Assistance program).

[71] Includes service persons under Chapter 34 (GI Bill) of the "Readjustment Benefits" education and training program. Service persons with over 180 days of active duty, any part of which was before January 1, 1977, are eligible to participate in this program.

[72] Includes post-Vietnam-era veterans, under Chapter 32, of the post-Vietnam-era "Veterans Education Account." Provides education and training assistance payments to veterans and service persons with no active duty time before January 1, 1977. Funding is provided through participants' contributions while on active duty and through transfers from the U.S. Department of Defense (DOD). Participants' contributions, up to a maximum of $2,700, are deposited to the fund prior to discharge. When the participant enters training, the monthly disbursement from his or her account is matched two for one from funds provided by DOD. Additional amounts in the form of incentive bonuses may also be provided by DOD funds. The U.S. Department of Veterans Affairs funds are not appropriated for this program, so these data represent obligations, which are funded through other agencies appropriations.

[73] Public Law 98–525, enacted October 19, 1984 (New GI Bill), established two new peacetime educational programs: an assistance program for veterans who enter active duty during the period beginning July 1, 1985, and ending on June 30, 1988, and an assistance program for certain members of the Selected Reserve.

[74] Chapter 30, also called the Montgomery Bill, and the new GI Bill are for eligible veterans who have agreed to have their military pay reduced $100 per month for their first 12 months of active duty in order to participate in this program. The "Readjustment Benefits" account under the U.S. Department of Veterans Affairs pays only the basic allowance, up to a maximum of $300 per month, for full-time training. "Supplemental Benefits" are paid by the U.S. Department of Defense (DOD).

[75] Chapter 106 is for members of the Selected Reserve. The reserve components include the Army, Navy, Air Force, Marine Corps Reserve, Army National Guard and Air National Guard under the U.S. Department of Defense (DOD), and the Coast Guard Reserve, which is under the U.S. Department of Transportation (DOT) when it is not operating as a service in the Navy. Eligible persons can receive up to $140 per month for full-time training. The DOD and DOT pay for this program, and the U.S. Department of Veterans Affairs administers it.

[76] Includes dependents of veterans under Chapter 35, the "Readjustment Benefits" education and training program. Provides education and training benefits to dependents of veterans who died of a service-connected disability or whose service-connected disability is rated permanent and total.

[77] These payments have been made to state education agencies for a number of years but were not a separate budget item until FY 88.

[78] The U.S.I.A. was called the "International Communication Agency" in FYs 80 and 81.

[79] This program was in the "Educational and Cultural Affairs" program in FYs 80–83, and became an independent program in FY 84.

[80] This program was combined with the "educational and cultural affairs" program in FY 77.

[81] Public Law 99–661 established this program to operate the scholarship program in tribute to the former Senator from Arizona. The Foundation awards scholarships and fellowships to outstanding graduate and undergraduate students who intend to pursue careers or advanced degrees in science or mathematics. The Foundation may also award honoraria to outstanding individuals who have made significant contributions to improve the instruction of science and mathematics in secondary schools.

[82] Appropriations for this program began in FY 76.

[83] Public Law 99–498 established this Institute as an independent non-profit corporation administered by a Board of Trustees. The Institute provides Native Americans with an opportunity to obtain a postsecondary education in various fields of Indian art and culture.

[84] Public Laws 99–500 and 99–591 established the James Madison Memorial Fellowship Foundation to operate a fellowship program to encourage graduate study of the American Constitution. First year of appropriations was FY 88.

[85] This program was transferred to the U.S. Department of Transportation in FY 68 from the U.S. Department of Housing and Urban Development.

[86] This program was established by the Juvenile Justice and Delinquency Prevention Act of 1974 to provide education and training and to provide leadership in improving correctional programs and practices in prisons. FY 75 had large outlays because of the construction of buildings and facilities.

[87] Appropriations for this program began in FY 70. This program is part of the Federal-Aid Highway Act of 1970, Public Law 91–605.

[88] The Federal Aviation Administration, originally an independent agency, was transferred to the U.S. Department of Transportation in FY 67.

[89] Appropriations began in FY 72. No funds have been appropriated since FY 82.

[90] First year of appropriations was FY 70.

[91] The National Service Trust Act of 1993 established a new agency, the Corporation for National and Community Service. On October 1, 1993 ACTION became part of the Corporation for National and Community Service. ACTION was established on July 1, 1971. This agency brings together a number of volunteer programs. Some of these funds were formerly in the Office of Economic Opportunity.

Footnotes—Continued

[92] These programs included the Service Learning Programs, University Year for ACTION, Volunteers in Service to America, Youth Challenge program, and the National Student Volunteer Program in FY 1975. In FY 80, programs included were the University Year for ACTION, Young Volunteers for ACTION, and National Service Learning programs. In fiscal year 1985, the program included the Service Learning programs, and in FYs 89 to 94, programs included were the Literacy Corps and the Student Community Services program. In FY 94, FY 95, and FY 96 the AmeriCorp program was included. This program provides education grants of up to $4,725 per year, for up to 2 years, to help pay for college or to repay student loans for people age 17 years or older who perform community service before, during or after postsecondary education.

[93] The Federal Emergency Management Agency was created on March 25, 1979, representing a combination of five existing agencies. The two largest were the Defense Civil Preparedness Agency in the U.S. Department of Defense and the Federal Preparedness Agency in the General Services Administration. The funds for the Federal Emergency Management Agency in FY 70 to FY 75 were in the other agencies.

[94] First year of appropriations was FY 68.

[95] First appropriations for the "other training programs" were in the late 1960s. These programs include the Fall-Out Shelter Analysis, Blast Protection Design through 1992. Starting in FY 1993, earthquake training and safety for teachers and administrators for grades 1 through 12 are included.

[96] The disaster relief program repairs and replaces damaged and destroyed school buildings. In FY 94 and FY 95 funds were for the repairs due to the Northridge Earthquake in California. In FY 94, $37.2 million was spent on school districts; $4.2 million was spent on community colleges and $43.8 million spent on universities. In FY 95, $74.4 million was spent on school districts; $8.4 million on community colleges and $87.6 million on colleges and universities.

[97] This program was transferred from the General Services Administration to the National Archives and Records Administration in April 1985.

[98] This program makes grants for the promotion of scholarly, cultural, and artistic exchanges between Japan and the United States. Appropriations began in FY 76.

[99] The National Archives and Records Administration became an independent agency in April 1985.

[100] This program was established by the act of July 20, 1970, Public Law 91–345.

[101] This program was established by Congress to conduct and support research and scholarships in the fields of peace, arms control, and conflict resolution. This program began operation in February 1986.

[102] Includes federal obligations for research and development centers administered by colleges and universities. FYs 95 and 96 are estimated.

[103] Total outlays for FYs 65 and 70 include the "Research and Training" program. FY 75 includes the "National Institute of Education" program. FYs 80 to 96 include outlays for the Office of Educational Research and Improvement.

—Data not available or not applicable.

NOTE.—Some data have been revised from previously published figures. To the extent possible, amounts reported represent outlays rather than obligations.

SOURCE: U.S. Department of Education, National Center for Education Statistics, compiled from data appearing in U.S. Office of Management and Budget, *Budget of the U.S. Government,* fiscal years 1967 to 1997; National Science Foundation, *Federal Funds for Research and Development,* fiscal years 1965 to 1996; and unpublished data obtained from various federal agencies. (This table was prepared June 1996.)

Table 357.—Estimated federal support for education, by agency and type of ultimate recipient: Fiscal year 1996

[In millions of dollars]

Agency	Total	Local education agencies	State education agencies	College students	Institutions of higher education	Federal	Multiple types of recipients	Other [1]
1	2	3	4	5	6	7	8	9
Total [2]	$96,445.6	$20,446.8	$5,182.7	$18,655.7	$30,596.4	$3,132.3	$10,425.2	$8,006.6
Total program funds - on-budget	$70,857.0	$20,446.8	$4,662.2	$8,226.0	$21,347.5	$3,132.3	$10,425.2	$2,617.1
Department of Education	30,405.0	11,659.0	3,968.8	5,260.2	4,989.3	527.4	2,035.8	1,964.5
Department of Agriculture	9,073.2	8,116.2	76.4	—	467.1	18.6	—	394.9
Department of Commerce	97.1	—	—	—	97.1	—	—	—
Department of Defense	3,722.3	172.8	—	209.6	1,812.2	1,324.4	203.4	—
Department of Energy	2,720.3	7.2	—	1.9	2,710.7	—	0.5	—
Department of Health and Human Services	12,823.8	353.4	—	1,160.6	7,114.5	153.0	4,042.3	—
Department of Housing and Urban Development	0.8	—	—	—	0.8	—	—	—
Department of the Interior	672.0	41.8	9.1	30.5	135.5	410.9	44.2	—
Department of Justice	195.3	—	—	—	4.6	190.7	—	—
Department of Labor	4,105.5	—	594.9	—	9.5	—	3,501.1	—
Department of State	53.2	—	—	—	1.5	51.2	—	0.5
Department of Transportation	106.7	—	—	0.3	50.2	44.4	2.9	9.0
Department of Treasury	50.3	—	—	—	1.3	49.0	—	—
Department of Veterans Affairs	1,445.2	—	13.0	1,430.2	2.0	—	—	—
Other agencies and programs								
Agency for International Development	262.5	—	—	—	15.3	—	—	247.2
Appalachian Regional Commission	9.7	—	—	—	2.2	—	7.5	—
Barry Goldwater Scholarship and Excellence in Education Foundation	3.0	—	—	—	—	—	3.0	—
Corporation for National and Community Service	221.8	—	—	—	—	—	221.8	—
Environmental Protection Agency	112.7	—	—	—	112.7	—	—	—
Estimated education share of federal aid to the District of Columbia	88.6	75.8	—	—	10.6	—	2.2	—
Federal Emergency Management Agency	70.6	20.6	—	—	50.0	—	—	—
General Services Administration	—	—	—	—	—	—	—	—
Harry S Truman scholarship fund	4.0	—	—	—	—	—	4.0	—
Institute of American Indian and Alaskan Native Culture and Arts Development	11.0	—	—	—	—	—	11.0	—
James Madison Memorial Fellowship Foundation	2.0	—	—	—	—	—	2.0	—
Japanese-United States Friendship Commission	2.0	—	—	—	—	—	2.0	—
Library of Congress	243.0	—	—	—	—	243.0	—	—
National Aeronautics and Space Administration	1,622.7	—	—	—	1,617.0	—	5.6	—
National Archives and Records Administration	106.1	—	—	—	—	106.1	—	—
National Commission on Libraries and Information Science	1.0	—	—	—	—	—	—	1.0
National Endowment for the Arts	4.8	—	—	—	—	—	4.8	—
National Endowment for the Humanities	91.6	—	—	—	—	—	91.6	—
National Science Foundation	2,244.6	—	—	117.6	2,127.0	—	—	—
Nuclear Regulatory Commission	15.5	—	—	—	15.5	—	—	—
Smithsonian Institution	11.9	—	—	—	—	0.8	11.1	—
U.S. Arms Control and Disarmament Agency	—	—	—	—	—	—	—	—
U.S. Information Agency	246.2	—	—	15.0	—	12.8	218.4	—
U.S. Institute of Peace	10.0	—	—	—	—	—	10.0	—
Other agencies	1.0	—	—	—	1.0	—	—	—
Off-budget support and nonfederal funds generated by federal legislation	25,588.6	—	520.5	10,429.7	9,248.9	—	—	5,389.5

[1] Other recipients include Indian tribes, private nonprofit agencies, and banks.

[2] Includes on-budget support, off-budget support, and nonfederal funds generated by federal legislation. Excludes federal tax expenditures.

—Data not available or not applicable.

NOTE.—Outlays by type of recipient are estimated based on obligation data. Because of rounding, details may not add to totals.

SOURCE: U.S. Department of Education, Office of the Undersecretary, unpublished tabulations; U.S. Office of Management and Budget, *Budget of the U.S. Government, Fiscal Year 1997;* National Science Foundation, *Federal Funds for Research and Development, Fiscal Years 1994, 1995, and 1996;* and unpublished data obtained from various federal agencies. (This table was prepared June 1996.)

Table 358.—Federal on-budget funds obligated for programs administered by the U.S. Department of Education: Fiscal years 1980 to 1996

[In thousands of dollars]

Program	1980	1985	1990	1991	1992	1993	1994	1995[1]	1996[2]
1	2	3	4	5	6	7	8	9	10
Total	**$14,102,165**	**$18,818,201**	**$25,214,923**	**$28,543,858**	**$34,966,632**	**$33,748,670**	**$36,644,942**	**$46,139,000**	**$47,050,000**
Elementary and secondary education	4,239,022	4,732,864	7,169,693	8,061,767	8,606,349	8,565,459	8,729,009	8,830,000	7,275,000
Grants for the disadvantaged	3,204,664	3,745,855	5,383,960	6,233,448	6,717,712	6,659,203	7,038,334	7,200,000	6,032,000
School improvement programs	788,918	748,000	1,524,001	1,555,406	1,587,369	1,600,013	1,368,108	1,343,000	1,026,000
Bilingual education	169,540	171,605	188,152	197,885	224,911	225,693	239,805	206,000	155,000
Indian education	75,900	67,404	73,580	75,028	76,357	80,550	82,762	81,000	62,000
School assistance in federally affected areas	812,873	695,746	815,573	785,807	835,394	760,456	911,716	783,000	742,000
Maintenance and operations	690,000	665,000	717,354	738,746	744,491	713,108	787,263	715,000	721,000
Construction	110,873	23,037	22,929	38,961	43,155	5,291	8,584	2,000	21,000
Disaster assistance	12,000	7,709	75,290	8,100	47,748	42,057	115,869	66,000	—
Education for the handicapped	1,555,253	2,666,056	3,480,122	4,695,615	4,750,048	4,752,116	5,965,688	5,767,000	5,879,000
State grant programs	815,805	1,245,219	1,258,871	2,214,902	1,980,432	1,842,956	2,779,228	2,467,000	3,125,000
Early childhood education[3]	38,745	27,625	280,341	387,282	480,599	476,180	661,665	661,000	307,000
Special centers, projects, and research	55,075	53,430	72,966	117,333	109,976	139,265	101,605	132,000	—
Captioned films and media services	17,778	35,670	15,191	16,326	16,593	17,571	18,608	19,000	—
Personnel training	55,375	68,025	70,838	69,288	89,753	90,120	104,012	91,000	—
Handicapped rehabilitation service and research	572,475	1,236,087	1,781,915	1,890,484	2,072,695	2,186,024	2,300,570	2,397,000	2,447,000
Vocational education and adult programs	1,153,743	856,271	1,138,674	800,661	1,774,664	1,575,268	1,456,185	1,461,000	1,223,000
Basic programs[4]	744,653	725,624	858,716	472,275	1,253,148	1,049,834	950,244	1,004,000	1,186,000
Consumer and homemaking	63,169	33,138	34,517	18,210	48,989	35,872	33,895	1,000	—
Program improvement and supportive services	162,512	5,202	—	—	—	—	—	—	—
State planning and advisory councils	13,423	7,584	7,923	8,803	9,325	8,928	9,087	9,000	—
Adult education, grants to states	153,724	84,723	188,280	201,032	235,650	309,810	254,724	299,000	26,000
Other[5]	16,262	—	49,238	100,341	227,552	170,824	208,235	148,000	11,000
Postsecondary student financial assistance	5,108,534	8,534,205	11,112,068	12,477,771	17,008,333	16,065,617	17,400,855	26,956,000	30,041,000
Educational opportunity grants[6]	2,534,378	3,558,440	4,919,264	5,867,941	6,274,116	6,764,683	7,092,393	6,484,000	8,342,000
Work-study	596,065	599,467	615,269	607,922	621,139	625,043	620,878	620,000	617,000
Perkins loan program	322,749	219,850	157,415	175,325	157,518	183,262	177,413	187,000	20,000
Federal Family Education Loan program[7]	1,597,877	4,130,920	5,341,039	5,733,383	9,855,159	8,380,619	8,444,937	10,461,000	8,756,000
Other student assistance programs[8]	57,465	25,528	79,081	93,650	100,401	112,010	1,065,234	9,204,000	12,306,000
Direct aid to postsecondary institutions	277,068	329,714	341,634	445,258	518,380	518,908	740,677	780,000	773,000
Aid to minority and developing institutions	114,680	140,374	99,812	111,506	130,215	130,743	211,054	231,000	15,000
Special programs for the disadvantaged	147,389	174,940	241,822	333,752	388,165	388,165	529,623	549,000	[9]758,000
Cooperative education	14,999	14,400	—	—	—	—	—	—	—
Higher education facilities	268,493	194,556	84,305	84,599	92,923	81,026	49,888	46,000	30,000
Construction loans and insurance	35,362	33,188	30,000	29,277	38,095	46,472	20,607	15,000	12,000
Interest subsidy grants	24,626	24,968	38,741	39,866	41,181	22,647	18,188	21,000	5,000
College housing loans	208,505	136,400	15,564	15,456	13,647	11,907	11,093	10,000	13,000
Other higher education programs	34,927	74,340	188,999	187,039	198,993	201,734	129,951	120,000	4,000
International education and foreign languages[10]	19,977	32,050	86,337	91,100	107,812	114,761	—	—	—
Fund for Improvement of Postsecondary Education[11]	12,000	12,710	99,450	87,826	87,831	86,257	129,554	116,000	([12])
Other	2,950	29,580	3,212	8,113	3,350	716	397	4,000	4,000
Public library services	101,218	116,027	132,583	142,252	148,208	144,380	149,591	150,000	125,000
Public library services	66,451	75,000	82,505	83,897	83,898	83,227	83,227	83,000	—
Interlibrary cooperation	—	18,000	19,551	19,908	19,908	19,749	19,749	24,000	—
Public library construction	—	16,027	14,837	18,554	17,179	14,871	21,074	24,000	7,000
Research libraries	5,992	6,000	6,593	5,855	5,855	5,808	5,808	—	—
Other	28,775	1,000	9,097	14,038	21,368	20,725	19,733	19,000	118,000
Payments to special institutions	273,860	253,622	292,736	306,833	327,521	320,455	321,753	340,000	291,000
American Printing House for the Blind	4,349	5,500	5,663	6,136	5,900	6,298	6,463	7,000	5,000
National Technical Institute for the Deaf	19,799	31,400	35,594	37,598	39,278	40,964	41,836	43,000	40,000
Gallaudet College	49,409	59,092	67,643	72,261	76,540	77,589	78,435	80,000	72,000
Howard University	200,303	157,630	183,836	190,838	205,803	195,604	195,019	210,000	174,000
Departmental accounts	277,174	364,800	458,536	556,256	705,819	763,251	789,629	906,000	667,000
Educational research and improvement	51,415	60,556	87,074	140,367	267,569	283,078	294,323	327,000	250,000
Departmental management account	223,857	300,885	370,844	415,469	438,246	480,166	495,249	579,000	417,000
Other	1,875	3,349	—	—	—	—	—	—	—
Trust funds	27	10	618	420	4	7	57	—	—

[1] Revised from previously published data.

[2] Estimated.

[3] Includes preschool incentive grants.

[4] Includes programs of national significance and special programs for the disadvantaged.

[5] Includes national programs for research, demonstrations, evaluation and technical assistance, literacy training for homeless adults, and some other small programs.

[6] Includes Pell Grants, Supplemental Education Opportunity Grants, State Student Incentive Grants, and Income Contingent Loans.

[7] Formerly the Guaranteed Student Loan program.

[8] Includes Federal Direct Student Loan program starting in fiscal year 1994.

[9] Dollar amount also includes "Fund for Improvement of Postsecondary Education" program.

[10] This program starting in fiscal year 1994 is included under the program, "Fund for Improvement of Postsecondary Education."

[11] International education and foreign languages are included under this program starting in fiscal year 1994.

[12] This program is included under the "Special programs for the disadvantaged" program.

—Data are not available or not applicable.

NOTE.—Because of rounding, details may not add to totals. Data presented in this tabulation are obligations, which differ from outlay figures reported in other tables in this chapter.

SOURCE: U.S. Office of Management and Budget, *Budget of the United States Government,* fiscal years 1982 to 1997. (This table was prepared May 1996.)

Table 359.—U.S. Department of Education outlays, by level of education and type of recipient: Fiscal years 1980 to 1996

[In millions of dollars]

Year and area of education	Total	Local education agencies	State education agencies	College students	Institutions of higher education	Federal	Multiple types of recipients	Other [1]
1	2	3	4	5	6	7	8	9
1980 total	**$13,137.8**	**$5,313.7**	**$1,103.2**	**$2,137.4**	**$2,267.2**	**$249.8**	**$693.8**	**$1,372.7**
Elementary/secondary	6,629.1	5,309.4	662.2	34.2	22.0	62.5	513.4	25.5
Postsecondary education	5,682.2	—	99.5	2,103.2	2,166.5	—	—	1,313.0
Other programs	747.7	4.3	341.5	—	—	187.3	180.4	34.2
Education research and statistics	78.7	—	—	—	78.7	—	—	—
1982 total	**14,109.3**	**5,425.8**	**1,414.2**	**1,610.2**	**1,951.8**	**268.3**	**535.4**	**2,903.6**
Elementary/secondary	6,456.3	5,420.8	593.8	48.9	21.9	2.6	340.3	27.9
Postsecondary education	6,418.8	—	196.6	1,561.3	1,847.7	—	—	2,813.2
Other programs	1,152.0	5.0	623.8	—	—	265.7	195.1	62.5
Education research and statistics	82.2	—	—	—	82.2	—	—	—
1984 total	**15,534.7**	**5,256.5**	**1,879.0**	**2,193.4**	**2,167.4**	**330.2**	**516.7**	**3,191.4**
Elementary/secondary	6,220.8	5,252.4	536.0	55.5	35.3	22.9	259.9	58.8
Postsecondary education	7,341.2	—	211.5	2,137.9	1,972.5	—	—	3,019.3
Other programs	1,813.1	4.1	1,131.5	—	—	307.3	256.8	113.3
Education research and statistics	159.6	—	—	—	159.6	—	—	—
1986 total	**17,740.1**	**6,435.1**	**1,823.3**	**2,685.9**	**2,637.2**	**265.4**	**625.8**	**3,267.5**
Elementary/secondary	7,552.0	6,432.1	558.5	68.3	45.2	2.2	372.0	73.8
Postsecondary education	8,444.9	—	215.6	2,617.6	2,523.0	—	—	3,088.7
Other programs	1,674.2	3.0	1,049.2	—	—	263.2	253.8	105.0
Education research and statistics	69.0	—	—	—	69.0	—	—	—
1988 total	**18,326.9**	**6,614.8**	**2,234.6**	**3,103.4**	**2,519.5**	**319.4**	**838.8**	**2,696.3**
Elementary/secondary	8,098.4	6,606.3	717.9	66.2	39.5	23.8	616.7	28.0
Postsecondary education	8,247.1	—	184.60	3,037.2	2,437.6	—	—	2,587.7
Other programs	1,939.0	8.5	1,332.1	—	—	295.6	222.1	80.6
Education research and statistics	42.4	—	—	—	42.4	—	—	—
1990 total	**23,198.6**	**8,000.7**	**2,490.3**	**3,859.6**	**3,649.8**	**441.4**	**912.2**	**3,844.4**
Elementary/secondary	9,681.3	7,995.0	700.3	80.5	85.4	113.1	650.7	56.3
Postsecondary education	11,176.0	—	261.6	3,779.1	3,475.0	—	—	3,660.4
Other programs	2,251.8	5.7	1,528.5	—	—	328.3	261.5	127.8
Education research and statistics	89.5	—	—	—	89.5	—	—	—
1992 total	**26,116.0**	**9,834.7**	**2,883.2**	**4,090.7**	**4,107.4**	**418.3**	**1,189.4**	**3,592.4**
Elementary/secondary	12,057.7	9,830.1	1,011.0	92.9	232.7	49.8	762.3	78.8
Postsecondary education	11,323.6	—	245.5	3,997.7	3,719.9	—	—	3,360.5
Other programs	2,579.9	4.6	1,626.6	—	—	368.5	427.0	153.1
Education research and statistics	154.8	—	—	—	154.8	—	—	—
1993 total	**30,478.2**	**10,459.3**	**3,123.0**	**5,274.8**	**5,264.0**	**404.5**	**1,200.2**	**4,752.4**
Elementary/secondary	13,059.0	10,451.5	1,261.0	110.5	281.9	51.0	823.3	79.8
Postsecondary education	14,660.7	—	225.9	5,164.3	4,749.9	—	—	4,520.6
Other programs	2,526.4	7.8	1,636.1	—	—	353.5	376.9	152.0
Education research and statistics	232.2	—	—	—	232.2	—	—	—
1994 total	**30,274.0**	**10,935.6**	**3,264.8**	**5,161.1**	**5,031.3**	**504.5**	**1,258.2**	**4,118.5**
Elementary/secondary	13,769.2	10,929.2	1,354.0	159.9	275.2	60.9	902.1	87.9
Postsecondary education	13,432.0	—	53.0	5,001.2	4,479.3	—	—	3,898.5
Other programs	2,796.0	6.4	1,857.8	—	—	443.6	356.1	132.1
Education research and statistics	276.8	—	—	—	276.8	—	—	—
1995 total	**31,414.0**	**11,210.9**	**3,585.9**	**4,967.7**	**5,019.2**	**485.4**	**1,349.2**	**4,795.9**
Elementary/secondary	14,029.0	11,203.4	1,410.0	190.5	170.1	70.3	946.9	37.9
Postsecondary education	14,243.0	—	250.8	4,777.2	4,570.0	—	—	4,645.0
Other programs	2,863.0	7.4	1,925.2	—	—	415.1	402.3	113.0
Education research and statistics	279.0	—	—	—	279.0	—	—	—
1996 total	**30,405.0**	**11,659.0**	**3,968.8**	**5,260.2**	**4,989.3**	**527.4**	**2,035.8**	**1,964.5**
Elementary/secondary	15,416.0	11,652.0	1,762.4	185.5	170.2	63.4	1,544.7	37.9
Postsecondary education	11,419.0	—	47.3	5,074.6	4,483.0	—	—	1,813.8
Other programs	3,234.0	7.0	2,159.1	—	—	464.0	491.1	112.8
Education research and statistics	336.0	—	—	—	336.0	—	—	—

[1] Other recipients include Indian tribes, private nonprofit agencies, and banks.
—Data are not available or not applicable.

NOTE.—Outlays by type of recipient are estimated based on obligation data. Some data have been revised from previously published figures. Because of rounding, details may not add to totals.

SOURCE: U.S. Office of Management and Budget, *Budget of the U.S. Government,* Fiscal Years 1982 to 1997, and *Catalog of Federal Domestic Assistance;* National Science Foundation, *Federal Funds for Research and Development,* Fiscal Years 1980 to 1995; and unpublished data obtained from various federal agencies. (This table was prepared June 1996.)

Table 360.—U.S. Department of Education obligations for major programs, by state or other area: Fiscal year 1995

[In thousands]

State or other area	Total	Grants for the disad-vantaged [1]	Block grants to states for school improve-ment [2]	School assist-ance in federally affected areas [3]	Vocational and adult education [4]	Education for the handi-capped [5]	Bilingual edu-cation [6]	Indian edu-cation	Higher and continuing education [7]	Student financial assist-ance [8]	Public library pro-grams [9]	Rehabili-tation services [10]	Goals 2000 [11]
1	2	3	4	5	6	7	8	9	10	11	12	13	14
Total	**$24,713,604**	**$7,172,237**	**$1,062,672**	**$671,707**	**$1,362,074**	**$3,116,710**	**$204,058**	**$75,027**	**$1,215,321**	**$7,358,439**	**$130,711**	**$2,129,820**	**$214,829**
Alabama	440,213	128,941	17,236	4,167	26,241	51,327	214	1,215	43,017	118,587	2,001	45,666	1,602
Alaska	136,832	25,363	5,266	64,392	5,144	10,115	1,151	6,965	2,723	5,843	552	7,662	1,656
Arizona	431,724	106,516	16,015	65,399	20,871	39,638	7,167	8,232	11,457	122,077	2,118	32,205	30
Arkansas	245,492	79,036	10,373	1,621	15,463	28,857	254	118	15,478	61,533	1,517	27,569	3,672
California	2,580,239	832,630	118,812	58,102	140,624	301,648	71,297	4,917	97,023	745,262	12,763	196,899	262
Colorado	278,419	69,808	13,115	7,281	16,207	33,217	4,076	432	14,142	88,070	2,097	25,661	4,312
Connecticut	199,189	55,722	10,410	5,015	12,482	40,331	2,011	24	8,350	42,712	1,898	16,753	3,481
Delaware	64,864	16,655	5,256	68	5,464	9,118	275	0	5,105	12,934	1,018	7,672	1,299
District of Columbia	335,327	21,109	5,159	1,056	5,415	1,330	1,476	0	222,847	64,399	570	11,489	477
Florida	1,022,864	304,566	46,195	11,800	61,216	154,221	7,528	60	30,629	283,523	6,774	100,382	15,961
Georgia	561,323	173,817	26,991	6,481	38,459	69,390	589	0	38,434	140,799	3,234	60,768	2,361
Hawaii	89,852	19,809	5,257	18,868	6,479	7,293	1,153	0	6,950	13,973	652	8,028	1,390
Idaho	110,494	27,062	5,248	4,425	6,954	11,622	1,540	255	3,983	37,252	627	11,068	458
Illinois	965,142	327,916	46,011	9,550	53,115	135,154	7,795	80	39,175	244,871	5,641	79,739	16,096
Indiana	460,156	113,142	20,109	1,675	31,514	66,853	212	9	15,897	162,579	2,979	43,452	1,734
Iowa	241,169	52,324	10,067	185	15,088	32,946	576	115	14,235	90,425	1,518	22,804	887
Kansas	311,494	59,694	9,523	8,556	12,766	27,861	903	319	12,305	153,983	1,347	21,025	3,212
Kentucky	373,196	133,099	16,237	1,117	24,168	46,576	100	0	16,947	86,490	2,124	40,531	5,808
Louisiana	533,405	194,266	22,239	5,945	27,481	47,914	2,055	455	27,037	149,527	1,751	46,716	8,019
Maine	129,461	29,510	5,257	2,656	12,082	30,542	998	124	6,003	27,369	676	12,586	1,658
Maryland	328,453	88,597	16,605	8,649	19,908	46,805	1,234	154	20,508	87,229	2,316	31,037	5,412
Massachusetts	516,436	126,138	18,469	4,301	24,277	76,366	3,282	255	22,872	196,776	2,733	40,925	42
Michigan	941,097	319,510	40,675	6,735	48,009	183,716	1,186	3,071	29,237	213,820	4,112	76,565	14,462
Minnesota	353,501	85,678	16,789	5,040	20,889	51,016	1,672	4,115	15,825	114,525	1,829	36,094	30
Mississippi	352,855	127,060	14,085	3,462	18,012	34,601	100	1,123	19,084	98,657	1,630	33,681	1,360
Missouri	415,170	115,526	19,802	6,504	27,348	58,853	920	42	16,577	120,096	2,423	47,041	37
Montana	123,053	26,427	5,253	21,760	5,924	10,070	2,587	3,843	7,704	29,828	812	8,398	450
Nebraska	154,745	31,051	6,060	6,869	8,359	19,565	709	348	5,527	60,267	1,041	14,382	567
Nevada	73,313	19,564	5,319	3,324	6,702	13,163	486	863	2,222	10,486	903	8,854	1,427
New Hampshire	75,824	16,727	5,254	875	6,414	12,689	280	0	3,219	20,992	788	8,586	0
New Jersey	519,558	145,617	26,526	11,323	30,819	109,368	2,816	104	17,080	128,009	4,373	41,075	2,448
New Mexico	242,779	61,206	8,014	38,213	9,889	23,468	6,288	6,180	9,998	58,342	1,157	17,226	2,798
New York	1,948,936	632,977	75,419	15,686	75,221	204,539	29,144	1,461	50,559	711,394	7,583	117,662	27,290
North Carolina	540,594	135,690	23,770	8,401	39,470	75,365	429	2,314	38,817	138,961	3,675	65,906	7,796
North Dakota	90,895	17,890	5,245	11,702	5,466	7,108	1,511	1,185	5,120	27,457	593	7,610	8
Ohio	1,097,689	307,509	43,793	3,814	57,482	218,237	224	29	26,912	332,456	4,938	98,579	3,715
Oklahoma	347,533	85,716	13,175	19,883	19,283	33,075	7,323	13,544	18,623	102,420	1,747	32,719	25
Oregon	244,631	79,138	11,191	2,982	15,163	34,740	2,706	1,331	10,173	55,901	1,590	25,681	4,035
Pennsylvania	1,261,464	316,544	44,636	3,033	56,340	110,176	2,214	0	30,738	575,703	5,799	100,650	15,631
Rhode Island	98,344	22,023	5,258	2,514	6,626	12,759	972	34	3,802	36,040	738	7,567	8
South Carolina	333,527	93,744	14,066	6,233	22,839	45,008	100	26	20,259	90,327	1,596	38,055	1,275
South Dakota	137,322	20,077	5,244	14,699	5,570	9,473	1,699	2,757	4,342	64,497	600	7,937	427
Tennessee	420,616	123,584	19,166	3,097	29,685	62,924	228	0	26,220	103,435	2,370	49,869	37
Texas	1,826,529	627,329	82,176	26,903	99,930	217,848	16,177	162	57,469	502,530	7,517	151,966	36,522
Utah	198,606	34,190	8,379	6,631	12,614	26,755	1,191	996	8,610	76,055	1,080	18,808	3,296
Vermont	70,495	16,338	5,255	12	5,290	6,661	267	97	4,650	22,505	455	7,685	1,281
Virginia	467,012	101,656	20,899	30,568	30,919	71,441	1,147	11	26,823	132,986	2,921	47,642	0
Washington	418,884	113,253	18,808	23,873	22,989	57,305	2,551	4,952	19,987	109,407	2,761	36,634	6,364
West Virginia	190,207	70,712	7,913	79	12,048	23,486	0	0	9,162	43,799	917	21,314	778
Wisconsin	433,263	125,832	19,876	6,747	25,729	56,409	510	2,118	19,507	128,606	2,345	43,901	1,683
Wyoming	66,456	16,283	5,150	7,126	5,146	7,358	349	591	2,803	14,240	532	6,508	370
Indian tribe setaside	43,338	0	1,256	0	0	28,767	0	0	0	0	2,508	10,271	536
Undistributed	100,493	15,291	328	80,948	400	0	0	314	0	2,494	0	0	719
Outlying areas													
American Samoa	14,478	4,998	2,111	0	376	3,127	100	0	659	2,174	89	800	45
Federated States of Micronesia	204	0	0	0	100	0	0	0	30	0	0	0	74
Guam	22,389	4,866	3,422	0	789	7,488	552	0	1,816	1,439	254	1,763	0
Marshall Islands	155	0	0	0	100	0	0	0	30	0	0	0	25
North Mariana Islands	6,766	2,372	822	0	375	1,632	0	0	153	638	87	662	25
Palau	1,204	0	13	0	100	746	0	0	31	1	76	212	25
Puerto Rico	700,733	261,631	25,253	1,179	47,317	3,706	945	0	21,356	292,973	1,854	44,461	59
Trust Territory of the Pacific	958	0	0	0	0	0	100	0	858	0	0	0	0
Virgin Islands	22,245	8,510	2,423	173	920	4,948	373	0	1,730	1,261	111	1,704	93

[1] Title I formerly called Chapter 1, Education Consolidation and Improvement Act of 1981 includes Grants to Local Education Agencies, Migrant Education—Basic State Grants, Program for Neglected and Delinquent Children, Capital Expenses, State Improvement Grants, and Even Start—State Educational Agencies.

[2] Title VI formerly called Chapter 2 includes Education Consolidation and Improvement Act of 1981, Dwight D. Eisenhower Professional Development Grants, Drug-Free Schools and Communities—State Grants, Education for Homeless Children and Youth, Christa McAuliffe Fellowships, and Innovative Education Program Strategies.

[3] Impact Aid—Basic Support Payments and Impact Aid—Payments for Children with Disabilities.

[4] Includes Vocational Education—Basic Grants to States, State Councils, Tech-Prep Education, Adult Education-State Administered Basic Grant Program, and State Literacy Resource Centers.

[5] Includes Special Education—Grants to States (Part B, Individuals with Disabilities Education Act), Preschool Incentive Grants to States, Special Education—Grants for Infants and Families with Disabilities, and Education of Children with Disabilities in State Operated or Supported Schools.

[6] Includes Emergency Immigrant Education Program and Bilingual Education State Grants.

[7] Includes Institutional Aid to Strengthen Higher Education Institutions serving significant numbers of low-income students, Other Special Programs for the Disadvantaged, Cooperative Education, Fund for the Improvement of Postsecondary Education, Fellowships and Scholarships, and annual interest subsidy grants for facilities construction.

[8] Includes Pell Grants, State Student Incentive Grants, Guaranteed Student Loan interest subsidies, and Postsecondary Review Program.

[9] Includes Public Library Services, Public Library Construction and Technology Enhancement, and Interlibrary Cooperation and Resource Sharing.

[10] Includes Rehabilitation Services—Vocational Rehabilitation Grants to States, Supported Employment Services for Individuals with Severe Disabilities, Rehabilitation Services—Client Assistance Program, Independent Living—State Grants, and Program of Protection and Advocacy of Individual Rights.

[11] Includes State and Local Systemic Improvement.

NOTE.—Data reflect revisions to figures in the *Budget of the United States Government, Fiscal Year 1997*. To the extent possible, data represent obligations rather than outlays. Because of the exclusion of certain programs, totals in this table are lower than those reported in other tables. Because of rounding, details may not add to totals.

SOURCE: U.S. Department of Education, National Center for Education Statistics, based on unpublished tabulations from the Office of Management and Budget; and U.S. Department of Commerce, Bureau of the Census, *Federal Expenditures by State for Fiscal Year 1995*. (This table was prepared April 1996.)

Table 361.—U.S. Department of Education obligations for major programs, by state or other area: Fiscal year 1994

[In thousands]

State or other area	Total	Grants for the disad-vantaged [1]	Block grants to states for school improve-ment [2]	School assist-ance in federally affected areas [3]	Vocational and adult education [4]	Education for the handi-capped [5]	Bilingual edu-cation [6]	Indian edu-cation	Higher and continuing education [7]	Student financial assist-ance [8]	Public library pro-grams [9]	Rehabili-tation services [10]	Goals 2000 [11]
1	2	3	4	5	6	7	8	9	10	11	12	13	14
Total	**$24,465,205**	**$6,883,656**	**$1,032,040**	**$736,574**	**$1,360,771**	**$3,415,767**	**$224,246**	**$73,887**	**$1,142,490**	**$7,375,058**	**$124,050**	**$2,035,216**	**$61,449**
Alabama	446,703	122,402	16,808	4,829	27,314	50,096	1,309	1,005	41,174	134,937	1,923	44,905	0
Alaska	140,161	18,247	4,984	76,172	5,367	10,089	525	6,879	2,470	7,052	466	7,459	451
Arizona	409,294	100,910	15,057	64,973	21,431	36,734	7,750	8,807	11,831	107,840	2,159	30,469	1,333
Arkansas	240,676	75,692	9,900	1,909	15,850	27,244	250	107	13,268	67,065	1,269	27,152	970
California	2,836,294	822,081	115,874	64,330	144,353	530,178	76,068	5,016	89,458	774,854	12,299	191,520	10,263
Colorado	286,821	68,191	12,871	7,983	16,569	37,710	4,743	774	12,742	102,887	1,591	19,699	1,062
Connecticut	191,729	54,228	10,719	7,190	13,237	40,016	1,064	28	8,721	37,471	1,598	16,519	940
Delaware	56,804	14,087	5,028	73	5,672	8,899	250	0	3,810	10,154	994	7,440	398
District of Columbia	295,509	22,012	7,480	1,242	5,677	5,749	2,359	199	208,672	30,034	568	11,516	0
Florida	950,013	290,780	44,764	13,817	63,741	143,226	4,966	62	23,324	259,743	6,430	95,233	3,926
Georgia	549,326	161,269	26,451	7,455	39,933	64,405	611	0	34,950	154,116	2,562	57,572	0
Hawaii	89,861	18,392	5,057	22,377	6,717	8,341	1,399	0	6,431	11,533	1,405	7,800	409
Idaho	109,946	25,563	5,071	4,764	7,067	13,794	1,716	204	3,941	36,176	898	10,753	0
Illinois	949,469	301,431	44,604	10,993	55,145	135,536	7,732	84	39,671	267,970	4,201	78,062	4,040
Indiana	448,402	104,291	20,878	1,993	32,826	64,188	500	18	15,607	165,400	2,168	40,534	0
Iowa	243,680	49,523	10,642	169	15,401	32,174	840	114	14,335	97,307	1,383	21,792	0
Kansas	281,129	52,973	9,721	10,505	13,154	26,542	1,061	285	11,571	132,296	1,317	20,858	846
Kentucky	365,342	125,951	15,082	1,290	24,873	45,035	432	0	15,163	94,626	1,777	39,668	1,445
Louisiana	505,172	184,603	20,125	7,014	28,405	45,790	2,204	477	25,881	146,129	2,560	39,971	2,015
Maine	88,234	28,878	5,085	2,831	1,462	1,125	1,472	75	5,623	27,855	792	12,541	496
Maryland	320,449	84,028	17,001	10,374	20,390	51,694	1,453	167	19,598	81,638	2,309	30,381	1,417
Massachusetts	523,546	122,859	19,826	5,226	25,352	85,987	4,034	260	22,032	193,189	2,664	40,278	1,840
Michigan	831,850	298,658	38,164	6,767	50,102	85,737	2,569	2,965	28,379	238,596	4,204	72,173	3,536
Minnesota	352,926	81,651	17,111	5,630	21,569	48,350	1,105	3,943	15,993	118,539	2,190	35,487	1,357
Mississippi	370,494	121,419	12,710	4,041	18,490	61,857	459	1,047	18,445	97,120	1,730	33,176	0
Missouri	423,929	112,582	19,770	5,926	28,146	56,003	599	44	15,850	134,593	2,485	46,277	1,654
Montana	123,889	25,555	5,073	24,231	6,108	10,261	3,278	3,577	6,930	30,498	595	7,784	0
Nebraska	152,575	31,596	6,322	8,151	8,694	18,679	743	846	5,304	59,314	942	11,984	0
Nevada	73,869	18,738	5,062	3,792	6,976	14,708	505	1,007	1,924	11,309	849	8,595	402
New Hampshire	82,815	14,640	5,039	1,029	6,641	21,456	382	0	3,315	21,113	770	8,429	0
New Jersey	500,974	153,203	26,580	11,393	32,035	85,165	2,210	106	16,475	131,378	2,893	39,537	0
New Mexico	235,504	58,392	7,321	37,501	10,103	21,848	9,216	5,433	8,630	58,945	996	16,391	726
New York	2,070,584	611,923	69,587	18,526	78,144	350,692	34,972	1,460	51,106	724,563	7,360	115,257	6,995
North Carolina	522,302	127,877	23,840	9,623	40,916	71,534	401	2,327	37,119	139,325	2,875	64,454	2,011
North Dakota	92,302	17,114	5,031	12,885	5,732	6,928	2,551	1,313	4,460	27,900	647	7,343	399
Ohio	817,265	286,764	42,040	4,500	60,131	8,518	449	36	23,892	289,678	4,492	96,767	0
Oklahoma	349,487	81,094	12,914	22,260	19,879	38,966	9,625	12,328	16,540	103,850	1,486	29,415	1,129
Oregon	245,683	71,641	11,157	3,637	15,708	31,290	3,408	1,204	9,983	70,109	1,451	25,071	1,024
Pennsylvania	961,335	300,838	43,172	3,598	59,635	108,832	1,304	0	31,928	304,144	4,941	98,971	3,973
Rhode Island	98,978	21,800	5,066	3,050	6,903	12,419	1,517	42	3,967	35,626	875	7,281	434
South Carolina	325,942	88,301	14,028	7,363	23,753	43,042	75	0	19,829	90,566	1,567	37,418	0
South Dakota	116,599	19,907	5,042	15,121	5,790	9,151	1,736	2,646	3,463	45,099	812	7,834	0
Tennessee	426,470	118,033	18,711	3,520	30,940	59,575	159	0	25,033	118,169	2,758	47,930	1,640
Texas	1,920,503	610,832	76,604	31,396	104,939	378,742	15,209	166	51,779	495,260	8,122	147,453	0
Utah	213,727	31,955	9,014	6,342	12,623	25,949	1,259	744	8,133	98,195	1,206	18,307	0
Vermont	63,785	13,919	5,024	14	5,526	6,301	248	110	4,536	19,570	626	7,512	399
Virginia	526,326	99,891	21,494	36,401	31,998	127,946	1,412	12	25,806	133,194	2,780	45,392	0
Washington	408,321	103,709	18,915	26,829	24,136	54,503	3,575	4,823	19,736	112,946	2,051	35,551	1,546
West Virginia	183,285	63,431	7,407	91	12,451	22,262	0	0	8,965	46,657	1,022	21,000	0
Wisconsin	415,314	115,384	19,701	7,325	26,635	55,365	347	2,333	18,188	124,995	2,280	42,761	0
Wyoming	65,569	14,083	5,022	8,288	5,390	7,297	298	816	2,243	14,833	750	6,549	0
Indian tribe setaside	89,222	35,514	1,385	0	0	49,907	0	0	0	0	2,415	0	0
Undistributed	270,398	10,677	0	78,311	1,381	0	0	0	0	179,403	0	625	0
Outlying areas													
American Samoa	13,744	4,537	1,420	0	381	5,168	75	0	191	1,114	88	769	0
Federated States of Micronesia	159	0	0	0	0	0	0	0	159	0	0	0	0
Guam	21,615	4,408	3,317	0	784	6,883	156	0	2,450	1,434	95	2,040	47
Marshall Islands	370	0	0	0	0	0	0	0	370	0	0	0	0
Northern Marianas	9,881	2,449	1,351	0	371	3,355	0	0	1,178	454	87	638	0
Palau	3,187	1,682	424	0	220	156	327	0	145	1	76	157	0
Puerto Rico	719,924	253,399	20,927	1,387	6,232	24,428	917	0	18,150	355,000	2,039	35,120	2,325
Trust Territory of the Pacific	13,331	0	0	0	421	12,775	75	0	61	0	0	0	0
Virgin Islands	22,208	7,671	3,264	135	954	5,169	346	0	1,563	1,298	158	1,650	0

[1] Chapter 1, Education Consolidation and Improvement Act of 1981 includes Grants to Local Education Agencies, Migrant Education—Basic State Grants, Educationally Deprived Children—State Administration, Program for Neglected and Delinquent Children, Capital Expenses, State Improvement Grants, and Even Start—State Educational Agencies.

[2] Includes Chapter 2, Education Consolidation and Improvement Act of 1981, Eisenhower Mathematics and Science Education—State Grants, Drug-Free Schools and Communities—State Grants, Education of Homeless Children and Youth, Christa McAuliffe Fellowships, Foreign Language Assistance, and State Block Grants.

[3] Includes Maintenance and Operations (Impact Aid/Disaster Assistance).

[4] Includes Vocational Education—Basic Grants to States, Community Based Organizations, Consumer and Homemaking Education, State Councils, Tech-Prep Education, Adult Education-State Administered Basic Grant Program, and State Literacy Resource Centers.

[5] Includes Special Education—Grants to States (Part B, Individuals with Disabilities Education Act), Preschool Incentive Grants to States, Special Education—Grants for Infants and Families with Disabilities, and Education of Children with Disabilities in State Operated or Supported Schools.

[6] Also includes Emergency Immigrant Education Program and Transition Program for Refugee Children.

[7] Includes Institutional Aid to Strengthen Higher Education Institutions serving significant numbers of low-income students, Other Special Programs for the Disadvantaged, Cooperative Education, Fund for the Improvement of Postsecondary Education, Fellowships and Scholarships, and annual interest subsidy grants for facilities construction.

[8] Includes Pell Grants, State Student Incentive Grants, Guaranteed Student Loan interest subsidies, and Postsecondary Review Program.

[9] Includes Public Library Services, Public Library Construction and Technology Enhancement, and Interlibrary Cooperation and Resource Sharing.

[10] Includes Rehabilitation Services—Vocational Rehabilitation Grants to States, Basic State Grants, Supported Employment Services for Individuals with Severe Disabilities, Rehabilitation Services—Client Assistance Program, Independent Living—State Grants, and Program of Protection and Advocacy of Individual Rights.

[11] Includes State and Local Systemic Improvement.

NOTE.—Data reflect revisions to figures in the *Budget of the United States Government, Fiscal Year 1996*. To the extent possible, data represent obligations rather than outlays. Because of the exclusion of certain programs, totals in this table are lower than those reported in other tables. Because of rounding, details may not add to totals.

SOURCE: U.S. Department of Education, National Center for Education Statistics, based on unpublished tabulations from the Office of Management and Budget; and U.S. Department of Commerce, Bureau of the Census, *Federal Expenditures by State for Fiscal Year 1994*. (This table was prepared March 1995.)

Table 362.—Appropriations for Title I and Title VI, Elementary and Secondary Education Act (ESEA) [1] of 1994, by state or other area: 1994–95 and 1995–96

[In thousands]

State or other area	Title I total, school year 1994–95 [2]	Title I, [3] school year 1995–96 [4]							Title VI [5]	
		Total	Total local education grants	Basic grants	Concentration grants	Neglected and delinquent children	Migrant children	Other [6]	1994 appropriations for 1994–95	1995 appropriations for 1995–96
1	2	3	4	5	6	7	8	9	10	11
Total [7]	$7,012,929	$7,214,160	$6,698,356	$5,968,235	$663,137	$39,311	$305,475	$171,018	$369,500	$347,250
Alabama	122,981	128,941	123,533	109,339	14,194	475	2,555	2,378	5,859	5,329
Alaska	25,354	25,363	14,723	13,630	1,093	174	9,923	543	1,833	1,724
Arizona	101,431	106,404	96,885	85,076	11,808	684	6,837	1,998	5,476	5,445
Arkansas	76,771	78,984	73,847	65,467	8,380	246	3,487	1,404	3,451	3,208
California	823,629	832,630	717,138	635,585	81,553	4,445	91,970	19,078	42,626	40,033
Colorado	69,650	69,756	64,861	59,857	5,004	163	3,426	1,307	4,875	4,794
Connecticut	57,569	55,664	51,443	48,389	3,055	638	2,160	1,423	4,010	3,813
Delaware	15,332	16,551	15,243	14,162	1,082	136	402	770	1,833	1,724
District of Columbia	24,357	21,109	19,455	17,080	2,375	690	193	772	1,833	1,724
Florida	297,267	304,566	273,962	245,742	28,220	1,422	23,568	5,614	16,290	15,759
Georgia	162,021	173,817	165,285	148,180	17,105	870	4,607	3,054	9,567	9,204
Hawaii	18,844	19,809	19,103	17,446	1,658	120	0	586	1,833	1,724
Idaho	25,968	27,062	21,537	19,876	1,661	111	4,812	602	1,833	1,725
Illinois	320,020	327,812	317,237	285,230	32,007	1,433	1,771	7,370	16,042	14,853
Indiana	107,371	113,142	107,176	99,708	7,468	830	2,776	2,360	7,952	7,303
Iowa	50,063	52,168	50,199	47,771	2,428	313	306	1,349	4,076	3,709
Kansas	54,058	59,694	51,613	48,269	3,345	571	6,418	1,092	3,697	3,469
Kentucky	126,307	133,099	122,910	108,929	13,981	721	6,897	2,570	5,316	4,855
Louisiana	185,261	194,266	186,888	164,072	22,816	847	1,906	4,625	6,762	6,150
Maine	29,272	29,510	25,243	23,586	1,658	183	3,465	618	1,833	1,724
Maryland	86,289	88,441	84,680	78,783	5,896	1,421	265	2,075	6,352	6,055
Massachusetts	133,324	125,630	118,857	109,564	9,293	851	2,725	3,197	7,157	6,858
Michigan	305,686	319,510	300,398	271,337	29,061	961	11,974	6,177	13,441	12,492
Minnesota	82,756	85,678	80,874	75,090	5,785	204	2,337	2,263	6,558	6,259
Mississippi	121,649	127,060	122,733	108,047	14,686	330	1,342	2,656	4,106	3,760
Missouri	114,418	117,658	113,094	102,067	11,027	699	814	3,051	7,326	6,872
Montana	25,755	26,271	24,871	22,225	2,646	85	707	608	1,833	1,724
Nebraska	31,911	30,947	27,381	25,475	1,906	218	2,293	1,054	2,411	2,233
Nevada	18,961	19,502	18,239	16,698	1,541	190	503	569	1,833	1,789
New Hampshire	15,395	16,629	15,756	14,758	999	179	98	597	1,833	1,724
New Jersey	155,336	145,617	137,637	126,918	10,719	2,500	948	4,532	9,716	9,260
New Mexico	58,486	61,206	58,311	51,202	7,109	381	1,242	1,271	2,527	2,451
New York	620,865	629,845	602,132	540,050	62,083	3,101	5,700	18,911	23,018	21,432
North Carolina	128,349	135,690	128,185	118,659	9,526	892	4,232	2,382	8,821	8,535
North Dakota	17,271	17,786	16,578	14,921	1,658	56	516	636	1,833	1,724
Ohio	288,738	307,509	296,610	266,258	30,352	2,017	1,882	7,000	15,267	14,183
Oklahoma	81,715	85,716	82,398	73,137	9,261	471	1,286	1,561	4,712	4,402
Oregon	76,379	79,138	65,310	60,744	4,566	781	11,741	1,306	4,182	3,930
Pennsylvania	311,997	316,544	299,889	273,703	26,187	744	5,525	10,386	15,296	14,376
Rhode Island	22,517	22,023	20,774	18,736	2,038	265	153	831	1,833	1,724
South Carolina	88,941	93,744	90,445	81,517	8,928	1,096	567	1,636	5,060	4,647
South Dakota	20,129	19,973	18,629	16,905	1,724	111	604	629	1,833	1,724
Tennessee	119,155	123,584	120,562	106,568	13,994	656	99	2,267	6,726	6,375
Texas	616,149	627,277	570,954	504,723	66,231	1,424	43,428	11,471	26,981	25,634
Utah	32,577	34,138	31,981	30,199	1,781	389	1,131	637	3,598	3,361
Vermont	14,701	16,338	14,712	13,713	999	120	945	561	1,833	1,724
Virginia	101,709	102,077	98,469	90,896	7,573	886	787	1,935	8,239	7,768
Washington	105,478	113,253	97,221	90,065	7,156	832	13,286	1,913	7,266	6,944
West Virginia	64,163	70,712	69,040	60,860	8,180	288	100	1,285	2,484	2,200
Wisconsin	117,600	125,832	121,375	113,589	7,785	991	644	2,822	7,306	6,827
Wyoming	14,279	16,283	15,448	14,355	1,094	112	175	548	1,833	1,724
Other activities										
Bureau of Indian Affairs	35,514	41,324	41,324	0	0	0	0	0	0	0
Migrant coordination activities	6,600	6,000	0	0	0	0	6,000	0	0	0
Even Start Migrant, Indian, and Territory setaside	4,568	5,101	0	0	0	0	0	5,101	0	0
Even Start Evaluation/Technical Assistance	1,782	1,400	0	0	0	0	0	1,400	0	0
Even Start/State Literacy State Literacy Initiative	3,817	1,000	0	0	0	0	0	1,000	0	0
Competitive grants	0	5,000	5,000	0	0	0	0	0	0	0
Outlying areas										
American Samoa	4,537	4,998	4,978	0	0	0	0	21	469	417
Guam	4,476	4,866	4,846	0	0	0	0	20	1,095	974
Northern Marianas	2,563	2,372	2,362	0	0	0	0	10	267	238
Puerto Rico	253,399	261,631	249,546	219,080	30,465	990	3,948	7,147	6,419	5,839
Trust Territory of the Pacific	1,725	0	0	0	0	0	0	0	137	0
Virgin Islands	7,747	8,510	8,474	0	0	0	0	35	902	802

[1] Elementary and Secondary Education Act was most recently revised through the Improving America's Schools Act (IASA) of 1994.
[2] Data are based on fiscal year 1995 budget authorizations. Excludes $13,100,000 for evaluation and studies; and $4,960,000 for rural technical assistance (Rural TACS).
[3] Formerly Chapter 1.
[4] Data are based on fiscal year 1996 budget authorizations. Excludes $3,664,000 for evaluation and studies.
[5] Formerly Chapter 2.

[6] Includes capital expenses, Even Start, and state program improvement grants.
[7] Total includes other activities and outlying areas.

NOTE.—Because of rounding, details may not add to totals.

SOURCE: U.S. Department of Education, Budget Service, Elementary, Secondary, and Vocational Education Analysis Division; and unpublished data. (This table was prepared April 1996.)

Table 363.—Federal science and engineering obligations to colleges and universities, by agency and state: Fiscal year 1994 [1]

[In thousands]

State or other area	Total	Department of Agriculture	Department of Defense	Department of Education	Department of Energy	Environmental Protection Agency	Department of Health and Human Services	National Aeronautics and Space Administration	National Science Foundation	Other [2]
1	2	3	4	5	6	7	8	9	10	11
United States	$17,801,310	$939,076	$2,216,723	$155,571	$3,387,486	$144,642	$6,890,100	$1,553,872	$2,191,307	$322,533
Alabama	213,348	25,501	18,424	4,055	3,844	1,906	115,038	25,729	16,170	2,681
Alaska	40,289	3,681	1,576	325	473	128	2,107	13,413	11,937	6,649
Arizona	242,939	10,718	20,673	3,941	5,217	2,834	65,643	50,911	79,263	3,739
Arkansas	57,856	22,897	5,653	3,641	299	298	17,669	976	5,167	1,256
California	3,584,333	37,292	201,902	14,563	1,041,929	9,909	972,195	972,912	299,707	33,924
Colorado	347,647	13,615	21,843	4,308	8,906	2,351	131,643	22,047	115,665	27,269
Connecticut	258,814	6,454	11,490	1,090	11,898	584	200,346	1,651	21,037	4,264
Delaware	35,277	5,553	6,924	2,178	937	1,086	4,945	987	9,503	3,164
District of Columbia	124,264	1,700	23,710	3,796	2,756	463	71,893	7,618	8,973	3,355
Florida	305,444	22,098	42,468	4,420	17,072	2,254	127,735	20,683	56,194	12,520
Georgia	316,744	28,071	72,783	3,211	19,909	10,593	128,800	12,089	31,125	10,163
Hawaii	73,607	12,716	3,719	1,110	3,167	0	19,473	8,582	15,016	9,824
Idaho	26,502	9,104	749	806	468	789	2,488	389	6,481	5,228
Illinois	1,116,594	24,693	49,140	8,597	633,981	950	248,338	10,928	133,718	6,249
Indiana	207,133	23,166	13,217	2,196	16,804	1,010	89,712	5,358	50,403	5,267
Iowa	201,567	27,186	6,478	1,598	33,932	2,461	89,467	6,115	16,984	17,346
Kansas	72,154	14,493	3,052	2,170	4,701	3,369	29,533	2,847	10,415	1,574
Kentucky	83,905	23,709	2,467	1,603	4,831	482	38,763	1,684	9,939	427
Louisiana	140,832	18,014	21,583	1,324	12,605	5,169	60,400	3,703	10,368	7,666
Maine	22,575	9,200	1,769	513	214	928	2,054	179	4,221	3,497
Maryland	957,386	14,995	492,369	3,706	14,642	4,936	338,406	33,312	48,725	6,295
Massachusetts	1,149,215	22,547	416,770	3,974	83,909	6,140	386,056	51,538	165,211	13,070
Michigan	433,431	27,557	37,709	2,239	13,424	10,224	236,374	19,067	81,991	4,846
Minnesota	228,602	20,805	25,990	2,674	6,165	2,711	130,430	2,557	33,964	3,306
Mississippi	72,120	28,722	7,412	1,889	5,046	320	14,572	2,181	9,250	2,728
Missouri	261,041	29,846	7,443	2,634	4,311	768	187,395	4,777	20,985	2,882
Montana	34,933	10,357	1,638	1,395	414	616	5,493	1,359	12,585	1,076
Nebraska	55,209	16,629	3,714	602	809	259	20,492	1,774	10,527	403
Nevada	31,374	4,024	205	261	4,114	5,083	7,277	597	7,268	2,545
New Hampshire	64,945	4,889	2,423	295	1,497	1,033	35,074	9,751	8,812	1,171
New Jersey	332,286	12,559	33,726	750	115,658	4,827	95,284	6,506	53,924	9,052
New Mexico	706,799	8,231	49,295	2,828	584,356	218	27,303	23,143	10,462	963
New York	1,463,307	30,064	70,891	10,326	391,070	4,089	717,710	23,928	208,331	6,898
North Carolina	502,963	38,212	26,393	4,082	9,535	13,155	334,580	8,317	54,284	14,405
North Dakota	33,338	12,467	556	1,024	7,007	1,462	3,444	437	3,006	3,935
Ohio	371,520	22,621	61,544	5,625	7,461	7,113	196,000	23,644	40,717	6,795
Oklahoma	77,091	16,993	10,018	2,182	3,215	1,113	18,214	8,592	14,148	2,616
Oregon	163,475	20,730	10,368	5,633	9,299	3,985	72,465	3,808	30,223	6,964
Pennsylvania	824,908	24,119	180,135	6,922	22,060	3,488	445,155	21,548	110,137	11,344
Rhode Island	66,489	3,872	10,477	185	2,551	1,199	21,954	3,408	18,900	3,943
South Carolina	97,197	17,506	6,406	1,137	18,252	556	32,278	1,373	14,813	4,876
South Dakota	17,738	7,937	53	139	0	194	2,206	2,565	4,174	470
Tennessee	296,240	26,219	14,962	2,258	103,029	919	125,587	6,610	15,084	1,572
Texas	725,552	50,238	86,889	7,763	27,430	10,721	413,424	36,651	85,573	6,863
Utah	152,271	9,709	29,252	2,377	3,893	2,270	67,683	13,912	20,493	2,682
Vermont	41,086	7,107	798	1,499	563	204	26,293	313	4,158	151
Virginia	311,236	22,736	26,577	5,277	80,695	1,472	108,191	22,231	32,040	12,017
Washington	366,473	27,446	31,845	2,740	17,433	1,305	212,156	9,741	51,098	12,709
West Virginia	83,878	8,793	1,480	857	4,893	3,240	8,208	23,427	29,769	3,211
Wisconsin	313,925	24,926	36,097	4,765	19,126	2,924	154,908	14,325	52,236	4,618
Wyoming	18,649	5,793	2,407	205	383	40	911	1,130	6,715	1,065
Outlying areas	74,809	20,566	1,261	1,883	1,303	494	26,335	2,549	19,418	1,000
American Samoa	1,299	1,293	0	6	0	0	0	0	0	0
Guam	3,427	2,313	211	0	0	0	568	0	130	205
Puerto Rico	64,936	12,755	1,050	1,847	1,303	494	24,861	2,549	19,288	789
Trust Territory of the Pacific	2,323	2,158	0	30	0	0	135	0	0	0
Virgin Islands	2,824	2,047	0	0	0	0	771	0	0	6

[1] Dollars reflect actual obligations during the fiscal year regardless of when the funds were actually spent by a recipient institution. Data include obligations to federally funded research and development centers administered by colleges and universities.

[2] Includes U.S. Department of Commerce, U.S. Department of Housing and Urban Development, U.S. Department of the Interior, Agency for International Development, U.S. Department of Labor, U.S. Department of Transportation, and Nuclear Regulatory Commission.

NOTE.—Totals exclude loans to individuals, such as the Federal Family Education Loan Program sponsored by the U.S. Department of Education, and federal training and development activities, as well as funds allocated to state agencies, even though the final recipient of such funds is known to be an academic institution. Tuition support programs such as Pell Grants are included in these figures.

SOURCE: National Science Foundation, *Federal Support to Universities, Colleges, and Nonprofit Institutions, Fiscal Year 1994.* (This table was prepared May 1996.)

Table 364.—Summary of federal funds for research, development, and R & D plant: Fiscal years 1988 to 1996

[In millions]

Item	Actual							Estimates		Percent change, 1995 to 1996
	1988	1989	1990	1991	1992	1993	1994	1995	1996	
1	2	3	4	5	6	7	8	9	10	11
Total outlays for research, development, and R & D plant	$56,556.6	$61,476.4	$64,276.5	$64,292.3	$65,719.0	$68,385.8	$68,335.9	$69,661.1	$70,012.7	0.5
Research and development	54,739.4	59,450.4	62,246.8	61,130.4	62,934.5	65,241.3	66,158.8	67,399.9	67,652.9	0.4
R & D plant	1,817.2	2,026.1	2,029.7	3,162.0	2,784.5	3,144.5	2,177.1	2,261.2	2,359.8	4.4
Total obligations for research, development, and R & D plant	58,992.2	63,570.9	65,950.9	64,990.5	68,577.2	70,414.7	69,427.0	73,028.7	70,906.0	−2.9
Research and development obligations	56,935.1	61,405.8	63,667.3	61,295.2	65,592.6	67,314.0	67,255.8	70,093.9	68,842.4	−1.8
Performers										
Federal intramural [1]	14,280.9	13,184.5	16,002.5	15,238.1	15,690.1	16,556.2	16,139.1	16,962.3	16,287.3	−4.0
Industrial firms	26,719.2	30,484.4	29,378.3	26,420.6	29,744.8	30,326.1	30,454.4	31,771.1	31,159.8	−1.9
FFRDCs [2] administered by industrial firms	1,911.3	1,960.0	2,237.6	2,068.3	2,009.8	1,451.3	1,293.5	1,192.3	1,287.3	8.0
Universities and colleges	7,827.7	8,672.0	9,142.2	10,168.5	10,271.2	11,156.1	11,828.7	12,103.1	12,177.6	0.6
FFRDCs [2] administered by universities and colleges	3,473.9	3,497.1	3,466.4	3,603.8	3,855.5	3,666.5	3,292.9	3,479.7	3,514.7	1.0
Other nonprofit institutions	1,682.6	1,999.1	2,249.6	2,637.4	2,803.6	2,811.9	2,929.6	3,068.6	2,916.2	−5.0
FFRDCs [2] administered by nonprofit institutions	505.6	522.0	632.3	679.4	745.6	753.4	735.5	777.8	792.2	1.9
State and local governments	142.1	167.4	213.9	215.1	184.1	320.3	325.4	446.9	456.4	2.1
Foreign	391.8	919.4	344.7	263.9	287.9	272.2	256.6	292.0	250.9	−14.1
Research obligations	18,650.0	20,765.4	21,738.9	23,968.4	24,490.6	26,890.5	27,440.4	27,803.9	28,270.9	1.7
Performers										
Federal intramural [1]	5,338.4	5,981.5	5,953.3	6,539.3	6,615.7	7,360.1	7,488.2	7,427.5	7,417.2	−0.1
Industrial firms	2,642.5	2,875.1	3,199.9	3,406.5	3,451.2	4,018.9	4,063.5	4,062.6	4,193.9	3.2
FFRDCs [2] administered by industrial firms	455.2	519.8	542.7	624.6	592.4	795.8	737.2	704.4	711.1	1.0
Universities and colleges	7,022.9	7,793.2	8,141.5	8,867.5	9,060.7	9,844.1	10,323.5	10,657.0	10,932.5	2.6
FFRDCs [2] administered by universities and colleges	1,564.8	1,703.4	1,808.1	2,160.9	2,351.8	2,347.6	2,181.1	2,212.6	2,262.9	2.3
Other nonprofit institutions	1,299.8	1,519.7	1,662.2	1,925.9	2,049.6	2,041.3	2,094.9	2,113.5	2,132.1	0.9
FFRDCs [2] administered by nonprofit institutions	82.9	109.5	148.2	170.9	139.9	173.4	178.0	174.5	173.5	−0.5
State and local governments	103.1	121.2	126.4	129.3	109.3	211.8	230.8	306.4	311.8	1.7
Foreign	140.4	142.1	156.5	143.4	120.0	97.4	143.3	145.4	136.0	−6.5
Fields of science										
Life sciences	7,724.5	8,495.1	8,837.8	9,622.0	9,910.5	10,772.1	11,078.8	11,400.9	11,662.9	2.3
Psychology	389.8	421.7	448.6	482.4	298.1	550.7	550.2	581.8	584.5	0.5
Physical sciences	3,317.3	3,705.2	3,808.7	4,235.3	4,439.2	4,427.0	6,792.7	5,988.2	6,253.0	4.4
Environmental sciences	1,607.0	1,773.3	2,174.1	2,149.8	2,207.6	2,608.5	2,032.0	1,941.1	2,054.8	5.8
Mathematics and computer sciences	642.9	735.5	840.7	903.7	1,150.3	1,225.4	1,242.3	1,498.7	1,564.8	4.4
Engineering	3,956.3	4,442.0	4,335.2	4,944.5	4,977.0	5,499.4	4,023.3	4,536.9	4,290.8	−5.4
Social sciences	485.8	551.1	630.0	727.3	689.7	674.9	655.0	740.8	740.7	(3)
Other sciences	526.5	641.6	663.7	903.4	806.3	1,132.5	1,066.1	1,115.5	1,119.6	0.4
Basic research obligations	9,473.6	10,602.0	11,285.6	12,170.8	12,489.9	13,399.1	13,552.9	13,569.1	14,037.4	3.5
Performers										
Federal intramural [1]	2,050.3	2,370.7	2,366.0	2,446.5	2,397.0	2,605.1	2,505.0	2,468.0	2,505.8	1.5
Industrial firms	596.9	773.2	887.5	949.9	920.3	959.2	1,109.1	891.5	983.1	10.3
FFRDCs [2] administered by industrial firms	133.0	166.7	175.4	209.1	187.8	237.3	237.6	251.2	255.0	1.5
Universities and colleges	4,868.3	5,221.4	5,548.2	6,064.5	6,331.8	6,798.5	7,024.0	7,224.4	7,477.4	3.5
FFRDCs [2] administered by universities and colleges	989.8	1,098.1	1,227.3	1,306.2	1,394.1	1,437.8	1,336.0	1,359.8	1,394.0	2.5
Other nonprofit institutions	728.6	838.9	924.1	1,015.5	1,097.2	1,164.9	1,125.7	1,116.3	1,153.1	3.3
FFRDCs [2] administered by nonprofit institutions	17.7	42.2	59.2	80.8	65.5	71.3	73.9	79.6	82.5	3.6
State and local governments	42.7	43.6	50.4	49.1	42.4	71.7	75.2	111.8	120.5	7.8
Foreign	46.3	47.4	47.6	49.1	53.8	53.3	66.1	66.4	65.9	−0.7
Fields of science										
Life sciences	4,501.8	4,915.7	5,177.5	5,433.6	5,841.7	6,288.8	6,429.8	6,610.8	6,845.5	3.5
Psychology	177.8	187.1	215.1	225.5	122.6	246.8	247.4	259.9	264.1	1.6
Physical sciences	2,199.6	2,506.5	2,661.5	2,881.5	2,951.4	2,907.1	3,649.2	3,295.5	3,447.6	4.6
Environmental sciences	872.7	1,016.9	1,274.6	1,263.5	1,303.6	1,533.5	997.2	999.4	1,015.1	1.6
Mathematics and computer sciences	313.2	349.8	406.9	426.1	481.4	511.3	503.6	547.6	569.1	3.9
Engineering	1,006.2	1,183.7	1,101.5	1,233.7	1,249.8	1,207.4	1,061.7	1,157.6	1,173.1	1.3
Social sciences	146.8	154.6	146.0	161.4	139.9	194.1	191.7	201.8	207.1	2.6
Other sciences	255.5	291.7	302.3	545.6	399.4	510.1	472.4	496.4	515.8	3.9
Applied research obligations	9,176.4	10,163.3	10,453.3	11,797.6	12,000.7	13,491.4	13,887.5	14,234.8	14,233.5	(3)
Performers										
Federal intramural [1]	3,288.1	3,610.8	3,587.3	4,092.8	4,218.7	4,755.0	4,983.2	4,959.5	4,911.3	−1.0
Industrial firms	2,045.6	2,101.8	2,312.4	2,456.6	2,530.9	3,059.7	2,954.4	3,171.0	3,210.8	1.3
FFRDCs [2] administered by industrial firms	322.2	353.2	367.3	415.5	404.6	558.6	499.6	453.2	456.1	0.6
Universities and colleges	2,154.6	2,571.8	2,593.4	2,803.0	2,728.9	3,045.5	3,299.3	3,432.6	3,455.0	0.7
FFRDCs [2] administered by universities and colleges	575.0	605.4	580.8	854.7	957.6	909.8	845.1	852.7	868.9	1.9
Other nonprofit institutions	571.2	680.8	738.1	910.4	952.5	876.4	969.2	997.2	979.0	−1.8
FFRDCs [2] administered by nonprofit institutions	65.2	67.3	89.0	90.1	74.5	102.2	104.0	94.8	91.0	−4.0
State and local governments	60.4	77.6	76.1	80.2	66.9	140.1	155.5	194.6	191.3	−1.7
Foreign	94.1	94.6	109.0	94.3	66.2	44.1	77.2	79.0	70.1	−11.3
Fields of science										
Life sciences	3,222.7	3,579.4	3,660.3	4,188.4	4,068.8	4,483.3	4,649.0	4,790.1	4,817.4	0.6
Psychology	212.0	234.5	233.5	258.9	175.6	303.9	302.9	321.9	320.4	−0.5
Physical sciences	1,117.7	1,198.8	1,147.2	1,353.9	1,467.7	1,519.8	3,143.5	2,692.7	2,805.4	4.2
Environmental sciences	734.3	756.3	899.3	886.3	904.0	1,075.0	1,034.8	941.7	1,039.6	10.4
Mathematics and computer sciences	329.6	389.7	433.9	477.6	678.9	714.1	738.7	951.1	995.8	4.7
Engineering	2,950.0	3,258.3	3,233.7	3,710.8	3,727.1	4,292.0	2,961.6	3,379.3	3,117.7	−7.7
Social sciences	339.0	396.4	484.0	566.0	549.8	480.8	463.3	538.9	533.6	−1.0
Other sciences	271.0	350.0	361.5	357.8	406.8	622.4	593.8	619.1	603.8	−2.5

**Table 364.—Summary of federal funds for research, development, and R & D plant:
Fiscal years 1988 to 1996—Continued**

[In millions]

Item	Actual							Estimates		
	1988	1989	1990	1991	1992	1993	1994	1995	1996	Percent change, 1995 to 1996
1	2	3	4	5	6	7	8	9	10	11
Development obligations	38,285.1	40,640.4	41,928.4	37,326.8	41,102.0	40,423.5	39,815.4	42,290.0	40,571.5	−4.1
Performers										
Federal intramural [1]	8,942.5	7,203.0	10,049.2	8,698.8	9,074.4	9,196.2	8,650.9	9,534.9	8,870.2	−7.0
Industrial firms	24,076.7	27,609.3	26,178.4	23,014.1	26,293.6	26,307.2	26,390.9	27,708.6	26,965.9	−2.7
FFRDCs [2] administered by industrial firms	1,456.1	1,440.2	1,694.9	1,443.7	1,417.4	655.5	556.3	487.9	576.2	18.1
Universities and colleges	804.8	878.8	1,000.5	1,301.0	1,210.6	1,312.0	1,505.2	1,446.1	1,245.1	−13.9
FFRDCs [2] administered by universities and colleges	1,909.1	1,793.6	1,658.3	1,442.9	1,503.7	1,318.9	1,111.8	1,267.1	1,251.8	−1.2
Other nonprofit institutions	382.8	479.5	587.4	711.5	753.9	770.6	834.8	955.1	784.1	−17.9
FFRDCs [2] administered by nonprofit institutions	422.7	412.4	484.0	508.5	605.7	580.0	557.6	603.3	618.7	2.6
State and local governments	39.0	46.3	87.5	85.8	74.8	108.5	94.7	140.5	144.7	3.0
Foreign	251.4	777.3	188.1	120.5	167.9	174.8	113.3	146.6	114.9	−21.7
R & D plant obligations	2,057.1	2,165.1	2,283.6	3,695.4	2,984.6	3,100.7	2,171.2	2,934.8	2,063.6	−29.7
Performers										
Federal intramural [1]	319.6	329.5	359.9	461.1	506.2	432.0	392.6	576.1	365.4	−36.6
Industrial firms	719.5	900.4	884.0	1,889.2	1,014.4	1,048.2	746.8	1,276.1	705.7	−44.7
FFRDCs [2] administered by industrial firms	204.3	212.3	231.0	279.6	202.2	124.4	119.4	104.0	92.9	−10.7
Universities and colleges	245.8	204.9	155.8	253.3	241.5	361.4	209.0	315.1	210.9	−33.1
FFRDCs [2] administered by universities and colleges	535.3	489.9	495.8	624.6	579.5	619.5	608.8	558.3	578.7	3.7
Other nonprofit institutions	23.7	14.2	121.3	154.6	393.9	415.6	20.9	32.3	23.4	−27.8
FFRDCs [2] administered by nonprofit institutions	6.2	8.4	31.4	19.7	46.3	65.5	72.9	71.3	85.1	19.4
State and local governments	0.3	1.4	0.5	0.6	0.5	0.5	0.8	1.6	1.6	0.3
Foreign	2.4	4.2	3.9	12.8	0.0	33.4	0.2	0.0	0.0	0.0

[1] Includes costs associated with the administration of intramural and extramural programs by federal personnel as well as actual intramural performance.

[2] Federally funded research and development centers.

[3] Percentage less than .05 percent.

NOTE.—Some data have been revised from previously published figures. Because of rounding, details may not add to totals.

SOURCE: National Science Foundation, *Federal Funds for Research and Development,* various years. (This table was prepared May 1996.)

Table 365.—Federal obligations to colleges and universities for research and development, by field: United States and outlying areas, 1980 to 1994

Field of science or engineering	1980	1981	1986	1988	1989	1990 [1]	1991 [1]	1992 [1]	1993 [1]	1994 [1]
1	2	3	4	5	6	7	8	9	10	11
Total, all fields	$4,160,543	$4,410,931	$6,456,743	$7,719,237	$8,523,190	$9,008,083	$10,031,058	$10,844,500	$10,923,070	$11,768,416
Engineering, total	612,456	792,223	998,312	1,129,303	1,157,047	474,709	543,530	587,404	683,676	702,397
Aeronautical	28,044	31,056	42,257	47,946	66,096	45,965	44,207	48,539	50,114	82,826
Astronautical	4,634	4,875	24,147	32,516	42,276	11,803	20,977	21,407	13,402	16,071
Chemical	22,210	27,667	50,379	67,647	45,829	56,845	67,968	63,900	67,234	58,293
Civil	48,130	58,300	35,402	30,947	43,026	37,306	34,064	30,756	44,252	55,969
Electrical	86,916	115,011	212,175	251,336	240,638	53,162	60,299	68,416	69,045	74,686
Mechanical	42,593	37,954	56,416	60,551	71,137	52,652	54,674	60,748	67,471	52,118
Metallurgy and materials	63,057	52,815	101,457	121,228	146,253	81,678	91,686	76,926	180,553	164,272
Engineering, other	316,872	464,545	476,079	517,132	501,792	135,298	169,655	216,712	191,605	198,162
All sciences, total	3,548,087	3,618,708	5,458,431	6,589,934	7,366,143	8,533,374	9,487,528	10,257,166	10,239,360	11,065,982
Physical sciences	507,884	500,657	770,254	859,764	979,037	890,444	1,022,807	1,134,579	1,022,880	1,135,704
Astronomy	52,736	54,835	78,435	89,791	103,271	98,804	115,212	149,417	139,579	214,549
Chemistry	170,048	165,189	255,593	281,573	299,417	272,929	295,576	325,224	321,105	324,213
Physics	249,661	250,342	379,289	426,005	505,723	453,538	518,840	544,200	511,036	539,758
Physical sciences, other	35,439	30,291	56,937	62,395	70,626	65,173	93,179	115,738	51,160	57,184
Mathematical sciences	53,987	53,668	96,405	119,217	134,998	109,587	125,893	140,544	131,875	76,793
Computer sciences	37,585	37,493	82,691	84,424	123,197	99,214	113,545	124,962	137,893	162,286
Environmental sciences	379,453	330,079	468,882	474,695	554,917	522,767	572,584	622,748	632,792	744,996
Atmospheric sciences	86,486	95,112	124,657	132,379	131,959	139,914	149,426	171,557	162,385	236,503
Geological sciences	109,523	101,207	118,401	131,913	152,449	147,517	173,492	172,185	181,384	186,542
Oceanography	92,079	91,863	121,855	129,473	163,035	117,636	94,448	107,897	103,472	116,229
Environmental sciences, other	91,365	41,897	103,969	80,930	107,474	117,700	155,218	171,109	185,551	205,722
Life sciences	2,137,751	2,290,587	3,463,114	4,349,268	4,730,663	4,773,434	5,319,947	5,629,395	5,566,756	6,310,555
Agricultural sciences	111,739	134,660	143,249	155,772	180,908	181,453	193,763	207,817	184,308	180,718
Biological sciences	1,085,602	1,192,756	1,849,516	2,345,433	2,558,987	2,578,470	2,820,183	2,950,701	2,931,726	3,191,832
Environmental biology	13,137	14,636	86,088	97,126	108,584	104,053	124,218	130,633	109,351	171,381
Medical sciences	885,898	904,963	1,325,157	1,689,606	1,829,888	1,853,979	2,102,127	2,252,375	2,253,419	2,689,314
Life sciences, other	41,375	43,572	59,104	61,331	52,296	55,479	79,656	87,869	87,952	77,310
Psychological sciences	86,459	87,734	138,338	186,924	209,344	225,987	258,886	254,311	277,667	318,832
Biological aspects	28,269	26,273	39,049	53,287	66,959	71,705	80,438	75,307	8,542	3,792
Social aspects	31,129	28,846	38,589	52,113	59,502	66,960	82,257	75,285	4,754	7,357
Psychological sciences, other	27,061	32,615	60,700	81,524	82,883	87,322	96,191	103,719	264,371	307,683
Social sciences	203,948	197,695	172,148	184,539	218,404	250,366	303,798	301,056	267,080	279,575
Anthropology	7,757	5,543	6,455	5,972	7,054	7,061	8,768	9,015	8,474	8,115
Economics	51,414	56,704	43,764	48,039	51,806	58,441	60,142	70,582	68,102	60,478
History	1,688	1,069	1,508	1,527	1,665	1,890	2,116	2,166	2,014	0
Linguistics	2,997	2,745	2,481	3,248	3,402	3,055	3,383	3,684	3,554	0
Political science	5,890	5,122	5,003	5,926	6,988	7,415	8,287	8,894	7,687	6,625
Sociology	34,903	38,136	34,580	55,204	75,404	96,240	113,829	104,430	35,666	30,602
Social sciences, other	99,299	88,376	78,357	64,623	72,085	76,264	107,273	102,285	141,583	173,755
Other sciences	141,020	120,795	266,599	331,103	415,583	1,661,575	1,770,068	2,049,571	2,202,417	2,037,241
Residual amounts	0	0	0	0	0	0	0	70	34	37

[1] All U.S. Department of Defense data are reported as other sciences.

NOTE.—Some data have been revised from previously published figures.

SOURCE: National Science Foundation, Science Resources Studies Division, unpublished data. (This table was prepared May 1996.)

Table 366.—U.S. Department of Agriculture obligations for child nutrition programs, by state or other area: Fiscal years 1994 and 1995

[In thousands]

State or other area	Total, fiscal year 1994	Fiscal year 1995								
		Total	Special milk	School lunch [1]	School breakfast	State administra-tive expenses	Commodities and cash in lieu of commodities [2]	Child and adult care	Summer food service	Nutrition education and training
1	2	3	4	5	6	7	8	9	10	11
Total	$7,768,161	$8,362,921	$20,649	$4,587,635	$1,181,816	$93,583	$742,844	$1,470,171	$255,954	$10,269
Alabama	154,926	161,661	38	93,076	20,206	1,847	16,216	25,433	4,685	158
Alaska	20,303	21,225	5	12,355	1,638	378	1,416	5,366	3	63
Arizona	132,265	141,671	178	75,771	19,695	1,556	10,866	29,649	3,818	138
Arkansas	95,127	97,920	33	52,863	15,846	1,295	9,604	15,177	3,009	93
California	940,962	996,563	852	582,713	144,465	10,819	70,499	167,757	18,294	1,164
Colorado	82,560	86,904	121	42,498	6,322	1,218	8,592	26,316	1,704	134
Connecticut	54,620	62,948	492	34,105	7,519	817	6,545	11,123	2,236	112
Delaware	21,625	22,619	44	9,494	2,473	397	1,980	7,677	491	63
District of Columbia	20,407	21,964	13	13,522	3,277	336	1,503	2,841	411	63
Florida	395,496	414,622	136	248,317	61,056	4,209	34,883	44,430	21,142	448
Georgia	255,972	273,973	39	159,372	46,522	2,611	26,848	29,777	8,541	262
Hawaii	31,603	33,551	8	19,551	4,334	447	3,763	4,769	617	63
Idaho	30,497	32,162	208	19,374	2,954	444	4,160	4,201	759	63
Illinois	277,206	299,757	2,649	174,230	25,996	3,265	26,430	52,901	13,846	440
Indiana	118,543	124,866	333	70,284	14,081	1,473	16,012	20,797	1,675	210
Iowa	71,155	74,481	186	40,081	6,025	961	10,958	15,394	769	107
Kansas	87,244	91,398	150	39,784	8,688	1,138	8,292	32,373	878	96
Kentucky	130,885	136,412	123	78,688	23,575	1,518	13,646	15,540	3,184	138
Louisiana	228,522	234,257	58	125,663	36,095	3,238	18,753	43,531	6,733	185
Maine	30,112	32,865	123	15,559	2,779	463	3,041	10,093	745	63
Maryland	106,453	116,514	405	60,253	12,331	1,429	9,976	28,970	2,978	173
Massachusetts	125,834	133,231	516	65,757	14,784	1,717	11,487	35,023	3,747	201
Michigan	188,997	211,255	1,020	112,462	23,102	2,294	19,456	48,407	4,158	355
Minnesota	144,829	150,547	1,074	58,146	9,585	2,266	13,696	63,267	2,338	176
Mississippi	144,657	150,102	10	86,811	24,977	1,809	11,791	20,857	3,734	114
Missouri	137,082	148,563	433	78,990	19,840	1,705	15,381	28,361	3,658	195
Montana	24,210	25,591	46	12,503	2,153	461	2,428	7,486	452	63
Nebraska	53,416	58,413	225	23,756	3,264	1,050	6,064	23,378	613	63
Nevada	25,524	27,796	120	16,207	4,174	370	2,800	3,161	902	63
New Hampshire	17,234	18,296	215	9,988	1,771	389	2,759	2,769	343	63
New Jersey	141,022	152,008	1,006	91,084	12,431	1,664	14,974	24,035	6,546	267
New Mexico	84,928	91,372	9	39,113	9,848	1,626	5,360	29,298	6,050	68
New York	554,838	583,279	1,211	333,558	74,425	5,711	47,082	83,858	36,793	640
North Carolina	211,594	225,646	134	122,353	35,497	2,526	22,470	38,400	4,028	239
North Dakota	24,897	25,104	66	9,487	1,272	507	2,442	10,914	354	63
Ohio	227,041	244,491	944	137,760	28,040	2,873	25,671	44,330	4,463	409
Oklahoma	113,223	118,610	98	63,039	17,090	1,578	10,875	23,851	1,954	126
Oregon	75,608	83,270	222	38,321	9,572	1,062	7,081	25,739	1,163	110
Pennsylvania	232,624	245,960	839	142,926	25,062	2,599	26,474	33,749	13,901	410
Rhode Island	18,055	19,677	125	11,567	1,500	317	1,777	2,980	1,348	63
South Carolina	136,709	144,621	33	81,758	25,505	1,462	12,346	16,564	6,817	137
South Dakota	26,002	28,021	46	14,323	2,590	455	3,120	6,449	976	63
Tennessee	150,313	160,606	30	90,748	24,633	1,782	16,481	22,635	4,113	185
Texas	725,389	742,563	99	427,322	117,379	8,298	61,671	109,606	17,433	755
Utah	70,972	73,008	73	32,495	3,930	1,068	7,401	26,031	1,915	93
Vermont	12,893	14,196	107	6,360	1,448	336	1,352	4,289	241	63
Virginia	137,872	151,544	221	86,354	20,955	1,091	17,356	22,138	3,209	219
Washington	127,421	135,961	263	68,856	15,631	1,695	12,402	34,379	2,543	192
West Virginia	56,802	60,502	41	33,055	11,704	747	5,254	8,238	1,401	63
Wisconsin	99,671	108,580	1,653	60,429	5,670	1,330	14,290	22,564	2,453	191
Wyoming	18,498	14,831	14	7,166	1,165	324	1,551	4,494	54	63
Administrative costs	0	6,755	0	0	0	0	6,755	0	0	0
Department of Defense dependents schools	5,933	5,942	0	4,561	0	0	1,382	0	0	0
Outlying areas										
American Samoa	63	63	0	0	0	0	0	0	0	63
Guam	4,097	4,483	0	2,578	803	213	587	302	0	0
Northern Marianas	63	72	0	0	0	0	72	0	0	0
Puerto Rico	161,239	159,370	0	112,121	26,957	1,514	10,961	3,585	4,092	140
Freely Associated States	0	0	0	0	0	0	0	0	0	0
Trust Territory	87	152	0	0	0	14	72	0	0	66
Virgin Islands	5,889	6,617	4	4,232	421	314	474	678	431	63
Undistributed [3]	196,154	353,492	3,558	133,897	138,760	561	15,265	44,241	17,211	-2

[1] Special Meal Assistance program is combined with "School Lunch" program.
[2] Commodities are based on preliminary food orders for fiscal year 1995.
[3] Undistributed amount reflects the difference between preliminary state earnings reports and federal obligations as of September 30, 1995.

NOTE.—Data are based on obligations as reported September 30, 1995. Negative amounts occur when program receipts exceed the obligations. Because of rounding, details may not add to totals.

SOURCE: U.S. Department of Agriculture, Food and Nutrition Service, Budget Division, unpublished data. (This table was prepared March 1996.)

Table 367.—U.S. Department of Health and Human Services allocations for Head Start and enrollment in Head Start, by state or other area: Fiscal years 1992, 1993, 1994, and 1995

State or other area	1992 Head Start allocations (in thousands)	1992 Head Start enrollment [1]	1993 Head Start allocations (in thousands)	1993 Head Start enrollment [2]	1994 Head Start allocations (in thousands)	1994 Head Start enrollment [3]	1995 Head Start allocations (in thousands)	1995 Head Start enrollment [4]
1	2	3	4	5	6	7	8	9
Total	$2,120,862	621,078	$2,683,158	713,943	$3,215,946	740,493	$3,402,946	750,696
Alabama	40,021	13,012	46,937	14,106	54,282	14,525	57,542	14,552
Alaska	4,434	1,067	5,316	1,143	6,295	1,209	6,534	1,209
Arizona	20,729	6,179	35,503	9,189	44,416	9,846	47,208	10,029
Arkansas	22,297	8,213	26,337	8,792	30,719	9,065	32,681	9,244
California	219,423	52,658	305,180	67,684	371,227	70,995	392,331	72,650
Colorado	19,353	6,604	25,505	7,672	31,787	8,118	35,757	8,576
Connecticut	18,694	5,311	22,066	5,561	26,061	5,660	27,022	5,625
Delaware	4,454	1,333	5,265	1,455	5,815	1,455	6,027	1,574
District of Columbia	9,673	2,639	11,631	2,841	12,854	2,841	14,329	2,913
Florida	67,552	20,567	92,741	25,333	118,976	27,398	125,508	27,623
Georgia	52,225	16,080	66,499	18,594	81,974	19,445	85,792	19,523
Hawaii	7,547	1,974	8,882	2,183	9,939	2,260	10,312	2,226
Idaho	6,745	1,658	8,329	1,850	9,574	1,912	10,009	1,841
Illinois	99,852	28,802	117,770	30,268	139,137	30,537	148,120	31,579
Indiana	31,054	10,213	37,979	11,107	46,558	11,730	48,871	11,739
Iowa	16,484	5,266	20,111	5,758	23,430	5,946	25,539	6,199
Kansas	14,175	4,705	17,885	5,389	22,095	5,793	24,772	6,158
Kentucky	38,053	12,467	45,318	13,791	54,364	14,071	58,383	14,267
Louisiana	48,205	15,804	62,996	18,677	75,876	19,344	78,691	19,344
Maine	9,476	3,132	11,011	3,361	12,610	3,439	13,118	3,439
Maryland	27,043	7,594	32,073	8,338	38,810	8,509	42,023	8,874
Massachusetts	42,348	10,159	49,615	10,929	57,264	10,794	61,129	10,990
Michigan	82,321	26,174	107,451	29,960	126,686	30,701	132,990	30,936
Minnesota	24,373	7,136	30,823	8,167	36,930	8,576	38,281	8,576
Mississippi	71,861	22,343	83,560	24,036	92,012	24,110	95,493	24,150
Missouri	35,641	11,972	45,641	13,592	55,979	14,063	58,752	14,064
Montana	6,436	1,961	8,211	2,226	9,563	2,304	9,772	2,304
Nebraska	10,284	3,154	12,322	3,465	14,342	3,644	15,456	3,764
Nevada	4,000	1,073	6,341	1,593	8,017	1,793	8,315	1,793
New Hampshire	4,080	1,016	4,895	1,131	5,699	1,156	6,379	1,232
New Jersey	54,532	11,688	63,902	12,773	71,189	12,898	74,610	13,016
New Mexico	13,655	4,958	18,954	6,055	24,241	6,397	27,269	6,821
New York	153,858	34,688	181,968	37,829	215,678	39,062	226,840	39,491
North Carolina	44,259	14,083	54,263	15,296	66,643	15,695	71,603	16,161
North Dakota	4,283	1,458	5,666	1,653	6,723	1,738	6,966	1,738
Ohio	84,964	29,132	110,420	32,567	133,913	33,919	139,497	34,215
Oklahoma	24,078	8,977	32,274	10,625	39,073	11,165	40,705	11,165
Oregon	17,760	3,885	21,782	4,431	27,080	4,638	29,086	4,698
Pennsylvania	82,449	22,414	99,688	24,866	119,354	25,672	126,251	26,149
Rhode Island	6,964	2,293	8,328	2,380	10,060	2,476	10,453	2,434
South Carolina	27,716	9,025	33,063	9,709	40,772	10,142	44,021	10,415
South Dakota	5,421	1,691	6,629	1,894	7,985	2,025	8,258	2,025
Tennessee	39,271	12,481	47,993	13,859	58,610	14,380	61,630	14,213
Texas	113,612	36,394	172,536	49,110	213,394	51,521	223,309	51,925
Utah	10,669	3,403	13,208	3,822	15,832	4,028	18,145	4,334
Vermont	4,556	1,129	5,339	1,260	5,957	1,271	7,636	1,486
Virginia	33,134	9,455	39,440	10,650	46,411	10,993	48,896	11,147
Washington	27,533	6,361	37,558	7,799	45,968	8,260	53,385	8,803
West Virginia	18,959	5,842	22,303	6,317	26,014	6,402	27,626	6,522
Wisconsin	31,052	9,665	40,956	11,247	49,461	11,953	52,633	12,171
Wyoming	3,371	1,128	4,149	1,245	4,925	1,323	5,099	1,313
Migrant programs	[5] 153,755	[5] 44,770	108,011	33,886	130,409	35,063	138,802	35,243
American Indian/Alaskan Native programs	—	—	74,800	17,973	90,793	18,738	95,130	18,821
Special projects	—	—	—	—	76	—	—	—
Outlying areas								
Puerto Rico	95,629	29,031	113,047	31,306	127,066	32,145	132,423	32,118
Pacific Territories	6,253	5,439	7,613	5,779	9,019	5,849	9,309	5,849
Virgin Islands	4,294	1,422	5,074	1,421	6,009	1,501	6,228	1,430

[1] The distribution of enrollment by age was: 7 percent were 5 years old and over; 63 percent were 4-year-olds; 27 percent were 3-year-olds; and 3 percent were under 3 years of age. Handicapped children accounted for 13.4 percent in Head Start programs. The racial/ethnic composition was: American Indian/Alaskan Native, 4 percent; Hispanic, 23 percent; black, 37 percent; white, 33 percent; and Asian, 3 percent.

[2] The distribution of enrollment by age was: 6 percent were 5 years old and over; 64 percent were 4-year-olds; 27 percent were 3-year-olds; and 3 percent were under 3 years of age. Handicapped children accounted for 13.2 percent in Head Start programs. The racial/ethnic composition was: American Indian/Alaskan Native, 4 percent; Hispanic, 24 percent; black, 36 percent; white, 33 percent; and Asian, 3 percent.

[3] The distribution of enrollment by age was: 6 percent were 5 years old and over; 64 percent were 4-year-olds; 27 percent were 3-year-olds; and 3 percent were under 3 years of age. Handicapped children accounted for 13.0 percent in Head Start programs.

The racial/ethnic composition was: American Indian/Alaskan Native, 4 percent; Hispanic, 24 percent; black, 36 percent; white, 33 percent; and Asian, 3 percent.

[4] The distribution of enrollment by age was: 7 percent were 5 years old and over; 61 percent were 4-year-olds; 28 percent were 3-year-olds; and 4 percent were under 3 years of age. Handicapped children accounted for 13.1 percent in Head Start programs. The racial/ethnic composition was: American Indian/Alaskan Native, 4 percent; Hispanic, 25 percent; black, 36 percent; white, 33 percent; and Asian, 3 percent.

[5] Includes American Indian/Alaskan Native and Migrant programs.

—Not applicable.

NOTE.—Because of rounding, details may not add to totals.

SOURCE: U.S. Department of Health and Human Services, Office of Human Development Services. (This table was prepared May 1996.)

Table 368.—Public school students receiving federally funded free or reduced price lunches, by selected school characteristics: School year 1993–94

School characterisics	Percent of students participating in program			
	Total	Elementary	Secondary	Combined [1]
1	2	3	4	5
Total	**33.2**	**38.8**	**22.0**	**39.1**
Community type				
Central city	44.9	52.1	29.0	52.2
Urban fringe/large town	24.0	28.6	15.4	24.0
Rural/small town	32.2	36.6	22.9	40.1
School size (students)				
Less than 150	38.6	38.4	35.8	50.3
150–299	38.1	39.5	28.4	51.8
300–499	37.0	38.8	26.2	37.3
500–749	33.5	36.0	22.3	34.7
750 or more	29.7	42.5	20.6	34.3
Minority students				
Less than 5%	22.0	22.4	17.0	28.6
5 to 19%	18.9	22.2	11.7	30.8
20 to 49%	32.0	38.1	20.1	38.5
50% or more	57.3	65.5	38.9	60.6

[1] Includes schools beginning with grade 6 or below and ending with grade 9 or above.

NOTE.—Some data have been revised from previously published figures.

SOURCE: U.S. Department of Education, National Center for Education Statistics, "Schools and Staffing Survey, 1993–94." (This table was prepared September 1996.)

Table 369.—Public and private school students receiving federally funded Chapter 1 [1] services, by selected school characteristics: School year 1993–94

School characteristics	Percent of students participating in program								
	All schools	Public				Private			
		Total	Elementary	Secondary	Combined [2]	Total	Elementary	Secondary	Combined [2]
1	2	3	4	5	6	7	8	9	10
Total	**13.1**	**14.3**	**18.5**	**6.1**	**13.6**	**3.3**	**4.6**	**1.9**	**1.4**
Community type									
Central city	17.0	19.4	24.2	9.2	14.3	4.4	6.7	2.5	0.8
Urban fringe/large town	9.3	10.2	13.2	4.7	8.3	2.2	2.7	0.9	1.9
Rural/small town	13.2	13.9	18.4	5.2	15.0	2.7	3.5	2.5	1.8
School size (students)									
Less than 150	9.8	16.7	20.0	11.1	15.7	3.8	3.3	8.1	3.8
150–299	13.1	16.7	19.2	7.6	11.6	5.1	6.2	4.1	1.4
300–499	14.7	16.3	18.0	7.0	13.0	2.6	3.7	0.9	0.8
500–749	14.7	15.5	17.6	6.0	18.3	2.0	3.8	1.1	0.3
750 or more	11.3	11.7	20.1	5.8	11.4	1.3	4.5	0.8	0.4
Minority students									
Less than 5%	7.8	8.8	11.7	3.7	9.7	1.7	2.4	0.6	0.8
5 to 19%	6.0	6.6	8.6	2.3	14.3	2.1	3.0	1.6	0.9
20 to 49%	10.2	10.8	14.6	3.3	13.6	2.7	2.7	3.7	1.7
50% or more	27.8	29.0	35.8	14.9	18.0	10.0	12.4	2.5	5.2

[1] Chapter 1 was reauthorized under the Improving America's Schools Act (IASA) of 1994 and is now called Title I.

[2] Includes schools beginning with grade 6 or below and ending with grade 9 or above.

NOTE.—Some data have been revised from previously published figures.

SOURCE: U.S. Department of Education, National Center for Education Statistics, "Schools and Staffing Survey, 1993–94." (This table was prepared September 1996.)

CHAPTER 5
Outcomes of Education

This chapter contains tables comparing educational attainment and work force characteristics. The data show labor force participation and income levels of high school dropouts and high school and college graduates. Population characteristics are provided for many of the measures to help evaluate disparities among various demographic groups. The first set of tables contains data from the Bureau of the Census on educational attainment and income of the labor force, and data from the Bureau of Labor Statistics on employment and unemployment. These tables provide information on the educational attainment of the labor force, by occupation, sex, and race/ethnicity; income, by level of education attained; and unemployment rates, by levels of education attained, sex, and race/ethnicity.

The second group of tables was compiled from Bureau of Labor Statistics data on high school dropouts and graduates. These data show the labor force participation and college enrollment of high school students within the year after they leave school. The tabulations also provide comparative labor force participation and unemployment rates for graduates and dropouts. Additional information on college enrollment rates by race/ethnicity and sex have been included to help form a more complete picture of high school outcomes.

The third set of tables has been prepared from the National Center for Education Statistics survey, Recent College Graduates, and from a Bureau of the Census survey on earnings and education. These tables provide data on employment outcomes for high school and college graduates. A table provides a salary comparison by field of college degree for the entire population. Trends in salaries received by college graduates also are featured in this section.

Statistics on educational attainment of the entire population are in Chapter 1. More detailed data on the number of high school and college graduates are contained in Chapters 2 and 3. Chapter 3 contains trend data on the proportion of high school graduates going to college. Additional data on the income of persons by educational attainment may be obtained from the Bureau of the Census in the *Current Population Reports,* Series P–60. The Bureau of Labor Statistics has a series of publications dealing with the educational characteristics of the labor force. Further information on survey methodologies is in the "Guide to Sources" in the appendix and in the publications cited in the source notes.

Opinions

One life goal consistently rated "very important" by young men and women was "being successful in work." A survey of 1992 high school seniors found that 89 percent of the men and 90 percent of the women rated "being successful in work" as a "very important goal." Two of the other most highly rated goals in the 1992 survey were "finding steady work" ("very important" for 87 percent of men and 89 percent of women) and "having strong friendships" ("very important" for 80 percent of both men and women). Two years later in 1994, these values continued to be highly rated by the former high school seniors. Another value that was highly rated two years after high school was "Providing better opportunities for my children" which was cited by 91 percent of the seniors as "very important." (table 371).

Labor Force

Adults with higher levels of education were more likely to participate in the labor force than those with less education. About 81 percent of adults with a bachelor's degree participated in the labor force in 1995 compared with 65 percent of persons who were high school graduates. Only 40 percent of those 25 and older who were not high school graduates were in the labor force. The labor force participation rates for blacks, age 25 and older with higher education levels were higher than the average for all people with similar levels of education. However, the labor force participation rates for blacks under age 25 were lower than the average of persons with similar education backgrounds (table 372).

Persons with lower levels of educational attainment were more likely to be unemployed than those who had higher levels of educational attainment. The 1995 unemployment rate for adults (25 years old and over) who had not completed high school was 9.0 percent compared with 4.8 percent for those with 4 years of high school and 2.4 percent for those with a bachelor's degree or higher. Young people tended to have higher unemployment rates than persons 25 and over, even after allowing for level of educational attainment (table 374).

One year after graduating from college in 1989–90, 84 percent of those receiving bachelor's degrees were employed (74 percent full time and 10 percent part time), 4 percent were unemployed, and 12 percent were not in the labor force (tables 380 and 381). Of the 12 percent of 1989–90 graduates not in the labor force, about two-thirds enrolled in further education (table 381).

Income

Between 1989 and 1994, median annual income of male full-time workers, when adjusted for inflation, decreased generally. However, there was no significant change for women overall, and there was an slight increase in the median income for women with a bachelor's degree or higher level of education. Income of men who were year-round full-time workers with 4 or more years of college dropped by 2 percent compared with a 12 percent drop for men with 1 to 3 years of high school. Income for men who had completed 4 years of high school also dropped by 12 percent (table 375).

Women's incomes are much lower than men's incomes, even after adjusting for level of education. The average 1994 incomes for full-time year-round workers with a bachelor's degree were $43,663 for men and $31,741 for women.

Dropouts and Graduates

The difficulties in entering the job market for dropouts, and youth in general, are highlighted by comparing their labor force and unemployment status. Only 68 percent of 1994–95 dropouts were in the labor force (employed or looking for work), and 30 percent of them were unemployed. Of the 1995 high school graduates who were not in college, 80 percent were in the labor force, and 21 percent of those in the labor force were unemployed (tables 377 and 378).

About 61 percent of the college graduates of the class of 1989–90 had jobs in professional, managerial, and technical areas in 1991. Twenty-three percent were employed in nonprofessional, nonmanagerial, and nontechnical areas (table 381).

A 1992 assessment of literacy skills for adults found that about 22 percent of the adult population lacked the ability to perform simple arithmetic operations, and 21 percent could not locate a simple piece of information in a short text excerpt. Only about one-fifth of the population could solve mathematical problems requiring 2 or more steps or integrate information from complex passages (table 385).

Figure 23.-Unemployment rates of persons 25 years old and over, by highest level of education attained: 1995

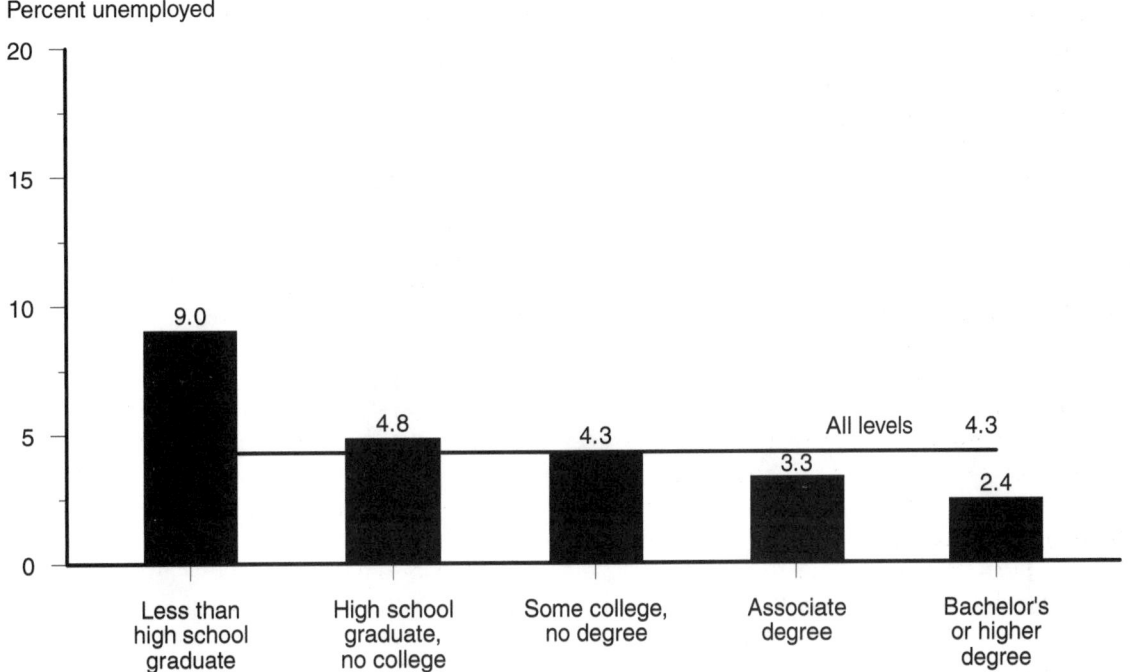

Percent unemployed

SOURCE: U.S. Department of Labor, Bureau of Labor Statistics, Office of Employment and Unemployment Statistics, unpublished data.

Figure 24.-Labor force status of 1994–95 high school graduates and dropouts: October 1995

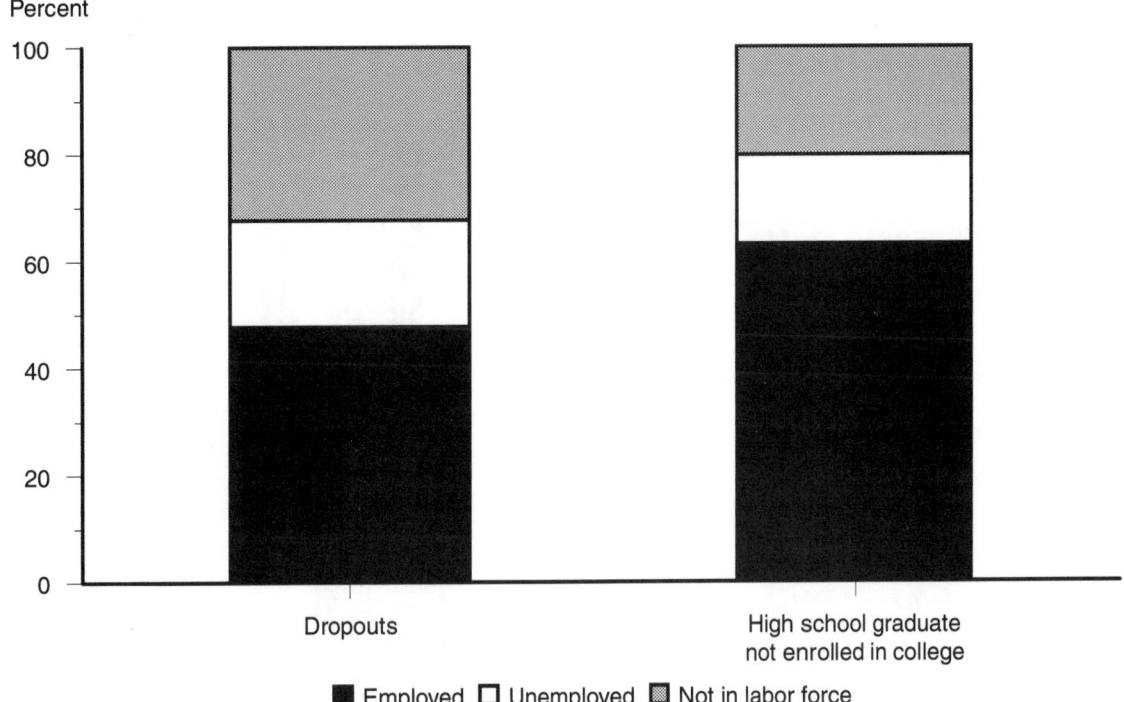

Percent

■ Employed □ Unemployed ▨ Not in labor force

SOURCE: U.S. Department of Labor, Bureau of Labor Statistics, "Employment Status of School Age Youth, High School Graduates and Dropouts, 1995."

Figure 25.-Median annual earnings of workers 25 years old and over, by highest degree attained and sex: 1994

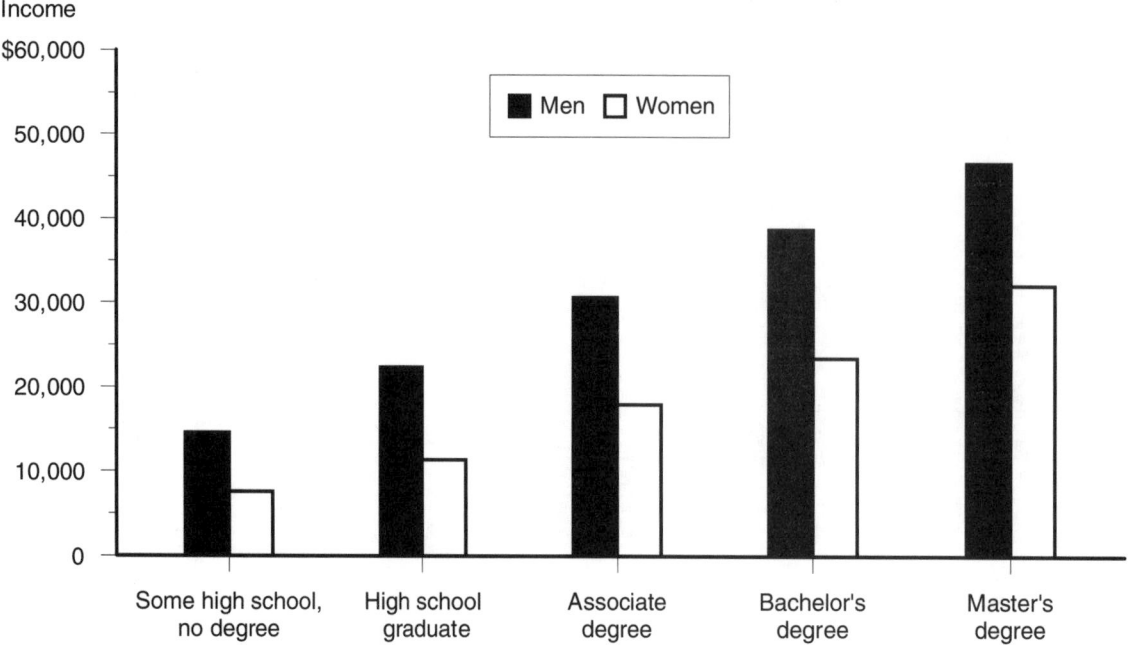

SOURCE: U.S. Department of Commerce, Bureau of the Census, *Current Population Reports*, Series P-60, *Monthly Income of Households, Families, and Persons in the United States: 1994.*

Figure 26.-Salaries of recent bachelor's degree recipients 1 year after graduation, by field: 1987 and 1991

[In constant 1991 dollars]

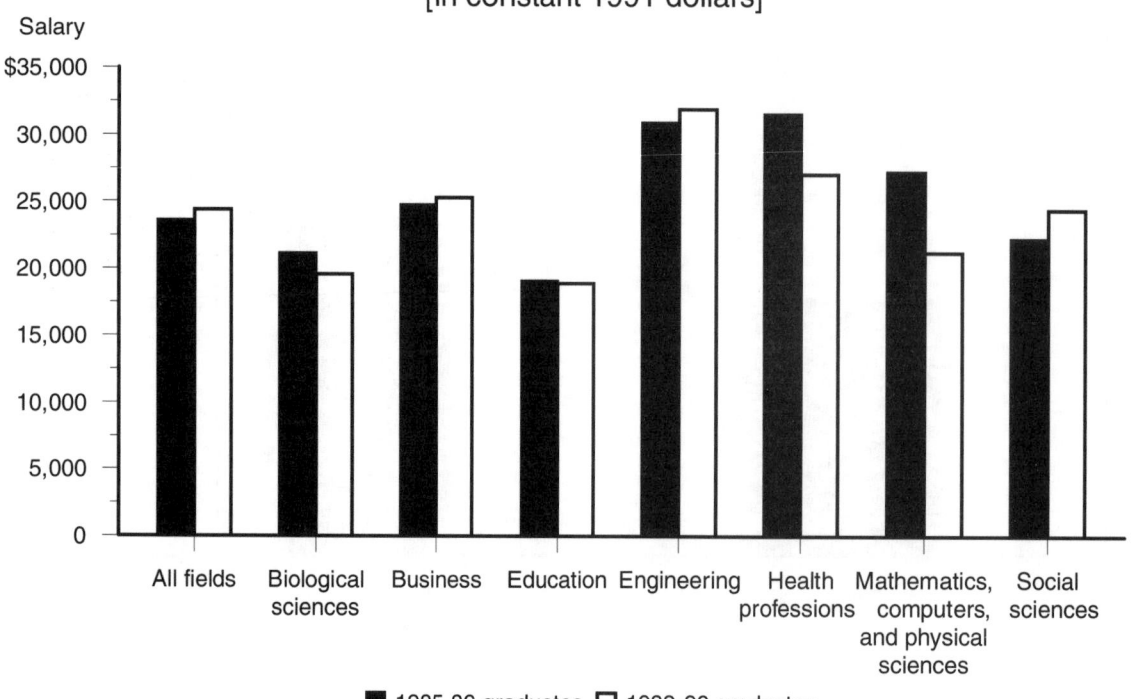

SOURCE: U.S. Department of Education, National Center for Education Statistics, "Recent College Graduates" surveys, 1987 and 1991.

Table 370.—Percent of 18- to 25-year-olds reporting drug use during the past 30 days and the past year: 1972 to 1994

Drug	1972	1974	1976	1977	1979	1982	1985	1988	1990	1991	1992	1993	1994 [1]
1	2	3	4	5	6	7	8	9	10	11	12	13	14
Percent reporting drug use during past 30 days													
Any illicit use	—	—	—	—	37.1	30.4	25.1	17.8	14.9	15.4	13.0	13.5	13.3
Marijuana	27.8	25.2	25.0	27.4	35.4	27.4	21.9	15.5	12.7	13.0	11.0	11.1	12.1
Hallucinogens	—	2.5	1.1	2.0	4.4	1.7	1.8	1.9	0.8	1.2	1.3	1.3	1.8
Cocaine	—	3.1	2.0	3.7	9.3	6.8	7.5	4.5	2.2	2.0	1.8	1.5	1.2
Heroin	—	—	—	—	—	—	0.3	0.1	0.1	0.1	0.2	0.1	—
Nonmedical use of:													
Stimulants	—	3.7	4.7	2.5	3.5	4.7	3.8	2.4	1.2	0.8	0.7	0.9	0.5
Sedatives	—	1.6	2.3	2.8	2.8	2.6	1.6	0.9	0.7	0.7	0.6	0.6	0.1
Tranquilizers	—	1.2	2.6	2.4	2.1	1.6	1.6	1.0	0.5	0.6	0.6	0.6	0.4
Analgesics	—	—	—	—	1.0	1.0	2.0	1.5	1.2	1.4	1.2	1.4	1.2
Alcohol	—	69.3	69.0	70.0	75.9	70.9	70.7	65.3	63.3	63.6	59.2	59.3	63.1
Cigarettes	—	48.8	49.4	47.3	42.6	39.5	36.6	35.2	31.5	32.2	31.9	29.0	34.6
Percent reporting drug use during past year													
Any illicit use	—	—	—	—	49.4	43.4	41.0	31.9	28.7	29.1	26.4	26.6	24.6
Marijuana	—	34.2	35.0	38.7	46.9	40.4	36.3	27.9	24.6	24.5	22.7	22.9	21.8
Hallucinogens	—	6.1	6.0	6.4	9.9	6.9	4.0	5.6	3.9	4.7	4.8	4.9	5.1
Cocaine	—	8.1	7.0	10.2	19.6	18.8	15.6	12.1	7.5	7.7	6.3	5.0	3.6
Heroin	—	0.8	0.6	1.2	0.8	—	0.6	0.3	0.5	0.3	0.5	0.3	0.1
Nonmedical use of:													
Stimulants	—	8.0	8.8	10.4	10.1	10.8	9.8	6.4	3.4	3.3	2.3	3.0	1.3
Sedatives	—	4.2	5.7	8.2	7.3	8.7	5.1	3.3	2.0	1.9	1.7	1.1	0.6
Tranquilizers	—	4.6	6.2	7.8	7.1	5.9	6.4	4.6	2.4	2.6	3.0	2.0	1.9
Analgesics	—	—	—	—	5.2	4.4	6.8	5.5	4.1	5.3	4.8	4.1	3.5
Alcohol	—	77.1	77.9	79.8	86.6	87.1	86.4	81.7	80.2	82.8	77.7	79.0	78.5
Cigarettes	—	—	—	—	46.7	47.2	43.9	44.7	39.7	41.2	41.1	38.3	41.1

[1] Due to changes in the survey instrument and administration, 1994 estimates are not comparable to previous years.

—Data not available or low precision; no estimate reported.

SOURCE: U.S. Department of Health and Human Services, Substance Abuse and Mental Health Services Administration, "National Household Survey on Drug Abuse: Population Estimates 1994," 1995. (This table was prepared April 1996.)

Table 371.—Percent of 1972, 1982, and 1992 high school seniors who felt that certain life values were "very important," by sex: 1972 to 1994

	Percent of 1972 seniors						Percent of 1982 seniors						Percent of 1992 seniors				
	1972		1974 (2 years after high school)		1976 (4 years after high school)		1982		1984 (2 years after high school)		1986 (4 years after high school)		1992		1994 (2 years after high school)		
Value	Male	Female	Male	Female	Male	Female	Male	Female	Male	Female	Male	Female	Male	Female	Total	Male	Female
1	2	3	4	5	6	7	8	9	10	11	12	13	14	15	16	17	18
Being successful in work	86.5	83.0	81.2	74.9	80.3	69.7	88.2	85.5	88.7	84.2	84.0	77.2	89.0	89.6	90.1	89.9	90.3
Finding steady work	82.3	73.7	74.7	59.9	79.3	62.1	88.0	84.4	87.4	83.3	84.2	76.3	87.1	88.6	89.7	88.7	90.7
Having lots of money	26.0	9.8	17.8	9.1	17.7	9.4	41.3	24.1	35.8	20.9	27.8	16.9	45.3	29.4	35.2	39.5	30.9
Being a leader in the community	14.9	8.0	8.5	4.4	9.2	4.2	11.3	5.9	13.7	6.4	9.5	4.5	—	—	—	—	—
Correcting inequalities	22.5	31.1	16.6	18.2	16.2	17.1	11.8	11.7	13.3	13.9	10.7	10.9	17.0	23.6	—	—	—
Having children	—	—	—	—	—	—	37.0	47.0	42.7	56.3	41.4	56.2	39.0	49.2	—	—	—
Having a happy family life	78.6	85.7	83.1	86.7	84.2	86.4	81.6	86.3	86.1	90.2	86.8	87.8	—	—	—	—	—
Providing better opportunities for my children	66.6	66.2	59.5	61.6	59.8	58.8	71.0	68.7	72.1	69.9	68.4	67.4	74.5	76.5	90.5	90.3	90.8
Living closer to parents or relatives	6.8	8.2	8.3	12.4	7.7	11.9	15.0	15.7	15.6	20.1	12.9	19.8	15.2	18.7	—	—	—
Moving from area	14.3	14.6	8.3	7.4	6.7	6.4	14.4	12.8	10.5	9.1	9.0	7.4	20.7	20.1	—	—	—
Having strong friendships	81.2	78.7	76.5	74.7	76.1	72.1	80.4	79.1	80.1	79.7	76.5	75.0	79.8	80.0	87.6	88.1	87.0
Having leisure time	—	—	60.9	55.1	65.4	60.1	70.2	68.8	74.5	72.0	70.1	68.9	65.3	62.0	—	—	—

—Question not asked.

SOURCE: U.S. Department of Education, National Center for Education Statistics, "National Longitudinal Study," "High School and Beyond" surveys, and "National Education Longitudinal Study," second and third followup surveys. (This table was prepared June 1995.)

Table 372.—Labor force participation of persons 16 years old and over, by age, sex, race/ethnicity, and highest level of education: 1995

Age, sex, and race/ethnicity	Labor force participation rate [1]						Employment/population ratio [2]					
	Total	Less than high school graduate [3]	High school graduate	College			Total	Less than high school graduate [3]	High school graduate	College		
				Some college, no degree	Associate degree	Bachelor's degree or higher				Some college, no degree	Associate degree	Bachelor's degree or higher
1	2	3	4	5	6	7	8	9	10	11	12	13
16 to 19 years old [4]	53.5	46.8	70.3	63.8	71.4	57.8	44.2	37.1	60.0	58.4	63.4	54.1
Men	54.8	48.6	73.9	62.7	63.4	52.2	44.7	38.1	62.6	56.9	47.1	46.0
Women	52.2	44.9	66.9	64.6	74.9	66.8	43.8	35.9	57.4	59.6	70.6	66.9
White [5]	57.1	50.6	72.5	66.3	77.8	49.2	48.8	41.7	63.9	61.5	71.2	49.2
Black [5]	39.9	33.5	62.3	49.4	40.3	43.9	25.7	20.0	42.5	40.2	13.6	44.2
Hispanic [6]	45.4	38.8	65.5	61.0	99.1	66.5	34.4	27.8	53.3	52.4	83.6	53.7
20 to 24 years old [4]	76.6	62.9	81.2	74.1	85.5	85.5	69.7	51.2	72.4	69.4	81.1	80.8
Men	83.1	81.1	90.0	76.1	86.7	86.3	75.4	68.2	80.6	71.3	82.7	80.6
Women	70.3	42.3	71.2	72.2	84.5	85.1	64.0	32.0	63.0	67.6	79.8	81.0
White [5]	78.7	66.0	83.0	75.8	86.5	87.1	72.7	55.6	75.3	71.8	82.4	82.6
Black [5]	68.7	49.5	74.3	69.0	81.3	81.4	56.5	31.8	60.0	60.5	74.5	74.3
Hispanic [6]	71.9	65.7	75.9	74.1	82.2	80.8	63.7	56.6	66.5	67.2	79.7	74.5
25 and older	66.7	39.9	65.4	72.6	79.2	81.0	63.8	36.4	62.3	69.5	76.6	79.0
Men	76.0	52.1	76.5	80.2	87.2	85.8	72.7	47.5	72.9	77.0	84.3	83.9
Women	58.3	29.2	56.4	65.8	73.2	75.4	55.7	26.6	53.7	62.8	70.8	73.3
White [5]	66.7	40.0	64.8	71.7	78.8	80.6	64.1	36.7	62.1	69.0	76.3	78.7
Black [5]	66.0	36.2	69.7	78.4	83.8	85.6	61.1	31.7	64.0	72.5	80.0	82.8
Hispanic [6]	67.5	55.3	74.3	79.0	81.5	83.1	62.4	49.5	69.2	74.2	77.1	80.2

[1] Percent of the civilian population who are employed or seeking employment.
[2] Number of persons employed as a percent of civilian population.
[3] Includes persons reporting no school years completed.
[4] Excludes persons enrolled in school.
[5] Includes persons of Hispanic origin.
[6] Hispanics may be of any race.

SOURCE: U.S. Department of Labor, Bureau of Labor Statistics, Office of Employment and Unemployment Statistics, Industry and Occupation tables, unpublished data. (This table was prepared April 1996.)

Table 373.—Occupation of employed persons 25 years old and over, by educational attainment and sex: 1995

Sex and occupation	Total employed, in thousands	Percentage distribution, by years of school completed							
		Total	Less than one year of high school	High school		College			
				1–4 years of high school, no diploma	High school graduate	Some college, no degree	Associate degree	Bachelor's degree	More than a bachelor's degree
1	2	3	4	5	6	7	8	9	10
All persons									
All occupational groups	106,037	100.0	3.7	6.7	33.0	19.3	8.7	18.8	9.9
Managerial and professional specialty	33,317	100.0	0.4	1.4	13.0	14.2	8.7	35.6	26.8
Executive, administrative, and managerial	16,345	100.0	0.7	2.1	20.6	20.3	8.4	33.1	14.8
Professional specialty occupations	16,971	100.0	0.2	0.6	5.6	8.2	9.1	37.9	38.4
Teachers, except college and university	4,148	100.0	0.1	0.6	5.0	6.2	3.1	47.9	37.2
Teachers, college and university	774	100.0	0.0	0.0	1.3	1.9	1.9	14.7	80.2
Technical, sales, and administrative support	30,772	100.0	0.8	3.5	36.0	26.5	11.3	18.3	3.6
Technicians and related support	3,472	100.0	0.2	1.2	19.7	25.3	23.8	24.1	5.6
Sales occupations	11,758	100.0	1.4	5.0	33.3	23.4	7.9	24.0	5.0
Administrative support, including clerical	15,543	100.0	0.6	2.9	41.6	29.0	11.0	12.7	2.1
Service occupations	12,421	100.0	7.9	12.8	43.2	20.1	7.5	7.1	1.3
Precision production, craft, and repair	12,094	100.0	5.0	11.0	47.8	20.3	9.0	5.8	1.1
Operators, fabricators, and laborers	14,483	100.0	9.3	15.6	50.4	15.4	4.8	4.0	0.6
Farming, forestry, and fishing	2,949	100.0	18.9	11.8	39.1	13.7	5.2	9.4	1.8
Men									
All occupational groups	57,420	100.0	4.5	7.2	32.1	18.6	7.7	19.1	10.9
Managerial and professional specialty	17,510	100.0	0.6	1.4	11.6	14.0	6.6	35.7	30.1
Executive, administrative, and managerial	9,439	100.0	0.9	2.2	17.5	18.6	7.3	36.3	17.2
Professional specialty occupations	8,072	100.0	0.2	0.5	4.8	8.5	5.9	35.0	45.1
Teachers, except college and university	1,049	100.0	0.2	0.2	4.1	6.0	3.1	44.1	42.1
Teachers, college and university	431	100.0	0.0	0.0	0.9	2.1	1.2	11.1	84.7
Technical, sales, and administrative support	11,118	100.0	1.2	3.2	27.3	25.3	10.2	26.6	6.3
Technicians and related support	1,686	100.0	0.1	1.5	17.6	26.0	20.0	27.3	7.3
Sales occupations	6,398	100.0	1.4	3.4	26.7	23.9	7.8	30.0	6.8
Administrative support, including clerical	3,034	100.0	1.3	3.8	34.1	27.9	9.6	18.9	4.5
Service occupations	4,723	100.0	8.1	9.3	39.0	23.1	8.6	10.0	1.9
Precision production, craft, and repair	11,014	100.0	4.9	11.0	47.8	20.4	9.3	5.7	1.0
Operators, fabricators, and laborers	10,741	100.0	8.7	14.7	49.9	16.4	5.2	4.3	0.7
Farming, forestry, and fishing	2,314	100.0	20.4	12.5	38.3	13.2	4.8	9.1	1.6
Women									
All occupational groups	48,617	100.0	2.7	6.0	34.1	20.1	10.0	18.4	8.7
Managerial and professional specialty	15,806	100.0	0.2	1.3	14.5	14.4	11.1	35.4	23.2
Executive, administrative, and managerial	6,906	100.0	0.4	2.0	24.9	22.6	9.9	28.8	11.4
Professional specialty occupations	8,900	100.0	0.1	0.7	6.3	8.0	12.0	40.5	32.4
Teachers, except college and university	3,099	100.0	0.1	0.7	5.3	6.3	3.1	49.1	35.5
Teachers, college and university	343	100.0	0.0	0.0	1.7	1.7	2.9	19.2	74.6
Technical, sales, and administrative support	19,654	100.0	0.6	3.7	40.9	27.1	11.9	13.6	2.1
Technicians and related support	1,786	100.0	0.3	0.9	21.7	24.6	27.4	21.0	4.1
Sales occupations	5,360	100.0	1.3	6.8	41.3	22.9	8.0	16.8	2.9
Administrative support, including clerical	12,509	100.0	0.4	2.7	43.5	29.3	11.4	11.2	1.6
Service occupations	7,698	100.0	7.8	15.0	45.8	18.3	6.8	5.3	1.0
Precision production, craft, and repair	1,080	100.0	5.9	11.9	48.2	19.1	6.5	6.9	1.5
Operators, fabricators, and laborers	3,742	100.0	10.9	17.9	51.7	12.5	3.4	3.2	0.5
Farming, forestry, and fishing	636	100.0	13.4	9.1	42.1	15.7	6.8	10.4	2.7

NOTE.—Because of rounding, details may not add to totals.

SOURCE: U.S. Department of Labor, Bureau of Labor Statistics, Office of Employment and Unemployment Statistics, Industry and Occupation tables, unpublished data. (This table was prepared April 1996.)

Table 374.—Unemployment rate of persons 16 years old and over, by age, sex, race/ethnicity, and highest degree attained: 1992, 1994, and 1995

Sex, race/ethnicity, and highest degree attained	Percent unemployed, 1992 [1]				Percent unemployed, 1994 [1]				Percent unemployed, 1995 [1]			
	16- to 24-year-olds [2]			25 years old and over	16- to 24-years-old [2]			25 years old and over	16- to 24-years-old [2]			25 years old and over
	Total	16 to 19 years	20 to 24 years		Total	16 to 19 years	20 to 24 years		Total	16 to 19 years	20 to 24 years	
1	2	3	4	5	6	7	8	9	10	11	12	13
All persons												
All education levels	14.3	21.7	12.0	6.1	12.5	17.6	9.7	4.8	12.1	17.3	9.1	4.3
Less than a high school graduate	24.9	27.8	22.3	11.4	21.0	21.5	19.9	9.8	20.2	20.8	18.6	9.0
High school graduate, no college	13.9	18.8	12.5	6.8	11.9	14.5	10.9	5.4	12.0	14.7	10.8	4.8
Some college, no degree	9.6	11.5	9.3	6.0	7.9	9.2	7.5	4.7	6.7	8.4	6.3	4.3
Associate degree	6.0	14.6	5.8	4.7	5.4	—	5.5	3.8	5.3	11.2	5.1	3.3
Bachelor's degree or higher	6.5	—	6.5	3.2	5.2	—	5.2	2.6	5.5	6.5	5.5	2.4
Men												
All education levels	15.1	22.0	13.0	6.4	13.2	19.0	10.2	4.8	12.5	18.4	9.2	4.3
Less than a high school graduate	23.6	26.8	21.1	11.4	20.8	22.5	17.5	9.3	19.9	21.6	15.9	8.8
High school graduate, no college	14.7	19.5	13.5	7.3	12.0	15.3	10.9	5.5	11.7	15.3	10.4	4.8
Some college, no degree	9.4	10.6	9.2	6.1	8.4	10.1	8.0	4.5	6.8	9.3	6.3	4.0
Associate degree	—	—	—	—	5.7	—	5.7	3.8	4.9	25.8	4.8	3.3
Bachelor's degree or higher	7.7	—	7.7	3.3	6.1	—	6.1	2.5	6.3	11.8	6.3	2.3
Women												
All education levels	13.3	21.4	10.9	5.7	11.6	16.2	9.2	4.9	11.7	16.1	9.0	4.4
Less than a high school graduate	27.1	29.3	24.8	11.4	21.3	20.2	25.2	10.5	20.8	19.9	24.4	9.2
High school graduate, no college	13.0	18.0	11.4	6.2	11.9	13.7	11.0	5.2	12.3	14.2	11.4	4.7
Some college, no degree	9.8	12.2	9.4	5.8	7.4	8.5	7.1	5.0	6.6	7.7	6.3	4.6
Associate degree	—	—	—	—	5.2	—	5.3	3.8	5.5	5.7	5.5	3.3
Bachelor's degree or higher	5.5	—	5.5	3.0	4.5	—	4.5	2.7	5.0	—	4.9	2.7
White [3]												
All education levels	12.0	18.4	10.0	5.5	10.6	15.1	8.1	4.3	10.2	14.5	7.7	3.9
Less than a high school graduate	21.5	24.0	19.2	10.7	18.1	18.7	16.8	8.9	17.2	17.7	15.9	8.3
High school graduate, no college	11.5	15.6	10.3	6.0	9.9	11.8	9.1	4.7	10.0	11.9	9.2	4.2
Some college, no degree	7.8	9.5	7.5	5.4	6.6	7.9	6.2	4.2	5.8	7.3	5.3	3.7
Associate degree	—	—	—	—	4.8	—	4.8	3.4	4.8	8.5	4.7	3.1
Bachelor's degree or higher	6.3	—	6.3	3.0	5.2	—	5.2	2.4	5.1	—	5.1	2.3
Black [3]												
All education levels	28.8	41.8	24.8	10.9	24.5	35.2	19.5	8.6	23.9	35.7	17.7	7.4
Less than a high school graduate	44.4	49.4	40.1	15.1	39.8	39.6	40.3	13.5	39.1	40.4	35.8	12.4
High school graduate, no college	26.6	37.2	24.1	12.3	23.1	31.4	20.6	9.9	22.5	31.8	19.3	8.2
Some college, no degree	21.6	26.1	21.0	10.3	15.8	21.4	14.9	8.1	13.0	18.7	12.2	7.5
Associate degree	—	—	—	—	12.0	—	12.1	5.8	10.7	66.4	8.5	4.6
Bachelor's degree or higher	7.6	—	7.6	4.4	5.0	—	5.1	3.5	8.7	—	8.6	3.2
Hispanic origin [4]												
All education levels	16.7	26.5	13.7	9.8	15.7	24.5	11.8	8.3	15.5	24.1	11.5	7.6
Less than a high school graduate	20.3	29.0	16.5	12.8	20.5	27.9	14.5	11.1	20.2	28.2	13.7	10.4
High school graduate, no college	14.7	23.2	12.4	9.0	13.8	20.5	12.0	7.6	14.1	18.7	12.3	6.8
Some college, no degree	11.4	18.8	10.5	8.4	10.2	14.3	9.2	6.9	10.4	14.1	9.4	6.1
Associate degree	—	—	—	—	9.2	—	9.3	5.9	4.3	15.6	3.0	5.5
Bachelor's degree or higher	10.3	—	10.3	5.0	4.9	—	4.9	4.2	7.4	19.4	7.8	3.5

[1] The unemployment rate is the percent of individuals in the labor force who are not working and who made specific efforts to find employment sometime during the prior 4 weeks. The labor force includes both employed and unemployed persons.

[2] Excludes persons enrolled in school.

[3] Includes persons of Hispanic origin.

[4] Persons of Hispanic origin may be of any race.

—Data not available or less than 0.1 percent.

SOURCE: U.S. Department of Labor, Bureau of Labor Statistics, Office of Employment and Unemployment Statistics, unpublished data. (This table was prepared May 1996.)

Table 375.—Median annual income of year-round full-time workers 25 years old and over, by level of education completed and sex: 1989 to 1994

Sex and year	Total	Elementary/secondary			College						
		Less than 9th grade [1]	9th to 12th grade, no diploma [2]	High school graduate [3]	Some college, no degree [4]	Associate degree [5]	Bachelor's degree or higher [6]				
							Total [6]	Bachelor's [7]	Master's [8]	Professional [8]	Doctorate [8]
1	2	3	4	5	6	7	8	9	10	11	12
						Current dollars					
Men											
1989	$30,465	$17,555	$21,065	$26,609	$31,308	—	$41,892	$38,565	—	—	—
1990	30,733	17,394	20,902	26,653	31,734	—	42,671	39,238	—	—	—
1991	31,613	17,623	21,402	26,779	31,663	$33,817	45,138	40,906	$49,734	$73,996	$57,187
1992 [9]	32,057	17,294	21,274	27,280	32,103	33,433	45,802	41,355	49,973	76,220	57,418
1993	32,359	16,863	21,752	27,370	32,077	33,690	47,740	42,757	51,867	80,549	63,149
1994	33,440	17,532	22,048	28,037	32,279	35,794	49,228	43,663	53,500	75,009	61,921
Women											
1989	20,570	12,188	13,923	17,528	21,631	—	28,799	26,709	—	—	—
1990	21,372	12,251	14,429	18,319	22,227	—	30,377	28,017	—	—	—
1991	22,043	12,066	14,455	18,836	22,143	25,000	31,310	29,079	34,949	46,742	43,303
1992 [9]	23,139	12,958	14,559	19,427	23,157	25,624	32,304	30,326	36,037	46,257	45,790
1993	23,629	12,415	15,386	19,963	23,056	25,883	34,307	31,197	38,612	50,211	47,248
1994	24,399	12,430	15,133	20,373	23,514	25,940	35,378	31,741	39,457	50,615	51,119
						Constant 1994 dollars					
Men											
1989	$36,411	$20,981	$25,176	$31,802	$37,418	—	$50,068	$46,091	—	—	—
1990	34,848	19,723	23,701	30,222	35,983	—	48,384	44,492	—	—	—
1991	34,398	19,176	23,288	29,138	34,453	$36,796	49,115	44,510	$54,116	$80,515	$62,226
1992 [9]	33,862	18,268	22,472	28,816	33,911	35,316	48,381	43,684	52,787	80,512	60,651
1993	33,188	17,295	22,309	28,071	32,898	34,553	48,962	43,852	53,195	82,612	64,766
1994	33,440	17,532	22,048	28,037	32,279	35,794	49,228	43,663	53,500	75,009	61,921
Women											
1989	24,584	14,567	16,640	20,949	25,853	—	34,419	31,922	—	—	—
1990	24,234	13,891	16,361	20,772	25,203	—	34,444	31,768	—	—	—
1991	23,985	13,129	15,729	20,496	24,094	27,203	34,069	31,641	38,028	50,860	47,118
1992 [9]	24,442	13,688	15,379	20,521	24,461	27,067	34,123	32,034	38,066	48,862	48,368
1993	24,234	12,733	15,780	20,474	23,646	26,546	35,185	31,996	39,601	51,497	48,458
1994	24,399	12,430	15,133	20,373	23,514	25,940	35,378	31,741	39,457	50,615	51,119
						Number with income (in thousands)					
Men											
1989	44,596	2,425	3,312	16,392	9,028	—	13,439	7,473	—	—	—
1990	44,406	2,250	3,315	16,394	9,113	—	13,334	7,569	—	—	—
1991	44,199	1,807	3,083	15,025	8,034	2,899	13,350	8,456	3,073	1,147	674
1992 [9]	44,752	1,815	3,009	14,722	8,067	3,203	13,937	8,719	3,178	1,295	745
1993	45,873	1,790	3,083	14,604	8,493	3,557	14,346	9,178	3,131	1,231	808
1994	47,566	1,895	3,057	15,109	8,783	3,735	14,987	9,636	3,225	1,258	868
Women											
1989	28,056	906	1,830	11,785	6,217	—	7,318	4,465	—	—	—
1990	28,636	847	1,861	11,810	6,462	—	7,655	4,704	—	—	—
1991	29,474	733	1,819	10,959	5,633	2,523	7,807	5,263	2,025	312	206
1992 [9]	30,346	734	1,659	11,039	5,904	2,655	8,355	5,604	2,192	334	225
1993	30,683	765	1,576	10,513	6,279	3,067	8,483	5,735	2,166	323	260
1994	31,379	696	1,675	10,785	6,256	3,210	8,756	5,901	2,174	398	283

[1] Includes fewer than 9 years education for 1989 and 1990.
[2] Includes 1 to 3 years high school for 1989 and 1990.
[3] Includes 4 years of high school for 1989 and 1990, and equivalency certificates for the other years.
[4] Includes 1 to 3 years of college and associate degrees for 1989 and 1990.
[5] Not reported separately for 1989 and 1990.
[6] Includes 4 or more years of college for 1989 and 1990.
[7] Includes 4 years of college for 1989 and 1990.
[8] Data not collected in 1989 and 1990.

[9] Data are based on 1990 census controls.
—Data not available or not applicable.

NOTE.—Due to rounding, numbers may not add to totals.

SOURCE: U.S. Department of Commerce, Bureau of the Census, *Current Population Reports*, Series P-60, "Money Income of Households, Families, and Persons in the United States," and "Income, Poverty, and Valuation of Noncash Benefits," various years. (This table was prepared June 1996.)

Table 376.—Total annual money earnings and median income of persons 25 years old and over,[1] by educational attainment and sex: 1994

Sex, earnings, and age	Total	Less than 9th grade	Some high school (no diploma)	High school graduate (includes equiva-lency)	Some college, no degree	Associate degree	College				
								Bachelor's degree or more			
							Total	Bachelor's degree	Master's degree	Profes-sional degree	Doctor's degree
1	2	3	4	5	6	7	8	9	10	11	12
					Number, in thousands						
Men, 25 years old and over											
Total	79,463	6,829	7,691	25,378	13,795	5,138	20,631	13,132	4,591	1,713	1,195
With earnings	77,546	6,507	7,286	24,704	13,573	5,046	20,429	12,997	4,558	1,691	1,183
					Percentage distribution of men with earnings						
Total	100.0	100.0	100.0	100.0	100.0	100.0	100.0	100.0	100.0	100.0	100.0
$1 to $4,999 or loss	5.8	12.1	11.2	5.8	4.8	3.9	3.1	3.4	2.6	2.7	1.7
$5,000 to 9,999	10.2	30.7	19.8	10.1	7.5	5.8	3.1	3.7	2.2	1.9	2.5
$10,000 to $14,999	11.8	24.0	20.3	13.0	10.2	8.4	5.3	5.9	4.1	4.0	4.5
$15,000 to $24,999	21.2	21.4	25.9	26.6	22.7	20.5	12.1	14.1	10.2	7.2	5.0
$25,000 to $34,999	16.8	6.7	12.8	19.9	20.6	19.7	14.5	16.3	13.3	9.5	7.5
$35,000 to $49,999	16.1	2.9	6.4	15.3	19.4	23.7	20.7	21.9	20.8	13.0	17.5
$50,000 to $74,999	11.1	1.6	2.3	7.0	10.7	13.3	21.9	20.1	26.1	19.2	28.7
$75,000 and over	7.0	0.6	1.2	2.3	4.1	4.7	19.4	14.7	20.7	42.6	32.6
Median income	$25,465	$11,324	$14,584	$22,387	$26,768	$30,643	$42,027	$38,701	$46,635	$61,739	$57,478
					Number, in thousands						
Women, 25 years old and over											
Total	86,975	7,118	8,874	31,072	15,561	6,756	17,594	12,181	4,226	715	472
With earnings	81,829	6,183	7,943	29,110	14,911	6,573	17,109	11,773	4,166	709	462
					Percentage distribution of women with earnings						
Total	100.0	100.0	100.0	100.0	100.0	100.0	100.0	100.0	100.0	100.0	100.0
$1 to $4,999 or loss	19.7	27.3	26.9	21.8	18.4	14.9	13.1	14.9	9.5	9.3	5.4
$5,000 to 9,999	21.0	47.1	37.4	22.3	17.1	13.4	8.0	9.2	5.5	3.8	5.4
$10,000 to $14,999	14.9	14.9	17.6	18.1	15.7	13.6	8.0	9.3	4.9	6.8	6.1
$15,000 to $24,999	20.2	8.3	12.5	22.6	24.7	25.3	17.9	19.9	13.8	14.7	11.0
$25,000 to $34,999	11.8	1.6	3.5	9.5	13.7	17.6	19.3	18.9	21.7	14.2	14.1
$35,000 to $49,999	7.8	0.4	1.3	4.1	7.1	11.1	19.0	17.2	25.2	15.4	17.3
$50,000 to $74,999	3.4	0.3	0.5	1.0	2.5	3.2	10.6	8.3	14.7	14.4	26.4
$75,000 and over	1.3	0.1	0.2	0.6	0.9	0.9	4.1	2.4	4.8	21.4	13.9
Median income	$12,766	$6,865	$7,618	$11,390	$14,585	$17,954	$26,237	$23,405	$32,069	$35,806	$40,793

[1] Includes full-time and part-time workers.

NOTE.—Because of rounding, details may not add to totals.

SOURCE: U.S. Department of Commerce, Bureau of the Census, *Current Population Reports*, Series P-60, No. 189, "Income, Poverty, and Valuation of Noncash Benefits: 1994." (This table was prepared May 1996.)

Table 377.—College enrollment and labor force status of 1994 and 1995 high school graduates 16 to 24 years old, by sex and race/ethnicity: October 1994 and October 1995

[Numbers in thousands]

Item	Civilian noninstitutional population			Civilian labor force [1]					Not in labor force
							Unemployed		
	Number	Percent	Percent of high school graduates	Number	Labor force participation rate	Employed	Number	Unemployment rate	
1	2	3	4	5	6	7	8	9	10
1994 high school graduates [2]									
Total	2,517	100.0	100.0	1,495	59.4	1,257	238	15.9	1,022
Men	1,244	49.4	49.4	792	63.6	665	127	16.0	452
Women	1,273	50.6	50.6	704	55.3	592	111	15.8	570
White [3]	2,065	82.0	82.0	1,252	60.6	1,108	144	11.5	813
Black [3]	318	12.6	12.6	175	53.0	100	75	42.8	143
Hispanic origin [4]	178	7.1	7.1	114	64.0	81	32	28.5	64
Enrolled in college, October 1994	1,559	100.0	61.9	723	46.4	642	82	11.3	836
Men	754	48.4	30.0	359	47.7	319	40	11.1	394
Women	805	51.6	32.0	364	45.2	322	42	11.4	441
2-year	530	34.0	21.1	324	61.2	283	42	12.8	205
4-year	1,029	66.0	40.9	399	38.7	359	40	10.1	630
Full-time students	1,427	91.6	56.7	609	42.7	537	72	11.8	818
Part-time students	131	8.4	5.2	114	86.9	104	10	8.6	17
White [3]	1,313	84.2	52.2	640	48.7	379	61	9.5	674
Black [3]	162	10.4	6.4	55	33.9	41	14	(5)	107
Hispanic origin [4]	87	5.6	3.5	46	55.3	40	7	(5)	41
Not enrolled in college, October 1994 ...	959	100.0	38.1	772	80.3	616	156	20.3	187
Men	491	51.2	19.5	432	88.1	346	87	20.1	58
Women	468	48.8	35.6	340	72.6	270	70	20.5	128
White [3]	752	78.4	29.9	612	81.4	529	85	13.5	140
Black [3]	156	16.3	6.2	120	77.4	59	61	50.7	36
Hispanic origin [4]	91	9.5	3.6	67	74.3	42	26	(5)	23
1995 high school graduates [6]									
Total	2,599	100.0	100.0	1,546	59.5	1,284	262	16.9	1,053
Men	1,238	47.6	47.6	749	60.5	602	147	19.6	489
Women	1,361	52.4	52.4	797	58.6	682	115	14.4	564
White [3]	2,088	80.3	80.3	1,278	61.2	1,096	182	14.2	810
Black [3]	356	13.7	13.7	202	56.9	144	59	29.1	153
Hispanic origin [4]	288	11.1	11.1	161	55.9	96	65	40.5	127
Enrolled in college, October 1995	1,610	100.0	61.9	756	47.0	659	97	12.8	853
Men	775	48.1	29.8	358	46.1	305	52	14.7	417
Women	835	51.9	32.1	398	47.7	354	45	11.2	436
2-year	559	34.7	21.5	359	64.1	299	60	16.7	201
4-year	1,050	65.2	40.4	397	37.8	360	37	9.4	653
Full-time students	1,450	90.0	55.8	626	43.2	541	85	13.5	824
Part-time students	159	9.9	6.1	130	81.7	118	12	9.6	29
White [3]	1,308	81.2	50.3	636	48.6	569	67	10.6	672
Black [3]	183	11.4	7.0	77	41.9	56	21	27.0	106
Hispanic origin [4]	155	9.6	6.0	69	44.6	40	29	(/5/)	86
Not enrolled in college, October 1995 ...	990	100.0	38.1	790	79.8	625	165	20.9	200
Men	463	46.8	17.8	391	84.5	297	94	24.1	72
Women	527	53.2	20.3	399	75.7	328	70	17.7	128
White [3]	780	78.8	30.0	642	82.4	528	115	17.9	137
Black [3]	173	17.5	6.7	126	72.9	88	38	30.3	47
Hispanic origin [4]	133	13.4	5.1	92	68.9	56	36	39.0	41

[1] The labor force includes all employed persons plus those seeking employment. The labor force participation rate is the percentage of persons either employed or seeking employment.

[2] Includes persons who graduated from high school between January and October 1994.

[3] Includes persons of Hispanic origin.

[4] Persons of Hispanic origin may be of any race.

[5] Data not shown where base is less than 75,000.

[6] Includes persons who graduated from high school between January and October 1995.

NOTE.—Data are based upon sample surveys of the civilian noninstitutional population. Percents are only shown when the base is 75,000 or greater. Even though the standard errors are large, smaller estimates are shown to permit users to combine categories in various ways. Because of rounding, details may not add to totals.

SOURCE.—U.S. Department of Labor, Bureau of Labor Statistics, "College Enrollment and Work Activity of 1995 High School Graduates." (This table was prepared May 1996.)

Table 378.—Labor force status of 1979–80 to 1994–95 high school dropouts 16 to 24 years old, by sex and race/ethnicity: October 1980 to October 1995

[Numbers in thousands]

Year, sex, and race [1]	Dropouts [1]		Dropouts in civilian labor force [2]						Not in labor force
	Number	Percent of total	Number	Labor force participation rate	Employed		Unemployed		
					Number	Percent of dropouts	Number	Unemployment rate	
1	2	3	4	5	6	7	8	9	10
All dropouts									
1979–80 dropouts in October [2]	739	100.0	471	63.7	322	43.6	149	31.6	268
1984–85 dropouts in October [2]	612	100.0	413	67.5	266	43.5	147	35.6	199
1985–86 dropouts in October [2]	562	100.0	359	63.9	259	46.1	100	27.9	203
1986–87 dropouts in October [2]	502	100.0	333	66.4	207	41.2	126	37.8	169
1987–88 dropouts in October [2]	552	100.0	327	59.2	240	43.5	87	26.7	225
1988–89 dropouts in October [2]	446	100.0	292	65.4	210	47.1	82	28.0	154
1989–90 dropouts in October [2]	405	100.0	280	69.0	189	46.7	90	32.3	125
1990–91 dropouts in October [2]	380	100.0	235	61.8	140	36.9	95	40.3	145
1991–92 dropouts in October [2]	406	100.0	242	59.6	147	36.3	95	39.1	164
1992–93 dropouts in October [2]	399	100.0	254	63.8	187	47.0	67	26.3	145
1993–94 dropouts in October [2]	510	100.0	311	61.1	219	42.9	93	29.8	198
1994–95 dropouts in October [2]	604	100.0	409	67.7	288	47.7	121	29.6	195
Men									
1979–80 dropouts in October [2]	422	57.1	305	72.3	212	50.2	93	30.5	117
1984–85 dropouts in October [2]	321	52.5	261	81.3	163	50.8	98	37.5	60
1989–90 dropouts in October [2]	215	53.1	173	80.2	110	51.2	63	36.2	42
1990–91 dropouts in October [2]	189	49.7	142	75.0	92	48.8	50	35.0	47
1991–92 dropouts in October [2]	189	46.6	130	69.1	85	45.2	45	34.7	59
1992–93 dropouts in October [2]	213	53.4	156	73.5	132	61.8	25	15.9	57
1993–94 dropouts in October [2]	259	50.8	198	76.5	151	58.2	47	23.9	61
1994–95 dropouts in October [2]	339	56.1	251	74.0	179	52.8	72	28.7	88
Women									
1979–80 dropouts in October [2]	317	42.9	166	52.4	110	34.7	56	33.7	151
1984–85 dropouts in October [2]	291	47.5	152	52.2	103	35.4	49	32.2	139
1989–90 dropouts in October [2]	190	46.9	107	56.3	79	41.6	28	26.1	83
1990–91 dropouts in October [2]	191	50.3	93	48.8	48	25.2	45	48.4	98
1991–92 dropouts in October [2]	218	53.7	112	51.4	62	28.6	50	44.3	106
1992–93 dropouts in October [2]	186	46.6	98	52.6	56	30.1	42	42.9	88
1993–94 dropouts in October [2]	251	49.2	113	45.2	68	27.1	45	40.0	137
1994–95 dropouts in October [2]	265	43.9	157	59.5	109	41.1	49	30.9	107
White [3]									
1979–80 dropouts in October [2]	580	78.5	392	67.6	286	49.3	106	27.0	188
1984–85 dropouts in October [2]	458	74.8	330	72.1	214	46.7	116	35.2	128
1989–90 dropouts in October [2]	303	74.8	211	69.8	156	51.4	56	26.3	92
1990–91 dropouts in October [2]	273	71.8	177	65.1	109	40.0	68	38.5	96
1991–92 dropouts in October [2]	319	78.6	190	59.7	128	40.3	62	32.5	129
1992–93 dropouts in October [2]	304	76.2	209	68.8	159	52.2	50	24.1	95
1993–94 dropouts in October [2]	382	74.9	252	66.0	177	46.3	75	29.8	130
1994–95 dropouts in October [2]	448	74.2	312	69.8	227	50.8	85	27.2	135
Black [3]									
1979–80 dropouts in October [2]	146	19.8	73	50.0	33	22.6	40	(4)	73
1984–85 dropouts in October [2]	132	21.6	69	52.3	39	29.5	30	(4)	63
1989–90 dropouts in October [2]	86	21.2	56	65.3	26	29.9	30	(4)	30
1990–91 dropouts in October [2]	98	25.8	54	55.0	28	28.4	26	(4)	44
1991–92 dropouts in October [2]	66	16.3	35	(4)	7	(4)	28	(4)	31
1992–93 dropouts in October [2]	80	20.1	34	42.9	21	26.2	13	(4)	46
1993–94 dropouts in October [2]	100	19.6	48	47.9	34	34.1	14	(4)	52
1994–95 dropouts in October [2]	109	18.0	66	61.0	40	36.4	27	(4)	42
Hispanic [5]									
1979–80 dropouts in October [2]	91	12.3	60	65.9	43	47.3	17	(4)	31
1984–85 dropouts in October [2]	106	17.3	73	68.9	40	37.7	33	(4)	33
1989–90 dropouts in October [2]	67	16.5	32	(4)	22	(4)	10	(4)	35
1990–91 dropouts in October [2]	61	16.1	48	(4)	30	(4)	18	(4)	13
1991–92 dropouts in October [2]	80	19.7	40	49.9	23	28.4	17	(4)	40
1992–93 dropouts in October [2]	60	15.0	43	(4)	28	(4)	15	(4)	17
1993–94 dropouts in October [2]	108	21.2	51	47.5	31	28.6	20	(4)	57
1994–95 dropouts in October [2]	174	28.8	119	68.6	84	48.5	35	29.3	55

[1] Persons who dropped out of school between October of the earlier year and October of the later year.

[2] The labor force includes all employed persons plus those seeking employment. The labor force participation rate is the percentage of persons either employed or seeking employment. The unemployment rate is the percent of persons in the labor force who are seeking employment.

[3] Includes persons of Hispanic origin.

[4] Data not shown where base is less than 75,000.

[5] Persons of Hispanic origin may be of any race.

NOTE.—Data are based upon sample surveys of the civilian noninstitutional population. Includes dropouts from any grade, including a small number from elementary and middle schools. Percents are only shown when the base is 75,000 or greater. Even though the standard errors are large, smaller estimates are shown to permit users to combine categories in various ways. Because of rounding, details may not add to totals.

SOURCE: U.S. Department of Labor, Bureau of Labor Statistics, *College Enrollment of High School Graduates*, various years. (This table was prepared May 1996.)

Table 379.—Employment of 12th graders, by selected student characteristics: 1992

Employment characteristics	Total	Sex		Race/ethnicity					Socioeconomic status[1]				Location of school attended		
		Male	Female	White	Black	Hispanic	Asian	American Indian	Low	Middle low	Middle high	High	Urban	Suburban	Rural
1	2	3	4	5	6	7	8	9	10	11	12	13	14	15	16

Percentage distribution

Average hours worked per week during senior year

Total	100.0	100.0	100.0	100.0	100.0	100.0	100.0	100.0	100.0	100.0	100.0	100.0	100.0	100.0	100.0
Did not work during year	31.8	33.0	30.7	27.6	47.4	38.9	43.3	45.0	38.2	29.8	28.2	32.5	35.6	29.4	31.6
1 to 5 hours	6.8	6.0	7.6	7.0	4.9	6.0	9.5	5.6	5.2	5.5	5.8	10.1	6.7	6.6	7.2
6 to 10 hours	9.8	8.9	10.7	11.2	6.5	5.3	6.7	5.6	6.7	8.3	10.6	12.6	9.4	9.6	10.6
11 to 15 hours	12.7	11.1	14.4	14.1	7.2	11.3	9.3	6.2	9.5	11.9	13.7	15.0	12.2	13.6	12.1
16 to 20 hours	16.1	15.0	17.2	17.3	11.9	13.3	13.5	12.5	13.4	18.6	18.4	14.0	14.3	18.3	14.9
More than 20 hours	22.7	26.0	19.5	22.8	22.1	25.2	17.7	22.3	27.1	25.9	23.3	15.8	21.7	22.5	23.7
21 to 25 hours	9.8	10.2	9.5	10.0	8.8	10.7	8.1	12.0	10.2	10.9	10.8	8.0	9.5	10.6	9.1
26 to 30 hours	5.6	6.5	4.8	5.5	6.4	6.6	4.4	3.8	6.8	6.4	5.9	3.4	5.3	5.7	5.8
31 to 35 hours	2.5	3.1	1.9	2.6	2.4	2.4	0.8	5.0	3.6	3.2	2.4	1.3	2.3	2.5	2.7
36 to 40 hours	3.3	4.2	2.4	3.3	2.9	4.1	3.7	0.9	4.3	4.2	2.7	2.1	3.3	2.4	4.3
More than 40 hours	1.5	2.0	1.0	1.5	1.7	1.4	0.8	0.7	2.2	1.4	1.6	1.0	1.3	1.4	1.8

Most recent type of work for employed students

Total	100.0	100.0	100.0	100.0	100.0	100.0	100.0	100.0	100.0	100.0	100.0	100.0	100.0	100.0	100.0
Lawn work or odd jobs	2.2	4.2	0.3	2.5	0.8	0.9	1.7	5.3	2.3	2.0	2.1	2.5	1.3	2.2	2.9
Food service	24.0	22.2	25.7	22.8	34.8	24.8	22.9	24.6	28.0	26.6	25.1	18.6	23.6	23.1	25.4
Delivery person	1.6	2.5	0.6	1.5	1.9	1.1	3.2	1.3	0.8	1.7	1.3	2.1	1.5	1.7	1.5
Babysitter or child care	4.3	0.6	7.9	4.8	2.4	2.2	5.0	1.1	3.2	3.9	4.5	5.4	4.9	4.4	3.9
Camp counselor/life guard	0.7	0.8	0.7	0.9	0.0	0.5	0.6	0.0	0.2	0.3	0.9	1.3	0.8	0.9	0.5
Farm worker	2.2	4.4	0.1	2.7	0.0	1.1	1.0	3.7	3.3	1.6	1.1	1.1	0.2	1.3	5.5
Mechanic	1.4	2.8	0.0	1.5	0.7	1.5	1.0	1.4	2.0	1.8	1.5	0.6	1.0	1.3	1.9
Grocery clerk or cashier	14.5	12.5	16.4	14.8	15.9	11.6	8.5	25.7	15.5	16.6	14.5	12.3	14.2	13.4	16.4
Beautician	0.2	0.1	0.3	0.1	1.1	0.3	0.6	0.0	0.6	0.2	0.1	0.1	0.2	0.2	0.3
House cleaning	0.9	0.7	1.1	0.8	0.8	2.0	0.6	0.0	1.5	0.6	1.2	0.6	0.7	0.6	1.4
Construction	2.0	4.0	0.1	2.1	1.0	1.9	0.9	2.0	2.6	2.3	1.9	1.4	1.4	1.8	2.7
Office or clerical	6.9	2.9	10.7	6.3	9.2	8.7	12.1	5.8	6.3	6.0	7.2	8.0	9.0	6.8	5.4
Health services	1.6	0.9	2.3	1.6	2.1	1.1	1.0	4.5	2.5	2.0	1.4	0.9	1.5	1.6	1.7
Salesperson	11.8	9.8	13.7	12.0	8.7	11.9	15.0	7.9	7.2	8.8	12.5	15.8	13.4	14.1	7.3
Warehouse worker	2.1	3.9	0.4	2.2	1.3	1.7	2.0	2.3	1.7	2.5	1.9	2.1	2.0	2.3	1.9
Other	23.5	27.7	19.6	23.5	19.3	28.8	25.4	18.3	22.0	21.4	22.3	27.4	24.4	24.6	21.3

Most recent hourly wage for employed students

Total	100.0	100.0	100.0	100.0	100.0	100.0	100.0	100.0	100.0	100.0	100.0	100.0	100.0	100.0	100.0
Less than $4.25 per hour	9.9	7.2	12.4	10.3	8.3	8.8	7.9	5.8	12.2	11.4	9.0	8.0	7.9	7.5	14.8
$4.25 to $6.00 per hour	77.5	75.6	79.2	76.7	80.9	81.1	77.0	79.3	79.0	76.8	80.0	74.8	80.1	77.0	75.8
$6.01 to $8.00 per hour	7.7	10.3	5.3	8.0	5.8	6.1	10.7	6.7	5.3	8.3	6.8	9.3	7.3	9.2	6.1
$8.01 or more per hour	5.0	6.9	3.2	5.1	5.0	4.0	4.5	8.3	3.5	3.5	4.1	7.9	4.8	6.3	3.4

[1] Socioeconomic status was measured by a composite score on parental education and occupations, and family income. The "Low" SES group is the lowest quartile.

NOTE.—Some data have been revised from previously published figures.

SOURCE: U.S. Department of Education, National Center for Education Statistics, "National Education Longitudinal Study of 1988," Second Followup survey. (This table was prepared August 1995.)

Table 380.—Full-time-employment status of bachelor's degree recipients 1 year after graduation, by field of study: 1976 to 1991

Field of study	Percent employed full-time					Percent employed full-time in a job closely related to field of study					Percent employed full-time in nonprofessional job [1]				
	1974–75 graduates in May 1976	1979–80 graduates in May 1981	1983–84 graduates in June 1985	1985–86 graduates in June 1987	1989–90 graduates in April 1991	1974–75 graduates in May 1976	1979–80 graduates in May 1981	1983–84 graduates in June 1985	1985–86 graduates in June 1987	1989–90 graduates in April 1991	1974–75 graduates in May 1976	1979–80 graduates in May 1981	1983–84 graduates in June 1985	1985–86 graduates in June 1987	1989–90 graduates in April 1991
1	2	3	4	5	6	7	8	9	10	11	12	13	14	15	16
Total	67	71	73	74	74	35	38	38	38	39	10	12	13	14	13
Professional/technical fields	77	80	82	81	80	51	51	47	47	48	9	10	13	11	11
Arts and sciences fields	56	56	56	62	64	18	17	15	25	26	12	14	15	15	14
Other	65	74	75	74	73	36	43	47	36	38	9	19	12	17	13
Newly qualified to teach	66	75	73	68	74	43	56	54	47	58	7	8	9	9	6
Not newly qualified to teach	67	71	73	74	73	33	36	36	37	36	12	13	13	14	14
Professional/technical fields	80	81	82	82	83	52	49	47	47	48	10	10	13	11	12
Engineering	79	84	84	83	84	57	55	53	46	50	4	2	3	5	3
Business and management	84	83	85	85	83	49	44	41	40	42	15	14	19	17	16
Health	75	77	75	76	86	71	66	70	65	83	2	4	2	3	1
Education [2]	66	67	63	73	67	22	29	24	57	39	12	18	16	9	11
Public affairs and services	—	77	74	72	66	—	46	31	37	49	—	10	15	20	9
Arts and sciences fields	57	56	56	63	64	17	16	15	25	23	13	15	15	15	15
Biological sciences	56	45	43	42	50	26	18	17	15	26	6	8	11	11	8
Physical sciences and mathematics [3]	50	58	51	76	72	19	29	20	48	48	6	8	7	9	7
Psychology	61	56	57	66	59	22	17	12	22	22	18	17	16	19	14
Social sciences	59	61	61	61	68	12	10	13	12	16	15	21	14	17	20
Humanities	56	55	59	59	59	12	14	17	19	11	17	18	19	19	21
Other	68	75	77	75	73	36	43	42	36	37	10	20	14	21	14
Communications	—	71	76	77	75	—	31	31	33	29	—	24	16	18	17
Miscellaneous	66	76	77	74	73	35	46	46	38	38	11	19	13	23	13

[1] Includes those not working in technical, managerial, or administrative types of jobs who reported that they did not need a college degree to obtain their job.

[2] Includes those who have not finished all requirements for teaching certification or were previously qualified to teach.

[3] Includes computer sciences.

—Data not available.

NOTE.—Data are from sample surveys of recent college graduates. Notes on methodology are included in the Guide to Sources. Data exclude bachelor's recipients from U.S. Service Schools. Deceased graduates and graduates living at foreign addresses at the time of the survey are not included.

SOURCE: U.S. Department of Education, National Center for Education Statistics, "Recent College Graduates" surveys. (This table was prepared August 1993.)

Table 381.—Employment status of 1989–90 bachelor's degree recipients 1 year after graduation, by field of study and occupational area: 1991

[Percentage distribution]

Occupational area in April 1991	All fields of study	Professional/technical fields						Arts and sciences				Other fields[1]
		Business and management	Education	Engineering	Health professions	Public affairs/ social services	Biological sciences	Mathematics, computer, and physical sciences	Social sciences	Humanities	Psychology	
1	2	3	4	5	6	7	8	9	10	11	12	13
Total	100	100	100	100	100	100	100	100	100	100	100	100
Employed	84	89	91	87	97	84	65	79	80	78	73	85
Business	21	45	4	7	3	3	10	7	22	13	15	28
Educators	13	1	73	1	1	3	7	9	6	18	10	3
Engineers	5	1	(2)	61	(2)	(2)	1	5	1	(2)	(2)	4
Health professionals	5	(2)	1	(2)	91	(2)	8	1	1	(2)	5	1
Public affairs/social services	3	(2)	(2)	(2)	(2)	57	1	(2)	6	2	15	1
Biological scientists	1	1	1	1	(2)	(2)	4	(2)	1	1	(2)	(2)
Computer, physical scientist, mathematician	1	1	(2)	(2)	(2)	(2)	(2)	7	(2)	(2)	(2)	(2)
Communications	2	1	(2)	(2)	(2)	1	1	(2)	2	9	1	14
Technicians	6	3	(2)	8	(2)	(2)	13	29	5	4	3	8
Other	3	3	1	2	(2)	(2)	5	7	4	2	1	(2)
Nonprofessional, nonmanagerial, and nontechnical	23	33	11	6	3	21	16	14	33	30	24	27
Unemployed[3]	4	5	2	3	(2)	3	2	4	4	4	5	6
Not in labor force[4]	12	6	6	9	2	13	33	16	15	18	21	9
Enrolled in school[5]	8	2	2	6	(2)	4	29	13	11	12	16	5

[1] Includes agriculture and natural resources, architecture and environmental design, area and ethnic studies, communications, consumer/personal/miscellaneous services, home economics, industrial arts, law, liberal/general studies, library and archival sciences, military sciences, multi/interdisciplinary studies, personal and social development, and trade and industrial.
[2] Less than 0.5 percent.
[3] Percent looking for work.
[4] Percent not looking for work.
[5] Enrolled full-time or part-time.

NOTE.—Because of rounding, details may not add to totals.

SOURCE: U.S. Department of Education, National Center for Education Statistics, "Recent College Graduates, 1991" survey. (This table was prepared July 1993.)

Table 382.—Percent of 1989–90 bachelor's degree recipients pursuing further education within 1 year after graduation, by type of enrollment and undergraduate major: 1991

Undergraduate major field of study	Ever enrolled since graduation	Ever enrolled full-time	Ever enrolled and employed	Ever enrolled and not employed	Enrolled in degree program beyond bachelor's
1	2	3	4	5	6
All bachelor's graduates	35	17	24	11	24
Professional/technical fields	28	17	22	6	18
Engineering	32	18	23	9	23
Business and management	21	13	16	5	12
Health professions	27	16	22	5	20
Education	38	27	33	5	29
Public affairs and social services	35	13	28	7	22
Arts and sciences fields	46	17	28	18	34
Biological sciences	64	17	30	34	47
Physical sciences, mathematics, and computer sciences	40	17	24	16	30
Psychology	50	19	31	20	40
Social sciences	42	16	28	14	30
Humanities	43	17	28	15	28
Other [1]	29	15	21	9	18
Highest degree graduate expects to obtain					
Bachelor's degree	15	10	13	3	3
Master's degree	31	18	24	6	20
Doctor's degree	58	21	36	22	49
First-professional degree	68	9	27	41	61

[1] Includes agriculture and natural resources, architecture and environmental design, area and ethnic studies, consumer/personal/miscellaneous services, home economics, industrial arts, law, liberal/general studies, library and archival sciences, military sciences, multi/interdisciplinary studies, personal and social development, and trade and industrial.

NOTE.—Data are from a sample survey of recent college graduates. Notes on methodology are included in the Guide to Sources. Data exclude bachelor's degree recipients from U.S. Service Schools. Deceased graduates and graduates living at foreign addresses at the time of the survey are not included.

SOURCE: U.S. Department of Education, National Center for Education Statistics, "Recent College Graduates, 1991" survey. (This table was prepared May 1993.)

Table 383.—Average annual salary of bachelor's degree recipients employed full-time 1 year after graduation, by field of study: 1976 to 1991

Field of study	Average salary [1] of 1974–75 degree recipients in February 1976		Average salary [1] of 1979–80 degree recipients in May 1981		Average salary [1] of 1983–84 degree recipients in June 1985		Average salary of 1985–86 degree recipients in June 1987		Average salary of 1989–90 degree recipients in April 1991	Percentage change in constant dollars, 1976 to 1991	Percentage change in constant dollars, 1987 to 1991
	Current dollars	Constant 1991 dollars	Current dollars	Constant 1991 dollars	Current dollars	Constant 1991 dollars	Current dollars	Constant 1991 dollars	Current dollars		
1	2	3	4	5	6	7	8	9	10	11	12
Total	$7,600	$18,200	$15,200	$22,800	$17,700	$22,400	$20,400	24,400	$23,600	29.7	–3.3
Engineering	12,200	29,200	22,400	33,600	24,100	30,500	26,600	31,900	30,900	5.8	–3.1
Business and management	10,200	24,400	16,300	24,400	18,700	23,700	21,100	25,300	24,700	1.2	–2.4
Health professions	8,600	20,600	17,300	25,900	20,800	26,300	22,600	27,000	31,500	52.9	16.7
Education [2]	6,300	15,100	11,500	17,200	13,800	17,500	15,800	18,900	19,100	26.5	1.1
Public affairs and social services	—	—	13,700	20,500	15,100	19,100	17,700	21,200	20,800	—	–1.9
Biological sciences	6,500	15,600	14,500	21,700	15,100	19,100	16,400	19,600	21,100	35.3	7.7
Physical sciences, mathematics, and computer sciences	7,000	16,800	16,300	24,400	17,500	22,200	22,500	27,000	27,200	61.9	0.7
Psychology	—	—	12,500	18,700	14,600	18,500	17,300	20,800	19,200	—	–7.7
Social sciences	6,700	16,000	14,000	21,000	15,800	20,000	20,300	24,400	22,200	38.8	–9.0
Humanities	5,800	13,900	12,600	18,900	14,000	17,700	16,200	19,400	19,100	37.4	–1.5
Communications	—	—	—	—	16,200	20,500	—	—	—	—	—
Miscellaneous	6,800	16,300	15,100	22,600	18,600	23,500	17,600	21,100	20,800	27.6	–1.4

[1] Reported salaries of full-time workers under $2,600 in 1976, $4,200 in 1981, and $5,000 in 1985 were excluded from the tabulations.

[2] Most educators work 9- to 10-month contracts.

—Data not available.

NOTE.—Data exclude bachelor's recipients from U.S. Service Schools and graduates living at foreign addresses at the time of the survey. Constant dollar adjustments based on the Consumer Price Index.

SOURCE: U.S. Department of Education, National Center for Education Statistics, "Recent College Graduates" surveys. (This table was prepared May 1993.)

Table 384.—Participation of young adults in voluntary organizations, by selected characteristics: 1984 to 1986 and 1992 to 1994

Young adult characteristics	Any voluntary activity	Percent participating in voluntary organizations								Percentage distribution of volunteer hours per week				
		Sports teams or clubs	Church activities	Union, farm, trade, or professional associations	Educational organizations	Youth organizations	Political clubs	Organized volunteer work[1]	Other voluntary group	None[2]	Less than 2 hours	2 to 4 hours	4 to 6 hours	6 hours or more
1	2	3	4	5	6	7	8	9	10	11	12	13	14	15
1984 to 1986[3]														
Total	—	36.0	32.2	17.7	—	9.2	6.2	5.8	9.6	—	—	—	—	—
Sex														
Male	—	46.8	29.3	20.3	—	11.7	6.7	5.3	9.7	—	—	—	—	—
Female	—	25.8	34.9	15.3	—	6.9	5.8	6.2	9.4	—	—	—	—	—
Race/ethnicity														
White, non-Hispanic	—	36.5	30.6	18.2	—	8.7	5.9	5.5	9.7	—	—	—	—	—
Black, non-Hispanic	—	31.9	44.2	14.9	—	12.0	8.2	6.8	10.3	—	—	—	—	—
Hispanic	—	34.6	32.4	15.8	—	9.5	6.9	4.3	7.1	—	—	—	—	—
Asian	—	41.4	31.0	27.3	—	10.8	5.9	14.1	10.3	—	—	—	—	—
American Indian	—	41.1	30.0	19.7	—	11.6	9.6	4.2	7.8	—	—	—	—	—
Socioeconomic status														
Low	—	29.2	30.9	12.2	—	7.0	3.4	4.5	6.9	—	—	—	—	—
Low-middle	—	34.5	31.4	15.6	—	8.7	4.5	4.8	8.6	—	—	—	—	—
High-middle	—	39.9	35.4	21.8	—	10.6	7.8	6.9	10.6	—	—	—	—	—
High	—	43.1	33.9	22.4	—	10.7	9.9	7.4	13.0	—	—	—	—	—
1992 to 1994[4]														
Total	37.2	7.2	11.8	1.8	6.0	10.3	3.0	10.4	7.3	62.7	15.2	7.9	5.8	8.3
Sex														
Male	36.8	9.5	11.1	1.9	4.6	11.2	2.9	8.3	7.3	63.2	14.7	7.7	5.6	8.8
Female	37.9	4.9	12.7	1.6	7.1	9.4	3.2	12.6	7.3	62.2	15.8	8.2	6.1	7.9
Race/ethnicity														
White, non-Hispanic	38.5	7.5	11.3	2.0	5.8	10.3	3.1	11.6	7.8	61.5	17.1	8.0	5.5	7.9
Black, non-Hispanic	35.9	6.3	15.8	1.1	6.4	11.5	3.1	5.8	6.2	64.1	9.6	8.1	7.7	10.6
Hispanic	31.7	6.3	11.2	0.8	6.5	9.6	2.3	6.7	5.4	68.4	9.8	7.3	6.0	8.5
Asian	35.8	5.7	10.5	1.4	7.1	8.1	3.4	13.0	8.4	64.2	14.9	8.7	4.3	8.0
American Indian	34.1	12.1	14.6	3.6	6.1	11.9	3.8	5.1	3.9	65.9	8.7	6.3	8.1	11.1
Socioeconomic status														
Low	26.4	5.0	10.4	0.9	4.0	7.4	1.5	5.9	5.0	73.6	8.2	5.8	4.5	7.9
Low-middle	30.4	6.3	10.8	1.3	3.9	8.3	2.1	7.1	6.3	69.6	11.0	6.0	5.9	7.5
High-middle	38.6	7.0	13.0	2.0	5.8	10.9	3.3	9.2	7.5	61.4	16.9	7.9	6.1	7.8
High	51.1	9.2	14.7	2.7	9.7	14.2	4.9	18.0	10.3	48.9	24.6	11.4	5.9	9.2

[1] E.g., hospital volunteer.
[2] Not a volunteer.
[3] Sample survey in 1986 based on people who were high school seniors in spring 1980. Respondents to the survey were asked about their voluntary participation in selected organizations over the previous 24-month period.
[4] Sample survey in 1994 based on people who were high school seniors in spring 1992. Respondents to the survey were asked about their voluntary participation in selected organizations over the previous 24-month period.

—Data not available or not applicable.

NOTE.—Some persons participated in more than one organization.

SOURCE: U.S. Department of Education, National Center for Education Statistics, "High School and Beyond, Third Followup" and "National Education Longitudinal Study, Third Followup." (This table was prepared July 1995.)

Table 385.—Literacy skills of adults, 16 years old and over, by selected characteristics: 1992

Selected characteristics	Prose literacy[1]						Document literacy[2]						Quantitative literacy[3]					
	Average score	Percent of adults with proficiency at level					Average score	Percent of adults with proficiency at level					Average score	Percent of adults with proficiency at level				
		1	2	3	4	5		1	2	3	4	5		1	2	3	4	5
1	2	3	4	5	6	7	8	9	10	11	12	13	14	15	16	17	18	19
Total	272	21	27	32	17	3	267	23	28	31	15	3	271	22	25	31	17	4
Sex																		
Male	272	22	26	31	18	4	269	23	27	31	17	3	277	21	23	31	20	5
Female	273	20	28	33	17	3	265	23	30	31	14	2	266	23	28	31	15	3
Age																		
16 to 18 years old	271	16	35	38	11	1	274	15	34	38	12	1	268	20	35	33	12	1
19 to 24 years old	280	14	29	37	18	2	280	14	29	37	18	2	277	16	28	37	16	2
25 to 39 years old	284	15	24	34	22	5	282	16	25	35	21	4	283	17	23	33	21	5
40 to 54 years old	286	15	23	34	22	5	278	17	27	33	19	3	286	16	22	33	23	6
55 to 64 years old	260	26	31	30	12	1	249	30	34	26	8	1	261	25	30	30	13	2
65 years old and older	230	44	32	19	5	1	217	53	32	13	2	0	227	45	26	20	7	2
Race/ethnicity																		
White	286	14	25	36	21	4	280	16	27	34	19	3	287	14	24	35	21	5
Black	237	38	37	21	4	0	230	43	36	18	3	0	224	46	34	17	3	0
Asian or Pacific Islander	242	36	25	25	12	2	245	34	25	28	12	2	256	30	23	27	16	4
American Indian	254	25	39	28	7	1	254	27	37	29	7	0	250	33	32	28	7	1
Hispanic, Mexican	206	54	25	16	5	0	205	54	25	16	4	0	205	54	25	17	4	0
Hispanic, Cuban	211	53	24	17	6	1	212	48	30	16	6	2	223	46	20	25	6	3
Hispanic, Puerto Rican	218	47	32	17	3	0	215	49	29	18	3	0	212	51	28	17	3	1
Hispanic, Central/South American	207	56	22	17	4	0	206	53	25	16	4	0	203	53	25	18	4	0
Hispanic, other	260	25	27	33	13	2	254	28	26	32	12	2	246	31	25	31	11	1
Highest level of education																		
Still in high school	271	16	36	37	11	0	274	15	35	38	12	1	269	19	35	32	12	1
0 to 8 years	177	75	20	4	0	0	170	79	18	3	0	0	169	76	18	5	1	0
9 to 12 years	231	42	38	17	2	0	227	46	37	15	2	0	227	45	34	17	3	0
GED	268	14	39	39	7	0	264	17	42	34	7	0	268	16	38	35	10	1
High school diploma	270	16	36	37	10	1	264	20	38	33	9	1	270	18	33	37	12	1
Some college	294	8	23	45	22	3	290	9	27	42	20	2	295	8	23	42	23	4
Associate degree	308	4	19	41	32	4	299	6	23	43	25	3	307	4	19	43	29	5
Bachelor's degree	322	4	11	35	40	10	314	4	15	37	36	8	322	4	12	35	38	12
Graduate studies/degree	336	2	7	28	47	16	326	3	10	34	41	12	334	2	9	30	42	17
Region																		
Northeast	270	22	28	31	16	3	264	24	29	30	14	2	267	24	25	31	16	4
Midwest	279	16	28	35	18	3	274	19	30	33	16	2	280	17	26	34	19	4
South	267	23	28	30	15	3	262	26	29	29	14	2	265	25	27	29	15	4
West	276	20	23	33	21	4	271	22	24	32	18	3	276	20	22	32	20	5
Prison population	246	31	37	26	6	0	240	33	38	25	4	0	236	40	32	22	6	1

[1] Prose literacy is the ability to understand and use information contained in various kinds of textual material. A level 1 score of 0 to 225 requires the reader to locate a single piece of information in a short text. A level 2 score of 226 to 275 requires the reader to locate a single piece of information in the text with several distractors or to make low-level inferences. A level 3 score of 276 to 325 requires the reader to make literal or synonymous matches between the text and information given in the task, or to make low-level inferences. A level 4 score of 326 to 375 requires the reader to perform multiple-feature matches and to integrate or synthesize information from complex passages. A level 5 score of 376 to 500 requires the reader to search for information in dense text which contains a number of distractors.

[2] Document literacy reflects the knowledge and skills used to process information from documents. A level 1 score of 0 to 225 requires the reader to locate pieces of information based on a literal match. A level 2 score of 226 to 275 requires the reader to match a single piece of information among several distractors. A level 3 score of 276 to 325 requires the reader to integrate multiple pieces of information from one or more documents. A level 4 score of 326 to 375 requires the performance of multiple-feature matches, cycling through documents, and integrating informa-

tion. A level 5 score of 376 to 500 requires the reader to search through complex displays that contain multiple distractors, to make high-level text-based inferences.

[3] Quantitative literacy is the ability to perform numerical operations in everyday life. A level 1 score of 0 to 225 requires the reader to perform a single, relatively simple, arithmetic operation. A level 2 score of 226 to 275 requires the reader to perform a single operation using numbers that are either stated in the task or easily located in the material. A level 3 score of 276 to 325 requires the reader to use two or more numbers to solve the problem. A level 4 score of 326 to 375 requires the reader to perform two or more sequential operations or a single operation in which the quantities are found in different types of displays. A level 5 score of 376 to 500 requires the reader to perform multiple operations sequentially. They must extract the features of the problem from text or rely on background knowledge to determine the quantities or operations needed.

SOURCE: U.S. Department of Education, National Center for Education Statistics, National Adult Literacy Survey, Adult Literacy in America, 1992, prepared by Educational Testing Service. (This table was prepared February 1994.)

CHAPTER 6
International Comparisons of Education

This chapter offers a broad perspective on education across the nations of the world. It also provides an international context for examining the condition of education in the United States. Historically, the National Center for Education Statistics (NCES) was not active in collecting international data, but recently NCES has expanded its role by serving as the national research center for the International Association for the Evaluation of Educational Achievement (IEA) Reading Literacy Study and funding international research studies comparing mathematics and science education. These studies include the Third International Mathematics and Science Study (TIMSS) and the Second International Assessment of Educational Progress, which provides comparative data for 9- and 13-year-olds. In addition, NCES is cooperating with international agencies in the compilation of statistics and the development of education indicators.

The data in this chapter were drawn from material prepared by the United Nations Educational, Scientific, and Cultural Organization (UNESCO), the Institute of International Education, the Organization for Economic Cooperation and Development (OECD), and the International Assessment of Educational Progress (IAEP). The basic summary data on enrollments, teachers, enrollment ratios, and finances were synthesized from information appearing in Education at a Glance published by OECD. Even though OECD tabulations are very carefully prepared, international data users should be cautioned about the many problems of definition and reporting involved in the collection of data about the educational systems in the world.

This chapter provides information from the International Assessment of Educational Progress (IAEP), sponsored by the Educational Testing Service (ETS), the U.S. Department of Education and the National Science Foundation. The mathematics and science performance of 13-year-old students in 20 countries, and 9-year-old students in 14 countries, was studied through assessments administered during 1990–91. Some countries assessed nationally representative samples of the two age groups; others limited their assessments to specific geographic areas or language groups.

A different perspective is provided by data on the enrollment of foreign students in U.S. institutions of higher education. These data from the Institute of International Education provide information on the number of foreign students and their countries of origin.

Further information on survey methodologies is in the "Guide to Sources" in the appendix and in the publications cited in the source notes.

Population

The percent of young people in a population can influence the proportion of national income allocated to each student. Countries with a greater proportion of young people must set aside larger proportions of domestic product for their education. Among the OECD countries, Turkey has by far the largest percentage of young people ages 5 to 13 at 19.9 percent. The closest followers are Ireland at 17.2 percent, and Portugal at 13.7 percent. Countries with relatively small numbers of persons in this age group include Germany at 8.9 percent, and Denmark at 9.9 percent. The proportion of 5- to 13-year-olds in the U.S was 12.8 percent, which was higher than most other OECD countries (table 386).

Enrollments

In 1993, over 1 billion students were enrolled in schools around the world. Of these students, 622 million were in elementary-level programs, 341 million were in secondary programs, and 78 million were in higher education programs (table 388).

Between 1980 and 1993, enrollments grew rapidly, particularly in the less developed areas of the world. Elementary enrollment changes ranged from increases of 38 percent in Africa and 22 percent in Central and South America to a 3 percent decrease in Europe.

Enrollment increases at the secondary level were more dramatic, especially in Africa (97 percent), Central and South America (43 percent) and Asia (38 percent). Secondary-level enrollment decreased in Europe by 3 percent and in Northern by 4 percent America (U.S., Canada, and Greenland).

Pupil/teacher ratios in elementary and secondary schools vary widely from country to country. Developed countries with relatively low elementary ratios in 1992 were Italy and Denmark (10.9) Countries with relatively high ratios included Ireland (25.6) and the Netherlands (23.6) (table 390).

At the postsecondary level, Africa (124 percent) and Asia (118 percent) had the largest increases followed by Oceania (88 percent) and Central and South America (66 percent). These postsecondary increases are a result of large growth in the school attendance rates and sizable rises in population (table 388). Enrollment rates varied among countries partially due to differing definitions of postsecondary education and what age it begins. In 1991, among the OECD countries, the United States had the largest proportion of 18- to 21-year-olds enrolled in postsecondary education at 36.4 percent, followed by Belgium (30.4 percent) and Canada (29.7 percent). For the 22 to 25 age group, Norway's enrollment is highest at 18.9 percent, Denmark follows at 18.3 percent, and the United States is third at 16.7 percent. Ireland had an enrollment rate of 4 percent (table 387).

In 1994–95 there were 453,000 foreign students studying at U.S. colleges and universities. This was 3,000 more than the year before, or a 1 percent increase. Approximately 58 percent of the students were from South and East Asian countries (table 408).

Education Systems

Of the 20 countries which participated in the 1991 International Assessment of Educational Progress (IAEP), 16 have national curricula. Only Canada, Switzerland, and Brazil join the United States in having state or provincial control of education For the countries participating in the assessment, the average length of the school year ranged from approximately 172 days in Portugal to approximately 251 days in China. The average amount of instruction per school day varied from under 4 hours in Hungary and Fortaleza, Brazil, to a little over 6 hours in France (table 392).

Achievement

Mathematics

In the 1991 IAEP mathematics assessment of 9-year-olds from 10 nations that tested nationally representative populations, students from Korea, Hungary, Taiwan, the (former) Soviet Union, and Israel all had average test scores that were significantly higher than those from the United States. In the assessment of the 13-year-old students in which 15 nations tested nationally representative populations, the average test scores of U.S. students were higher than only one country, Jordan. There was no significant difference between the test scores of U.S. stu-

dents and those of students from Slovenia and Spain. The remaining 10 countries all had average test scores that were significantly higher than those of U.S. students (tables 393 and 395).

An analysis of the 1991 IAEP scores on different mathematics topics reveals that U.S. 9-year-old students scored well in the area of data analysis, statistics, and probability. In this area, the average test score of the U.S. 9-year-olds was the same or higher than students in all the other countries which tested comprehensive populations, except for Korea. The U.S. 13-year-olds' average test score in data analysis, statistics, and probability was lower than those of the students in many of the countries testing comprehensive populations. The exceptions were Spain, Slovenia, and Jordan, where the test scores were lower than those of the U.S. 13-year-olds (tables 394 and 396).

Science

In the 1991 IAEP science assessment of 9-year-olds, 10 nations tested nationally representative populations. The average science scores of U.S. students were significantly lower than those of Korean students, but about the same as students from Taiwan, Canada, Hungary, Spain and the (former) Soviet Union. The IAEP assessment of 13-year-old science students involved 14 nations testing nationally representative populations. Students from 7 of the participating nations had average science scores that were higher than those of U.S. 13-year-old students, 4 had scores that were about the same, and 2 countries, Ireland and Jordan had lower scores. (Note: In this international assessment of education, the standard errors are relatively large. In the interest of allowing for meaningful comparisons between countries, the IAEP tables in the *Digest of Education Statistics* list standard errors) (tables 398 and 399).

When the results of the 1991 IAEP science assessments are analyzed by subject matter, U.S. 9-year-olds excelled in the earth and space sciences. In this area, U.S. students had average test scores that were significantly higher than their counterparts in Korea and Taiwan, but about the same as Hungary (tables 397).

Geography

On a 1991 International Assessment of Educational Progress in geography, students from Hungary performed at a significantly higher level on the 24 geography items than their counterparts from the other eight countries in the study (Canada, Ireland, Korea, Scotland, Slovenia, the former Soviet Union, Spain, and the United States (table 391).

Reading

On a reading literacy assessment of 9- and 14-year-olds in 32 countries, students in Finland were among the best readers at both levels. Students in the United States produced relatively high scores at the 9-year-old level. Among the 14-year-olds, students in the United States also scored in the high performing group, along with students from France, Sweden, New Zealand, Hungary, Iceland, Switzerland, and Hong Kong. American students performed considerably better at the 9-year-old level relative to the other participating countries than at the 14-year-old level (tables 401 and 402).

Degrees

Ratios of bachelor's degrees conferred per hundred 22- or 23-year-olds in 1992 ranged from 6 in Turkey and 7 in Austria and Finland to 32 in Canada and 27 in the United States. Over 50 percent of all bachelor's degrees were awarded to women in Australia, Canada, Denmark, the Netherlands, New Zealand, Norway, Spain, Sweden, and the United States (table 403).

Countries have been paying more attention lately to the percent of graduates in the math and science fields. For undergraduate degrees awarded in science, math and computer science, and engineering, most OECD countries report rates from 15 to 35 percent. Finland, Belgium, and Germany all are over 30 percent, while Spain and Canada are closer to 15 percent. The proportion of graduate degrees in math and science ranged even wider. Among the countries with the highest proportions were Japan (54 percent), Sweden (44 percent), and Austria (37 percent). Among the countries with the lowest proportions were the United States (14 percent), Australia (14 percent), and New Zealand (19 percent) (tables 404 and 405).

Finances

In general, higher income countries have a larger expenditure per student than lower income countries. At both primary and secondary levels of education, Norway, Sweden, and the United States ranked at the upper end. For primary education, Sweden spent $4,840 per student and the United States spent $5,600, and for secondary education, Austria, Norway, Sweden, and the United States had expenditures over $6,000 per student. Switzerland, United States, Japan, and the United Kingdom spent relatively large amounts per student in higher education, with each having expenditures per student over $10,000 (table 406).

A comparison of public expenditures on education as a percent of gross domestic product (GDP) in OECD countries shows that national investment in education ranged from 3.6 percent of GDP in Japan to 6.7 percent in Sweden (table 407).

Figure 27.-Percentage change in enrollment, by area of the world and level of education: 1980 to 1993

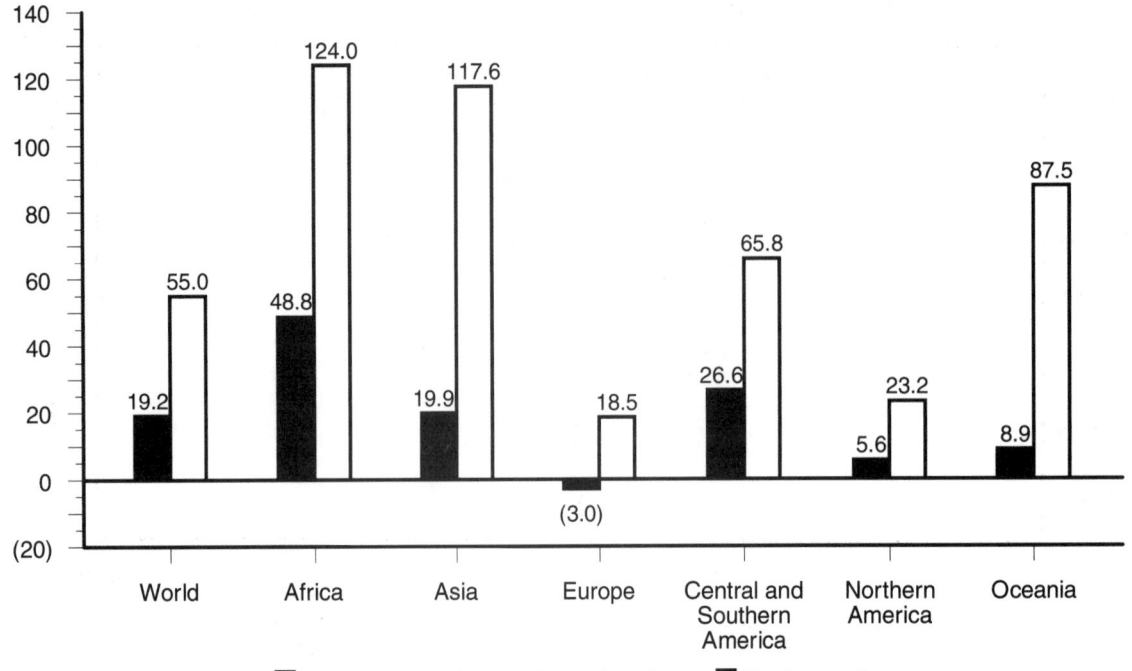

■ Elementary and secondary education □ Postsecondary

SOURCE: United Nations Educational, Scientific, and Cultural Organization, Paris, *Statistical Yearbook*, various years.

Figure 28.-Public expenditures for education as a percentage of gross national product: Selected countries, 1992

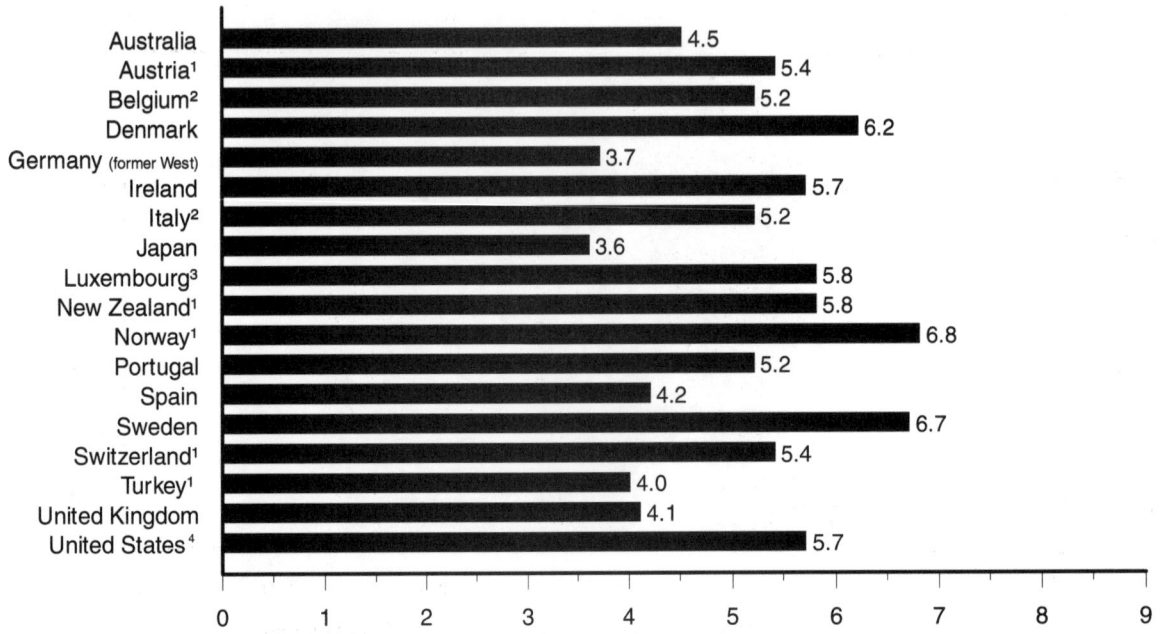

[1] 1991 data.
[2] 1990 data.
[3] 1989 data.
[4] Excludes preprimary data.

SOURCE: Organization for Economic Cooperation and Development, *Education at a Glance*, and unpublished data.

Figure 29.-Distribution of mathematics proficiency scores of 13-year-olds, by country: 1991

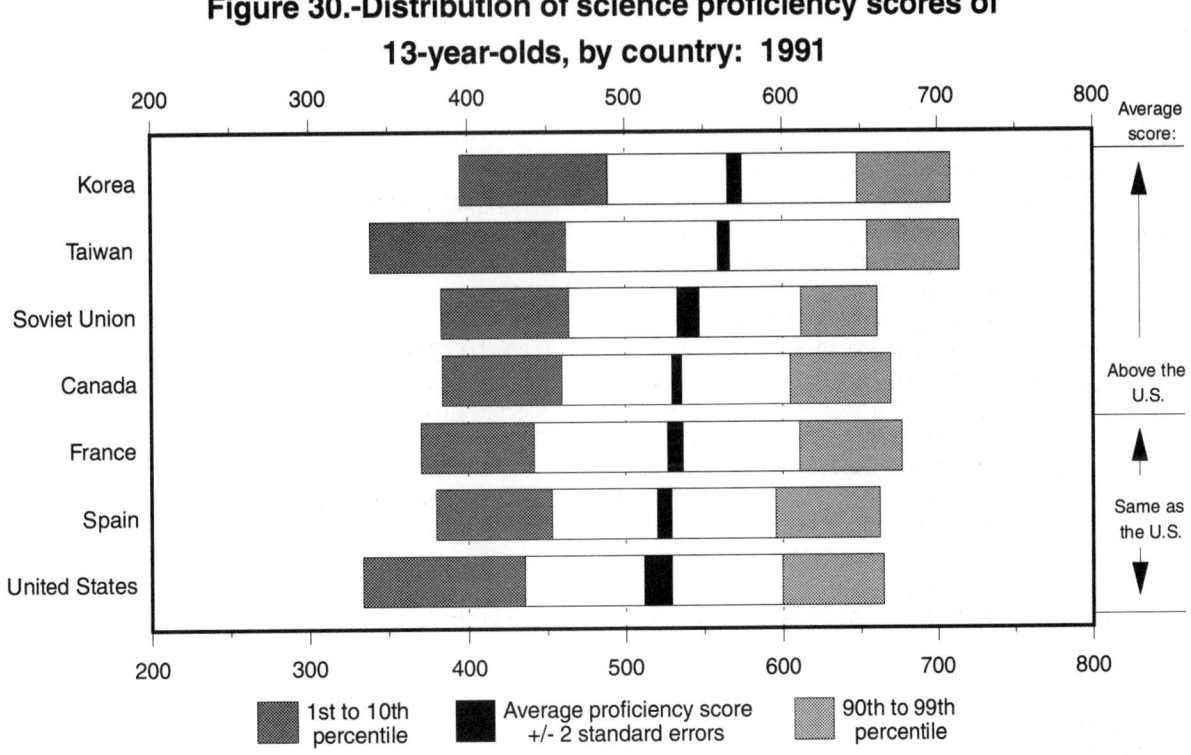

SOURCE: Educational Testing Service, International Assessment of Educational Progress, unpublished tabulations, 1992.

Figure 30.-Distribution of science proficiency scores of 13-year-olds, by country: 1991

SOURCE: Educational Testing Service, International Assessment of Educational Progress, unpublished tabulations, 1992.

Figure 31.-Bachelor's degree recipients as a percent of population in the appropriate age group for selected countries, by sex: 1991

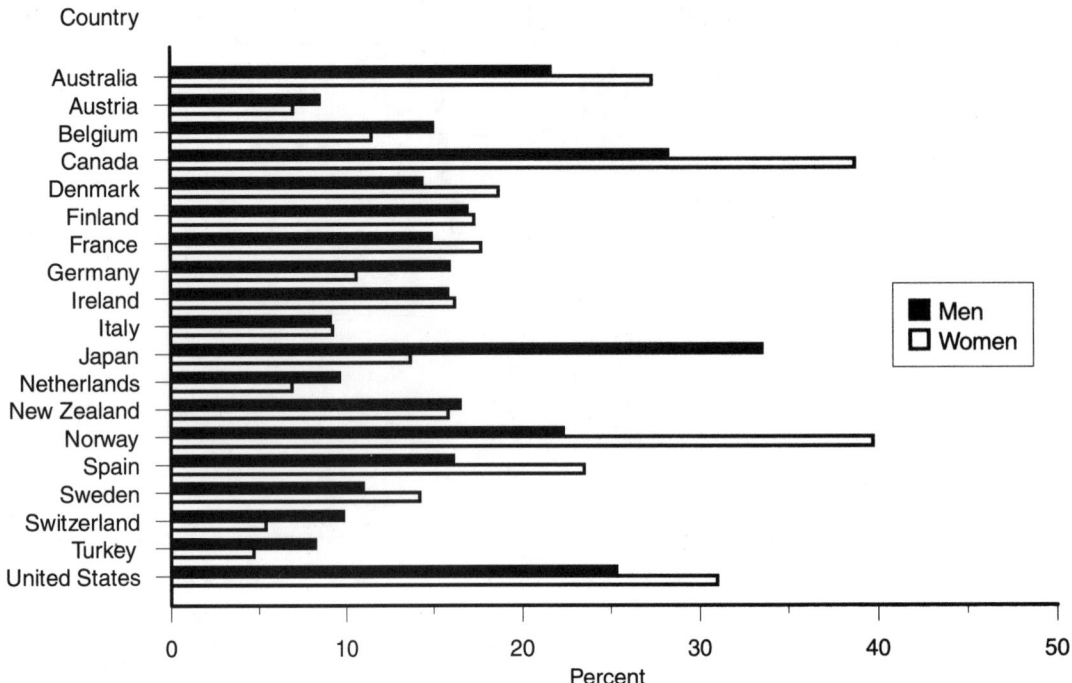

SOURCE: Organization for Economic Cooperation and Development, unpublished data.

Table 386.—School-age populations as a percent of total population: Selected countries, 1985, 1990, and 1991

Country	5- to 13-year-olds as a percent of total population			14- to 17-year-olds as a percent of total population		
	1985	1990	1991	1985	1990	1991
1	2	3	4	5	6	7
Australia	14.5	13.1	13.0	6.6	6.4	6.1
Austria	10.9	10.4	10.5	6.4	5.1	4.9
Belgium	11.4	10.9	10.9	5.8	5.1	4.9
Canada	12.8	12.4	12.5	6.1	5.5	5.5
Denmark	12.0	10.1	9.9	5.8	5.7	5.5
Finland	11.5	11.8	11.6	5.6	4.9	5.0
France	12.8	12.1	12.1	6.2	5.8	5.5
Germany (former West)	9.1	8.7	8.9	6.1	4.1	4.0
Greece	—	—	—	—	5.5	—
Iceland	15.7	15.0	—	6.7	6.8	—
Ireland	17.9	17.5	17.2	7.7	8.0	7.7
Italy	12.7	10.3	10.1	6.5	6.0	5.9
Japan	14.0	11.8	11.5	6.2	6.5	6.4
Luxembourg	10.2	10.1	—	5.5	4.4	—
Netherlands	12.0	10.7	10.7	6.8	5.4	5.1
New Zealand	15.3	13.5	13.4	7.5	6.7	6.4
Norway	12.5	11.0	11.0	6.4	5.8	5.5
Portugal	15.3	14.3	13.7	6.9	6.8	6.9
Spain	15.0	12.9	12.4	6.8	6.8	6.7
Sweden	11.3	10.2	10.2	5.4	5.2	5.0
Switzerland	10.6	10.1	10.1	5.8	4.8	4.7
Turkey	20.6	20.6	19.9	8.7	8.9	8.9
United Kingdom	11.4	11.1	11.3	6.3	5.2	4.9
United States	12.6	12.8	12.8	6.2	5.4	5.3

—Data not available.

SOURCE: Organization for Economic Cooperation and Development, *Education at a Glance*, and unpublished data. (This table was prepared May 1995.)

Table 387.—Percent of population enrolled in secondary and postsecondary institutions, by age group: Selected countries, 1985, 1990, and 1991

Country	Secondary schools, 14 to 17 years old			Postsecondary institutions								
				18 to 21 years old			22 to 25 years old			26 to 29 years old		
	1985	1990	1991	1985	1990	1991	1985	1990	1991	1985	1990	1991
1	2	3	4	5	6	7	8	9	10	11	12	13
Australia	—	—	91.4	—	—	28.9	7.2	—	11.6	—	—	7.6
Belgium	91.7	—	94.6	24.5	—	30.4	7.2	—	9.1	1.5	—	1.7
Canada	92.5	95.8	94.0	25.5	28.9	29.7	9.5	11.4	12.2	3.0	3.4	3.5
Denmark	89.9	90.0	90.0	7.4	7.4	8.2	16.3	17.9	18.3	8.2	9.3	9.5
Finland	89.8	98.2	—	9.3	13.6	—	17.3	20.7	—	7.9	10.2	—
France	93.0	95.1	95.4	19.4	24.6	26.6	10.0	11.8	12.7	4.3	3.9	4.0
Germany (former West)	94.7	94.2	93.6	8.8	8.5	9.1	15.5	15.9	16.3	8.9	10.4	10.6
Ireland	83.6	87.2	89.7	15.2	20.3	20.5	2.8	4.3	4.3	—	—	—
Japan	95.7	95.7	96.1	—	—	—	—	—	—	—	—	—
Netherlands	93.0	92.5	92.7	14.4	17.9	19.1	11.9	13.4	14.5	5.7	4.7	4.7
New Zealand	74.4	84.2	88.4	14.9	20.8	23.2	9.6	13.8	16.1	—	—	—
Norway	90.0	93.2	93.5	8.6	13.6	14.5	13.9	17.4	18.9	6.2	7.4	8.2
Portugal	—	—	69.1	5.8	—	11.3	5.4	—	6.6	2.3	—	2.2
Spain	67.3	79.1	81.6	14.9	21.2	21.5	10.6	13.5	14.2	4.0	4.5	5.3
Sweden	91.3	91.4	91.6	7.9	8.7	9.3	11.3	11.4	11.8	6.5	6.1	6.2
Switzerland	88.9	89.8	90.0	5.7	6.4	6.6	10.6	12.1	12.8	5.2	6.4	7.0
Turkey	—	32.6	33.9	—	7.4	7.9	—	4.6	4.9	—	2.3	2.1
United Kingdom	77.7	83.3	84.2	—	16.1	17.6	—	4.7	6.2	—	—	3.4
United States [1]	92.1	92.9	92.9	33.0	36.2	36.4	14.5	17.1	16.7	8.2	8.5	9.1

[1] Postsecondary includes higher education only.
—Data not available.

SOURCE: Organization for Economic Cooperation and Development, *Education at a Glance*, and unpublished data. (This table was prepared May 1995.)

Table 388.—Selected statistics for countries [1] with populations over 10 million, by continent: 1980, 1990, and 1993

Country	Population in millions			Persons per square kilometer in 1993	First level [2]					
					Enrollment in thousands			Enrollment ratio [6]		
	1980	1990	1993		1980	1990	1993	1980	1990	1993
1	2	3	4	5	6	7	8	9	10	11
World total [7]	4,444.4	5,284.8	5,543.6	41	539,471	593,177	622,059	95	99	99
Africa										
Algeria [8]	18.7	24.9	26.7	11	3,119	4,189	[9]4,436	94	100	[9]103
Angola	7.0	9.2	10.3	8	1,301	990	—	175	91	—
Cameroon	8.7	11.5	12.5	26	1,379	1,964	1,824	98	101	87
Cote D'Ivoire	8.2	12.0	13.3	41	1,025	1,415	1,554	79	71	69
Egypt [8]	43.7	56.3	60.3	60	4,663	6,964	7,732	73	94	97
Ethiopia	36.4	47.4	51.9	[9]45	2,131	2,466	[9]1,856	34	31	[9]23
Ghana	10.7	15.0	16.4	69	[16]1,378	1,945	—	80	77	—
Kenya [8]	16.6	23.6	26.4	45	3,927	5,392	5,643	115	95	91
Madagascar [8]	9.1	12.6	13.9	24	1,724	1,571	1,505	136	87	73
Morocco	19.4	24.3	25.9	58	2,172	2,484	[9]2,728	83	67	[9]73
Mozambique [8]	12.1	14.2	15.1	19	[19]1,387	1,260	1,227	99	66	60
Nigeria [8]	72.0	96.2	105.3	114	13,760	13,777	[9]15,870	119	86	[9]93
South Africa	29.2	37.1	39.7	32	[12,24]4,737	6,952	[22]5,758	[12]103	109	111
Sudan [8]	18.7	24.6	26.6	11	1,464	2,043	—	50	50	—
Uganda	13.1	17.9	19.9	85	[23]1,292	[23]2,470	[23]2,456	[23]50	[23]70	[23]67
United Republic of Tanzania	18.6	25.6	28.0	32	[24]3,368	[24]3,379	[24]3,737	93	70	70
Zaire	27.0	37.4	41.2	18	4,196	4,562	4,939	92	70	68
Zimbabwe	7.1	9.9	10.7	27	1,235	2,116	2,376	85	116	119
Asia										
Afghanistan [8]	16.1	15.0	17.7	27	1,116	[13]726	787	34	[13]25	31
Bangladesh	88.2	108.1	115.2	800	8,240	11,940	—	61	79	—
China [8]	998.9	1,155.3	1,196.4	125	146,270	122,414	124,212	113	127	118
India	688.9	850.6	901.5	274	73,873	99,118	108,201	83	98	102
Indonesia	151.0	182.8	191.7	101	25,537	29,754	[9]29,599	107	115	[9]114
Iran, Islamic Republic of [8]	39.3	58.9	64.2	39	4,799	9,370	9,863	87	110	105
Iraq	13.0	18.1	19.5	44	2,616	3,328	[9]2,857	113	111	[9]91
Japan	116.8	123.5	124.5	330	11,827	9,373	8,769	101	100	102
Kazakstan	14.9	16.7	17.0	6	—	—	1,227	—	—	86
Korea, North (DPR)	18.3	21.8	23.0	191	—	[21]1,543	—	—	[21]104	—
Korea, South (Republic of)	38.1	42.9	44.1	445	5,658	4,869	[29]4,099	110	105	[29]98
Malaysia	13.8	17.9	19.2	58	2,009	2,456	2,719	93	93	93
Myanmar (former Burma)	33.8	41.8	44.6	66	4,148	5,385	—	91	105	—
Nepal [8]	14.9	19.3	20.8	148	1,068	2,789	[9]3,035	84	103	[9]109
Pakistan	85.3	121.9	132.9	167	[19]5,474	[19]8,856	—	39	44	—
Philippines	48.3	60.8	64.8	216	[20]8,518	10,427	[29]10,899	112	113	[29]111
Saudi Arabia	9.6	16.0	17.1	8	927	1,877	[9]2,026	61	73	[9]75
Sri Lanka [8]	14.8	17.2	17.9	273	2,081	2,112	2,013	103	105	106
Syrian Arab Republic	8.7	12.3	13.7	74	1,556	2,452	2,625	100	109	105
Thailand [8]	46.7	55.6	57.6	112	7,393	6,957	[9]6,758	99	99	[9]98
Turkey	44.4	56.1	59.6	76	5,656	6,862	[9]6,708	96	110	[9]103
Uzbekistan	15.9	20.4	21.9	49	—	—	1,853	—	—	80
Vietnam [8]	53.7	66.7	71.3	215	7,887	8,862	9,725	109	103	111
Yemen	8.2	11.3	13.2	25	703	[32]1,671	—	[33]65	[33]88	—
Europe										
Belarus	9.6	10.2	10.2	49	750	615	635	104	95	96
Czechoslovakia (former) [8]	15.3	15.6	15.6	—	1,904	1,924	[35]867	92	94	—
Czech Republic	10.3	10.3	10.3	—	—	546	521	—	96	99
Slovakia	5.0	5.3	5.3	—	—	—	346	—	—	101
France	53.9	56.7	57.5	104	4,610	4,149	4,061	111	108	106
Germany [36]	78.3	79.4	80.9	227	3,636	3,431	3,524	—	101	97
Greece	9.6	10.2	10.4	79	901	813	—	103	98	—
Hungary	10.7	10.4	10.2	110	1,162	1,131	1,009	96	95	95
Italy	56.4	57.0	57.1	190	4,423	3,056	2,863	100	97	98
Netherlands [8]	14.1	15.0	15.3	374	1,333	1,082	[9]1,046	100	102	[9]97
Poland	35.6	38.1	38.3	118	4,167	5,189	5,194	100	98	98
Romania	22.2	23.2	23.0	97	3,237	1,253	[9]1,201	102	91	[9]86
Russian Federation	138.5	147.9	147.8	9	6,009	7,596	[29]7,849	102	109	[29]109
Spain	37.5	39.3	39.5	78	3,610	2,820	2,448	109	107	104
Ukrainian S.S.R.	50.0	51.6	51.6	85	3,595	3,991	2,659	102	89	87
United Kingdom	56.3	57.4	57.9	237	4,911	4,533	[9,39]5,023	103	104	[9,39]112
Yugoslavia, Federal Republic	9.5	10.2	10.6	—	—	467	—	—	72	[9]72
North America										
Canada	24.6	27.8	28.8	3	2,185	2,340	[9]2,438	99	101	[9]105
Cuba [8]	9.7	10.6	10.9	98	1,469	888	983	106	99	104
Mexico	67.1	84.5	90.0	46	14,666	14,402	14,469	122	115	112
United States [41]	227.2	249.4	257.8	28	21,076	22,392	23,212	101	104	104
South America										
Argentina	28.1	32.5	33.8	12	3,917	[25]4,999	4,990	106	[25]108	107
Brazil [8]	121.3	148.5	156.5	18	22,598	28,944	[9]30,106	99	109	[9]111
Chile	11.1	13.2	13.8	18	2,185	1,991	2,066	109	100	98
Colombia	26.5	32.3	34.0	30	4,168	4,247	4,599	124	110	119
Ecuador	8.0	10.3	11.0	39	1,534	1,846	[9]1,987	117	116	[9]123
Peru	17.3	21.6	22.9	18	3,161	3,855	[29]4,030	114	118	119
Venezuela	15.1	19.5	20.9	23	[43]3,158	[43]4,053	[9,43]4,222	93	96	[9]96
Oceania										
Australia	[45]14.6	[45]16.9	[45]17.6	2	1,718	1,583	1,634	112	108	108

[1] Selection based on total population for midyear 1993.

[2] First level enrollment generally consists of elementary school, grades 1–6.

[3] Second level enrollment includes general education, teacher training (at the second level), and technical and vocational education. This level generally corresponds to secondary education in the United States, grades 7–12.

[4] Third level enrollment includes college and university enrollment, and technical and vocational education beyond the high school level. There is considerable variation in reporting from country to country.

[5] In many countries, a child may be exempt from school attendance if there is no suitable school within a reasonable distance of his/her home.

[6] Data are the total enrollment of all ages in the school level divided by the population of the specific age groups which correspond to the school level. Adjustments have been made for the varying lengths of first and second level programs. Because some countries have many students from outside the normal age range, ratios may exceed 100.

[7] Enrollment totals and ratios exclude Democratic People's Republic of Korea. Data do not include adult education or special education provided outside regular schools.

[8] Classification of first and/or second levels have been revised. Data by level may not be comparable over time.

[9] Data for 1992.

[10] Data exclude Ecole Nationale d'Administration et de Magistrature (ENAM).

[11] Eastern Cameroon.

[12] Data for 1986.

[13] Data for 1989.

[14] Excludes all private institutions.

[15] Data for 1985.

[16] Data refer to public education only.

[17] Data for 1979.

[18] Data for 1984.

[19] Includes education preceding the first level.

[20] Data for 1981.

[21] Data for 1987.

[22] Data do not include Transkei, Bophuthatswana, Venda, or Ciskei.

[23] Data refer to government maintained and aided schools only.

[24] Data refer to Tanzania mainland only.

Table 388.—Selected statistics for countries [1] with populations over 10 million, by continent: 1980, 1990, and 1993—Continued

Second level [3]						Third level [4]						Age for compulsory attendance [5]
Enrollment in thousands			Enrollment ratio [6]			Enrollment in thousands			Enrollment ratio [6]			
1980	1990	1993	1980	1990	1993	1980	1990	1993	1980	1990	1993	
12	13	14	15	16	17	18	19	20	21	22	23	24
268,187	**315,412**	**341,063**	**47**	**52**	**55**	**50,578**	**68,560**	**78,374**	**12.1**	**13.6**	**15.5**	**—**
1,028	2,176	[9]2,305	33	61	[9]61	—	286	[9]303	5.9	11.4	[9]11.4	6–15
191	186	—	20	12	—	2	7	—	0.4	0.8	—	7–15
234	500	648	18	28	32	[10]12	33	—	1.6	3.2	—	[11]6–12
222	—	—	19	23	25	20	[12]24	—	2.9	[13]3.1	—	7–13
2,929	5,507	6,133	50	76	76	716	[14]708	—	16.1	17.5	[9]17.1	6–14
[15]666	866	[9]721	8	13	[9]11	14	34	—	0.4	0.8	—	7–13
693	[13]830	—	41	37	—	8	10	—	1.6	1.4	—	6–14
428	[15]458	—	20	[15]21	25	13	[13]31	—	0.9	1.6	—	—
[17]234	—	—	[18]30	17	14	23	36	[9]43	2.6	3.1	[9]3.5	6–13
797	1,124	[9]1,208	26	34	[9]35	112	[15]181	—	5.9	10.1	10.3	7–16
[20]108	160	164	5	8	7	1	[21]2	5	0.1	[15]0.1	0.4	7–14
2,346	3,123	[9]4,032	21	24	[9]29	150	[13]336	—	2.2	[13]4.0	—	6–12
—	2,743	—	[12]55	68	77	—	[22]439	[9,24]490	—	12.8	[9]13.4	—
384	732	—	16	23	—	29	[13]60	—	1.7	3.0	—	—
[23]87	[23]268	[23]261	[23]5	[23]12	[23]11	6	18	24	0.5	[23]1.1	[23]1.3	—
[24]79	[24]167	[24]197	3	5	5	[15]5	[13]5	—	—	[15]0.3	—	7–14
862	[9]1,097	1,341	24	[15]23	24	28	[25]61	—	1.2	1.9	—	6–12
75	661	640	8	49	45	8	49	[9]62	1.3	5.2	[9]6.1	7–15
137	—	—	10	[13]8	15	[12]22	24	—	—	[13]1.7	—	7–15
2,659	3,593	—	18	19	—	240	434	—	2.8	3.8	—	6–10
56,778	51,054	53,837	46	48	55	[26]1,161	[26]2,147	4,505	1.2	1.7	3.8	7–16
32,748	[15]44,485	64,116	30	44	49	3,545	4,951	—	5.2	7.8	—	[27]6–14
5,722	10,965	[9]10,969	29	44	[9]43	[18]980	[9]1,885	[9]1,973	—	[9]10.0	[9]10.2	7–13
2,718	5,085	7,059	42	54	66	[15,18]184	[16]312	[16]437	—	9.1	15.1	6–10
1,033	[25]1,167	[9]1,145	57	47	[9]44	107	[25]210	—	8.7	[25]12.6	—	6–12
9,558	11,026	—	93	97	—	2,412	[13]2,683	—	30.5	[15]27.8	—	6–15
—	—	—	—	—	90	260	290	272	34.1	40.1	41.6	—
—	[21,31]2,468	—	—	—	—	—	[21]390	—	—	—	—	5–15
4,286	4,560	[29]4,569	78	90	[29]96	[30]648	1,691	2,099	14.7	38.6	[29]50.8	6–12
1,084	1,420	1,573	48	56	59	58	124	—	4.1	7.2	—	6–14
1,066	[21]1,359	—	22	23	—	[21]202	[9]195	[9]244	—	[21]4.8	—	5–10
512	709	[9]855	21	31	[9]35	[16]34	94	—	2.7	4.9	—	6–11
2,166	3,983	—	14	21	—	[15]268	[13]305	—	[15]2.5	2.6	—	7–13
2,929	4,034	[29]4,804	64	73	79	1,276	1,709	—	24.4	27.4	26.2	7–13
349	893	[9]1,073	29	44	[9]49	62	154	[9]193	7.1	11.6	[9]13.7	—
1,267	2,082	2,247	55	74	74	[26]43	[12]62	—	2.7	5.2	[29]6.1	5–15
604	914	923	46	52	47	140	222	—	16.9	17.8	[9]17.6	6–11
1,920	2,230	[9]2,718	29	30	[9]37	[15]1,027	[13]952	[9]1,156	12.7	[13]15.7	[9]18.7	7–15
2,218	3,808	[9]4,300	35	54	[9]61	246	750	1,143	5.4	12.9	[9]15.7	6–14
—	[13]3,652	3,136	—	—	94	278	344	—	29.6	31.6	—	6–11
—	—	—	42	33	35	[31]115	[13]186	—	2.1	1.5	1.5	—
73	[33]421	—	[33]4	[33]31	—	8	[25,38]23	—	[33]1.0	[25,38]2.9	—	—
760	968	994	98	93	92	177	192	178	39.0	47.4	44.1	[34]6–17
781	864	—	89	83	—	197	190	—	17.4	17.0	—	6–16
—	—	1,120	—	—	86	120	118	129	17.5	16.0	15.5	—
—	—	658	—	—	89	—	—	73	—	—	17.1	—
5,014	5,522	5,737	85	99	106	1,077	1,699	2,075	25.3	39.6	49.5	6–16
[37,38]8,457	7,398	7,796	—	98	101	1,624	2,049	1,875	27.2	33.9	35.6	6–18
740	851	—	81	99	—	121	195	—	17.1	25.9	—	6–15
357	514	529	70	79	81	101	102	134	14.1	14.0	16.9	6–16
5,308	5,118	4,716	72	79	81	1,118	1,452	1,682	27.0	30.8	37.3	6–13
[38]1,391	1,402	[9]1,370	93	120	[9]123	360	479	[9]507	29.3	39.8	[9]44.8	5–16
1,674	1,888	2,109	77	81	84	589	545	694	18.1	21.7	25.5	7–14
871	2,838	[9]2,452	71	92	[9]82	193	[13]165	[9]236	12.1	[13]8.5	[9]11.8	6–14
12,991	13,956	13,732	96	94	88	5,700	5,100	4,587	46.1	52.2	45.3	—
3,977	4,755	4,734	87	105	113	698	1,222	[9]1,371	23.2	36.7	[9]41.1	6–15
3,406	3,408	4,125	94	93	80	880	895	—	41.6	46.5	—	[34]6–17
5,342	4,336	[9]4,537	83	86	[9]92	827	1,258	[9]1,528	19.1	29.1	[9]37.4	5–16
—	788	[9]832	—	63	[9]65	—	[9]133	[9]143	—	[9]18.0	[9]18.9	7–15
2,323	2,292	[9]2,392	88	101	[9]104	[40]1,173	1,917	2,011	51.6	94.7	[9]102.9	6–16
1,146	1,002	726	81	89	77	152	242	[9]198	17.3	20.9	[9]18.1	6–11
4,742	6,704	6,977	48	55	58	930	1,311	1,358	14.2	14.1	13.8	6–14
21,945	19,313	21,055	94	96	97	12,097	13,820	14,305	58.0	77.7	76.2	7–16
[20]1,366	[25]1,974	—	56	[25]69	—	491	[21]959	—	21.8	[9]40.7	40.5	6–14
2,819	3,499	[9]4,086	34	39	[9]43	1,409	[42]1,540	[42]1,595	11.1	11.3	11.5	7–14
538	720	653	52	73	67	145	255	327	12.3	20.5	26.7	6–13
1,733	[9]2,378	2,796	41	[9]55	62	272	[13]475	—	9.1	[15]11.3	—	6–14
592	[15]730	[9]814	53	55	[9]55	270	207	—	34.9	20.0	—	6–14
1,203	1,698	[29]1,776	59	67	65	306	682	[9]778	17.3	33.1	[9]40.1	6–12
[44]222	[44]281	[9,44]299	21	35	[9]35	307	550	—	20.6	29.0	—	5–15
1,100	1,278	1,282	71	82	84	324	485	964	25.4	35.5	41.9	6–16

[25] Data for 1988.
[26] Includes full-time students only.
[27] Data pertain to the majority of states.
[28] General education only.
[29] Data for 1994.
[30] Data do not include Air & Correspondence courses.
[31] Includes correspondence courses.
[32] Data for Former Democratic Yemen do not include schools for nomads.
[33] Former Yemen Arab Republic only.
[34] Grade levels changed for compatibility with ISCED.
[35] Data are a combination of data for the Czech Republic and Slovakia.
[36] Data include both former East and West Germany.
[37] Excludes technical education, consisting of both on the job training and school education.
[38] Data do not include apprenticeships and health care training.
[39] Includes infant classes in primary schools, previously considered as preprimary education.
[40] Excludes trade and vocational programs.

[41] Population data are from the U.S. Bureau of the Census, Current Population Reports, Population Estimates. Enrollment totals and ratios are based on data compiled by the National Center for Education Statistics and the U.S. Bureau of the Census. First level includes grades 1 through 6 (ages 5–10), second level includes grades 7 through 12 (ages 11–16), and third level includes ages 20–24.
[42] Excludes post-graduate level.
[43] Data refer to grades 1 to 9 (basic education).
[44] Data refers to grades 10 and 11.
[45] Includes Norfolk Island.
—Data not available.

NOTE.—Some data have been revised from previously published figures.

SOURCE: United Nations Educational, Scientific, and Cultural Organization (UNESCO), Paris, Statistical Yearbook, various years; U.S. Department of Commerce, Bureau of the Census, Current Population Reports, Series P-20; and U.S. Department of Education, National Center for Education Statistics, Common Core of Data and "Fall Enrollment in Institutions of Higher Education" surveys, and Integrated Postsecondary Education Data System (IPEDS), "Fall Enrollment" survey. (This table was prepared May 1996.)

Table 389.—Estimated population, school enrollment, teachers, and public expenditures for education in major areas of the world: 1980, 1990, 1992, and 1993

| Item | World total [1] | Major areas of the world | | | | | |
		Africa [2]	Asia [3]	Europe [4]	Central and South America [5]	Northern America [5]	Oceania [6]
1	2	3	4	5	6	7	8
1980							
Population, all ages, [7] in thousands	4,444,361	475,666	2,642,110	692,997	358,440	252,461	22,687
Enrollment, all levels, [8] in thousands	858,235	80,146	494,052	132,101	87,216	59,904	4,815
First (primary) level	539,471	64,249	335,871	48,669	65,319	22,611	2,752
Second level [9]	268,187	14,355	144,495	66,810	16,967	23,914	1,647
Third level [10]	50,578	1,543	13,687	16,623	4,930	13,379	416
Teachers, all levels, [8] in thousands	38,124	2,406	19,466	8,233	3,732	4,015	272
First (primary) level	18,854	1,712	10,830	2,343	2,261	1,579	129
Second level [9]	15,525	600	7,477	4,573	1,083	1,679	112
Third level [10]	3,745	94	1,159	1,317	388	757	31
Public expenditures on education, in millions of U.S. dollars	$526,700	$22,900	$103,500	$200,600	$34,200	$155,100	$10,400
As a percent of gross national product	4.9	5.3	4.4	[11] 5.1	3.9	5.2	5.6
1990							
Population, all ages, [7] in thousands	5,284,843	632,672	3,186,447	721,739	439,719	277,838	26,428
Enrollment, all levels, [8] in thousands	977,149	108,274	564,914	131,805	104,974	61,971	5,211
First (primary) level	593,177	80,815	361,881	47,504	75,479	24,774	2,724
Second level [9]	315,412	24,509	179,989	65,408	22,079	21,569	1,859
Third level [10]	68,560	2,950	23,045	18,893	7,416	15,627	628
Teachers, all levels, [8] in thousands	46,793	3,809	24,069	9,399	5,154	4,031	331
First (primary) level	22,614	2,411	12,670	2,697	3,006	1,686	144
Second level [9]	19,216	1,241	9,680	5,180	1,520	1,450	146
Third level [10]	4,964	157	1,719	1,522	628	896	42
Public expenditures on education, in millions of U.S. dollars	$1,017,000	$26,000	$227,100	$368,000	$47,100	$330,200	$18,600
As a percent of gross national product	4.9	5.7	4.2	[11] 5.0	4.1	5.4	5.6
1992							
Population, all ages, [7] in thousands	5,457,896	669,631	3,295,787	724,826	456,588	283,803	27,261
Enrollment, all levels, [8] in thousands	1,018,220	116,438	590,319	132,033	109,242	64,730	5,458
First (primary) level	610,842	86,149	370,556	47,606	77,980	25,744	2,806
Second level [9]	333,651	27,000	193,743	65,076	23,383	22,541	1,908
Third level [10]	73,728	3,289	26,020	19,351	7,879	16,445	744
Teachers, all levels, [8] in thousands	48,448	4,121	24,748	9,654	5,421	4,162	342
First (primary) level	23,395	2,628	12,881	2,786	3,190	1,763	148
Second level [9]	19,868	1,322	10,016	5,322	1,559	1,498	152
Third level [10]	5,185	170	1,852	1,547	672	902	42
Public expenditures on education, in millions of U.S. dollars	$1,231,900	$24,700	$300,600	$469,900	$56,700	$360,500	$19,500
As a percent of gross national product	5.1	5.9	4.3	5.4	4.4	5.6	5.8
1993							
Population, all ages, [7] in thousands	5,543,607	688,786	3,349,520	725,679	465,065	286,867	27,690
Enrollment, all levels, [8] in thousands	1,041,496	120,412	605,844	131,696	112,368	65,609	5,568
First (primary) level	622,059	88,615	377,148	47,296	80,008	26,140	2,852
Second level [9]	341,063	28,340	198,919	64,697	24,187	22,984	1,936
Third level [10]	78,374	3,456	29,777	19,703	8,173	16,485	780
Teachers, all levels, [8] in thousands	49,501	4,229	25,355	9,756	5,606	4,204	350
First (primary) level	23,778	2,661	13,046	2,833	3,279	1,806	153
Second level [9]	20,291	1,389	10,256	5,377	1,626	1,489	155
Third level [10]	5,431	179	2,053	1,546	700	910	43
Public expenditures on education, in millions of U.S. dollars	$1,176,000	$26,200	$289,800	$391,100	$66,600	$382,100	$20,200
As a percent of gross national product	5.1	6.2	4.3	5.2	4.6	5.6	6.0

[1] Enrollment and teacher data exclude the Democratic People's Republic of Korea. Expenditure data exclude Albania, Cambodia, Democratic People's Republic of Korea, Lao People's Democratic Republic, Lebanon, Mongolia, Mozambique, South Africa, and Viet Nam.

[2] Excludes Rodrigues and other small islands.

[3] Excludes the former U.S.S.R., the Democratic People's Republic of Korea, and Arab states, but includes both the Asian and the European portions of Turkey.

[4] Includes the former U.S.S.R.

[5] Northern America includes Bermuda, Canada, Greenland, St. Pierre, Miquelon and the United States of America. Hawaii is included in Northern America rather than Oceania. Central and South America includes the rest of America.

[6] Includes American Samoa, Australia, Guam and New Zealand.

[7] Estimate of midyear population.

[8] Excludes special and adult education provided outside regular schools. Data prior to 1992 exclude preprimary.

[9] Includes general, teacher training and vocational education.

[10] Includes universities and other institutions of higher education.

[11] This figure is for Europe, not including the former U.S.S.R.

SOURCE: United Nations Educational, Scientific, and Cultural Organization, Paris, *Statistical Yearbook*, various years. (This table was prepared May 1996.)

Table 390.—Pupils per teacher in public and private elementary and secondary schools, by level of education: Selected countries, 1985 to 1992

Country	Elementary					Junior high schools					Senior high schools				
	1985	1989	1990	1991	1992	1985	1989	1990	1991	1992	1985	1989	1990	1991	1992
1	2	3	4	5	6	7	8	9	10	11	12	13	14	15	16
Australia [1]	[1]13.8	—	—	18.0	[2]18.4	—	—	—	—	—	3.2	—	—	11.9	—
Austria	11.3	11.5	11.6	11.6	12.2	9.2	7.9	7.7	7.6	7.7	15.2	12.6	12.4	11.9	11.6
Belgium	—	—	—	9.3	13.7	—	—	—	—	—	—	—	—	4.6	—
Canada	18.1	16.9	17.1	—	—	16.0	15.5	15.5	—	—	16.0	15.5	15.3	—	—
Denmark	12.7	12.2	11.2	11.1	[3]10.9	10.2	8.4	9.3	9.2	[3]9.1	14.8	13.6	13.3	12.6	[3]10.4
France	—	—	—	22.7	[4]20.4	—	—	—	—	—	—	—	—	5.6	—
Germany (former West)	20.7	20.3	20.3	21.4	[5]19.6	16.9	14.7	14.6	14.8	[5]14.6	23.7	21.9	21.0	20.4	[5]19.0
Ireland	—	—	—	—	25.6	—	—	—	—	—	7.2	8.0	8.3	8.6	—
Italy	12.8	10.8	10.7	10.9	10.9	9.6	8.7	8.5	8.3	9.0	10.8	10.7	10.7	10.5	8.8
Japan	—	21.5	[1]20.8	[1]20.3	[6]19.8	—	19.4	18.6	17.7	[6]16.8	—	[1]16.4	16.2	16.2	[6]16.4
Luxembourg	—	13.7	—	—	—	—	86.6	—	—	—	—	5.2	—	—	—
Netherlands	20.2	19.2	19.2	19.0	[7]23.6	12.7	12.6	12.4	10.2	—	—	—	—	—	—
New Zealand	20.1	19.7	19.1	18.4	18.5	—	—	—	—	—	—	—	—	—	—
Norway	—	—	—	10.7	—	—	—	—	8.7	—	—	—	—	8.1	—
Portugal	—	—	—	13.3	—	—	—	—	0.1	—	—	—	—	5.2	—
Spain	26.8	22.9	21.2	19.7	21.2	21.4	19.5	18.8	17.8	17.6	15.3	15.1	14.8	14.7	15.9
Sweden	11.6	10.7	10.6	10.4	11.9	10.8	10.6	10.2	10.6	10.6	13.1	12.2	11.9	11.9	16.0
Turkey	31.1	30.7	30.6	30.5	29.3	41.3	50.0	48.4	49.7	47.5	11.0	12.2	12.1	13.1	13.2
United Kingdom	19.7	22.0	22.0	22.2	20.8	—	18.5	18.5	18.6	15.9	11.1	17.2	13.9	13.7	[8]14.8
United States	17.0	15.6	15.6	15.5	—	16.5	16.0	15.9	16.1	16.8	16.2	16.0	15.8	15.6	15.0

[1] Public schools only.

[2] Teachers include principals, deputy principals and senior teachers mainly involved in administrative tasks.

[3] Full-time and part-time teachers are estimates. Distribution by school level (primary and lower secondary levels) is also an estimate. Kindergartens are classified as public institutions.

[4] The number of full-time equivalent teachers does not take into account the additional hours given by teachers. In public secondary education institutions, an increase of 6.6 per cent of total full-time equivalents would be observed if the additional hours were taken into account. The number of teachers in independent private secondary education institutions are entirely estimates. About 18 per cent of all the pedagogical and support staff, and about 7 per cent of all the staff employed in educaton have been estimated.

[5] Most components are estimates.

[6] Principals and vice-principals are included in "Teachers" while other staff is included in "Support staff." Full-time equivalents of part-time teachers are not calculated, since there are no valid and reliable data available on the basis of which such calculations can be made.

[7] Teaching staff do not include direction staff.

[8] Figures on teachers at lower secondary education are included in upper secondary education.

—Data not available.

SOURCE: Organization for Economic Cooperation and Development, "Education at a Glance," various years; and unpublished data. (This table was prepared April 1996.)

Table 391.—Geography proficiency of 13-year-olds in educational systems participating in the International Assessment of Educational Progress: 1991

Country	Average percent correct			
	All geography items [1] (s.e.)	Geographic skills and tools [2] (s.e.)	Physical geography items [3] (s.e.)	Cultural geography items [4] (s.e.)
1	2	3	4	5
Hungary	69.8 (0.6)	76.3 (0.5)	67.8 (0.7)	65.0 (0.7)
Slovenia	65.3 (0.6)	67.9 (0.5)	63.6 (0.7)	64.3 (0.9)
Canada [5]	63.0 (0.5)	69.5 (0.4)	61.0 (0.6)	58.2 (0.6)
Soviet Union (former) [6]	62.6 (1.1)	72.2 (0.9)	61.2 (1.0)	53.4 (1.8)
United States	61.9 (0.8)	69.4 (0.6)	58.3 (1.0)	58.1 (1.0)
Spain [7]	60.1 (0.7)	62.4 (0.9)	58.9 (0.7)	58.9 (1.1)
Korea	59.7 (0.5)	67.8 (0.5)	52.1 (0.7)	60.3 (0.6)
Ireland	58.5 (0.6)	62.7 (0.6)	59.5 (0.8)	52.3 (0.8)
Scotland	58.3 (0.6)	66.2 (0.5)	57.1 (0.8)	50.6 (0.8)

[1] All 24 geographic items.

[2] Eight items testing ability to use maps, charts, and globes.

[3] Nine items testing knowledge of location of physical features and concepts of climate.

[4] Seven items testing knowledge of cultural entities and interactions between people and their environment.

[5] Eight provinces.

[6] Schools in 14 republics where instruction is in Russian.

[7] Schools where instruction is in Spanish, in all regions except Cataluna.

NOTE.—s.e.=standard error.

SOURCE: U.S. Department of Education, National Center for Education Statistics, International Assessment of Educational Progress, Learning About The World, 1992. (This table was prepared May 1993.)

Table 392.—Characteristics of educational systems participating in the International Assessment of Educational Progress: 1991

Country	Ethnic homogeneity [1]	Age for starting school	Average days in school year [2]	Average minutes of instruction in school day [2]	National curriculum	Percent of schools with one or more problems [2,3]
1	2	3	4	5	6	7
Populations (comprehensive)						
Canada [4]	No	6	188 (0.2)	304 (0.8)	No	13 (1.3)
France	Yes	6	174 (1.7)	370 (3.4)	Yes	29 (4.9)
Hungary	Yes	6	177 (1.5)	223 (1.3)	Yes	32 (4.2)
Ireland [5]	Yes	6	173 (0.9)	323 (4.4)	Yes	39 (5.8)
Israel [5]	No	6	215 (2.2)	278 (6.5)	Yes	46 (6.7)
Jordan	Yes	6	191 (0.9)	260 (2.9)	Yes	63 (5.3)
Korea	Yes	6	222 (2.5)	264 (2.4)	Yes	24 (4.9)
Scotland	Yes	5	191 (0.9)	324 (2.3)	Yes	23 (4.0)
Slovenia	Yes	7	190 (1.5)	248 (2.5)	Yes	50 (5.3)
Spain [6]	No	6	188 (2.3)	285 (3.2)	Yes	33 (5.0)
(Former) Soviet Union [7]	No	6 or 7	198 (2.1)	243 (2.6)	Yes	72 (5.1)
Switzerland [8]	No	6 or 7	207 (3.2)	305 (7.4)	No	11 (3.5)
Taiwan	No	6	222 (2.5)	318 (6.9)	Yes	10 (2.8)
United States	No	6	178 (0.4)	338 (5.0)	No	5 (2.2)
Populations (with exclusions or low participation)						
Brazil, Fortaleza	No	7	183 (1.1)	223 (9.8)	No	62 (5.3)
Brazil, Sao Paulo	No	7	181 (0.2)	271 (9.3)	No	60 (4.6)
China	Yes	6.5 or 7	251 (2.1)	305 (7.1)	Yes	43 (6.3)
England	Yes	5	192 (1.8)	300 (4.4)	Yes	24 (8.3)
Italy [9]	Yes	6	204 (0.5)	289 (5.0)	Yes	18 (5.1)
Mozambique, Maputo, and Beira	No	7	193 (0.0)	272 (0.0)	Yes	92 (0.0)
Portugal	Yes	6	172 (1.1)	334 (6.5)	Yes	56 (7.9)

[1] 90 percent of entire population from one ethnic group.
[2] For 13–year-olds.
[3] Problems included: overcrowded classrooms, inadequate facilities and maintenance, shortages of textbooks and other educational materials, student absenteeism, lack of discipline, and vandalism of school property.
[4] Four provinces assessed 9-year-olds. Nine provinces assessed 13-year-olds.
[5] Schools where instruction is in Hebrew.
[6] Schools where instruction is in Spanish, in all regions except Cataluna.
[7] Schools in 14 republics, where instruction is in Russian.

[8] Fifteen Cantons.
[9] Emilia-Romagna province only.

NOTE.—Standard errors appear in parentheses.

SOURCE: U.S. Department of Education, National Center for Education Statistics, International Assessment of Educational Progress, *Learning Science* and *Learning Mathematics*, by Educational Testing Service. (This table was prepared February 1992.)

Table 393.—Classroom, home, and mathematics activities of 9-year-olds in educational systems participating in the International Assessment of Educational Progress: 1991

Country	Average percent correct on mathematics test	Percent of students who read for fun every day	Percent of students with 2 hours or more homework daily	Percent of students who do math exercises by themselves often	Percent of students who work with math tools often [1]	Percent of students who watch TV 5 hours or more daily
1	2	3	4	5	6	7
Populations (comprehensive)						
Korea	75 (0.6)	25 (1.2)	22 (1.1)	23 (1.0)	11 (1.0)	9 (0.7)
Hungary	68 (0.6)	50 (1.6)	25 (1.4)	69 (1.0)	20 (1.0)	16 (1.2)
Taiwan	68 (0.8)	29 (1.3)	31 (1.2)	47 (1.3)	30 (1.1)	8 (0.8)
(Former) Soviet Union [2]	66 (1.3)	63 (1.3)	31 (1.3)	62 (1.2)	21 (1.0)	18 (0.7)
Israel [3]	64 (0.7)	57 (1.4)	35 (1.5)	42 (1.5)	21 (1.2)	24 (1.1)
Spain [4]	62 (1.0)	55 (1.4)	29 (1.8)	60 (1.7)	23 (1.7)	17 (1.4)
Ireland	60 (0.8)	45 (1.4)	18 (1.5)	51 (1.6)	14 (1.1)	23 (1.5)
Canada [5]	60 (0.5)	48 (0.8)	13 (0.6)	48 (1.0)	13 (0.6)	22 (0.8)
United States	58 (1.0)	45 (1.5)	20 (1.2)	44 (1.5)	19 (1.3)	26 (1.6)
Slovenia	56 (0.6)	63 (1.5)	15 (1.1)	61 (1.4)	20 (1.3)	8 (0.6)
Populations (with exclusions or low participation)						
Italy [6]	68 (0.9)	51 (1.9)	17 (1.5)	42 (2.1)	18 (1.3)	9 (0.8)
Scotland	66 (0.9)	43 (1.6)	4 (0.6)	48 (1.5)	13 (1.5)	23 (1.5)
England	59 (1.9)	51 (2.6)	9 (1.2)	47 (2.8)	18 (1.5)	23 (2.0)
Portugal	55 (0.9)	60 (2.2)	20 (1.7)	32 (2.1)	17 (1.7)	20 (1.5)

[1] Tools are counting blocks, geometric shapes, and geometric solids.
[2] Schools in 14 republics, where instruction is in Russian.
[3] Schools where instruction is in Hebrew.
[4] Schools where instruction is in Spanish, in all regions except Cataluna.
[5] Four provinces.
[6] Emilia-Romagna province only.

NOTE.—Standard errors appear in parentheses.

SOURCE: U.S. Department of Education, National Center for Education Statistics, International Assessment of Educational Progress, *Learning Mathematics*, by Educational Testing Service. (This table was prepared February 1992.)

Table 394.—Mathematics test scores of 9-year-olds in educational systems participating in the International Assessment of Educational Progress: 1991

Country	Average percent correct			Percentile scores						Topic averages					Process averages		
	Total	Male	Female	1	5	10	90	95	99	Numbers and operations	Measurement	Geometry	Data analysis, statistics, and probability	Algebra and functions	Conceptual understanding[1]	Procedural knowledge[2]	Problem solving[3]
1	2	3	4	5	6	7	8	9	10	11	12	13	14	15	16	17	18
IAEP average	63.3	—	—	—	—	—	—	—	—	61.2	67.2	63.9	67.6	61.8	63.2	66.7	58.5
Populations (comprehensive)																	
Korea	74.8 (0.6)	77.2 (0.7)	72.4 (0.8)	26.2 (0.9)	41.0 (3.7)	50.8 (4.7)	93.4 (0.0)	95.1 (0.0)	98.4 (0.0)	74.6 (0.6)	73.0 (0.8)	75.4 (0.7)	79.3 (0.6)	72.1 (0.7)	75.0 (0.6)	78.7 (0.6)	68.8 (0.6)
Hungary	68.2 (0.6)	68.2 (0.8)	68.2 (0.8)	20.4 (2.3)	33.3 (4.5)	40.7 (1.2)	90.2 (2.5)	93.4 (0.0)	98.4 (0.0)	67.5 (0.7)	71.6 (0.7)	68.6 (0.7)	63.4 (0.8)	72.4 (0.8)	68.2 (0.7)	70.8 (0.7)	64.4 (0.7)
Taiwan	68.1 (0.8)	68.4 (0.8)	67.8 (0.9)	19.2 (1.6)	32.1 (4.6)	41.0 (1.8)	91.8 (1.7)	95.1 (0.0)	98.4 (0.0)	67.1 (0.8)	69.3 (0.8)	69.2 (0.8)	72.8 (0.8)	64.2 (0.8)	68.5 (0.8)	76.1 (0.8)	55.7 (0.8)
(Former) Soviet Union[4]	65.9 (1.3)	66.4 (1.2)	65.4 (1.4)	20.0 (0.6)	30.8 (1.0)	37.7 (0.7)	90.2 (0.7)	93.4 (2.3)	98.4 (0.0)	65.7 (1.3)	71.3 (1.0)	64.4 (1.3)	60.1 (1.5)	67.8 (1.3)	63.0 (1.3)	72.0 (1.2)	61.7 (1.4)
Israel[5]	64.4 (0.7)	66.0 (0.8)	62.7 (0.9)	21.3 (0.4)	30.4 (2.8)	38.6 (3.1)	86.9 (2.1)	91.8 (0.0)	96.7 (0.0)	63.6 (0.8)	69.9 (0.7)	58.8 (0.9)	63.9 (1.0)	66.8 (0.7)	62.6 (0.8)	68.3 (0.8)	61.6 (0.8)
Spain[6]	61.9 (1.0)	61.9 (1.3)	61.8 (1.1)	18.8 (0.6)	26.8 (1.8)	32.8 (2.0)	86.9 (0.0)	90.2 (2.4)	96.7 (0.0)	61.3 (1.1)	60.8 (0.8)	60.1 (1.1)	69.3 (1.1)	58.3 (1.1)	60.8 (1.0)	66.1 (1.0)	57.3 (1.1)
Ireland	60.0 (0.8)	59.9 (0.9)	60.1 (1.1)	16.0 (3.3)	24.6 (0.4)	31.2 (1.5)	85.0 (3.9)	90.2 (0.0)	95.1 (0.0)	58.0 (0.9)	64.2 (0.8)	57.9 (0.9)	65.2 (0.8)	59.4 (1.0)	59.3 (0.8)	63.9 (0.8)	55.5 (0.9)
Canada[7]	59.9 (0.5)	59.9 (0.7)	60.0 (0.6)	19.6 (1.6)	28.3 (2.5)	35.7 (1.5)	83.6 (0.0)	88.5 (0.0)	93.4 (2.8)	55.0 (0.6)	65.4 (0.5)	64.7 (0.6)	72.3 (0.5)	56.4 (0.6)	60.4 (0.5)	61.1 (0.6)	57.4 (0.5)
United States	58.4 (1.0)	58.7 (1.1)	58.0 (1.2)	18.0 (1.1)	24.6 (0.0)	29.5 (2.1)	83.6 (0.0)	90.2 (2.3)	96.7 (1.6)	54.3 (1.1)	63.2 (1.0)	56.9 (1.0)	72.8 (1.1)	55.3 (1.0)	59.7 (1.0)	59.5 (1.1)	54.5 (1.0)
Slovenia	55.8 (0.6)	55.8 (0.7)	55.9 (0.7)	18.9 (0.8)	27.7 (1.8)	34.0 (0.8)	79.3 (0.3)	84.5 (0.0)	93.1 (0.0)	52.7 (0.6)	62.4 (0.6)	63.1 (0.8)	54.2 (0.8)	57.8 (0.6)	56.3 (0.6)	57.6 (0.6)	52.3 (0.7)
Populations (with exclusions or low participation)																	
Italy[8]	67.8 (0.9)	69.5 (1.0)	65.9 (1.1)	23.0 (2.0)	34.4 (1.6)	42.6 (0.3)	90.2 (1.7)	93.4 (4.9)	98.4 (0.0)	67.3 (0.9)	73.3 (0.9)	64.6 (1.1)	71.1 (0.9)	60.8 (1.3)	67.8 (0.9)	72.5 (0.9)	60.6 (1.1)
Scotland	65.7 (0.9)	65.8 (1.1)	65.6 (1.1)	23.0 (0.1)	32.8 (0.0)	39.3 (2.8)	89.8 (4.6)	93.3 (2.7)	96.7 (4.6)	62.1 (1.0)	71.3 (0.9)	68.5 (0.8)	73.9 (0.8)	63.1 (1.2)	66.3 (0.8)	67.9 (1.0)	61.8 (0.8)
England	59.5 (1.9)	58.5 (1.5)	60.3 (2.9)	17.2 (2.1)	26.7 (1.6)	32.8 (0.5)	86.9 (2.5)	91.8 (3.3)	96.7 (0.0)	53.6 (2.1)	67.2 (1.6)	67.0 (1.5)	70.4 (1.7)	56.9 (2.1)	60.7 (1.7)	59.2 (2.0)	57.9 (1.9)
Portugal	55.5 (0.9)	56.8 (1.1)	54.2 (1.1)	16.7 (1.9)	26.2 (0.5)	31.6 (0.8)	81.7 (2.6)	86.9 (0.0)	93.4 (1.6)	54.4 (1.1)	58.3 (0.7)	55.6 (1.2)	57.1 (1.0)	54.6 (1.0)	55.7 (0.9)	59.5 (1.1)	49.2 (1.0)
Populations (Canadian)																	
Quebec-French	64.5 (0.7)	65.1 (0.8)	64.0 (0.8)	23.0 (0.0)	32.8 (0.6)	40.7 (4.5)	85.3 (0.0)	88.5 (1.3)	95.1 (0.0)	59.1 (0.8)	68.1 (0.7)	72.8 (0.7)	76.8 (0.7)	63.6 (0.8)	64.6 (0.6)	66.2 (0.9)	62.0 (0.8)
Quebec-English	62.5 (0.8)	62.9 (0.9)	62.0 (1.0)	18.0 (0.0)	29.5 (0.4)	36.1 (1.7)	86.9 (0.9)	90.2 (0.0)	96.7 (0.0)	58.5 (0.9)	69.1 (0.7)	64.1 (0.9)	73.2 (0.7)	57.5 (0.8)	63.5 (0.8)	63.9 (0.8)	58.7 (0.8)
British Columbia	61.9 (0.5)	61.8 (0.7)	62.0 (0.6)	18.2 (1.3)	29.5 (2.3)	36.1 (3.1)	85.3 (0.0)	90.2 (0.2)	96.7 (0.0)	58.7 (0.6)	67.4 (0.5)	62.4 (0.5)	72.3 (0.6)	56.5 (0.5)	62.1 (0.4)	63.7 (0.6)	59.1 (0.6)
New Brunswick-English	59.8 (0.7)	60.3 (0.9)	59.3 (0.9)	17.5 (3.5)	26.7 (0.0)	33.9 (3.6)	83.6 (0.0)	88.5 (5.5)	95.1 (0.0)	56.1 (0.8)	66.0 (0.7)	63.1 (1.0)	69.3 (0.8)	54.6 (0.7)	61.2 (0.7)	61.1 (0.8)	55.7 (0.7)
Ontario-English	56.8 (0.7)	56.3 (0.9)	57.2 (0.9)	18.0 (0.0)	24.6 (2.4)	31.2 (1.5)	81.1 (4.6)	85.7 (3.1)	93.4 (0.0)	52.0 (0.8)	63.3 (0.7)	60.0 (0.9)	69.5 (0.7)	52.2 (0.7)	57.6 (0.7)	57.6 (0.8)	54.3 (0.7)
Ontario-French	54.5 (0.6)	54.7 (0.7)	54.3 (0.6)	18.0 (2.7)	26.3 (0.4)	31.2 (0.0)	77.1 (1.0)	82.0 (0.0)	90.2 (5.3)	48.2 (0.6)	60.0 (0.7)	61.7 (0.7)	67.6 (0.7)	55.1 (0.6)	55.9 (0.6)	54.4 (0.6)	52.4 (0.7)

[1] Conceptual understanding questions analyzed students' abilities in understanding of mathematical facts and concepts.

[2] Procedural knowledge tasks required students to apply knowledge and concepts in solving routine problems using procedures taught in the classroom.

[3] Problem solving questions required the student to apply several skills to a unique situation. These tasks usually involved multiple steps.

[4] Schools in 14 republics, where instruction is in Russian.

[5] Schools where instruction is in Hebrew.

[6] Schools where instruction is in Spanish, in all regions except Cataluna.

[7] Four provinces.

[8] Emilia-Romagna province only.

—Data not available.

NOTE.—Standard errors appear in parentheses.

SOURCE: U.S. Department of Education, National Center for Education Statistics, International Assessment of Educational Progress, Learning Mathematics, by Educational Testing Service. (This table was prepared February 1992.)

Table 395.—Classroom, home, and mathematics activities of 13-year-olds in educational systems participating in the International Assessment of Educational Progress: 1991

Country	Average percent correct on mathematics test	Percent of students who read for fun every day	Percent of students with 2 hours or more homework daily	Percent of students who watch TV 5 hours or more daily	Percent of students who do math exercises by themselves every day	Percent of students who take a math quiz at least once a week	Percent of students with positive attitudes towards mathematics
1	2	3	4	5	6	7	8
Populations (comprehensive)							
Korea	73 (0.6)	11 (0.8)	41 (1.7)	11 (0.9)	17 (1.0)	28 (1.9)	71 (1.3)
Taiwan	73 (0.7)	19 (1.2)	41 (1.3)	10 (0.7)	32 (1.1)	87 (1.1)	79 (0.9)
Switzerland [1]	71 (1.3)	51 (1.1)	20 (1.3)	7 (0.8)	47 (1.9)	40 (2.5)	85 (1.1)
(Former) Soviet Union [2]	70 (1.0)	47 (1.3)	52 (1.6)	17 (1.0)	40 (1.7)	52 (1.5)	76 (1.8)
Hungary	68 (0.8)	44 (1.2)	58 (1.3)	13 (1.0)	37 (1.6)	17 (1.3)	85 (0.8)
France	64 (0.8)	40 (1.2)	55 (1.6)	5 (0.7)	—	64 (1.3)	81 (1.0)
Israel [3]	63 (0.8)	40 (1.7)	50 (1.9)	20 (1.2)	12 (1.1)	36 (2.2)	90 (0.8)
Canada [4]	62 (0.6)	38 (0.9)	27 (1.0)	14 (0.7)	50 (1.1)	53 (0.9)	94 (0.4)
Scotland	61 (0.9)	38 (1.5)	14 (1.1)	24 (1.3)	48 (2.1)	17 (1.3)	91 (0.7)
Ireland	61 (0.9)	41 (1.3)	63 (1.9)	9 (0.9)	54 (1.5)	19 (1.5)	88 (1.0)
Slovenia	57 (0.8)	42 (1.2)	28 (1.7)	4 (0.5)	41 (1.4)	28 (1.5)	83 (1.0)
Spain [5]	55 (0.8)	36 (1.3)	64 (1.5)	10 (0.8)	39 (1.6)	31 (1.7)	89 (1.0)
United States	55 (1.0)	28 (1.3)	29 (1.8)	20 (1.7)	50 (2.7)	68 (2.1)	90 (1.1)
Jordan	40 (1.0)	24 (1.3)	56 (2.0)	7 (0.8)	34 (1.4)	68 (1.5)	77 (1.5)
Populations (with exclusions or low participation)							
China [6]	80 (1.0)	28 (1.5)	44 (1.8)	7 (0.5)	78 (1.6)	63 (2.2)	79 (2.1)
Italy [7]	64 (0.9)	47 (1.3)	79 (1.3)	5 (0.7)	10 (0.7)	19 (1.6)	86 (0.9)
England	61 (2.2)	41 (3.2)	33 (2.8)	14 (2.2)	21 (2.5)	28 (5.8)	91 (1.2)
Portugal	48 (0.8)	44 (1.8)	30 (1.6)	11 (1.0)	30 (1.6)	21 (1.8)	84 (1.1)
Brazil, Sao Paulo	37 (0.8)	33 (1.5)	45 (1.9)	19 (1.2)	35 (1.4)	44 (1.5)	83 (1.0)
Brazil, Fortaleza	32 (0.6)	41 (1.3)	48 (1.8)	21 (1.5)	31 (1.6)	56 (1.9)	86 (1.1)
Mozambique, Maputo and Beira	28 (0.3)	41 (1.6)	42 (1.8)	20 (1.2)	62 (1.6)	94 (1.0)	88 (1.0)

[1] Fifteen cantons.
[2] Schools in 14 republics, where instruction is in Russian.
[3] Schools where instruction is in Hebrew.
[4] Nine provinces.
[5] Schools where instruction is in Spanish, in all regions except Cataluna.
[6] Twenty provinces and independent cities.
[7] Emilia-Romagna province only.

—Data not available.

NOTE.—Standard errors appear in parentheses.

SOURCE: U.S. Department of Education, National Center for Education Statistics, International Assessment of Educational Progress, *Learning Mathematics,* by Educational Testing Service. (This table was prepared February 1992.)

Table 396.—Mathematics test scores of 13-year-olds in educational systems participating in the International Assessment of Educational Progress: 1991

Country	Average percent correct			Percentile scores						Topic averages					Process averages		
	Total	Male	Female	1	5	10	90	95	99	Numbers and operations	Measurement	Geometry	Data analysis, statistics, and probability	Algebra and functions	Conceptual understanding [1]	Procedural knowledge [2]	Problem solving [3]
1	2	3	4	5	6	7	8	9	10	11	12	13	14	15	16	17	18
IAEP average	58.3	—	—	—	—	—	—	—	—	61.0	46.9	62.2	69.1	54.2	60.6	58.4	55.9
Populations (comprehensive)																	
Korea	73.4 (0.6)	74.4 (0.9)	72.2 (1.0)	20.0 (0.0)	33.3 (1.5)	41.3 (1.5)	96.0 (0.0)	97.3 (1.9)	100.0 (0.0)	77.4 (0.6)	59.5 (0.9)	77.4 (0.6)	81.2 (0.7)	70.8 (0.8)	78.3 (0.5)	73.4 (0.7)	68.5 (0.7)
Taiwan	72.7 (0.7)	73.1 (0.9)	72.4 (0.9)	18.7 (1.4)	26.7 (0.0)	35.0 (3.0)	97.3 (1.3)	98.7 (0.0)	100.0 (0.0)	74.7 (0.6)	63.7 (0.9)	76.6 (0.8)	81.2 (0.6)	69.2 (0.9)	74.7 (0.7)	74.7 (0.7)	68.6 (0.8)
Switzerland [4]	70.8 (1.3)	72.8 (1.5)	68.7 (1.1)	30.7 (1.2)	42.7 (0.8)	50.7 (1.9)	93.3 (1.3)	94.7 (0.0)	98.7 (0.0)	73.6 (1.0)	62.0 (1.5)	76.6 (1.3)	81.8 (1.1)	62.7 (1.9)	71.7 (1.1)	69.0 (1.4)	71.9 (1.3)
(Former) Soviet Union [5]	70.2 (1.0)	70.0 (1.3)	70.3 (0.9)	20.9 (2.4)	35.2 (1.4)	42.7 (0.8)	92.0 (0.0)	94.7 (0.0)	98.7 (0.0)	69.2 (1.0)	59.7 (1.1)	77.6 (1.0)	76.1 (1.0)	71.9 (1.1)	70.3 (1.0)	73.2 (1.2)	66.7 (1.0)
Hungary	68.4 (0.8)	68.5 (1.0)	68.3 (0.9)	21.3 (0.9)	32.4 (2.3)	38.7 (1.3)	93.3 (0.0)	96.0 (0.0)	98.7 (0.0)	69.4 (0.7)	55.1 (1.0)	73.3 (0.8)	75.9 (0.8)	69.8 (0.9)	69.8 (0.7)	70.8 (0.8)	64.2 (0.8)
France	64.2 (0.8)	65.5 (0.9)	62.8 (0.9)	22.7 (3.0)	30.7 (0.8)	37.3 (1.0)	89.3 (0.0)	92.0 (5.3)	97.3 (1.3)	65.0 (0.7)	52.7 (1.0)	73.1 (0.8)	79.3 (0.7)	57.0 (1.0)	67.4 (0.7)	65.7 (0.9)	59.3 (0.8)
Israel [6]	63.1 (0.8)	64.4 (0.9)	61.8 (1.1)	21.3 (1.6)	30.7 (1.0)	37.3 (0.2)	87.8 (2.6)	91.8 (4.3)	96.0 (3.9)	64.8 (0.7)	47.2 (1.1)	65.8 (1.0)	74.8 (0.6)	64.7 (1.0)	63.8 (0.8)	65.3 (0.9)	59.8 (0.9)
Canada [7]	62.0 (0.6)	63.0 (0.7)	60.9 (0.6)	21.3 (0.6)	32.0 (0.0)	37.3 (0.0)	86.7 (0.0)	90.7 (0.0)	97.3 (1.3)	65.6 (0.6)	49.9 (0.6)	68.1 (0.7)	76.4 (0.6)	52.7 (0.7)	65.1 (0.6)	61.9 (0.7)	58.9 (0.5)
Scotland	60.6 (0.9)	60.4 (1.0)	60.8 (1.1)	21.3 (0.8)	29.0 (2.8)	34.7 (0.0)	86.7 (0.0)	90.7 (0.0)	96.0 (0.0)	59.7 (0.8)	51.0 (1.2)	69.6 (0.9)	79.1 (0.8)	52.8 (1.2)	61.8 (0.9)	59.2 (1.0)	60.9 (0.9)
Ireland	60.5 (0.9)	62.6 (1.2)	58.4 (1.1)	17.8 (1.3)	26.8 (1.7)	33.3 (2.0)	86.7 (0.0)	90.7 (0.0)	96.0 (4.2)	65.1 (1.0)	49.4 (1.0)	59.9 (1.1)	71.8 (1.0)	55.6 (1.1)	61.5 (0.8)	62.0 (1.2)	57.9 (0.8)
Slovenia	57.1 (0.8)	58.1 (1.0)	56.1 (1.0)	21.3 (0.0)	27.1 (3.9)	32.9 (0.1)	82.7 (0.2)	88.0 (2.6)	94.7 (0.0)	62.2 (0.7)	43.1 (0.9)	63.1 (1.0)	63.6 (0.8)	51.8 (1.0)	58.5 (0.7)	59.0 (0.8)	53.7 (0.8)
Spain [8]	55.4 (0.8)	57.1 (1.1)	53.8 (0.8)	20.3 (1.6)	28.6 (0.5)	32.9 (0.0)	78.4 (0.8)	84.7 (1.3)	91.9 (2.0)	60.1 (0.6)	37.9 (0.8)	60.0 (1.2)	67.7 (0.8)	52.5 (1.2)	58.4 (0.7)	55.8 (0.9)	51.9 (0.8)
United States	55.3 (1.0)	55.8 (1.1)	54.8 (1.3)	17.3 (3.8)	24.0 (0.6)	29.3 (0.0)	82.7 (1.3)	90.7 (0.1)	97.3 (0.0)	61.0 (1.0)	39.5 (1.0)	54.3 (1.0)	72.2 (1.0)	49.2 (1.6)	57.4 (0.9)	56.0 (1.3)	52.3 (1.0)
Jordan	40.4 (1.0)	41.4 (1.2)	39.1 (1.9)	13.3 (0.0)	17.6 (1.2)	21.3 (1.5)	65.3 (3.1)	75.7 (3.3)	89.3 (5.2)	42.8 (1.0)	32.0 (1.0)	43.5 (1.0)	45.7 (1.0)	38.1 (1.3)	44.9 (0.9)	38.5 (1.2)	37.9 (1.0)
Populations (with exclusions or low participation)																	
China [9]	80.2 (1.0)	81.7 (1.0)	78.5 (1.1)	37.0 (2.2)	49.3 (2.7)	57.3 (3.3)	96.0 (1.3)	98.7 (1.3)	100.0 (0.0)	84.9 (0.9)	71.3 (1.5)	80.2 (1.1)	75.4 (1.2)	82.4 (0.9)	81.6 (1.0)	83.0 (0.9)	75.6 (1.2)
England	60.6 (2.2)	60.8 (3.0)	60.4 (2.2)	18.7 (1.9)	27.4 (3.3)	34.5 (3.7)	89.3 (3.9)	93.3 (1.3)	97.3 (1.0)	58.5 (2.0)	51.2 (2.5)	70.3 (2.4)	79.5 (1.8)	54.0 (2.8)	62.0 (2.1)	59.0 (2.6)	60.8 (2.0)
Italy [10]	64.0 (0.9)	65.8 (1.1)	62.1 (0.9)	23.0 (1.3)	32.4 (0.9)	36.5 (1.5)	88.0 (0.0)	91.8 (0.5)	96.0 (0.0)	63.8 (0.8)	62.8 (1.1)	75.3 (1.0)	71.7 (0.8)	52.6 (1.2)	66.6 (0.8)	62.1 (1.1)	63.3 (0.9)
Portugal	48.3 (0.8)	48.9 (1.3)	47.9 (0.9)	17.3 (0.9)	23.9 (1.3)	28.0 (0.5)	74.7 (0.9)	80.6 (1.7)	89.7 (2.6)	52.1 (0.8)	31.9 (0.7)	49.0 (1.3)	68.6 (1.0)	43.1 (1.1)	51.5 (0.9)	47.1 (1.0)	46.4 (0.7)
Brazil, Sao Paulo	37.0 (0.8)	37.9 (0.9)	36.2 (0.9)	10.3 (2.1)	16.7 (1.0)	18.7 (0.9)	62.7 (0.7)	70.7 (1.5)	82.7 (0.7)	40.9 (0.8)	24.1 (0.5)	34.3 (1.5)	49.7 (1.0)	35.6 (1.1)	38.5 (1.0)	36.5 (1.1)	36.0 (0.6)
Brazil, Fortaleza	32.4 (0.6)	35.2 (0.9)	30.5 (0.6)	10.9 (0.4)	14.7 (0.6)	17.3 (0.3)	56.8 (2.1)	65.3 (0.6)	80.8 (3.5)	35.8 (0.7)	20.5 (0.5)	28.6 (0.8)	43.8 (0.8)	32.3 (0.9)	35.3 (0.7)	30.8 (0.8)	31.0 (0.5)
Mozambique, Maputo, and Beira	28.3 (0.3)	28.8 (0.5)	27.8 (0.3)	11.5 (1.1)	16.2 (1.6)	18.7 (0.1)	44.6 (1.4)	50.0 (3.2)	60.0 (2.2)	33.8 (0.4)	20.1 (0.3)	29.2 (0.5)	35.4 (0.6)	20.5 (0.5)	34.0 (0.4)	22.9 (0.4)	28.2 (0.4)
Populations (Canadian)																	
Quebec-French	68.7 (0.7)	69.8 (1.0)	67.5 (0.8)	29.3 (1.4)	39.7 (1.8)	45.3 (2.8)	89.3 (0.0)	93.3 (0.0)	96.4 (2.7)	72.3 (0.6)	56.4 (1.0)	78.1 (0.8)	81.1 (0.6)	58.4 (1.0)	72.6 (0.7)	68.0 (0.8)	65.3 (0.8)
Saskatchewan-French	67.5 (1.0)	68.8 (1.5)	66.3 (1.4)	32.0 (1.3)	36.0 (2.9)	46.5 (3.7)	87.8 (3.9)	90.7 (2.5)	96.0 (1.3)	73.9 (1.0)	53.8 (1.2)	69.2 (1.0)	76.0 (0.7)	61.6 (1.4)	70.1 (1.2)	69.3 (1.0)	62.9 (1.1)
British Columbia	66.2 (0.7)	66.8 (0.8)	65.4 (1.0)	25.3 (0.7)	35.6 (2.1)	41.3 (0.6)	90.7 (4.0)	94.7 (3.6)	97.3 (1.3)	69.3 (0.7)	54.1 (0.9)	69.6 (0.9)	79.9 (0.7)	60.2 (0.8)	68.5 (0.7)	68.0 (0.8)	61.8 (0.7)
Quebec-English	65.7 (0.9)	65.7 (1.6)	65.7 (0.8)	23.0 (2.5)	33.8 (3.9)	41.3 (1.3)	90.7 (0.0)	94.7 (2.4)	98.7 (0.0)	68.7 (0.9)	53.5 (1.1)	70.6 (1.0)	78.1 (1.0)	59.6 (1.1)	68.3 (0.9)	66.6 (1.0)	61.9 (1.0)
Alberta	64.0 (0.8)	64.5 (0.8)	63.4 (0.8)	23.5 (2.6)	33.3 (0.0)	38.7 (3.5)	88.0 (0.3)	92.0 (1.8)	97.3 (0.0)	68.6 (0.7)	54.3 (0.9)	67.2 (0.8)	80.0 (0.7)	52.1 (0.9)	68.3 (0.7)	62.6 (0.8)	61.0 (0.7)
Manitoba-French	63.1 (0.6)	64.5 (1.1)	61.9 (0.8)	26.7 (2.7)	34.7 (2.4)	41.3 (0.0)	85.3 (0.0)	89.3 (0.0)	94.7 (0.0)	67.1 (0.7)	48.5 (0.7)	66.6 (0.8)	75.0 (0.8)	58.5 (0.7)	64.6 (0.7)	66.0 (0.7)	58.2 (0.6)
Saskatchewan-English	62.0 (0.7)	63.2 (0.9)	60.7 (1.0)	21.3 (1.3)	29.7 (4.5)	37.3 (5.8)	86.7 (3.8)	90.7 (0.0)	96.0 (0.0)	66.1 (0.6)	49.6 (0.9)	62.9 (1.2)	78.3 (0.7)	54.6 (0.8)	64.0 (0.7)	64.4 (0.8)	57.2 (0.7)
New Brunswick-French	60.6 (0.4)	60.5 (0.6)	60.7 (0.6)	20.3 (1.3)	30.2 (3.1)	36.0 (0.0)	85.1 (1.3)	89.3 (3.0)	93.3 (0.0)	65.4 (0.5)	46.5 (0.5)	64.5 (0.5)	72.3 (0.5)	54.3 (0.4)	63.7 (0.4)	62.6 (0.4)	55.3 (0.4)
Nova Scotia	59.7 (0.6)	60.7 (0.9)	58.8 (0.8)	20.0 (0.0)	29.3 (1.2)	35.1 (1.5)	85.3 (0.0)	89.7 (0.0)	97.3 (0.0)	62.9 (0.6)	47.3 (0.8)	63.7 (0.7)	73.9 (0.7)	53.5 (0.8)	61.8 (0.6)	60.2 (0.6)	57.1 (0.6)
Newfoundland	58.9 (0.6)	57.8 (0.7)	59.9 (0.8)	18.7 (1.3)	29.3 (0.4)	34.7 (0.0)	88.0 (5.8)	88.0 (0.0)	96.0 (2.7)	61.9 (0.6)	45.1 (0.7)	65.1 (0.9)	72.4 (0.7)	52.7 (0.6)	61.8 (0.6)	60.3 (0.7)	54.3 (0.6)
Ontario-English	58.3 (0.8)	59.3 (1.0)	57.4 (0.9)	20.0 (1.2)	29.3 (0.0)	34.7 (0.0)	84.0 (2.0)	89.3 (1.3)	96.0 (1.3)	61.8 (0.8)	46.2 (0.9)	63.4 (1.0)	73.6 (0.8)	49.5 (1.0)	60.8 (0.8)	58.5 (0.9)	55.5 (0.8)
Manitoba-English	58.0 (0.8)	58.0 (0.9)	57.9 (1.0)	20.0 (1.7)	28.0 (2.7)	33.3 (4.2)	82.7 (0.0)	86.7 (0.0)	96.0 (3.5)	62.5 (0.7)	45.6 (0.9)	58.4 (0.9)	73.6 (0.9)	50.8 (1.0)	60.5 (0.8)	58.8 (0.9)	54.4 (0.7)
New Brunswick-English	57.7 (0.5)	58.3 (0.7)	57.1 (0.7)	20.0 (0.0)	27.5 (1.6)	33.3 (0.0)	82.7 (0.0)	89.3 (2.0)	96.0 (0.0)	62.4 (0.5)	51.3 (0.6)	62.4 (0.6)	71.0 (0.6)	43.2 (0.6)	61.4 (0.5)	55.4 (0.6)	56.4 (0.5)
Ontario-French	53.5 (0.6)	53.5 (0.8)	53.5 (0.8)	18.7 (0.2)	25.3 (1.1)	32.0 (0.0)	76.0 (3.0)	82.7 (0.0)	92.0 (2.3)	58.0 (0.6)	38.8 (0.7)	59.0 (1.0)	69.0 (0.7)	44.7 (0.9)	56.6 (0.7)	54.1 (0.8)	49.6 (0.6)

[1] Conceptual understanding questions analyzed students' abilities in understanding of mathematical facts and concepts.

[2] Procedural knowledge tasks required students to apply knowledge and concepts in solving routine problems using procedures taught in the classroom.

[3] Problem-solving questions required the student to apply several skills to a unique situation. These tasks usually involved multiple steps.

[4] Fifteen cantons.

[5] Schools in 14 republics, where instruction is in Russian.

[6] Schools where instruction is in Hebrew.

[7] Nine provinces

[8] Schools where instruction is in Spanish, in all regions except Cataluna.

[9] Twenty provinces and independent cities.

[10] Emilia-Romagna province only.

—Data not available.

NOTE.—Standard errors appear in parentheses.

SOURCE: U.S. Department of Education, National Center for Education Statistics, International Assessment of Educational Progress, Learning Mathematics, by Educational Testing Service. (This table was prepared February 1992.)

Table 397.—Science test scores of 9-year-olds in educational systems participating in the International Assessment of Educational Progress: 1991

Country	Average percent correct			Percentile scores						Topic averages				Process averages		
	Total	Male	Female	1	5	10	90	95	99	Life sciences	Physical sciences	Earth and space sciences	Nature of science	Exhibit basic knowledge of science facts and concepts (Knows)	Combine factual knowledge with rules and formulas (Uses)	Able to draw conclusions on the basis of available data (Integrates)
1	2	3	4	5	6	7	8	9	10	11	12	13	14	15	16	17
IAEP average	62.1	—	—	—	—	—	—	—	—	63.3	58.6	64.1	63.9	63.9	62.7	56.9
Populations (comprehensive)																
Korea	67.9 (0.5)	70.4 (0.7)	65.1 (0.5)	32.8 (4.9)	44.8 (0.4)	50.0 (0.0)	84.5 (0.0)	87.9 (0.0)	93.1 (3.4)	69.1 (0.5)	68.2 (0.5)	62.4 (0.6)	70.7 (0.6)	67.3 (0.5)	70.1 (0.5)	64.5 (0.5)
Taiwan	66.7 (0.5)	68.5 (0.6)	64.6 (0.7)	27.6 (1.3)	39.7 (0.0)	44.8 (7.2)	86.2 (0.0)	89.7 (0.0)	94.8 (0.0)	65.3 (0.6)	68.1 (0.5)	66.6 (0.7)	67.4 (0.6)	65.3 (0.6)	69.5 (0.6)	63.6 (0.6)
United States	64.7 (0.9)	65.5 (1.1)	63.8 (0.8)	25.9 (0.3)	36.2 (1.7)	43.1 (5.1)	84.5 (0.0)	87.9 (0.0)	93.1 (0.0)	65.2 (0.9)	57.5 (0.8)	70.6 (1.1)	70.7 (1.0)	67.0 (1.0)	65.2 (0.9)	57.9 (0.8)
Canada[1]	62.8 (0.4)	63.6 (0.4)	62.0 (0.5)	27.6 (0.5)	37.9 (1.1)	43.1 (0.0)	81.0 (0.0)	84.5 (0.0)	91.4 (0.0)	63.3 (0.4)	57.7 (0.4)	66.8 (0.4)	67.3 (0.5)	63.4 (0.4)	65.3 (0.4)	56.4 (0.4)
Hungary	62.5 (0.5)	63.4 (0.6)	61.6 (0.6)	26.9 (1.7)	38.5 (0.7)	44.8 (0.0)	79.3 (0.0)	84.2 (2.9)	89.7 (0.0)	64.7 (0.6)	56.3 (0.6)	68.2 (0.5)	62.0 (0.6)	66.1 (0.5)	61.1 (0.5)	57.4 (0.7)
Spain[2]	61.7 (0.7)	63.4 (0.9)	59.7 (0.7)	27.6 (3.1)	36.2 (0.0)	41.8 (1.6)	81.0 (0.0)	84.5 (0.0)	89.7 (0.0)	65.7 (0.7)	54.1 (0.7)	62.7 (0.7)	65.1 (1.0)	66.7 (0.7)	60.3 (0.7)	53.8 (0.8)
(Former) Soviet Union[3]	61.5 (1.2)	62.7 (1.4)	60.4 (1.2)	29.3 (4.2)	39.7 (1.5)	43.1 (1.4)	79.3 (4.8)	86.2 (2.4)	93.1 (4.8)	63.8 (1.4)	58.1 (1.7)	63.1 (1.4)	60.2 (1.4)	63.9 (1.4)	62.3 (1.1)	54.7 (1.4)
Israel[4]	61.2 (0.7)	63.0 (0.9)	59.4 (0.7)	27.6 (0.3)	36.2 (1.4)	41.4 (0.0)	81.0 (0.0)	86.2 (0.0)	93.1 (0.0)	61.4 (0.8)	59.8 (0.6)	60.6 (0.7)	64.1 (0.9)	61.0 (0.8)	63.0 (0.6)	57.7 (0.8)
Slovenia	57.7 (0.5)	58.3 (0.6)	57.0 (0.6)	27.8 (0.8)	35.1 (0.2)	40.4 (0.4)	75.4 (0.0)	79.0 (0.0)	86.0 (1.5)	59.4 (0.5)	56.6 (0.5)	58.3 (0.7)	54.1 (0.6)	60.3 (0.5)	57.0 (0.5)	52.9 (0.7)
Ireland	56.5 (0.7)	58.2 (1.0)	54.8 (0.9)	22.9 (1.4)	29.3 (1.6)	36.2 (1.3)	75.9 (0.0)	81.0 (1.8)	89.7 (5.2)	54.7 (0.8)	53.8 (0.7)	62.9 (0.8)	59.5 (0.8)	57.2 (0.8)	57.4 (0.7)	53.0 (0.8)
Populations (with exclusions or low participation)																
Italy[5]	66.9 (0.9)	67.9 (1.0)	65.8 (1.0)	31.0 (1.7)	41.4 (3.3)	48.3 (0.3)	86.2 (1.7)	89.7 (1.7)	94.8 (0.0)	71.3 (0.9)	61.0 (0.9)	66.8 (0.9)	66.9 (1.1)	71.6 (0.9)	66.1 (0.9)	58.2 (1.1)
England	62.9 (0.9)	63.8 (1.3)	62.0 (1.2)	24.1 (4.1)	36.2 (0.9)	41.4 (0.0)	82.8 (0.0)	86.2 (2.8)	93.1 (0.0)	62.4 (0.9)	60.1 (0.9)	66.3 (1.1)	66.0 (1.1)	64.5 (1.0)	63.6 (0.9)	58.2 (1.0)
Scotland	62.2 (0.7)	61.9 (0.7)	62.5 (1.0)	27.6 (0.0)	36.8 (3.0)	43.1 (0.0)	81.0 (0.0)	84.5 (0.0)	89.7 (0.0)	61.3 (0.7)	59.1 (0.8)	65.1 (0.7)	67.7 (1.0)	62.5 (0.6)	62.7 (0.7)	60.4 (0.8)
Portugal	54.8 (0.7)	56.3 (0.9)	53.3 (0.9)	26.3 (3.8)	33.3 (3.2)	37.9 (0.0)	72.4 (0.0)	79.0 (5.6)	86.2 (3.9)	58.1 (0.8)	50.0 (0.6)	57.3 (0.9)	52.4 (1.1)	58.4 (0.9)	54.1 (0.7)	48.5 (0.8)
Populations (Canadian)																
British Columbia	65.9 (0.6)	66.1 (0.6)	65.6 (0.6)	29.3 (4.6)	41.4 (0.0)	46.6 (3.6)	82.8 (0.0)	86.2 (0.0)	91.4 (0.0)	66.4 (0.7)	59.6 (0.7)	72.1 (0.9)	69.9 (0.8)	68.2 (0.6)	66.9 (0.6)	58.6 (0.8)
Quebec-English	63.0 (0.7)	64.3 (0.9)	61.7 (0.8)	29.3 (2.0)	37.9 (0.0)	43.1 (2.0)	82.8 (0.0)	86.2 (0.0)	91.4 (0.0)	63.9 (0.8)	57.3 (0.6)	66.8 (0.8)	67.9 (0.8)	65.1 (0.8)	64.4 (0.6)	55.7 (0.8)
Quebec-French	62.8 (0.5)	63.2 (0.7)	62.4 (0.5)	32.8 (5.2)	40.7 (3.6)	44.8 (0.6)	79.3 (0.0)	84.5 (0.0)	89.7 (4.9)	63.3 (0.6)	59.1 (0.6)	63.0 (0.6)	69.0 (0.7)	61.1 (0.5)	66.9 (0.6)	57.9 (0.6)
Ontario-English	62.5 (0.5)	63.6 (0.6)	61.4 (0.7)	27.6 (0.0)	36.2 (2.6)	43.1 (3.1)	81.0 (0.0)	86.2 (3.4)	91.4 (0.0)	63.0 (0.6)	56.6 (0.5)	68.4 (0.6)	66.2 (0.7)	64.3 (0.6)	64.1 (0.5)	55.1 (0.5)
New Brunswick-English	61.6 (0.4)	61.9 (0.5)	61.3 (0.6)	24.1 (0.0)	34.5 (3.2)	41.4 (0.0)	81.0 (0.0)	84.5 (0.0)	91.4 (0.0)	61.3 (0.4)	56.9 (0.4)	67.2 (0.5)	65.4 (0.5)	63.1 (0.4)	63.4 (0.4)	54.5 (0.5)
Ontario-French	56.3 (0.5)	56.5 (0.7)	56.1 (0.5)	28.9 (3.5)	34.5 (0.0)	39.7 (0.0)	74.1 (0.0)	79.3 (1.8)	86.2 (0.0)	54.9 (0.5)	53.7 (0.5)	60.5 (0.5)	60.3 (0.7)	55.1 (0.5)	59.7 (0.5)	51.7 (0.6)

[1] Four provinces.
[2] Schools where instruction is in Spanish, in all regions except Cataluna.
[3] Schools in 14 republics, where instruction is in Russian.
[4] Schools where instruction is in Hebrew.
[5] Emilia-Romagna province only.

—Data not available.

NOTE.—Standard errors appear in parentheses.

SOURCE: U.S. Department of Education, National Center for Education Statistics, International Assessment of Educational Progress, *Learning Science*, by Educational Testing Service. (This table was prepared February 1992.)

Table 398.—Classroom, home, and science activities of 9-year-olds in educational systems participating in the International Assessment of Educational Progress: 1991

Country	Average percent correct on science test	Percent of students who read for fun every day	Percent of students who read about science often	Percent of students who never conduct experiments	Percent of students with 2 hours or more homework daily	Percent of students who watch TV 5 hours or more daily
1	2	3	4	5	6	7
Populations (comprehensive)						
Korea	68 (0.5)	25 (1.4)	21 (1.1)	19 (1.1)	20 (1.2)	10 (0.8)
Taiwan	67 (0.5)	32 (1.3)	17 (1.0)	10 (0.8)	29 (1.4)	12 (0.8)
United States	65 (0.9)	47 (1.8)	32 (1.5)	22 (1.3)	19 (1.4)	25 (1.6)
Canada [1]	63 (0.4)	48 (0.9)	20 (0.7)	27 (1.0)	12 (0.6)	22 (0.7)
Hungary	63 (0.5)	52 (1.5)	36 (1.3)	40 (1.3)	29 (1.5)	15 (1.2)
Spain [2]	62 (0.7)	54 (1.9)	39 (1.7)	40 (2.2)	28 (1.6)	20 (1.8)
(Former) Soviet Union [3]	62 (1.2)	65 (1.8)	33 (2.2)	44 (1.2)	27 (1.8)	17 (1.1)
Israel [4]	61 (0.7)	55 (1.3)	27 (1.3)	14 (1.1)	36 (1.7)	24 (1.2)
Slovenia	58 (0.5)	61 (1.2)	40 (1.5)	21 (1.1)	15 (1.2)	10 (0.8)
Ireland	57 (0.7)	50 (1.5)	24 (1.3)	50 (2.0)	16 (1.3)	22 (1.6)
Populations (with exclusions or low participation)						
Italy [5]	67 (0.9)	50 (1.6)	22 (1.6)	50 (1.8)	27 (1.2)	9 (1.1)
England	63 (0.9)	49 (1.8)	21 (2.0)	11 (1.3)	10 (1.1)	22 (1.9)
Scotland	62 (0.7)	46 (2.1)	22 (1.5)	28 (2.6)	5 (0.8)	24 (1.4)
Portugal	55 (0.7)	62 (1.6)	18 (1.9)	22 (1.6)	22 (1.6)	18 (1.6)

[1] Four provinces.
[2] Schools where instruction is in Spanish, in all regions except Cataluna.
[3] Schools in 14 republics, where instruction is in Russian.
[4] Schools where instruction is in Hebrew.
[5] Emilia-Romagna province only.

NOTE.—Standard errors appear in parentheses.

SOURCE: U.S. Department of Education, National Center for Education Statistics, International Assessment of Educational Progress, *Learning Science,* by Educational Testing Service. (This table was prepared February 1992.)

Table 399.—Classroom, home, and science activities of 13-year-olds in educational systems participating in the International Assessment of Educational Progress: 1991

Country	Average percent correct on science test	Percent of students who read for fun every day	Percent of students with 2 hours or more homework daily	Percent of students who watch TV 5 hours or more daily	Percent of students who never conduct experiments	Percent of students who take a science quiz at least once a week	Percent of students with positive attitudes towards science
1	2	3	4	5	6	7	8
Populations (comprehensive)							
Korea	78 (0.5)	11 (0.8)	38 (1.5)	10 (0.8)	35 (1.7)	21 (1.6)	27 (1.3)
Taiwan	76 (0.4)	17 (1.1)	44 (1.3)	7 (0.7)	25 (1.3)	67 (1.2)	51 (1.2)
Switzerland [1]	74 (0.9)	49 (1.2)	21 (1.3)	7 (0.6)	36 (1.7)	18 (1.2)	59 (1.5)
Hungary	73 (0.5)	44 (1.3)	61 (1.5)	16 (1.1)	31 (1.7)	27 (1.6)	69 (1.2)
(Former) Soviet Union [2]	71 (1.0)	48 (1.1)	52 (1.6)	19 (1.3)	13 (0.8)	88 (1.2)	66 (1.4)
Slovenia	70 (0.5)	43 (1.5)	27 (1.4)	5 (0.6)	22 (1.5)	18 (1.0)	78 (1.2)
Israel [3]	70 (0.7)	40 (1.4)	49 (1.4)	20 (1.2)	35 (1.4)	28 (1.9)	62 (1.6)
Canada [4]	69 (0.4)	36 (0.9)	26 (0.9)	15 (0.7)	13 (0.7)	26 (1.1)	62 (1.0)
France	69 (0.6)	39 (1.5)	55 (1.6)	4 (0.5)	20 (1.7)	47 (1.4)	55 (1.3)
Scotland	68 (0.6)	37 (1.4)	15 (1.5)	23 (1.3)	3 (0.3)	11 (1.0)	66 (1.2)
Spain [5]	68 (0.6)	34 (1.5)	62 (1.9)	11 (0.9)	51 (2.3)	42 (2.6)	78 (1.4)
United States	67 (1.0)	29 (1.4)	31 (1.6)	22 (1.7)	25 (1.9)	69 (2.0)	57 (2.1)
Ireland	63 (0.6)	40 (1.3)	66 (1.6)	9 (0.9)	27 (2.1)	18 (1.1)	57 (1.4)
Jordan	57 (0.7)	22 (1.0)	54 (2.0)	10 (0.9)	26 (1.4)	73 (1.8)	82 (1.0)
Populations (with exclusions or low participation)							
Italy [6]	70 (0.7)	45 (1.4)	78 (1.2)	7 (0.8)	59 (1.9)	9 (1.0)	73 (1.4)
England	69 (1.2)	36 (1.8)	26 (2.8)	23 (1.7)	2 (0.6)	8 (0.9)	66 (2.9)
China [7]	67 (1.1)	28 (1.4)	35 (2.1)	2 (0.4)	29 (2.4)	42 (2.2)	74 (1.7)
Portugal	63 (0.8)	47 (1.2)	30 (1.7)	11 (0.9)	48 (1.7)	34 (2.0)	71 (1.4)
Brazil, Sao Paulo	53 (0.6)	31 (1.1)	48 (1.9)	18 (1.1)	35 (1.6)	45 (1.2)	69 (1.3)
Brazil, Fortaleza	46 (0.6)	41 (1.2)	50 (2.0)	20 (1.5)	44 (1.9)	55 (1.9)	74 (1.3)

[1] Fifteen cantons.
[2] Schools in 14 republics, where instruction is in Russian.
[3] Schools where instruction is in Hebrew.
[4] Nine provinces.
[5] Schools where instruction is in Spanish, in all regions except Cataluna.
[6] Emilia-Romagna province only.

[7] Twenty provinces and independent cities.

NOTE.—Standard errors appear in parentheses.

SOURCE: U.S. Department of Education, National Center for Education Statistics, International Assessment of Educational Progress, *Learning Science,* by Educational Testing Service. (This table was prepared February 1992.)

Table 400.—Science test scores of 13-year-olds in educational systems participating in the International Assessment of Educational Progress: 1991

Country	Average percent correct			Percentile scores						Topic averages				Process averages		
	Total	Male	Female	1	5	10	90	95	99	Life sciences	Physical sciences	Earth and space sciences	Nature of science	Exhibit basic knowledge of science facts and concepts (Knows)	Combine factual knowledge with rules and formulas (Uses)	Able to draw conclusions on the basis of available data (Integrates)
1	2	3	4	5	6	7	8	9	10	11	12	13	14	15	16	17
IAEP average	66.9	—	—	—	—	—	—	—	—	68.0	64.4	66.9	70.9	72.6	65.4	64.9
Populations (comprehensive)																
Korea	77.5 (0.5)	79.6 (0.6)	75.0 (0.7)	35.9 (0.0)	50.0 (0.0)	57.8 (3.8)	93.8 (0.0)	95.3 (0.0)	98.4 (0.0)	80.3 (0.5)	75.8 (0.5)	74.8 (0.5)	78.8 (0.6)	83.9 (0.5)	77.2 (0.4)	72.7 (0.6)
Taiwan	75.6 (0.4)	76.3 (0.6)	74.9 (0.6)	28.6 (3.6)	42.2 (0.0)	51.6 (0.0)	93.8 (0.0)	95.3 (0.0)	98.4 (0.0)	77.9 (0.5)	74.8 (0.4)	72.2 (0.5)	76.4 (0.6)	81.4 (0.5)	74.7 (0.4)	72.3 (0.5)
Switzerland[1]	73.7 (0.9)	76.4 (1.1)	70.9 (0.8)	35.9 (2.9)	50.0 (5.7)	57.8 (0.6)	92.2 (0.0)	95.3 (0.0)	98.4 (0.0)	74.3 (0.9)	70.3 (0.9)	74.5 (0.8)	79.8 (1.0)	77.1 (0.9)	71.6 (0.8)	74.6 (1.1)
Hungary	73.4 (0.5)	75.6 (0.6)	71.4 (0.7)	33.3 (1.9)	45.3 (1.0)	51.6 (0.0)	92.2 (0.0)	95.3 (0.0)	98.4 (0.0)	77.3 (0.5)	70.1 (0.6)	72.2 (0.6)	75.3 (0.7)	82.5 (0.5)	71.1 (0.5)	69.9 (0.7)
(Former) Soviet Union[2]	71.3 (1.0)	72.9 (1.1)	69.6 (1.1)	31.3 (0.6)	43.8 (0.0)	51.6 (0.0)	89.1 (2.3)	92.2 (2.7)	96.9 (0.0)	73.0 (1.0)	70.8 (1.0)	73.0 (0.9)	68.0 (1.2)	78.8 (1.1)	69.8 (0.8)	67.6 (1.3)
Slovenia	70.3 (0.5)	72.5 (0.7)	68.2 (0.6)	34.4 (2.2)	43.8 (0.0)	50.0 (0.0)	89.1 (0.0)	92.2 (0.0)	96.9 (3.8)	73.1 (0.6)	67.3 (0.5)	70.1 (0.6)	72.5 (0.6)	80.2 (0.5)	68.0 (0.5)	66.0 (0.6)
Israel[3]	69.7 (0.7)	71.6 (0.8)	68.0 (0.8)	34.4 (0.1)	42.2 (0.0)	47.6 (3.9)	89.1 (0.0)	92.2 (0.0)	96.9 (0.0)	65.4 (0.7)	69.8 (0.7)	67.5 (0.8)	78.5 (0.7)	70.5 (0.7)	68.4 (0.8)	71.1 (0.8)
Canada[4]	68.8 (0.4)	70.5 (0.5)	67.1 (0.4)	32.8 (0.0)	43.8 (0.0)	48.4 (1.7)	87.5 (0.0)	90.6 (0.0)	95.3 (0.0)	68.5 (0.4)	64.9 (0.4)	67.9 (0.4)	79.0 (0.5)	71.7 (0.4)	66.1 (0.4)	71.0 (0.5)
France	68.6 (0.6)	70.7 (0.7)	66.5 (0.7)	31.3 (1.8)	40.6 (2.1)	45.3 (1.7)	89.1 (0.0)	92.2 (0.0)	96.9 (0.0)	67.5 (0.6)	66.8 (0.6)	66.8 (0.6)	75.7 (0.7)	71.4 (0.6)	66.3 (0.6)	70.1 (0.8)
Scotland	67.9 (0.6)	69.6 (0.7)	66.3 (0.9)	28.6 (2.5)	39.1 (0.0)	45.3 (0.0)	87.5 (2.6)	90.6 (5.4)	96.9 (5.2)	67.3 (0.7)	65.7 (0.7)	64.1 (0.8)	76.8 (0.7)	72.3 (0.7)	65.8 (0.6)	67.7 (0.8)
Spain[5]	67.5 (0.6)	69.2 (0.6)	66.0 (0.7)	35.1 (0.5)	42.6 (1.3)	48.4 (0.2)	85.9 (2.4)	89.1 (0.0)	95.3 (0.0)	70.3 (0.6)	64.1 (1.0)	68.5 (0.7)	70.0 (0.7)	76.3 (0.7)	65.2 (0.6)	64.3 (0.8)
United States	67.0 (1.0)	69.4 (1.2)	64.5 (0.9)	28.1 (2.0)	39.3 (2.9)	43.8 (5.1)	85.9 (0.0)	90.6 (0.0)	95.3 (0.0)	69.1 (1.0)	61.6 (1.1)	67.0 (0.9)	75.6 (1.3)	72.8 (1.0)	65.1 (0.9)	65.4 (0.3)
Ireland	63.3 (0.6)	66.1 (0.9)	60.8 (0.8)	27.4 (2.3)	35.9 (0.0)	40.6 (2.3)	84.4 (3.2)	89.1 (0.0)	95.3 (0.0)	61.0 (0.6)	60.7 (0.7)	65.5 (0.8)	71.4 (0.7)	66.0 (0.7)	62.0 (0.6)	63.4 (0.7)
Jordan	56.6 (0.7)	57.1 (0.8)	55.9 (1.3)	23.4 (0.0)	30.2 (2.9)	35.9 (0.0)	78.1 (1.6)	84.4 (2.1)	92.2 (3.5)	58.6 (0.7)	53.8 (0.8)	60.7 (0.9)	56.1 (0.9)	65.3 (0.7)	56.6 (0.8)	49.2 (0.9)
Populations (with exclusions or low participation)																
England	68.7 (1.2)	70.3 (1.6)	67.1 (1.8)	31.3 (0.0)	39.1 (0.0)	44.3 (3.3)	89.1 (0.0)	92.2 (0.0)	98.4 (3.5)	68.2 (1.2)	66.6 (1.2)	65.9 (1.5)	76.5 (1.4)	72.1 (1.2)	66.8 (1.2)	69.0 (1.5)
China[6]	67.2 (1.1)	69.4 (1.2)	64.8 (1.1)	28.1 (3.5)	40.6 (0.6)	45.3 (1.6)	87.5 (1.6)	92.2 (2.2)	96.9 (1.6)	63.8 (1.1)	67.6 (1.4)	70.2 (1.4)	69.7 (1.1)	68.2 (1.1)	67.1 (1.1)	66.6 (1.1)
Italy[7]	69.9 (0.7)	72.2 (0.8)	67.6 (0.8)	31.3 (2.7)	43.8 (4.4)	48.4 (0.0)	89.1 (0.0)	92.2 (0.0)	95.3 (0.0)	71.8 (0.7)	67.0 (0.7)	70.8 (0.7)	72.7 (0.7)	76.7 (0.7)	66.9 (0.7)	69.6 (0.8)
Portugal	62.6 (0.8)	65.0 (1.0)	60.3 (0.8)	28.1 (2.7)	37.3 (1.6)	42.2 (3.1)	84.4 (0.0)	89.1 (0.0)	93.8 (1.6)	65.9 (0.8)	58.4 (0.7)	61.1 (0.9)	67.7 (1.2)	69.8 (0.8)	60.9 (0.7)	59.5 (1.1)
Brazil, Sao Paulo	52.7 (0.6)	56.3 (0.8)	49.6 (0.7)	23.4 (1.2)	29.7 (0.7)	33.3 (0.8)	74.5 (3.9)	81.3 (1.7)	92.2 (2.7)	56.3 (0.8)	48.8 (0.5)	55.8 (0.7)	52.5 (0.8)	60.4 (0.9)	51.9 (0.5)	47.5 (0.7)
Brazil, Fortaleza	46.4 (0.6)	49.1 (0.7)	44.3 (0.8)	21.8 (2.1)	27.3 (1.1)	31.3 (0.0)	67.2 (0.6)	73.4 (0.1)	85.9 (2.5)	51.3 (0.7)	42.6 (0.6)	48.6 (0.7)	44.8 (0.9)	55.5 (0.8)	45.4 (0.5)	40.5 (0.8)
Populations (Canadian)																
Alberta	74.1 (0.4)	76.4 (0.6)	71.8 (0.5)	35.9 (0.5)	48.4 (0.0)	54.7 (0.0)	90.6 (0.0)	93.8 (0.0)	96.9 (0.0)	72.3 (0.5)	71.3 (0.5)	73.7 (0.5)	84.0 (0.5)	75.7 (0.5)	72.0 (0.4)	76.4 (0.6)
British Columbia	72.4 (0.5)	73.5 (0.6)	71.4 (0.6)	35.9 (1.6)	46.9 (0.0)	53.1 (0.0)	89.1 (0.0)	92.2 (0.0)	95.3 (0.0)	70.2 (0.5)	70.7 (0.5)	72.1 (0.6)	80.7 (0.6)	76.4 (0.5)	69.6 (0.5)	74.0 (0.6)
Quebec-French	71.4 (0.5)	73.1 (0.6)	69.5 (0.6)	34.4 (3.1)	46.9 (1.6)	53.1 (1.3)	89.1 (0.0)	92.2 (0.0)	96.9 (0.0)	72.5 (0.5)	67.1 (0.6)	70.4 (0.6)	80.2 (0.6)	74.3 (0.6)	68.8 (0.5)	73.5 (0.7)
Saskatchewan-English	70.1 (0.6)	72.0 (0.7)	68.2 (0.6)	32.8 (1.6)	43.8 (0.0)	50.0 (0.0)	89.1 (0.0)	92.2 (0.0)	96.9 (0.0)	70.5 (0.6)	65.1 (0.7)	71.5 (0.7)	79.8 (0.6)	74.0 (0.6)	68.2 (0.5)	70.2 (0.8)
Quebec-English	69.2 (0.5)	71.2 (0.7)	67.1 (0.7)	32.8 (0.0)	43.8 (0.0)	48.4 (2.2)	87.5 (0.0)	92.2 (0.0)	96.9 (3.8)	69.0 (0.5)	64.8 (0.6)	68.1 (0.6)	80.6 (0.6)	72.9 (0.6)	66.4 (0.5)	71.1 (0.7)
Nova Scotia	68.7 (0.4)	70.2 (0.7)	67.0 (0.6)	31.3 (4.7)	42.2 (7.0)	48.4 (1.6)	87.5 (2.2)	90.6 (0.0)	95.3 (0.0)	68.0 (0.5)	65.8 (0.4)	68.9 (0.5)	76.4 (0.9)	71.8 (0.4)	67.7 (0.4)	67.8 (0.8)
Manitoba-English	68.6 (0.6)	70.3 (0.7)	66.9 (0.7)	29.7 (4.1)	39.1 (1.6)	45.3 (2.3)	87.5 (2.2)	92.2 (0.0)	95.3 (1.6)	67.5 (0.6)	64.9 (0.6)	70.5 (0.6)	77.3 (0.7)	72.6 (0.6)	66.8 (0.5)	68.3 (0.7)
Ontario-English	67.0 (0.6)	68.6 (0.8)	65.5 (0.5)	29.7 (1.1)	42.2 (4.8)	46.9 (0.0)	85.9 (2.2)	90.6 (2.7)	95.3 (0.0)	66.4 (0.6)	63.0 (0.7)	65.8 (0.6)	78.1 (0.7)	69.8 (0.6)	64.2 (0.6)	69.4 (0.8)
Manitoba-French	66.6 (0.7)	69.5 (1.1)	64.2 (0.6)	32.8 (2.2)	42.2 (2.7)	46.9 (0.0)	85.9 (0.0)	89.1 (0.0)	93.8 (3.1)	65.2 (0.6)	64.4 (0.8)	67.4 (0.7)	73.3 (0.9)	69.7 (0.8)	64.1 (0.7)	68.2 (1.0)
New Brunswick-English	66.3 (0.4)	67.9 (0.5)	64.8 (0.5)	29.6 (0.3)	39.1 (0.0)	45.3 (0.0)	85.9 (0.0)	89.1 (0.0)	95.3 (3.5)	66.2 (0.4)	62.8 (0.4)	65.8 (0.5)	74.9 (0.4)	69.7 (0.4)	64.6 (0.4)	66.5 (0.5)
Newfoundland	66.1 (0.5)	68.7 (0.7)	63.7 (0.6)	31.3 (0.0)	39.1 (0.0)	45.3 (0.0)	87.5 (2.2)	90.6 (0.0)	95.3 (0.0)	64.8 (0.6)	62.4 (0.5)	68.5 (0.7)	75.1 (0.6)	69.9 (0.6)	64.6 (0.5)	65.7 (0.6)
Saskatchewan-French	64.8 (0.6)	66.2 (1.1)	63.4 (1.3)	32.8 (3.5)	45.3 (3.8)	50.0 (3.8)	82.8 (3.0)	87.5 (2.7)	92.2 (1.6)	63.9 (1.1)	59.8 (1.1)	68.7 (0.9)	74.4 (1.1)	67.8 (1.1)	62.1 (0.8)	67.0 (1.2)
New Brunswick-French	63.6 (0.3)	64.2 (0.6)	63.1 (0.5)	29.7 (0.0)	37.5 (0.0)	43.8 (0.0)	82.8 (3.5)	87.5 (0.0)	93.8 (0.0)	62.0 (0.4)	62.2 (0.4)	64.5 (0.4)	69.0 (0.5)	63.5 (0.5)	63.4 (0.3)	64.1 (0.5)
Ontario-French	60.3 (0.5)	62.2 (0.7)	58.5 (0.7)	29.0 (2.6)	37.5 (0.0)	40.6 (1.8)	81.3 (0.6)	84.4 (0.0)	92.2 (0.0)	60.7 (0.6)	56.2 (0.6)	61.2 (0.6)	68.1 (0.8)	62.1 (0.7)	58.8 (0.5)	61.2 (0.7)

[1] Fifteen cantons.
[2] Schools in 14 provinces, where instruction is in Russian.
[3] Schools where instruction is in Hebrew.
[4] Nine provinces.
[5] Schools where instruction is in Spanish, in all regioins except Cataluna.
[6] Twenty provinces and independent cities.
[7] Emilia-Romagna province only.
— Data not available.

NOTE.—Standard errors appear in parentheses.

SOURCE: U.S. Department of Education, National Center for Education Statistics, International Assessment of Educational Progress, Learning Science, by Educational Testing Service. (This table was prepared February 1992.)

Table 401.—Reading literacy test scores of 9-year-olds: Selected countries, 1992

Country	Grade tested	Mean age	Overall mean score (s.e.)[1]	Narrative[2] 1st quartile	Narrative[2] mean score (s.e.)[1]	Narrative[2] 3rd quartile	Expository[3] mean score (s.e.)[1]	Documents[4] mean score (s.e.)[1]
1	2	3	4	5	6	7	8	9
Finland	3	9.7	569 (3.4)	508	568 (3.0)	602	569 (3.1)	569 (4.0)
United States	4	10.0	547 (2.8)	476	553 (3.1)	619	538 (2.6)	550 (2.7)
Sweden	3	9.8	539 (2.8)	467	536 (2.6)	592	542 (2.7)	539 (3.2)
France	4	10.1	531 (4.0)	467	532 (4.1)	580	533 (4.1)	527 (3.9)
Italy	4	9.9	529 (4.3)	468	533 (4.0)	576	538 (4.0)	517 (4.9)
New Zealand	5	10.0	528 (3.3)	452	534 (3.5)	594	531 (3.1)	521 (3.3)
Norway	3	9.8	524 (2.6)	455	525 (2.8)	576	528 (2.3)	519 (2.8)
Iceland[5]	3	9.8	518 (0.0)	448	518 (0.0)	571	517 (0.0)	519 (0.0)
Hong Kong	4	10.0	517 (3.9)	431	494 (4.1)	548	503 (3.4)	554 (4.2)
Singapore	3	9.3	515 (1.0)	450	521 (1.1)	567	519 (1.0)	504 (1.0)
Switzerland	3	9.7	511 (2.7)	438	506 (2.6)	566	507 (2.7)	522 (2.8)
Ireland	4	9.3	509 (3.6)	445	518 (3.7)	571	514 (3.2)	495 (3.8)
Belgium[6]	4	9.8	507 (3.2)	439	510 (3.3)	558	505 (2.8)	506 (3.5)
Greece	4	9.3	504 (3.7)	447	514 (3.8)	567	511 (3.6)	488 (3.8)
Spain	4	10.0	504 (2.5)	429	497 (2.4)	543	505 (2.3)	509 (2.7)
Germany (former West)	3	9.4	503 (3.0)	421	491 (2.8)	543	497 (2.9)	520 (3.2)
Canada[7]	3	8.9	500 (3.0)	437	502 (3.5)	566	499 (2.7)	500 (2.8)
Germany (former East)	3	9.5	499 (4.3)	414	482 (4.2)	531	493 (3.6)	522 (5.0)
Hungary	3	9.3	499 (3.1)	437	496 (2.9)	541	493 (3.1)	509 (3.5)
Slovenia	3	9.7	498 (2.6)	435	502 (2.7)	570	489 (2.5)	503 (2.5)
Netherlands	3	9.2	485 (3.6)	425	494 (3.3)	539	480 (3.4)	481 (3.9)
Cyprus	4	9.8	481 (2.3)	421	492 (2.4)	548	475 (2.3)	476 (2.1)
Portugal	4	10.4	478 (3.6)	419	483 (3.3)	531	480 (3.0)	471 (4.5)
Denmark	3	9.8	475 (3.5)	386	463 (3.4)	539	467 (3.5)	496 (3.6)
Trinidad/Tobago	4	9.6	451 (3.4)	383	455 (3.6)	502	458 (3.4)	440 (3.3)
Indonesia	4	10.8	394 (3.0)	351	402 (2.8)	436	411 (3.2)	369 (3.0)
Venezuela	4	10.1	383 (3.4)	322	378 (3.2)	426	396 (3.3)	374 (3.7)

[1] s.e.=standard error.

[2] Narrative prose is continuous text in which the writer's aim is to tell a story.

[3] Expository prose is continuous text designed to describe factual information to the reader.

[4] Documents are structured information presented in the form of charts, tables, maps, graphs, lists, or sets of instructions.

[5] Iceland tested all students, therefore standard errors are not applicable.

[6] Only French-speaking students were tested.

[7] British Columbia only.

SOURCE: International Association for the Evaluation of Educational Achievement, *How in the World Do Students Read?, 1992*. (This table was prepared April 1993.)

Table 402.—Reading literacy test scores of 14-year-olds: Selected countries, 1992

Country	Grade tested	Mean age	Overall mean score (s.e.) [1]	Narrative [2] mean score (s.e.) [1]	Expository [3] 1st quartile	Expository [3] mean score (s.e.) [1]	Expository [3] 3rd quartile	Documents [4] mean score (s.e.) [1]
1	2	3	4	5	6	7	8	9
Finland	8	14.7	560 (2.5)	559 (2.8)	493	541 (2.2)	575	580 (2.5)
France	9	15.4	549 (4.3)	556 (4.2)	484	546 (4.3)	580	544 (4.2)
Sweden	8	14.8	546 (2.5)	556 (2.6)	469	533 (2.4)	576	550 (2.4)
New Zealand	10	15.0	545 (5.6)	547 (5.7)	457	535 (5.7)	597	552 (5.3)
Hungary	8	14.1	536 (3.3)	530 (3.1)	469	536 (3.6)	577	542 (3.2)
Iceland [5]	8	14.8	536 (0.0)	550 (0.0)	472	548 (0.0)	617	509 (0.0)
Switzerland	8	14.9	536 (3.2)	534 (3.4)	466	525 (3.2)	572	549 (3.0)
Hong Kong	9	15.2	535 (3.7)	509 (3.7)	480	540 (3.8)	576	557 (3.8)
United States	9	15.0	535 (4.8)	539 (4.9)	456	539 (5.6)	599	528 (4.0)
Singapore	8	14.4	534 (1.1)	530 (1.1)	476	539 (1.2)	574	533 (1.1)
Slovenia	8	14.7	532 (2.3)	534 (2.6)	471	525 (2.2)	576	537 (2.2)
Germany (former East)	8	14.4	526 (3.5)	512 (3.9)	464	523 (3.5)	566	543 (2.9)
Denmark	8	14.8	525 (2.1)	517 (2.0)	458	524 (2.2)	573	532 (2.1)
Portugal	9	15.6	523 (3.1)	523 (2.5)	469	523 (3.4)	556	523 (3.4)
Canada [6]	8	13.9	522 (3.0)	526 (3.1)	449	516 (3.1)	569	522 (2.7)
Germany (former West)	8	14.6	522 (4.4)	514 (4.9)	453	521 (4.5)	573	532 (3.9)
Norway	8	14.8	516 (2.3)	515 (2.1)	464	520 (2.4)	569	512 (2.4)
Italy	8	14.1	515 (3.4)	520 (3.6)	459	524 (3.2)	565	501 (3.3)
Netherlands	8	14.3	514 (4.9)	506 (4.8)	442	503 (4.7)	546	533 (5.3)
Ireland	9	14.5	511 (5.2)	510 (5.3)	439	505 (5.3)	555	518 (4.9)
Greece	9	14.4	509 (2.9)	526 (2.9)	450	508 (3.1)	548	493 (2.6)
Cyprus	9	14.8	497 (2.2)	516 (2.2)	427	492 (2.4)	536	482 (2.0)
Spain	8	14.2	490 (2.5)	500 (3.0)	435	495 (2.6)	536	475 (2.0)
Belgium [7]	8	14.3	481 (4.9)	484 (5.1)	415	477 (4.8)	522	483 (4.7)
Trinidad/Tobago	9	14.4	479 (1.7)	482 (1.7)	408	485 (1.8)	537	472 (1.7)
Thailand	9	15.2	477 (6.2)	468 (6.6)	429	486 (5.9)	533	478 (6.2)
Philippines	8	14.5	430 (3.9)	421 (3.6)	378	439 (4.1)	472	430 (3.9)
Venezuela	9	15.5	417 (3.1)	407 (2.9)	381	433 (3.3)	482	412 (3.0)
Nigeria [8,9]	9	15.3	401 (—)	402 (—)	351	406 (—)	441	394 (—)
Zimbabwe [9]	9	15.5	372 (3.8)	367 (3.3)	326	374 (3.6)	411	373 (4.6)
Botswana	9	14.7	330 (2.0)	340 (1.6)	294	339 (1.9)	371	312 (2.4)

[1] s.e.=standard error.
[2] Narrative prose is continuous text in which the writer's aim is to tell a story.
[3] Expository prose is continuous text designed to describe factual information to the reader.
[4] Documents are structured information presented in the form of charts, tables, maps, graphs, lists, or sets of instructions.
[5] Iceland tested all students, therefore standard errors are not applicable.
[6] British Columbia only.

[7] Only French-speaking students were tested.
[8] Insufficient data to calculate the design effect.
[9] Sampling response rate of schools was below 80 percent.
—Data not available.

SOURCE: International Association for the Evaluation of Educational Achievement, *How in the World Do Students Read?*, 1992. (This table was prepared April 1993.)

Table 403.—Number of bachelor's degree recipients per 100 persons of the theoretical age of graduation, [1] by sex: Selected countries: 1989 to 1992

Country	Men and women				Men				Women			
	1989	1990	1991	1992	1989	1990	1991	1992	1989	1990	1991	1992
1	2	3	4	5	6	7	8	9	10	11	12	13
Australia	20.8	—	24.4	26.3	19.3	—	21.6	22.0	22.3	—	27.3	30.8
Austria	6.7	7.8	7.8	—	7.7	8.7	8.5	—	5.6	7.0	7.0	—
Belgium	—	—	13.3	—	—	—	15.0	—	—	—	11.5	—
Canada	30.2	31.8	33.3	32.2	26.9	27.6	28.2	26.9	33.5	36.0	38.7	37.7
Denmark	12.9	15.0	22.1	16.5	11.5	13.2	14.4	17.6	14.4	16.8	18.7	26.9
Finland	—	—	—	6.5	—	—	—	7.8	—	—	—	5.2
France	13.9	14.9	16.3	—	13.8	14.7	14.9	—	14.0	15.1	17.7	—
Germany (former West)	13.2	12.9	13.3	—	16.1	15.7	15.9	—	10.1	10.0	10.6	—
Ireland	16.3	17.5	16.0	17.4	—	16.9	15.8	17.7	—	18.2	16.2	17.1
Italy	—	—	—	—	—	—	—	—	—	—	—	—
Japan	—	21.8	23.7	23.4	—	30.9	33.5	32.3	—	12.3	13.7	14.1
Netherlands	10.2	8.0	8.3	17.8	12.3	9.4	9.6	17.6	7.9	6.5	6.9	18.0
New Zealand	15.7	15.1	16.1	18.0	16.4	15.7	16.5	17.7	15.0	14.6	15.8	18.3
Norway	—	—	—	19.4	—	—	—	14.8	—	—	—	24.2
Portugal	—	—	—	—	—	—	—	—	—	—	—	—
Spain	—	—	—	8.0	—	—	—	5.8	—	—	—	10.4
Sweden	13.1	12.2	12.5	11.4	11.1	10.5	11.0	9.6	15.1	14.0	14.2	13.3
Switzerland	7.7	7.8	7.6	—	10.1	10.3	9.8	—	5.3	5.1	5.4	—
Turkey	6.3	6.5	6.5	6.0	7.9	8.2	8.2	7.4	4.7	4.7	4.7	4.4
United Kingdom	—	—	—	20.4	—	—	—	21.1	—	—	—	19.7
United States	27.8	28.1	28.1	27.4	26.1	25.9	25.3	24.7	29.6	30.5	31.0	30.3

[1] In most countries the theoretical age of graduation was 22 or 23. The range was from 21 to 25. The number of bachelor's degree recipients may be of any age.
— Data not available.

SOURCE: Organization for Economic Cooperation and Development, *Education at a Glance.* (This table was prepared July 1996.)

Table 404.—Percent of undergraduate degrees awarded in science: Selected countries, 1985, 1990, and 1991

Country	All science degrees			Natural sciences			Mathematics and computer science			Engineering		
	1985	1990	1991	1985	1990	1991	1985	1990	1991	1985	1990	1991
1	2	3	4	5	6	7	8	9	10	11	12	13
Australia	—	—	21.6	—	—	15.9	—	—	—	—	—	5.7
Austria	16.8	19.6	20.1	5.0	5.3	5.9	4.1	5.2	4.8	7.7	9.0	9.5
Belgium	14.7	—	32.2	4.6	—	4.3	1.7	—	1.7	8.4	—	26.3
Canada	17.1	16.4	15.5	4.9	6.0	5.7	4.5	4.2	3.7	7.7	6.2	6.1
Denmark	22.5	26.1	27.6	6.3	4.4	6.1	—	—	0.1	16.2	21.7	21.4
Finland	39.3	33.5	34.5	7.7	4.1	4.2	6.3	5.9	6.6	25.3	23.4	23.7
Germany (former West)	23.8	31.3	31.5	5.0	7.2	7.3	2.3	3.5	3.9	16.5	20.5	20.2
Ireland	28.8	34.1	28.5	12.8	14.1	12.4	4.0	6.3	4.4	12.0	13.7	11.6
Italy	19.5	19.7	19.8	8.1	7.6	7.5	3.1	3.9	3.8	8.3	8.3	8.5
Japan	22.7	23.5	23.5	2.4	2.4	2.4	—	—	—	20.3	21.0	21.1
Netherlands	21.8	21.1	21.4	8.5	7.1	6.5	1.2	1.6	1.6	12.1	12.4	13.3
New Zealand	20.5	19.5	16.3	11.7	8.2	7.1	5.5	5.5	4.0	3.3	5.8	5.2
Norway	6.1	12.9	12.3	2.5	2.1	1.8	1.8	0.6	0.6	1.8	10.2	9.9
Portugal	—	24.3	—	6.5	6.7	—	—	7.0	—	—	10.5	—
Spain	13.9	15.0	15.4	5.5	5.7	5.3	1.3	2.6	2.9	7.0	6.7	7.1
Sweden	15.4	24.0	24.3	2.6	4.1	4.2	1.6	4.7	4.9	11.3	15.2	15.2
Switzerland	20.2	23.0	22.7	10.3	11.2	11.0	2.1	3.7	3.8	7.9	8.1	7.9
Turkey	23.0	20.6	21.3	3.6	4.6	4.9	1.6	2.1	2.3	17.8	13.8	14.1
United States	21.7	16.9	15.9	6.3	5.1	5.1	5.5	4.0	3.6	9.8	7.8	7.2

—Data not available.

SOURCE: Organization for Economic Cooperation and Development, unpublished data. (This table was prepared May 1995.)

Table 405.—Percent of graduate degrees awarded in science: Selected countries, 1985, 1990, and 1991

Country	All science degrees			Natural sciences			Mathematics and computer science			Engineering		
	1985	1990	1991	1985	1990	1991	1985	1990	1991	1985	1990	1991
1	2	3	4	5	6	7	8	9	10	11	12	13
Australia	—	—	13.9	—	—	9.6	—	—	—	—	—	4.3
Austria	43.3	37.7	37.4	14.2	12.3	13.4	7.3	4.6	6.1	21.7	20.8	17.9
Canada	19.7	20.0	19.7	7.5	7.8	7.7	2.8	3.4	3.4	9.4	8.8	8.7
Denmark	16.0	22.2	22.9	4.1	5.8	5.4	2.7	4.8	4.5	9.2	11.6	13.0
Finland	47.6	30.6	29.2	24.0	14.7	12.4	6.3	5.4	4.6	17.2	10.5	12.2
Germany (former West)	27.7	33.2	33.9	18.7	23.5	23.3	1.8	2.3	2.2	7.2	7.4	8.4
Ireland	31.4	34.5	28.4	18.9	19.5	15.7	2.6	5.8	4.1	9.9	9.3	8.6
Japan	50.1	54.6	54.2	9.5	9.5	9.5	—	—	—	40.5	45.1	44.7
Netherlands	—	28.9	29.9	20.6	17.7	16.7	—	1.5	1.6	7.5	9.7	11.6
New Zealand	45.1	22.6	19.3	24.6	13.8	11.5	5.4	4.7	3.6	15.1	4.0	4.2
Norway	40.1	33.4	33.8	17.9	8.0	7.9	3.5	2.1	2.5	18.7	23.3	23.4
Spain	35.6	26.9	26.6	28.6	19.7	19.1	1.8	1.4	2.5	5.1	5.7	5.0
Sweden	48.0	48.5	44.4	21.2	19.4	15.1	6.8	9.2	8.2	20.0	19.9	21.1
Switzerland	30.7	30.2	32.6	20.3	22.0	23.1	2.8	1.7	1.8	7.6	6.5	7.6
Turkey	35.8	24.0	21.7	6.6	7.6	6.4	2.8	3.3	2.8	26.3	13.2	12.4
United States	13.5	14.5	13.8	4.5	4.2	3.8	2.8	3.4	3.2	6.3	6.9	6.7

—Data not available.

SOURCE: Organization for Economic Cooperation and Development, unpublished data. (This table was prepared May 1995.)

Table 406.—Public education expenditures per student, by level of student: Selected countries, 1985 to 1992

[In constant 1992 dollars]

Country	Primary				Secondary				Higher education			
	1985	1990	1991	1992	1985	1990	1991	1992	1985	1990	1991	1992
1	2	3	4	5	6	7	8	9	10	11	12	13
Austria	$3,451	$3,526	$3,681	$4,010	$3,943	$4,632	$4,821	$6,420	$6,557	$6,369	$6,635	$5,820
Belgium	2,232	2,131	2,206	2,390	5,279	4,805	5,151	5,150	7,098	6,178	6,423	6,590
Denmark	3,570	4,446	4,529	4,220	5,045	5,301	5,540	4,940	8,570	8,332	7,916	6,710
France	—	—	2,669	2,900	—	—	4,780	5,430	—	—	4,903	6,020
Germany	—	—	—	2,980	—	—	—	4,260	—	—	—	—
Japan	—	—	—	3,530	—	—	—	3,900	—	—	—	11,850
Ireland	1,323	1,429	1,588	1,770	2,277	2,403	2,563	2,770	5,173	5,527	5,755	7,270
Norway	3,404	3,878	4,002	4,480	4,817	5,153	5,538	6,200	7,857	8,629	8,658	8,720
Portugal	1,330	1,931	2,174	—	1,759	—	2,435	—	3,732	—	6,346	—
Spain	1,439	1,800	1,917	2,030	1,998	2,706	2,812	3,140	1,907	3,156	3,340	3,770
Sweden [1]	—	5,271	5,635	4,840	—	6,292	6,835	6,050	—	8,669	8,819	7,120
Switzerland [1]	—	—	5,611	3,560	—	—	6,761	—	—	—	15,124	12,900
Turkey	—	—	582	—	—	—	519	—	—	—	2,879	—
United Kingdom	2,336	2,897	2,878	3,120	3,864	5,499	4,383	4,390	—	—	9,911	10,370
United States	4,364	5,223	5,333	5,600	5,282	6,546	6,667	6,470	10,221	12,013	12,157	11,880

[1] Change in definition in 1992.
—Data not available.

NOTE.—Data adjusted to U.S. dollars using the purchasing power pariety (PPP) index.

SOURCE: Organization for Economic Cooperation and Development, *Education at a Glance,* and unpublished data. (This table was prepared May 1995.)

Table 407.—Public expenditures for education as a percentage of gross domestic product: Selected countries, 1985 to 1992

Country	All levels							Primary education						Secondary education						Higher education						
	1985	1987	1988	1989	1990	1991	1992	1985	1987	1988	1989	1990	1991	1985	1987	1988	1989	1990	1991	1985	1987	1988	1989	1990	1991	1992
1	2	3	4	5	6	7	8	9	10	11	12	13	14	15	16	17	18	19	20	21	22	23	24	25	26	27
Australia	6.0	5.6	5.5	—	—	4.6	4.5	1.8	1.6	1.6	—	—	1.5	2.1	1.9	1.9	—	—	1.5	1.8	1.8	1.8	—	—	1.5	1.8
Austria	5.7	5.7	5.5	5.3	5.2	5.4	—	1.0	1.0	1.0	0.9	0.9	1.0	2.8	2.8	2.7	2.6	2.5	2.6	1.0	1.1	1.1	1.1	1.1	1.1	—
Belgium	6.4	5.9	5.6	5.7	5.2	—	—	1.1	1.0	1.0	0.9	0.9	—	3.0	2.6	2.5	2.5	2.3	—	1.0	1.0	0.9	0.9	0.9	—	—
Denmark	6.2	6.2	6.4	6.4	6.2	6.1	6.2	1.7	1.7	1.7	1.7	1.7	1.7	2.8	2.9	2.9	2.9	2.7	2.7	1.2	1.2	1.3	1.3	1.3	1.3	1.3
Germany (former West)	4.6	4.4	4.3	—	—	4.1	3.7	0.6	0.6	0.6	—	—	0.5	2.2	2.1	2.0	—	—	1.9	1.0	1.0	1.0	—	—	0.9	1.0
Ireland	5.9	6.2	5.6	5.3	5.2	5.4	5.7	1.7	1.8	1.6	1.6	1.5	1.6	2.4	2.5	2.3	2.2	2.1	2.2	0.9	1.1	1.0	1.0	1.0	1.1	1.4
Italy	4.7	4.8	4.9	5.0	5.2	—	—	1.2	1.1	1.1	1.2	1.1	—	2.0	2.2	2.2	2.3	2.2	—	0.6	0.7	0.8	0.7	1.0	—	—
Japan	—	—	—	—	—	—	3.6	—	—	—	—	—	—	—	—	—	—	—	—	—	—	—	—	—	—	0.3
Luxembourg	—	6.0	6.0	5.8	—	—	—	—	2.1	2.1	2.0	—	—	—	2.5	2.5	2.4	—	—	—	0.2	0.2	0.2	—	—	—
New Zealand	—	5.3	5.2	6.3	—	5.8	—	—	1.5	1.4	1.7	—	1.5	—	1.3	1.2	1.5	—	1.3	—	1.5	1.6	1.8	—	2.0	—
Norway	5.6	6.2	6.4	6.5	6.4	6.8	—	1.7	1.9	1.9	1.8	1.6	1.7	2.7	2.8	2.9	2.8	2.7	2.8	0.8	0.9	1.0	1.1	1.2	1.3	—
Portugal	—	4.3	—	4.8	4.8	5.5	5.2	2.1	2.1	2.3	2.1	2.1	2.2	1.8	1.9	1.4	1.6	1.6	2.0	0.6	0.7	0.8	0.9	0.9	0.9	0.9
Spain	3.6	3.7	3.9	4.2	4.4	4.5	4.2	1.2	1.1	1.1	1.1	1.0	1.0	1.8	1.9	2.1	2.2	2.3	2.4	0.4	0.5	0.6	0.6	0.7	0.8	0.9
Sweden	—	6.0	5.9	5.5	5.7	6.1	6.7	—	2.2	2.2	2.0	2.0	2.2	0.0	2.7	2.5	2.4	2.5	2.7	—	1.0	1.0	0.9	1.1	1.1	1.0
Switzerland	5.1	5.0	5.1	—	—	5.4	—	2.9	2.8	2.8	—	—	1.4	1.3	1.2	1.3	—	—	2.4	1.0	1.0	1.0	—	—	1.2	—
Turkey	—	—	—	—	—	4.0	—	—	—	—	—	—	1.9	—	—	—	—	—	1.0	—	—	—	—	—	1.0	—
United Kingdom	—	—	—	—	—	—	—	—	1.3	1.3	1.3	1.3	1.3	2.2	2.3	2.3	2.2	2.3	2.2	1.1	1.0	0.9	0.9	0.9	1.0	0.1
United States	—	—	—	—	—	—	5.7	1.5	1.6	1.7	1.8	1.8	1.8	1.9	1.9	1.9	1.9	2.0	2.0	1.3	1.4	1.4	1.2	1.5	1.5	1.6

—Data not available.

SOURCE: Organization for Economic Cooperation and Development, unpublished data. (This table was prepared May 1995.)

Table 408.—Foreign students enrolled in institutions of higher education in the United States and outlying areas, by continent, region, and selected countries of origin: 1980–81 to 1994–95

Continent, region, and country	1980–81		1985–86		1989–90		1990–91		1991–92		1992–93		1993–94		1994–95	
	Number	Per-cent	Number	Per-cent	Number	Per-cent	Number	Per-cent	Number	Per-cent	Number	Per-cent	Number	Per-cent	Number	Per-cent
1	2	3	4	5	6	7	8	9	10	11	12	13	14	15	16	17
Total	311,880	100.0	343,780	100.0	386,850	100.0	407,530	100.0	419,590	100.0	438,620	100.0	449,704	100.0	452,635	100.0
Africa	38,180	12.2	34,190	9.9	24,570	6.4	23,800	5.8	21,900	5.2	20,520	4.7	20,569	4.6	20,724	4.6
Eastern Africa	6,260	2.0	6,730	2.0	7,330	1.9	7,590	1.9	7,040	1.7	6,950	1.6	7,093	1.6	7,139	1.6
Central Africa	1,130	0.4	1,540	0.4	1,800	0.5	1,650	0.4	1,690	0.4	1,470	0.3	1,472	0.3	1,430	0.3
North Africa	7,310	2.3	5,980	1.7	4,740	1.2	4,540	1.1	4,090	1.0	3,730	0.9	3,614	0.8	3,522	0.8
Southern Africa	1,480	0.5	2,360	0.7	2,750	0.7	2,840	0.7	2,660	0.6	2,560	0.6	2,563	0.6	2,672	0.6
West Africa	22,000	7.1	17,580	5.1	7,950	2.1	7,180	1.8	6,400	1.5	5,800	1.3	5,804	1.3	5,943	1.3
Nigeria	17,350	5.6	13,710	4.0	4,480	1.2	3,710	0.9	3,160	0.8	2,490	0.6	2,285	0.5	2,147	0.5
Europe	25,330	8.1	34,310	10.0	46,040	11.9	49,640	12.2	53,710	12.8	58,010	13.2	62,442	13.9	64,811	14.3
Eastern Europe	1,670	0.5	1,770	0.5	3,360	0.9	4,780	1.2	6,890	1.6	9,800	2.2	12,929	2.9	15,906	3.5
Western Europe	23,660	7.6	32,540	9.5	42,680	11.0	44,860	11.0	46,820	11.2	48,210	11.0	49,496	11.0	48,905	10.8
France	—	—	3,680	1.1	5,340	1.4	5,630	1.4	5,580	1.3	5,660	1.3	5,976	1.3	5,843	1.3
Germany, Federal Republic of [1]	3,310	1.1	4,730	1.4	6,750	1.7	7,000	1.7	7,570	1.8	7,880	1.8	8,508	1.9	8,592	1.9
Greece	3,750	1.2	4,440	1.3	4,430	1.1	4,360	1.1	4,490	1.1	4,350	1.0	4,144	0.9	3,699	0.8
Spain	—	—	1,740	0.5	3,640	0.9	4,300	1.1	4,590	1.1	5,160	1.2	5,246	1.2	5,126	1.1
United Kingdom	4,440	1.4	5,940	1.7	7,100	1.8	7,300	1.8	7,470	1.8	7,630	1.7	7,828	1.7	7,786	1.7
Latin America	49,810	16.0	45,480	13.2	48,090	12.4	47,580	11.7	43,200	10.3	43,250	9.9	45,246	10.1	47,239	10.4
Caribbean	10,650	3.4	11,100	3.2	12,580	3.3	12,610	3.1	11,120	2.7	10,270	2.3	10,672	2.4	11,286	2.5
Central America	12,970	4.2	12,740	3.7	16,540	4.3	15,950	3.9	12,820	3.1	13,460	3.1	13,886	3.1	14,923	3.3
Mexico	6,730	2.2	5,460	1.6	6,540	1.7	6,740	1.7	6,650	1.6	7,580	1.7	8,021	1.8	9,003	2.0
South America	26,190	8.4	21,640	6.3	18,970	4.9	19,020	4.7	19,250	4.6	19,530	4.5	20,708	4.6	21,030	4.6
Brazil	—	—	2,840	0.8	3,730	1.0	3,900	1.0	4,260	1.0	4,540	1.0	4,977	1.1	5,017	1.1
Colombia	—	—	4,010	1.2	3,320	0.9	3,180	0.8	2,930	0.7	2,850	0.6	3,077	0.7	3,208	0.7
Venezuela	11,750	3.8	7,040	2.0	2,740	0.7	2,890	0.7	3,130	0.7	3,440	0.8	3,742	0.8	4,092	0.9
Middle East	84,710	27.2	52,720	15.3	37,330	9.6	33,420	8.2	31,210	7.4	30,240	6.9	29,509	6.6	30,246	6.7
Iran	47,550	15.2	14,210	4.1	7,440	1.9	6,260	1.5	4,930	1.2	4,090	0.9	3,621	0.8	2,896	0.6
Jordan	6,140	2.0	6,590	1.9	5,250	1.4	4,320	1.1	3,700	0.9	3,260	0.7	2,826	0.6	2,431	0.5
Lebanon	6,770	2.2	7,090	2.1	4,450	1.2	3,900	1.0	3,080	0.7	2,540	0.6	2,165	0.5	1,835	0.4
Saudi Arabia	10,440	3.3	6,900	2.0	4,110	1.1	3,590	0.9	3,550	0.8	3,750	0.9	3,721	0.8	4,075	0.9
Turkey	—	—	2,460	0.7	3,400	0.9	4,080	1.0	4,560	1.1	4,980	1.1	5,474	1.2	6,716	1.5
North America [2]	14,790	4.7	16,030	4.7	18,590	4.8	18,950	4.6	19,780	4.7	21,550	4.9	23,288	5.2	23,394	5.2
Canada	14,320	4.6	15,410	4.5	17,870	4.6	18,350	4.5	19,190	4.6	20,970	4.8	22,655	5.0	22,747	5.0
Oceania	4,180	1.3	4,030	1.2	4,010	1.0	4,230	1.0	3,870	0.9	4,300	1.0	3,857	0.9	4,327	1.0
South and East Asia	94,640	30.3	156,830	45.6	208,110	53.8	229,830	56.4	245,810	58.6	260,670	59.4	264,693	58.9	261,789	57.8
East Asia	51,650	16.6	80,720	23.5	127,320	32.9	146,020	35.8	158,490	37.8	168,410	38.4	171,279	38.1	168,190	37.2
China	2,770	0.9	13,980	4.1	33,390	8.6	39,600	9.7	42,940	10.2	45,130	10.3	44,381	9.9	39,403	8.7
Hong Kong	9,660	3.1	10,710	3.1	11,230	2.9	12,630	3.1	13,190	3.1	14,020	3.2	13,752	3.1	12,935	2.9
Japan	13,500	4.3	13,360	3.9	29,840	7.7	36,610	9.0	40,700	9.7	42,840	9.8	43,770	9.7	45,276	10.0
Korea, Republic of	6,150	2.0	18,660	5.4	21,710	5.6	23,360	5.7	25,720	6.1	28,520	6.5	31,076	6.9	33,599	7.4
Taiwan	19,460	6.2	23,770	6.9	30,960	8.0	33,530	8.2	35,550	8.5	37,430	8.5	37,581	8.4	36,407	8.0
South Central Asia	14,540	4.7	25,800	7.5	38,840	10.0	42,370	10.4	46,810	11.2	50,430	11.5	48,941	10.9	47,836	10.6
India	9,250	3.0	16,070	4.7	26,240	6.8	28,860	7.1	32,530	7.8	35,950	8.2	34,796	7.7	33,537	7.4
Pakistan	2,990	1.0	5,440	1.6	7,070	1.8	7,730	1.9	8,120	1.9	8,020	1.8	7,299	1.6	6,989	1.5
South East Asia	28,450	9.1	50,310	14.6	41,950	10.8	41,440	10.2	40,510	9.7	41,830	9.5	44,461	9.9	45,763	10.1
Indonesia	3,250	1.0	8,210	2.4	9,390	2.4	9,520	2.3	10,250	2.4	10,920	2.5	11,744	2.6	11,872	2.6
Malaysia	6,010	1.9	23,020	6.7	14,110	3.6	13,610	3.3	12,650	3.0	12,660	2.9	13,718	3.1	13,617	3.0
Philippines	—	—	3,920	1.1	4,540	1.2	4,270	1.0	3,950	0.9	3,700	0.8	3,528	0.8	3,472	0.8
Singapore	—	—	3,930	1.1	4,440	1.1	4,500	1.1	4,760	1.1	4,860	1.1	4,823	1.1	4,473	1.0
Thailand	6,550	2.1	6,940	2.0	6,630	1.7	7,090	1.7	7,690	1.8	8,630	2.0	9,537	2.1	10,889	2.4
Stateless [3]	240	0.1	190	0.1	110	(4)	80	(4)	120	(4)	80	(4)	100	(4)	105	(4)

[1] 1990–91 and later years data are for Germany, which includes the former Federal Republic of Germany and the former Democratic Republic of Germany.
[2] Excludes Mexico and Central America, which are included with Latin America.
[3] Home country unknown or undeclared.
[4] Less than .05 percent.
—Data not available.

NOTE.—Data are for "nonimmigrants," i.e., students who have not migrated to this country. Because of rounding, details may not add to totals.

SOURCE: Institute of International Education, Open Doors, various years; and unpublished data. (Latest edition copyright © 1995 by the Institute of International Education. All rights reserved.) (This table was prepared April 1996.)

CHAPTER 7
Library Resources and Technology

This chapter contains statistics on libraries and on the use of information technologies. These data show the extent of America's access to information technologies outside of formal classroom activities. The data also provide a capsule description of the magnitude and availability of library resources. Access to information has been widely cited as the key to success in a growing number of endeavors. Thus, how information is made available and to whom become matters of concern.

The first section of the chapter has tables dealing with public libraries, public and private school libraries, and college and university libraries. They contain data on collections, population served, staff, and expenditures. Two tables provide institutional-level information for the largest public libraries and the largest college libraries in the country.

The second half of the chapter provides information on the availability and use of technology. For example, the proportion of children using computers at school may be compared over time. Also included are data on the use of home computers by adults and school children, with comparisons among various demographic groups.

Related data may be found in various sections of this report. For example, statistics on the number of degrees conferred in computer and information sciences and library sciences are in chapter 3. Further information on survey methodologies are in the "Guide to Sources" and in the publications cited in the source notes.

Resources

In 1990–91, 96 percent of all public schools and 87 percent of all private schools had libraries or media centers. About 59,000 librarians and 41,000 library aides provided service in public schools during the 1990–91 school year. There was an average of 931 students per librarian at public elementary schools and 1,052 students per librarian at public secondary schools. At private elementary schools, there was an average of 636 students per librarian (table 409).

In 1993, there were 8,929 public libraries in the United States with 656 million books and serial volumes. The annual attendance per capita was 4.0 and the reference transactions per capita was 1.1 (table 415).

Technology

The use of computers has become widespread in the workplace. In October 1993, 46 percent of all workers used computers on the job. More frequent use of computers was associated with higher levels of education and higher incomes. Only 34 percent of the high school graduates and 10 percent of the high school dropouts used computers compared to 71 percent of those with master's degrees. Among those who did use computers, the master's degree recipients were more likely to use the computers for a wider variety of applications than high school graduates. The most common uses of computers on the job were: bookkeeping/invoicing (45 percent), word processing (44 percent), communications (39 percent), analysis/spreadsheets (36 percent), and data bases (35 percent). Workers in the 25- to 49-year-old age range were more likely to use computers than younger or older workers. Elementary and secondary teachers were less likely to use computers than persons employed in other managerial or professional fields (table 416).

The total computer usage rate of students at school increased from 27 percent in 1984, to 43 percent in 1989, to 59 percent in October 1993. The rate at the 1–8 grade level increased from 52 percent in 1989 to 69 percent in 1993. The computer usage rate in 1993 was 58 percent for students in high school and 55 percent for students in college. Sizable percentages of students used computers at home, though fewer actually used them for schoolwork. About 25 percent of elementary school children used computers at home and about 11 percent used them for schoolwork. Students at the high school and undergraduate level were about twice as likely as the elementary school children to use home computers for schoolwork. In general, students in higher income families were more likely to use computers at home and use them for schoolwork than were students from lower income families. About 13 percent of the high school students in the $25,000 to $29,999 household income group used computers at home for school work compared to 45 percent in the $75,000 and over income group (table 418).

Expenditures

Total expenditures for college libraries rose by 30 percent between 1988–89 and 1993–94. However, the proportion of college budgets spent on libraries fell slightly from 2.4 percent in 1988–89 to 2.3 percent in 1993–94 (table 333).

Figure 32.-Student use of computers at school, by level of instruction: October 1989 and 1993

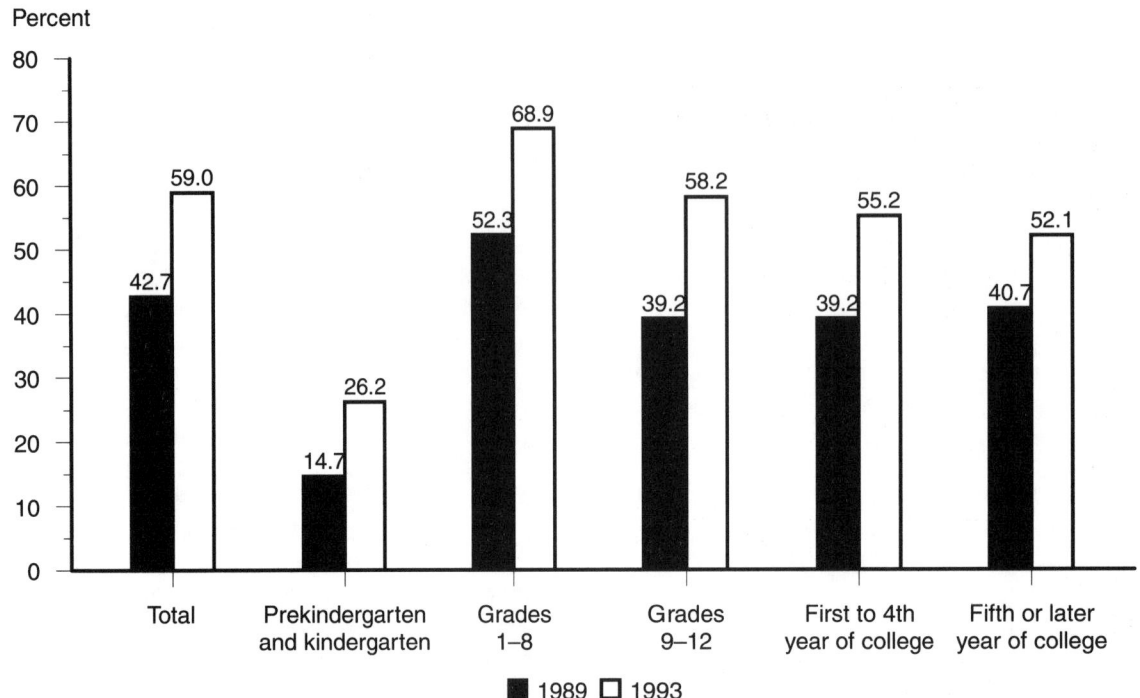

SOURCE: U.S. Department of Commerce, Bureau of the Census, Current Population Survey, October 1989 and 1993, and unpublished data.

Table 409.—Selected statistics of public and private school libraries/media centers, by level and size of school: 1990–91

School level and size	Public schools						Private schools				
	Number of library/media centers	Percent of schools with library/media centers	Librarians and other professional media staff		Library/media center aides		Number of library/media centers	Percent of schools with library/media centers	Librarians and other professional media staff		Library/media center aides
			Number	Student/staff ratio					Number	Student/staff ratio	
1	2	3	4	5	6		7	8	9	10	11
All schools	76,545	95.8	58,738	967	41,480		21,431	86.8	9,497	492	4,341
Fewer than 300 pupils	22,032	89.5	9,603	600	6,974		16,897	84.1	5,058	459	2,337
300 to 499 pupils	22,733	98.0	16,607	863	10,779		2,876	98.4	2,085	534	993
500 to 699 pupils	16,032	99.1	13,801	1,026	9,266		988	99.8	1,115	526	530
700 to 999 pupils	9,343	99.1	9,265	1,108	7,017		459	98.3	747	505	282
1,000 to 1,999 pupils	5,736	98.9	8,317	1,169	6,554		211	100.0	492	556	199
2,000 or more pupils	669	100.0	1,145	1,886	890		(¹)	(¹)	(¹)	(¹)	(¹)
Elementary	54,387	96.9	36,803	931	26,950		13,296	86.1	4,159	636	2,653
Fewer than 300 pupils	15,250	92.1	6,123	613	4,907		11,017	84.0	2,767	593	1,710
300 to 499 pupils	18,657	98.6	12,980	856	8,870		1,765	98.0	917	734	720
500 to 699 pupils	12,848	99.3	10,534	1,051	7,221		411	99.5	327	741	173
700 to 999 pupils	6,039	99.3	5,380	1,177	4,211		103	92.8	148	597	50
1,000 or more pupils	1,593	97.7	1,786	1,117	1,741		—	—	—	—	—
Secondary	18,705	94.8	19,441	1,052	13,019		2,301	94.1	2,355	377	805
Fewer than 300 pupils	4,925	86.7	2,621	596	1,468		1,184	89.1	868	203	174
300 to 499 pupils	3,284	95.7	2,987	840	1,640		497	100.0	562	347	150
500 to 699 pupils	2,835	98.3	2,904	938	1,823		286	100.0	369	459	238
700 to 999 pupils	3,055	98.6	3,582	1,007	2,583		191	100.0	266	578	100
1,000 to 1,999 pupils	3,937	99.4	6,202	1,181	4,615		143	100.0	290	664	143
2,000 or more pupils	669	100.0	1,145	1,886	890		(¹)	(¹)	(¹)	(¹)	(¹)
Combined	3,453	85.4	2,494	877	1,511		5,834	85.8	2,983	383	883
Fewer than 300 pupils	1,857	78.1	859	505	599		4,696	83.1	1,423	357	453
300 to 499 pupils	792	93.0	640	1,251	269		614	98.2	606	404	123
500 to 699 pupils	349	100.0	363	929	222		291	100.0	419	416	119
700 to 999 pupils	249	97.6	303	961	223		165	100.0	333	406	132
1,000 or more pupils	206	99.5	329	1,339	198		68	100.0	202	401	56

¹Data reported under 1,000 to 1,999 category.
—Data not available.

NOTE.—Data are derived from a sample survey and are subject to sampling error. Because of rounding, details may not add to totals.

SOURCE: U.S. Department of Education, National Center for Education Statistics, "Schools and Staffing Survey." (This table was prepared April 1994.)

Table 410.—Percent of public schools having access to selected telecommunication capabilities, by location of access site and level of school: 1994 and 1995

Telecommunications capabilities	Percent of schools having access	Percent of schools with telecommunications access, by location [1]				
		Administrative offices	Teacher workrooms	Classrooms	Computer labs	Library/media centers
1	2	3	4	5	6	7
All public schools, 1994						
Computer with any telecommunication capabilities via local area network	56	67	17	38	59	60
Computer with any telecommunication capabilities via modem	57	55	9	28	38	56
Broadcast television	70	36	31	83	41	84
Cable television	74	31	24	70	39	85
Closed circuit television	25	49	31	94	59	89
Two-way video with 2–way audio	6	27	14	63	21	61
One-way video with two-way audio or computer link	10	28	14	58	36	67
All public schools, 1995						
Computer with any telecommunication capabilities via local area network	77	73	20	45	71	64
Computer with any telecommunication capabilities via modem	76	61	10	30	41	64
Computer with any telecommunication capabilities via wide area network	61	58	14	35	41	68
Broadcast television	71	35	28	82	47	88
Cable television	76	33	25	72	42	91
Closed circuit television	28	50	32	91	60	89
Two-way video with 2–way audio	13	24	17	57	37	69
One-way video with two-way audio or computer link	7	26	15	63	41	54

[1] Location estimates are based on those schools having access to each type of telecommunication capability. Percents of schools reporting telecommunication locations do not sum to 100 because many schools have access in more than one location.

NOTE.—Data are derived from a sample survey and are subject to sampling error.

SOURCE: U.S. Department of Education, National Center for Education Statistics, Fast Response Survey System, *Survey on Advanced Telecommunications in U.S. Public Schools, K-12;* and *Advanced Telecommunications in U.S. Public Elementary and Secondary Schools, 1995.* (This table was prepared September 1996.)

Table 411.—Percent of public schools and school classrooms having access to the Internet, by school characteristics: 1994 and 1995

School characteristics	Estimated number of schools, 1995	Percent of schools having access to Internet		Percent of instructional rooms [1] having access to Internet		Mean number of all computers, [2] per school 1995	Percent of computers [2] with Internet access, 1995	Number of computers [2] with Internet access in schools with Internet access					
								Mean number of computers, 1995	Percent distribution of computers, 1995				
		1994	1995	1994	1995				1 computer	2 to 5 computers	6 to 9 computers	10 or more computers
1	2	3	4	5	6	7	8	9	10	11	12	13
All public schools	**77,853**	**35**	**50**	**3**	**9**	**72**	**14**	**12**	**35**	**38**	**6**	**21**
Instructional level [3]												
Elementary	57,705	30	46	3	10	60	13	9	40	37	5	18
Secondary	18,083	49	65	4	8	112	13	16	25	39	9	27
Size of enrollment												
Less than 300	20,673	30	39	3	11	41	15	7	34	42	8	16
300 to 999	50,044	35	52	3	10	71	15	12	38	35	6	21
1,000 or more	7,136	58	69	3	4	164	8	15	19	45	5	31
Metropolitan status												
City	17,906	40	47	4	8	84	11	11	29	39	6	26
Urban fringe	18,464	38	59	4	8	83	13	12	38	34	6	22
Town	19,539	29	47	3	10	72	16	14	36	35	6	22
Rural	21,944	35	48	3	10	54	14	9	36	42	6	16
Percent of students eligible for free or reduced-price lunch												
Less than 11 percent	13,192	—	62	—	9	77	15	14	29	38	6	26
11 to 30 percent	21,876	—	59	—	10	78	15	13	35	33	7	25
31 to 70 percent	28,017	—	47	—	8	68	12	9	40	40	5	15
71 percent or more	14,651	—	31	—	5	65	10	9	32	43	4	21

[1] Includes all classrooms, computer labs, and library/media centers.
[2] Includes computers used for instructional or administrative purposes.
[3] Excludes combined elementary/secondary schools because of small sample size.
—Data not available.

NOTE.—Data are derived from a sample survey and are subject to sampling error. Details may not add to totals because of rounding for weighted estimates.

SOURCE: U.S. Department of Education, National Center for Education Statistics, Fast Response Survey System, *Survey on Advanced Telecommunications in U.S. Public Schools, K-12;* and *Advanced Telecommunications in U.S. Public Elementary and Secondary Schools, 1995.* (This table was prepared September 1996.)

Table 412.—General statistics of college and university libraries: 1974–75 to 1991–92

Item	1974–75[1]	1975–76[1]	1976–77[1]	1978–79[1]	1981–82	1984–85	1987–88	1991–92
1	2	3	4	5	6	7	8	9
Number of libraries	2,972	2,987	3,058	3,122	3,104	3,322	3,438	3,274
Total enrollment, in thousands[2]	10,322	11,291	11,121	11,392	12,372	12,242	12,767	14,359
Full-time-equivalent enrollment, in thousands[2]	7,805	8,480	8,313	8,348	9,015	8,952	9,230	10,361
Collections, thousands of units								
Number of volumes at end of year	447,059	468,033	481,442	519,895	567,826	631,727	718,504	749,429
Number of volumes added during year	23,242	22,977	22,367	21,608	19,507	20,658	21,907	20,982
Number of serial subscriptions[3]	4,434	4,618	4,670	4,775	4,890	6,317	6,416	6,966
Library staff, in full-time equivalents								
Total staff in regular positions[3]	56,836	56,852	57,087	58,416	58,476	58,476	67,251	67,166
FTE enrollment per FTE staff	137.3	149.2	145.6	142.9	154.2	153.1	137.2	154.3
Librarians and professional staff	23,530	23,104	23,308	23,676	23,816	21,822	25,115	26,341
Other paid staff	33,306	33,748	33,779	34,740	34,660	38,026	40,733	40,421
Contributed services	—	—	—	—	—	—	1,403	404
Student assistants	—	—	—	—	—	—	33,821	29,075
Hours of student and other assistance, in thousands	34,687	36,725	39,950	39,552	40,068	28,360	—	—
Library operating expenditures (excluding capital outlay)								
Operating expenditures, total, in thousands	$1,091,784	$1,180,128	$1,259,637	$1,502,158	$1,943,769	$2,404,524	$2,770,075	$3,648,654
Operating expenditures per FTE student	140	139	152	180	216	269	300	352
Operating expenditures per FTE student in constant 1991–92 dollars	373	347	357	363	317	351	358	352
Salaries[4]	592,568	649,374	698,090	824,438	1,081,894	1,156,138	1,451,551	1,889,368
Hourly wages	61,474	66,175	68,683	79,535	100,847	—	—	—
Fringe benefits	—	—	—	—	—	231,209	—	—
Preservation	22,206	22,375	22,521	25,274	30,351	32,939	34,144	43,126
Collections	327,904	357,544	373,699	450,180	561,199	750,282	891,281	1,197,293
Print materials	—	—	—	—	—	—	—	420,930
Serial subscriptions	—	—	—	—	—	—	—	639,128
Microforms	—	—	—	—	—	—	—	43,666
Audiovisual materials	—	—	—	—	—	—	—	23,879
Machine readable materials	—	—	—	—	—	—	—	29,093
Other collection expenditures	—	—	—	—	—	—	—	40,596
Other library operating expenditures	87,632	84,660	96,643	122,731	169,478	233,957	393,099	518,867
Operating expenditures, total, in percents	100.0	100.0	100.0	100.0	100.0	100.0	100.0	100.0
Salaries[4]	54.3	55.0	55.4	54.9	55.7	48.1	52.4	51.8
Hourly wages	5.6	5.6	5.5	5.3	5.2	—	—	—
Fringe benefits	—	—	—	—	—	9.6	—	—
Preservation	2.0	1.9	1.8	1.7	1.6	1.4	1.2	1.2
Collections	30.0	30.3	29.7	30.0	28.9	31.2	32.2	32.8
Other library operating expenditures	8.0	7.2	7.7	8.2	8.7	9.7	14.2	14.2
Library operating expenditures as percent of total institutional expenditures for educational and general purposes	3.9	3.8	3.8	3.7	3.5	3.4	3.2	3.0

[1] Includes data for U.S. territories.
[2] Fall enrollment for the academic year specified.
[3] Data are for end of year.
[4] Includes expenditures for fringe benefits (except for 1984–85 and 1987–88) and salary equivalents of contributed services staff.
—Data not available.

NOTE.—Because of rounding, details may not add to totals.

SOURCE: U.S. Department of Education, National Center for Education Statistics, *Library Statistics of Colleges and Universities,* various years; and Integrated Postsecondary Education Data Survey, "Academic Library Survey." (This table was prepared August 1995.)

Table 413.—Selected statistics on the collections, staff, and operating expenditures of 50 large college and university libraries: 1988

Institution	Rank order, by number of volumes	Number of volumes at end of year, in thousands	Full-time-equivalent staff		Operating expenditures, in thousands	
			Total	Professional	Total	Salaries and wages
1	2	3	4	5	6	7
Harvard University (Mass.)	1	11,497	1,049	325	$37,196	$20,464
Yale University (Conn.)	2	9,144	707	195	32,010	12,584
University of Illinois, Urbana Campus	3	7,377	536	146	16,337	8,662
University of California, Berkeley	4	7,191	740	168	27,524	17,620
University of Michigan, Ann Arbor	5	6,133	677	143	21,621	10,693
University of Texas, Austin	6	5,889	584	136	17,463	9,436
University of California, Los Angeles	7	5,812	711	209	28,447	15,800
Columbia University, Main Division (N.Y.)	8	5,741	641	166	22,196	12,082
University of Chicago (Ill.)	9	4,865	349	74	13,954	6,217
University of Wisconsin, Madison	10	4,804	504	139	18,161	9,754
University of Minnesota, Twin Cities	11	4,651	484	122	17,740	8,824
Indiana University, Bloomington	12	4,530	431	104	11,486	6,618
Ohio State University, Main Campus	13	4,254	454	118	15,784	8,444
Cornell University (N.Y.)	14	4,189	414	120	12,986	6,915
Princeton University (N.J.)	15	4,071	375	105	15,660	8,038
Rutgers University, New Brunswick (N.J.)	16	4,054	384	82	14,948	8,351
University of Washington	17	3,724	447	109	14,350	7,786
Duke University (N.C.)	18	3,669	320	94	12,178	6,012
University of Arizona	19	3,622	328	84	10,943	5,453
University of North Carolina, Chapel Hill	20	3,520	413	117	15,884	7,686
University of Pennsylvania	21	3,500	368	108	13,780	7,400
Michigan State University	22	3,302	331	78	11,517	5,900
Stanford University (Calif.)	23	3,187	407	80	18,213	10,488
University of Southern California	24	3,170	344	64	11,860	7,390
University of Virginia, Main Campus	25	3,003	343	96	14,119	6,703
New York University	26	2,988	361	108	15,550	7,593
University of Iowa	27	2,931	274	86	11,491	5,718
University of Pittsburgh, Main Campus (Penn.)	28	2,713	342	83	10,110	5,310
University of Florida	29	2,702	405	106	12,954	7,278
University of Georgia	30	2,688	322	76	10,428	4,984
University of Rochester (N.Y.)	31	2,598	231	61	8,820	3,678
University of Kansas, Main Campus	32	2,585	260	77	9,061	4,251
Northwestern University (Ill.)	33	2,574	288	79	8,979	5,321
State University of New York, Buffalo, Main Campus	34	2,493	272	90	10,703	5,500
University of California, Santa Barbara	35	2,476	247	62	10,334	5,882
Southern Methodist University (Texas)	36	2,415	141	49	5,619	2,404
University of Missouri, Columbia	37	2,411	235	56	6,601	3,617
University of Oklahoma, Norman Campus	38	2,396	209	55	5,192	2,267
University of Hawaii, Manoa	39	2,365	247	73	8,587	4,925
Louisiana State U. & A&M & Hebert Laws Center	40	2,343	283	62	7,983	3,949
Johns Hopkins University (Md.)	41	2,330	308	82	12,007	5,756
Arizona State University	42	2,315	366	95	12,510	5,457
University of Delaware	43	2,296	220	57	7,655	3,093
Purdue University, Main Campus (Ind.)	44	2,242	268	59	7,966	4,102
Wayne State University (Mich.)	45	2,234	266	74	10,395	4,457
University of California, Davis	46	2,227	320	68	14,989	7,619
Syracuse University, Main Campus (N.Y.)	47	2,217	271	68	8,106	3,821
University of Colorado, Boulder	48	2,186	222	50	7,805	4,235
Massachusetts Institute of Technology	49	2,181	265	87	9,443	5,097
Washington University (Missouri)	50	2,170	230	66	9,558	3,853

SOURCE: U.S. Department of Education, National Center for Education Statistics, unpublished data. (This table was prepared May 1993.)

Table 414.—General statistics of public libraries, by population of legal service area: 1993

Item	Population of legal service area						
	Total	Under 10,000	10,000 to 49,999	50,000 to 99,999	100,000 to 249,999	250,000 to 499,999	500,000 and over
1	2	3	4	5	6	7	8
Number of public library service outlets	**16,939**	**5,746**	**4,131**	**1,833**	**2,061**	**1,144**	**2,013**
Central libraries	8,887	5,415	2,494	495	316	85	71
Branch libraries	7,017	251	1,281	1,115	1,553	981	1,836
Bookmobiles	1,035	80	356	223	192	78	106
Collections, in thousands							
Books and serial volumes [1]	655,919	90,749	160,126	81040	93,297	70,891	159,816
Audio and video materials and films	30,479	2,903	7,282	3,925	4,401	3,017	8,948
Serial subscriptions	1,776	259	449	210	234	162	461
Paid staff, in full-time equivalents							
Librarians	37,349	5,404	9,586	4,686	5,178	3,811	8,685
Librarians with ALA-MLS [2]	24,825	995	5,589	3,297	3,899	3,197	7,848
Other staff	74,560	4,801	17,473	10,167	12,196	9,061	20,861
Finances, in thousands							
Total operating income	$5,068,950	$334,846	$1,137,033	$660,076	$779,154	$630,148	$1,527,693
	Percentage distribution						
Source of income							
Total	100.0	100.0	100.0	100.0	100.0	100.0	100.0
Federal	1.1	1.3	0.8	0.9	1.2	1.2	1.4
State	12.5	9.4	10.8	12.7	10	12.3	15.7
Local	78.0	74.5	79.5	79.5	81.7	80.8	73.9
Other	8.4	14.9	8.9	6.9	7.1	5.7	9.1

[1] Some data are different from other tables due to a different population base.

[2] ALA-MLS=A master's degree from a graduate library education program accredited by the American Library Association (ALA).

NOTE.—Because of rounding, details may not add to totals. Totals may be underestimated due to nonresponse.

SOURCE: U.S. Department of Education, National Center for Education Statistics, *Public Libraries in the United States: 1993.* (This table was prepared July 1996.)

Table 415.—Public libraries, books and serial volumes, annual attendance, and reference transactions, by state: 1993

State	Number of public libraries	Number of books and serial volumes [1] (in thousands)	Number of books and serial volumes per capita	Library visits per capita [2]	Circulation per capita [2]	Public library reference transactions per capita [3]	State	Number of public libraries	Number of books and serial volumes [1] (in thousands)	Number of books and serial volumes per capita	Library visits per capita [2]	Circulation per capita [2]	Public library reference transactions per capita [3]
1	2	3	4	5	6	7	1	2	3	4	5	6	7
United States	**8,929**	**656,031**	**2.7**	**4.0**	**6.5**	**1.1**							
Alabama	208	7,057	1.9	2.7	3.8	0.5	Missouri	148	18,181	3.9	4.2	8.1	0.9
Alaska	85	1,879	3.1	4.1	6.2	0.7	Montana	83	2,422	3.0	3.6	6.1	0.7
Arizona	39	7,212	2.0	4.6	6.9	1.3	Nebraska	269	4,778	3.8	—	7.9	—
Arkansas	36	4,661	2.1	2.3	4.1	0.4	Nevada	26	2,686	2.0	3.4	5.0	0.8
California	169	59,171	1.9	4.5	5.0	1.4	New Hampshire	229	4,761	4.6	5.5	8.0	0.7
Colorado	120	9,327	2.6	4.4	7.8	1.2	New Jersey	310	28,796	3.8	4.8	5.8	0.8
Connecticut	194	12,794	4.2	6.6	8.2	1.2	New Mexico	69	3,435	3.1	3.9	6.8	0.7
Delaware	29	1,225	1.8	3.2	4.4	0.5	New York	758	68,339	3.8	5.0	6.8	1.3
District of Columbia ...	1	1,874	3.1	3.7	3.3	2.0	North Carolina	74	13,094	2.0	3.3	5.8	0.8
Florida	100	20,683	1.6	—	4.9	—	North Dakota	78	1,901	3.5	5.2	6.9	0.6
Georgia	54	13,068	1.9	2.8	4.6	0.6	Ohio	250	39,920	3.6	5.2	11.9	1.6
Hawaii	1	2,985	2.3	2.8	5.4	1.2	Oklahoma	110	5,577	2.2	3.9	6.4	0.9
Idaho	107	2,930	3.3	4.9	7.8	0.8	Oregon	124	6,473	2.4	—	9.4	0.8
Illinois	606	34,265	3.4	5.4	7.6	1.3	Pennsylvania	448	24,140	2.1	2.8	4.7	0.6
Indiana	238	19,141	3.7	5.5	9.9	1.1	Rhode Island	51	3,704	4.0	5.3	6.3	0.0
Iowa	517	10,794	3.9	5.0	9.0	0.6	South Carolina	40	6,088	1.7	2.9	4.1	0.9
Kansas	320	8,825	4.3	4.9	9.3	1.3	South Dakota	113	2,327	4.2	5.2	8.9	—
Kentucky	116	7,068	1.9	2.6	5.3	0.3	Tennessee	137	8,031	1.6	2.7	4.1	0.8
Louisiana	65	9,478	2.2	2.6	4.4	0.6	Texas	498	31,472	2.0	2.9	4.6	1.0
Maine	225	4,831	4.9	5.2	7.6	—	Utah	69	4,561	2.5	—	8.6	—
Maryland	24	13,276	2.7	2.3	9.7	1.1	Vermont	201	2,366	4.8	—	7.2	—
Massachusetts	374	27,770	4.7	—	7.0	—	Virginia	90	15,275	2.5	4.5	7.5	1.0
Michigan	377	23,637	2.5	3.5	5.3	0.8	Washington	70	13,531	2.7	—	10.2	—
Minnesota	132	12,333	2.8	4.6	9.5	1.4	West Virginia	97	4,428	2.4	3.5	4.8	0.9
Mississippi	47	5,065	2.0	2.7	3.2	0.4	Wisconsin	380	16,094	3.2	5.8	8.7	1.1
							Wyoming	23	2,302	4.9	5.3	8.2	0.9

[1] Some data are different from other tables due to a different population base.

[2] The total number of persons entering the library for whatever purpose during the year.

[3] A reference transaction is an information contact which involves the knowledge, use, recommendations, interpretation or instructions in the use of one or more information sources by a member of the library staff.

—Response rate less than 70 percent.

NOTE.—Totals may be underestimated due to nonresponse.

SOURCE: U.S. Department of Education, National Center for Education Statistics, *Public Libraries in the United States: 1993.* (This table was prepared July 1996.)

Table 416.—Percent of workers, 18 years old and over, using computers on the job, by selected characteristics and computer activities: October 1993

Selected characteristics	Percent using computers at work	Number using computers at work, in thousands	Percent of on-the-job computer workers using specific computer applications [1]										
			Analysis/ spreadsheets	Book-keeping, invoicing, and inventory	Communications [2]	CAD [3]	Data bases	Desktop publishing/ graphics	Education	Programming	Sales and telemarketing	Word processing	Using 4 or more categories
1	2	3	4	5	6	7	8	9	10	11	12	13	14
Total	45.8	51,106	36.1	45.0	38.7	7.6	34.5	22.3	15.7	13.1	16.2	44.4	40.7
Age													
18 to 24	34.4	4,965	25.0	45.3	27.1	6.0	27.1	15.9	10.4	11.2	19.9	34.7	29.8
25 to 29	48.3	8,424	37.2	45.2	38.7	7.7	35.0	22.8	14.3	13.9	17.0	45.7	41.8
30 to 39	50.7	14,969	38.8	45.4	40.4	8.7	36.0	25.0	15.8	14.9	16.4	45.0	42.9
40 to 49	51.3	13,854	38.6	45.1	42.0	7.9	36.8	23.4	18.5	12.9	14.5	47.5	43.4
50 to 59	43.9	6,881	34.5	44.3	38.8	6.4	33.3	20.4	15.8	11.2	15.0	43.9	39.2
60 or older	27.2	2,014	28.0	42.7	31.6	4.5	27.4	15.0	14.0	9.3	16.9	40.0	33.9
Educational attainment and sex													
Not high school graduate	10.0	1,190	19.1	54.4	20.4	3.8	22.2	9.9	9.6	8.8	20.6	16.0	21.8
High school graduate	34.2	13,307	23.7	52.5	29.4	4.4	25.8	13.3	9.5	8.9	17.6	30.8	29.9
Some college	50.4	11,548	33.5	49.5	38.5	7.3	33.9	20.6	13.0	11.3	18.0	40.9	40.0
Associate degree	58.2	5,274	37.5	47.0	39.7	7.9	34.7	21.7	13.8	14.2	14.9	41.6	40.7
Bachelor's degree	68.8	13,162	46.9	40.0	45.1	10.4	41.5	28.8	19.4	16.7	17.0	54.8	49.2
Master's degree	71.2	4,628	47.9	29.3	48.5	10.0	41.9	35.3	31.0	18.1	10.4	63.8	52.1
Doctor's or professional degree	66.9	1,999	42.8	27.9	45.9	7.6	39.2	28.3	21.3	15.2	5.2	66.5	46.2
Male	40.3	24,414	41.1	45.2	39.4	11.1	35.2	25.3	14.8	17.0	18.1	40.7	43.0
Not high school graduate ...	8.5	642	20.2	56.0	20.9	5.6	19.8	10.9	9.1	9.6	16.2	12.2	21.1
High school graduate	24.2	4,942	23.4	52.0	24.6	7.2	19.6	12.9	7.7	9.6	17.7	17.3	25.4
Some college	42.8	5,086	35.8	50.4	37.1	10.4	33.4	22.0	12.8	15.6	20.9	32.1	40.0
Associate degree	52.6	2,358	41.8	46.8	39.3	13.3	36.0	26.2	14.7	19.1	16.8	36.6	41.9
Bachelor's degree	69.8	7,324	52.3	42.6	47.1	13.8	43.4	31.6	16.6	21.0	20.9	53.8	53.2
Master's degree	75.4	2,601	56.0	34.1	51.7	13.0	46.8	37.8	25.2	22.5	13.8	63.3	57.2
Doctor's or professional degree	66.5	1,461	45.0	29.2	46.0	8.6	38.7	29.9	20.9	17.9	5.2	63.7	47.9
Female	52.4	26,692	31.6	44.8	38.1	4.4	33.8	19.6	16.5	9.5	14.5	47.8	38.6
Not high school graduate ...	12.5	547	17.8	52.5	19.9	1.7	25.1	8.7	10.3	7.9	25.8	20.5	22.6
High school graduate	45.2	8,365	23.8	52.8	32.2	2.8	29.4	13.6	10.5	8.6	17.5	38.8	32.5
Some college	58.6	6,461	31.6	48.7	39.7	4.8	34.3	19.4	13.1	8.0	15.7	47.9	40.0
Associate degree	63.7	2,916	34.0	47.1	40.0	3.5	33.6	18.1	13.1	10.2	13.5	45.7	39.6
Bachelor's degree	67.6	5,838	40.2	36.8	42.5	6.1	39.2	25.3	22.9	11.5	12.0	56.1	44.1
Master's degree	66.5	2,027	37.4	23.2	44.3	6.0	35.6	32.1	38.5	12.4	6.0	64.4	45.5
Doctor's or professional degree	68.2	538	36.8	24.1	45.4	4.8	40.8	24.1	22.3	7.7	5.2	74.3	41.5
Race/ethnicity													
White, non-Hispanic	48.7	43,020	37.2	45.8	39.3	7.8	35.2	23.0	15.9	13.4	16.7	45.9	41.8
Black, non-Hispanic	36.2	4,016	27.5	38.3	37.3	5.8	31.2	16.8	15.7	10.9	12.9	35.5	34.1
Hispanic	29.3	2,492	29.1	45.6	32.1	6.5	27.6	18.7	13.3	10.8	16.0	33.6	32.9
Other	43.9	1,578	39.7	39.4	37.2	8.9	33.5	22.6	12.9	15.2	10.2	44.5	39.0
Occupational group													
Managerial and professional specialty	67.7	21,044	46.5	39.3	45.7	10.6	40.3	31.1	22.2	16.7	11.6	56.7	49.7
Executive, administrative, and managerial	72.3	10,645	54.5	54.3	49.0	8.1	44.3	29.6	15.9	14.9	18.4	58.3	55.6
Professional specialty occupations	68.3	7,712	43.2	26.6	45.8	15.4	40.7	33.2	16.1	20.0	5.4	54.2	45.2
Teachers, except college and university	49.1	2,091	18.9	16.4	28.0	5.5	20.1	30.0	69.6	11.2	2.3	52.0	36.2
Teachers, college and university	72.5	597	44.0	15.8	48.9	11.2	33.4	34.9	47.0	23.8	2.2	77.4	51.1
Technical, sales, and administrative support	65.5	22,316	31.2	50.7	36.5	5.1	33.4	17.3	11.9	10.9	22.6	42.0	38.7
Technicians and related support	69.9	2,592	41.5	29.0	38.1	13.1	37.9	21.2	11.0	28.8	4.7	37.4	37.9
Sales occupations	48.8	6,220	34.1	59.9	33.6	4.7	31.5	18.5	11.0	8.2	53.7	34.8	43.5
Administrative support, including clerical	76.7	13,505	27.9	50.6	37.5	3.7	33.3	16.0	12.4	8.7	11.7	46.2	36.6
Service occupations	14.7	2,126	15.2	31.3	31.5	2.7	20.9	7.5	9.1	6.6	11.6	20.5	18.7
Precision production, craft, and repair	23.2	2,976	32.0	45.3	29.2	9.9	26.1	16.4	11.0	14.4	9.6	20.6	28.2
Operators, fabricators, and laborers	14.9	2,382	15.3	51.8	18.3	6.1	17.0	12.5	6.5	7.1	9.6	11.4	16.4
Farming, forestry, and fishing	8.5	262	27.5	65.3	16.4	1.8	27.3	16.2	8.6	7.6	10.4	28.2	31.7
Family income [4]													
Less than $20,000	25.1	5,224	24.4	46.6	28.8	5.1	27.4	15.5	12.1	9.4	18.7	33.1	30.6
$20,000 to $29,999	38.4	7,337	29.3	48.9	35.3	6.1	31.1	19.2	13.8	11.2	17.8	38.6	36.7
$30,000 to $39,999	45.7	8,911	32.3	47.1	35.7	6.9	31.5	20.6	15.1	11.8	15.0	40.7	37.1
$40,000 to $49,999	51.9	7,027	34.2	45.4	37.3	7.3	33.0	20.6	15.6	12.9	13.4	42.2	38.2
$50,000 to $74,999	60.6	12,643	40.4	43.4	42.2	8.9	37.5	24.4	17.8	14.6	15.2	47.6	43.7
$75,000 or more	65.9	8,994	49.3	40.6	47.8	9.5	42.1	29.5	17.0	16.3	17.5	57.9	52.2

[1] Individuals may be counted in more than one computer activity.
[2] Includes bulletin boards and electronic mail.
[3] Computer assisted design.
[4] Excludes persons whose income data were not available.

NOTE.—Data are based on a sample survey of households and are subject to sampling and nonsampling error.

SOURCE: U.S. Department of Commerce, Bureau of the Census, Current Population Survey, October 1993, unpublished data. (This table was prepared March 1994.)

Table 417.—Access to and use of home computers, by selected characteristics of students and other users: October 1993

Selected characteristics	Percent with computers at home	Percent using computers at home	Distribution of frequency of use per week for persons using computers in home				Percent of persons whose home computer has specific components [1]				Percent of computer users using specific applications [2]					
			6 or 7 days	4 or 5 days	2 or 3 days	1 day or less	Hard disk	Printer	Color monitor	Fax or modem	Communications [3]	School assignments	Education programs	Games	Job-related	Word processing
1	2	3	4	5	6	7	8	9	10	11	12	13	14	15	16	17
Total, all persons	**27.1**	**17.6**	**14.7**	**17.1**	**33.3**	**34.9**	**80.7**	**75.8**	**68.2**	**38.5**	**33.5**	**28.3**	**34.6**	**34.9**	**23.8**	**53.2**
Age																
Less than 25	30.8	21.0	11.1	15.5	36.2	37.3	79.5	75.2	69.1	36.2	8.4	48.9	38.1	57.2	3.1	37.7
25 to 29	23.4	16.6	16.8	18.4	33.4	31.3	83.5	68.5	66.3	44.2	48.0	22.6	30.0	21.1	35.2	63.4
30 to 39	30.7	21.0	16.2	17.9	33.2	32.7	82.3	74.0	70.3	42.3	51.2	15.6	34.2	22.2	38.6	61.9
40 to 49	36.4	23.0	16.9	17.9	30.9	34.3	80.9	79.4	69.6	39.0	48.6	15.7	33.5	19.1	39.1	65.1
50 to 59	27.1	15.8	17.7	19.8	27.9	34.7	80.2	79.2	65.0	37.1	50.9	9.5	30.8	19.5	37.2	64.7
60 or older	10.5	4.6	20.7	16.7	28.7	33.9	80.2	77.5	60.0	33.2	51.4	3.3	27.4	19.7	26.5	59.4
Family income																
Less than $20,000	9.2	5.6	19.2	15.7	31.3	33.8	72.4	64.6	57.8	28.6	32.3	34.7	33.0	33.7	16.2	50.2
$20,000 to $29,999 ...	18.5	11.3	16.6	16.6	33.9	32.9	74.6	73.0	62.8	32.1	33.8	28.4	37.8	36.8	21.2	50.2
$30,000 to $39,999 ...	26.5	16.9	14.0	16.8	34.2	35.0	76.8	72.7	66.7	33.7	33.6	27.5	35.3	35.4	22.2	49.2
$40,000 to $49,999 ...	35.2	22.9	13.9	16.6	33.8	35.7	81.6	77.2	71.4	37.5	31.4	26.0	32.8	35.4	21.0	48.9
$50,000 to $74,999 ...	47.3	31.6	13.5	17.6	33.2	35.7	82.5	78.6	70.4	41.7	33.3	28.5	34.2	35.4	25.2	53.8
$75,000 or more	62.8	42.4	14.3	17.9	33.0	34.8	87.6	80.1	72.2	46.1	35.3	26.9	35.0	33.6	29.1	60.2
Total, all students	**36.1**	**26.5**	**12.4**	**16.3**	**36.3**	**35.1**	**80.6**	**76.3**	**69.9**	**37.5**	**11.8**	**55.1**	**39.1**	**55.1**	**5.7**	**41.8**
Preprimary	29.6	15.3	4.7	10.7	39.5	45.0	82.3	72.0	69.6	40.9	0.7	4.1	62.0	86.6	0.0	5.1
1st to 8th grade	31.9	24.3	9.9	14.1	37.9	38.1	79.9	75.2	72.1	36.9	2.6	43.6	48.2	86.4	0.0	28.0
9th to 12th grade	37.2	28.1	11.6	17.7	37.3	33.3	77.7	78.0	69.7	34.6	7.1	73.0	26.6	32.9	2.3	47.6
Undergraduate	44.7	32.4	16.2	19.2	31.8	32.8	81.5	78.1	66.8	36.3	26.5	70.6	26.8	16.3	12.1	62.0
Graduate	60.4	51.8	25.5	21.4	33.2	20.0	89.4	77.9	67.8	50.3	47.8	69.5	39.2	21.9	37.0	80.1
Sex																
Male	36.2	26.9	15.1	17.0	34.1	33.7	81.0	76.1	70.5	38.7	12.7	54.1	39.4	57.8	6.1	40.1
Preprimary	28.5	14.8	6.0	13.1	37.3	43.6	82.7	71.1	71.0	41.3	0.4	5.8	61.3	90.7	0.0	4.4
1st to 8th grade	31.8	24.5	11.6	14.3	36.6	37.5	80.6	75.1	72.1	36.2	2.2	40.5	47.4	88.8	0.0	26.0
9th to 12th grade ...	36.6	27.6	15.0	19.7	33.4	31.9	77.5	77.8	69.7	36.5	8.5	72.5	27.4	34.3	2.3	45.1
Undergraduate	48.7	36.1	20.2	19.8	30.0	30.0	82.1	78.8	68.2	40.7	29.4	72.1	27.8	18.3	12.5	61.9
Graduate	62.6	55.2	31.0	20.7	30.2	18.1	89.7	75.0	69.2	51.8	53.6	71.6	42.1	25.1	42.4	80.6
Female	36.0	26.2	9.6	15.5	38.5	36.5	80.2	76.5	69.4	36.3	10.8	56.2	38.8	52.3	5.4	43.6
Preprimary	30.9	15.8	3.4	8.2	41.9	46.5	82.0	73.0	68.2	40.6	1.0	2.2	62.7	82.3	0.0	5.8
1st to 8th grade	32.1	24.2	8.0	13.8	39.4	38.7	79.2	75.2	72.1	37.6	3.1	46.9	49.1	83.9	0.0	30.2
9th to 12th grade ...	37.9	28.6	8.1	15.6	41.4	34.9	77.9	78.2	69.7	32.6	5.7	73.5	25.8	31.5	2.3	50.1
Undergraduate	41.5	29.4	12.3	18.6	33.5	35.6	80.9	77.5	65.6	32.0	23.7	69.0	25.8	14.3	11.8	62.1
Graduate	58.4	48.8	19.9	22.1	36.1	21.8	89.2	80.7	66.4	48.9	41.8	67.5	36.2	18.7	31.6	79.7
Race/ethnicity																
White, non-Hispanic ..	43.3	32.2	11.9	16.0	35.8	36.3	81.1	77.6	70.1	38.0	11.4	55.2	38.4	55.6	5.7	42.6
Preprimary	35.8	19.0	4.4	11.8	37.4	46.4	83.7	72.7	70.2	41.7	0.7	4.3	62.0	87.1	0.0	5.7
1st to 8th grade	39.6	30.8	9.7	13.8	37.1	39.5	80.5	76.8	72.3	37.5	2.7	43.8	47.2	87.0	0.0	28.9
9th to 12th grade ...	46.2	35.1	10.9	16.6	38.1	34.4	78.2	79.5	69.8	35.5	7.1	73.5	25.5	31.8	2.1	48.7
Undergraduate	49.4	35.5	15.8	19.3	31.2	33.7	81.9	79.2	67.0	36.4	26.1	71.2	25.5	15.5	13.2	64.0
Graduate	61.4	52.8	25.1	22.1	32.5	20.3	89.3	78.1	67.3	50.1	47.3	70.8	39.3	21.0	36.2	82.1
Black, non-Hispanic ...	16.1	10.8	13.8	16.8	37.0	32.4	73.8	64.8	68.4	34.5	14.2	53.0	50.8	56.3	7.4	33.9
Preprimary	12.3	4.1	5.9	2.9	53.6	37.7	67.9	59.2	66.9	39.3	0.0	0.0	76.7	85.7	0.0	0.0
1st to 8th grade	13.1	8.9	10.6	16.9	42.8	29.7	73.6	60.7	70.6	33.8	3.2	44.8	64.9	84.5	0.0	22.6
9th to 12th grade ...	14.6	10.3	12.6	22.0	29.0	36.4	71.4	59.7	61.5	21.2	3.7	67.9	36.1	40.4	5.6	27.2
Undergraduate	27.0	19.1	18.7	13.9	33.0	34.4	76.1	75.2	70.7	41.3	37.2	60.6	40.3	27.5	9.3	56.7
Graduate	56.7	47.6	21.7	18.8	32.2	27.3	82.3	75.3	69.5	48.6	37.4	60.3	35.8	24.9	47.9	60.2
Hispanic	15.2	10.3	13.9	21.1	39.6	25.5	74.7	73.0	63.0	32.7	17.2	54.9	34.7	51.2	5.2	35.3
Preprimary	11.7	5.6	7.9	6.8	36.7	48.6	70.5	75.5	53.8	29.7	0.0	0.0	39.6	71.1	0.0	0.0
1st to 8th grade	12.1	7.4	11.2	16.1	42.8	29.9	72.3	70.4	65.3	31.2	0.8	38.9	40.4	84.7	0.0	17.6
9th to 12th grade ...	14.4	9.6	13.7	33.2	29.6	23.5	71.5	76.9	67.4	31.2	15.8	68.7	27.7	41.3	2.4	47.1
Undergraduate	27.3	21.9	15.0	22.4	42.1	20.5	78.2	70.5	55.5	31.4	30.8	73.1	30.3	12.7	5.8	47.5
Graduate	56.3	52.2	28.5	16.5	44.4	10.6	95.1	84.9	77.9	58.8	69.8	71.8	39.6	37.7	43.5	75.4
Family income																
Less than $20,000	15.2	10.9	18.5	16.0	34.1	31.3	74.9	65.9	57.9	29.2	20.4	62.0	35.3	44.0	8.4	47.6
$20,000 to $29,999 ...	25.5	18.6	13.4	16.8	38.6	31.2	72.7	71.8	63.7	31.1	13.0	53.3	41.2	51.5	7.0	38.6
$30,000 to $39,999 ...	34.3	25.1	11.9	15.4	38.2	34.6	76.3	73.2	67.5	32.8	11.5	55.3	41.0	54.1	6.9	36.9
$40,000 to $49,999 ...	42.6	31.5	10.9	16.7	37.0	35.3	80.4	78.8	74.0	36.0	8.9	53.2	38.1	61.3	4.8	35.7
$50,000 to $74,999 ...	55.9	42.0	10.5	17.3	34.1	38.1	82.8	79.9	73.4	41.8	10.1	54.1	38.1	56.9	4.4	41.9
$75,000 or more	73.7	54.1	12.1	15.2	37.2	35.5	87.8	80.5	74.6	43.6	10.4	54.5	40.8	57.9	4.9	46.7

[1] Data are for the most recently purchased computer for families with more than one computer. Percent based on persons who have a computer in their home.

[2] Individuals may be counted in more than one computer activity.

[3] Includes bulletin boards and electronic mail.

NOTE.—Data are based on a sample survey of households and are subject to sampling and nonsampling error.

SOURCE: U.S. Department of Commerce, Bureau of the Census, Current Population Survey, October 1993, unpublished data. (This table was prepared May 1994.)

Table 418.—Student use of computers, by level of instruction and selected characteristics: October 1984, 1989, and 1993

Student and school characteristics	October 1984 Total	October 1989						October 1993					
		Total	Prekindergarten and kindergarten	Grades 1 to 8	Grades 9 to 12	1st to 4th year of college	5th or later year of college	Total	Prekindergarten and kindergarten	Grades 1 to 8	Grades 9 to 12	1st to 4th year of college	5th or later year of college
1	2	3	4	5	6	7	8	9	10	11	12	13	14
Percent of students using computers at school													
Total	**27.3**	**42.7**	**14.7**	**52.3**	**39.2**	**39.2**	**40.7**	**59.0**	**26.2**	**68.9**	**58.2**	**55.2**	**52.1**
Sex													
Male	29.0	43.5	13.9	52.9	38.7	42.1	47.0	59.4	25.9	69.5	56.5	57.5	56.7
Female	25.5	41.9	15.6	51.7	39.8	36.8	34.9	58.7	26.5	68.4	60.0	53.3	47.8
Race/ethnicity													
White, non-Hispanic	30.0	45.7	17.0	58.4	40.6	40.0	39.6	61.6	29.4	73.7	59.9	54.9	49.8
Black, non-Hispanic	16.8	32.6	7.4	35.7	36.0	35.1	35.2	51.5	16.5	56.5	54.5	56.9	57.9
Hispanic	18.6	34.9	10.1	40.2	33.6	32.4	37.8	52.3	19.2	58.4	54.1	51.9	53.7
Other	28.6	42.7	8.5	47.0	41.4	43.9	58.0	59.0	23.5	65.7	57.3	60.9	69.4
Household income													
Less than $5,000	18.7	36.7	8.5	40.4	35.6	40.1	53.5	51.2	19.6	55.0	50.6	61.7	66.7
$5,000 to 9,999	21.0	36.1	9.2	40.3	32.7	40.5	60.2	53.3	24.4	60.3	51.9	53.9	56.2
$10,000 to 14,999	22.4	38.4	14.6	44.4	39.1	30.8	55.2	56.4	20.1	64.7	56.7	50.7	76.1
$15,000 to 19,999	25.9	41.5	11.9	50.9	34.8	39.6	44.0	58.1	23.8	67.5	57.4	51.2	58.5
$20,000 to 24,999	26.7	42.4	14.6	51.8	40.1	32.5	44.4	56.4	23.7	64.3	53.0	57.4	52.4
$25,000 to 29,999	30.5	46.1	16.1	56.4	43.8	40.4	42.1	60.0	28.0	70.1	60.3	51.5	58.0
$30,000 to 34,999	30.5	44.2	17.4	56.8	37.8	37.1	33.3	59.1	23.7	69.6	59.7	51.7	45.3
$35,000 to 39,999	32.3	45.2	16.1	58.3	41.5	34.5	45.3	60.7	27.1	72.1	61.7	49.2	47.9
$40,000 to 49,999	32.8	44.7	15.4	59.7	36.7	38.1	35.4	59.3	28.5	70.3	57.2	53.9	48.6
$50,000 to 74,999	35.5	47.0	16.2	61.2	44.6	43.4	31.8	62.6	28.6	75.6	61.5	57.4	44.2
$75,000 or more	36.0	51.2	21.2	67.0	45.8	49.6	31.0	64.6	33.5	78.7	62.5	60.9	47.7
Control of school													
Public	27.4	43.3	16.4	51.9	39.0	37.5	41.3	60.2	30.1	68.6	58.1	53.9	54.1
Private	26.5	38.9	11.8	56.6	42.6	46.3	39.7	52.1	18.7	72.5	60.7	60.7	48.0
Percent of students using computers at home													
Total	**11.5**	**18.8**	**10.2**	**17.8**	**20.7**	**21.3**	**33.4**	**27.0**	**15.6**	**24.7**	**28.7**	**32.8**	**52.6**
Sex													
Male	14.0	20.7	11.0	18.7	23.9	25.4	36.0	27.4	15.1	24.8	28.2	36.6	56.1
Female	9.0	17.0	9.3	16.9	17.4	18.0	31.1	26.6	16.1	24.6	29.2	29.7	49.5
Race/ethnicity													
White, non-Hispanic	13.7	22.7	12.2	22.3	25.3	23.6	35.6	32.8	19.4	31.4	35.9	36.0	53.6
Black, non-Hispanic	4.9	7.3	3.7	6.8	8.5	9.1	18.6	10.9	4.2	9.0	10.4	19.4	48.1
Hispanic	3.6	7.5	3.4	6.6	8.2	11.5	27.1	10.4	5.7	7.5	9.8	22.0	52.2
Other	9.0	18.8	9.9	16.6	21.6	23.7	24.7	28.7	17.0	23.2	37.0	33.0	47.1
Household income													
Less than $5,000	2.9	8.4	4.5	4.1	6.6	17.7	29.4	9.7	1.1	4.1	6.8	25.6	45.2
$5,000 to 9,999	3.2	5.4	1.0	2.7	4.4	14.2	28.4	8.0	0.9	4.5	5.3	21.3	45.6
$10,000 to 14,999	5.0	7.2	1.9	6.2	6.5	11.8	26.5	11.4	4.6	6.4	8.7	29.8	50.0
$15,000 to 19,999	7.5	11.3	3.2	9.2	13.6	15.8	33.6	15.1	6.9	10.9	14.1	28.9	43.0
$20,000 to 24,999	9.9	12.9	6.8	11.6	13.6	16.9	32.2	16.8	7.4	13.1	17.9	27.7	49.6
$25,000 to 29,999	12.8	17.0	11.9	16.5	17.1	19.2	29.6	21.1	12.3	19.3	22.0	26.1	47.0
$30,000 to 34,999	15.8	17.7	8.0	17.6	20.2	19.4	30.7	24.1	18.7	20.5	29.1	26.4	44.4
$35,000 to 39,999	19.4	21.4	8.7	22.2	25.1	22.1	26.5	27.1	13.0	26.3	28.1	32.7	52.7
$40,000 to 49,999	20.4	25.7	14.8	27.5	27.7	21.7	40.7	32.2	21.6	32.9	33.9	32.5	45.9
$50,000 to 74,999	24.2	31.6	20.6	33.8	34.3	27.6	41.1	43.0	25.5	45.3	46.4	40.1	58.2
$75,000 or more	22.1	43.8	25.2	50.9	53.4	33.9	41.4	56.1	38.2	62.3	61.0	47.0	64.7
Control of school													
Public	11.2	17.9	8.3	16.8	19.7	20.7	32.2	25.3	12.1	23.0	27.2	31.9	50.0
Private	13.8	24.4	13.4	27.7	35.9	23.8	35.9	37.4	22.4	41.5	47.2	36.9	57.7
Percent of students using computers at home for school work													
Total	**4.6**	**8.9**	**0.6**	**6.3**	**12.2**	**13.7**	**23.9**	**14.9**	**0.6**	**10.8**	**20.9**	**23.1**	**36.6**
Sex													
Male	5.9	9.5	0.6	6.3	13.6	16.0	25.9	14.8	0.9	10.1	20.5	26.3	40.3
Female	3.3	8.3	0.6	6.2	10.8	11.7	22.0	15.0	0.4	11.5	21.4	20.5	33.2
Race													
White, non-Hispanic	5.4	10.7	0.6	7.7	15.2	15.1	25.5	18.2	0.8	13.8	26.5	25.7	37.8
Black, non-Hispanic	2.3	3.4	0.9	2.7	4.0	6.2	12.6	5.7	—	4.0	6.9	11.5	30.1
Hispanic	1.4	3.6	—	2.8	4.4	6.4	24.8	5.6	—	2.9	6.7	15.9	36.8
Other	3.8	9.1	—	5.8	13.4	15.5	14.8	16.0	1.1	9.3	27.0	23.7	29.2
Household income													
Less than $5,000	1.0	5.0	—	1.5	4.1	12.6	23.8	6.7	—	2.5	4.0	18.7	36.0
$5,000 to 9,999	1.5	3.2	—	0.6	2.6	10.3	26.5	4.8	—	1.1	3.6	16.1	35.5
$10,000 to 14,999	1.9	3.5	0.7	1.8	3.6	8.1	19.3	7.3	—	2.6	5.6	25.9	34.6
$15,000 to 19,999	3.0	4.5	—	2.1	5.2	9.3	30.2	8.6	0.4	4.7	10.8	18.7	31.0
$20,000 to 24,999	3.1	5.7	0.3	3.8	7.6	10.5	23.8	9.8	0.7	5.1	12.6	22.9	35.0
$25,000 to 29,999	5.1	6.4	0.3	4.1	8.2	12.3	19.7	10.4	1.1	6.3	13.4	19.5	34.9
$30,000 to 34,999	4.9	8.0	0.1	5.7	12.0	12.8	19.8	13.0	0.8	8.1	21.9	18.0	35.1
$35,000 to 39,999	7.1	10.5	1.2	7.9	15.0	15.9	18.7	15.4	0.8	12.4	21.0	22.6	37.2
$40,000 to 49,999	9.2	11.9	0.7	9.7	17.1	14.3	29.4	17.1	1.1	14.7	24.2	22.2	32.1
$50,000 to 74,999	11.5	15.2	0.8	12.7	21.2	17.5	28.5	23.2	1.0	19.7	35.0	27.0	38.2
$75,000 or more	9.8	22.0	2.4	21.9	34.2	21.2	22.2	30.4	0.8	29.4	45.2	30.6	41.5
Control of school													
Public	4.5	8.5	0.6	5.9	11.5	13.1	22.2	14.2	0.5	10.1	19.8	22.7	34.7
Private	5.4	11.4	0.5	9.4	23.6	15.8	27.1	18.8	1.0	17.8	35.4	24.8	40.1

—Data not available.

NOTE.—Data are based on a sample survey of households and are subject to sampling and nonsampling error.

SOURCE: U.S. Department of Commerce, Bureau of the Census, Current Population Survey, October 1984, 1989, and 1993, unpublished data. (This table was prepared April 1994.)

Guide to Tabular Presentation

This section is intended to assist the reader in following the basic structure of the *Digest* tables and to provide a legend for some of the common symbols and indexes used throughout the book. Unless otherwise noted, all data are for the 50 states and the District of Columbia.

Table Components

Title Describes the table content concisely.

Unit Indicator Informs the reader of the measurement united in the table—"In thousands," "In millions of dollars," etc. Noted below the title unless several units are used, in which case the unit indicators are generally given in the spanner or individual column heads.

Spanner Describes a group of two or more columns.

Column head Describes specific column.

Stub Describes a row or a group of rows. Each stub is followed by a number of dots (leaders) or by a semicolon if no data appears in the data fields.

Field The area of the table which contains the data elements.

Rules in the field

Single horizontal rules indicate
— that the data below the line add to the figure immediately above the line, or
— in the case of derived figures (e.g., percents, medians) that the datum above the line represents a cumulative figure.

Double horizontal rules demarcate groups of related rows.

Single vertical rules delineate columns.

Double vertical rules divide the table into sections with unique stubs.

Example of Table Structure

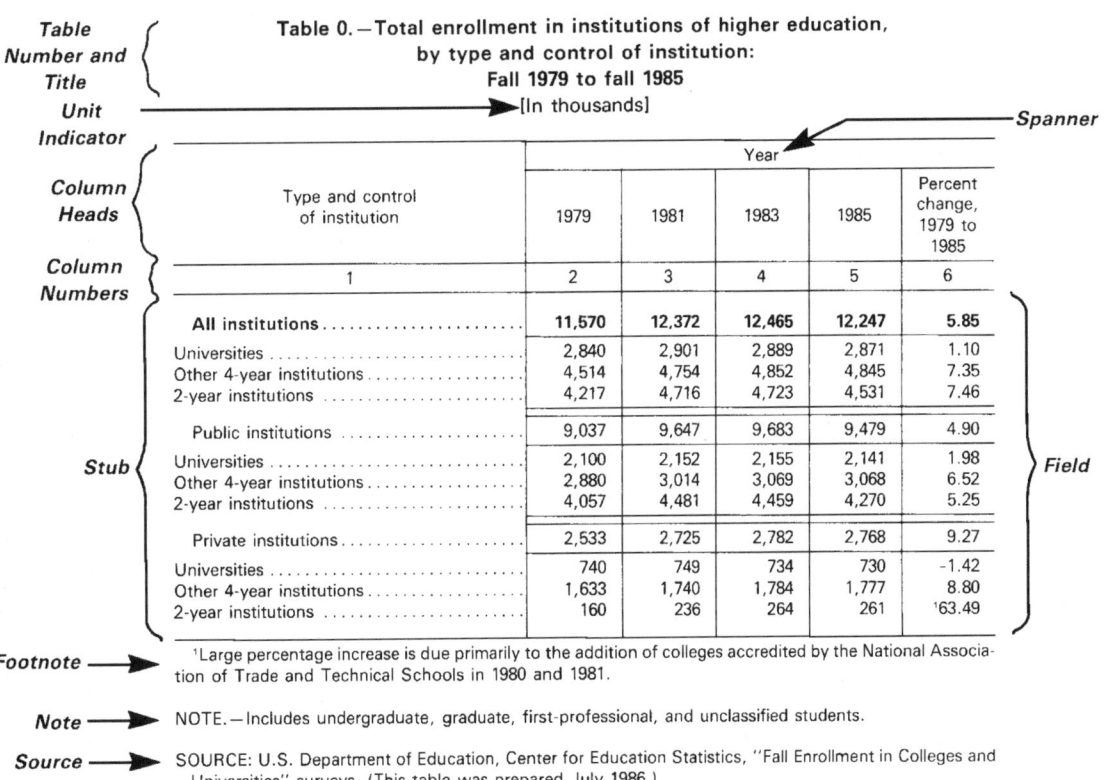

Table 0.—Total enrollment in institutions of higher education, by type and control of institution: Fall 1979 to fall 1985

[In thousands]

Type and control of institution	Year				Percent change, 1979 to 1985
	1979	1981	1983	1985	
1	2	3	4	5	6
All institutions	11,570	12,372	12,465	12,247	5.85
Universities	2,840	2,901	2,889	2,871	1.10
Other 4-year institutions	4,514	4,754	4,852	4,845	7.35
2-year institutions	4,217	4,716	4,723	4,531	7.46
Public institutions	9,037	9,647	9,683	9,479	4.90
Universities	2,100	2,152	2,155	2,141	1.98
Other 4-year institutions	2,880	3,014	3,069	3,068	6.52
2-year institutions	4,057	4,481	4,459	4,270	5.25
Private institutions	2,533	2,725	2,782	2,768	9.27
Universities	740	749	734	730	-1.42
Other 4-year institutions	1,633	1,740	1,784	1,777	8.80
2-year institutions	160	236	264	261	[1]63.49

[1]Large percentage increase is due primarily to the addition of colleges accredited by the National Association of Trade and Technical Schools in 1980 and 1981.

NOTE.—Includes undergraduate, graduate, first-professional, and unclassified students.

SOURCE: U.S. Department of Education, Center for Education Statistics, "Fall Enrollment in Colleges and Universities" surveys. (This table was prepared July 1986.)

Footnote Describes a unique circumstance relating to a specific item within the table. Usually listed below the bottom rule of the table.

Note Furnishes general information that relates to the entire table.

Source The document or reference from which the data are drawn. This note may also include the organizational unit responsible for preparing the data.

Descriptive Terms

Average A number that is used to represent the "typical value" of a group of numbers. It is regarded as a measure of "location" or "central tendency" of a group of numbers.

Arithmetic mean is the most commonly used average. It is derived by summing the individual item values of a particular group and dividing that sum by the number of items. This value is often referred to simply as the "mean" or "average."

Median is the measure of central tendency that occupies the middle position in a rank order of values. It generally has the same number of items above it as below it. If there is an even number of items in the group, the median is the average of the middle two items.

Per capita, or per person, figure represents an average computed for every person in a specified group, or population. It is derived by dividing the total for an item (such as income or expenditures) by the number of persons in the specified population.

Index number A value that provides a means of measuring, summarizing, and communicating the nature of changes that occur from time to time or from place to place. An index is used to express changes in prices over periods of time but may also be used to express differences between related subjects at a single point in time.

The *Digest* most often uses the Consumer Price Index to compare purchasing power over time.

To compute a price index, a base year or period is selected. The base year price is then designated as the base or reference price to which the prices for other years or periods are related.

A method of expressing the price relationship is:

$$\text{Index number} = \frac{\text{Price of a set of one or more items for related year}}{\text{Price of the same set of items for base year}} \times 100$$

When 100 is subtracted from the index number, the result equals the percent change in price from the base year.

Current and constant dollars are used in a number of tables to express finance data. Unless otherwise noted, all figures are in current dollars, not adjusted for inflation. Constant dollars provide a measure of the impact of inflation on the current dollars.

Current dollar figures reflect actual prices or costs prevailing during the specified year(s).

Constant dollar figures attempt to remove the effects of price changes (inflation) from statistical series reported in dollar terms.

The constant dollar value for an item is derived by dividing the base year price index (for example, the Consumer Price Index for 1986) by the price index for the year of data to be adjusted and multiplying by the item to be adjusted. The result is an adjusted dollar value as it would presumably exist if prices were the same as the base year—in other words, as if the dollar had constant purchasing power. Any changes in the constant dollar amounts would reflect only changes in the real values.

NOTE: Tables may not include data for all years implied in table titles.

Guide to Sources
Sources and Comparability of Data

The information presented in this report was obtained from many sources, including federal and state agencies, private research organizations, and professional associations. The data were collected using many research methods, including surveys of a universe (such as all colleges) or of a sample, compilations of administrative records, and statistical projections. *Digest* users should take particular care when comparing data from different sources. Differences in procedures, timing, phrasing of questions, interviewer training, and so forth mean that the results from the different sources may not be strictly comparable. Following the general discussion of data accuracy below, descriptions of the information sources and data collection methods are presented, grouped by sponsoring organization. More extensive documentation of a particular survey's procedures does not imply more problems with the data, only that more information is available.

Accuracy of Data

The accuracy of any statistic is determined by the joint effects of "sampling" and "nonsampling" errors. Estimates based on a sample will differ somewhat from the figures that would have been obtained if a complete census had been taken using the same survey instruments, instructions, and procedures. In addition to such sampling errors, all surveys, both universe and sample, are subject to design, reporting, and processing errors and errors due to nonresponse. To the extent possible, these nonsampling errors are kept to a minimum by methods built into the survey procedures. In general, however, the effects of nonsampling errors are more difficult to gauge than those produced by sampling variability.

Sampling Errors

The samples used in surveys are selected from a large number of possible samples of the same size that could have been selected using the same sample design. Estimates derived from the different samples would differ from each other. The difference between a sample estimate and the average of all possible samples is called the sampling deviation. The standard or sampling error of a survey estimate is a measure of the variation among the estimates from all possible samples and, thus, is a measure of the precision with which an estimate from a particular sample approximates the average result of all possible samples.

The sample estimate and an estimate of its standard error permit us to construct interval estimates with prescribed confidence that the interval includes the average result of all possible samples. If all possible samples were selected under essentially the same conditions and an estimate and its estimated standard error were calculated from each sample, then: (1) approximately 2/3 of the intervals from one standard error below the estimate to one standard error above the estimate would include the average value of all possible samples; and (2) approximately 19/20 of the intervals from two standard errors below the estimate to two standard errors above the estimate would include the average value of all possible samples. We call an interval from two standard errors below the estimate to two standard errors above the estimate a 95 percent confidence interval.

To illustrate this concept, consider the table of standard errors and 95 percent confidence intervals for estimates from the 1989–90 Beginning Postsecondary Students Survey (table A1). For the estimate that 28.1 percent of all female students in a vocational certificate program completed the program in 9 months or less, the table shows that the standard error is 3 percent. Therefore, we can create a 95 percent confidence interval which is approximately 22.1 to 34.1 (28.1 percent + 2 times 3 percent).

Analysis of standard errors can help assess how valid a comparison between two estimates might be. The standard error of a difference between two independent sample estimates is equal to the square root of the sum of the squared standard errors of the estimates. The standard error (se) of the difference between independent sample estimates "a" and "b" is:

$$se_{a,b} = (se_a^2 + se_b^2)^{1/2}$$

It should be noted that most of the standard error estimates presented in subsequent sections and in the original documents are approximations. That is, to derive estimates of standard errors that would be applicable to a wide variety of items and could be prepared at a moderate cost, a number of approximations were required. As a result, the standard error estimates provide a general order of magnitude rather than the exact standard error for any specific item. The preceding discussion on sampling variability was directed toward a situation concerning one or two estimates. Determining the accuracy of statistical projections is more difficult. In general, the further away the projection date is from the date of the actual data being used for the projection, the greater the probable error in the projections. If, for instance, annual data from 1970 to 1992 are being used to project enrollment in institutions of higher education, the further beyond 1992 one projects, the more variability in the projection. One will be less sure of the 2000 enrollment projection than of the 1995 projection. A detailed discussion of the projections methodology is contained in *Projections of Education Statistics to 2006* (National Center for Education Statistics, 1996).

Nonsampling Errors

Universe and sample surveys are subject to nonsampling errors. Nonsampling errors may arise when respondents or interviewers interpret questions differently, when respondents must estimate values, or when coders, keyers, and other processors handle answers differently, when persons who should be included in the universe are not, or when persons fail to respond (completely or partially). Nonsampling errors usually, but not always, result in an understatement of total survey error and thus an overstatement of the precision of survey estimates. Since estimating the magnitude of nonsampling errors often would require special experiments or access to independent data, these nonsampling errors are seldom available.

To compensate for nonresponse, adjustments of the sample estimates are often made. An adjustment made for either type of nonresponse, total or partial, is often referred to as an imputation, which is often a substitution of the "average" questionnaire response for the nonresponse. Imputations are usually made separately within various groups of sample members which have similar survey characteristics. Imputation for item nonresponse is usually made by substituting for a missing item the response to that item of a respondent having characteristics that are similar to those of the nonrespondent.

Although the magnitude of nonsampling error in the data compiled in this *Digest* is frequently unknown, idiosyncrasies that have been identified are noted on the appropriate tables.

Department of Education

National Center for Education Statistics (NCES)

Beginning Postsecondary Student Longitudinal Study

The Beginning Postsecondary Student Longitudinal Study (BPS) provides information concerning persistence, progress, and attainment from initial time of entry into postsecondary education through leaving and entering the workforce. BPS includes traditional and nontraditional (e.g., older) students and is representative of all beginning students in postsecondary education. BPS follows first-time, beginning students for at least 6 years at 2–year intervals, collecting student data, postsecondary transcripts, and financial aid reports. By starting with a cohort that has already entered postsecondary education, and following it for 6 years, BPS will be able to determine to what extent, if any, students who start postsecondary education later differ in their progress, persistence, and attainment.

Further information on the Beginning Postsecondary Student Longitudinal Survey may be obtained from:

Paula R. Knepper
Data Development and Longitudinal Studies Group
National Center for Education Statistics
555 New Jersey Avenue NW
Washington, DC 20208–5652

Common Core of Data

NCES uses the Common Core of Data (CCD) survey to acquire and maintain statistical data from each of the 50 states, the District of Columbia, and the outlying areas. Information about staff and students is collected annually at the school, LEA (local education agency or school district), and state levels. Information about revenues and expenditures is also collected at the state level.

Data are collected for a particular school year (July 1 through June 30) via survey instruments sent to the states by October 15 of the subsequent school year. States have 2 years in which to modify the data originally submitted.

Since the CCD is a universe survey, the CCD information presented in this edition of the Digest is not subject to sampling errors. However, nonsampling errors could come from two sources— nonreturn and inaccurate reporting. Almost all of the states submit the six CCD survey instruments each year, but submissions are sometimes incomplete or too late for publication.

Understandably, when 57 education agencies compile and submit data for approximately 85,000 public schools and 15,000 local school districts, misreporting can occur. Typically, this results from varying interpretation of NCES definitions and differing recordkeeping systems. NCES attempts to minimize these errors by working closely with the Council of Chief State School Officers (CCSSO) and its Committee on Evaluation and Information Systems (CEIS).

The state education agencies report data to NCES from data collected and edited in their regular reporting cycles. NCES encourages the agencies to incorporate into their own survey systems the NCES items they do not already collect so that those items will also be available for the subsequent CCD survey. Over time, this has meant fewer missing data cells in each state's response, reducing the need to impute data.

NCES subjects data from the education agencies to a comprehensive edit. Where data are determined to be inconsistent, missing, or out of range, NCES contacts the education agencies for verification. NCES-prepared state summary forms are returned to the state education agencies for verification. States are also given an opportunity to revise their state-level aggregates from the previous survey cycle.

Questions concerning the Common Core of Data can be directed to:

John Sietsema
Surveys and Cooperative Systems Group
National Center for Education Statistics
555 New Jersey Avenue NW
Washington, DC 20208–5651

Federal Support for Education

NCES prepares an annual compilation of federal funds for education. Data for U.S. Department of Education programs come from the *Budget of the U.S. Government.* Budget offices of other federal agencies provide information for all other federal program support except for research funds, which are obligations reported by the National Science Foundation in *Federal Funds for Research and Development.* Some data are estimated, based on reports from the federal agencies contacted and the *Budget of the U.S. Government.*

Except for money spent on research, outlays were used to report program funds to the extent possible. Some tables are obligations as noted in the title of the table. Some federal program funds not commonly recognized as education assistance are also included in the totals reported. For example, portions of federal funds paid to some states and counties as shared revenues resulting from the sale of timber and minerals from public lands have been estimated

as funds used for education purposes. Parts of the funds received by states (in 1980) and localities (throughout the period) under the General Revenue Sharing Program are also included, as are portions of federal funds received by the District of Columbia. The share of these funds allocated to education was assumed equal to the share of general funds expended for elementary and secondary education by states and localities in the same year as reported by the U.S. Bureau of the Census in its annual publication, *Governmental Finances.*

All state intergovernmental expenditures for education were assumed earmarked for elementary/secondary education. Contributions of parent governments of dependent school systems to their public schools amounted to approximately 9 percent of local government revenues and local government revenue sharing in each year. Therefore, 9 percent of local government revenue-sharing funds were assumed allocated each fiscal year to elementary and secondary education. Parent government contributions to public school systems were obtained from the U.S. Bureau of the Census, *Finances of Public School Systems.* The amount of state revenue-sharing funds allocated for postsecondary education in 1980 was assumed to be 13 percent, the proportion of direct state expenditures for institutions of higher education reported in Governmental Finances for that year.

The share of federal funds for the District of Columbia assigned to education was assumed equal to the share of the city's general fund expenditures for each level of education.

For the job training programs conducted by the Department of Labor, only estimated sums spent on classroom training have been reported as educational program support.

During the 1970s, The Office of Management and Budget (OMB) prepared annual reports on federal education program support. These were published in *Budget of the United States Government [Special Analyses].* The information presented in this report is not, however, a continuation of the OMB series. A number of differences in the two series should be noted. OMB required all federal agencies to report outlays for education-related programs using a standardized form, thereby assuring agency compliance in reporting. The scope of education programs reported here differs from OMB. Off-budget items such as the annual volume of guaranteed student loans were not included in OMB's reports. Finally, while some mention is made of an annual estimate of federal tax expenditures, OMB did not include them in its annual analysis of federal education support. Estimated federal tax expenditures for education are the difference between current federal tax receipts and what these receipts would be without existing education deductions to income allowed by federal tax provisions.

Recipients' data are estimated based on *Estimating Federal Funds for Education: A New Approach Applied to Fiscal Year 1980,* U.S. Department of Education, "Federal Support for Education, Fiscal Years 1980 to 1984," and Catalog of Federal Domestic Assistance. The recipients' data are estimated and tend to undercount institutions of higher education (IHEs), students, and local education agencies (LEAs). This is because some of the federal programs have more than one recipient receiving funds. In these cases, the recipients were put into a "mixed recipients" category, because there was no way to disaggregate the amount each recipient received.

High School and Beyond

High School and Beyond (HS&B) is a national longitudinal survey of 1980 high school sophomores and seniors. The base-year survey was a probability sample of 1,015 high schools with a target number of 36 sophomores and 36 seniors in each of the schools. A total of 58,270 students participated in the base-year survey. Substitutions were made for noncooperating schools—but not for students—in those strata where it was possible. Overall, 1,122 schools were selected in the original sample and 811 of these schools participated in the survey. An additional 204 schools were drawn in a replacement sample. Student refusals and absences resulted in an 82 percent completion rate for the survey.

Several small groups in the population were oversampled to allow for special study of certain types of schools and students. Students completed questionnaires and took a battery of cognitive tests. In addition, a sample of parents of sophomores and seniors (about 3,600 for each cohort) was surveyed.

HS&B first follow-up activities took place in the spring of 1982. The sample design of the first follow-up survey called for the selection of approximately 30,000 persons who were sophomores in 1980. The completion rate for sophomores eligible for on-campus survey administration was about 96 percent. About 89 percent of the students who left school between the base year and first follow-up surveys (dropouts, transfer students, and early graduates) completed the first follow-up sophomore questionnaire.

As part of the first follow-up survey of HS&B, transcripts were requested in fall 1982 for an 18,152 member subsample of the sophomore cohort. Of the 15,941 transcripts actually obtained, 1,969 were excluded because the students had dropped out of school before graduation, 799 were excluded because they were incomplete, and 1,057 were excluded because the student graduated before 1982 or the transcript indicated neither a dropout status nor graduation. Thus 12,116 transcripts were utilized for the overall curriculum analysis presented in this publication. All courses in each transcript were assigned a six-digit code based on *A Classification of Secondary School Courses* (developed by Evaluation Technologies, Inc. under contract with NCES). Credits earned in each course were expressed in Carnegie units. (The Carnegie unit is a standard of measurement that represents one credit for the completion of a 1-year course. To receive credit for a course, the student must have received a passing grade—"pass," "D," or higher.) Students who transferred from public to private schools or from private to public schools between their sophomore and senior years were eliminated from public/private analyses.

In designing the senior cohort first follow-up survey, one of the goals was to reduce the size of the retained sample, while still keeping sufficient numbers of minorities to allow important policy analyses. A total of 11,227 (94 percent) of the 11,995 persons subsampled completed the questionnaire. Information was obtained about the respondents' school and employment experiences, family status, and attitudes and plans.

The sample for the second follow-up, which took place in spring 1984, consisted of about 12,000 members of the senior cohort and about 15,000 members of the sophomore cohort. The completion rate for the senior cohort was 91 percent, and the completion rate for the sophomore cohort was 92 percent.

HS&B third follow-up data collection activities were performed in spring of 1986. Both the sophomore and senior cohort samples for this round of data collection were the same as those used for the second follow-up survey. The completion rates for the sophomore and senior cohort samples were 91 percent and 88 percent, respectively.

Table A2 contains the maximum number of cases that are available for the tabulations of the specific classification variables used throughout this publication.

The standard error (se) of an individual percentage (p) based on HS&B data can be approximated by the formula

$$se_p = DEFT\,[p(100-p)/n]^{1/2}$$

where n is the sample size and DEFT, the square root of the design effect, is a factor used to adjust for the particular sample design used in HS&B. Table A3 provides the DEFT factors for different HS&B samples and subsamples.

In evaluating a difference between two independent percentages, the standard error of the difference may be conservatively approximated by taking the square root of the sum of the squared standard errors of the two percentages. For example, in the

1986 follow-up of 1980 sophomores, 84.0 percent of the men and 77.2 percent of the women felt that being successful in work was "very important," a difference of 6.8 percentage points. Using the formula and the sample sizes from table A2 and the DEFT factors from table A3, the standard errors of the two percentages being compared are calculated to be:

$$1.43[(84.0)(16.0)/(5,391)]^{1/2} = .714$$
$$1.43[(77.2)(22.8)/(5,857)]^{1/2} = .784$$

The standard error of the difference is therefore

$$(.714^2 + .784^2)^{1/2} = (.510 + .615)^{1/2} = 1.06$$

The sampling error (95 chances in 100) of the difference is approximately double the standard error, or approximately 2.1 percentage points, and the 95 percent confidence interval for the difference is 6.8 + 2.1, or 4.7 to 8.9 percentage points.

The standard error estimation procedure outlined above does not compensate for survey item nonresponse, which is a source of nonsampling error. (Table A2 reflects the maximum number of responses that could be tabulated by demographic characteristics.) For example, of the 10,925 respondents in the 1984 follow-up survey of 1980 high school graduates, 372, or 3.4 percent, did not respond to the particular question on whether they had ever used a pocket calculator. Item nonresponse varied considerably. A very low nonresponse rate of 0.1 percent was obtained for a question asking whether the respondent had attended a postsecondary institution. A much higher item nonresponse rate of 12.2 percent was obtained for a question asking if the respondent had used a micro or minicomputer in high school. Typical item nonresponse rates ranged from 3 to 4 percent.

The Hispanic analyses presented in this report relied on students' self-identification as members of one of four Hispanic subgroups: Mexican, Mexican-American, Chicano; Cuban; Puerto-Rican, Puertorriqueno, or Boricua; or other Latin American, Latino, Hispanic, or Spanish descent.

An NCES series of technical reports and data file users manuals provides additional information on the survey methodology.

Further information on the High School and Beyond survey may be obtained from:

Aurora M. D'Amico
Data Development and Longitudinal Studies Group
National Center for Education Statistics
555 New Jersey Avenue NW
Washington, DC 20208–5652

1990 High School Transcript Study Tabulations

This study involved analysis of transcripts of 1990 high school graduates from 330 schools. The analyses were based on approximately 21,500 1990 graduates selected for the National Assessment of Educational Progress (NAEP) in 1990. The study collected information such as course lists, graduation requirements, and the definition of units of credit and grades, on a school-level basis.

Similar studies were conducted of course taking patterns of 1987 and 1982 graduates. The 1987 data are based on approximately 22,799 transcripts from 433 schools obtained as part of the 1987 High School Transcript Study. The 1982 data are based on approximately 12,000 transcripts collected by the High School and Beyond Project.

Because the 1982 High School and Beyond study used a different method for identifying handicapped students than did the 1987 and 1990 transcript studies, and in order to make the statistical summaries as comparable as possible, all the counts and percentages in this report are restricted to students whose records indicate that they had not participated in a special education program. This restriction lowers the number of 1990 graduates represented in the tables to 20,866.

Further information can be obtained from:

Steve Gorman
Education Assessment Division
National Center for Education Statistics
555 New Jersey Avenue NW
Washington, DC 20208–5653

Integrated Postsecondary Education Data System

The Integrated Postsecondary Education Data System (IPEDS) surveys approximately 11,000 postsecondary institutions, including universities and colleges, as well as institutions offering technical and vocational education beyond the high school level. This survey, which began in 1986, replaced the Higher Education General Information Survey (HEGIS).

IPEDS consists of eight integrated components that obtain information on who provides postsecondary education (institutions), who participates in it and completes it (students), what programs are offered and what programs are completed, and both the human and financial resources involved in the provision of institutionally based postsecondary education. Specifically, these components include: Institutional Characteristics, including instructional activity; Fall Enrollment, including age and residence; Enrollment in Occupationally Specific Programs; Completions; Finance; Staff; Salaries of Full-Time Instructional Faculty; and Academic Libraries.

The higher education portion of this survey is a census of accredited 2– and 4–year colleges. Prior to 1993, data from the technical and vocational institutions were collected through a sample survey. Beginning in 1993, all data are gathered in a census of all postsecondary institutions. The tabulations on "Institutional Characteristics" developed for this edition of the *Digest* are based on lists of all institutions and are not subject to sampling errors.

Prior to the establishment of IPEDS in 1986, HEGIS acquired and maintained statistical data on the characteristics and operations of institutions of higher education. Implemented in 1966, HEGIS was an annual universe survey of institutions accredited at the college level by an agency recognized by the Secretary of the U.S. Department of Education. These institutions were listed in NCES's *Education Directory, Colleges and Universities.*

The trend tables presented in this report draw on HEGIS surveys which solicited information concerning institutional characteristics, faculty salaries, finances, enrollment, and degrees. Since these surveys were distributed to all higher education institutions, the data presented are not subject to sampling error. However, they are subject to nonsampling error, the sources of which varied with the survey instrument. Information concerning the nonsampling error of the enrollment and degrees surveys draws extensively on the "HEGIS Post-Survey Validation Study" conducted in 1979.

Further information on IPEDS may be obtained from:

Roslyn A. Korb
Surveys and Cooperative Systems Group
National Center for Education Statistics
555 New Jersey Avenue NW
Washington, DC 20208–5652

Institutional Characteristics

This survey provides the basis for the universe of institutions presented in the *Directory of Postsecondary Institutions.* The universe comprises institutions that met certain accreditation criteria and offered at least a 1-year program of college-level studies leading toward a degree. All of these institutions were certified as eligible by the U.S. Department of Education's Division of Eligibility and Agency Evaluation. The survey collects basic information necessary to classify the institutions including control, level, and kinds of programs; information on tuition, fees, and room and board charges; and unduplicated full-year enrollment counts and instructional activity.

Fall Enrollment

This survey has been part of the HEGIS and IPEDS series since 1966. The enrollment survey response rate is relatively high; the 1994 response rate was 96 percent. Major sources of nonsampling error for this survey as identified in the 1979 report, were classification problems, the unavailability of needed data, interpretation of definitions, the survey due date, and operational errors. Of these, the classification of students appears to have been the main source of error. Institutions had problems in correctly classifying first-time freshmen and other first-time students for both full-time and part-time categories. These problems occurred most often at 2-year institutions (private and public) and private 4-year institutions. In the 1977–78 HEGIS validation studies, the classification problem led to an estimated overcount of 11,000 full-time students and an undercount of 19,000 part-time students. Although the ratio of error to the grand total was quite small (less than 1 percent), the percentage of errors was as high as 5 percent for detailed student levels and even higher at certain aggregation levels.

Beginning with fall 1986, the survey system was redesigned with the introduction of the Integrated Postsecondary Education Data System (IPEDS) (see above). The IPEDS system comprises all postsecondary institutions, but also maintains comparability with earlier surveys by allowing HEGIS institutions to be tabulated separately. The survey allows (in alternating years) for the collection of age and residence data.

Salaries, Tenure, and Fringe Benefits of Full-Time Instructional Faculty

This institutional survey has been conducted for most years from 1966–67 to 1987–88, and annually since 1989–90. Although the survey form changed a number of times during those years, only comparable data are presented in this report.

Between 1966–67 and 1985–86 this survey differed from other HEGIS surveys in that imputations were not made for nonrespondents. Thus, there is some possibility that the salary averages presented in this report may differ from the results of a complete enumeration of all colleges and universities. Beginning with the surveys for 1987–88, the IPEDS data tabulation procedures included imputations for survey nonrespondents. The response rate for the 1994–95 survey was 95 percent for higher education institutions, or 92 percent overall. Because of the higher response rate for public colleges, it is probable that the public colleges' salary data are more accurate than the data for private colleges. Although data from these surveys are not subject to sampling error, sources of nonsampling error may include computational errors and misclassification in reporting and processing. NCES reviews individual colleges' data for internal and longitudinal consistency and contacts the colleges to check inconsistent data.

Completions

This survey was part of the HEGIS series throughout its existence. However, the degree classification taxonomy was revised in 1970–71, 1982–83, and 1991–92. Collection of degree data has been maintained through the IPEDS system.

Though information from survey years 1970–71 through 1981–82 is directly comparable, care must be taken if information before or after that period is included in any comparison. Degrees-conferred trend tables arranged by the 1991–92 classification are included in the *Digest* to provide consistent data from 1970–71 to 1993–94. Data in this edition on associate and other formal awards below the baccalaureate, by field of study, cannot be made comparable with figures prior to 1982–83. The nonresponse rate did not appear to be a significant source of nonsampling error for this survey. The return rate over the years has been high, with the higher education response rate for the 1993–94 survey at 97 percent. The overall response rate including the noncollegiate institutions is 89 percent. Because of the high return rate for the institutions of higher education, nonsampling error caused by imputation is also minimal.

The major sources of nonsampling error for this survey were differences between the NCES program taxonomy and taxonomies used by the colleges, classification of double majors, operational problems, and survey timing. In the 1979 HEGIS validation study, these sources of nonsampling contributed to an error rate of 0.3 percent overreporting of bachelor's degrees and 1.3 percent overreporting of master's degrees. The differences, however, varied greatly among fields. Over 50 percent of the fields selected for the validation study had no errors identified. Categories of fields that had large differences were business and management, education, engineering, letters, and psychology. It was also shown that differences in proportion to the published figures were less than 1 percent for most of the selected fields that had some errors. Exceptions to these were: master's and Ph.D. programs in labor and industrial relations (20 percent and 8 percent); bachelor's and master's programs in art education (3 percent and 4 percent); bachelor's and Ph.D. programs in business and commerce, and in distributive education (5 percent and 9 percent); master's programs in philosophy (8 percent); and Ph.D. programs in psychology (11 percent).

Financial Statistics

This survey was part of the HEGIS series and has been continued under the IPEDS system. Changes were made in the financial survey instruments in fiscal years (FY) 1976, 1982, and 1987. The FY 76 survey instrument contained numerous revisions to earlier survey forms and made direct comparisons of line items very difficult. Beginning in FY 82, Pell Grant data were collected in the categories of federal restricted grants and contracts revenues and restricted scholarships and fellowships expenditures. The introduction of IPEDS in the FY 87 survey included several important changes to the survey instrument and data processing procedures. While these changes were significant, considerable effort has been made to present only comparable information on trends in this report and to note inconsistencies. Finance tables for this publication have been adjusted by subtracting the largely duplicative Pell Grant amounts from the later data to maintain comparability with pre-FY 82 data.

Possible sources of nonsampling error in the financial statistics include nonresponse, imputation, and misclassification. The response rate has been about 85 to 90 percent for most of the years reported. The response rate for the FY 1994 survey was 95 percent.

Two general methods of imputation were used in HEGIS. If the prior year's data were available for a nonresponding institution, these data were inflated using the Higher Education Price Index and adjusted according to changes in enrollments. If no previous year's data were available, current data were used from peer institutions selected for location (state or region), control, level, and enrollment size of institution. In most cases estimates for nonreporting institutions in IPEDS were made using data from peer institutions.

Beginning with FY 87, the IPEDS survey system included all postsecondary institutions, but maintained comparability with earlier surveys by allowing 2- and 4-year HEGIS institutions to be tabulated separately. The finance data tabulated for this publication reflect totals for the HEGIS or higher education institutions only. For FY 87 through FY 91, in order to maintain comparability with the historical time series of HEGIS institutions, data were combined from two of the three different survey forms that make up the IPEDS survey system. The vast majority of the data were tabulated from Form 1, which was used to collect information from public and private nonprofit 2- and 4-year colleges. Form 2, a condensed form, was used to gather data for the 2-year proprietary institutions. Because of the differences in the data requested on the two forms, several assumptions were made about the Form 2 reports so that their figures could be included in the institutions of higher education totals.

In IPEDS, the Form 2 institutions were not asked to separate appropriations from grants and contracts, nor state from local sources of funding. For the Form 2 institutions, all the federal revenues were assumed to be federal grants and contracts and all of the state and local revenues were assumed to be restricted state grants and contracts. All other Form 2 sources of revenue, except for tuition and fees and sales and services of educational activities, were included under "other." Similar adjustments were made to the expenditure accounts. The Form 2 institutions reported instruction and scholarship and fellowship expenditures only. All other educational and general expenditures were allocated to academic support.

To reduce reporting error, NCES uses national standards for reporting finance statistics. These standards are contained in *College and University Business Administration: Administrative Services* (1974 Edition), and the *Financial Accounting and Reporting Manual for Higher Education* (1990 Education), published by the National Association of College and University Business Officers; *Audits of Colleges and Universities* (as amended August 31, 1974), by the American Institute of Certified Public Accountants; and *HEGIS Financial Reporting Guide* (1980), by NCES. Wherever possible, definitions and formats in the survey form are consistent with those in these four accounting texts.

Staff

The fall staff data presented in this publication were collected by NCES, through the IPEDS system, which collected data from postsecondary institutions, including all 2- and 4-year higher education institutions. The NCES collects staff data biennially in odd numbered years in institutions of postsecondary education.

The IPEDS "Fall Staff" questionnaires were mailed out by NCES; the respondents reported the number of employees in their institutions as of January 15, 1994. The "Fall Staff" questionnaires were mailed out by NCES between October and November 1993; the respondents reported the employment statistics in their institution that cover the payroll period closest to October 1 of the survey year.

The "Fall Staff" survey had an overall response rate of 87 percent. The response rate for higher education institutions was 92 percent.

The International Assessment of Educational Progress

The International Assessment of Educational Progress (IAEP), sponsored by the U.S. Department of Education and the National Science Foundation and conducted by the Educational Testing Service, surveyed the mathematics and science performance of 13-year-old students in 20 countries, and 9-year-old students in 14 countries during 1990–91. Some countries drew samples from virtually all children in the appropriate age group; others confined their as-

sessments to specific geographic areas, language groups, or grade levels.

From each population at each level, a random sample of 3,300 students from about 110 different schools was selected; half were assessed in science and half in mathematics. During March 1991, a total of about 175,000 9- and 13-year-olds (those born in calendar years 1981 and 1977, respectively) were tested in 13 different languages.

The achievement tests given to 9-year-olds included 62 questions in mathematics and 60 questions in science. For the 13-year-olds, the test included 76 questions in mathematics and 72 questions in science. Students at each age spent additional time responding to questions about their backgrounds and home and school experiences. A school questionnaire was also completed by school administrators.

The statistical significance of differences in performance between participating countries was determined through use of the Bonferroni multiple comparison procedure. The procedure allows for the probability of falsely declaring a significant difference to 5 percent across the entire set of possible comparisons between pairs of countries.

For more information about this survey contact:

Eugene Owen
Data Development and Longitudinal Studies Group
National Center for Education Statistics
555 New Jersey Avenue NW
Washington, DC 20208–5653

National Adult Literacy Survey

The National Adult Literacy Survey was created as a new measure of literacy and funded by the Department of Education. It is the third and largest assessment of adult literacy funded by the federal government. The aim of the survey is to profile the English literacy of adults in the United States based on their performance across a wide array of tasks that reflect the types of materials and demands they encounter in their daily lives.

To gather the information on adults' literacy skills, trained staff interviewed nearly 13,600 individuals aged 16 and older during the first eight months of 1992. These participants had been randomly selected to represent the adult population in the country as a whole. Black and Hispanic households were oversampled to ensure reliable estimates of literacy proficiencies and to permit analyses of the performance of these subpopulations. In addition, some 1,100 inmates from 80 federal and state prisons were interviewed to gather information on the proficiencies of the prison population. In total, over 26,000 adults were surveyed.

Each survey participant was asked to spend approximately an hour responding to a series of diverse literacy tasks as well as questions about his or her demographic characteristics, educational background, reading practices, and other areas related to literacy. Based on their responses to the survey tasks, adults received proficiency scores along three scales which reflect varying degrees of skill in prose, document and quantitative literacy. The results of the survey were published in a report, *Adult Literacy in America* in September 1993.

Further information on the National Adult Literacy Survey may be obtained from:

Andrew Kolstad
Education Assessment Division
National Center for Education Statistics
555 New Jersey Avenue NW
Washington, DC 20208–5653

National Assessment of Educational Progress

The National Assessment of Educational Progress (NAEP) is a series of cross-sectional studies designed and initially implemented in 1969. NAEP has gathered information about selected levels of educational achievement across the country. NAEP has surveyed the educational attainments by age and grade (9-, 13-, and 17-year-olds, and 4th-, 8th-, and 12th-graders), and young adults (ages 25–35) in 10 learning areas. Different learning areas have been assessed periodically, and all areas have been reassessed in order to measure possible changes in educational achievement.

The assessment data presented in this publication were derived from tests designed and conducted by the Education Commission of the States (1969–1983) and by the Educational Testing Service (1983 to present). Three-stage probability samples have been used. The primary sampling units have been stratified by region and, within region, by state, size of community, and, for the two smaller sizes of community strata, by socioeconomic level. The first stage of sampling entails defining and selecting primary sampling units (PSU's). For each age/grade level (4,8, and 12) the second stage entails enumerating, stratifying, and randomly selecting schools, both public and private, within each PSU selected at the first stage. The third stage involves randomly selecting students within a school for participation in NAEP. Assessment exercises have been administered either to individuals or to small groups of students by specially trained personnel.

After NAEP data are scored, they are weighted in accordance with the population structure and adjusted for nonresponse. Analyses include computing the percentage of students giving various responses and using Item Response Theory (IRT) technology to estimate levels of achievement for the nation and various subpopulations. IRT technology enables the assessment of a sample of students in a learning area or subarea on a single scale even if different students have been administered different exercises. The underlying principle is that when a number of items require similar skills, the regularities observed across patterns of response can often be used to characterize both respondents and tasks in terms of a relatively small number of variables. When aggregated through appropriate mathematical formulas, these variables capture the dominant features of the data.

Sample sizes for the reading proficiency portion of the 1991–92 NAEP study were 4,944 for the 9-year-olds, 3,965 for the 13-year-olds, and 4,447 for the 17-year-olds. Sample sizes for the 1991–92 NAEP science study and the 1991–92 NAEP math study were: 7,335 for 9-year-olds, 5,909 for 13-year-olds, and 4,359 for 17-year-olds. Response rates were 94, 91, and 83 percent, respectively. Data on standard errors for the 1991–92 studies can be found in Tables A4, A5, and A6.

Sample sizes for the reading proficiency portion of the 1989–90 NAEP study were 4,268 for the 9-year-olds, 4,609 for the 13-year-olds, and 2,689 for the 17-year-olds. Response rates were 93 percent, 90 percent, and 82 percent, respectively. Response rates for earlier years (1970–71, 1974–75, and 1979–80) were generally lower. For example, the lowest response rate for the 9-year-olds was 88 percent in 1974–75, and the lowest response rate over all was 70 percent for the 17-year-olds in 1974–75.

The 1993–94 U.S. history assessment data in this report are based on a nationally representative sample of 5,499 4th-graders, 8,767 8th-graders, and 7,818 12th-graders. The response rates were: 90 percent for 4th-graders, 90 percent for 8th-graders, and 89 percent for 12th-graders.

The 1991–92 writing assessment was administered to 7,166 4th-graders, 11,112 8th-graders, and 11,532 12th-graders. Student response rates for the 1992–93 writing assessment were 93 percent for the 4th-graders, 89 percent for the 8th-graders, and 81 percent for the 12th-graders. Sample sizes varied depending on the test items and the scoring method used.

In 1991–92, a science assessment was administered to 7,335 4th-graders, 5,909 8th-graders, and 4,359 12th-graders. The response rates were 94 percent for the 4th-graders, 91 percent for the 8th-graders, and 83 percent for the 12th-graders.

The 1993–94 geography assessment was administered to 5,507 4th-graders, 6,878 8th-graders, and 6,234 12th-graders. The response rates for the assessment were 93 percent for the 4th-graders, 93 percent for the 8th-graders, and 90 percent for the 12th-graders.

In 1990, representative state-level data were produced for mathematics at the 8th-grade level. This was the first time NAEP had produced data on a state-by-state level. In 1992, state-level assessments were conducted in 4th-and 8th-grade mathematics and 4th-grade reading.

Information from NAEP is subject to both nonsampling and sampling error. Two possible sources of nonsampling error are nonparticipation and instrumentation. Certain populations have been oversampled to assure samples of sufficient size for analysis. Instrumentation nonsampling error could result from failure of the test instruments to measure what is being taught and, in turn, what is being learned by the students.

For further information on NAEP, contact:

Gary W. Phillips
Education Assessment Division
National Center for Education Statistics
555 New Jersey Avenue NW
Washington, DC 20208–5653

National Education Longitudinal Study of 1988

The National Education Longitudinal Study of 1988 (NELS:88) is the third major longitudinal study sponsored by the National Center for Education Statistics. The two studies that preceded NELS:88, the National Longitudinal Study of the High School Class of 1972 (NLS-72) and High School and Beyond (HS&B) in 1980, surveyed high school seniors (and sophomores in HS&B) through high school, postsecondary education, and work and family formation experiences. Unlike its predecessors, NELS:88 begins with a cohort of 8th-grade students. In 1988, some 25,000 eighth-graders, their parents, their teachers, and their school principals were surveyed. Follow-ups were conducted in 1990, 1992, and 1994, when a majority of these students were in 10th and 12th grades, and then 2 years after their scheduled high school graduation. A similar follow-up is being conducted in 1997.

NELS:88 is designed to provide trend data about critical transitions experienced by young people as they develop, attend school, and embark on their careers. It will complement and strengthen state and local efforts by furnishing new information on how school policies, teacher practices, and family involvement affect student educational outcomes (i.e., academic achievement, persistence in school, and participation in postsecondary education). For the base year, NELS:88 includes a multifaceted student questionnaire, four cognitive tests, a parent questionnaire, a teacher questionnaire, and a school questionnaire.

To ensure that private schools, rural schools, and schools with high minority membership were adequately represented, sampling was first conducted at the school level and then at the student level within schools. Additionally, oversamples of students with Hispanic and Asian or Pacific Island heritage were drawn. The base year data are drawn from a nationally representative sample of 1,000 schools (800 public schools; and 200 private schools, including parochial institutions). Within this school sample, 25,000 eighth-grade students were selected at random.

In 1990, when the students were in 10th grade, the students, school dropouts, their teachers, and their school principals were surveyed. The 1988 survey of parents was not a part of the 1990 follow-up. In 1992, when the students were in 12th grade the second follow-up conducted surveys of students, dropouts, parents, teachers, and school principals. Also, information on the students' transcripts, the schools' course offerings, and enrollments were collected, and there was a school effects survey. Tables A7 and A8 present the respondent counts and design effects of NELS:88 and the 1990 and 1992 follow-ups.

Further information about the NELS:88 survey can be obtained from:

Jeffrey A. Owings
Data Development and Longitudinal Studies Group
National Center for Education Statistics
555 New Jersey Avenue NW
Washington, DC 20208–5651

National Household Education Survey

The National Household Education Survey (NHES) is a data collection system that is designed to address a wide range of education-related issues. Surveys were conducted in the spring of 1991 and in the spring of 1993. It will be conducted in the spring of 1995 and biennially thereafter.

The NHES targets specific populations for detailed data collection. While the survey is not designed to develop an in-depth research database, it is intended to provide more detailed data on the topics and populations of interest than are collected through supplements to other household surveys.

The NHES is designed as a telephone survey of the noninstitutional civilian population of the U.S. Households are selected for the survey using random digit dialing (RDD) methods. Data are collected using computer assisted telephone interviewing (CATI) procedures.

The methodology for any single fielding of the NHES is linked to the research issues under study, the level of data required to address these issues, and how precise the estimates generated from the survey data need to be in order to meet the objectives of the study. However, while the specifications for each annual survey will vary, there are general features of the NHES methodology that will stay relatively constant from one survey to the next.

NCES envisions the continued use of RDD methods to select the sample for the NHES in the future. Although the sample size for a particular component of the survey may vary somewhat from year to year, NCES expects to screen between 60,000 and 75,000 households for the annual surveys.

The topics addressed by the NHES:91 were early childhood education and adult education. About 60,000 households were screened for the NHES:91. In the Early Childhood Education component, about 14,000 parents/guardians of 3- to 8-year olds completed interviews about their children's early educational experiences. Included in this component were participation in nonparental care/education, characteristics of programs and care arrangements, and early school experiences including delayed kindergarten entry and retention in grade. In addition to questions about care/education arrangements and school, parents are asked about activities children engaged in with parents and other family members inside and outside the home. Information on family, household, and child characteristics was also collected.

In the NHES:91 Adult Education component, about 9,800 persons 16 years of age and older, identified as having participated in an adult education activity in the previous 12 months, were questioned about their activities. Data were collected on programs and up to four courses, including the subject matter duration, sponsorship, purpose, and cost. A smaller sample of nonparticipants (about 2,800) also completed interviews about barriers to participation. Information on the household and the adult's background and current employment also was collected. In the NHES:95 survey, of the 23,969 adults sampled for the adult education component, 80 percent (19,722) completed the interview.

In the NHES:93, nearly 64,000 households were screened. Approximately 11,000 parents of 3- to 7-year olds completed interviews for the School Readiness component. Topics included in this component were the developmental characteristics of preschoolers, school adjustment and teacher feedback to parents for kindergartners and primary students, center-based program participation, early school experiences, home activities with family members, and health status. Extensive family and child background characteristics, including parent language and education, income, receipt of public assistance, and household composition, were collected to permit the identification of at-risk children.

In the School Safety and Discipline component, about 12,700 parents of children in grades 3 through 12, and about 6,500 youth in grades 6 through 12, were interviewed about their school experiences. Topics included the school learning environment, discipline policy, safety at school, victimization, the availability and use of alcohol/drugs, and alcohol/drug education. Peer norms for behavior in school and substance use were also included in this topical component. Extensive family and household background information was collected, as well as characteristics of the school attended by the child. In the NHES:95 survey, the Early Childhood Program Participation component provides information on infants,' toddlers,' and preschoolers' participation in a variety of early care and education settings, including both home-based and center-based arrangements. The survey component also includes data on kindergarten and primary school history and experiences.

For more information contact:

Kathryn A. Chandler,
Surveys and Cooperative Systems Group
National Center for Education Statistics
555 New Jersey Avenue, NW
Washington, DC 20208–5651

National Longitudinal Study

The National Longitudinal Study (NLS) of the high school class of 1972 began with the collection of base-year survey data from a sample of about 19,000 high school seniors in spring of 1972. Five more follow-up surveys of these students were conducted in 1973, 1974, 1976, 1979, and 1986. The NLS was designed to provide the education community with information on the transitions of young adults from high school through postsecondary education and the workplace.

The sample design for the NLS is a stratified, two-stage probability sample of students from all schools, public and private, in the 50 states and the District of Columbia with a 12th-grade enrollment during the 1971–72 school year. During the first stage of sampling, about 1,070 schools were selected for participation in the base-year survey. As many as 18 students were selected at random from each of the sample schools. Both the size of the school and student samples were increased during the first follow-up survey. Beginning with the first follow-up and continuing through the fourth follow-up, about 1,300 schools participated in the survey and slightly under 23,500 students were sampled. The response rates for each of the different rounds of data collection have been 80 percent or higher.

Sample retention rates across the survey years have been quite high. For example, of the individuals responding to the base-year questionnaire, the percentages who responded to the first, second, third, and fourth follow-up questionnaires were about 94, 93, 89, and 83 percent, respectively.

Further information may be obtained from:

Surveys and Cooperative Systems Group
National Center for Education Statistics
555 New Jersey Avenue NW
Washington, DC 20208–5652

National Postsecondary Student Aid Study

The National Postsecondary Student Aid Study (NPSAS) is a comprehensive nationwide study of how students and their families pay for postsecondary education. It covers national representative samples of undergraduates, graduates, and first-professional students; students attending less than 2–year institutions, 2– to 3–year schools, 4–year colleges, and major universities. Participants included students who do not receive aid and their parents as well as students who do receive financial aid and their parents. Study results are used to help determine future federal policy regarding student financial aid. The study is conducted every three years.

The first NPSAS was conducted during the 1986–87 school year. Data were gathered from about 1,130 colleges, universities, and other postsecondary institutions; 55,000 students; and 16,000 parents. These data provided information on the cost of postsecondary education, the distribution of financial aid, and the characteristics of both aided and nonaided students and their families.

As a part of the 1992–93 NPSAS, information on more than 78,000 undergraduates and graduate students enrolled during the school year was collected at 1,100 postsecondary institutions. The sample included students enrolled at any time between July 1, 1992 and June 30, 1993. About 66,000 students and a subsample of their parents were interviewed by telephone. Table A9 presents standard errors for undergraduates enrolled full-time and part-time in fall 1992, by aid status and source of aid during 1992–93, and control and level of institution.

Further information may be obtained from:

Andrew G. Malizio
Data Development and Longitudinal Studies Group
National Center for Education Statistics
555 New Jersey Avenue NW
Washington, DC 20208–5652

National Survey of Postsecondary Faculty

The National Survey of Postsecondary Faculty (NSOPF), a survey of instructional faculty in higher education institutions, was conducted for the first time in the 1987–88 academic year by NCES. The study consisted of three major components: the Institutional Survey, a stratified random sample of 480 institutional-level respondents, with a response rate of 88 percent; the Faculty Survey, a stratified random sample of 11,013 eligible faculty members within the participating institutions, with a response rate of 76 percent; and the Department Chair Survey, a stratified random sample of 3,029 eligible department chairpersons (or their equivalent) within the participating 2– and 4–year institutions, with a response rate of 80 percent.

Institutions were selected from nonproprietary U.S. postsecondary institutions that grant a 2–year (A.A.) or higher degree, and have been accredited by organizations recognized by the U.S. Department of Education. Included in this group are religious, medical, and other specialized institutions. This survey universe consisted of 3,159 institutions from the 1987 IPEDS.

The 1988 NSOPF gathered information on the backgrounds, responsibilities, workloads, salaries, benefits, and attitudes of full- and part-time instructional faculty in higher education institutions. Additional information was collected on faculty composition, turnover and recruitment, and retention and tenure policies from institutional and department-level respondents.

The second cycle of the National Study of Postsecondary Faculty (NSOPF-93) was limited to surveys of faculty and institutions, but with a substantially expanded sample of 974 public and private nonproprietary higher education institutions and 31,354 faculty. Unlike NPSOF-88, which was limited to faculty whose regular assignment included instruction, the faculty universe for NSOPF-93 was expanded to include anyone who was designated as faculty, whether or not their responsibilities included instruction, and other (non faculty) personnel with instructional responsibilities. Under this definition, researchers and administrators and other institutional staff who hold faculty positions, but who do not teach, were included in the sample. The definition of the institution universe for NSOFP-93 was identical to the one used in NSOPF-88.

For more information contact:

Linda J. Zimbler
Surveys and Cooperative Systems Group
National Center for Education Statistics
555 New Jersey Avenue NW
Washington, DC 20208–5652

Projections of Education Statistics

Since 1964, NCES has published projections of key statistics for elementary and secondary schools and institutions of higher education. These projections include statistics such as enrollments, instructional staff, graduates, earned degrees, and expenditures. The Projections reports include several alternative projection series and a methodology section describing the techniques and assumptions used to prepare them. Data in this edition of the Digest reflect the middle alternative projection series.

Differences between the reported and projected values are, of course, almost inevitable. An evaluation of past projections revealed that, at the elementary and secondary level, projections of enrollments have been quite accurate: mean absolute percentage differences for enrollment were less than 1 percent for projections from 1 to 5 years in the future, while those for teachers were less than 4 percent. At the higher education level, projections of enrollment have been fairly accurate: mean absolute percentage differences were 5 percent or less for projections from 1 to 5 years into the future.

Since projections of time series are subject to errors both by the nature of statistics and the properties of projection methodologies, users are cautioned not to place too much confidence in the numerical values of the projections. Important, but unforeseeable, economic and social changes may lead to differences, particularly at the higher education level. Rather, projections are to be considered as indicators of broad trends.

For further information about projection methodology and accuracy, contact:

Debra E. Gerald
Data Development and Longitudinal Studies Group
National Center for Education Statistics
555 New Jersey Avenue NW
Washington, DC 20208–5654

Library Statistics Program

Nationwide, public library statistics are collected using the Public Libraries Survey and disseminated annually through the Federal-State Cooperative System for public library data (FSCS). Descriptive statistics are produced for nearly 9,000 public libraries. The Public Libraries Survey includes information about staffing; operating income and expenditures; type of governance; type of administrative structure; size of collection; and service measures such as reference transactions, public service hours, interlibrary loans, circulation, and library visits. In FSCS, respondents supply the information electronically, and data are edited and tabulated in machine-readable form.

The respondents are 8,929 public libraries identified in the 50 states and the District of Columbia by state library agencies. At the state level, FSCS is administered by State Data Coordinators, appointed by the Chief Officer of each State Library Agency. The State Data Coordinator collects the requested data from local public libraries and submits these data to NCES. An annual training conference sponsored by NCES is provided for the State Data Coordinators. A steering committee representing State Data Coordinators and other public library constituents is active in the development of FSCS data elements and software. Technical assistance to states is provided by phone and in person by the FSCS steering committee and by NCES staff and contractors. All 50 states and the District of Columbia have submitted data which are available for individual public libraries and are also aggregated to state and national levels.

Since 1990, data collections have been collected electronically. The most recent software is called DECPLUS. It includes identifying information on all known public libraries and their outlets, all state libraries, and some library systems and cooperatives. Beginning in 1994, this resource will be available for drawing samples for special surveys on such topics as literacy, access for the disabled, and library construction.

Under the Academic Libraries Survey (ALS), NCES surveyed academic libraries on a 3–year cycle between 1966 and 1992. Since 1988, ALS has been a component of the Integrated Postsecondary Education Data System and is on a 2–year cycle. ALS provides data on about 3,500 academic libraries. In aggregate, these data provide an overview of the status of academic libraries nationally and statewide. The survey collects data on the libraries in the entire universe of accredited higher education institutions and on the libraries in nonaccredited institutions with a program of 4 years or more. ALS produces descriptive statistics on academic libraries in postsecondary institutions in the 50 states, the District of Columbia and the outlying areas.

The School Library Statistics Survey collected data on school libraries/media centers in 1990–91. This survey asked questions on libraries in public and private schools as part of the Schools and Staffing Survey (SASS). These questionnaires were revised and a sample survey of about 7,600 schools was conducted during school year 1993–94. The library components of the 1990–91 SASS include: number of students served and number of professional staff and aides; at the district level, number of full-time equivalent librarians/media specialists, vacant positions, positions abolished, and approved positions; and amount of librarian input in establishing curriculum. The 1993–94 survey was much more extensive and added questions concerning media centers and collections of libraries.

Additional information on these academic and school library studies is available from:

Jeff Williams
Surveys and Cooperative Systems Group
National Center for Education Statistics
555 New Jersey Avenue NW
Washington, DC 20208–5652

Survey of Recent College Graduates

Since 1976, NCES has conducted six surveys of baccalaureate and master's degree recipients 1 year after graduation. The Recent College Graduates surveys have concentrated on those graduates entering the teaching profession. The surveys link major field of study with outcomes such as whether the respondent entered the labor force or was seeking additional education. Data on labor force includes employment status (unemployed, part-time or full-time employed), occupation, salary, career potential, relation to major field of study, and need for a college degree. To obtain accurate results on teachers, graduates with a major in education are oversampled. The latest 2 surveys continued to oversample education majors, but increased the sampling of graduates with majors in other fields.

The survey involves a two-stage sampling procedure. First, the universe of institutions awarding bachelor's and master's degrees is stratified by number or percentage of degrees awarded to education graduates and by control of institution (public or private). A sample of institutions within each strata is then selected. Second, for each of the selected institutions, a list of their graduates by major field of study is obtained and a sample of graduates is drawn by major field of study. Graduates in certain major fields of study (e.g., education, mathematics, physical sciences) are sampled at higher rates than graduates in others fields. Roughly one year after graduation the sample of graduates is located, contacted by mail or telephone, and asked to respond to the questionnaire.

The locating process is more detailed than in most surveys. Nonresponse rates are directly related to the time, effort, and resources used in locating graduates rather than to graduates' refusals to participate. Despite the difficulties in locating graduates, response rates for recent studies are comparable to studies without locating problems. The data presented in this report provide valuable information not available elsewhere about college outcomes.

The 1976 survey of 1974–75 college graduates was the first and smallest of the series. The sample consisted of 211 schools, of which 200 (96 percent) responded. Of the 5,854 graduates in the sample, 4,350 responded, for a response rate of 79 percent.

The 1981 survey was somewhat larger, with a coverage of 297 institutions and 15,852 graduates. Responses were obtained from 283 institutions, for an institutional response rate of 95 percent, and from 9,312 graduates (716 others were determined to be out of scope), for a response rate of 74 percent.

The 1985 survey sampled 404 colleges and 18,738 graduates of whom 17,853 were found to be in scope. Responses were obtained from 13,200 students, for a response rate of 78 percent. The response rate for the colleges was 98 percent. The 1987 survey form was sent to 21,957 graduates. Responses were received from 16,878, for a response rate of 79.7 percent.

The 1991 RCG study involved a sample of 18,135 graduates of 400 bachelor's and master's degree-granting institutions. The 18,135 graduates consisted of 16,172 bachelor's degrees recipients and 1,963 master's degree recipients between July 1, 1989 and June 30, 1990. Random samples of graduates were selected from lists stratified by field of study. Graduates in education, mathematics, and the physical sciences were sampled at a higher rate, as were minority graduates to provide a sufficient number of these graduates for analysis purposes. The graduates included in the sample were selected in proportion to the institution's number of graduates. The institutional response rate was 95 percent and the graduate response rate was 83 percent.

Table A10 contains sample sizes for number of graduates, by field, for the 1976, 1981, 1985, 1987, and 1991 surveys.

Further information on this survey may be obtained from:

Peter Stowe
Surveys and Cooperative Systems Group
National Center for Education Statistics
555 New Jersey Avenue NW
Washington, DC 20208–5652

Public School Principal Survey on Safe, Disciplined, and Drug-Free Schools

This sample survey used the NCES Fast Response Survey System (FRSS), which is designed to gather timely information for policy makers. The survey was conducted in 1991 by Westat, Inc. A national sample of 830 public school principals, representing a response rate of 94 percent, answered questions regarding the extent of discipline problems within their schools. They were also questioned about the nature and effectiveness of their schools' current policies and drug education programs.

This survey categorized principals by instructional level (elementary, secondary), type of school location (city, urban fringe, town, rural), enrollment size (less than 300, 300 to 999, 1,000 or more), region (Northeast, Central, Southeast, and West), and percentage of students receiving free or reduced-price lunches (10 percent or less, 11 to 40 percent, 41 percent or more).

For more information about this survey contact:

Judi Carpenter
Surveys and Cooperative Systems Group
National Center for Education Statistics
555 New Jersey Avenue NW
Washington, DC 20208–5651

Public School Kindergarten Teachers' Views on Children's Readiness for School

This sample survey of 1,448 public school kindergarten teachers was conducted as part of a national early childhood assessment system for National Education Goal One: "By the year 2000, all American children will start school ready to learn." The survey obtained data on kindergarten teachers' views of children's readiness and on the teacher's classroom practices.

For more information about this survey contact:

Judi Carpenter
Surveys and Cooperative Systems Group
National Center for Education Statistics
555 New Jersey Avenue NW
Washington, DC 20208–5651

Advanced Telecommunications in U.S. Public Elementary and Secondary Schools, 1995

Current information regarding the availability and use of telecommunications, and in particular, access to the Internet, was requested by this sample survey. The data were gathered from a nationally representative sample of 917 public elementary and secondary schools in fall 1995. The survey was commissioned in response to the National Information Infrastructure (NII) set forth by the President to encourage an acceleration of the goal to connect all of the nation's school classrooms, as well as libraries, hospitals, and law enforcement agencies, to the "Information Superhighway."

For more information about this survey contact:

Judi Carpenter
Surveys and Cooperative Systems Group
National Center for Education Statistics
555 New Jersey Avenue, NW
Washington, DC 20208–5651

Schools and Staffing Survey

The Schools and Staffing Survey (SASS) is a set of linked questionnaires that covers public school districts, public and private schools, principals, and teachers, as its core components. SASS was first conducted for the National Center for Education Statistics by the Bureau of the Census during the 1987–88 school year. SASS subsequently was conducted in 1990–91 and in 1993–94. The next SASS is scheduled for school year 1998–99. SASS is a mailed questionnaire with telephone followup that collects data on the nation's public and private elementary and secondary teaching force, characteristics of schools and school principals, demand for teachers, and school/school district policies. The 1990–91 and 1993–94 SASS also collected data on Bureau of Indian Affairs (BIA) schools. The SASS data are collected through a sample survey of schools, the school districts associated with sampled schools, school principals, and teachers. The 1993–94 SASS expanded as well to cover school libraries and librarians, and field tested an administrative student records questionnaire.

The 1993–94 SASS estimates are based upon a sample consisting of approximately 9,900 public schools, 3,300 private schools, and 5,500 public school districts associated with the public schools in sample. From these schools, about 57,000 public school teachers and 11,500 private school teachers were selected for the 1993–94 SASS teacher survey.

The public school sample for the 1993–94 SASS was based upon the 1991–92 school year Common Core of Data (CCD), the compilation of all the nation's public school districts and public schools. CCD is collected annually from state education agencies. The frame includes regular public schools, Department of Defense-operated military base schools in the United States, and nonregular schools such as special education, vocational, and alternative schools. SASS is designed to provide national estimates for public and private school characteristics and state estimates for school districts, public schools, principals, and teachers. The teacher survey is designed as well to allow comparisons between new and experienced teachers, and between bilingual/ESL teachers and other teachers.

The private school sample for the 1993–94 SASS was selected from the 1991–92 Private School Universe Survey (PSS), supplemented with list updates from states and some associations available in time for sample selection. PSS collects basic data on all of the nation's private schools from two sources: the list frame and the area search frame. The list frame was compiled from a set of private school associations that provide NCES with their membership lists and states that gather lists of private schools. The area search frame consisted of schools not included on the list frame that were compiled from local sources in a sample of counties around the United States. Private school estimates are available at the national level and by type of private school.

The Teacher Demand and Shortage (school district) and School Principal Questionnaires were mailed out first in October 1993, along with School Library/Media Center and Library Media Specialist/Librarian Questionnaires. The weighted response rate for the Teacher Demand and Shortage Questionnaire was 93.9 percent. Weighted response rates for the Public School Principal Questionnaire and the Private School Questionnaire were 96.6 percent and 87.6 percent, respectively.

In December 1993, public, private, and BIA school questionnaires were mailed out. The public, private, and BIA teacher questionnaires were sent out in several batches, between mid-December 1993 and early February 1994. Weighted response rates for the Public School Questionnaire and the Private School Questionnaire were 92.3 percent and 83.2 percent, respectively. Five percent of public schools and 9 percent of private schools did not provide a list of teachers in their schools and were thus ineligible for sampling. Weighted response rates were 88.2 percent for public school teachers and 80.2 percent for private school teachers.

Item response rates were varied, but generally high, ranging from 67 to 100 percent for the TDS, 65 to 100 percent for public school principal questions, 55 to 100 percent for private school principal items, 83 to 100 percent for public school items, 61 to 100 percent for private school survey items, 71 to 100 percent for public school teacher items, and 69 to 100 percent for private school teacher items.

Public-use and restricted-use microdata files are available on CD-ROM or 9–track tape. Summary data from the 1993–94 SASS can be found in *Schools and Staffing in the United States: Selected Data for Public and Private Schools, 1993–94* (NCES 95–191). More detailed results from the 1993–94 SASS are published in *Schools and Staffing in the United States: A Statistical Profile, 1993–94* (NCES 96–124). Data by state are available in *SASS by State - 1993–94 Schools and Staffing Survey Selected State Results* (NCES 96–312). Further information about the sample may be obtained from *1993–94 Schools and Staffing Survey: Sample Design and Estimation* (NCES 96–086). Data from previous SASS collections are published in the 1987–88 and 1990–91 *Profile* (NCES 92–127 and 93–146, respectively), as well as the 1987–88 and 1990–91 versions of the sample design report (NCES 91–127 and 93–449, respectively).

For more information about this survey or to order reports, contact:

Kerry Gruber
Surveys and Cooperative Systems Group
National Center for Education Statistics
555 New Jersey Avenue NW
Washington, DC 20208–5651

Office for Civil Rights

Civil Rights Survey of Elementary and Secondary Schools

The Office for Civil Rights (OCR), U.S. Department of Education, conducts biennial surveys of public school districts and of schools within those districts. Data are obtained on the characteristics of pupils enrolled in public schools throughout the Nation. Such information is required under Title VI of the Civil Rights Act of 1964, Title IX of the Education Amendments of 1972, and Section 504 of the Rehabilitation Act of 1973 to enable OCR to carry out its compliance responsibilities. The 1990 survey included the 100 largest public school districts, those of special interest (i.e., court order, compliance review), and a stratified random sample of approximately 3,500 districts representing approximately 40,000 schools. School, district, and national data are currently available.

Further information is available from:

Peter McCabe
Office for Civil Rights
U.S. Department of Education
330 C Street SW
Washington, DC 20202

The Office of Special Education and Rehabilitative Services

Annual Report to Congress on the Implementation of the Education of the Handicapped Act

The Individual with Disabilities Education Act (IDEA), formerly the Education of the Handicapped Act (EHA) requires the Secretary of Education to transmit to Congress annually a report describing the progress in serving the nation's handicapped children. The annual report contains information on children served by the public schools under the provisions of Part B of the IDEA and for children served in state-operated programs (SOP) for the handicapped under Chapter I of the Elementary and Secondary Education Act (ESEA). Statistics on children receiving special education and related services in various settings and school personnel providing such services are reported in an annual submission of data to the Office of Special Education and Rehabilitative Services (OSERS), by the 50 states, the District of Columbia, and the outlying areas. The child count information is based on the number of handicapped children receiving special education and related services on December 1st of each year.

Since each participant in programs for the handicapped is reported to OSERS, the data are not subject to sampling error. However, nonsampling error can occur from a variety of sources. Some states follow a noncategorical approach to the delivery of special education services, but produce counts by handicapping condition because EHA-B requires it. In those states that do categorize their handicapped students, definitions and labeling practices vary.

Further information on the Annual Report to Congress may be obtained from:

Office of Special Education Programs
Office of Special Education and Rehabilitative
 Services
330 C Street SW
Washington, DC 20202

National Longitudinal Transition Study of Special Education Students

As part of the 1983 amendments to the Education of the Handicapped Act (EHA), Congress requested that the U.S. Department of Education conduct a national longitudinal study of the transition of secondary special education students to determine how they fare in terms of education, employment, and independent living. A 5–year study was mandated, which was to include youth from ages 13 to 21 who were in special education at the time they were selected and who represented all 11 federal disability categories. Data were drawn from extensive telephone interviews with parents, from school records, and from a survey of educators in secondary schools attended by youth in the study.

The study was conducted by SRI International and began in April, 1987. The National Transition Study involves a nationally representative sample of more than 8,000 secondary-age youth with disabilities. A sample of 450 school districts was randomly selected from the universe of approximately 14,000 school districts serving secondary special education students. An additional replacement sample of 176 additional districts was selected due to a low rate of agreement to participate from the initial group of districts. Participation in the study was invited from the approximately 80 special schools serving secondary-age deaf, blind, and deaf-blind schools. A total of approximately 300 school districts and 25 special schools agreed to have youth selected for the study.

For further information about this study, contact:

Office of Special Education and Rehabilitative
 Services
Office of Special Education Programs
330 C Street SW
Washington, DC 20202

Other Governmental Agencies

Bureau of the Census

Current Population Survey

Current estimates of school enrollment, as well as social and economic characteristics of students, are based on data collected in the Census Bureau's monthly household survey of about 60,000 households. The monthly Current Population Survey (CPS) sample consists of 729 areas comprising 1,973 counties, independent cities, and minor civil divisions throughout the 50 states and the District of Columbia. The sample was initially selected from the 1980 census files and is periodically updated to reflect new housing construction.

The monthly CPS deals primarily with labor force data for the civilian noninstitutional population (i.e., excluding military personnel and their families living on post and inmates of institutions). In addition, in October of each year, supplemental questions are asked about highest grade completed, level and grade of current enrollment, attendance status, number and type of courses, degree or certificate objective, and type of organization offering instruction for each member of the household. In March of each year, supplemental questions on income are asked. The responses to these questions are combined with answers to two questions on educational attainment: highest grade of school ever attended, and whether that grade was completed.

The estimation procedure employed for the monthly CPS data involves inflating weighted sample results to independent estimates of characteristics of the civilian noninstitutional population in the United States by age, sex, and race. These independent estimates are based on statistics from decennial censuses; statistics on births, deaths, immigration, and emigration; and statistics on the population in the armed services. Generalized standard error tables are provided in the Current Population Reports. The data are subject to both nonsampling and sampling errors.

Further information is available in the *Current Population Reports*, Series P-20, or by contacting:

Education and Social Stratification Branch
Population Division
Bureau of the Census
U.S. Department of Commerce
Washington, DC 20233

School Enrollment

Each October, the Current Population Survey (CPS) includes supplemental questions on the enrollment status of the population 3 years old and over. The main sources of nonsampling variability in the responses to the supplement are those inherent in the survey instrument. The question of current enrollment may not be answered accurately for various reasons. Some respondents may not know current grade information for every student in the household, a problem especially prevalent for households with members in college or in nursery school. Confusion over college credits or hours taken by a student may make it difficult to determine the year in which the student is enrolled. Problems may occur with the definition of nursery school (a group or class organized to provide educational experiences for children), where respondents' interpretations of "educational experiences" vary.

Examples of sampling variability in the estimates of school enrollment rates are given in Table A11. Questions concerning the CPS "School Enrollment" survey may be directed to:

Education and Social Stratification Branch
Bureau of the Census
U.S. Department of Commerce
Washington, DC 20233

Educational Attainment

Data on years of school completed are derived from two questions on the Current Population Survey (CPS) instrument. Formal reports documenting educational attainment are produced by the Bureau of the Census using March CPS results. The latest report is Educational Attainment in the United States, March 1994 and 1993, Series P-20, No. 476, which is available from the Government Printing Office.

In addition to the general constraints of the CPS, some data indicate that the respondents have a tendency to overestimate the educational level of members of their household. Some inaccuracy is due to a lack of the respondent's knowledge of the exact educational attainment of each household member and the hesitancy to acknowledge anything less than a high school education. Another cause of nonsampling variability is the change in the numbers in the armed services over the years. In 1970, 25 percent of all males 20 and 21 years old were in the armed services. By 1974, this had decreased to less than 10 percent. The exclusion of members of the armed services appears to increase the proportion of the CPS population with some college and decrease the proportion of those who finished high school but went no further. After 1974, there was more stability in the proportion of young men in the military.

Beginning with the data for March 1980, tabulations have been controlled to the 1980 census. Examples of the sampling variability in the estimates of educational attainment are given in Table A12. The figures shown in the table hold for total or white population estimates only. The variability in estimates for

subgroups (region, household relationships, etc.) can be estimated using the tables presented in Current Population Reports.

Questions concerning "Educational Attainment in the United States" may be directed to:

Education and Social Stratification Branch
Bureau of the Census
U.S. Department of Commerce
Washington, DC 20233

Government Finances

The Census Bureau conducts an annual survey of Government Finances as authorized by law under Title 13, United States Code, Section 182. This survey covers the entire range of government finance activities: revenue, expenditure, debt, and assets. Revenues and expenditures comprise actual receipts and payments of a government and its agencies, including government-operated enterprises, utilities, and public trust funds. The expenditure reporting categories comprise all amounts of money paid out by a government and its agencies with the exception of amounts for debt retirement and for loan, investment, agency, and private trust transactions.

Most of the federal government statistics for 1994 are based on figures that appear in The Budget of the United States Government for the Fiscal Year 1995. Since the classification used by the Census Bureau for reporting state and local government finance statistics differs in a number of important respects from the classification used in the United States Budget, it was necessary to adjust the federal data. For this report, federal budget expenditures include interest accrued, but not paid, during the fiscal year; Census data on interest are on a disbursement basis.

The state government finances for 1991 are based primarily on the annual Census Bureau survey of state finances for fiscal year 1991. Census staff compiled figures from official records and reports of the various states for most of the state financial data.

The sample of local governments is drawn from the 1987 Census of Governments and consists of certain local governments taken with certainty plus a sample below the certainty level.

The statistics in this Census report, Governmental Finances, that are based wholly or partly on data from the sample are subject to sampling error. State government finance data are not subject to sampling error. Estimates of major United States totals for local governments are subject to a computed sampling variability of less than one-half of I percent. The estimates are also subject to the inaccuracies in classification, response, and processing which would occur if a complete census had been conducted under the same conditions as the sample.

Further information can be obtained from:

Governments Division
Bureau of the Census
U.S. Department of Commerce
Washington, DC 20233

1990 Census of Population - Education in the United States

This report is based on a part of the decennial census which consists of questions asked of a 1–in-6 sample of persons and housing units in the United States. This sample was asked more detailed questions about income, occupation and housing costs in addition to general demographic information.

School Enrollment

Persons classified as enrolled in school reported attending a "regular" public or private school or college at any time between February 1, 1990 and the time listed. Questions asked were whether the institution attended was public or private, and level of school in which the student was enrolled.

Educational Attainment

Data for educational attainment were tabulated for persons 15 years and over, and classified according to the highest grade completed or the highest degree received. Instructions were also given to include the level of the previous grade attended or the highest degree received for persons currently enrolled in school.

Poverty status

To determine poverty status, answers to income questions were used and compared to the appropriate poverty threshold. All persons except institutionalized persons, persons in military group quarters and in college dormitories, and unrelated persons under 15 years old were considered. If total income of each family or unrelated individual in the sample was less than the corresponding cutoff, that family or individual was classified as "below the poverty level."

Further information can be obtained from:

Population Division
Bureau of the Census
U.S. Department of Commerce
Washington, DC 20233

National Institute on Drug Abuse

The National Institute on Drug Abuse of the U.S. Department of Health and Human Services is the primary supporter of the long-term study entitled "Monitoring the Future: A Continuing Study of the Lifestyles and Values of Youth," conducted at the University of Michigan, Institute for Social Research. One component of the study deals with student drug abuse. Results of a national sample survey have been published annually since 1975. Approximately 125 to 135 schools have participated each year. With the exception of 1975 when about 9,400 students participated in the survey, the annual senior samples are comprised of roughly 17,000 students. They complete self-administered questionnaires given to them in their classrooms by University of Michigan personnel. Beginning in 1991, similar surveys of nationally representative samples of 8th- and 10th grade samples have been conducted annually. The 10th grade samples involve about 15,000 students in 125 schools each year, while the 8th grade samples have approximately 18,000 students in 160 schools. Over the years, the response rate has varied from 77 to 84 percent. Table A15 provides examples of the survey's sampling error.

Understandably, there will be some reluctance to admit illegal activities. Also, students who were out of school on the day of the survey were nonrespondents. The survey did not include high school dropouts. The inclusion of these two groups would tend to increase the proportion of individuals who had used drugs. A 1983 study found that the inclusion of the absentees could increase some of the drug usage estimates by as much as 2.7 percent. (Details on that study and its methodology were published in *Drug Use Among American High School Students, College Students, and Other Young Adults,* by Lloyd D. Johnston, Patrick M. O'Malley, and Jerald G. Bachman, available from the National Clearinghouse on Drug Abuse Information, 5600 Fishers Lane, Rockville, MD 20857.)

Further information on this survey may be obtained from:

National Institute of Drug Abuse
Division of Epidemiology and Statistical Analysis
5600 Fishers Lane
Rockville, MD 20857

National Science Foundation

Survey of Earned Doctorates Awarded in the United States

The Survey of Earned Doctorates Awarded in the United States has collected basic statistics from the universe of doctoral recipients in the United States each year since 1958. It has been supported by five federal agencies: the National Science Foundation, in conjunction with the U.S. Department of Education; the National Endowment for the Humanities; the U. S. Department of Agriculture; and the National Institute of Health.

A survey form is distributed, with the assistance of graduate deans, to each person completing the requirements for a doctorate. Of the approximately 40,000 persons eligible for the survey, approximately

95 percent respond. The questionnaire obtains information on sex, race/ethnicity, marital status, citizenship, handicaps, dependents, specialty field of doctorate, educational institutions attended, time spent in completion of doctorate, financial support, educational debt, postgraduation plans, and educational attainment of parents. The data are collected, edited, and published by the National Academy of Sciences.

For further information contact:

Science and Engineering Education and
Human Resources Program
Division of Science Resources Studies
National Science Foundation
4201 Wilson Boulevard
Arlington, Virginia 22230

Federal Obligations to Universities, Colleges and Nonprofit Institutions

Each year, the National Science Foundation collects data on obligations to colleges and universities from federal agencies. Obligations differ from expenditures in that funds obligated during one fiscal year may be spent by the recipient in later years. Obligation amounts include direct federal support, so that amounts subcontracted to other institutions are included. Those funds received through subcontracts from prime contractors are excluded. Also excluded from the data are certain types of financial assistance, such as the Department of Education's Guaranteed Student Loan Program and obligations to the U.S. service academies. For purposes of tabulations in this publication, university-administered federally funded research and development centers (FFRDCs) have been included in appropriate state totals.

The universe of academic institutions for this survey is based on the Integrated Postsecondary Education Data Survey conducted by the National Center for Education Statistics (see above). Institutions without federal support were excluded and some systems were combined into single reporting units.

Further information on this survey may be obtained from *Federal Support to Universities, Colleges, and Nonprofit Institutions,* published by the National Science Foundation, or by contacting:

Science and Engineering Activities Program
Division of Science Resources Studies
National Science Foundation
4201 Wilson Boulevard
Arlington, Virginia 22230

Survey of Scientific and Engineering Expenditures at Universities and Colleges

The National Science Foundation's annual academic survey collects data on research and development expenditures in the sciences and engineering from a sample of 459 institutions in the United States and outlying areas. Those institutions were selected from the universe of 595 schools that grant a graduate science or engineering degree and/or perform activities for which at least $50,000 has been funded from separately budgeted R&D expenditures. In addition, the survey includes 19 university-affiliated, federally funded research and development centers (FFRDCs).

The 459 institutions sampled for FY 1991, include all doctorate-granting institutions, all historically black colleges and universities with any R&D expenditures, and a random sample of all other institutions. The response rate was 97 percent. Data presented are assembled from the most recently completed survey and represent the latest totals available as of August 1992.

Further information on this survey may be obtained from *Academic Science/Engineering, R&D Funds,* published by the National Science Foundation, or by contacting:

Science and Engineering Activities Program
Division of Science Resources Studies
National Science Foundation
4201 Wilson Boulevard
Arlington, Virginia 22230

Other Organization Sources

American College Testing Program

The American College Testing (ACT) Assessment is designed to measure educational development in the areas of English, mathematics, social studies, and natural sciences. The ACT Assessment is taken by college-bound high school students and the test results are used to predict how well students might perform in college.

Prior to the 1984–85 school year, national norms were based on a 10 percent sample of the students taking the test. Since then, national norms are based on the test scores of all students taking the test. Moreover, beginning with 1984–85, these norms have been based on the most recent ACT scores available from students scheduled to graduate in the spring of the year. Duplicate test records are no longer used to produce national figures.

Separate ACT standard scores are computed for English, mathematics, social studies, science reasoning, and, as of October 1989, reading. ACT standard scores are reported for each subject area on a scale from 1 to 36. The four ACT standard scores have a mean (average) of about 19 and a standard deviation of about 6 for college-bound students nationally. A composite score is obtained by taking the simple average of the four standard scores and is an indication of student's overall academic development across these subject areas. Beginning with the October 1989 test date, a new version of the ACT was introduced.

It should be noted that college-bound students who take the ACT Assessment are not representative of college-bound students nationally. First, students who live in the Midwest, Rocky Mountains and Plains, and the South are overrepresented among ACT-tested students as compared with college-bound students nationally. Second, ACT-tested students tend to enroll in public colleges and universities more frequently than do college-bound students nationally.

For further information, contact:

The American College Testing Program
2201 North Dodge Street
P.O. Box 168
Iowa City, IA 52243

American Federation of Teachers

The American Federation of Teachers (AFT) has reported national and state average salaries and earnings for teachers, other school employees, government workers, and professional employees over the past 25 years. The AFT's survey of state departments of education obtains information on minimum salaries, experienced teachers reentering the classroom, and teacher age and experience. Most data from the survey are reported as received, although some data are confirmed by telephone. These data are available in the AFT's annual report *Salary and Analysis of Salary Trends.* While this serves as the primary vehicle for reporting the results of the AFT's annual survey of state departments of education, several other data sources are also used in the report.

Further information on this survey can be obtained from:

American Federation of Teachers
555 New Jersey Avenue NW
Washington, DC 20001

College Entrance Examination Board

The Admissions Testing Program of the College Board comprises a number of college admissions tests, including the Preliminary Scholastic Assessment Test (PSAT) and the Scholastic Assessment Test (SAT). High school students participate in the testing program as sophomores, juniors, or seniors— some more than once during these 3 years. If they have taken the tests more than once, only the most recent scores are tabulated. The PSAT and SAT report subscores in the areas of mathematics and verbal ability.

The SAT results are not representative of high school students or college-bound students nationally

since the sample is self-selected. Generally, tests are taken by students who need the results to attend a particular college or university. The state totals are greatly affected by the requirements of its state colleges. Public colleges in a number of states require ACT scores rather than SAT scores. Thus, the proportion of students taking the SAT in these states is very low and is inappropriate for any comparison. In recent years, more than 1 million high school students have taken the examination annually.

Further information on the SAT can be obtained from:

College Entrance Examination Board
Educational Testing Service
Princeton, NJ 08541

Council for Aid to Education

The Council for Aid to Education, Inc., (CFAE) is a not-for-profit corporation funded by contributions from business. CFAE largely provides consulting and research services on voluntary support to corporations and information services to education institutions. Each year CFAE conducts a survey of colleges and universities and private elementary and secondary schools to obtain information on the amounts, sources, and purposes of private gifts, grants, and bequests received during the academic year.

In the 1991–92 study, survey forms were sent to approximately 2,900 colleges and universities and 1,280 responded. The response rates were much higher for the 4–year colleges than for the 2–year colleges. For example, 89 percent of the doctoral-level institutions and 55 percent of the comprehensive and general baccalaureate colleges participated in the survey, but only 12 percent of the 2–year colleges responded. CFAE estimates that about 84 percent of all voluntary support is reported in the survey because of the high participation of institutions receiving large amounts of funding.

Survey forms are reviewed by CFAE for internal consistency before preparing a computerized database. Institutional reports of voluntary support data from the CFAE "Survey of Voluntary Support of Education" are more comprehensive and detailed than the related data in the "Financial Statistics of Institutions of Higher Education" survey conducted by NCES. The results from the "Survey of Voluntary Support of Education" are published in the annual *Voluntary Support of Education,* which may be purchased from CFAE.

Further information is available from:

Director of Research
Council for Aid to Education, Inc.
51 Madison Avenue
Suite 2200
New York, NY 10010

Council of Chief State School Officers

The Council of Chief State School Officers (CCSSO) is a nonprofit organization of the 57 public officials who head departments of public education in every state, the outlying areas, the District of Columbia, and the Department of Defense Dependents Schools. In 1985, the CCSSO founded the State Education Assessment Center to provide a locus of leadership by the states to improve the monitoring and assessment of education. *State Education Indicators, 1993* is the principal report of the Assessment Center's program of indicators on education. Most of the data are obtained from a member questionnaire; the remainder of the data are obtained from federal government agencies. Information on mathematics education was taken from *CCSSO, State Policies on Science and Mathematics Evaluation, 1992.*

For additional information, contact:

Wayne Martin
State Education Assessment Center
Council of Chief State School Officers
One Massachusetts Avenue, NW
7th Floor
Washington, DC 20001

Council of State Directors of Programs for the Gifted

The Council of State Directors of Programs for the Gifted is composed of the director or individual in the leadership position for gifted education in each of the 50 states, the District of Columbia, and the outlying areas. The Council has conducted many surveys in the past and most recently conducted two comprehensive state surveys in order to produce a profile of gifted education throughout the Nation. These data are reported in the 1985, 1987, 1990 and 1994 "State of the States Gifted and Talented Education" reports. This edition of the *Digest* uses data from the 1993–94 school year.

Further information is available from:

Evie Hiatt, President
Council of State Directors of Programs for the Gifted
Care of Texas Education Agency
Division of Adult Education
1701 North Congress
Austin, Texas 78701

Education Commission of the States

The Education Commission of the States (ECS) Clearinghouse collects information on laws and standards in the field of education and reports them periodically in "Clearinghouse Notes." The Commission collects information about administrators, principals, and teachers. It also examines policy areas, such as assessment and testing, collective bargain-

ing, early childhood issues, quality education, and school schedules. The information is collected by reading state newsletters, tracking state legislation, and surveying state education agencies. Data are verified by the individual states when necessary. Even though ECS monitors state activity on a continuous basis, it updates the reports only when there is significant change in state activity.

Further information is available from:

Chris Pipho
Education Commission of the States
1860 Lincoln Street, Suite 300
Denver, CO 80295

Gallup Poll

Each year the Gallup Poll conducts the "Public Attitudes Toward the Public Schools" survey, funded by Phi Delta Kappa. The survey includes interviews with adults representing the civilian noninstitutional population 18 years old and over.

The sample used in the 27th annual survey was made up of a total of 1,311 respondents and is described as a modified probability sample of the nation. Personal, in-home interviewing was conducted in representative communities.

The survey is a sample survey and is subject to sampling error. The size of error depends largely on the number of respondents providing data. Table A16 shows the approximate sampling errors associated with different percentages and sample sizes for the survey. Table A17 provides approximate sampling errors for comparisons of two sample percentages.

For example, an estimated percentage of about 10 percent based on the responses of 1,000 sample members has an approximate sampling error of 2 percent at the 95 percent confidence level. The sampling error for the difference in two percentages (50 percent versus 41 percent) based on two samples of 750 members and 400 members, respectively, is about 8 percent at the 95 percent confidence level.

Further information on this survey can be obtained from:

Neville Robertson
Phi Delta Kappa
P.O. Box 789
Bloomington, IN 47402–0789

Independent Sector

In 1992, Independent Sector commissioned the Gallup Poll to conduct a national survey on the giving and volunteering behavior of Americans. This survey is part of a series of surveys that will be conducted every 2 years. The information was obtained from in-home personal interviews conducted from April 3 to May 17, 1992, with a representative national sample of 2,671 adult Americans 18 or more years old. The sampling procedure did not include those with incomes above $200,000 because they constitute such a small percentage of the population.

The results from this survey are published in *Giving and Volunteering in the United States* and may be purchased from:

Independent Sector
1828 L Street NW
Washington, DC 20036

International Association for the Evaluation of Educational Achievement (IEA)

The International Association for the Evaluation of Educational Achievement, known as the IEA, is comprised of research centers and scholars from around the world whose aim is to investigate education problems common among countries. In 1988, the IEA General Assembly, composed of the research institutes participating in IEA projects, decided to undertake a study of reading literacy. The study held its first National Research Coordinator (NRC) meeting in November 1988. The construction and pilot testing of instruments was conducted in the period from November 1988 to July 1990. The main testing took place in the period October 1990 to April 1991 depending on the school year in each country. Thirty-two school systems were involved in the IEA Reading Literacy Study. Data were collected from 210,059 students, 10,518 teachers, and 9,073 schools. All students took reading tests for two sessions totaling 75 minutes at the 9–year-old level and two sessions totaling 85 minutes at the 14–year-old population. All students responded to a background questionnaire about their reading at home and at school. Teachers and school principals responded to questionnaires about themselves, their teaching and the school organization. Each national center (NCES was the center for the United States) completed a National Case Study Questionnaire.

For more information, contact:

Marilyn Binkley, NRC USA
National Center for Education Statistics
555 New Jersey Avenue, NW
Washington, DC 20208–5650

Institute of International Education

Each year the Institute of International Education (IIE) conducts a survey of the number of foreign students studying in American colleges and universities and reports these data in *Open Doors*, an annual publication. All of the regionally accredited institutions in the *Education Directory, Colleges and Universities* published by NCES are surveyed by IIE. The data

presented in the *Digest* are drawn from the IIE survey which requests the total enrollment of foreign students in an institution and information on student characteristics, such as country of origin. For the 1994–95 survey, 2,684 out of 2,758 (97.3 percent) institutions reported data for the survey.

Additional information can be obtained from the publication *Open Doors* or by contacting:

Todd M. Davis
Institute of International Education
809 United Nations Plaza
New York, NY 10017–3580

Metropolitan Life Insurance Company

The Metropolitan Life Survey of the American Teacher for the Metropolitan Life Insurance Company was conducted by Louis Harris and Associates. This survey was designed to measure the experiences of new public school teachers who began their first year of teaching in the 1990–91 school year. It includes questions on their experiences with students, administrators, other teachers, and parents. There were three surveys of this cohort of new teachers. The first survey was conducted during the summer of 1990 to measure the expectations of new graduates from teaching schools immediately prior to their first year of teaching in public schools. The second survey compared how these new teachers' experiences in their first year of teaching affected their attitudes, and how the actual experience of teaching compared with their prior expectations. The current survey focuses on these teachers' experience two years into their teaching career. It includes questions which allow comparisons on their attitudes toward teaching now versus one and two years ago.

A total of 1,000 teachers who began their first year of teaching in the public schools in the 1990–91 school year were surveyed. The sample was designed to be representative of all new teachers in the public schools who graduated from teaching colleges in 1990 and taught for the first time in a public school in the 1990–91 school year.

The sample was drawn from lists of 1990 graduates from a probability sample of colleges listed by the American Association of Colleges for Teacher Education. Graduates who did not teach full-time in public schools in 1990–91 were excluded from the sample.

The priority for fielding the sample was as follows: first, any respondents from the second phase of the study (after the first year of teaching); second, any respondents from the first phase (before teaching) who were not also included in the second phase; finally, any remaining teachers from the original sample group who were not used in the first phase.

All interviews were conducted by telephone in May and June 1992.

For more information contact:

Metropolitan Life Survey of the American Teacher
Metropolitan Life Insurance Company
One Madison Avenue
New York, NY 10010

National Association of State Scholarship and Grant Programs

The National Association of State Scholarship and Grant Programs (NASSGP) is an association of states with general programs of scholarship or grant assistance for undergraduate study. Executive officers responsible for grant program administration represent each state in the Association. *The 26th Annual Survey Report: 1994–95 Academic Year* is produced the by the New York State Higher Education Services Corporation, and data are reported for all 50 states, the District of Columbia, and Puerto Rico.

For more information on this survey, contact:

Charles Treadwell
New York State Higher Education Services
  Corporation
99 Washington Avenue, Room 1438
Albany, NY 12255
Attention: NASSGAP

National Education Association

The National Education Association (NEA) reports enrollment, expenditure, revenue, graduate, teacher, and instructional staff salary data in its annual publication, *Estimates of School Statistics.* Each year NEA prepares regression-based estimates of financial and other education statistics and submits them to the states for verification. Generally about 30 states adjust these estimates based on their own data. These preliminary data are published by NEA along with revised data from previous years. States are asked to revise previously submitted data as final figures become available. The most recent publication contains all changes reported to the NEA.

Status of the American Public School Teacher

The "Status of the American Public School Teacher" survey is conducted every 5 years by the National Education Association (NEA). The survey was designed by the NEA Research Division and initially administered in 1956. The intent of the survey is to solicit information covering various aspects of public school teachers' professional, family, and civic lives.

Participants for the survey are selected using a two-stage sample design, with the first-stage stratum determined by the number of students enrolled in the districts. Selection probabilities are determined so that the resulting sample is self-weighting. In 1990–91, questionnaires were sent to a sample of 1,981 of the nation's approximately 2,400,000 public school teachers. With an initial and four follow-up mailings, 1,499 questionnaires were returned, of which 145 were not usable. The sample was adjusted to 1,836 to reflect the 145 unusable responses. The response rate was 73.7 percent.

Possible sources of nonsampling errors are nonresponses, misinterpretation, and—when comparing data over years—changes in the sampling method and instrument. Misinterpretation of the survey items should be minimal, as the sample responding is not from the general population but one knowledgeable about the area of concern. Also, the sampling procedure changed after 1956 and some wording of items has changed over the different administrations.

Since sampling is used, sampling variability is inherent in the data. An approximation to the maximum standard error for estimating the population percentages is 1.4 percent. To estimate the 90 percent confidence interval for population percentages, the maximum standard error of 1.4 percent is multiplied by 1.65 (1.4 x 1.65). The resulting percentage (2.3) is added and subtracted from the population estimate to establish upper and lower bounds for the confidence interval. For example, if a sample percentage is 60 percent, there is a 90 percent chance that the population percentage lies between 57.7 percent and 62.3 percent (60 percent + 2.3 percent).

Questions concerning the "Status of the American Public School Teacher" survey may be directed to:

National Education Association–Research
1201 16th Street NW
Washington, DC 20036

Organization for Economic Cooperation and Development

The Organization for Economic Cooperation and Development (OECD) publishes analyses of national policies in education, training, and economics in more than 20 countries. The countries surveyed are: Australia, Austria, Belgium, Canada, Czeck and Slovak Federal Republic, Denmark, Finland, France, Germany, Hungary, Ireland, Italy, Japan, Luxembourg, Netherlands, New Zealand, Norway, Portugal, Spain, Sweden, Switzerland, Turkey, United Kingdom, United States, and the former Yugoslavia.

Since only developed nations, mostly European, are included in these studies, the range of analysis is limited. However, OECD data allow for some detailed international comparison of financial resources or other education variables to be made for this selected group of countries.

In the past several years, OECD has revised its data collection procedures to highlight current education issues. The Centre for Educational Research and Innovation (CERI) has developed an Indicators of Education Systems (INES) project involving representatives of the OECD countries and the OECD Secretariat to improve international education statistics. Large improvements in data quality and comparability among OECD countries have resulted from the country to country interaction sponsored through the INES project. The most recent publication in this series is *Education at a Glance* (1995).

More complete information on INES may be obtained from:

Norberto Bottani
INES/OECD
2, rue Andre-Pascal
75775 Paris CEDEX 16
France

Research Associates of Washington

Research Associates annually compiles the Higher Education Price Index (HEPI) which measures average changes in prices of goods and services purchased by colleges and universities through current-fund educational and general expenditures. Sponsored research and auxiliary enterprises are not priced by the HEPI.

The HEPI is based on the prices (or salaries) of faculty and of administrators and other professional service personnel; clerical, technical, service, and other nonprofessional personnel; and contracted services, such as data processing, communication, transportation, supplies and materials, equipment, books and periodicals, and utilities. These represent the items purchased for current operations by colleges and universities. Prices for these items are obtained from salary surveys conducted by various national higher education associations, the American Association of University Professors, the Bureau of Labor Statistics, and the National Center for Education Statistics; and from components of the Consumer Price Index (CPI) and the Producer Price Index (PPI) published by the U.S. Department of Labor, Bureau of Labor Statistics.

The quantities of these goods and services have been kept constant based on the 1971–72 buying pattern of colleges and universities. The weights assigned the various items priced, which represent their relative importance in the current-fund educational and general budget, are estimated national averages. Variance in spending patterns of individual institutions from these national averages reduces only

slightly the applicability of the HEPI to any given institutional situation. Modest differences in the weights attached to expenditure categories have little effect on overall index values. This is because the HEPI is dominated by the trend in faculty salaries and similar salary trends for other personnel hired by institutions, which absorbs or diminishes the effects of price changes in other items purchased in small quantities.

For more information, contact:

Research Associates
Kent Halstead
2605 Klingle Road, NW
Washington, DC 20008

United Nations Educational, Scientific, and Cultural Organization

The United Nations Educational, Scientific, and Cultural Organization (UNESCO) conducts annual surveys of education statistics of its member countries. Besides official surveys, data are supplemented by information obtained by UNESCO through other publications and sources. Each year more than 200 countries reply to the UNESCO surveys. In some cases, estimates are made by UNESCO for particular items such as world and continent totals. While great efforts are made to make them as comparable as possible, the data still reflect the vast differences among the countries of the world in the structure of education. While there is some agreement about the reporting of first- and second-level data, the third level (postsecondary education) presents numerous substantial problems. Some countries report only university enrollment while other countries report all postsecondary, including vocational and technical schools and correspondence programs. A very high proportion of some countries' third-level students attend institutions in other countries. While definition problems are many in this sort of study, other survey problems should not be overlooked. The member countries that provide data to UNESCO are responsible for their validity. Thus, data for particular countries are subject to nonsampling error and perhaps sampling error as well. Some countries may furnish only rough estimates, while data from other countries may be very accurate. Other difficulties are caused by the varying periodicity of data collection among the countries of the world. In spite of such problems, many researchers use UNESCO data because they are the best available for such a large group of countries. Users should examine footnotes carefully to recognize some of the data limitations.

More complete information may be obtained from the *Statistical Yearbook* published by UNESCO or from:

Office of Statistics
UNESCO
7, Place de Fontenoy
75700 Paris
France

Table A1.—Standard errors for enrollment and completion status of first-time postsecondary students starting during the 1989–90 academic year, by degree objective and other student characteristics: 1994

Student characteristics	2-year college students starting in 1989–90						Students seeking bachelor's degrees in 1989–90					
	Attained by 1994[1]				No degree by 1994		Highest degree completed, not enrolled for bachelor's degree[2]				Still enrolled for bachelor's[3]	No degree, not enrolled[4]
	Total	Certificate	Associate	Bachelor's	Enrolled	Not enrolled	Total, degree	Certificate	Associate	Bachelor's		
Total	**1.9**	**1.3**	**1.7**	**1.0**	**1.5**	**2.0**	**1.3**	**0.5**	**0.9**	**1.4**	**1.0**	**1.2**
Male	2.6	1.8	1.9	1.4	2.4	2.9	1.9	0.7	1.0	1.7	1.5	1.7
Female	2.8	1.9	2.6	1.3	1.8	2.9	1.7	0.8	1.3	1.9	1.2	1.6
Race												
White, non-Hispanic	2.2	1.6	1.9	1.1	1.5	2.2	1.5	0.6	1.0	1.6	1.0	1.3
Black, non-Hispanic	6.6	4.9	4.3	2.2	4.8	7.5	4.1	1.2	3.1	3.3	2.8	4.1
Hispanic	6.2	4.9	4.4	3.0	6.7	7.0	5.5	3.3	2.2	4.8	4.6	5.5
Asian/Pacific Islander	—	—	—	—	—	—	5.9	0.6	3.1	6.0	4.8	6.4
Socioeconomic status in 1989–90												
Low (25 percent)	4.7	3.6	2.6	1.0	3.0	4.9	4.7	3.2	2.9	3.7	3.6	4.9
Middle (50 percent)	2.7	1.8	2.0	1.3	2.3	2.9	1.9	0.8	1.1	2.0	1.6	1.9
High (25 percent)	3.3	2.1	3.3	2.3	2.5	3.0	1.8	0.7	1.1	1.8	1.3	1.4
Dependent student family income in 1989–90												
Less than $20,000	4.4	3.3	3.9	2.1	3.7	4.4	2.8	0.5	1.6	2.6	2.3	3.0
$20,000 to $39,999	4.2	2.9	3.3	2.5	3.2	4.0	2.3	1.1	1.3	2.1	1.9	2.2
$40,000 to $59,999	4.8	3.0	4.3	2.6	3.2	4.7	2.6	1.3	1.2	2.4	1.7	2.5
$60,000 or more	6.2	2.9	6.7	3.8	5.6	5.9	2.5	0.6	2.0	3.0	2.2	1.7
Diploma/delayed entry status[5]												
Diploma, did not delay	2.3	1.6	2.3	1.7	2.0	2.2	1.4	0.5	0.8	1.5	1.0	1.2
Diploma, delayed entry	2.9	2.4	1.9	0.8	2.2	3.1	3.8	2.3	2.7	2.7	3.7	4.3
No diploma	5.7	4.8	3.1	1.3	2.9	6.3	6.1	2.0	1.4	5.1	6.8	9.1
Age (as of 12/31/89)												
18 years or younger	2.6	1.7	2.6	2.0	2.1	2.7	1.5	0.6	0.9	1.5	1.1	1.3
19 years	4.5	3.4	3.8	1.2	3.9	4.8	3.1	1.1	1.3	2.9	2.9	3.1
20 to 29 years	3.8	3.1	2.3	1.1	3.1	4.3	4.9	3.4	3.9	3.6	4.5	5.8
30 years or over	4.5	3.5	2.5	0.6	2.9	4.4	5.9	1.8	4.5	3.3	7.0	8.6
Marital status												
Never married	2.2	1.5	1.9	1.4	1.9	2.4	1.4	0.6	1.0	1.5	1.0	1.2
Married	4.6	3.6	2.5	1.3	2.7	5.1	5.8	1.6	1.2	5.3	6.2	7.5
Divorced, widowed, separated	6.8	6.7	2.5	1.0	4.6	7.8	9.0	0.6	7.8	5.3	10.5	11.8
Expected degree level for 2-year students												
Less than 2 years	6.7	6.4	2.5	0.0	5.8	7.4	—	—	—	—	—	—
2 to 4 years	4.5	3.7	2.6	1.0	3.1	4.4	—	—	—	—	—	—
Bachelor's or higher	2.3	1.5	2.1	1.4	1.8	2.5	—	—	—	—	—	—
Average hours worked per week while enrolled												
None	4.7	4.2	3.1	2.0	2.9	5.0	2.5	0.8	1.3	2.5	1.8	2.5
1 to 20 hours	4.8	2.9	4.0	2.5	2.9	4.3	2.2	0.6	1.2	2.2	1.6	1.9
More than 20 hours	2.2	1.6	1.8	1.2	1.9	2.5	1.9	0.9	1.0	1.9	1.4	—
Received financial aid during 1989–90												
Yes	3.1	2.2	2.3	1.9	2.3	3.2	1.5	0.4	0.6	1.6	0.9	1.4
No	2.3	1.6	2.1	1.0	1.7	2.5	2.1	0.9	1.6	2.0	1.6	1.8

[1] Highest degree attained at any institution. Students who have attained may also be enrolled.

[2] Status as of 1994. Includes those students who are no longer working towards a bachelor's degree, but who had completed another type of degree or award.

[3] Status as of 1994. Includes students who had completed another type of degree or award (associate degree: 11.8 percent, certificate: 2.7 percent) but are still working toward a bachelor's degree.

[4] Status as of 1994. Enrollment can be full-time or part-time. Includes students who are still enrolled, but are no longer working toward a bachelor's degree.

[5] Students were considered to have a diploma only if they had a regular high school diploma. Students with a GED or other high school credentials were considered to have no diploma.

—Data not available or not applicable.

NOTE.—Data reflect completion and enrollment status by spring 1994 of first-time postsecondary students starting in academic year 1989–90.

SOURCE: U.S. Department of Education, National Center for Education Statistics, Beginning Postsecondary Student Longitudinal Survey, 1994. (This table was prepared September 1996.)

Table A2.—Respondent counts for selected High School and Beyond surveys

Classification variable and subgroup	Followup survey of 1980 sophomores in 1982	Followup survey of 1980 seniors in 1982	Followup survey of 1980 sophomores in 1984	Followup survey of 1980 seniors in 1984	Followup survey of 1980 sophomores in 1986	Followup survey of 1980 seniors in 1986
Total respondents (unweighted)	**25,830**	**11,227**	**11,463**	**10,925**	**11,248**	**10,536**
Sex						
Male	12,717	5,213	5,514	5,058	5,391	4,832
Female	13,113	6,014	5,949	5,867	5,857	5,704
Race/ethnicity						
White, non-Hispanic	17,295	5,180	7,285	5,057	7,194	5,246
Black, non-Hispanic	3,338	2,724	1,651	2,625	1,585	2,726
Hispanic	4,439	2,749	1,795	2,654	1,745	1,950
Asian or Pacific Islander	413	367	425	355	413	356
American Indian or Alaskan Native	248	191	253	185	246	200
Other or unclassified	97	16	54	49	65	58
Socioeconomic status composite (SES)[1]						
Low	6,752	3,940	2,831	3,857	2,751	3,668
Low-middle	6,234	2,390	2,624	2,314	2,559	2,289
High-middle	6,134	2,168	2,849	2,107	2,817	1,995
High	6,341	1,988	3,086	1,936	3,044	1,900
Unclassified	369	741	73	711	77	684
Father's highest level of education						
Less than high school	5,179	—	—	—	—	—
High school graduate[2]	11,961	—	—	—	—	—
College graduate[3]	5,169	—	—	—	—	—
Don't know/missing	3,521	—	—	—	—	—
High school program (self-reported)						
Academic	10,152	4,145	6,547	4,007	—	3,899
General	8,789	3,829	3,468	3,764	—	3,602
Vocational	6,664	2,660	3,611	2,581	—	2,481
Unclassified	225	593	56	573	—	554
High school type						
Public	—	9,969	8,647	9,727	—	9,385
Catholic	—	964	2,479	911	—	876
Other private	—	294	337	287	—	275
Postsecondary education status[4]						
Full-time	—	—	4,466	—	—	—
Part-time	—	—	3,275	—	—	—
Never enrolled	—	—	3,678	—	—	—
Missing/unclassified	—	—	44	—	—	—
October 1980 postsecondary education attendance status						
Part-time 2-year public institution	—	—	—	—	—	352
Part-time 4-year public institution	—	—	—	—	—	152
Full-time 2-year public institution	—	—	—	—	—	1,312
Full-time 4-year public institution	—	—	—	—	—	1,986
Full-time 4-year private institution	—	—	—	—	—	1,015
Not a student	—	—	—	—	—	4,523
Other and missing	—	—	—	—	—	1,196
Postsecondary education plans						
No plans	—	—	—	—	—	1,623
Attend vocational/technical school	—	—	—	—	—	1,835
Attend college less than four years	—	—	—	—	—	1,528
Earn bachelor's degree	—	—	—	—	—	2,631
Earn advanced degree	—	—	—	—	—	2,265
Missing	—	—	—	—	—	654
Participation in high school extracurricular activities[5]						
Never participated	—	—	—	—	—	1,024
Participated as a member	—	—	—	—	—	4,104
Participated as a leader	—	—	—	—	—	4,457

[1] The SES index is a composite of five equally weighted measures: father's education, mother's education, family income, father's occupation, and presence of certain items in the respondent's household.

[2] Includes attendance at a vocational, trade, or business school, or 2-year college; or attendance at a 4-year college resulting in less than a bachelor's degree.

[3] Includes those with a bachelor's or higher level degree.

[4] Postsecondary education status was determined by students' enrollment in academic or vocational study during the four semesters—fall 1982, spring 1983, fall 1983, and spring 1984—following their scheduled high school graduation. Students who enrolled in full-time study in each of the four semesters were classified as full time. Students who were enrolled in part-time study in any of the four semesters and those who were enrolled in full-time study in fewer than four semesters were classified as part time. Stu-

dents who had neither enrolled on a full-time nor part-time basis in each of the four semesters were classified as never enrolled.

[5] Responses to questions concerning participation in each of 15 different extracurricular activity areas (i.e., varsity sports, debate, band, subject-matter clubs, etc.) were used to classify students' overall level of participation in extracurricular activities. The difference between the sum of the three category respondent counts and the total sample size is due to missing data.

—Data not applicable.

NOTE.—Data from students who dropped out of school between the 10th and 12th grades were not used in analyses of sophomore samples.

Table A3.—Design effects (DEFF) and root design effects (DEFT) for selected High School and Beyond surveys and subsamples

Subsample characteristic	Followup survey of 1980 sophomores in 1984	Followup survey of 1980 seniors in 1984	Followup survey of 1980 sophomores in 1986	Followup survey of 1980 seniors in 1986
Total sample	**2.40 (1.54)**	**2.87 (1.69)**	**2.19 (1.47)**	**2.28 (1.50)**
Sex				
Male	—	—	2.07 (1.43)	2.13 (1.45)
Female	—	—	2.06 (1.43)	2.26 (1.50)
Race/ethnicity				
White and other	2.06 (1.42)	2.09 (1.44)	1.92 (1.38)	1.70 (1.30)
Black	2.22 (1.47)	2.26 (1.50)	2.19 (1.47)	2.40 (1.54)
Hispanic	3.15 (1.73)	3.72 (1.92)	3.11 (1.76)	4.06 (2.01)
Socioeconomic status composite (SES)				
Low	1.91 (1.37)	2.28 (1.50)	1.83 (1.35)	2.31 (1.51)
Middle	1.95 (1.39)	1.81 (1.34)	2.06 (1.42)	2.02 (1.42)
High	2.05 (1.42)	1.93 (1.38)	1.92 (1.38)	1.71 (1.30)

—Not available

NOTE.—The average design effect for the 1980 sophomore cohort first followup (1982) survey is 3.59(1.89) and the average design effect for the 1980 senior first followup (1982) survey is 2.64(1.62).

Table A4.—Standard errors for the NAEP reading proficiency study: 1971 to 1992

Item	Standard error for estimate (mean) [1]			Standard error for percent of students reading at or above anchor level 200						Standard error for percent of students reading at or above anchor level 250					
	1971	1990	1992	1971	1975	1980	1988	1990	1992	1971	1975	1980	1988	1990	1992
9-year-olds															
Total	1.0	1.2	0.9	1.0	0.8	1.0	1.3	1.3	1.1	0.6	0.6	0.8	1.1	1.0	0.8
White	0.9	1.3	1.0	1.0	0.8	0.7	1.6	1.4	1.2	0.7	0.7	0.9	1.5	1.2	1.0
Black	1.7	2.9	2.2	1.5	1.5	1.9	2.9	3.4	2.2	0.5	0.3	0.6	1.2	1.5	0.8
Hispanic	—	2.3	3.1	—	3.0	2.6	3.3	2.7	3.5	—	0.5	1.4	2.3	2.0	2.3
13-year-olds															
Total	0.9	0.8	1.2	0.5	0.4	0.4	0.6	0.6	0.7	1.1	1.0	1.1	1.3	1.0	1.4
White	0.7	0.9	1.2	0.3	0.2	0.2	0.6	0.6	0.6	0.9	0.9	0.8	1.5	1.2	1.4
Black	1.2	2.2	2.3	1.7	1.3	1.7	2.2	2.3	2.7	1.2	1.6	2.0	2.3	3.5	2.7
Hispanic	—	2.3	3.5	—	2.3	2.4	2.6	2.4	3.5	—	3.6	2.6	4.4	2.9	5.1
17-year-olds															
Total	1.2	1.1	1.1	0.3	0.3	0.3	0.3	0.3	0.4	0.9	0.7	0.9	0.8	1.0	0.8
White	1.0	1.2	1.4	0.2	0.1	0.1	0.3	0.2	0.3	0.7	0.6	0.6	0.9	1.1	0.9
Black	1.7	2.3	2.1	1.5	1.8	1.7	1.0	1.3	1.6	1.6	1.6	2.0	2.4	2.8	2.3
Hispanic	—	3.6	3.7	—	2.4	1.8	2.4	2.1	2.3	—	4.1	3.1	4.8	4.7	4.0

[1] Item response theory is used as a basis to estimate performance at the three levels on a common scale from 0 to 500.

—Data not available.

Table A5.—Standard errors for the NAEP writing, history, and civics proficiency studies: 1976 to 1992

Item	Standard error for estimated (mean) [1] writing performance						Standard error for estimated (mean) [1] history performance, 1988			Standard error for estimated percent correct in civics					
	4th grade		8th grade		11th grade		4th grade	8th grade	12th grade	13-year-olds			17-year-olds		
	1984	1992	1984	1992	1984	1992				1976	1982	1988	1976	1982	1988
Total	**1.5**	**1.5**	**2.0**	**1.3**	**1.6**	**1.4**	**0.9**	**0.7**	**1.0**	**0.2**	**0.4**	**0.4**	**0.3**	**0.5**	**0.5**
Male	2.8	1.7	2.3	1.9	1.4	1.2	1.2	1.0	1.3	0.2	0.4	0.6	0.3	0.6	0.7
Female	3.1	1.7	2.4	1.3	2.5	2.0	1.0	0.8	1.1	0.3	0.4	0.4	0.3	0.5	0.6
White	1.9	1.7	2.1	1.3	1.8	1.2	1.0	0.8	1.2	0.2	0.3	0.5	0.3	0.4	0.6
Black	5.0	3.8	5.7	4.0	3.6	3.2	1.9	1.5	1.7	0.3	0.4	0.6	0.5	0.5	1.0
Hispanic	5.8	3.6	6.4	2.2	6.6	3.8	1.7	1.9	1.8	0.6	0.5	1.8	0.8	1.2	1.7

[1] Item response theory used as a basis to estimate performance at the three levels on a common scale from 0 to 400.

Table A6.—Standard errors for the NAEP mathematics and science proficiency studies: 1977 to 1992

Item	Standard error for percent of students at or above—											
	Mathematics proficiency anchor level 250			Mathematics proficiency anchor level 300			Science proficiency anchor level 200			Science proficiency anchor level 250		
	1978	1982	1992	1978	1982	1992	1977	1982	1992	1977	1982	1992
9-year-olds												
Total	0.7	1.0	0.9	0.1	0.1	0.3	1.1	1.9	1.2	0.7	1.8	1.0
White	0.9	1.1	1.0	0.2	0.1	0.3	0.7	2.0	0.9	0.7	2.1	1.1
Black	0.6	0.8	1.4	0.1	0.1	0.1	1.5	2.7	3.5	0.6	1.3	1.4
Hispanic	2.5	1.7	2.5	0.5	0.0	0.5	3.1	6.1	4.3	1.7	2.7	1.8
13-year-olds												
Total	1.2	1.2	1.1	0.7	0.9	1.0	0.7	0.8	0.5	1.1	1.6	1.1
White	0.9	0.9	1.1	0.7	1.0	1.3	0.5	0.6	0.4	0.9	1.4	1.3
Black	2.1	2.5	2.7	0.5	1.0	0.7	2.4	2.4	2.8	1.7	1.9	2.8
Hispanic	2.9	2.5	2.7	1.0	1.0	1.2	2.4	3.3	2.6	1.8	5.1	2.9
17-year-olds												
Total	0.5	0.5	0.5	1.1	1.3	1.3	0.2	0.5	0.5	0.7	1.0	1.2
White	0.3	0.3	0.4	1.1	1.4	1.4	0.1	0.2	0.3	0.4	0.9	1.0
Black	1.7	1.5	2.5	1.6	1.5	3.9	1.3	1.9	1.8	1.5	2.1	3.7
Hispanic	2.3	1.9	2.2	2.7	2.2	4.9	1.7	2.9	2.6	1.7	2.7	6.6

Table A7.—Respondent counts for the National Educational Longitudinal Study: 1988, 1990, and 1992

Classification variable and subgroup	Base year, 1988	First followup 1990	Second followup 1992
Total respondents (unweighted)	**24,599**	**20,706**	**21,188**
Sex			
Male	12,241	10,462	10,713
Female	12,358	10,244	10,475
Race/ethnicity			
White, non-Hispanic	16,317	13,837	14,024
Black, non-Hispanic	3,009	2,218	2,260
Hispanic	3,171	2,751	2,922
Asian or Pacific Islander	1,527	1,302	1,406
American Indian or Alaskan Native	299	259	266
Other or unclassified	276	399	310
Socioeconomic status composite (SES)			
Low	5,934	4,556	4,395
Low-middle	5,788	4,472	4,501
High-middle	5,836	4,378	4,516
High	7,030	5,262	5,437
Unclassified	11	2,038	2,339
High school program (self-reported)			
Academic	7,298	6,420	7,567
General	3,369	7,990	6,125
Vocational	4,161	1,806	1,911
Unclassified	9,771	4,490	5,585
High school type			
Public	19,396	16,813	15,145
Catholic	2,602	1,012	934
Other private	2,601	1,602	1,530
Not enrolled	—	1,043	2,725
Missing	—	236	854
Postsecondary education plans			
No plans	2,685	2,483	2,646
Attend vocational/technical school	2,102	2,323	2,072
Attend college less than 4 years	3,078	3,074	2,457
Earn bachelor's degree	10,251	5,874	5,631
Earn advanced degree	6,268	5,269	5,580
Missing	215	1,683	2,802
School academic clubs and extracurricular activities			
Never participated	21,516	15,292	17,117
Participated as a member	2,798	5,144	3,355
Participated as a leader	285	270	716

—Not applicable.

Table A8.—Design effects (DEFF) and root design effects (DEFT) for selected National Educational Longitudinal Survey samples

Subsample characteristic	Base year 1988		First follow-up 1990		Second follow-up 1992	
	Mean DEFF	Mean DEFT	Mean DEFF	Mean DEFT	Mean DEFF	Mean DEFT
All students	2.54	1.56	3.802	1.912	3.668	1.881
Dropouts	—	—	4.705	1.997	2.919	1.686
Sex						
Male	1.98	1.39	3.456	1.817	3.094	1.729
Female	1.93	1.38	3.324	1.783	3.238	1.785
Race/ethnicity						
White and other	2.25	1.48	3.101	1.729	3.084	1.737
Black	1.65	1.27	3.804	1.867	2.938	1.654
Hispanic	2.06	1.41	2.643	1.591	2.772	1.626
Asian/Pacific Islander	2.00	1.40	2.758	1.609	2.511	1.562
American Indian/Alaskan Native	—	—	2.066	1.362	3.292	1.687
Socioeconomic status composite (SES)						
Low	1.58	1.25	2.797	1.644	2.931	1.680
Middle	1.66	1.28	3.138	1.732	2.516	1.569
High	1.84	1.34	3.576	1.817	3.849	1.921
High school type						
Public	2.27	1.48	3.147	1.736	3.116	1.733
Catholic	2.70	1.59	2.619	1.513	2.545	1.564
Other private	8.80	1.83	6.529	2.391	6.049	2.334
Community type						
Urban	—	—	3.463	1.842	3.742	1.897
Suburban	—	—	3.412	1.788	2.998	1.705
Rural	—	—	2.634	1.571	3.311	1.687

—Data not available.

Table A9.—Standard errors for undergraduates enrolled full-time and part-time in fall 1989, by aid status and source of aid during 1989–90, and control and level of institution

Control and level of institution	Nonaided	Receiving aid, by source				
		Any aid	Federal	State	Institutional	Other
		Full-time students				
All institutions	**0.82**	**0.82**	**0.80**	**0.77**	**0.65**	**0.35**
Public	1.01	1.01	0.94	0.98	0.66	0.43
4-year doctoral	1.38	1.38	1.25	1.20	0.91	0.73
Other 4-year	1.78	1.78	1.63	2.11	1.16	0.72
2-year	2.14	2.14	2.03	1.89	1.44	0.73
Less than 2-year	5.20	5.20	6.42	2.55	2.19	5.36
Private, nonprofit	1.20	1.20	1.18	1.48	1.35	0.70
4-year doctoral	1.70	1.70	1.66	1.94	1.61	1.09
Other 4-year	1.59	1.59	1.62	2.12	1.95	0.97
2-year	3.33	3.33	3.10	3.98	3.99	2.80
Less than 2-year	3.74	3.74	4.73	8.78	8.81	2.89
Private, proprietary	1.19	1.19	1.39	1.53	1.66	0.59
2-year and above	1.65	1.65	1.86	2.93	2.53	0.93
Less than 2-year	1.69	1.69	2.01	1.32	2.11	0.56
		Part-time students				
All institutions	**0.96**	**0.96**	**0.61**	**0.46**	**0.44**	**0.55**
Public	1.05	1.05	0.66	0.49	0.52	0.59
4-year doctoral	1.53	1.53	1.31	0.85	0.65	0.81
Other 4-year	1.70	1.70	1.12	0.81	0.90	0.91
2-year	1.35	1.35	0.83	0.62	0.67	0.76
Less than 2-year	8.23	8.23	3.17	4.47	1.36	4.02
Private, nonprofit	1.69	1.69	1.24	1.27	0.88	1.51
4-year doctoral	1.95	1.95	1.74	1.73	0.91	2.03
Other 4-year	2.34	2.34	1.59	1.73	1.21	2.07
2-year	5.19	5.19	5.64	3.65	3.53	1.95
Less than 2-year	10.58	10.58	10.55	3.90	4.52	11.17
Private, proprietary	4.55	4.55	4.69	2.33	1.51	1.17
2-year and above	4.21	4.21	5.28	3.22	3.52	1.89
Less than 2-year	6.60	6.59	6.65	3.14	1.23	1.45

Table A10.—Respondent counts of full-time workers from the Recent College Graduate survey: 1976 to 1991

Field of study	Number employed full time				
	1974–75 graduates in May 1976	1979–80 graduates in May 1981	1983–84 graduates in April 1985	1985–86 graduates in April 1987	1989–90 graduates in April 1991
Total respondents (unweighted)	**2,464**	**5,521**	**6,799**	**15,024**	**9,451**
Professions	1,840	4,260	3,730	8,987	3,825
Arts and sciences	514	811	2,586	4,869	2,256
Other	110	450	483	1,168	3,370
Newly qualified to teach	1,337	2,469	1,109	2,546	1,966
Not newly qualified to teach	1,127	3,052	5,690	12,478	7,485
Professions	601	1,841	2,809	7,043	2,549
Engineering	80	270	601	915	411
Business and management	290	749	1,532	2,407	1,598
Health	72	252	387	3,106	281
Education [1]	141	464	146	521	188
Public affairs and services	18	106	143	94	71
Arts and sciences	433	770	2,430	4,369	2,006
Biological sciences	83	116	243	380	179
Physical sciences and mathematics	40	103	1,062	1,782	466
Psychology	64	105	189	366	316
Social sciences	107	252	449	780	813
Humanities	139	194	487	1,061	232
Other	93	441	451	1,066	2,930
Communications	7	73	240	392	217
Miscellaneous	86	368	211	674	2,713

[1] Includes those who had not finished all requirements for teaching certification or were previously qualified to teach.

Table A11.—Estimated enrollment rates and standard errors in the October Current Population Survey

Base of percentage, in thousands	Estimated percentage				
	2 or 98	5 or 95	10 or 90	25 or 75	50
	Total or white persons				
100	2.1	3.3	4.6	6.6	7.6
250	1.3	2.1	2.9	4.2	4.8
500	1.0	1.5	2.0	2.9	3.4
1,000	0.7	1.0	1.4	2.1	2.4
2,500	0.4	0.7	0.9	1.3	1.5
5,000	0.3	0.5	0.6	0.9	1.1
10,000	0.2	0.3	0.5	0.7	0.8
25,000	0.13	0.2	0.3	0.4	0.5
50,000	0.09	0.15	0.2	0.3	0.3
100,000	0.07	0.10	0.05	0.2	0.2
150,000	0.05	0.12	0.12	0.2	0.2
	Black or Hispanic persons				
75	2.6	4.1	5.6	8.1	9.3
100	2.3	3.5	4.8	7.0	8.1
250	1.4	2.2	3.1	4.4	5.1
500	1.0	1.6	2.2	3.1	3.6
1,000	0.7	1.1	1.5	2.2	2.5
2,500	0.5	0.7	1.0	1.4	1.6
5,000	0.3	0.5	0.7	1.0	1.1
10,000	0.2	0.4	0.5	0.7	0.8
15,000	0.2	0.3	0.4	0.6	0.7
20,000	0.2	0.2	0.3	0.5	0.6

Table A12.—Estimated educational attainment rates and standard errors in the March Current Population Survey

Estimate	Base of percentage in thousands	Standard error	90 percent confidence interval [1]		90 percent confidence interval [1]	
			Lower bound	Upper bound	Lower bound	Upper bound
2 or 98	100	2.00	0.0	5.3	0.0	5.9
	100,000	0.06	1.9	2.1	1.9	2.10
10 or 90	100	4.30	2.9	17.1	1.6	18.4
	100,000	0.14	9.8	10.2	9.7	10.3
50	100	7.20	38.1	61.9	35.9	64.1
	100,000	0.20	49.7	50.3	49.6	50.4

[1] The confidence interval for the larger values can be found by taking the complement of that shown, e.g., for 98 it would be 94.1 to 100 for 95 percent confidence.

Table A13.—Estimated standard errors for selected estimates of persons from the "Participation in Adult Education" CPS supplement

Estimate	Standard error	90 percent confidence interval		90 percent confidence interval	
		Lower bound	Upper bound	Lower bound	Upper bound
10	4.5	3	17	1	19
50	10.2	33	67	30	70
500	30.0	451	550	441	559
50,000	253.0	49,583	50,417	49,504	50,496

Table A14.—Estimated participation rates and standard errors in the "Participation in Adult Education" CPS supplement

Estimate	Base of percentage in thousands	Standard error	90 percent estimate confidence interval [1]		90 percent estimate confidence interval [1]	
			Lower bound	Upper bound	Lower bound	Upper bound
1 to 99	50	2.40	0.0	5.0	0.0	6.7
	5,000	0.20	0.7	1.3	1.6	2.4
10 or 90	50	7.10	0.0	21.7	0.0	23.9
	5,000	0.70	8.8	11.2	8.6	11.4
50	50	11.80	30.5	69.5	26.9	73.1
	5,000	1.20	48.0	52.0	47.6	52.4

[1] The confidence interval for the larger values can be found by taking the complement of that shown, e.g., for 99 it would be 93.3 to 100 for 95 percent confidence.

Table A15.—Percent of seniors who had ever used selected drugs and 95 percent confidence limits: 1986 [1]

Drug	Lower limit	Observed estimate	Upper limit
Alcohol	89.7	91.3	92.7
Marijuana/hashish	48.7	50.9	53.1
LSD	6.3	7.2	8.2
PCP	3.8	4.8	6.0
Cocaine	15.5	16.9	18.4
Heroin	0.8	1.1	1.4

[1] Approximate sample size = 15,200.

Table A16.—Sampling errors (95 percent confidence level) for percentages estimated from the Gallup Poll: 1992 and 1993

Percent	Size of sample						
	1,500	1,000	750	600	400	200	100
	Recommended allowance for sampling error of a percentage						
Percentages near 10 or 90	2	2	3	3	4	5	8
Percentages near 20 or 80	3	3	4	4	5	7	10
Percentages near 30 or 70	3	4	4	5	6	8	12
Percentages near 40 or 60	3	4	5	5	6	9	12
Percentages near 50	3	4	5	5	6	9	13
Percentages near 60	3	4	5	5	6	9	12
Percentages near 70	3	4	5	5	6	8	12
Percentages near 80	3	3	4	4	5	7	10
Percentages near 90	2	2	3	3	4	5	8

Table A17.—Sampling errors (95 percent confidence level) for the difference in two percentages estimated from the Gallup Poll: 1992 and 1993

Size of sample	Size of sample					
	1,500	1000	750	600	400	200
	Recommended allowance for sampling error of a difference in percentages (percentages near 80 or 20)					
1,500	4					
1,000	4	5				
750	5	5	5			
600	5	5	6	6		
400	6	6	6	7	7	
200	8	8	8	8	9	10
	Recommended allowance for sampling error of a difference in percentages (percentages near 50)					
1,500	5					
1,000	5	6				
750	6	6	7			
600	6	7	7	7		
400	7	8	8	8	9	
200	10	10	10	10	11	13

Table A18.—Approximate sampling errors (95 percent confidence level) for percentages estimated from Metropolitan Life "Survey of the American Teacher, 1987"

Percentage	Size of sample					
	2000	1500	1000	500	200	100
	Recommended allowance for sampling error of a percentage					
Percentages near 10 or 90	1	2	2	3	4	6
Percentages near 20 or 80	2	2	2	4	6	8
Percentages near 30 or 70	2	2	3	4	6	9
Percentages near 40 or 60	2	3	3	4	7	10
Percentages near 50	2	3	3	4	7	10

Table A19.—Approximate sampling errors (95 percent confidence level) for the differences in two percentages estimated from the Metropolitan Life "Survey of the American Teacher, 1987"

Sample sizes of two groups being compared	Recommended allowance for sampling error of a difference in percentages				
	Percentage result at 10% or 90%	Percentage result at 20% or 80%	Percentage result at 30% or 70%	Percentage result at 40% or 60%	Percentage result at 50%
2,000 vs. 1,000	2	3	4	4	4
1,000 vs. 1,000	3	4	4	4	4
1,000 vs. 200	5	6	7	7	8
1,000 vs. 100	6	8	9	10	10
200 vs. 100	7	10	11	12	12

Table A20.—Maximum differences required for significance (90 percent confidence level) between sample subgroups of the "Status of the American Public School Teacher" survey

Size of one subgroup	Size of other subgroup						
	100	200	300	400	500	600	700
100	11.6	10.1	9.5	9.2	9.0	8.9	8.8
200	10.1	8.2	7.5	7.1	6.9	6.7	6.6
300	9.5	7.5	6.7	6.3	6.0	5.8	5.7
400	9.2	7.1	6.3	5.8	5.5	5.3	5.2
500	9.0	6.9	6.0	5.5	5.2	5.0	4.8
600	8.9	6.7	5.8	5.3	5.0	4.7	4.6
700	8.8	6.6	5.7	5.2	4.8	4.6	4.4

Definitions

Academic support This category of college expenditures includes expenditures for support services that are an integral part of the institution's primary missions of instruction, research, or public service. Includes expenditures for libraries, galleries, audio/visual services, academic computing support, ancillary support, academic administration, personnel development, and course and curriculum development.

Achievement test An examination that measures the extent to which a person has acquired certain information or mastered certain skills, usually as a result of specific instruction.

Administrative support staff Includes personnel dealing with salary, benefits, supplies, and contractual fees for the office of the principal, full-time department chairpersons, and graduation expenses.

Agriculture Courses designed to improve competencies in agricultural occupations. Included is the study of agricultural production, supplies, mechanization and products, agricultural science, forestry, and related services.

American College Testing Program (ACT) The ACT assessment program measures educational development and readiness to pursue college-level coursework in English, mathematics, natural science, and social studies. Student performance on the tests does not reflect innate ability and is influenced by a student's educational preparedness.

Appropriation (federal funds) Budget authority provided through the congressional appropriation process that permits federal agencies to incur obligations and to make payments.

Appropriation (institutional revenues) An amount (other than a grant or contract) received from or made available to an institution through an act of a legislative body.

Associate degree A degree granted for the successful completion of a sub-baccalaureate program of studies, usually requiring at least 2 years (or equivalent) of full-time college-level study. This includes degrees granted in a cooperative or work-study program.

Auxiliary enterprises This category includes those essentially self-supporting operations which exist to furnish a service to students, faculty, or staff, and which charge a fee that is directly related to, although not necessarily equal to, the cost of the service. Examples are residence halls, food services, college stores, and intercollegiate athletics.

Average daily attendance (ADA) The aggregate attendance of a school during a reporting period (normally a school year) divided by the number of days school is in session during this period. Only days on which the pupils are under the guidance and direction of teachers should be considered days in session.

Average daily membership (ADM) The aggregate membership of a school during a reporting period (normally a school year) divided by the number of days school is in session during this period. Only days on which the pupils are under the guidance and direction of teachers should be considered as days in session. The average daily membership for groups of schools having varying lengths of terms is the average of the average daily memberships obtained for the individual schools.

Bachelor's degree A degree granted for the successful completion of a baccalaureate program of studies, usually requiring at least 4 years (or equivalent) of full-time college-level study. This includes degrees granted in a cooperative or work-study program.

Books Non-periodical printed publications bound in hard or soft covers, or in loose-leaf format, of at least 49 pages, exclusive of the cover pages; juvenile nonperiodical publications of any length found in hard or soft covers.

Budget authority (BA) Authority provided by law to enter into obligations that will result in immediate or future outlays. It may be classified by the period of availability (1-year, multiple-year, no-year), by the timing of congressional action (current or permanent), or by the manner of determining the amount available (definite or indefinite).

Business Program of instruction that prepares individuals for a variety of activities in planning, organizing, directing, and controlling business office systems and procedures.

Carnegie unit A standard of measurement that represents one credit for the completion of a 1-year course.

Catholic school A private school over which a Roman Catholic church group exercises some control or provides some form of subsidy. Catholic schools for the most part include those operated or supported by: a parish, a group of parishes, a diocese, or a Catholic religious order.

Central cities The largest cities, with 50,000 or more inhabitants, in a Metropolitan Statistical Area (MSA). A smaller city within a MSA may also qualify if it has at least 25,000 inhabitants or has a population of one-third or more of that of the largest city and a minimum population of 25,000. An exception occurs where two cities have contiguous boundaries and constitute, for economic and social purposes, a single community of at least 50,000, the smaller of which must have a population of at least 15,000.

Class size The membership of a class at a given date.

Classroom teacher A staff member assigned the professional activities of instructing pupils in self-contained classes or courses, or in classroom situations. Usually expressed in full-time equivalents.

Cohort A group of individuals that have a statistical factor in common, for example, year of birth.

College A postsecondary school which offers general or liberal arts education, usually leading to an associate, bachelor's, master's, doctor's, or first-professional degree. Junior colleges and community colleges are included under this terminology.

Combined elementary and secondary school A school which encompasses instruction at both the elementary and the secondary levels. Includes schools starting with grade 6 or below and ending with grade 9 or above.

Computer science A group of instructional programs that describes computer and information sciences, including computer programming, data processing, and information systems.

Constant dollars Dollar amounts that have been adjusted by means of price and cost indexes to eliminate inflationary factors and allow direct comparison across years.

Consumer, personal, and miscellaneous services A group of instructional programs that describes the fundamental skills a person is normally thought to need in order to function productively in society.

Some examples are child development, consumer education, and family relations.

Consumer Price Index (CPI) This price index measures the average change in the cost of a fixed market basket of goods and services purchased by consumers.

Consumption That portion of income which is spent on the purchase of goods and services rather than being saved.

Control of institutions A classification of institutions of elementary/secondary or higher education by whether the institution is operated by publicly elected or appointed officials (public control) or by privately elected or appointed officials and derives its major source of funds from private sources (private control).

Credit The unit of value, awarded for the successful completion of certain courses, intended to indicate the quantity of course instruction in relation to the total requirements for a diploma, certificate, or degree. Credits are frequently expressed in terms such as "Carnegie units," "semester credit hours," and "quarter credit hours."

Current dollars Dollar amounts that have not been adjusted to compensate for inflation.

Current expenditures (elementary/secondary) The expenditures for operating local public schools, excluding capital outlay and interest on school debt. These expenditures include such items as salaries for school personnel, fixed charges, student transportation, school books and materials, and energy costs. Beginning in 1980–81, expenditures for State administration are excluded.

Current expenditures per pupil in average daily attendance Current expenditures for the regular school term divided by the average daily attendance of full-time pupils (or full-time equivalency of pupils) during the term. See also Current expenditures and Average daily attendance.

Current-fund expenditures (higher education) Money spent to meet current operating costs, including salaries, wages, utilities, student services, public services, research libraries, scholarships and fellowships, auxiliary enterprises, hospitals, and independent operations. Excludes loans, capital expenditures, and investments.

Current-fund revenues (higher education) Money received during the current fiscal year from revenue which can be used to pay obligations currently due, and surpluses reappropriated for the current fiscal year.

Current Population Survey See Guide to Sources.

Disposable personal income Current income received by persons less their contributions for social insurance, personal tax, and nontax payments. It is the income available to persons for spending and saving. Nontax payments include passport fees, fines and penalties, donations, and tuitions and fees paid to schools and hospitals operated mainly by the government. See also Personal income.

Doctor's degree An earned degree carrying the title of Doctor. The Doctor of Philosophy degree (Ph.D.) is the highest academic degree and requires mastery within a field of knowledge and demonstrated ability to perform scholarly research. Other doctorates are awarded for fulfilling specialized requirements in professional fields, such as education (Ed.D.), musical arts (D.M.A.), business administration (D.B.A.), and engineering (D.Eng. or D.E.S.). Many doctor's degrees in academic and professional fields require an earned master's degree as a prerequisite. First-professional degrees, such as M.D. and D.D.S., are not included under this heading.

Educational and general expenditures The sum of current funds expenditures on instruction, research, public service, academic support, student services, institutional support, operation and maintenance of plant, and awards from restricted and unrestricted funds.

Educational attainment The highest grade of regular school attended and completed.

Elementary education/programs Learning experiences concerned with the knowledge, skills, appreciations, attitudes, and behavioral characteristics which are considered to be needed by all pupils in terms of their awareness of life within our culture and the world of work, and which normally may be achieved during the elementary school years (usually kindergarten through grade 8 or kindergarten through grade 6), as defined by applicable state laws and regulations.

Elementary school A school classified as elementary by state and local practice and composed of any span of grades not above grade 8. A preschool or kindergarten school is included under this heading only if it is an integral part of an elementary school or a regularly established school system.

Elementary/secondary school As reported in this publication, includes only regular schools (i.e., schools that are part of State and local school systems, and also most not-for-profit private elementary/secondary schools, both religiously affiliated and nonsectarian). Schools not reported include subcollegiate departments of institutions of higher education, residential schools for exceptional children, Federal schools for American Indians, and Federal schools on military posts and other Federal installations.

Employment Includes civilian, noninstitutional persons who: 1) worked during any part of the survey week as paid employees; worked in their own business, profession, or farm; or worked 15 hours or more as unpaid workers in a family-owned enterprise; or 2) were not working but had jobs or businesses from which they were temporarily absent due to illness, bad weather, vacation, labor-management dispute, or personal reasons whether or not they were seeking another job.

Endowment A trust fund set aside to provide a perpetual source of revenue from the proceeds of the endowment investments. Endowment funds are often created by donations from benefactors of an institution, who may designate the use of the endowment revenue. Normally, institutions or their representatives manage the investments, but they are not permitted to spend the endowment fund itself, only the proceeds from the investments. Typical uses of endowments would be an endowed chair for a particular department or for a scholarship fund. Endowment totals tabulated in this book also include funds functioning as endowments, such as funds left over from the previous year and placed with the endowment investments by the institution. These funds may be withdrawn by the institution and spent as current funds at any time. Endowments are evaluated by two different measures, book value and market value. Book value is the purchase price of the endowment investment. Market value is the current worth of the endowment investment. Thus, the book value of a stock held in an endowment fund would be the purchase price of the stock. The market value of the stock would be its selling price as of a given day.

Engineering Instructional programs that describe the mathematical and natural science knowledge gained by study, experience, and practice and applied with judgment to develop ways to utilize the materials and forces of nature economically for the benefit of mankind. Include programs that prepare individuals to support and assist engineers and similar professionals.

English A group of instructional programs that describes the English language arts, including composition, creative writing, and the study of literature.

Enrollment The total number of students registered in a given school unit at a given time, generally in the fall of a year.

Expenditures Charges incurred, whether paid or unpaid, which are presumed to benefit the current fiscal year. For elementary/secondary schools, these include all charges for current outlays plus capital outlays and interest on school debt. For institutions of higher education, these include current outlays plus capital outlays. For government, these include charges net of recoveries and other correcting transactions other than for retirement of debt, investment in securities, extension of credit, or as agency transaction. Government expenditures include only external transactions, such as the provision of perquisites or other payments in kind. Aggregates for groups of governments exclude intergovernmental transactions among the governments.

Expenditures per pupil Charges incurred for a particular period of time divided by a student unit of measure, such as average daily attendance or average daily membership.

Extracurricular activities Activities that are not part of the required curriculum and that take place outside of the regular course of study. As used here, they include both school-sponsored (e.g., varsity athletics, drama and debate clubs) and community-sponsored (e.g., hobby clubs and youth organizations like the Junior Chamber of Commerce or Boy Scouts) activities.

Family A group of two persons or more (one of whom is the householder) related by birth, marriage, or adoption and residing together. All such persons (including related subfamily members) are considered as members of one family.

Federal funds Amounts collected and used by the federal government for the general purposes of the government. There are four types of federal fund accounts: the general fund, special funds, public enterprise funds, and intragovernmental funds. The major federal fund is the general fund, which is derived from general taxes and borrowing. Federal funds also include certain earmarked collections, such as those generated by and used to finance a continuing cycle of business-type operations.

Federal sources Includes federal appropriations, grants, and contracts, and federally-funded research and development centers (FFRDCs). Federally subsidized student loans and Pell Grants are not included.

First-professional degree A degree that signifies both completion of the academic requirements for beginning practice in a given profession and a level of professional skill beyond that normally required for a bachelor's degree. This degree usually is based on a program requiring at least 2 academic years of work prior to entrance and a total of at least 6 academic years of work to complete the degree program, including both prior-required college work and the professional program itself. By NCES definition, first-professional degrees are awarded in the fields of dentistry (D.D.S or D.M.D.), medicine (M.D.), optometry (O.D.), osteopathic medicine (D.O.), pharmacy (D.Phar.), podiatric medicine (D.P.M.), veterinary medicine (D.V.M.), chiropractic (D.C. or D.C.M.), law (J.D.), and theological professions (M.Div. or M.H.L.).

First-professional enrollment The number of students enrolled in a professional school or program which requires at least 2 years of academic college work for entrance and a total of at least 6 years for a degree. By NCES definition, first-professional enrollment includes only students in certain programs. (See First-professional degree for a list of programs.)

Fiscal year The yearly accounting period for the Federal Government, which begins on October 1 and ends on the following September 30. The fiscal year is designated by the calendar year in which it ends; e.g., fiscal year 1988 begins on October 1, 1987, and ends on September 30, 1988. (From fiscal year 1844 to fiscal year 1976, the fiscal year began on July 1 and ended on the following June 30.)

Foreign languages A group of instructional programs that describes the structure and use of language that is common or indigenous to people of the same community or nation, the same geographical area, or the same cultural traditions. Programs cover such features as sound, literature, syntax, phonology, semantics, sentences, prose, and verse, as well as the development of skills and attitudes used in communicating and evaluating thoughts and feelings through oral and written language.

Full-time enrollment The number of students enrolled in higher education courses with total credit load equal to at least 75 percent of the normal full-time course load.

Full-time-equivalent (FTE) enrollment For institutions of higher education, enrollment of full-time students, plus the full-time equivalent of part-time students. The full-time equivalent of the part-time students is estimated using different factors depending on the type and control of institution and level of student.

Full-time instructional faculty Those members of the instruction/research staff who are employed full time as defined by the institution, including faculty with released time for research and faculty on sabbatical leave. Full-time counts exclude faculty who are employed to teach less than two semesters, three quarters, two trimesters, or two 4-month sessions; replacements for faculty on sabbatical leave or those on leave without pay; faculty for preclinical and clinical medicine; faculty who are donating their services; faculty who are members of military organizations and paid on a different pay scale from civilian employees; academic officers, whose primary duties are administrative; and graduate students who assist in the instruction of courses.

Full-time worker In educational institutions, an employee whose position requires being on the job on school days throughout the school year at least the number of hours the schools are in session. For higher education, a member of an educational institution's staff who is employed full time.

General administration support services Includes salary, benefits, supplies, and contractual fees for boards of education staff and executive administration. Excludes state administration.

General Educational Development (GED) program Academic instruction to prepare persons to take the high school equivalency examination. See GED recipient.

GED recipient A person who has obtained certification of high school equivalency by meeting State requirements and passing an approved exam, which is intended to provide an appraisal of the person's achievement or performance in the broad subject matter areas usually required for high school graduation.

General program A program of studies designed to prepare students for the common activities of a citizen, family member, and worker. A general program of studies may include instruction in both academic and vocational areas.

Geographic region 1) One of four regions used by the Bureau of Economic Analysis of the U.S. Department of Commerce, the National Assessment of Educational Progress, and the National Education Association, as follows: (The National Education Association designated the Central region as Middle region in its classification.)

Northeast

Connecticut
Delaware
District of Columbia
Maine
Maryland
Massachusetts
New Hampshire
New Jersey
New York
Pennsylvania
Rhode Island
Vermont

Central (Middle)

Illinois
Indiana
Iowa
Kansas
Michigan
Minnesota
Missouri
Nebraska
North Dakota
Ohio
South Dakota
Wisconsin

Southeast

Alabama
Arkansas
Florida
Georgia
Kentucky
Louisiana
Mississippi
North Carolina
South Carolina
Tennessee
Virginia
West Virginia

West

Alaska
Arizona
California
Colorado
Hawaii
Idaho
Montana
Nevada
New Mexico
Oklahoma
Oregon
Texas
Utah
Washington
Wyoming

2) One of the regions or divisions used by the U.S. Bureau of the Census in Current Population Survey tabulations, as follows:

Northeast

(New England)
Maine
New Hampshire
Vermont
Massachusetts
Rhode Island
Connecticut

(Middle Atlantic)
New York
New Jersey
Pennsylvania

South

(South Atlantic)
Delaware
Maryland
District of Columbia
Virginia
West Virginia
North Carolina
South Carolina
Georgia
Florida

(East South Central)
Kentucky

Midwest

(East North Central)
Ohio
Indiana
Illinois
Michigan
Wisconsin

(West North Central)
Minnesota
Iowa
Missouri
North Dakota
South Dakota
Nebraska
Kansas

West

(Mountain)
Montana
Idaho
Wyoming
Colorado
New Mexico
Arizona
Utah
Nevada

(Pacific)
Washington

Tennessee
Alabama
Mississippi

Oregon
California
Alaska
Hawaii

(West South Central)
Arkansas
Louisiana
Oklahoma
Texas

Government appropriation An amount (other than a grant or contract) received from or made available to an institution through an act of a legislative body.

Government grant or contract Revenues from a government agency for a specific research project or other program.

Graduate An individual who has received formal recognition for the successful completion of a prescribed program of studies.

Graduate enrollment The number of students who hold the bachelor's or first-professional degree, or the equivalent, and who are working towards a master's or doctor's degree. First-professional students are counted separately. These enrollment data measure those students who are registered at a particular time during the fall. At some institutions, graduate enrollment also includes students who are in postbaccalaureate classes but not in degree programs. In specified tables, graduate enrollment includes all students in regular graduate programs and all students in postbaccalaureate classes but not in degree programs (unclassified postbaccalaureate students).

Graduate Record Examination (GRE) Multiple-choice examinations administered by the Educational Testing Service and taken by college students who are intending to attend certain graduate schools. The tests are offered in a variety of subject areas. Ordinarily, a student will take only the exam that applies to the intended field of study.

Graduation Formal recognition given an individual for the successful completion of a prescribed program of studies.

Gross domestic product (GDP) The total national output of goods and services valued at market prices. GDP can be viewed in terms of expenditure categories which include purchases of goods and services by consumers and government, gross private domestic investment, and net exports of goods and services. The goods and services included are largely those bought for final use (excluding illegal transactions) in the market economy. A number of inclusions, however, represent imputed values, the most important of which is rental value of owner-occupied housing. GDP, in this broad context, measures the output attributable to the factors of production—labor and property—supplied by U.S. residents.

Handicapped Those children evaluated as having any of the following impairments, who because of these impairments need special education and related services. (These definitions apply specifically to data from the U.S. Office of Special Education and Rehabilitative Services presented in this publication.)

Deaf Having a hearing impairment which is so severe that the student is impaired in processing linguistic information through hearing (with or without amplification) and which adversely affects educational performance.

Deaf-blind Having concomitant hearing and visual impairments which cause such severe communication and other developmental and educational problems that the student cannot be accommodated in special education programs solely for deaf or blind students.

Hard of hearing Having a hearing impairment, whether permanent or fluctuating, which adversely affects the student's educational performance, but which is not included under the definition of "deaf" in this section.

Mentally retarded Having significantly subaverage general intellectual functioning, existing concurrently with defects in adaptive behavior and manifested during the developmental period, which adversely affects the child's educational performance.

Multihandicapped Having concomitant impairments (such as mentally retarded-blind, mentally retarded-orthopedically impaired, etc.), the combination of which causes such severe educational problems that the student cannot be accommodated in special education programs solely for one of the impairments. Term does not include deaf-blind students but does include those students who are severely or profoundly mentally retarded.

Orthopedically impaired Having a severe orthopedic impairment which adversely affects a student's educational performance. The term includes impairment resulting from congenital anomaly, disease, or other causes.

Other health impaired Having limited strength, vitality, or alertness due to chronic or acute health problems such as a heart condition, tuberculosis, rheumatic fever, nephritis, asthma, sickle cell anemia, hemophilia, epilepsy, lead poisoning, leukemia, or diabetes which adversely affects the student's educational performance.

Seriously emotionally disturbed Exhibiting one or more of the following characteristics over a long period of time, to a marked degree, and adversely affecting educational performance: an inability to learn which cannot be explained by intellectual, sensory, or health factor; an inability to build or maintain satisfactory interpersonal relationships with peers and teachers; inappropriate types of behavior or feelings under normal circumstances; a general pervasive mood of unhappiness or depression; or a tendency to develop physical symptoms or fears associated with personal or school problems. This term does not include children who are socially maladjusted, unless they also display one or more of the listed characteristics.

Specific learning disabled Having a disorder in one or more of the basic psychological processes involved in understanding or in using spoken or written language, which may manifest itself in an imperfect ability to listen, think, speak, read, write, spell, or do mathematical calculations. The term includes such conditions as perceptual handicaps, brain injury, minimal brain dysfunction, dyslexia, and developmental aphasia. The term does not include children who have learning problems which are primarily the result of visual, hearing, or environmental, cultural, or economic disadvantage.

Speech impaired Having a communication disorder, such as stuttering, impaired articulation, language impairment, or voice impairment, which adversely affects the student's educational performance.

Visually handicapped Having a visual impairment which, even with correction, adversely affects the student's educational performance. The term includes partially seeing and blind children.

Higher education Study beyond secondary school at an institution that offers programs terminating in an associate, baccalaureate, or higher degree.

Higher education institutions (alternative classification)

Doctoral-granting Characterized by a significant level and breadth of activity in commitment to doctoral-level education as measured by the number of doctorate recipients and the diversity in doctoral-level program offerings.

Comprehensive Characterized by diverse postbaccalaureate programs (including first-professional) but not engaged in significant doctoral-level education.

General baccalaureate Characterized by primary emphasis on general undergraduate, baccalaureate-level education. Not significantly engaged in postbaccalaureate education.

Specialized Baccalaureate or postbaccalaureate institution emphasizing one area (plus closely related specialties), such as business or engineering. The programmatic emphasis is measured by the percentage of degrees granted in the program area.

2-year Conferring at least 75 percent of its degrees and awards for work below the bachelor's level.

New These institutions, though not necessarily newly organized, are new additions to the Higher Education General Information Survey universe. When degree and award data become available, they will be reclassified.

Non-degree-granting Offering undergraduate or graduate study but not conferring degrees or awards. In this volume, these institutions are included under Specialized.

Higher education institutions (traditional classification)

4-year institution An institution legally authorized to offer and offering at least a 4-year program of college-level studies wholly or principally creditable toward a baccalaureate degree. In some tables, a further division between universities and other 4-year institutions is made. A "university" is a postsecondary institution which typically comprises one or more graduate professional schools (also see University). For purposes of trend comparisons in this volume, the selection of universities has been held constant for all tabulations after 1982. "Other 4-year institutions" would include the rest of the nonuniversity 4-year institutions.

2-year institution An institution legally authorized to offer and offering at least a 2-year program of college-level studies which terminates in an associate degree or is principally creditable toward a baccalaureate degree. Also includes some institutions that have a less than 2-year program, but were designated as institutions of higher education in the Higher Education General Information Survey.

Higher Education Price Index A price index which measures average changes in the prices of goods and services purchased by colleges and universities through current-fund education and general expenditures (excluding expenditures for sponsored research and auxiliary enterprises).

High school   A secondary school offering the final years of high school work necessary for graduation, usually including grades 10, 11, 12 (in a 6–3–3 plan) or grades 9, 10, 11, and 12 (in a 6–2–4 plan).

High school program   A program of studies designed to prepare students for their postsecondary education and occupation. Three types of programs are usually distinguished—academic, vocational, and general. An academic program is designed to prepare students for continued study at a college or university. A vocational program is designed to prepare students for employment in one or more semiskilled, skilled, or technical occupations. A general program is designed to provide students with the understanding and competence to function effectively in a free society and usually represents a mixture of academic and vocational components.

Historically black colleges and universities   Accredited institutions of higher education established prior to 1964 with the principal mission of educating black Americans. Federal regulations (20 USC 1061 (2)) allow for certain exceptions of the founding date.

Household   All the persons who occupy a housing unit. A house, apartment, or other group of rooms, or a single room, is regarded as a housing unit when it is occupied or intended for occupancy as separate living quarters, that is, when the occupants do not live and eat with any other persons in the structure, and there is direct access from the outside or through a common hall.

Housing unit   A house, an apartment, a mobile home, a group of rooms, or a single room that is occupied as separate living quarters.

Imaginative writing   This type of writing can take a variety of forms, such as stories, poems, plays, or lyrics. It represents a special approach to sharing experiences and understanding the world and ourselves. In this form of writing, special attention is given to rhythm and tone; the use of anecdote; the presence of metaphor and simile; shifts in plots; and the unexpected use of words, phrases, or punctuation.

Income tax   Taxes levied on net income, that is, on gross income less certain deductions permitted by law. These taxes can be levied on individuals or on corporations or unincorporated businesses where the income is taxed distinctly from individual income.

Independent operations   A group of self-supporting activities under control of a college or university. For purposes of financial surveys conducted by the National Center for Education Statistics, this category is composed principally of Federally Funded Research and Development Centers (FFRDC).

Informative writing   This type of writing is used to share information and to convey messages, directions, and ideas. It often involves reporting or retelling events or experiences that have already occurred.

Institutional support   The category of higher education expenditures that includes day-to-day operational support for colleges, excluding expenditures for physical plant operations. Examples of institutional support include general administrative services, executive direction and planning, legal and fiscal operations, and community relations.

Instruction   That category including expenditures of the colleges, schools, departments, and other instructional divisions of higher education institutions and expenditures for departmental research and public service which are not separately budgeted. Includes expenditures for both credit and noncredit activities. Excludes expenditures for academic administration where the primary function is administration (e.g., academic deans).

Instruction (elementary and secondary)   Instruction encompasses all activities dealing directly with the interaction between teachers and students. Teaching may be provided for students in a school classroom, in another location such as a home or hospital, and in other learning situations such as those involving co-curricular activities. Instruction may be provided through some other approved medium such as television, radio, telephone, and correspondence. Instruction expenditures include: salaries, employee benefits, purchased services, supplies, and tuition to private schools.

Instructional staff   Full-time-equivalent number of positions, not the number of different individuals occupying the positions during the school year. In local schools, includes all public elementary and secondary (junior and senior high) day-school positions that are in the nature of teaching or in the improvement of the teaching-learning situation. Includes consultants or supervisors of instruction, principals, teachers, guidance personnel, librarians, psychological personnel, and other instructional staff. Excludes administrative staff, attendance personnel, clerical personnel, and junior college staff.

Instructional support services   Includes salary, benefits, supplies, and contractual fees for staff providing instructional improvement, educational media (library and audiovisual), and other instructional support services.

Junior high school A separately organized and administered secondary school intermediate between the elementary and senior high schools, usually including grades 7, 8, and 9 (in a 6–3–3 plan) or grades 7 and 8 (in a 6–2–4 plan).

Labor force Persons employed as civilians, unemployed (but looking for work), or in the armed services during the survey week. The "civilian labor force" comprises all civilians classified as employed or unemployed.

Land-grant colleges The First Morrill Act of 1862 facilitated the establishment of colleges through grants of land or funds in lieu of land. The Second Morrill Act in 1890 provided for money grants and for the establishment of black land-grant colleges and universities in those states with dual systems of higher education.

Local education agency See School district.

Mandatory transfer A transfer of current funds that must be made in order to fulfill a binding legal obligation of the institution. Included under mandatory transfers are debt service provisions relating to academic and administrative buildings, including (1) amounts set aside for debt retirement and interest and (2) required provisions for renewal and replacement of buildings to the extent these are not financed from other funds.

Master's degree A degree awarded for successful completion of a program generally requiring 1 or 2 years of full-time college-level study beyond the bachelor's degree. One type of master's degree, including the Master of Arts degree, or M.A., and the Master of Science degree, or M.S., is awarded in the liberal arts and sciences for advanced scholarship in a subject field or discipline and demonstrated ability to perform scholarly research. A second type of master's degree is awarded for the completion of a professionally oriented program, for example, an M.Ed. in education, an M.B.A. in business administration, an M.F.A. in fine arts, an M.M. in music, an M.S.W. in social work, and an M.P.A. in public administration. A third type of master's degree is awarded in professional fields for study beyond the first-professional degree, for example, the Master of Laws (L.L.M.) and Master of Science in various medical specializations.

Mathematics A group of instructional programs that describes the science of numbers and their operations, interrelations, combinations, generalizations, and abstractions and of space configurations and their structure, measurement, transformations, and generalizations.

Mean test score The score obtained by dividing the sum of the scores of all individuals in a group by the number of individuals in that group.

Metropolitan population The population residing in Metropolitan Statistical Areas (MSAs). See Metropolitan Statistical Area.

Metropolitan Statistical Area (MSA) A large population nucleus and the nearby communities which have a high degree of economic and social integration with that nucleus. Each MSA consists of one or more entire counties (or county equivalents) that meet specified standards pertaining to population, commuting ties, and metropolitan character. In New England, towns and cities, rather than counties, are the basic units. MSAs are designated by the Office of Management and Budget. An MSA includes a city and, generally, its entire urban area and the remainder of the county or counties in which the urban area is located. An MSA also includes such additional outlying counties which meet specified criteria relating to metropolitan character and level of commuting of workers into the central city or counties. Specified criteria governing the definition of MSAs recognized before 1980 are published in Standard Metropolitan Statistical Areas: 1975, issued by the Office of Management and Budget. New MSAs were designated when 1980 counts showed that they met one or both of the following criteria:

1. Included a city with a population of at least 50,000 within their corporate limits, or

2. Included a Census Bureau-defined urbanized area (which must have a population of at least 50,000) and a total MSA population of at least 100,000 (or, in New England, 75,000).

Migration Geographic mobility involving a change of usual residence between clearly defined geographic units, that is, between counties, States, or regions.

Minimum-competency testing Measuring the acquisition of competence or skills to or beyond a certain specified standard.

National Assessment of Educational Progress (NAEP) See Guide to Sources.

Newly qualified teacher Persons who: 1) first became eligible for a teaching license during the period of the study referenced or who were teaching at the time of survey but were not certified or eligible for a teaching license; and 2) had never held full-time, regular teaching positions (as opposed to substitute) prior to completing the requirements for the degree which brought them into the survey.

Nonmetropolitan residence group The population residing outside Metropolitan Statistical Areas. See Metropolitan Statistical Area.

Nonresident alien A person who is not a citizen of the United States and who is in this country on a temporary basis and does not have the right to remain indefinitely.

Nonsupervisory instructional staff Persons such as curriculum specialists, counselors, librarians, remedial specialists, and others possessing education certification but not responsible for day-to-day teaching of the same group of pupils.

Normal school A normal school was an institution which was engaged primarily in the preparation of teachers for positions in elementary and secondary schools. Prior to 1900, normal schools were often secondary schools with teacher training programs. During the early 20th century, normal schools gradually developed into higher education institutions.

Obligations Amounts of orders placed, contracts awarded, services received, or similar legally binding commitments made by Federal agencies during a given period that will require outlays during the same or some future period.

Occupational home economics Courses of instruction emphasizing the acquisition of competencies needed for getting and holding a job or preparing for advancement in an occupational area using home economics knowledge and skills.

Occupied housing unit Separate living quarters with occupants currently inhabiting the unit.

Off-Budget Federal entities Organizational entities, federally owned in whole or in part, whose transactions belong in the budget under current budget accounting concepts but that have been excluded from the budget totals under provisions of law.

Operation and maintenance services Includes salary, benefits, supplies, and contractual fees for supervision of operations and maintenance, operating buildings (heating, lighting, ventilating, repair, and replacement), care and upkeep of grounds and equipment, vehicle operations and maintenance (other than student transportation), security, and other operations and maintenance services.

Other foreign languages and literatures Any instructional program in foreign languages and literatures not described in tables 239 and 240, including language groups and individual languages such as the non-Semitic African languages, Native Amer-

ican languages, the Celtic languages, Pacific language groups, the Ural-Altaic languages, Basque, and others.

Other support services Includes salary, benefits, supplies, and contractual fees for business support services, central support services, other support services not otherwise classified.

Other support services staff All staff not reported in other categories. This group includes media personnel, social workers, bus drivers, security, cafeteria workers, and other staff.

Outlays The value of checks issued, interest accrued on the public debt, or other payments made, net of refunds and reimbursements.

Part-time enrollment The number of students enrolled in higher education courses with a total credit load less than 75 percent of the normal full-time credit load.

Per capita income The mean income computed for every man, woman, and child in a particular group. It is derived by dividing the total income of a particular group by the total population in that group.

Personal income Current income received by persons from all sources minus their personal contributions for social insurance. Classified as "persons" are individuals (including owners of unincorporated firms), nonprofit institutions serving individuals, private trust funds, and private noninsured welfare funds. Personal income includes transfers (payments not resulting from current production) from government and business such as social security benefits and military pensions but excludes transfers among persons.

Persuasive writing This type of writing attempts to bring about some action or change. Its primary purpose is to influence others. It is concerned with the positions, beliefs, and attitudes of the readers.

Physical plant assets Includes the values of land, buildings, and equipment owned, rented, or utilized by colleges. Does not include those plant values which are a part of endowment or other capital fund investments in real estate. Excludes construction in progress.

Postbaccalaureate enrollment The number of graduate and first-professional students working towards advanced degrees and of students enrolled in graduate-level classes but not enrolled in degree programs. See also Graduate enrollment and First-professional enrollment.

Postsecondary education The provision of formal instructional programs with a curriculum designed primarily for students who have completed the requirements for a high school diploma or equivalent. This includes programs of an academic, vocational, and continuing professional education purpose, and excludes avocational and adult basic education programs.

Private school or institution A school or institution which is controlled by an individual or agency other than a State, a subdivision of a State, or the Federal Government, which is usually supported primarily by other than public funds, and the operation of whose program rests with other than publicly elected or appointed officials.

Property tax The sum of money collected from a tax levied against the value of property.

Proprietary institution An educational institution that is under private control but whose profits derive from revenues subject to taxation.

Public school or institution A school or institution controlled and operated by publicly elected or appointed officials and deriving its primary support from public funds.

Pupil-teacher ratio The enrollment of pupils at a given period of time, divided by the full-time-equivalent number of classroom teachers serving these pupils during the same period.

Racial/ethnic group Classification indicating general racial or ethnic heritage based on self-identification, as in data collected by the Bureau of the Census or on observer identification, as in data collected by the Office for Civil Rights. These categories are in accordance with the Office of Management and Budget standard classification scheme presented below:

White A person having origins in any of the original peoples of Europe, North Africa, or the Middle East. Normally excludes persons of Hispanic origin except for tabulations produced by the Bureau of the Census, which are noted accordingly in this volume.

Black A person having origins in any of the black racial groups in Africa. Normally excludes persons of Hispanic origin except for tabulations produced by the Bureau of the Census, which are noted accordingly in this volume.

Hispanic A person of Mexican, Puerto Rican, Cuban, Central or South American, or other Spanish culture or origin, regardless of race.

Asian or Pacific Islander A person having origins in any of the original peoples of the Far East,

Southeast Asia, the Indian subcontinent, or the Pacific Islands. This area includes, for example, China, India, Japan, Korea, the Philippine Islands, and Samoa.

American Indian or Alaskan Native A person having origins in any of the original peoples of North America and maintaining cultural identification through tribal affiliation or community recognition.

Remedial education Instruction for a student lacking those reading, writing, or math skills necessary to perform college-level work at the level required by the attended institution.

Resident population Includes civilian population and armed forces personnel residing within the United States. Excludes armed forces personnel residing overseas.

Revenue All funds received from external sources, net of refunds, and correcting transactions. Noncash transactions such as receipt of services, commodities, or other receipts "in kind" are excluded as are funds received from the issuance of debt, liquidation of investments, and nonroutine sale of property.

Salary The total amount regularly paid or stipulated to be paid to an individual, before deductions, for personal services rendered while on the payroll of a business or organization.

Sales and services Revenues derived from the sales of goods or services that are incidental to the conduct of instruction, research, or public service. Examples include film rentals, scientific and literary publications, testing services, university presses, and dairy products.

Sales tax Tax imposed upon the sale and consumption of goods and services. It can be imposed either as a general tax on the retail price of all goods and services sold or as a tax on the sale of selected goods and services.

Scholarships and fellowships This category of college expenditures applies only to money given in the form of outright grants and trainee stipends to individuals enrolled in formal coursework, either for credit or not. Aid to students in the form of tuition or fee remissions is included. College Work-Study funds are excluded and are reported under the program in which the student is working. In the tabulations in this volume, Pell Grants are not included in this expenditure category.

Scholastic Aptitude Test (SAT) An examination administered by the Educational Testing Service and used to predict the facility with which an individual will progress in learning college-level academic subjects.

School A division of the school system consisting of students in one or more grades or other identifiable groups and organized to give instruction of a defined type. One school may share a building with another school or one school may be housed in several buildings.

School administration support services Includes salary, benefits, supplies, and contractual fees for the office of the principal, full-time department chairpersons, and graduation expenses.

School climate The social system and culture of the school, including the organizational structure of the school and values and expectations within it.

School district An education agency at the local level that exists primarily to operate public schools or to contract for public school services. Synonyms are "local basic administrative unit" and "local education agency."

Science The body of related courses concerned with knowledge of the physical and biological world and with the processes of discovering and validating this knowledge.

Secondary instructional level The general level of instruction provided for pupils in secondary schools (generally covering grades 7 through 12 or 9 through 12) and any instruction of a comparable nature and difficulty provided for adults and youth beyond the age of compulsory school attendance.

Secondary school A school comprising any span of grades beginning with the next grade following an elementary or middle-school (usually 7, 8, or 9) and ending with or below grade 12. Both junior high schools and senior high schools are included.

Secondary enrollment The total number of students registered in a school beginning with the next grade following an elementary or midde-school (usually 7, 8, or 9) and ending with or below grade at a given time.

Senior high school A secondary school offering the final years of high school work necessary for graduation.

Serial volumes Publications issued in successive parts, usually at regular intervals, and as a rule, intended to be continued indefinitely. Serials include periodicals, newspapers, annuals, memoirs, proceedings, and transactions of societies.

Social studies A group of instructional programs that describes the substantive portions of behavior, past and present activities, interactions, and organizations of people associated together for religious, benevolent, cultural, scientific, political, patriotic, or other purposes.

Socioeconomic status (SES) For the High School and Beyond study and the National Longitudinal Study of the High School Class of 1972, the SES index is a composite of five equally weighted, standardized components: father's education, mother's education, family income, father's occupation, and household items. The terms high, middle, and low SES refer to the upper, middle two, and lower quartiles of the weighted SES composite index distribution.

Special education Direct instructional activities or special learning experiences designed primarily for students identified as having exceptionalities in one or more aspects of the cognitive process or as being underachievers in relation to general level or model of their overall abilities. Such services usually are directed at students with the following conditions: (1) physically handicapped; (2) emotionally handicapped; (3) culturally different, including compensatory education; (4) mentally retarded; and (5) students with learning disabilities. Programs for the mentally gifted and talented are also included in some special education programs. See also Handicapped.

Standardized test A test composed of a systematic sampling of behavior, administered and scored according to specific instructions, capable of being interpreted in terms of adequate norms, and for which there is data on reliability and validity.

Standardized test performance The weighted distributions of composite scores from standardized tests used to group students according to performance.

Standard Metropolitan Statistical Area (SMSA) See Metropolitan Statistical Area (MSA).

Student An individual for whom instruction is provided in an educational program under the jurisdiction of a school, school system, or other education institution. No distinction is made between the terms "student" and "pupil," though "student" may refer to one receiving instruction at any level while "pupil" refers only to one attending school at the elementary or secondary level. A student may receive instruction in a school facility or in another location, such as at home or in a hospital. Instruction may be provided by direct student-teacher interaction or by some other approved medium such as television, radio, telephone, and correspondence.

Student support services Includes salary, benefits, supplies, and contractual fees for staff providing attendance and social work, guidance, health, psychological services, speech pathology, audiology, and other support to students.

Subject-matter club Organizations that are formed around a shared interest in a particular area of study and whose primary activities promote that interest. Examples of such organizations are math, science, business, and history clubs.

Supervisory staff Principals, assistant principals, and supervisors of instruction. Does not include superintendents or assistant superintendents.

Tax base The collective value of objects, assets, and income components against which a tax is levied.

Tax expenditures Losses of tax revenue attributable to provisions of the Federal income tax laws that allow a special exclusion, exemption, or deduction from gross income or provide a special credit, preferential rate of tax, or a deferral of tax liability affecting individual or corporate income tax liabilities.

Technical education A program of vocational instruction that ordinarily includes the study of the sciences and mathematics underlying a technology, as well as the methods, skills, and materials commonly used and the services performed in the technology. Technical education prepares individuals for positions—such as draftsman or lab technician—in the occupational area between the skilled craftsman and the professional person.

Total expenditure per pupil in average daily attendance Includes all expenditures allocable to per pupil costs divided by average daily attendance. These allocable expenditures include current expenditures for regular school programs, interest on school debt, and capital outlay. Beginning in 1980–81, expenditures for State administration are excluded and expenditures for other programs (summer schools, community colleges, and private schools) are included.

Trade and industrial occupations The branch of vocational education which is concerned with preparing persons for initial employment or with updating or retraining workers in a wide range of trade and industrial occupations. Such occupations are skilled or semiskilled and are concerned with layout designing, producing, processing, assembling, testing, maintaining, servicing, or repairing any product or commodity.

Transcript An official list of all courses taken by a student at a school or college showing the final grade received for each course, with definitions of the various grades given at the institution.

Trust funds Amounts collected and used by the Federal Government for carrying out specific purposes and programs according to terms of a trust agreement or statute, such as the social security and unemployment trust funds. Trust fund receipts that are not anticipated to be used in the immediate future are generally invested in interest-bearing Government securities and earn interest for the trust fund.

Tuition and fees A payment or charge for instruction or compensation for services, privileges, or the use of equipment, books, or other goods.

Unclassified students Students who are not candidates for a degree or other formal award, although they are taking higher education courses for credit in regular classes with other students.

Unadjusted dollars See **current dollars.**

Undergraduate students Students registered at an institution of higher education who are working in a program leading to a baccalaureate degree or other formal award below the baccalaureate, such as an associate degree.

Unemployed Civilians who had no employment but were available for work and: 1) had engaged in any specific jobseeking activity within the past 4 weeks; 2) were waiting to be called back to a job from which they had been laid off; or 3) were waiting to report to a new wage or salary job within 30 days.

U.S. Service Schools These institutions of higher education are controlled by the U.S. Department of Defense and the U.S. Department of Transportation. The ten institutions counted in the NCES surveys of higher education institutions include: the Air Force Institute of Technology, Community College of the Air Force, Naval Postgraduate School, Uniformed Services University of the Health Sciences, U.S. Air Force Academy, U.S Army Command And General Staff College, U.S. Coast Guard Academy, U.S. Merchant Marine Academy, U.S. Military Academy, and the U.S. Naval Academy.

University An institution of higher education consisting of a liberal arts college, a diverse graduate program, and usually two or more professional schools or faculties and empowered to confer degrees in various fields of study. For purposes of maintaining trend data in this publication, the selection of university institutions has not been revised since 1982.

Visual and performing arts A group of instructional programs that generally describes the historic development, aesthetic qualities, and creative processes of the visual and performing arts.

Vocational education Organized educational programs, services, and activities which are directly related to the preparation of individuals for paid or unpaid employment, or for additional preparation for a career, requiring other than a baccalaureate or advanced degree.

Vocational home economics Vocational courses of instruction emphasizing the acquisition of competencies needed for getting and holding a job or preparing for advancement in an occupational area using home economics knowledge or skills.

Index of Table Numbers

A

Academic programs in high school, 132–134, 135, 136, 144

Accounting, degrees conferred, 241–245

Achievement tests. See Assessment

Activities
elementary school, 140
college faculty, 223, 224
high school, 141, 143, 144
kindergarten, 49, 140
young adults, 384

Additions to plant value, higher education, 347

Administration expenditures
elementary and secondary schools, 158–160, 163, 164
institutions of higher education, 332–336, 338–342, 346

Administrative units (school districts), 88–92

Adult basic education, 352

Adult education participants in, 350, 351

Adult and vocational education, 208, 241–243, 350, 351, 353
Federal funds for, 356, 358, 360, 361

Affiliation, religious
elementary and secondary schools, 58–61, 137–139, 141–143
institutions of higher education, 176

Age
enrollment, 6, 7
for compulsory school attendance, 149
of college students, 171–173, 182, 206–208

Agriculture
degrees conferred, 10, 241–248, 250–253, 257, 258, 260, 261, 263, 264, 266, 267, 271
enrollment, higher education, 208, 209
faculty in higher education, 226–228
formal awards, organized occupational curricula, 241–243
units earned by high school graduates, 134

Alcohol use by students or adults, 145–148, 370

All levels of education, 1–37

American Indians
activities, 141–143
attendance patterns, 150
attitudes about schools, 139, 151
courses taken by high school students, 133–137
degrees conferred, 256–270, 293–299, 302
educational attainment, 12

enrolled in colleges and universities, 202–206, 312
enrolled in public schools, 44
expected occupations, 138
financial aid, 312
high school program, 132
testing, 109, 113, 124, 126

Annual expenditure per pupil, public schools, 38, 87, 91, 165, 166, 406

Annual salary. See Salaries.

Applications, college, 181

Applied research funds, 332–336, 338–342, 346, 354, 364, 365

Architecture
degrees conferred, 241–248, 250–253, 257, 258, 260, 261, 263, 264, 266, 267, 272
enrollment, higher education, 208

Area studies, degrees conferred, 241–248, 250–253, 257, 258, 260, 261, 263, 264, 266, 267

Art, degrees conferred, 241–248, 250–253, 257, 258, 260, 261, 263, 264, 266, 267, 292

Asian or Pacific Islander
activities, 141–144
attendance patterns, 150
attitudes about schools, 139, 151
courses taken by high school students, 133–137
degrees conferred, 256–270, 293–299, 302
educational attainment, 12
enrolled in colleges and universities, 202–206, 312
enrolled in public schools, 44
expected occupations, 138
financial aid, 312
high school program, 132
testing, 109, 113, 114, 124, 126

Assessment
American College Testing, 131
Graduate Record Examination, 308
international, 391–402
minimum-competency, 153, 154
National Assessment of Educational Progress, 105–123
National Education Longitudinal Study, 124
Scholastic Assessment Test, 125–130

Associate degrees, 9, 11, 167, 168, 212–214, 239–243, 249–253, 256–258

Athletics, participation in school activities, 141, 143, 144

Attendance patterns, 150

Attitudes about
education, 21–28, 68, 73–75

U.S. Department of Education Online Library

Public Access via Internet
through the
National Library of Education's INet System

Individuals with access to the Internet can tap a rich collection of education related information at the U.S. Department of Education (ED), including:

- General Information about the Department's Mission, Organization, Key Staff, and Programs
- Information about Key Departmental Initiatives, such as GOALS 2000, Technology, Family Involvement, School-to-Work Programs, and Elementary and Secondary Schoolwide Projects
- Full-text Publications for Teachers, Parents, and Researchers
- Statistical Tables, Charts, and Data Sets
- Research Findings and Syntheses
- Directories of Effective Programs and Exemplary Schools
- Directories of Information Centers and Sources of Assistance
- Student Financial Aid Information
- Press Releases
- Status of Legislation and Budget
- Selected Speeches and Testimony by the Secretary of Education
- Grant Announcements and Applications
- Event Calendars
- Announcements of New Publications and Data Sets
- Searchable ED Staff Directory
- Links to Public Internet Resources at ERIC Clearinghouses, Regional Laboratories, R&D Centers, and other ED-Funded Institutions
- Links to other Education-Related Internet Resources

The Department's Internet Online Library is maintained by the National Library of Education (NLE) in the Office of Educational Research and Improvement (OERI) on its Institutional Communications Network (INet).

Latest Developments

The GOALS 2000 legislation reauthorized OERI and created the National Library of Education (NLE), which is responsible for assembling and providing access to a comprehensive collection of education information, as well as promoting resource sharing and cooperation among libraries and other providers of education information. INet and ERIC are core components of a distributed electronic repository which NLE plans to develop in close collaboration with the National Education Dissemination System (NEDS), which also was established in OERI's reauthorization.

Latest Developments (continued)

In response to customer demand we are making much more information available in hypertext markt language (HTML) format on our World Wide Web server. In September we unveiled a new, completely redesigned WWW home page which was very well-received. *Government Executive* (11/95) called it "among the classiest--and most useful--of all federal sites." Point Communications rates us among the top 5% of Web sites. In October we logged more than 1.3 million accesses from 75 countries.

Access via Internet

Although WWW is the access method of choice for 75% of our customers, we are committed to providing access to as much of our information as possible through Gopher, FTP, and E-Mail for those users who still depend on those methods. We are committed to providing text-only equivalents to all graphical features to accommodate visually impaired users.

Our **WWW Server** can be accessed at URL (uniform resource locator):
> **http://www.ed.gov/**

The **Gopher Server's** address is:
> **gopher.ed.gov**

> or select **North America-->USA-->General-->U.S. Department of Education** from the All/Other Gophers menu on your system

FTP users can access the information by ftping to:

> **ftp.ed.gov** (log on anonymous)

E-mail users can get our catalog and instructions on the usafe of our Mail server by sending e-mail to:
> **almanac@inet.ed.gov**
> in the body of the message type **send catalog**
> (avoid the use of signature blocks)

Please note that no public telnet access is available. You must either have an appropriate WWW, Gopher, or FTP client at your site or be able to telnet to a public access client elsewhere.

Questions and Comments

If you have any suggestions or questions about the contents of the WWW, Gopher, FTP, and Mail servers, please use one of the following addresses:

E-mail:	**inetmgr@inet.ed.gov**	Snail Mail:	**INet Project Manager**
	gopheradm@inet.ed.gov		**National Library of Education**
	webmaster@inet.ed.gov		**U.S. Department of Education/OERI**
Telephone:	**(202) 219-2266**		**555 New Jersey Ave., N.W., Rm. 214**
Fax:	**(202) 219-1817**		**Washington, D.C. 20208-5725**

Selected Publications of the National Center for Education Statistics

Adult Literacy in America
GPO #065-000-00588-3, $12

Advanced Telecommunications in U.S. Public Schools, K-12
GPO #065-000-00743-6, $4.50

America's High School Sophomores: A 10-Year Comparison
GPO #065-000-00572-7, $7.50

America's Teachers: Profile of a Profession
GPO #065-000-00567-1, $13

Approaching Kindergarten: A Look at Preschoolers in the United States
GPO #065-000-00807-6, $3

Arts in Public Elementary and Secondary Schools
GPO #065-000-00811-4, $5.50

Characteristics of Students Who Borrow to Finance Their Postsecondary Education
GPO #065-000-00719-3, $7

The Condition of Education 1996
GPO #065-000-00871-8, $25

The Cost of Higher Education: Findings from the Condition of Education 1995
GPO #065-000-00861-1, $2

The Educational Progress of Hispanic Students: Findings from the Condition of Education 1995
GPO #065-000-00799-1, $2.25

The Educational Progress of Women: Findings from the Condition of Education 1995
GPO #065-000-00831-9, $1.25

The Educational Progress of Black Students: Findings from the Condition of Education 1994
GPO #065-000-00762-2, $2

High School Students Ten Years After "A Nation At Risk": Findings from the Condition of Education 1994
GPO #065-000-00761-4, $2

America's Teachers Ten Years After "A Nation At Risk": Findings from the Condition of Education 1994
GPO #065-000-00763-1, $2

Curricular Differentiation in Public High Schools
GPO #065-000-00723-1, $3.75

Digest of Education Statistics, 1996
GPO #065-000-00904-8, $44

Dropout Rates in the United States, 1994
GPO #065-000-00887-4, $10

Education in the States and Nations
GPO #065-000-00873-4, $22

Historically Black Colleges and Universities, 1976-1994
GPO #065-000-00903-0, $9

Literacy Behind Prison Walls
GPO #065-000-00716-9, $13

NAEP 1992 Trends in Academic Progress
GPO #065-000-00672-3, $41

1992 Mathematics Report Card for the Nation and the States
GPO #065-000-00559-0, $22

NAEP 1994 Reading Report Card for the Nation and the States
GPO #065-000-00845-9, $13

NAEP 1994 Geography Report Card
GPO #065-000-00872-6, $10

NAEP 1994 U.S. History Report Card
GPO #065-000-00865-3, $10

Profile of the American High School Sophomore, 1990
GPO #065-000-00726-6, $18

Patterns of Teacher Compensation: Statistical Analysis
GPO #065-000-00835-1, $11

Private Schools in the U.S.: A Statistical Profile, 1990-91
GPO #0657000-00739-8, $14

Profile of Undergraduates in U.S. Postsecondary Education Institutions: 1992-93
GPO #065-000-00802-5, $12

Programs at Higher Education Institutions for Disadvantaged Precollege Students
GPO #065-000-00833-5, $6.50

Projections of Education Statistics to 2006
GPO #065-000-00853-0, $14

Public School Teacher Cost Differences Across the United States
GPO #065-000-00812-2, $9

Reading Literacy in the United States
GPO #065-000-00875-1, $9

Schools and Staffing in the United States: A Statistical Profile, 1993–94 Survey (SASS)—SASS by State
GPO #065-000-00889-1, $15

Understanding Racial-Ethnic Differences in Secondary School Science and Mathematics Achievement
GPO #065-000-00747-9, $6

Undergraduates Who Work While Enrolled in Postsecondary Education: 1989-90
GPO #065-000-00678-2, $6

Urban Schools: The Challenge of Location and Poverty
GPO #065-000-00869-6, $14

Vocational Education in the United States: The Early 1990's
GPO #065-000-00820-3, $21

Youth Indicators: 1996
GPO #065-000-00898-0, $12

—Free from OERI—

"At-Risk" Eighth-Graders Four Years Later
NCES #95-736

How Much Time Do Public and Private School Teachers Spend in Their Work?
NCES #94-709

Programs and Plans of the National Center for Education Statistics
NCES #95-133

Student Strategies To Avoid Harm at School
NCES #95-203

Student Victimization at School
NCES #95-204

Some publications are produced annually: *The Condition of Education* in June; *Dropout Rates in the United States* in September; *Digest of Education Statistics* in November; and *Projections of Education Statistics* in December. Please check with the **Order Desk** at the **U.S. Government Printing Office** for information on the latest edition. The telephone number is **202–512–1800.** The **U.S. Government Printing Office** (GPO) order blank is on the back.

1996

United States Government
INFORMATION
PUBLICATIONS ★ PERIODICALS ★ ELECTRONIC PRODUCTS

Order Processing Code:
* 7903

Charge your order.
It's easy!

Please type or print.

Fax your orders to: (202) 512–2250
Phone your orders to: (202) 512–1800

Mail to: Superintendent of Documents
P.O. Box 371954
Pittsburgh, PA 15250–7954

Qty.	Stock Number	Title	Price Each	Total Price

The total cost of my order is $ _____. Price includes regular shipping and handling and is subject to change. International customers please add 25%.

Total | |

Company or personal name   (Please type or print)

Additional address/attention line

Street address

City, State, Zip code

Daytime phone including area code

Purchase order number (optional)

Check method of payment:

❏ Check payable to Superintendent of Documents
❏ GPO Deposit Account ⬚⬚⬚⬚⬚⬚–⬚
❏ VISA   ❏ MasterCard

⬚⬚⬚⬚⬚⬚⬚⬚⬚⬚⬚⬚⬚⬚⬚⬚⬚⬚⬚⬚

⬚⬚⬚⬚ (expiration date)   *Thank you for your order!*

Authorizing signature   8/96

Important: Please include this completed order form with your payment. Photocopies of form are acceptable.

ISBN 0-16-048916-4

9 780160 489167   90000